Design Integration
Using Autodesk Revit® 2027

Daniel John Stine

SDC
PUBLICATIONS

SDC Publications
P.O. Box 1334
Mission, KS 66222
913-262-2664
www.SDCpublications.com
Publisher: Stephen Schroff

Examination Copies
Books received as examination copies are for review purposes only and may not be made available for student use. Resale of examination copies is prohibited.

Electronic Files
Any electronic files associated with this book are licensed to the original user only. These files may not be transferred to any other party.

Trademarks
Autodesk®, **AutoCAD®**, **Maya®, mental ray®, Revit®, 3ds Max®** are registered trademarks or trademarks of Autodesk, Inc., and/or its subsidiaries and/or affiliates in the USA and/or other countries. All other trademarks are trademarks of their respective holders.

Disclaimer
The author and publisher of this book have used their best efforts in preparing this book. These efforts include the development, research and testing of the material presented. The author and publisher shall not be liable in any event for incidental or consequential damages with, or arising out of, the furnishing, performance, or use of the material.

ISBN-13: 978-1-63057-802-2
ISBN-10: 1-63057-802-9

Printed and bound in the United States of America.

Foreword

The intent of this book is to provide the student with a well-rounded knowledge of Autodesk Revit tools and techniques for use in both academia and industry.

As an instructor, the author understands that many students in a classroom setting have varying degrees of computer experience. To help level the "playing field" the first chapter, located on the publisher's website, is devoted to an introduction to computers. Much of the basics are covered, from computer hardware and software to file management procedures, including step-by-step instruction on using a flash drive.

Chapters 2 through 5 cover many of the Revit basics needed to successfully and efficiently work in the software. Once the fundamentals are covered, the remaining chapters walk the reader through a building project which is started from scratch so nothing is taken for granted by the reader or the author.

This book was designed for the building design industry. All three "flavors" of the Revit platform are introduced in this textbook. This approach gives the reader a broad overview of the Building Information Modeling (BIM) process. The topics cover the design integration of most of the building disciplines: Architectural, Interior Design, Structural, Mechanical, Plumbing and Electrical. Civil is not covered but adding topography to your model is.

Throughout the book the student develops a two-story law office. The drawings start with the floor plans and develop all the way to photo-realistic renderings similar to the one on the cover of this book. Along the way, the building's structure, ductwork, plumbing and electrical (power and lighting) are modeled.

The reader will have a thorough knowledge of many of the Revit basics needed to be productive in a classroom or office environment. Even if you will only be working with one "flavor" of Revit in your chosen profession, this book will give you important knowledge on how the other disciplines will be doing their work and valuable insight on the overall process.

Online Content:
The chapter-starter files, models of the law office project completed up to the point of the current chapter, can be found online at the publisher's website (see the inside front cover for more information). This allows instructors/students to jump around in the text, or to skip chapters. For example, an Interior Design class might model the building (walls, doors, windows, ceilings) and skip the structural chapter in order to focus on space layout.

Finally, a draft copy of *Roof Study Workbook* is also provided for use by the owner of the book. This document includes some information on controlling the top surface of the roof in Revit.

Errata:
Please check the publisher's website from time to time for any errors or typos found in this book after it went to the printer. Simply browse to www.SDCpublications.com, and then navigate to the page for this book. Click the **View/Submit errata** link in the upper right corner of the page. If you find an error, please submit it so we can correct it in the next edition.

You may contact the publisher with comments or suggestions at service@SDCpublications.com.
Please do not email with Revit questions unless they relate to a problem with this book.

Software required:
To successfully complete the exercises in this book you will need to have access to Autodesk *Revit*, a 30-day trial of which can be downloaded from Autodesk's website. Additionally, qualifying students may download the free student version of the software from **students.autodesk.com**. Both versions are fully functional versions of the software. The reader will also need access to the free *Autodesk Design Review 2017* DWFx viewer and markup application. This is a free download from Autodesk.com.

Instructors:
An Instructor's resource guide is available with this book. It contains:

- Answers to the questions at the end of each chapter
- Outline of tools and topics to be covered in each lesson's lecture
- Images of suggested student printouts to use for grading
- Suggestions for additional student work (for each lesson)

About the Author:
Daniel John Stine, AIA, CSI, CDT, IES, WELL AP, is a distinguished Wisconsin-registered architect with over two decades of professional experience, currently serving as the Director of Design Technology at Lake|Flato, a leading architecture firm based in San Antonio, Texas. Dan is an active member of the national AIA Committee on the Environment (COTE) Leadership Group, where his expertise significantly contributes to advancing sustainable architectural practices.

Dan's remarkable contributions to the field include pioneering the integration of Building Information Modeling (BIM) for lighting analysis with ElumTools, early-stage energy modeling using Autodesk Insight, and immersive experiences through virtual reality (VR) and augmented reality (AR) technologies with platforms like HTC Vive, Oculus Rift, Fuzor, Enscape, and Microsoft HoloLens 2. He has also co-developed the Electrical Productivity Pack for Revit, a tool that enhances electrical design efficiency, marketed by ATG under the CTC Software brand. His innovative work has caught the attention of industry giants Dell and Autodesk, leading to feature videos that showcase his impactful contributions to architecture and design technology.

Dan is an esteemed speaker who has shared his insights on BIM, design technology, and sustainable design at prestigious international forums across the USA, Mexico, Canada, Europe, Asia, and Australia, including Autodesk University, RTC/BILT, and various AIA national and state conferences. His engagement with the global architectural community led to a special invitation from Autodesk to collaborate on future Revit features at their largest R&D facility in Shanghai, China, in 2017.

Dedicated to educating the next generation of architects, Dan holds a teaching position at North Dakota State University, where he mentors graduate architecture students. His academic contributions span lectures and workshops at universities across the United States, fostering growth and innovation in both architecture and interior design education. Dan's affiliations with professional organizations like the American Institute of Architects, Construction Specifications Institute, Illuminating Engineering Society, and the Autodesk Developer Network underscore his commitment to excellence and innovation in the architectural field. Through his teaching and pioneering work, Dan continues to shape the future of architectural design and technology.

Dan writes about design on his blog, BIM Chapters, and in his textbooks published by SDC Publications:

- *Residential Design Using Autodesk Revit 2027*
- *Commercial Design Using Autodesk Revit 2027*
- *Design Integration Using Autodesk Revit 2027 (Architecture, Structure and MEP)*
- *Interior Design Using Autodesk Revit 2027 (with co-author Aaron Hansen)*
- *Autodesk Revit 2021 Architectural Command Reference*
- *Residential Design Using AutoCAD 2027*
- *Commercial Design Using AutoCAD 2027*
- *Chapters in Architectural Drawing (with co-author Steven H. McNeill, AIA, LEED AP)*
- *Interior Design Using Hand Sketching, SketchUp and Photoshop (also with Steven H. McNeill)*
- *SketchUp 2024 for Interior Designers (with co-author Maria Delgado, PhD)*

You may contact the publisher with comments or suggestions at **service@SDCpublications.com**

BIM Chapters (Author's Blog):
http://bimchapters.blogspot.com

X/Twitter
@DanStine_MN

LinkedIn
https://www.linkedin.com/in/danstinemn

Certification Study Guides

The author of this book has also prepared the following certification study guides that students can use to achieve successful results when taking certification exams, which can help make the difference when trying to secure that dream job!

- *Microsoft Office Specialist Excel Associate 365/2019 Exam Preparation*
- *Microsoft Office Specialist Word Associate 365/2019 Exam Preparation*
- *Microsoft Office Specialist PowerPoint Associate 365/2019 Exam Preparation*
- *Autodesk Revit for Architecture Certified User Exam Preparation (Revit 2027 Edition)*
- *Autodesk AutoCAD Certified User Study Guide (2024 Edition)*

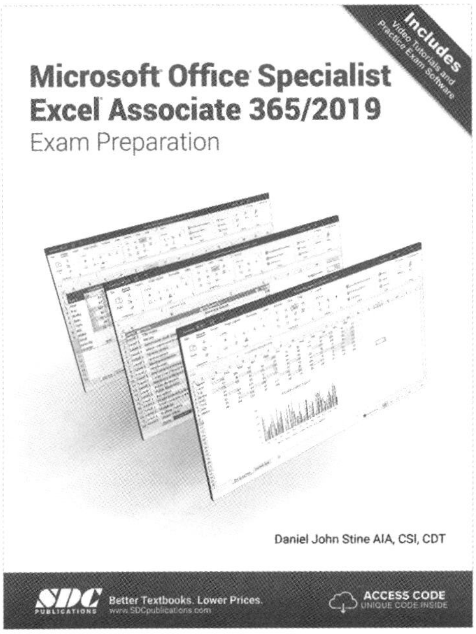

Notes:

Table of Contents

Exclusive Online Content

See the inside-front cover of this book for download instructions and your unique access code.

Bonus Videos

This book comes with several short videos, approximately 3-5 minutes long, which can be watched in order while working through this book. The full index of video titles can be found on the next page.

These videos are supplementary and not required to complete the exercises in this book. Rather, the videos are intended to cover many of the fundamental Revit topics in a different context to help the reader better understand this important material. A few videos cover intermediate topics, such as the sloped "cloud" ceiling shown in the image to the right.

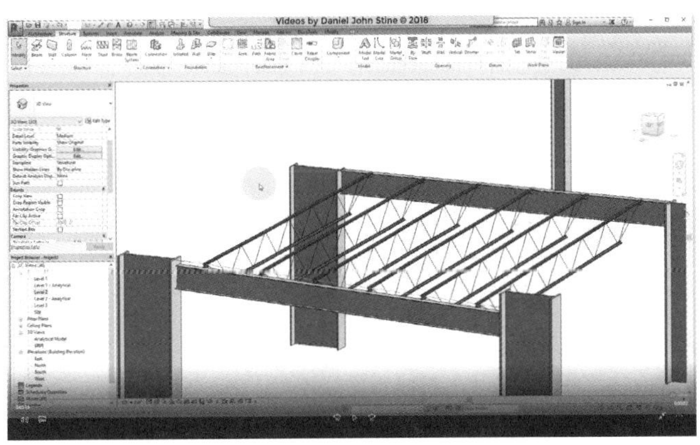

Bonus Videos Index:

The image below is a view of the model developed in this tutorial.

Cutaway view of project created from scratch by reader! Notice the walls, windows, curtain wall, doors, cabinets, roof, floors, ceilings, furniture, structure, electrical and HVAC elements.

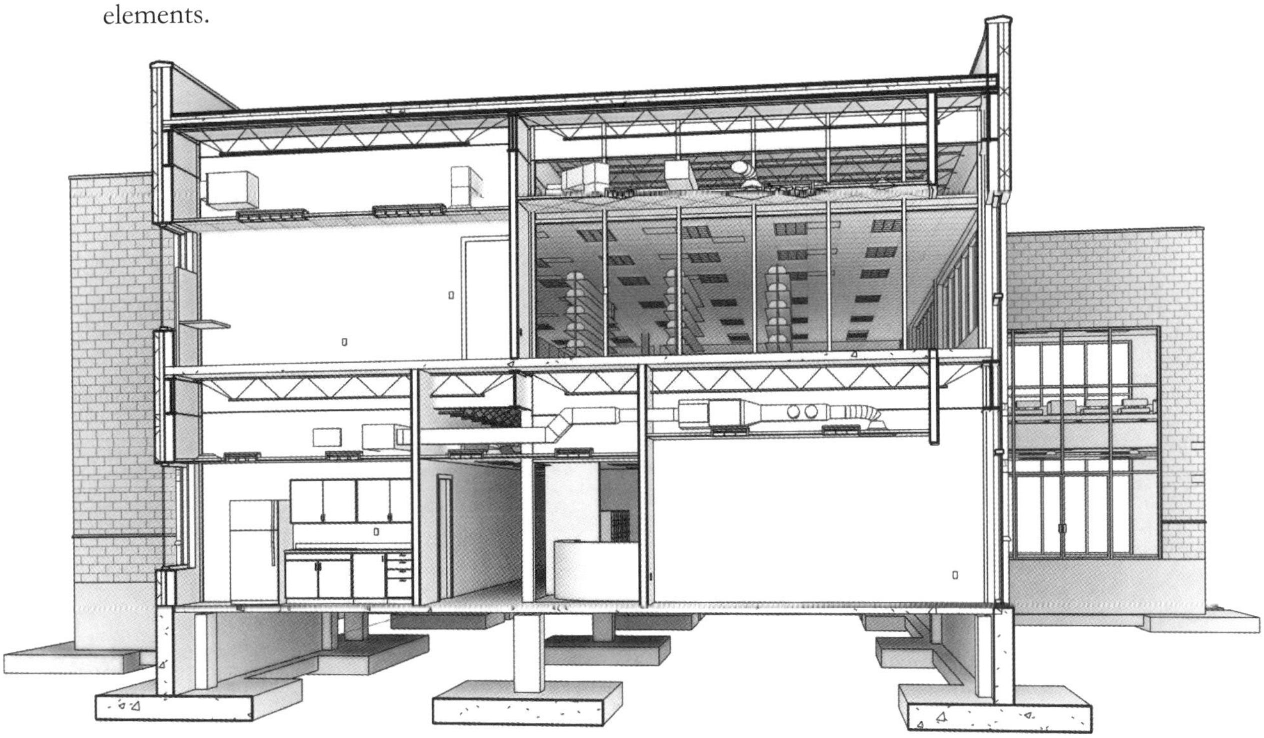

Notes:

Lesson 1
Getting Started with Autodesk Revit:

This chapter will introduce you to Autodesk® Revit®. You will study the User Interface and learn how to open and exit a project, and adjust the drawing view on the screen. It is recommended that you spend an ample amount of time learning this material, as it will greatly enhance your ability to progress smoothly through subsequent chapters.

Exercise 1-1:
What is Revit?

What is Autodesk Revit used for?

Autodesk Revit (Architecture, Structure, and MEP) is the world's first fully parametric building design software. This revolutionary software, for the first time, truly takes architectural computer-aided design beyond simply being a high-tech pencil. Revit is a product of Autodesk, makers of AutoCAD, Civil 3D, Forma, Inventor, 3DS Max, Maya, and many other popular design programs.

Revit can be thought of as the foundation of a larger process called **Building Information Modeling** (BIM). The BIM process revolves around a virtual, information-rich 3D model. In this model, all major building elements are represented and include information such as manufacturer, model, cost, phase, and more. Once a model has been developed in Revit, third-party add-ins and applications can be used to further leverage the data. Some examples are Facilities Management, Analysis (e.g., energy, wind, structural, and lighting), Construction Sequencing, Cost Estimating, Code Compliance, and much more!

Revit can be an invaluable tool to designers when leveraged to its full potential. The iterative design process can be implemented using specialized Revit features, such as *Phasing* and *Design Options*. Material selections can be developed and attached to various elements in the model, allowing a single change to switch the wood from oak to maple throughout the project. The power of (live) schedules may be used to accurately determine quantities and document various parameters contained within content (this is the "I" in BIM, which stands for Information). Finally, the three-dimensional nature of a Revit-based model allows the designer to present compelling visualizations, including still images and animations. These graphics help to more clearly communicate the design intent to clients and stakeholders. This book will cover many of these tools and techniques to **assist** in the creative process.

What is a parametric building modeler?

Revit is a program designed from the ground up to be a parametric architectural design platform. The term parametric describes a process by which an element is modified, and an adjacent element(s) is automatically modified to maintain a previously established relationship. For example, if a wall is moved, perpendicular walls will lengthen or shorten to remain attached to the related wall. Additionally, elements attached to the wall will move, such as wall cabinets, doors, windows, and air grilles.

Revit stands for **Rev**ise **Inst**antly; a change made in one view is automatically updated in all other views, schedules, and sheets. For example, if you move a door in an interior elevation view, the floor plan will automatically update. Or, if you delete a door, it will be deleted from all other views and schedules.

A major goal of Revit is to eliminate many of the repetitive and mundane tasks traditionally associated with CAD programs, allowing more time for design, coordination, and visualization. For example, all sheet numbers, elevation tags, and reference bubbles are automatically updated when they are changed anywhere in the project. Therefore, it is difficult to find a mis-referenced detail tag.

The best way to understand how a parametric model works is to describe the Revit project file. A single Revit file contains your entire building project. Even though you mostly draw in 2D views, you are actually drawing in 3D. In fact, the entire building project is a 3D model. From this 3D model, Revit generates (live) 2D elevations, 2D sections, and perspective views. Therefore, when you delete a door in an elevation view, you are actually deleting it from the 3D model, from which all 2D views are generated and automatically updated.

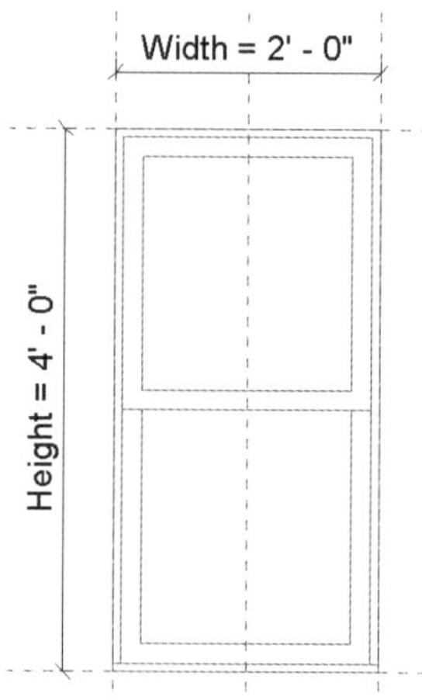

Window model size controlled by parameters *Width* and *Height*

Another way in which Revit is a parametric building modeler is that **parameters** can be used to control the size and shape of geometry. For example, a window model can have two *parameters* that control the window's size. Thus, from a window's properties, it is possible to control the size of the window without using any of Revit's modify tools, such as *Scale* or *Move*. Furthermore, the *parameter* settings (i.e., width and height in this example) can be saved within the window model (called a *Family*). You could have the 2′ x 4′ settings saved as "Type A" and the 2′ x 6′ as "Type B." Each saved list of values is called a *Type* within the *Family*. Thus, this one double-hung window *Family* could represent an unlimited number of rectangular window sizes! You will learn more about this later in the book.

What Disciplines does Revit Support?

Revit supports **Architecture, Interior Design, Structure**, and **MEP** (Mechanical, Electrical, and Plumbing). You can download the free trial from autodesk.com. Students may download a free, renewable 1-year version of Revit and other Autodesk products at www.autodesk.com/education.

Revit is not meant to support professional site design. Civil engineers and surveyors use tools such as Autodesk AutoCAD Civil 3D for accurate site grading, road and parking lot design, and related documentation.

Now is as good a time as any to make sure the reader understands that Revit is not, and has never been, backward compatible. This means there is no *Save As* option to revert to a previous version of Revit. Also, an older version of Revit cannot open a file, project, or family saved in a newer format. So, make sure you consider what version your school or employer is currently standardized on before upgrading any projects or content. Revit will automatically upgrade an older format when opened in a newer version of the software. This is a one-time process that can take several minutes.

Revit model of an existing building, with architecture, structural, mechanical, plumbing and electrical all modeled.
Image courteous of LHB, Inc. www.LHBcorp.com

3D model of lunchroom created in *Interior Design Using Autodesk Revit by Stine*

Download Autodesk Content

Content originally provided with Revit, such as doors, windows, toilets, etc., is no longer downloaded to your hard drive during the software installation. Instead, the content is downloaded as needed from the **Insert → Load Autodesk Family** tool. An internet connection will be required to place content. Optionally, all content may be downloaded, see: https://autode.sk/30EJYkX

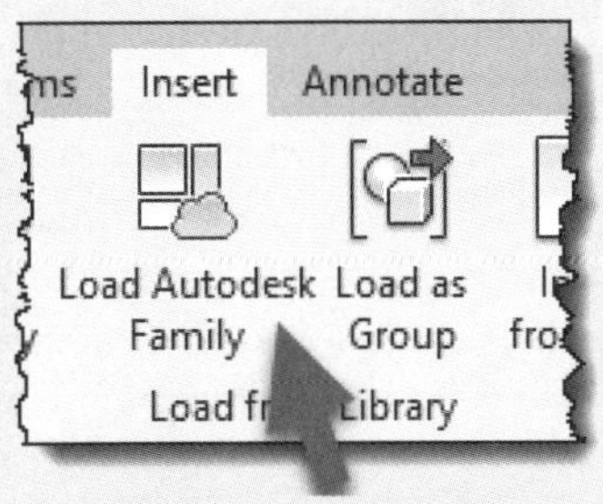

Lobby rendering from *Interior Design Using Autodesk Revit*

Why use Revit?

Many people ask, "Why use Revit versus other programs?" The answer can certainly vary depending on the situation and particular needs of an individual or organization.

Generally speaking, this is why most companies use Revit:

- Many designers and drafters are using Revit to streamline repetitive drafting tasks and focus more on designing and detailing a project.
- Revit is a widely used program and offers many features for designing buildings. Revit is constantly being developed, and Autodesk provides incremental upgrades and patches regularly; Revit 2027 was released about a year after the previous version.
- Multiple firms can collaborate and coordinate closely in Revit. The models can also be hosted in the cloud, via Autodesk Forma (previously BIM 360).
- Revit was designed specifically for architectural design and includes features like:
    - *Autodesk Renderer* Photo Realistic Rendering
    - Phasing: model changes over time
    - Design Options: model changes during the same time period
    - Live schedules
    - Cloud Rendering via *Autodesk cloud services*
    - Conceptual Energy Analysis via *Autodesk cloud services*
    - Daylighting Analysis via *Autodesk cloud services*

A few basic Revit concepts

The following is a brief overview of the basic organization of Revit as a software application. You should not get too hung up on these concepts and terms, as they will make more sense as you work through the tutorials in this book. This discussion is simply laying the groundwork, so you have a general frame of reference on how Revit works.

The Revit platform has three fundamental types of elements:

- Model Elements
- Datum Elements
- View-Specific Elements

Model Elements

Think of *Model Elements* as things you can put your hands on once the building has been constructed. They are typically 3D but can sometimes be 2D. There are two types of *Model Elements*:

- **Host Elements**: walls, floors, slabs, roofs, ceilings.

- **Model Components**: Stairs, Doors, Furniture, Casework, Beams, Columns, Pipes, Ducts, Light Fixtures, Model Lines, etc.

    - Some *Model Components* require a host before they can be placed within a project. For example, a window can only be placed in a host, which could be a wall, roof, or floor, depending on how the element was created. If the host is deleted, all hosted or dependent elements are automatically deleted.

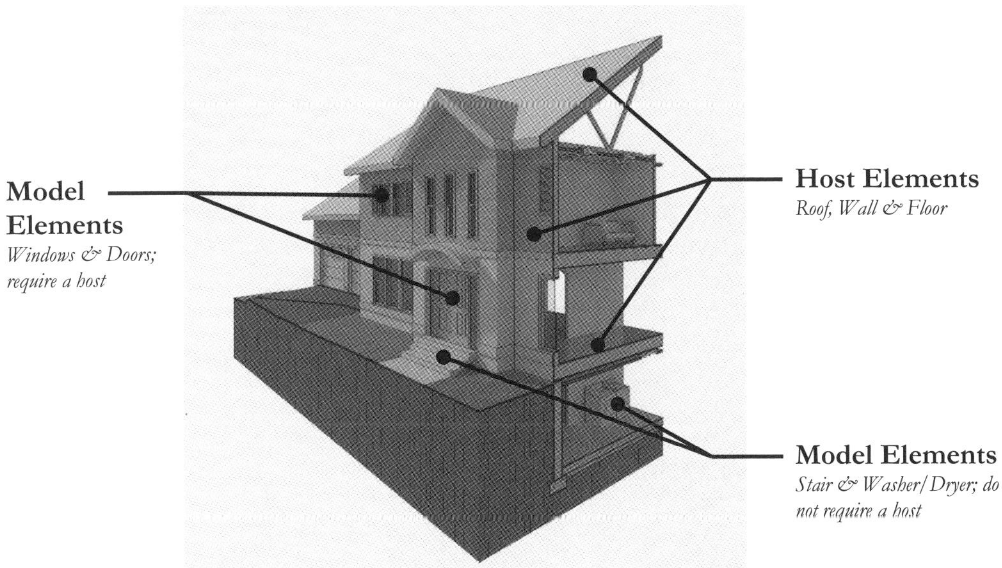

Datum Elements

Datum Elements are reference planes within the building that graphically and parametrically define the location of various elements within the model. These are the three types of *Datum Elements,* all of which define 3D planes:

- **Grids**
  - Typically laid out in a plan view to locate structural elements such as columns and beams, as well as walls. Grids show up in plan, elevation, and section views. Moving a grid in one view moves it in all other views, as it is the same element. (See the next page for an example of a grid in plan view.)
- **Levels**
  - Used to define vertical relationships, mainly surfaces that you walk on. They only show up in elevation, section, and 3D views. Most elements are placed relative to a *Level*; when the *Level* is moved, those elements move with it (e.g., doors, windows, casework, ceilings).
- **Reference Planes**
  - These are similar to grids in that they show up in plan, elevation, or sections. They do not have reference bubbles at the end like grids. Revit breaks many tasks down into simple 2D tasks, which result in 3D geometry. *Reference Planes* are used to define 2D surfaces on which to work within the 3D model. They can be placed in any view, horizontally, vertically, or at an angle.

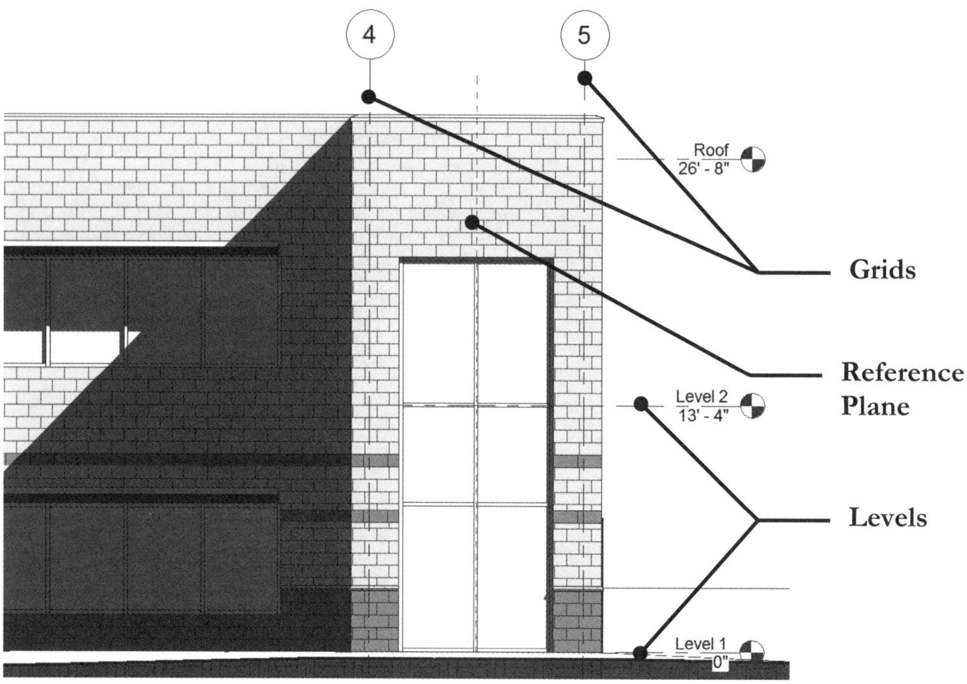

View-Specific Elements

As the name implies, the items about to be discussed only show up in the specific view in which they are created. For example, notes and dimensions added to the architectural floor plans will not appear in the structural floor plans. These elements are all 2D and primarily serve as communication tools to accurately document the building for construction or presentations.

- **Annotation elements** (text, tags, symbols, dimensions)
    - Size automatically set and changed based on selected view scale
- **Details** (detail lines, filled regions, 2D detail components)

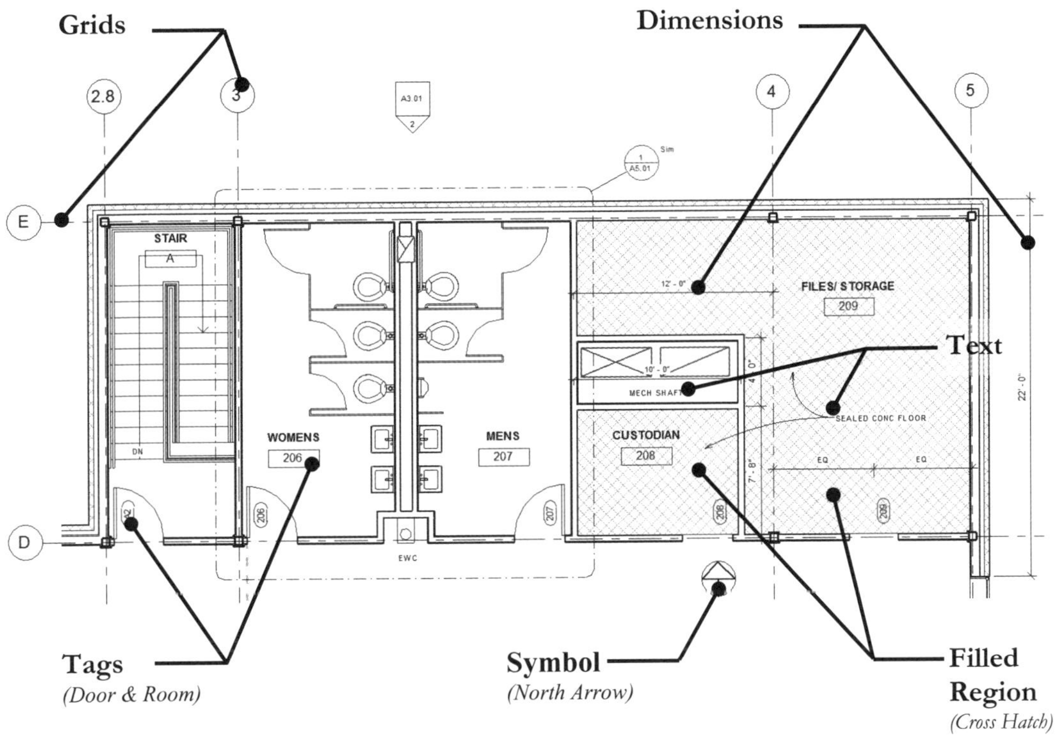

> **File Types (and extensions):**
> Revit has four primary file types that you will work with as a Revit user. Each file type, as with any Microsoft Windows-based program, has a specific three-letter file name extension; that is, after the name of the file on your hard drive, you will see a period and three letters:
>
> | | |
> |---|---|
> | .RVT | Revit project files; the file most used (also for backup files) |
> | .RFA | Revit family file; loadable content for your project |
> | .RTE | Revit template; a project starter file with office standards preset |
> | .RFT | Revit family template; a family starter file with parameters |

The Revit platform has three fundamental ways in which to work with the elements (for display and manipulation):

- Views
- Schedules
- Sheets

The following is a cursory overview of the main ideas you need to know. This is not an exhaustive study on views, schedules, and sheets.

Views

Views, accessible from the *Project Browser*, are where most work is done in Revit. Think of views as slices through the building, both horizontal (plans) and vertical (elevations and sections).

- **Plans**
  - A *Plan View* is a horizontal slice through the building. You can specify the location of the **cut plane**, which determines if certain windows show up or how much of the stair is seen. A few examples are architectural floor plan, reflected ceiling plan, site plan, structural framing plan, HVAC floor plan, electrical floor plan, lighting [ceiling] plan, etc. The images below show this concept; the image on the left is the 3D BIM. The middle image shows the portion of the building above the cut plane removed. Finally, the last image on the right shows the plan view in which you work and place on a sheet.

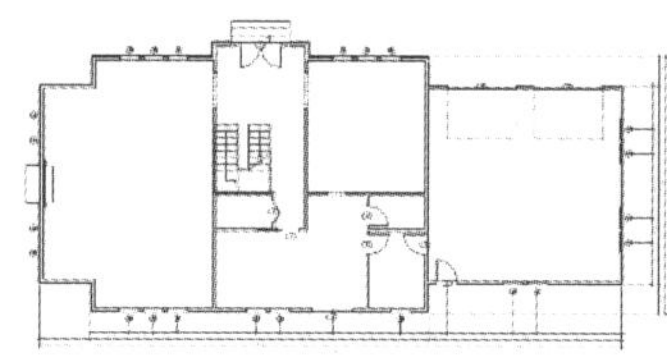

- **Elevations**
  - An "exterior" elevation is a vertical slice, but where the slice lies outside the floor plan, as in the middle image below. Each elevation created is listed in the *Project Browser*. The image on the right is an example of a South exterior elevation view, which is a "live" view of the 3D model. If you select a window here and delete it, the floor plans will update instantly.

  - Similarly, an "interior" elevation is a vertical slice, but inside the building. This interior view is cropped at the perimeter of a given room.

- **Sections**
  - Similar to elevations, sections are also vertical slices. However, these slices cut through the building. A section view can be cropped down to become a wall section or even look just like an elevation. The images below show the slice, the portion of the building in the foreground removed, and then the actual view created by the slice. A setting exists for each section view to control how far into that view you can see. The example on the right is "seeing" deep enough to show the doors on the interior walls.

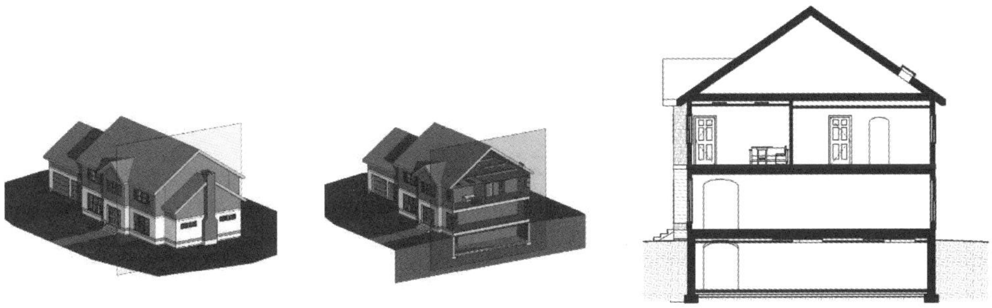

- **3D and Camera**
  - In addition to the traditional "flattened" 2D views that you will typically work in, you are able to see your designs more naturally via 3D and Camera views. A 3D view is simply an orthogonal view of the project viewed from the exterior. A Camera view is a perspective view; cameras can be created both inside and outside of the building. Like the 2D views, these 3D/Camera views can be placed on a sheet for printing and presenting. Revit provides a number of tools to help explore the 3D view, such as Section Box, Steering Wheel, Temporary Hide and Isolate, and Render.

    The image on the left is a 3D view in "shade mode" with shadows enabled. The image on the right is a camera view set up inside the building; the view is set to "hidden line" rather than shaded, and the camera is at eye level.

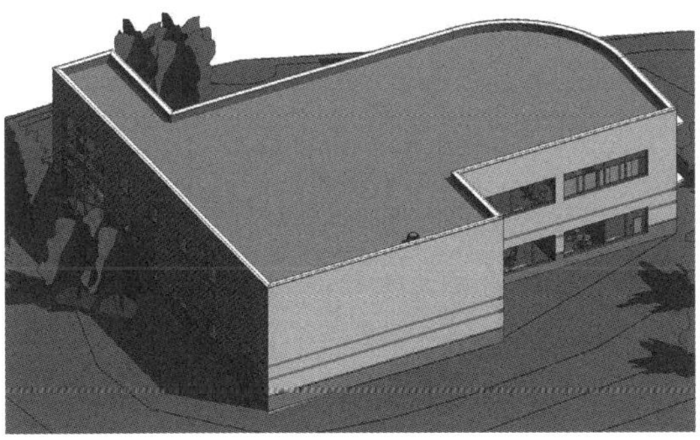
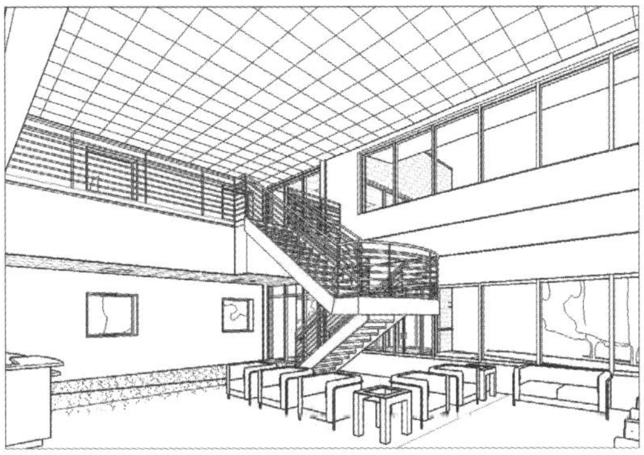

Schedules

Schedules are lists of information generated from content placed or modeled within the project. A schedule can be created, such as the door schedule shown below, that lists selected data for each door in the project. Revit allows you to work directly in the schedule views. Any change in a schedule view is applied directly to the element being scheduled. Again, if a door were deleted from this schedule, it would be instantly removed from the project.

DOOR AND FRAME SCHEDULE													
DOOR NUMBER	DOOR				FRAME		DETAIL			GLAZING	FIRE RATING	HDWR GROUP	
	WIDTH	HEIGHT	MATL	TYPE	MATL	TYPE	HEAD	JAMB	SILL				
1000A	3' - 8"	7' - 2"	WD		HM		11/A8.01	11/A8.01					
1046	3' - 0"	7' - 2"	WD	D10	HM	F10	11/A8.01	11/A8.01 SIM				34	
1047A	6' - 0"	7' - 10"	ALUM	D15	ALUM	SF4	6/A8.01	6/A8.01	1/A8.01 SIM	1" INSUL		2	CARD READER N. LEAF
1047B	8' - 0"	7' - 2"	WD	D10	HM	F13	12/A8.01	11/A8.01 SIM			60 MIN	85	MAG HOLD OPENS
1050	3' - 0"	7' - 2"	WD	D10	HM	F21	8/A8.01	11/A8.01		1/4" TEMP		33	
1051	3' - 0"	7' - 2"	WD	D10	HM	F21	8/A8.01	11/A8.01		1/4" TEMP		33	
1052	3' - 0"	7' - 2"	WD	D10	HM	F21	8/A8.01	11/A8.01		1/4" TEMP		33	
1053	3' - 0"	7' - 2"	WD	D10	HM	F21	8/A8.01	11/A8.01		1/4" TEMP		33	
1054A	3' - 0"	7' - 2"	WD	D10	HM	F10	8/A8.01	11/A8.01		1/4" TEMP	-	34	
1054B	3' - 0"	7' - 2"	WD	D10	HM	F21	8/A8.01	11/A8.01		1/4" TEMP	-	33	
1055	3' - 0"	7' - 2"	WD	D10	HM	F21	8/A8.01	11/A8.01		1/4" TEMP	-	33	
1056A	3' - 0"	7' - 2"	WD	D10	HM	F10	9/A8.01	9/A8.01			20 MIN	33	
1056B	3' - 0"	7' - 2"	WD	D10	HM	F10	11/A8.01	11/A8.01			20 MIN	34	
1056C	3' - 0"	7' - 2"	WD	D10	HM	F10	20/A8.01	20/A8.01			20 MIN	33	
1057A	3' - 0"	7' - 2"	WD	D10	HM	F10	8/A8.01	11/A8.01			20 MIN	34	
1057B	3' - 0"	7' - 2"	WD	D10	HM	F30	9/A8.01	9/A8.01		1/4" TEMP	20 MIN	33	
1058A	3' - 0"	7' - 2"	WD	D10	HM	F10	9/A8.01	9/A8.01			-	33	

Sheets

You can think of sheets as the pieces of paper on which your views and schedules will be printed. Views and schedules are placed on sheets and then arranged. Once a view has been placed on a sheet, its reference bubble is automatically filled out, and that view cannot be placed on any other sheet. The setting for each view, called "view scale," controls the size of the drawing on each sheet; it also controls the size of text and dimensions.

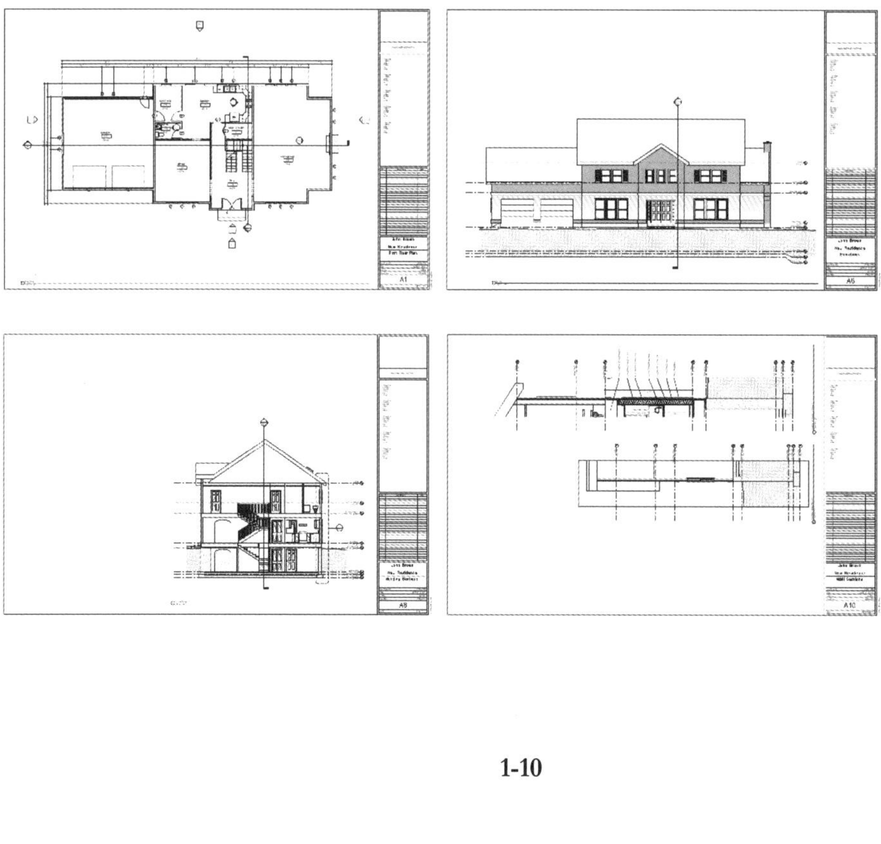

Exercise 1-2:
Overview of the Revit User Interface

Revit is a powerful and sophisticated program. Because of its robust feature set, it has a measurable learning curve, though its intuitive design makes it easier to learn than other CAD-based programs. However, like most things, when broken down into smaller pieces, we can easily learn to harness the power of Revit. That is the goal of this book.

This section will walk through the different aspects of the User Interface (UI). As with any program, understanding the user interface is key to using its features.

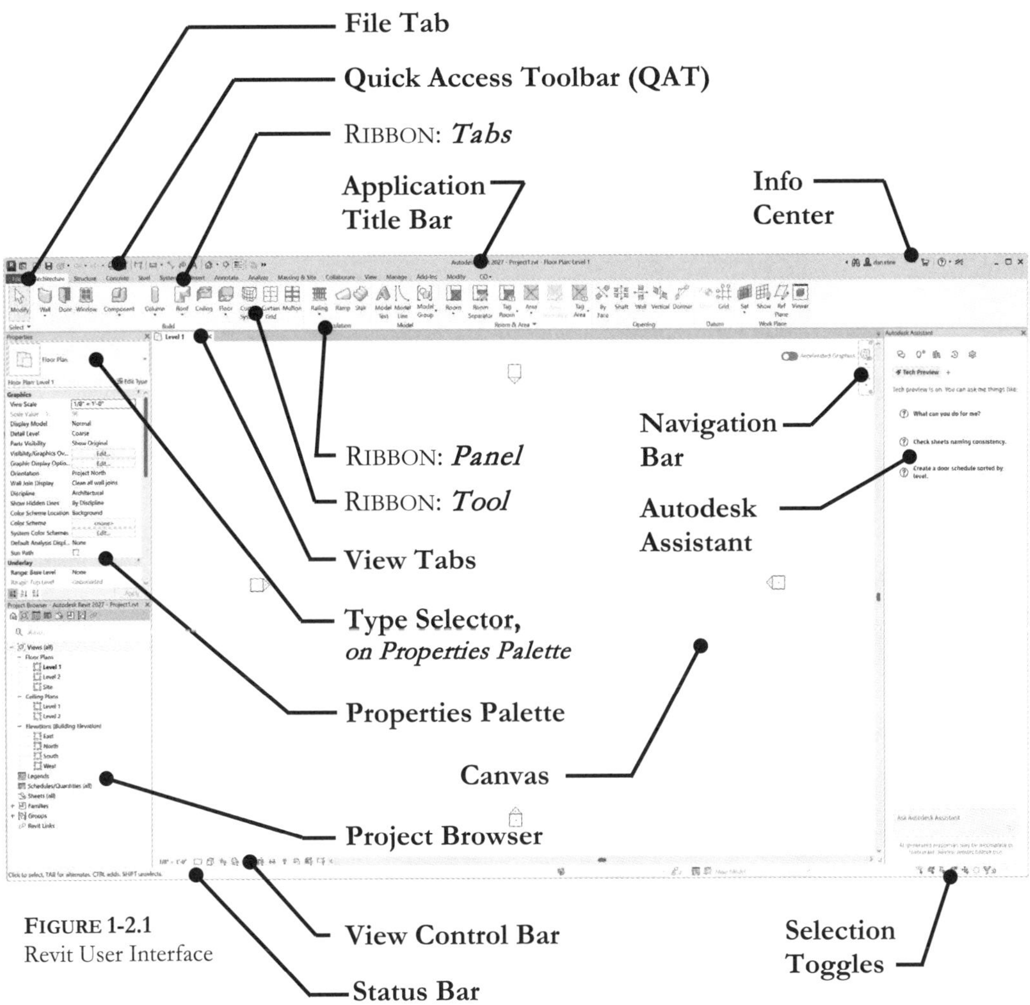

FIGURE 1-2.1
Revit User Interface

The Revit User Interface

TIP: See the online videos on the User Interface.

Application Title Bar

In addition to the *Quick Access Toolbar* and *Info Center*, which are covered in the next few sections, you are also presented with the product name, version, and the current file & view name in the center. As previously noted, the version is important as you do not want to upgrade unless you have coordinated with other staff and/or consultants; everyone must be using the same version of Revit.

File Tab

Access to *File* tools such as *Save*, *Plot*, *Export,* and *Print* (both hardcopy and electronic printing). You also have access to tools that control the Revit application as a whole, not just the current project, such as *Options* (see the end of this section for more on *Options*).

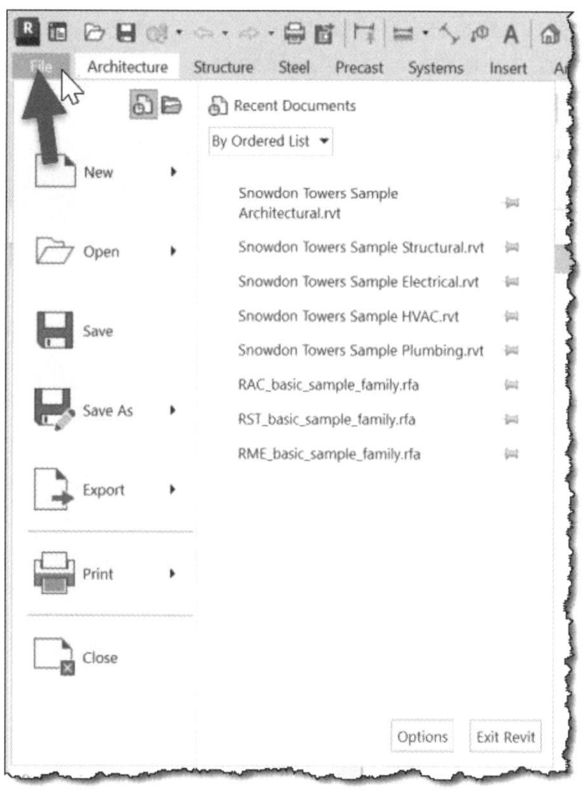

Recent and Open Documents:

These two icons (from the *File tab*) toggle the entire area on the right to show either the recent documents you have been in (icon on the left) or a list of the documents you currently have open.

In the *Recent Documents* list, you click a listed document to open it. This saves time as you do not have to click *Open* → *Project* and browse for the document (*Document* and *Project* mean the same thing here). Finally, clicking the "Pin" icon keeps that project from dropping off the list as additional projects are opened.

In the *Open Documents* list, the "active" project you are working in is listed first; clicking another project switches you to that open project.

The list on the left, in the *File Tab* shown on the previous page, represents three different types of buttons: *button, drop-down button,* and *split button.* Save and Close are simply **buttons**. Save-As and Export are **drop-down buttons** that reveal a group of related tools. If you click or hover your cursor over one of these buttons, you will get a list of tools on the right. Finally, **split buttons** have two actions depending on which part of the button you click on; hovering over the button reveals the two parts (see the bottom image to the right). The main area is the most used tool; the arrow reveals additional related options.

Button

Drop-down Button

Split Button

Quick Access Toolbar

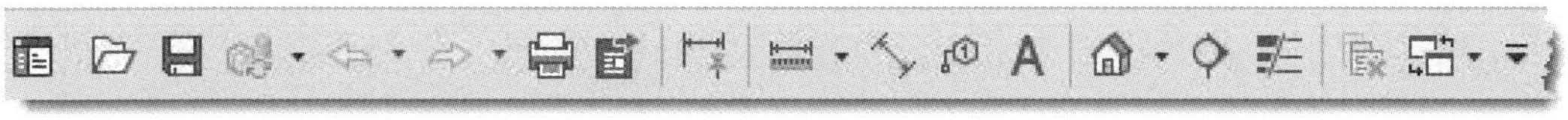

Referred to as *QAT* in this book, this single toolbar provides access to often used tools (Home, *Open, Save, Undo, Redo, Measure, Tag,* etc.). It is always visible regardless of what part of the *Ribbon* is active.

The *QAT* can be positioned above or below the *Ribbon,* and any command from the *Ribbon* can be added to it; simply right-click any tool on the *Ribbon* and select *Add to Quick Access Toolbar.* Moving the *QAT* below the *Ribbon* gives you much more room to add your favorite commands from the *Ribbon.* Clicking the larger down-arrow to the far right reveals a list of common tools that can be toggled on and off.

The first icon returns to the Home screen shown when Revit first opens. Some icons on the QAT have a down arrow on the right, which, when clicked, reveals a list of related tools. In the case of *Undo* and *Redo*, you can undo (or redo) several actions at once.

Ribbon – Architecture Tab

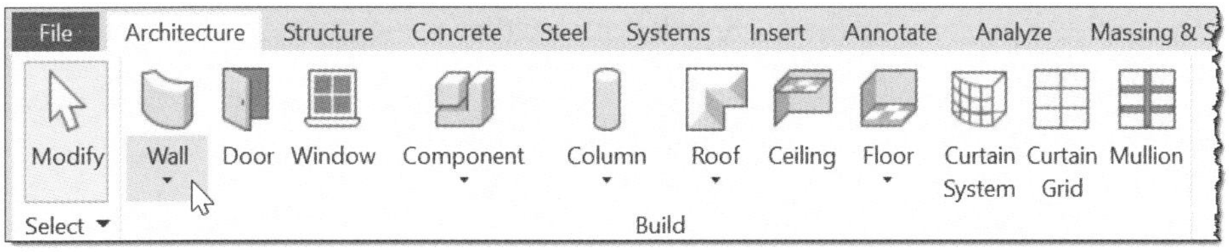

The *Architecture* tab on the *Ribbon* contains most of the tools the architect needs to model a building, essentially the things you can put your hands on when the building is done.

Each tab starts with the *Modify* tool, i.e., the first button on the left. This tool puts you into “selection mode,” allowing you to select elements to modify. Clicking this tool cancels any active command and unselects elements. With the *Modify* tool selected, you may select elements to view their properties or edit them. Note that the *Modify* tool, which is a button, is different than the *Modify* tab on the *Ribbon.*

The *Ribbon* has three types of buttons: *button*, *drop-down button,* and *split*, as covered on the previous page. In the previous image, you can see that the *Wall* tool is a **split button**. Most of the time, you would simply click the top part of the button to draw a wall. Clicking the down-arrow part of the button, for the *Wall* tool example, gives you the option to draw a *Wall, a Structural Wall, a Wall by Face, a Wall Sweep, or* a *Reveal.*

***TIP:** The Model Text tool is only for placing 3D text in your model, not for adding notes!*

Ribbon – Annotate Tab

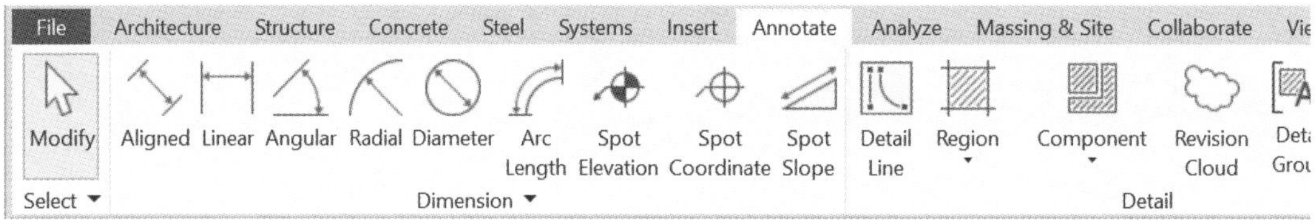

To view this tab, simply click the label "Annotate" near the top of the *Ribbon*. This tab presents a series of tools that allow you to add notes, dimensions, and 2D "embellishments" to your model in a specific view, such as a floor plan, elevation, or section. All of these tools are **view-specific**, meaning a note added in the first floor plan will not show up anywhere else, not even another first floor plan: for instance, a first floor electrical plan.

Notice in the image above that the Dimension panel label has a down arrow next to it. Clicking the down arrow reveals an **extended panel** with additional related tools.

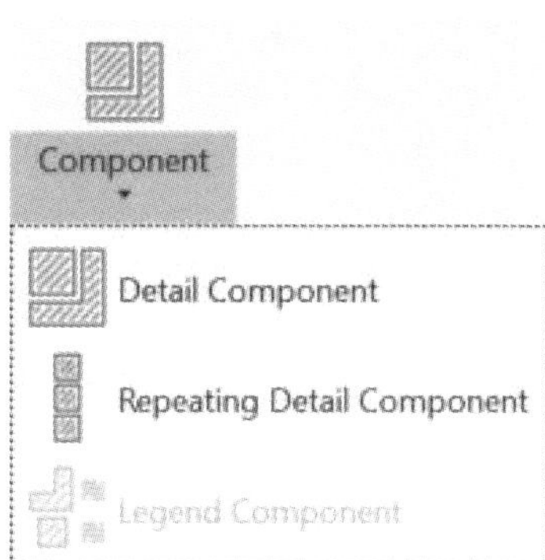

Finally, notice the *Component* tool in the image above; it is a **split button** rather than a *drop-down button*. Clicking the top part of this button will initiate the *Detail Component* tool. Clicking the bottom part of the button opens the fly-out menu, revealing related tools. Once you select an option from the fly-out, that tool becomes the default for the top part of the split button for the remainder of the current Revit session (see the image to the right).

Ribbon – Modify Tab

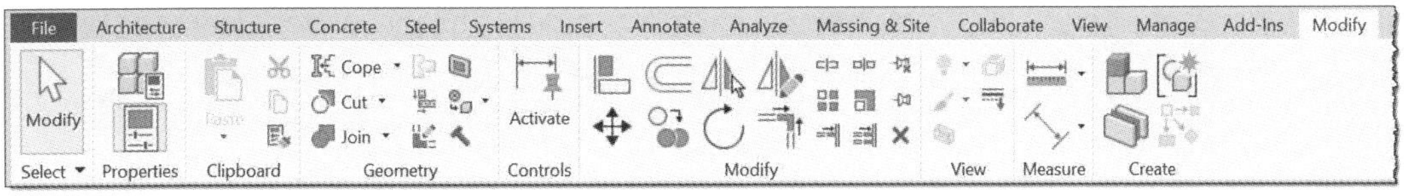

Several tools for manipulating and deriving information from the current model are available on the *Modify* tab. Additional *Modify* tools are automatically appended to this tab when elements are selected in the model (see *Modify Contextual Tab* on the next page).

TIP: Do not confuse the Modify tab with the Modify tool when following instructions in this book.

Ribbon – View Tab

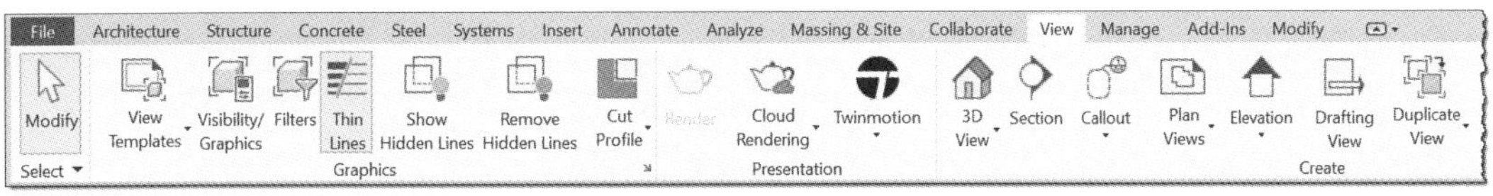

The tools on the *View* tab allow you to create new views of your 3D model, including 2D views (e.g., floor plans, elevations, and sections) and 3D views (e.g., isometric and perspective views).

The *View* tab also gives you tools to control how views look, including which elements are shown (e.g., Plumbing Fixture, Furniture, or Section Marks) and line weights.

NOTE: Line weights are controlled at a project-wide level but may be overridden.

Finally, notice the little arrow in the lower-right corner of the *Graphics* panel. When you see an arrow like this, you can click on it to open a dialog box with settings that relate to the panel's tool set (*Graphics* in this example). Hovering over the arrow reveals a tooltip that tells you which dialog box will be opened.

Ribbon – Modify Contextual Tab

The *Modify* tab is displayed when certain tools are active or elements are selected in the model; this is called a *contextual tab*. The first image below shows the *Place Wall* tab, which presents various options while adding walls. The next example shows the *Modify Walls* contextual tab, which is accessible when one or more walls are selected.

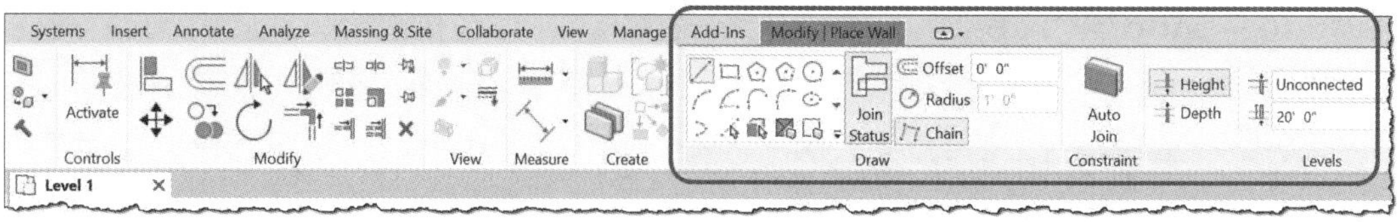

Place Wall contextual tab – visible when the Wall tool is active.

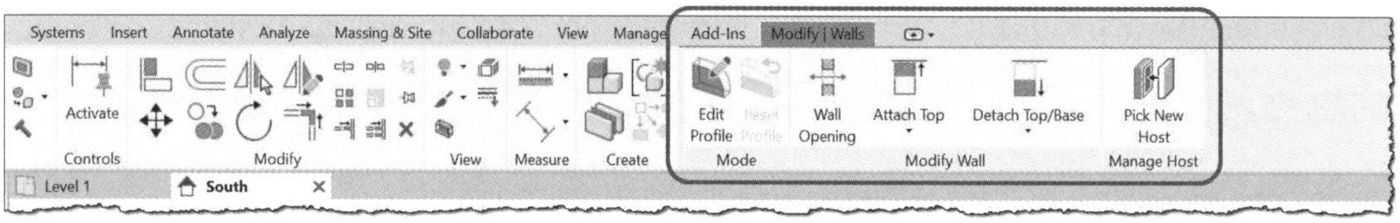

Modify Walls contextual tab – visible when a wall is selected.

Ribbon – Customization

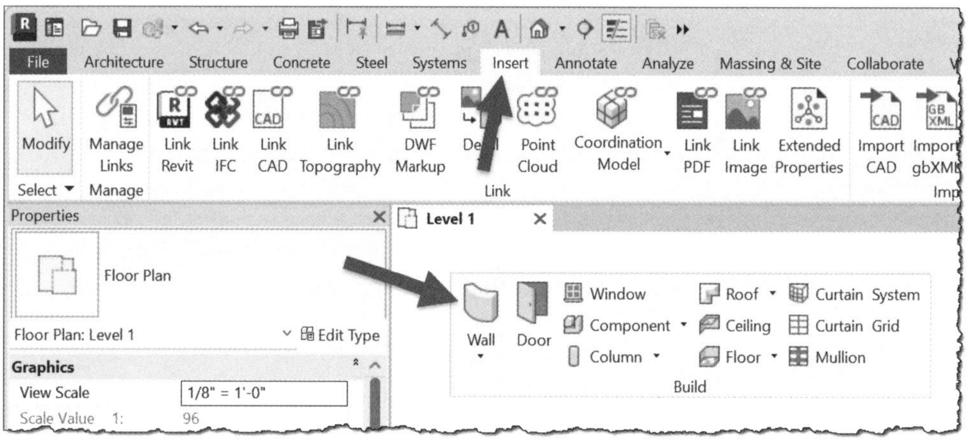

There isn't much customization that can be done to the *Ribbon*. One of the only things you can do is pull a panel off the *Ribbon* by clicking and holding down the left mouse button on the titles listed, e.g., "Link" or "Build," across the bottom. This panel can be placed within the *drawing window* or on another screen if you have a dual monitor setup.

The image above shows the *Build* panel, from the *Architecture* tab, detached from the *Ribbon* and floating within the drawing window. Notice that the *Insert* tab is active. Thus, you have constant access to the *Build* tools while accessing other tools. Note that the *Build* panel is not available on the *Architecture* tab as it is literally moved, not just copied.

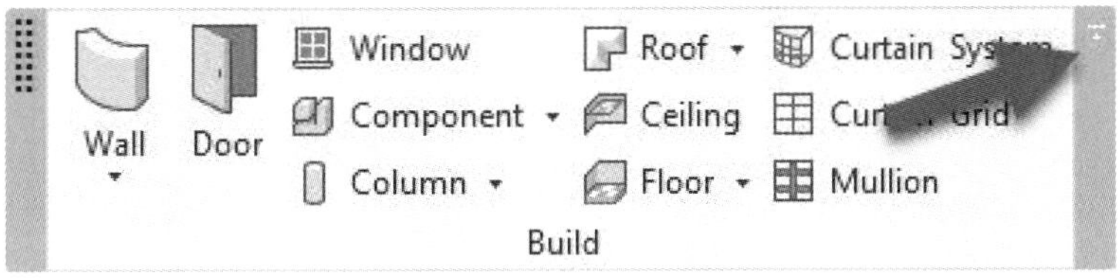

When you need to move a detached panel back to the *Ribbon,* do the following: hover over the detached panel until the sidebars appear, then click the "Return panels to ribbon" icon in the upper right (as shown in the image above). Panels cannot be moved to other tabs.

> ***FYI:*** *Whenever the resolution of your monitor is too low or you don't have the Revit application maximized on the screen, the buttons may be modified to take up less room on the Ribbon; typically, the words are removed. Compare the image to the right with the Build panel above.*
>
> 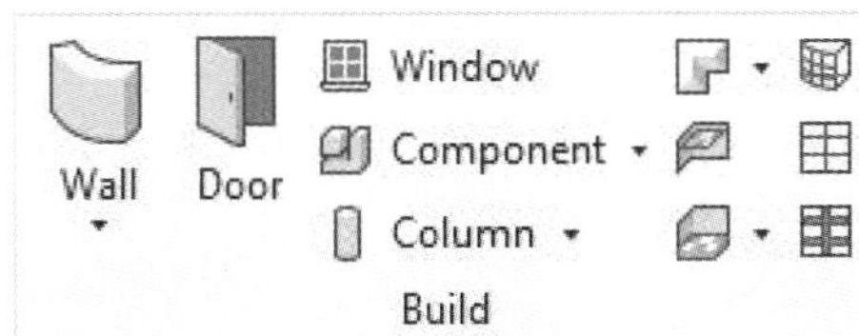
>

If you install a Revit add-in on your computer, you will likely see a new tab appear on the Ribbon. Some add-ins are free, while others require a subscription. If an add-in only has one tool, it will likely be added to the catch-all tab called Add-Ins (shown in the image below). Some firms have custom tools they developed, and may have their own tab, like LF Tools.

Tab Visibility

This is not really customizing the User Interface, but in the Options dialog, there are several adjustments one can make, such as turning off tabs and tools not used.

> **TIP:** When Revit is first opened, you are prompted to indicate your role, or what type of work you do. This will turn off tabs here.

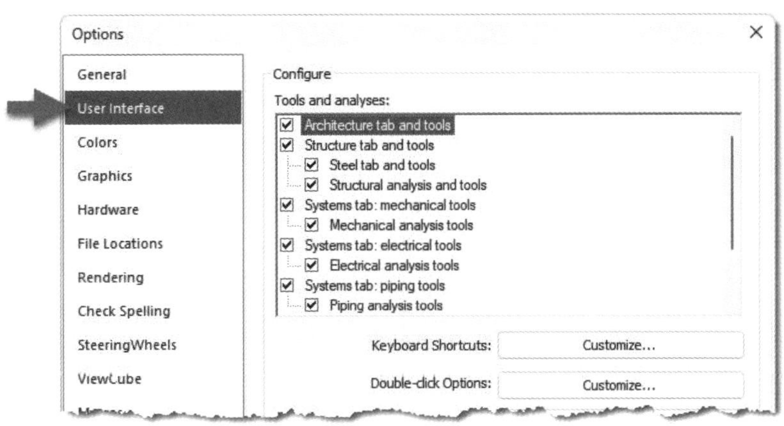

Ribbon – States

The *Ribbon* can be displayed in one of four states:

- Full Ribbon (default)
- Minimize to Tabs
- Minimize to Panel Tiles
- Minimize to Panel Buttons

The intent of this feature is to increase the size of the available drawing window. It is recommended, however, that you leave the *Ribbon* fully expanded while learning to use the program. The images in this book show the fully expanded state. The images below show the other three options. When using one of the minimized options, you simply hover (or click) your cursor over the Tab or Panel to temporarily reveal the tools.

FYI: Double-clicking on a Ribbon tab will also toggle the states.

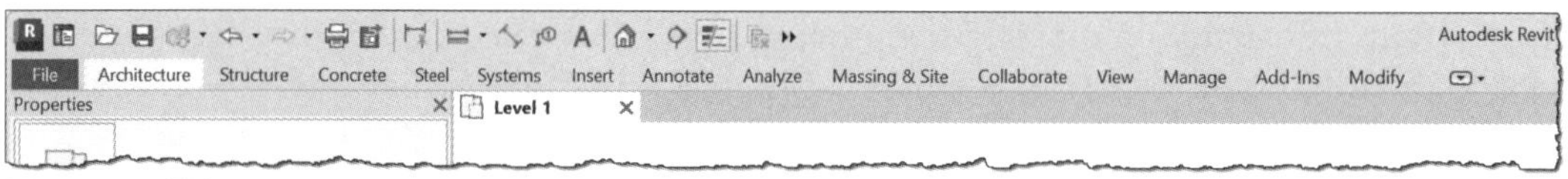

Minimize to Tabs

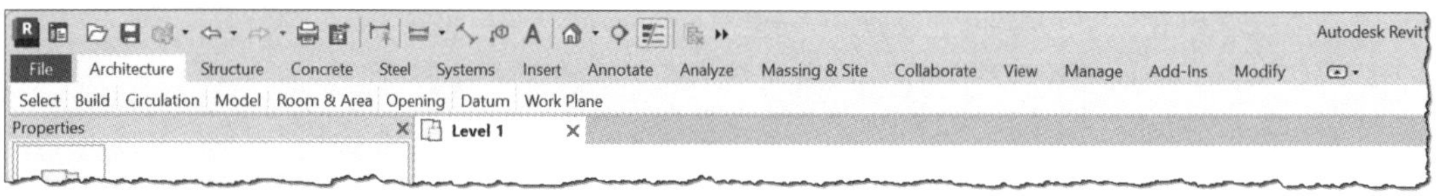

Minimize to Panel Tiles

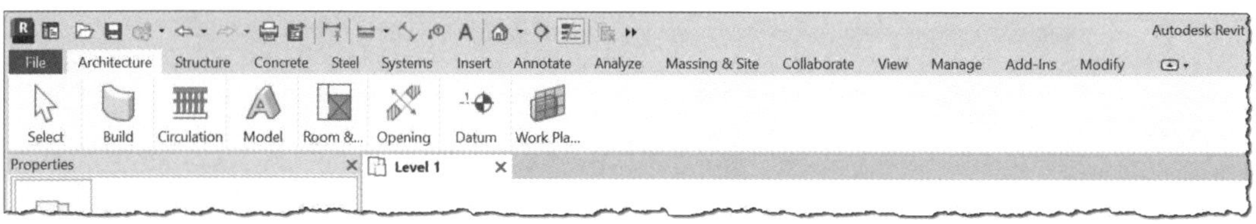

Minimize to Panel Buttons

> **Elevation Marker**
>
> This item is not actually part of the Revit UI but is visible in the drawing window by default through the various templates you can start with, so it's worth mentioning at this point. The four elevation markers point to each side of your project and ultimately indicate the drawing sheet where you'll find an elevation drawing of each side of the building. All you need to know right now is that you should generally place your building in the center of the four elevation markers shown in each plan view; DO NOT delete them, as doing so will remove the related view from the Project Browser.
>
> 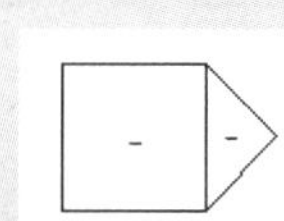

Ribbon – References in this Book

When the exercises refer to tools in the Ribbon, a consistent approach is used to eliminate unnecessary wording and save space. Take a moment to understand this so that things go smoothly for you later.

Throughout the textbook, you will see an instruction similar to the following:

23. Select **Architecture → Build → Wall**

This means click the ***Architecture*** tab, and within the ***Build*** panel, select the ***Wall*** tool. Note that the *Wall* tool is actually a split button, but a subsequent tool was not listed, so you are to click on the primary part of the button. Compare the above example to the one below:

23. Select **Architecture → Build → Wall → Structural Wall**

The above example shows that you should click the down arrow on the Wall tool to select the *Structural Wall* option.

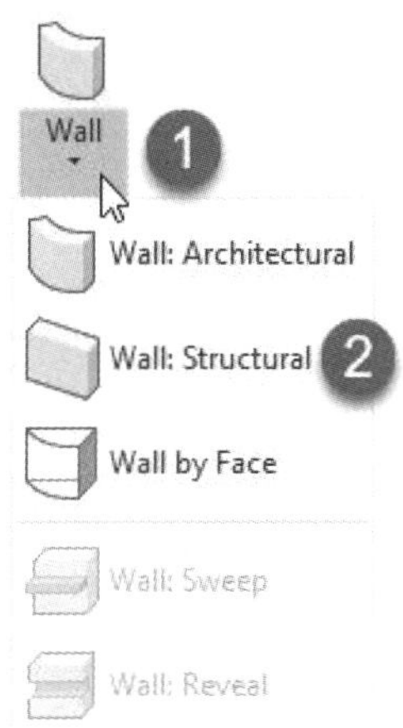

Thus, the general pattern is this:

Tab → Panel → Tool → drop-down list item

#1 *Tab:* This will get you to the correct area within the *Ribbon.*

#2 *Panel:* This will narrow down your search for the desired tool.

#3 *Tool:* Specific tool to select and use.

Drop-down list item: This is specified only for drop-down buttons and sometimes for split buttons.

The image below shows the order in which the instructions for selecting a tool are given; note that you do not actually click the panel title.

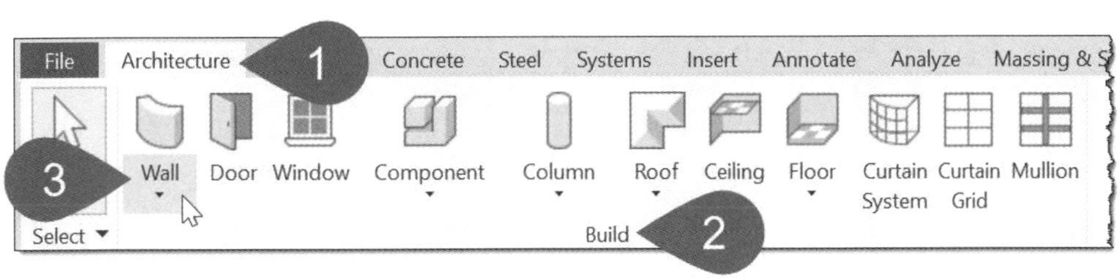

Options Bar

Note that the previous version of Revit had a contextual area just below the Ribbon, and above the View Tabs, called the Options Bar. This has been removed from Revit, and all related features have been moved to the Ribbon and/or Properties Palette.

Properties Palette – Element Type Selector

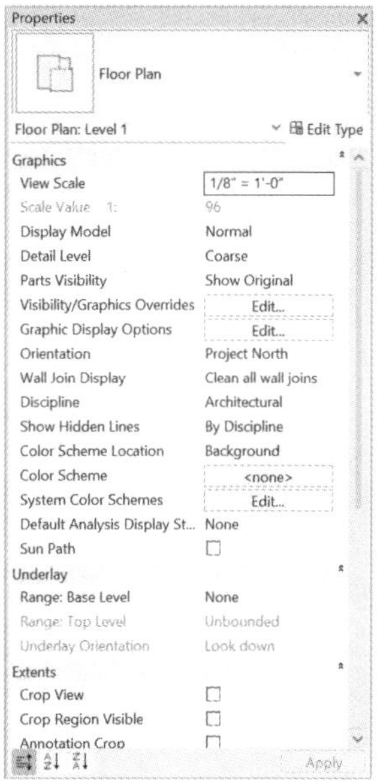

Properties Palette; nothing selected

The *Properties Palette* provides instant access to settings related to the element selected or about to be created. When nothing is selected, it shows information about the current view. When multiple elements are selected, the common parameters are displayed.

The *Element Type Selector* is an important part of the *Properties Palette.* Whenever you are adding elements or have them selected, you can select from this list to determine how a wall to be drawn will look, or how a wall previously drawn should look (see lower left image). If a wall type needs to change, you never delete it and redraw it; you simply select it and pick a new type from the *Type Selector.*

The **Selection Filter** drop-down list below the *Type Selector* shows the type and quantity of the currently selected elements. When multiple elements are selected, you can narrow the properties to a single element type (aka Category), such as *wall.* Notice that the image below shows seven doors are in the current selection set. Selecting **Doors (7)** will cause the *Palette* to only show *Door* properties, even though many other elements are selected (and remain selected).

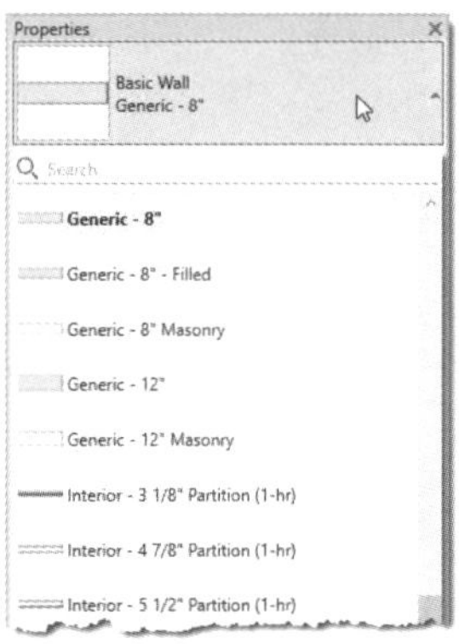

Type Selector; Wall tool active or a Wall is selected

Selection Filter; multiple elements selected

The width of the *Properties Palette* and the center column position can be adjusted by dragging the cursor over that area. You may need to do this at times to see all the information. However, making the *Palette* too wide will reduce the usable drawing area.

The *Properties Palette* should be left open; if you accidentally close it, you can reopen it by **View → Window → User Interface → Properties** or by typing **PP** on the keyboard.

Project Browser

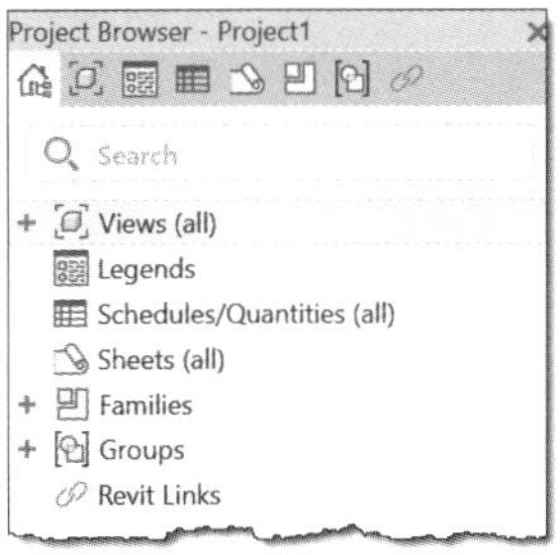

Primary nodes in project browser

The *Project Browser* is the "Grand Central Station" of the Revit project database. All the views, schedules, sheets, and content are accessible through this hierarchical list. The first image on the left shows the seven major categories; any item with a "plus" next to it contains subcategories or items (each with a filter icon across the top – Home is the default).

Double-clicking a View, Legend, Schedule, or Sheet opens it for editing; the current item open for editing is bold (**Level 1** in the example to the left). An empty box indicates the view is not placed on a sheet. Right-clicking displays a pop-up menu with options such as *Delete* and *Copy*.

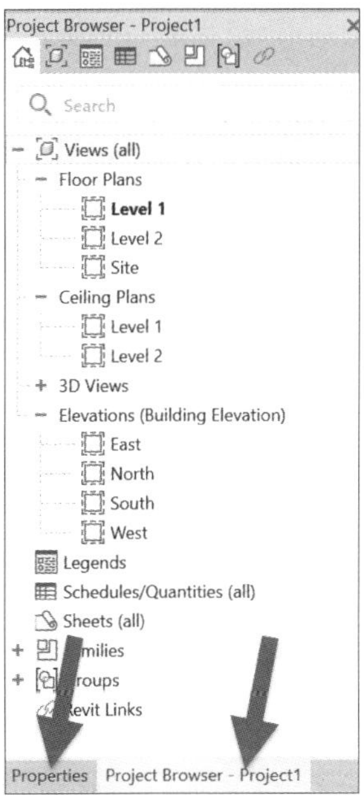

Alternative configuration

Right-click on *Views (all)*, at the top of the *Project Browser*, and you will find a **Search** option in the pop-up menu. This can be used to search for a *View*, *Family*, etc., a useful tool when working on a large project with 100s of items to sift through.

Like the *Properties Palette*, the width of the *Project Browser* can be adjusted. When the two are stacked above each other, they both move together. You can also stack the two directly on top of each other; in this case, you will see a tab for each at the bottom, as shown in the second image to the left.

The *Project Browser* should be left open; if you accidentally close it by clicking the "X" in the upper right, you can reopen it by

View → Window → User Interface → Project Browser.

The *Project Browser* and *Properties Palette* can be repositioned on a second monitor, if you have one, when you want more room to work in the drawing window.

Status Bar

This area will display, on the far left, information about the current command or list information about a selected element. The right-hand side of the *Status Bar* shows the number of elements selected. The small funnel icon to the left of the selection number can be clicked to open the *Filter* dialog box, which lets you narrow your current selection to a specific category; for example, you could select the entire floor plan and then filter it down to just the doors. This is different than the *Selection Filter* in the *Properties Palette,* which keeps everything selected.

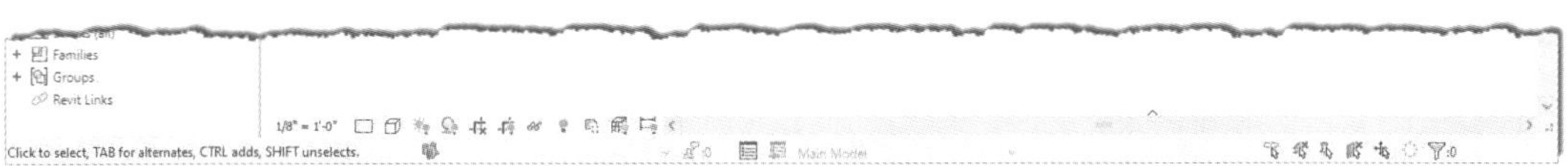

On the *Status Bar*, the first five icons on the right, shown in the image below, control how elements are **selected**. From left to right, these are:

- Select Links
- Select Underlay Elements
- Select Pinned Elements
- Select Elements by Face
- Drag Elements on Selection

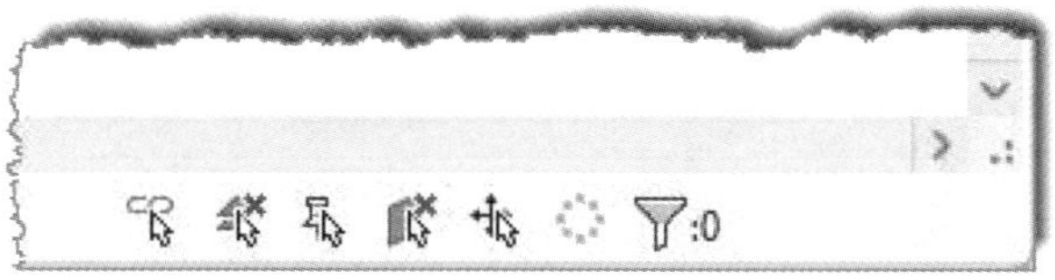

Hover your cursor over an icon for the name and for a brief description of what it does. These are toggles that are on or off; **the red 'X' in the upper right of each icon means you cannot select that type of element within the model**. These controls help prevent accidentally moving or deleting things. Keep these toggles in mind if you are having trouble selecting something; you may have accidentally toggled one of these on.

Finally, the two drop-down lists toward the center of the Status Bar control, Design Options and Worksets (see the image on the previous page). Design Options facilitate multiple design solutions in the same area, and *Worksets* enable more than one designer to be in the model at a time.

View Control Bar

This feature gives you convenient access to tools that control each view's display settings (e.g., scale, shadows, detail level, graphics style). The options vary slightly between view types: 2D view, 3D view, Sheet, and Schedule. The important thing to know is that these settings only affect the current view, the one listed on the *Application Title Bar*. Most of these settings are available in the *Properties Palette*, but this toolbar cannot be turned off (i.e., hidden) as the *Properties Palette* can.

Context Menu

The *context menu* appears near the cursor whenever you right-click (see image at right). The options on that menu will vary depending on what tool is active or what element is selected.

Canvas (aka Drawing Window)

This is where you manipulate the Building Information Model (BIM). Here you will see the current view (plan, elevation, or section), schedule, or sheet. Any changes made are instantly propagated to the entire database.

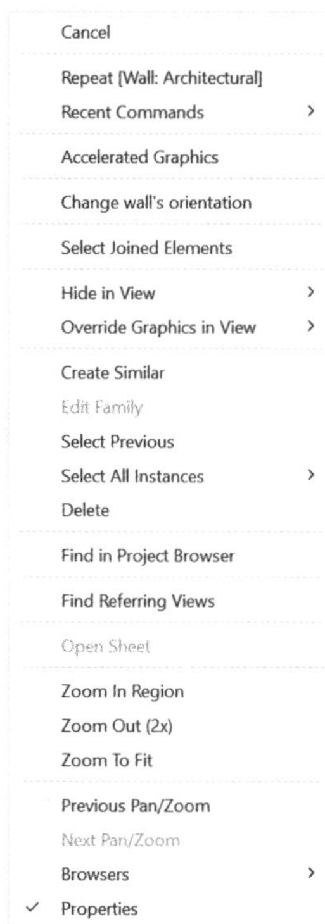

Context menu example with a wall selected

Autodesk Assistant (with Autodesk AI)

This feature has primarily been an advanced help feature across Autodesk products. But that changes significantly with the integration of **Autodesk AI**. While the early version of this AI tool offers model interrogation and some creation and editing options, the feature will surely enable significant advancements in creativity, efficiency, and accuracy within Revit specifically and the AEC industry in general. Remember, AI can make mistakes!

Example prompts:

- What can you do for me?
- Check sheets naming consistency
- Create a door schedule sorted by level

A summary of rooms was requested in the example shown here.

Revit Options

There are several User Interface settings that are not tied to the current model. That is, these settings apply to the installation of Revit on your computer, rather than to just one model or project file. A few of these settings will be briefly discussed here. It is recommended that you don't make any changes here right now.

Click on **Options** in the *File* tab. The options under File Locations specify where Revit finds templates and content. In the Hardware section, verify that your graphics card and display driver meet Autodesk's minimum requirements. If Revit is crashing or exhibits strange behavior, it often relates to your graphics driver. You can bypass this problem by turning off *Use Hardware Acceleration*, but this will make Revit run slower when panning and zooming.

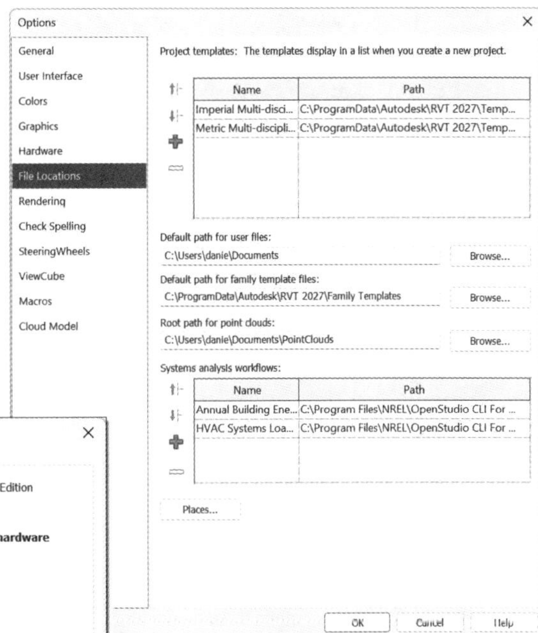

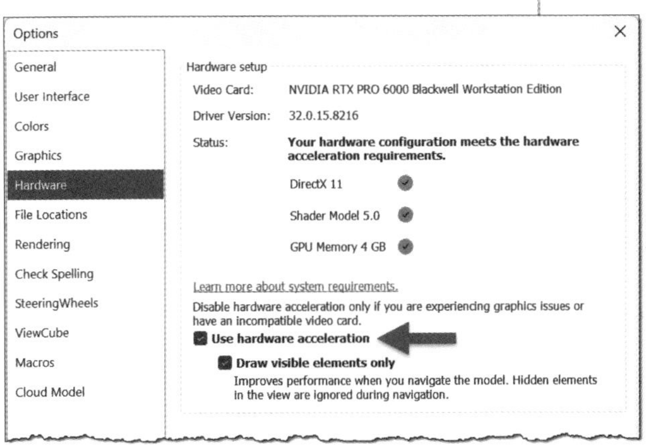

Efficient Practices

The *Ribbon* and menus are really helpful when learning a program like Revit; however, most experienced users rarely use them! The process of moving the mouse to the edge of the screen to select a command, then back to where you were, is very inefficient, especially for those who do this all day, five days a week. Here are a few ways experienced BIM operators work:

- Use the wheel on the mouse to Zoom (spin the wheel), Pan (press and hold the wheel button while moving the mouse), and Zoom Extents (double-clicking the wheel button). All this can be done while in another command; so, if you are in the middle of drawing walls and need to zoom in to see which point you are about to Snap to, you can do it without canceling the Line command and without losing focus on the area you are designing by having to click an icon near the edge of the screen.

- Revit conforms to many of the Microsoft Windows operating system standards. Most programs, including Revit, have several standard commands that can be accessed via keyboard shortcuts. Here are a few examples (press both keys at the same time):
    - Ctrl + S — Save — *(saves the current model)*
    - Ctrl + A — Select All — *(selects everything in the text editor)*
    - Ctrl + Z — Undo — *(undoes the previous action)*
    - Ctrl + X — Cut — *(Cut to Windows clipboard)*
    - Ctrl + C — Copy — *(does not replace Revit's Copy tool)*
    - Ctrl + V — Paste — *(used to copy between models/views/levels)*
    - Ctrl + Tab — Change View — *(toggles between open views)*
    - Ctrl + P — Print — *(opens print dialog)*
    - Ctrl + N — New — *(create new project file)*
    - F7 — Spelling — *(launch spell check feature)*
    - ENTER — Previous Command — *(repeat previous command)*

- If you recall, the *Open Documents* area, on the *File Tab,* lists all the views that are currently open on your computer. By clicking one of the names in the list, you "switch" to that view. A shortcut is to press **Ctrl + Tab** to quickly cycle through the open drawings.

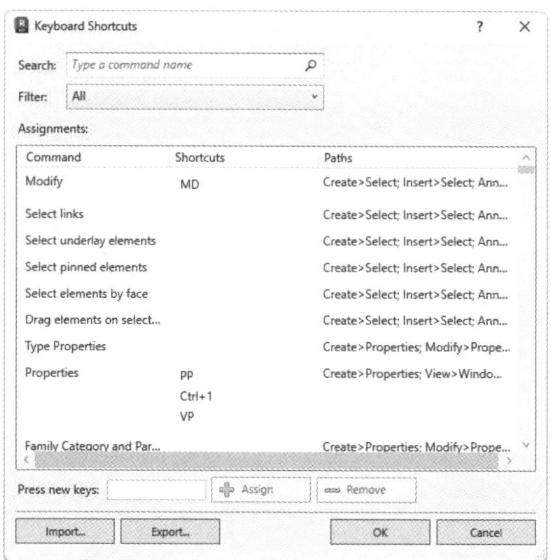

Keyboard shortcuts dialog

- Many Revit commands also have keyboard shortcuts. So, with your right hand on the mouse (and not moving from the "design" area), your left hand can type **WA** when you want to draw a Wall, for example. You can see all the preloaded shortcuts and add new ones by clicking *View (tab)* → *User Interface (drop-down)* → *Keyboard Shortcuts.*

It should be noted that any customized keyboard shortcuts are specific to the computer you are working on, not the project. You can use the *Export* button (see image to the right) to save the entire keyboard shortcuts list to a file, and then *Import* it into another computer's copy of Revit.

View Tabs

Revit displays a tab for each open view. Clicking a tab is a quick way to switch between open views. Click the "X" in each view tab to close that view. Drag a tab to change its position. Tabs can also be pulled outside of the main Revit application window – even to a second monitor. In the second image below, the schedule could be filling a second computer screen while reviewing the same information in the floor plan.

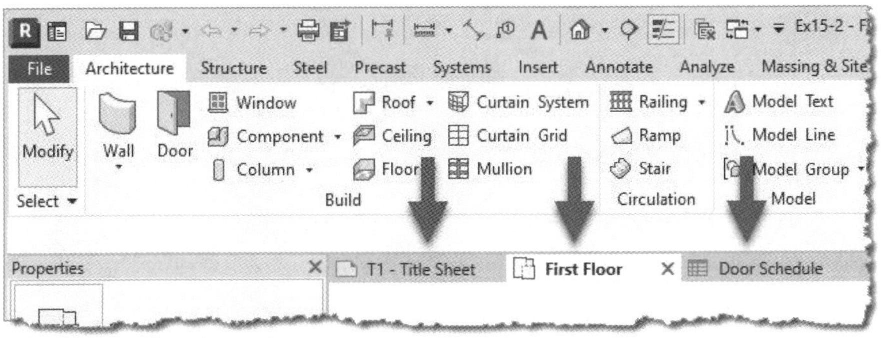

View Tabs; one for each open view

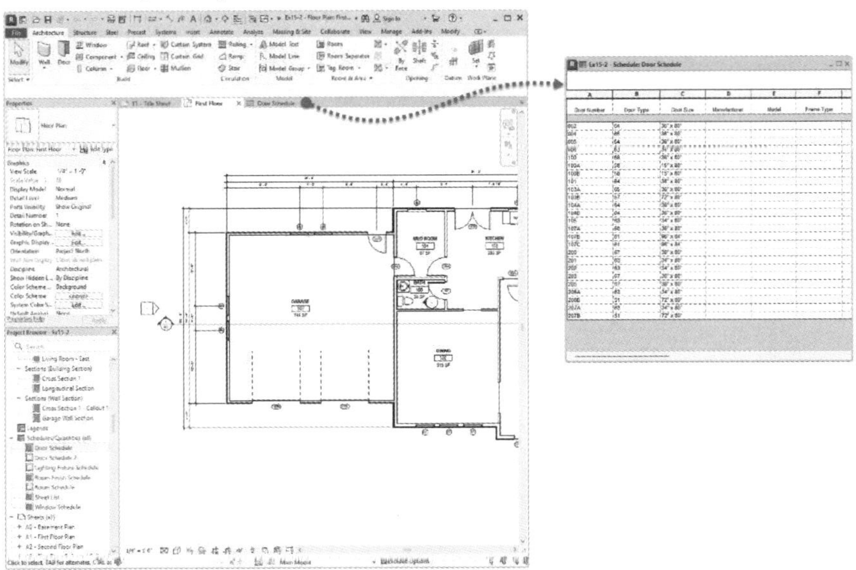

View Tabs can be pulled outside of the main Revit application window, even to a second screen

This concludes your brief overview of the Revit user interface. Many of these tools and operations will be covered in more detail throughout the book.

Exercise 1-3:
Open, Save, and Close a Revit Project

To *Open* **Revit 2027** in Windows 11, select Start and then click Revit 2027 or search for it.

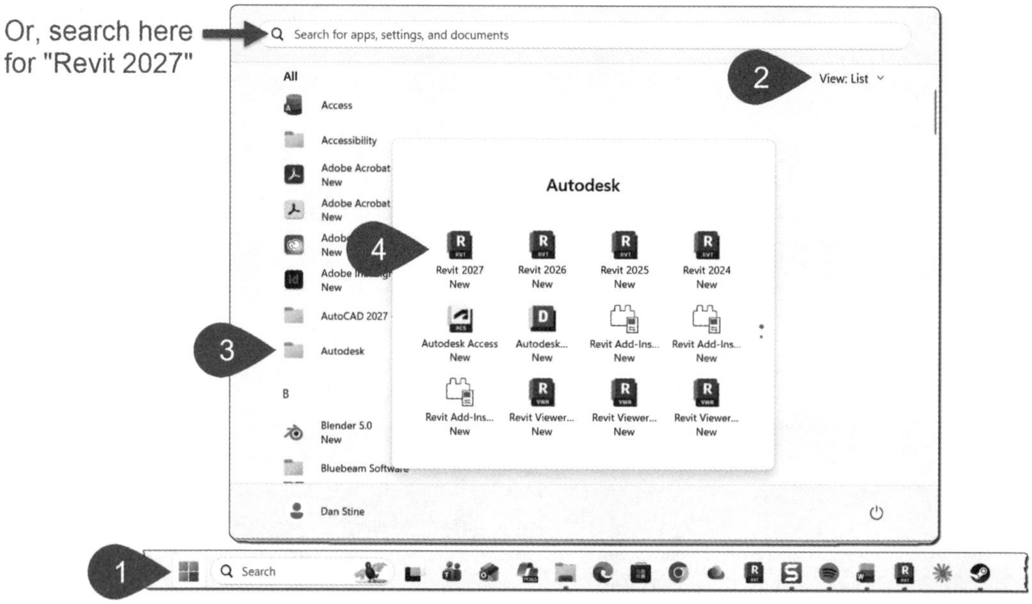

Or double-click the Revit icon on your desktop.

How to Open a Revit Project

By default, Revit opens to the Home screen, which displays thumbnails of recent projects you have worked on. Clicking the thumbnail opens the project.

1. Click the **Open** button under *Models* as shown to the right.

FYI: If the preview is for a *Central* file (aka Worksharing) it will automatically open a *Local* file. Worksharing allows multiple people to work in the same file.

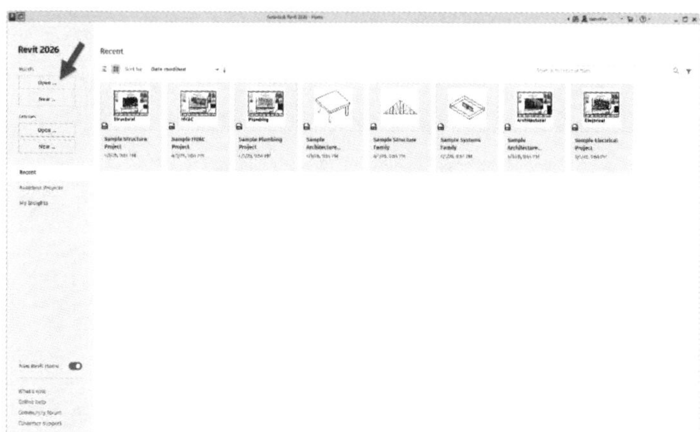

FIGURE 1-3.1 Revit Home screen

Next, you will open an existing Revit project file. You will select a sample file provided online at SDCpublications.com; see the inside front cover for more information.

2. Click the drop-down box at the top of the *Open* dialog (Figure 1-3.2). Browse to your downloaded files (provided files must be downloaded from www.SDCpublications.com; see the backside of the front cover of this book for more info).

   *TIP: If you cannot access the online sample files, you can substitute any Revit file you can find. Some sample files may be found here on your computer's hard drive: C:\Program Files\Autodesk\Revit 2027\Samples, or via **File** (tab) → **Open** (fly-out) → **Sample Files**.*

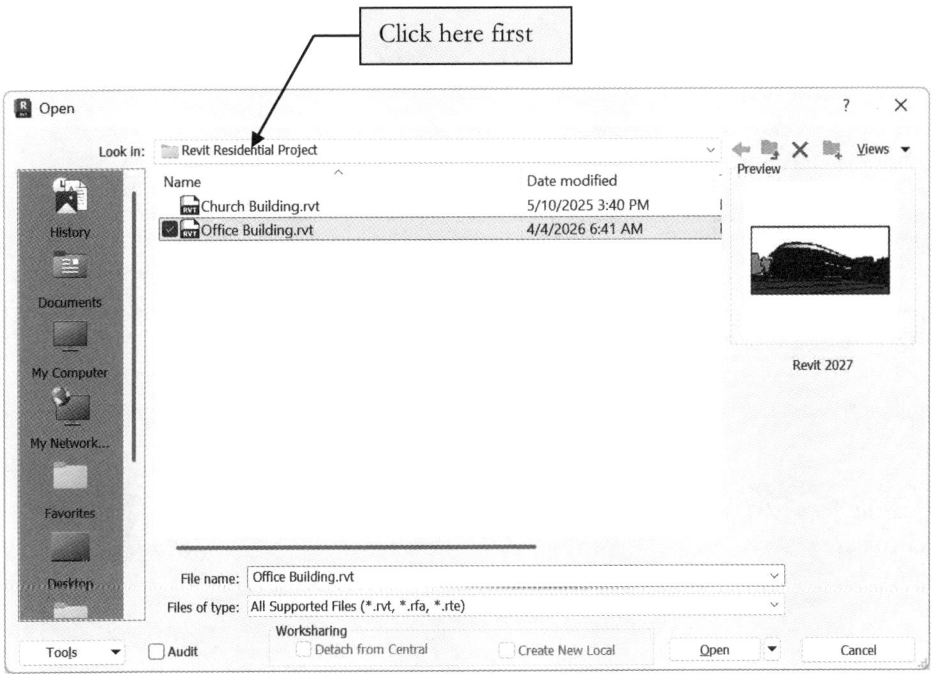

FIGURE 1-3.2 Open dialog; downloaded content from SDCpublications.com

3. Select the file named **Office Building.rvt** and click **Open**.

FYI: Notice the preview of the selected file. This will help you select the correct file before taking the time to open it.

The *Office Building.rvt* file is now open, and the last saved view is displayed in the drawing window (Figure 1-3.3).

FIGURE 1-3.3 Sample file "Office Building.rvt"

FYI: The Autodesk Assistant can be closed if additional screen space is needed. To open it later: **View → User Interface → Autodesk Assistant**.

The *File Tab* lists the projects and views currently open on your computer (Figure 1-3.4).

4. Click **File Tab → Open Documents (icon)** (Figure 1-3.4).

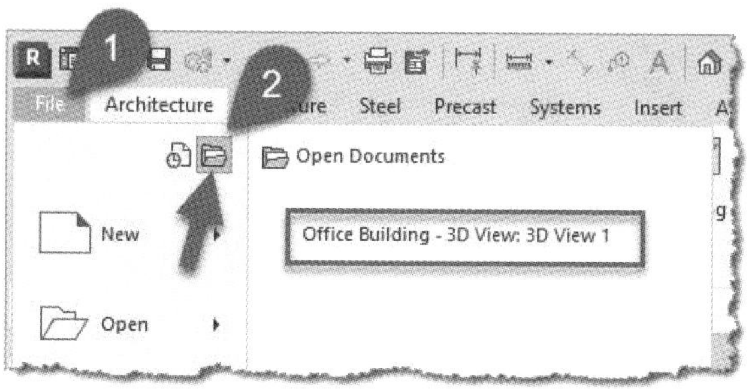

FIGURE 1-3.4 File Tab: Open Documents view

Notice that the *Office Building.rvt* project file is listed. Next to the project name is the name of a view open on your computer (e.g., floor plan, elevation).

Additional views will be added to the list as you open them. Each view has the project name as a prefix. The current view, the view you are working in, is always at the top of the list. You can toggle between open views from this menu by clicking on them, but this is normally done via the View tabs above the drawing window.

Opening Another Revit Project

Revit allows you to have more than one project open at a time.

5. Click **Open** from the *Quick Access Toolbar.*

6. Per the instructions previously covered, browse the downloaded online files.

7. Select the file named **Church Building.rvt** and click **Open** (Figure 1-3.5).

   TIP: If you cannot locate the online files, substitute one of the Autodesk sample files.

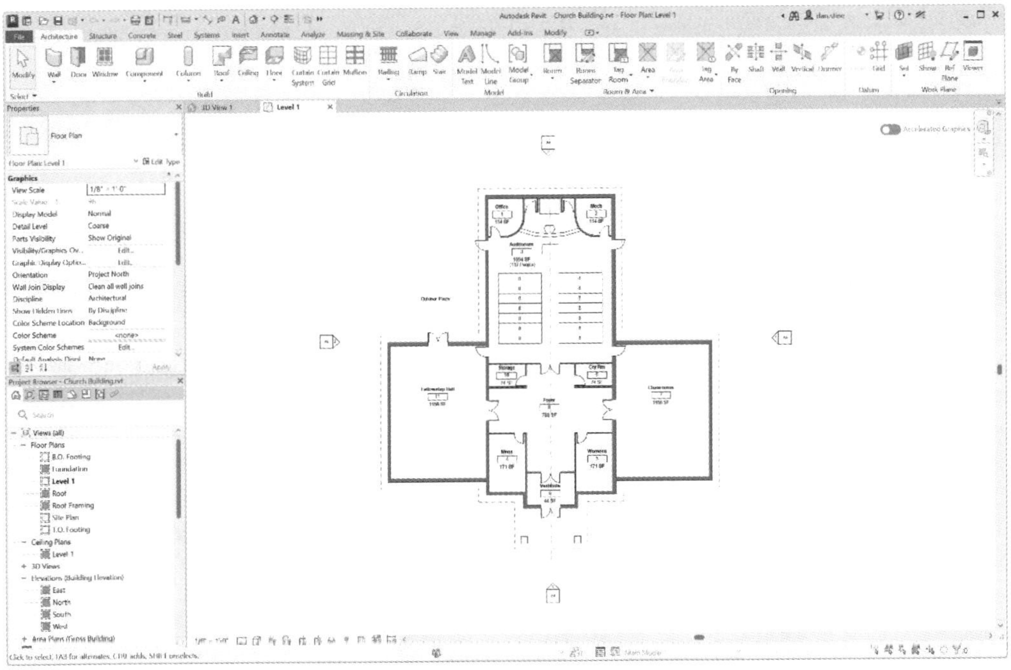

FIGURE 1-3.5 Sample file "Church Building.rvt"

8. Click **Open Documents** from the *File Tab* (Figure 1-3.6).

Notice that the *Church Building.rvt* project is now listed along with a view: Floor Plan: Level 1.

Try toggling between projects by clicking on *Office Building.rvt – 3D View: 3D View 1.*

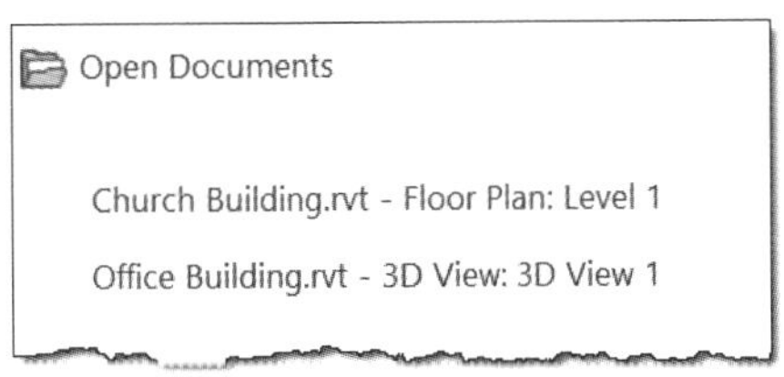

FIGURE 1-3.6 Open Documents

Close a Revit Project

9. Select **File Tab → Close**; click **No** if prompted to save.

This will close the current project/view. If more than one view is open for a project, only the current view will close. The project and the other open views will not close until you get to the last open view.

10. Repeat the previous step to close the other project file.

If you made changes and have not saved your project yet, you will be prompted to save your project before Revit closes the view. **Do not save at this time**. When all open project files are closed, you find yourself back in the *Revit Home* screen – which is where you started.

Saving a Revit Project

At this time, you will not actually save a project.

To save a project file, simply select *Save* from the *Quick Access Toolbar.* You can also select *Save* from the *File Tab* or press *Ctrl* + *S* on the keyboard.

You should get in the habit of saving often to avoid losing work due to a power outage or program crash. Revit offers a reminder to save; the notification is based on how long it has been since your last save. The **Save Time Interval** is set in *Options.*

You can also save a copy of the current project by selecting **Save As** from the File Tab. Once you use the Save As command, you are in the new project file, and the file you started in is closed.

Closing the Revit Program

Finally, from the *File Tab,* select **Exit Revit**. This will close any open projects/views and shut down Revit. Again, you will be prompted to save, if needed, before Revit closes the view. **Do not save at this time**.

You can also click the "X" in the upper-right corner of the *Application* window to close Revit.

Exercise 1-4:
Creating a New Project

Open **Autodesk Revit.**

Creating a New Project File

The steps required to set up a new Revit model project file are very simple.

To manually create a new project (maybe you just finished working on a previous assignment and want to start the next one):

1. Select **New** under "Models" on the Home Screen (not New "Families").

FYI: *If the Home screen is not visible, you can also select File tab → New → Project.*

After clicking *New,* you will get the ***New Project*** dialog box (Figure 1-4.1).

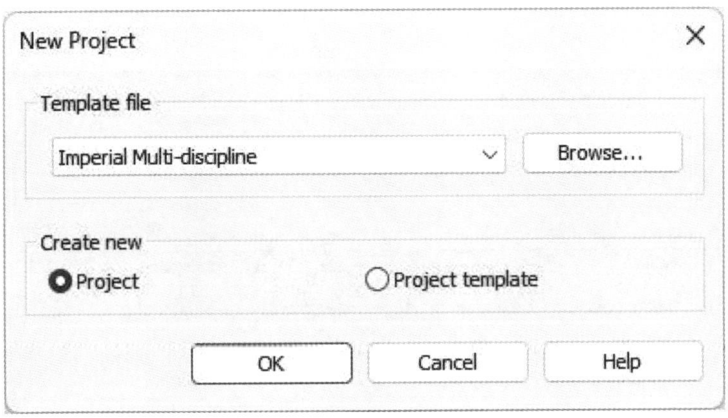

FIGURE 1-4.1 New Project dialog box

The *New Project* dialog box lets you specify the template file you want to use, or not use a template at all via the <None> option (which is not recommended). You can also specify whether you want to create a new project or a new template file.

2. Select the **Imperial Multi-discipline** option in the drop-down list. Leave *Create new* set to **Project** (Figure 1-4.1).

3. Click **OK**. You now have a new unnamed/unsaved project file.

To name an unnamed project file you simply *Save*. The first time an unnamed project file is saved you will be prompted to specify the name and location for the project file.

4. Select **File → Save** from the *Ribbon*.

5. Specify a **name** and **location** for your new project file.
   Your instructor may specify a location or folder for your files if in a classroom setting.

What is a Template File?

A template file allows you to start your project with specific content and certain settings preset the way you like or need them.

For example, you can have the units set to *Imperial* or *Metric*. You can have the door, window and wall families you use most loaded and eliminate other less often used content. Also, you can have your company's title block preloaded and even have all the sheets for a project set up.

A custom template is a must for design firms and contractors using Revit and will prove useful to the student they become more proficient with the program.

> ***Be Aware:***
> It will be assumed from this point forward that the reader understands how to create, open and save project files. Please refer back to this section as needed. If you still need further assistance, ask your instructor for help.

Exercise 1-5:
Using Zoom and Pan to View Your Drawings

Learning to *Pan* and *Zoom* in and out of a drawing is essential for accurate and efficient design, drafting, and visualization. We will review these commands now so you are ready to use them with the first design exercise.

Open **Revit**.

You will select a sample file from the SDC Publications-provided online files.

1. Select **Open** from the *Quick Access Toolbar.*

2. Browse to the **downloaded online files**.

3. Select the file named **Church Building.rvt** and click **Open** (Figure 1-5.1).

   TIP: If you cannot locate the online files, substitute any of the training files that come with Revit, found at C:\Program Files\Autodesk\Revit 2027\Samples.

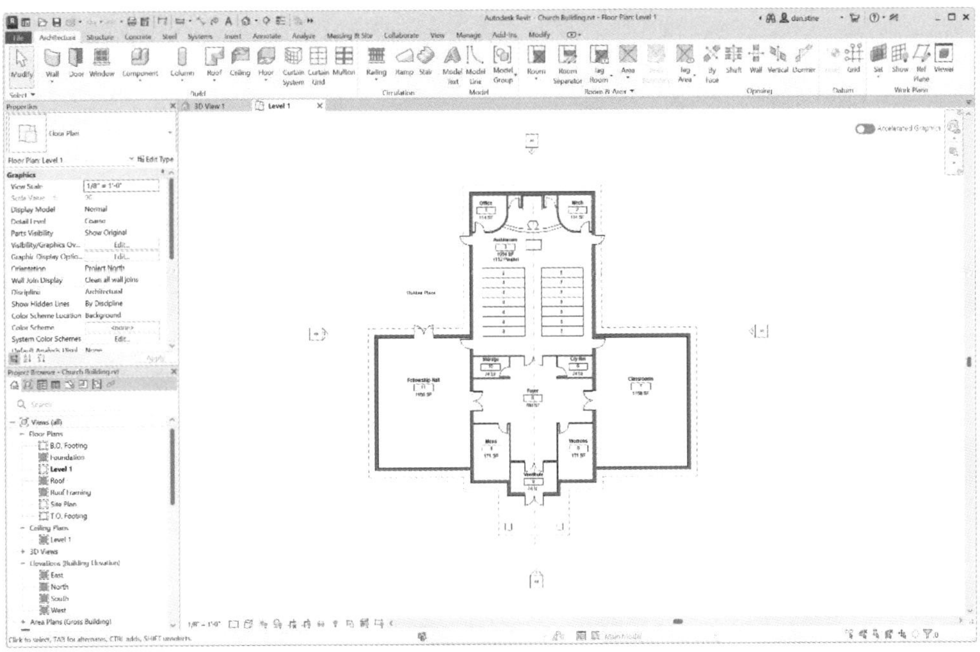

FIGURE 1-5.1 Church Building.rvt project

If the default view that is loaded is not **Floor Plan: Level 1**, double-click on **Level 1** under **Views\Floor Plans** in the *Project Browser*. Level 1 will be bold when it is the active or current view in the drawing window.

Using Zoom and Pan Tools

You can access the *Zoom* tools from the ***Navigation Bar*** or use the *scroll wheel* on your mouse.

The *Zoom* icon contains several zoom-related tools:

- The default (i.e., visible) icon is *Zoom in Region*, which allows you to window an area to zoom into.
- The *Zoom* icon is a **split button**.
- Clicking the down-arrow part of the button reveals a list of related *Zoom* tools.
- You will see the drop-down list on the next page.

Zoom In

4. Select the top portion of the *Zoom* icon (see image to right).

5. Drag a window over your plan view (Figure 1-5.2).

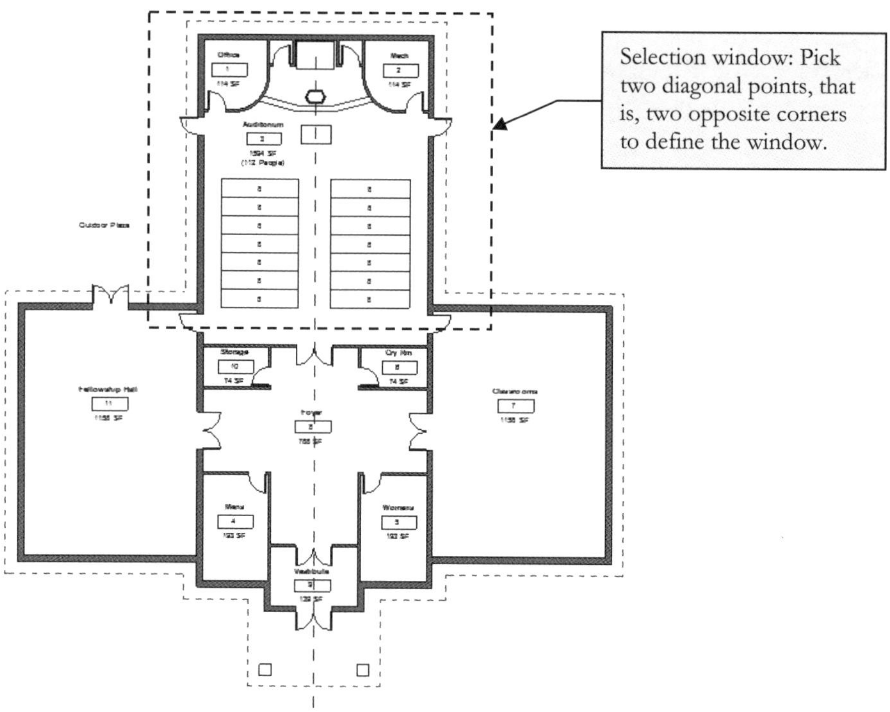

FIGURE 1-5.2 Zoom In window

You should now be zoomed in to the specified area (Figure 1-5.3).

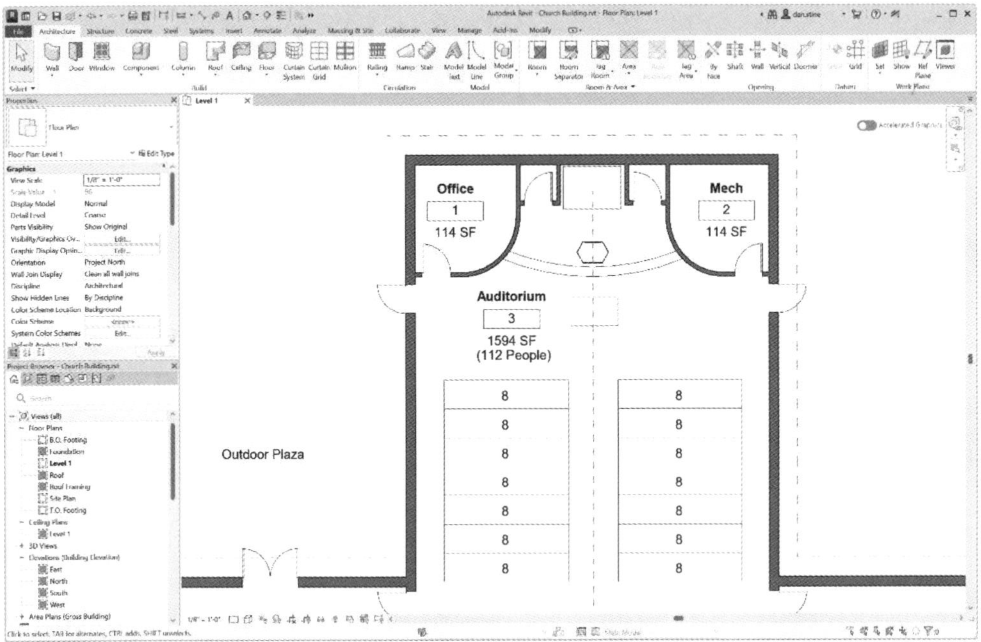

FIGURE 1-5.3 Zoom In results

Zoom Out

6. Click the down-arrow next to the zoom icon (Figure 1-5.4). Select **Previous Pan/Zoom**.

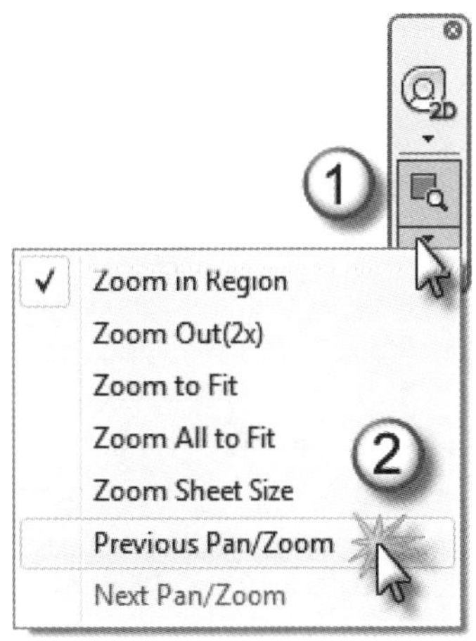

FIGURE 1-5.4 Zoom Icon drop-down

You should now be back where you started. Each time you select this icon, you are resorting to a previous view state. Sometimes you have to select this option multiple times if you did some panning and multiple zooms.

7. **Zoom** into a smaller area, and then **Pan**, i.e., adjust the portion of the view seen, by holding down the scroll wheel button.

The Pan tool just changes the portion of the model you see on the screen; it does not actually move it.

Take a minute and try the other *Zoom* tools to see how they work. When finished, click **Zoom to Fit** before moving on.

TIP: *You can double-click the wheel button on your mouse to* Zoom Extents *in the current view.*

Default 3D View

Clicking on the *Default 3D View* icon on the *QAT* loads a 3D View. This allows you to quickly switch to a 3D view.

8. Click on the **Default 3D View** icon.

9. Go to the **Open Documents** listing in the *File Tab* and notice that the *3D View* and the *Floor Plan* view are both listed at the bottom.

   ***REMEMBER:** You can toggle between views here.*

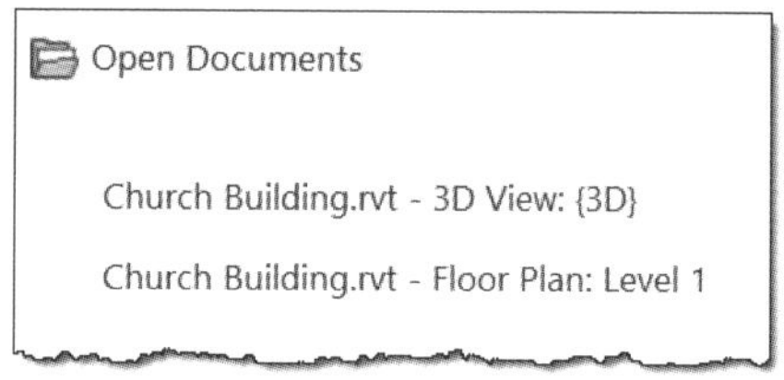

10. Click the **Esc** key to close the *File Tab.*

ViewCube

The *ViewCube* provides convenient control over the 3D view. This technology has been implemented across many of Autodesk's programs to make the process seamless for its customers.

11. You should notice the ***ViewCube*** in the upper right corner of the drawing window (Figure 1-5.5). If not, you can turn it on by clicking *View → Windows → User Interface → ViewCube.*

    ***TIP:** The ViewCube is only visible in 3D views.*

Hovering your cursor over the *ViewCube* engages it. As you move about the *Cube,* you see various areas highlight. If you click, you will be taken to that highlighted area in the drawing window. You can also click and drag your cursor on the *Cube* to "roll" the model in an unconstrained fashion. Click and drag the mouse on the disk below the Cube to spin the model without rolling. Finally, you have a few options in a right-click menu, and the **Home** icon, just above the *Cube*, gets you back to where you started if things get disoriented!

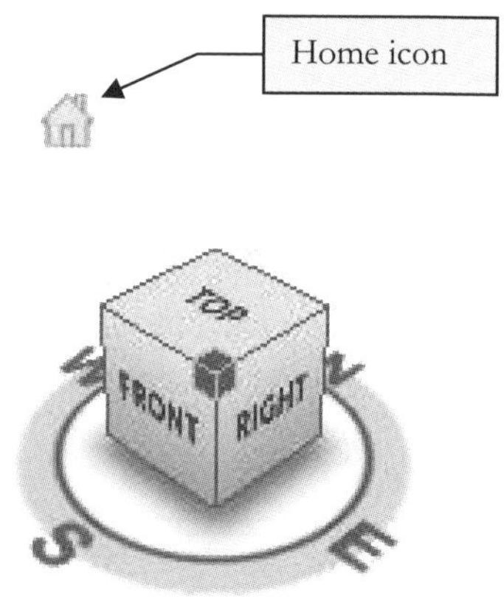

FIGURE 1-5.5 ViewCube

12. Give the *ViewCube* a try, then click the **Home** icon when you are done.

***REMEMBER:** The* Home *icon only shows up when your cursor is over the ViewCube.*

Navigation Wheel

Similar to the *ViewCube*, the *Navigation Wheel* helps you navigate your model. With the *Navigation Wheel,* you can walk through your model, going down hallways and turning into rooms. Revit has not advanced to the point where the doors will open for you; thus, you walk through closed doors or walls as if you were a ghost!

The *Navigation Wheel* is activated by clicking the upper icon on the *Navigation Bar.*

Unfortunately, it is way too early in your Revit endeavors to learn to use the *Navigation Wheel.* You can try this in the chapter on creating photorealistic renderings and camera views. You would typically use this tool in a camera view.

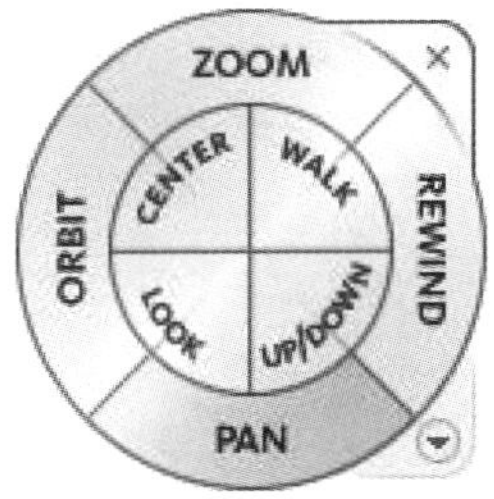

FIGURE 1-5.6 Navigation Wheel

13. **Close** the *Church Building* project **without** saving.

Using the Scroll Wheel on the Mouse

The scroll wheel on the mouse is a must for those using BIM software. In Revit, you can *Pan* and *Zoom* without even clicking a zoom icon. You simply **scroll the wheel to zoom** and **hold the wheel button down to pan**. This can be done while in another command (e.g., while drawing walls). Another nice feature is that the drawing zooms into the area near your cursor, rather than zooming only at the center of the drawing window. Give this a try before moving on. Once you get the hang of it, you will not want to use the icons. Also, double-clicking the wheel button zooms *to Fit* so everything is visible on the screen.

Exercise 1-6:
Using Revit's Help System

This section of your introductory chapter will provide a quick overview of Revit's *Help System*. This will allow you to study topics in more detail if you want to know how something works beyond the introductory scope of this textbook.

1. Click the **round question mark** icon in the upper-right corner of the screen.

You are now in Revit's Help site (Figure 1-6.1). This is a website which opened in your web browser. The window can be positioned side-by-side with Revit, which is especially nice if you have a dual-screen computer system. This interface requires an internet connection. As a website, Autodesk can add and revise information at any time, unlike files stored on your hard drive. This also means the site can change quite a bit, potentially making the following overview outdated. If the site has changed, just follow along as best you can for the next three pages.

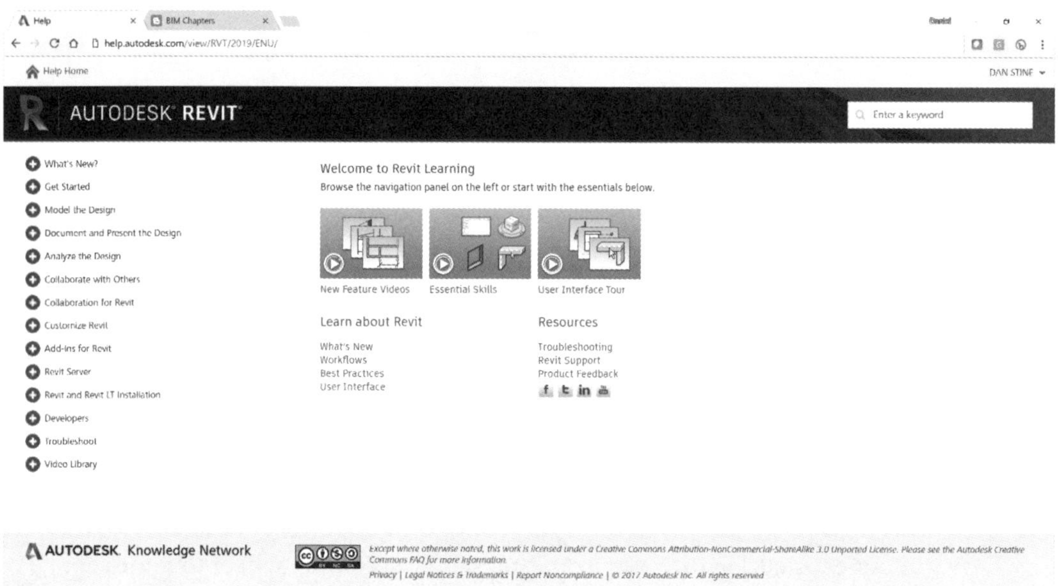

FIGURE 1-6.1 Autodesk Help site

Tip: Remember that the **Autodesk Assistant** can also be used to learn more about specific commands, and, with its AI-powered capabilities, it can even execute some of them for you.

In the upper right, you can click the search field and search the *Help System* for a word or phrase. You may also click any one of the links to learn more about the topic listed. The next few steps will show you how to access the *Help System's* content on the Revit user interface, a topic you have just studied.

2. On the left, click the **plus symbol** next to **Get Started.**

3. Now, click the **plus symbol** next to **User Interface** (Figure 1-6.2).

Notice the tree structure on the left. You can use this to quickly navigate the help site.

4. Finally, click directly on **Ribbon.**

You now see information about the *Ribbon* as shown in the image below. Notice additional links are provided below on the current topic. You can use the browser's *Back* and *Forward* buttons to move around in the *Help System.*

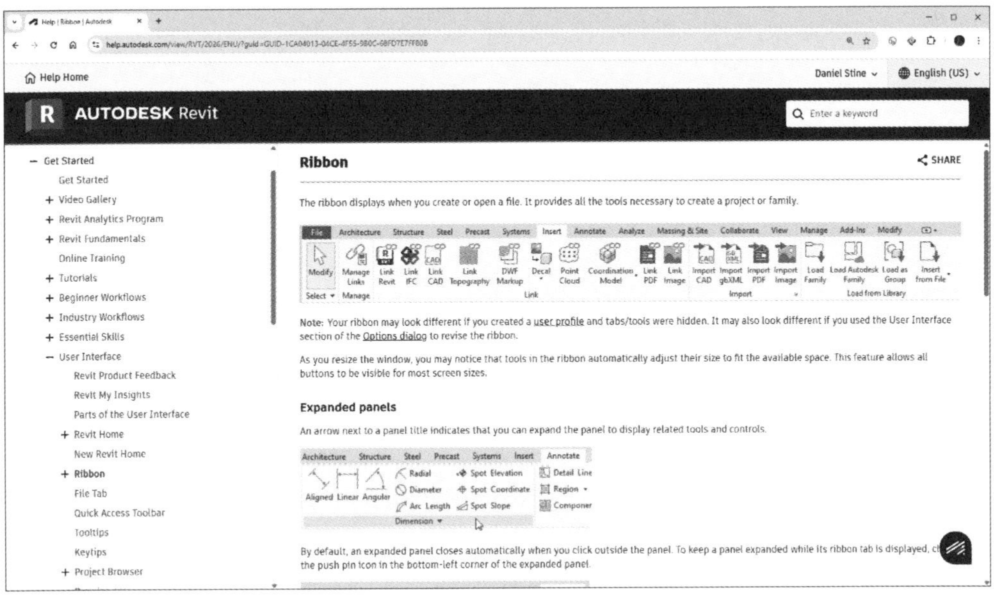

FIGURE 1-6.2 Help window; Ribbon overview

Next, you will try searching the Revit *Help System* for a specific Revit feature. This is a quick way to find information if you have an idea of what it is you are looking for.

5. In the upper right corner of the current *Help System* web page, click in the search text box and then type **gutter.**

6. Press **Enter** on the keyboard.

The search results are shown in Figure 1-6.3. Each item in the list is a link that will take you to information on that topic.

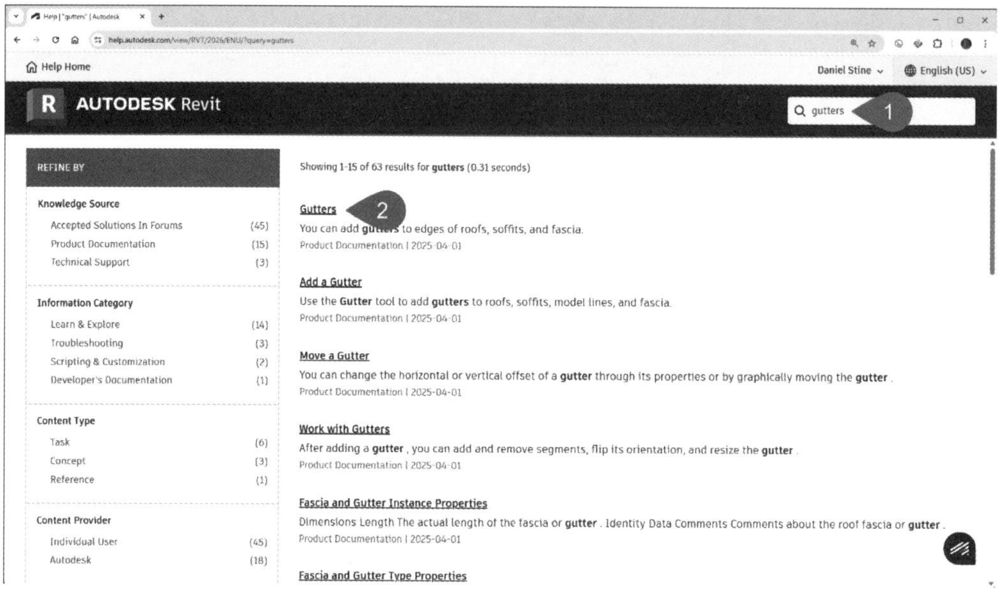

FIGURE 1-6.3 Help search results

The *Help System* can be used to complement this textbook. It is a reference resource, not a tutorial. As you work through the tutorials in this book, you may want to use the Help System to fill in the blanks if you have trouble or want more information on a topic.

Exercise 1-7:
Introduction to Autodesk Drive

We will finish this chapter with a look at Autodesk Drive, which is an integral foundation for much of Autodesk's **Cloud Services**. You do not necessarily need to use Autodesk's cloud services to complete this book successfully.

Here is how Autodesk describes *Autodesk Drive* on their website:

Autodesk Drive is a cloud storage solution that allows individuals and small teams to organize, preview, and share any type of design or model data.

You can use Autodesk Drive to:

- Upload data to a personal cloud drive.
- Organize and manage your data into folders.
- View 2D and 3D designs and models within the browser on any device.
- Share files & folders with others for viewing, editing, uploading, and managing data.
- You can also access, view, and edit data that others have shared with you.
- With Desktop Connector installed, you can also view and organize files stored in Drive from your desktop and desktop applications.

The Cloud, Defined

Before we discuss *Autodesk Drive* with more specificity, let's define what the *Cloud* is. **The Cloud is a service, or collection of services, which exists partially or completely online.** This is different from the *Internet*, which mostly involves downloading static information, in that you are creating and manipulating data. Most of this happens outside of your laptop or desktop computer.

The cloud gives the average user access to massive amounts of storage space, computing power, and software they could not otherwise afford if they had to actually own, install, and maintain these resources in their office, school, or home. In one sense, this is similar to a *Tool Rental Center*, in that the average person could not afford, nor would it be cost-effective to own, a jackhammer. However, for a fraction of the cost of ownership and maintenance, we can rent it for a few hours. In this case, everyone wins!

Creating an Autodesk Account

The first thing an individual needs to do in order to gain access to *Autodesk Drive* is create a free Autodesk account at drive.autodesk.com. If you are already using an Autodesk product, you likely already have an Autodesk account.

This account is for an individual person, not a computer, not an installation of Revit or AutoCAD, nor does it come from your employer or school. Each person who wishes to access *Autodesk Drive* services must create an account, which will give them a unique username and password.

Generally speaking, there are two ways you can access *Autodesk Drive* cloud services:

- Autodesk Drive website
- Within Revit or AutoCAD; local computer

Autodesk Drive Website

When you have documents stored in the *Cloud,* you can access them via your web browser. Here you can manage your files, view them without the full application (some file formats are not supported), and share them. These features use advanced browser technology, so make sure your browser is up to date; Chrome works well.

Using the website, you can upload files from your computer to store in the *Cloud.* To do this, create or open a Folder, then click the **Upload** option (Fig. 1-7.1).

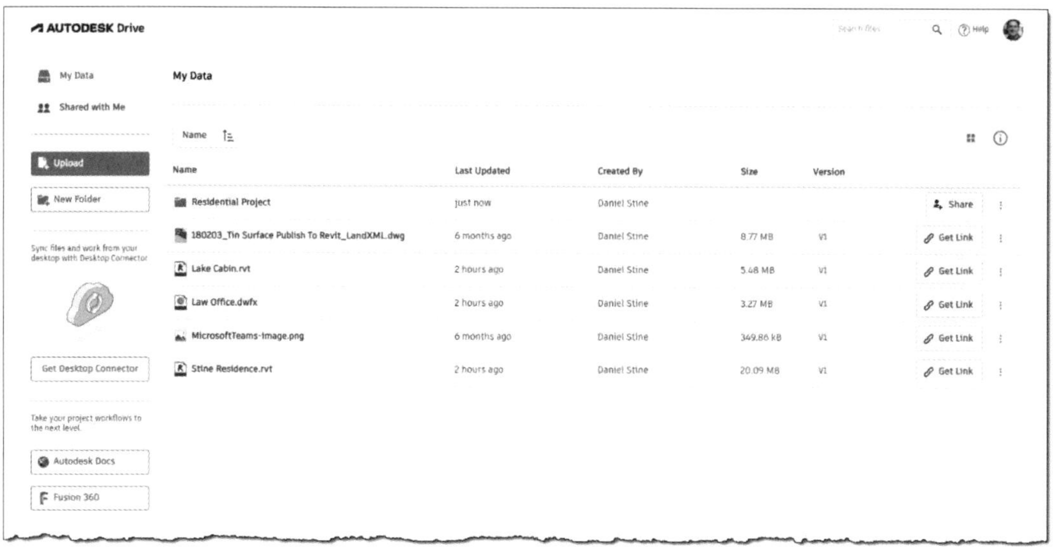

FIGURE 1-7.1 Viewing files stored in the cloud

Tip: If using a modern browser, you can drag and drop documents onto the window. This is a great way to create a secure backup of your documents.

You can share files stored in the *Cloud* with others. Simply hover over a file within *Autodesk DRIVE* and click the **Get Link** icon to see the Share dialog (Figure 1-7.2). Anyone with this link can view and download the shared files (if Allow Downloads is toggled on).

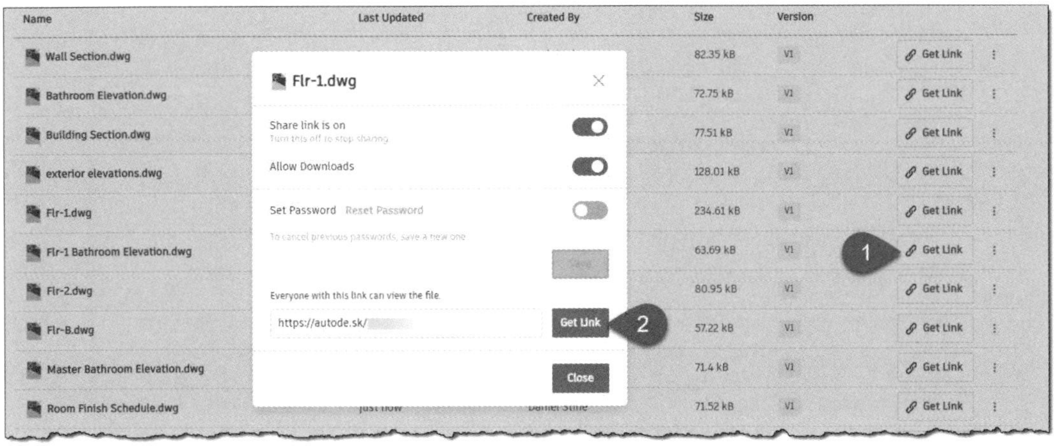

FIGURE 1-7.2 Sharing files stored in the cloud

Installing Autodesk Desktop Connector

To sync the Autodesk Drive files with your local computer and work directly on these files, you must first download Autodesk Desktop Connector. This tool creates an environment similar to OneDrive or Dropbox, but with enhanced features supporting Autodesk-specific CAD and BIM workflows.

To install Desktop Connector, first close any open Autodesk products, such as AutoCAD. Then click the **Get Desktop Connector** button (Fig. 1-7.1) to access the download page. Download the latest version and install it.

Files are now synced locally and appear in This PC in Windows Explorer (Fig. 1-7.3).

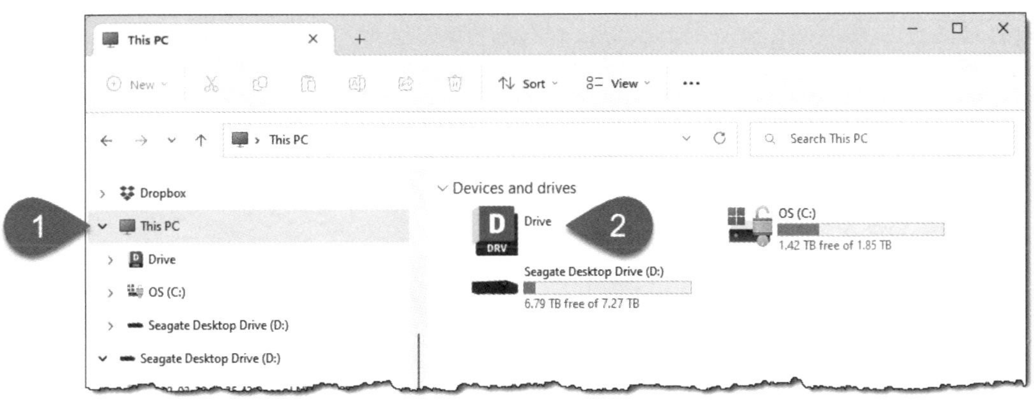

FIGURE 1-7.3 Accessing Drive files via Desktop Connector

The same cloud-based files appear locally, as shown below (Fig. 1-7.4).

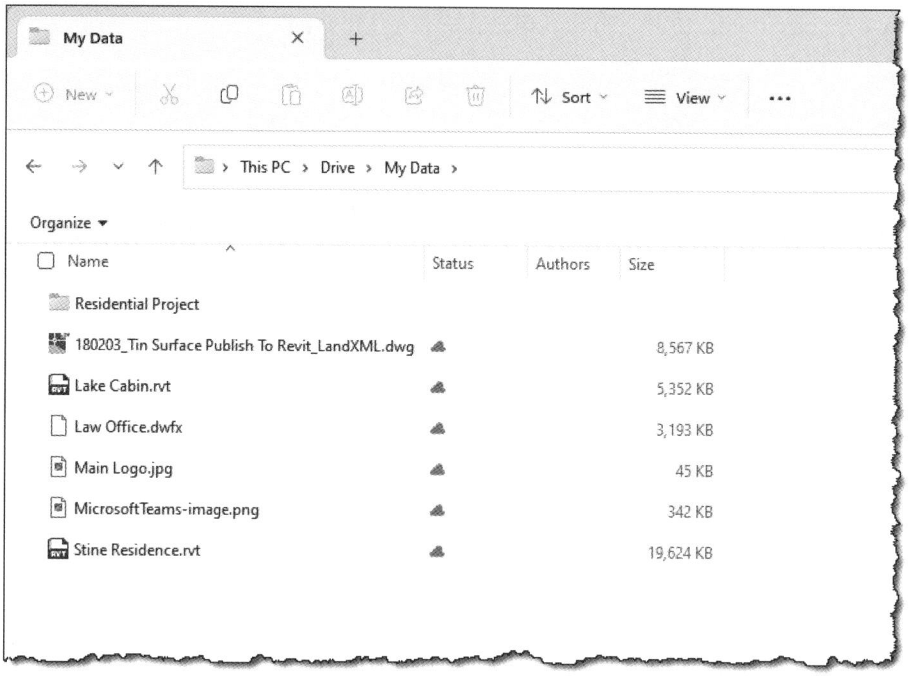

FIGURE 1-7.4 Accessing Drive files via Desktop Connector

Accessing Autodesk DRIVE within your CAD/BIM application

Another way to access your cloud-stored data is from within your Autodesk application, such as Revit or AutoCAD. This is typically the most convenient, as you can open, view, and modify your drawings. Once logged in, you will also have access to any *Cloud Services* available to you from within the application, such as rendering services or *Green Building Studio.*

To sign into your *Autodesk Account* within your application, simply click the **Sign In** option in the notification area in the upper right corner of the window. You will need to enter your student email address and password, or your work/personal email if you are not a student. When properly logged in, you will see your username or email address listed, as shown in Figure 1-7.5 below. Note: you are most likely already signed in, as this is required to use most Autodesk products.

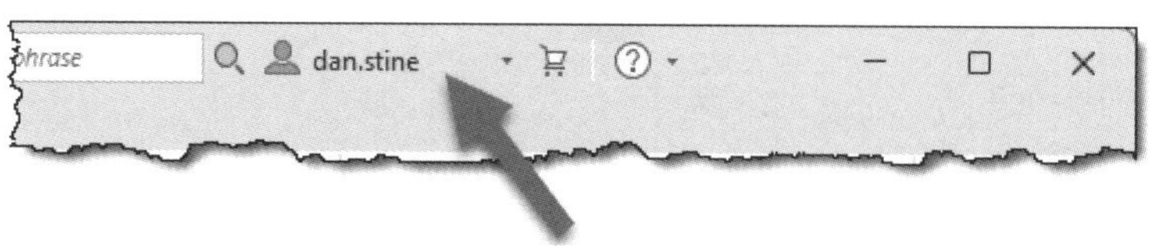

FIGURE 1-7.5 Example of user logged into their Autodesk account

The files within Autodesk Drive may be accessed via the **Open** dialog, as shown in Figure 1-7.6 below. Working on the files in this location ensures they are automatically backed up every time you save your work.

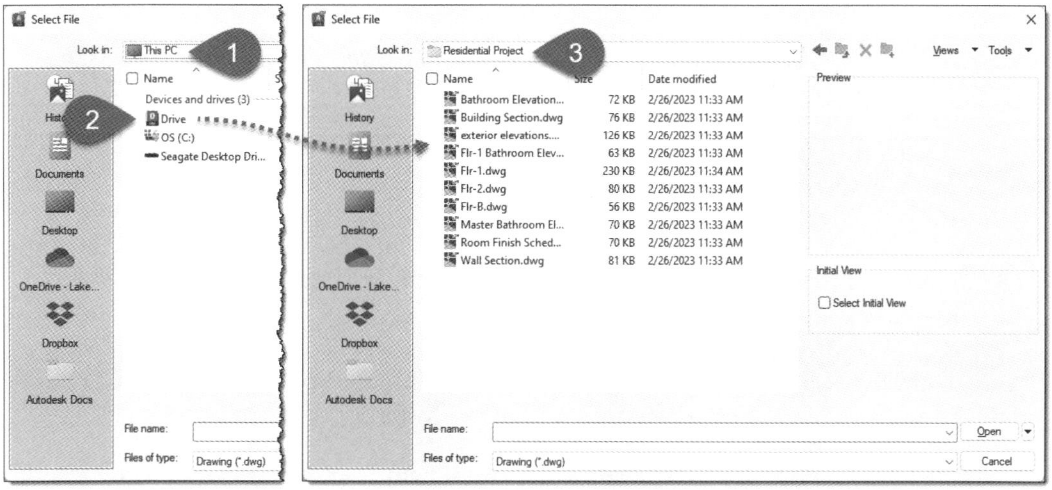

FIGURE 1-7.6 Accessing Autodesk Drive within AutoCAD or Revit

Notice that once a file has been modified, you can tell by the **Version** being incremented in Autodesk Drive when viewed in your browser, as shown below (Fig. 1-7.7).

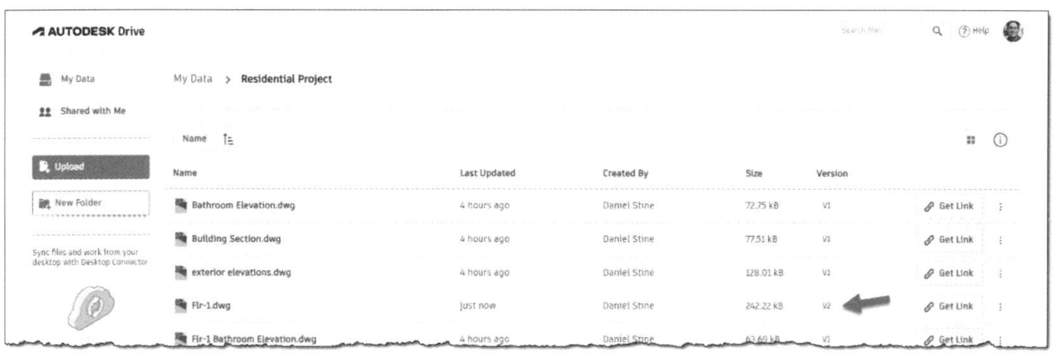

FIGURE 1-7.7 Accessing Autodesk Drive within AutoCAD or Revit

When using AutoCAD and when sharing files with others via Drive, only one person may modify a DWG file at a time. Similarly, when working with Revit models, an additional paid service called **Forma Design Collaboration** (previously BIM 360 Collaborate Pro) is required for multiple users to work within the same BIM.

As you work through this book, it is recommended that you save all your work in the Cloud via Autodesk Drive, so you have a safe, secure location for your files. These files can then be accessed from several locations via the two methods discussed here. It is still important to maintain a separate copy of your files on a flash drive, a portable hard drive, or in another cloud-based service such as *Dropbox*. This will be important if your main files ever become corrupt. You should manually back up your files to your backup location so a corrupt file does not automatically corrupt your backups.

TIP: If you have a file that will not open, try one of the following:

- In AutoCAD: Open AutoCAD and then, from the *Application Menu*, select Drawing Utilities → Recover → **Recover**. Then browse to your file and open it. AutoCAD will try to recover the drawing file. This may require some things to be deleted, but it is better than losing the entire file.

- In Revit: Open Revit and then, from the *Application Menu*, select Open, browse to your file, and select it. Click the **Audit** checkbox, then click Open. Revit will attempt to repair any problems with the project database. Some elements may need to be deleted, but this is better than losing the entire file.

Be sure to check out the Autodesk website to learn more about Forma Design Collaboration and the growing number of cloud services Autodesk is offering.

Self-Exam:

The following questions can be used as a way to check your knowledge of this lesson. The answers can be found at the bottom of this page.

1. The *View* tab allows you to save your project file. (T/F)

2. You can zoom in and out using the wheel on a wheel mouse. (T/F)

3. Revit is a parametric architectural design program. (T/F)

4. A ______________ file allows you to start your project with specific content and certain settings preset the way you like or need them.

5. Autodesk Drive allows you to save your files safely in the ____________ .

Review Questions:

The following questions may be assigned by your instructor as a way to assess your knowledge of this section. Your instructor has the answers to the review questions.

1. The *Ribbon* dynamically changes to show options that complement the current operation. (T/F)

2. Revit is strictly a 2D drafting program. (T/F)

3. The Projects/Views listed in the *Open Documents* list allow you to see which Projects/Views are currently open. (T/F)

4. When you use the *Pan* tool you are actually moving the drawing, not just changing what part of the drawing you can see on the screen. (T/F)

5. Revit was not originally created for architecture. (T/F)

6. The icon with the floppy disk picture () allows you to _________________ a project file.

7. Clicking on the ____________ next to the *Zoom* icon will list additional zoom tools not currently shown in the *View* toolbar. 

8. You do not see the *ViewCube* unless you are in a ________________ view.

9. Creating an *Autodesk* user account is free. (T/F)

10. The *Views/Schedules cannot be positioned outside of the Revit application window.* (T/F)

SELF-EXAM ANSWERS:
1 – F, **2** – T, **3** – T, **4** – Template, **5** – Cloud

Notes:

Autodesk User Certification Exam
Be sure to check out Appendix A for an overview of the official Autodesk User Certification Exam and the available study book and software, sold separately, from SDC Publications and this author.

Successfully passing this exam is a great addition to your resume and could help set you apart and help you land a great a job. People who pass the official exam receive a certificate signed by the CEO of Autodesk, the makers of Revit.

Lesson 2
Quick Start: Small Office:

In this lesson, you'll receive a straightforward overview of how Autodesk Revit works. The very basics of creating the primary components of a floor plan will be covered: Walls, Doors, Windows, Roof, Annotation, and Dimensioning. You will see the amazing "out-of-the-box" features in Revit: powerful yet easy to use. It should get you very excited about learning this software program. Future lessons will cover these features in more detail as we learn other editing tools and related skills along the way.

Exercise 2-1:
Walls, Grids, and Dimensions

In this exercise, you will draw the walls, starting with the exterior. Read the directions carefully; everything you need to do is clearly listed.

Exterior Walls

1. Start a new project named **Small Office** per the following instructions:

   a. **Home Screen → Models → New…**

   b. Click **Browse…** (Figure 2-1.1)

   c. Select the template file named **Commercial-Default.rte**. *(You should be brought to the correct folder automatically.)*

   d. Click **Open**.

   e. With the template file just selected and *Create new* "Project" selected, click **OK** (Figure 2-1.1).

   See Lesson 1 for more information on creating a new project.

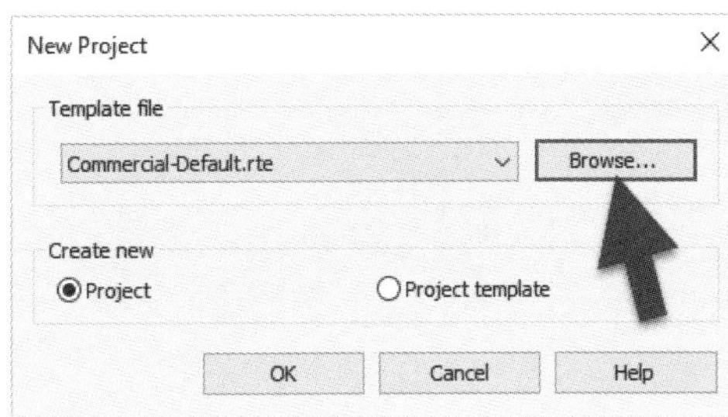

FIGURE 2-1.1 New Project

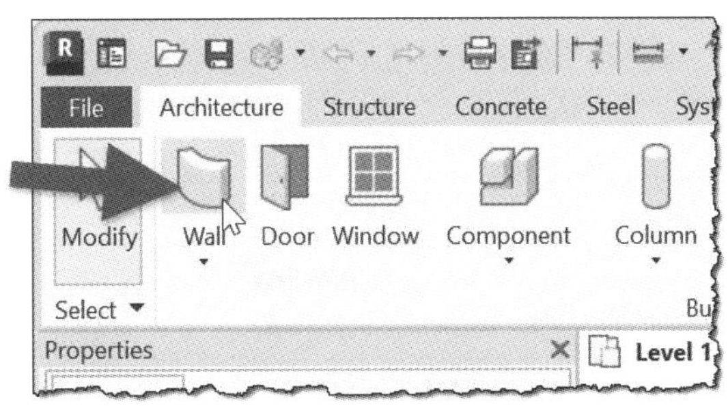

FIGURE 2-1.2 Wall tool

2. Select **Architecture → Build → Wall** on the *Ribbon*. (See Figure 2-1.2.)

Notice that the *Ribbon* and *Properties Palette* have been updated to display settings for walls. Next, you will modify those settings.

***FYI:** By default, the bottoms of new walls will be at the current floor level, and the tops of the walls are set via the Ribbon as shown in the next step.*

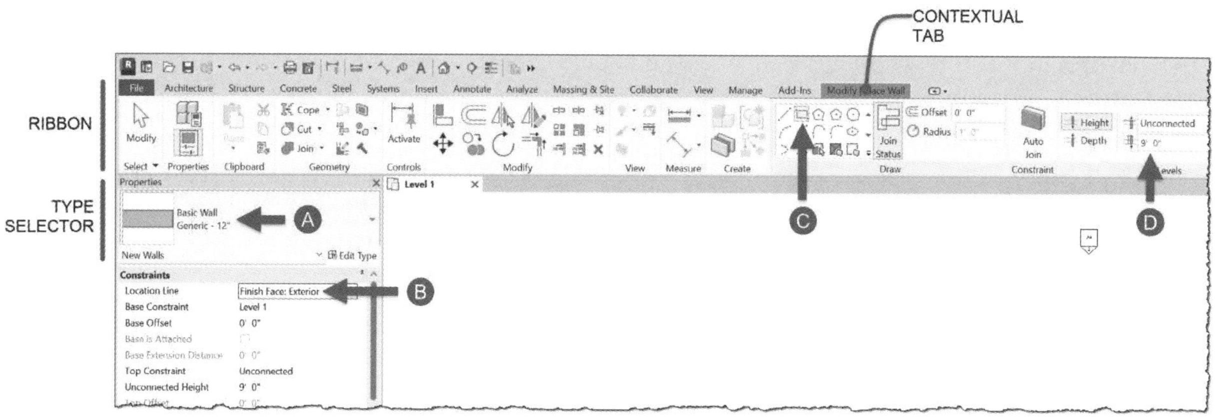

FIGURE 2-1.3 Ribbon, Properties, and Type Selector

3. Modify the *Type Selector, Properties,* and *Ribbon* as follows (Figure 2-1.3):

   a. *Type Selector:* Click in this area and select *Basic Wall:* **Generic – 12″**.

   b. *Location Line:* Set this to **Finish Face: Exterior**.

   c. Click the **Rectangle** icon in the *Draw* panel on the *Ribbon. (This allows you to draw four walls at once [i.e., a rectangle], rather than one wall at a time.)*

   d. *Height:* Change the height from 14′-0″ to **9′-0″**.

You are now ready to draw the exterior walls.

4. In the *Drawing Window*, click in the upper left corner.

   ***TIP:** Make sure to draw within the four elevation markers (see image to the right).*

5. Start moving the mouse down and to the right. **Click** when the two temporary on-screen listening dimensions are approximately **100′** (East to West) and **60′** (front to back).

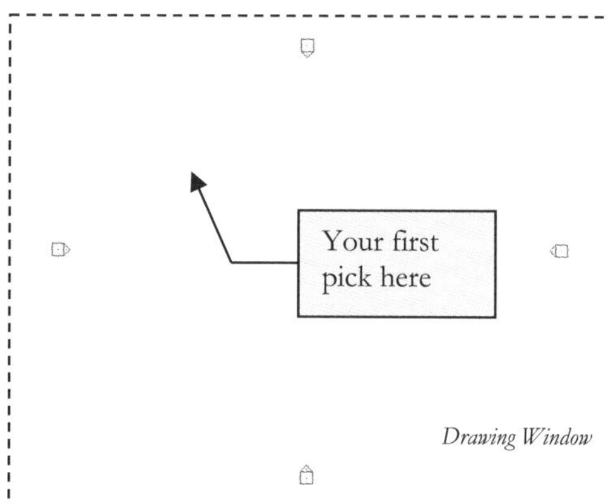

Getting the dimensions exact isn't important, as they will be revised later.

Your drawing should look similar to Figure 2-1.4; similar in that the dimensions do not have to be exact right now, and the building's location relative to the four elevation tags may vary slightly.

The *Temporary Dimensions* are displayed until the user invokes the next action. While the dimensions are displayed, you can click on the dimension text and adjust the wall dimensions. Also, by default, the *Temporary Dimensions* reference the center of the wall – you can change this by simply clicking on the grips located on each *Witness Line*; each click toggles the witness line location between center, exterior face, and interior face.

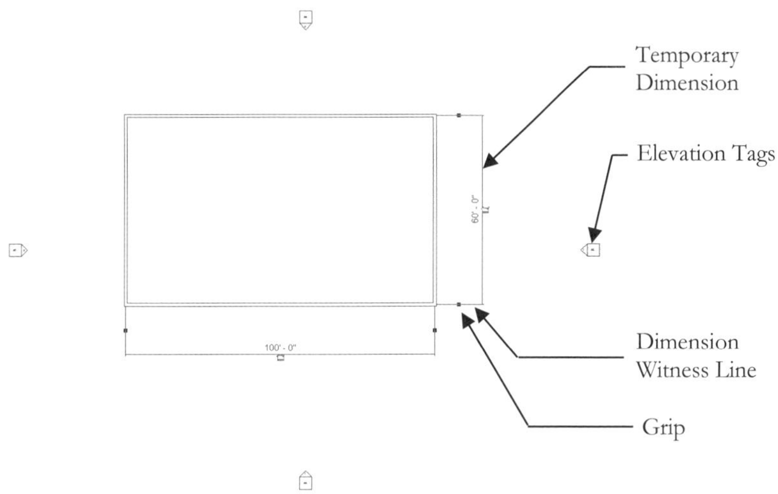

FIGURE 2-1.4 Exterior walls

In the next few steps, you will create grid lines and establish a relationship between the walls and the grids so that moving a grid moves the wall with it.

Grids:

Grids are used to position structural columns and beams in a building. Adding a grid involves selecting the *Grid* tool and then picking two points in the drawing window.

6. Click **Modify** on the *Ribbon* (to finish using the *Wall* tool) and then select the **Architecture → Datum → Grid**.

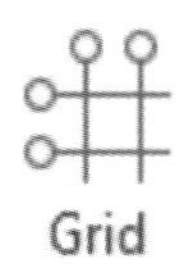

   FYI: The same Grid *tool is also found on the* Structure *tab.*

Next, you will draw a vertical grid off to the left of your building. Once you have drawn all the grids, you will use a special tool to align the grid with the walls and lock that relationship.

7. [*first pick*] **Click** down and to the left of your building as shown in Figure 2.1-5.

   FYI: 'Click' always means left-click, unless a right-click is specifically called for.

8. [*second pick*] Move the cursor straight up (i.e., vertically), making sure you see a dashed cyan line, which indicates you are snapped to the vertical plane, and the angle dimension reads 90 degrees. Just past the North edge of the building (as shown in Figure 2.1-5), **click**.

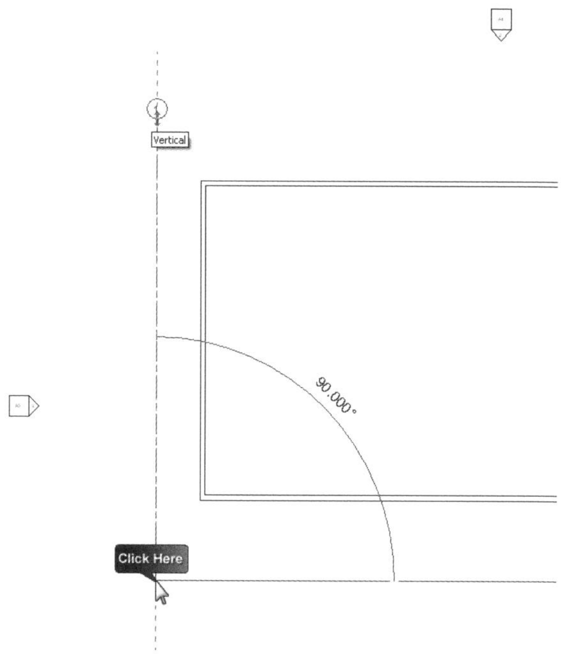

FIGURE 2-1.5 Drawing a grid

You have now drawn your first grid line. Next, you will draw four more grid lines: two horizontal and two vertical.

NOTE: The Grid tool will remain active until you start another tool or select Modify (selecting Modify allows you to select other elements in the drawing window).

9. Draw another vertical grid approximately centered on your building. BEFORE YOU PICK THE FIRST POINT, make sure you see a dashed horizontal cyan reference line indicating the grid line will align with the previous grid line (you will see this before clicking the mouse at each end of the grid line), then go ahead and pick both points (Figure 2-1.6).

10. Draw the remaining grid lines shown in Figure 2-1.6. Again, do not worry about the exact location of the grid lines, just make sure the ends align with each other.

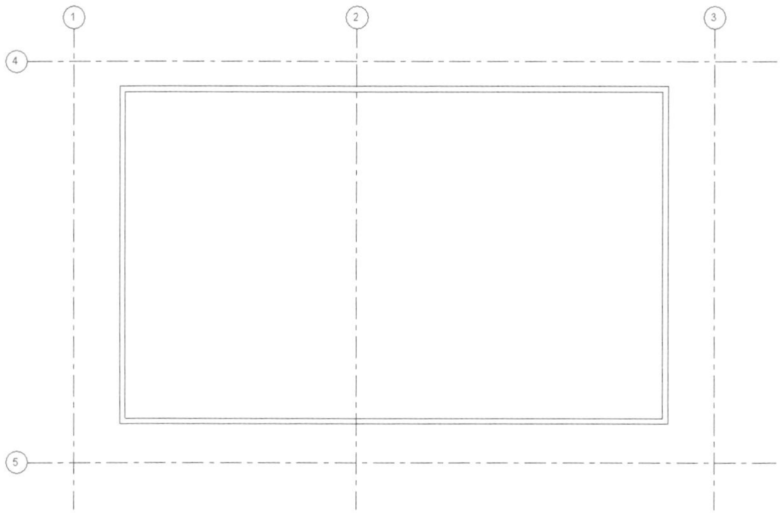

FIGURE 2-1.6 Grids added

Next, you will modify the two horizontal grid lines to have letters instead of numbers.

11. Zoom in on the grid bubble for the upper horizontal grid line.
12. Click *Modify* and then click on the grid line to select it.
13. With the grid line selected, click on the dark blue text within the bubble.
14. Type **A** and press *Enter* on the keyboard (Figure 2-1.7).
15. Click **Modify** again.
16. Change the other horizontal grid to **B**.

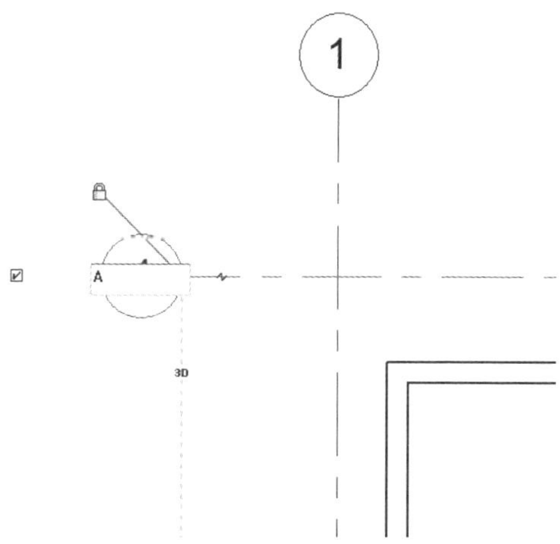

FIGURE 2-1.7 Grid edit

Align

Next, you will use the *Align* tool to reposition the grid lines so they "align" with the exterior face of the adjacent walls. The steps are simple: select the *Align* tool from the *Ribbon*; pick the reference line (i.e., the exterior wall face); and then select the item to move (i.e., the grid line). This tool works on many Revit objects!

17. Select **Modify → Modify → Align** from the *Ribbon.*

REMINDER: Ribbon instructions are Tab → Panel → Tool

18. [*Align: first pick*] With the *Align* tool active, notice the prompt on the *Status Bar*, select **Wall faces** on the *Ribbon*, next to the label "Prefer", and then select the exterior face of the wall adjacent to grid line 1.

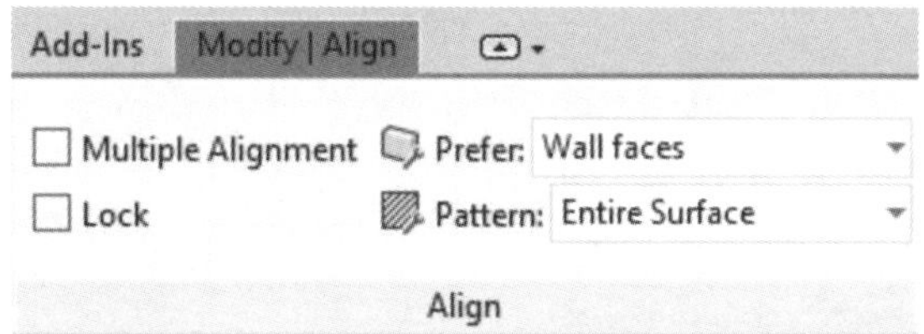

19. [*Align: second pick*] Select **grid line 1**. Be sure to see the next step before doing anything else!

The grid line should now be aligned with the exterior wall face. Immediately after using the *Align* tool, you have the option of "locking" that relationship; you will do that next. The ability to lock this relationship is only available until the next tool is activated. After that, you would need to use the *Align* tool again.

20. Click the un-locked **padlock** symbol to "lock" the relationship between the grid line and the wall (see Figure 2-1.8).

21. Use the steps just outlined to **Align** and **Lock** the remaining grid lines with their adjacent walls. Do not worry about the location of grid line 2 (i.e., the vertical grid in the center).

    Tip: Always select the element that should NOT move first. If you get it wrong, just use Undo and try again.

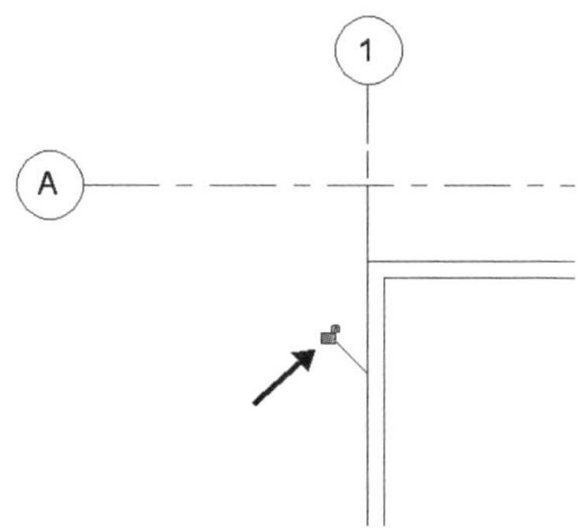

FIGURE 2-1.8 Align "lock"

Dimensions

Next, you will add dimensions to the grid lines and use them to drive the location of the walls and grids and learn how to lock them.

22. Select **Modify** and then **right-click** anywhere within the *Drawing Window*; click **Zoom To Fit**.

23. Select **Annotate → Dimensions → Aligned** tool.

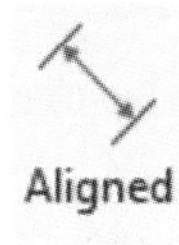

At this point, the *Dimension* tool is active. Notice the various controls available on the *Ribbon*. You can set things like the dimension style (via the *Element Type Selector*) and the kind of dimension (linear, angle, radius, etc.), and which portion of the wall to *Prefer* (e.g., face, center, core face).

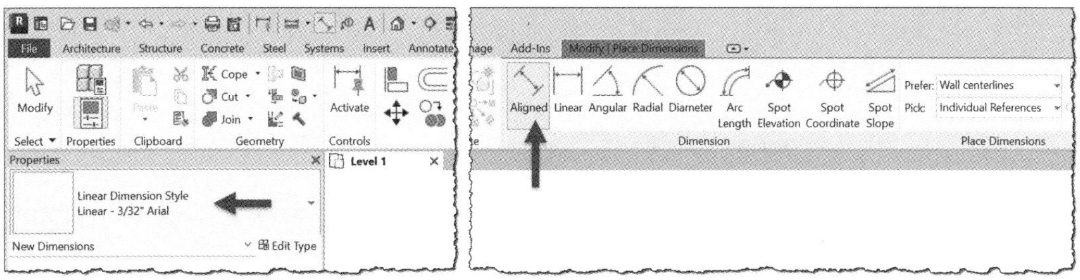

24. With the *Ribbon* and *Properties Palette* as shown above, which should be the default settings, **select grid line 1**.

   FYI: *The grid line will pre-highlight before you select it, helping ensure you select the correct item (e.g., the grid line versus the wall). Be careful not to select the wall.*

25. Now **select grid line 2** and then **select grid line 3**.

Your last pick point is to decide where the dimension line should be positioned.

26. Click in the location shown in Figure 2-1.9 to position the dimension line.

   TIP: *Do not click near any other objects, or Revit will continue the dimension string to that item.*

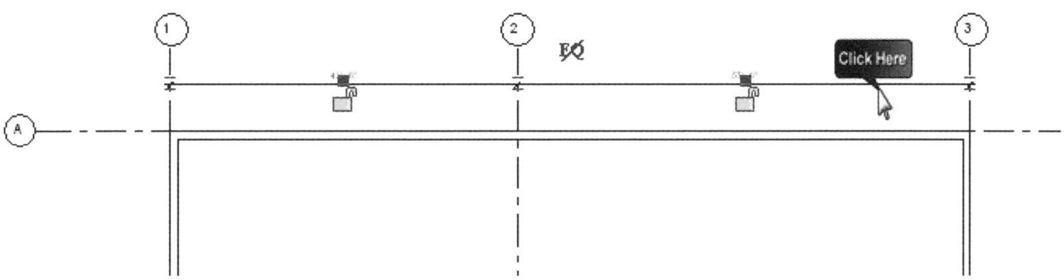

FIGURE 2-1.9 Adding dimensions

Notice that while the dimension string is selected, you see an EQ symbol with a slash through it. This symbol indicates that the individual components of the dimension string are not equal in length. The next step will show you how easy it is to make these dimensions equal!

27. With the dimension string selected, click the EQ symbol located near the middle of the dimension.

The grid lines are now equally spaced (Figure 2-1.10), and this relationship will be maintained until the EQ symbol is selected again to toggle the "dimension equality" feature off.

> ***NOTE:** When dimension equality is turned off or a dimension is deleted, the grid line will not return to its original location; Revit does not remember its original location.*

Typically, you would not want to click the padlock icons here, as that would lock the current dimension and prevent the grid lines from being moved at all.

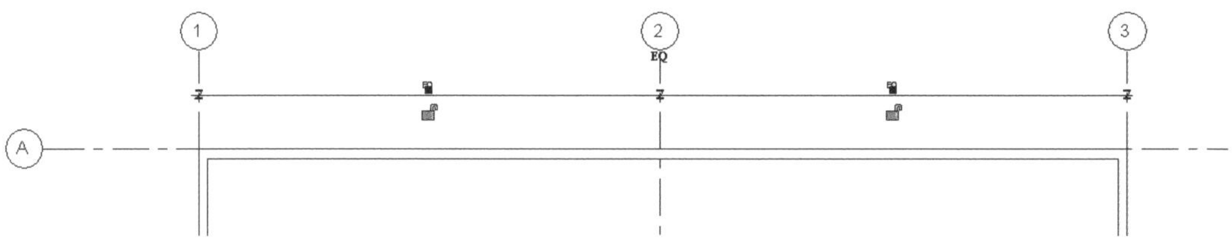

FIGURE 2-1.10 Toggling dimension equality

Next, you will add an "overall building" dimension from grid line 1 to grid line 3. This dimension can be used to drive the overall size of your building (always keeping grid line 2 equally spaced).

28. Using the **Aligned** *Dimension* tool, add a dimension from grid line 1 to grid line 3 and then pick to position the dimension line (Figure 2-1.11).

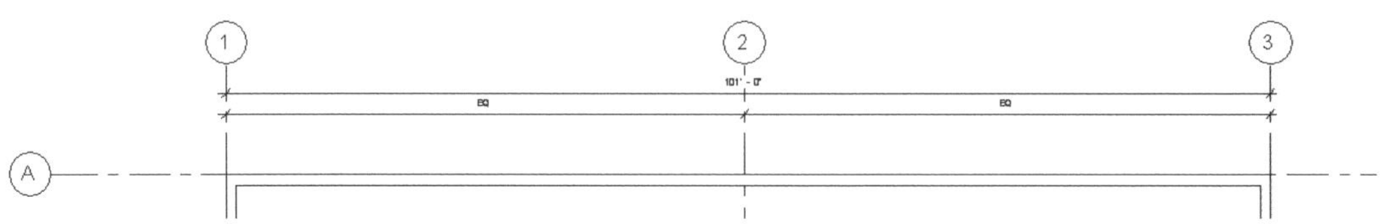

FIGURE 2-1.11 Overall building dimension added

When using a dimension to drive the location of geometry, select the item you want to move, then select the dimension text to enter the new value. You cannot just select the dimension because Revit does not know whether you want the left, right, or both grid lines to move. The only thing you can do, graphically, by selecting the dimension directly is "lock" that dimension by clicking on the padlock symbol, and then click the blue dimension text to add a suffix if desired. Next, you will adjust the overall building size.

29. Click **Modify** (or press the *Esc* key twice) to make sure you cancel or finish the *Dimension* tool and that nothing is selected.

30. **Select grid line 3**.

31. With grid line 3 selected, click the overall building dimension text and type **101**, and then press *Enter*.

    FYI: *Notice that Revit assumes feet if you do not provide a foot or inch symbol.*

32. Repeating the previous steps, add a dimension between grid lines A and B, and then adjust the model so the dimension reads **68′-0″**.

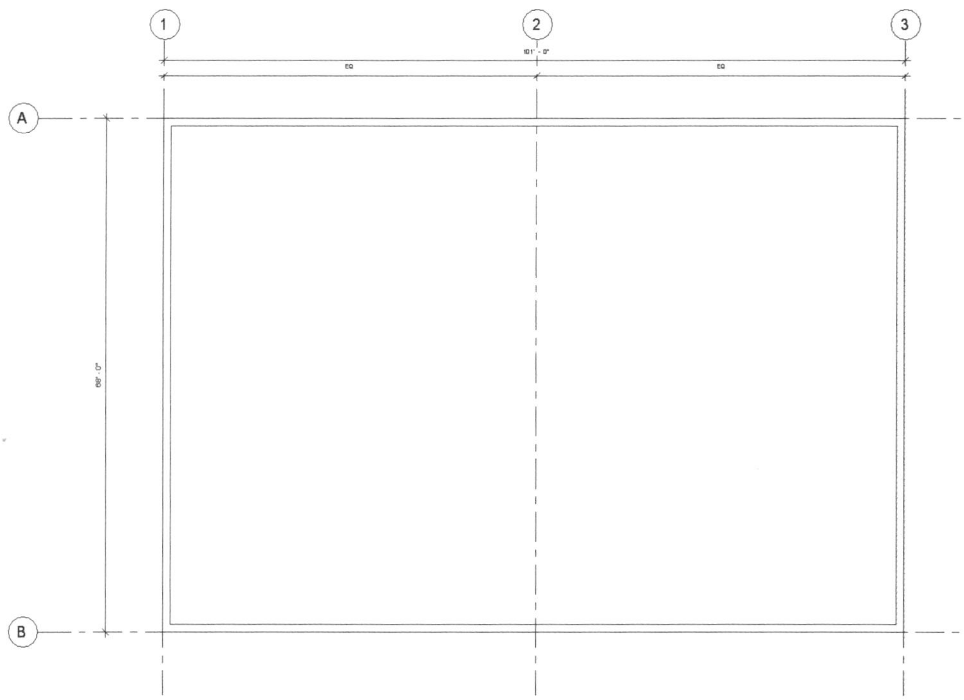

FIGURE 2-1.12 Building size established

Your project should now look similar to Figure 2-1.12. You should notice that dimensions must “touch” two or more items (the grid lines in this case). Also, because the walls were aligned and locked to the grids, moving the grids caused the walls to move.

The last thing you will do before moving on to the interior walls is replace the generic walls with more specific ones. This would be a common situation in a design firm; a generic wall is added as a “place holder” until the design is refined to the point where the exterior wall system is selected.

The process for swapping a wall is very simple: select the wall and pick a different option from the *Type Selector*. The next steps will do this and also show you how to quickly select all exterior walls so you can change them all at once!

33. Click **Modify** and then hover your cursor over one of the exterior walls so it highlights. (Do not click yet.)

34. *With an exterior wall highlighted,* i.e., pre-selected, take your hand off the mouse and tap the **Tab** key until all four walls pre-highlight.

    FYI: The Tab *key cycles through the various items below your cursor. The current options should include one wall, a chain of walls, and a grid line.*

35. *With all four walls highlighted,* **click** to select them.

36. *With all four walls selected,* pick *Basic Wall:* **Exterior – Brick on CMU** from the *Type Selector* on the *Properties Palette.*

    Tip: *If you receive any errors, refer back to step 3 and ensure the Location Line option is set correctly in the Properties Palette.*

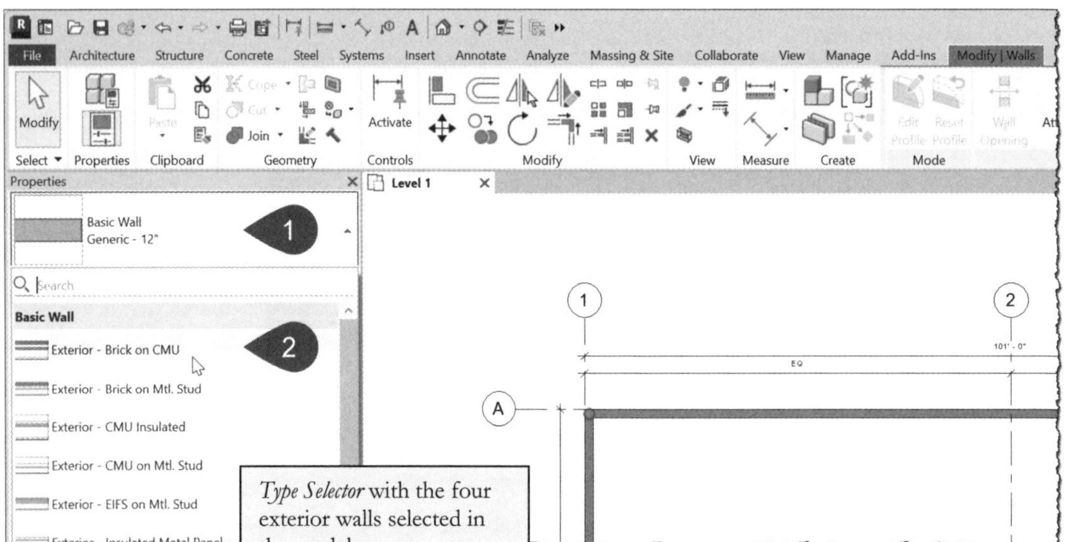

Type Selector with the four exterior walls selected in the model.

Detail Level

Revit lets you control how much detail is shown in walls.

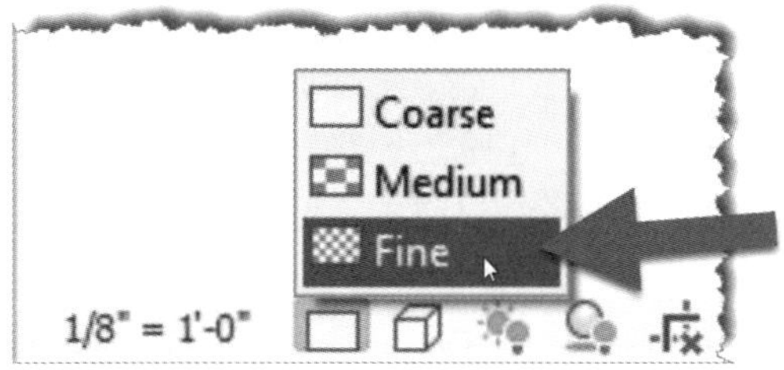

37. On the *View Control Bar*, located in the lower left corner of the *Drawing Window*, set the *Detail Level* to **Fine**.

As you can see in the two images below, *Coarse* simply shows the outline of a wall type, and *Fine* shows the individual layers of the wall's materials (i.e., brick, insulation, concrete block, etc.).

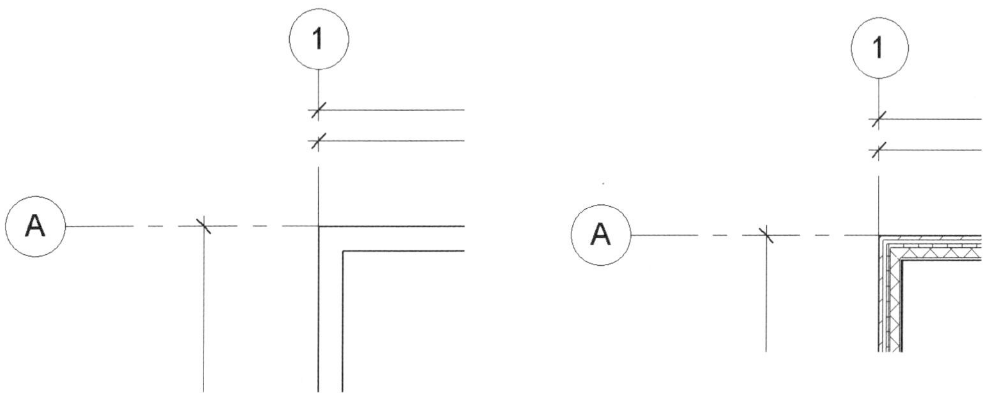

FIGURE 2-1.13 Detail level – coarse (left) vs. fine (right)

Now that you have the exterior walls established, the grid lines properly placed, and their relationships locked in the project, you can now proceed with the layout of the interior spaces.

Interior Walls

38. With the **Wall** tool selected, modify the *Ribbon* and *Properties Palette* to the following (also, see image on the following page):

    a. *Type Selector:* set to <u>*Basic Wall:*</u> **Interior – 4 7/8" Partition (1-hr)**.

    b. *Location Line:* Set this to **Wall Centerline.**

    c. *Turn off Chain.*

    d. *Height:* **Roof**

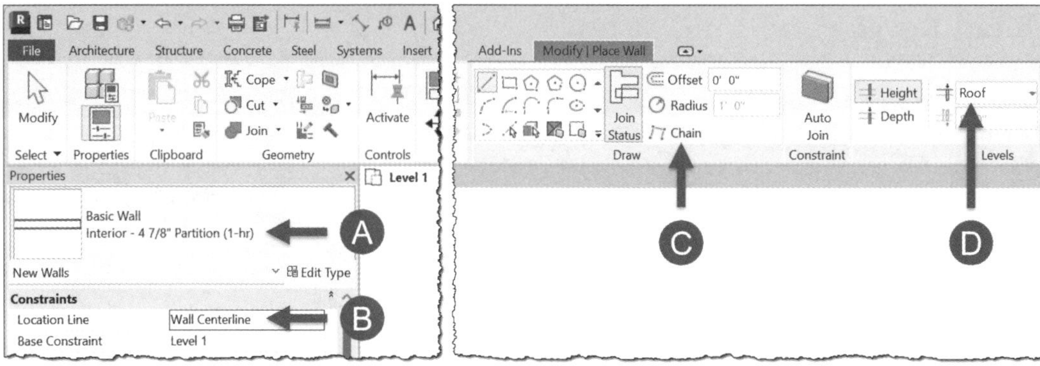

39. Draw a wall from the West wall (i.e., "vertical" wall on the left) to the East wall (on the right). See Figure 2-1.14.

    a. Make sure your cursor "snaps" to the wall before clicking.

    b. Before clicking the second point of the wall, make sure the dashed cyan line is visible so you know the wall will be truly horizontal.

    c. The exact position of the wall is not important at this point as you will adjust it in the next step.

    d. With the temporary dimensions still active, proceed to the next step.

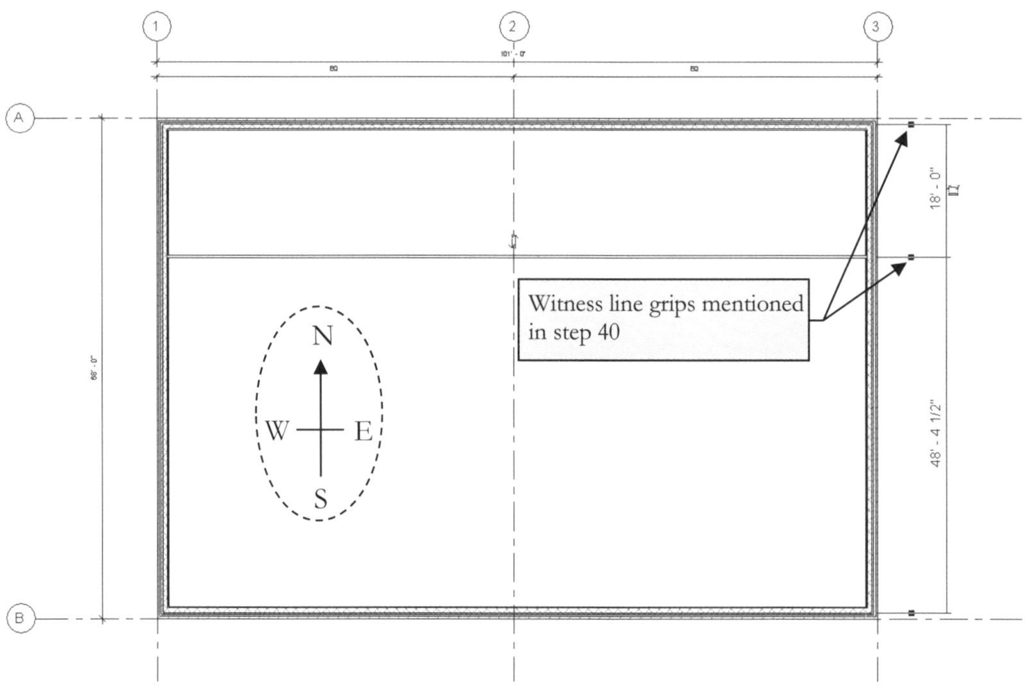

FIGURE 2-1.14 Adding interior walls – compass added for reference only

40. Click the **witness line grips** (see Figure 2-1.14) until the "clear" space of the room is listed (see Figure 2-1.15).

41. Now click the blue text of the temporary dimension, type **22**, and then press *Enter* (Figure 2-1.15).

42. Click **Modify** to finish the current task.

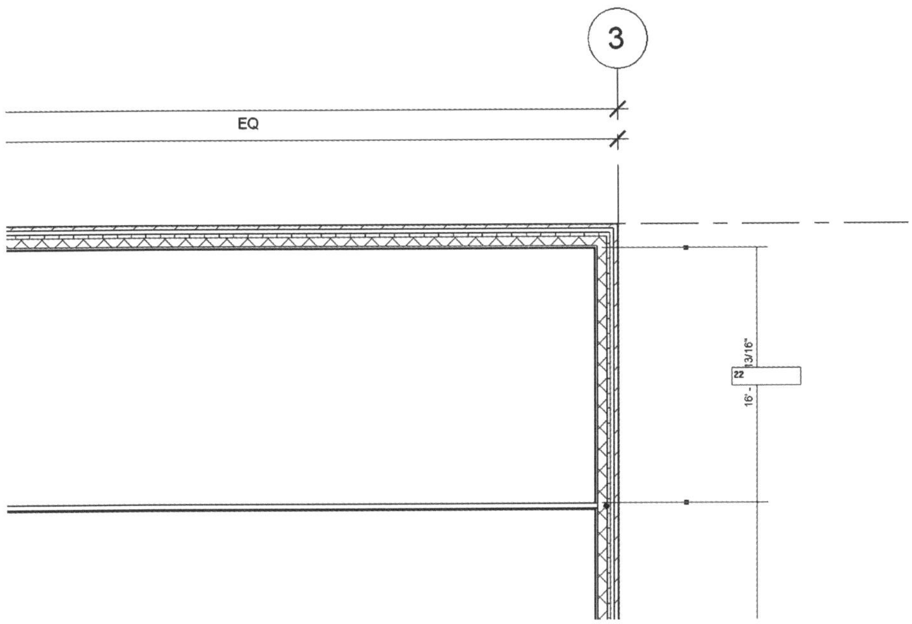

FIGURE 2-1.15 Repositioning interior wall via temporary dimensions

The clear space between the interior wall and the north wall is now 22′-0″. Next, you will add additional interior walls to create equally spaced rooms in this area.

43. Using the same settings as the interior wall just added, draw five (5) vertical walls as shown in Figure 2-1.16.

    a. Make sure they are orthogonal (i.e., the dashed cyan line is visible before picking the wall's endpoint).

    b. Make sure you "snap" to the perpendicular walls (at the start and endpoint of the walls you are adding).

    c. Do not worry about the exact position of the walls.

    ***TIP:** Unselect Chain on the Ribbon if not already unselected.*

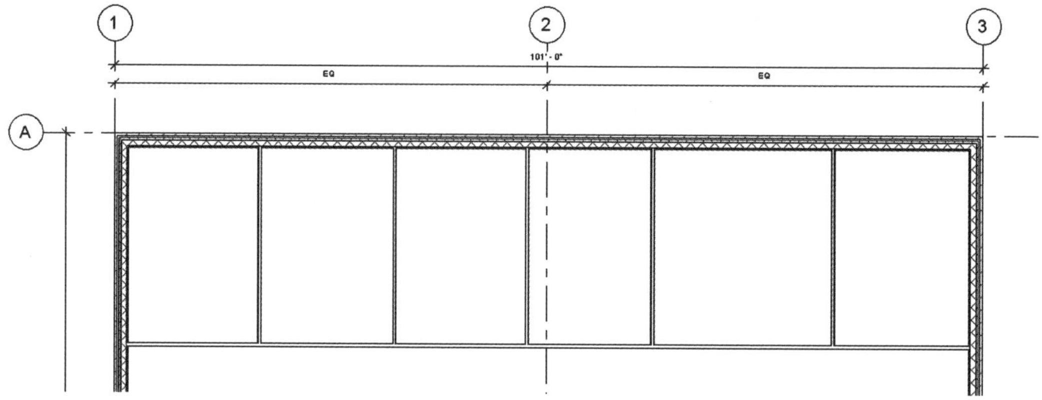

FIGURE 2-1.16 Adding additional interior walls

In the next step, you will use a dimension string to reposition the walls so they are equally spaced. This process is similar to what you did to reposition grid line 2. However, you have to specify which part of the wall you want to dimension to (center, face, core center, core face).

FYI: *The "core" portion of a wall system typically consists of the structural element(s) such as the concrete block (in your exterior walls) or the metal studs (in your interior walls).*

44. Select **Annotate → Dimension → Aligned** tool on the *Ribbon.*

45. On the *Ribbon*, set *Prefer* to **Wall Faces**.

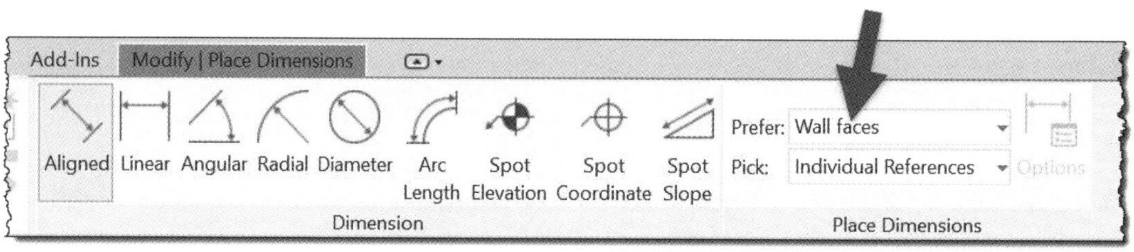

This setting will force Revit to only look for the face of a wall system. You can select either face depending on which side of the wall you favor with your cursor. This feature lets you confidently pick specific references without needing to continually zoom in and out all over the floor plan.

46. Select the interior face of the West wall to start your dimension string.

The next several picks will need to reference the wall centerlines. Revit allows you to toggle the wall position option on the fly via the *Ribbon.*

47. Change the setting to **Wall Centerlines**.

48. The next five picks will be on the five "vertical" interior walls. Make sure you see the dashed reference line centered on the wall, indicating that you are about to select the correct reference plane.

49. Change the wall location setting back to **Wall Faces** and select the interior face of the East wall (the wall at grid line 3).

50. Your last pick should be away from any elements to position the dimension string somewhere within the rooms (Figure 2-1.17).

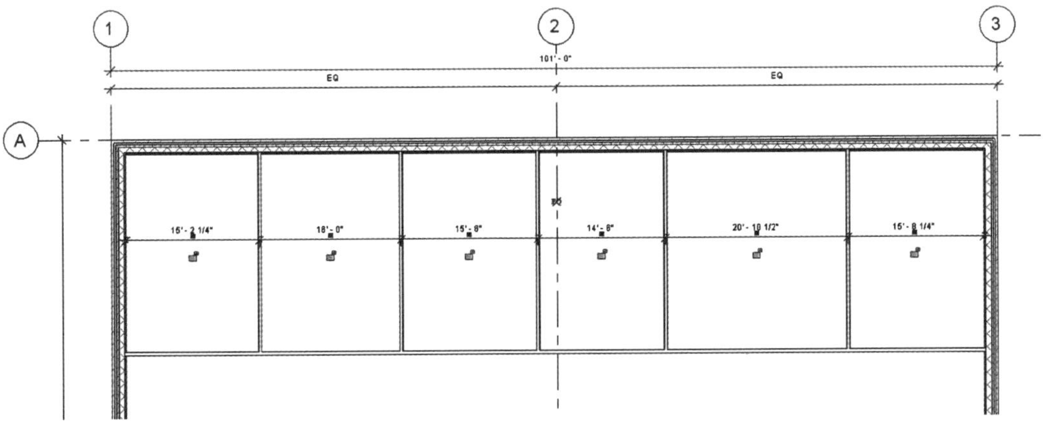

FIGURE 2-1.17 Adding a dimension string

51. Click the  symbol to reposition the interior walls.

52. Click **Modify** (or press the Esc key twice).

The interior walls are now equally spaced (Figure 2-1.18)!

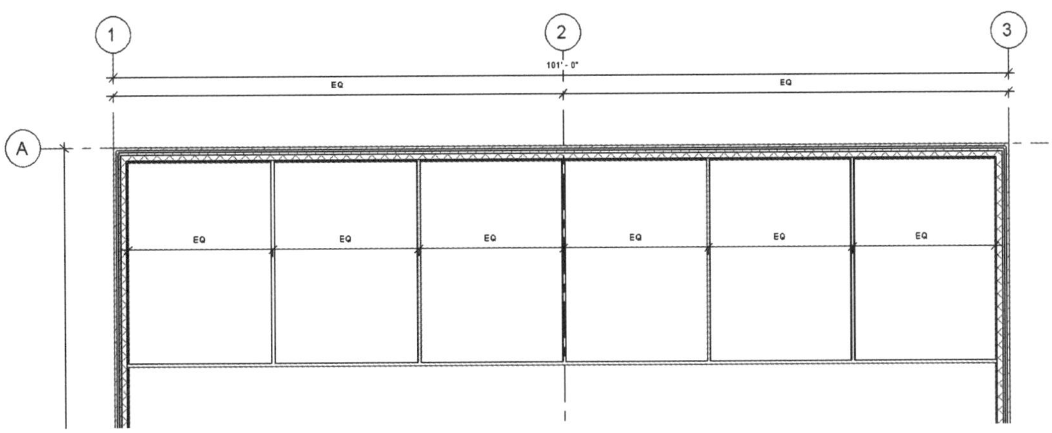

FIGURE 2-1.18 Enabling dimension equality

53. Add a vertical "clear" dimension to indicate the depth of the rooms. Set *Prefer* to **Wall Faces** for both ends of the dimension line. See Figure 2-1.19.

54. Click the **padlock** symbol (🔓) to tell Revit this dimension should not change (Figure 2-1.19).

55. Click **Modify**.

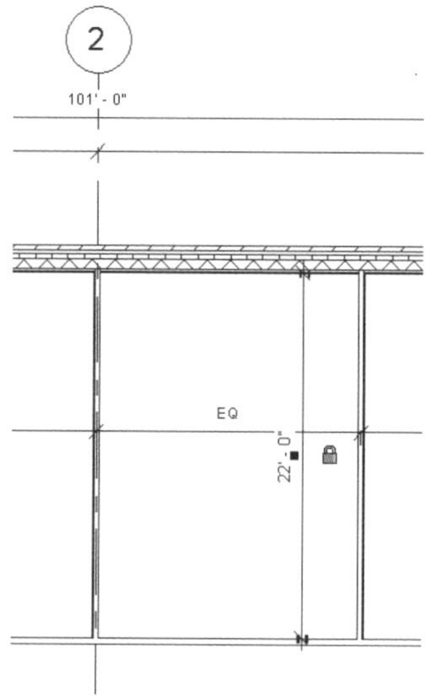

FIGURE 2-1.19
Locking dimensions

Next, you will adjust the overall building dimensions and notice how the various parametric relationships you established cause the model to update!

56. Click **grid line 3** and change the overall dimension from 101 to **40**, by clicking on the dimension text and then pressing *Enter.*

TIP: *When adjusting the building footprint via the dimensions, you need to select the grid line, not the east wall, because the dimension references the grid line.*

Notice the interior walls have adjusted to remain equal, and grid line 2 is still centered between grids 1 and 3 (Figure 2-1.20).

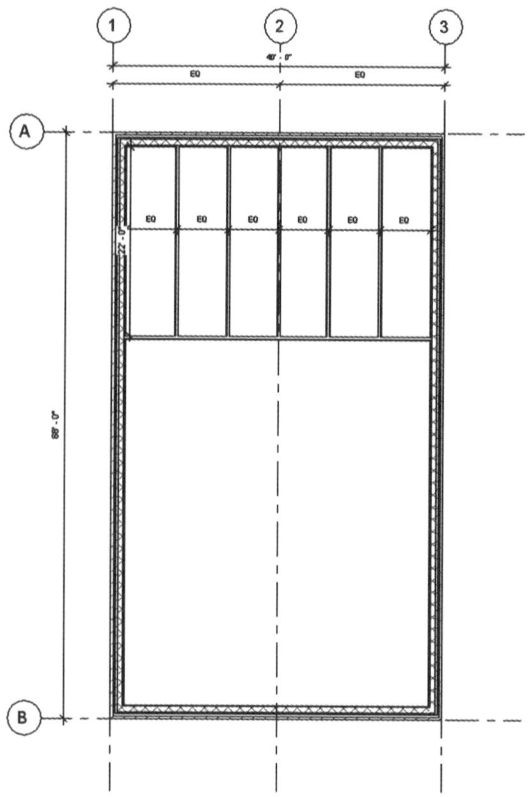

FIGURE 2-1.20 Adjusting dimensions

57. Change the 40′-0″ dimension to **110′-0″**.

58. Select grid line A and change the 68′-0″ dimension to **38′-0″**.

Your model should now look similar to Figure 2-1.21. Notice that the interior wall maintained its 22′-0″ clear dimension because the interior wall has a dimension that is locked to the exterior wall, and the exterior wall has an alignment that is locked to grid line A.

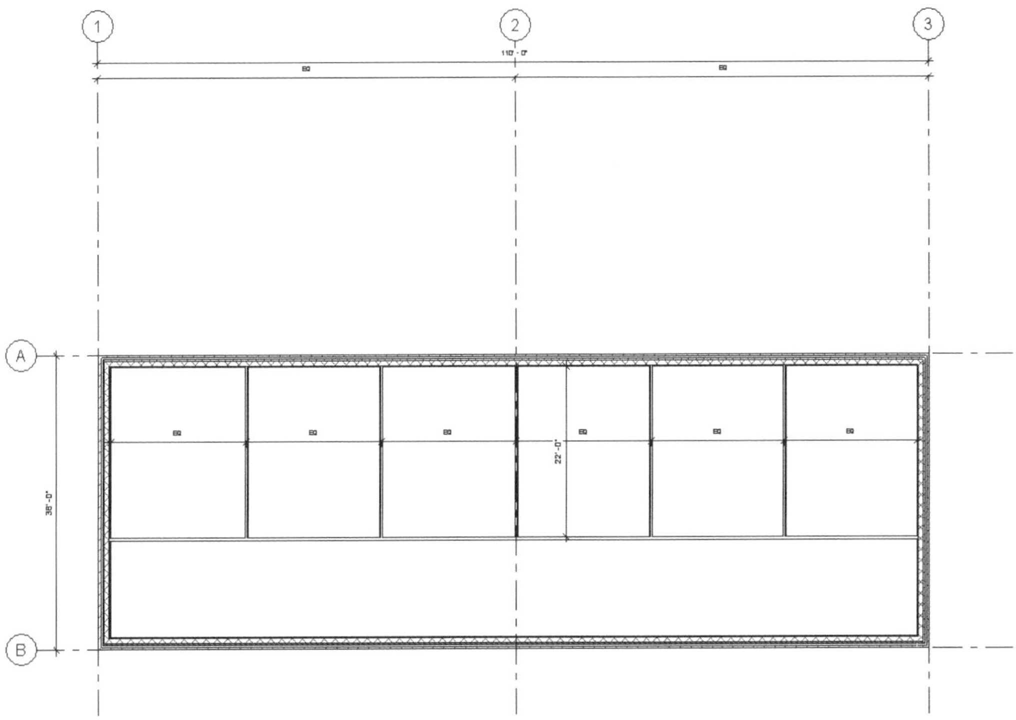

FIGURE 2-1.21 Adjusting dimensions

59. Click the **Undo** icon on the *QAT* to restore the 68′ dimension.

Your building should now be 110′-0″ x 68′-0″.

60. **Save** your project as ***Small Office.rvt***.

TIP: You can use the Measure tool to list the distance between two points. This is helpful when you want to quickly verify the clear dimension between walls. Simply click the icon and snap to two points and Revit will temporarily display the distance. You can also click "chain" on the Ribbon and have Revit add up the total length of several picks.

Exercise 2-2:
Doors

In this exercise, you will add doors to your small office building.

1. Open **Small Office.rvt** created in Exercise 2-1.

Placing Doors

2. Select **Architecture → Build → Door** tool on the *Ribbon* (Figure 2-2.1).

Notice that the *Ribbon and Properties Palette* have been updated to display options related to Doors. Next, you will modify those settings.

The *Type Selector* indicates the door style, width, and height. Clicking in this area lists all the doors pre-loaded into the current project (Fig. 2-2.2).

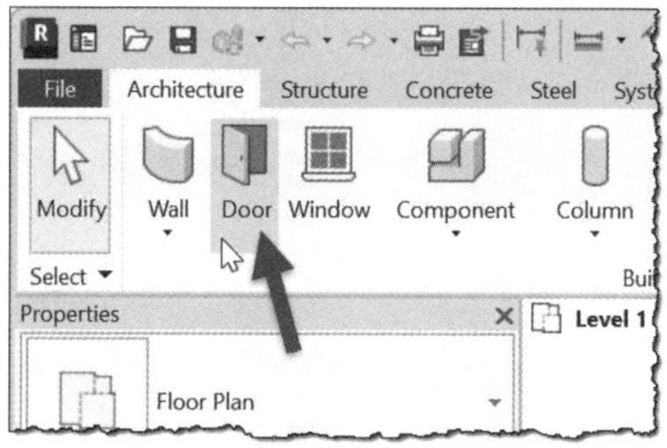

FIGURE 2-2.1 Door tool

The default template project that you started from has several sizes for a single flush door. Notice, in Figure 2-2.2, that there are two standard heights in the list. The 80″ (6′-8″) doors are the standard residential height, and the 84″ (7′-0″) doors are the standard commercial door height.

3. Change the *Element Type Selector* to *<u>Single-Flush:</u>* **36″ x 84″**, and click **Tag on Placement** on the *Ribbon* (it should have a blue background when active).

4. Move your cursor over a wall and position the door as shown in **Figure 2-2.3**. (Do <u>not</u> click yet.)

Notice that the swing of the door changes depending on what side of the wall your cursor is on.

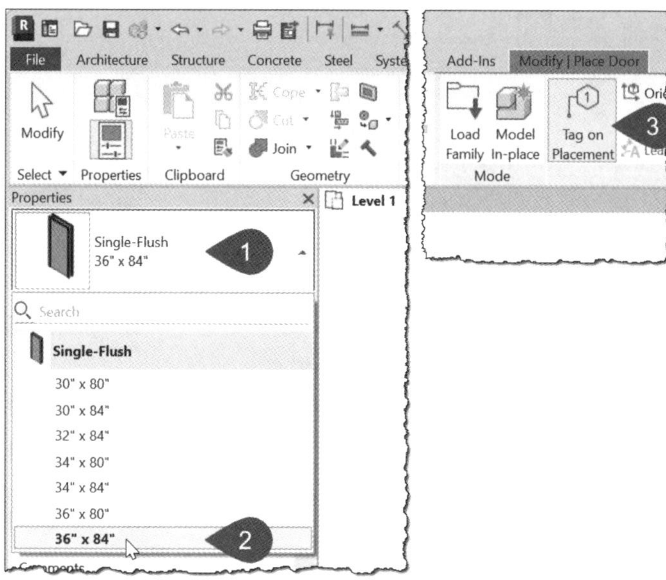

FIGURE 2-2.2 Type selector: Doors

Also, notice Revit displays temporary dimensions to help you place the door in the correct location.

5. Click to place the door. Revit automatically trims the wall and adds a door tag.

   TIP: Press the spacebar before clicking to flip the door swing if needed.

6. While the door is still selected, click on the *change swing (control arrows)* symbol to make the door swing against the wall if it is not already (Figure 2-2.4).

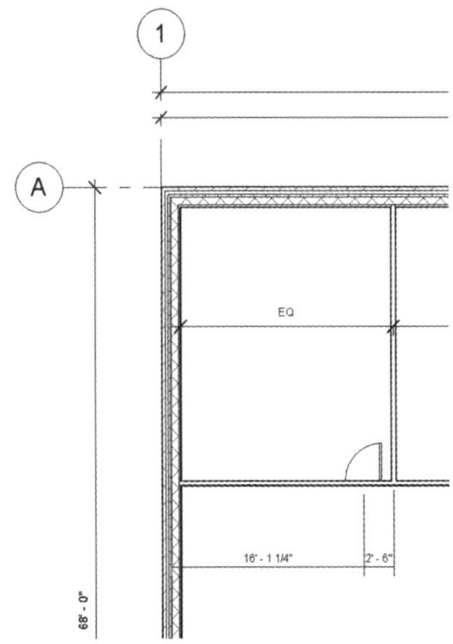

FIGURE 2-2.3 Adding door

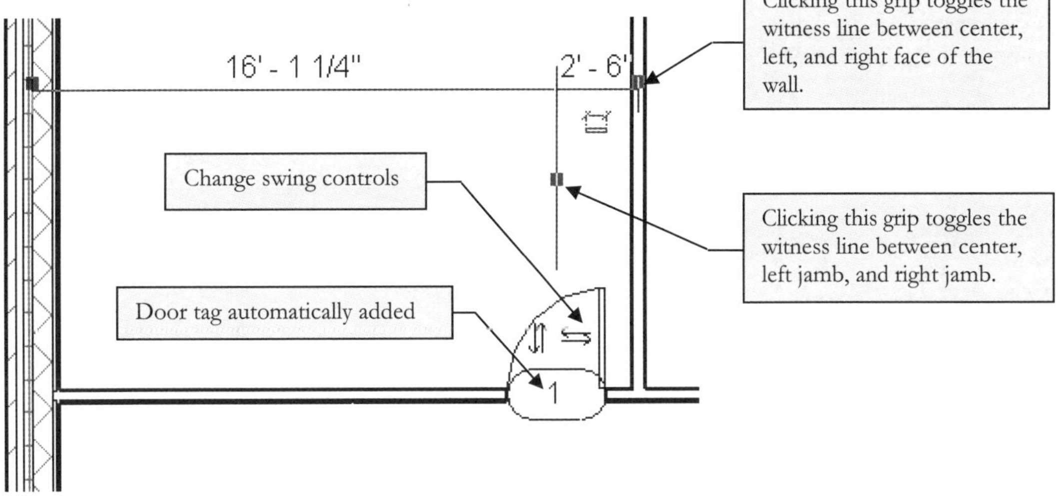

FIGURE 2-2.4 Door just placed

Next, you will reposition the door relative to the adjacent wall.

7. Click **Modify** to finish the *Door* tool.

8. Click the door (not the door tag) you just placed to select it.

9. Click the **witness line grips** multiple times until the temporary dimension references the right side (door jamb) and the wall face as shown in Figure 2-2.5.

TIP: You can also click and drag the witness line grip to another wall or line if the default location isn't what you need.

10. Click on the dimension text, type **4"**, and press *Enter.* Make sure you add the inch symbol, or you will get feet rather than inches (Figure 2-2.5).

    Tip: For this chapter, this will be the typical dimension for all doors directly adjacent to a wall, as shown here.

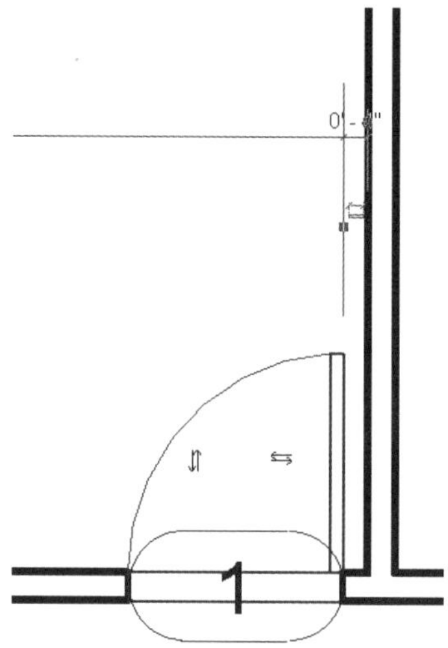

FIGURE 2-2.5 Edit door location

Unfortunately, the Revit door *Families* loaded in the commercial template do not have frames. So the 4" dimension just entered provides for a 2" frame and 2" of wall. The Autodesk-provided online content does provide some doors with frames. It is possible to create just about any door-and-frame combination using the *Family Editor.* The *Family Editor* is a special mode in Autodesk Revit that lets you create geometry and custom parametric content, including doors with sidelights, transoms, and more!

Mirroring Doors

The *Mirror* command will now be used to quickly create another door on the opposite side of the adjacent perpendicular wall.

11. With the door selected, click the **Mirror - Pick Axis** on the *Modify Tab.*

12. On the *Ribbon*, ensure **Copy** is activated (highlighted). If the copy option was not selected, then the door would be relocated, rather than copied.

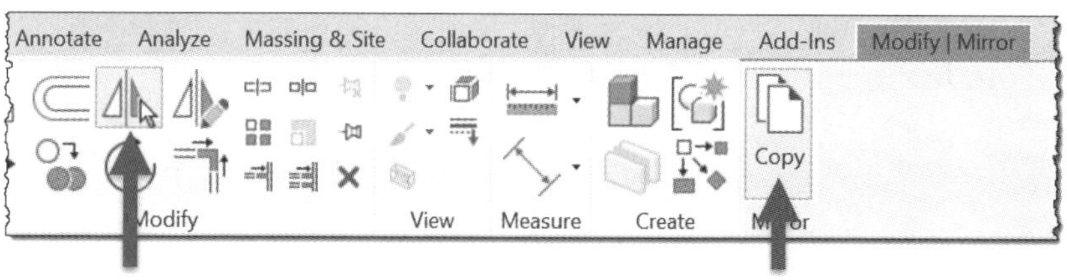

13. With the door selected and the *Mirror* command active, hover the cursor over the adjacent wall until the dashed reference line appears centered on the wall, keep moving the mouse until you see this, and then click. (Figure 2-2.6)

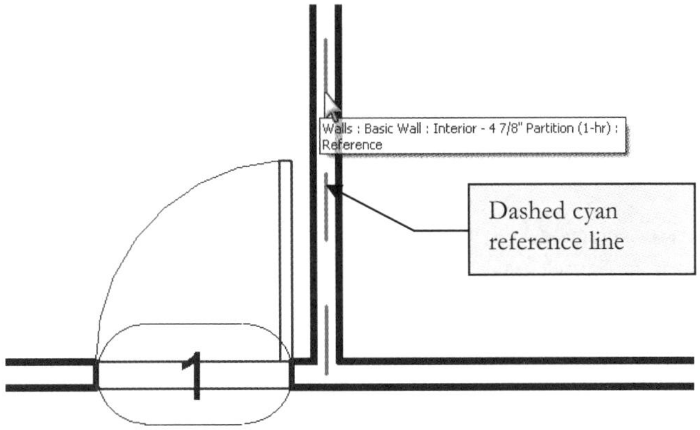

FIGURE 2-2.6 Mirroring a door

As shown in Figure 2-2.7, the door has been mirrored to the correct location.

Revit does not automatically add door tags to mirrored or copied doors. These will be added later.

TIP: *The size of the door tag is controlled by the view's scale.*

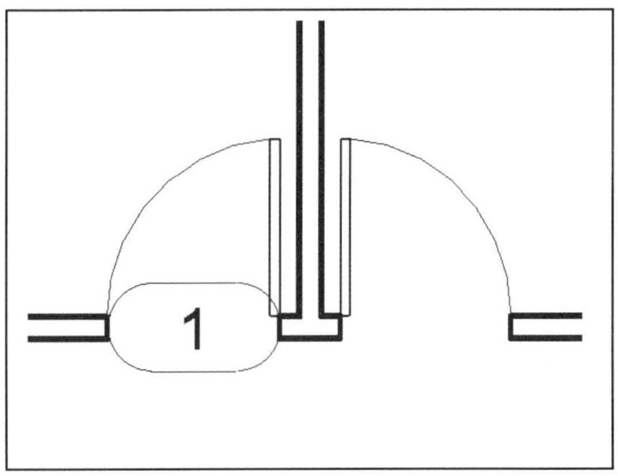

FIGURE 2-2.7 Door mirrored

Copying Doors

Now you will copy the two doors to the remaining rooms.

14. Click to select the first door (not the door tag) and then press and hold the **Ctrl** key. *While holding the Ctrl key,* click to add the second door to the selection set.

15. With the two doors selected, click the **Copy** tool.

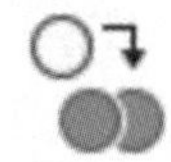

16. On the *Ribbon*, select **Multiple** (if not already checked).

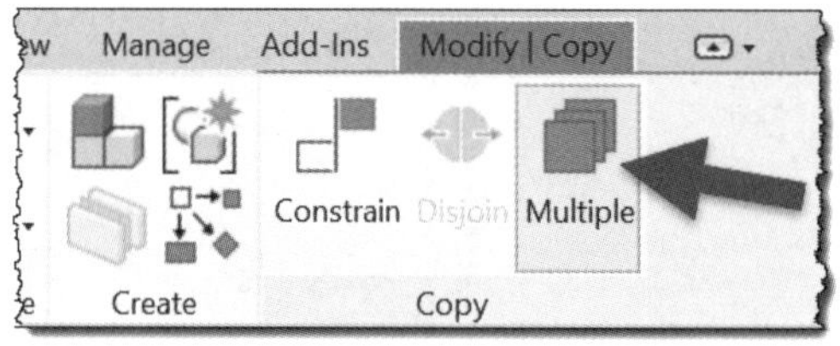

At this point, you need to pick two points: a "copy from here" point and a "copy to there" point. The first point does not have to be directly on the elements(s) to be copied. The next step will demonstrate this: you will pick the midpoint of the wall adjacent to the two doors (first pick), then pick the midpoint of the wall where you want a set of doors (second pick). With "multiple" checked, you can continue selecting "second points" until you finish making copies (press *Esc* or *Modify* to end the command).

17. Pick three points:

    a. *First pick:* midpoint/centerline of wall (see Figure 2-2.8);

    b. *Second pick:* midpoint/centerline of wall shown in Figure 2-2.9;

    c. *Third pick:* midpoint/centerline of wall shown in Figure 2-2.9.

18. Pick **Modify** to end *Copy*.

The doors are now copied.

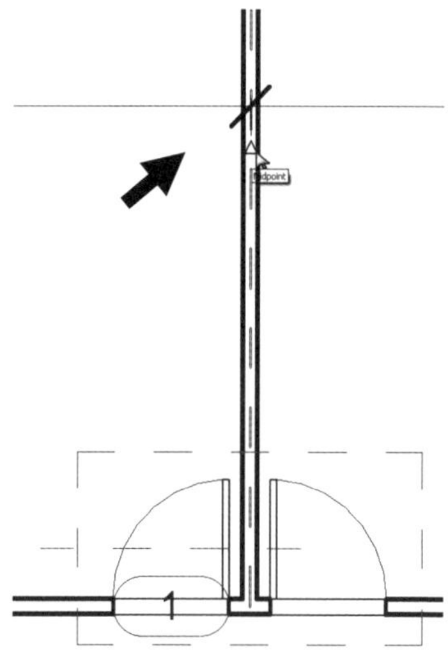

FIGURE 2-2.8 Copy – first point with midpoint symbol visible

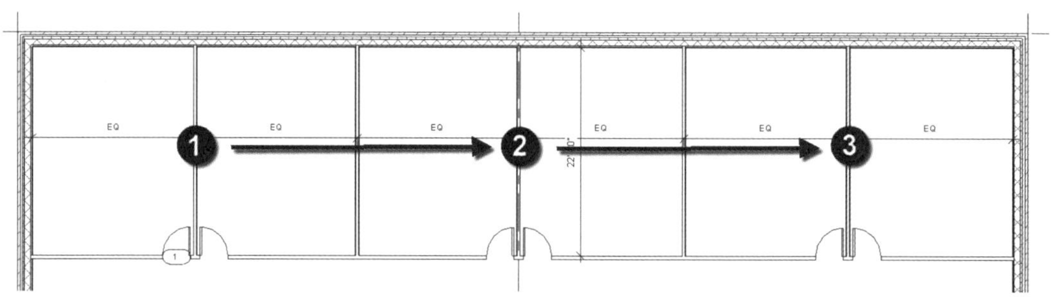

FIGURE 2-2.9 Numbers indicate pick-points listed in step #17

You will now add two exterior doors using the same door type.

19. Using the **Door** tool, add two exterior doors approximately located per Figure 2-2.10. Match the swing and hand shown.

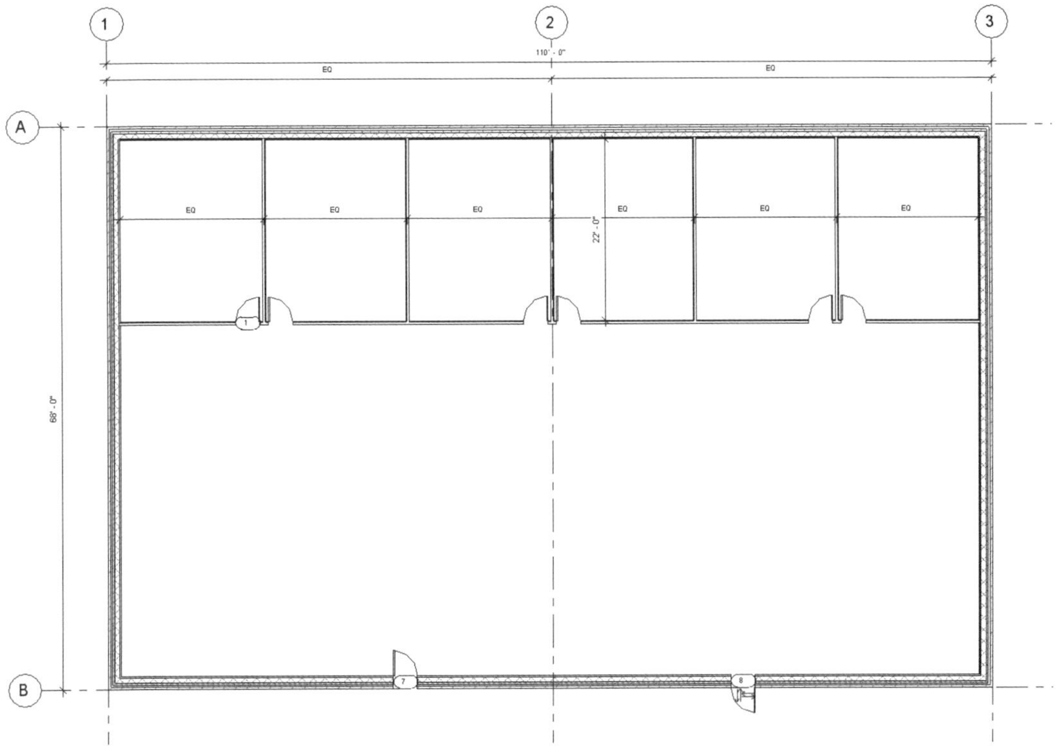

FIGURE 2-2.10 Adding exterior doors

Tag All (Not Tagged)

Revit provides a command to quickly add a tag (e.g., a door tag) to any door that does not have one in the current view. The tag might need to be moved or rotated once placed, but this still saves time and reduces the risk of missing a door tag.

20. Select **Annotate → Tag → Tag All.**

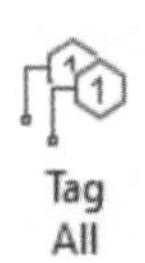

21. In the *Tag All Not Tagged* dialog box, check the box for **Doors** under *Category* and set *Tag Orientation* to **Vertical**. Click **OK** (see image on next page).

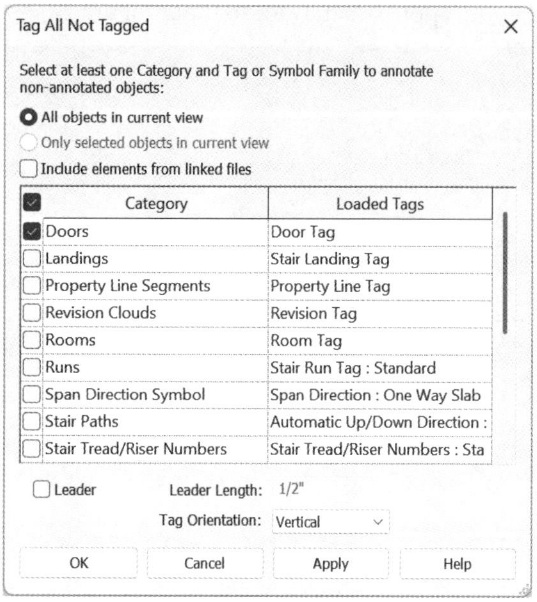

All the doors should now be tagged in your floor plan.

FYI: *Door tags can be deleted at any time and added again later at any time. Tags simply display information in the element they tag – thus, no information about the element is deleted; the building information integrity remains intact.*

Deleting Doors

Next, you will learn how to delete a door when needed. This process will work for most elements in Revit (e.g., walls, windows, text, etc.).

22. Click **Modify**.

23. Click on door number 7 (the exterior door on the left, not the door tag) and press the **Delete key** on your keyboard.

As you can see, the door has been deleted, and the opening in the wall is automatically filled in. Also, a door tag can only exist when attached to a door; therefore, the door tag was deleted.

One last thing to note: Revit numbers doors in the order they were placed (regardless of level). Doors are not automatically renumbered when one is deleted, unless the *Numbering* feature on the Manage tag is used. Also, doors can be renumbered to just about anything you want.

24. **Save** your project *(Small Office.rvt)*.

Exercise 2-3:
Windows

In this exercise, you will add windows to your small office building.

1. Open **Small Office.rvt** created in Exercise 2-2.

Placing Windows

2. Select **Architecture → Build → Window**.

Notice that the *Ribbon* and *Properties Palette* have changed to show options related to windows. Next, you will modify those settings.

The *Type Selector* indicates the window style, width, and height. Clicking the down arrow to the right lists all the windows loaded in the current project.

3. With the *Window* tool active, do the following (Figure 2-3.1):

   a. Change the *Type Selector* to *Fixed:* **36" x 48"**.

   b. On the *Ribbon*, verify *Tag on Placement* is toggled **off**.

   c. Note the **Sill Height** value in the *Properties Palette.*

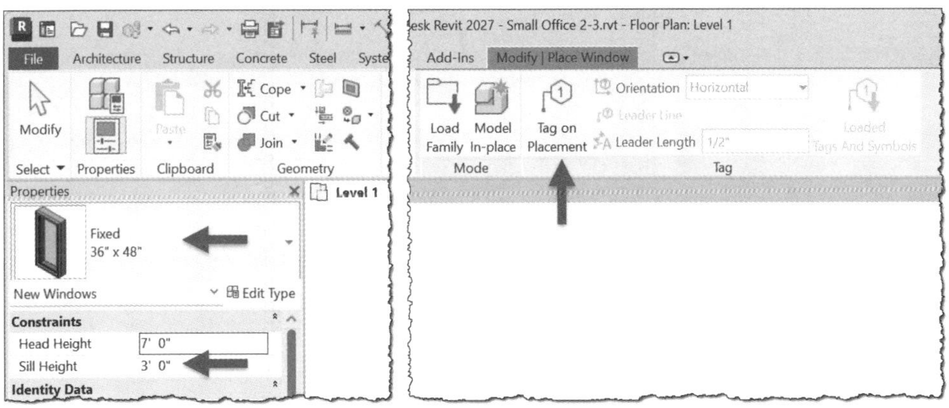

FIGURE 2-3.1 Ribbon and Properties Palette: Window tool active

4. Move your cursor over a wall and place **two windows** as shown in **Figure 2-3.2**. *Notice that the window's position changes depending on which side of the wall your cursor is on.*

FYI: *The window sill height is controlled by the Properties Palette, which you will study later in this book. For now, the default dimension was used.*

5. Adjust the **temporary dimensions** per the following:
   a. Dimensions per Figure 2-3.2.
   b. Use the witness line grip to adjust the witness line position.

   ***REMEMBER:** The selected item moves when temporary dimensions are adjusted. Pick the left window to set the 6'-0" dimension and the right for the 8'-0" dimension.*

6. Using the **Copy** command, in a way similar to copying the doors in the previous exercise, copy the two windows into each office as shown in Figure 2-3.3. (Do not worry about exact dimensions.)

7. **Save** your project *(Small Office.rvt)*.

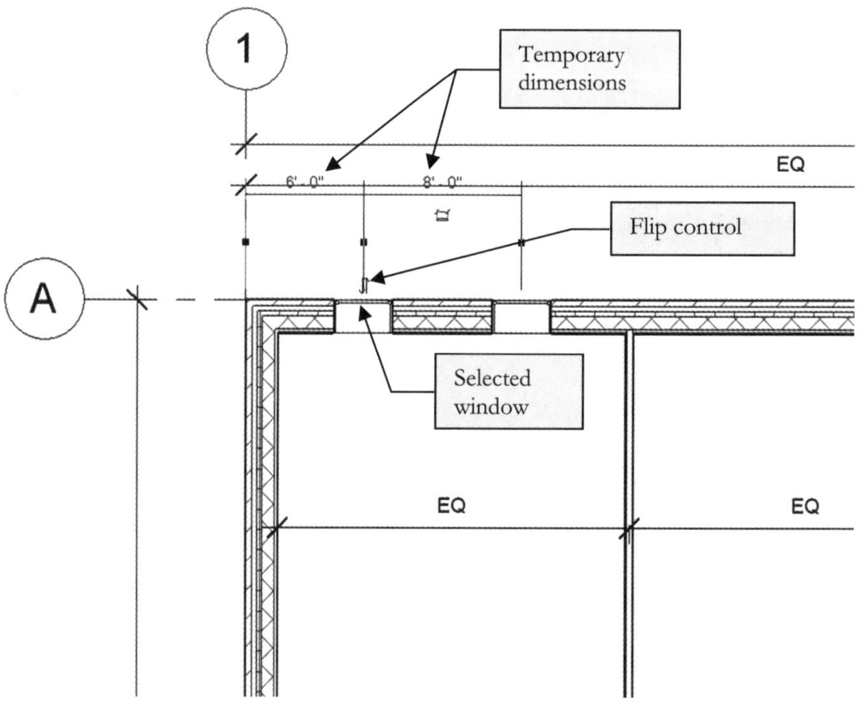

FIGURE 2-3.2 Adding windows – temporary dimensions still active

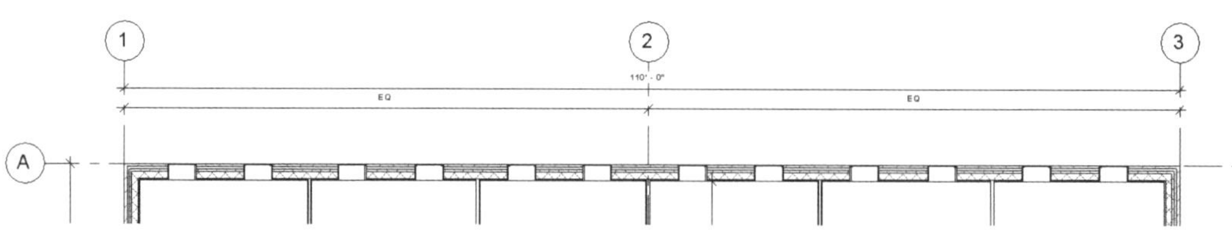

FIGURE 2-3.3 Windows added to north wall

The windows will not adjust with the grid lines and interior walls; it is possible to add dimensions and get this to work. If you tried to change the overall dimension from 110′ to 40′ again, Revit would let you know it needed to delete some windows before the change could be made. Like doors, windows need their host to exist.

The windows can all be adjusted via the temporary dimensions. The selected window has the largest width available in the project (based on the template file from which the project was started), but it is not a masonry dimension. However, additional window sizes can be added on the fly at any time. Additionally, you can create your own template file that has the doors, windows, walls, etc., that you typically need for the kind of design work you do.

In addition to the preloaded windows, several window styles are available via the *Load Autodesk Family* tool (e.g., dbl-hung, casement, etc.). It is also possible to create just about any window design in the *Family Editor*.

Object Snap Symbols:

By now, you should be well aware of the snaps that Revit suggests as you move your cursor around within the drawing window.

If you hold your cursor still for a moment while a snap symbol is displayed, a tooltip will appear on the screen. However, when you become familiar with the snap symbols, you can pick sooner (Figure 2-3.4).

The TAB key cycles through the available snaps near your cursor.

The keyboard shortcut turns off the other snaps for one pick. For example, if you type SE on the keyboard while in the Wall command, Revit will only look for an endpoint for the next pick.

Finally, typing SO (snaps off) turns all snaps off for one pick.

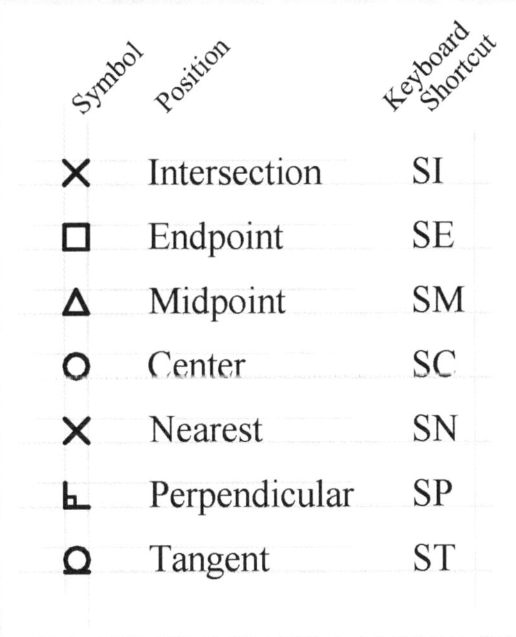

FIGURE 2-3.4 Snap Reference Chart

Exercise 2-4:
Roof

You will now add a simple roof to your building.

1. Open **Small Office.rvt** created in Exercise 2-3.

The first thing you will do is take a quick look at a 3D view of your building and notice an adjustment that needs to be made to the exterior walls.

2. Click the **Default 3D View** icon on the *QAT*.

The 3D icon switches you to the default 3D view in the current project. Your view should look similar to Figure 2-4.1. Notice the exterior walls are not high enough, which is due to a previous decision to set the wall height to 9′-0″. Next you will change this, which can be done in the plan view or the current 3D view.

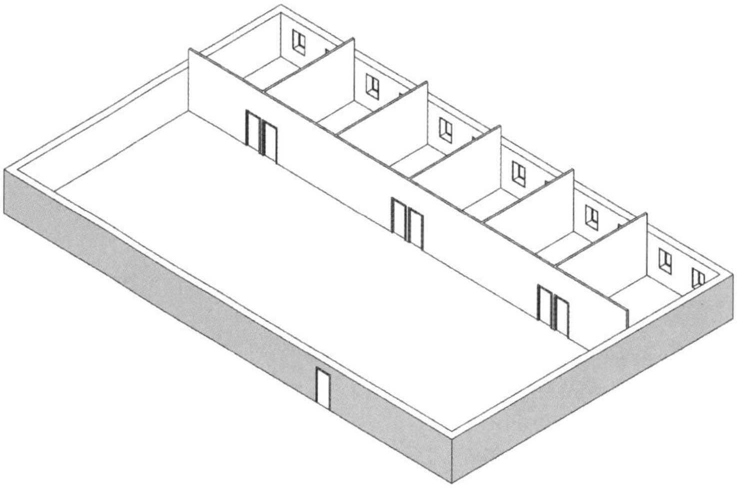

FIGURE 2-4.1 3D view of small office

3. In the 3D view, hover your cursor over one of the exterior walls to pre-highlight it, then (before clicking) press the **Tab** key to pre-highlight a "chain of walls" (i.e., all the exterior walls), and then **click** to select them.

Next, you will access the properties of the selected walls to adjust the wall height. In Revit, most design decisions can be adjusted at any time.

4. Change the following in the *Properties Palette*:
   a. *Top Constraint:* **Up to level: Roof**
   b. *Top Offset:* **2′-0″**
   c. Click **Apply** (Figure 2-4.2B).

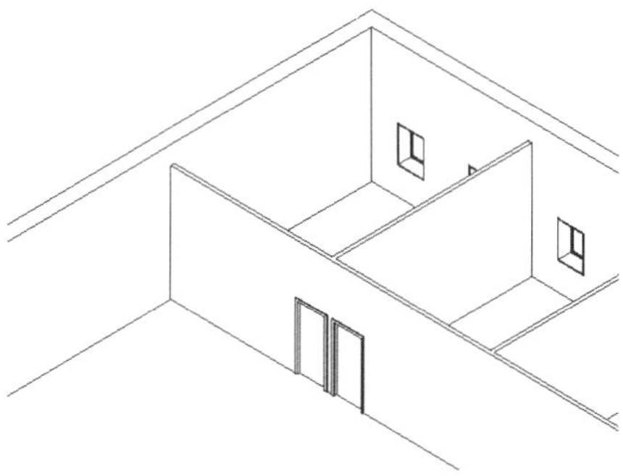

FIGURE 2-4.2A Exterior wall heights adjusted

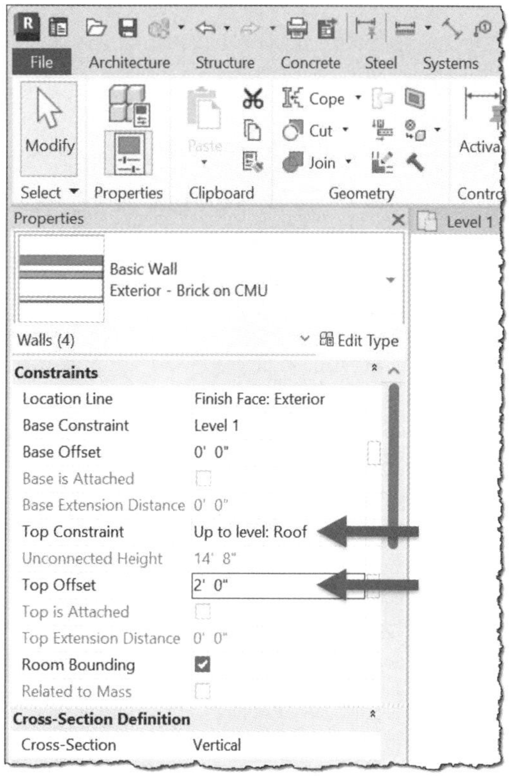

FIGURE 2-4.2B Selected wall properties

Setting the top of the wall to be associated with a *Level* establishes a parametric relationship that causes the wall height to automatically adjust if the level datum is adjusted (e.g., from 12′-0″ to 14′-0″).

Plus, the *Top Offset* at 2′-0″ creates a 2′-0″ parapet that will always be 2'-0" high, regardless of the roof elevation setting. However, there are instances when you would want the height to be fixed.

Properties Palette: All settings related to the selected wall appear here; these are called instance parameters.

Sketching a Roof

Now that the exterior walls are the correct height, you will add the roof. This building will have a flat roof located at the roof level.

5. Double-click **Level 1** (floor plan) in the *Project Browser* to switch back to that view.

6. Click **Architecture → Build → Roof** (Figure 2-4.3).

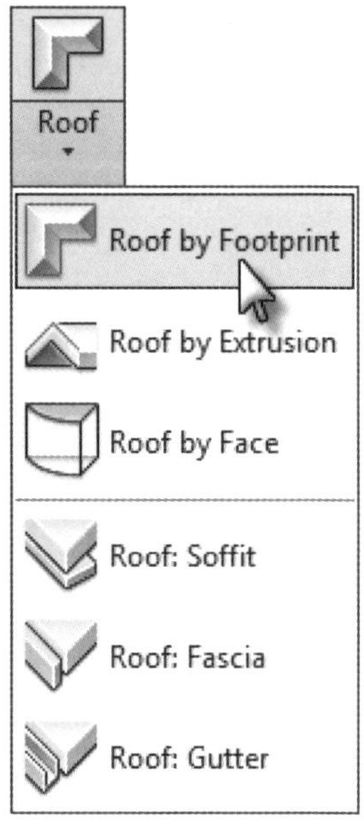

FIGURE 2-4.3 Roof tool

The fly-out prompts you to choose the method you want to use to create the roof.

7. Click **Roof by Footprint**.

   FYI: If you get a prompt to move the completed roof to "Level 2" level, that means you probably started this chapter with the wrong Revit project template.

At this point, you have entered *Sketch Mode,* where the Revit model is grayed out, so the perimeter you are about to sketch stands out.

Also, notice that the *Ribbon* and *Properties Palette* have been temporarily replaced with Sketch options for the roof (Figure 2-4.4).

8. Click **Extend Into Wall** and make sure **Defines Slope** is not checked on the *Ribbon* (Figure 2-4.4).

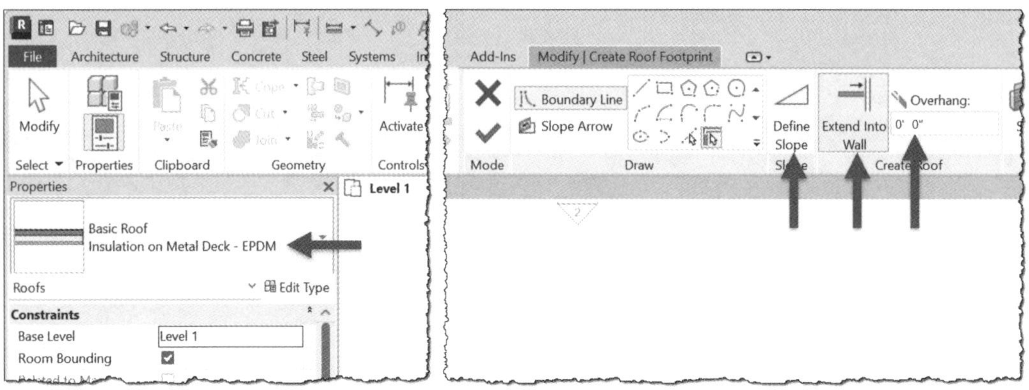

FIGURE 2-4.4 Roof sketch tools

9. Select the exterior walls:

   a. Hover your cursor over one of the exterior walls to pre-highlight the wall.

   b. Press **Tab** to select a "Chain of Walls" (i.e., all the exterior walls).

   c. Favoring the interior side of the wall, **click** to select the exterior walls, which will add the sketch lines.

At this point, you should have four magenta sketch lines, one on each wall, which represent the perimeter of the roof you are creating. When sketching a roof footprint, ensure lines do not overlap and that corners are cleaned up with the Trim command, if required. Your sketch lines require no additional edits because of the way you added them (i.e., Pick chain of walls using Tab + Select).

Notice for the roof sketch, you need to adjust the level at which the roof will be created. By default, the top surface of the roof element will be parametrically aligned with the current level (i.e., Level 1 in this case). You will change this to the roof level.

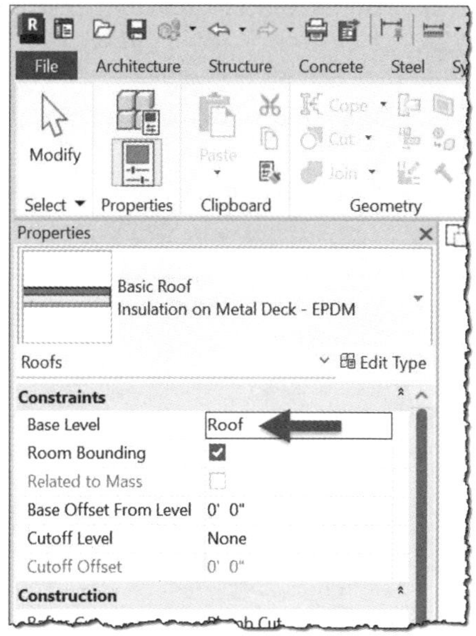

FIGURE 2-4.5 Roof instance properties

10. Set *Base Level* to **Roof** (Figure 2-4.5).

Now you are ready to finish the roof and exit sketch mode.

11. Click the **green check mark** on the *Ribbon*. 

12. If prompted, click **Yes** to the join geometry option (Figure 2-4.6).

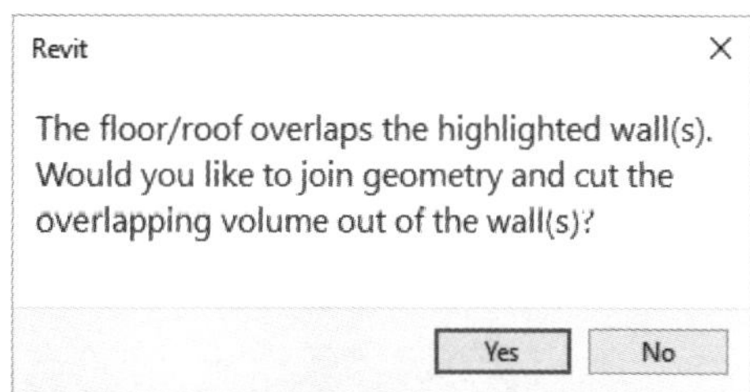

FIGURE 2-4.6 Join geometry prompt

The join geometry option will make the line work look correct in sections. If you clicked "No," the wall and roof lines would overlap, making them look messy.

The roof is now created and, in section, will extend through the finishes to the concrete block because "extend into wall" was selected when the sketch lines were added. Also, because you used the "Pick Walls" option on the *Ribbon* (which was the default), the roof edge will move with the exterior walls.

13. To see the roof, click the **Default 3D View** icon.

14. To adjust the 3D view, press and hold the **Shift** key while pressing the **wheel button** and dragging the mouse around.

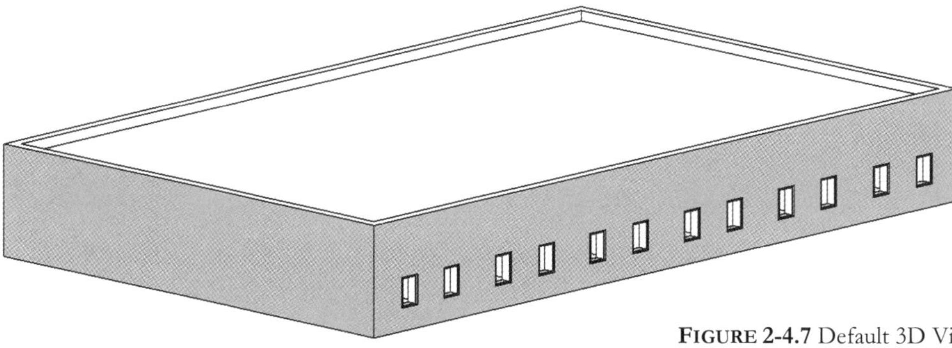

FIGURE 2-4.7 Default 3D View

15. Click the **X** on the {3D} drawing tab to close that view. This will close the 3D view but not the project or the Level 1 view.

REMEMBER: *Clicking the* ***X*** *in the upper right of the application title bar will close Revit, but it will prompt you to save first if needed.*

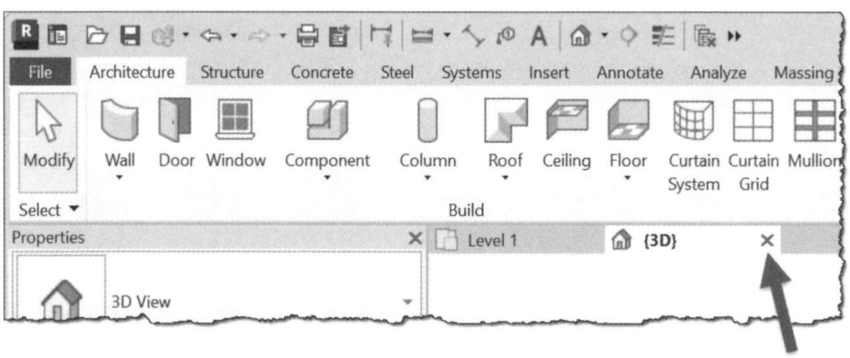

16. **Save** your project.

Exercise 2-5:
Annotation, Room Tags & Schedules

Adding text is very simple in Revit. In this exercise, you will add a title below the floor plan. You will also place rooms and room tags.

Placing Text

1. Open **Small Office.rvt** created in Exercise 2-4.

2. Make sure your current view is **Level 1**. The word "Level 1" will be bold under the *Floor Plans* heading in your *Project Browser*. If Level 1 is not current, simply double-click on the Level 1 text in the *Project Browser*.

3. Select **Annotate → Text → Text** tool on the *Ribbon*.

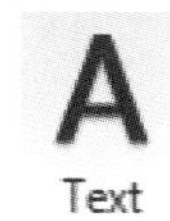

Once again, notice the *Ribbon* has changed to display some options related to the active tool (Figure 2-5.1).

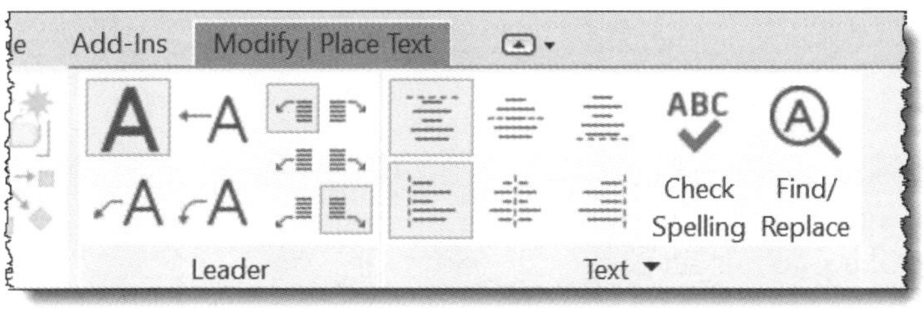

FIGURE 2-5.1 Ribbon with Text tool active

The *Type Selector* indicates the text style (which determines the font style, height and more); users can create additional text styles. From this *Contextual Tab*, on the Ribbon, your alignment (i.e., Left justified, Centered or Right justified) can also be set.

4. Set the *Ribbon* settings to match those shown above, and **Click** below the floor plan to place the text (Figure 2-5.2).

5. Type **OFFICE BUILDING – Option A**, then click somewhere in the plan view to finish the text (do not press *Enter*).

The text height, in the *Type Selector*, refers to the size of the text on a printed piece of paper. For example, if you print your plan you should be able to place a ruler on the text and read ¼″ when the text is set to ¼″ in the *Type Selector*.

Text size can be a complicated process in CAD programs; Revit makes it very simple. All you need to do is change the **view scale** for **Level 1** and Revit automatically adjusts the text and annotation to match that scale – so it always prints ¼″ tall on the paper.

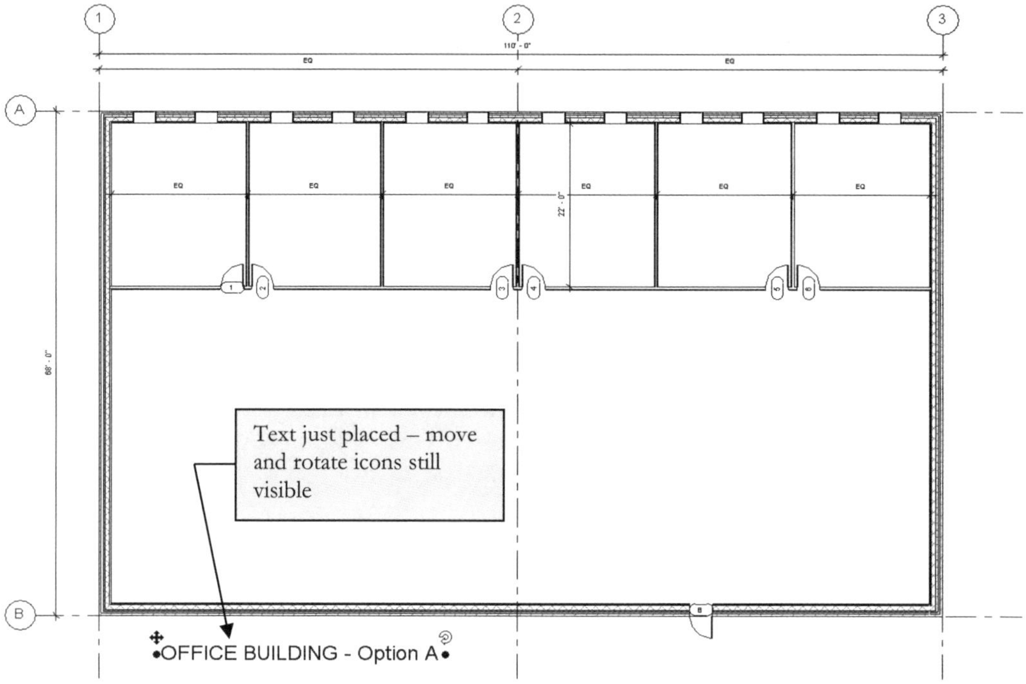

FIGURE 2-5.2 Placing text

You will not change the scale now, but it can be done via the *View Control Bar* (Figure 2-5.3). If you want to try changing it, just make sure it is set back to 1/8″ = 1′-0″ when done.

You should now notice that your text and even your door and window symbols are half the size they used to be when changing from 1/8″ to 1/4″.

You should understand that this scale adjustment will only affect the current view (i.e., Level 1). If you switched to Level 2 (if you had one), you would notice it is still set to 1/8″=1′-0″. This is nice because you may, on occasion, want one plan at a larger scale to show more detail.

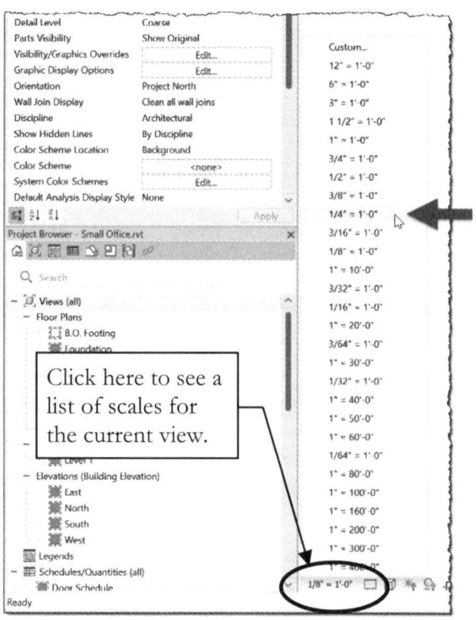

FIGURE 2-5.3 Set View Scale

Placing Room and Room Tags

Placing *Room Tags* must be preceded by placing a *Room*. A *Room* element is used to define a space and to hold information about it (e.g., floor finish, area, department, etc.).

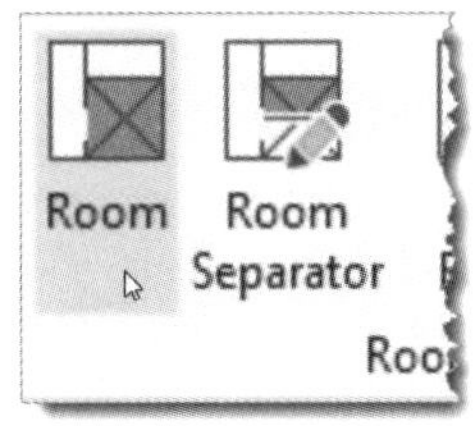

The *Room* feature searches for areas enclosed by walls; a valid area is pre-highlighted before you click to create it.

By default, Revit automatically places a Room Tag at the cursor location when you click to add a *Room* element.

6. Select **Architecture → Room & Area → Room**.

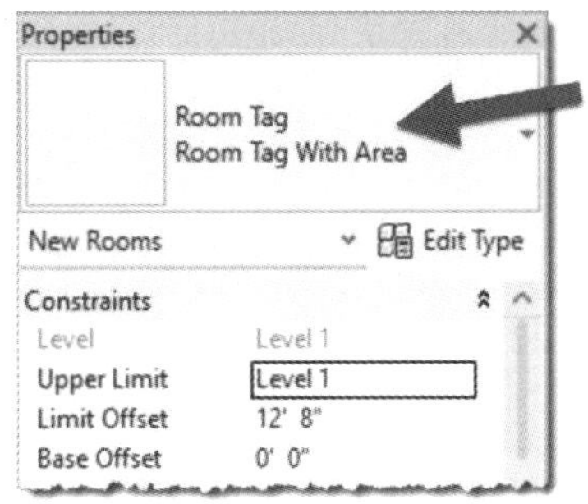

7. Set the *Type Selector* to **Room Tag: Room Tag With Area** and make sure **Tag on placement** is selected on the *Ribbon*.

8. Click within each room in the order shown in Figure 2-5.4; watch for the dashed reference line to align the tags.

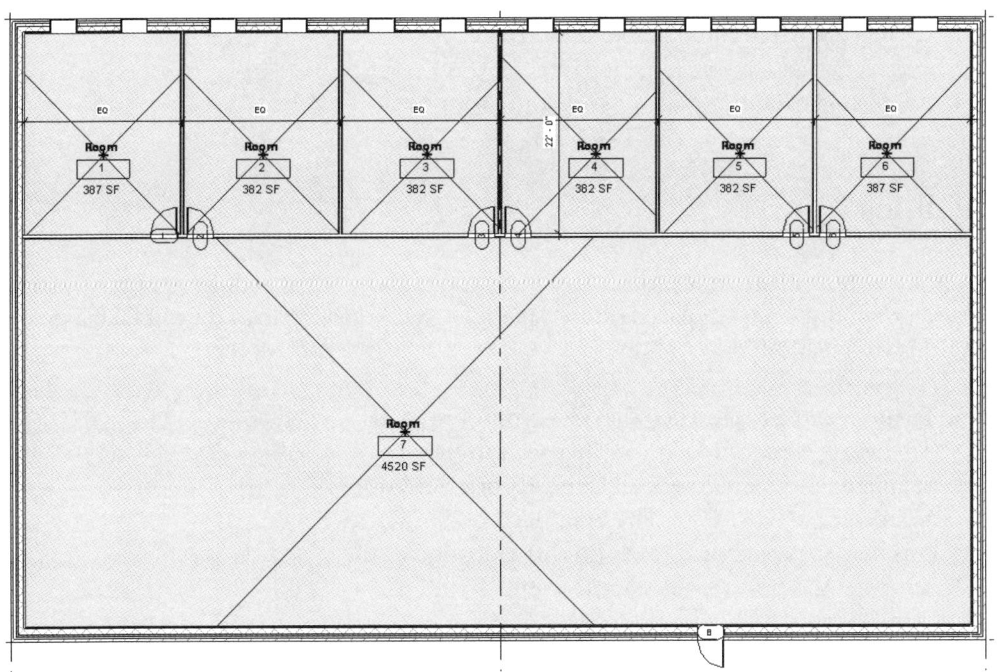

FIGURE 2-5.4 Placing rooms and room tags

While the *Room* tool is active, any previously placed rooms in the model are shaded light blue so you can see which spaces already have them. The large "X" is also part of the room. When the *Room* tool is not active, you can hover the cursor over the approximate location of the "X" until it pre-highlights, then you can click to select the room. With the *Room* object selected, you can add information to it via the *Properties Palette* or delete.

9. Click **Modify** to end the current tool.

Notice the rooms are not visible, and the "X" is gone. Also, notice the *Room Tag* selected shows the following information stored within the *Room* object: Name, Number, and Area.

FYI: *The area updates automatically when the walls move.*

Next, you will change the room names.

10. Click on the *Room Tag* for **room number 1** to select it.

When a *Room Tag* is selected, the name and number text is editable, but the area text is not.

11. Click on the room name text, type **OFFICE**, and then press **Enter** on the keyboard.
12. Change rooms 2-4 to also be named **OFFICE**.
13. Change the large room name to **LOBBY**.
14. Leave two rooms (5 and 6) as "Room" for now.

Schedules

The template you started your project from had room and door schedules set up. So, from the first door and room you placed, these schedules started filling in! You will take a quick look at this to finish out this section.

15. In the *Project Browser*, click the "+" symbol next to *Schedules/Quantities* to expand that section (if required) and then double-click on **Room Schedule** to open that view. ***FYI:*** The blue-filled box indicates this item is placed on a sheet (in this case, due to the template the project was started from).

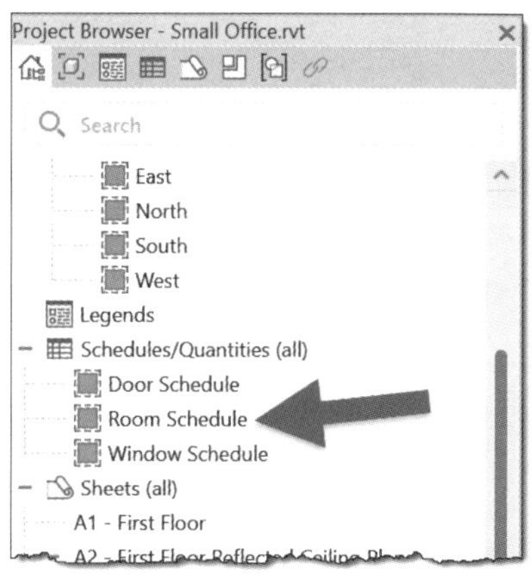

The room schedule is a tabular view of the Revit model. This information is "live" and can be changed directly in the schedule, which will immediately update the model elements (Figure 2-5.5).

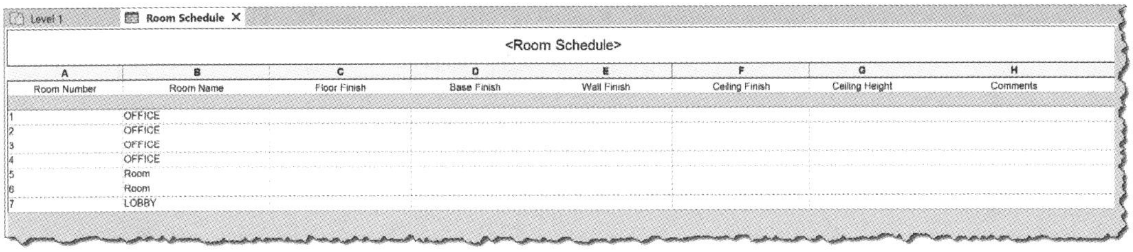

<Room Schedule>

A	B	C	D	E	F	G	H
Room Number	Room Name	Floor Finish	Base Finish	Wall Finish	Ceiling Finish	Ceiling Height	Comments
1	OFFICE						
2	OFFICE						
3	OFFICE						
4	OFFICE						
5	Room						
6	Room						
7	LOBBY						

FIGURE 2-5.5 Room Schedule

Next, you will change the two rooms named "room," and see that the floor plan is automatically updated!

16. Click in the *Room Name* column for room number 5 and change the text to read **MEN'S TOILET RM.**

17. Click in the *Room Name* column for room number 6 and change the text to read **WOMEN'S TOILET RM.**

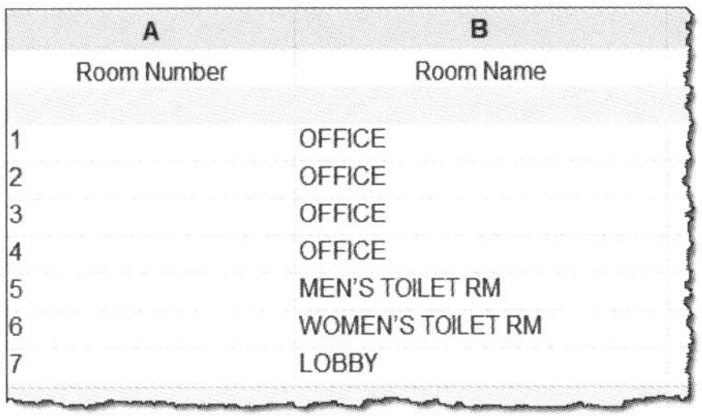

A	B
Room Number	Room Name
1	OFFICE
2	OFFICE
3	OFFICE
4	OFFICE
5	MEN'S TOILET RM
6	WOMEN'S TOILET RM
7	LOBBY

18. Click the "X" next to the Room Schedule view tab to close it.

19. Switch to *Level 1* (if required) and **zoom in** on rooms 5 and 6 (Figure 2-5.6).

Notice that the room names have been updated because the two views (floor plan and schedule) are listing information from the same "parameter value" in the project database.

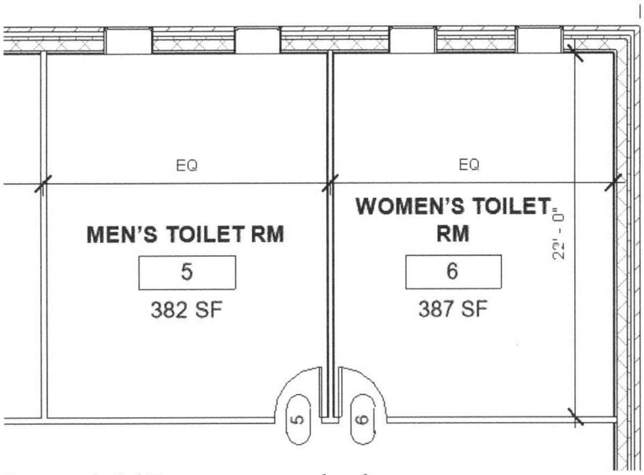

FIGURE 2-5.6 Room names updated

TIP: You can zoom in and out in a schedule by holding down the **CTRL** key and **scrolling the wheel** on your mouse. Use **CTRL + 0** to reset the view.

20. Open and Close the door schedule to view its current status.

21. **Save** your project.

Exercise 2-6:
Printing

The last thing you need to know to round out your basic Revit knowledge is how to print the current view.

Printing the current view:

1. In the *Level 1* view, right-click anywhere and select **Zoom to Fit**.

2. Select **File Tab → Print**.

3. Adjust your settings to match those shown in **Figure 2-6.1**.

   - Select a printer, from the list, that you have access to.
   - Set *Print Range* to **Visible portion of current window**.

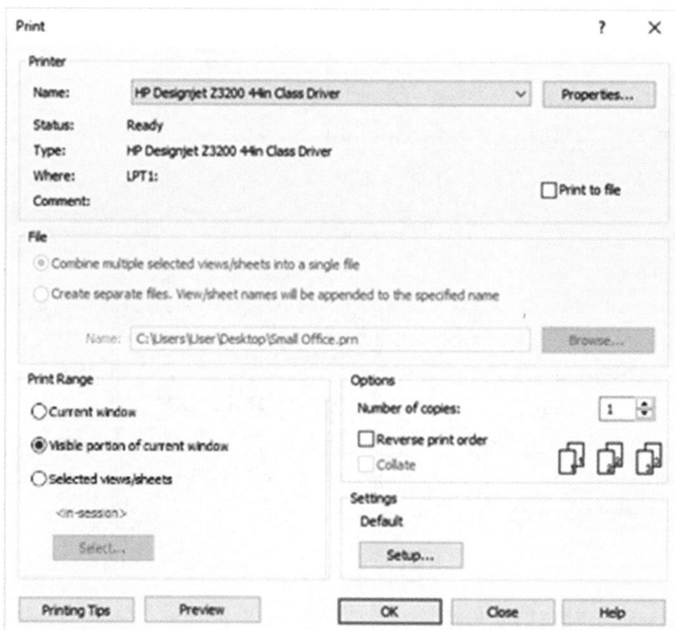

FIGURE 2-6.1 Print dialog

4. Click on the **Setup** button to adjust additional print settings.

5. Adjust your settings to match those shown in **Figure 2-6.2**.

   - *Set Zoom to:* **Fit to page**

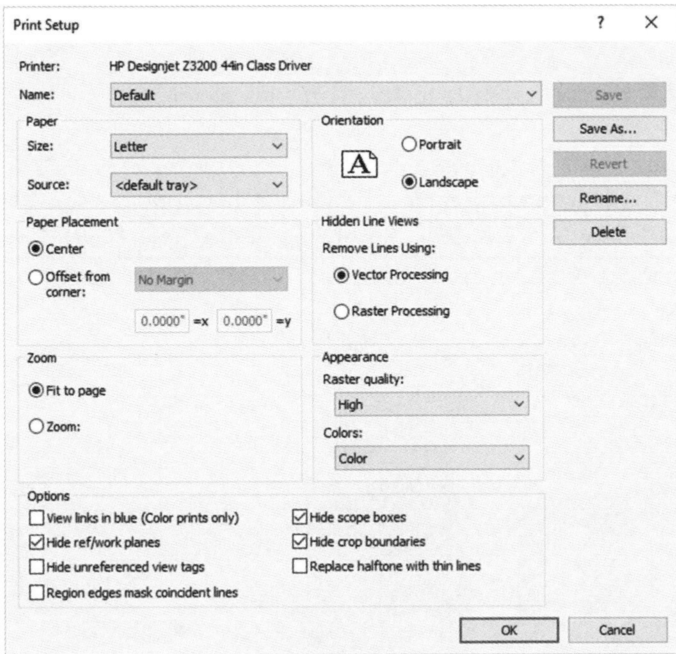

FIGURE 2-6.2 Print Setup dialog

6. Click **OK** to close the *Print Setup* dialog and return to *Print.*

7. Click the **Preview** button in the lower left corner. This will save paper and time by verifying the drawing will be correctly positioned on the page (Figure 2-6.3).

8. Click the **Print** button at the top of the preview window.

9. Click **OK** to print to the selected printer.

FYI: *Notice you do not have the option to set the scale (i.e., 1/8" = 1'-0"). If you recall from our previous exercise, the scale is set in the properties for each view. If you want a quick half-scale print you can change the zoom factor to 50%. You could also select "Fit to page" to get the largest image possible but not to scale.*

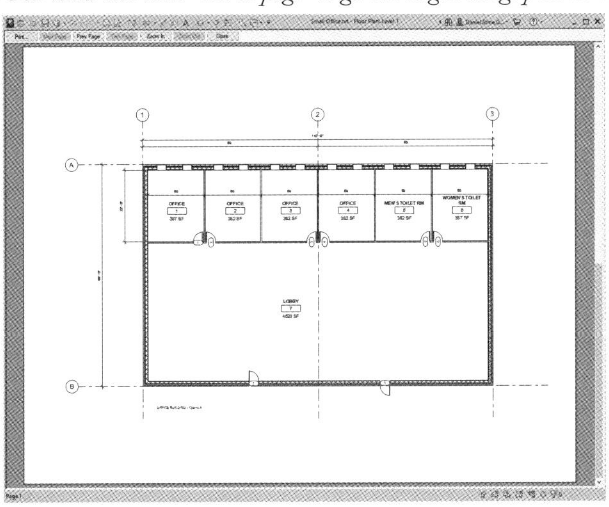

FIGURE 2-6.3 Print Preview

Printer versus Plotter?

Revit can print to any printer or plotter installed on your computer.

A <u>Printer</u> is an output device that uses smaller paper (e.g., 8½″x11″ or 11″x17″). A <u>Plotter</u> is an output device that uses larger paper; plotters typically have one or more rolls of paper ranging in size from 18″ wide to 36″ wide. A roll feed plotter has a built-in cutter that can – for example – cut paper from a 36″ wide roll to make a 24″x36″ sheet.

Plotter with three paper rolls

Color **printer** / copier

In addition to physically printing on paper, it is also possible to export a PDF file using Revit's built-in tool. This is accessed from **File → Export → PDF** or via the *Quick Access Toolbar* (see image to right). The PDF file can be emailed to clients, contractors, consultants, and more. The PDF file is also a good way to save progress versions of your drawings.

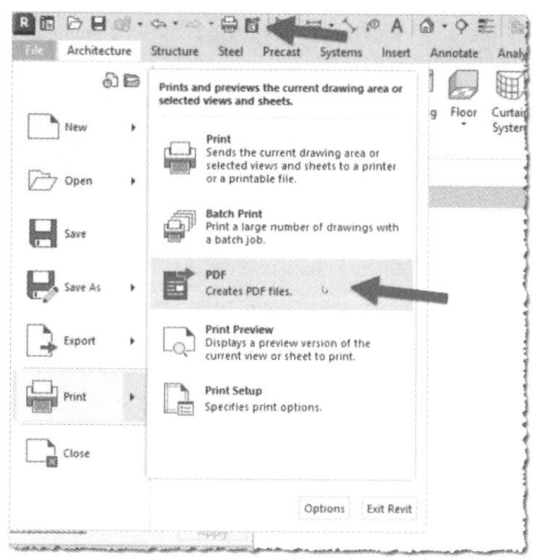

Export sheets and/or views to a PDF file

Self-Exam:

The following questions can be used as a way to check your knowledge of this lesson. The answers can be found at the bottom of this page.

1. The *Measure* tool is used to dimension drawings. (T/F)
2. Revit will automatically trim the wall lines when you place a door. (T/F)
3. Snap will help you to draw faster and more accurately. (T/F)
4. A 6′-8″ door is a standard door height in ____________ construction.
5. While using the wall tool, the height can be quickly adjusted on the

   __________________ *Bar.*

Review Questions:

The following questions may be assigned by your instructor as a way to assess your knowledge of this section. Your instructor has the answers to the review questions.

1. The *View Scale* for a view is set by clicking the scale listed on the *View Control Bar.* (T/F)
2. Dimensions are placed with only two clicks of the mouse. (T/F)
3. The relative size of text in a drawing is controlled by the *View Scale.* (T/F)
4. You can quickly switch to a different view by clicking on a View tab. (T/F)
5. You cannot select which side of the wall a window is offset to. (T/F)
6. The __________ key cycles through the available snaps near your cursor.
7. The _____________ tool can be used to list the distance between two walls without drawing a dimension.
8. While in the *Door* tool you can change the door style and size via the

   ______________________ within the *Properties Palette.*

SELF-EXAM ANSWERS:
1 – F, **2** – T, **3** – T, **4** – Residential, **5** – Options

Notes:

Lesson 3
Overview of Linework and Modify Tools:

It may seem odd to you that, in an industry-leading 3D design program, you will begin by learning to draw and edit 2D lines and shapes. However, any 3D object requires, at a minimum, detailed information in at least two of the three dimensions. Once two dimensions are defined, Autodesk® Revit® can begin to automate much of the third dimension for you. Many building components and features will require you to draw the perimeter using 2D lines.

Many of the edit tools that are covered in this lesson are the same tools that are used to edit the 3D building components.

Exercise 3-1:
Lines and Shapes

Drawing Lines:

You will draw many 2D lines in Autodesk Revit, typically in what is called *Sketch* mode. Two-dimensional lines in Autodesk Revit are extremely precise drawing elements. This means you can create very accurate drawings. Lines, or any drawn object, can be as precise as 8 decimal places (i.e., 24.999999999) or 1/256.

Autodesk Revit is a vector-based program. That means each drawn object is stored in a numerical database. When geometry needs to be displayed on the screen, Autodesk Revit reads the project database to determine what to show. This ensures that the line will be very accurate at any scale or zoom magnification.

A raster-based program, in contrast to vector based, is comprised of dots that infill a grid. The grid can vary in density and is typically referred to as resolution (e.g., 600x800, 1600x1200, etc.). This file type is used by graphics programs that typically deal with photographs, such as Adobe Photoshop. There are two reasons this type of file is not appropriate for Computer-Aided Design (CAD) programs:

- A raster-based line, for example, is composed of many dots on a grid, representing the line's width. When you zoom in, magnifying the line, it starts to become pixilated, meaning you actually start to see each dot on the grid. In a vector file you can "infinitely" zoom in on a line, and it will never become pixilated because the program recalculates the line each time you zoom in.

- A CAD program, such as Revit, only needs to store the start and end coordinates for each wall. For example, the dots needed to draw the wall are calculated on-the-fly for the current screen resolution, whereas a raster file must store each dot that represents the full length and width of the line, or lines in the wall, for example. This can vary from a few hundred dots to several thousand dots, depending on the resolution, for the same line.

The following graphic illustrates this point:

Vector vs. Raster Lines:

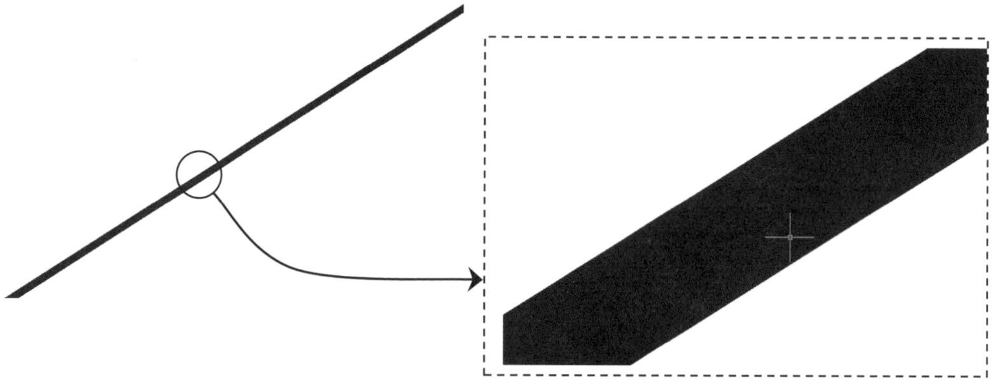

FIGURE 3-1.1 Vector Line Example
File Size: approx. 33kb

FIGURE 3-1.1A Vector Line Enlarged 1600%

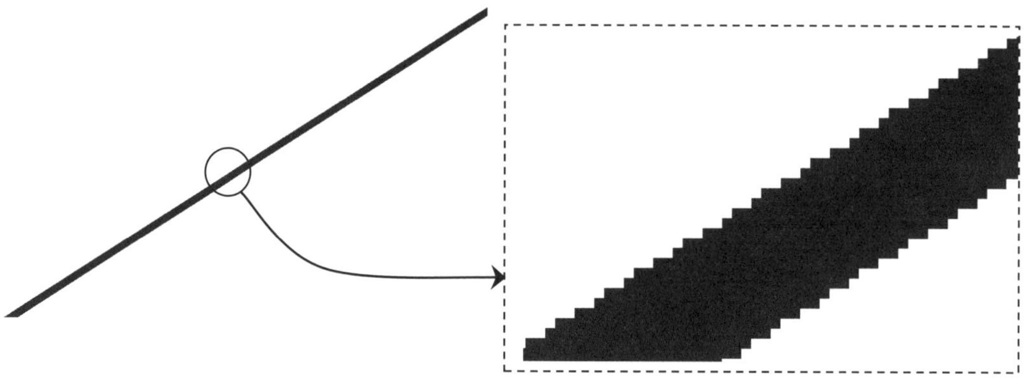

FIGURE 3-1.2 Raster Line Example
File Size: approx. 4.4MB

FIGURE 3-1.2A Raster Line Enlarged 1600%

The Detail Lines Tool:

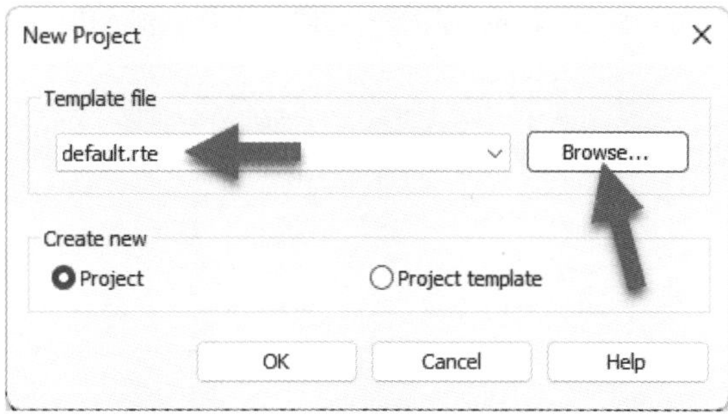

You will now study the *Detail Lines* tool.

1. **Open** Revit.

Each time you start Revit, you are in the *Recent Files* view. This view is closed automatically when a new or existing project is opened.

2. Start a new project: select **File Tab → New → Project**, click **Browse**, select **default.rte**, and then click **Open** and then **OK**.
    a. Or, click **New…** (Models) from the *Home* screen.

The drawing window is set to the *Level 1 Floor Plan* view. The 2D drafting will be done in a drafting view. Next you will learn how to create one of these views.

3. Select **View → Create → Drafting View**.
(Remember: this means *Tab → Panel → Icon* on the *Ribbon*.)

4. In the *New Drafting View* dialog box, type **Ex 3-1** for the *Name* and set the *Scale* to **3/4″ = 1′-0″** by clicking the down-arrow at the right (Figure 3-1.3).

FIGURE 3-1.3 New Drafting View dialog

You are now in the new view and the *Project Browser* will contain a node labeled *Drafting Views (Detail)*. Here, each *Drafting View* created will be listed.

5. In the *Project Browser*, click the plus symbol next to the label **Drafting Views (Detail)**; this will display the *Drafting Views* that exist in the current project (Figure 3-1.4).

You are now ready to start looking at the *Detail Lines* tool:

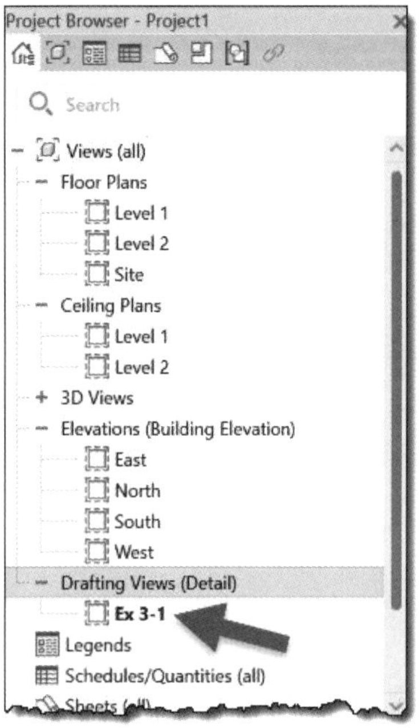

FIGURE 3-1.4 Project Browser: Drafting Views

6. Select the ***Annotate*** tab on the *Ribbon*.

7. On the *Detail* panel, select **Detail Line** (Figure 3-1.5).
   TIP: Do not use the "Model Line" tool on the Architecture tab.

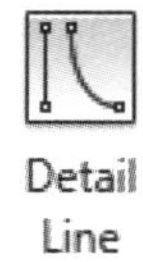

8. **Draw a line** from the lower left corner of the screen to the upper right corner of the screen, by simply clicking two points on the screen within the drawing window (Figure 3-1.6).

   NOTE: Do not drag or hold your mouse button down; just click.

After clicking your second point, you should notice the length and the angle of the line are graphically displayed; this information is temporary and will disappear when you move your cursor.

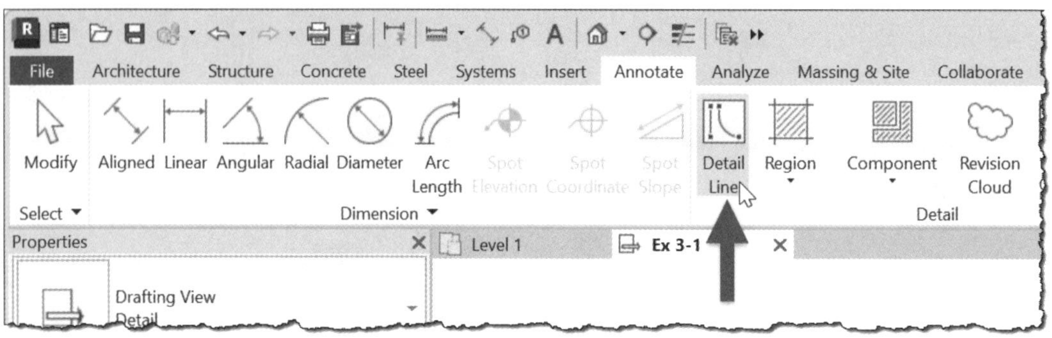

FIGURE 3-1.5 Annotate tab

You should also notice that the *Detail Line* tool is still active, which means you could continue to draw additional lines on the screen.

9. After clicking your second point, select the ***Modify*** tool from the left side of the *Ribbon*.

Selecting *Modify* cancels the current tool and allows you to select portions of your drawing for information or editing. Revit conveniently places the *Modify* tool in the same location on each tab, so it is always available no matter which tab on the *Ribbon* is active.

***TIP:** Pressing the Esc key twice reverts Revit back to Modify mode.*

Did You Make a Mistake?

Whenever you make a mistake in Revit you can use the **UNDO** command, via the *QAT*, to revert to a previous drawing state. You can perform multiple UNDOs all the way to your previous *Save*.
Similarly, if you press Undo a few too many times, you can use **REDO**.

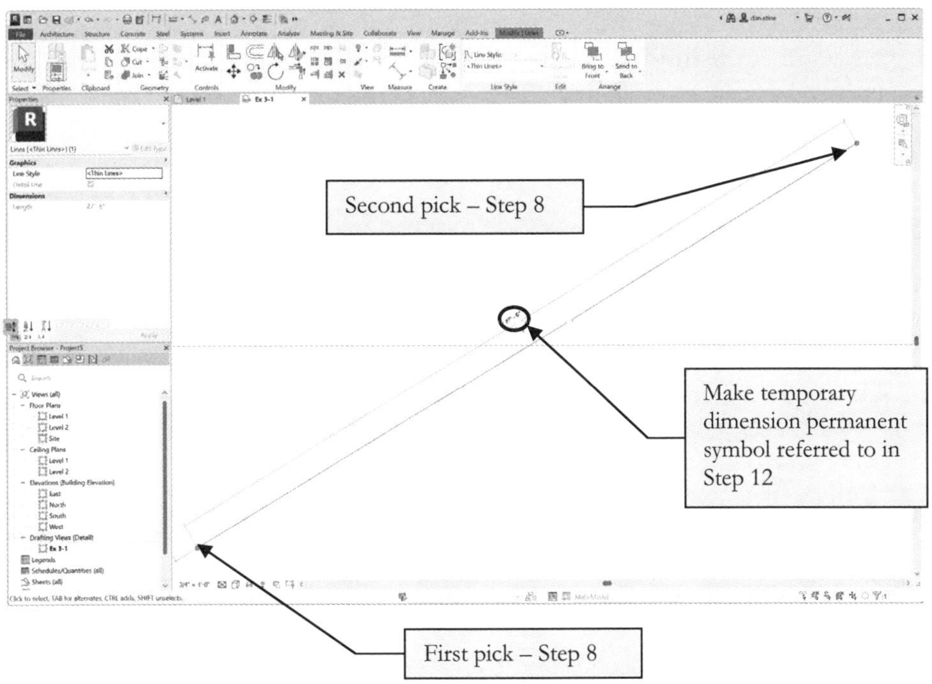

FIGURE 3-1.6 Your first detail line; exact dimensions are not important at this point.

Notice in the image above that while the *Detail Line* tool is active, the *Modify | Place Detail Line* contextual tab is shown. As soon as you click the *Modify* button or press Esc, the tab reverts to the basic *Modify* tab.

This constitutes your first line! However, as you are probably aware, it is not very accurate in terms of length and angle. Your line will likely be a different length due to where you picked your points and the size and resolution of your monitor.

Typically, you need to provide information such as length and angle when drawing a line; you rarely pick arbitrary points on the screen as you did in the previous steps. Revit allows you to get close with the on-screen dimension and angle information. Most of the time, you also need to accurately pick your starting point. For example, how far one line is from another, or picking the exact middle point on another line.

Having said that, however, the line you just drew still has precise numbers associated with its length and angle; this information is displayed after the line is drawn. The dimension and angle information is displayed until you begin drawing another line or select another tool. You can also select the line. While the dimensions are still visible, you can use them to modify the line's length and angle; you will try that later.

10. If not already selected, click the **Modify** tool from the *Ribbon.*

Notice that the temporary dimensions have disappeared.

While you are in *Modify* mode, you can select lines and objects in the current view.

11. Now **select the line** by clicking the mouse button with the cursor directly over the line.

FYI: Always use the left button unless the right button is specifically mentioned.

Notice that the temporary dimensions have returned.

The following step shows how to make a temporary dimension permanent:

If, at any point, you want to make a temporary dimension permanent, you simply click the "make this temporary dimension permanent" symbol near the dimension. You will try this now.

12. With the diagonal line still selected, click the "make this temporary dimension permanent" symbol near the dimension (Figure 3-1.6).

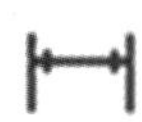

13. Select **Modify** to unselect the line.

The dimension indicating the length of the line is now permanent (Figure 3-1.7). The value of your dimension will not be the same as the one in this book as the size of your monitor and the exact points picked can vary greatly.

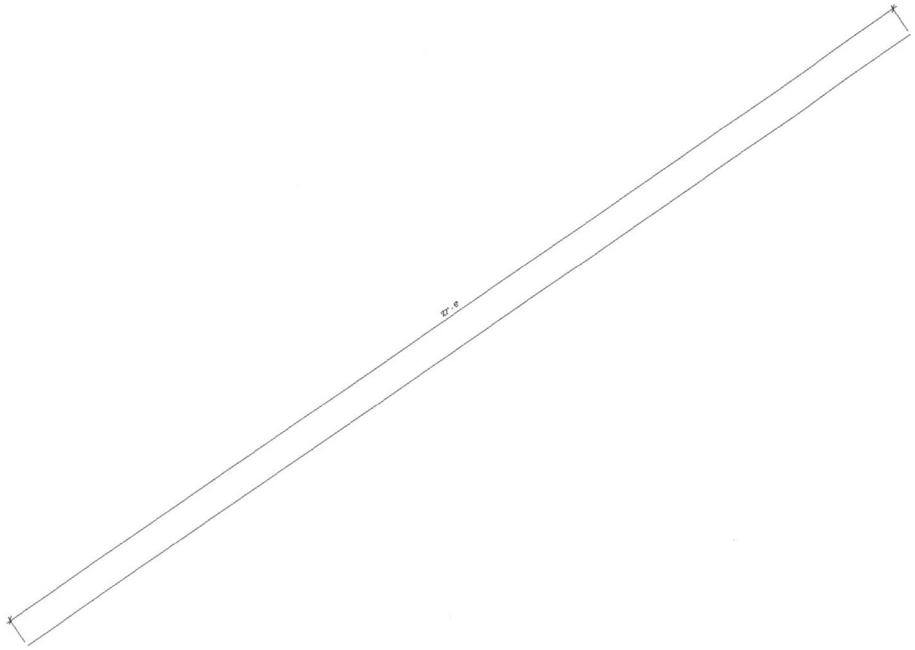

FIGURE 3-1.7 Temp dimension converted to permanent dimension

The following shows how to change the length of the line:

Currently, the line is approximately 20 - 30′ long (27′-6″ in Figure 3-1.7). If you want to change the length of the line to 22′-6″, you select the line and then change the dimension text, which in turn changes the line length. This can also be done with the temporary dimensions; the key is that the line has to be selected. You will try this next.

FYI: *Your detail line length will vary slightly depending on the size and resolution of your computer monitor, as you will be seeing more or less of the drawing area. This also assumes you have not performed any zooming, including spinning the wheel button on your mouse. If your line is way off, you should Undo or start over so the next several steps work out as intended.*

14. In *Modify* mode, select the diagonal line.

15. With the line currently selected, click on the dimension-text.

A dimension-text edit box appears directly over the dimension, within the drawing window. Whatever you type as a dimension changes the line to match.

16. Type **22 6** (i.e., 22 *space* 6) and press **Enter** (Figure 3-1.8).

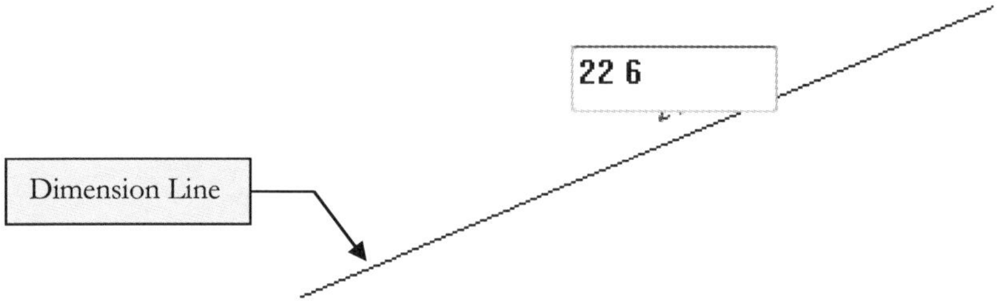

FIGURE 3-1.8 Editing dimension to change line length

You should have noticed the line's length changed. Revit assumes you want the line to change length equally at both ends, so the midpoint does not move. Try changing the dimension to 100′ and then Undo.

Locking Dimensions:

Revit allows you to *Lock* a dimension, which prevents the dimension and line length from changing. You will investigate this now to help avoid problems later.

17. Make sure the line is *not* selected; to do this, press Esc or click *Modify*.

18. Select the dimension, not the line, and note the following about the selected dimension (Figure 3-1.9).

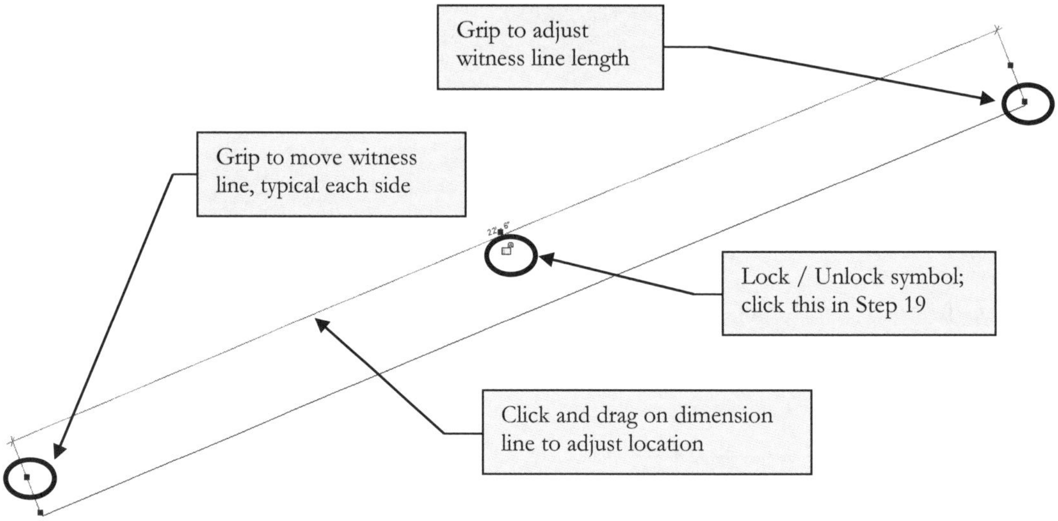

FIGURE 3-1.9 Selected dimension

19. Click on the **Lock/Unlock** padlock symbol to lock the dimension (Figure 3-1.9). 

The dimension is now locked. Again, this means that you cannot change the dimension OR the line, though you can move it. The dimension is attached to the line so that changing one affects the other. Next, you will see what happens when you try to modify the dimension while it is locked.

Any time the line or dimension is selected, you will see the lock or unlock symbol in the locked position. 

FYI: Clicking the dimension's padlock icon anytime it is visible will toggle the setting between locked and unlocked.

20. Select **Modify** to unselect the *Dimension.*

21. Select the line (not the dimension).

22. Click on the dimension text and attempt to modify the line length to **21′**.

As you can see, Revit will not let you edit the text.

Even though your current view is showing a relatively small area, i.e., your *Drafting View,* it is actually an infinite drawing board.

In architectural CAD drafting, everything is drawn to true life size, or full scale, ALWAYS! If you are drawing a building, you might draw an exterior wall that is 600′-0″ long. If you are drawing a window detail, you might draw a line that is 8″ long. In either case, you are entering that line's actual length.

You could, of course, have an 8″ line and a 600′-0″ line in the same *Drafting View*. Either line would be difficult to see at the current drawing magnification (i.e., approximately 22′ x 16′ area; also recall that your diagonal line is 27′-6″ long). So, you would have to zoom in to see the 8″ line and zoom out to see the 600′-0″ line. Next, you will get to try this.

When the diagonal line is selected, notice the *Properties Palette* lists the type of entity selected (i.e., Lines), the *Style* (i.e., Thin Lines), and the *Length* (i.e., 22′-6″). See Chapter 1 for more information on the *Properties Palette* and how to open it if you accidentally closed it.

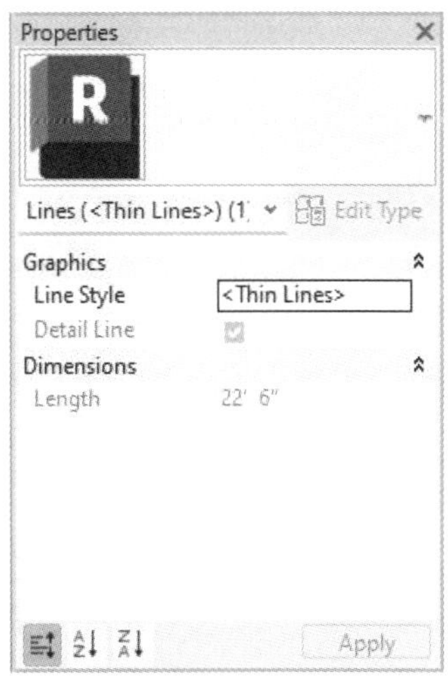

FIGURE 3-1.10 Properties Palette with diagonal line selected

Draw an 8″ Line:

The next steps will walk you through drawing an 8″ horizontal line. Revit provides multiple ways to do this. You will try one of them now.

23. Select **Annotate → Detail → Detail Line**.

24. Pick a point somewhere in the upper left corner of the drawing window.

25. Start moving the mouse towards the right and generally horizontal until you see a dashed reference line extending in each direction of your line appear on the screen, as in Figure 3-1.11.

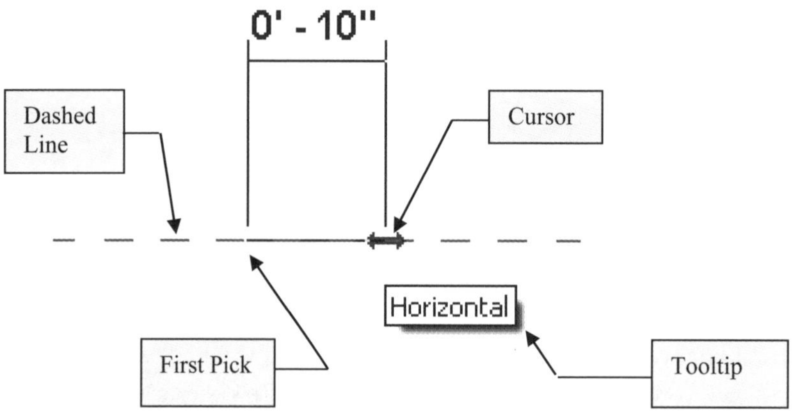

FIGURE 3-1.11 Drawing a line with the help of Revit

TIP: You will see a dashed horizontal line and a tooltip when the line is horizontal.

As you move the mouse left and right, you will notice that Revit displays various dimensions that let you quickly draw your line at these often-used increments. See the next exercise to learn more about how to control the increments shown.

26. With the dashed line and *tooltip* visible on the screen, take your hand off the mouse, so you do not accidentally move it, and type **8″** and then press **Enter**.

    TIP: Remember, you have to type the inch symbol; Revit always assumes you mean feet unless you specify otherwise. A future lesson will review the input options in more detail.

You have just drawn a line with a precise length and angle!

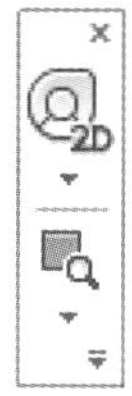

27. Use the ***Measure*** tool to verify it was drawn correctly. Click *Modify* → *Measure* → *Measure (down arrow)* → *Measure Between Two References*

28. Use the ***Zoom In Region*** tool to enlarge the view of the 8″ line via the *Navigation Bar* (image to the right).

29. Now use the ***Zoom to Fit*** or ***Previous Pan/Zoom*** tools so that both lines are visible again.

Draw a 600′ Line:

30. Select the ***Detail Line*** tool and pick a point in the lower right corner of the drawing window.

31. Move the cursor straight up from your first point so that the line snaps to the vertical and the dashed line appears (Figure 3-1.12).

32. With the dashed line and *tooltip* visible on the screen, take your hand off the mouse so you do not accidentally move it; type **600** and then press **Enter**.

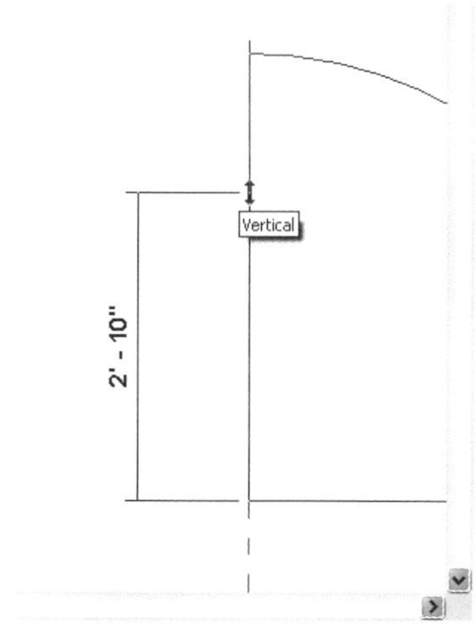

FIGURE 3-1.12 Drawing another Detail Line; 600′-0″ vertical line – lower right

TIP #1: Notice this time you did not have to type the foot symbol (′).

TIP #2: You do not need to get the temporary dimension close to reading 600′; the temporary dimension is ignored when you type in a value.

33. Press the **Esc** key twice to exit the *Detail Line* tool and return to the *Modify* mode.

Because the visible portion of the drawing area is only about 16′ tall, you obviously would not expect to see a 600′ line. You need to change the drawing's magnification by zooming out to see it.

34. Use ***Zoom to Fit*** to see the entire drawing (Fig. 3-1.13).

TIP: Double-click your wheel button to Zoom Extents.

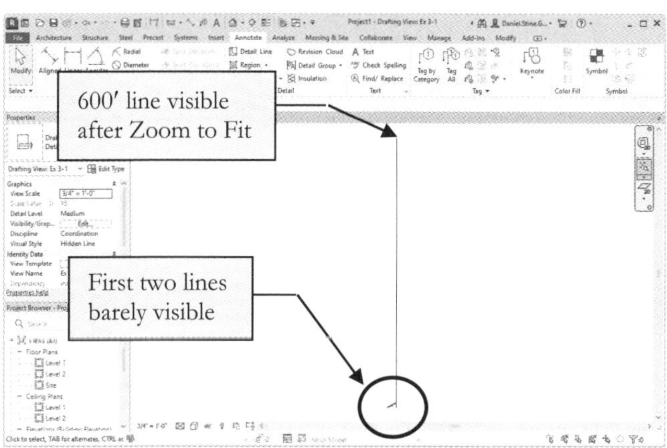

FIGURE 3-1.13 Detail view with three lines

Drawing Shapes:

Revit provides several tools for drawing common shapes such as squares, rectangles, circles, and ellipses. These tools can be found on the *Ribbon* while the *Detail Line* tool is active. You will take a look at *Rectangle* and *Circle* now.

Creating a Rectangle:

35. Use ***Previous Pan/Zoom***, or *Zoom Region*, to get back to the original view where the diagonal line spans the screen.

36. Select the ***Detail Line*** tool.

Notice the *Ribbon* and *Properties Palette* have changed to show various options related to *Detail Lines* (Figure 3-1.14).

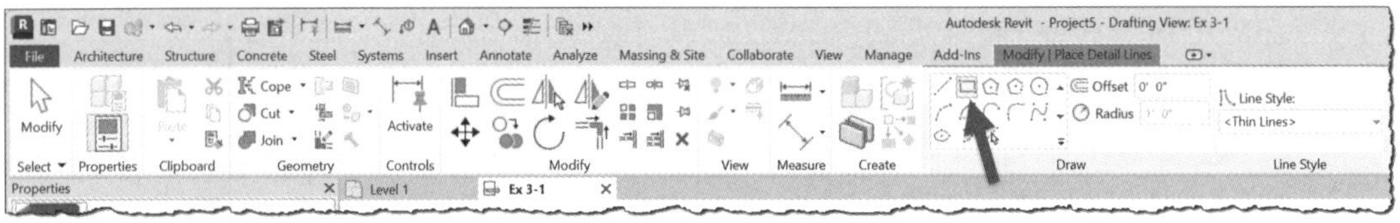

FIGURE 3-1.14 Place Detail Lines contextual Tab on Ribbon

37. Select the **Rectangle** tool from the *Ribbon.*

TIP: Hover your cursor over the icon to see the tooltip until you learn what tools the icons represent.

38. Pick the "**first corner point**" somewhere near the lower center of the drawing window (Figure 3-1.15).

Notice that the temporary dimensions display a dimension for both width and height. At this point, you can pick a point on the screen, trying to get the dimensions correct before clicking the mouse button. If you do not get the rectangle drawn correctly, you can click each dimension-text and change the dimension while the temporary dimensions are displayed; see the next two steps for the rectangle dimensions.

39. Draw a 2′-8″ x 4′-4″ rectangle using the temporary dimensions displayed on the screen; if you do not draw it correctly, do the following:

    a. Click the dimension-text for the horizontal line, then type **2′-8″** and then press **Enter**.

    b. Type **4′-4″** and then press **Enter** for the vertical dimension.

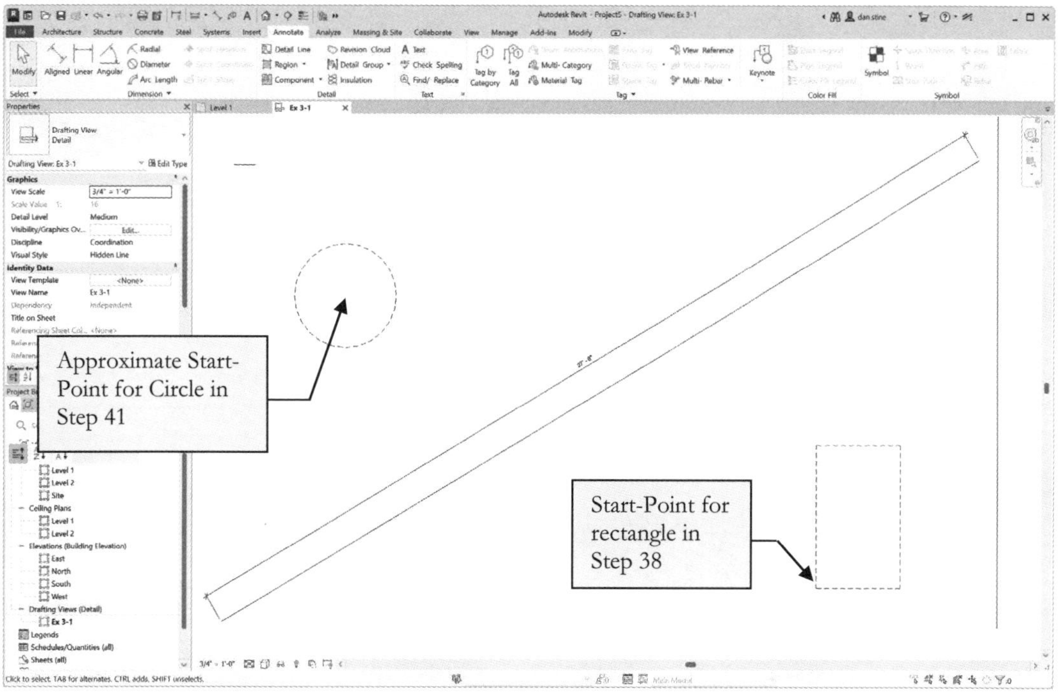

FIGURE 3-1.15 Drawing with Rectangle and Circle to be added (shown dashed for clarity)

Creating a Circle:

40. With the *Detail Line* tool active, select **Circle** from the *Ribbon* (Figure 3-1.16).

41. You are now prompted to pick the center point for the circle; pick a point approximately as shown in Figure 3-1.15.

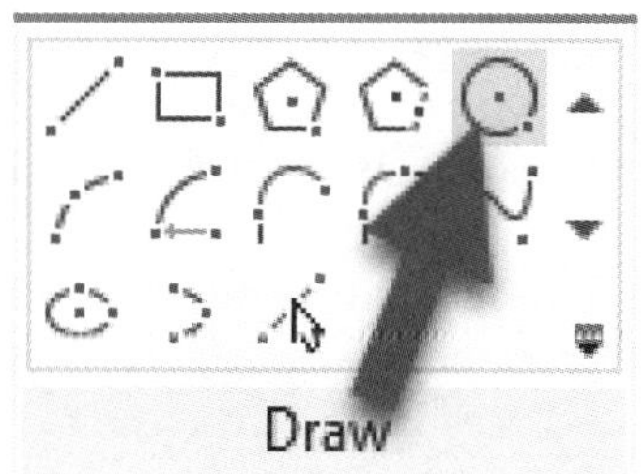

FIGURE 3-1.16 Detail Line shapes

You should now see a dynamic circle and a temporary dimension attached to your cursor, which allows you to visually specify the circle's size. Move your mouse around to see that you could arbitrarily pick a point on the screen to create a quick circle if needed, then proceed to Step 42 where you will draw a circle with a radius of 1'-6⅝".

42. Type **1 6 5/8** and then press **Enter** (Figure 3-1.17).

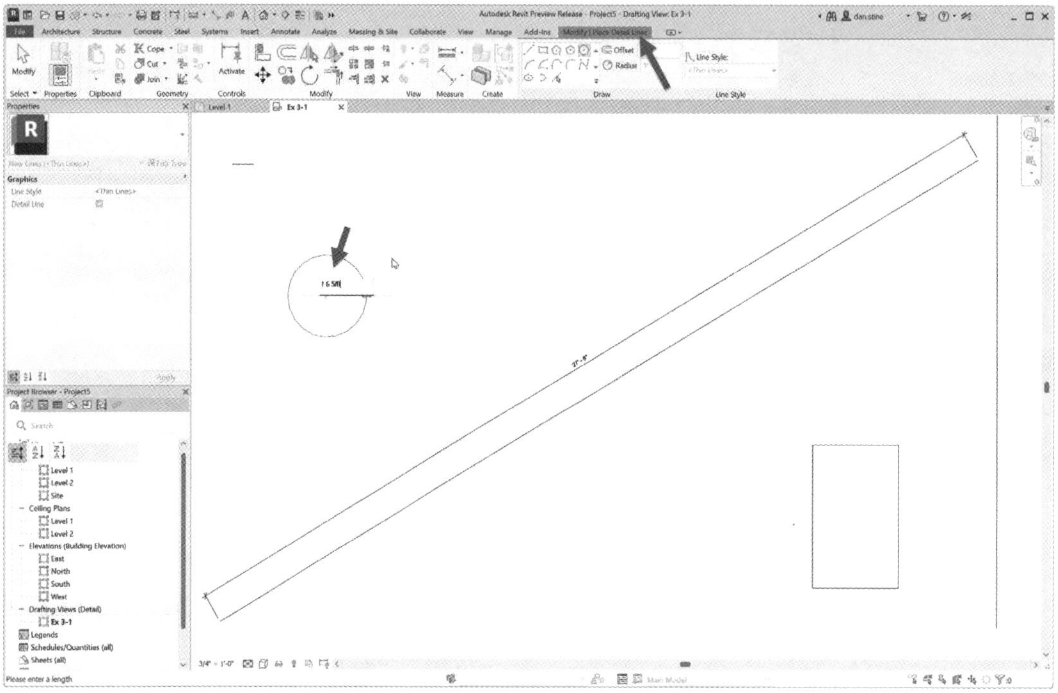

FIGURE 3-1.17 Drawing with Rectangle and Circle added

Notice in the image above, the *Detail Line* is still active because the *contextual tab*, **Modify | Place Detail Lines**, is visible and the *Status Bar* is prompting to "Click to enter circle center." You need to press **Esc** or click *Modify* to cancel the command; clicking another command will also cancel the current command.

43. **Select the circle** and notice a temporary dimension appears indicating the circle's radius. Press **Esc** to unselect it (Figure 3-1.18).

    TIP: This temporary dimension can be used to change the radius of the circle while the circle is selected.

44. **Save** your project as "**ex3-1.rvt**".

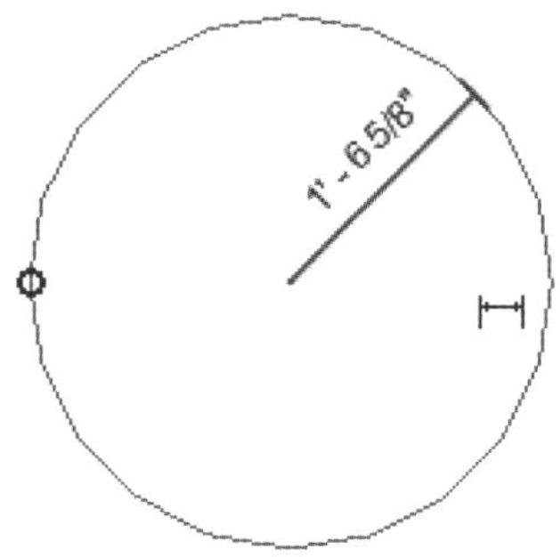

FIGURE 3-1.18
Circle selected

Exercise 3-2:
Snaps

Snaps are tools that allow you to accurately pick a point on an element. For example, when drawing a line you can use *Object Snap* to select, as the start-point, the endpoint or midpoint of another line or wall.

This feature is absolutely critical to drawing accurate technical drawings. Using this feature allows you to be confident you are creating perfect intersections, corners, etc. (Figure 3-2.1).

Object Snaps Options:

You can use *Object Snaps* in one of two ways.

- "Normal" mode
- "Temporary Override" mode

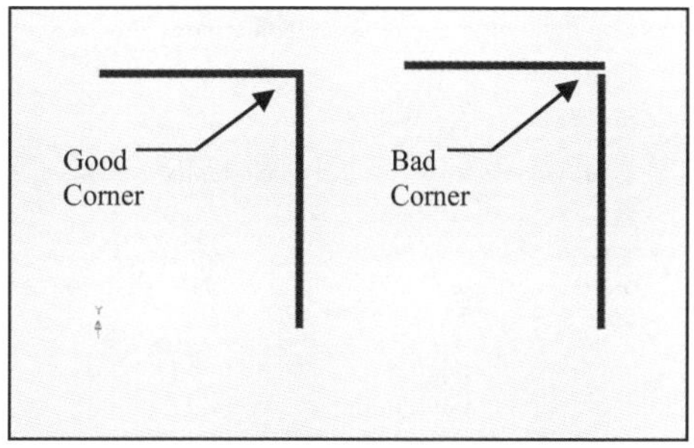

FIGURE 3-2.1 Typical problem when *Snaps* are not used

"Normal" *SNAP* mode is a feature that constantly scans the area near your cursor when Revit is looking for user input. You can configure which types of points to look for.

NOTE: *The term "normal" is not a Revit term, rather it is simply a description used in this book to differentiate this portion of the Snaps feature from the Temporary Override portion discussed next.*

Using a "Temporary Override" *Object Snap* for individual pick-points allows you to quickly select a particular point on an element. This option will temporarily disable the other *Object Snap* settings, which means you tell Revit to just look for the endpoint on an object, for the next pick-point only, rather than the three or four types being scanned for by the "normal" *Object Snaps* feature.

Overview of the Snaps Dialog Box:

Revit provides a *Snaps* dialog box where you specify which *Object Snaps* you want enabled. Next you will take a look at it.

1. Open project **Ex3-1** and select **Manage → Settings → Snaps**.

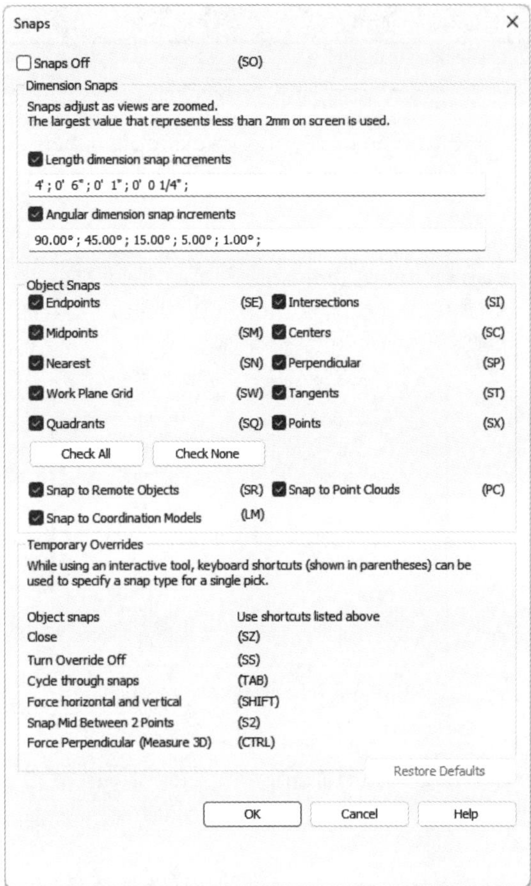

FIGURE 3-2.2 Snaps dialog box; default settings

You should now see the *Snaps* dialog box (Figure 3-2.2). Take a minute to study the various settings that you can control with this dialog box. Notice the check box at the top that allows you to turn this feature off completely.

Dimension Snaps

This controls the automatic dimensions that Revit suggests when you are drawing. Following the given format you could add or remove increments. If you are zoomed in close, only the smaller increments are used.

Object Snaps

This controls the "normal" *Object Snaps* that Revit scans for while you are drawing. Unchecking an item tells Revit not to scan for it anymore. Currently, all *Object Snaps* are enabled (Figure 3-2.2).

Temporary Overrides

This area is really just information on how to use Temporary Overrides.

While drawing you will occasionally want to tell Revit you only want to *Snap* to an Endpoint for the next pick. Instead of opening the *Snaps* dialog and un-checking every *Object Snap* except for Endpoint, you can specify a *Temporary Override* for the next pick. You do this by typing the two letters, in parentheses, in the *Object Snaps* area of the *Snaps* dialog (Figure 3-2.2).

2. Make sure the *Snaps Off* option is unchecked in the upper-left corner of the dialog box; this turns Snaps completely off.

3. Click on the **Check All** button to make sure all *Snaps* are checked.

4. Click **OK** to close the *Snaps* dialog box.

Understanding Snap Symbols:

Again, you should be well aware of the *Object Snap* symbols that Revit displays as you move your cursor about the drawing window while you are in a tool like *Wall* and Revit is awaiting your input or pick-point.

If you hold your cursor still for a moment, while a snap symbol is displayed, a tooltip will appear on the screen. However, when you become familiar with the snap symbols you can pick sooner, rather than waiting for the tooltip to display (Figure 3-2.3).

The TAB key cycles through the available snaps near your cursor.

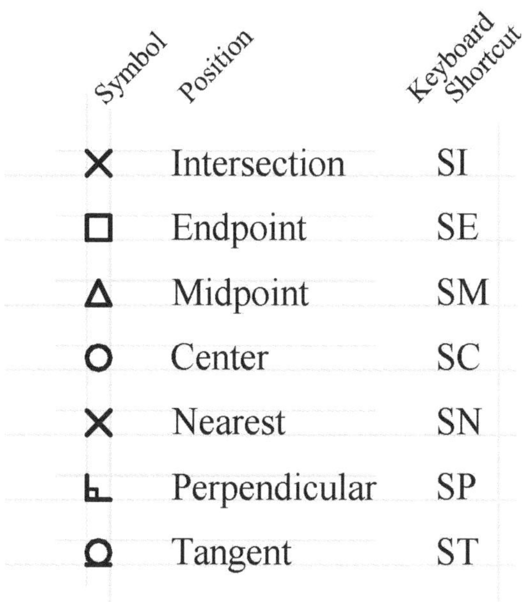

FIGURE 3-2.3 Snap symbols

Finally, typing **SO** turns all snaps off for one pick.

FYI: *The Snaps shown in Figure 3-2.2 are for Revit in general, not just the current project. This is convenient; you don't have to adjust to your favorite settings for each Project or View, existing or new.*

Setting Object Snaps:

You can set Revit to have just one or all Snaps running at the same time. Let us say you have Endpoint and Midpoint set to be running. While using the *Wall* tool, you move your cursor near an existing wall. When the cursor is near the end of the wall you will see the Endpoint symbol show up; when you move the cursor towards the middle of the line you will see the Midpoint symbol show up.

The next step shows you how to tell Revit which Object Snaps you want it to look for. First you will save a new copy of your project.

5. Select **File Tab → Save-As → Project**.

6. Name the project **ex3-2.rvt**.

7. As discussed previously, open the ***Snaps*** dialog box.

8. Make sure only the following *Snaps* are checked:
    a. Endpoints
    b. Midpoints
    c. Centers
    d. Intersections
    e. Perpendicular

9. Click **OK** to close the dialog box.

For More Information:

For more on using Snaps, search Revit's *Help System* for **Snaps**. Then double-click **Snap Points** or any other items found by the search.

Now that you have the *Snaps* adjusted, you will give this feature a try.

10. Using the ***Detail Line*** tool, move your cursor to the lower-left portion of the diagonal line (Figure 3-2.4).

11. Hover the cursor over the line's endpoint (without picking); when you see the *Endpoint* symbol you can click to select that point.

Just So You Know

It is important that you see the *SNAP* symbol before clicking. Also, once you see the symbol you should be careful not to move the mouse too much.

These steps will help to ensure accurate selections.

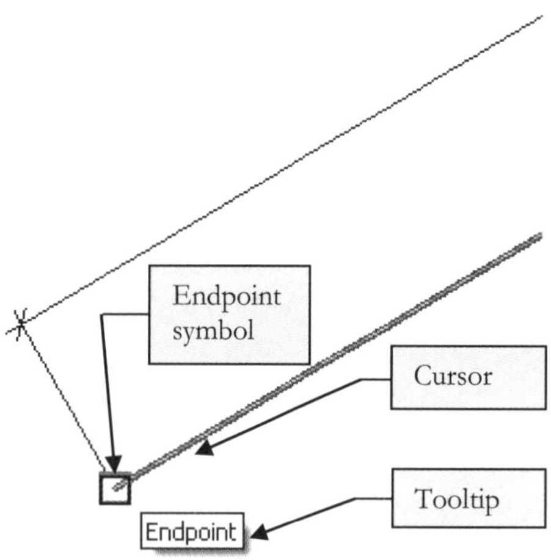

FIGURE 3-2.4 Endpoint SNAP symbol visible

While still in the Detail Line tool, you will use Snaps to draw lines and sketch accurately.

12. Draw the additional lines shown in **Figure 3-2.5** using the appropriate *Object Snap,* changing the selected Snaps as required to select the required points.

TIP #1: At any point while the Line tool is active, you can open the SNAP dialog box and adjust its settings. This will not cancel the Line command.

TIP #2: Also, remember you can press Tab to cycle through the various snap options below or near your cursor.

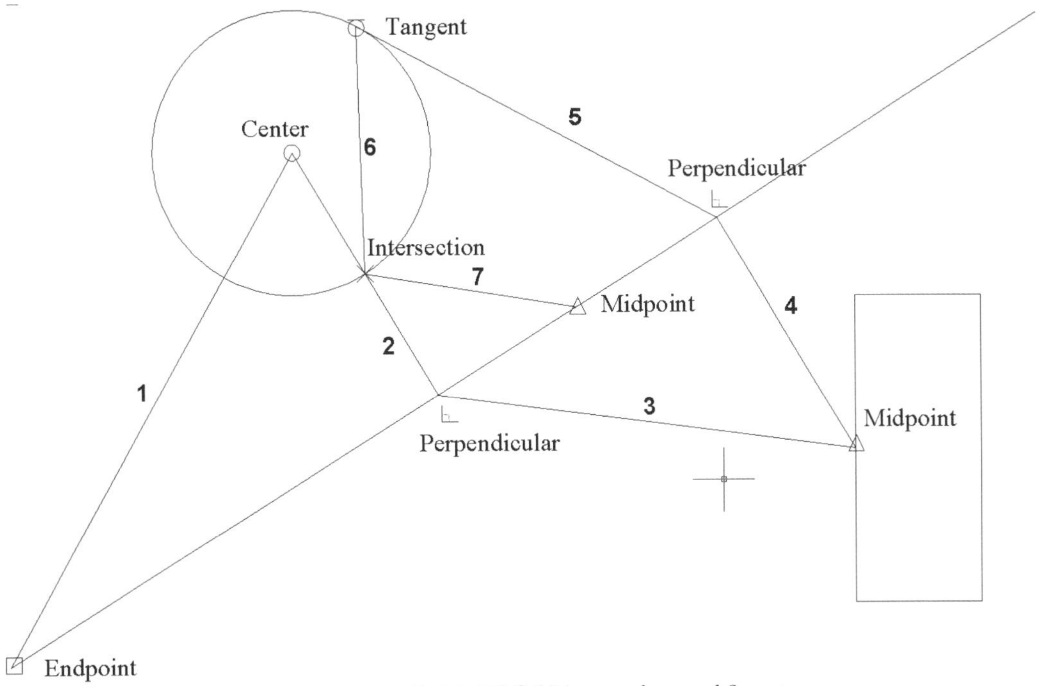

FIGURE 3-2.5 Lines to draw and Snap to use

13. **Save** your project.

Your drawing might look slightly different depending on where you drew the rectangle and circle in the previous steps.

> **This is a Residential Example?**
>
> OK, this is not really an architectural example yet. However, the point here is to focus on the fundamental concepts and not architecture just yet.

Save Reminders:

Revit is configured to remind you to save every 30 minutes to prevent you from losing any work (Figure 3-2.6).

It is recommended that you do not simply click *Cancel*; instead, click the **Save the project** option.

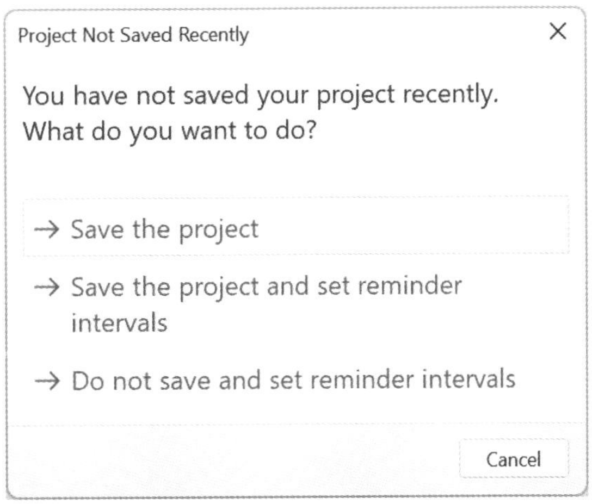

FIGURE 3-2.6 Save reminder

Exercise 3-3:
Edit Tools

The *edit tools* are often used in Revit. A lot of time is spent tweaking designs and making code and client-related revisions.

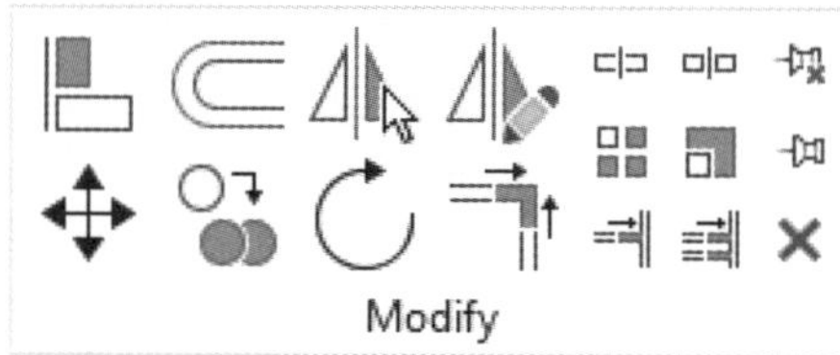

FIGURE 3-3.1 Modify panel

Example: you use the *design tools* (e.g., Walls, Doors, Windows) to initially draw the project. Then you use the *edit tools* to *Move* a wall so a room becomes larger, *Mirror* a cabinet so it faces in a different direction, or *Rotate* the furniture per the owner's instructions.

You will usually access the various edit tools from the Modify tab on the *Ribbon*. You can probably visualize what most of the commands do by the graphics on the icons; see Figure 3-3.1. When you hover over an icon, the tool name will appear. The two letters shown to the right are its keyboard shortcut; pressing those two keys, one at a time, activates that tool.

In this exercise, you will get a brief overview of a few of the edit tools by manipulating the tangled web of lines you have previously drawn.

1. **Open** project **ex3-2.rvt** from the previous lesson.

2. **Save-As "ex3-3.rvt"**.

FYI: You will notice that instructions or tools that have already been covered in this book will have fewer "step-by-step" instructions.

Delete Tool:

It is no surprise that the *Delete* tool is a necessity; things change and mistakes are made. You can *Delete* one element at a time or several. Deleting elements is very easy: you select the elements, and then pick the *Delete* icon. You will try this on two lines in your drawing.

3. While holding the **Ctrl** key, select the lines identified in **Figure 3-3.2**.

   TIP: See the section below Figure 3-3.2 on Selecting Entities.

4. Select **Delete** from the *Ribbon* (or press the **Delete** key on the keyboard).

The lines are now deleted from the project.

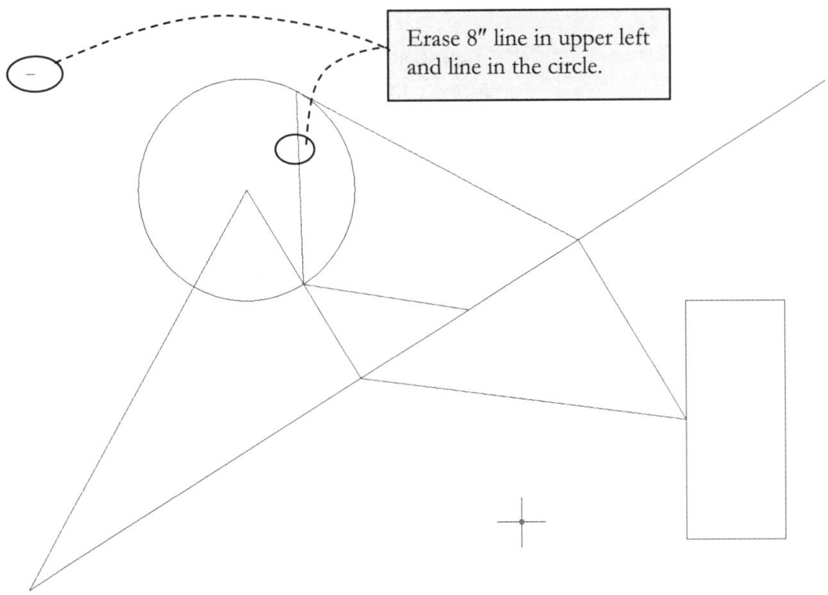

FIGURE 3-3.2 Lines to be erased

Selecting Objects:

At this time, we will digress and take a quick look at the various techniques for selecting entities in Revit. Most tools work the same way when selecting elements.

When selecting entities, you have two primary ways to select them:

- Individually select entities one at a time
- Select several entities at a time with a window

You can use one or a combination of both methods to select elements when using the *Copy* tool.

Individual Selections:
When prompted to select entities to copy or delete, for example, you simply move the cursor over the element and click; holding the **Ctrl** key you can select multiple objects. Then you typically click the tool you wish to use on the selected items. Press **Shift** and click on an item to subtract it from the current selection set.

Continued on next page

Window Selections:
Similarly, you can pick a *window* around several elements to select them all at once. To select a *window*, rather than selecting an object as previously described, you select one corner of the *window* you wish to define. That is, you pick a point in "space" and hold the mouse button down. Now, as you move the mouse, you will see a rectangle on the screen that represents the windowed area you are selecting; when the *window* encompasses the elements you wish to select, release the mouse.

You actually have two types of windows you can select. One is called a **window** and the other is called a **crossing window**.

Window:
This option allows you to select only the objects that are completely within the *window*. Any lines that extend out of the *window* are not selected.

Crossing Window:
This option allows you to select all the entities that are completely within the *window* and any that extend outside the *window*.

Using Window versus Crossing Window:
To select a *window* you simply pick and drag from left to right to form a rectangle (Figure 3-3.3a).

Conversely, to select a *crossing window*, you pick and drag from right to left to define the two diagonal points of the window (Figure 3-3.3b).

Selecting a chain of lines (hover, tab, click):
Revit provides a quick and easy way to select a chain of lines, that is, a series of lines (or walls) whose endpoints are perfectly connected. You simply hover your cursor over one line so it highlights, then press the Tab key once, and then click the mouse button. This trick can be used to quickly select all the exterior walls on a building, for example.

Turning off **Drag Element on Selection** on the *Status Bar* helps to avoid accidentally clicking directly on an element and moving it rather than starting the intended first corner of a selection window.

Remember, all these draw, modify and select tools have direct application to working with Revit's 3D building components, not just the 2D geometry being covered in this chapter.

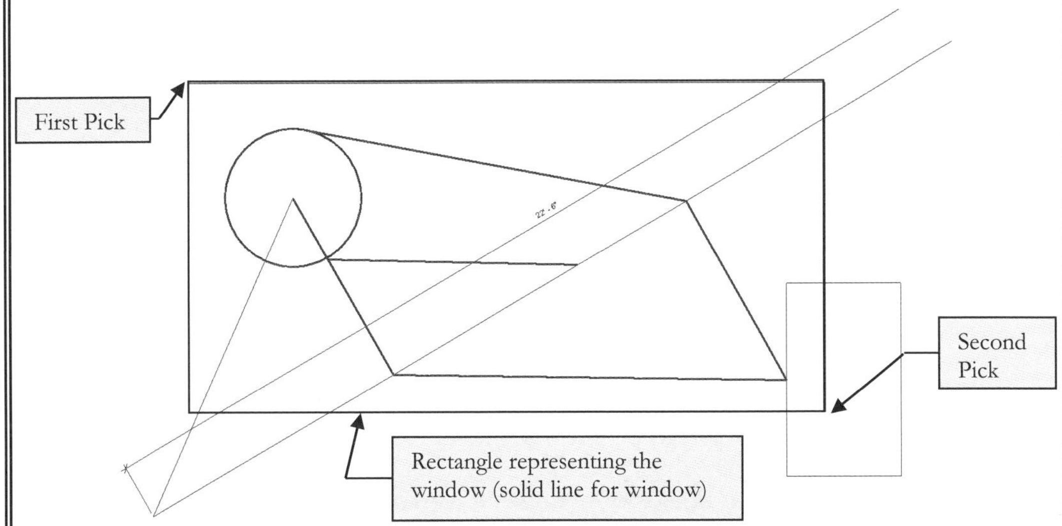

FIGURE 3-3.3A Six items selected using *window;* only the lines completely within the window are selected.

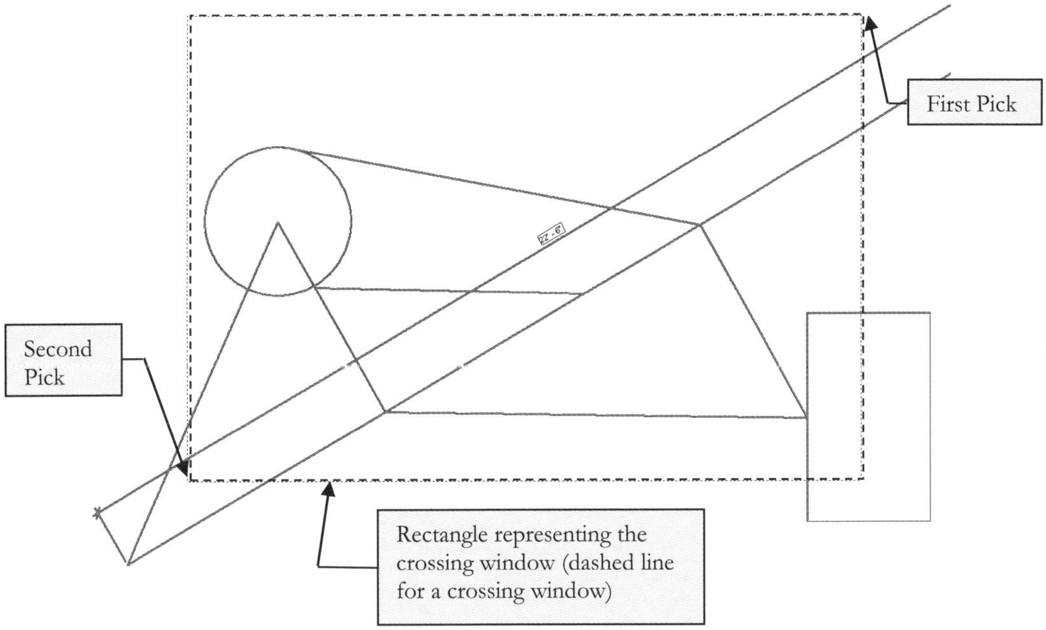

FIGURE 3-3.3B Everything selected using a *crossing window;* all lines within crossing are selected.

Copy Tool:

The *Copy* tool allows you to accurately duplicate an element(s). You select the items you want to copy and then pick two points that represent an imaginary vector, which provides both length and angle, defining the path used to copy the object. You can also type in the length if there are no convenient points to pick in the drawing. You will try both methods next.

5. **Select the circle**.

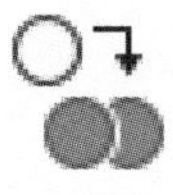

6. Select **Copy** from the *Ribbon*.

Notice the prompt on the Status Bar: Click to enter move start point.

7. Pick the **center** of the **circle** (Figure 3-3.4).

   FYI: *You actually have three different Snaps you can use here: Center, Endpoint, and Intersection. All occur at the exact same point.*

Notice the prompt on the Status Bar: Click to enter move end point.

8. Pick the **endpoint** of the angled line in the lower left corner (Figure 3-3.4).

   FYI: *If you want to make several copies of the circle, select* Multiple *on the Ribbon.*

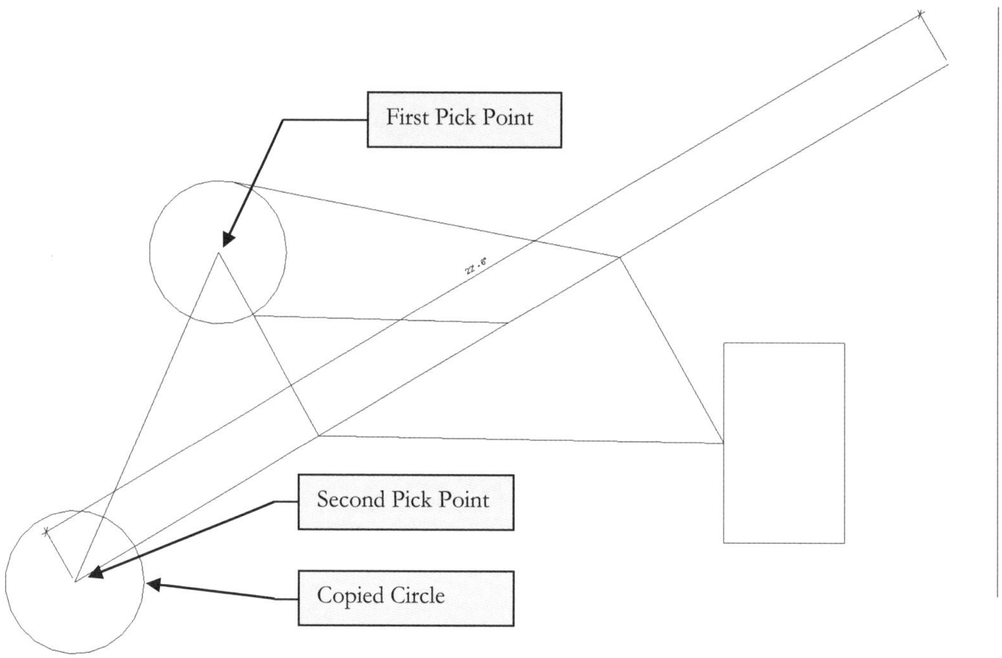

FIGURE 3-3.4 Copied circle; also indicates points selected

9. **Select the rectangle** *(all four lines).*

   TIP: Try the "hover, tab, click" method discussed on page 3-22.

10. Select **Copy**.

11. Pick an arbitrary point on the screen. In this scenario, it makes no difference where you pick; you will see why in a moment.

At this point, move the mouse in the direction you want to copy the rectangle until the correct angle is displayed, then type the distance instead of picking a second point on the screen.

12. Move the mouse towards the upper right until 45 degrees displays, then type **6′** and then press **Enter** (Figure 3-3.5).

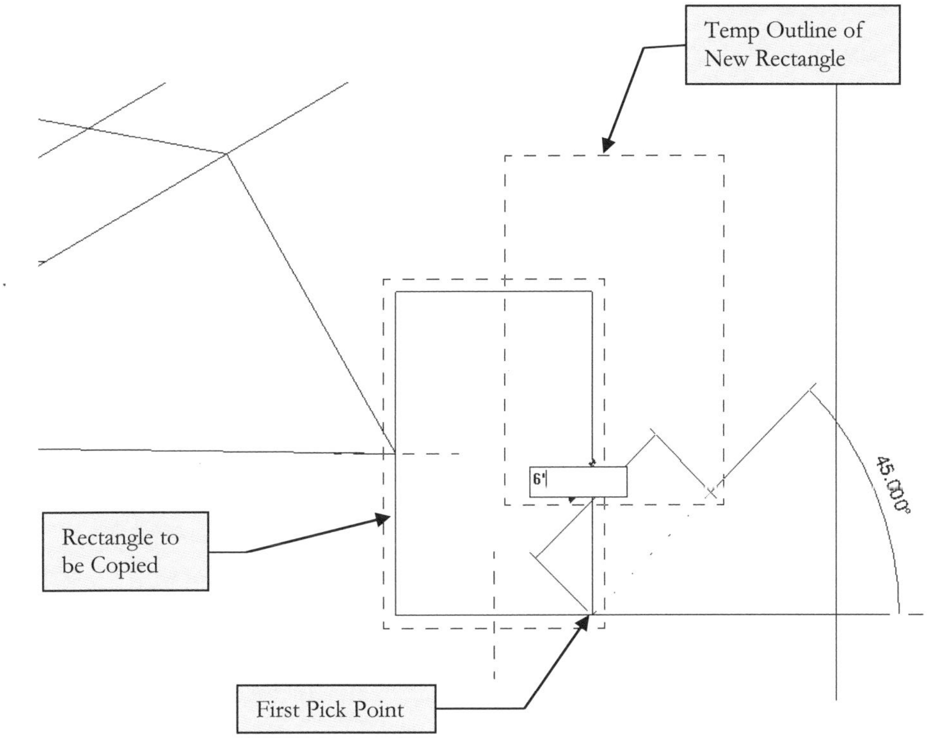

FIGURE 3-3.5 Copying rectangle; angle set visually and distance typed in

NOTE: Your drawing may look a little different from this one because it is not completely to scale.

Move Tool:

The *Move* tool works exactly like the *Copy* tool except, of course, you move the element(s) rather than copy it. Given the similarity to the previously covered tool, the *Move* tool will not be covered now. You are encouraged to try it yourself; just Undo your experiments before proceeding.

Rotate Tool:

With the *Rotate* tool, you can arbitrarily or accurately rotate one or more objects in your drawing. When you need to rotate accurately, you can pick points that define the angle, assuming points exist in the drawing to pick, or you can type a specific angle.

Rotate involves the following steps:

- Select element(s) to be rotated
- Select *Rotate*
- Determine if the Center of Rotation symbol is where you want it.
    - If you want to move it:
        - Simply drag it, or
        - Click *Place* on the *Ribbon*
- Select a point to define a reference line and begin rotation.
- Pick a second point using one of the following methods:
    - By selecting other objects or using the graphic angle display *or*
    - You can type an angle and press **Enter**.

13. **Select the new rectangle** you just copied *(all four lines)*.

14. Select **Rotate** on the *Ribbon*.

Notice that the "Center of Rotation" grip, by default, is located in the center of the selected elements. This is the point about which the rotation will occur. See Figure 3-3.6.

You will not change the "Center of Rotation" at this time.

15. Pick a point directly to the right of the "Center of Rotation" grip; this tells Revit you want to rotate the rectangle relative to the horizontal plane (Figure 3-3.6).

Now, as you move your mouse up or down, you will see the temporary angle dimension displayed. You can move the mouse until the desired angle is displayed, then click to complete the rotation, or type the desired angle and press **Enter**. If you recall, the *Snaps* dialog box controls the angle increments Revit displays; they are all whole numbers. So if you need to rotate something 22.45 degrees, you must type it as Revit will never display that number as an option.

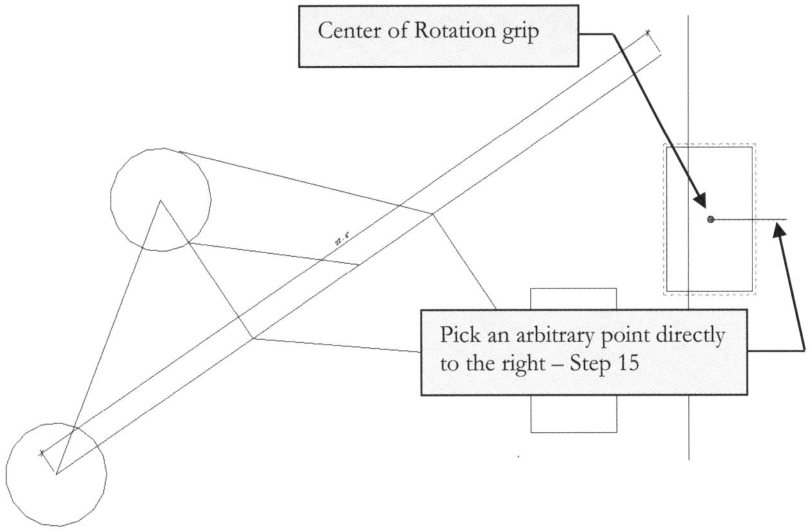

FIGURE 3-3.6 Rotate tool; first step – select lines and then click Rotate

16. Move the mouse up and to the left until 90 degrees is displayed and then click to complete the rotation (Figure 3-3.7).

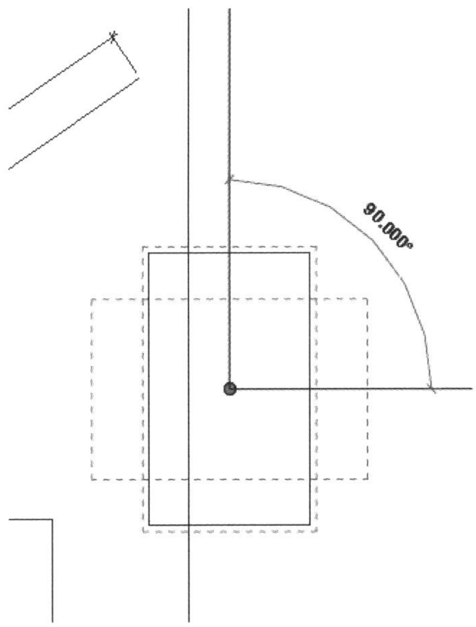

FIGURE 3-3.7 Rotate tool; last step – select angle visually or type angle

The previous steps just rotated the rectangle 90 degrees counter-clockwise about its center point (Figure 3-3.8).

17. Select the **Undo** icon. 

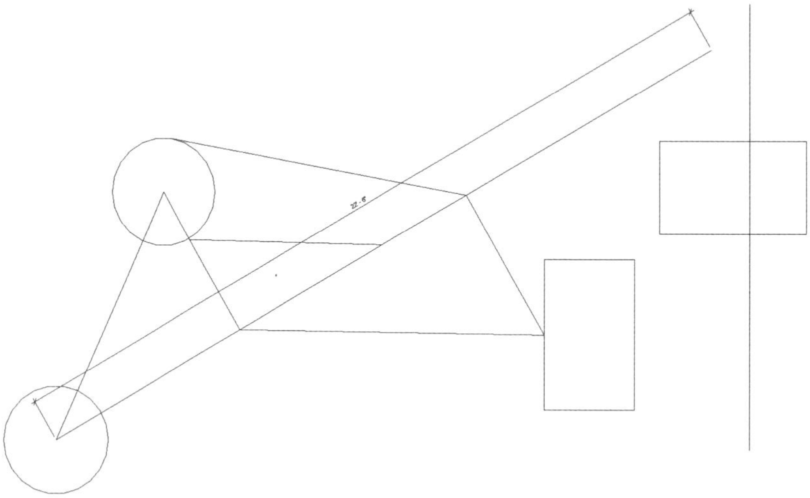

FIGURE 3-3.8 Rotate tool; rectangle rotated about its center point

Now you will do the same thing, but with a different angle and a different "Center of Rotation."

18. **Select the rectangle** and then pick **Rotate.**

19. Click and drag the "Center of Rotation" grip to the left and *Snap* to the midpoint of the vertical line (Figure 3-3.9).

    TIP: You can also click the **Place** *button on the Ribbon (see the image to the right).*

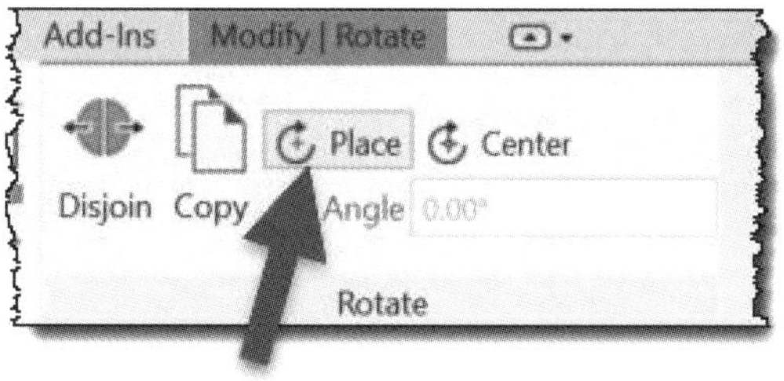

20. Pick a point to the right, creating a horizontal reference line.

21. Start moving your mouse downward, then type **22.5** and then press **Enter** (Figure 3-3.10).

The rectangle is now rotated 22.5 degrees clockwise (Figure 3-3.11).

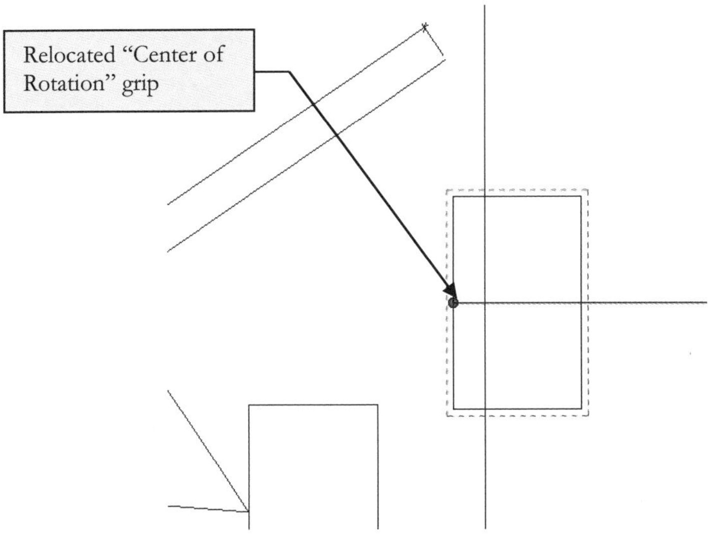

FIGURE 3-3.9 Rotate tool; relocated Center of Rotation grip

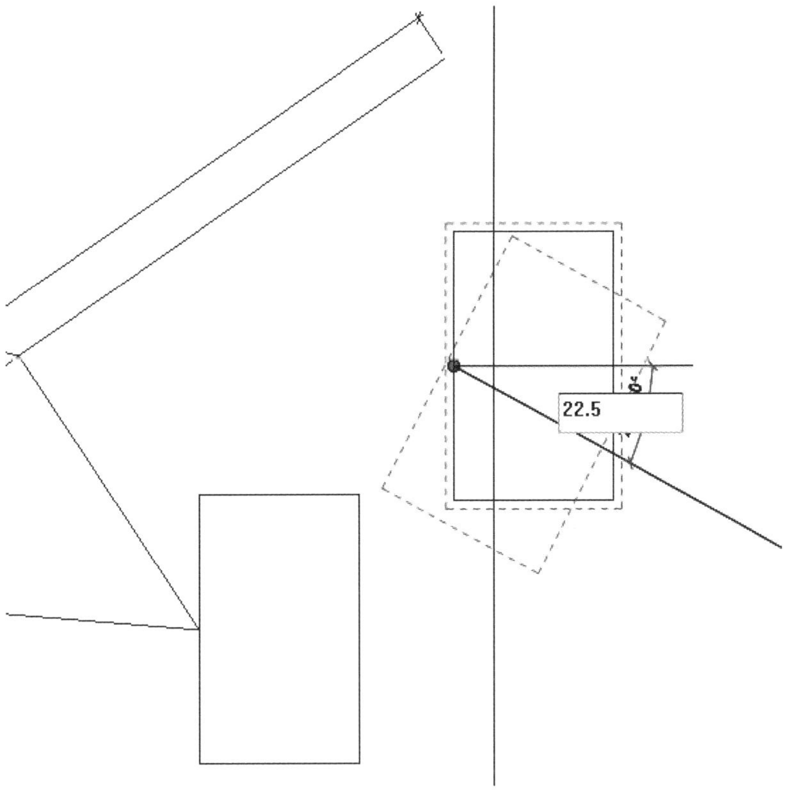

FIGURE 3-3.10 Rotate tool; typing in exact angle

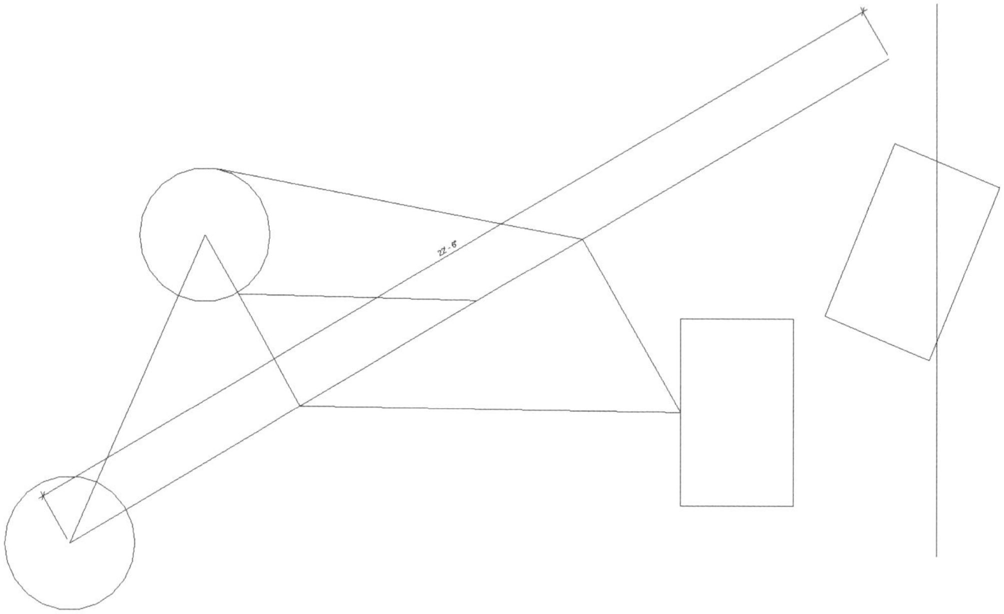

FIGURE 3-3.11 Rotate tool; rectangle rotated 22.5 degrees

Scale Tool:

The *Scale* tool has steps similar to the *Rotate* tool. First, you select what you want to scale or resize, specify a scale factor, and then you pick the base point. The scale factor can be specified by selecting points on the screen or by entering a numerical scale factor (e.g., 2 or .5, where 2 is twice the original size and .5 is half the original size).

Next, you will use the *Scale* tool to adjust the size of the circle near the bottom.

Before you resize the circle, use the Modify tool/mode to measure its diameter. Select the circle and view its temporary dimensions. After resizing the circle, you will refer back to the temporary dimensions to note the change. This step is meant to teach you how to verify the accuracy and dimensions of entities in Revit.

22. Select the bottom circle.

23. Select the **Scale** icon from the *Ribbon*.

On the *Ribbon,* you will specify a numeric scale factor of .5 to resize the circle to half its original size.

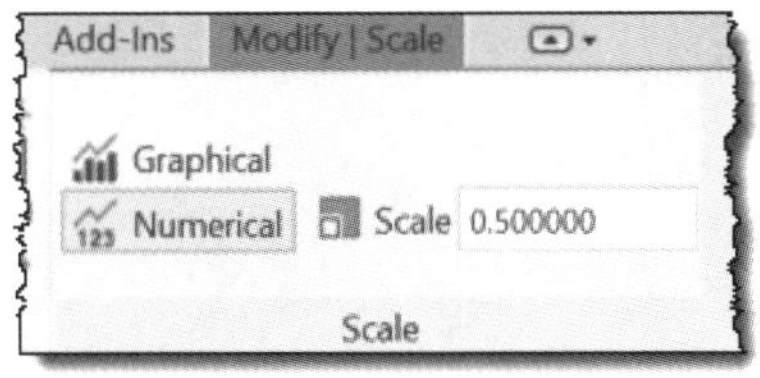

24. Click **Numerical** and then type **.5** in the textbox *(see the Ribbon to the right).*

You are now prompted **Click to enter origin** on the *Status Bar.* This is the base point about which the circle will be scaled; see examples in Figure 3-3.13 on the next page.

25. Click the center of the circle.

You just used the *Scale* tool to change the circle's radius from 1-6 5/8 to 9 5/16. A scale factor of .5 reduces the entities to half their original scale (Figure 3-3.12).

> **Selecting the Correct Center of Rotation *(Base Point)*:**
> You need to select the appropriate *Center of Rotation,* or Base Point, for both the *Scale* and *Rotate* commands to get the results desired. A few examples are shown in Figure 3-3.13. The dashed line indicates the original position of the entity being modified. The black dot indicates the base point selected.

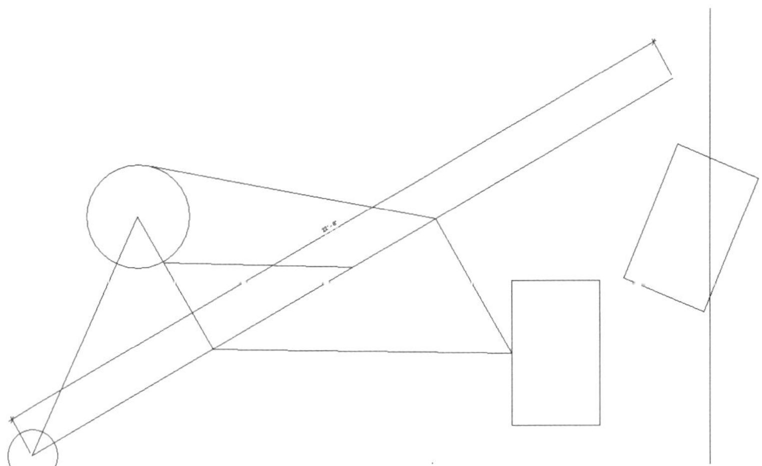

FIGURE 3-3.12 Resize circle; notice it is half the size of the other circle

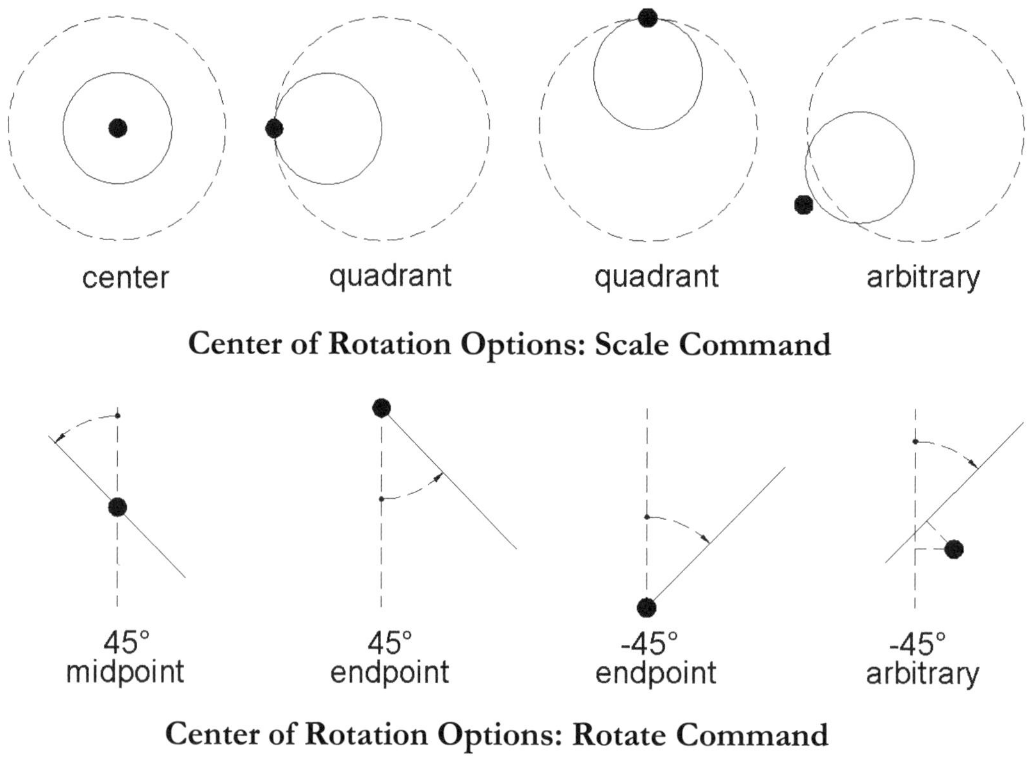

FIGURE 3-3.13 Center of Rotation Options and the various results

This will conclude the brief tour of the *Edit* tools. Do not forget, even though you are editing 2D lines, the edit tools work the same way on 3D elements such as walls, floors, roofs, etc. Exception: you cannot *Scale* walls, doors, etc.; these objects have to be modified by other methods. You would not typically change the door thickness when changing its width and height, as would happen if you could use the *Scale* tool on it.

As you surely noticed, the *Modify* panel on the *Ribbon* has a few other tools that have not been investigated yet. Many of these will be covered later in this book.

26. **Save** the project. Your project should already be named "ex3-3.rvt" per Step 2 above.

Exercise 3-4:
Annotations

Annotations, or text and notes, allow the designer and technician to accurately describe the drawing. Here you will take a quick look at this feature set. There is a chapter, later in the book, dedicated to annotation which covers these tools in greater detail.

Annotations:

Adding annotations to a drawing can be as essential as the drawing itself. Often the notes describe a part of the drawing that would be difficult to discern from the drawing alone.

For example, a wall framing drawing showing a bolt may not indicate, graphically, how many bolts are needed or at what spacing. The note might say "*5/8" anchor bolt at 24" O.C.*"

Next you will add text to your drawing.

1. **Open** project **ex3-3.rvt** from the previous lesson.

2. **Save-As** "**ex3-4.rvt**".

3. Use **Zoom** if required to see the entire drawing, except for the 600' line which can run off the screen.

4. Select **Annotate → Text → Text.**

   Note that the *Model Text* tool on the *Architecture* tab is only for drawing 3D text; *Drafting Views* are only 2D so that command is not even an option currently.

From the *Text* icon tooltip (see image to the right) you can see that the keyboard shortcut for the *Text* tool is **TX**. Thus, at any time you can type T and then X to activate the *Text* tool; if you have another command active, Revit will cancel it.

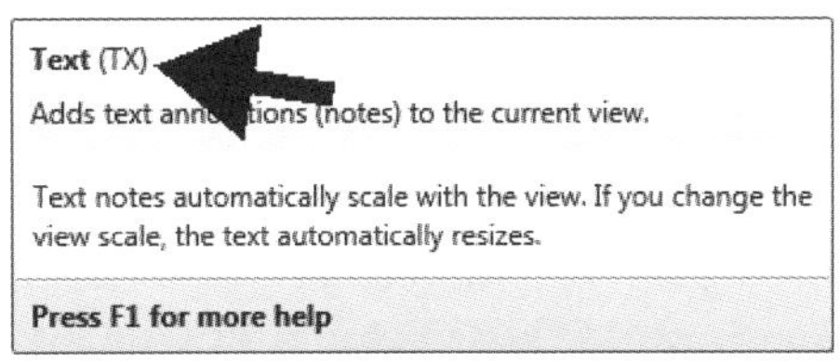

Text icon's tooltip (hover cursor over icon)

Experienced and efficient designers use a combination of keyboard shortcuts and mouse clicks to save time. For example, while your left hand is typing TX, your right hand can be moving toward the location where you want to insert the text. This process is generally more efficient than switching between tabs on the *Ribbon* and clicking icons, or fly-out icons which require yet another click of the mouse.

Notice the current *prompt* on the *Status Bar* at the bottom of the screen; you are asked to "Click to start text or click and drag rectangle to create wrapping text." By clicking on the screen you create one line of text, starting at the point picked, and press **Enter** to create additional lines. By clicking and dragging a rectangle you specify a window, primarily for the width, which causes Revit to automatically move text to the next line. When the text no longer fits within the window it is pushed below, or what is called "text wrapping" (Figure 3-4.1).

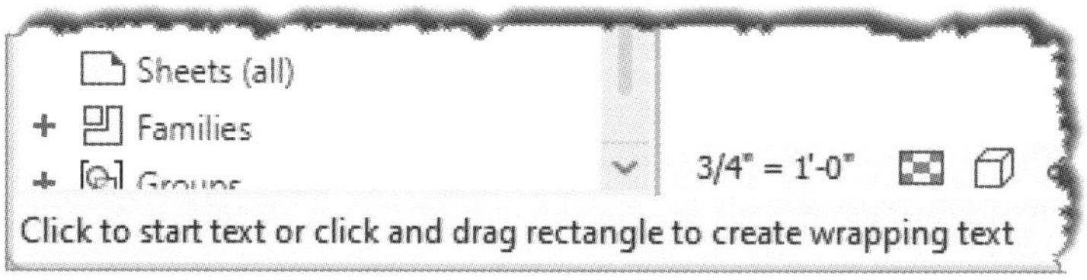

FIGURE 3-4.1 Status Bar while Text tool is active

You should also notice the various text options available on the *Ribbon* while the *Text* tool is active (Figure 3-4.2). You have two text heights loaded from the template file you started with, text justification icons (Left, Center, Right) and the option to attach leaders, or pointing arrows, to your drawings. The *Text* tool will be covered in more detail later in this book.

FYI: *The text heights shown (i.e., ¼", 3/32" via Type Selector) are heights the text will be when printed on paper, regardless of the view scale.*

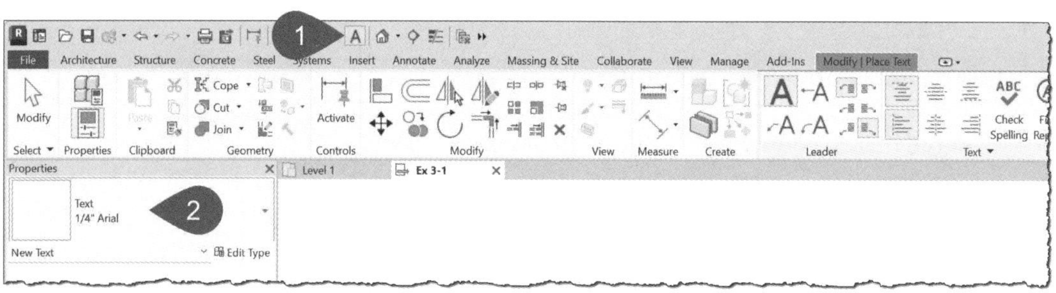

FIGURE 3-4.2 Ribbon and Properties Palette with the Text tool active

5. Pick a point in the upper left portion of the view as shown in Figure 3-4.3.

6. Type "**Learning Revit is fun!**"

7. Click anywhere in the view, except on the active text, to finish the *Text* command; pressing **Enter** will only add new lines.

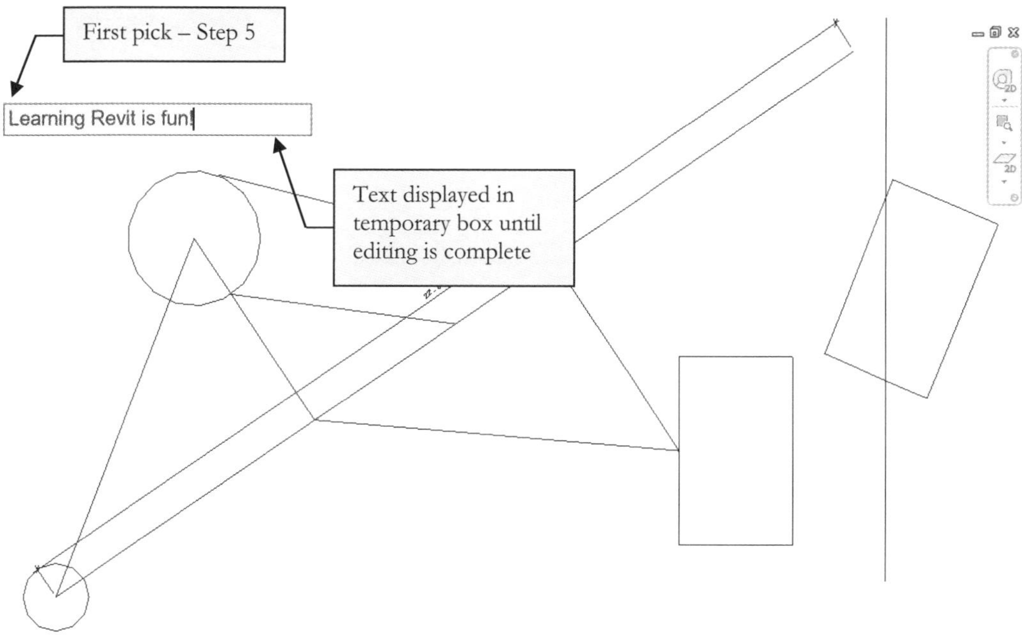

FIGURE 3-4.3 Text tool; picking first point and typing text.

As soon as you complete the text edit, the text will still be selected, and the *Move* and *Rotate* symbols will be displayed near the text; this allows you to more quickly *Move* or *Rotate* the text after it is typed (Figure 3-4.4).

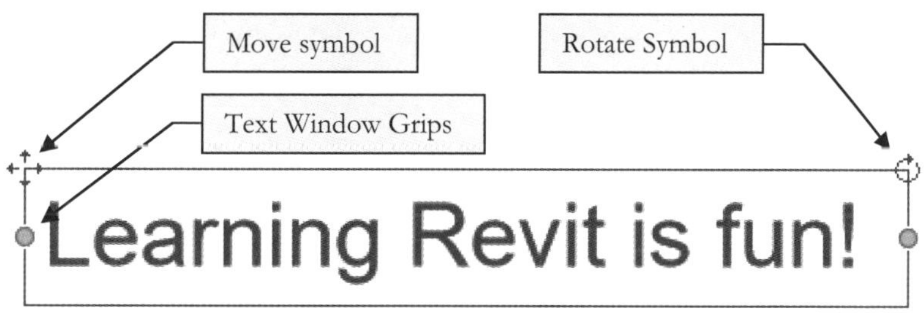

FIGURE 3-4.4 Text tool; text typed with Move and Rotate symbols showing.

8. Finish the *Text* tool completely by pressing *Modify* or clicking in the drawing.

***TIP:** Notice that the text is no longer selected, the symbols are gone, and the contextual tab disappears from the Ribbon.*

Your text should generally look similar to Figure 3-4.5.

9. Print your drawing; refer back to page 2-15 for basic printing information. Your print should fit the page and look similar to Figure 3-4.5.

10. **Save** your project.

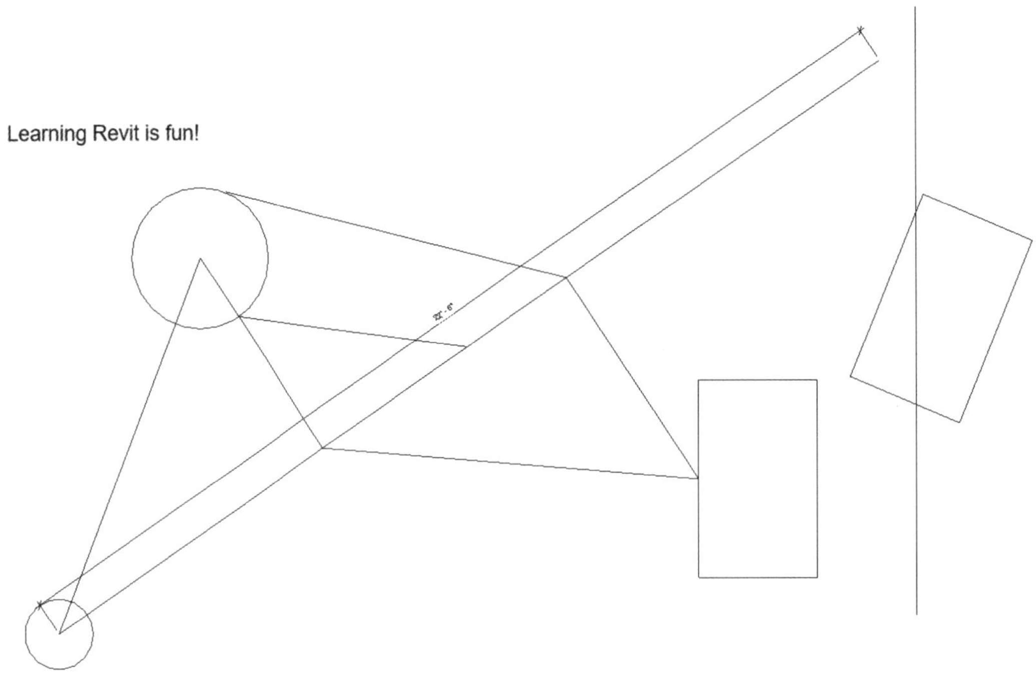

FIGURE 3-4.5 Text tool; text added to current view

Self-Exam:

The following questions can be used as a way to check your knowledge of this lesson. The answers can be found at the bottom of the page.

1. Revit is only accurate to three decimal places. (T/F)

2. The triangular-shaped Snap symbol represents the Midpoint snap. (T/F)

3. You can move or rotate text via its modify symbols when text is selected. (T/F)

4. Use the _____________ tool to duplicate objects.

5. When selecting objects, use the ______________________ to select all the objects in the selection window and all objects that extend through it.

Review Questions:

The following questions may be assigned by your instructor as a way to assess your knowledge of this section. Your instructor has the answers to the review questions.

1. Revit is a raster-based program. (T/F)

2. The "Center of Rotation" you select for the *Rotate* and *Scale* commands is not important. (T/F)

3. Entering 16 for a distance actually means 16′-0″ to Revit. (T/F)

4. Use the *Detail Line* tool, with ________________ selected on the *Ribbon*, to create squares.

5. You can change the height of the text from the *Type Selector*. (T/F)

6. Pressing the ______________ key cycles you through the snap options.

7. Where do the two predefined text heights come from? ________________

8. Specifying degrees with the *Rotate* tool, you must type the number when Revit does not display the number you want; the increments shown on-screen are set in the

   _________________________ dialog box.

9. List all the Snap points available on a circle (ex. Line: endpoint, midpoint,

   nearest): ____.

10. The Snaps Off option must not be checked in the Snaps dialog box to automatically and accurately select snap points while drawing. (T/F)

SELF-EXAM ANSWERS:
1 – F, **2** – T, **3** – T, **4** – Copy, **5** – Crossing Window

Notes:

Lesson 4
Drawing 2D Architectural Objects:

This lesson is intended to give you practice drawing in Autodesk® Revit®; while doing so, you will become familiar with the various shapes and sizes of the more common symbols used in a residential design.

Do not forget that learning to draw 2D is important in Autodesk Revit. You often define 3D items, like walls, in 2D floor plans, while Autodesk Revit takes care of the third dimension automatically. Additionally, you will often want to embellish a view with 2D lines; for example, the exterior elevation, which is a 2D projection of a 3D model.

If you have used other design programs, such as AutoCAD or AutoCAD Architecture, these lessons will help you understand how to draw in Autodesk Revit, which uses a more visual, graphic-based input system.

Each drawing will be created in its own *Drafting View*.

For some of the symbols to be drawn, you will have step-by-step instructions and a study on a particular tool that would be useful in the creation of that object. Other symbols to be drawn are for practice by repetition and do not provide step-by-step instructions.

Do NOT draw the dimensions provided; they are for reference only.

Exercise 4-1:
Sketching Rectilinear Objects

Overview:

All the objects you will draw in this exercise consist entirely of straight lines, either orthogonal or angular.

As previously mentioned, all the objects MUST BE drawn in SEPARATE *Drafting Views*. Each object will have a specific name provided, which is to be used to name the *Drafting View*. All views will be created in one Revit project file, which should be saved in your personal folder created for this course.

view name: Bookcase

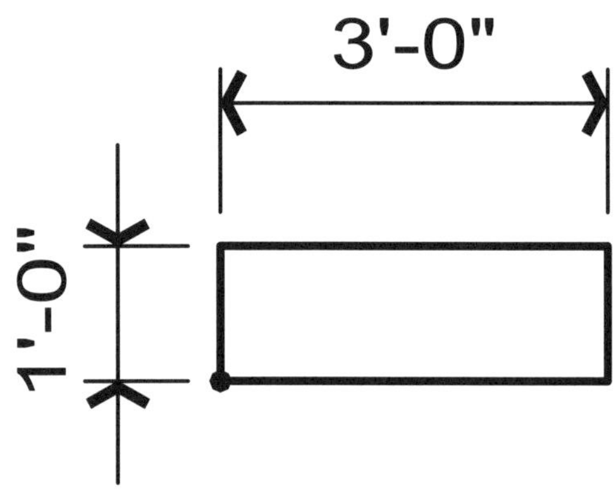

This is a simple rectangle that represents the size of a bookcase.

1. **Open** a new project; **Save** the project as **Ex4-1.rvt**.
   Tip: use the *default.rte* template again.

2. Create a new *Drafting View* named **Bookcase** (Figure 4-1.1) *(from the View tab).*

3. Select **Detail Line** from the *Annotate* tab.

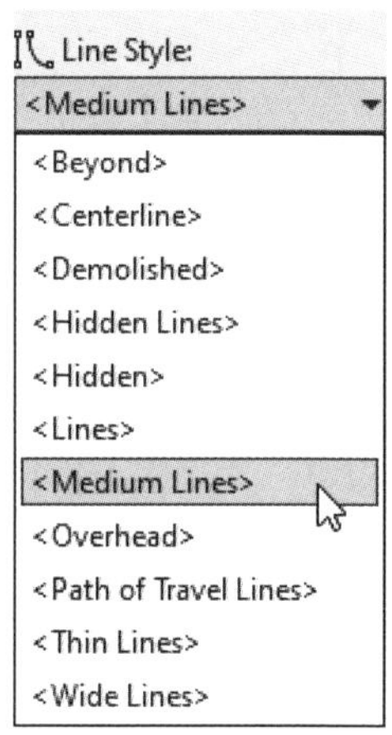

By default, the current line thickness is set to *Thin Lines.* You can see this on the *Ribbon* when the *Detail Line* tool is active. You will change this to *Medium* next.

4. Set the line thickness to **Medium Lines** (Figure 4-1.2; also see image to the right).

   NOTE: Use this setting for all the drawings in this chapter.

5. Click the **Rectangle** button on the *Ribbon* (Figure 4-1.2).

6. **Draw a rectangle**, per the dimensions shown above, generally in the center of the drawing window.

   TIP: You should be able to accurately draw the rectangle using the temporary dimensions; if not, click on the dimension text to change it.

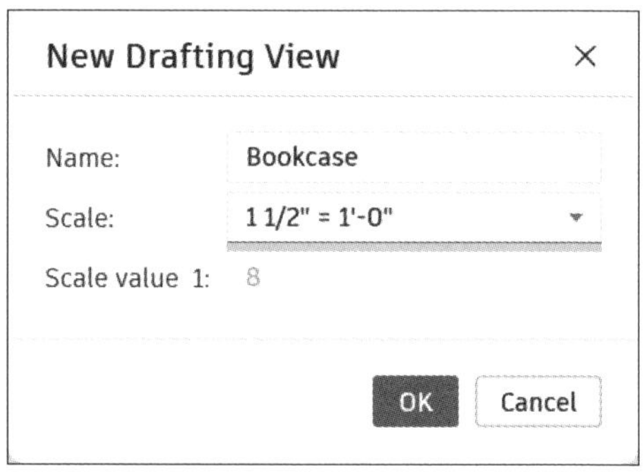

FIGURE 4-1.1 New Drafting View dialog

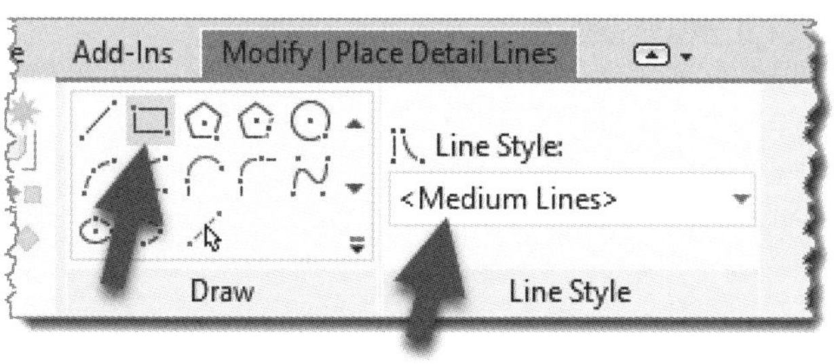

FIGURE 4-1.2 Ribbon; Medium Lines and Rectangle selected

view name: Coffee Table

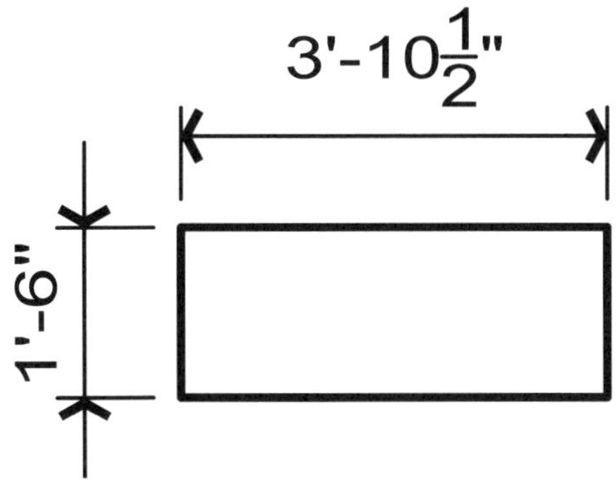

7. Create a new *Drafting View.*

   NOTE: *This step will be assumed for the rest of the drawings in this exercise.*

8. Similar to the steps listed above, plus the suggestions mentioned below, create the coffee table shown to the left.

Draw the rectangle as closely as possible using the visual aids; you should be able to get the 1′-6″ dimension correct. Then click on the text for the temporary horizontal dimension and type in 3′-10 1/2″.

<u>Entering fractions</u>: the 3′-10½″ can be entered in one of four ways.

o	3 10.5	*Notice there is a space between the feet and inches.*
o	3 10 1/2	*Two spaces separate the feet, inches and fractions.*
o	0 46.5	*This is all in inches; that is 3′-10½″ = 46.5″.*
o	46.5″	*Omit the feet and use the inches symbol.*

view name: Desk-1

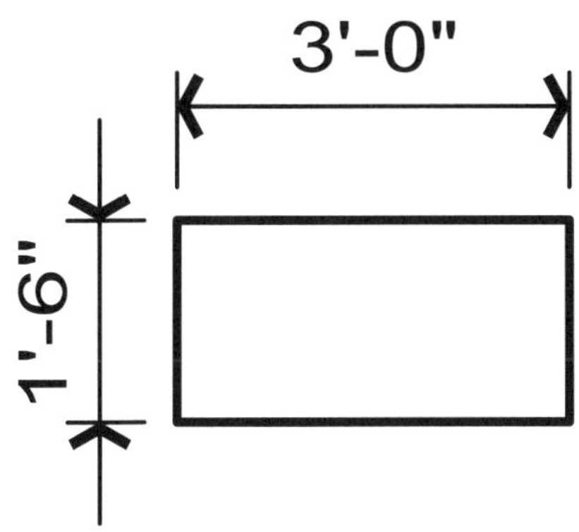

9. Draw the *Desk* in its own view, similar to the steps outlined above.

TIP: *You should double-check your drawing's dimensions using the* Measure *tool. Pick the icon from the* Modify *tab and then pick two points. A temporary dimension will display.*

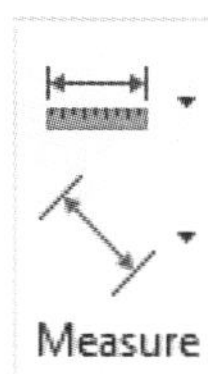

view name: **Night Table**

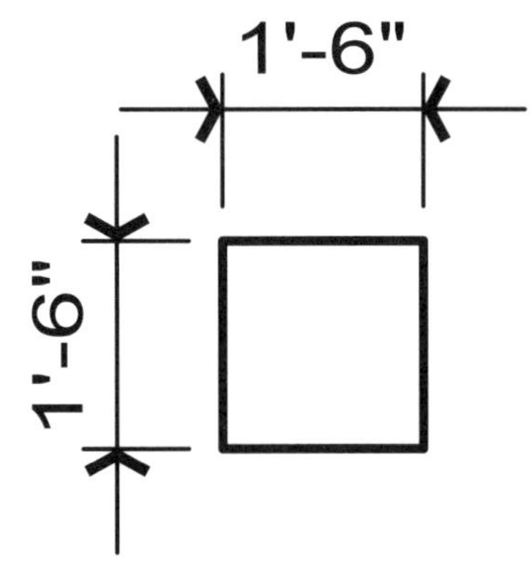

Obviously, you could draw this quickly per the previous examples. However, you will look at copying a Drafting View and modifying an existing drawing.

You will use the *Move* tool to stretch the 3′-0″ wide desk down to a 1′-6″ wide night table.

First, you will look at *Drafting Views* and how they are organized in the *Project Browser*, and then you will copy the *Desk-1 Drafting View* to start the *Night Table* drawing/view.

10. Locate the ***Drafting Views*** section in the *Project Browser* and expand it by clicking on the "plus" symbol.

Notice that the three views you previously created are listed (Figure 4-1.3). The *Desk-1* view is shown with bold text because it is the current view. All *Drafting Views* are listed here and can be renamed, copied, or deleted at any time by right-clicking on the item in the list. You will copy the *Desk-1* view next.

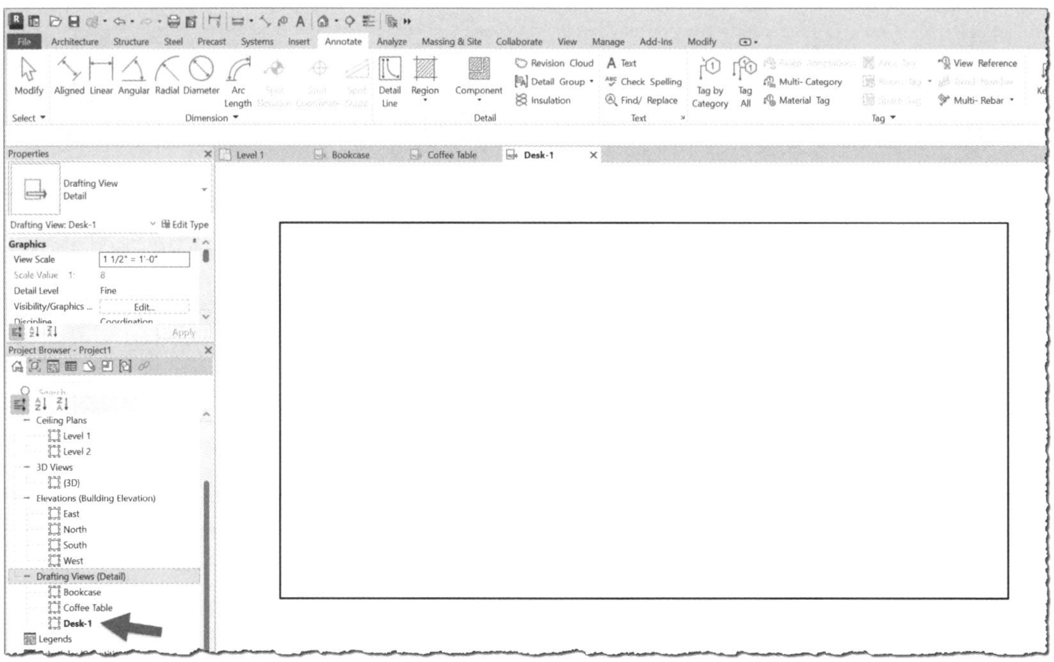

FIGURE 4-1.3 Project Browser: Drafting Views section expanded

11. Right-click on the *Desk-1* view (Figure 4-1.4).

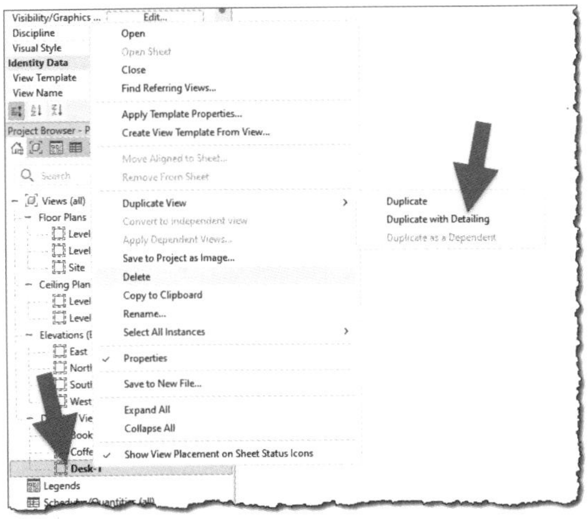

FIGURE 4-1.4 Drafting Views list – Right click on Desk-1 view for menu

Next, you will select *Duplicate with Detailing*, which will copy the *View* and the *View's* contents, whereas the *Duplicate* option will only copy the *View* and its settings, but without any line work.

12. Select **Duplicate View → Duplicate with Detailing** from the pop-up menu (Figure 4-1.4).

You now have a new View named *Copy of Desk-1* in the *Drafting Views* list. This *View* is open and current.

13. **Right-click** on the new view name, ***Copy of Desk-1***, and select **Rename** from the pop-up menu.

14. Type **Night Table** and then press **Enter** (Figure 4-1.5).

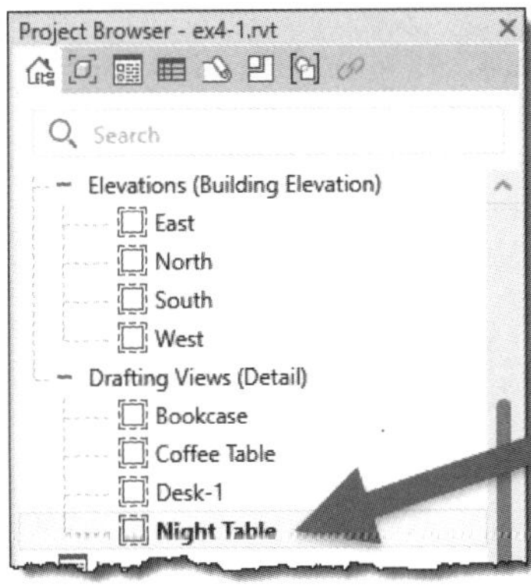

FIGURE 4-1.5 Rename View dialog – Night Table entered

You are now ready to modify the copy of the *Desk-1* linework. You will use the *Move* tool to change the location of one of the vertical lines, which will cause the two horizontal lines to stretch with it. Autodesk Revit *Detail Lines* automatically have a parametric relationship to adjacent lines when their endpoints touch them.

15. Select the vertical line on the right and then click the **Move** icon on the *Ribbon.*

16. Pick the midpoint of the vertical line, then move the mouse 1′-6″ to the left and click again (Figure 4-1.6).

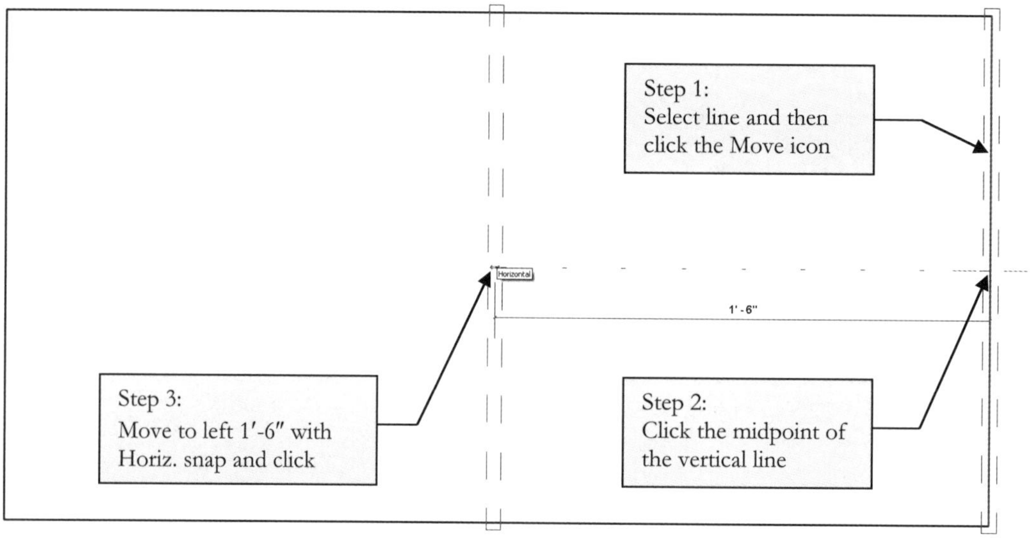

FIGURE 4-1.6 Move tool used to stretch a rectangle

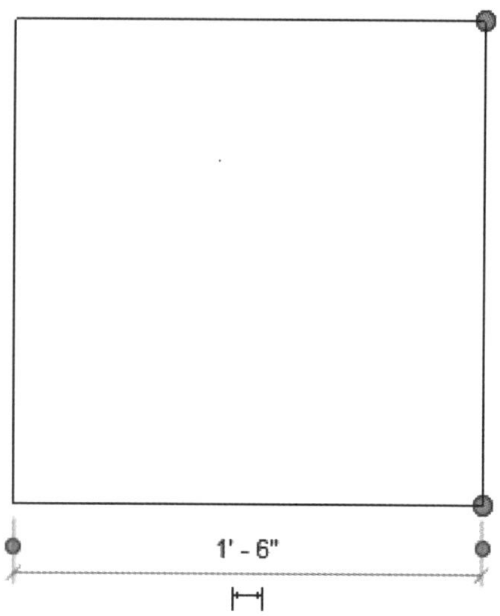

FIGURE 4-1.7 Stretched rectangle (using Move tool)

The rectangle is now resized to half its original width.

You will notice that the horizontal lines automatically adjust.

Revit assumes a special relationship between a line being edited and any line whose endpoint is directly touching it.

***TIP:** You can select "Disjoin" on the Ribbon while in the Move command if you don't want other lines to move or stretch with it. You will not do that here, though.*

17. **Save** your project.

view name: Dresser-1

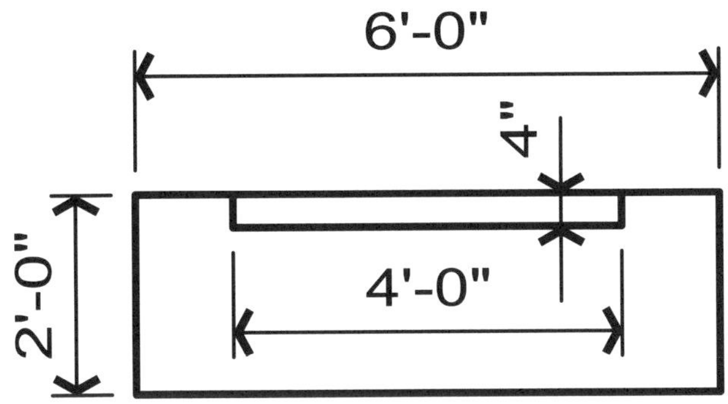

18. Draw the dresser using the following tip:

    TIP: Simply draw two rectangles. Move the smaller rectangle into place using the Move tool and Snaps.

view name: **Dresser-2**

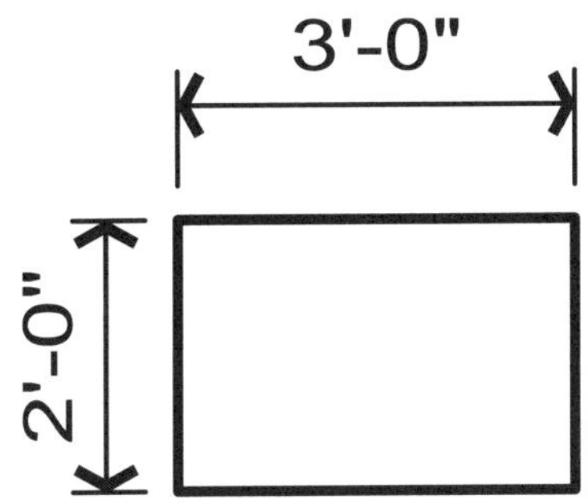

19. Draw this smaller dresser.

view name: **Desk-2**

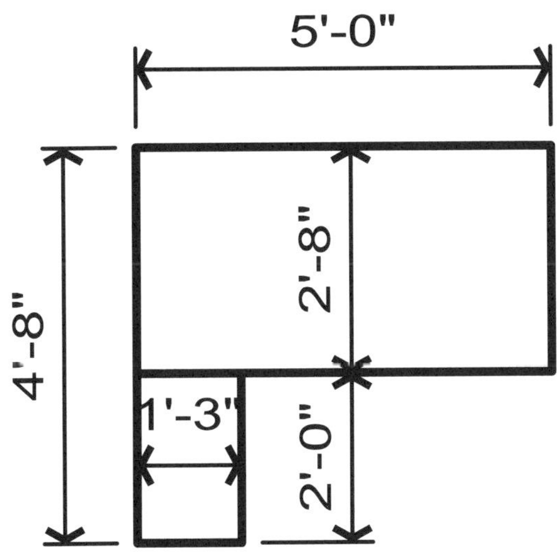

20. Draw this desk in the same way you drew *Dresser-1*.

view name: **File Cabinet**

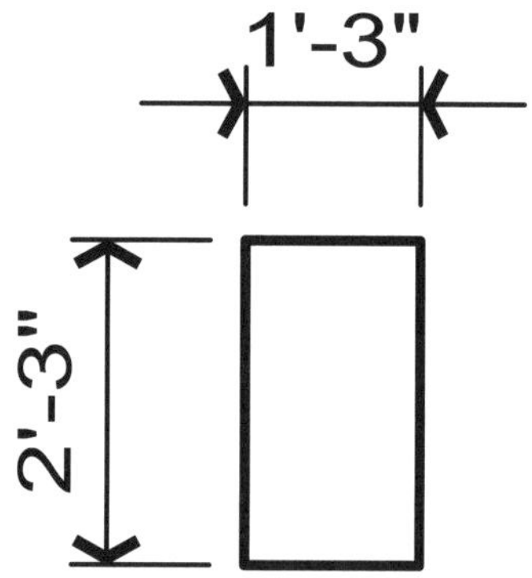

21. Draw this file cabinet.

view name: **Chair-1**

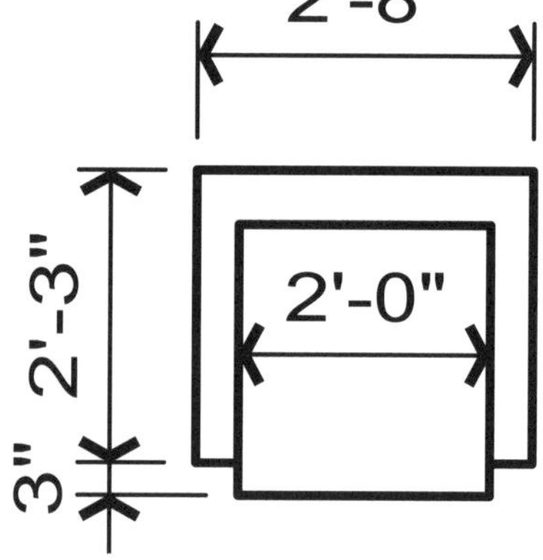

22. Draw this chair per the following tips:

Draw the 2′x2′ square first, and then draw three separate rectangles as shown to the right. Move them into place with *Move* and *Snaps*. Next, delete the extra lines so your drawing looks like the one shown on the left. Pay close attention to the dimensions!

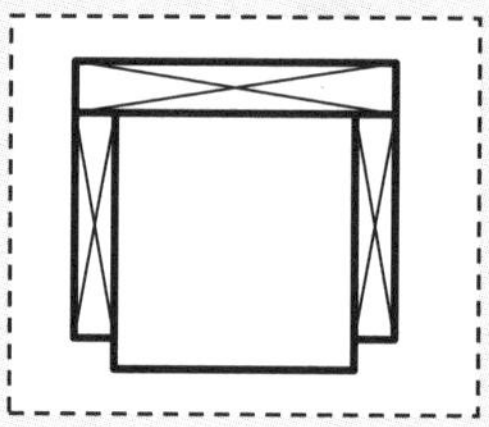

view name: **Sofa**

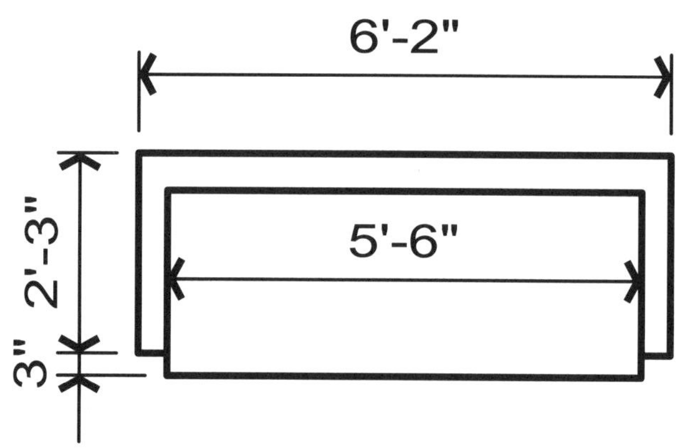

23. *Duplicate* and *Rename* the *Chair-1* view to start this drawing.

Tip: *See the next page for more information on creating this drawing.*

You can create the *Sofa* in a similar way that you created the *Night Table*; that is, you will use the *Move* tool. Rather than selecting a single vertical line, you will select all the lines on one side of the chair.

You can select all the lines on one side in a single step, rather than clicking each one individually while holding the Ctrl key. You will select using a *window* selection, not a *crossing window* selection.

24. **Select** all the lines on the right side (Figure 4-1.8).

TIP: Pick from left to right for a window *selection.*

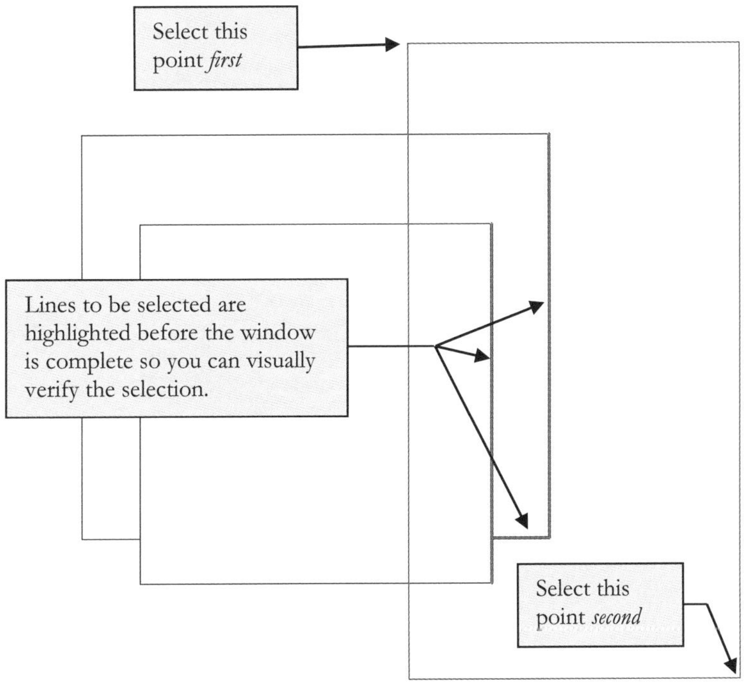

FIGURE 4-1.8 Stretch chair using Move tool

25. Use the ***Move*** tool to extend the chair into a sofa.

TIP: The difference between the chair width and the sofa width is the distance the lines are to be moved.

You have just successfully transformed the chair into a sofa! Do not forget to *Save* often to avoid losing work. Also, use the *Measure* tool to verify the accuracy of your drawing.

view name: **Bed-Double**

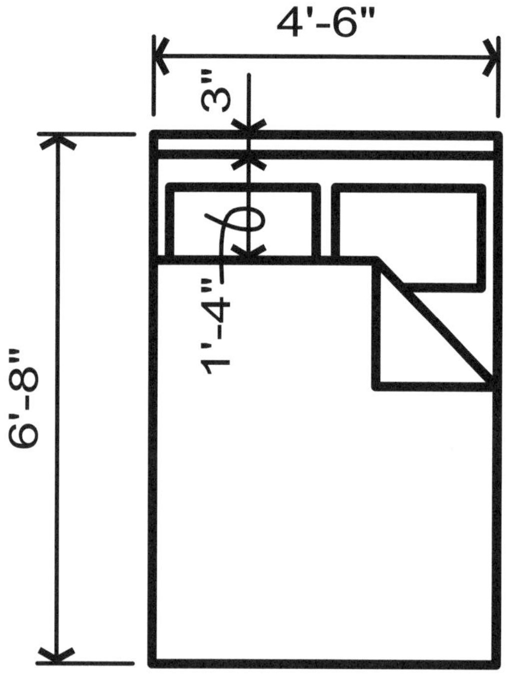

26. Draw this bed using lines and rectangles; the exact sizes of items not dimensioned are not important.

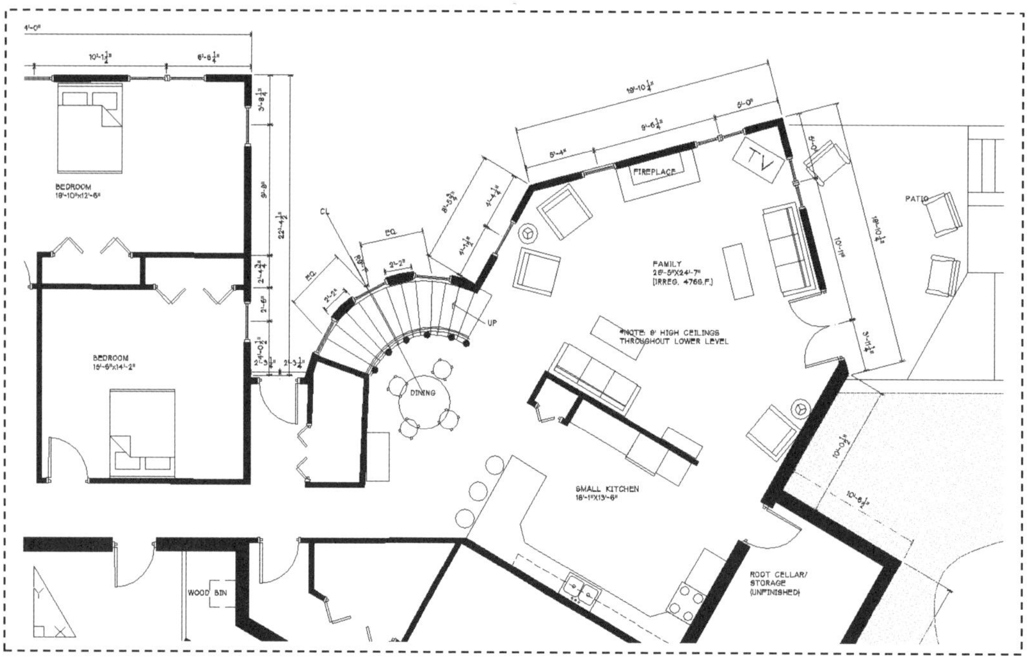

FIGURE 4-1.9 Floor Plan example using similar furniture to that drawn in this exercise.

Image courtesy of Stanius Johnson Architects
www.staniusjohnson.com

Exercise 4-2:
Sketching Objects with Curves

Similar to the previous exercise, you will draw several shapes; this time, they will have curves.

You will look at the various commands for creating curves, such as *Arc*, *Circle,* and *Fillet.*

Again, you will not draw the dimensions as they are for reference only; each drawing should be drawn in its own *Drafting View*. Name the view with the label provided.

Finally, you can ignore the black dot on each drawing below. This dot simply represents the location from which the symbol would typically be inserted or placed.

view name: Laundry-Sink

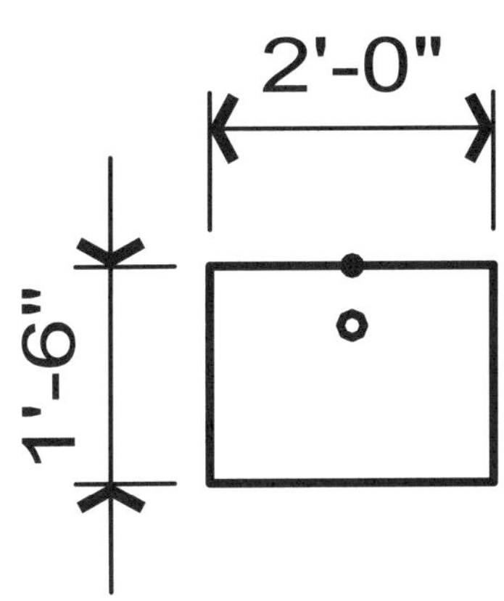

This is a simple rectangle representing the size of a laundry sink, with a circle representing the drain.

1. **Open** a new Revit project and name it **Ex4-2.rvt**.
2. Draw the rectangle shown; refer to Exercise 4-1 for more information.
3. Use the ***Measure*** tool to verify the size of your rectangle.

Next, you will draw a circle for the drain. The drain needs to be centered left and right and 5" from the back edge. The following steps show you one way to do this.

4. Select the ***Detail Line*** tool from the *Annotate* tab.
5. Select the ***Circle*** icon from the *Ribbon* (Figure 4-2.1).

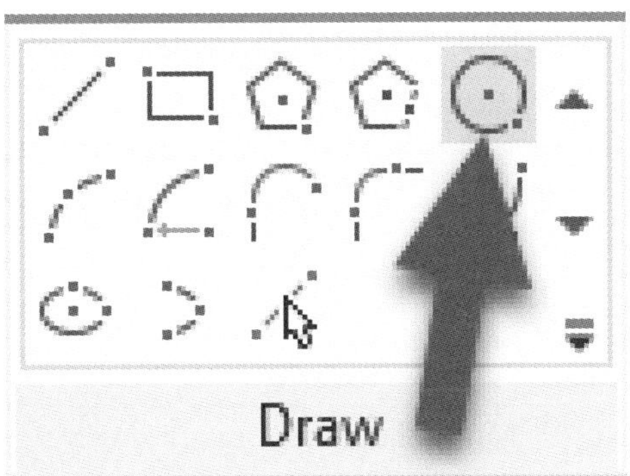

FIGURE 4-2.1 Sketch Options for detail lines

6. Pick the midpoint of the top line (Figure 4-2.2).

   FYI: This is the center of the circle.

7. Type **0 1** for the radius and press **Enter** (0 1 = 0′ – 1″).

   FYI: This creates a 2″ diameter circle.

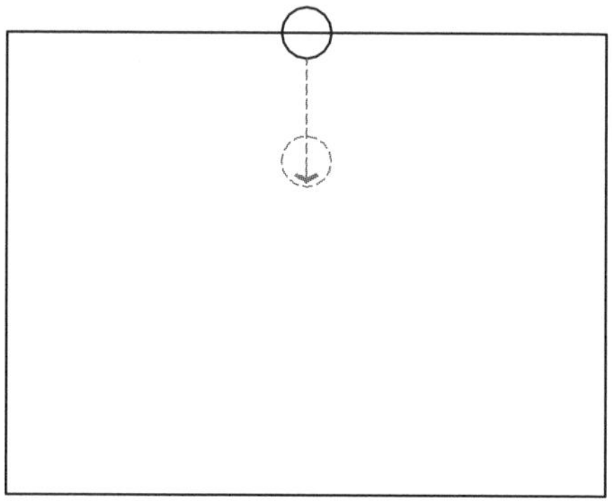

FIGURE 4-2.2 Creating a circle and moving it into place.

At this point, you may get an error indicating the "Line is too short" or "Element is too small on screen" (Figure 4-2.3). This is supposed to prevent a user, like yourself, from accidentally drawing a very small line when you click the mouse twice right next to each other, or trying to change the dimension of a previously drawn line to something less than 1/32″. If you get this error, you simply zoom in on your drawing more so that the circle is more prominently visible on the screen.

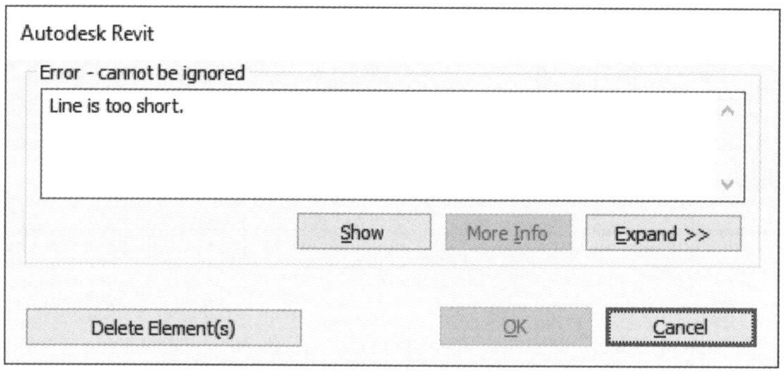

FIGURE 4-2.3 Possible Revit error message when creating the circle

8. If you did get the error message just described, click *Cancel*, *Zoom In* and then draw the circle again.

9. Select the circle and then the ***Move*** tool.

10. **Move** the circle straight down 5″ (Figure 4-2.2).

That's it! Do not forget to save your *Ex4-2* project often.

view name: **Dryer**

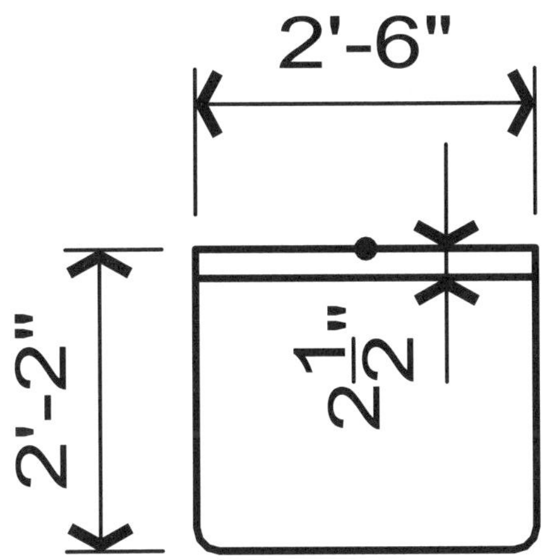

Here you will draw a dryer with rounded front corners. This, like all the other symbols in this lesson, is a plan view symbol, as in "viewed from the top."

11. Draw a 30″x26″ Rectangle.

12. Use the ***Measure*** tool to verify your dimensions.

Next, you will draw the line that is 2½″ from the back of the dryer. You will draw the line in approximately the correct position, then use the temporary dimensions to fine-tune the location.

13. Select the **Detail Line** tool and then pick a point approximately 3″ down from the upper-left corner; a temporary dimension will be displayed before you click your mouse button (Figure 4-2.4).

14. Complete the horizontal line by picking a point perpendicular to the vertical line on the right (Figure 4-2.4).

15. With the temporary dimensions still displayed, click the text for the 0′-3″ dimension, type **0 2.5**, and then press **Enter** (Figure 4-2.5).

16. Click ***Modify*** to clear the selection and make the *Temporary Dimensions* go away.

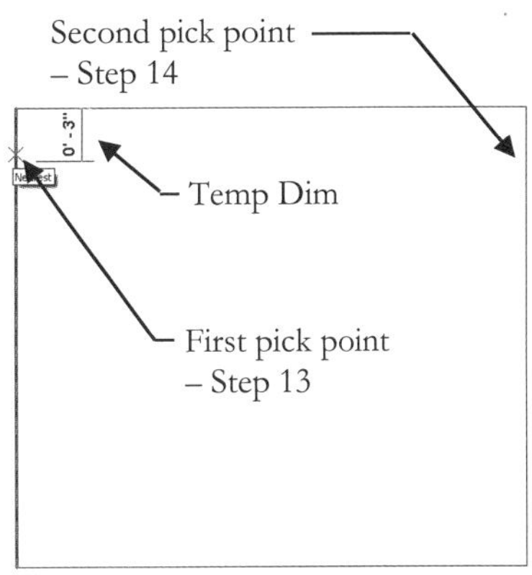

FIGURE 4-2.4 Drawing a line

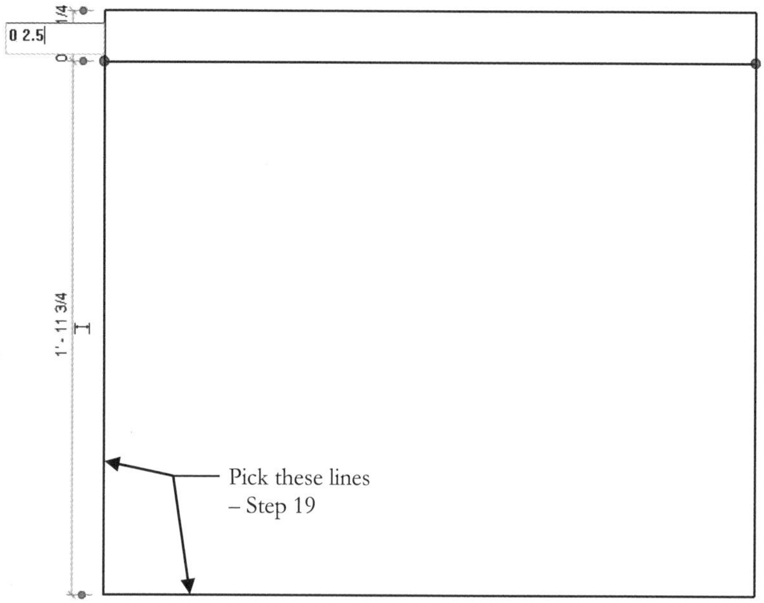

FIGURE 4-2.5 Adjusting new lines position via temporary dimensions

Next, you will round the corners. You still use the *Detail Line* tool, but use a *Draw* option called *Fillet Arc*, pronounced "Fill it." You will try this next.

17. With the ***Detail Lines*** tool active, select the **Fillet Arc** *Draw* option on the *Ribbon* (Figure 4-2.6).

18. Check **Radius** and enter **0′ 2″** in the text box on the *Ribbon* (Figure 4-2.6).

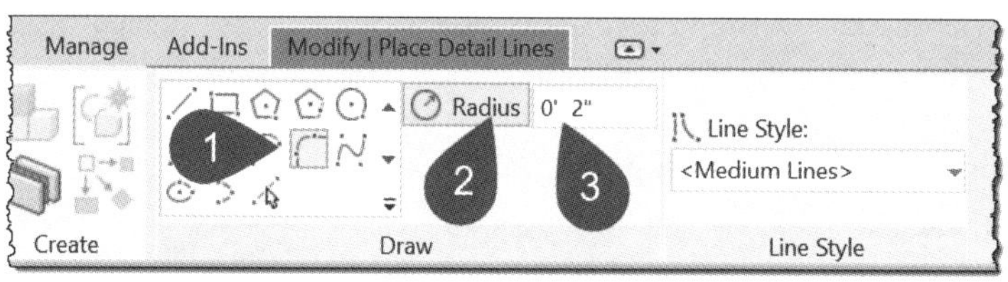

FIGURE 4-2.6 Ribbon and *Ribbon*; options for Detail Lines in Fillet mode

19. Pick the two lines identified in Figure 4-2.5.

The intersection of the two lines is where the arc is placed; notice the two lines you picked have been trimmed back to the new *Fillet Arc*.

20. Repeat the previous step to **Fillet** the other corner.

view name: Washer

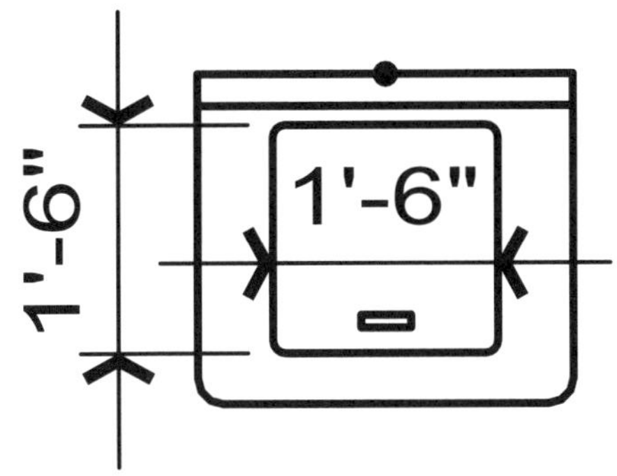

This drawing is identical to the *Dryer* except for the door added to the top. You can duplicate the *Dryer Drafting View* to get a jump start on this drawing.

To draw the door you will use the **Offset** option, which is part of the *Detail Line* tool.

The ***Offset*** tool is easy to use; to use it, you:

- Select the *Detail Line* tool
- Select the *Pick Lines* icon on the *Ribbon*
- Enter the *Offset* distance on the *Ribbon*
- Select near a line, and on the side to offset

21. Select the ***Detail Line*** tool.

22. Select the **Pick Lines** icon on the *Ribbon* (Figure 4-2.7).

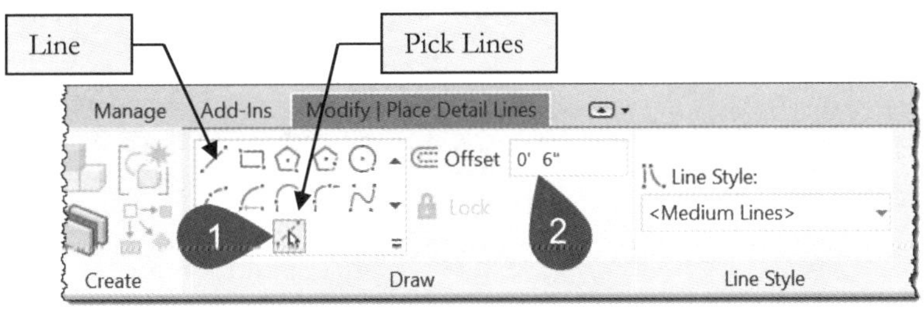

FIGURE 4-2.7 Ribbon and *Ribbon*: options for Detail Lines in Pick Lines mode

Note that the *Pick Lines* icon toggles you from *Draw* mode to *Pick Lines* mode. The *Pick Lines* mode allows you to use existing linework to quickly create new linework. You should notice that the available options on the Ribbon change after selecting *Pick Lines*; you can switch back by selecting the *Draw* icons on the *Ribbon* (Figure 4-2.7).

23. Enter **0′ 6″** for the *Offset* distance (Figure 4-2.7).

Next, you will need to select a line to offset. Which side of the line you click on will indicate the direction the line is offset. Revit provides a visual reference line indicating which side the line will be offset to and its location based on the offset distance entered.

Without clicking the mouse button, move your cursor around the drawing and notice the visual reference line. Move your mouse from side-to-side over a line to see the reference line move to correspond to the cursor location.

24. **Offset** the left vertical line towards the right.

TIP: Make sure you entered the correct offset distance in the previous step (Figure 4-2.8).

You will need to look at the washer drawing and the dryer drawing dimensions to figure out the door size.

25. **Offset** the other three sides; your sketch should look like Figure 4-2.9.

26. Use the ***Fillet Arc*** sketch mode, in the *Detail Line* tool, to create a 1″ radius on the four corners.

27. Click ***Modify*** to finish the current command.

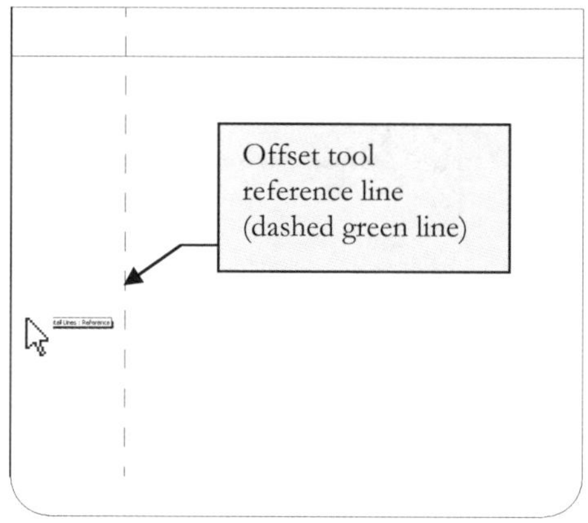

FIGURE 4-2.8 Offset left vertical line towards the right 6″

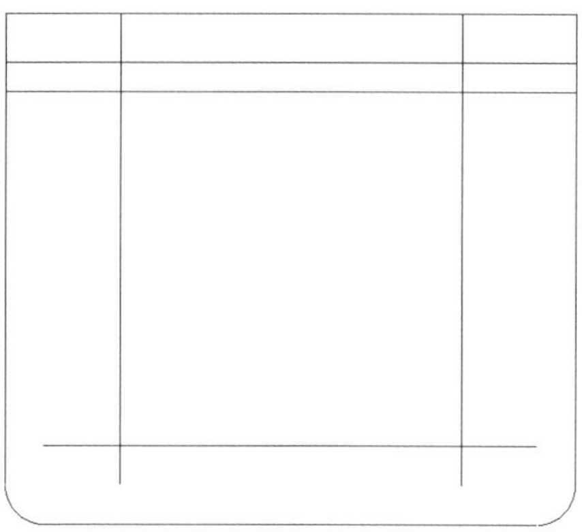

FIGURE 4-2.9 All four lines offset inward to create outline for washer door

All four corners should now be rounded off.

28. Draw a small 4″x1″ rectangle to represent the door handle. Draw it anywhere. Then using *Snaps*, move it to the midpoint of the bottom door edge, and then move the handle 2″ up.

29. **Save** your project. Make sure the view name is *Washer*.

TIP: Revit also provides an Offset *tool on the* Modify *tab of the* Ribbon. *The steps required are very similar to those just described.*

view name: **Range**

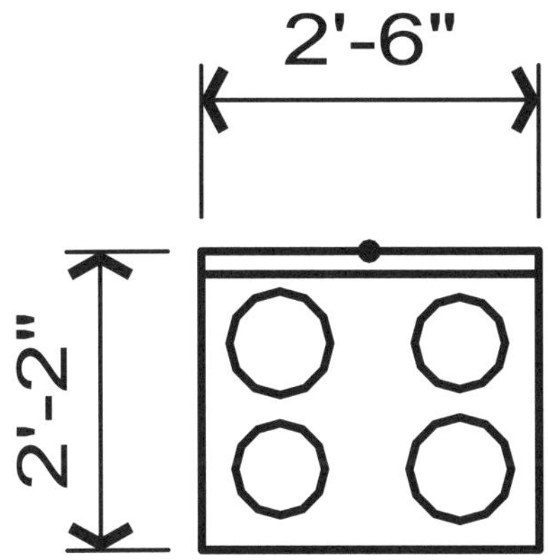

Now you will draw a kitchen *Range* with four circles that represent the burners.

In this exercise you will have to draw temporary lines, called *construction lines*, to create reference points needed to accurately locate the circles. Once the circles have been drawn, the construction lines can be erased.

30. Draw the range with a 2″ deep control panel at the back; refer to the steps described to draw the dryer if necessary.

31. Draw the four construction lines shown in Figure 4-2.10. Use the ***Ref Plane*** tool on the *Architecture* tab.

32. Draw two 9½″ Dia. circles and two 7½″ Dia. circles using the intersection of the construction lines to locate the centers of the circles (Figure 4-2.10).

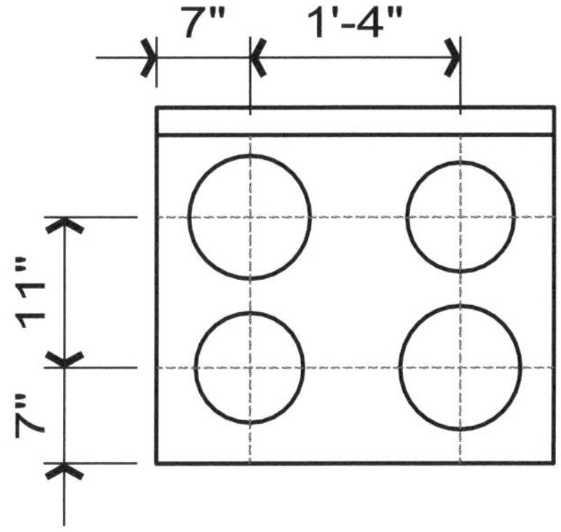

FIGURE 4-2.10 Range with four temporary construction lines (shown dashed for clarity)

TIP: Refer back to the Laundry-Sink for sketching circles.

33. **Erase** the four **Ref Plane** lines (construction lines).

34. **Save** your project.

TIP: When using the Measure *tool, you can select* Chain *on the* Ribbon *to have* Revit *calculate the total length of several picks. For example, you can quickly get the perimeter of a rectangle by picking each corner. Notice, as you pick points, the* Total Length *is listed on the* Ribbon.

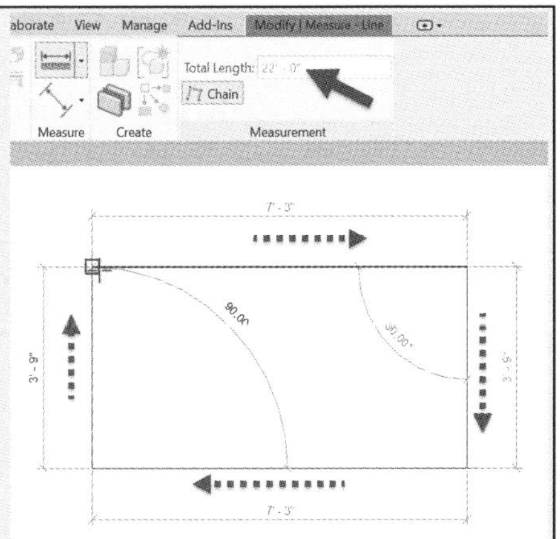

view name: **Chair-2**

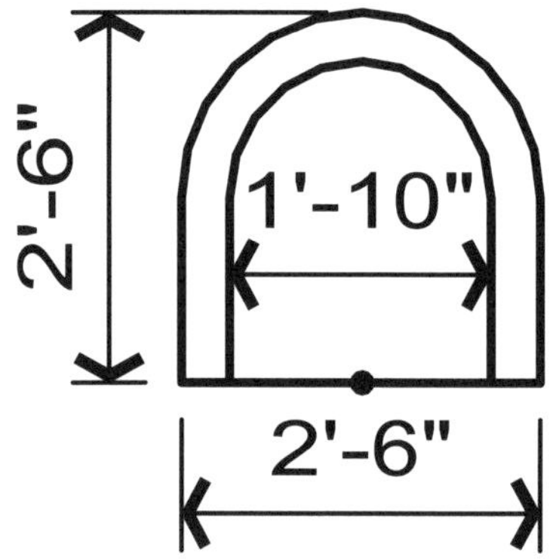

Now you will sketch another chair. You will use *Detail Line* with *Offset* and the *Arc* settings.

First, you will draw the arc at the perimeter.

35. Select *Detail Line* and then **Center – Ends Arc** from the *Ribbon* (Figure 4-2.1).

Notice on the *Status Bar,* you are prompted to "**Click to enter arc center.**"

36. *First Pick*: Pick a point somewhere in the middle of a new *Drafting View* named *Chair-2* (Figure 4-2.11).

You are now prompted, on the *Status Bar*, "**Drag arc radius to desired location.**"

37. *Second Pick*: Move the cursor towards the left, while snapped to the horizontal, until the temporary dimension reads **1′-3″** (Figure 4-2.11).

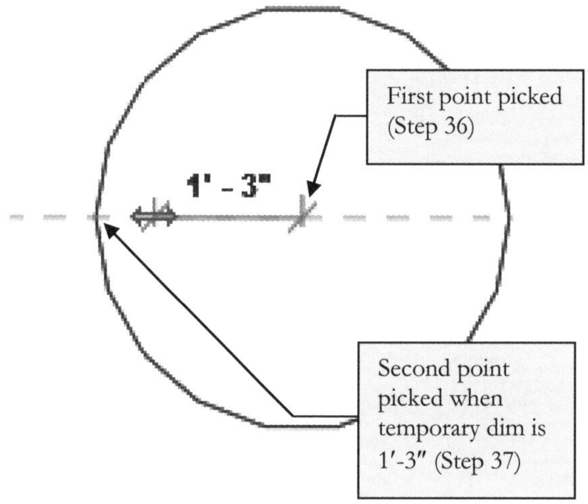

FIGURE 4-2.11 Sketching an arc; picking second point

NOTE: As you can see, Revit temporarily displays a full circle until you pick the second point. This is because Revit does not know which direction the arc will go or what the arc length will be. The full circle allows you to visualize where your arc will be (Figure 4-2.11).

38. *Third Pick*: Move the cursor to the right until the arc is 180 degrees and snapped to the horizontal again (Figure 4-2.12).

TIP: Notice that your cursor location determines which direction or side the arc is created; move the cursor around before picking the third endpoint to see how the preview arc changes on screen.

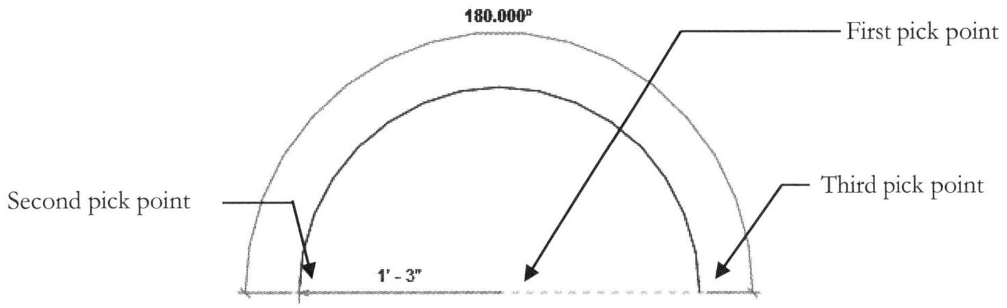

FIGURE 4-2.12 Pick points for arc command

Next, you will draw the three *Detail Lines* to complete the chair's perimeter.

39. Draw two vertical lines **1′-3″** long, attached to the arc endpoints.

    TIP: *Do not forget to use* Medium Lines *when sketching detail lines; if you forget, you can select the lines while in Modify mode and choose* Medium Lines *from the* Element Type Selector *on the* Ribbon.

40. Draw the **2′-6″** line across the bottom.

Notice the radius is 1′-3″. You did not have to enter that number because the three points you picked were enough information for Revit to determine it automatically.

If you had drawn the three lines in Steps 39 and 40 before the arc, you would not have had the required center point to pick while creating the arc. However, you could have drawn a temporary horizontal line across the top to set up a center pick that would allow you to draw the circle in its final location; or even better, use the **Start-End-Radius** *Detail Line* option.

You have now completed the chair's perimeter.

41. Use the ***Offset*** tool to offset the arc and two vertical lines the required distance to complete the sketch.

42. **Save** your project.

view name: **Love-Seat**

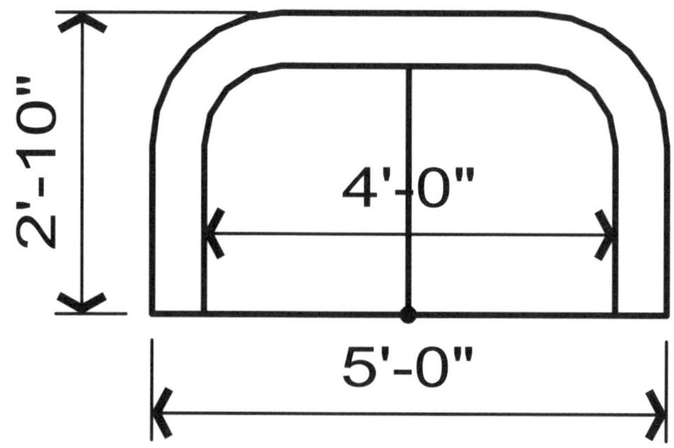

You should be able to draw this *Love-Seat* without any further instruction. Use the same radius as *Chair-2*.

You can create the drawing using a combination of the following tools:

- *Detail Line*
- *Fillet Arc*
- *Offset*
- *Move*

view name: **Tub**

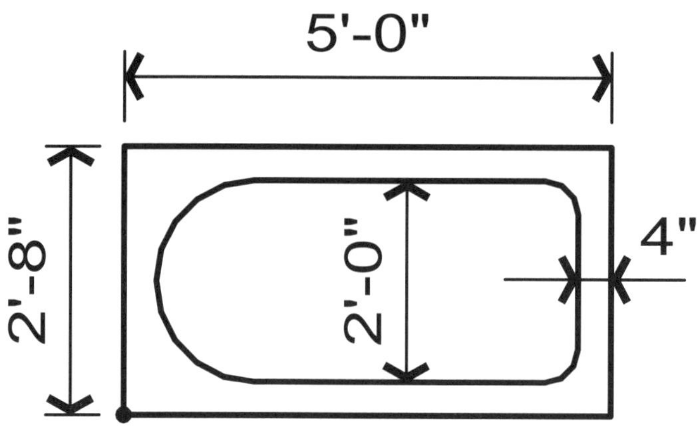

Now you will draw a bathtub. You will use several commands previously covered.

You will use the following tools:

- *Detail Line*
- *Fillet Arc*
- *Offset*
- *Move*

You may also wish to draw one or more construction lines to help locate things like the large radius, although it can be drawn without them.

view name: **Lav-1**

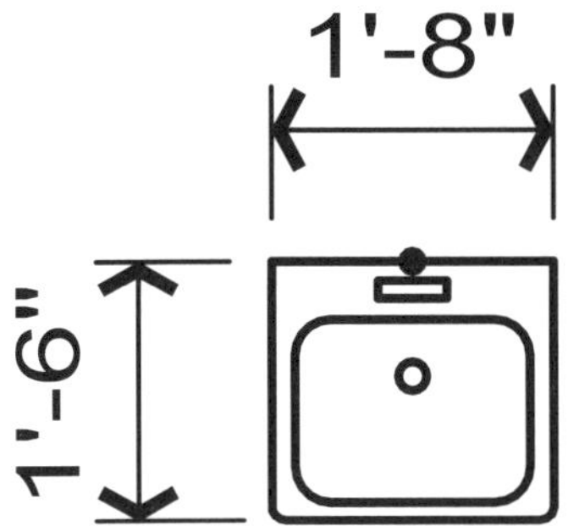

Draw this lavatory per the following specifications:

- Larger arcs shown shall have a 2½″ radius
- Smaller arcs shown shall have a 1″ radius, outside corners
- Sides and Front of sink to have 1½″ space, offset
- Back to have 4″ space, offset
- Small rectangle to be 4½″x1″ and 1½″ away from the back
- 2″ Dia. drain, 8″ from back

view name: **Lav-2**

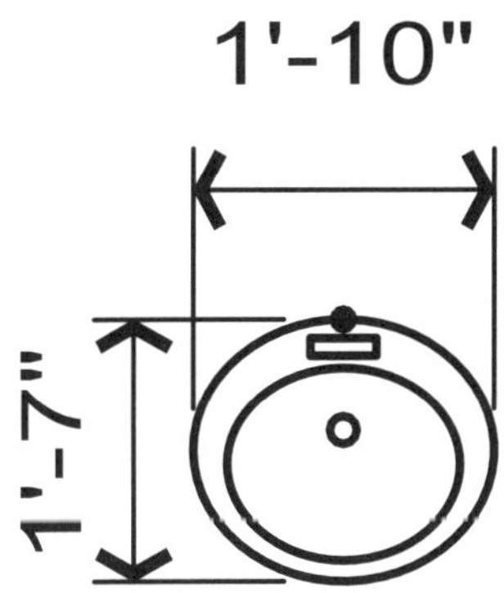

Next, you will draw another lavatory. This time, you will use the *Ellipse* tool.

43. Create a new *Drafting View.*

44. Select *Detail Lines* and then **Ellipse** from the *Ribbon* (Figure 4-2.1).

Notice the *Status Bar* prompt: "**Click to enter ellipse center**."

45. Pick near the middle of the screen.

46. With the cursor snapped to the vertical, point the cursor straight down and then type **0 9.5**; press **Enter**.

NOTE: 9½″ is half the HEIGHT, which is 1′-7″.

Now you need to specify the horizontal axis of the ellipse.

47. Again, snapping to the horizontal plane, position the cursor towards the right then type **0 11** and then press the **Enter** key.

NOTE: 11″ is half the width: 1′-10″.

That's all it takes to draw an ellipse!

48. ***Copy*** the ellipse vertically downward **3½"** (Figure 4-2.13).

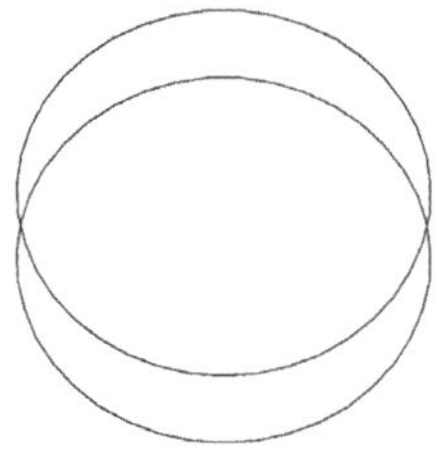

FIGURE 4-2.13 Ellipse copied downward 3½"

Next, you will use the *Scale* tool to reduce the size of the second ellipse. To summarize the steps involved:

- Select the ellipse to be resized
- Select the *Scale* icon
- Pick the origin
- Pick the opposite side of the ellipse
- Enter a new value for the ellipse.

49. Select the lower ellipse.

50. Select the **Scale** icon on the *Ribbon,* on the *Modify* tab.

Notice the *Status Bar* prompt: "**Pick to enter origin.**" The origin, or base point, is a point on, or relative to, the object that does not move.

51. *First Pick:* Pick the top edge, midpoint, of the selected ellipse (Figure 4-2.14).

52. *Second Pick:* Pick the bottom edge, midpoint, of the same ellipse (Figure 4-2.14).

53. Type **1 2** (i.e., 1'-2") and press **Enter**; this will be the new distance between the two points picked.

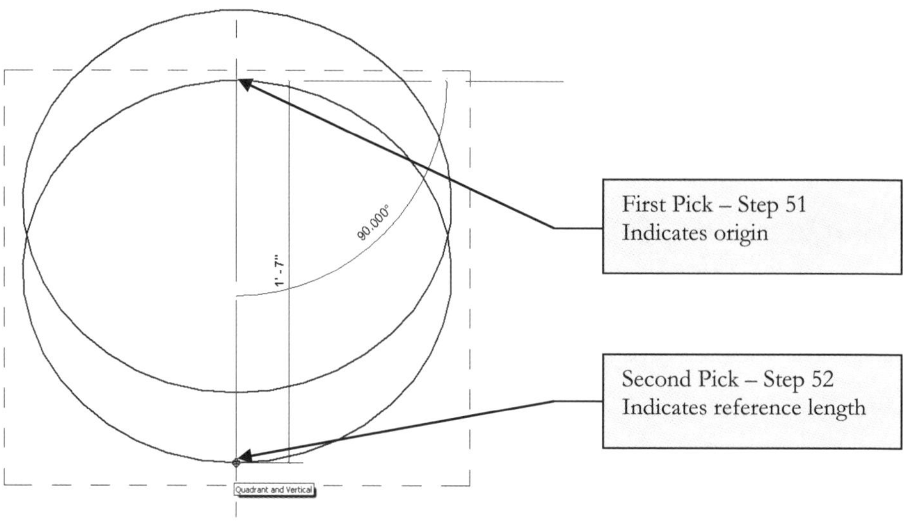

FIGURE 4-2.14 Scaling the ellipse

Next, you need to draw the faucet and drain. As it turns out, the faucet and drain for *Lav-1* are in the same position relative to the middle and back (black dot). So to save time, you will *Copy/Paste* these items from the *Lav-1* drafting view into the *Lav-2* view.

54. Open **Lav-1** *Drafting View.*

55. Select the entire *Lav-1* sketch.

56. Pick **Modify | Lines → Clipboard → Copy** while the *Lav-1* linework is selected.

57. Switch back to the *Lav-2* view and press **Ctrl + V** on the keyboard. Press both keys at the same time.

58. Pick a point to the side of the *Lav-2* sketch (Figure 4-2.15).

59. Select the faucet, the small rectangle, and the drain (i.e., the circle).

    TIP: Use a window *selection, picking from left to right.*

60. Select the ***Move*** tool; pick the middle/back of the *Lav-1* sketch and then pick the middle/back of the *Lav-2* sketch.

    NOTE: These two points represent the angle and distance to move the selected items.

61. **Erase** the extra *Lav-1* linework from the *Lav-2* view.

You should now have the faucet and drain correctly positioned in your *Lav-2* view.

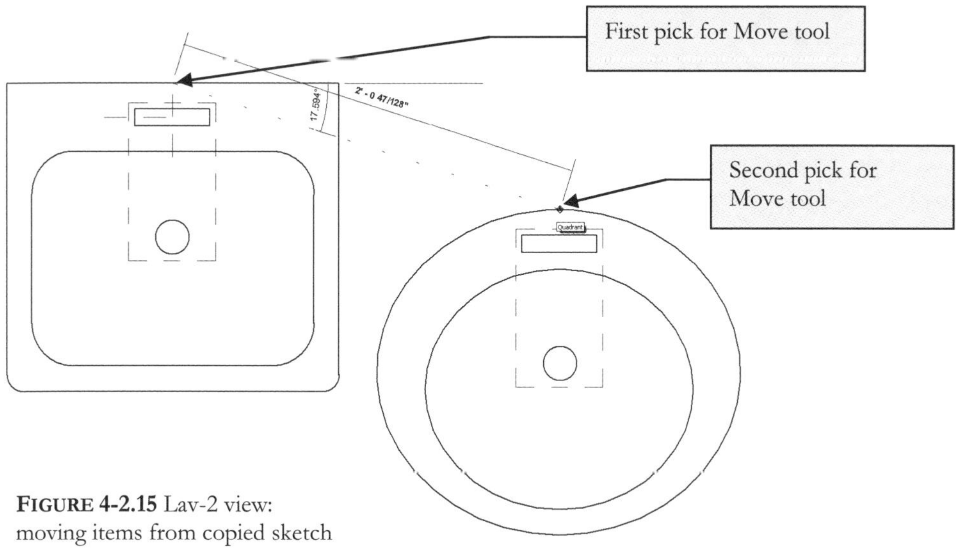

FIGURE 4-2.15 Lav-2 view: moving items from copied sketch

view name: **Sink-1**

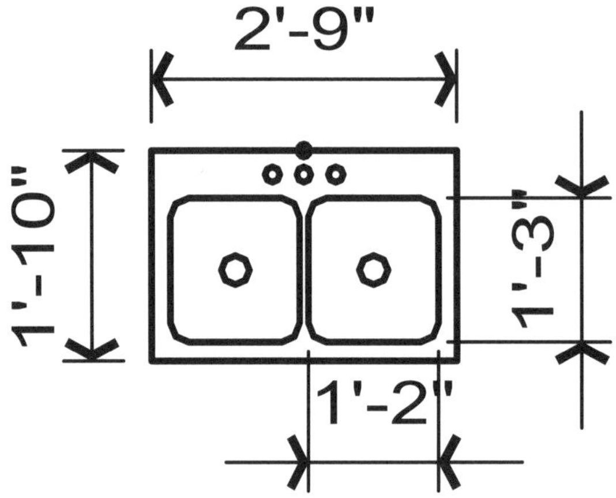

Draw this lavatory per the following specifications:

- 2″ space, offset at sides and front
- 3″ Dia. Circles centered in sinks
- 2″ rad. for Fillets
- 1½″ Dia. at faucet spaces; 3½″ apart

view name: **Water-Closet**

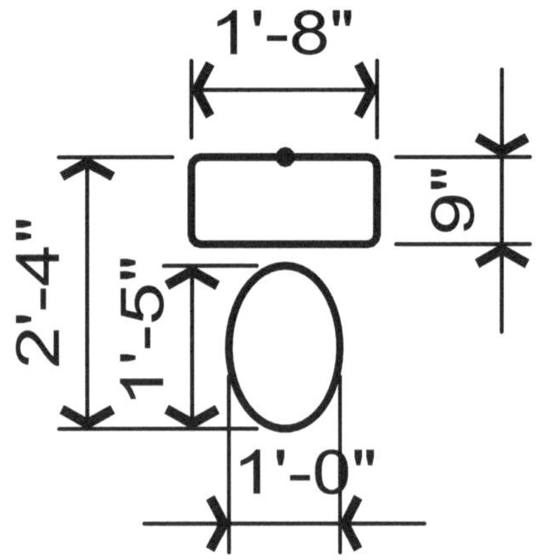

You should be able to draw this symbol without any help.

TIP: *Draw a construction line from the Origin (i.e., black dot) straight down 11″ (2′-4″ – 1′-5″ = 11″). This will give you a point to pick when drawing the ellipse.*

view name: **Tree**

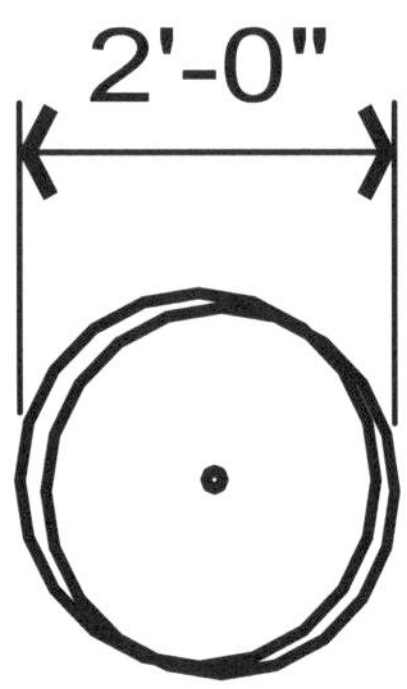

62. Draw one large circle and then copy it similar to this drawing.

63. Draw one small 1″ diameter circle at the approximate center.

64. **Save** your project.

view name: **Door-36**

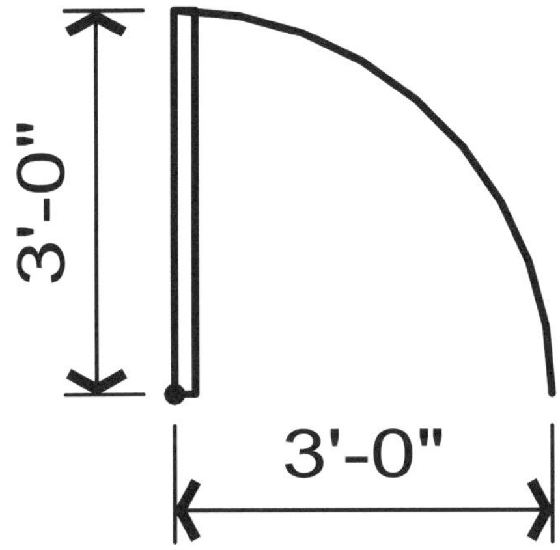

This symbol is used to show a door in a floor plan. The arc represents the path of the door as it opens and shuts.

A symbol like this, 90 degrees open, helps to avoid the door conflicting with something in the house like cabinets or a toilet. Existing doors are typically shown open 45 degrees so it is easier to visually discern new from existing.

Revit has an advanced door tool, so you would not actually draw this symbol very often. However, you may decide to draw one in plan that represents a gate in a reception counter or one in elevation to show a floor hatch. Refer back to Figure 4-1.9 for a floor plan example with door symbols.

65. Draw a **2″x3′-0″ rectangle**.

66. Draw an arc using **Center – Ends Arc**; select the three points in the order shown in Figure 4-2.16.

TIP: Be sure your third pick shows the cursor snapped to the horizontal plane.

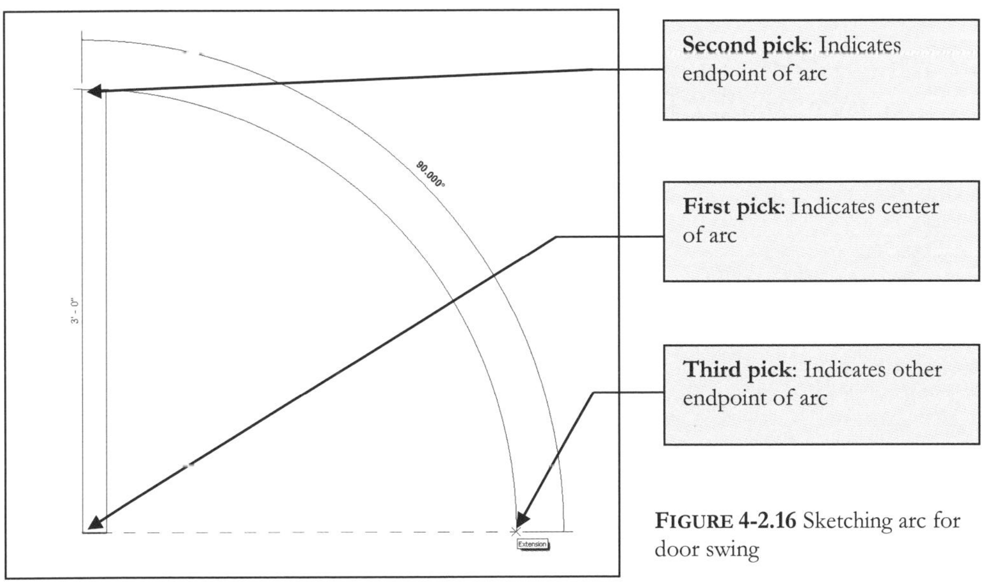

FIGURE 4-2.16 Sketching arc for door swing

view name: **Door2-36**

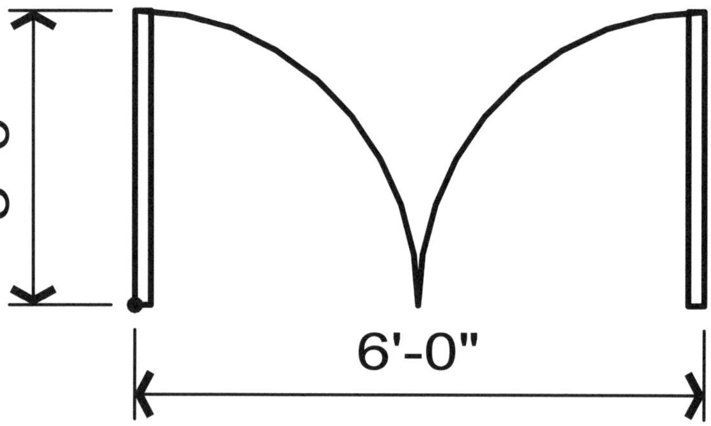

Here you will use a previous drawing and the *Mirror* tool to quickly create this drawing showing a pair of doors in a single opening.

67. Right-click on **Door-36** view label in the *Project Browser*; select "**Duplicate with detailing"** from the pop-up menu.

68. **Rename** the new *Detail View* **Door2-36.**

Next you will mirror both the rectangle and the arc. By default, Revit wants you to select a previously drawn line to be used as the "axis of reflection," but you do not have a line that would allow you to mirror the door properly to the left, so you have to pick the "*Draw Mirror Axis*" option on the *Ribbon.*

69. Select the rectangle and the arc, use a *crossing window* by picking from right to left, and then pick the **Modify | Lines → Modify → Mirror - Draw Axis** tool from the *Ribbon.*

70. Make sure ***Copy*** is selected on the *Ribbon.* See image to the right; this is the default.

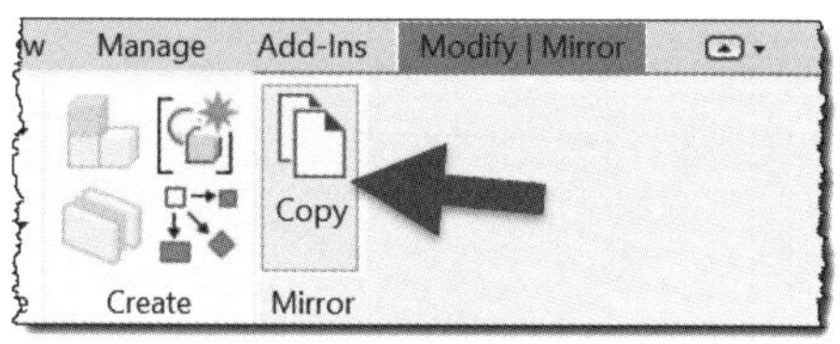

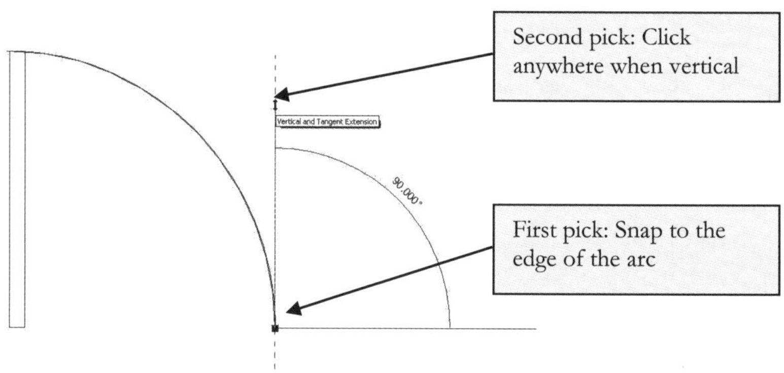

FIGURE 4-2.17 Creating axis of reflection

Notice the *Status Bar* is prompting you to "**Pick Start Point for Axis of Reflection**."

71. Pick the two points shown in **Figure 4-2.17**.

At this point the door symbol, the rectangle and arc, is mirrored and the *Mirror* tool is done.

72. Select ***Modify*** to end the command and unselect everything.

73. **Save** your project as "Ex4-2.rvt".

view name: Clg-Fan-1

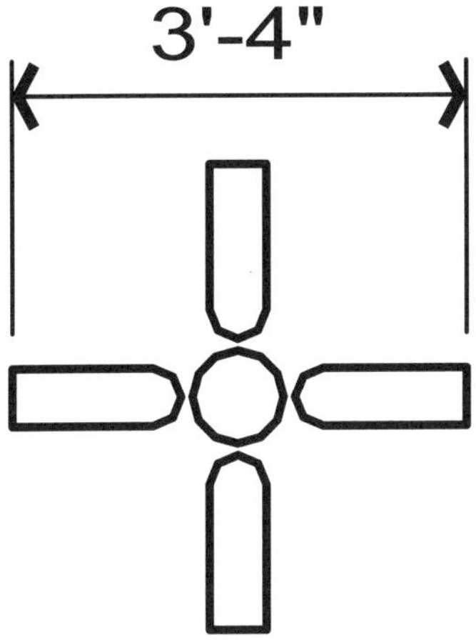

You will use the *Array* command while drawing this ceiling fan.

The *Array* command can be used to array entities in a rectangular pattern (e.g., columns on a grid) or in a polar pattern (i.e., in a circular pattern).

You will use the polar array to rotate and copy the fan blade all in one step!

74. Start a new drawing and create the portion of drawing shown in the figure to the right.

75. Select the fan blade and then select **Array** from the *Ribbon*.

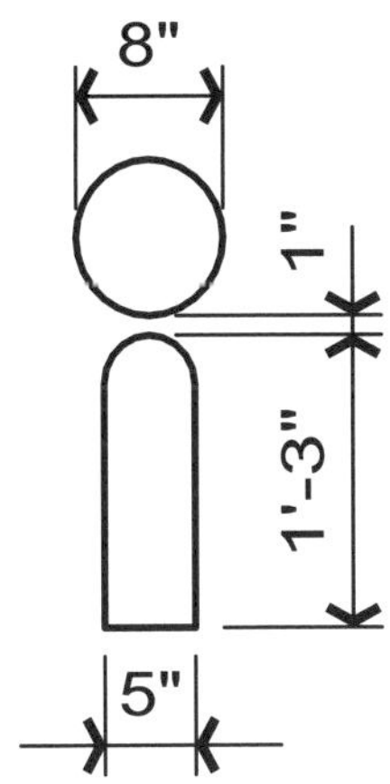

Similar to the *Rotate* tool, you will relocate the *Center of Rotation Symbol* to the center of the 8" circle. This will cause the fan blade to array around the circle rather than the center of the first fan blade.

76. Click *Radial* on the *Ribbon* and then click and *drag* the **Rotation grip** to the center of the 8″ circle (or click the *Place* button on the *Ribbon*); make sure Revit snaps to the center point before clicking (see Figure 4-2.19).

77. Make the following changes to the *Ribbon* (Figure 4-2.18).

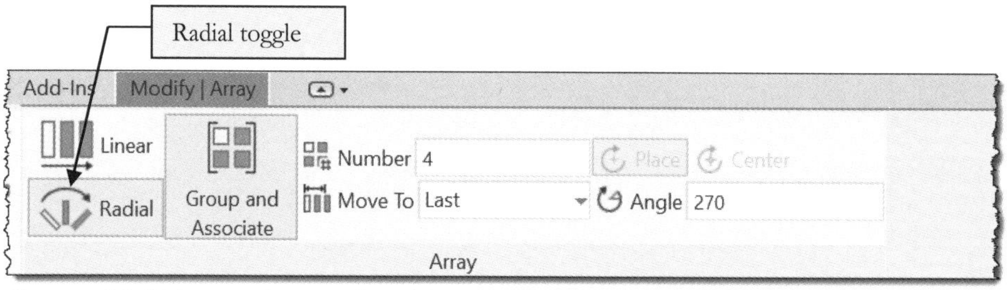

FIGURE 4-2.18 Array options on the Ribbon

78. After typing the angle in the *Ribbon*, press **Enter**.

You should now see the three additional fan blades and a temporary array number. This gives you the option to change the array number if desired.

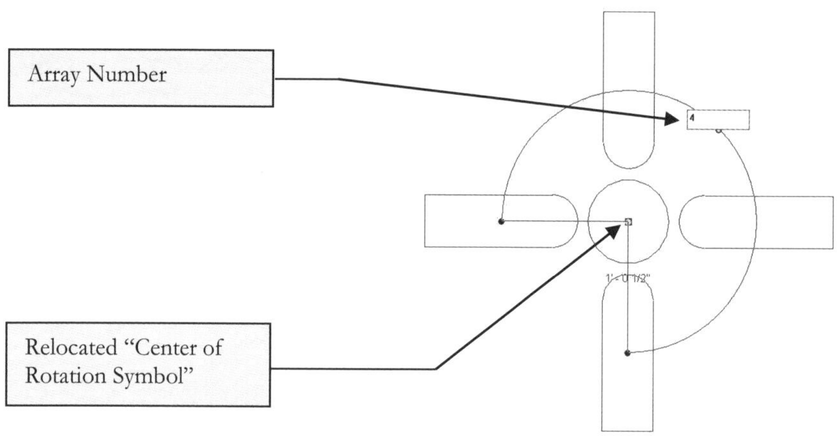

FIGURE 4-2.19 Arraying fan blades

79. Click **Modify** to complete the *Array* and finish the ceiling fan.

Because you left *Group and Associate* checked on the *Ribbon* when you created the array, you can select any part of a fan blade and the array number will appear, like a temporary dimension, and allow you to change the number. You can select *Ungroup* from the *Ribbon* to make each item individually editable as if you had drawn everything from scratch.

80. **Save** your project.

FYI: You can export each Drafting View to a file and import it back into any project file. It can then be placed as a symbol into floor plans. This would make for smaller files on large projects, such as a large hospital complex. The major downside is that you would not see anything in your 3D views for furniture. Thus, you will not likely use these for your Revit plans, but you will be able to utilize every skill learned in this section!

Self-Exam:

The following questions can be used as a way to check your knowledge of this lesson. The answers can be found at the bottom of the page.

1. Revit does not allow you to copy *Detail Views*. (T/F)

2. Entering 4 3.25 in Revit means 4'-3¼". (T/F)

3. Reference Planes (aka, construction lines) are useful drawing aids. (T/F)

4. Use the ______________ tool to sketch an oval shape.

5. When you want to make a previously drawn rectangle wider you would use

   the ______________ tool.

Review Questions:

The following questions may be assigned by your instructor as a way to assess your knowledge of this section. Your instructor has the answers to the review questions.

1. Use the *Offset* option to quickly create a parallel line(s). (T/F)

2. If Revit displays an error message indicating a line is too small to be drawn, you simply zoom in more and try again. (T/F)

3. Use the ______________ command to create a reverse image.

4. With the *Move* tool, lines completely within the selection window are actually only moved, not stretched. (T/F)

5. You can relocate the "center of rotation" when using *Radial Array*. (T/F)

6. Occasionally you need to draw an object and then move it into place to accurately locate it. (T/F)

7. The ______________ is an option within the *Detail Line* tool which allows you to create a rounded corner where two lines intersect.

8. When using the *Mirror* tool, you occasionally need to draw a temporary line that represents the *Axis of Reflection*. (T/F)

9. Which line style was required to be selected in the *Type Selector*, in the *Properties Palette*, for all the linework in this Lesson? ______________

10. In the *Detail Line* tool, how many options allow you to draw arcs? _______

SELF-EXAM ANSWERS:
1 – F, **2** – T, **3** – T, **4** – Ellipse, **5** – Move

Notes:

Lesson 5
Floor Plans:

In this lesson, you will draw the architectural floor plans of an office building. The office building will be further developed in subsequent chapters. It is recommended that you spend adequate time on this lesson, as later lessons build on this one.

Exercise 5-1:
Project Setup

The Project:

A **program statement** is created in the pre-design phase of a project. Working with the client or user group, the design team gathers as much information as possible about the project before starting to design.

The information gathered includes:

- Rooms: What rooms are required?
- Size: How big do the rooms need to be? For example, toilets for a convention center are much bigger than those for a dentist's office.
- Adjacencies: This room needs to be next to that room. For example, the public toilets need to be accessible from the public lobby.

Looking at the Program Schedule (Figure 5-1.1), on the next page, the reader can see a simple example of a program statement created in Revit, using its schedule feature. In this example, each room name is being grouped by department: Admin., Exec., Misc., Public, Staff. The actual designed area is then compared to the original programmed, or desired, area.

> *NOTE: The actual area would really be blank at this point in the project.*

Next, the *Area Check* column is used to identify any rooms that are way too big or small and would affect cost or function. Finally, any required adjacencies are spelled out.

With the project statement in hand, the design team can begin the design process. Although modifications may, and will, need to be made to the program statement, it is used as a goal to meet the client's needs.

This Program Schedule will not actually be created in Revit, though it is possible to do so even before anything has been drawn. The actual *Area* column would say "not enclosed" until the room was placed into the model.

PROGRAM SCHEDULE					
Name	Area	PROGRAM AREA	AREA CHECK	ADJACENCIES	Comments
ADMINISTRATION					
ADMIN ASSIST	385 SF	350 SF	1.099231		
OFFICE MANAGER	139 SF	150 SF	0.925591	ADMIN ASSIST	
	524 SF	500 SF			
EXECUTIVE					
EXEC CONF RM	525 SF	500 SF	1.049186	2ND FLOOR	
EXEC OFFICE	203 SF	200 SF	1.016296	CONF RM	
EXEC OFFICE	241 SF	200 SF	1.205583	CONF RM	
	969 SF	900 SF			
MISC					
CONF ROOM	330 SF	300 SF	1.098994	1ST FLOOR	
CUSTODIAN	70 SF	80 SF	0.870683		
FILES/ STORAGE	316 SF	300 SF	1.053266		
HALL	282 SF				
LAW LIBRARY	1614 SF	1500 SF	1.075987		
MECH & ELEC ROOM	433 SF	400 SF	1.081616		
STAIR	140 SF	150 SF	0.932319		
	3184 SF	2730 SF			
PUBLIC					
COAT CLOSET	36 SF	20 SF	1.806169	LOBBY	
ENTRY VESTIBULE	297 SF	300 SF	0.989502		
LOBBY	1577 SF	1500 SF	1.051604	TOILET RMS	
LOUNGE	297 SF	300 SF	0.989502	2ND FLR	
MENS	165 SF				
MENS	165 SF				
UPPER LOBBY	1101 SF	1000 SF	1.100529		
WAITING	212 SF	200 SF	1.061807		
WOMENS	165 SF				
WOMENS	165 SF				
	4180 SF	3320 SF			
STAFF					
ASSOCIATES OFFICE	294 SF	300 SF	0.980222	EXEC OFFICES	
BREAK RM	143 SF	150 SF	0.955858		
OFFICE	104 SF	120 SF	0.865974		
OFFICE	116 SF	120 SF	0.962979		
OPEN OFFICE	884 SF	1000 SF	0.883816		
PARALEGAL	504 SF	500 SF	1.007133		
WORK ROOM	329 SF	300 SF	1.097483		
	2374 SF	2490 SF			
	11230 SF	9940 SF			

FIGURE 5-1.1 Program Schedule

Project Snapshot

Below you will find a preview of the floor plans that will be developed in the text. Compare the room names with those shown in the Program Schedule.

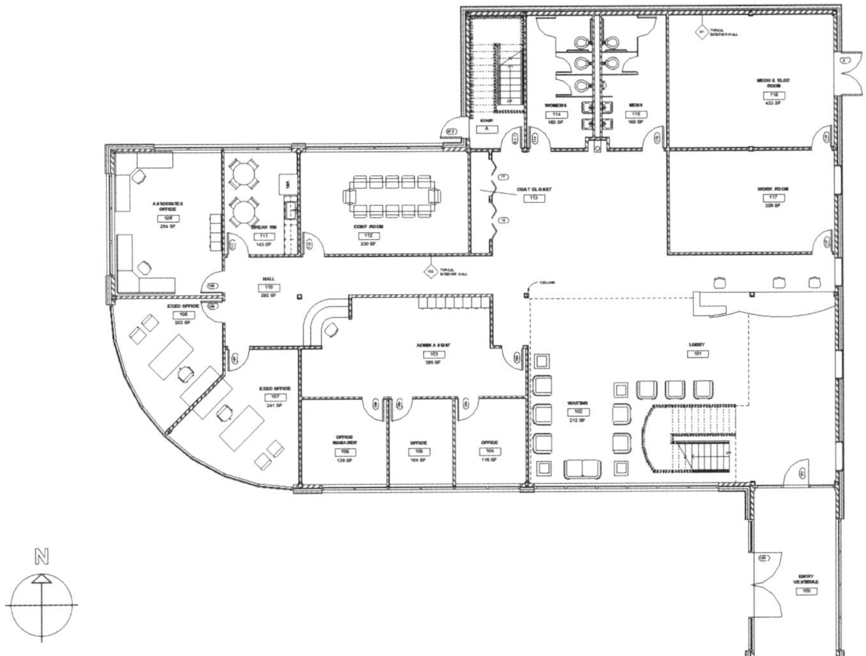

FIGURE 5-1.2 Level 1 floor plan

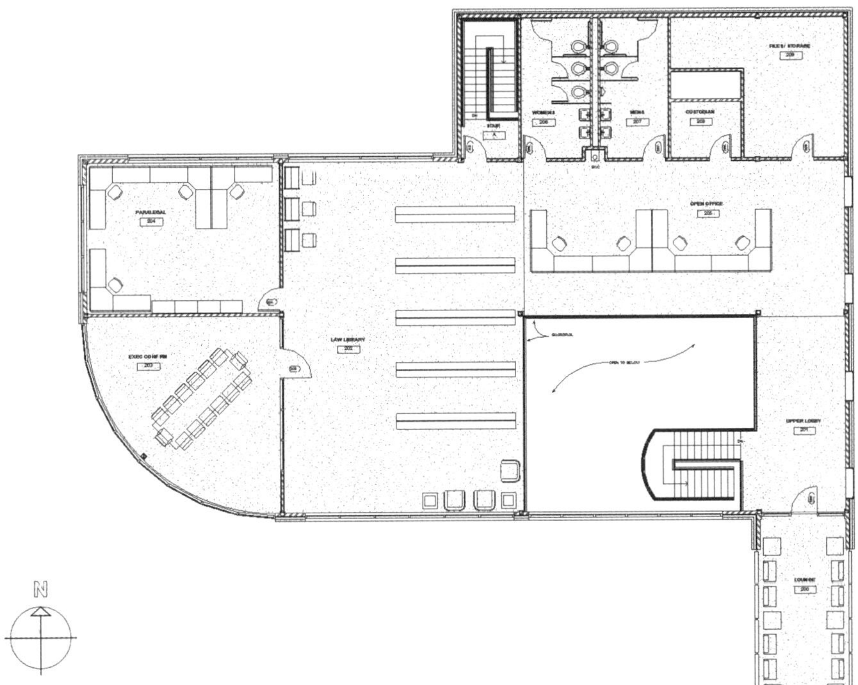

FIGURE 5-1.3 Level 2 floor plan

Project Timeline

The textbook generally follows the workflow a design firm would take when designing a building. After gathering the programming information, floor plans are first developed that align with the program. Next, the vertical relationships are studied; floors, ceilings and roofs are added along with the beams and joists. This helps to establish the required floor to floor heights.

Once these basic elements have been modeled, the elevations and a few primary sections can be studied. The floor plans are then further refined, developing toilet room layouts, furniture and casework. All these building objects in the model can then be scheduled in order to list information about each, such as manufacturer, model number and cost.

Mechanical and electrical systems are then distributed through the facility, all the while ensuring proper clearances exist while routing ducts and piping.

With the project basically complete, photorealistic renderings are created to present the project to others. Finally, all the drawings (i.e., views of the model) are then placed on sheets to create a set of construction documents.

Each new chapter will instruct the reader to open a partially completed file as a first step. This will help avoid any problems with previous exercises being skipped or not completed properly. Also, in the chapters on structural, mechanical and electrical, the beginning model files will have a portion of the work completed to reduce the amount of work required of the student and result in a more complete project. Additionally, a few custom components will be provided that are not found in the out-of-the-box content that comes with Revit. **Therefore, ensure the online files are available while working through the textbook so the required files are accessible. See the inside front cover of this book for more information.**

Creating the Project File:

A Building Information Model (BIM), as previously mentioned, consists of a single file. This file can be quite large. For example, the prestigious architectural design firm SOM used Revit to design the Freedom Tower in New York. As you can imagine, a skyscraper would be a large BIM file, whereas a single-family residence would be much smaller.

Large databases are just starting to enter the architectural design realm. However, banks, hospitals, and the like have been using them for years, even with multiple users!

When Revit is launched, the *Recent Files* view is loaded. Template files have several items set up and ready to use (e.g., some wall, door and window types). Starting with the correct template can save you a significant amount of time.

Revit provides a handful of templates with particular project types in mind. They are Commercial, Construction and Residential.

In this exercise you will use the Commercial template. It has several aspects of the project file already set up and ready for use. A few of these items will be discussed momentarily.

As your knowledge in Revit increases, you will be able to start refining a custom template, which probably will originate from a standard template. The custom template will have things like your firm's title block and a cover sheet with abbreviations, symbols and such, all set up and ready to go.

Next you will create a new project file.

1. On the Home screen, select ***New... under Models***

   Or, if the Ribbon is showing, select ***Application Menu → New → Project.***

You are now in the *New Project* dialog box. Rather than clicking **OK**, which would use a stripped-down default template, you will select **Browse** so you can select a specialized template (Figure 5-1.4).

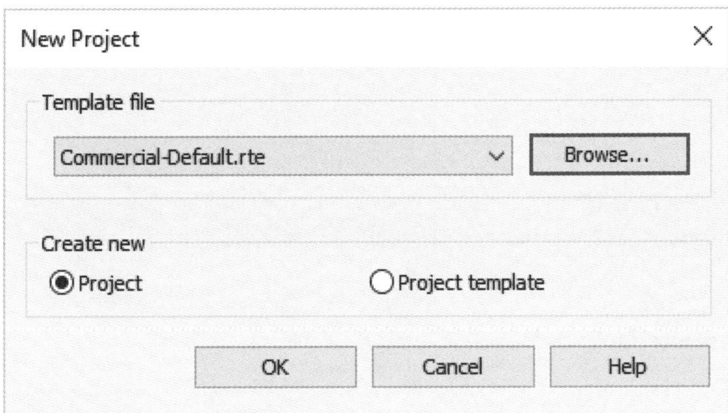

FIGURE 5-1.4 New Project dialog

2. Click the **Browse...** button.

3. It is VERY important you select the correct template: Select the template named **Commercial-Default.rte** from the list of available templates (Figure 5-1.5).

4. Click **Open** to select the highlighted template file.

5. Click **OK** to complete the *New Project* dialog.

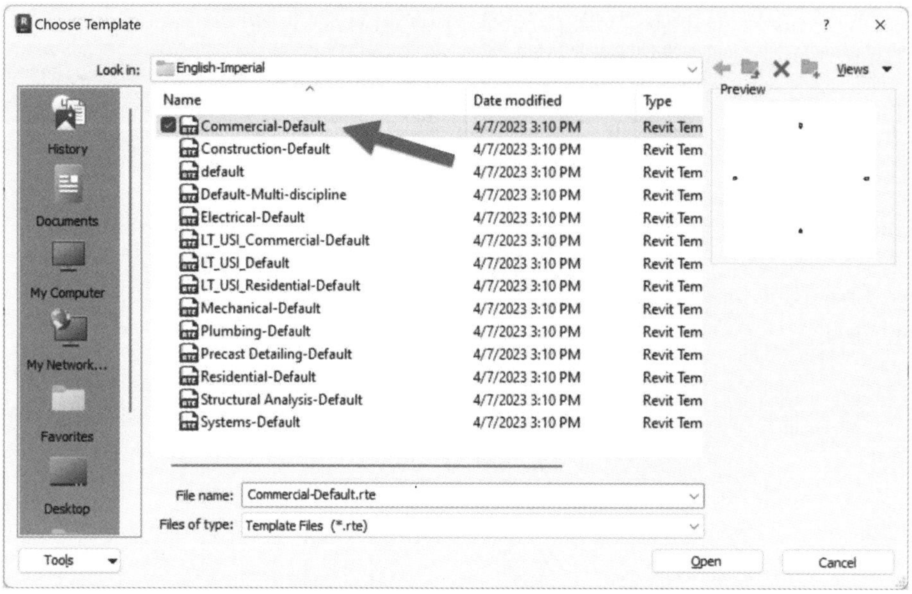

FIGURE 5-1.5 Choose Template dialog

You have just set up a project file that has sheets and schedules created and various building elements preloaded to save time when starting on a commercial project.

Next you will take a look at the predefined wall types that have been loaded.

6. Select **Architecture → Build → Wall.**

7. Click the *Type Selector* down-arrow on the *Properties Palette* (Figure 5-1.6).

Wall Types:

Notice the wall types that have been preloaded as part of the Commercial template. These wall types are a few of the types of walls one would expect to find on a basic commercial construction project.

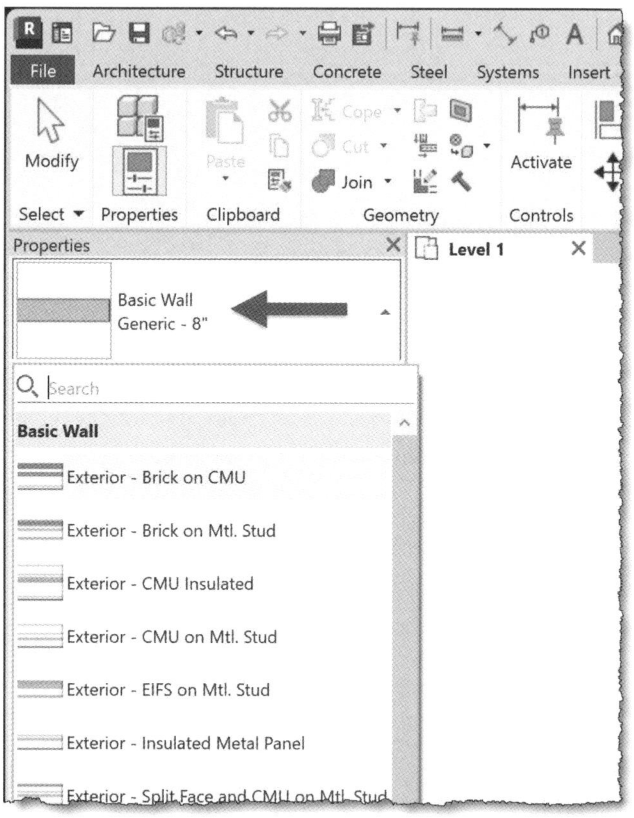

FIGURE 5-1.6 Preloaded wall types

The walls are mostly masonry and metal stud walls, both interior and exterior. If you look at the Residential template, you will see mostly wood stud wall types. Additionally, the thicknesses of materials can vary between Commercial and Residential; this is also accounted for in the templates. For example, gypsum board is typically ⅝″ thick on commercial projects whereas it is usually only ½″ on residential work.

To reiterate the concept, consider the following comparison between a typical commercial interior wall and a typical residential interior wall.

- <u>Typical Commercial Wall</u>
  - \+ ⅝″ Gypsum Board
  - \+ 3⅝″ Metal Stud
  - \+ ⅝″ Gypsum Board
  - = Total thickness: **4⅞″**

- <u>Typical Residential Wall</u>
  - \+ ½″ Gypsum Board
  - \+ 2x4 Wood Stud (3 ½″ actual)
  - \+ ½″ Gypsum Board
  - = Total Thickness: **4½″**

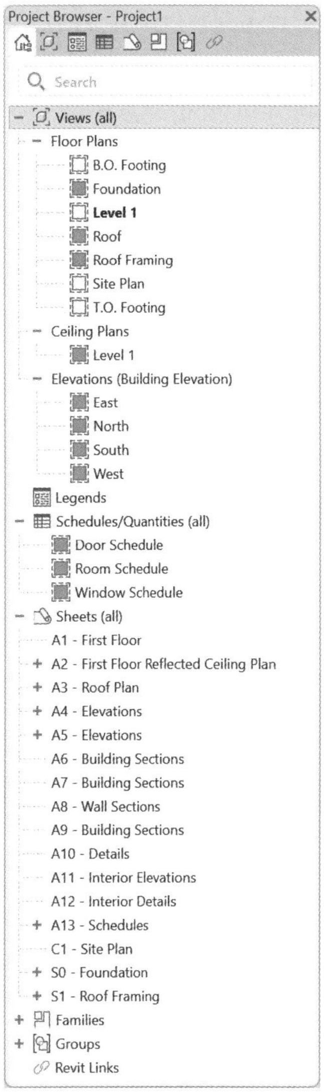

FIGURE 5-1.7 Project Browser: various items preloaded

Project Browser:

Take a few minutes to look at the *Project Browser* and notice the views and sheets that have been set up, via the template file selected (Figure 5-1.7).

Many of the views that you need to get started with the design of a commercial project are set up and ready to go (Figure 5-1.7).

For the architectural drawings, practically all the sheets typically found on a commercial project have been created; see Figure 5-1.7 under the *"Sheets (all)"* heading of the *Project Browser*. Also, notice the sheets with a "plus" symbol next to them. These are sheets that already have one or more views placed on them. You will study this more later, but a view, such as your East elevation view, is placed on a sheet at a scale you select. This means your title block sheets will have printable information as soon as you start sketching walls in one of your plan views.

You will be creating additional views and sheets for the other disciplines: structural, mechanical and electrical.

Project Information:

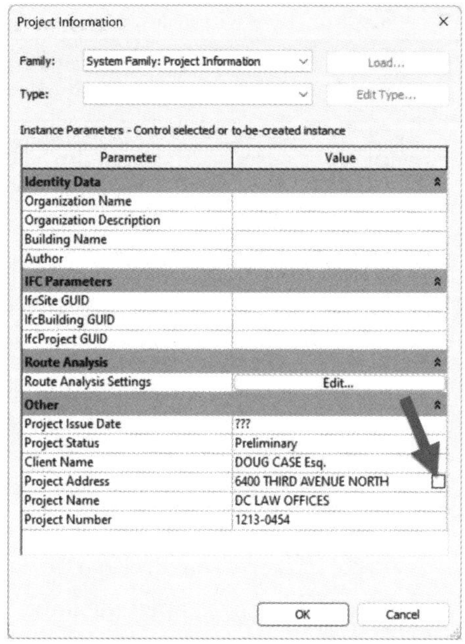

FIGURE 5-1.8
Project Information dialog

Revit provides a dialog to enter the basic project information. You will enter this information next.

8. Select **Manage → Settings → Project Information**.

9. Enter the *Project Information* shown in Figure 5-1.8.

FYI: For now you will enter three question marks for the date.

Project Issue Date:	**???**
Project Status:	**Preliminary**
Client Name:	**DOUG CASE Esq.**
Project Name:	**DC LAW OFFICES**
Project Number:	**1213-0454**

10. Click within the *Project Address* "Value" field, and then click the button that appears to the right (Figure 5-1.8).

11. Enter the project address shown in Figure 5-1.9.

FYI: This is the address where the law office is going to be built, not the client's current address.

Enter:
6400 THIRD AVENUE NORTH
MINNEAPOLIS, MN 55401

NOTE: You can enter any address you want to at this point; the address suggested is fictional.

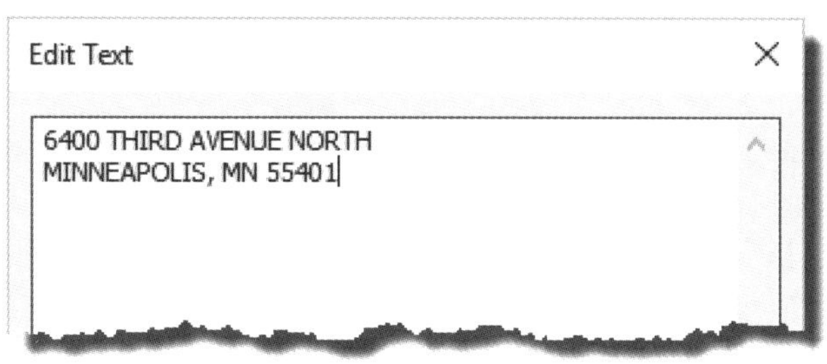

FIGURE 5-1.9 Adding Project Address (partial view)

12. Click **OK**.

13. Click the **Edit** button next to the *Route Analysis Settings.*

14. Review the options related to a tool that finds an exit path through the building (Figure 5-1.10) then click **Cancel** to close the dialog.

15. Click **OK** to close the *Project Information* dialog box.

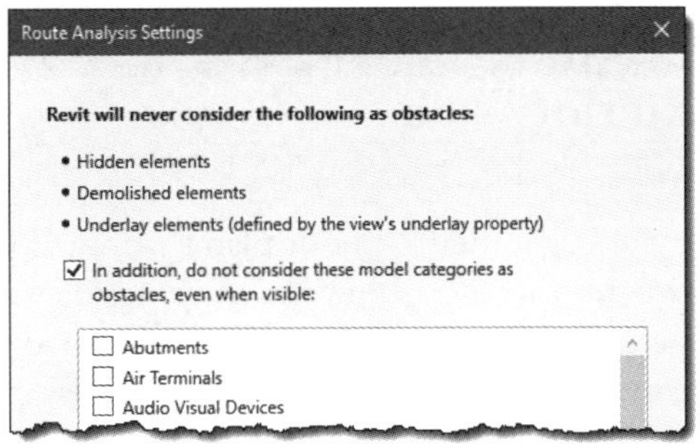

FIGURE 5-1.10 Adding Energy Data (partial view)

The project information is now saved in your Revit project database. Revit has already used some of this information to infill a portion of your title block on each of your sheets. You will verify this next.

16. Under the ***Sheets*** heading, in the *Project Browser*, double-click on the sheet **A1 – First Floor**.

17. **Zoom** in to the lower right area of title block (Figure 5-1.11).

Notice that much of the information is automatically filled in, which is true for every sheet!

Your project database is now set up.

18. **Save** your project as **Law Office.rvt**.

FIGURE 5-1.11 Sheet A1 – First Floor Plan: Title block with Project Information added automatically

Exercise 5-2:
Exterior Walls

You will begin the first floor plan by drawing the exterior walls. Like many projects, early on you might not be certain what the exterior walls are going to be. So, you will start out using the generic wall styles. Then you will change them to a more specific wall style once you have decided what the wall construction is.

Often, a building is designed with a specific site in mind. However, to keep in line with most drafting and design classes, where floor plans are studied before site plans, you will develop the floor plans now.

Adjust Wall Settings:

1. Switch to **Level 1** (floor plan) view; select the **Wall** tool from the *Architecture* tab.

2. Edit the *Ribbon* and *Properties Palette* as follows (Figure 5-2.1):

    a. *Wall style:* **Basic Wall: Generic – 12″**

    b. *Location Line:* **Finish Face; Exterior**

    c. *Chain:* **checked**

    d. *Height:* **Unconnected**

    e. *Height:* **30′ 0″**

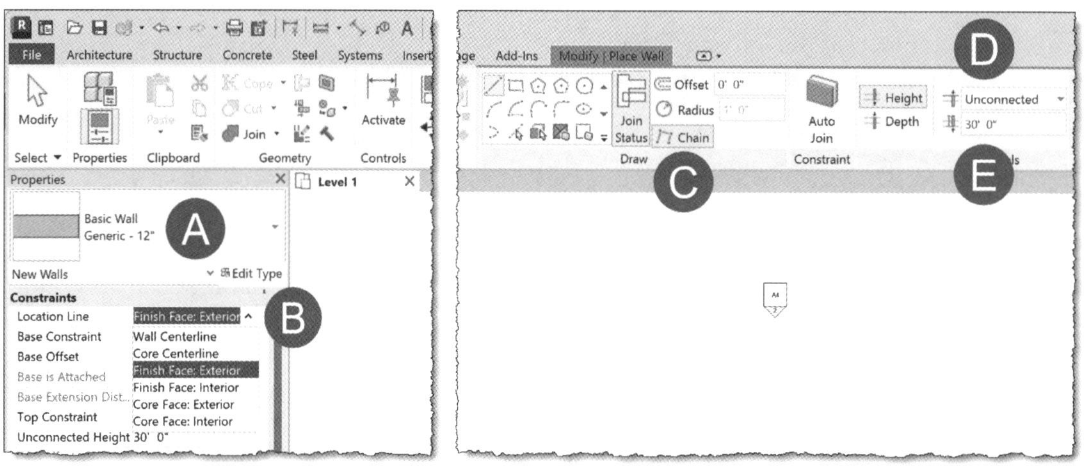

FIGURE 5-2.1 Ribbon and Properties Palette – Wall command active

The wall thickness of 12″ was selected because the exterior wall will be masonry with insulation, so it is wise to select a wall that is close to what you anticipate it will be. The height is set at 30′-0″ based on the design team's experience with this type of project and required space for higher ceilings, beams and ductwork. It can, and will, be changed later in the design process. The "unconnected" setting means the wall is a fixed height and will not adjust when any other floor levels, above the first floor, are adjusted. When drawing masonry walls, the exterior face of the building should be drawn to masonry coursing dimensions to reduce cutting and waste. Setting the *Location Line* to Finish Face; Exterior allows the coursing dimensions to be entered in for the length of the walls.

Draw the Exterior Walls:

3. **Draw** the walls shown in Figure 5-2.2. Do not draw the dimensions. Use the *Measure* tool to double-check your work. Center the building between the elevation tags (see Figure 2-1.4).

    a. Drawing the curved wall: Draw all the walls and leave the curved wall for last. Next, use the ***Fillet Arc*** option within the *Wall* tool and set the Radius to **26′-6″**; click the bottom wall first and then the left wall. Refer back to page 4-14 for a refresher on this process.

NOTE: If you draw in a clockwise fashion, your walls will have the exterior side of the wall correctly positioned. You can also use the spacebar to toggle which side the exterior face is on.

TIP: When using the Wall *tool, you can click* Chain *to continuously draw walls. When Chain is not selected you have to pick the same point twice: once where the wall ends and again where the next wall begins.*

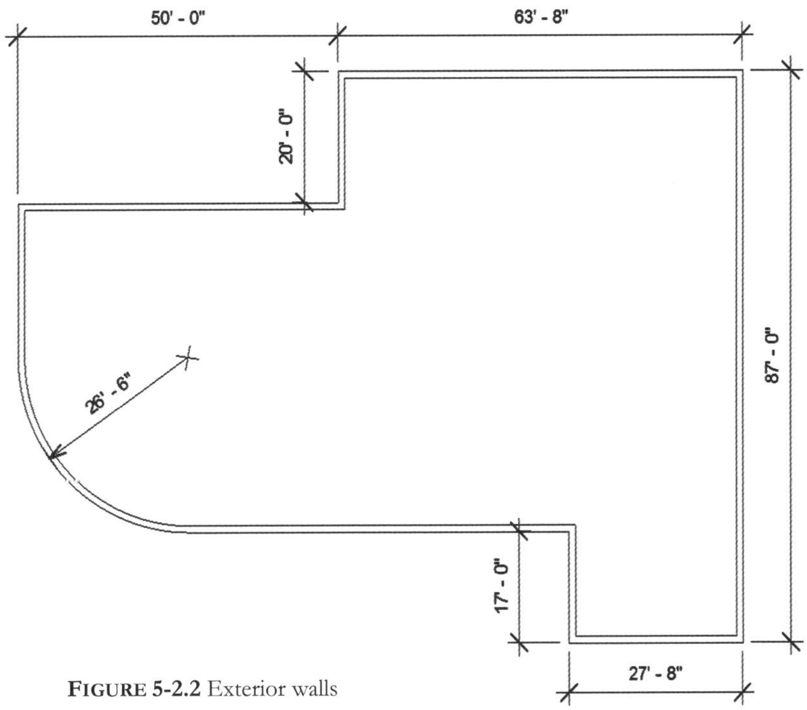

FIGURE 5-2.2 Exterior walls

Modifying Wall Dimensions:

Now that you have the exterior walls drawn, you might decide to adjust the building size for masonry coursing, or subtract square footage to reduce cost.

Editing walls in Revit is very easy. You can select a wall and edit the temporary dimensions that appear, or you can use the *Move* tool to change the position of a wall. Any walls whose endpoints touch the modified wall are also adjusted; they grow or shrink, automatically.

Next you will adjust the dimensions of the walls just drawn.

4. Click **Modify** and then select the far right wall (Figure 5-2.3).

5. Select the temporary dimensions text (26′-8″) and then type **14 0** (Figure 5-2.3).

   FYI: Remember that you do not need to type the foot or inch symbol; the space distinguishes between them.

   TIP: Whenever you want to adjust the model via temporary/permanent dimensions, you need to select the object you want to move first and then select the text (i.e., number) of the temporary/permanent dimension.

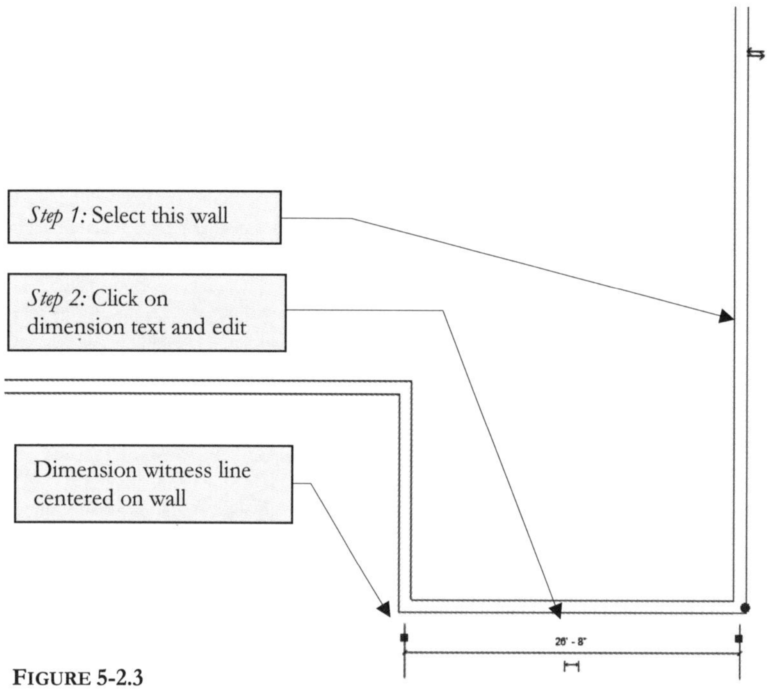

FIGURE 5-2.3
Editing temp wall dimensions

6. In the lower right corner of the floor plan, select the wall shown in Figure 5-2.4.

7. Edit the 17′-0″ dimension to **26′-0″**.

   TIP: Just type 26 and press Enter; Revit will assume feet when a single number is entered.

   FYI: You can edit the location of the witness lines if desired by going to Manage → Settings → Additional Settings → Annotations → Temporary Dimensions; here you can set the default to "face" rather than "centerlines." Do not make changes at this time.

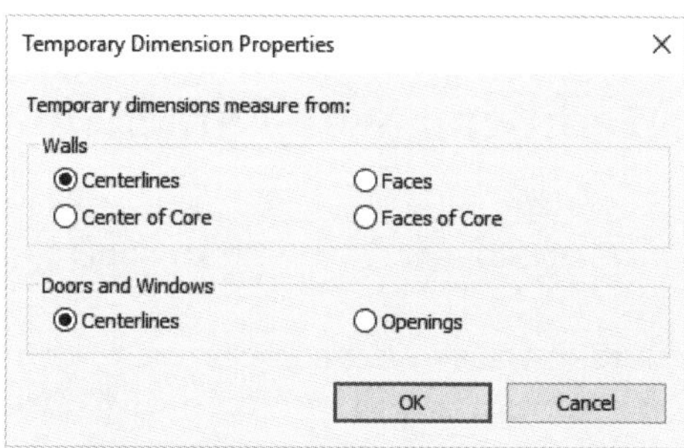

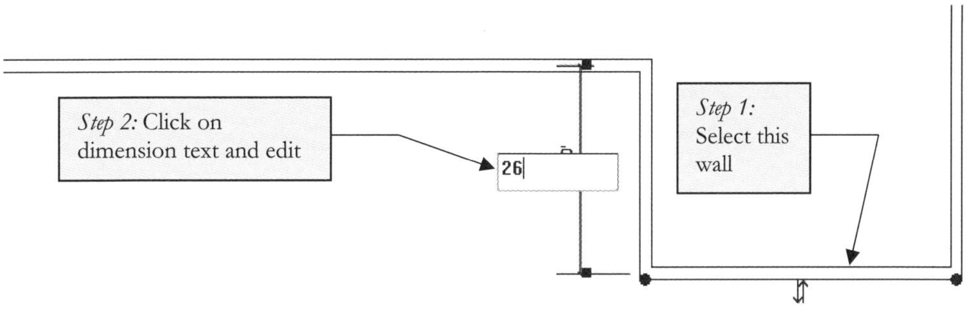

FIGURE 5-2.4 Editing exterior walls; lower right corner of floor plan

Because the temporary dimensions measure to the centerline of the walls, the reported dimension will not always match the original dimension you entered, which was based on the face of the wall rather than the centerline.

> ***TIP:*** *Concrete blocks, or CMU, come in various widths, and most are 16″ long and 8″ high. With drawing plans, there is a simple rule to keep in mind to make sure you are designing walls to coursing. This applies to wall lengths and openings within CMU walls.*
>
> *Dimension rules for CMU coursing in floor plans:*
>
> - ***E***′-0″ or ***E***′-8″ where ***E*** is any even number (e.g., 6′-0″ OR 24′-8″)
> - ***O***′-4″ where ***O*** is any odd number (e.g., 5′-4″)

Using the Align tool with walls:

Revit has a tool called *Align* that allows you to quickly make one wall align with another. After they are aligned, you have the option to *Lock* that relationship so the two walls will move together, which is great when you know you want two walls to remain aligned but might accidentally move one, for instance, while zoomed in and you cannot see the other wall.

8. Select the **Modify → Modify → Align** icon.

Notice the *Status Bar* is asking you to select a reference line or point. This is the wall, or linework, that is in the correct location; the other walls will be adjusted to match the reference plane.

9. Set *Prefer* to **Wall Faces** on the *Ribbon*, and then select the exterior face of the vertical wall shown in Figure 5-2.5.

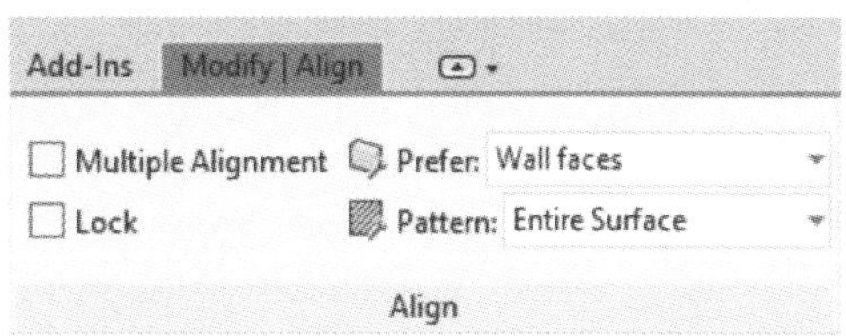

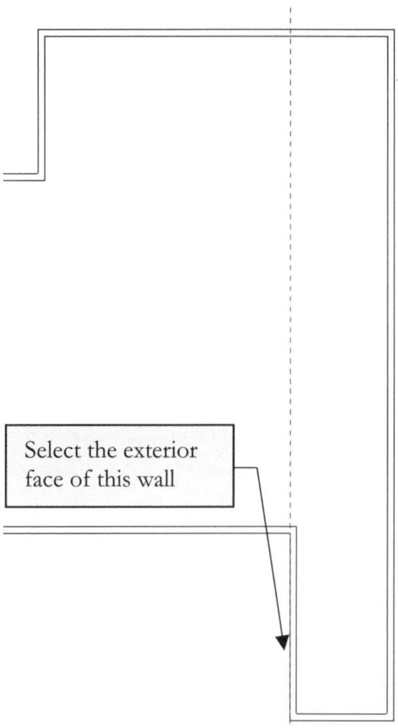

FIGURE 5-2.5
Align tool: wall selected

You should notice a temporary dashed line appear on screen. This will help you to visualize the reference plane.

Notice the *Status Bar* is prompting you to select an entity to align with the temporary reference plane.

10. Now, select the exterior face of the north (top) vertical wall (see Figure 5-2.6).

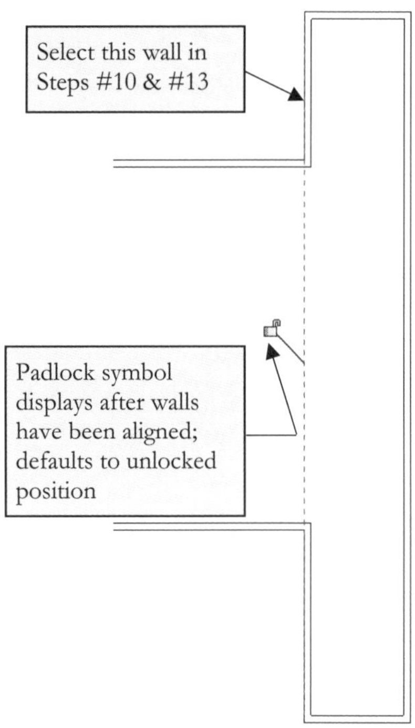

FIGURE 5-2.6
Align tool: select wall to be aligned

Note that if you would have selected the interior face of the wall, that side of the wall would have aligned with the reference plane rather than the exterior, as it is. If you made a mistake, click *Undo* and try it again.

Also, notice that you have a padlock symbol showing. Clicking the padlock symbol will cause the alignment relationship to be maintained (i.e., a parametric relationship). Next you will lock the alignment relationship and experiment with a few edits to see how modifying one wall affects the other.

11. Click on the **padlock** symbol (Figure 5-2.6).

The padlock symbol is now in the locked position.

12. Click **Modify** to unselect the walls.

13. Select the vertical wall identified in Figure 5-2.6.

Next, you will make a dramatic change so you can clearly see the results of that change on both "locked" walls.

14. Change the 14′-0″ dimension to **60′-0″** (Figure 5-2.7).

Notice that both walls moved together (Figure 5-2.7). Also notice that when either wall is selected the padlock is displayed, which helps in identifying "locked" relationships while you are editing the project. Whenever the padlock symbol is visible, you can click on it to unlock it or remove the aligned relationship.

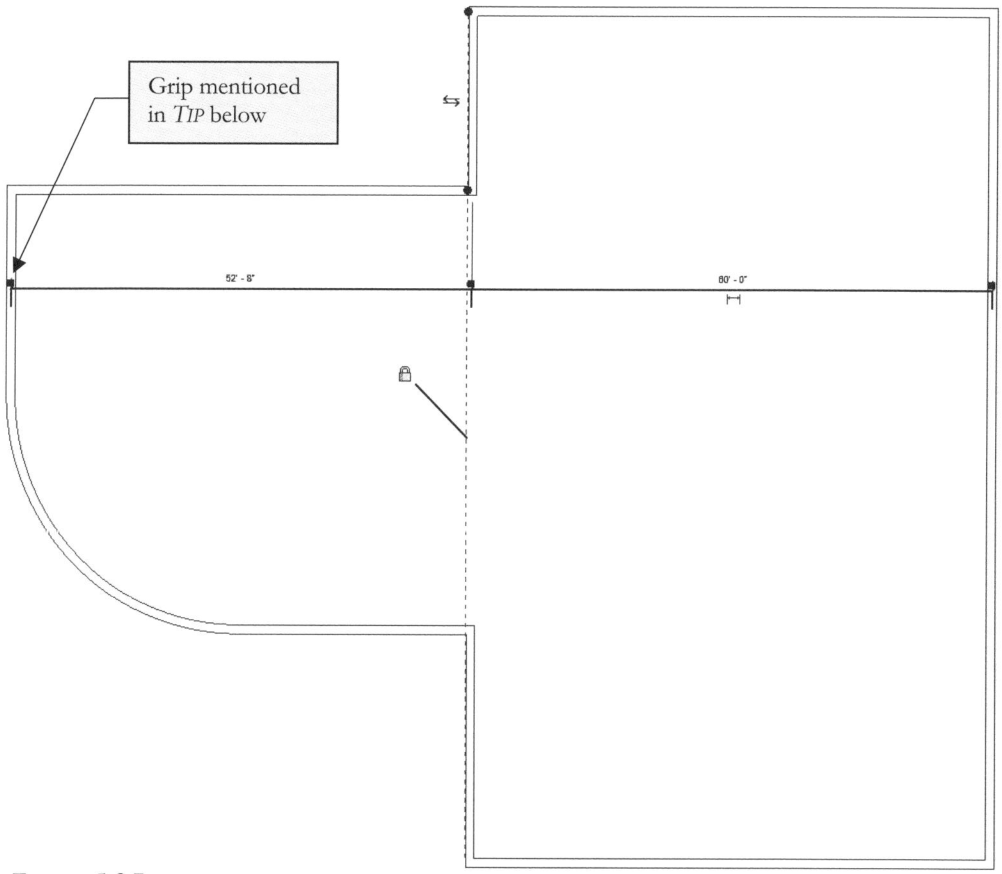

FIGURE 5-2.7
Wall edit: Both walls move together

TIP: Clicking the grip on the witness line of a temporary dimension *causes the witness line to toggle locations on the wall (i.e., exterior face, interior face or center). You can also drag the grip to a different wall.*

As it turns out, we don't need the two vertical walls aligned. So the next step instructs you to remove the alignment.

15. With one of the two vertical walls (that are locked in alignment with each other) selected, click the **padlock** icon to unlock it.

Next, you will make a few more wall modifications, on your own, to get the perimeter of the building in its final configuration and to masonry coursing.

16. Modify wall locations by selecting a wall and modifying the temporary dimensions; the selected wall is the one that moves to match Figure 5-2.8; do not draw the dimensions at this time.

    TIP #1: *Select the wall to be relocated before editing a dimension.*

    TIP #2: *Make sure you use the Measure tool to verify all dimensions before moving on! Also, do not delete the elevation tags.*

    TIP #3: *Utilize the TIP on the previous page to adjust the witness line location before editing the dimensions.*

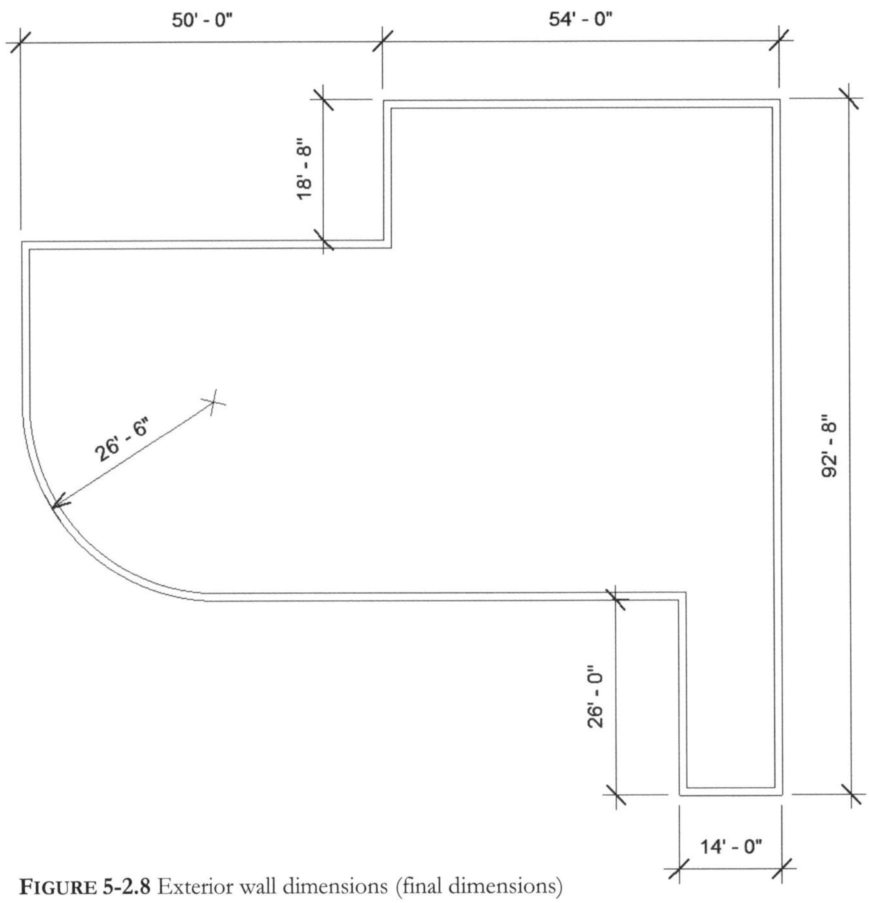

FIGURE 5-2.8 Exterior wall dimensions (final dimensions)

Changing a Wall Type:

In the following steps, you will learn how to change the generic walls into a more refined wall type. Basically, you select the walls you want to change and then pick a different wall type from the *Type Selector* on the *Ribbon*. Remember, the *Ribbon* and *Properties Palette* are context sensitive, which means the wall types are only listed in the *Type Selector* when you are using the *Wall* tool, or you have a wall selected.

17. Select all the walls in your **First Floor** plan view.

    TIP: You can select all the walls at once: click and drag the cursor to select a Window. Later in the book you will learn about "Filter Selection" which also aids in the selection process.

18. From the *Type Selector* on the *Properties Palette*, select **Exterior – Split Face and CMU on Mtl. Stud** (Figure 5-2.9).

19. Click **Modify** to unselect the walls.

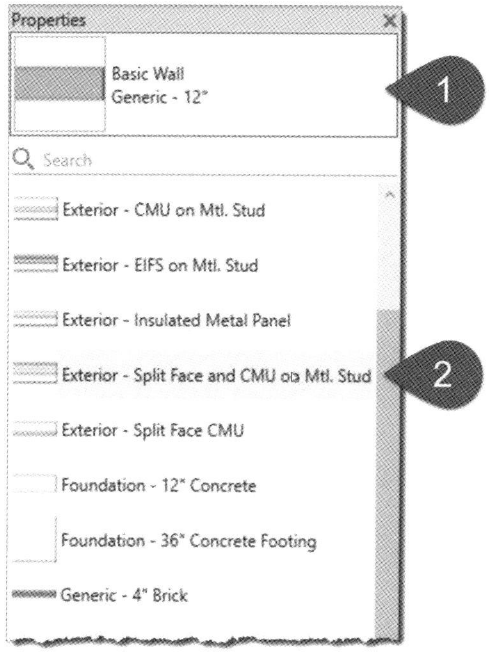

FIGURE 5-2.9 Type Selector

If you zoom in on the walls, you can see their graphic representation has changed a little. It will change more when you adjust the *View's Detail Level* near the end of this exercise. Typically, try to start with a wall closest to the one you think you will end up with; you may never even have to change the wall type.

Even though the wall did not change much graphically in this plan view, it did change quite a bit. In a 3D view, which you will look at in a moment, the wall now has horizontal accent bands and a wall cap or a parapet cap! The image to the right is a snapshot of the 30′-0″ tall wall you now have in your model.

It was important that the *Location Line* be set to "Finish Face: Exterior" when the walls were drawn. When the walls were just changed, the *Location Line* position did not move. Thus, all the exterior dimensions are still accurate. All the walls grew in thickness towards the interior.

Exploring the Exterior Wall Style:

As previously mentioned, Revit provides several predefined wall styles, from metal studs with gypsum board to concrete block and brick cavity walls.

Next, you will take a close look at the predefined wall type you are using for the exterior walls.

20. Select one of the exterior walls in your floor plan.

21. Draw your attention to the *Properties Palette*; type **PP** if it is not visible.

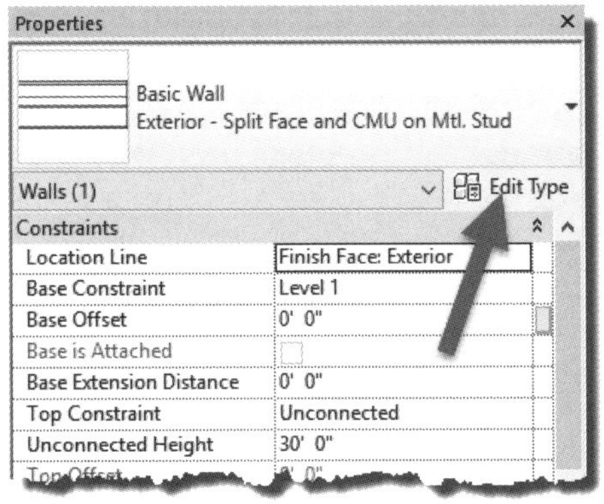

FIGURE 5-2.10
Element Properties icon

22. Select the ***Edit Type*** button (Figure 5-2.10).

23. You should be in the *Type Properties* dialog box. Click the ***Edit*** button next to the *Structure* parameter (Figure 5-2.11).

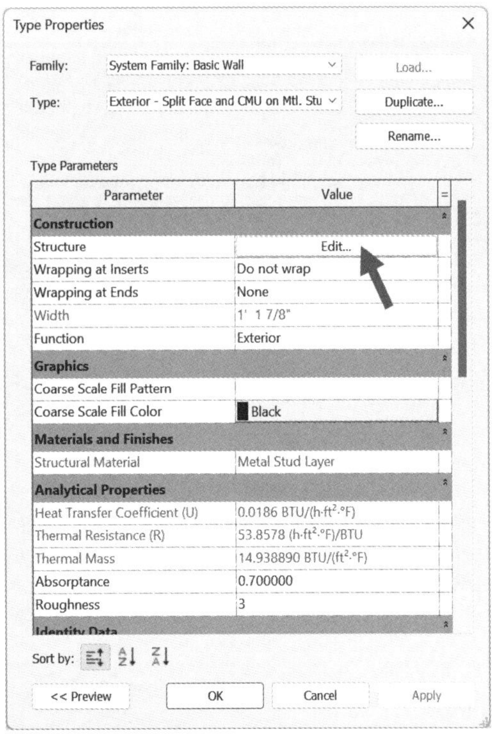

FIGURE 5-2.11 Type Properties

FYI: *Revit has two types of properties,* ***Instance*** *(shown in the Properties Palette) and* ***Type*** *(shown to the left):*

Instance Properties: This is information that can vary by instance (i.e., individual walls, doors, windows, etc.), for example, the height to the bottom of a window, or the fire rating of a wall or door. These values can vary from instance to instance.

Type Properties: This is information that is the same for every instance of a specific type. For example, the width and height of window type "W1" should be the same for all, and the width of wall type "S6" should be the same for all. Any changes to these values change all previous, and yet to be drawn, objects of that type in the model.

24. Finally, you are in the *Edit Assembly* dialog box. This is where you can modify the construction of a wall type. Click **<<Preview**, in the lower left, to display a preview of the selected wall type (Figure 5-2.12).

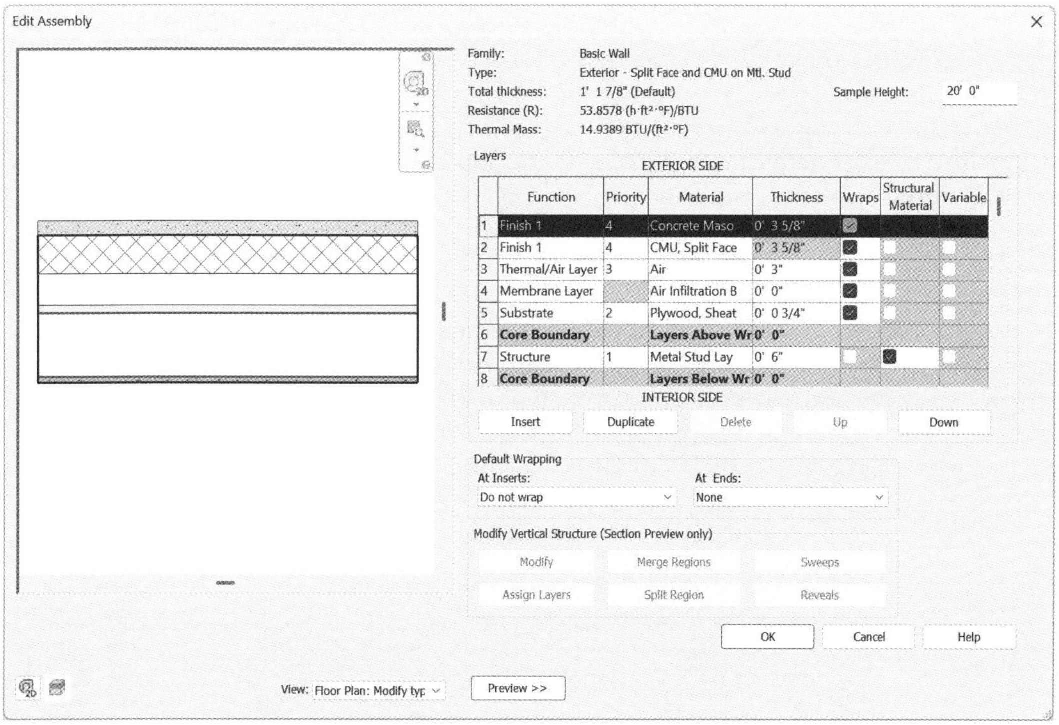

FIGURE 5-2.12 Edit Assembly

Here, the *Edit Assembly* dialog box allows you to change the composition of an existing wall.

Things to notice (Figure 5-2.12):

- Each row is called a *Layer*. By clicking on a *Layer* and picking the **up** or **down** buttons, you can reposition materials within the wall assembly. Clicking **Insert** adds a new material.

- The **exterior** side is labeled at the top and **interior** side at the bottom.

- You will see horizontal lines, or *Layers*, identifying the core material. The core boundary can be used to place walls and dimension walls. For example, the *Wall* tool will let you draw a wall with the interior or exterior core face as the reference line. On an interior wall you might dimension to the face of stud rather than to the finished face of gypsum board; this would give the contractor the information needed for the part of the wall they will build first.

- *R-Value* and *Thermal Mass* values are listed near the top of the screen. These are derived from the individual *Layers* within the wall assembly.

Next, you will see how the vertical elements within the wall are established. You will not be changing anything at this time, as this is only an exploration of the settings for our exterior wall being used.

25. Click the drop-down next to the word *View* and select **Section: Modify Type Attributes** (Figure 5-2.13 - Step #1).

Notice the preview now changes to show the wall in section. The height of this wall is determined by the "sample height" setting in the upper right of the *Edit Assembly* dialog. It is possible to zoom and pan within the preview window; first you must click within it.

26. Next, click the **Sweeps** button (Figure 5-2.13 – Step #2).

Notice the *Wall Sweeps* dialog shows there are four elements that are being imposed on the wall. A sweep is a 2D outline that is extruded horizontally along the length of a wall wherever it occurs. Its material and position in or on the wall can be adjusted via the columns to the right of each sweep. If you try adjusting these values, make sure you select Cancel or Undo before proceeding to the next step.

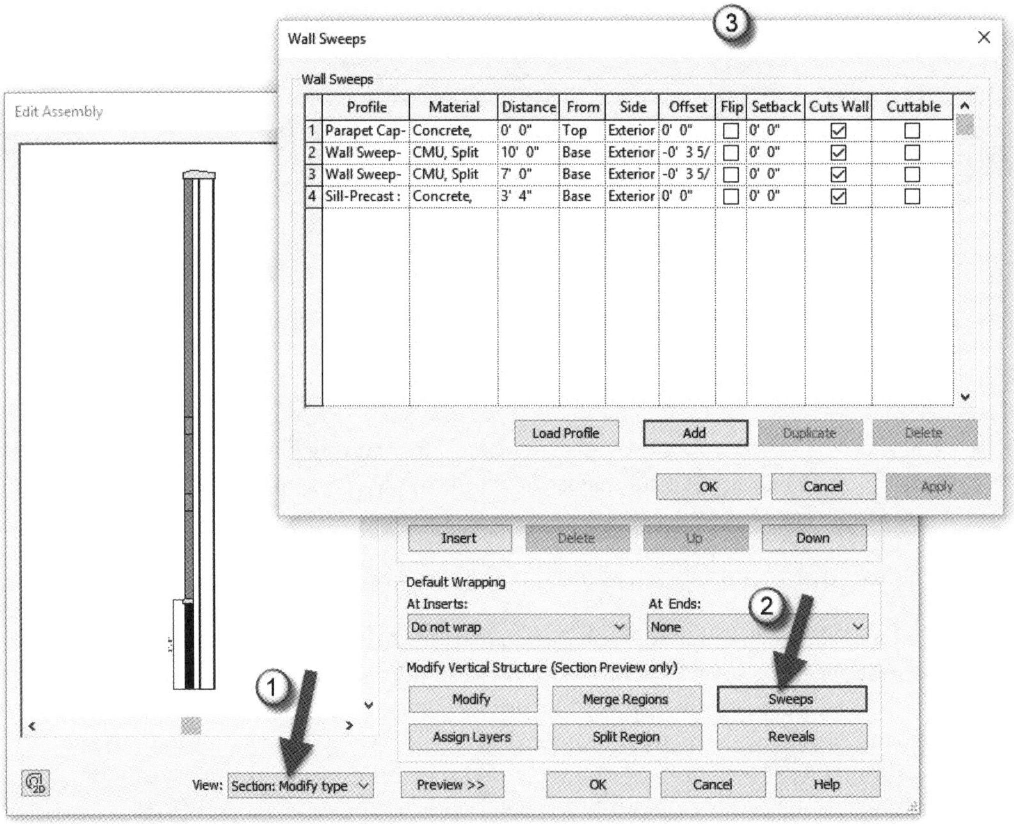

FIGURE 5-2.13 Wall Sweeps

27. Select **Cancel** to close all the open dialog boxes.

For many of the walls, Revit can display more refined linework and hatching within the wall. This is controlled by the *Detail Level* option for each view. You will change the *Detail Level* for the **First Floor** plan view next.

28. Click on the ***Detail Level*** icon in the lower left corner of the drawing window (Figure 5-2.14).

29. Select **Medium.**

    FYI: *This view adjustment is only for the current view, as are all changes made via the View Control Bar.*

FIGURE 5-2.14 Detail Level; Set to Medium

The typical commercial project floor plan scale is ⅛″ = 1′-0″ – this allows larger buildings to fit on a standard sheet (e.g., 22″ x 34″). However, the law office is a smaller building so the scale can be increased to ¼″ = 1′-0″ to show more detail.

30. Set the View Scale to **¼″ = 1′-0.″**

You may need to zoom in, but you should now see additional lines and some hatching for the various *Layers* within the wall. The two images below show the difference between *Coarse* and *Medium* settings. ***FYI:*** *The* View Scale *changes the size of the hatch pattern.* Give it a try, but set the scale back to ¼″ = 1′-0″ before proceeding.

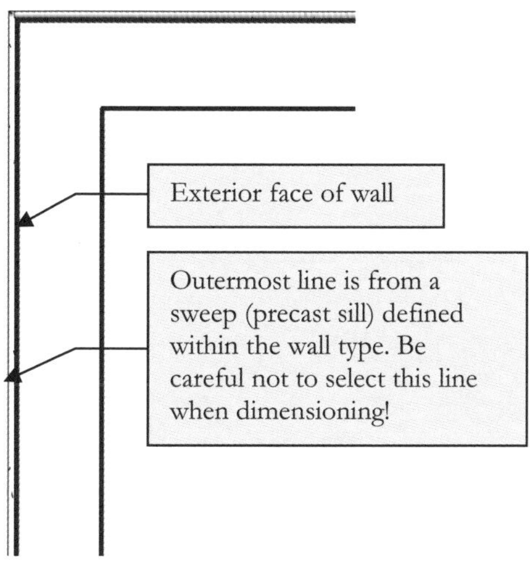

FIGURE 5-2.15A
Detail Level; Set to Coarse

FIGURE 5-2.15B
Detail Level; Set to Medium

If you did not pay close enough attention when drawing the walls originally, some of your walls may show the CMU to the inside of the building.

> ***TIP:*** *On the* View *tab you can select Thin Lines to temporarily turn off the line weights; this has no effect on plotting.*

31. Select **Modify** (or press **Esc**); select a wall. You will see a symbol appear that allows you to flip the wall orientation by clicking on that symbol (Figure 5-2.16).

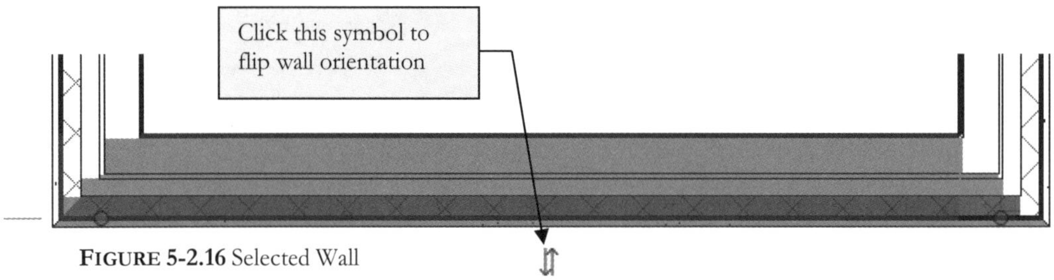

FIGURE 5-2.16 Selected Wall

32. Whether you need to adjust walls or not, click on the flip symbol to experiment with its operation.

> ***TIP:*** *The flip symbol is always on the exterior side, or what Revit thinks is the exterior side of the wall.*

33. If some walls do need to be adjusted so the CMU, and flip symbol, are to the exterior, do it now. You may have to select the wall(s) and use the *Move* tool to reposition the walls to match the required dimensions.

> ***TIP:*** *Walls are flipped about the Location Line, which can be changed via the Properties Palette when the wall is selected. So changing the Location Line to Wall Centerline before flipping the wall will keep the wall in the same position. Be sure to change the Location Line back to Exterior Face.*

TIP: *You can use the MOVE tool on the Ribbon to accurately move walls. The steps are the same as in the previous chapters!*

Follow these steps to move an object:

- Select the wall.
- Click the *Move* icon.
- Pick any point on the wall.
- Start the mouse in the correct direction, don't click.
- Start typing the distance you want to move the wall and press **Enter**.

34. You can see your progress nicely in a 3D view. Click the ***Default 3D View*** icon on the *Quick Access Toolbar*. The walls are shown shaded to make the image read better (Figure 5-2.17).

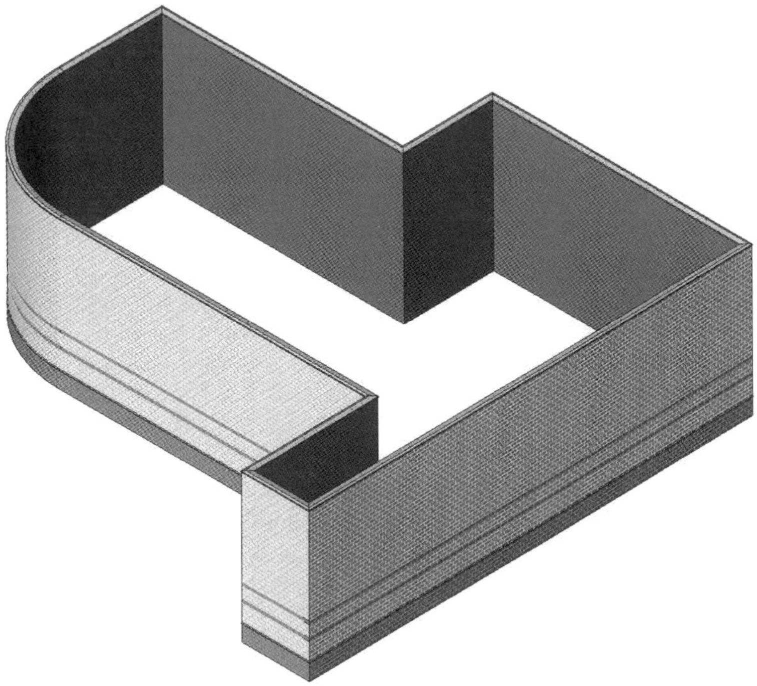

If you zoom in on the walls, you can see how much detail Revit can store in a wall type. By picking a few points, you defined the wall's width, height and exterior finish materials!

35. Close the **3D** view and switch back to the **First Floor** plan view.

36. **Save** your project.

TIP: Holding down the Shift *key while pressing the wheel button on the mouse allows you to fly around the building. You will have to experiment with how the mouse movements relate to the building's rotation. Selecting an item first causes that item to remain centered on the screen during orbit.*

Exercise 5-3:
Interior Walls

In this lesson you will draw the interior walls for the first and second floors. Using the line sketching and editing techniques you have studied in previous lessons, you should be able to draw the interior walls with minimal information.

Overview on How Plans Are Typically Dimensioned:

The following is an overview of how walls are typically dimensioned in a floor plan. This information is intended to help you understand the dimensions you will see in the exercises, as well as prepare you for the point when you dimension your plans (in a later lesson).

Stud walls, wood or metal, are typically dimensioned to the center of the walls; this can vary from region to region and from office to office. Some firms dimension to the face of stud. Here are a few reasons why you should dimension to the center of the stud rather than to the face of the gypsum board:

- The contractor is laying out the walls in a large "empty" area. The most useful dimension is to the center of the stud; that is where they will make a mark on the floor. If the dimension was to the face of the gypsum board, the contractor would have to stop and calculate the center of the stud, which is not always the center of the wall thickness; for example, a stud wall with one layer of gypsum board on one side and two layers of gypsum board over resilient channels on the other side of the stud.

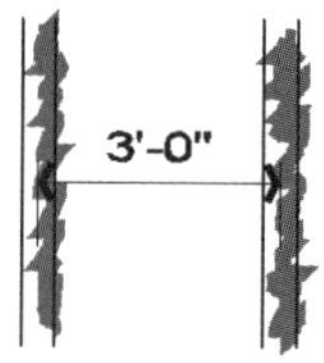

Dimension Example – Two Stud Walls

- When creating a continuous string of dimensions, the extra dimensions, text and arrows indicating the thickness of the walls would take up an excessive amount of room on the floor plans, space that would be better used by notes.

Occasionally you should dimension to the face of a wall rather than the center; here's one example:

- When indicating design intent or building code requirements, you should reference the exact points and surfaces. For example, if you have uncommonly large trim around a door opening, you may want a dimension from the edge of the door to the face of the adjacent wall. Another example would be the width of a hallway; if you want a particular width you would dimension between the two faces of the wall and add the text "clear" below the dimension to make it known, without question, that the dimension is not to the center of the wall.

Dimensions for masonry and foundation walls:

- Foundation and masonry walls are dimensioned to the nominal face and not the center. These types of walls are modular (e.g., 8″x8″x16″) so it is helpful, for both designer and builder, to have dimensions that relate to the masonry wall's coursing.

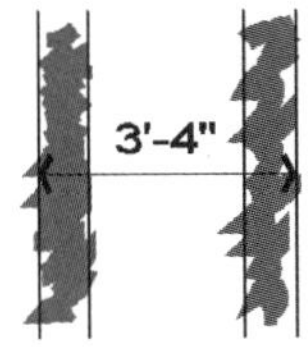

Dimension Example – Two masonry Walls

Dimensions from a stud wall to a masonry wall:

- The rules above apply for each side of the dimension line. For example, a dimension for the exterior CMU wall to an interior stud wall would be from the exterior face of the foundation wall to the center of the stud on the interior wall.

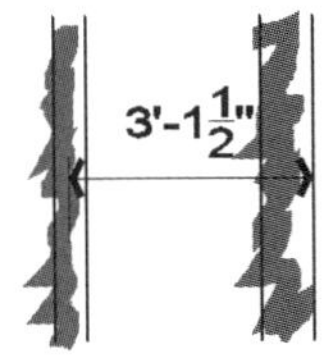

Dimension Example – Stud to masonry

Again, you will not be dimensioning your drawings right away, but Revit makes it easy to comply with the conventions above.

Drawing the First Floor Interior Walls:

Now that you have the perimeter drawn, you will draw a few interior walls. When drawing floor plans it is good practice to sketch out the various wall systems you think you will be using; this will help you determine what thickness to draw the walls. Drawing the walls at the correct thickness helps later when you are fine-tuning things.

One of the most typical walls on a commercial project consists of 3⅝″ metal studs (at 16″ O.C.) with one layer of gypsum board on each side, making a wall system that is 4⅞″ thick.

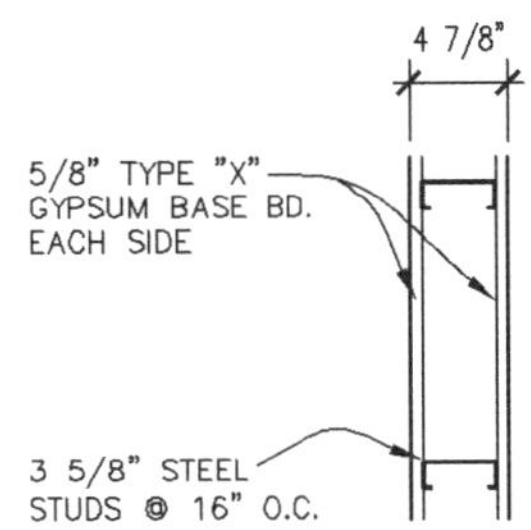

This composition can vary greatly. For example, you may need to add resilient channels to one side of the wall to enhance sound control; they are ⅞″ thick and are installed on the noisy side of the wall

Finishes: Gypsum board walls can be finished in a variety of ways. The most economical finish is usually one or more colors of paint. Other options include wall fabrics like high-end wall paper, which are used in executive offices and conference rooms; fiberglass liner panels which are used in janitor rooms and food service areas; veneer plaster which is used for durability, or high-impact gypsum board can also be used; tile, which is used in toilet rooms and showers, to name a few. These finishes are nominal and are not included in the thickness used to draw the wall.

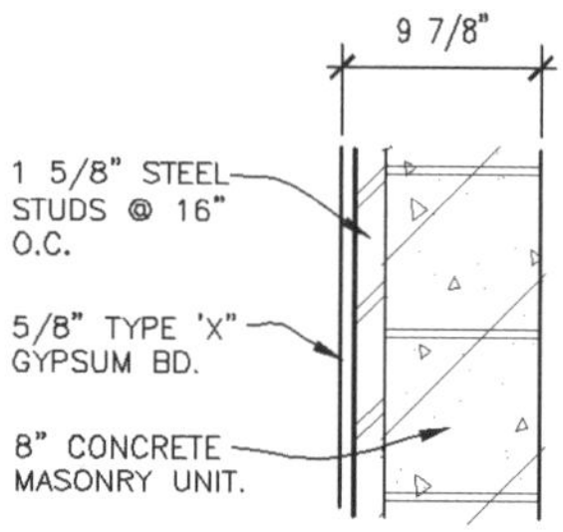

Concrete block, referred to as "CMU," walls are often used to construct stair and elevator shafts, high traffic or high abuse areas, and for security; filling the cores with concrete or sand can increase strength, sound control and even stop bullets. The most used size is 8″ wide CMU; 6″, 10″ and 12″ are also commonly used. Typically, 4″ and 6″ wide is used for aesthetics and 10″ and 12″ CMU for structural reasons.

Finishes: Concrete block can just be painted, or it can have special finishes, such as Glazed Block or Burnished Concrete Block, which cost more but are durable and are available in many colors. In offices, conference rooms and other more refined areas, concrete block walls are not desirable so they are covered with metal furring channels and gypsum board, especially in rooms where three walls are metal studs and only one would be CMU. The sooner this is taken into consideration, the better, as this can significantly affect space for furniture in a room. Another major furniture obstacle is fin-tube radiation at the exterior walls.

Walls often have several Life Safety issues related to them. Finishes applied to walls must have a certain flame spread rating, per local building code. Several walls are usually required to be fire rated, protecting one space from another in the event of a fire; these walls have restrictions on the amount of glass (windows + doors), type of door and window frames (wood vs. steel) and the need to extend the wall to the floor or roof deck above.

Revit's architecture and MEP tools can help to coordinate many of these things just mentioned. Walls can hold information about fire ratings and sound control. This information can then be presented in a schedule, or a feature called *View Filters* can be used to make the walls stand out.

Drawing the fin-tube radiation or displacement ventilation (i.e., the things that heat the room and take up space) in using Revit's MEP tools gives the architects and interior designers the information they need to design casework and furniture around those things.

Adjust Wall Settings:

1. In the Level 1 plan view; select **Wall** from the *Architecture* tab on the *Ribbon.*

2. Make the following changes to the wall options in the *Ribbon* and *Properties Palette* (similar to Figure 5-2.1):

    a. *Wall style:* **Interior – 4 7/8″ partition (1-hr)**

    b. *Height:* **Roof** (aka, *Top Constraint*)

    c. *Location Line:* **Wall Centerline**

All your interior walls will be **4 7/8″** for each floor, unless specifically noted otherwise.

3. Draw a horizontal, East to West, wall approximately as shown in Figure 5-3.1. Do not worry about the location; you will adjust its exact position in the next step.

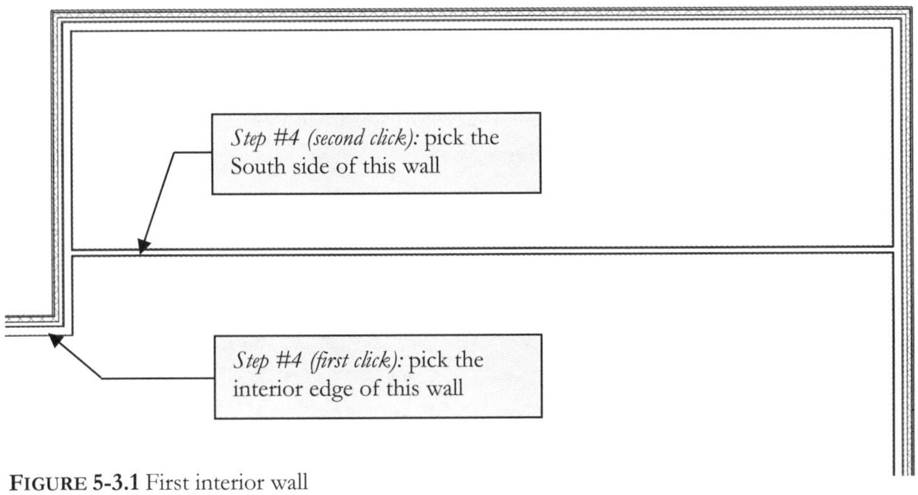

FIGURE 5-3.1 First interior wall

4. Use the ***Align*** tool to align the interior wall you just drew with the edge of the exterior wall (Figure 5-3.1). Set *Prefer* to Wall Faces on the *Ribbon*. When you are done, the wall should look like Figure 5-3.2.

FYI: You do not need to "lock" this alignment.

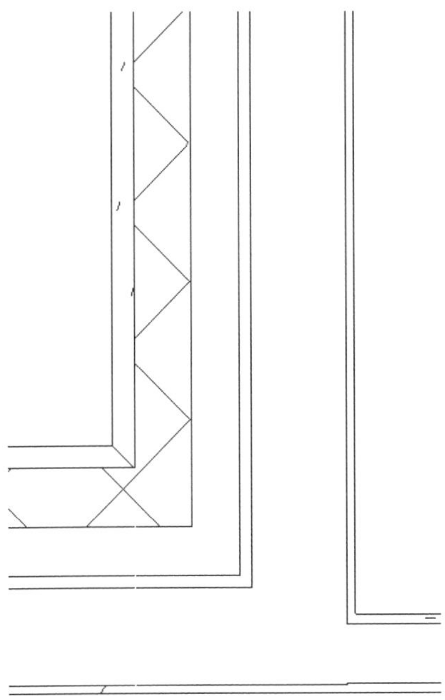

Notice the gypsum board is not the same thickness between the exterior and interior walls. You will adjust the **exterior wall** to the standard ⅝″ thickness for commercial projects.

5. Adjust the gypsum board (row 10) from ½″ to **⅝″**; refer back to page 5-18, Steps 20-24.

Because you edited a Type Parameter, all walls of type *Exterior - Split Face and CMU on Mtl. Stud* updated instantly to the new thickness. However, the interior wall now needs to be aligned again because it was not locked after aligning the two walls previously.

6. Use the ***Align*** tool to align the two walls again; zoom in if needed.

FIGURE 5-3.2 Aligned wall

Next, you will draw a handful of walls per the given dimensions. You will use the same partition type: 4⅞" partition (1-hr).

7. Draw the interior walls shown in Figure 5-3.3a and b; see the *TIPS* on the next two pages which should help you sketch the walls more accurately.
    a. Use **Trim**, **Copy**, **Split** and temporary dimensions, as needed.
    b. The centerlines show walls that align with each other. Do not draw the centerlines. ***TIP:*** *Use the Align tool.*
    c. The angled wall is centered on the curved wall and at a 45 degree angle. Start the wall by snapping to the midpoint of the curved wall and then draw the wall an arbitrary length, snapped to the 45 degree plane; then use the *Trim* tool to finish the other side.

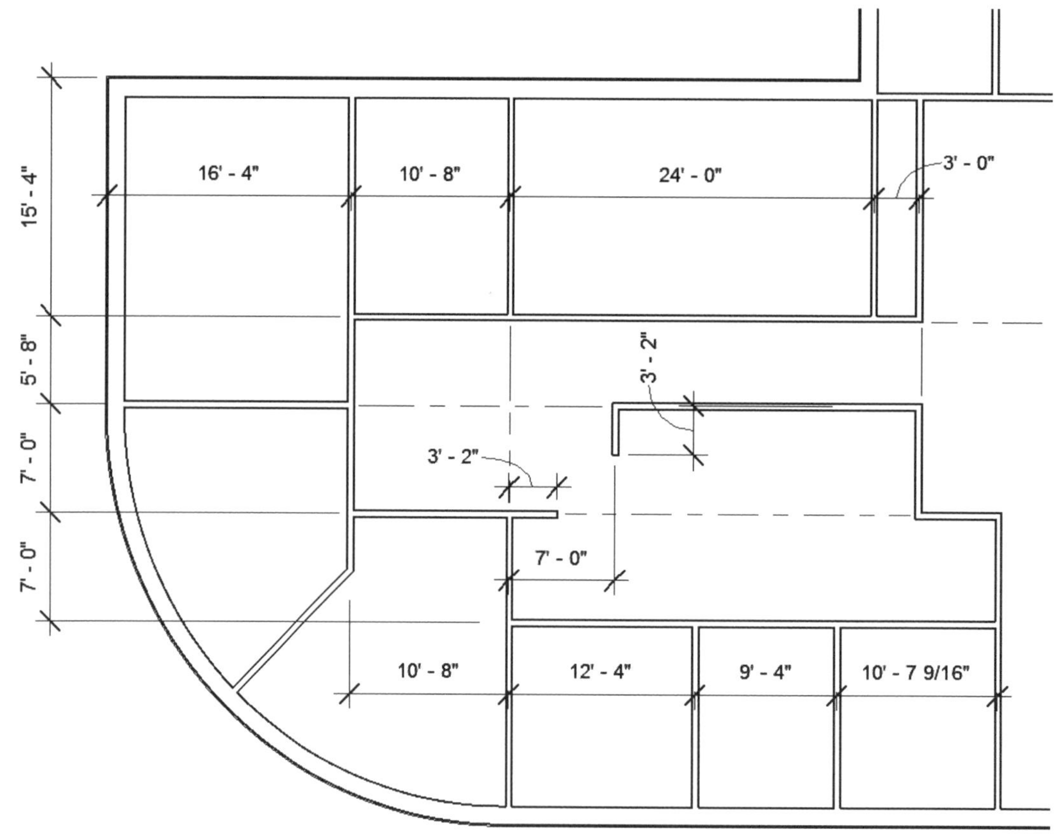

FIGURE 5-3.3A Layout dimensions for first floor interior walls – West

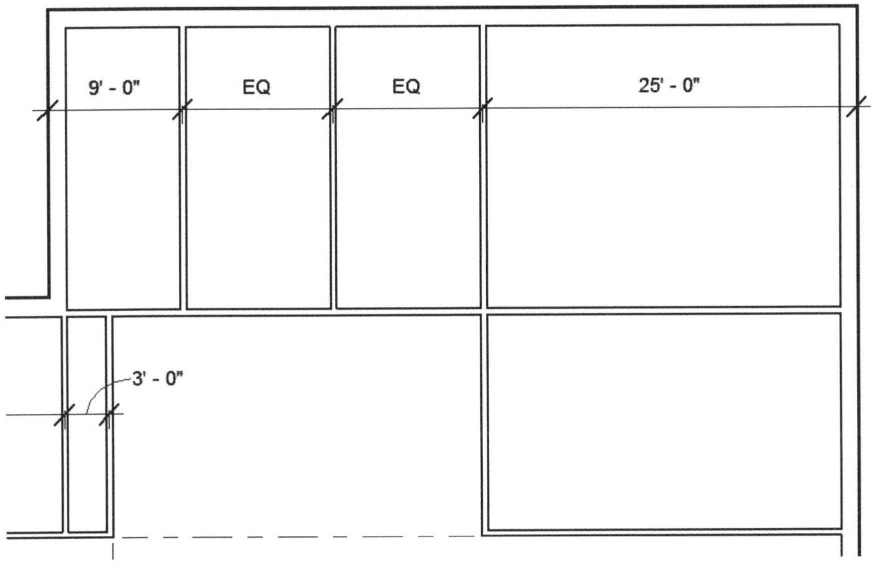

FIGURE 5-3.3B Layout dimensions for first floor interior walls – North-East

TIP – DIMENSION WITNESS LINE CONTROL:

When sketching walls, you can adjust the exact position of the wall after its initial placement. However, the temporary dimensions do not always reference the desired wall location (left face, right face or center). You will see how easy it is to adjust a dimension's *Witness Line* location so you can place the wall exactly where you want it.

First, you will be introduced to some dimension terminology. The two boxed notes below are only for permanent dimensions; the others are for both permanent and temporary.

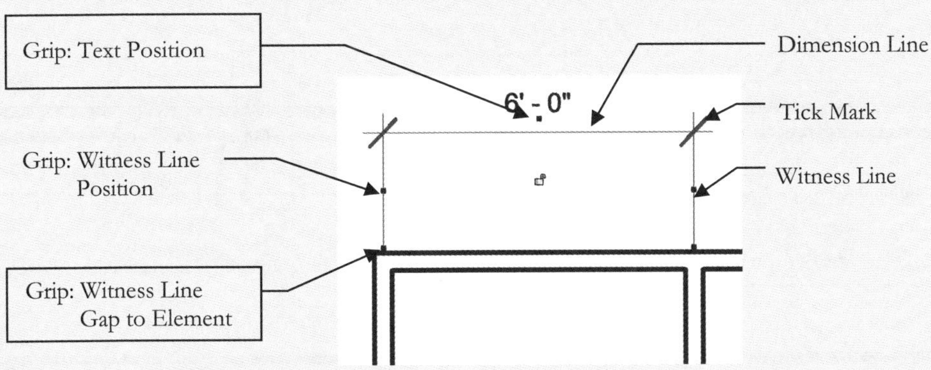

Next, you will adjust the *Witness Lines* so you can modify the inside clear dimension, between the walls, in the above illustration.

Continued on next page

TIP – DIMENSION WITNESS LINE CONTROL… *(Continued from previous page)*

When you select a wall, you will see temporary dimensions similar to the image below.

***NOTE:** Some elements do not display temporary dimensions; in that case, you can usually click the "Activate Controls" button on the Ribbon to see them.*

Clicking, not dragging, on the witness line grip causes the witness line to toggle between the location options (left face, right face, center). In the example below, the grip for each witness line has been clicked until both witness lines refer to the "inside" of the room.

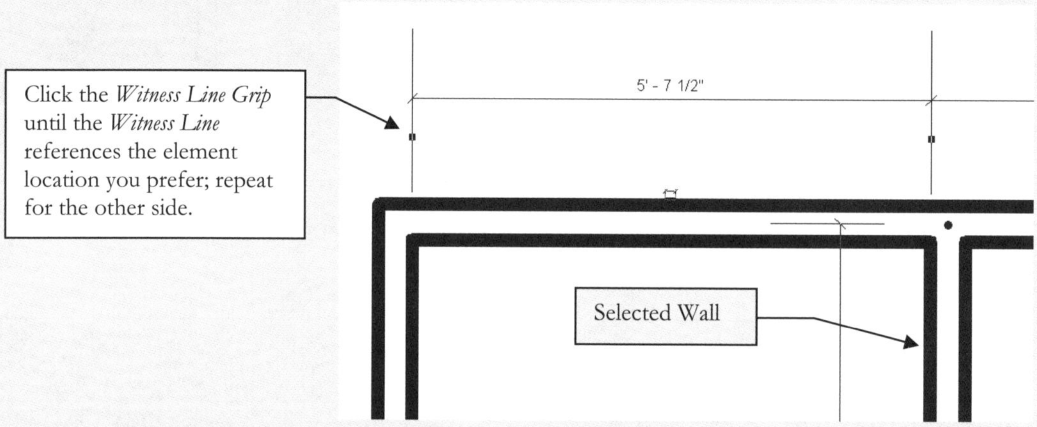

In the above example the temporary dimension could now be modified, which would adjust the location of the wall to a specific inside or clear dimension.

Not only can you adjust the *Witness Line* about a given element, you can also move the *Witness Line* to another element. This is useful because Revit's temporary dimensions for a selected element do not always refer to the desired element. You can relocate a *Witness Line* (temporary or permanent) by clicking and dragging the grip; see example below.

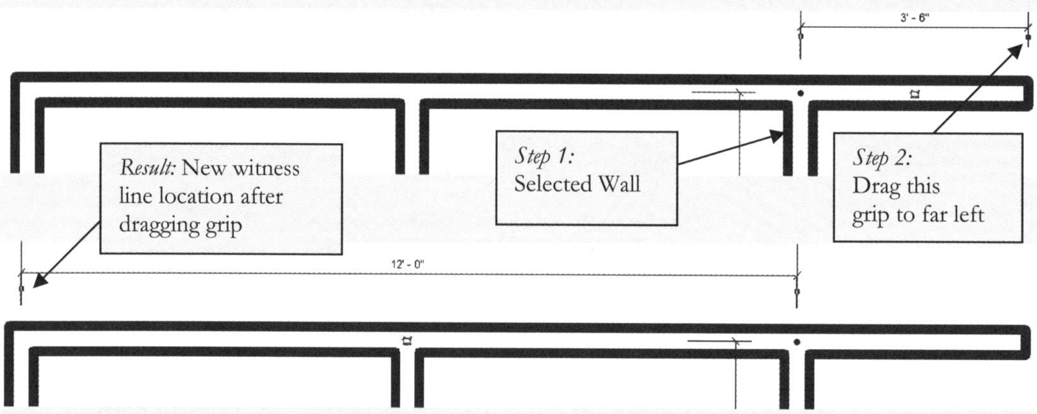

8. Use the *Measure* tool to double-check all dimensions.

The image below shows what your first floor plan should now look like:

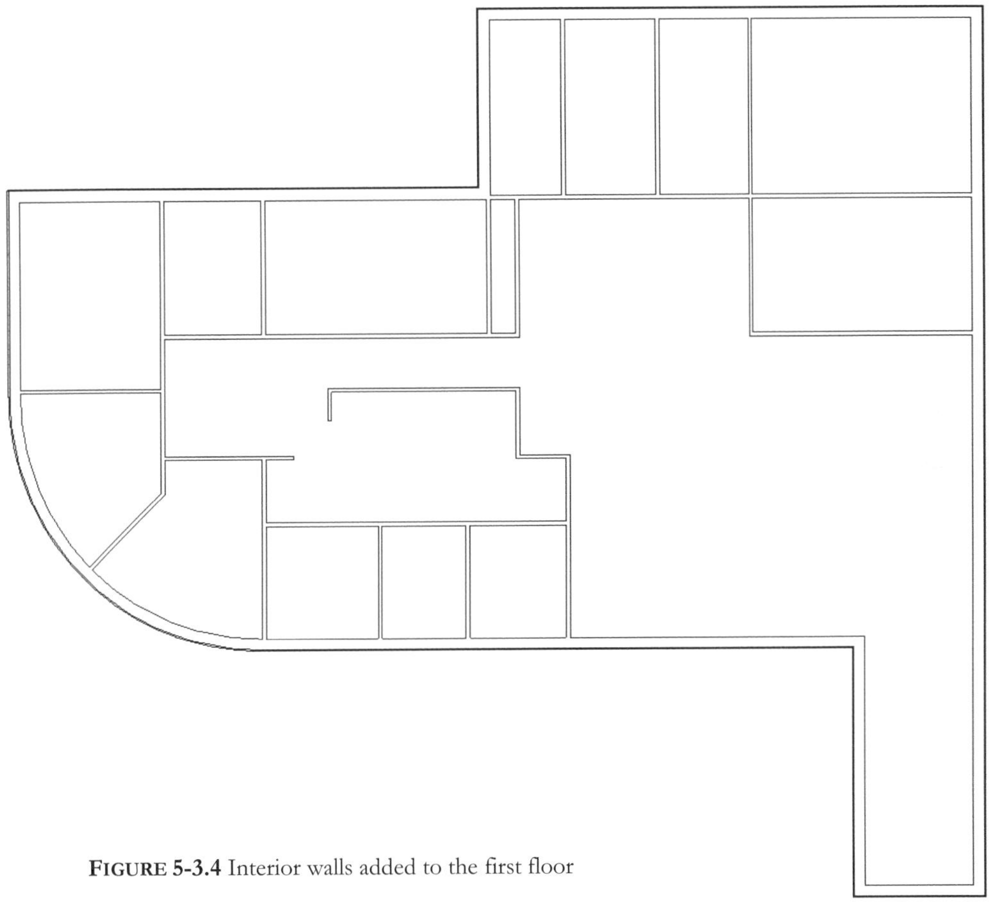

FIGURE 5-3.4 Interior walls added to the first floor

It is important to remember that the "flip control" symbol is displayed on the exterior side of the wall, even for interior walls, when the wall is selected. This corresponds to the Exterior Side and Interior Side designations with the wall type editor; this helps on interior walls that are not symmetrical. If your symbol is on the wrong side, click it to flip the wall and the symbol to the other side. All of your interior walls are symmetrical, so this is not necessary. You may have to move or align the wall so it is flush with the adjacent exterior wall.

Setting Up the Second Floor Plan:

Looking at the *Project Browser*, you should notice a second floor plan view does not exist. Setting one up involves two steps.

First, you need to create a Level datum in an elevation or section view. This serves as a reference plane which hosts several types of elements in Revit. For example, the bottoms of walls, doors, cabinets, etc. are parametrically assigned to a level. If the Level datum moves, everything attached to the level moves as well.

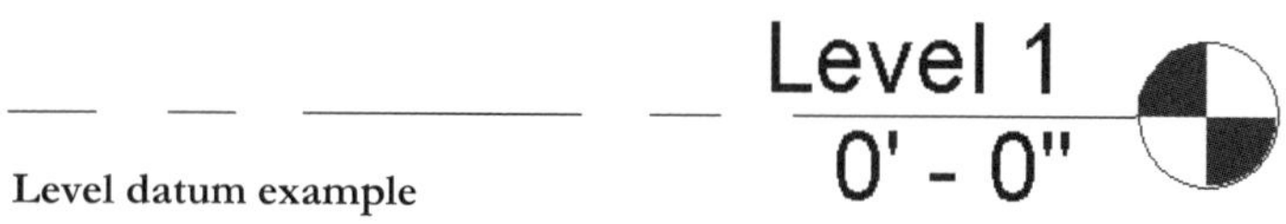

Level datum example

Second, you need to create a floor plan view and ceiling plan view that are associated to the new *Level*. It is possible to have multiple floor plan views based off of the same level; floor plan, code plan, finish plan, power plan, lighting plan, HVAC plan, plumbing plan, and framing plan. Each of these views represents a horizontal slice through the building and each will have its own notes and tags as well as visibility manipulations. For example, the structural framing plan does not need to see the casework and the architectural plan does not need to see the fire dampers.

Because you already have several walls whose tops are associated with the roof *Level* datum, you will simply rename it to be the second floor. After that you can create a floor plan view for that level. Finally, you will create a *Level* datum for the roof.

Typically, you only create *Levels* for surfaces you walk on.

9. Switch to the **South** elevation view via the *Project Browser* (see Figure 5-3.5). Double-click **South**.

You are now viewing the *South* elevation (see Figure 5-3.6). The *Level* datums should extend past the building on each side if you started your floor plan near the center of the elevation tags as originally instructed.

Levels can only be created and edited in elevations and sections.

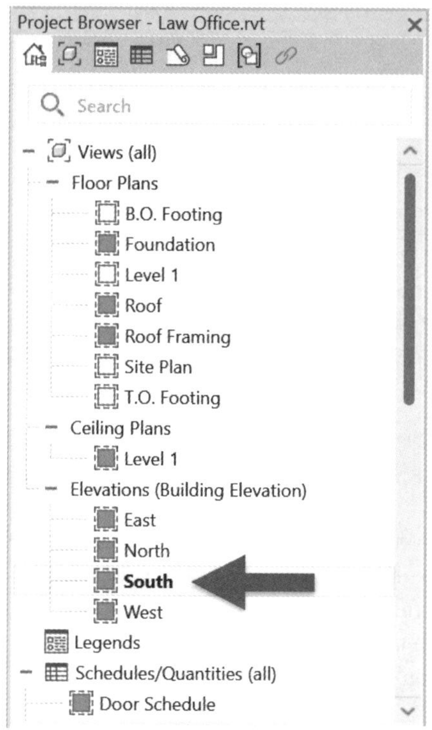

FIGURE 5-3.5 Opening the South elevation

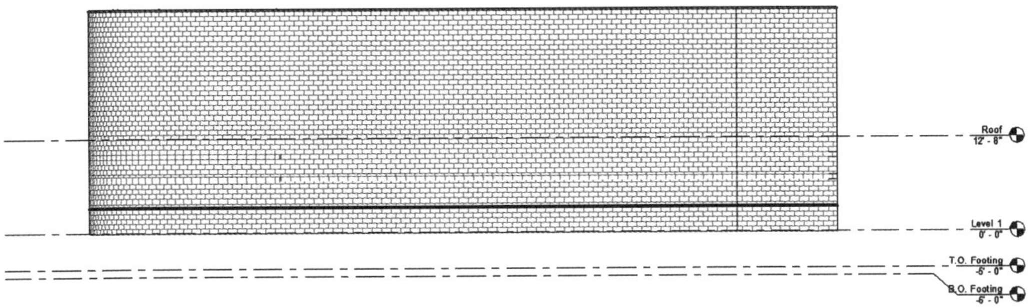

FIGURE 5-3.6 South elevation view showing walls and levels

10. Select the **Roof** *Level* datum.

11. Click on the roof text and enter **Level 2**; press **Enter**.

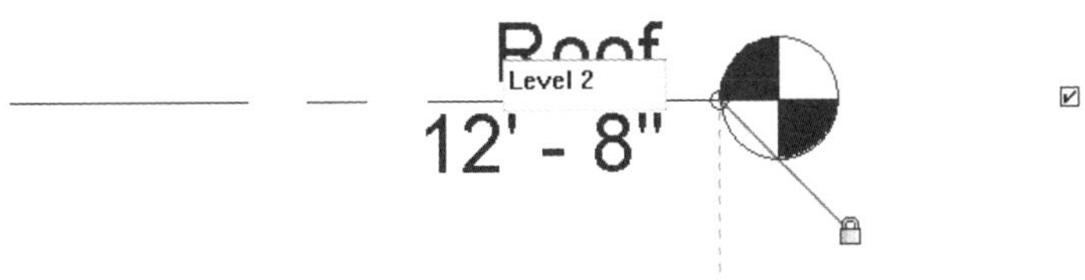

12. Click **Yes** to the prompt shown in the image below.

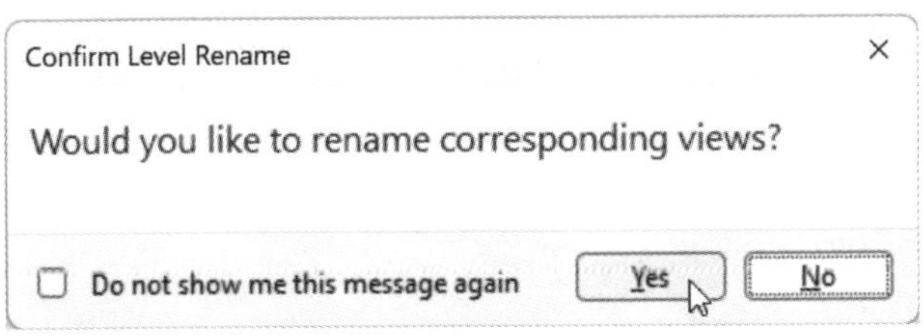

The ***Roof*** view under *Floor Plans*, in the *Project Browser*, has now been changed to **Level 2**.

13. Click on the 12′-8″ text, of the ***Level 2*** *datum*, and change it to **13′-4″**, then press **Enter**.

The second floor level is now set properly for our project. This value can be changed at any time during the project, but it is safer to set it as early as possible as some things do not automatically adjust, such as stairs.

Next you will create a new *Level* datum for the roof.

14. While still in the **South** elevation view, select

    Architecture → Datum → Level.

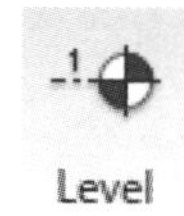

15. Draw a new **Level** per the following instructions:
    a. Check **Create Plan View** on the *Ribbon.*
    b. Pick from left to right.
    c. Align the ends with the ends of the levels below. They will snap into place before you click.
    d. Draw the *Level* datum anywhere above Level 2.
    e. Once drawn, edit the elevation text to be: **26′-8″**
    f. Change the title from *Level 3* to **Roof.**
    g. Click **Yes** to rename corresponding views.

When you select the **Roof** level datum in the **South** elevation, a dashed line and a padlock should appear. This indicates the Levels are locked together. If one moves, they all move.

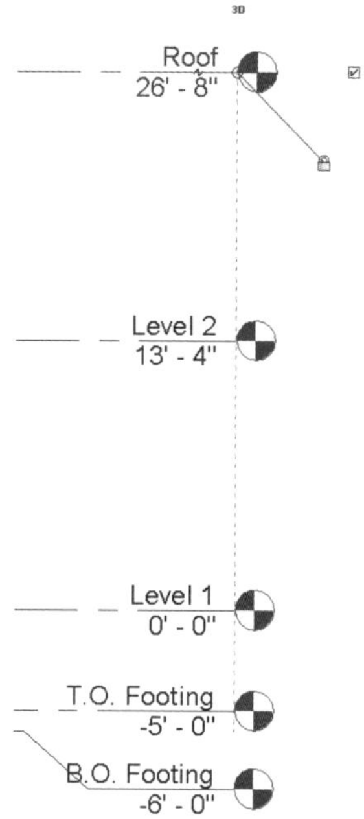

FIGURE 5-3.7
New roof level added

16. **Close** the **South** elevation view.

There are just two more house-cleaning items to do before drawing the Level 2 walls. First, the **Roof Framing** view is tied to the **Level 2** datum, so that will be deleted. You will create structural views later in the book. Second, you will apply a *View Template* to the **Level 2** view to make sure it is set up properly for a floor plan view; a *View Template* is a saved set of view parameters.

17. Right-click on the **Roof Framing** view listed under *Floor Plans* in the *Project Browser* and select **Delete** from the pop-up menu.

18. Right-click on **Level 2** and select **Apply Template Properties…** from the pop-up menu (see Figure 5-3.8).

You are now in the *Apply Template Properties* dialog box (Figure 5-3.9). Take a moment to notice the various settings it stores and is thus able to apply to the selected view.

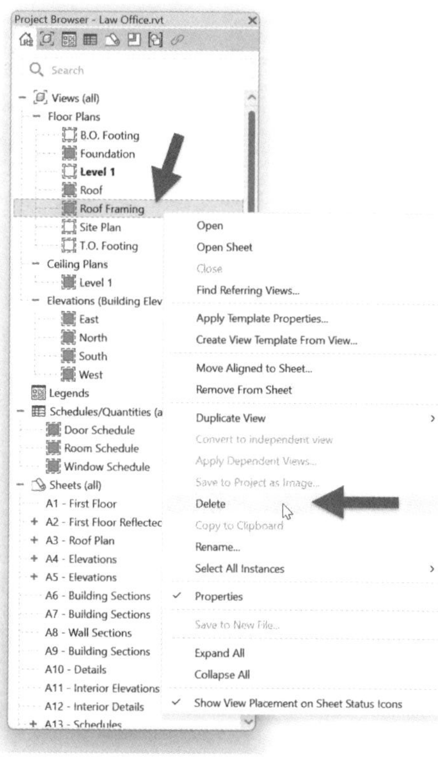

FIGURE 5-3.8 Apply View Template

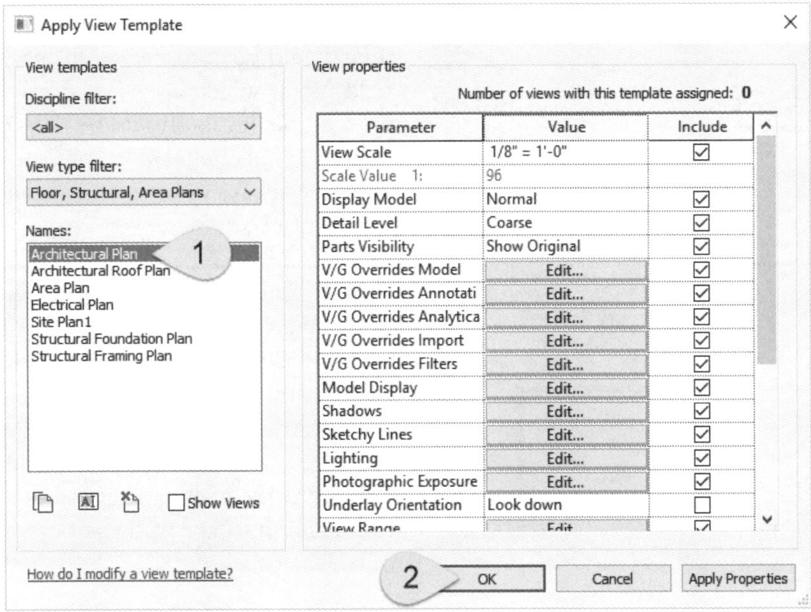

FIGURE 5-3.9 Apply View Template dialog box

19. Make sure **Architectural Plan** is selected on the left, and then click **OK**.

FYI: When applied this way, the View Template *only has a one-time effect on the selected view. That means, if the View Template is changed, the Views that have used it this way previously will not be updated. You would have to reapply the View Template to any views, if desired, after the View Template has been updated. You may select more than one View in the Project Browser and apply a View Template to all the selected Views at once. To create a permanent connection between a view and a view template, select the view template in the* Properties *palette while in the desired view.*

20. Open the **Level 2** view.

21. Set the *View Scale* to **1/4″ = 1′-0″** and the *Detail Level* to **Medium**.

Notice the exterior walls are already shown (Figure 5-3.10). If you recall, the exterior walls drawn on Level 1 were set to be 30′-0″ tall. Also, Level 2 is at 13′-4′ with a cut plane 4″-0″ above that; thus, Level 2 cuts the 30′-0″ at 17′-4″. This is why the exterior wall is shown and the interior walls are not; the interior walls are set to only extend up to Level 2, which was the Roof level initially. Finally, the Level 2 *view* is set to only look down to the Level 2 *datum* and not beyond. This is why we do not see the interior walls below even though we have not yet drawn a 3D element representing a floor. Next you will quickly explore these settings.

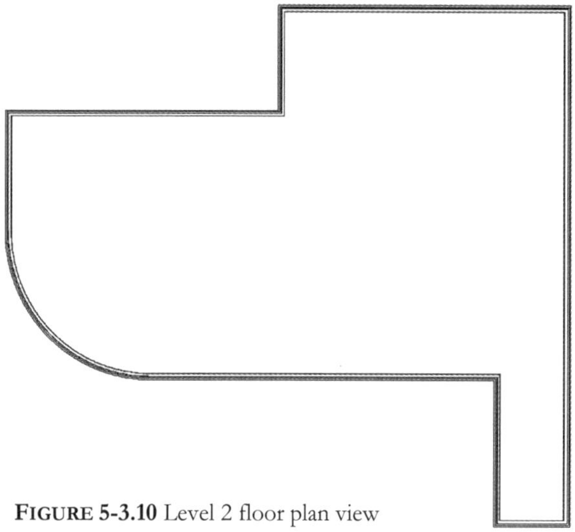

FIGURE 5-3.10 Level 2 floor plan view

It is ideal to draw walls similar to how they would be constructed in the field. Walls which are tall and extend up multiple levels should be drawn as one wall. This helps to ensure the walls are always in proper alignment from floor to floor.

On the other hand, if walls between floors align but are not connected, you would not likely want the wall to extend through the floor. If at some point in the design the walls needed to move out of alignment, it could be difficult if the wall had several hosted elements on it (i.e., wall cabinets, mirrors, urinals, etc.).

22. While in the *Level 2* view, make sure nothing is selected and note the *Properties Palette* is displaying the *Level 2 View Properties.*

23. In the *Properties Palette,* scroll down and click **Edit** next to *View Range.*

FIGURE 5-3.11 Level 2 floor plan view

Looking at Figure 5-3.11, notice the *Cut Plane* is set at 4′-0″, recalling that Level 2 is currently set at 13′-4″ and could change if needed. The *View Depth* setting determines how far down Revit looks into your 3D model. Often, the *Bottom* settings and *View Depth* are the same number; if not, anything between the *Bottom* settings and the *View Depth* setting gets an override to a linestyle called *Beyond.* You will learn more about this later.

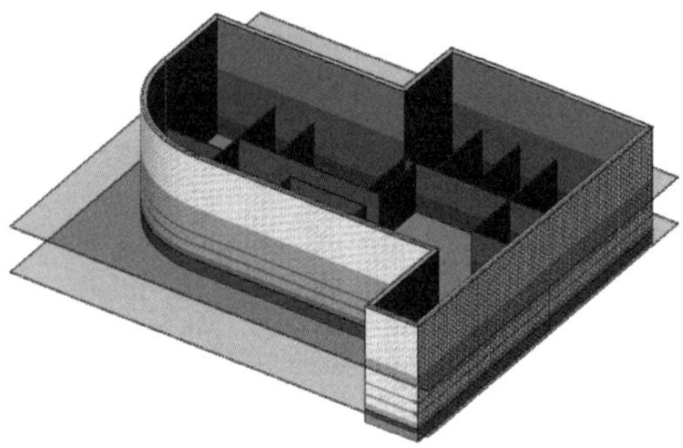

FIGURE 5-3.12 Cut planes

The image to the right is a graphic representation of the Level 1 and 2 Cut Planes on the Law Office model we are developing.

24. **Cancel** out of the *View Range* dialog box.

Second Floor Plan Interior Walls:

You are now ready to begin drawing the Level 2 interior walls. The first thing you will do is learn how to copy walls from the first floor to the second floor, as some walls are in the same location on both floors (e.g., the toilet room walls typically align so the plumbing stacks).

25. Open the **Level 1** floor plan view.

26. Holding the **Ctrl** key down allows you to select multiple objects. Select the walls highlighted in Figure 5-3.13.

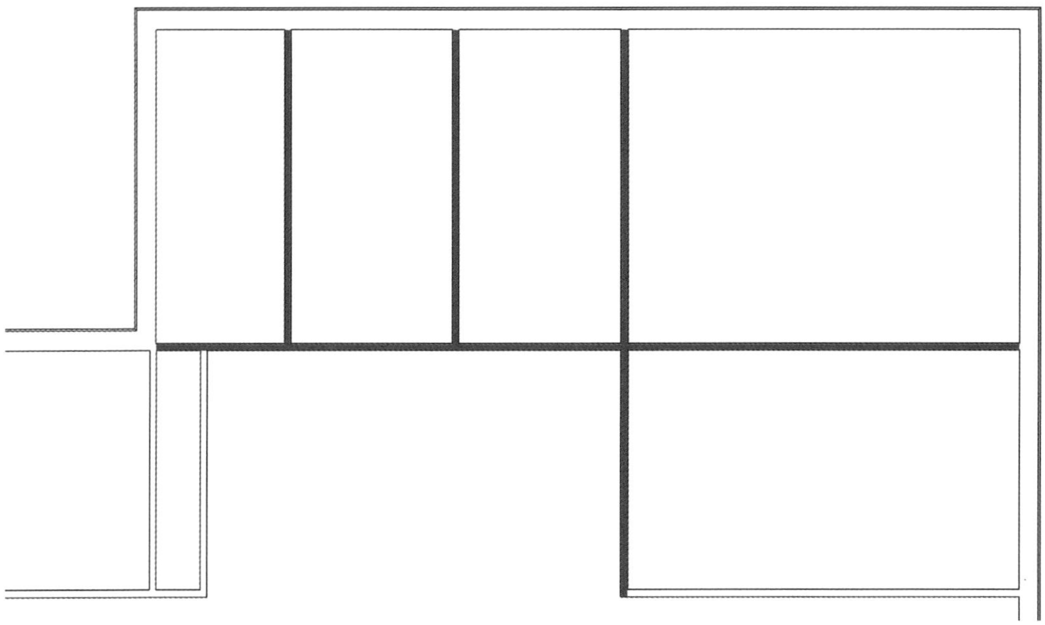

FIGURE 5-3.13 Level 1 walls to be copied to Level 2

27. With the four walls selected, click **Modify | Walls → Clipboard → Copy**.

    a. Notice in the lower right corner of the screen, Revit lists the number of elements currently selected (see image to the right).

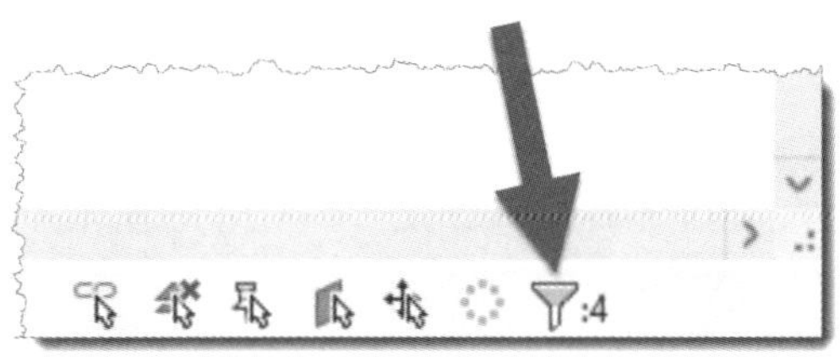

Next you will copy the walls in the clipboard to Level 2.

28. Click **Modify** to clear the current selection.

29. Switch to **Level 2** floor plan view.

30. Click **Modify → Clipboard → Paste → Aligned to Current View** (Figure 5-3.14).

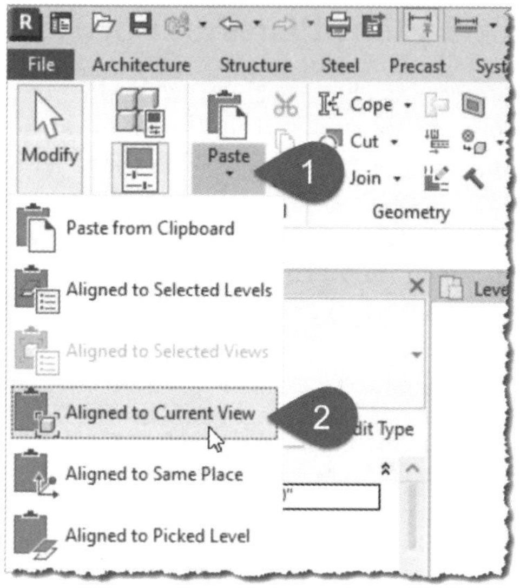

FIGURE 5-3.14 Paste from clipboard

The four walls have now been added to Level 2 in your Revit model (Figure 5-3.15).

Next you will learn how to trim the longer vertical wall back to the horizontal wall so all three vertical lines are the same length.

31. Click **Modify → Modify → Trim/ Extend Single Element**

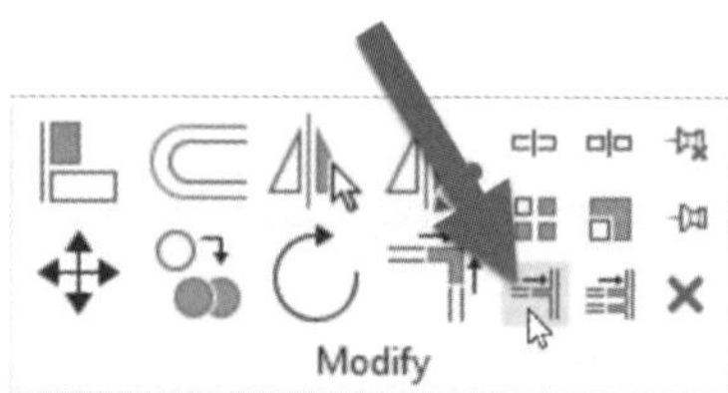

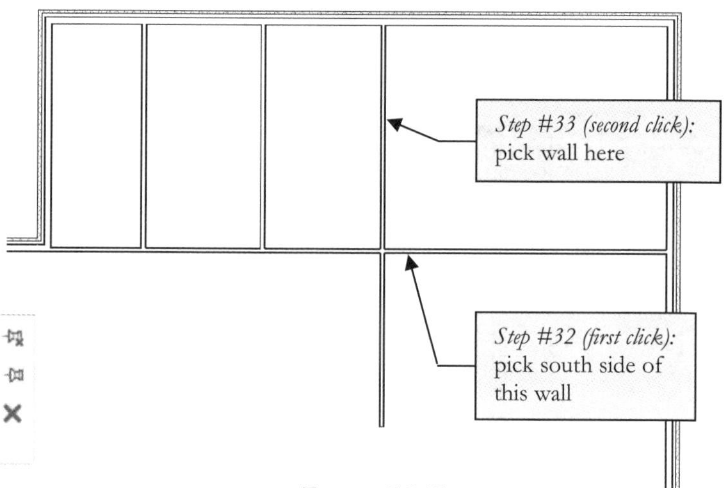

FIGURE 5-3.15
Level 2: Walls pasted from clipboard

32. Click the horizontal wall as the **trim boundary** (Figure 5-3.15).

33. Click the upper portion of the vertical wall (i.e., the portion you wish to keep) as shown in Figure 5-3.15.

The wall should now be trimmed to match the adjacent walls just copied. Another way to achieve the same results is to simply select the vertical wall and drag its end-grip back to the horizontal wall. If you want to try this, click **Undo** and make the same edit using this technique.

34. Select **Wall** from the *Architecture* tab on the *Ribbon.*

35. Make the following changes via the *Ribbon* and *Properties Palette*:
    a. *Wall style:* **Interior – 4 7/8" partition (1-hr)**
    b. *Height:* **Roof**
    c. *Location Line:* **Wall Centerline**

36. Draw the five walls shown in Figure 5-3.16. Do not add the dimensions at this time.

***REMEMBER:** Dimensions are from the exterior face of the exterior walls and the centerline of all interior walls.*

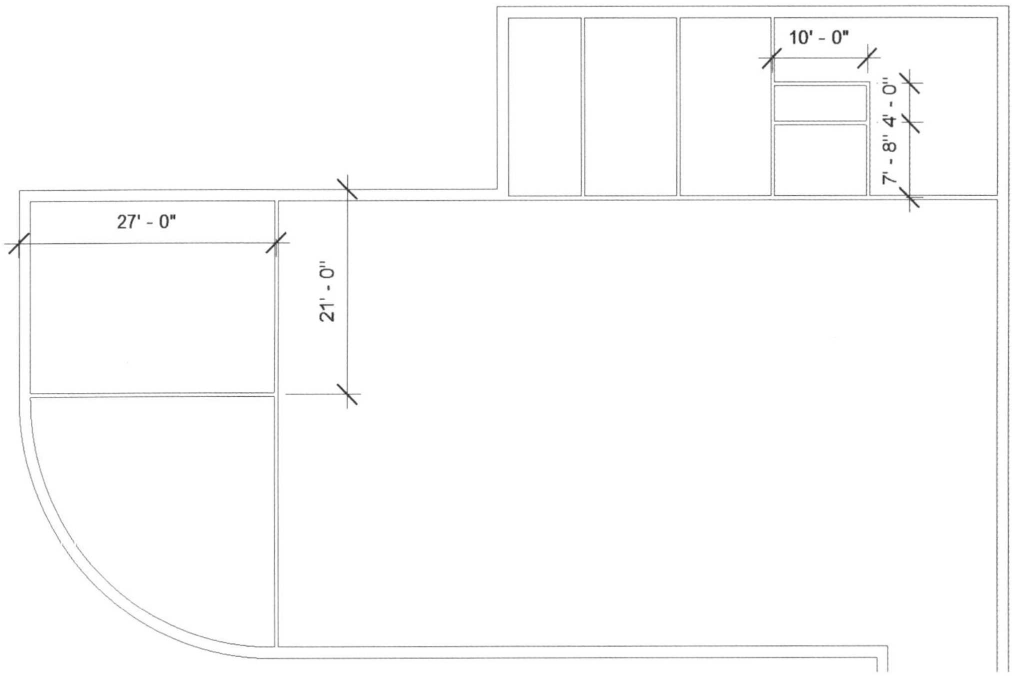

FIGURE 5-3.16 Level 2: Remaining wall to be added (detail level set to Coarse for clarity)

You now have all the major Level 1 and Level 2 walls placed in your Building Information Model (BIM). In the next exercise, you will add doors and windows.

37. **Save** your project.

Don't forget to back up your Revit project file regularly. This one file contains all your work; if it becomes corrupt or is accidentally overwritten you will have to start all over again! Well, at least that is what would happen in the real world. In this book you will get a new file to start with at the beginning of each chapter.

Exercise 5-4:
Doors, Windows and Curtain Walls

This lesson will take a closer look at inserting doors and windows.

Now that you have sketched the walls, you will add some doors. A door symbol indicates which side the hinges are on and the direction the door opens.

New doors are typically shown open 90 degrees in floor plans, which helps to avoid conflicts such as the door hitting an adjacent base cabinet. Additionally, to make it clear graphically, existing doors are shown open only 45 degrees.

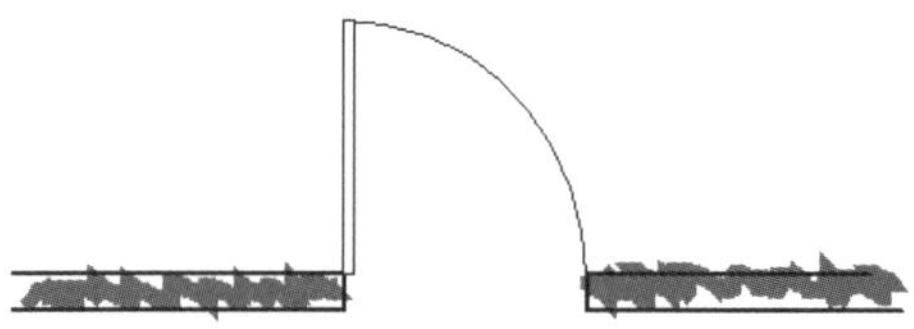

Door symbol Example – New Door drawn with 90 degree swing

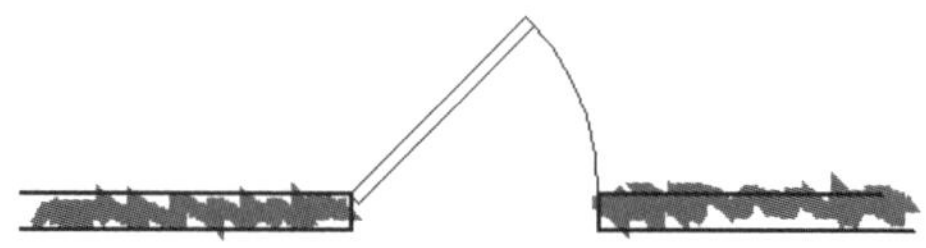

Door symbol Example – Existing Door shown with 45 degree swing

One of the most powerful features of any CAD program is its ability to reuse previously drawn content. With Revit, you can insert entire door systems (door, frame, trim, etc). You drew a 2D door symbol in Lesson 4; however, you will use Revit's powerful *Door* tool which is fully 3D.

For those new to drafting, you may find this comparison between CAD and hand-drafting interesting: when hand-drafting, one uses straight edges or a plastic template that has doors and other often used symbols to trace.

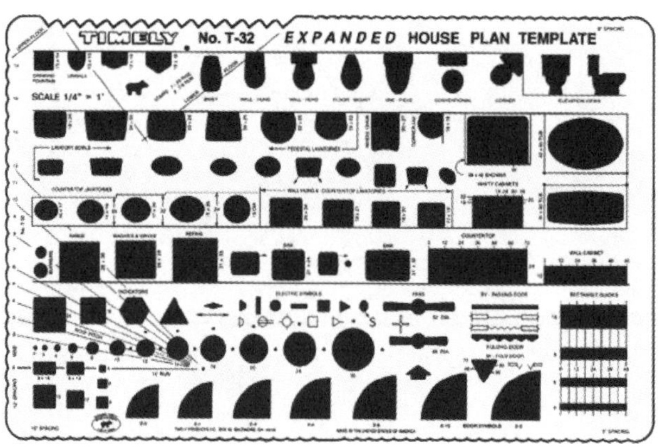

Hand Drafting Template – Plastic template with holes representing common residential shapes (at ¼″ – 1′-0″)

Image used by permission, Timely Templates

Doors in stud walls are dimensioned to the center of the door opening. On the other hand, and similar to dimensioning masonry walls, doors in masonry walls are dimensioned to the face. See example below.

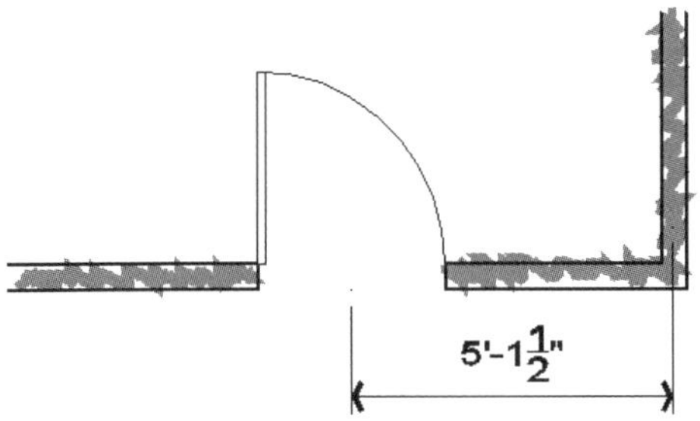

Door Dimension Example – Dimension to the center of the door opening

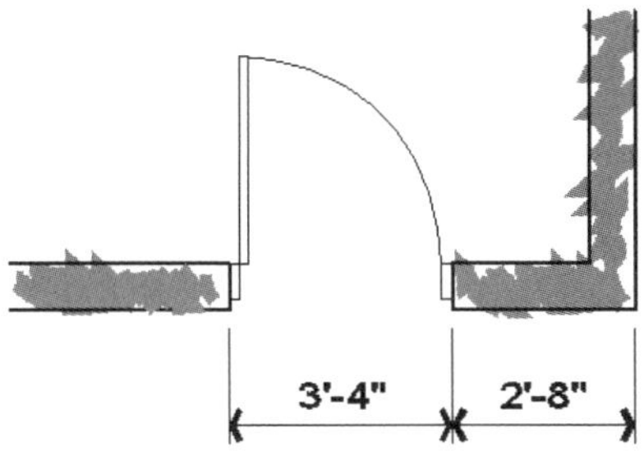

Door Dimension Example – Dimension the opening size and location

Accessible Doors

Most building codes in the US require that a door's clear opening is a minimum of 32″ wide. If you look at a typical commercial door that is open 90 degrees, you will notice that the stops on the door frame, the door thickness and the throw of the hinges all take space from the actual width of the door in the closed position; therefore, 36″ wide doors are typically used (see Figure 5-4.1).

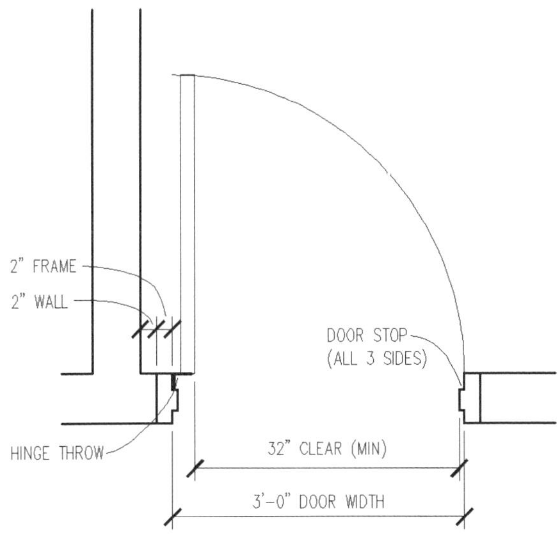

FIGURE 5-4.1
Details to know about accessible doors

Door Stops are usually an integral part of the hollow metal door frame. Their main function is to "stop" the door when being shut. However, they also provide visual privacy and can have sound or weather strips applied. Door stops are NOT typically drawn in floor plans.

Hinge Throw is the distance the door is projected out into the opening as the door is opened, which varies relative to the hinge specified.

The **2″ Wall** dimension is the amount of wall many designers provide between the frame and any adjacent wall. This helps to ensure that the door will open the full 90 degrees regardless of the door hardware selected.

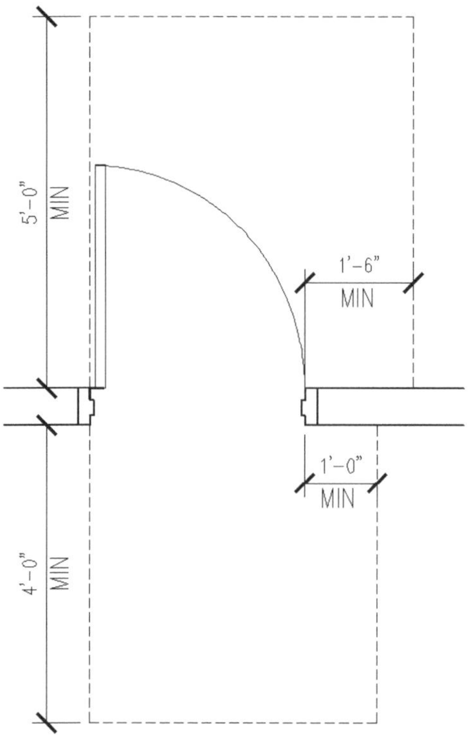

FIGURE 5-4.2
Clear floor space at accessible doors

Building Codes can vary regarding clearances required at a door, but most are pretty similar. Typically, doors that have BOTH a closer and a latch must have sufficient space for a handicapped person to operate the door.

Pull Side of a door that is required to be accessible typically needs to have 18″ clear from the edge of the door, not the outside edge of the frame, to any obstruction. An obstruction could be a wall, a base cabinet or furniture.

Push Side of a door that is required to be accessible typically needs to have 12″ clear from the edge of the door to any obstruction.

Most building codes and the Americans with Disabilities Act (ADA) require slightly different dimensions depending on approach, meaning is the person approaching the door perpendicular or parallel to the wall or door?

In this book, all doors adjacent to a wall will have a 2″ dimension between the wall and the edge of the door frame (per Figure 5-4.3), and all other doors will be dimensioned. A note to this effect is usually found in a set of Construction Documents, which significantly reduces the number of doors that need to be dimensioned.

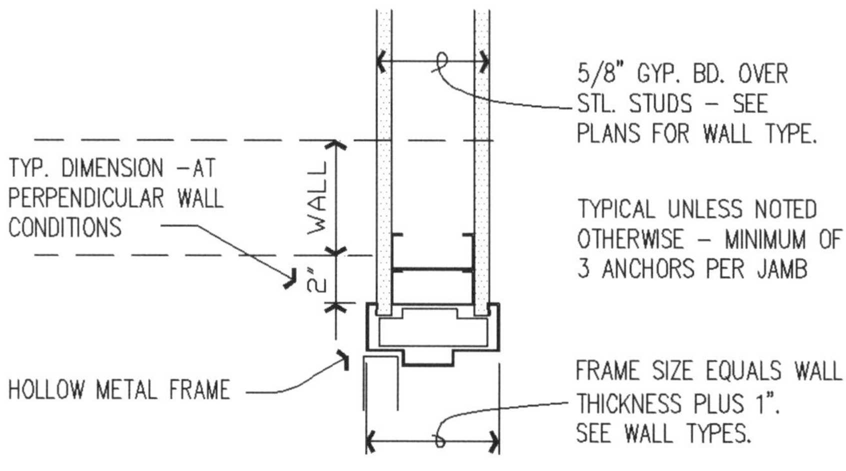

FIGURE 5-4.3 Typical hollow metal door jamb detail

Loading Additional Door Families:

Revit has done an excellent job providing several different door families. This makes sense, seeing as doors are an important part of an architectural project. Some of the provided families include bi-fold, double, pocket, sectional (garage), and vertical rolling, to name a few. In addition to the library groups found on your local hard drive, many more are available via the internet and the Get Autodesk Content command and the Insert tab, which requires an internet connection.

The default template you started with, "Commercial-Default.rte," only provides one door family. Each family typically contains multiple door sizes. If you want to insert additional styles, you will need to load additional *Families* from the library. The reason for this step is that, when you load a family, Revit actually copies the data into your project file. If every possible group was loaded into your project at the beginning, not only would it be hard to find what you want in a large list of doors, but the files would also be several megabytes in size before you even drew the first wall.

You will begin this section by loading a few additional *Families* into your project.

1. Open your project, if necessary.

2. Select **Insert → Load from Library → Load Autodesk Family** on the *Ribbon.*

Browse through the ***Doors*** category for a moment (Fig. 5-4.4). If the content has been manually downloaded, you can also browse to C:\ProgramData\Autodesk\RVT 2027\Libraries\English-Imperial\Doors.

Each preview represents a *Family*, each having one or more *Types* of varying sizes. Next, you will load (3) door *families* into your project.

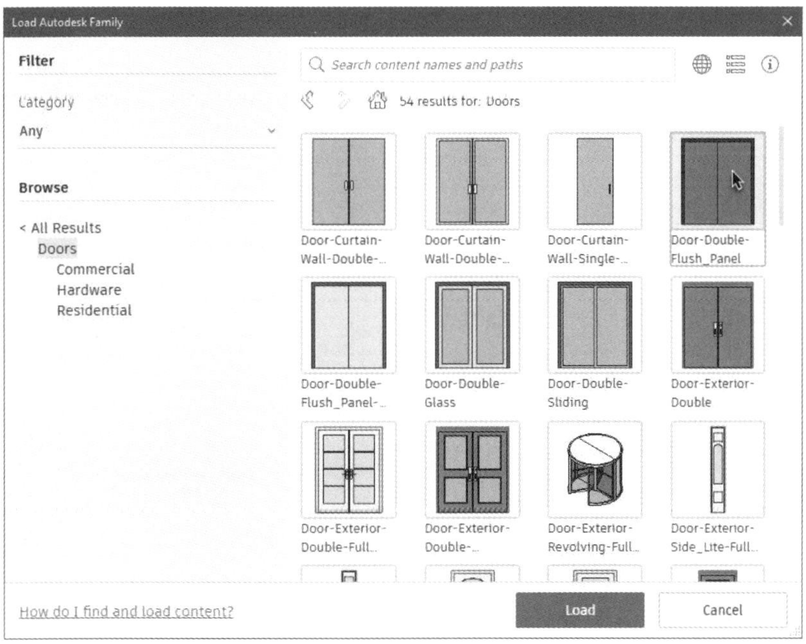

FIGURE 5-4.4 Door Families on hard drive

3. Select **Door-Double-Flush_Panel**, and then click **Load** (Figure 5-4.4).

This door family has a **Type Catalog** which allows users to limit how many Types are loaded into the project. In this commercial project we would not want to use 6'-8" doors as they are more suited for residential projects. **FYI:** The *Type Catalog* is a text file with the same name as the family—this file must be in the same folder as the family for Revit to "see" it.

4. In the *Type Catalog*, select **72" x 84"** and then click **OK** (Figure 5-4.5).

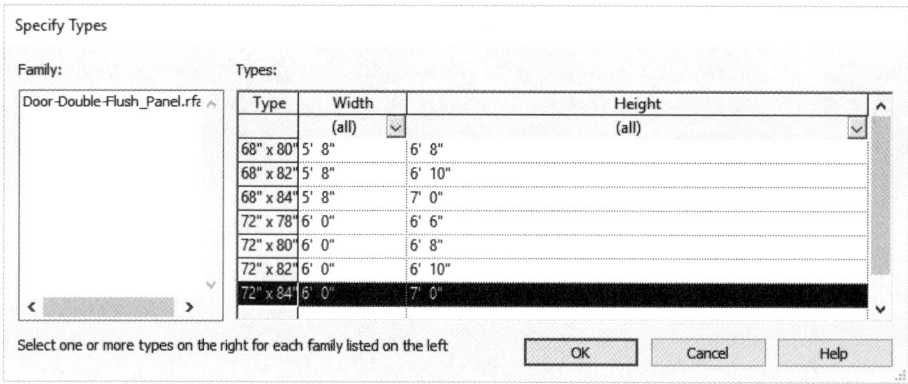

FIGURE 5-4.5 Type catalog for door family being loaded

As soon as you click *Open*, the selected family is copied into your current project and is available for placement.

5. Repeat Steps 2 – 4 to load the following door families:

   a. **Door-Curtain-Wall-Single-Glass**

   b. **Bifold-4 Panel.rfa**

      FYI: This file is missing in Revit 2027; Load from provided online files; see inside-front cover for download instructions.

6. In the *Project Browser*, filter to the *Families* category and then *Doors* to see the loaded door *families* (Figure 5-4.6).

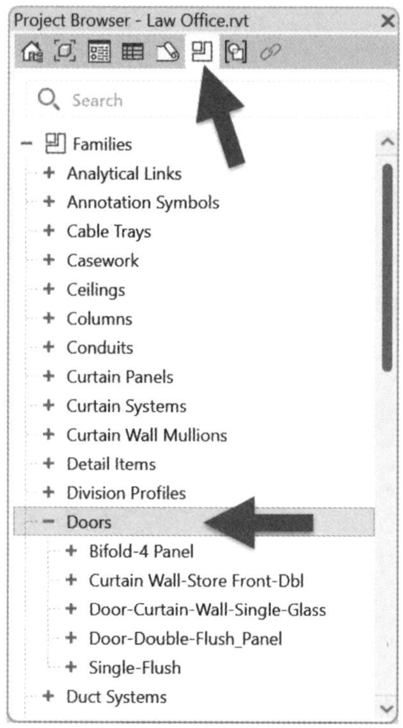

FIGURE 5-4.6 Loaded door families

If you expand the *Doors* sub-category itself in the *Project Browser*, you see the predefined door sizes associated with that family. Right-clicking on a door size allows you to rename, delete or duplicate it. <u>To add a door size, you duplicate and then modify properties for the new item.</u>

***FYI:** The curtain wall "doors" will not show up when using the Door tool. These doors only work in a wall type that is a curtain wall (more on this later).*

Placing Level 1 Doors:

Next, you will start inserting the doors into the first floor plan.

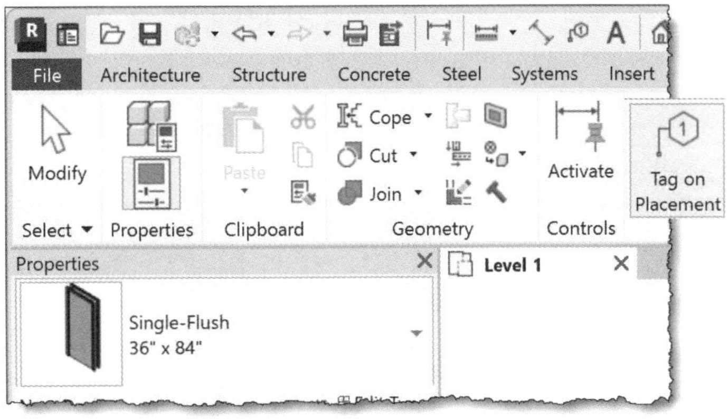

7. Select **Architecture → Door** and then pick **Single-Flush: 36″ x 84″** from the *Type Selector* on the *Properties Palette.* Also, select **Tag on Placement** on the *Ribbon.*

8. In the **Level 1** floor plan view, insert one door in the Northeastern-most room as shown in Figure 5-4.7.

   a. Set the distance between the door opening and the adjacent wall to **4″**. Refer back to Exercise 2-2 for a refresher on this. The 4″ dimension accounts for a 2″ portion of wall and 2″ door frame, which the Revit door families unfortunately do not show. See Figure 5-4.3.

FIGURE 5-4.7 First door placed on Level 1, Northeastern room

Immediately after the door is inserted, or when the door is selected, you can click on the horizontal or vertical flip-controls to position the door swing and hand as desired.

Since **Tag on placement** was selected on the *Ribbon,* Revit automatically adds a *Door Tag* near the newly inserted door. The door itself stores information about the door that can then be compiled in a door schedule. The doors are automatically numbered in the order they are placed. The number can be changed at any time to suit the designer's needs. Most architects and designers use "1x" or "1xx" (i.e., 12 or 120) numbers for the first floor and "2x" or "2xx" numbers for the second floor.

The *Door Tag* can be moved simply by clicking on it to select it, and then clicking and dragging it to a new location. You may need to press the **Tab** key to pre-highlight the tag before you can select it.

Also, with the *Door Tag* selected you can set the vertical or horizontal orientation and if a leader should be displayed when the tag is moved; it is done via the settings on the *Ribbon.*
NOTE: *The tag must be selected.*

9. With the newly inserted door selected, note the door's *Instance Properties* in the *Properties Palette.*

   TIP: *Type PP if the Properties Palette is not visible.*

FIGURE 5-4.8 Instance Properties for door

Notice, in Figure 5-4.8, you see the *Instance Parameters* which are options that vary with each door, e.g., Sill Height and Door Number (Mark). These parameters control selected or yet to be created items.

The *Type Parameters* are not visible in this dialog. To be sure you want to make changes that affect all doors of that type, Revit forces you to click the *"Edit Type"* button and make changes in the *Type Properties* dialog. Also, in the *Type Properties* dialog, you can add additional predefined door sizes to the "Single-Flush" door family by clicking the *Duplicate* button, providing a new name and changing the "size" dimensions for that new *Type.*

10. Click ***Modify*** to unselect the door.

11. Finish inserting the 17 additional doors for Level 1 (Figure 5-4.9). Use the following guidelines:

    a. Use the door styles shown in Figure 5-4.9; doors not labeled are to be **Single-Flush 36″ x 84″**.

b. While inserting doors, you can control the door swing by moving the cursor to one side of the wall or the other and by pressing the spacebar on the keyboard.

c. The order in which the doors are placed does not matter; this means your door numbers may not match the numbers shown in the book. You will modify these numbers later in the book.

d. Unless dimensioned, all doors are to be **4"** away from adjacent wall; see Figure 5-4.3. Do not draw dimensions.

e. Note that the image below has the *Detail Level* set to *Coarse*, the *Door Tags* turned off and the scale temporarily modified to make the image more readable. You do not need to make these adjustments. If you do, set them back before proceeding.

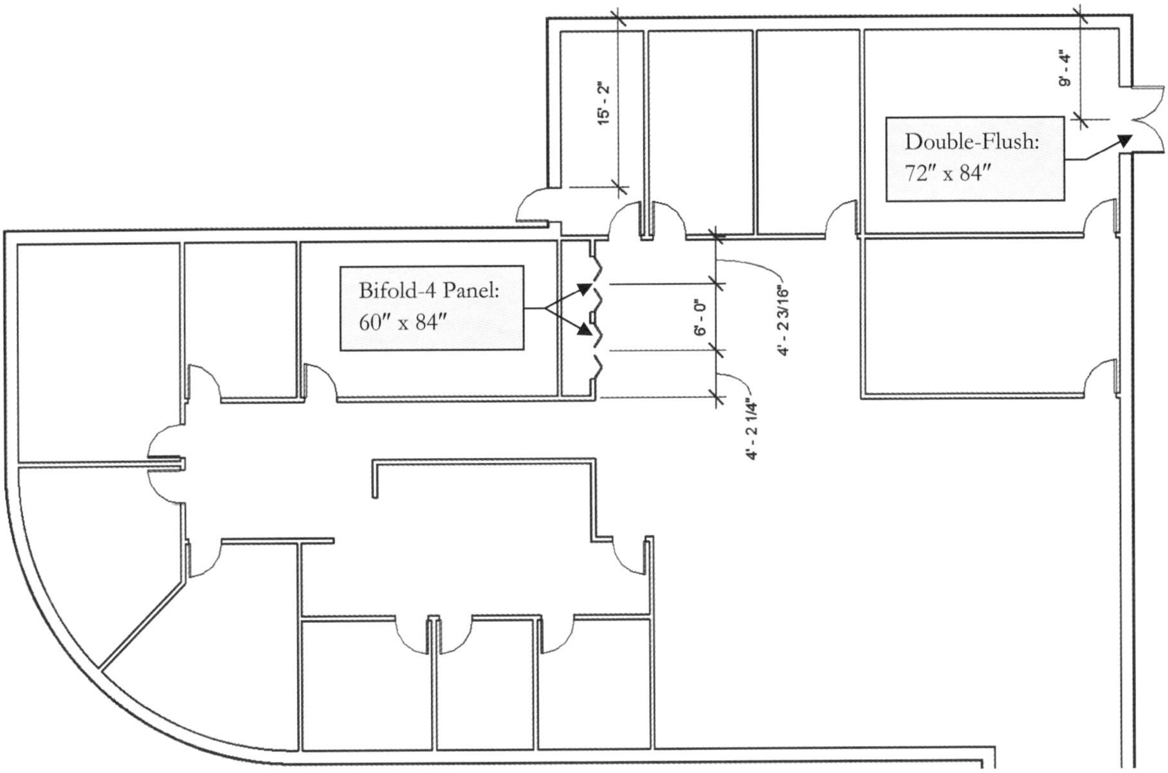

FIGURE 5-4.9 Level 1 doors to be inserted

Placing Level 2 Doors:

Next you will start inserting the doors into the second floor plan.

12. Place the 6 additional doors for Level 2, following the same guidelines as Level 1 (Figure 5-4.10).

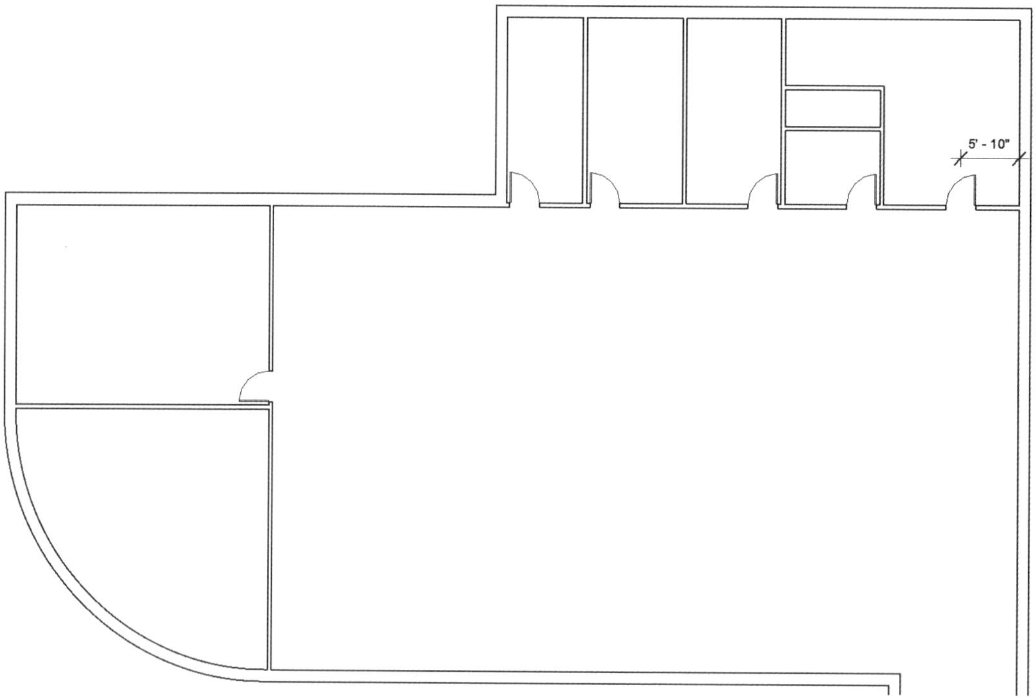

FIGURE 5-4.10 Level 2 doors to be inserted

A few additional doors will be added later. Note that the bottom of a door is automatically attached to the *Level* on which it is inserted. Also, because doors are 7′-0″ tall, they pass through the view's 4′-0″ *Cut Plane*. Some *Families*, like these doors, are set to show 2D linework, or *symbolic lines*, in place of the 3D objects when **cut** in plan view. This allows the arc to appear that represents the swing of the door. In a 3D elevation or section view, the 3D door object is shown, which is in the closed position in this case.

Note on Wall Openings:

Although your building does not contain any openings, you will learn about them before moving on to placing windows. An opening is similar to a door in that, when placed, it removes a portion of wall automatically, creating a circulation route. Also, like doors, openings come in different pre-defined shapes and sizes.

One common mistake is to break a wall so the floor plan appears to have an opening. However, when a section is cut through the opening, there is no wall above the opening. This is also problematic for the room tagging feature and the *Ceiling Placement* tool.

One of the keys to working successfully in Revit is to model the building project just like you would build it because that is the way Revit is designed to work.

One opening family type can be found in the *Openings* folder, called *Passage - Opening-Elliptical Arch*. The *Type Properties* dialog for it is shown below (Figure 5-4.11). Notice the various fields that can be filled in. For example, you could enter how much it would cost to construct an opening with an arched top in the *Cost* field.

> ***FYI:** Be sure to review the tools on the* Opening *panel, located on the* Architecture *tab as well.*

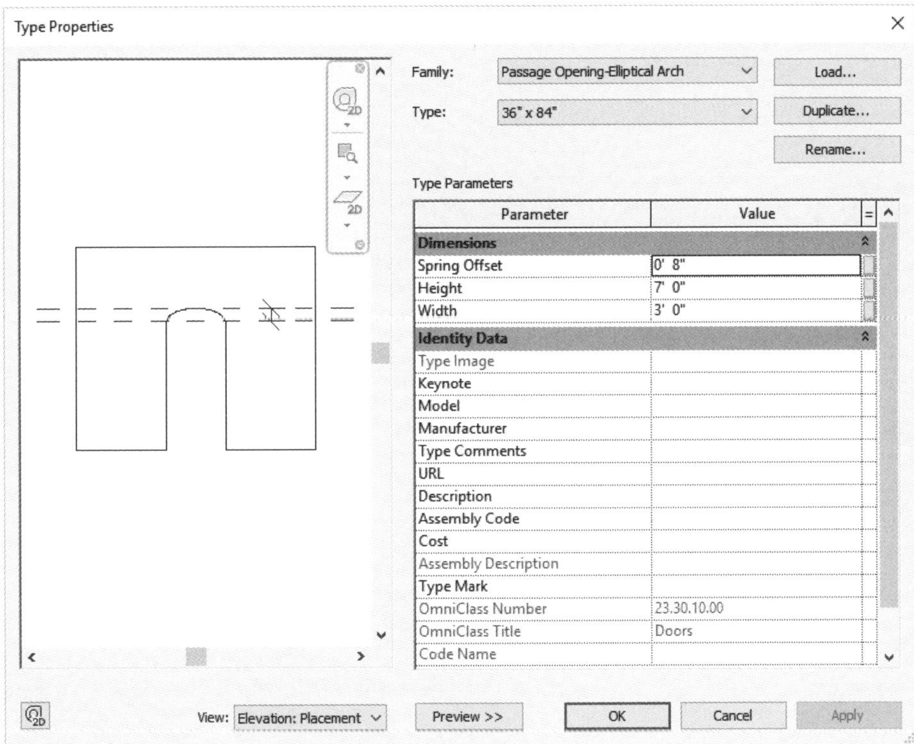

FIGURE 5-4.11 Properties for wall opening

Insert Windows:

Adding windows to your project is very similar to adding doors. The template file you started from has one family preloaded into your project; it is called Fixed. By contrast, the Residential template has three: Casement with Trim, Double Hung with Trim and Fixed with Trim. While in the *Window* tool and looking at the *Element Type Selector* drop-down, you will see the various sizes available for insertion. Additional *Families* can be loaded, similar to how you loaded the doors, although your project will only use the *Fixed* family and *Store Front* walls which are covered directly after the windows.

Most of the exterior fenestrations will be Store Front walls. However, a few windows, aka punched openings, will be placed along the east wall.

13. Switch to the **Level 1** floor plan view.

14. Using the ***Window*** tool, on the *Basics* tab, select **Fixed: 24″ x 48″** in the *Element Type Selector*.

FIGURE 5-4.12 Window type properties

We actually want a 48″ x 48″ window, but one does not exist. The next steps will walk you through the process of creating a new *Type* within the *Fixed* window family.

15. Select **Edit Type** from the *Properties Palette* (Figure 5-4.12).

16. Click **Duplicate**.

17. For the name of the new *Type*, enter **48″x 48″** and then click **OK** (Figure 5-4.13).

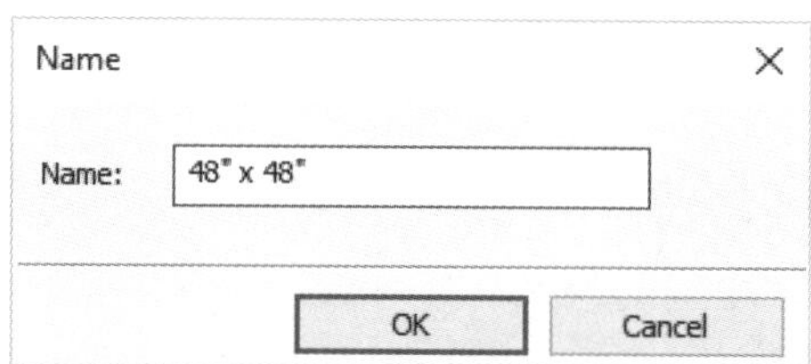

FIGURE 5-4.13 Name new family type

You now have a new *Type* named 48″ x 48″ but the parameters are still set for the 24″ x 48″ *Type* that was selected when you clicked *Duplicate*. Next you will adjust those settings.

18. Make sure the *Width* and *Height* are both set to **4′-0″** (Figure 5-4.14).

The sill height will be different for each floor, so you will not bother to change that setting.

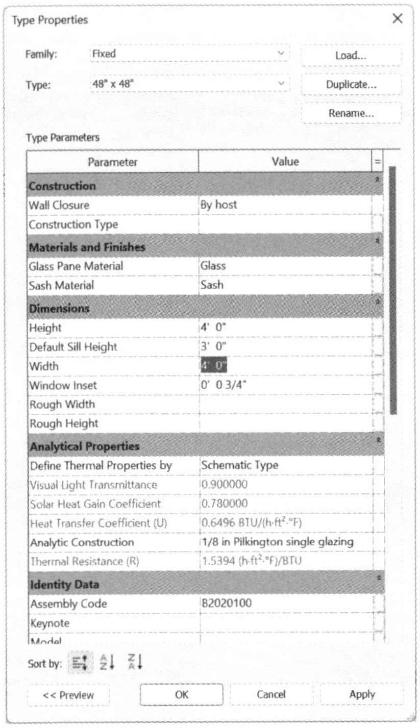

FIGURE 5-4.14 Window type properties

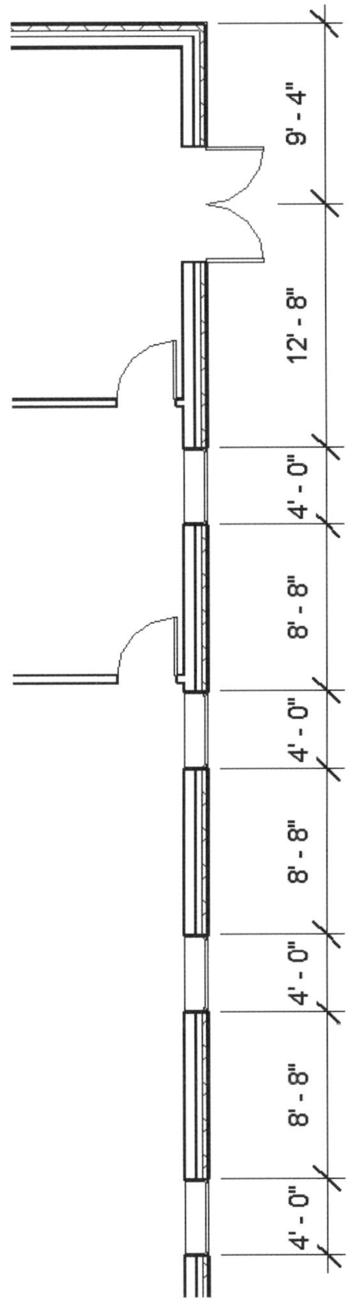

FIGURE 5-4.15
Level 1 windows to be added; North East corner of plan

19. Insert the windows as shown in **Figure 5-4.15**; be sure to adjust the window locations to match the dimensions shown. Do not add the dimensions.

20. Be sure to click towards the exterior side of the wall so the glass and window frame are on the exterior side of the wall. Use the flip controls if any correction is needed.

TIP: To edit location: Modify → Select window → Adjust temporary dimension witness lines → Edit temporary dimension text, just like repositioning doors.

With a window *Type,* not only is the window size pre-defined, but the vertical distance off the ground is as well. Next you will see where this setting is stored.

21. Select one of the windows that you just placed in the wall.

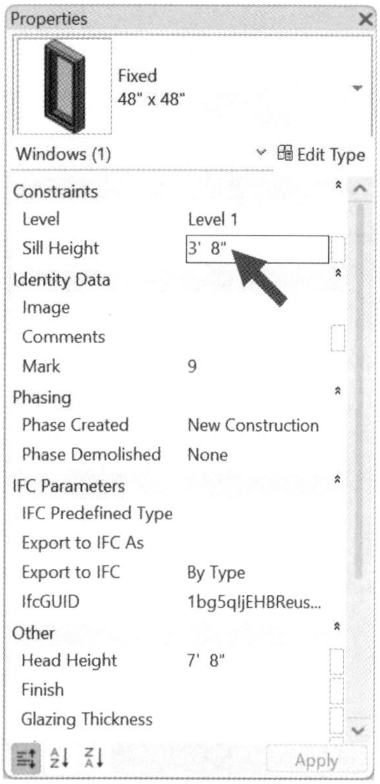

FIGURE 5-4.16 Window instance properties

As previously discussed, this dialog shows you the various settings for the selected item, a window in this case (Figure 5-4.16).

As you might guess, the same size window could have more than one sill height (i.e., distance from the floor to the bottom of the window). So, Revit lets you adjust this setting on a window by window basis.

Another setting you might have noticed by now is the *Phase Created.* This is part of what makes Revit a 4D program; the fourth dimension is time. Again, you might have several windows that are existing and two to three new ones in an addition, all the same size window. Revit lets you do that!

22. Set the *Sill Height* to **3′-8″** and click **OK**.

23. Repeat the previous step for the remaining three windows.

Copying Windows from Level 1 to Level 2:

In the next few steps you will copy the windows from Level 1 up to Level 2. You will use a slightly different technique than when you copied the walls.

24. Select the four windows on Level 1.

25. Click **Copy** in the *Clipboard* panel, not the *Modify* panel.

26. Without the need to leave the **Level 1** view, click **Modify → Clipboard → Paste → Aligned to Selected Levels** (Figure 5-4.18).

27. Click **Level 2** and then **OK** (Figure 5-4.17).

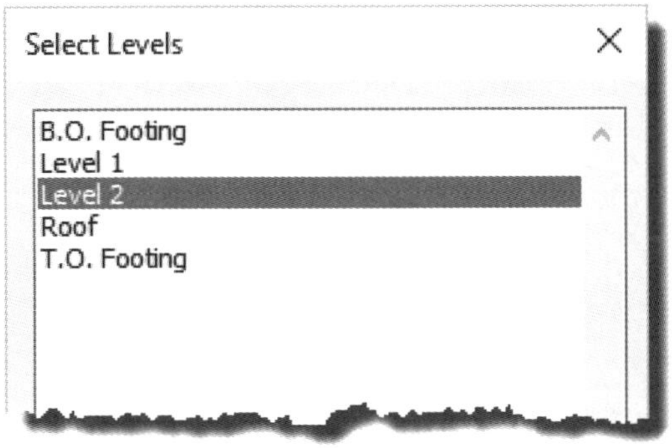

FIGURE 5-4.17 Paste aligned, level options

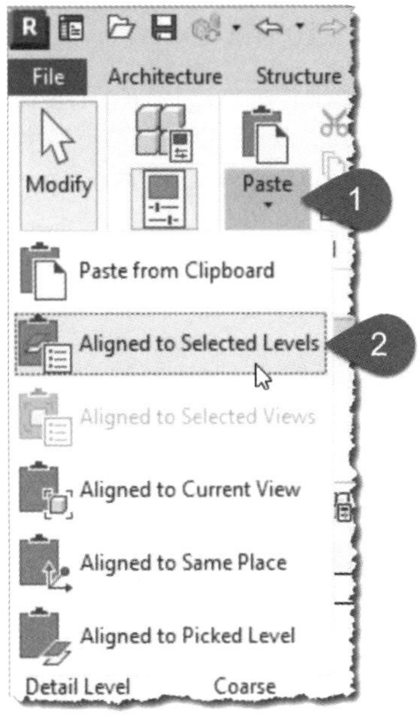

FIGURE 5-4.18
Select levels options

TIP: *On a high rise building it would be possible to select multiple levels and have the clipboard contents copied to multiple floors at once!*

28. Switch to **Level 2** to see the newly added windows.

29. Change the sill height for the **Level 2** windows to **3′-4″**.

CLEANING HOUSE

As previously mentioned, you can view the various *Families* and *Types* loaded into your project via the *Project Browser*. The more *Families* and *Types* you have loaded the larger your file is, whether or not you are using them in your project. Therefore, it is a good idea to get rid of any door, window, etc., that you know you will not need in the current project. You do not have to delete any at this time, but this is how you do it:

- In the *Project Browser*, navigate to Families → Windows → Fixed. Right-click on **36″ x 72″** and select **Delete**.

Another reason to delete types is to avoid mistakes. As you have seen, loading a door family brings in 6′-8″ and 7′-0″ tall doors. On a commercial project you would rarely use 6′-8″ tall doors, so it would be a good idea to delete them from the project so you do not accidentally pick them.

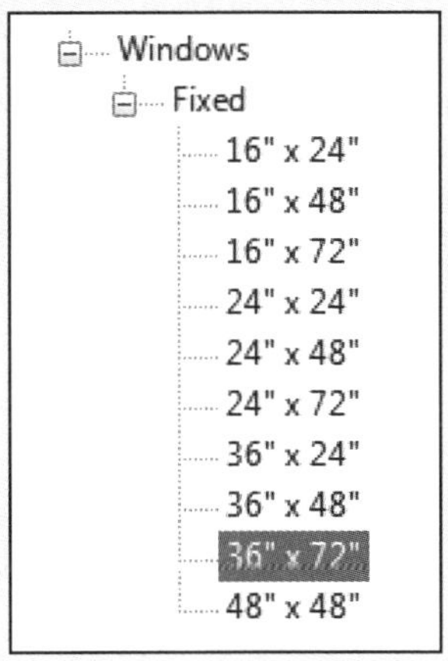

FIGURE: Project Browser

Placing Curtain Walls:

In addition to what are often referred to as punched openings, or the windows, Revit also provides a wall type called **Curtain Wall**. *Curtain Walls* are placed using the *Wall* tool, rather than the *Window* tool, but represent an expanse of glass.

If you select the *Wall* tool, you will see that the commercial template you started with provides three *Curtain Wall* types: Curtain Wall, Exterior Glazing and Storefront.

The first one, Curtain Wall, represents one extreme, that being a blank slate in which you totally design the mullion layout. When the wall is placed, you basically have a panel of glass the entire length and height of the wall.

The second wall type, Exterior Glazing, has the glass divided up, but does not provide any mullions. This would be like a butt-glazed system until mullions are added.

Thirdly, the Storefront wall type represents the other extreme where mullions are placed in both the horizontal and vertical direction at a specific spacing. The layout is locked down, i.e., pinned, and cannot be accidentally modified unless a mullion is manually un-pinned. For simplicity in this tutorial, this will be the system you use.

A Curtain Wall has four primary elements:

- Wall
- Panel
- Grid
- Mullion

Each of these elements must be individually selected in order to edit them. You often have to tap the **Tab** key to cycle through and select something specific; once the item is pre-highlighted, you click to select it.

The blank slate *Curtain Wall* wall type represents the simplest condition: the wall and a single panel that coincides with the wall (see Figure 5-4.19).

FIGURE 5-4.19 Curtain wall

To begin dividing up a curtain wall you need to add *Curtain Grids* (see Figure 5-4.20); Revit has a specific tool for this on the *Home* tab. When a *Curtain Grid* is added, the panel in which it was placed gets split.

The image to the right has:

8 Curtain Panels
4 Curtain Wall Grids
1 Wall

When a ***Curtain Grid*** is selected, you may adjust its location with the *Move* tool or the temporary dimensions.

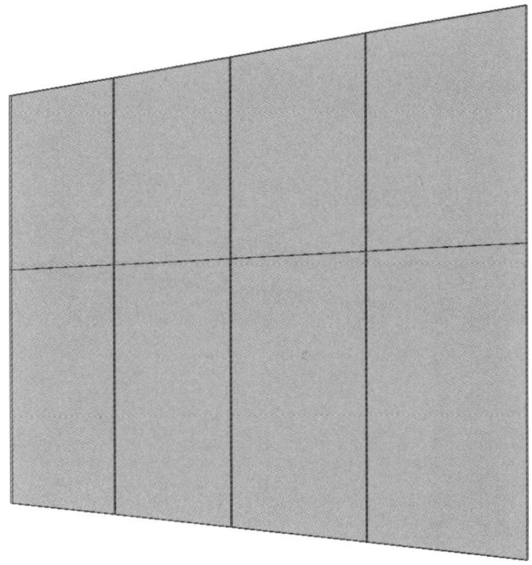

FIGURE 5-4.20 Curtain wall with grids added

When a **Curtain Panel** is selected, you can swap it out with other Revit elements such as walls and special curtain wall doors.

Once *Curtain Grids* have been placed, you may use the ***Mullion*** tool to place *Mullions* on *Curtain Grids.*

The image to the right shows *Mullions* at each of the four grids and along the perimeter. A portion of a *Mullion* was deleted at the bottom edge and a *Curtain Panel* was swapped out for a door (Figure 5-4.21).

The image to the right has:

7 Curtain Panels
4 Curtain Wall Grids
21 Curtain Wall Mullions
1 Door
1 Wall

FIGURE 5-4.21 Curtain wall with mullions added

Notice the large number of mullions in the list above. Mullions stop and start at each *Curtain Grid* intersection. This made it easy to select the mullion at the desired door opening location and simply delete it.

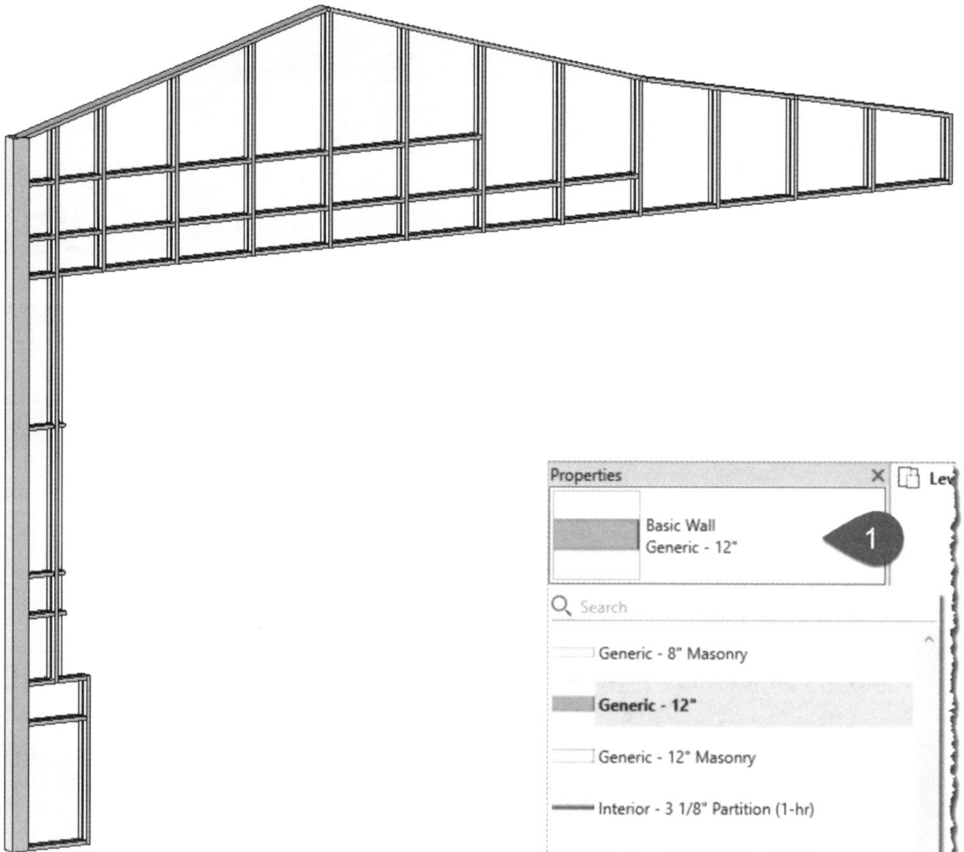

The next few steps will walk you through adding curtain walls to the Level 1 Floor Plan.

30. Switch to the **Level 1** floor plan view.

31. Select the ***Wall*** tool on the *Ribbon.*

32. Select the wall style named ***Storefront*** from the *Type Selector* (Figure 5-4.22).

Before drawing the *Storefront* wall type, you will review its properties.

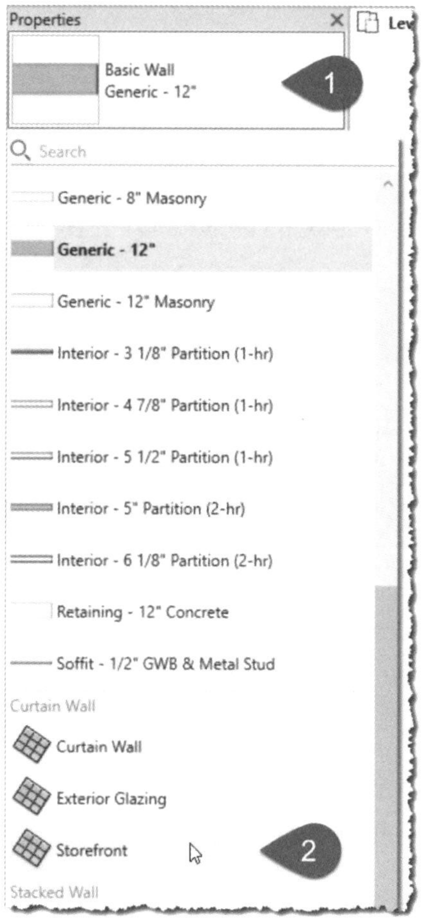

FIGURE 5-4.22
Curtain wall named Storefront

33. Note the *Instance Properties* via the *Properties Palette.*

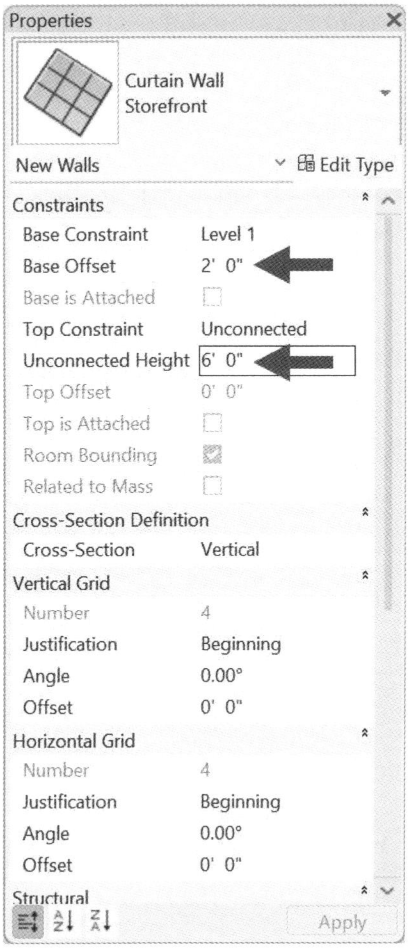

FIGURE 5-4.23 Storefront instance properties

Take a moment to notice a few things about the information presented (Figure 5-4.23).

The *Base Constraint* is equal to the floor plan level you are currently on. Keep in mind **Level 1** refers to the *Level datum* and not the name of the *view* that you are in.

The *Sill Height* is set by the *Base Offset* parameter and the *Head Height* is set by *Top Constraint.*

Because these are *Instance Parameters* they can vary from location to location within the project.

34. Make the following adjustments:
    a. *Base Offset:* **2′-0″**
    b. *Unconnected Height:* **6′-0″**

35. Click the ***Edit Type*** button to view the *Type Properties.*

> **TIP:** Notice the **Cross-Section** parameter in the list above. All walls in Revit can be Slanted, Tapered, or Vertical. Selecting slanted reveals another parameter to specify the angle of the wall. Curtainwall and stacked walls cannot be tapered.

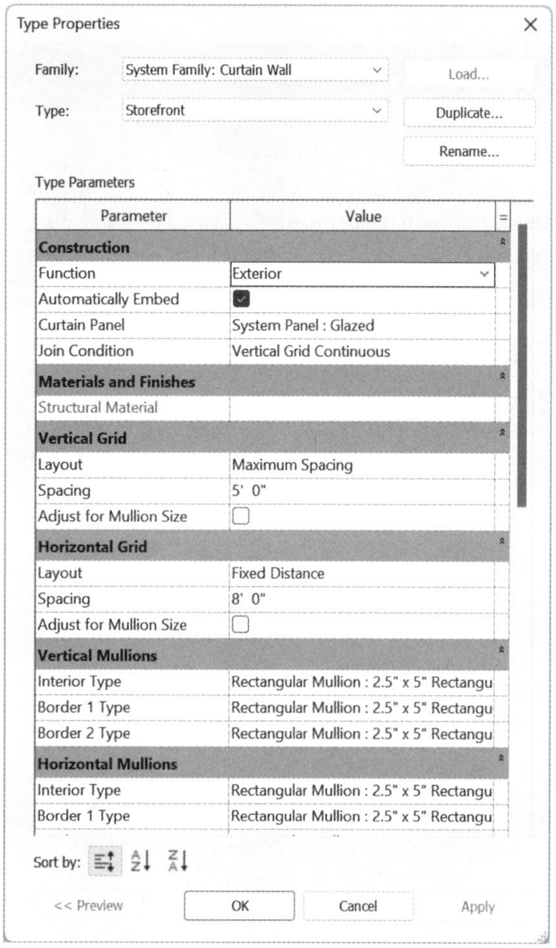

FIGURE 5-4.24 Storefront Type properties

Again, take a moment to notice a few things about the information presented (Figure 5-4.24).

Each wall type has a *Function* setting; this one is set to Exterior. Others may be set to Interior, Foundation, Retaining, Soffit, or Core-Shaft. This setting has an effect on how the wall is drawn and may be used by energy analysis programs.

Automatically Embed allows one wall to cut a hole in another, similar to what a door or window does when placed in a wall.

Various rules on the mullions and their spacing are adjustable here.

36. Press **OK** to close out of the open dialog box.

37. In the Northwest corner of the building, snap to the middle of the wall, **4′-0″** down from the corner and then click. (See Figures 5-4.25a and 5-4.26 for the location.)

38. Move your cursor straight downward, along the wall, and click when the temporary dimension reads **14′-0″** (see Figure 5-4.25b).

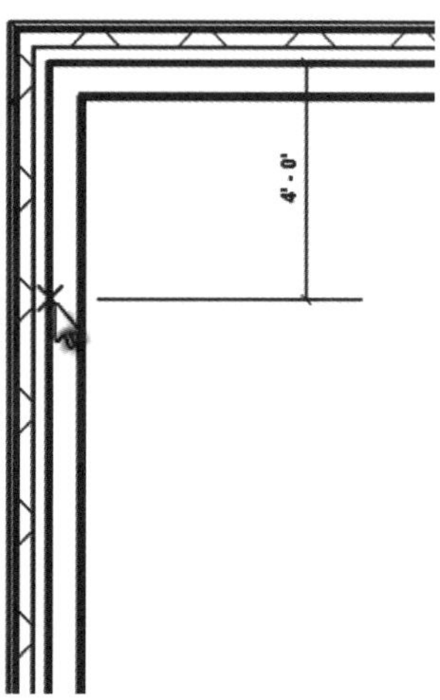

FIGURE 5-4.25A
Storefront – *first pick*

The Curtain Wall is now placed in the West wall (Figure 5-4.25c). The flip-control appears on the exterior side of the curtain wall when it is selected, similar to regular walls. If the flip-control is on the interior side of the wall, as in Figure 5-4.25c, click the control to flip the curtain wall so the glass favors the exterior side of the wall.

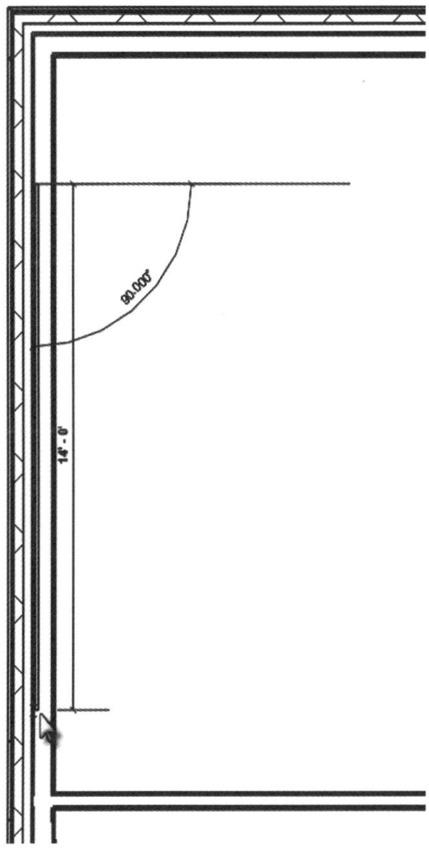

FIGURE 5-4.25B Storefront – *second pick*

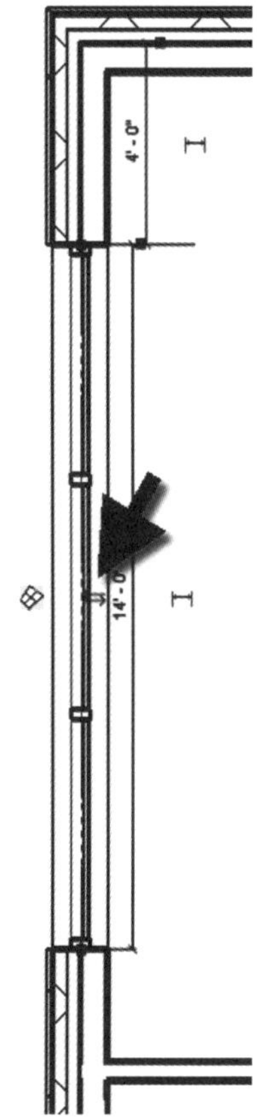

FIGURE 5-4.25C Storefront – selected

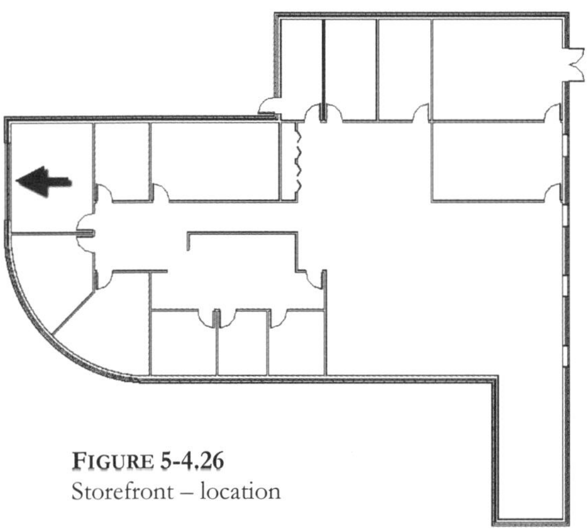

FIGURE 5-4.26
Storefront – location

You have now placed your first curtain wall. The next few steps will instruct you to add the remaining curtain walls. Several will be similar to the first one, with some occurring on each floor. However, at the main entry you will add two-story tall curtain walls that will extend past the second floor, which will then automatically show up in both floor plans.

Notice, in Figure 5-4.27, that the curtain wall already has mullions; this is based on the settings for the *Type* named "Storefront" we used.

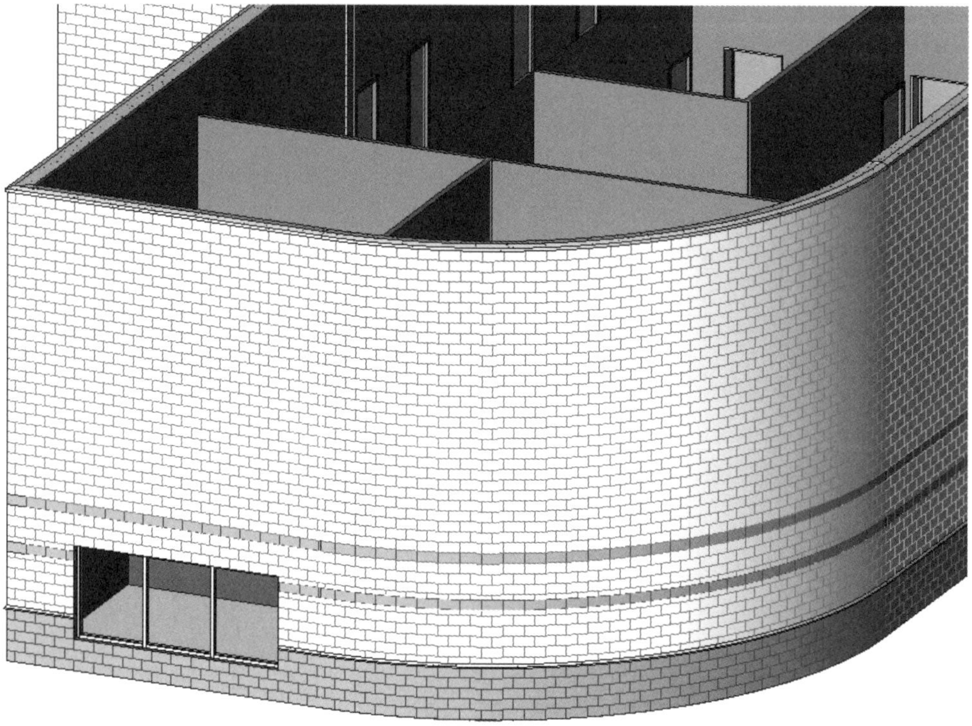

FIGURE 5-4.27 Storefront – shown in 3D view

39. Add four more **Storefront** type curtain walls using the same settings:
    a. See Figure 5-4.28 for locations.
    b. Do not add the dimensions at this time.

TIP: *Draw Detail Lines first to help position the edges of the curtain wall within the main wall.*

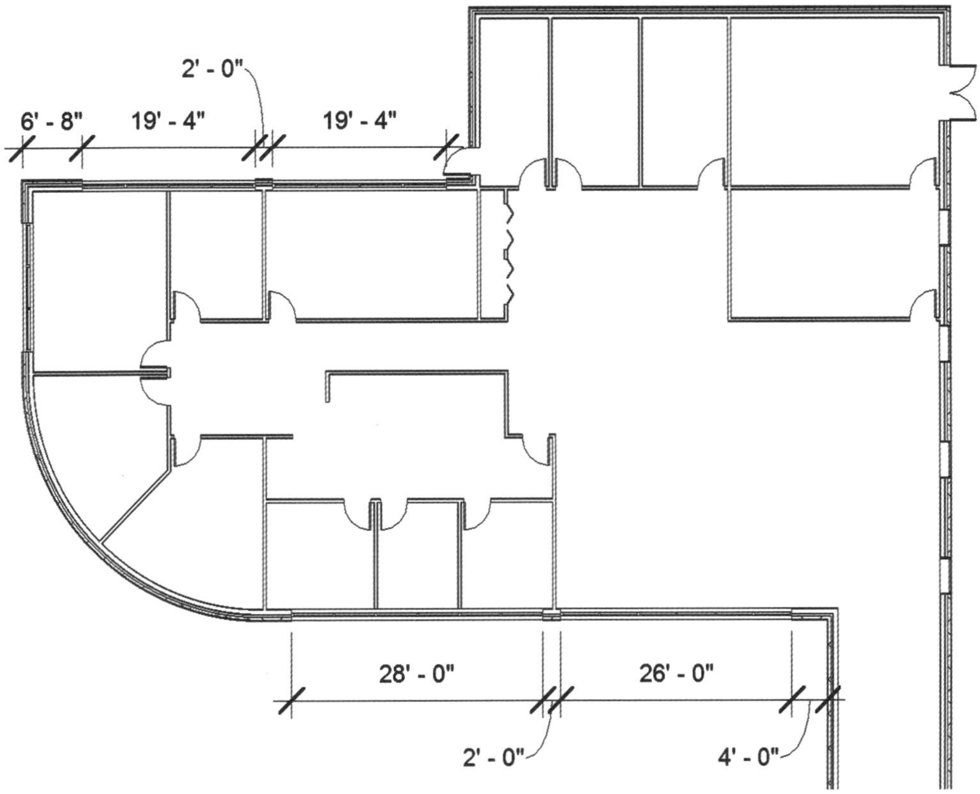

FIGURE 5-4.28 Storefront – additional Level 1 locations

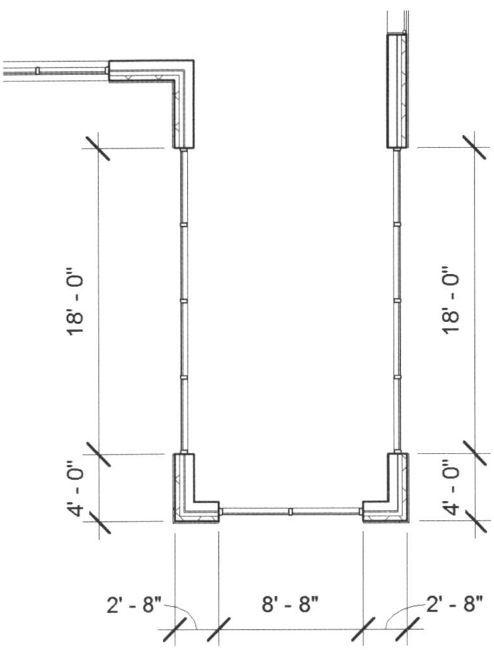

FIGURE 5-4.29
Storefront – additions at main entry

40. Add the three curtain walls at the main entry.

a. *Base Offset:* **0′-0″**

b. *Unconnected Height:* **21′-4″**

See Figure 5-4.29.

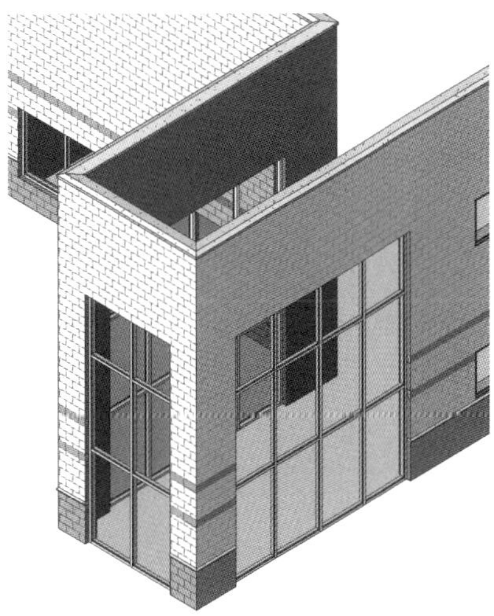

The mullions will be adjusted in the chapter that deals with creating and editing elevations.

Next, you will draw a curtain wall along the curved wall. This will also be a two-story tall wall. You will learn how it is possible to draw walls based on linework that exists within other elements, such as walls. This bypasses the need to pick the points to define the wall length, and angle if curved.

41. Place the curved curtain wall (Figure 5-4.30A):
    a. *Wall type:* Curtain wall: **Storefront**
    b. *Base Offset:* **0′-0″**
    c. *Unconnected Height:* **21′-4″**
    d. Select the "pick" tool in the *Draw* panel (Step #1 in image below).
    e. Click the centerline of the curved wall (Figure 5-4.30B).

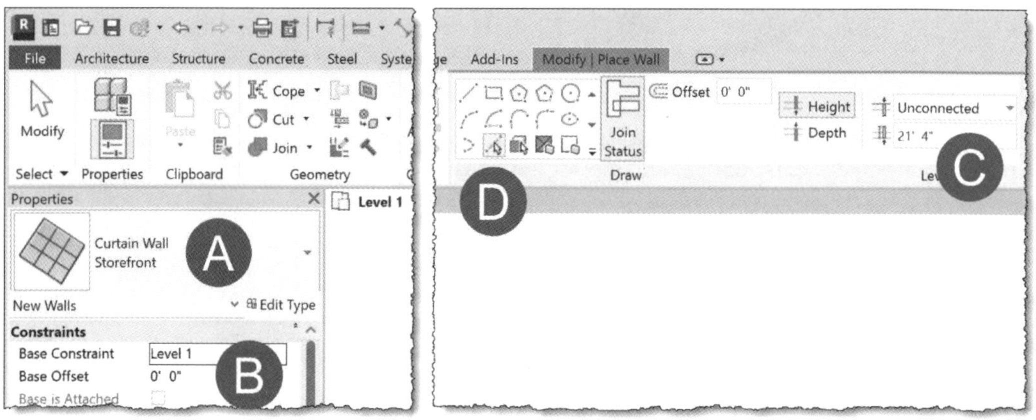

FIGURE 5-4.30A Curved Storefront – UI settings

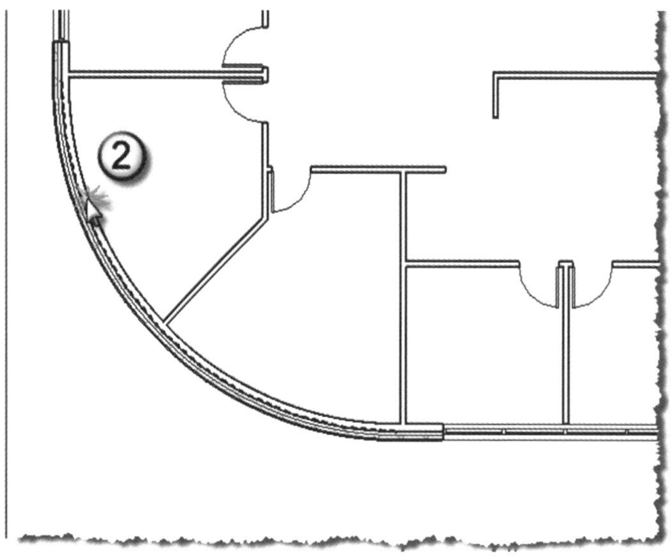

FIGURE 5-4.30B Curved Storefront – placement via the "pick" option

Because the curtain wall is the same length as the solid curved wall, the sweeps in the wall cannot be created; this is not a problem in this case. The curtain wall is not as tall as the solid wall, so some of the wall still exists above the curtain wall as seen in the image to the right.

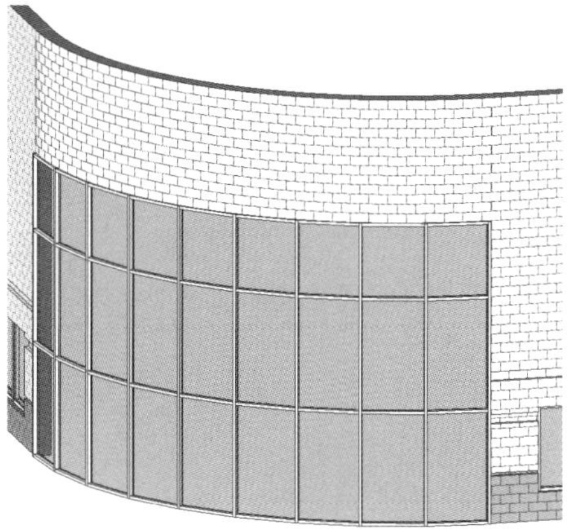

42. Click the "X" to close the warning.

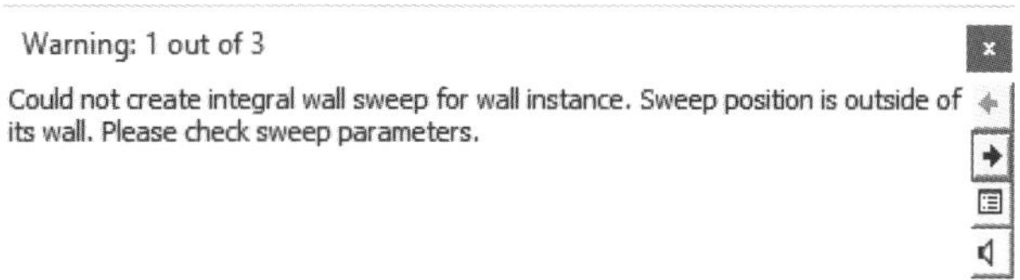

For some reason, the way Revit is programmed, the curtain wall may extend past the curved wall we selected so one quick correction is required *(next three steps)*.

43. Select the curtain wall; be sure to select the dashed line that represents the entire length of wall, not a mullion or curtain grid.

44. A round grip appears at the end of a wall when it is selected; right-click on the grip.

45. Select ***Disallow Join*** (Figure 5-4.32)

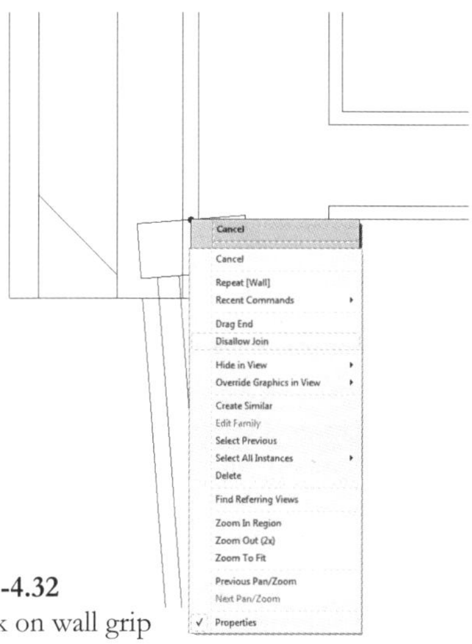

FIGURE 5-4.32
Right-click on wall grip

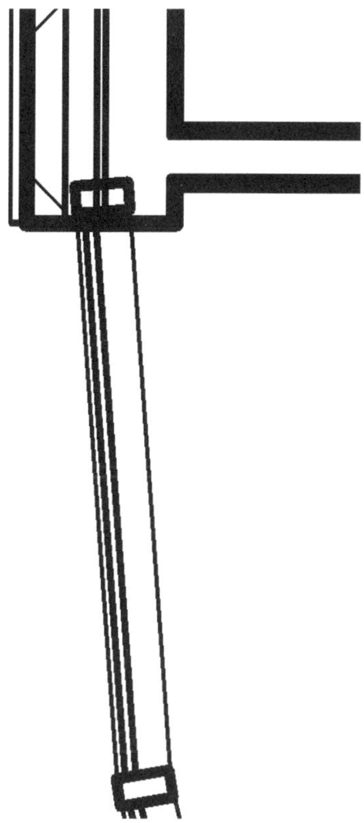

FIGURE 5-4.31
Storefront – problem at jamb

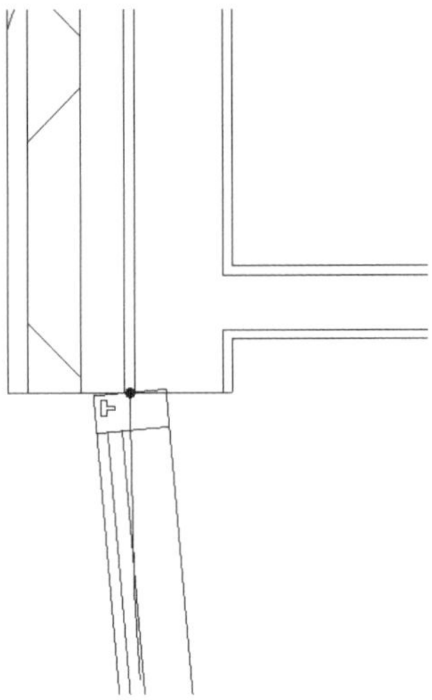

FIGURE 5-4.33
Relocated wall grip

46. Click and drag the grip down and snap to the endpoint of the vertical wall (Figure 5-4.33)

The curtain wall is now adjusted to the correct length. You are now ready to add the remaining curtain walls on Level 2.

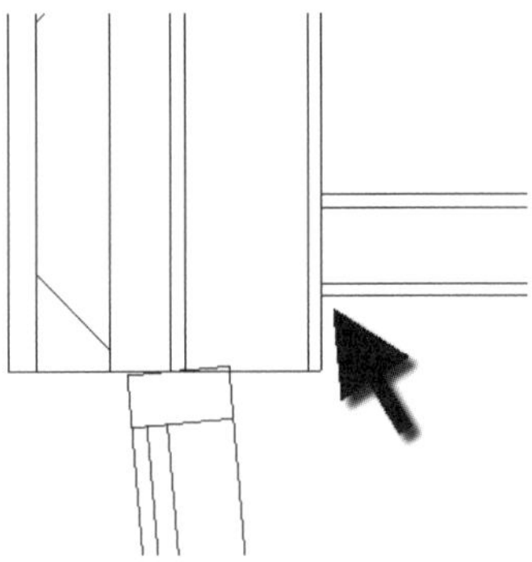

FIGURE 5-4.34
Disallow Join example

***TIP:** The Disallow Join feature works on regular walls. One popular use is when a new wall abuts an existing wall and you do not want them to join. For example, if the exterior wall were existing and the interior partition new, you would want a line to separate them as in Figure 5-4.34. You do not need to make this change to your model.*

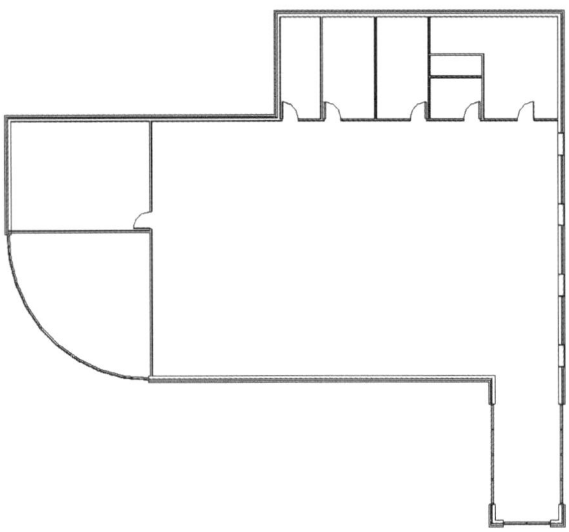

FIGURE 5-4.35
Level 2 – Two story curtain walls automatically seen

47. Switch to the **Level 2** floor plan view.

Notice the four curtain wall elements drawn 21′-4″ tall are visible right away in the **Level 2** view because they pass through this view's *Cut Plane.*

48. Using the techniques previously covered, copy and paste the five curtain walls from Level 1 to Level 2.
    a. See Figure 5-4.36.
    b. All dimensions and settings should remain the same as Level 1.

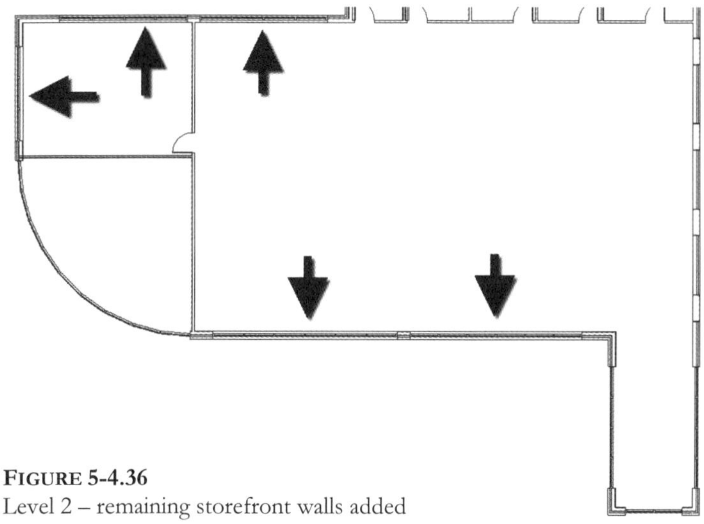

FIGURE 5-4.36
Level 2 – remaining storefront walls added

Your project now has a lot of glass to allow daylight to enter the building! Later in the text you will add sun shades to reduce the amount of hot summer sun that enters the office. Looking at the default **3D** view, you can see your building already starting to take shape.

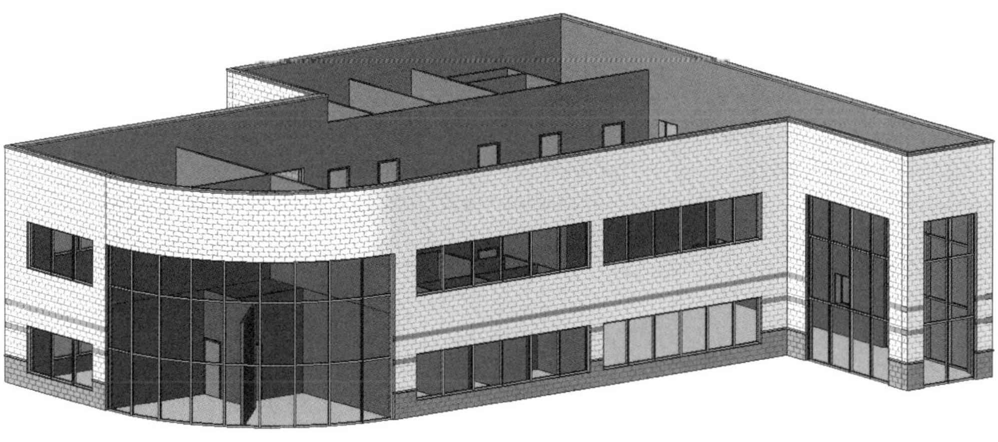

FIGURE 5-4.37
3D view – Showing Storefront added

Self-Exam:

The following questions can be used as a way to check your knowledge of this lesson. The answers can be found at the bottom of the page.

1. The *Ribbon* allows you to select the height your wall will be drawn at. (T/F)
2. It is not possible to draw a wall with the interior or exterior face of the core as the reference point. (T/F)
3. Objects cannot be moved accurately with the *Move* tool. (T/F)
4. The __________ tool, in the *Quick Access Toolbar*, has to be selected in order to select an object in your project.
5. A wall has to be ____________ to see its flip icon.

Review Questions:

The following questions may be assigned by your instructor as a way to assess your knowledge of this section. Your instructor has the answers to the review questions.

1. Revit comes with many predefined doors and windows. (T/F)
2. The *Project Information* dialog allows you to enter data about the project, some of which is automatically added to sheet titleblock. (T/F)
3. You can delete unused families and types in the *Project Browser*. (T/F)
4. It is not possible to add a new window type to a window family. (T/F)
5. It is not possible to select which side of the wall a window should be on while you are inserting the window. (T/F)
6. What tool will break a wall into two smaller pieces? ____________________
7. The ___________ tool allows you to match the surface of two adjacent walls.
8. Use the __________ key, on the keyboard, to flip the door swing while placing doors using the *Door* tool.
9. You adjust the location of a dimension's witness line by clicking on (or dragging) its ______________.
10. The _____________ file has a few doors, windows and walls preloaded in it.

SELF-EXAM ANSWERS:
1 – T, **2** – F, **3** – F, **4** – Modify, **5** – Selected

Lesson 6
Roofs, Floors & Ceilings:

Now that you have the floor plans developed to a point where only minor changes will occur, you can start thinking about the horizontal planes within the building: roofs, floors and ceilings.

In this text you will start with the roof. This is the first element most often modeled of the three elements covered in this chapter. It is first because, with the roof in place, the exterior of the building begins to take its final shape, specifically in 3D and camera views.

Floors and ceilings are then added so the building sections start to take shape. These elements, plus a consultation with the mechanical engineer on the approximate size of the ductwork, will help to determine the distance required between the floors and the roof.

The depth of the structural system is also an important factor when processing the horizontal conditions of your building. This will be covered in a later chapter but in reality would be considered parallel with the information covered in this chapter via the structural engineer.

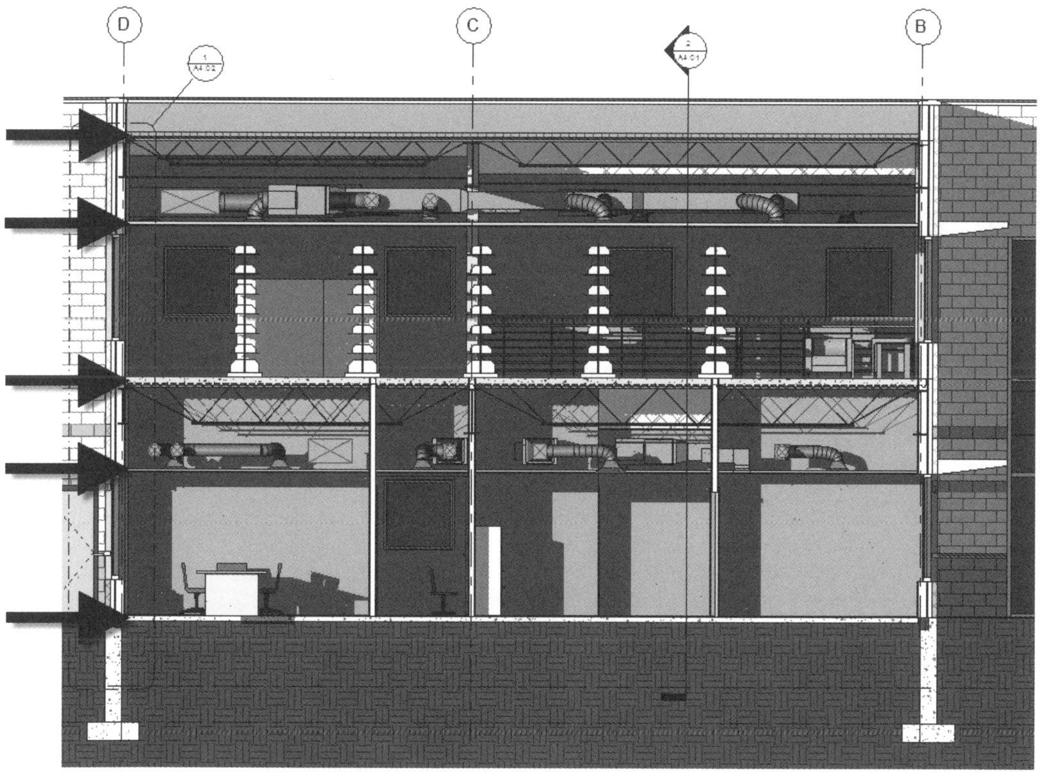

Building section showing floors, ceilings and the roof; notice structural and ductwork as well.

Exercise 6-1:
Introduction to the Roof Tool

In this lesson, you will look at the various ways to use the *Roof* tool to draw the more common roof forms used in architecture today. This exercise will be completed in a separate, newly created project. You will return to your main Revit project in the next chapter.

Start a New Revit Project:

You will start a new project for this lesson so you can quickly compare the results of using the *Roof* tool.

1. Start a new project using the **default.rte** template.

2. Switch to the **North** elevation view and rename the level named *Level 2* to **T.O. Masonry**. This will be the reference point for your roof. Click **Yes** to automatically rename the corresponding views.

   TIP: Just select the Level *datum and click on the level datum's text to rename.*

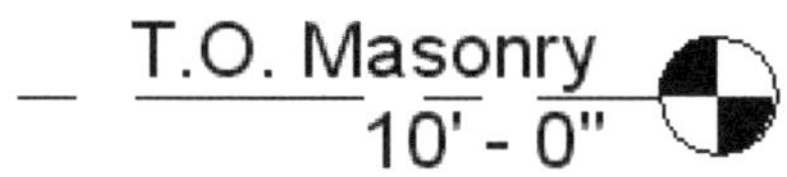

3. Switch to the ***Level 1 Floor Plan*** view.

Drawing the Buildings:

4. Set the Level 1 *"Detail Level"* to **Medium**, so the material hatching is visible within the walls.

   TIP: Use the View Control Bar at the bottom.

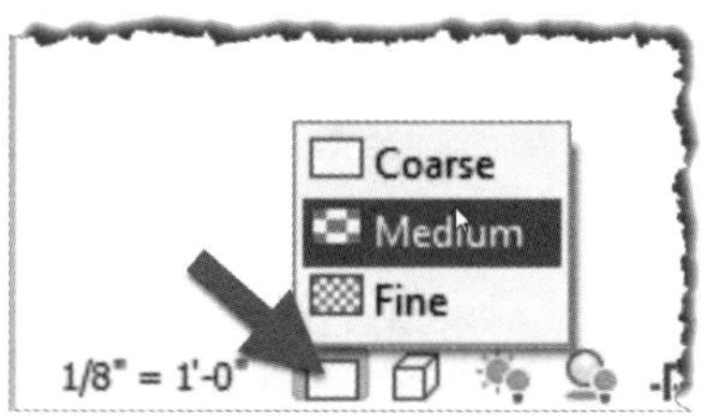

5. Using the ***Wall*** tool with the wall *Type* set to "**Exterior - Brick on Mtl. Stud**," and draw a **40′-0″ x 20′-0″** building (Figure 6-1.1).

   FYI: The default Wall height is OK; it should be 20'-0".

Be sure to draw the building within the elevation tags.

> ***TIP:*** *You can draw the building in a single step by selecting the* Rectangle *option on the Ribbon while using the* Wall *tool.*

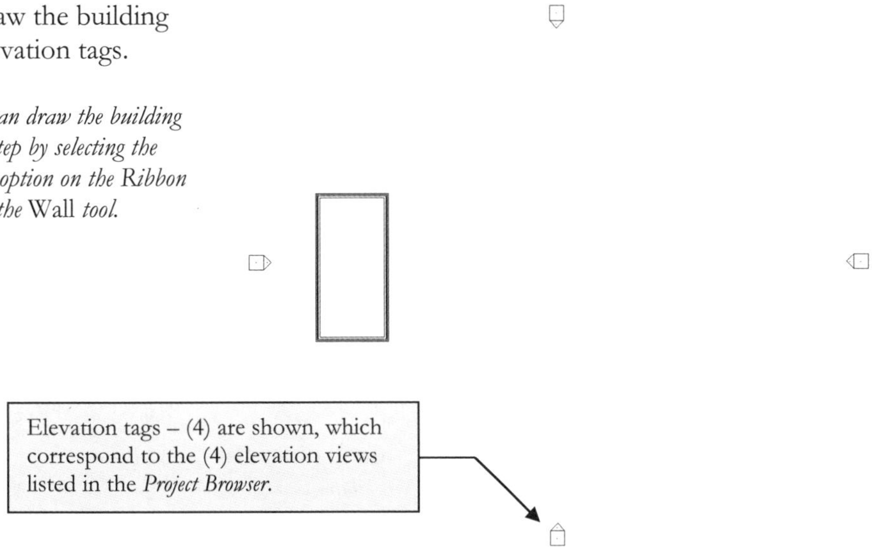

FIGURE 6-1.1 Bldg. and Elev. tags

You will copy the building to create a total of 4 buildings. You will draw a different type of roof on each one.

6. Drag a window around the walls to select them. Then use the **Array** command to set up four buildings **35′-0″ O.C.** (Figure 6-1.2). See the *Array Tip* below.

> ***TIP:*** *Zoom in and make sure the brick is on the exterior side of the wall. If not, you can select each wall and click its* flip *icon.*

> ***ARRAY TIP:*** *Select the first building, select Array, and then, just like the Copy command, define a copy 35′ to the right, then enter the number of copies.*

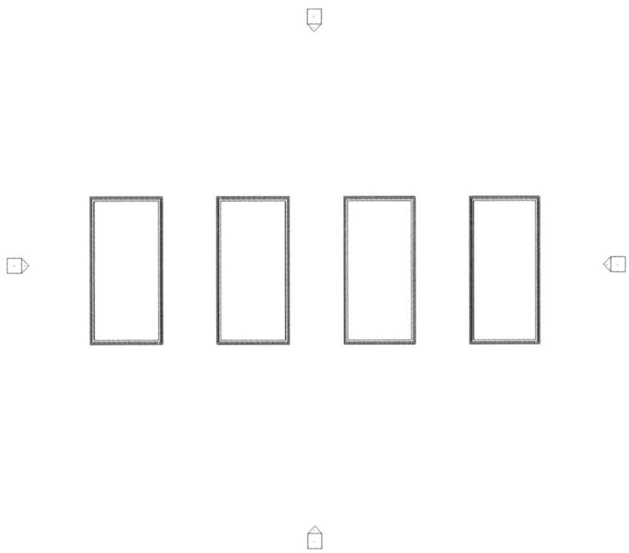

FIGURE 6-1.2 Four buildings

7. Select all of the buildings and click **Ungroup** from the *Ribbon*.

Hip Roof

The various roof forms are largely defined by the *"Defines slope"* setting. This is displayed in the *Ribbon* while the *Roof* tool is active. When a wall is selected, and the *"Defines slope"* option is selected, the roof above that portion of the wall slopes. You will see this more clearly in the examples below.

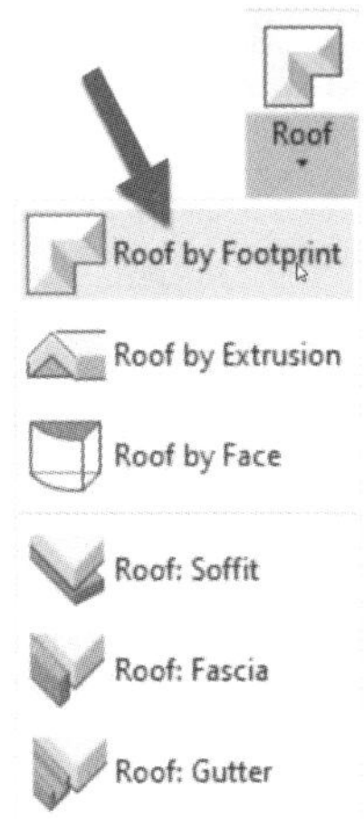

8. Switch to the **T.O. Masonry** *Floor Plan* view.

9. Select the **Architecture → Build → Roof** *(down-arrow)* → **Roof by Footprint** tool.

10. Set the overhang to **2'-0"** and make sure that the **Defines slope** option is activated (highlighted) on the *Ribbon.*

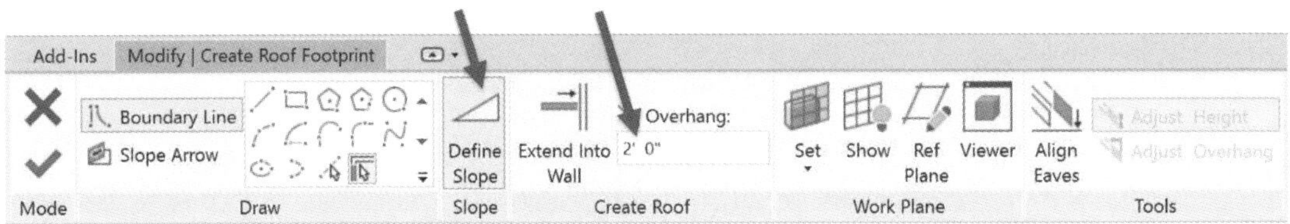

11. Select the four walls of the West (far left) building, clicking each wall one at a time.

    TIP: Make sure you select towards the exterior side of the wall; notice the review line before clicking.

12. Click **Finish Edit Mode** (i.e., the green check mark) on the *Ribbon* to finish the *Roof* tool.

13. Click the **Attach** button to attach the roof to the walls.

14. Switch to the **South** elevation (Figure 6-1.3).

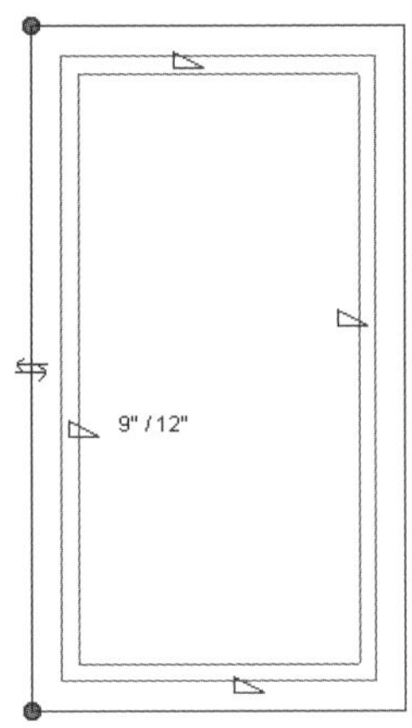

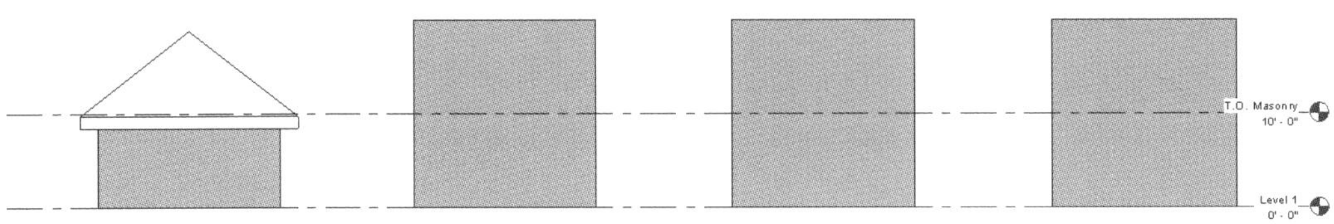

FIGURE 6-1.3 South elevation – Hip roof

You will notice that the default wall height is much higher than what we ultimately want. However, when the roof is drawn at the correct elevation, and you attach the walls to the roof, the walls automatically adjust to stop under the roof object. Additionally, if the roof is later raised or lowered, the walls will follow; you can try this in the South elevation view by simply using the *Move* tool. ***REMEMBER:** You can make revisions in any view.*

15. Switch to the **3D** view using the icon on the *QAT* (Figure 6-1.4).

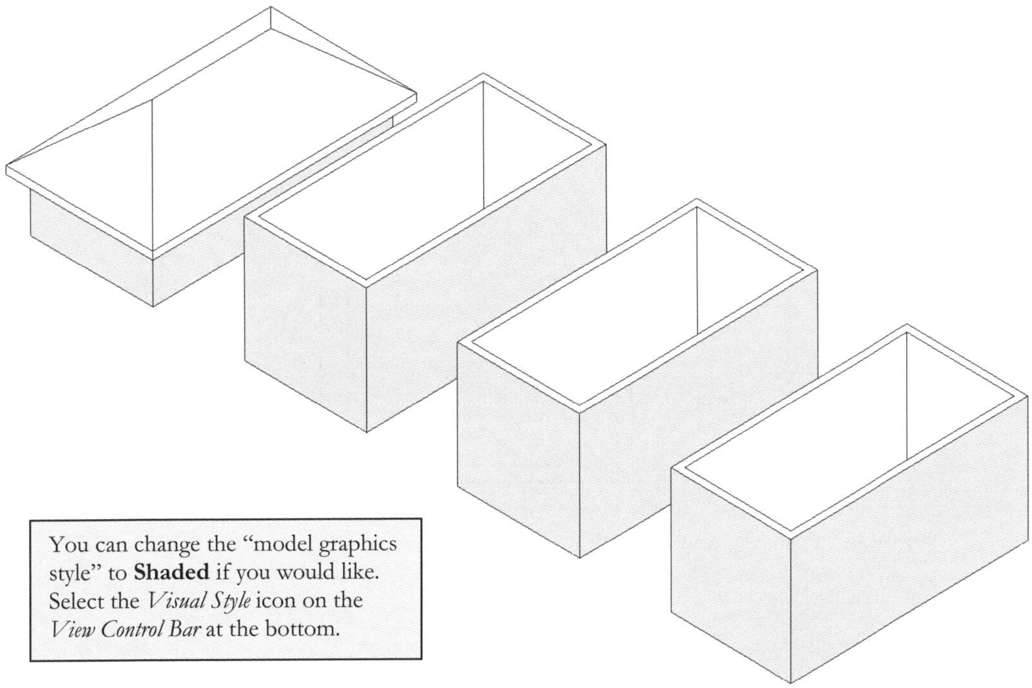

You can change the "model graphics style" to **Shaded** if you would like. Select the *Visual Style* icon on the *View Control Bar* at the bottom.

FIGURE 6-1.4 3D view – hip roof

Gable Roof

16. Switch back to the **T.O. Masonry** view (not the ceiling plan for this level).

17. Select the **Roof → Roof by Footprint** tool.

18. Set the overhang to **2′-0″** and make sure **Defines slope** is selected (highlighted) on the *Ribbon*.

19. Only select the two long (40′-0″) walls.

20. **Uncheck** the **Defines slope** option.

21. Select the remaining two walls (Figure 6-1.5).

22. Pick the **green check mark** on the *Ribbon* to finish the roof.

23. Select **Attach** to attach the walls to the roof.

24. Switch to the **South** elevation view (Figure 6-1.6).

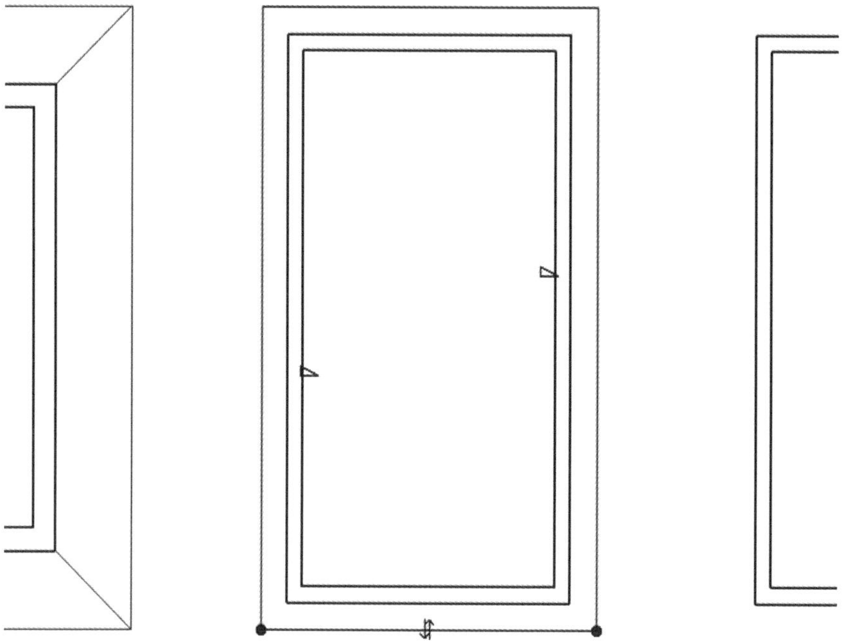

FIGURE 6-1.5 Gable – plan view

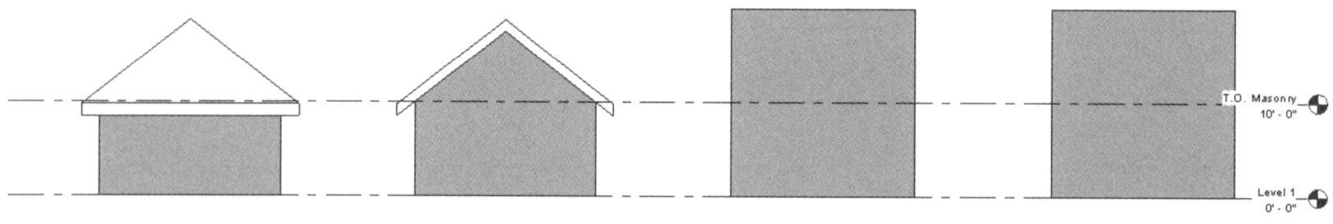

FIGURE 6-1.6 South elevation – gable roof

25. Switch to the **3D** view (Figure 6-1.7).

Notice the wall extends up to conform to the underside of the roof on the gable ends.

FYI: *You may be wondering why the roofs look odd in the floor plan view. If you remember, each view has its own* cut plane. *The* cut plane *happens to be lower than the highest part of the roof – thus, the roof is shown cut at the cut plane. If you go to Properties Palette → View Range (while nothing is selected) and then adjust the cut plane to be higher than the highest point of the roof, then you will see the roof's ridge line.*

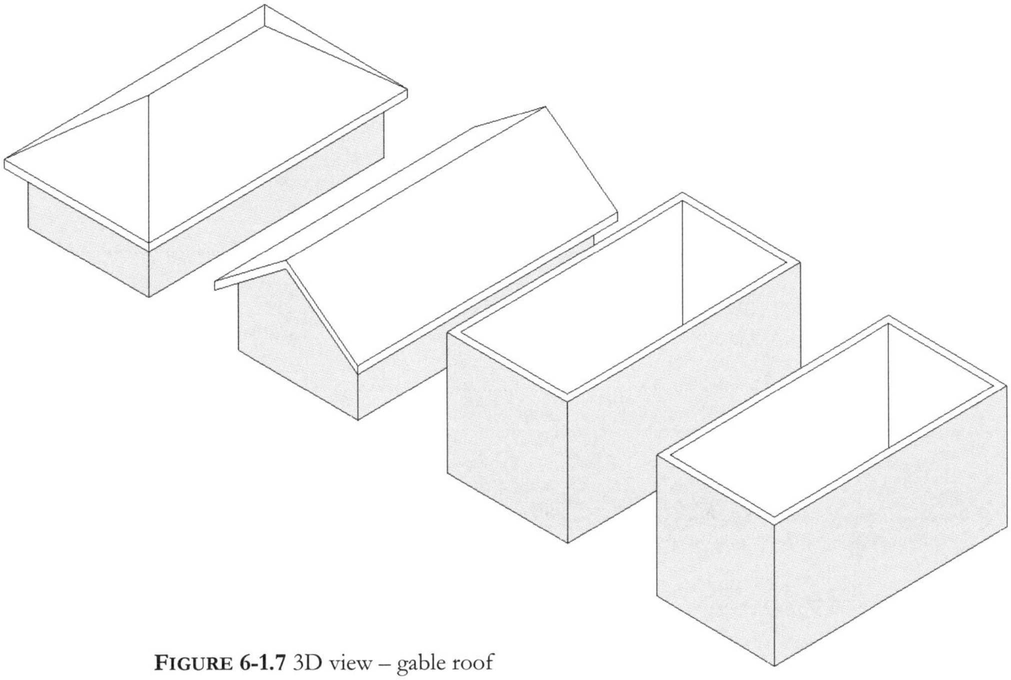

FIGURE 6-1.7 3D view – gable roof

Shed Roof

26. Switch back to the **T.O. Masonry** view.

27. Select the **Roof → Roof by Footprint** tool.

28. Check **Defines slope** on the *Ribbon.*

29. Set the overhang to **2′-0″** on the *Ribbon.*

30. Select the East wall (40′-0″ wall, right-hand side).

31. Toggle off **Defines slope** on the *Ribbon.*

32. Select the remaining three walls (Figure 6-1.8).

33. With nothing selected, set the **Slope**, aka roof pitch, to 3/12 (Figure 6-1.9) on the *Properties Palette.*

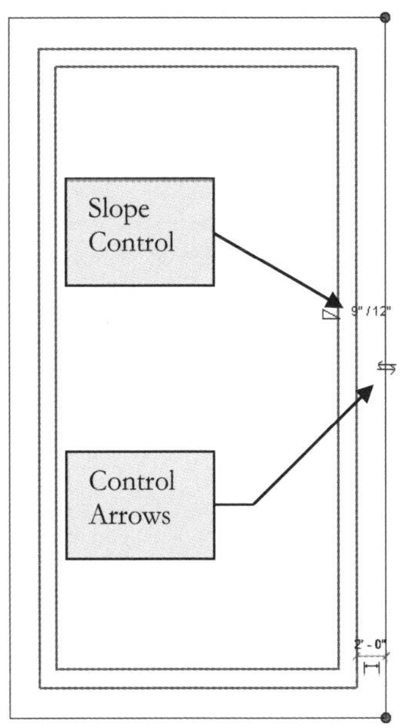

FIGURE 6-1.8 Selected walls

34. Click **Apply** on the *Properties Palette.*

35. Pick the **green check mark** on the *Ribbon* to finish the roof.

36. Select **Attach** to attach the walls to the roof.

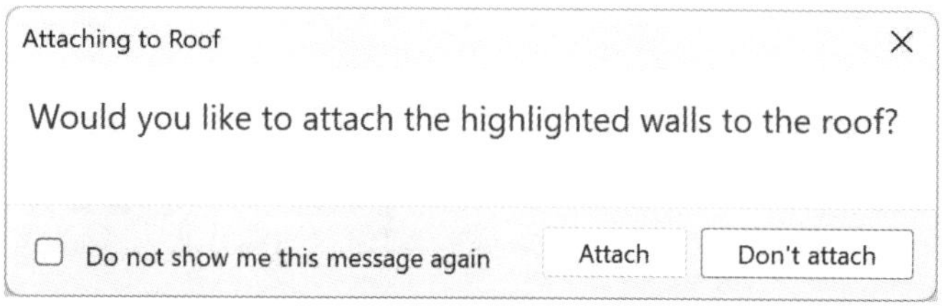

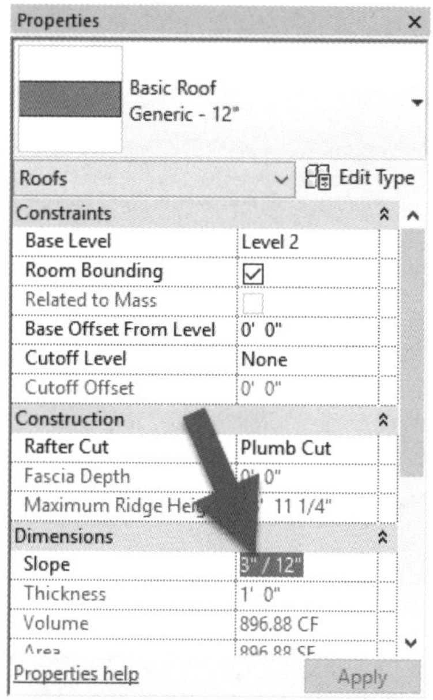

FIGURE 6-1.9
Properties for Roof tool

***FYI:** You can also change the slope of the roof by changing the Slope Control text (see Figure 6-1.8); just select the text and type a new number.*

***TIP:** You can use the Control Arrows, while the roof line is still selected, to flip the orientation of the roof overhang if you accidentally selected the wrong side of the wall and the overhang is on the inside of the building.*

37. Switch to the **South** elevation view (Figure 6-1.10).

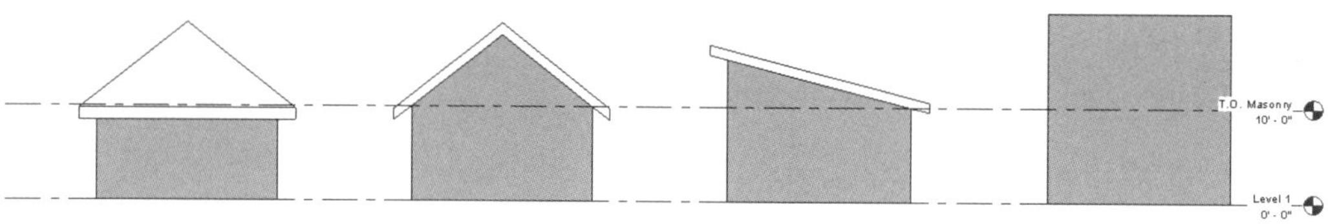

FIGURE 6-1.10 South elevation – shed roof

38. Switch to the ***Default 3D*** view (Figure 6-1.11).

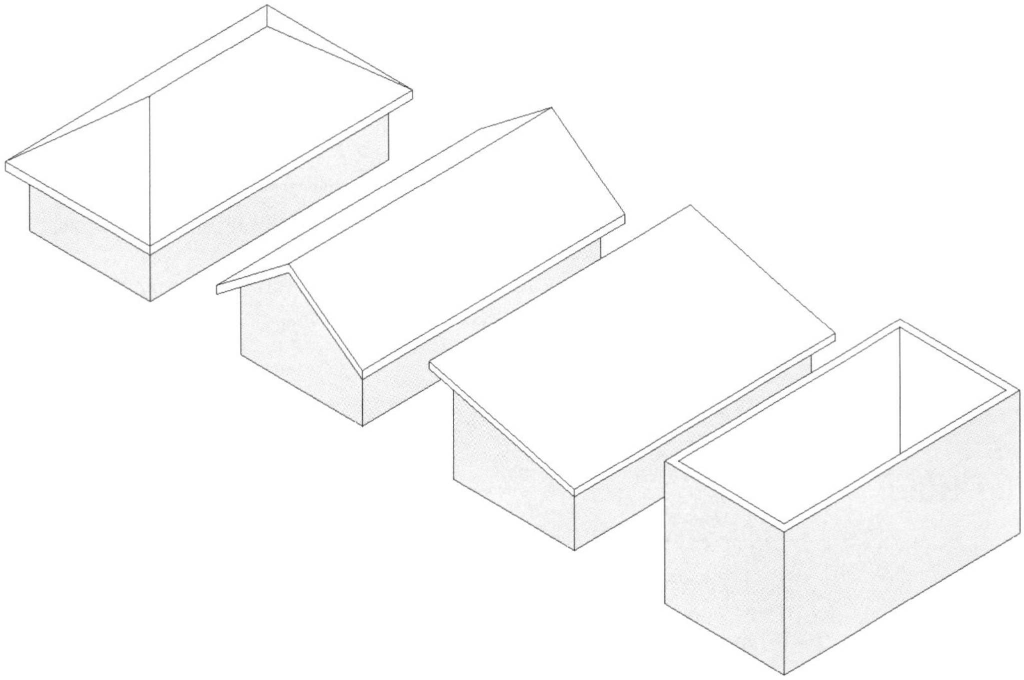

FIGURE 6-1.11 Default 3D view – shed roof

Once the roof is drawn, you can easily change the roof's overhang. You will try this on the shed roof. You will also make the roof slope in the opposite direction.

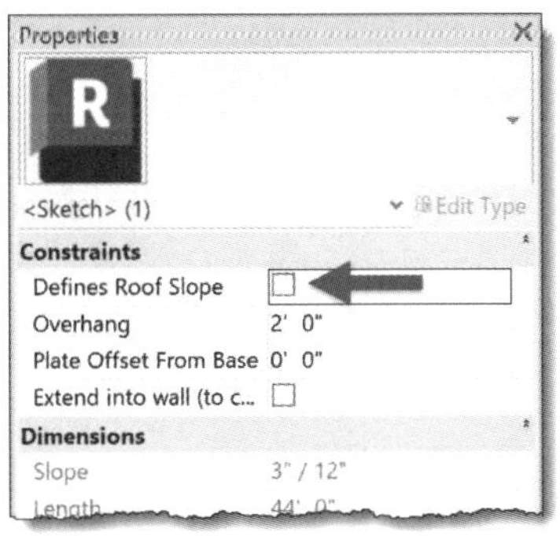

39. In **T.O. Masonry** view, select **Modify** from the *Ribbon*, and then select the shed roof.

40. Click **Edit Footprint** from the *Ribbon.*

41. Click on the East roof sketch-line to select it.

42. Uncheck **Defines slope** in properties.

43. Now select the West roofline and check **Defines slope**. Make sure the *Slope* is still set to **3"/12"**.

If you were to select the green check mark now, the shed roof would be sloping in the opposite direction. But, before you do that, you will adjust the roof overhang at the high side.

44. Click on the East roofline again to select it.

45. Change the overhang to **6′-0″** in properties.

Changing the overhang only affects the selected roofline.

46. Select the **green check mark**.

47. Switch to the South view to see the change (Figure 6-1.12).

Thus, you can see it is easier to edit an object than to delete it and start over. Just remember you have to be in sketch mode (i.e., *Edit Sketch*) to make changes to the roof. Also, when a sketch line is selected, its properties are displayed in the *Properties Palette.* That concludes the shed roof example.

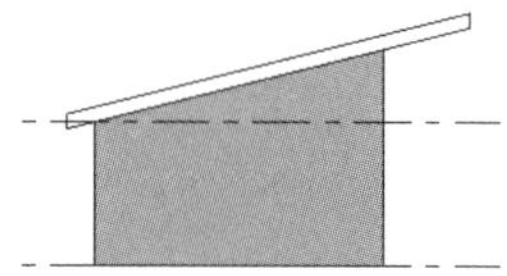

FIGURE 6-1.12 South elevation – shed roof (revised)

Flat Roof:

48. Switch back to the **T.O. Masonry** *Floor Plan* view.

49. Select the **Roof → Roof by Footprint** tool.

50. Set the overhang to **2′-0″** and make sure **Defines slope** is not active (i.e., un-highlighted) on the *Ribbon.*

51. Select all four walls, picking towards the exterior side of the wall.

52. Pick the **green check mark**.

53. Select **Attach** to attach the walls to the roof.

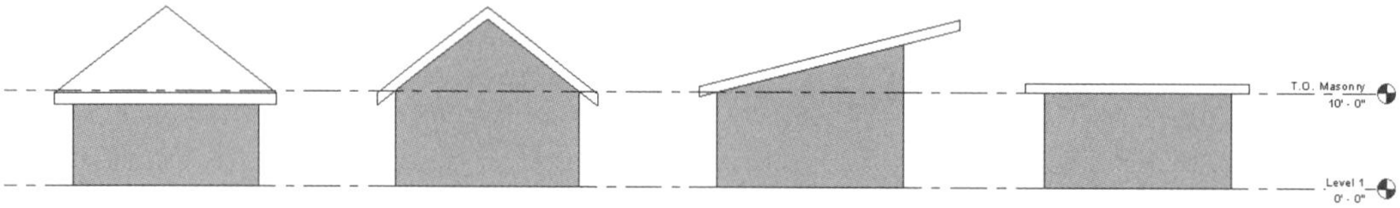

FIGURE 6-1.13 South elevation – flat roof

54. Switch to the South elevation view (Figure 6-1.13).

55. Also, take a look at the **Default 3D view** (Figure 6-1.14).

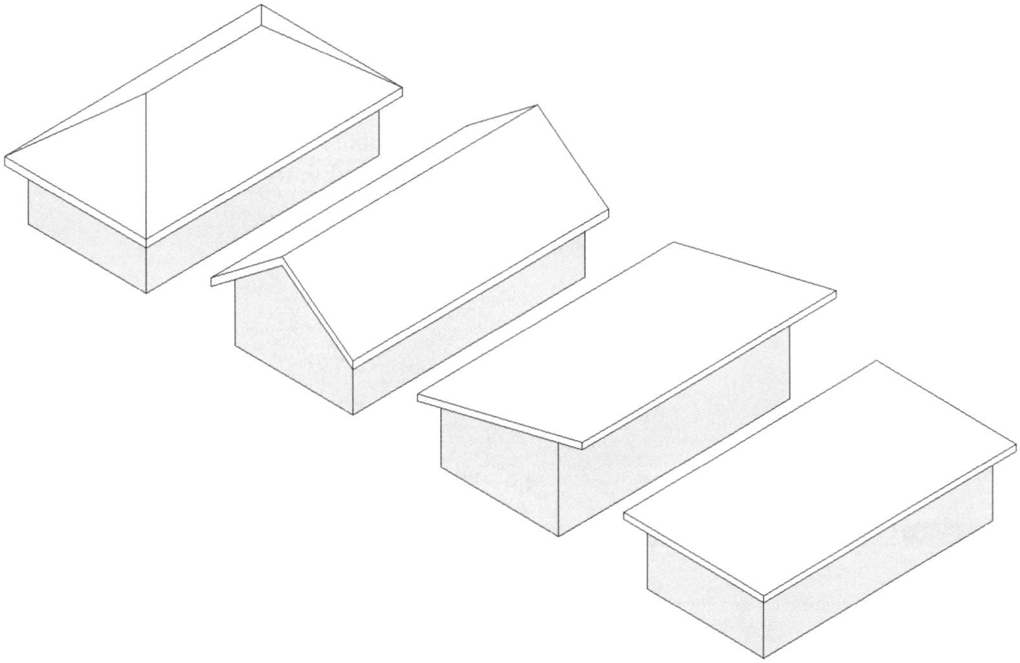

FIGURE 6-1.14 Default 3D view – flat roof

56. Save your project as **ex6-1.rvt**.

Want More?

Revit has additional tools and techniques available for creating more complex roof forms. However, that is beyond the scope of this book. If you want to learn more about roofs, or anything else, take a look at one of the following resources:

- Revit **Web Site:** www.autodesk.com
- Revit **Newsgroup** (potential answers to specific questions)
  www.augi.com; www.revitcity.com; www.autodesk.com; www.revitforum.org
- Revit **Blogs** information from individuals (some work for Autodesk and some don't)
  www.BIMchapters.blogspot.com, www.revitoped.com

Reference material: Roof position relative to wall

The remaining pages in this exercise are for reference only and do not need to be applied to your model. You are encouraged to study this information so you become more familiar with how the *Roof* tool works.

The following examples use a brick and concrete block wall. The image below shows the *Structure* properties for said wall type. Notice the only item within the *Core Boundary* section is the *Masonry – Concrete Block* (i.e., CMU), which is 7⅝″ thick (nominally 8″). Keep this in mind as you read through the remaining material.

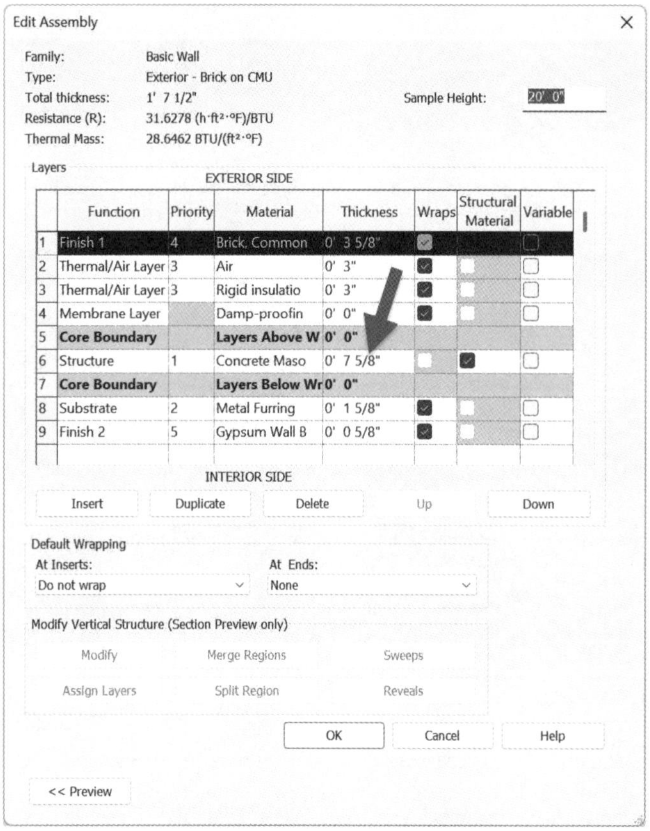

The following examples will show you how to control the position of the roof system relative to the wall below, both vertically and horizontally. The roof properties that dictate its position basically involve relationships between three things: the **Level Datum**, the exterior **Wall System**, and the bottom edge of the **Roof System**. There are several other properties (e.g., pitch, construction, fascia, etc.) related to the roof that will not be mentioned at the moment, so the reader may focus on a few basic principles.

The examples on this page show a sloped roof sketched with *Extend into wall (to core)* enabled and the *Overhang* set to 2′-0″. Because *Extend into wall (to core)* was selected, the bottom edge of the roof is positioned relative to the *Core Boundary* of the exterior wall rather than the finished face of the wall. See the discussion about the wall's *Core Boundary* on the previous page.

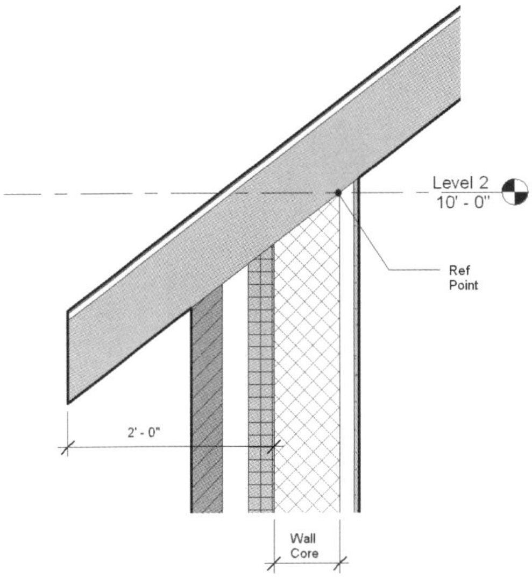

Extend to Core + Rafter

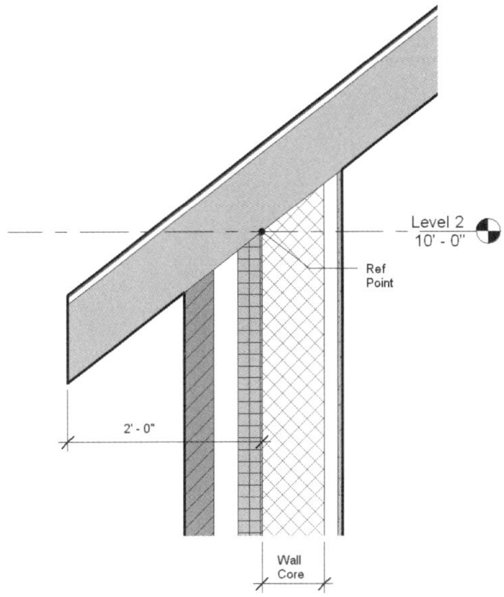

Extend to Core + Truss

Revit Roof Properties under Consideration:

Extend Into Wall: (To Core) This option was *highlighted* on the *Ribbon* while sketching the roof.

Rafter or Truss: This option is an *Instance Parameter* of the roof object; the example on the above left is set to *Rafter*, and the other is set to *Truss*.

NOTE: *The* Extend into Wall (to core) *option affects the relative relationship between the wall and the roof, as you will see by comparing this example with the one on the next page.*

Base Level: Set to *Level 2*: By associating various objects to a level, it is possible to adjust the floor elevation (i.e., *Level Datum*) and have doors, windows, floors, furniture, roofs, etc., all move vertically with that level.

Base Offset: From Level Set to *0′-0″*: This can be a positive or negative number and will remain unchanged even if the level moves.

The examples on this page show a sloped roof sketched with *Extend into wall (to core)* NOT enabled, and the *Overhang* still set to 2′-0″. Notice that the roof overhang is derived from the exterior face of the wall (as opposed to the Core Boundary face in the previous example, where *Extend into wall* was enabled).

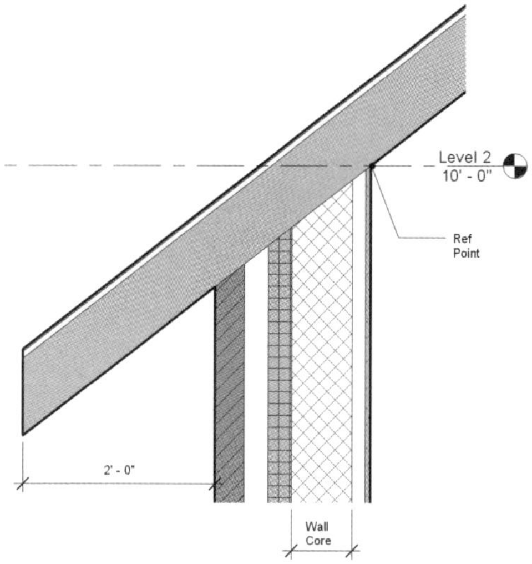

Rafter + not extended to core

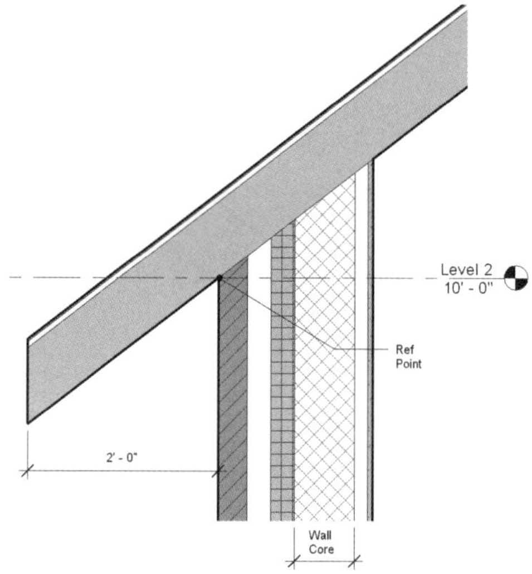

Truss + not extended to core

Revit Roof Properties under Consideration:

Extend Into Wall: (To Core) This option was *NOT highlighted* on the *Ribbon* when sketching the roof.

Rafter or Truss: This option is an *Instance Parameter* of the roof object; the example on the above left is set to *Rafter*, and the other is set to *Truss*.

Base Level: Set to *Level 2*. By associating various objects to a level, it is possible to adjust the floor elevation (i.e., *Level Datum*) and have doors, windows, floors, roofs, etc., all move vertically with that level.

Base Offset: From Level Set to *0′-0″*. This can be a positive or negative number and will remain unchanged even if the level moves.

As you can see from the previous examples, you would most often want to have *Extend to wall (to core)* selected while sketching a roof because it would not typically make sense to position the roof based on the outside face of brick or the inside face of gypsum board for commercial construction.

Even though you may prefer to have *Extend to wall (to core)* selected, you might like to have a 2′-0″ overhang relative to the face of the brick rather than the exterior face of concrete block. This can be accomplished in one of two ways:

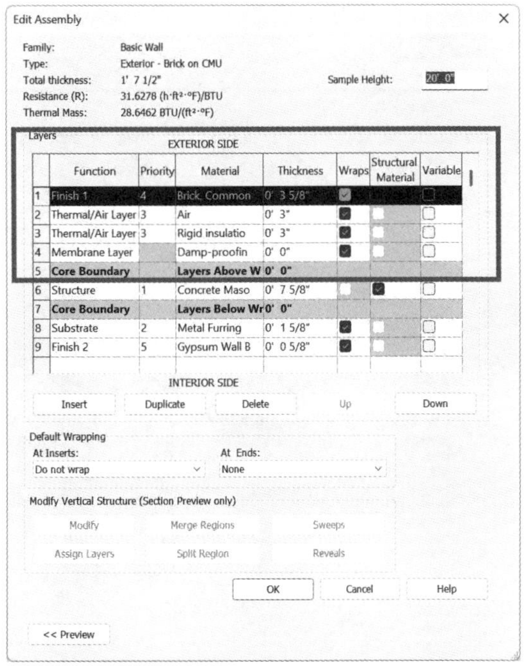

(A) You can modify the overhang while sketching the roof to include the wall thickness that occurs between the face of the wall and the face of the core: 2′-0″ + 9⅝″ = 2′-9⅝″. See the image to the right.

(B) The second option is to manually edit the sketch lines. You can add dimensions while in *Sketch* mode, select the sketch line to move, and then edit the dimension. The dimension can also be *Locked* to maintain the roof edge position relative to the wall. When you finish the sketch, the dimensions are hidden.

Energy Truss:

In addition to controlling the roof overhang, you might also want to control the roof properties to accommodate an energy truss with what is called an *energy heal*, which allows for more insulation to occur directly above the exterior wall.

To do this, you would use the *Extend into wall (to core) + Truss* option described above and then set the *Base Offset from Level* to 1′-0″ (for a 1′-0″ energy heal). See the image and the *Properties Palette* shown on the next page.

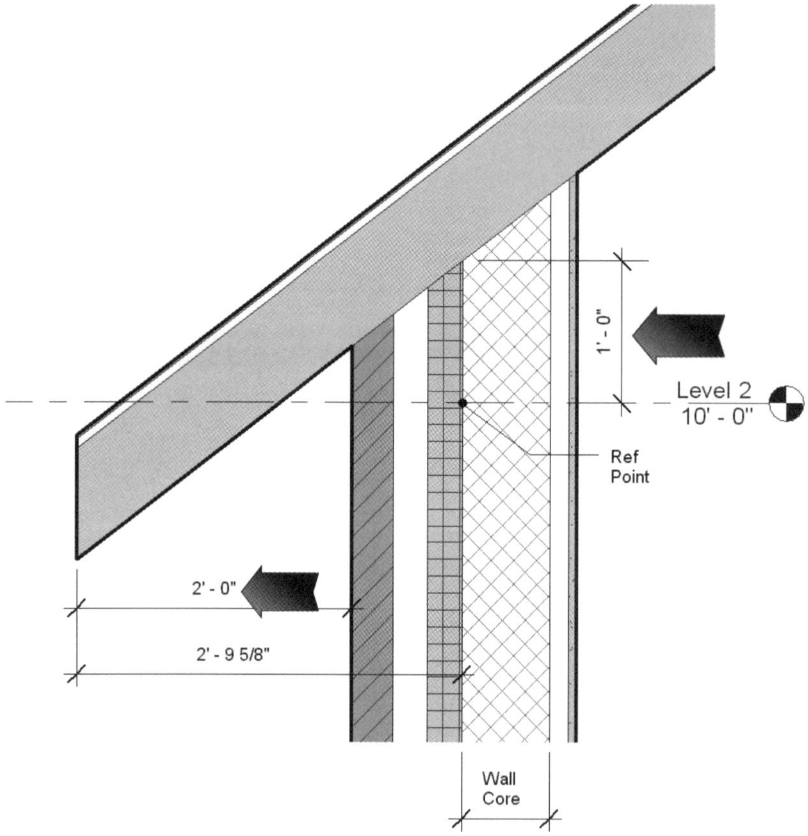

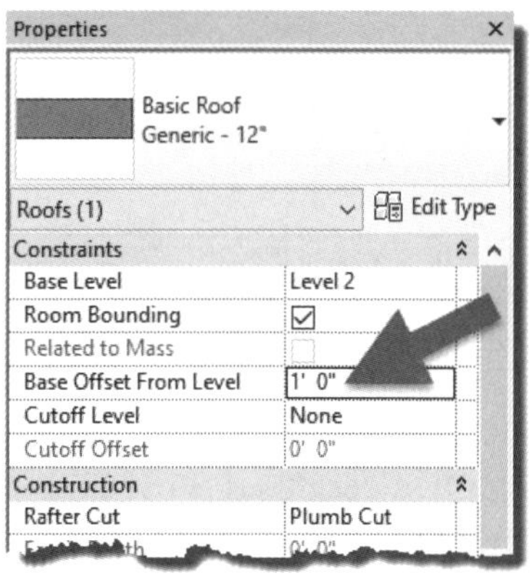

Many other properties and techniques exist for developing the roof of a project, such as the *Rafter Cut* and *Fascia Depth,* which control the fascia design. Also, you can apply a sweep to a roof edge to add a 1x fascia board around the building. These are intermediate-to-advanced concepts and will not be covered here.

This concludes the study of the *Roof* tool!

Exercise 6-2:
Law Office Roof

The template file you started with already has a **Roof** plan view created. However, you renamed that to Level 2 and then created a new *Roof* datum and corresponding views. If you recall, the *Roof* datum is at 26′-8″ (see page 5-34). This Roof plan view creates a working plane for the *Roof* tool; the thickness of your roof sits on top of the reference plane.

Create a Flat Roof:

1. Open your **Law Office** BIM file; use the Chapter 6 "starter file" if you had problems with the previous chapter (see the inside front cover for access to the online files).

2. Switch to the **Roof** plan view.

Your image should look something like Figure 6-2.1. The exterior walls you can see in the **Roof** plan view were created in Lesson 5; the specified height extends into the Roof's *View Range*. The interior walls are visible, but are shaded gray (i.e., halftone); this is because of a view setting called **Underlay**. The Underlay feature is used to visually coordinate items between floors. In the roof plan you might want to know where the wall between the two toilet rooms is to discern where the vent pipe will penetrate the roof.

You will be selecting the exterior walls to define the edge of the roof. Before you can finish a roof sketch, you must have the entire perimeter of the roof drawn with line endpoints connected. Revit allows you to sketch additional lines and use tools like *Trim* to complete the perimeter of the roof sketch if needed.

3. Select the ***Roof*** tool from the *Architecture* tab; click the down-arrow.

4. Select **Roof by Footprint** from the pop-up menu.

5. Make sure **Pick Walls** is selected *Ribbon: Architecture → Draw (panel)*.

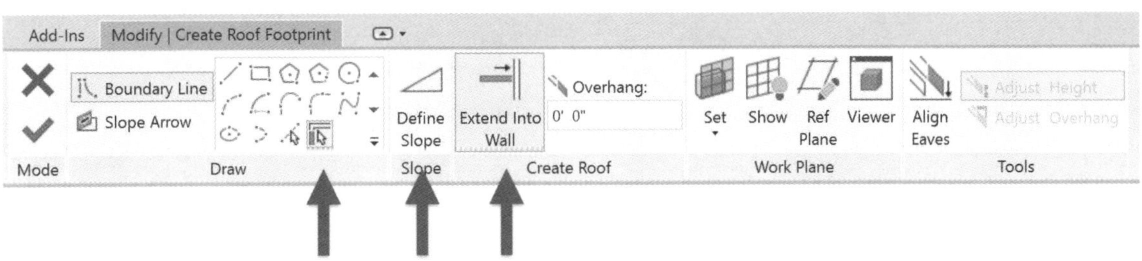

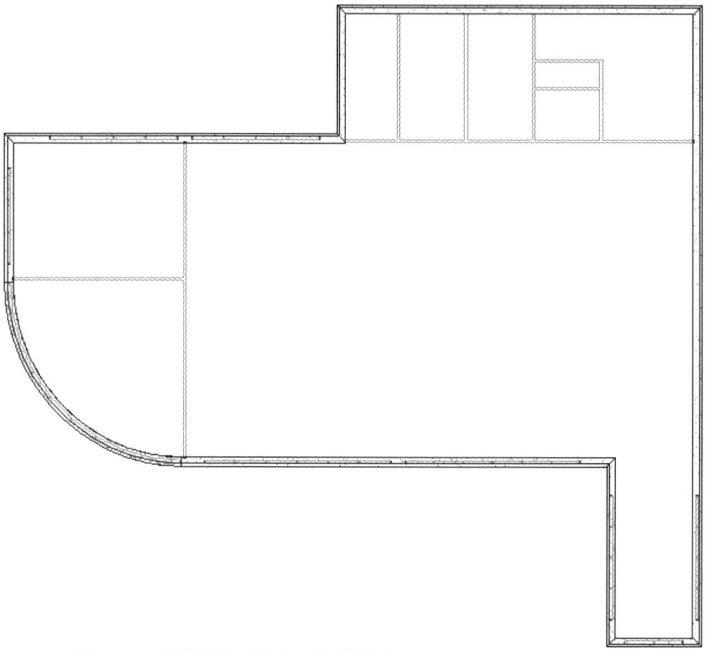

FIGURE 6-2.1 Roof Plan; initial view

6. Uncheck **Defines Slope** on the *Ribbon* to make a flat roof.

7. Change the drop-down selector, on the *Properties Palette*, to **New <Sketch>** (Figure 6-2.2).

These are the properties for the sketch lines, not the roof element (compare *Roofs Instance Properties*).

8. Notice if this were a sloped roof, you could change the roof pitch here if **Defines Roof Slope** were checked.

9. Change the drop-down back to **Roofs** so you can see the roof element properties.

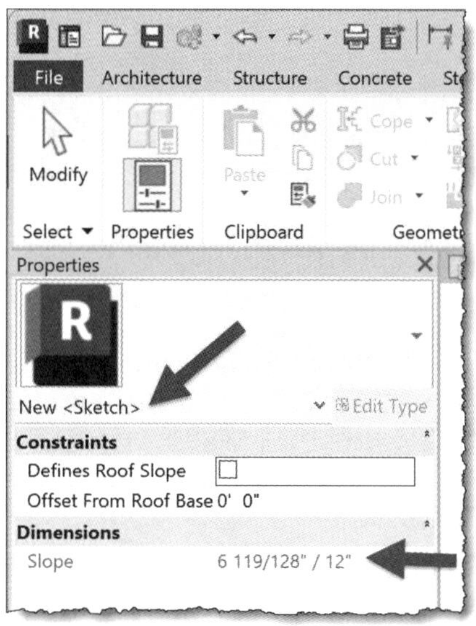

FIGURE 6-2.2 Roof Properties

10. Check **Extend to wall core** on the *Ribbon*.

We will digress for a moment to explain exactly what "extend to wall core" means. This will help ensure you create the roof correctly. First the properties of the wall will be exposed so you understand what constitutes a wall type core. Next, you will learn how this ties into the *Roof* tool. If you want to follow along, you can select *Cancel Roof* on the *Ribbon* and then repeat the previous steps before moving on to the next numbered steps.

Back on page 6-18 and following you explored the exterior wall style. There it pointed out where to view/edit the "structure" of the wall *Layers*, via the *Edit Assembly* dialog. The graphic below shows a variety of wall types with their wall cores highlighted. Within the *Edit Assembly* dialog, the highlighted Layer(s) fall within the *Core Boundary* section.

Generally speaking, the *Wall Core* represents the real-world structural portion of the wall. Walls can be both drawn and dimensioned based on the faces and centerline of the wall core. The *Wall Core* has a higher precedence when walls intersect. Revit automatically cleans up similar *Layers* within other wall types. Additionally, in the case of this exercise, the wall core is used in conjunction with creating the roof element. This is also true for floors as well.

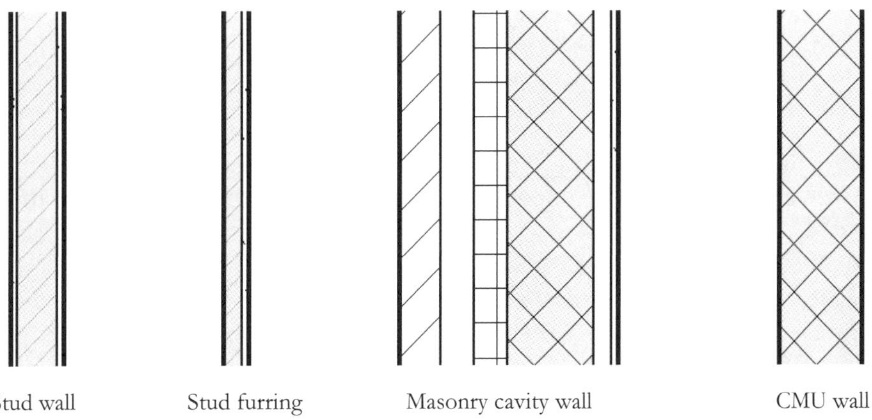

Notice a few things about the walls above before moving on. The two walls on the left have the metal stud *Layer* within the *Wall Core*, but the masonry cavity wall does not. In the first two, the studs are the structural element holding up the wall; in the latter the CMU holds up the wall and the metal studs are just used to fasten the gypsum board to it. Finally, the fourth wall contains one *Layer* which is the *Wall Core*. Every wall must have at least one *Layer* within the *Core Boundary*. An example of two *Layers* within the *Core Boundary* might be the studs and the sheathing which is used for shear, making both *Layers* part of the structural makeup of the wall. In this case you would never want any intersecting wall to interrupt the sheathing.

When using the *Roof* tool, it is possible to have Revit automatically sketch the roof's edge based on one of the two faces of a *Wall Core*. Therefore, it is important to select towards the side of the wall relating to the core face you want. The two images below show the two options possible when *Extend wall to core* is selected within the *Roof* tool.

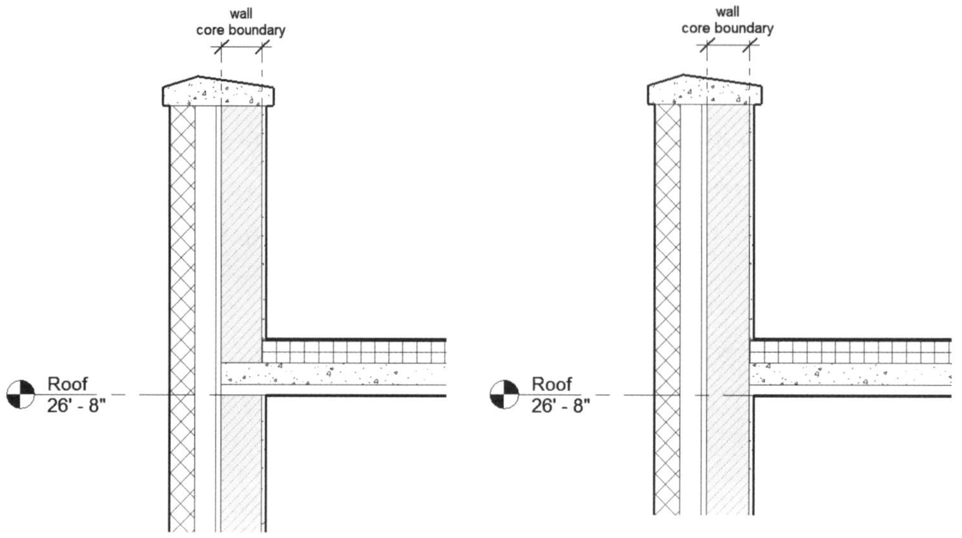

Roof tool: Extend to core options

Notice in both images above, the gypsum board *Layer* within the wall type is interrupted by the roof. You will employ the option on the left. However, either option is perfectly valid depending on how the building is intended to be constructed: a separate parapet or balloon framing.

In either case, due to the use of metal studs, the roof deck will be supported by steel beams at the perimeter. The structural system will be added in a later chapter. Revit does not care if a roof or floor is not properly supported, which is not the case with beams, as you will see in the upcoming structural section.

11. Select each of the exterior walls, favoring the exterior side when clicking the wall. Just before clicking, the dashed reference line should be at the exterior face of the wall core per the example shown in Figure 6-2.3.

TIP: Use the flip control *icon while the line is still selected if your dashed reference line is on the wrong side (i.e., interior).*

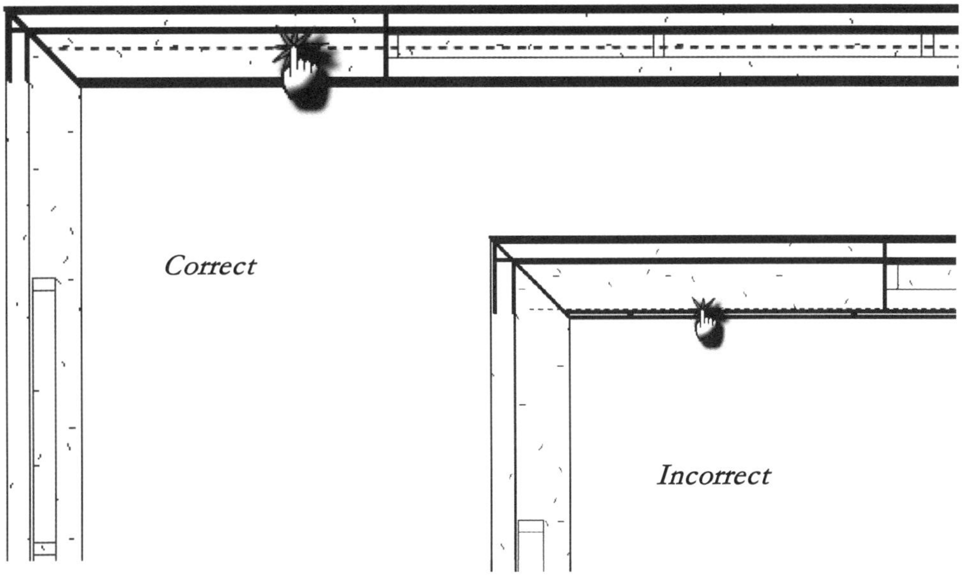

FIGURE 6-2.3 Roof Plan; four walls selected for sketching roof footprint

Note that the exterior walls, just selected, can be selected in any order.

All of the sketch lines should have automatically trimmed at the corners (Figure 6-2.4). If not, you would need to use the *Trim* tool to close the perimeter of the roof footprint. Many of your 2D drafting skills learned earlier in this book can be applied to this type of *Sketch* mode.

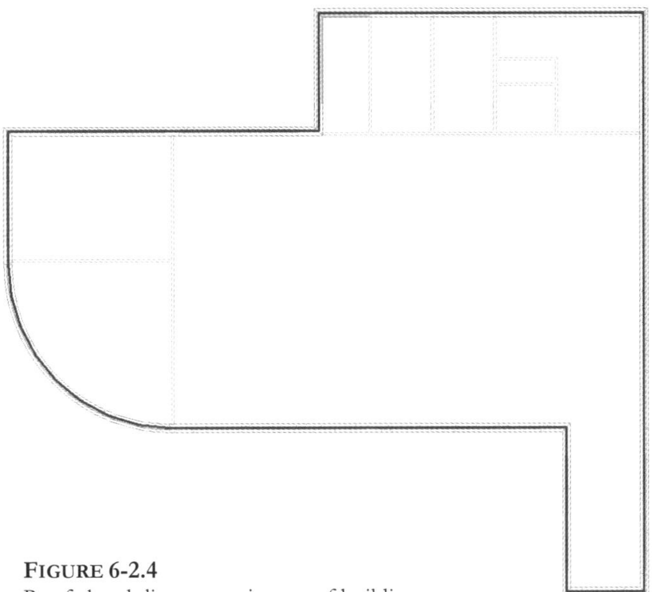

FIGURE 6-2.4
Roof sketch lines at perimeter of building

Take a moment and look at the *Properties Palette.* As already mentioned, the overall roof thickness sits on top of the *Level datum* of the view in which it was drawn. Typically, the *Roof Level datum* relates to the top of the steel beams, thus the roof occurs above that elevation.

Notice the parameter *Base Offset From Level.* This allows you to enter a distance in which to move the roof up from the *Base Level.* If you entered 2′-0″ and the roof level datum changed, the roof would still be 2′-0″ above the repositioned level datum.

Before completing the roof you will learn how to specify the *Roof Type.* This is similar to walls in that various *Layers* can be defined within the roof element.

12. Select **Edit Type** button on the *Properties Palette.* Notice the various *Parameters* and *Types* available; click **OK** to close without making any changes.

Notice in Figure 6-2.5 that the *Type* drop-down at the top lists five roof types.

13. Make sure the *Type Selector* is set to **Insulation on Metal Deck – EPDM** on the *Properties Palette.*

Now that the roof footprint is complete you can finish the roof.

14. Select **Finish Edit Mode** (green checkmark) from the *Ribbon.*

15. Click **Don't attach** to the prompt to attach walls below to the roof (Figure 6-2.6).

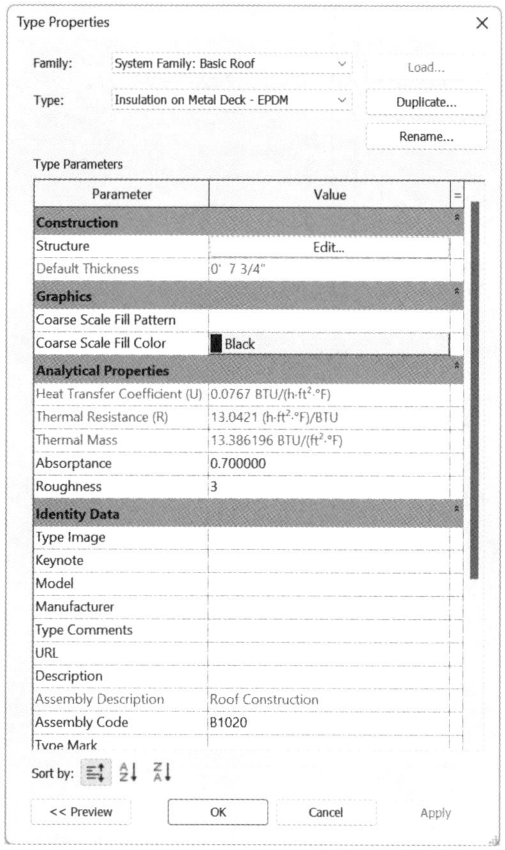

FIGURE 6-2.5 Roof type properties; selecting roof type

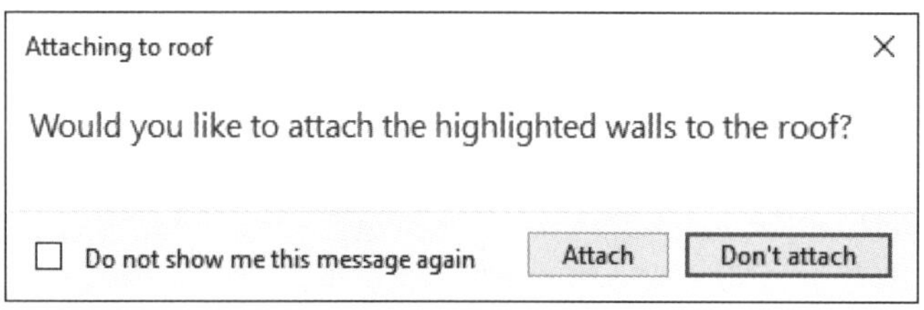

FIGURE 6-2.6 Roof Plan; attachment prompt

16. Click **Yes** to join the roof and exterior walls.

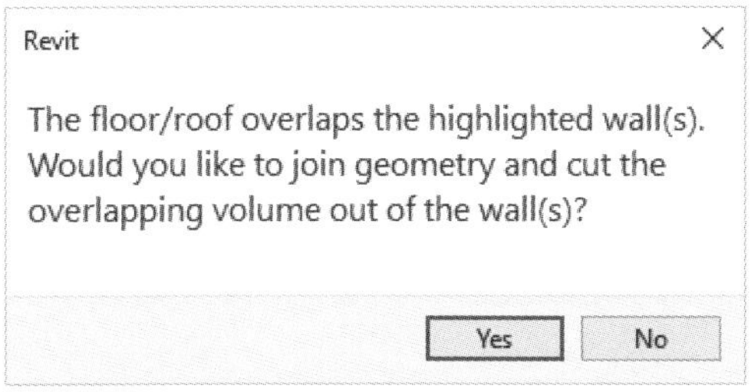

FIGURE 6-2.7 Roof Plan; join and cut prompt

Joining the roof and walls via this prompt is what interrupts the stud *Layer* as shown in the graphic on page 6-20.

17. Switch to your ***3D*** view via the *Quick Access Toolbar.*

Your project should look like Figure 6-2.8.

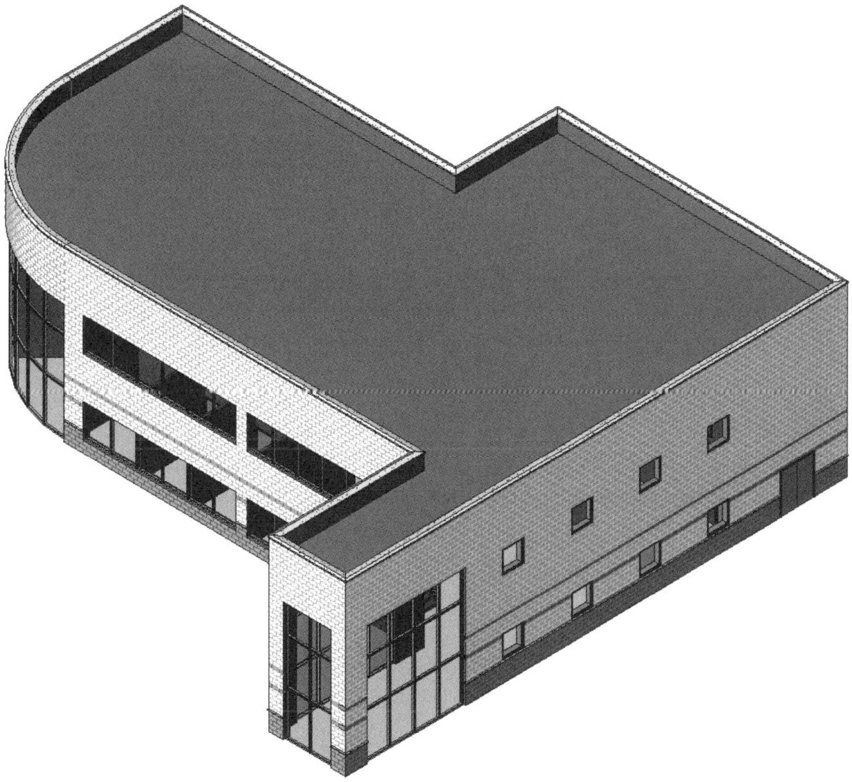

FIGURE 6-2.8 3D View; roof added

18. Switch back to your **Roof** floor plan view.

Despite the fact that you just added a roof, which is a solid 3D element, you might still see the second floor walls, depending on a specific view setting. When the **Underlay** feature is set, it will show the specified level on top of whatever is visible in the current view. At this point we would not want to see the Level 2 walls.

If the level 2 walls are showing in the roof plan view, do the following:

19. Make sure nothing is selected so the ***View Properties*** are showing in the *Properties Palette.*

20. Set the Underlay *Parameter* **Base Level** to **None** (Figure 6-2.9).

21. Click **Apply** to make the adjustment to the view.

The *Level 2* walls are now removed from the **Roof** plan view.

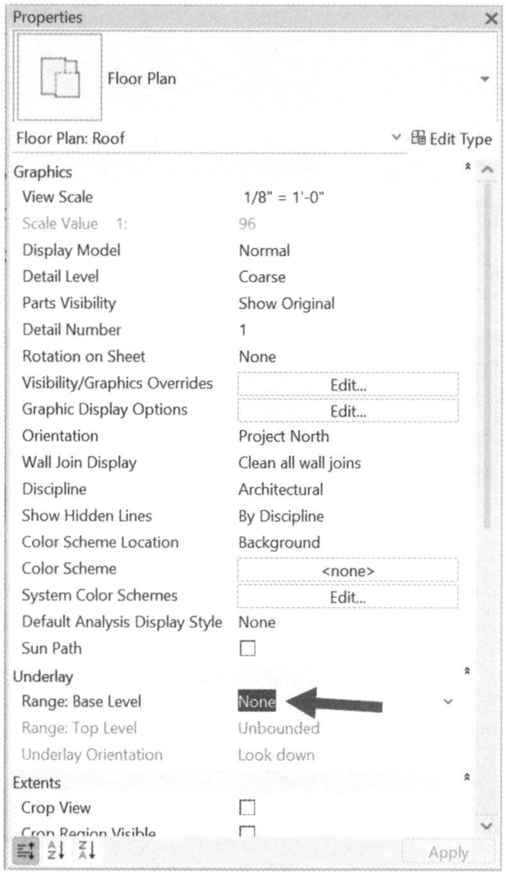

FIGURE 6-2.9 Roof plan view; view propertied

At some point in the project you would edit the roof surface to have the required sloped surfaces to shed rain water towards the roof drains. But those types of edits are best saved for later in the design process. If you spent the time to model that information now and then the client decided to make a big change, you would have to redo all that work.

22. **Save** your project.

TIP: You have probably figured this out by now: the last view open when you close the project will be the view that is opened the next time the project is opened.

Exercise 6-3:
Floor Systems

In this exercise you will add the Level 1 and Level 2 floors. The Level 1 floor is a slab-on-grade example, as the building has no basement, and Level 2 is a composite concrete and metal deck floor. Both of these floors are already defined in the project, which stems from the template from which it was started.

Level 1, Slab on Grade:

Sketching floors is a lot like sketching roofs; you can select walls to define the perimeter and draw lines to fill in the blanks and add holes, or cut outs, in the floor object.

1. **Open** your Revit project (Law Office).
2. Switch to the **Level 1** floor plan view if needed.
3. Select **Architecture → Build → Floor** (down-arrow) → **Floor**.
4. Click the ***Type Selector*** on the *Properties Palette.*
5. Set the *Type* to **4″ Concrete Slab** (if not already); see Figure 6-3.1.
6. Click **Apply** to accept the change.

Notice, in the *Properties Palette*, the *Height Offset From Level* which allows the slab to be moved up or down relative to the *Level* that hosts the slab.

Also, the *Phase Created* allows you to manage which portion of the building is existing and new. The law office project is all new, so you do not have to worry about any *Phase* settings.

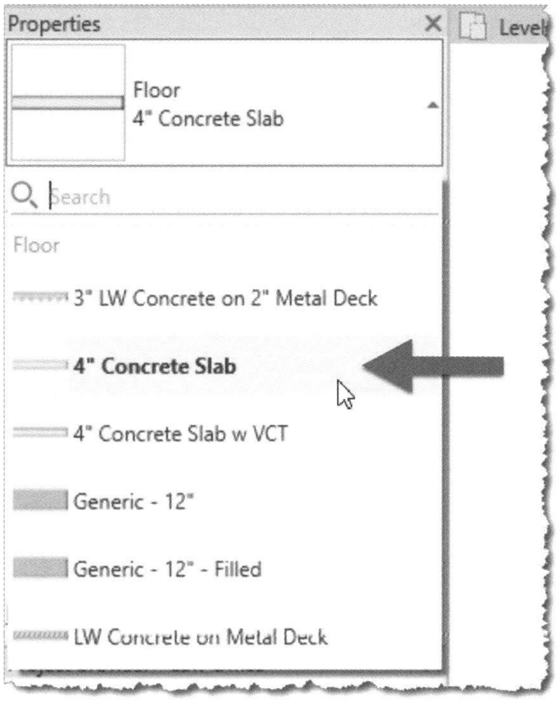

FIGURE 6-3.1 Floor tool; type selector

Similar to the *Roof Sketch* mode, you will be drawing the *Boundary Line* for the floor by picking walls. Ultimately your slab will stop at the foundation walls, but they have not been drawn yet so you will draw the slab to the interior face of core. Remember, for the roof you went to the exterior face of core.

7. Make sure the *Ribbon* matches the settings shown in Figure 6-3.2.
    a. *Boundary Line* selected
    b. *Pick Walls* icon selected
    c. *Extend into wall (to core)* checked

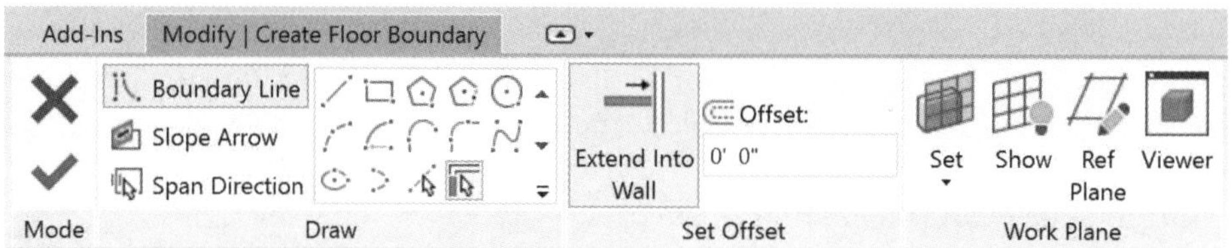

FIGURE 6-3.2 Floor tool; ribbon and settings

8. Select the interior side of each exterior wall, with the exception of the curtain wall (do not select it yet). See Figure 6-3.3.

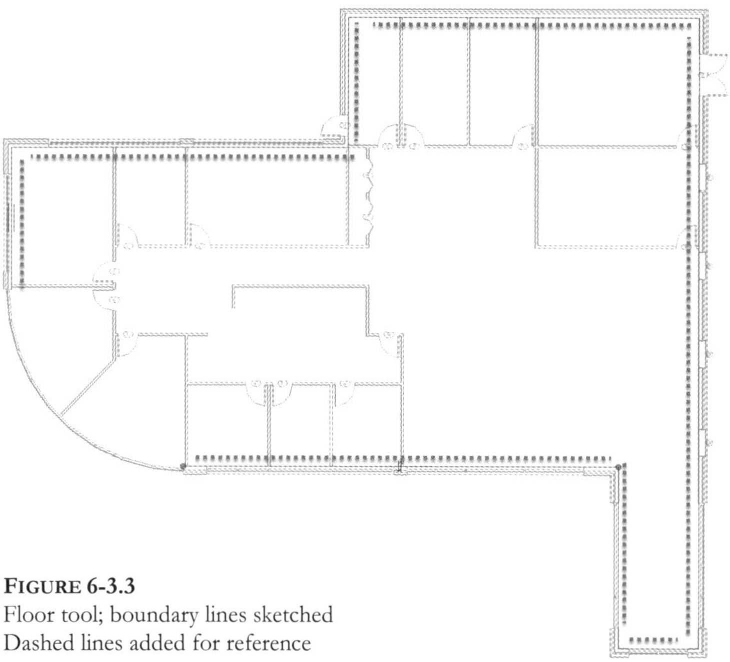

FIGURE 6-3.3
Floor tool; boundary lines sketched
Dashed lines added for reference

You will select the curtain wall in a moment. However, it is a different thickness and does not have a core like the other walls. So, when you pick the wall, the floor boundary sketch line will be centered on the curtain wall. You will have to manually sketch lines and trim them at each end of the curtain wall in order to properly enclose the floor boundary.

9. Select the curtain wall, which in turn adds a curved boundary line.

10. Zoom in to each end of the curtain wall, and select the ***Line*** icon from the *Draw* panel on the *Create Floor Boundary* tab.

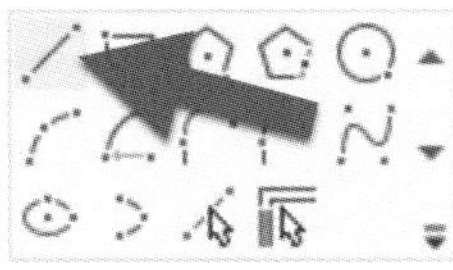

11. Sketch a line, using snaps, from the end of the curtain wall to the adjacent wall sketch line (Figure 6-3.4).

12. Use the ***Trim*** tool, while still in the *Floor Sketch* mode, to clean up any corners that are not perfect and/or connected. This is likely only going to be at the transition from the curved wall to the orthogonal walls.

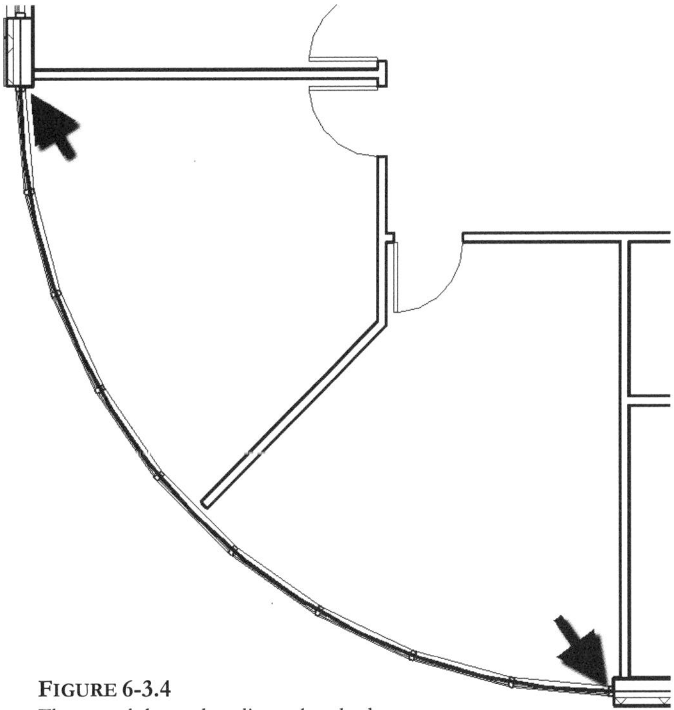

FIGURE 6-3.4
Floor tool; boundary lines sketched at curved curtain wall area

Now that you have the perimeter of the floor defined, you may finish the creation of the floor element.

13. Click the **green check mark** on the *Ribbon* to finish the floor.

TIP: If you get any errors, see the next page.

COMMON ERRORS FINISHING A FLOOR SKETCH:

If you get an error message when trying to finish a floor sketch, it is probably due to a problem with the sketched perimeter lines. Here are two common problems:

Perimeter not closed:
You cannot finish a floor if there is a gap, large or small, in the perimeter sketch.
Fix: Sketch a line to close the loop.

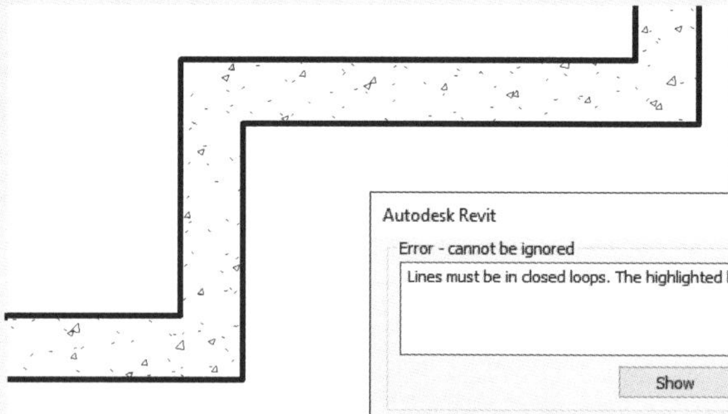

Sketch lines – perimeter not closed because line is missing

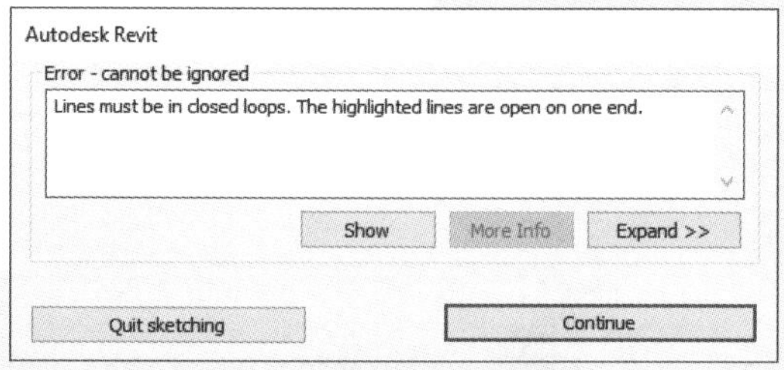

Error message after clicking finish sketch

Perimeter lines intersect:
You cannot finish a floor if any of the sketch lines intersect.
Fix: Use Trim to make it so all line endpoints touch.

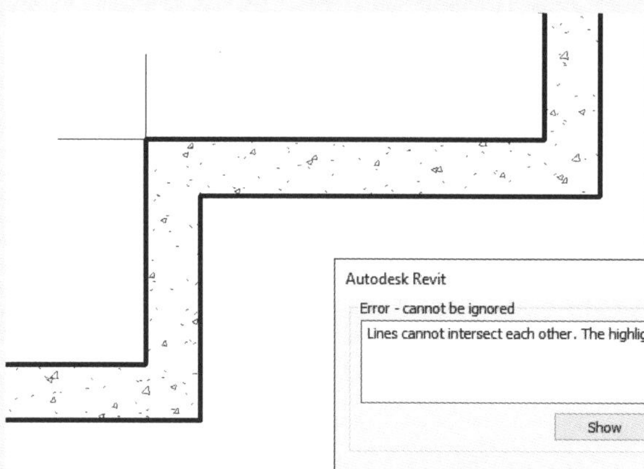

Sketch lines – lines extend past each other; not good

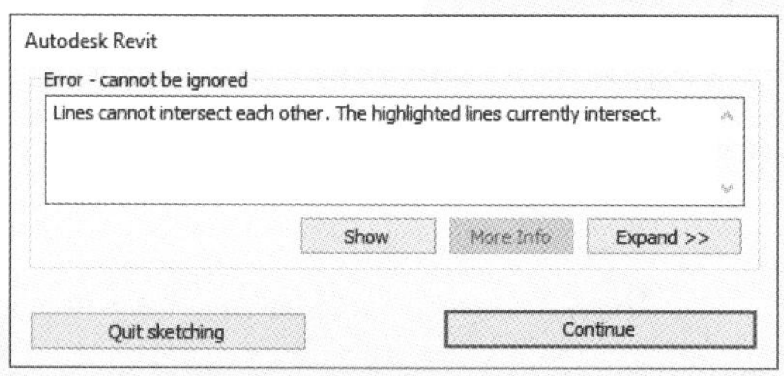

Error message after clicking finish sketch

The floor for Level 1 has now been created. However, because the surface pattern is hidden in this view, you cannot see it. The only place the floor is visible is at the two exterior door openings (Figure 6-3.5); this is the best place to select the slab by pressing **Tab** to get past the door and select the slab. You can also toggle on **Select Elements by Face** (via icons in the lower right corner) and then select the floor by clicking anywhere on it. Leaving this toggle on all the time can make it difficult to select other things, so you may want to toggle it back off when you don't need it anymore.

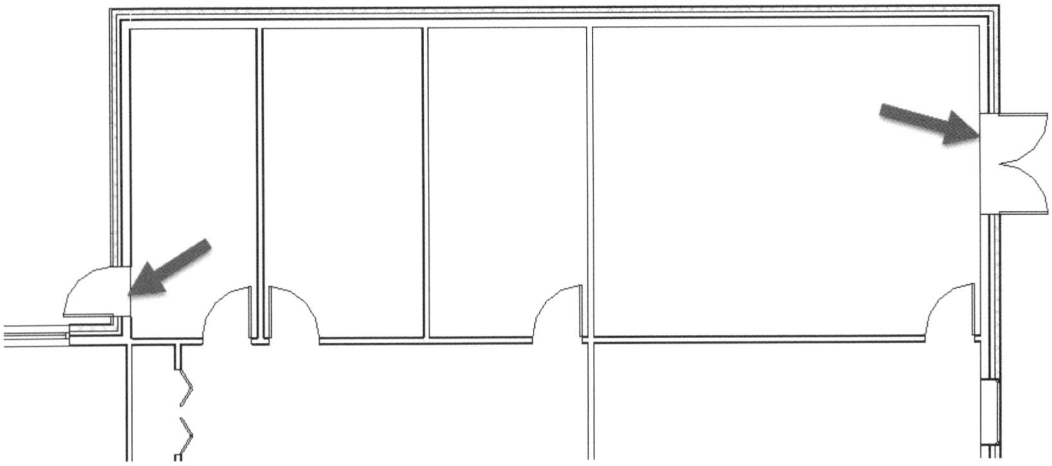

FIGURE 6-3.5 Level 1 floor plan; floor slab visible at exterior door openings

Often a surface pattern is not assigned to the structural slab. Instead, another floor is added in each room to define floor finishes later during the design process once the plan is fixed. A 1/8″ thick *Floor* can be created for each floor finish. The 1/8″ *Floor* is then added to each room, offset 1/8″ from the host level so it is on top of the structural slab. This method allows various surface patterns to be applied. If a surface pattern were added to the structural slab, it would be visible everywhere, such as toilet rooms, the lobby, and the mechanical room. The other benefit is the ability to schedule the floor finishes and get quantities. You can even add **formulas** to the schedules and get total cost for each flooring type!

Level 2, Concrete on Metal Deck:

Creating the second floor will be a little more involved than the first floor. This is because the upper floor requires several openings. For example, you need to define the openings for the stair shaft and the two-story lobby space. However, Revit makes the process very simple.

You will again use a predefined floor type for the Level 2 floor. The floor you will use is 5½″ thick: a 1½″ metal deck and the remaining is concrete. At this early stage in the project it may be helpful to modify the floor to have a *Layer* that represents a placeholder for the structural joists that hold up the floor. In section view, this can help better visualize the required space, before the structural engineers add their elements to the BIM.

14. Switch to the ***Level 2*** floor plan view.

15. Click to start the ***Floor*** tool (Floor: Architectural) on the *Ribbon.*

16. Set the *Type Selector* to **LW Concrete on Metal Deck**.

17. Click **Edit Type** on the *Properties Palette.*

18. Click **Edit,** next to the *Structure* parameter.

You are now in the *Edit Assembly* dialog; here you will temporarily add a *Layer* to serve as a placeholder for the bar joists (Figure 6-3.6). This process is identical for editing Revit walls and roofs!

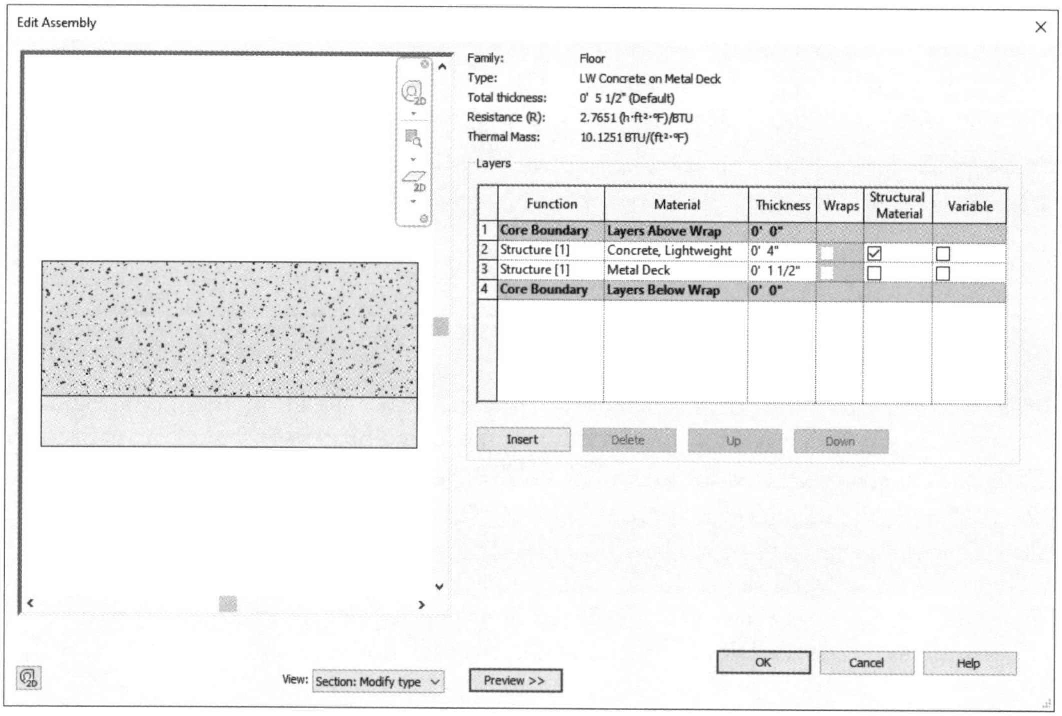

FIGURE 6-3.6 Edit assembly dialog for current floor type.

19. Click the **Insert** button.

The new *Layer* should have been placed below the bottom *Core Boundary* placeholder. This is fine for what we are attempting to do. You will also set the *Function* to "finish" so the walls are not adversely affected by this temporary element in the floor type.

20. Change the new *Layer* as follows (Figure 6-3.7):

    a. *Function:* **Finish 2**

    b. *Priority:* **5**

    c. *Material:* **<By Category>**

    d. *Thickness:* **1′-2″**

	Function	Priority	Material	Thickness	Wraps	Structu Mater
1	**Core Boundary**		**Layers Above Wrap**	**0' 0"**		
2	Structure	1	Concrete, Lightweig	0' 4"	☐	☑
3	Structure	1	Metal Deck	0' 1 1/2"	☐	☐
4	**Core Boundary**		**Layers Below Wrap**	**0' 0"**		
5	Finish 2	5	<By Category>	1' 2"	☐	☐

FIGURE 6-3.7 Floor properties: layer settings

21. Close the open dialog boxes (i.e., click **OK** two times).

You are now ready to start sketching the boundary of the Level 2 floor.

22. Using the *Pick Wall* icon, select the walls shown in Figure 6-3.8:

    a. Make sure *Extend into wall (to core)* is selected.

    b. Click to the exterior side of the exterior walls, opposite to what you did for Level 1.

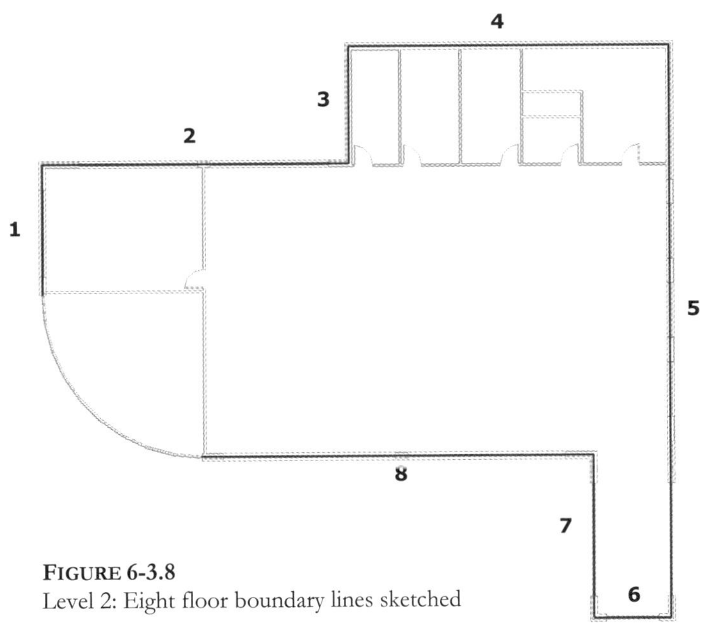

FIGURE 6-3.8
Level 2: Eight floor boundary lines sketched

23. Zoom into the North stair shaft, and make the edits shown in Figure 6-3.9.
    a. Use the *Line* and *Trim* tools from the *Ribbon*. Remember, these are the tools and techniques you mastered in Chapter 4.
    b. The 8′-4″ line should align with the top riser, in the North-South direction.

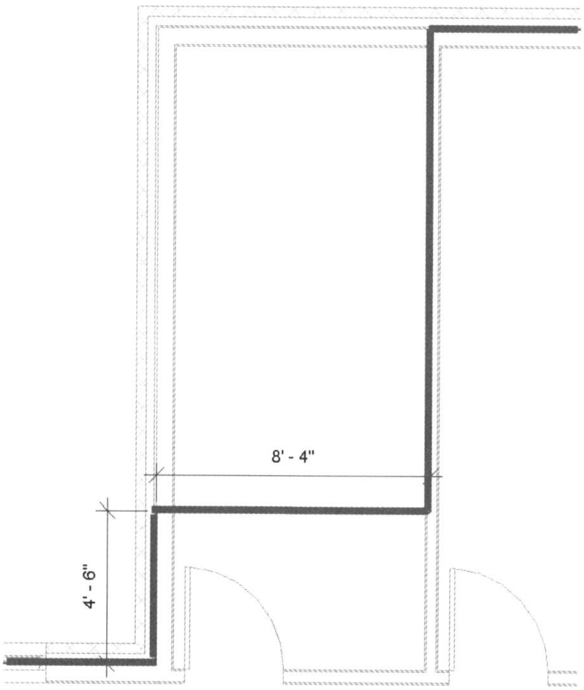

FIGURE 6-3.9
Level 2: Floor boundary at North stair

24. While still in *Sketch* mode for the Level 2 floor, pan to the right to show the area in Figure 6-3.10.

You will now define a hole in the floor for ductwork. On a real project, this may be added later in the project once the mechanical engineer gets involved and suggests the size of supply and return air ducts needed. You will add the hole now regardless.

25. Select the ***Pick Walls*** icon and with *Extend into wall (to core)* checked, select the shaft side of the four walls.
    a. Use the flip-control arrows for each sketch line if needed because the wrong side of the wall may have been selected.
    b. Use Trim to clean up the corners.

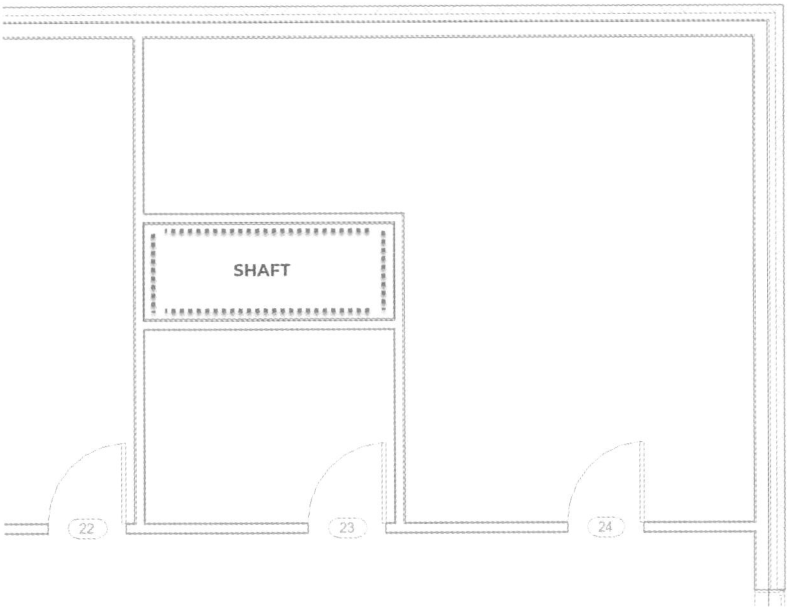

FIGURE 6-3.10 Level 2 (North-East corner): Floor boundary at shaft

Whenever a perimeter is drawn within another, it defines a hole.

Next you will define the floor boundary at the two-story lobby, which starts on Level 1.

26. Sketch the floor opening as shown in Figure 6-3.11:
    a. Use the *Split* tool on the sketch line along the exterior wall.
    b. Use the *Line* tool to sketch the floor opening per the dimensions shown.
    c. Use *Trim* as needed to clean up the corners.
    d. You do not have to add the dimensions, but you can if desired. They will be hidden when the floor is finished.

The last area to define is the curved edge at the curtain wall. On Level 1 the floor went under the curtain wall; on Level 2 the floor edge needs to be held back from the curtain wall, allowing room for it to pass by.

27. Using a similar technique as Level 1, sketch the Level 2 floor edge as shown in Figure 6-3.12.
    a. The curved line is 5″ in (towards the interior of the building) in relation to the adjacent sketch lines.

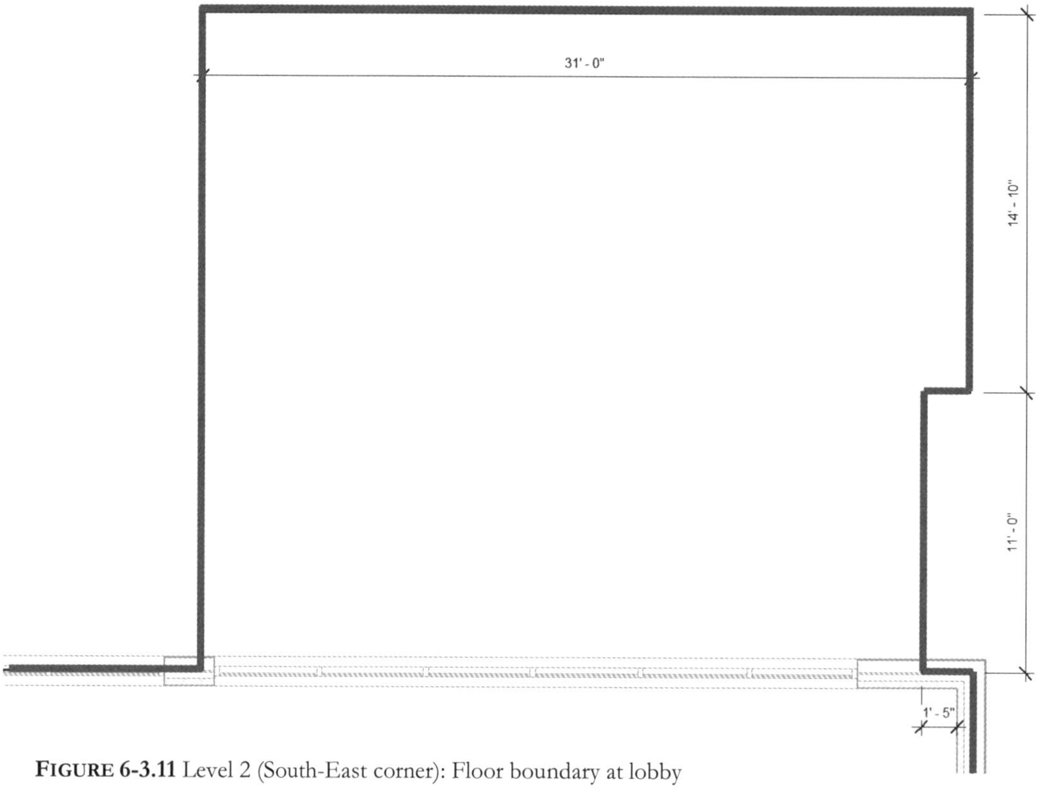

FIGURE 6-3.11 Level 2 (South-East corner): Floor boundary at lobby

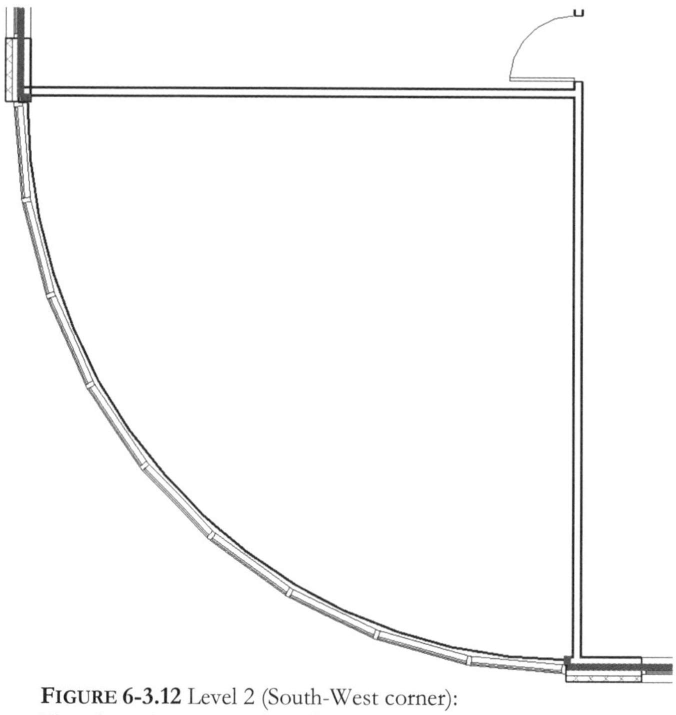

FIGURE 6-3.12 Level 2 (South-West corner):
Floor boundary at curtain wall

You are now ready to finish the floor sketch and let Revit create the 3D floor object in the BIM.

28. Click the green checkmark on the *Ribbon* to finish the floor sketch.

29. Click **Attach** to extending the floor below up to the new floor. If you get a warning, click 'Unjoin element'.

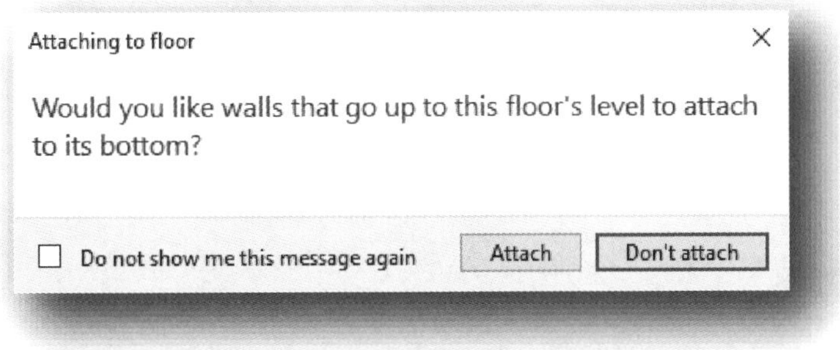

30. Click **Yes** to join and cut walls.

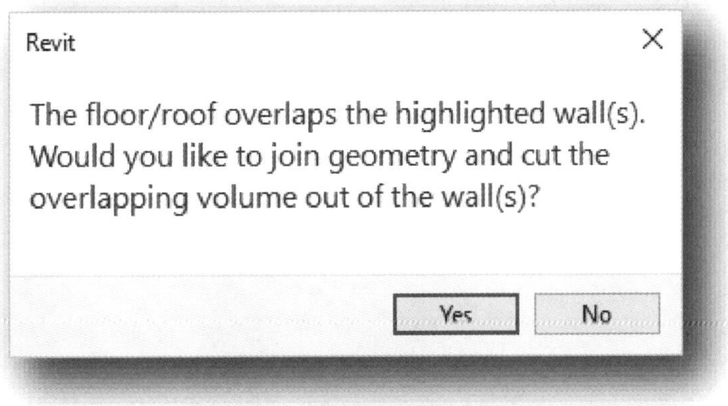

Notice, unlike the Level 1 slab, the LW Concrete on Metal Deck has a surface pattern defined, which shows up everywhere. You will leave this for now as it helps to see the extents of the floor in this early design phase of the project.

31. Switch to the ***Default 3D View***.

32. Use the ***ViewCube*** to move around the exterior of your building.

Notice you can see the Level 1 and Level 2 floors through the curtain wall glazing!

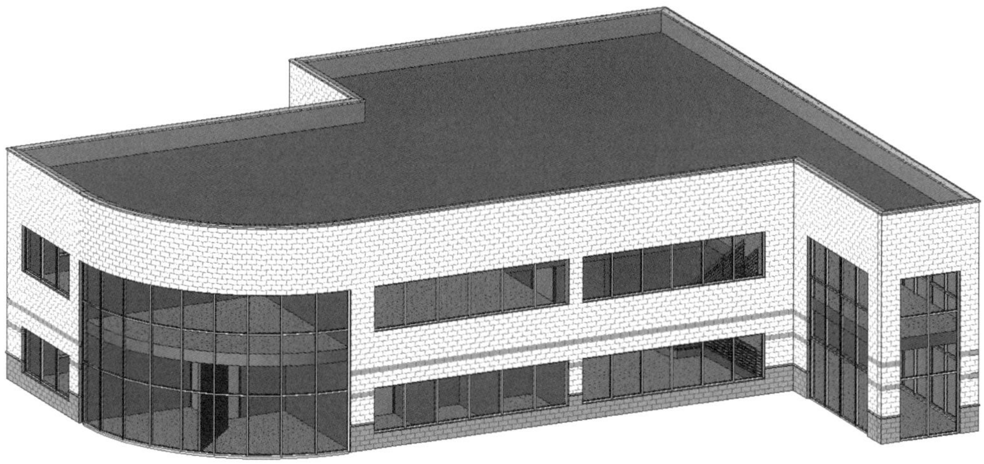

FIGURE 6-3.13 default 3D view: floors visible through glazing

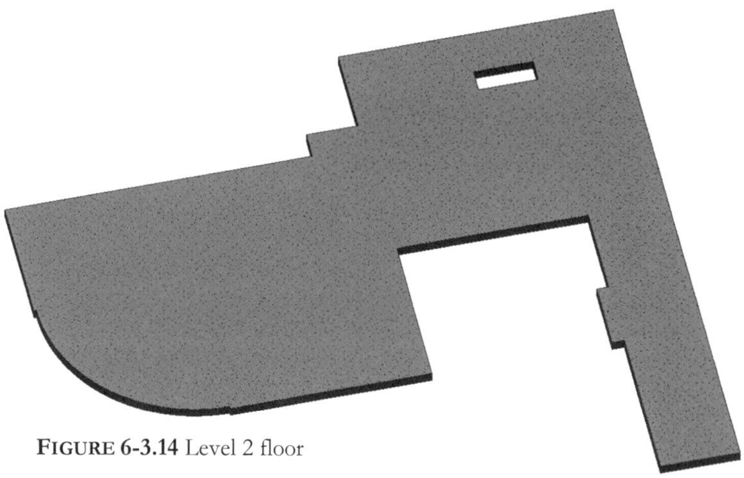

The image to the left was generated from the ***3D*** view above. Simply select the floor, click the sunglasses on the *View Control Bar*, then select *Isolate Element.*

FIGURE 6-3.14 Level 2 floor

33. **Save** your project.

Exercise 6-4:
Ceiling Systems

This lesson will explore Revit's tools for modeling ceilings. This will include drawing different types of ceiling systems.

Suspended Acoustical Ceiling Tile System:

1. **Open** your Law Office project.

2. Switch to the ***Level 1*** ceiling plan view, from the *Project Browser*; ceiling plans are just below the floor plans.

Notice the doors' and windows' visibility is automatically "turned" off in the ceiling plan views (Figure 6-4.2). Actually, the ceiling plan views have a cutting plane similar to floor plans, except they look up rather than down. You can see this setting by right-clicking on a view name in the *Project Browser* and then selecting **View Range** in the *Properties Palette.* The default value is 7′-6″. You might increase this if, for example, you had 10′-0″ ceilings and 8′-0″ high doors. Otherwise, the doors would show because the 7′-6″ cutting plane would be below the door height (Figure 6-4.1).

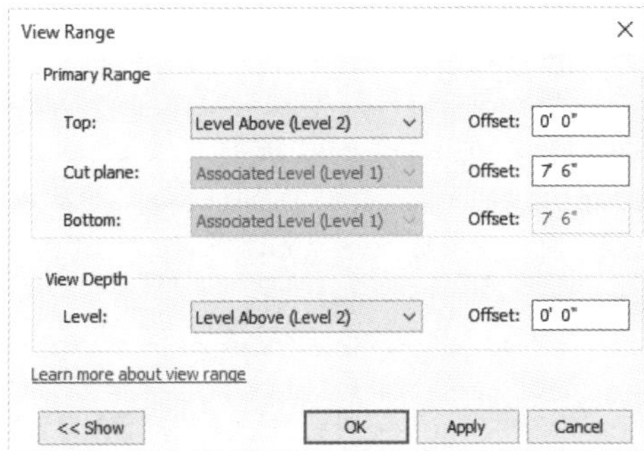

FIGURE 6-4.1 Properties: View Range settings

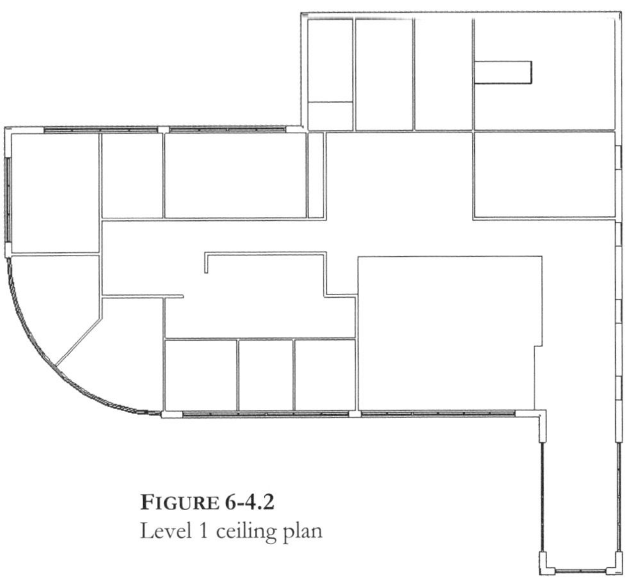

FIGURE 6-4.2
Level 1 ceiling plan

3. Select **Architecture → Build → Ceiling**.

You have four ceiling types, by default, to select from (Figure 6-4.3).

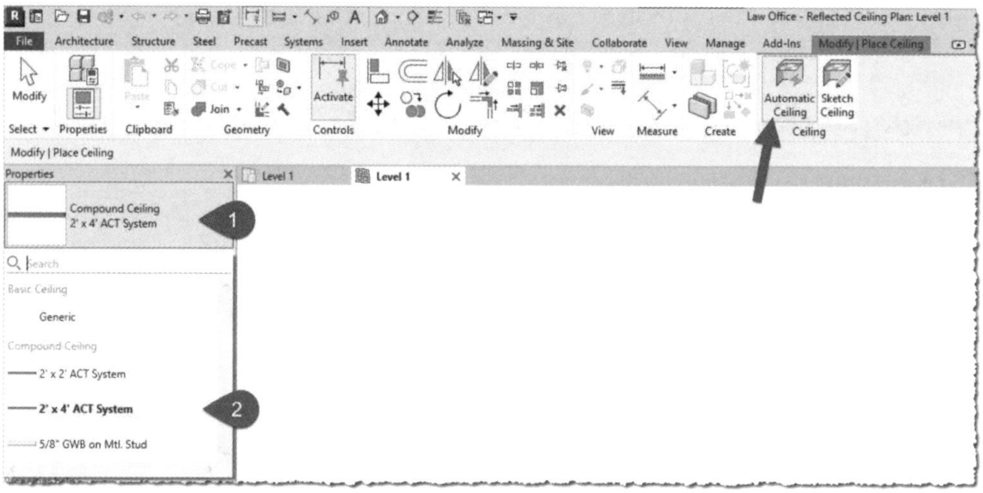

FIGURE 6-4.3 Ceiling: Ribbon options

4. Select *Compound Ceiling:* **2′x2′ ACT System**.

Next you will change the ceiling height. The default setting is 10′-0″ above the current level. You will change the ceiling height to 8′-0″; this will give plenty of space above the ceiling to the bottom of the joists, perhaps for recessed light fixtures and ductwork. This setting can be changed on a room-by-room basis. Hence, it is an instance parameter.

5. Ensure the *Properties Palette* is visible; type **PP** if not.

6. Set the *Height Offset From Level* setting to **8′-0″** (Figure 6-4.4).

You are now ready to place ceiling grids. This process cannot get much easier, especially compared to other CAD/BIM programs.

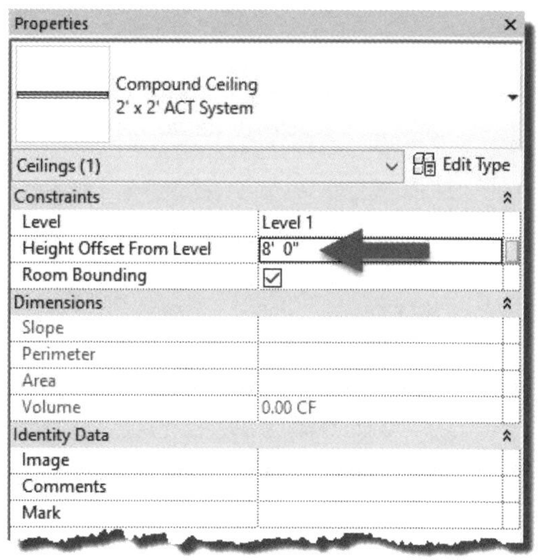

FIGURE 6-4.4 Ceiling: Properties

7. Move your cursor anywhere within the office in the North-West corner of the building. You should see the perimeter of the room highlighted.

8. Pick within that Northwest room; Revit places a grid in the room (Figure 6-4.5).

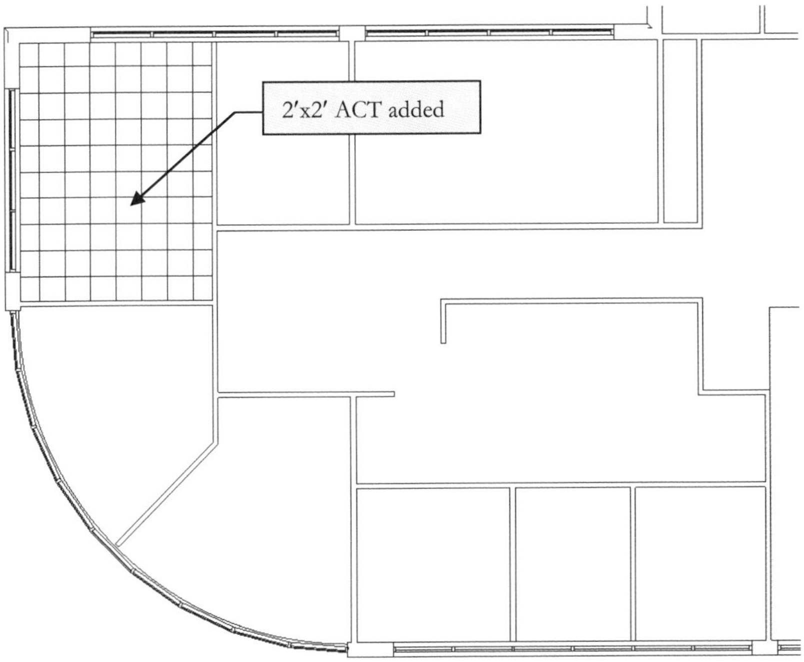

FIGURE 6-4.5: Level 1 Ceiling Plan view: 2′x2′ suspended acoustical ceiling tile added to office

You now have a 2′x2′ ceiling grid at 8′-0″ above the floor, Level 1 in this case. Later in the book, when you get to the exercise on cutting sections, you will see the ceiling with the proper height and thickness.

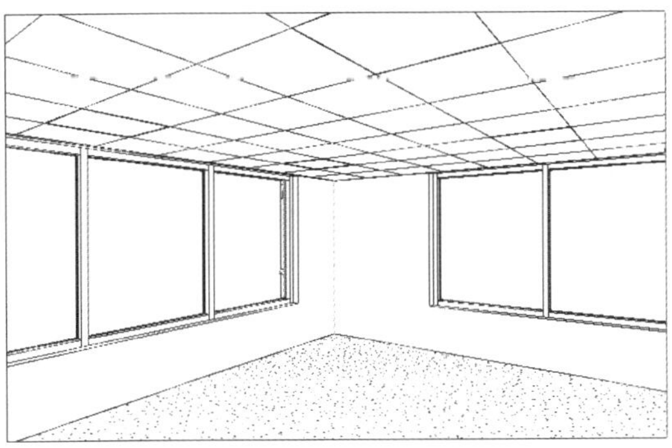

The image to the left is a *camera* view of the room you just added the ceiling to. You will learn how to create camera views in Chapter 15.

Next you will add the same ceiling system to several other Level 1 rooms.

9. Use the ***Ceiling*** tool to place 2′x 2′ acoustic ceiling tile (ACT) at 8′-0″ above finished floor (AFF) in the rooms shown (Figure 6-4.6).

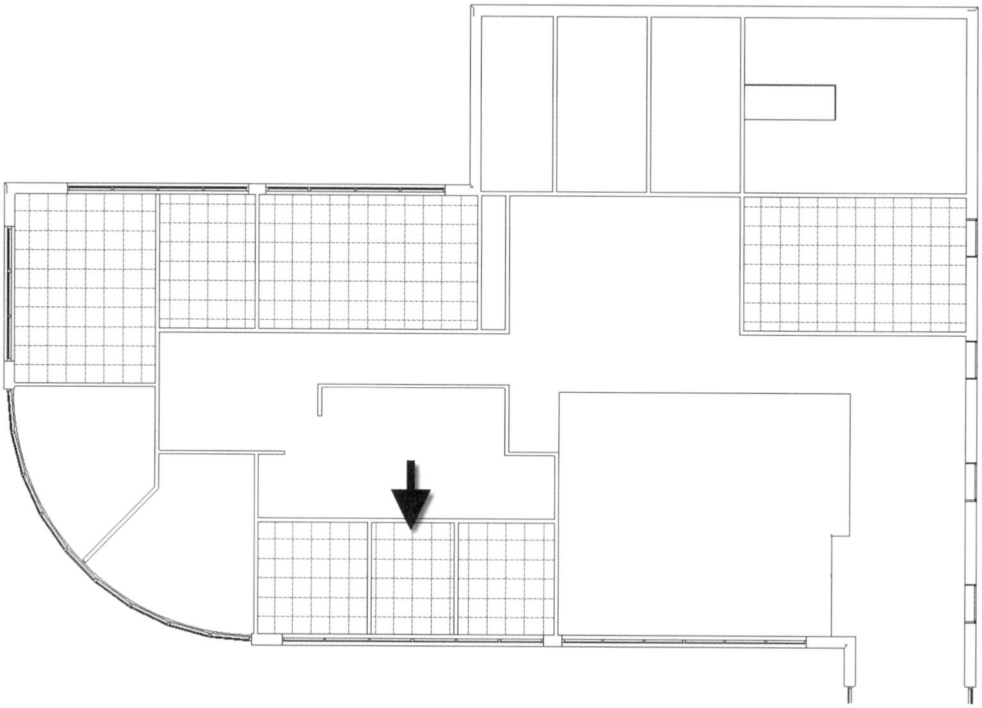

FIGURE 6-4.6: Level 1 Ceiling Plan view: 2′x2′ suspended acoustical ceiling tile added to rooms.

When you place a ceiling grid, Revit centers the grid in the room. The general rule of thumb is you should try to avoid reducing the tile size by more than half of a tile. You can see in Figure 6-4.6 that the East and West sides are small slivers for the center office on the South exterior wall. You will adjust this next.

10. Select **Modify** from the *Ribbon.*

11. **Select** the ceiling grid identified in Figure 6-4.6. Only one line will be highlighted.

12. Use the ***Move*** tool to move the grid 12″ to the East (Figure 6-4.7). ***Tip:*** If the grid does not move, ensure *Join* is not checked on the *Ribbon*. If it is, use 'Move' on another element (e.g. door) to clear the disjoin option and then return to this step.

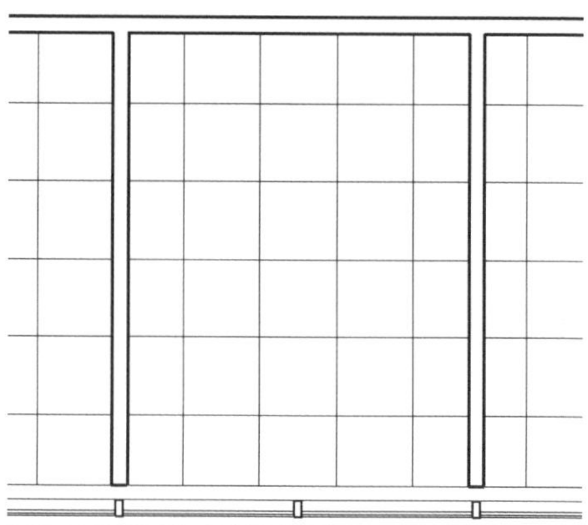

FIGURE 6-4.7
Level 1 Ceiling plan view: ceiling grid relocated.

Moving the grid does not move the ceiling element itself, only its surface pattern.

Next, you will look at drawing gypsum board ceiling systems. The process is identical to placing the grid system.

Gypsum Board Ceiling System:

You will create a new ceiling type for a gypsum board (Gyp. Bd.) ceiling. To better identify the areas that have a Gyp. Bd. ceiling, you will set the ceiling surface to have a stipple pattern. This will provide a nice graphical representation for the Gyp. Bd. ceiling areas. The ceiling you are about to create would lean more towards a commercial application. You will add this ceiling to toilet rooms, as it holds up better in locations with moisture and provides better security. The space above a Gyp. Bd. ceiling is not easily accessible as acoustical ceiling tile (ACT) is, so access panels are often required to access shutoff valves, VAVs, etc.

The first thing you will do is look at the Revit *Materials* which are assigned to elements throughout the model. Materials are used to manage the pattern applied to the surface of an element seen in elevation and the pattern applied when an element is cut in section. Additionally, a color can be selected for *Shaded with Edges* (Model Graphics Style). Later in the book, you will also learn how a rendering material can be added, which is used when creating a photorealistic rendering.

Several elements can reference the same material. For example, a door, trim, a custom ceiling, furniture, etc., could refer to the same wood material, which could be set to clear maple. If, at any point in the project, the *Material* for wood is changed to stained oak, all elements which reference it are updated. Thus, if several wood finishes or species are required, you would have to create multiple *Materials* in Revit.

13. Select **Manage → *Settings* → Materials**. *This is the list of materials you select from when assigning a material to each layer in a wall system, etc.*

14. Select *Gypsum Wall Board* in the *Name* list and then right-click; select **Duplicate Using Shared Assets**. Rename the new *Material* to **Gypsum Ceiling Board** (see Figure 6-4.8 and image to right).

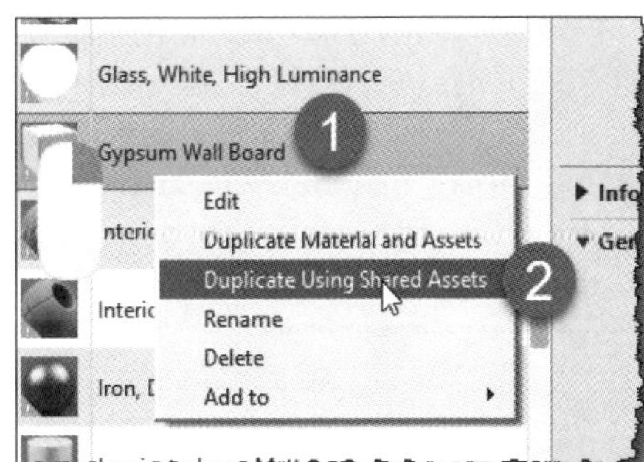

15. On the Graphics tab, in the *Surface Pattern\foreground* area, click **<none>** and select the *Drafting* pattern **Gypsum-Plaster** from the list, and then click **OK** (Figure 6-4.8).

The *Surface Pattern* setting is what will add the stipple pattern to the Gyp. Bd. ceiling areas. With this set to *none*, the ceiling has no pattern, like the basic ceiling type. Creating a new material allows you to separately control the surface pattern of Gyp. Bd. walls vs. ceilings. Walls do not have a surface pattern typically, whereas ceilings do.

Thus, if you wanted Carpet 1 finish to never have the stipple hatch pattern, you could change the surface pattern to *none* via the *Materials* dialog and not have to change each view's visibility override.

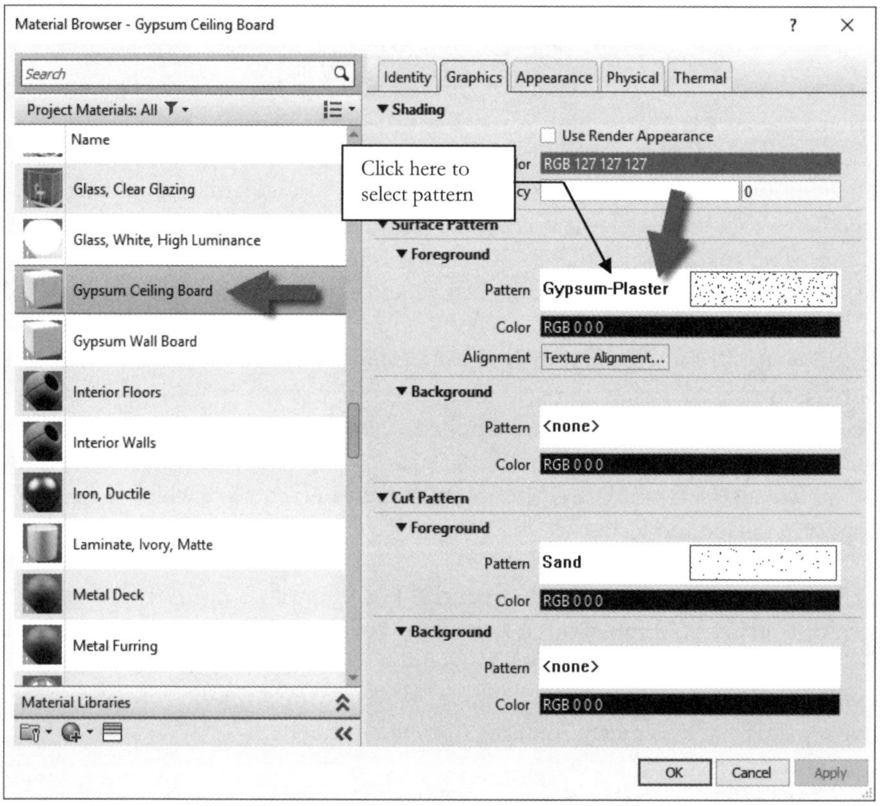

FIGURE 6-4.8 Materials dialog

You will learn more about this later, but if you switch to the *Appearance* tab, you will notice the appearance asset is still tied to the Gypsum Wall Board material. This means any changes made to how this material renders (i.e. photorealistic image) will also change the Gypsum Wall Board material. The arrow in the image below lets us know that this asset is shared by one other material in this project. Clicking the duplicate icon to the far right will make a new unique asset (using 'Duplicate Material and Assets' would have achieved the same result).

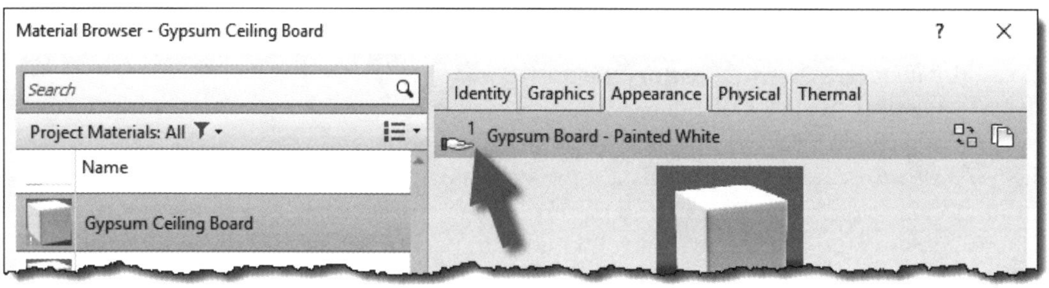

The template you started from does have one Gyp. Bd. Ceiling, but this is meant for a soffit or a small room where the ceiling is not suspended from the structure above; it has $3\frac{5}{8}''$ metal studs. You will use this ceiling as a starting point, and create a ceiling with $\frac{3}{4}''$ metal furring over $1\frac{1}{2}''$ metal studs/channels. All of this is then suspended by wires from the structure above; these wires are not modeled in Revit.

16. From the *Architecture* tab on the *Ribbon*, select **Ceiling**.

17. Set the *Type Selector* to **5/8″ GWB on Metal Stud**.

    FYI: You are selecting this because it is most similar to the ceiling you will be creating. GWB = Gypsum Wall Board

18. Click the **Edit Type** button.

19. Click *Duplicate* and type the name **Susp GB on Metal Stud**.

At this point you have a new ceiling type available to be placed in the model. However, it is exactly like the one you copied (i.e., 5/8″ GWB on Metal Stud). Next, you will modify the composition of your new ceiling type system family.

20. Select **Edit** next to the *Structure* parameter.

21. Create a *Layer* and set the values as follows (Fig. 6-4.9):

    a. **1½″ Mtl. Stud**

    b. **¾″ Mtl. Stud**

    c. **Gypsum Ceiling Board** *(This is the material you created in Step 13+.)*

    TIP: Use the Insert button to add a new Layer and then, with the new Layer selected, use the up and down buttons to reposition the Layer within the ceiling system.

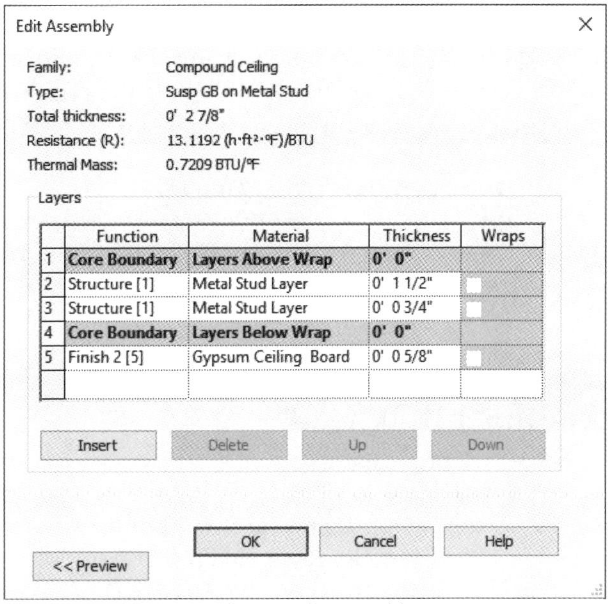

FIGURE 6-4.9 New ceiling – Edit assembly

22. Click **OK** two times to close the open dialog boxes.

    FYI: The ceiling assembly you just created represents a typical suspended Gyp. Bd. ceiling system. The Metal Studs are perpendicular to each other and suspended by wires, similar to an ACT system.

You are now ready to draw a gypsum board ceiling.

23. Make sure **Susp GB on Metal Stud** is selected in the *Type Selector* on the *Properties Palette.*

24. Set the ceiling height to **8′-0.″**

25. Pick the two toilet rooms as shown in **Figure 6-4.10**.

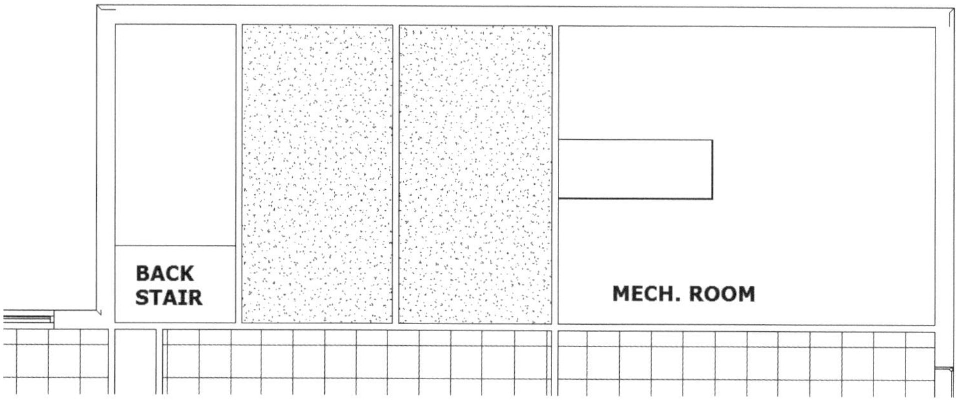

FIGURE 6-4.10 Gyp. Bd. Ceiling

You now have a gypsum board ceiling at 8′-0″ above the Level 1 floor slab. Notice the stipple pattern does a good job of highlighting the extents of the Gyp. Bd. Ceiling, as compared to the adjacent mechanical room which will not have a ceiling.

> ***DESIGN INTEGRATION TIP:*** *Once the structure and HVAC (i.e., ductwork) have been added, any ceilings will obscure those elements if they are lower in elevation. However, all those elements will show in the mechanical room. Showing the structure and HVAC is great for coordination and helps the contractor understand the project better. For instance, how difficult would it be to paint the Mechanical Room structure and ductwork.*

Adding a Bulkhead:

Next, you will place a ceiling in the hallway. However, you cannot simply pick the room to place the ceiling because Revit would fill in the adjacent lobby and office area. First, you will need to draw bulkheads to close these areas off at the ceiling level. They will not be visible in the floor plan view as they do not pass through its cut plane. A bulkhead is a portion of wall that hangs from the floor or structure above (see image to right) and creates a closed perimeter for a ceiling system to abut into. The bulkhead will create a perimeter that the *Ceiling* tool will detect for the proper ceiling placement.

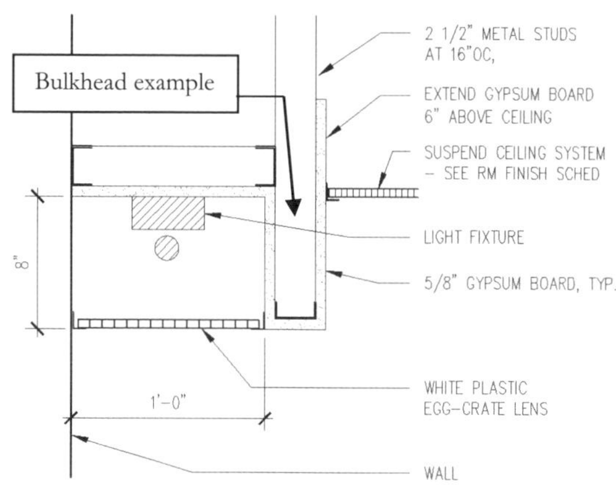

26. While still in the **Level 1** ceiling plan view, select the **Wall** *tool.*

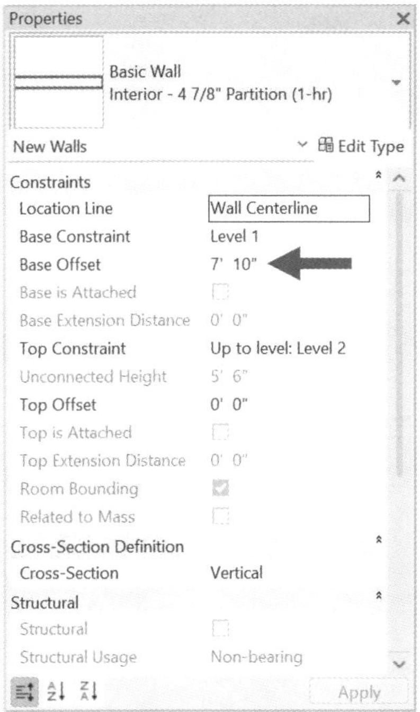

FIGURE 6-4.11 Bulkhead (wall) properties

27. In the *Type Selector*, set the wall type to **Interior – 4 7/8″ Partition (1-hr)**.

28. In the *Properties Palette*, set the <u>*Base Offset*</u> to **7′-10″**. *This will put the bottom of the wall to 7′-10″ above the current floor level, Level 1 in this case* (Figure 6-4.12).

29. Set the <u>*Top Constraint*</u> to **Up to level: Level 2** (Figure 6-4.11).

TIP: The next time you draw a wall, you will have to change the Base Offset back to 0′-0″ or your wall will be 7′-10″ off the floor; this is hard to remember!

30. **Draw the bulkhead**; make sure you snap to the adjacent walls (Figure 6-4.12).

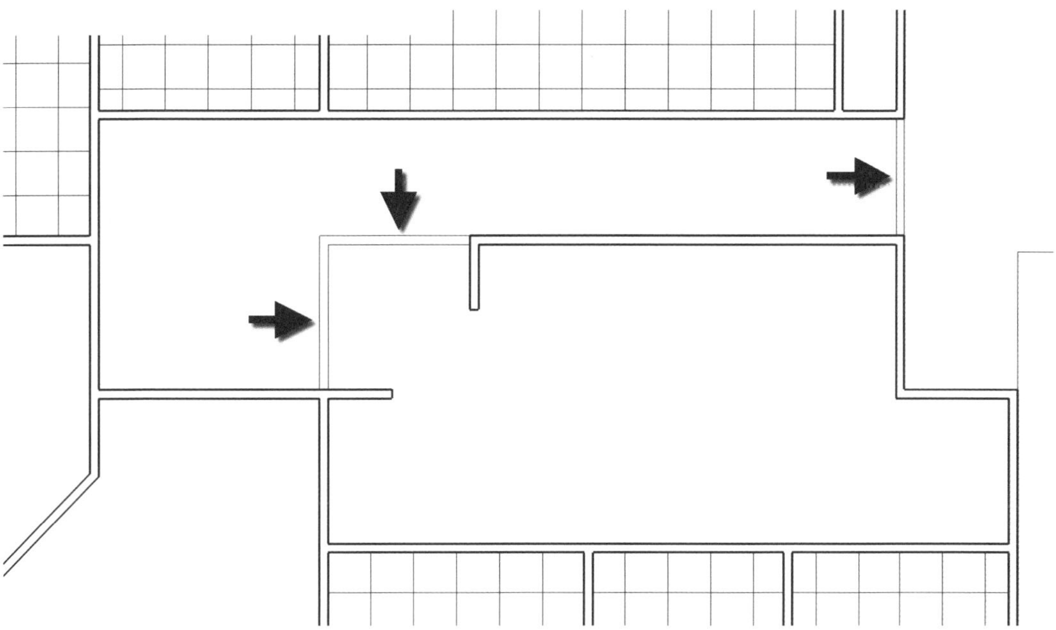

FIGURE 6-4.12 Bulkhead modeled

31. Select the ***Ceiling*** tool and hover your cursor over the hallway.

Notice, in Figure 6-4.13, how the bulkheads create a valid perimeter in the hallway. If the bulkhead bottom was 8′-2″ or the ceiling height was 7′-8″, Revit would not find this same perimeter. Take a moment and give it a try. Undo any changes before moving on.

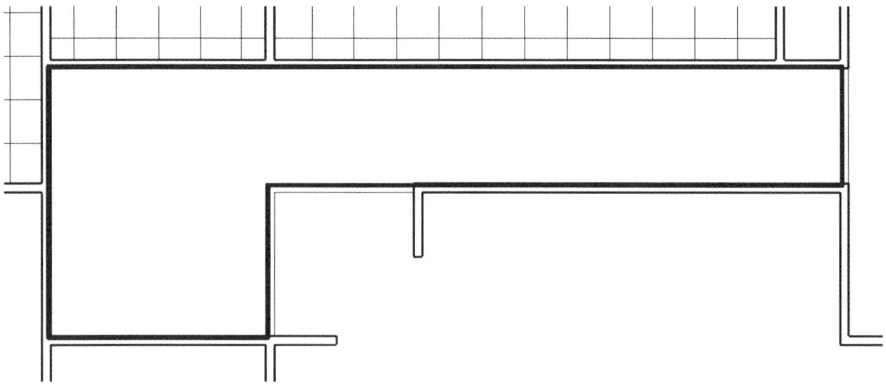

FIGURE 6-4.13 Ceiling perimeter highlighted

32. With the ceiling height set to **8′-0,″** click in the hallway to place the **2′x2′ ACT System**.

33. Reposition the grid as shown in Figure 6-4.14.
    a. Sometimes, with odd-shaped rooms like this, it can be impossible not to have small slivers of tiles.

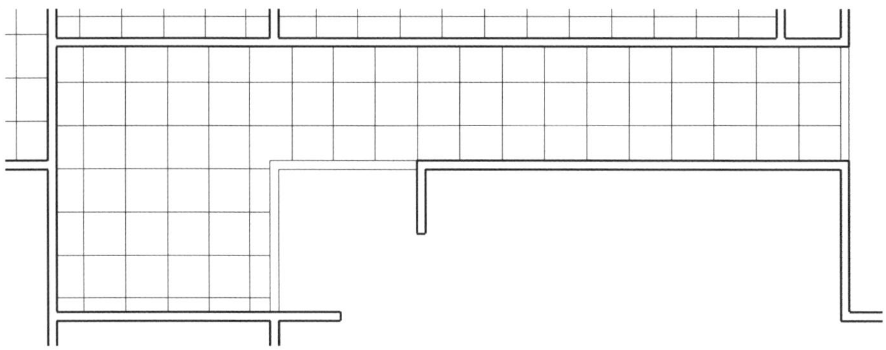

FIGURE 6-4.14 Hallway ceiling placed

DESIGN INTEGRATION TIP: *In addition to laying out the ceiling tile to minimize sliver tiles, the grid needs to accommodate the lighting design. In the hallway, a full tile is provided down the center with this in mind.*

34. Place the remaining bulkheads and 2′x2′ ACT ceilings per the image below; note the ceiling and bulkhead heights vary (Figure 6-4.15 – dashed stair added later in book).

35. Use the ***Align*** tool to make adjacent ceiling grids line up as shown; remember, select the item you do not want to move first.

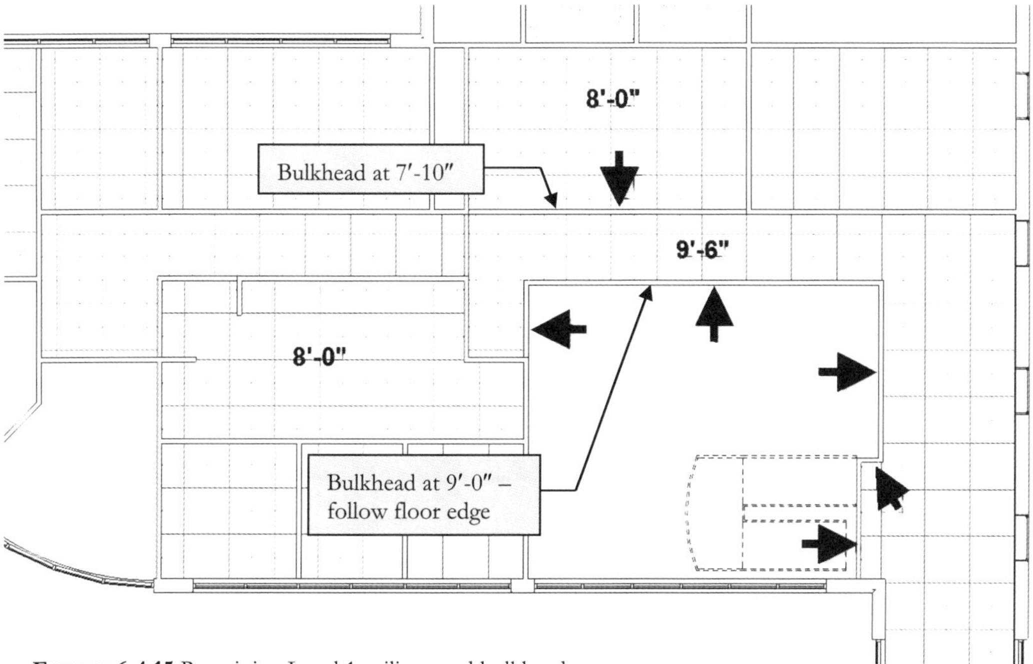

FIGURE 6-4.15 Remaining Level 1 ceilings and bulkheads

You are now ready to move on to the Level 2 reflected ceiling plan. First, you need to create a view in which to work.

36. Select **View → Create → Plan Views → Reflected Ceiling Plan**.

37. Select **Level 2** and then click **OK**.

38. Set the view scale to **1/4″ = 1′-0″**

> **Deleting a Ceiling Grid:**
>
> When selecting a ceiling grid, Revit only selects one line. This does not allow you to delete the ceiling grid. To delete: hover cursor over a ceiling grid line and press the **Tab** key until you see the ceiling perimeter highlight, then click the mouse. The entire ceiling will be selected. Press Delete.

You now have a Level 2 ceiling plan view in which to work. It is possible to make multiple plan or ceiling views of the same level (e.g., floor plan, finish plan, code plan, etc.)

39. Using the techniques previously covered, add the Level 2 ceilings per the information provided in Figure 6-4.16.

    a. Rotated ceiling:
        i. Select a grid line.
        ii. Use the ***Rotate*** tool.
        iii. **Move** the grid as shown.

    b. Bulkhead:
        i. Bottom at **8′-0″**
        ii. Draw with ***Arc*** tool or *Pick* with offset.
        iii. Show approx. **3′-0″** from exterior wall.

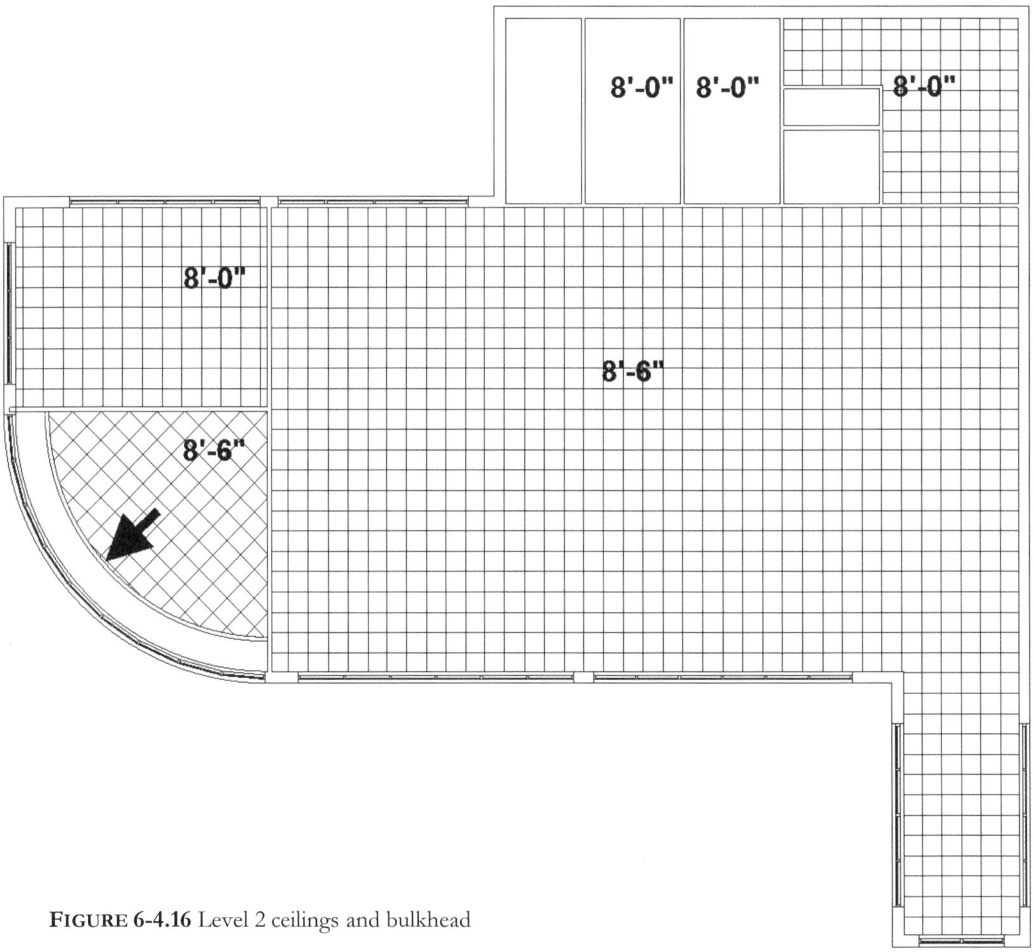

FIGURE 6-4.16 Level 2 ceilings and bulkhead

40. **Save** your project.

Self-Exam:

The following questions can be used as a way to check your knowledge of this lesson. The answers can be found at the bottom of the page.

1. You don't have to click *Finish Roof* when you are done defining a roof. (T/F)
2. The wall below the roof automatically conforms to the underside of the roof when you join the walls to the roof. (T/F)
3. The roof overhang setting is available from the *Ribbon*. (T/F)
4. To create a gable roof on a building with 4 walls, two of the walls should not have the ________________________ option checked.
5. Is it possible to change the reference point for a temporary dimension that is displayed while an object is selected? (Y/N)

Review Questions:

The following questions may be assigned by your instructor as a way to assess your knowledge of this section. Your instructor has the answers to the review questions.

1. When creating a roof using the "*create roof by footprint*" option, you need to create a closed perimeter. (T/F)
2. The **Defines slope** setting can be changed after the roof is "finished." (T/F)
3. The ceiling grid position cannot be modified. (T/F)
4. To delete a ceiling grid, you must first select the perimeter. (T/F)
5. While using the ***Roof*** tool, you can use the ____________ tool from the *Ribbon* to fill in the missing segments to close the perimeter.
6. You use the ___________ variable to adjust the vertical position of the roof relative to the current working plane (view).
7. Tool used to draw a bulkhead: ____________ .
8. You need to use the ___________________ to flip the roofline when you pick the wrong side of the wall and the overhang is shown on the inside.
9. A second, internal, perimeter creates a hole in the floor. (T/F)
10. Changing the name of a level tag (in elevation) causes Revit to rename all the corresponding views (plan, ceiling, etc.) if you answer yes to the prompt. (T/F)

SELF-EXAM ANSWERS:
1 - F, **2** – T, **3** – T, **4** – defines slope, **5** – Y

Notes:

Lesson 7
Vertical Circulation:

In this chapter, Revit's Stair, Railing, and Ramp tools will be covered. This can be one of the most challenging features in Revit, given the wide variety of stairs and railings around the world. These tools have some limitations and cannot accommodate all situations. In these cases, one might have to use Revit's In-Place families to model a highly customized stair and/or railing, or use another, more advanced 3D modeling tool to import it.

The first few "exercises" will provide a basic introduction to the stair and railing tools in Revit. There are no required steps for the law office project in these sections. However, it is highly recommended that this information be reviewed before completing the steps later in this chapter. **There are required steps in the last exercise in this chapter.**

Exercise 7-1:
Introduction to Stairs and Railings

Before delving into the details, this section provides a broad overview of Stairs and Railings in Revit.

This image is a photorealistic rendering of a stair and railing modeled in Revit. This example is from the author's textbook, *Interior Design Using Autodesk Revit.* Notice the railing occurs on both sides of all three "runs" of stairs and along the [second] floor edge.

Basic Stair and Railing Terminology

First, let's define some terms related to stairs and railings in Revit. These terms generally correspond to real-world architectural and construction terminology. However, the main goal here is to define the terms in the context of Revit.

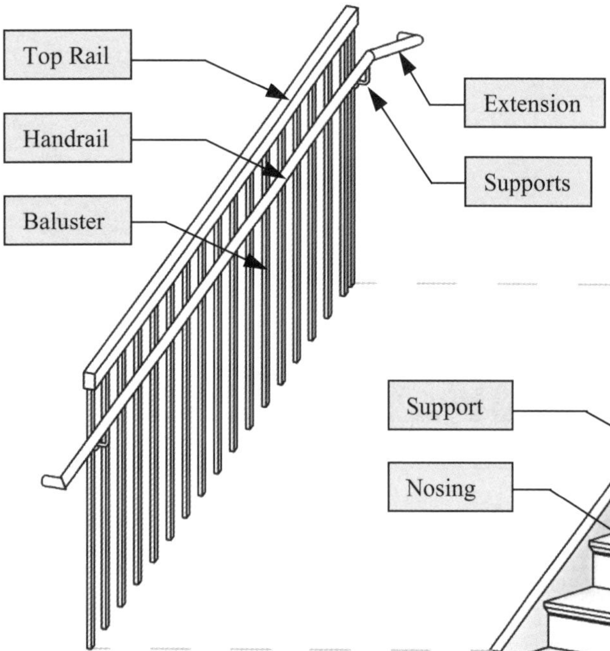

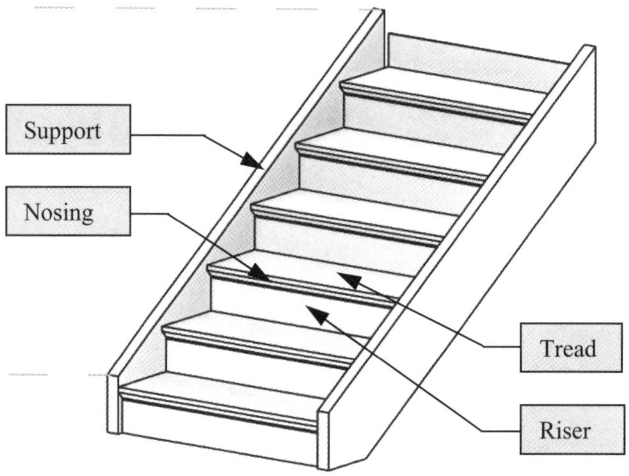

FIGURE 7-1.1a Basic Railing

FIGURE 7-1.1b Basic Stair

- Revit Stair Element
  - **Run**: a continuous section of stairs, consisting of Risers and Treads, between main floor levels and/or landings.
  - **Tread**: the flat horizontal part you step on.
  - **Riser**: the vertical portion that fills the gap between the treads. Not all stairs have risers.
  - **Nosing**: the outer edge, where the riser and tread come together.
  - **Landing**: intermediate horizontal surface (i.e., floor) between the main floor levels of a building. Building codes often require a landing when a stair "run" rises more than a certain distance, providing a safe place to rest.
  - **Supports** (aka Stringer): the structural elements supporting the treads and risers. For a commercial project, this is typically a steel tube or C-channel. A stair typically has a stringer on each side. For wider stairs, one or more stringers may be required. They either span between floors (e.g., from Level 1 to Level 2) or are anchored to an adjacent wall.

- **Cut Marks**: in a 2D plan view, the stair is cut where it intersects the view's cut plane—an angled line is added to graphically cut off the stair. This allows space below the stairs to be seen (e.g., a storage room and door under the stairs).
- **Stair Path** (Annotation)
  - **Down/Up arrows**: in a 2D plan view, the arrow graphically indicates the direction the stairs ascend or descend. The arrow is typically used in conjunction with text (see next definition).
  - **Down/Up Text**: Text used in conjunction with arrows to make it clear which direction the stairs are going, which would be difficult to determine without looking at other views (e.g., sections), which a printed set of drawings may not contain (e.g., a small remodel project).
    - **FYI**: The Arrow and Text are added automatically to a new stair but can be deleted. Thus, the Stair Path tool exists, on the Annotation tab, if they need to be added later.
- **Tread Number** (Annotation): This tool, on the Annotation tab, places a sequence of numbers along a stair "run" indicating the total number of risers or treads.

- Revit Railing Element
  - **Balusters**: vertical elements extending from the floor or stair up to the "top rail." For commercial projects, building codes state that a 4" sphere cannot pass through a railing system. **FYI:** Balusters are not needed if glass panels are used.
  - **Handrails**: continuous rounded element, attached to a wall or balusters with a "support," along a floor edge, a ramp or stair "run" which allows someone to place their hand on, to prevent falling.
  - **Guardrail**: A taller railing system, which may include a handrail, to prevent falling from a stair or floor edge. **FYI:** In the USA, when a guardrail is required, it must be at least 42 inches tall.
  - **Supports**: bracket used to attach the handrail to the wall or balusters.
  - **Top Rails**: continuous rail at the top of the railing system—supported by balusters.

Plan View Representation of Stairs

In Revit plan views, Stairs and their hosted Railings are not shown as true 3D elements being cut by the view's cut plane. Rather, they are a hybrid 2.5D representation that follows traditional architectural graphic standards for floor plans. An example of this is shown in Figure 7-1.2a. Notice all parts of the stairs and railing extend to the Cut Mark. Contrast this with Figure 7-1.2b, which is a true 3D view of the same stair; notice the railing is hardly visible, and there is no cut mark. The cut plane for both examples is 3'-0" as seen in Figure 7-1.2c.

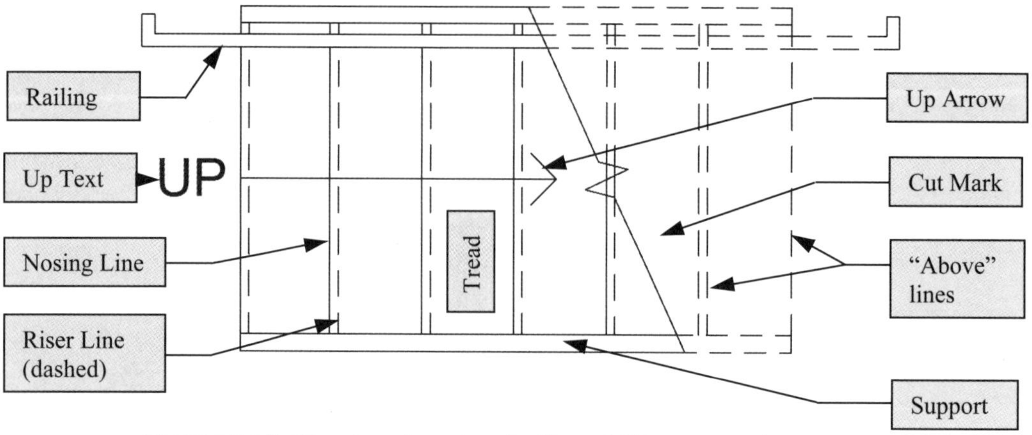

FIGURE 7-1.2a Plan view of a stair and railing – 2.5D representation

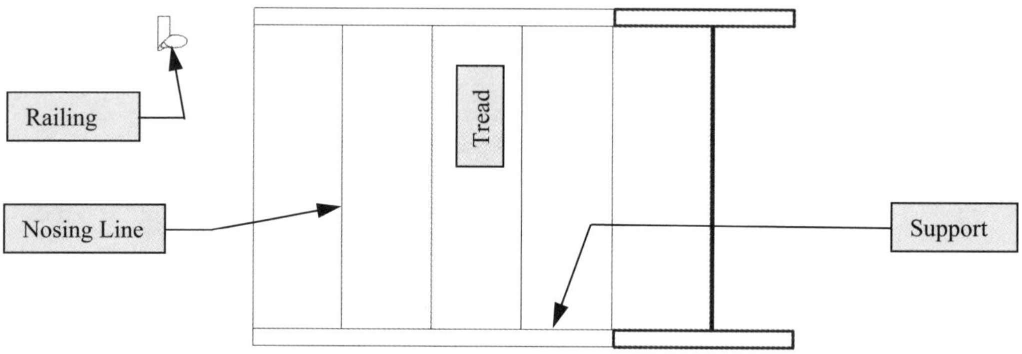

FIGURE 7-1.2b Plan view of a stair and railing – true 3D representation

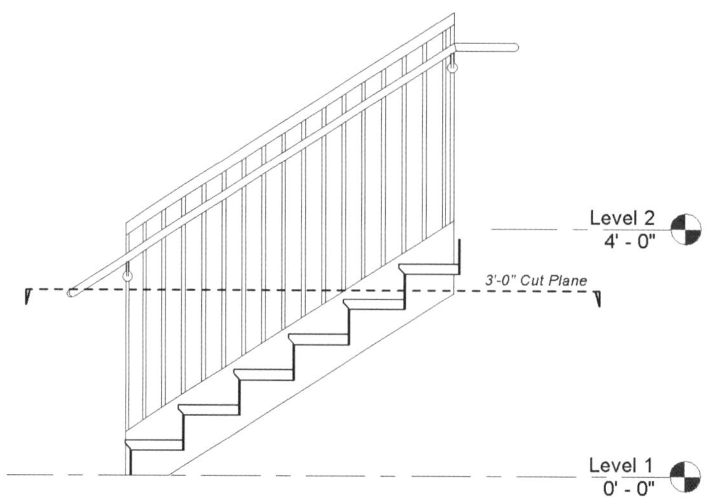

FIGURE 7-1.2c Stair in section with plan view's *cut plane* indicated

The Stair and Railing tools will be covered in more detail in the subsequent exercises in this chapter. But, first, here is a high-level introduction to the tools available in Revit.

Stair Tools

Revit has a single stair tool: **Stair by Component**.

Railing Tools

Revit has two main tools one can use to model railings:

- Sketch Path
- Place on Host

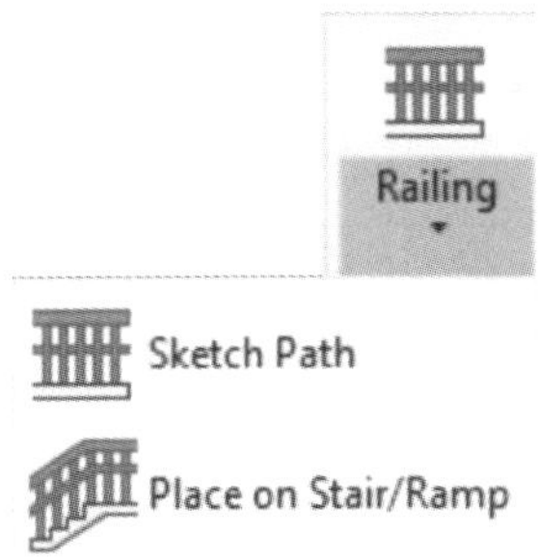

The **Sketch Path** tool allows a continuous section of railing to be added to the current level. The **Pick Host** command provides a quick way to add railings to a stair or railing, which is handy if they were deleted or not added during the stair/ramp creation.

In addition to these two Railing tools, railings can also be created while creating Stairs and Ramps. While in the Stair or Ramp command, selecting the **Railing** button on the Ribbon lets you specify which railing to use and how to position it (Figure 7-1.3). Revit will add a railing to both sides. Once created, one or both of the railings can be deleted. One tricky thing about the Pick Host tool is that it only works if the stair or ramp does not have any railings.

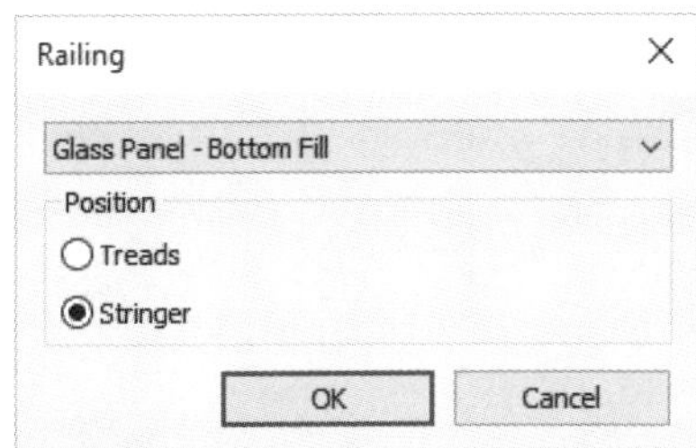

FIGURE 7-1.3
Specify how railing will be created

Basic Stair Types

Revit has three fundamentally different stair types, which are needed to properly model the various types of stairs typically found in construction.

Stair Types:

- Assembled Stair
- Monolithic Stair (aka Cast-In-Place)
- Precast Stair

Assembled Stair

Revit's Assembled Stair represents the most common type of stair construction: concrete pan and steel riser (Figure 7-1.4). A residential stair constructed of wood can also be accomplished with this option. With this type, Revit provides separate settings for the treads, risers, and supports.

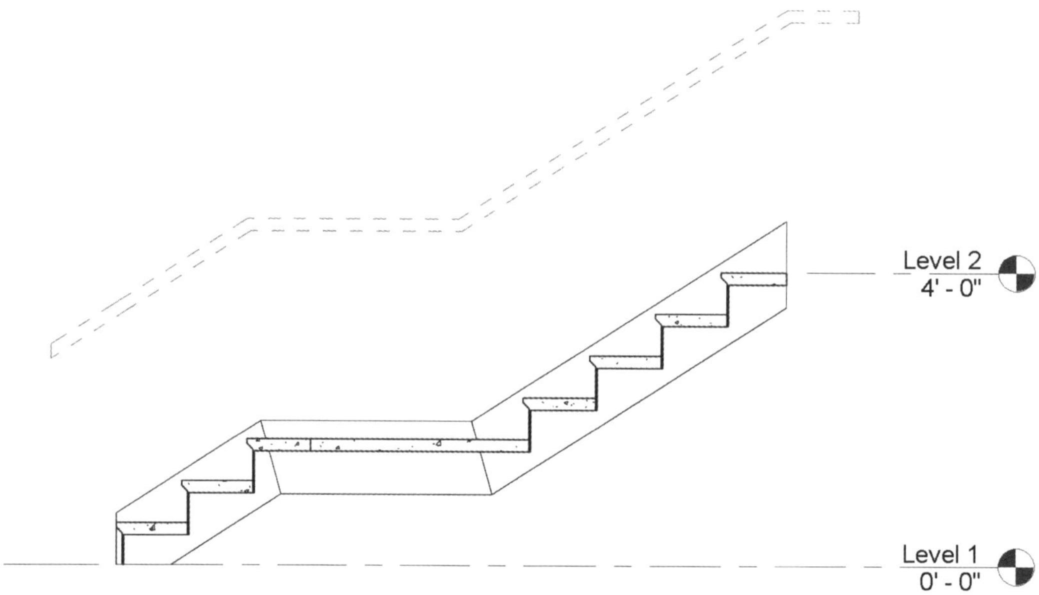

FIGURE 7-1.4 Assembled stair type example

Monolithic Stair (aka Cast-In-Place)

When a stair is constructed with cast-in-place concrete (CIP), the monolithic stair type should be used (Figure 7-1.5). This stair is often used outside the building (site design) or within the building whose primary structure is also CIP concrete. The properties for this type of stair vary a bit from the assembled stair type—for example, the minimum thickness and whether the bottom should slope or step can be specified. Structural designers can also add **Rebar** to this type of element.

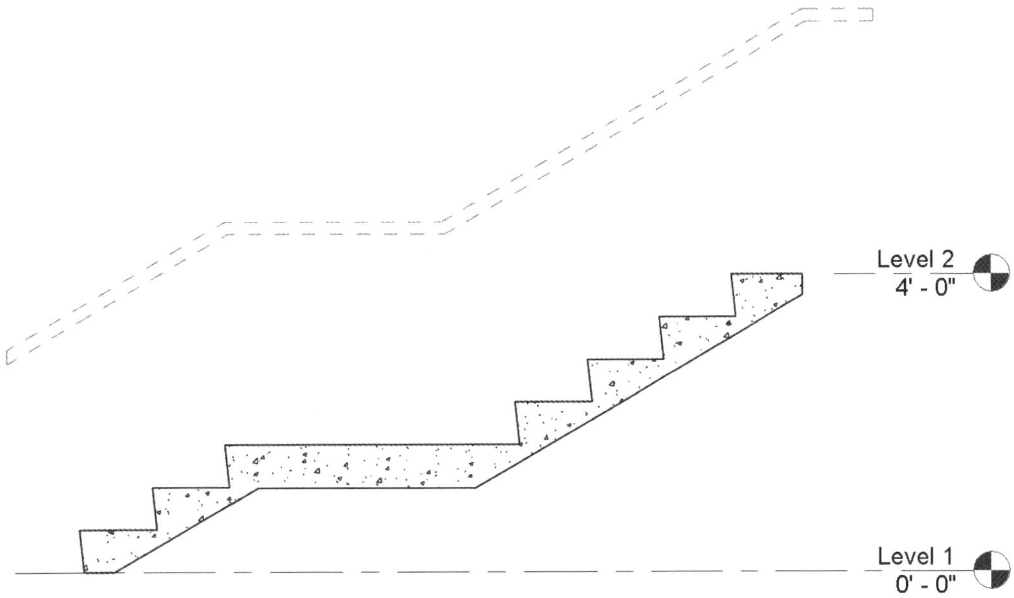

FIGURE 7-1.5 Monolithic stair type example

Precast Stair

When the various parts of a stair are manufactured off-site with concrete and then shipped to the job site, the Precast Stair type can be used to properly represent this special condition (Figure 7-1.6). Notice the special notches which are used to interconnect and support the individual parts. This stair type can also have Rebar added to it. **FYI:** This stair type can only be created using the *Stair by Component* command.

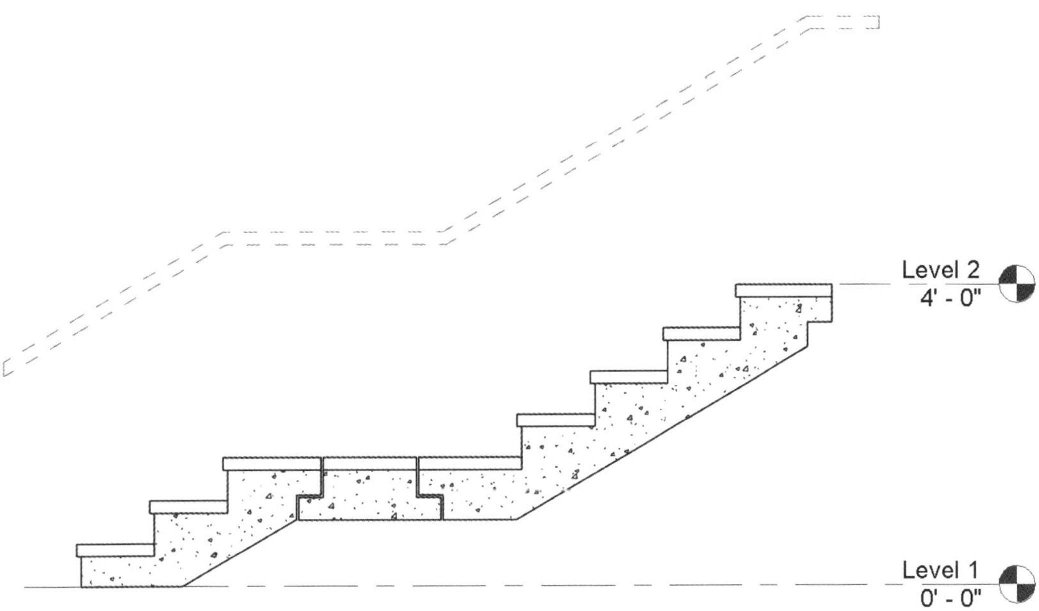

FIGURE 7-1.6 Precast stair type example

Because the parameters vary between stair types, it is often not a simple task to select a stair of one type (e.g. Assembled) and switch it to another (e.g. Monolithic) via the Type Selector. The stair needs to be modified or recreated from scratch to switch between types.

To see the difference between the **End with Riser** versus **End with Tread** options, compare Figure 7-1.2c, which is set to end with riser, with Figure 7-1.4 set to end with tread. In this example, the "end" is the top, and each option is common in construction. The 'end with riser' option is used if the stair stops right at the floor edge. The 'end with tread' option is used when the stair ends a distance away from the main floor and something similar to a landing is added to fill in the gap.

This image is another view of the stair and railing design shown at the beginning of this section. The railings at the level 2 floor edge are separate elements from the railings hosted to the stair.

Graphic Controls

There are a number of ways to manage the visibility of Stairs and Railings in Revit. For the most part, these options apply to all stairs and railings regardless of which tool was used to create them.

Object Styles (project wide settings)

The highest level of graphic control in a Revit project is **Manage → Object Styles** (Figure 7-1.7). Here, one can specify the line thickness and color for the various parts of a Stair (same for Railings). For Stairs and Railings, these settings only apply if there are no view specific overrides or filters. ***Tip:*** Compare the terms listed to the previous images.

Visibility/Graphic Overrides (view specific settings)

The graphics of Stairs/Railings can also be controlled on a view-by-view basis via the **Visibility/Graphics Overrides** dialog (Figure 7-1.8); while in a view, type **VV**. For example, maybe a Demolition plan or Code plan should show less detail…this can be achieved just in those views.

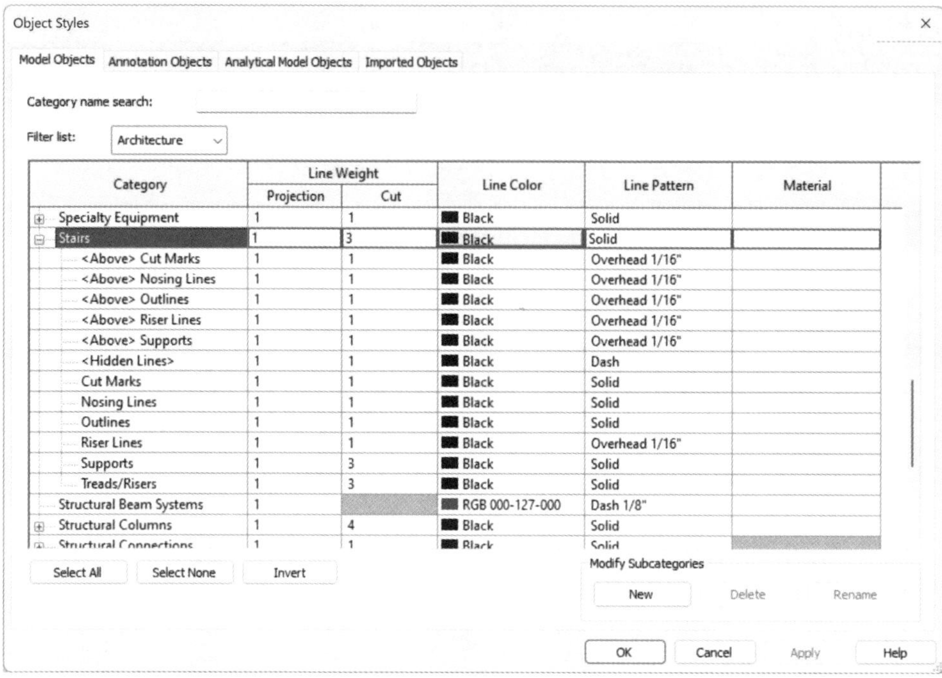

FIGURE 7-1.7 Object Styles dialog – project-wide graphics controls for stairs

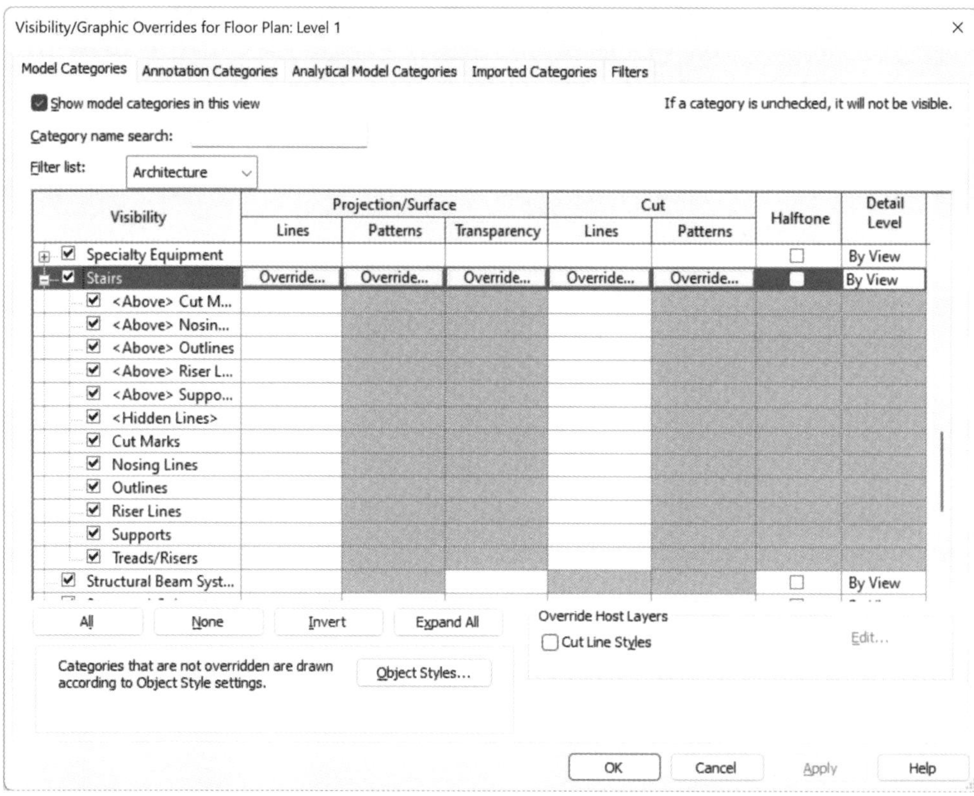

FIGURE 7-1.8 Visibility/Graphic Overrides dialog – view specific graphics controls for stairs

Calculate Tread/Riser Size

Although Revit automatically calculates the rise and tread dimensions for you, it is still a good idea to understand what is happening.

The **riser** is typically calculated to be as large as building codes will allow. Occasionally, a grand stair will have a smaller riser to create a more elegant stair.

Similarly, the **tread** is usually designed to be as small as allowable by building codes. This author worked on the design of a ski chalet where the treads were deeper than required by code for the comfort of those wearing ski boots in the building.

The largest riser and shortest tread create the steepest stair allowed. This takes up less floor space; see the next image. A stairway that is too steep is uncomfortable and unsafe.

Building codes vary by location; for this exercise, you will use 7″ (max.) for the risers and 12″ (min.) for the treads (11″ tread plus a 1″ nosing).

Codes usually require that each tread be the same size in a single run, likewise with risers.

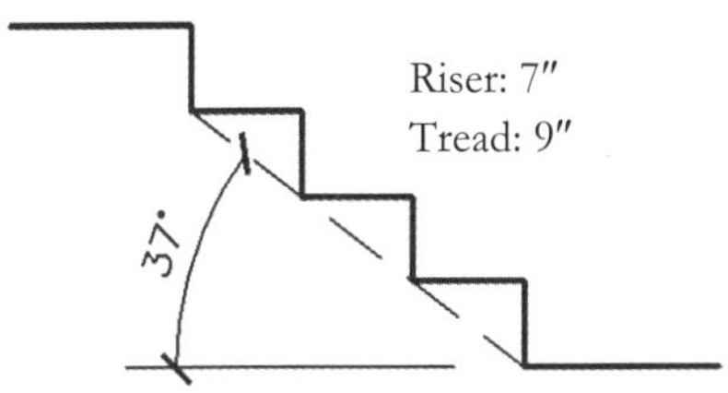

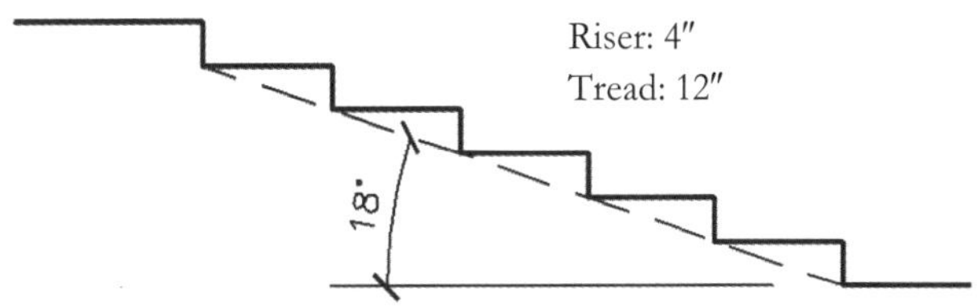

To calculate the number and size of the risers:

Given:

Risers: **7″** max.
Floor to floor height: **13′-4″**.

Calculate the number of risers:

13′-4″ divided by 7″ (or 160″ divided by 7″) = 22.857

Seeing as each riser has to be the same size we will have to round off to a whole number. You cannot round down because that will make the riser larger than the allowed maximum (13′-4″ / 22 = 7.3″). Therefore, you have to round up to 23. Thus: 13′-4″ divided by 23 = 6.957.

So you need **23** risers that are **6 15/16″** each.

Multistory Stairs

If a stair extends multiple stories (i.e. levels) in a building, Revit has a feature which will support this in some cases (but not all). When a stair is selected, click the **Select Levels** command on the Ribbon while in an elevation view—from here you select levels to extend the stair to. This really only works with straight run or U-shaped stairs (aka switchback stair).

In the image below (Figure 7-1.9), there are triple-run (left) and double-run (right) stairs. As a side note, the-triple-run stair might be used to minimize required floor space but requires enough vertical distance between floors as two of the runs overlap and can create headroom issues. When using the Multi-Story Stair feature in this case, the **double-run will work, but the triple-run will not**.

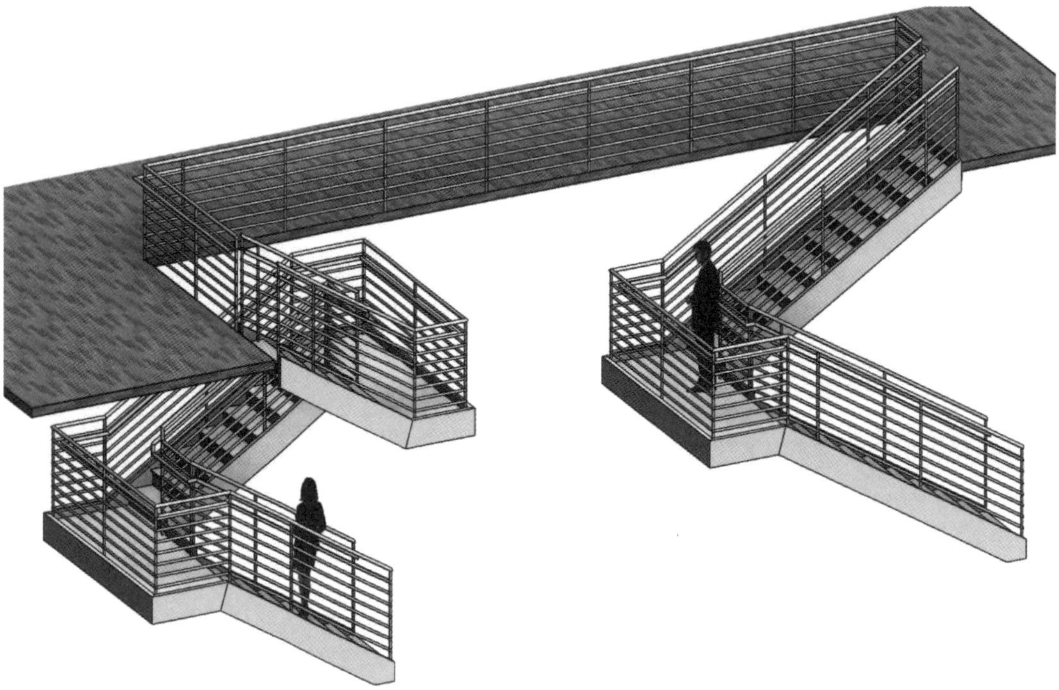

FIGURE 7-1.9 Two stair designs between level 1 and level 2

If the Multi-Story Stair feature is used on these two cases, we see the result in Figure 7-1.10. Because the stair is essentially arrayed vertically, and the triple-run starts and ends on the same side, we see a major issue. However, the double-run stair works correctly.

FIGURE 7-1.10 Stairs arrayed vertically using the Multistory Top Level parameter

Another problem with the new MS Story stair tool is it does not create half of the landings as shown in the image to the right (Figure 7-1.11). Often, in a stair shaft, the stair is all made of the same construction. The assumption with this tool, and the original stair tool, is that the primary floor construction, at each level, would extend into the stair shaft and define the landing at that location. While that may be done in some situations, it is not the norm.

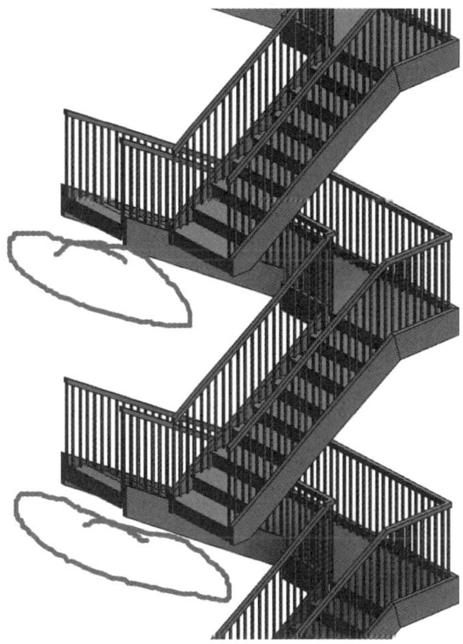

FIGURE 7-1.11 MS Stair missing landings

Conclusion

This concludes the basic introduction to Stairs and Railings in Revit. The next sections will dive deeper into each of these tools.

Exercise 7-2:
Stair by Component

Stair Types

When the *Stair by Component* command is selected, the **Type Selector** lists three options (Figure 7-2.1); this example is based on the Commercial-default template. At this point it is helpful to compare these three options with their corresponding entries in the **Project Browser** under Families - marked with #1 in Figure 7-2.2. The fourth item marked with #2, "stair," contains everything related to the older *Stair by Sketch* command. The remaining items are the "components" for this newer stair tool. These components are selected within the properties of the three main options highlighted here.

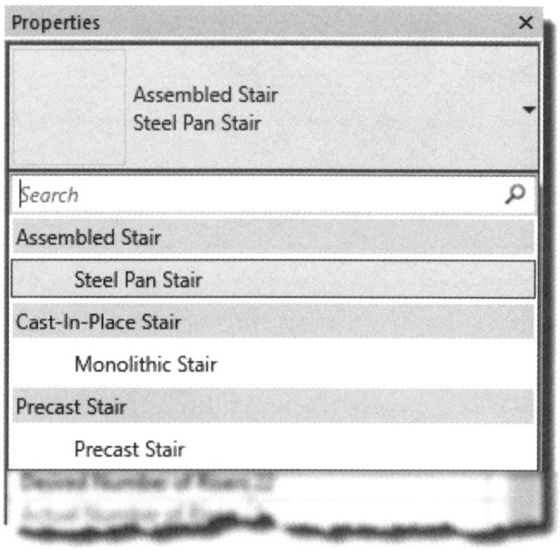

FIGURE 7-2.1 Type Selector; Stair by Component tool active

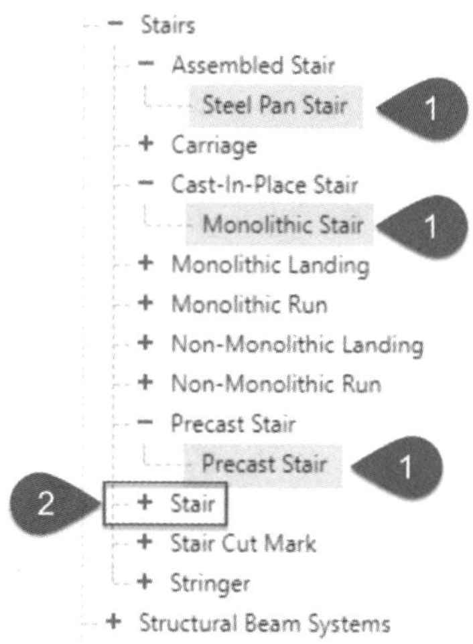

FIGURE 7-2.2 Family\Stairs in Project Browser

Stair Component Types

To see how a Stair by Component type, listed above, makes use of the **component types** take a look at the Type Properties for the "Steel Pan Stair" in Figure 7-2.3. The selected component types, which have been highlighted, can each be seen in the Project Browser as shown in Figure 7-2.4, also highlighted.

Unlike the Stair by Sketch, which contains all required properties in one Type Properties dialog (covered in the previous section), the Stair by Component has Type Properties for the entire stair (Steel Pan Stair in this example) and then Type Properties for the various components: Run Type, Landing Type, Supports and Cut Mark Type.

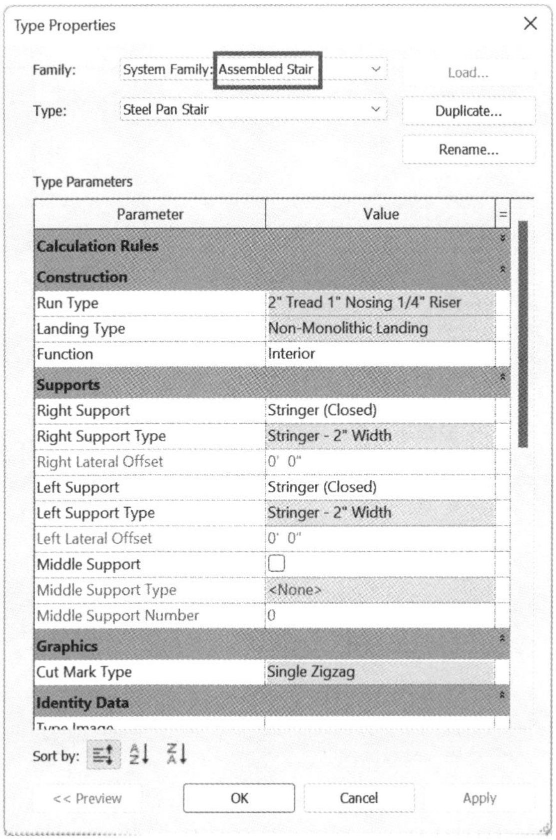

FIGURE 7-2.3 Steel Pan Stair type properties

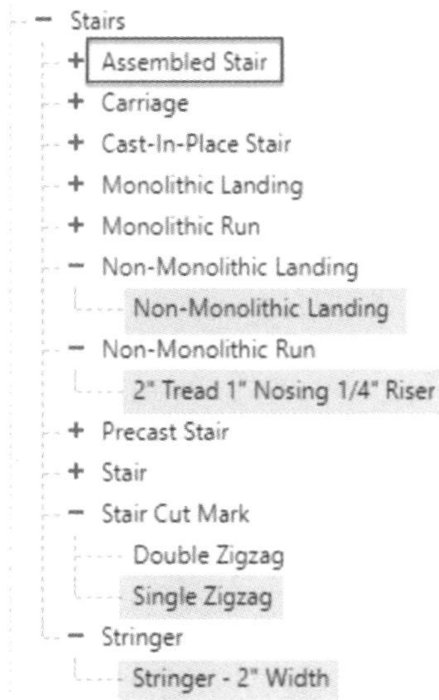

FIGURE 7-2.4 Component families used by Steel Pan Stair

Supports defined: Both a **Carriage** and a **Stringer** are able to support the stair. In Revit, a carriage is below the riser and treads while a stringer runs alongside them. A *Stair by Component* stair can have three supports, Left, Right and Middle, as seen in Figure 7-2.4. All three supports can be carriage-style but only the Left/Right can be stringers. **FYI:** There is some legacy terminology in Revit that is a bit confusing; a stringer is called "Closed" and a carriage is called "Open."

Examples of parameters associated with component types can be seen in Figure 7-2.5; here we see the *Run Type* named **2" Tread 1" Nosing ¼" Riser** and the *Right Support Type* named **Stringer – 2" Width**.

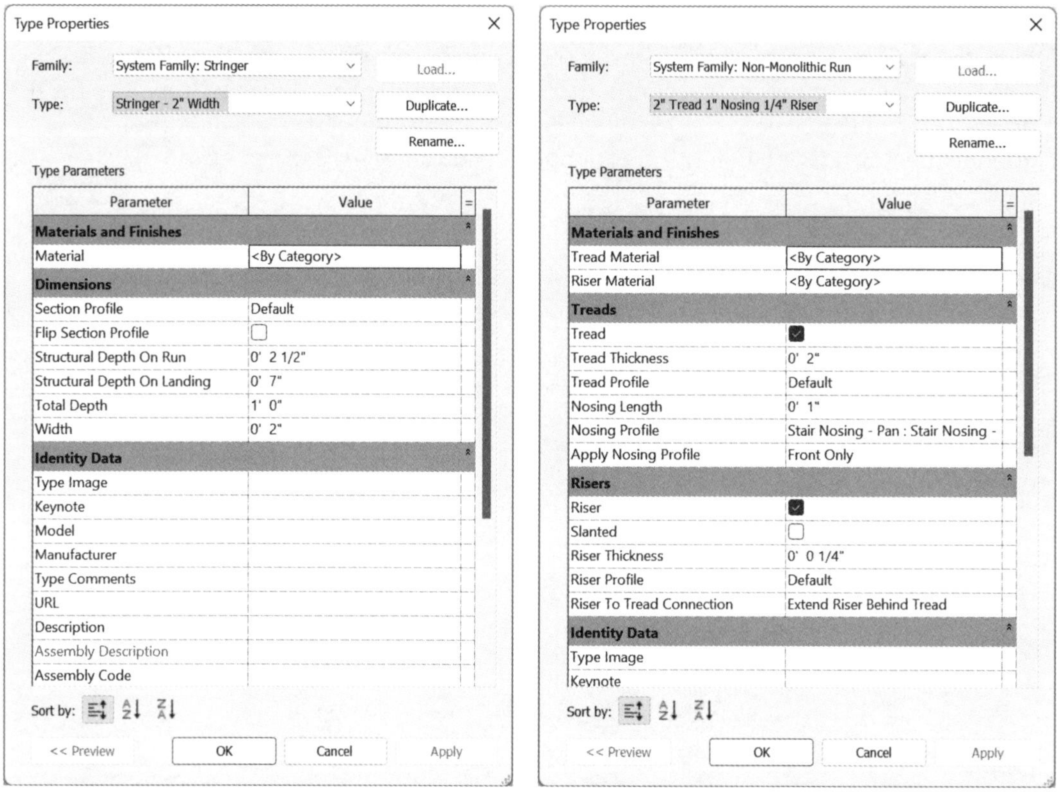

FIGURE 7-2.5 Type properties for two of the stair component types associated with 'Steel Pan Stair'

Notice in the image above that things like material and tread profile can be selected. This entire **Run Type** can be duplicated and modified when required—for example, a project has a simple utilitarian stair and a more formal open stair. Also notice that a profile can be selected for the supports: **Section Profile**. Thus, we can define a channel-shape which is fairly common in commercial construction. Remember, with the Stair by Sketch, the support can only be rectangular in shape.

All these settings will make more sense once you start using this tool. However, at this point you should have the basic understanding that there are properties for the entire stair system and then separate properties (i.e. types) for the individual components of the stair.

Creating Stairs using Stair by Component

While creating a stair with Stair by Component, the 3D "components" are created along the way. Using this tool, the individual sketch lines are not seen or editable (e.g., boundary and riser) like they are with the Stair by Sketch tool. This makes it easier to see what the stair will look like before clicking Finish Edit Mode. Also, because there are not sketch lines, it is possible to create a stair with multiple switch backs.

Here are the basic steps for the Stair tool:

- Start at the lowest level
- Select **Stair** tool
- Verify stair style in **Type Selector**
- Verify Base and Top Level settings in **Properties**
- Adjust settings on the **Ribbon (see** Figure 7-2.6 below)
    - Location Line
    - Offset (horizontal)
    - Stair Width
    - Landing creation
- **Pick points** to define one or more runs
- *Optional:* Add **Landing** to top or bottom if needed
    - select *Landing* on Ribbon while in the Stair by Component tool
- *Optional:* Select and delete individual **Support** elements
    - For example, if there is a door at an intermediate landing
    - Use the *Support* option to replace if needed

The image below shows the **Ribbon** while the Stair tool is active (Figure 7-2.6). Be sure to select the best option for Location Line. If in a stair shaft, one of the exterior support options is likely the more convenient option. Note that these settings can vary from run to run within the same stair instance.

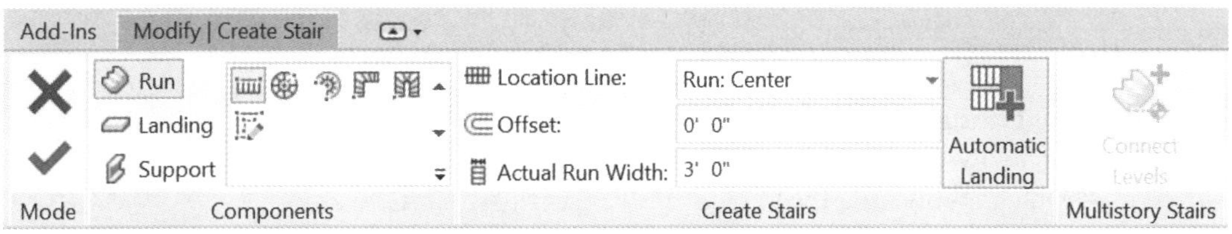

FIGURE 7-2.6 Ribbon options for Stair tool

Picking the points on-screen is similar to the Stair by Sketch tool. Two clicks can create a continuous single run from floor to floor, or, as shown in the image below, multiple clicks can create multiple runs. All along, Revit indicates how many risers remain before reaching the next level.

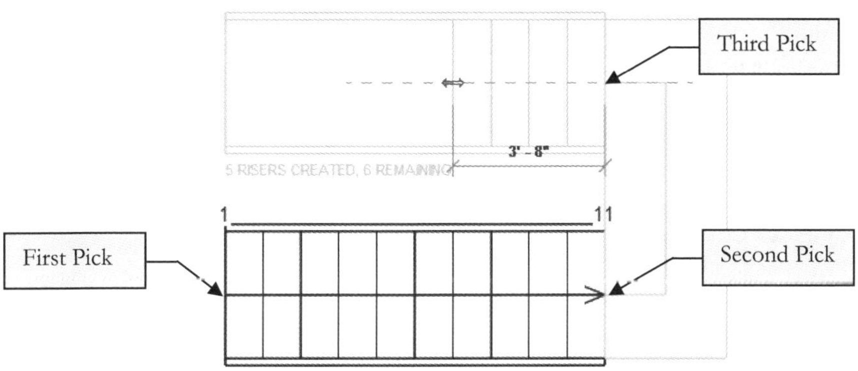

FIGURE 7-2.7 Creating stair with Stair by Component tool

Once the components are created and you are still in the Stair by Component tool, individual components can be selected.

Stair Landings

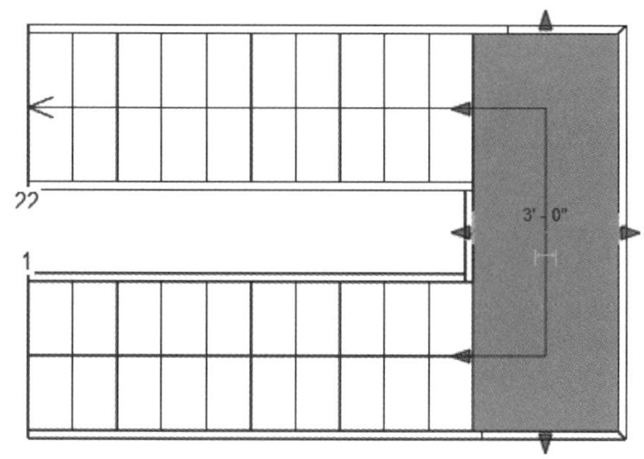

FIGURE 7-2.8 Stair by Component edit mode with landing selected

In the first image (Figure 7-2.8), the intermediate landing is selected. Notice there are six grips. There is one grip on each side and one grip at each stair run.

The next image (Figure 7-2.9) shows how the landing can be modified when adjusting the grips by clicking and dragging. In this example, the three circled grips were moved to change the size and shape of the intermediate landing.

Landings are only automatically added between runs when **Automatic Landing** is selected on the Ribbon. If additional landing construction is required at the top or bottom of the stair, select the **Landing** option (see Ribbon image below) and then sketch a closed loop which is touching the adjacent stair run.

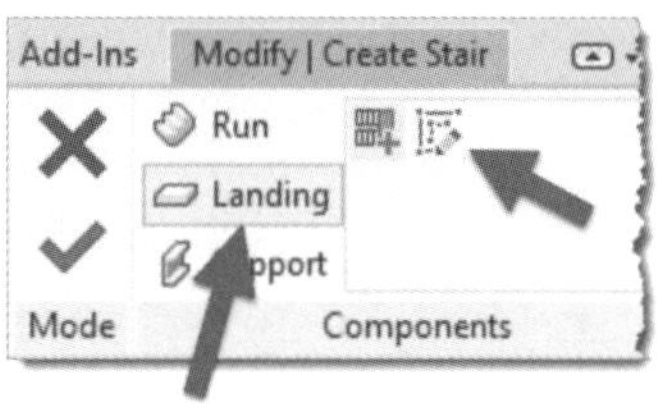

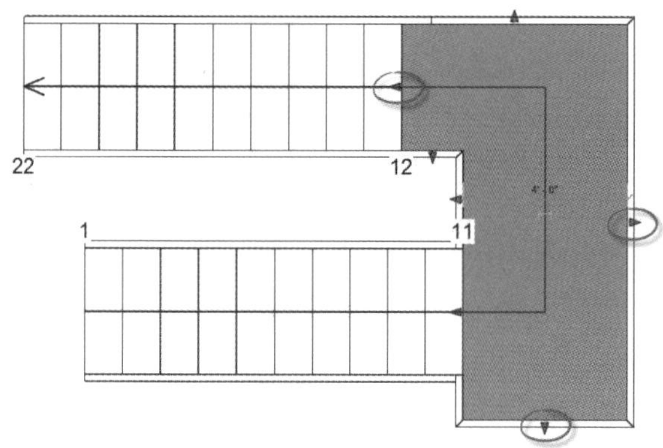

FIGURE 7-2.9 Landing adjusted using grips

The result is a landing with added supports on all three sides as seen in the upper part of Figure 7-2.10. Selecting the end support allows you to delete it. Notice how the side supports adjust from mitered to flush cut in the lower image once the support has been deleted.

When a landing is selected, its **Relative Height** and thickness are listed in the Properties Palette. Adjusting the elevation will automatically adjust the runs, plus the number entered will be changed to the closest riser position. However, the runs are not adjustable if any of them have been converted to a sketch (more on this in a moment).

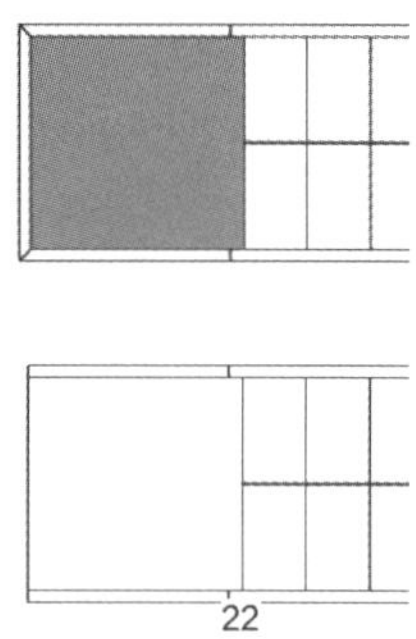

FIGURE 7-2.10 Added landing and support deleted

Non-rectilinear Landings:
The intermediate landings automatically created by Revit can be modified. While in Stair Edit mode, select the landing component as shown in the first image in Figure 7-2.11. Click the **Convert** command on the Ribbon.

At this point, a message appears indicating the conversion is irreversible. Click **Close** to complete the conversion. The landing portion of the stair is now a Sketch-based stair element.

With the landing still selected, click the **Edit Sketch** command on the Ribbon. The lines which define the perimeter of the landing, in plan-view, are now editable. Use **Draw** and **Modify** tools, such as Line, Circle, Arc, Split, Trim, Offset, etc. to adjust the footprint of the landing. An example of a modified landing can be seen in the second image to the right.

When finished editing the landing sketch, click the **green checkmark** to exit sketch mode. If the sketch is not a clean outline with any overlapping or crossing lines Revit will create the landing. Unlike other sketches, like floors, there cannot be multiple closed loops (e.g. in a floor, a loop within a loop would create a hole in the floor). If a sketch error is shown, Revit will highlight the problem area. Simply click Continue and fix the problem.

Click the green checkmark one more time to finish the entire stair instance; Revit will recreate any hosted railings as well. This can be seen in the last image to the right.

If the landing needs to be modified again, select the stair and click Edit Stair and then select the landing component and click Edit Sketch.

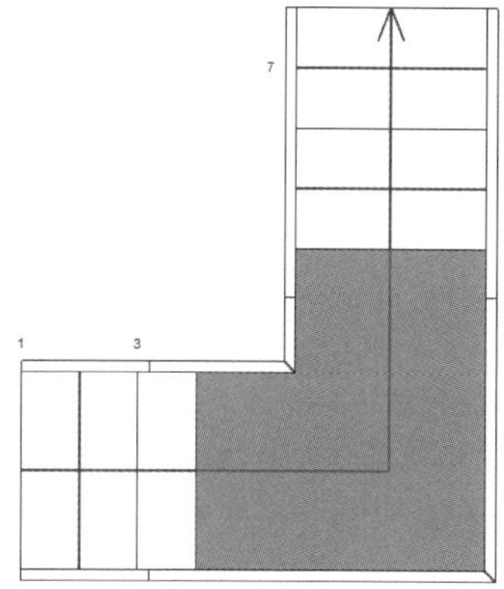

Original Landing

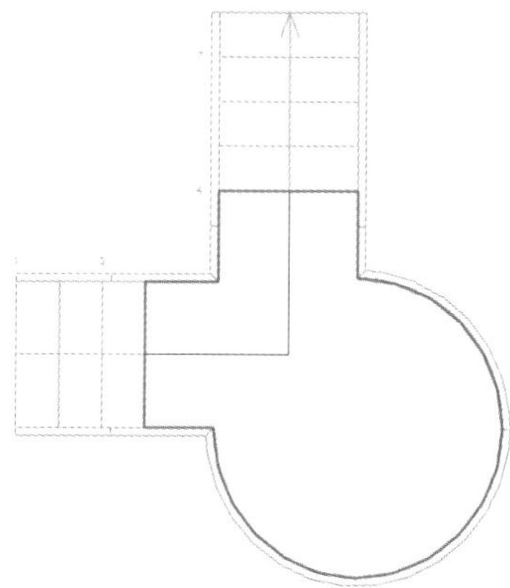

Convert to Sketch and Modify

Custom Landing Result

FIGURE 7-2.11 Custom Stair Landing

<u>**Landing Properties:**</u>
A landing can have its main properties defined by the Run, which is the default setting, or independently.

Selecting a landing and then looking at its Type Properties we see **Same as Run** is selected (Figure 7-2.12). This tells Revit to inherit several properties from the stair run that the landing is connected to within the *Stair by Component* instance.

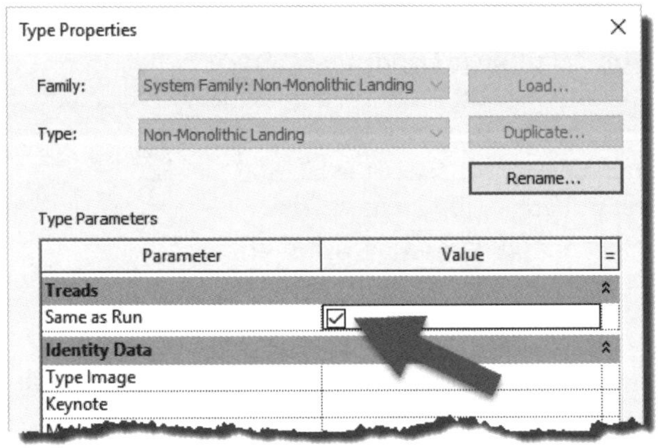

FIGURE 7-2.12 Landing type properties; 'Same as Run' checked

TIP: A component within the stair can be selected without entering edit mode. Simply hover your cursor over the component and then tap the **Tab** key and click to select once the component highlights.

When **Same as Run** is unchecked, several properties appear as shown in Figure 7-2.13.

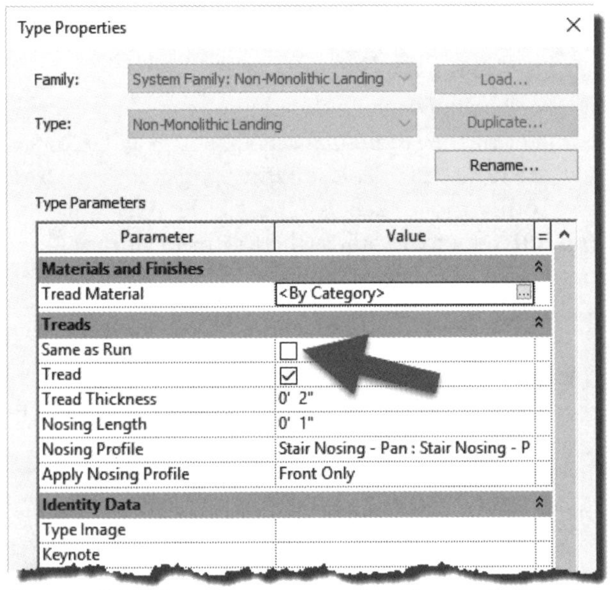

FIGURE 7-2.13 Landing type properties; 'Same as Run' unchecked

<u>**Landing Material:**</u>
In addition to controlling the various tread properties, notice that a **material** parameter is also now available when **Same as Run** is unchecked. If the landing requires a different floor finish, uncheck the **Same as Run** option and specify the material using the **Tread Material** parameter.

An example of the nosing and material matching the run can be seen in Figure 7-2.14.

FIGURE 7-2.14 Landing nosing and material example

Stair Supports

When a support (aka Stringer) is selected, there are three ways in which the end can be cut: Horizontal, Perpendicular and Vertical (Figure 7-2.15). The default is Vertical. This setting is only adjustable at the ends of a top or bottom run. Notice in the image that the setting can vary for each side of the stair.

These options for supports are more limiting than those for the Stair by Sketch tool. Looking back at that section, we see it is possible to control whether the stringer continues to slope or is flat, and its vertical dimension. With the Stair by Component tool we can only extend the stringer if there is a landing to host it.

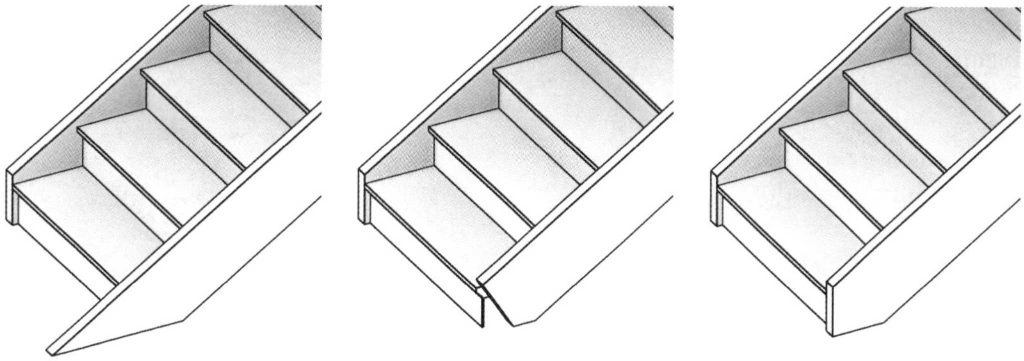

Horizontal *Perpendicular* *Vertical*

FIGURE 7-2.15 Three options for a support end cut: Horizontal, Perpendicular and Vertical, respectively

Revit generally does a good job at how supports transition. Sometimes there are issues as seen in the example below, on the left. This is not really Revit's fault. The issue is we did not give Revit enough room to make an appropriate transition. Once the landing has been adjusted, we see the buildable result on the right. As we will see later, this is true for railings as well.

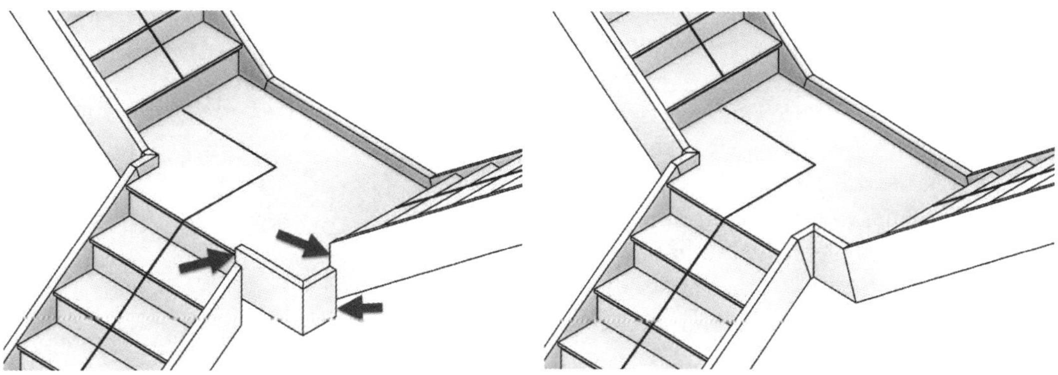

Support Transition Issues *Support Transition Correction*

FIGURE 7-2.16 Dealing with supports which do not transition correctly

The example in the previous image (Figure 7-2.16) shows two runs coming off of the same landing, up to the next level. The steps to accomplish this will be covered in the next section on stair runs.

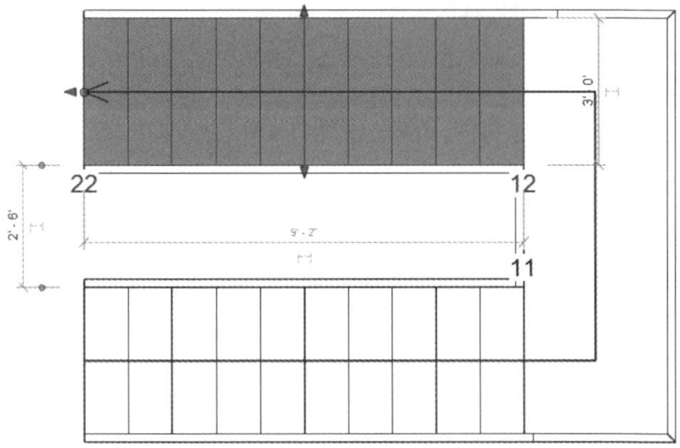

FIGURE 7-2.17 Stair run selected

Stair Runs

When an individual stair run is selected, there are a few adjustment options for the grips, as shown in Figure 7-2.17.

Dragging the side grips adjusts the stair's width only for the selected run. Each run can be a different width.

Dragging the top-end (or bottom-end) grip will depress the number of steps in the selected run. The opposite run will have the same number of steps added (or removed); see Fig. 7-2.18.

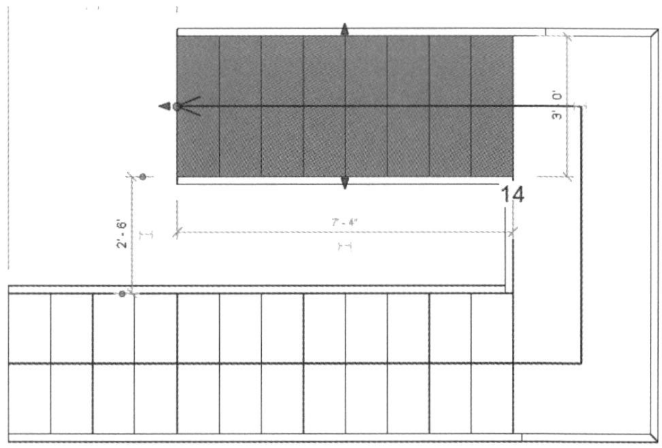

FIGURE 7-2.18 Stair run grip adjusted

A selected run can also be **nudged** using the Arrow keys. When nudging the stair away from the landing, Revit will automatically extend the landing to meet up with the new stair position.

Additional runs can be modeled within the same stair instance, as shown in the previous section. This may be for a grand stair or access to an adjacent roof level. Here is how this is done:

- While in edit mode, select the landing (Fig. 7-2.19)
- Copy the **Relative Height** to the clipboard; highlight and press **CTRL + C**
- Select the **Run** command on the *Ribbon* (Step #1, Fig. 7-2.20)

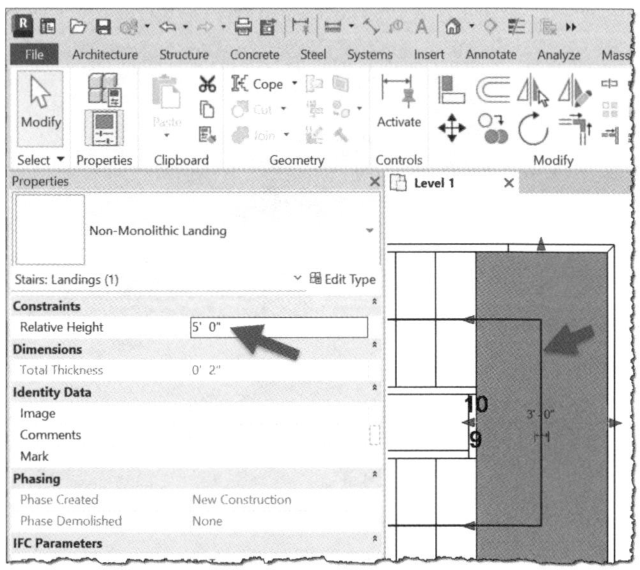

FIGURE 7-2.19 Height listed for selected landing

- Switch the *Properties Palette* drop-down to **Runs** (Step #2, Fig. 7-2.20)
- Paste the landing height into **Relative Base Height**; **CTRL + V** (Step #3, Fig. 7-2.20)
- Draw the stair run (Figure 7-2.21)

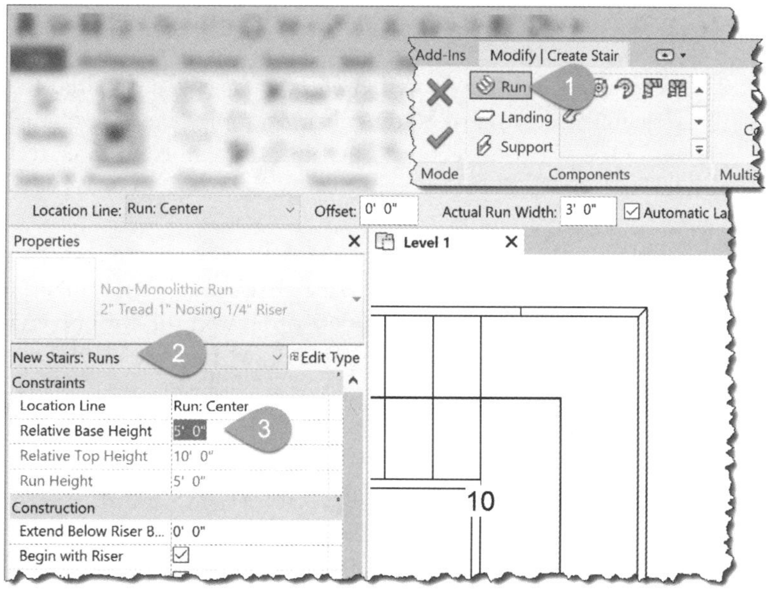

FIGURE 7-2.20 Adding an extra stair run from an intermediate landing

The result is a new run joined to the landing as seen in the two images that follow. Notice that the run arrow cannot connect multiple stair runs. Thus, make sure to model the desired primary path first. Also, if the secondary stair run needs to be repositioned, it will no longer be joined to the landing. However, the landing can be adjusted, and once it touches the run it will automatically join with it.

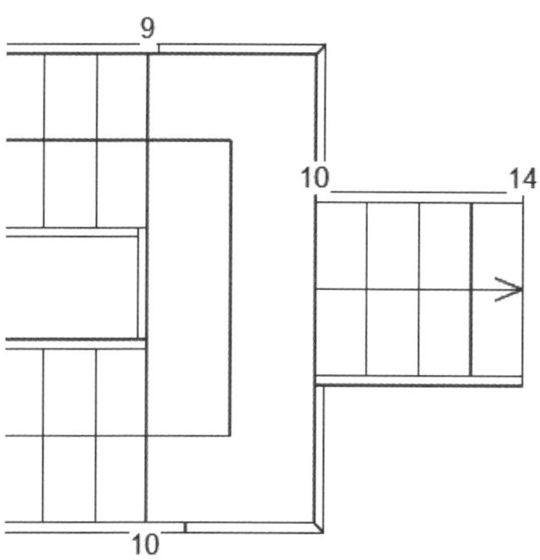

FIGURE 7-2.21 Extra run added to stair

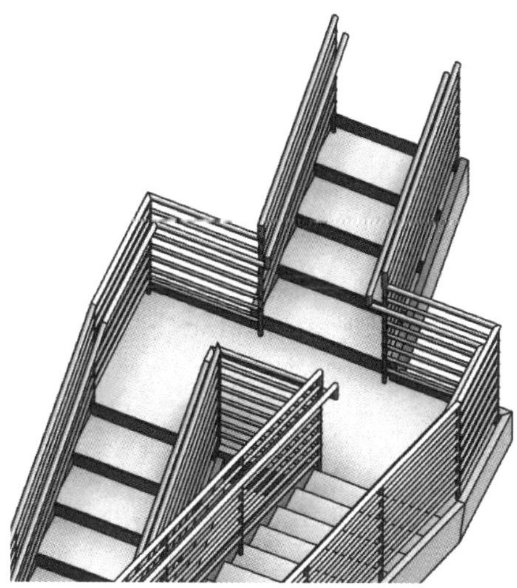

FIGURE 7-2.22 3D view of modified stair

Stair Limitations

There are a few limitations with *Stair by Component* compared to *Stair by Sketch* when it comes to modeling a stair run or landing. For example, the edge of the stair cannot be angled as shown in the previous section. The bottom tread is not able to be extended out and rounded either.

The way to deal with these limitations is to convert the stair component to a sketch-based run or landing. As covered a few pages back for a custom landing, with a stair run selected, while in edit mode, click the **Convert** option on the Ribbon. As the following message indicates, this is irreversible. The main drawbacks are not being able to drag grips to resize the components, but runs and landings still join properly. Thus, the drawbacks are minimal when compared to the need to model the stair correctly. Once a component is converted, select it and click **Edit Sketch** on the Ribbon to modify a run or landing. At this point you are two "edit modes" deep—meaning the green checkmark, for finish, must be clicked twice to fully complete the stair modification.

Stair Annotation

There are a few annotation tools related to Stair by Component to be aware of.

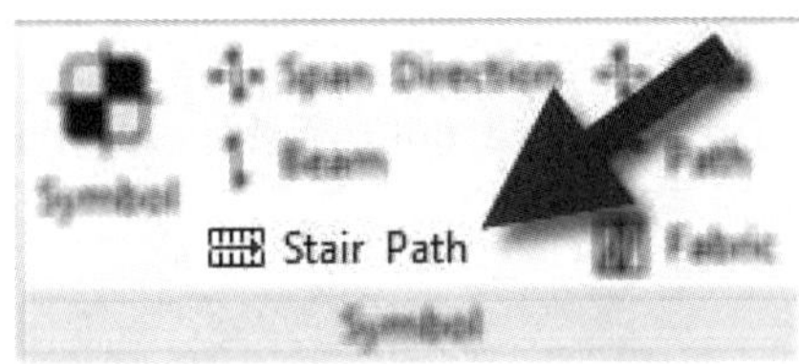

The **Stair Path** tool, found on the Annotation tab, adds the UP or DN text and an arrow. Keep in mind that every tool on this tab is 2D and view-specific. When a stair is created, the Stair Path annotation is automatically added to every plan view. When subsequent plan views are created (or copied without detailing), stair arrow annotations are not automatically added to those.

The Stair Path element can be selected and repositioned, or even deleted, in each view. If the annotation is deleted or a new plan-view is created, use the **Stair Path** tool to add it to a stair instance.

The visibility of the text and arrows can be controlled separately and per view. Figure 7-2.23 shows the **Visibility/Graphic Overrides** dialog with the Stair Paths category expanded on the Annotation Categories tab.

The text and arrow can be moved separately. The text, “UP” or “DN,” can be moved in any direction. The arrow can only be moved perpendicular to the run of the stair.

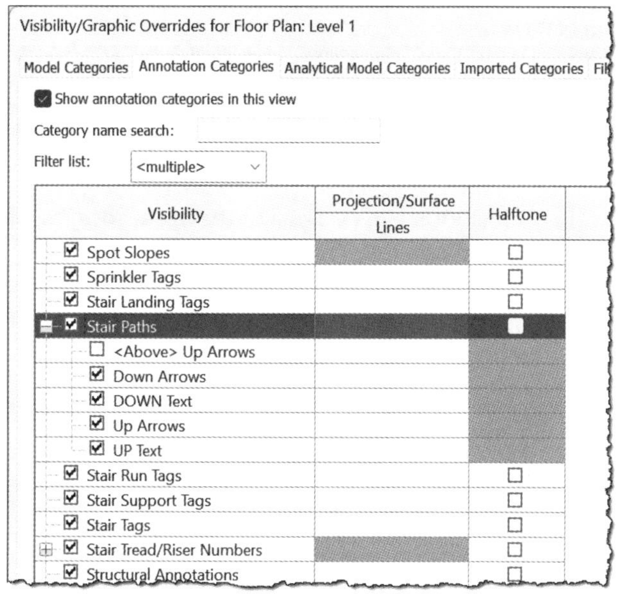

FIGURE 7-2.23 Stair path category

The **Tread Number** tool, also found on the Annotation tab, enumerates each tread for a selected run.

This tool is simple to use. To add tread numbers to a stair, start the command and select a stair run in a plan or section view. Each separate run must be selected, even within a single Stair instance. The numbers only appear in the current view.

An example of the results is shown in Figure 7-2.24 for both section and plan views.

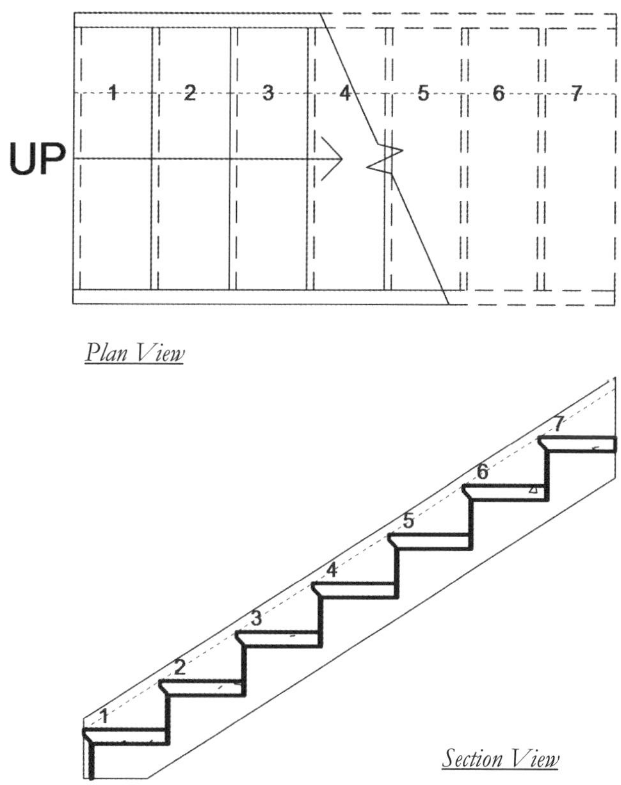

FIGURE 7-2.24 Tread Number tool results

Once placed, select it to access several formatting options via the Properties Palette. The Tread Number element is selected in Figure 7-2.24; notice the dashed line running through the numbers. When not selected, there is no visible line.

Warnings

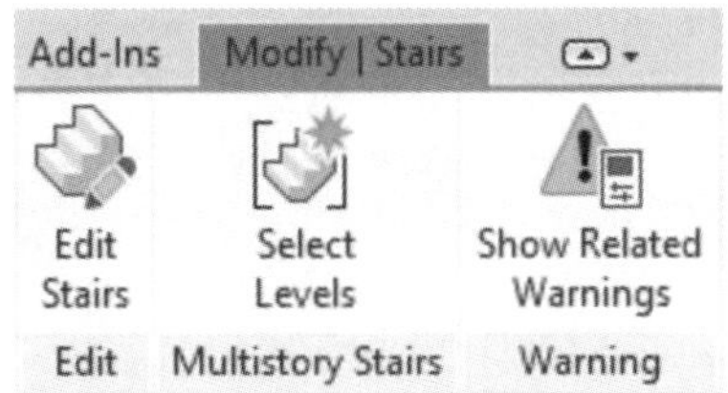

If a stair has a problem, for example, a stair instance does not reach a floor level, the **Show Related Warning** button will appear whenever that stair is selected.

Clicking this button opens a dialog that describes the problem, as shown in the image below (Figure 7-2.25). This can happen if a stair is created and there are "remaining" risers listed prior to clicking finish. Also, if a stair type is switched from non-monolithic to monolithic, this can appear.

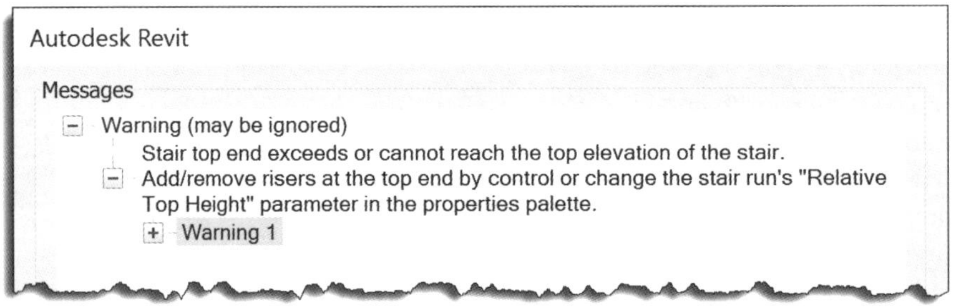

FIGURE 7-2.25 Warning message for selected stair

To see a full list of warnings for the entire model, select **Manage → Warnings** (Figure 7-2.26). This should be done occasionally to ensure there are no major issues with the model. Keeping this list free of major errors can improve the model's performance, as Revit is not constantly checking for this situation.

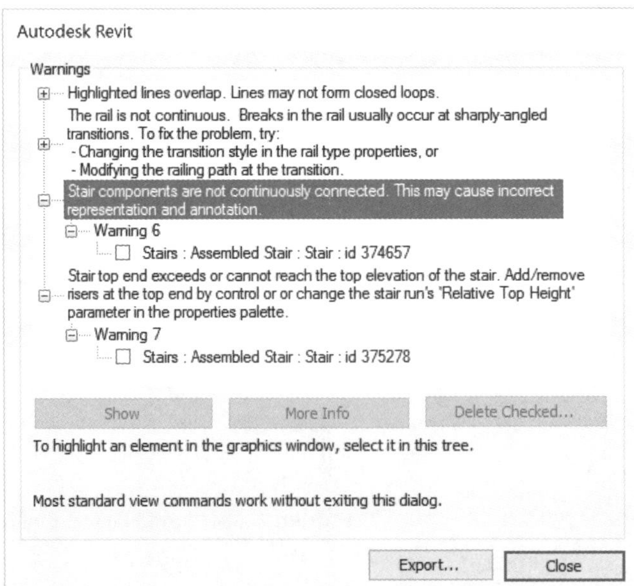

FIGURE 7-2.26 Warnings list for entire project

Exercise 7-3:
Introduction to Railings

This "exercise" will provide a basic introduction to the railing tool in Revit. There are no required steps for the law office project in this section. However, it is highly recommended that this information be reviewed before completing the steps later in this chapter.

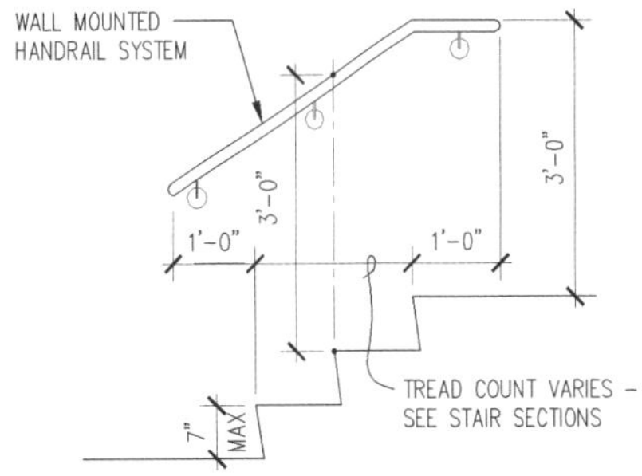

Railing Types

When the *Railing* command is selected, the railing Types in the current project are listed in the **Type Selector**. Compare this list to the same items listed in the **Project Browser** under Families\Railings\Railings. The items listed in the Project Browser can be Duplicated or Deleted.

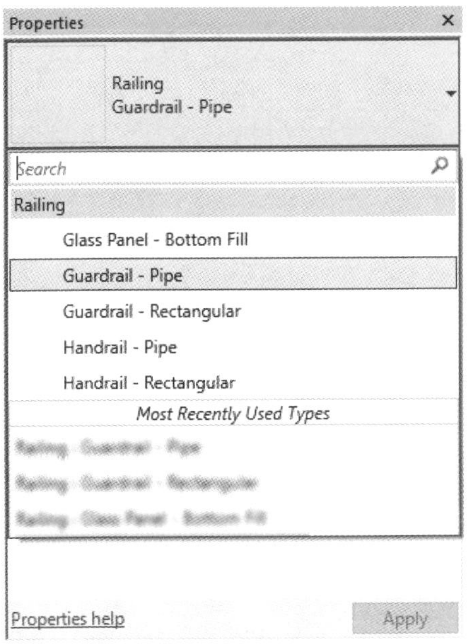

FIGURE 7-3.1 Type Selector; Railing tool active

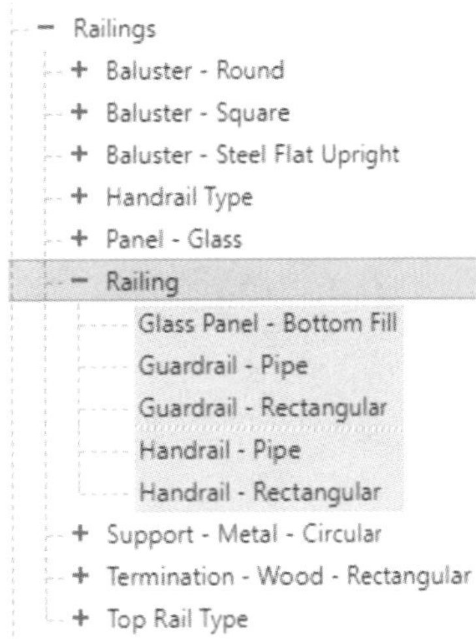

FIGURE 7-3.2 Family\Railing in Project Browser

Railing Component Types

Similar to Stairs, Railings have several high-level properties (i.e., Type Properties). These are shown in Figure 7-3.3. Notice the option to select a Top Rail and Handrail type. Also, there is an option for two handrails on the same railing. This allows a Handrail to be placed on both sides of a railing.

The options available in the Top Rail and Handrail component drop-down lists are based on the Types created in the current project. These options can be seen in the Project Browser as shown in Figure 7-3.4. These Types can be Duplicated or Deleted via the right-click menu.

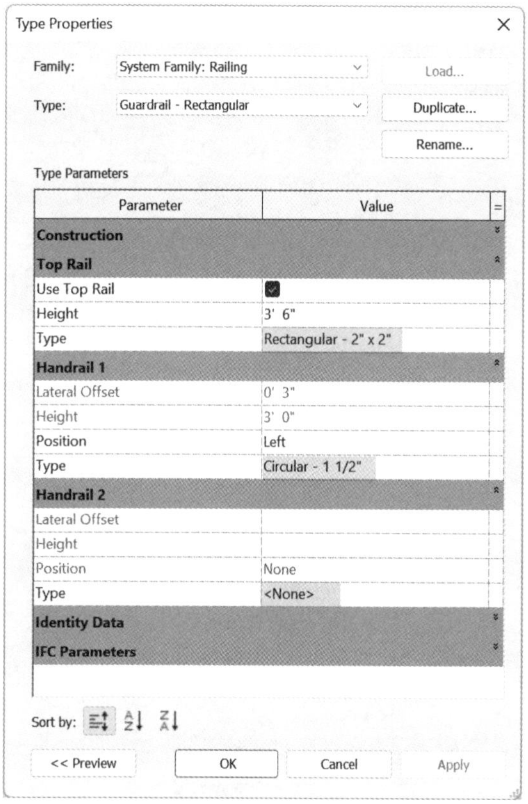

FIGURE 7-3.3 Guardrail – Rectangular railing properties

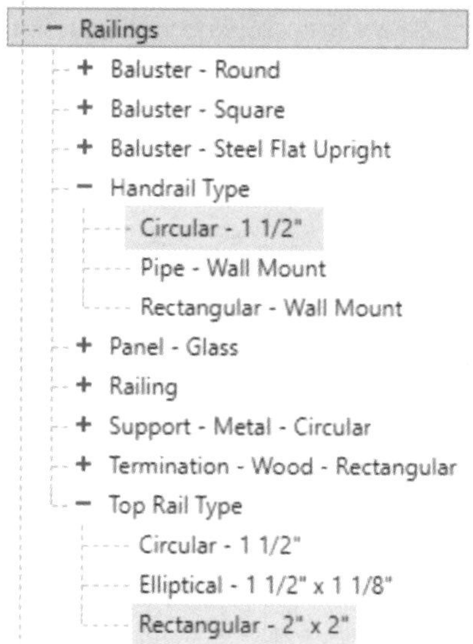

FIGURE 7-3.4 Component families used by railing

Conceptually, take note that a Top Rail and Handrail are more complex than just selecting a profile, as this will help you understand Revit's internal structure for these element types. The properties associated with the Top Rail and Handrail selected in the previous image can be seen in Figure 7-3.5.

In Revit, a Profile is a simple 2D closed outline—a series of connected lines and/or arcs. An example is shown in Figure 7-3.7. Similar to other families, profiles can be parameterized. Thus, this simple circle can represent multiple diameters. The Project Browser shown in Figure 7-3.6 shows two sizes (i.e., types) for this profile. Just like doors, these types can be duplicated and new sizes created without the need to create a new profile family. However, creating a new profile is easy: **New → Family → Profile.rft** template.

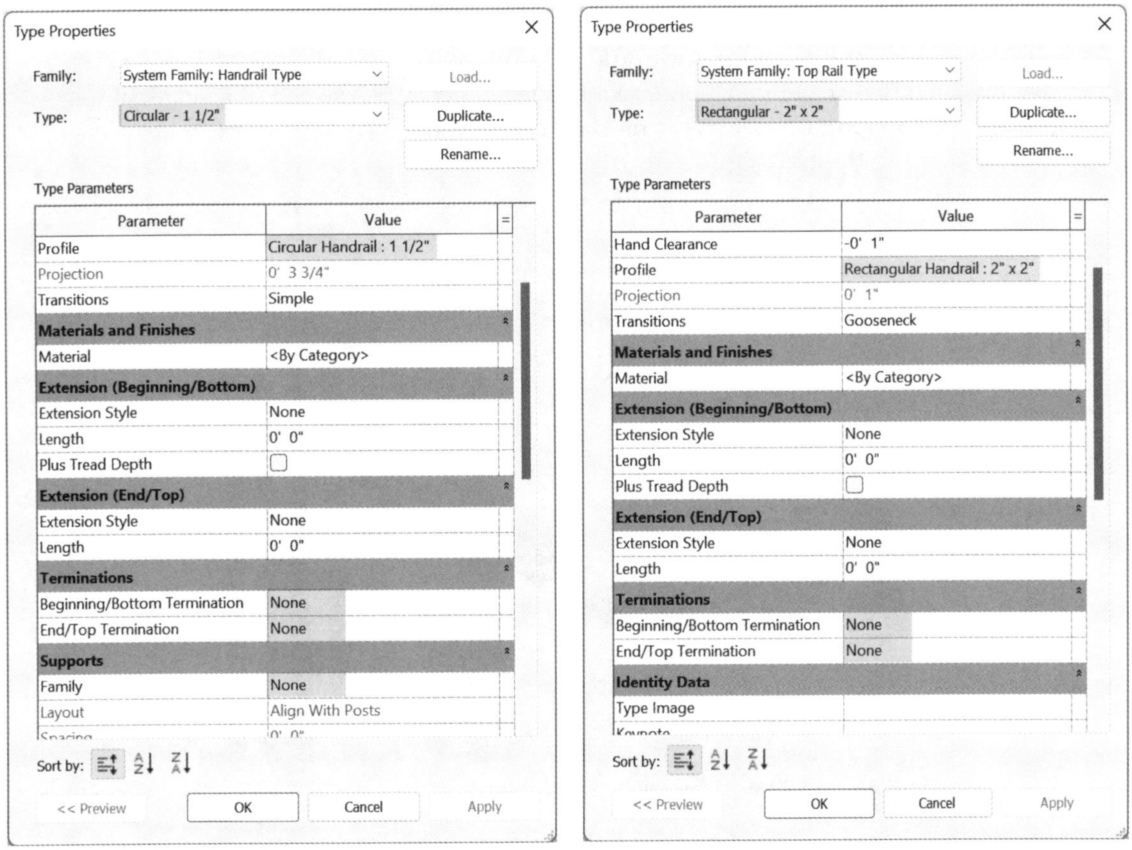

FIGURE 7-3.5 Type properties for two of the railing component types associated with "Guardrail – Rectangular"

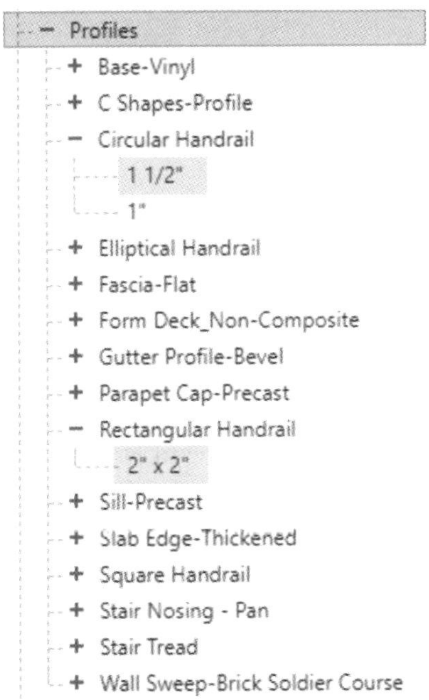

FIGURE 7-3.6 Profiles families used by handrail & top rail types

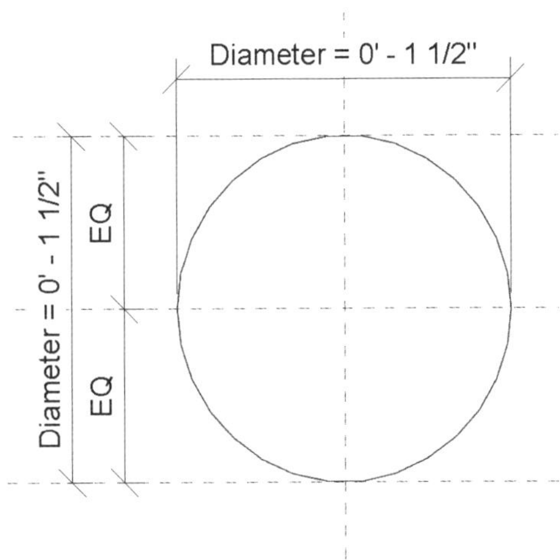

FIGURE 7-3.7 Profiles Circular handrail profile as seen in the family editor

In Figure 7-3.5, notice both Handrails and Top Rails have an option called **Terminations**. Handrails also have an option for **Supports**. In this example they are all set to "None." Figure 7-3.8 shows that a termination (aka escutcheon) occurs at the end of a Handrail (or Top Rail) and a Support is what holds the Handrail in place. Each of these items are separate families loaded into the current project.

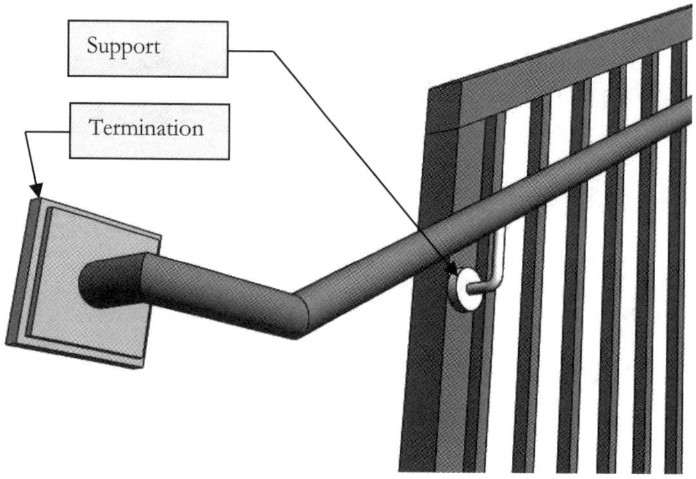

FIGURE 7-3.8 Termination and Supports example

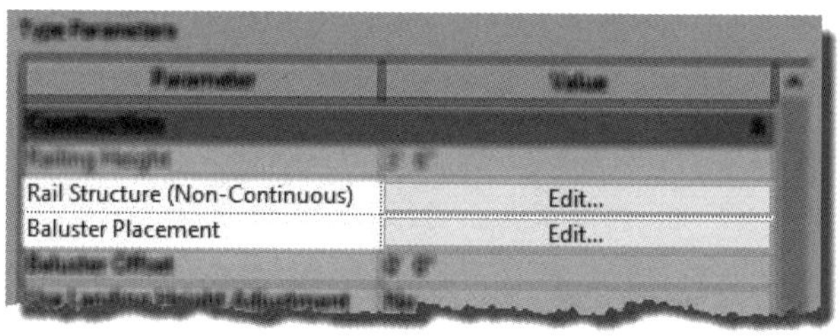

Now that the various components and nested families in a railing have been covered, we need to back up to the beginning and look at how the rest of the railing is defined. This is the pattern, either horizontal, vertical or both, that fills that area from the stair/floor up to the Top Rail. You are about to see two of the most complex dialogs in Revit! We will compare the settings between the two guardrail types Pipe and Rectangular to help understand how the various options and settings work.

Rail Structure (Non-Continuous)

When a railing has horizontal/parallel rails, in addition to the Top Rail and Handrail, they are defined in the **Edit Rails (Non-Continuous)** dialog shown in Figure 7-3.10. To access this dialog, select a railing, click Edit Type, and then click Edit next to Rail Structure (Non-Continuous).

Looking at Figure 7-3.9 we notice the "Pipe" railing only has vertical elements. Thus, the Edit Rails dialog is empty. Contrast this with the "Rectangular" railing type which is mainly composed of horizontal/parallel rails.

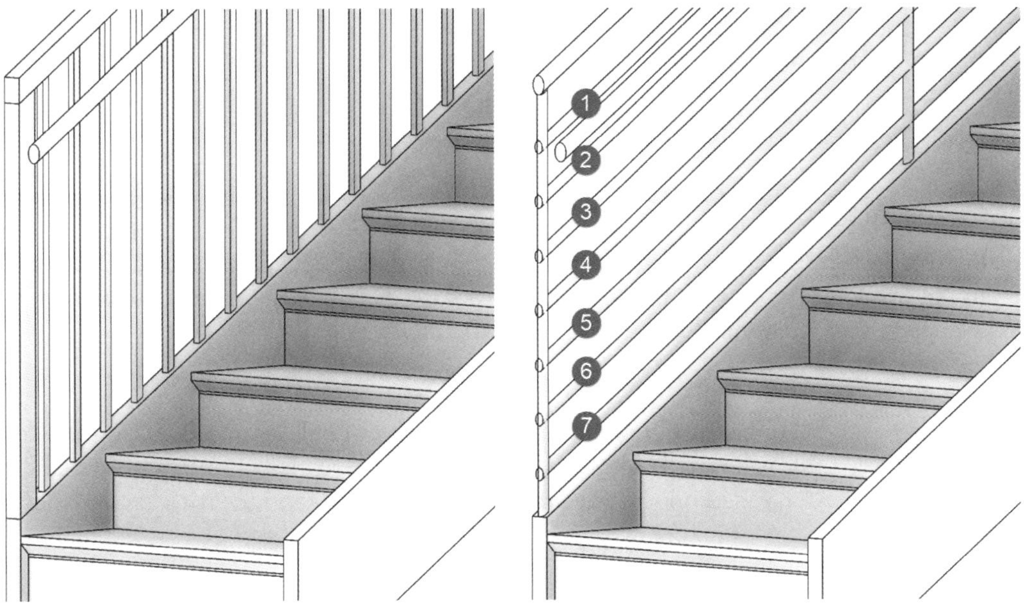

Guardrail - Rectangular *Guardrail - Pipe*

FIGURE 7-3.9 Graphically comparing two railing types found in the Commercial-Default project template

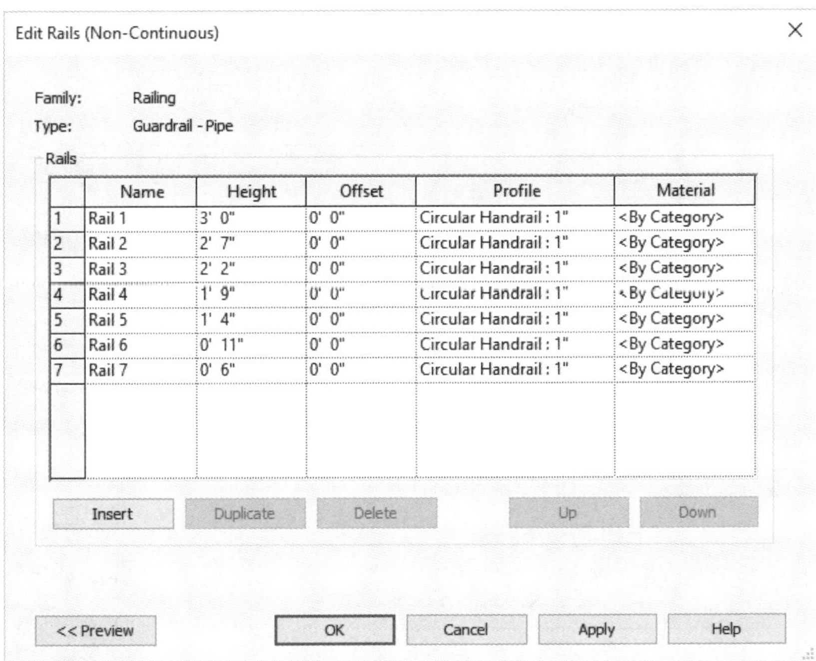

	Name	Height	Offset	Profile	Material
1	Rail 1	3' 0"	0' 0"	Circular Handrail : 1"	<By Category>
2	Rail 2	2' 7"	0' 0"	Circular Handrail : 1"	<By Category>
3	Rail 3	2' 2"	0' 0"	Circular Handrail : 1"	<By Category>
4	Rail 4	1' 9"	0' 0"	Circular Handrail : 1"	<By Category>
5	Rail 5	1' 4"	0' 0"	Circular Handrail : 1"	<By Category>
6	Rail 6	0' 11"	0' 0"	Circular Handrail : 1"	<By Category>
7	Rail 7	0' 6"	0' 0"	Circular Handrail : 1"	<By Category>

FIGURE 7-3.10 Defining horizontal elements within a railing

The numbers added to the "Rectangular" railing example, in Figure 7-3.9, correspond to the numbered rows in Figure 7-3.10. Notice each row has five settings as defined below.

Name
Each row can be named to help keep things organized. Each row must have a unique name. These named rows appear in the Edit Baluster Placement dialog covered in the next section.

Height
The Height of the rail is from the floor/landing or the front edge of the tread as shown in Figure 7-3.11. Compare the dimensions shown in this image to those listed in the Edit Rails dialog (Figure 7-3.10). Note that the height is to the top of the rail in each case. Dimensions from the tread edge and to the top of the Top Rail and Handrail relate to how building codes define stair, guardrail and handrail requirements.

Offset
This allows each rail to be offset horizontally from the main railing if needed. In previous versions of Revit this is how a handrail was defined. There are many creative ways this option can be used. Keep in mind there are two other "offset" options for a railing: the instance parameter *Tread/Stringer Offset* and the type parameter *Baluster Offset.*

Profile
This defines the shape continuously extruded along the handrail. Speaking of continuously, it is unclear why the dialog says "Non-Continuous"! Load and/or create additional Profiles in the current project for more options. Note that this could include something that looks like a stair stringer to maintain a consistent look when the railing at a stair transitions to a railing at an open floor edge (Figure 7-3.12).

Material
This defines the material applied to the shape created by the extruded profile.

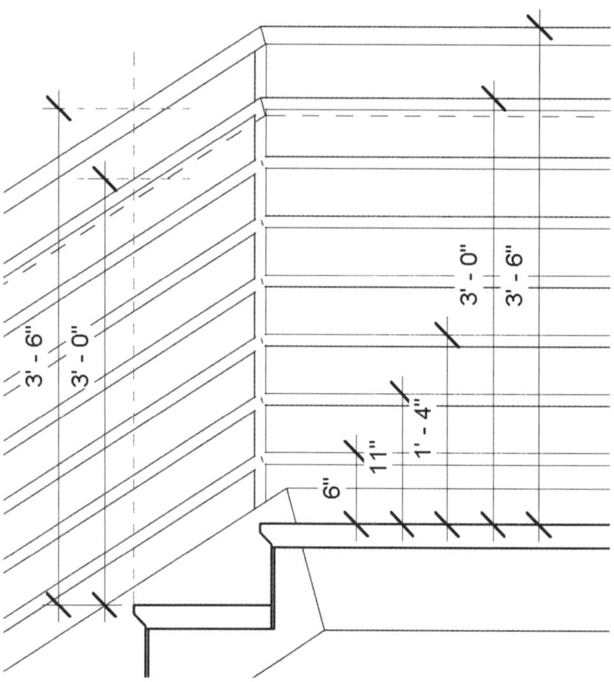

FIGURE 7-3.11 Railing rail dimensions

FIGURE 7-3.12
Railing with stringer

In the Edit Rails dialog, new rows can be inserted, and current rows can be duplicated or deleted. The order of the rows does not matter as the Height parameter dictates its position, but having them in the same relative order is helpful—thus the Up and Down buttons. Finally, expanding the preview option allows you to see the results without closing the dialog or clicking apply. However, clicking Apply will update the model without the need to close the dialog. This shows the changes in your model rather than a generic sample preview.

Baluster Placement

Where the *Rail Structure* dialog defines all the horizontal/parallel elements (except for top and handrail) the **Edit Baluster Placement** dialog defines all the vertical elements within a railing system. This dialog, as seen in Figure 7-3.13, has two main sections: **Main Pattern** and **Posts** as pointed out.

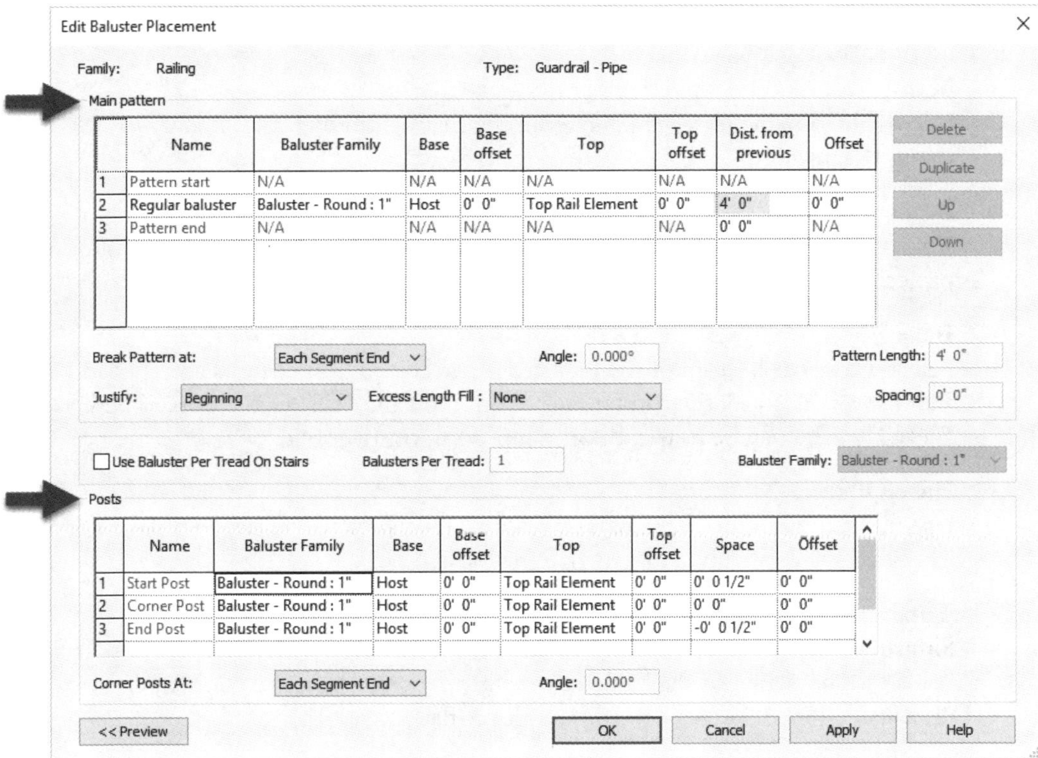

FIGURE 7-3.13 Edit Baluster Placement dialog; Guardrail – Pipe (4'-0" main pattern spacing)

Main Pattern

In the example above, for Guardrail – Pipe, there is not a "main pattern" per se. This is because the "main pattern" is defined by horizontal/parallel bars. Thus, in this example the Main Pattern is the "structural" supports for the railing system which are spaced 4'-0" (note the highlighted value in Figure 7-3.13). **FYI:** The 1" diameter pipe at 4'-0" on center may or may not be adequate to develop the code required lateral resistance at the top edge of the railing.

Comparing the two guardrail examples (Figure 7-3.9) we see the "Pipe" type has the "main pattern" spaced at **4'-0"** (Figure 7-3.13), whereas the "Rectangular" option spacing is only **4"** (Figure 7-3.14).

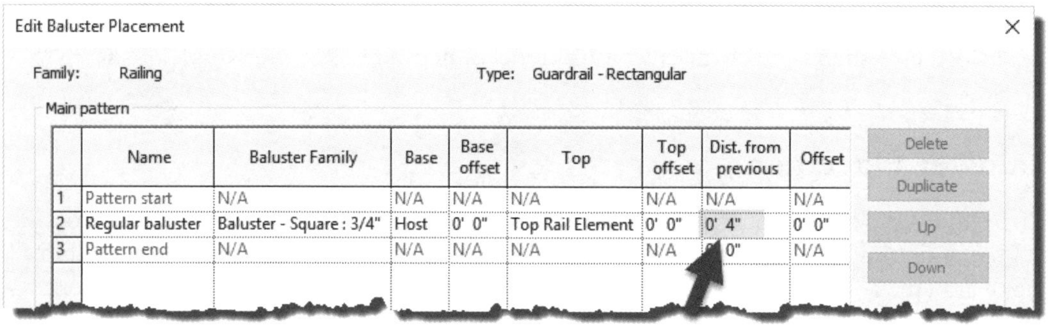

FIGURE 7-3.14 Edit Baluster Placement dialog; Guardrail – Rectangular (4" main pattern spacing)

Main Pattern settings per row:

- **Name**
  User-defined name for each baluster in the main pattern. This is mainly to help keep things organized.

- **Baluster Family**
  This drop-down lists all the baluster families (post or panel) loaded in the current project. Note that *None* is also an option.

- **Base**
  Select where the bottom of the baluster is placed. Built-in options are *Host* and *Top Rail Element.* Also, all the named rails (from the Edit Rails dialog) appear here as well. **FYI:** The host can be a stair, floor, ramp, roof, or toposolid.

- **Base Offset**
  Use this setting to move the baluster vertically relative to the selected *Base.* The value can be positive (for up) and negative (for down).

- **Top**
  Similar to the *Base* settings, the Top setting specifies the position of the top of the baluster. The height of the baluster can vary depending on the context, e.g., hosted on a stair (sloped) versus hosted on a floor (flat).

- **Top Offset**
  Use this setting to move the baluster vertically relative to the selected *Top.* The value can be positive (for up) and negative (for down).

- **Dist. From previous**
  Determines the spacing between the balusters.

- **Offset**
  Horizontally offset the baluster relative to the sketched path. The value can be positive and negative.

Both of these examples are simple and easy to understand. The example shown below depicts a more complex baluster pattern. Note that the Base and Top options selected relate to named rows in the Edit Rails dialog. This entire "main pattern" is repeated along the railing length. Note the **Justify** and **Excess Length Fill** settings as well.

FIGURE 7-3.15 Example of a more complex baluster pattern

Another variation on **baluster placement** is to place them **per tread** as shown in the example below, Figure 7-3.16. In this residential-type application, there are two balusters per tread. Notice the more elaborate newel post family selected as a starting post.

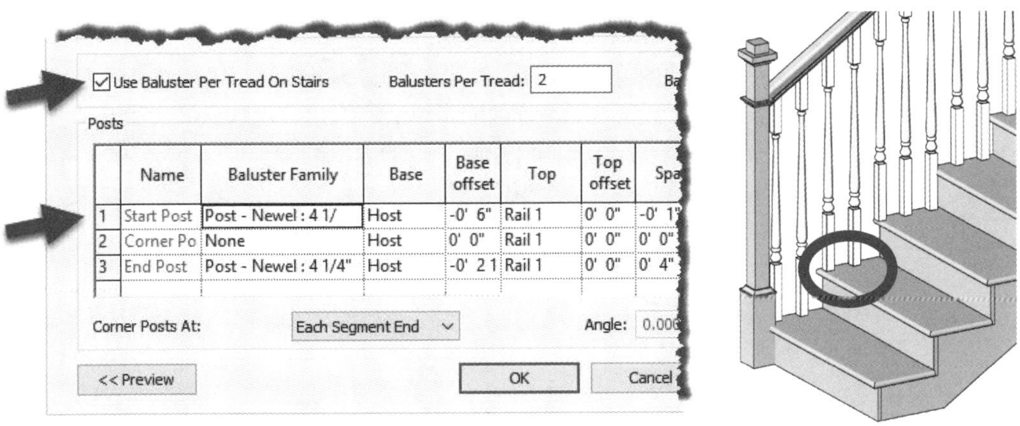

FIGURE 7-3.16 Baluster per tread

A **baluster family** is unique in that its top and bottom must be able to slope, at stairs, or be flat at a floor or landing. An example of the Baluster – Square family can be seen in the image below—shown in the family editor (Figure 7-3.17). Notice the **Top Cut Angle** and **Bottom Cut Angle** parameters. All of the required parameters are provided in the **Baluster – Post** family template file. If a new baluster family needs to be created, either copy (the RFA file) or start from the provided template.

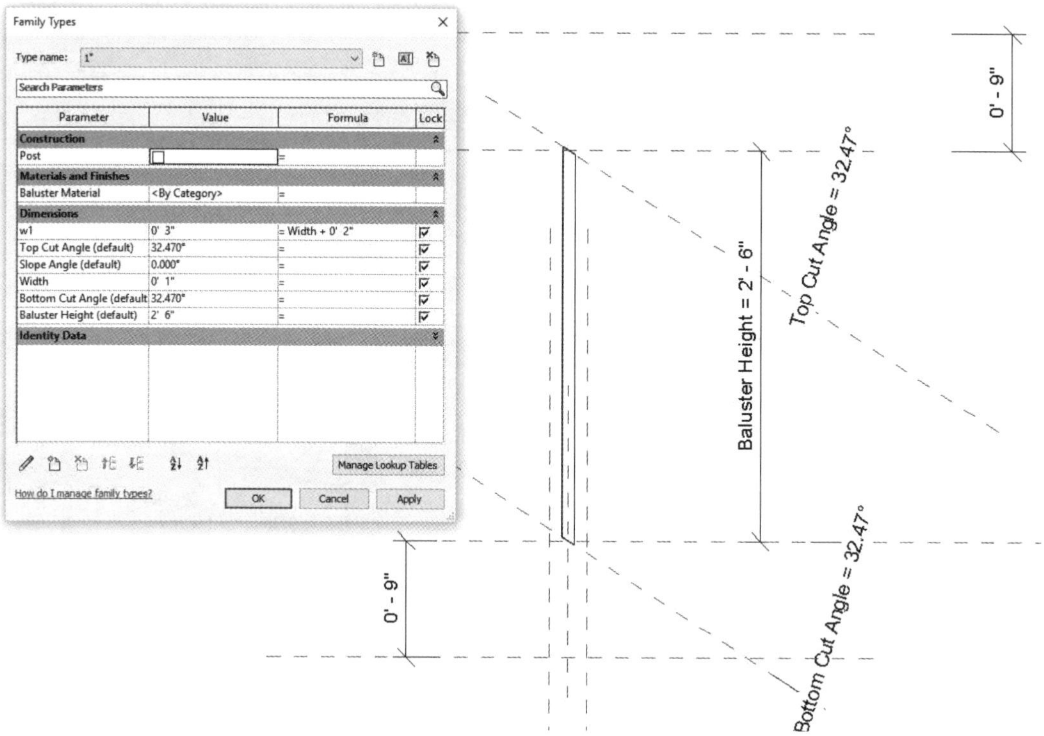

FIGURE 7-3.17 Baluster example in the family editor

For more information on Stairs and Railings in Revit:

- Visit the Autodesk Help website
- Visit www.revitforum.org, www.augi.com or https://forums.autodesk.com
- Check out **Tim Waldock's** in-depth posts on Revit's stairs and railings on his blog RevitCat: http://revitcat.blogspot.com/

Posts

The Posts section is more straightforward.

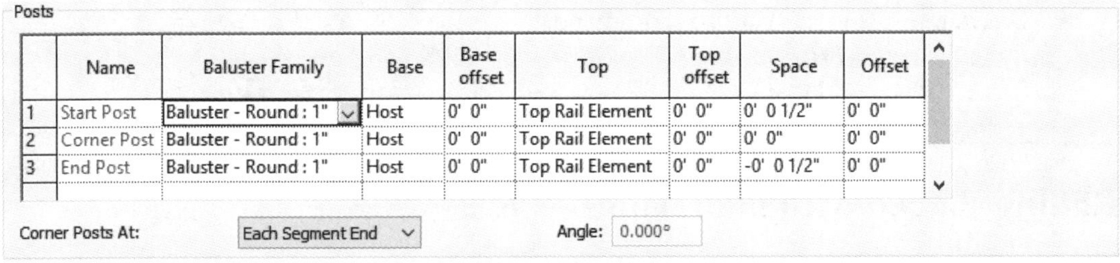

Posts

	Name	Baluster Family	Base	Base offset	Top	Top offset	Space	Offset
1	Start Post	Baluster - Round : 1"	Host	0' 0"	Top Rail Element	0' 0"	0' 0 1/2"	0' 0"
2	Corner Post	Baluster - Round : 1"	Host	0' 0"	Top Rail Element	0' 0"	0' 0"	0' 0"
3	End Post	Baluster - Round : 1"	Host	0' 0"	Top Rail Element	0' 0"	-0' 0 1/2"	0' 0"

Corner Posts At: Each Segment End — Angle: 0.000°

FIGURE 7-3.18 Posts section of Edit Baluster Placement dialog

Posts settings per row:

- **Name**
  There are only three built-in options named First, Corner and End.

- **Baluster Family**
  This drop-down lists all the baluster families (post or panel) loaded in the current project. Note that *None* and *Default* are also options.

- **Base**
  Select where the bottom of the post is placed. Built-in options are *Host* and *Top Rail Element.* Also, all the named rails (from the Edit Rails dialog) appear here as well.
  FYI: The host can be a stair, floor, ramp, roof or toposurface.

- **Base Offset**
  Use this setting to move the post vertically relative to the selected *Base.* The value can be positive (for up) and negative (for down).

- **Top**
  Similar to the *Base* settings, the Top setting specifies the position of the top of the post. The height of the post can vary depending on the context; e.g. hosted on a stair (sloped) versus hosted on a floor (flat).

- **Top Offset**
  Use this setting to move the post vertically relative to the selected *Top.* The value can be positive (for up) and negative (for down).

- **Space**
  Reposition the post along the length of the railing, if needed. One example might be to align the edge of the post with the vertical cut edge of the stringer below.

- **Offset**
  Horizontally offset the post relative to the sketched path. The value can be positive and negative.

Railing Tools

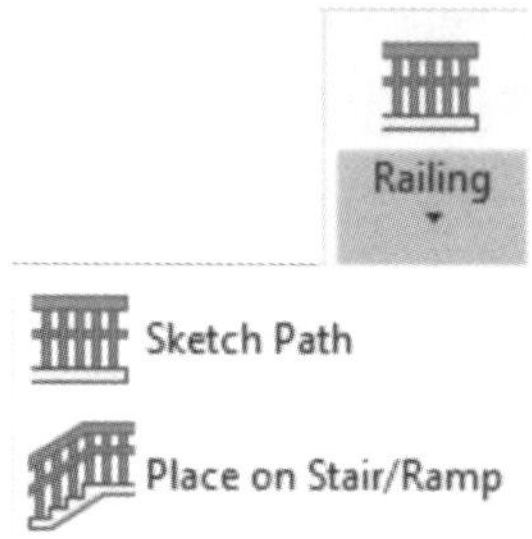

There are two main ways a railing can be added to a Revit project:

- In conjunction with the **Stair** or **Ramp** tools
- Separately, using the **Railing** commands
    a. Sketch Path
    b. Place on Host

Railing Placed with Stair Tool

When a new project is created using one of the default Revit templates, and a stair (or Ramp) is created, a railing is automatically placed on both sides. The image below (Figure 7-3.19) shows what the default results look like in a 3D view. These two railings are hosted by the stair and will update if the stair is modified. There are a number of things we can change to convey the design intent when needed.

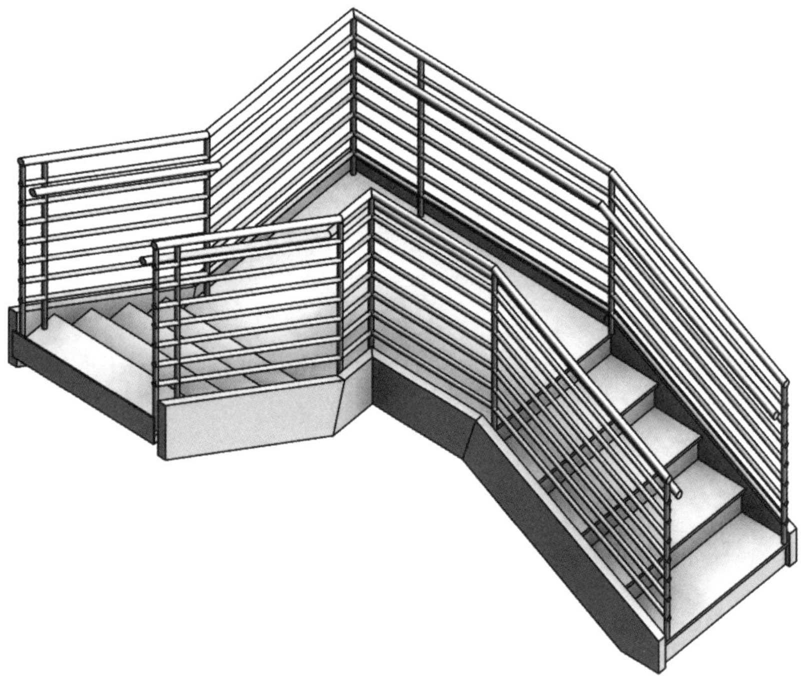

FIGURE 7-3.19 Default railing created with a new stair

> If all railings have been deleted, use the **Railing → Place on Host** tool to quickly recreate the railings hosted by the stair. This tool only works if all railings have been deleted from the stair.

There are two settings related to railings we can adjust prior to creating the Stair (or Ramp). While creating the stair, click the **Railing** button on the Ribbon. This opens the Railing dialog shown in Figure 7-3.2. Here the railings type can be changed and its position relative to the stringer and treads. Note that both of these settings can be changed later.

Given the railing is hosted by the stair there are only a few things that can be done to modify the path.

The railing system can be continued at the top or bottom (or both) of the stair as shown in the image below (Figure 7-3.21).

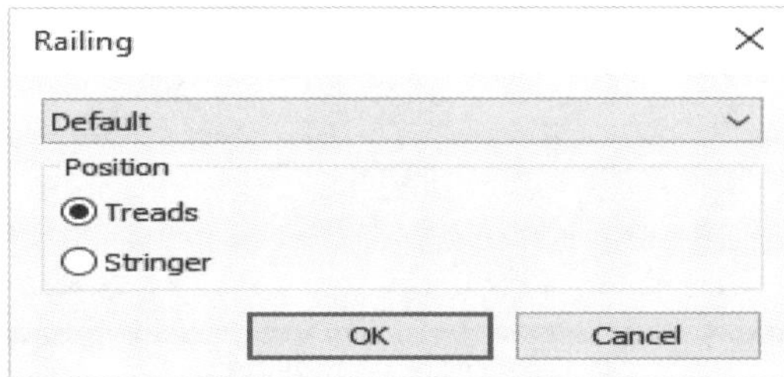

FIGURE 7-3.20 Railing options within stair tool

FIGURE 7-3.21 Extending railing at top of stair – along open floor edge

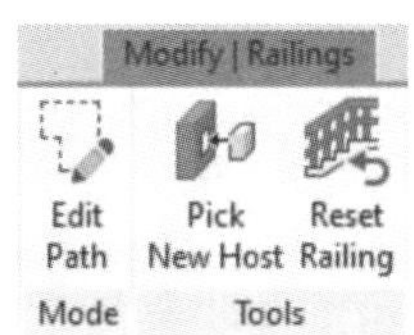

To do this (after the stair and railings are created):

- Start at the top or bottom level of the stair (or 3D view)
- Select the railing
- Click **Edit Path** on the *Ribbon*
- Select one of the **Draw** options (i.e., Line, Arc) from the *Ribbon*
- **Sketch** lines from the end of the stair hosted railing
- **Select** the newly sketched line (one at a time)
- Set the **Slope** option to **Flat** on the *Ribbon*
- See Figure 7-3.22

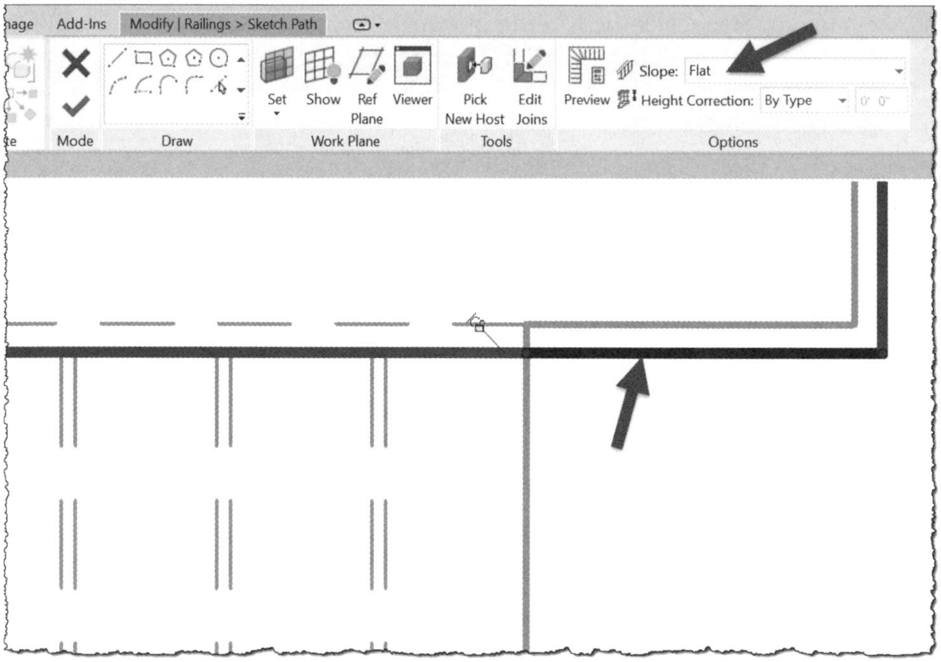

FIGURE 7-3.22 Extending railing at top of stair – along open floor edge

If the railing changes at the floor edge, for example the handrail stops or a stringer needs to be added to the railings as in Figure 7-3.12, then a separate railing element needs to be added—not part of the stair hosted railing. The trick in this case is adjusting the sketch lines so there is no odd overlap or gaps between the two railings.

When two sketch segments are selected, the Ribbon changes to show the **Rail Join** options. This can be changed if the transition between rails does not look as desired. This is similar to the **Edit Joins** tool on the Ribbon while in sketch mode.

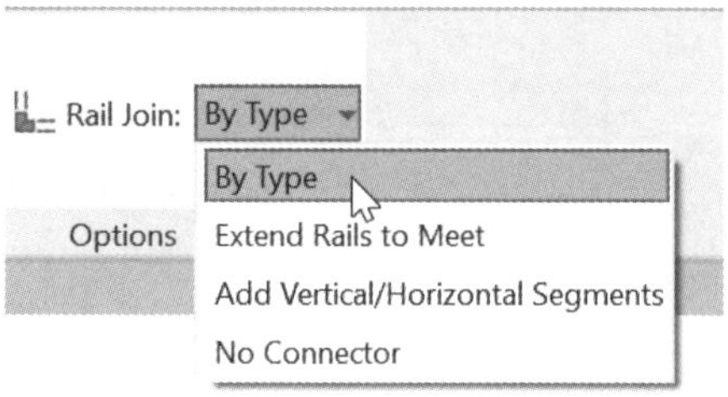

Railing → Sketch Path Tool

When a railing needs to be created apart from a stair or ramp, use the **Railing → Sketch Path** tool. When this command is selected, you simply sketch a path for the railing system to follow. If the railing has a Handrail, the side it is placed on is determined by which direction the sketch is created. While in sketch mode, click the **Preview** option to see the railing as it is to be sketched (similar to how Stair by Component works).

A sketched railing can be hosted to a floor—even a sloped floor. While in sketch mode, select the **Pick New Host** option on the Ribbon and then select the floor. The default host for a sketched railing is the level associated with the current plan-view.

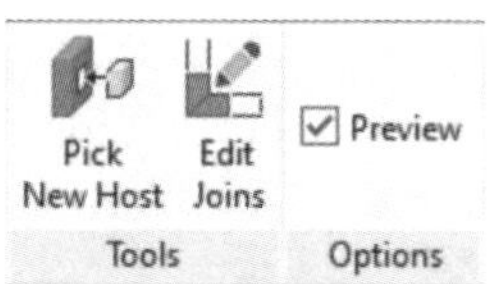

The next two topics, **Handrails** and **Top Rails**, are relatively new features associated with a Railing type in Revit. Prior to Revit 2013, these elements were defined within the Edit Rails dialog. Now they are their own sub-element and can be selected separately from the main railing in the model (tapping the Tab key may be required). It is helpful to know this in case you are working in older project files—even if they have been upgraded. These old-format railings do not allow the handrail or top rail to be selected.

Handrail

A Handrail in Revit is a component within the Railing type. It cannot be used on its own. Keep in mind that any changes made to a Handrail type will change it wherever it is used. It is easy to edit a Handrail type while working in the context of a specific railing type, not realizing the same Handrail type is used in another railing type. In some cases, the Handrail type needs to be duplicated to prevent changes from affecting other railing types.

Here are the main options related to a handrail type:

- Profile
- Material
- Extension (top and bottom)
- Terminations
- Supports (including spacing)

A few of these options have been adjusted to produce the results shown in Figure 7-3.23 (below). The steps required to accomplish this will be covered next.

FIGURE 7-3.23 Handrail with several parameter adjustments

Railing Type Settings:
First, we notice the Railing type is where the Handrail is specified (Figure 7-3.24). In this case, two railing types are used, one for **Handrail 1** and one for **Handrail 2**. Creating multiple Handrail types is required if you want to have a different profile or position them at a different height as shown in this example.

For a center railing on a wide stair, Handrail 1 and 2 might be the same type but with different positions (one Left and one Right). This would place a handrail, at the same height, on both sides of the railing.

In this case, for two railing heights, the **Position** is the same.

This double-handrail example is not uncommon in elementary-grade schools. The normal higher rail is for adults and the lower one for students.

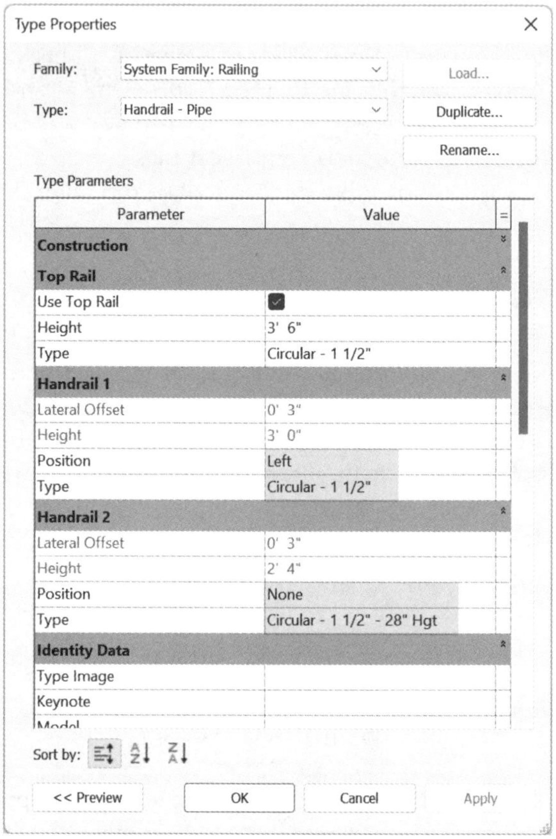

FIGURE 7-3.24 Handrail type and position

Creating a duplicate handrail is accomplished by **right-clicking** on a handrail type in the Project Browser and selecting **Duplicate** (Figure 7-3.25). Once a new type is created, the various properties covered on the next few pages can be adjusted as required.

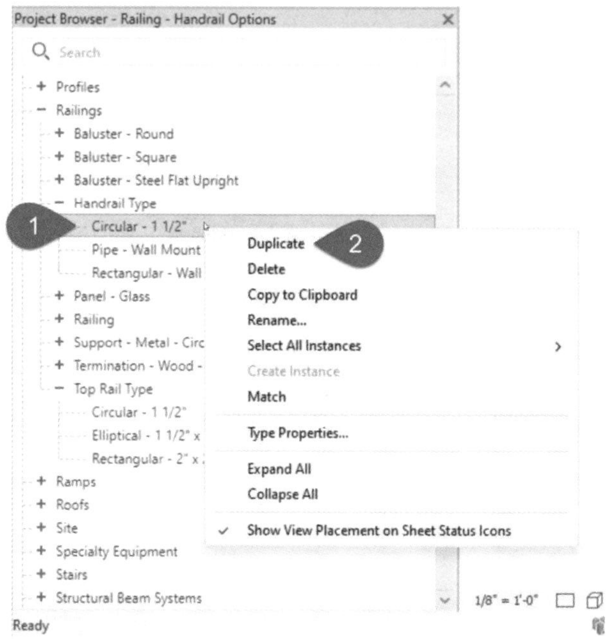

FIGURE 7-3.25 Duplicating a handrail type

Handrail 1 Properties:

The upper handrail, which is the default handrail as seen in Figure 7-3.9, has been modified per the following (see Figure 7-3.26).

- **Material:** Set to Wood
- **Extension Style:** Set to Wall (other options are None, Floor, Post). Default setting is None. This setting makes the handrail automatically return to the wall.
- **Length** (Bottom Extension): 1'-0". This will extend the length of the handrail from its default end, which aligns with the first riser. This is typically required to make the handrail comply with building codes.
- **Plus Tread Depth** (Bottom Extension): Checked. This makes the handrail continue along the slope the length of one tread. Checking this option makes the flat portion, controlled by the previous "Length" parameter, the correct height off the floor.

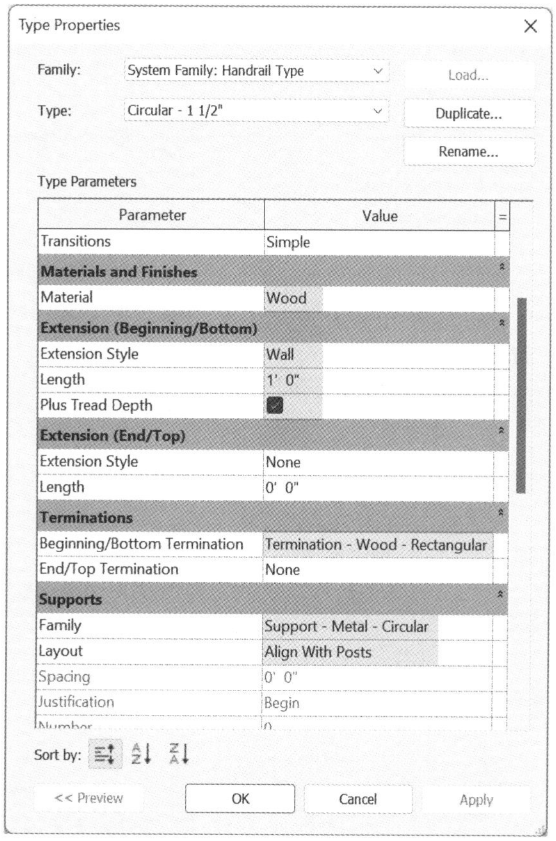

FIGURE 7-3.26 Upper handrail settings (i.e., Handrail 1)

- **Bottom Termination:** Termination – Wood – Rectangular. Places a family at the end of the handrail.
- **Family** (Supports): Support – Metal – Circular. Select the desired family for the handrail support.
- **Layout:** Align with Posts. Determines how the supports are placed/spaced. Other options are Fixed Distance, Fixed Number, Maximum Spacing and Minimum Spacing. Some of these options activate subsequent parameters such as Spacing and Justification.

The families listed for Terminations and Supports are created with a special subcategory designation Railing\Terminations and Railing\Supports.

Handrail 2 Properties:
The **lower handrail** is a duplicate of the previous handrail. Just the variations will be highlighted here (see Figure 7-3.27).

- **Height:** 2'-4"
- **Extension Style:** Set to Floor

The extension might more realistically just be set to wall like the upper handrail. However, this example helps to depict the options.

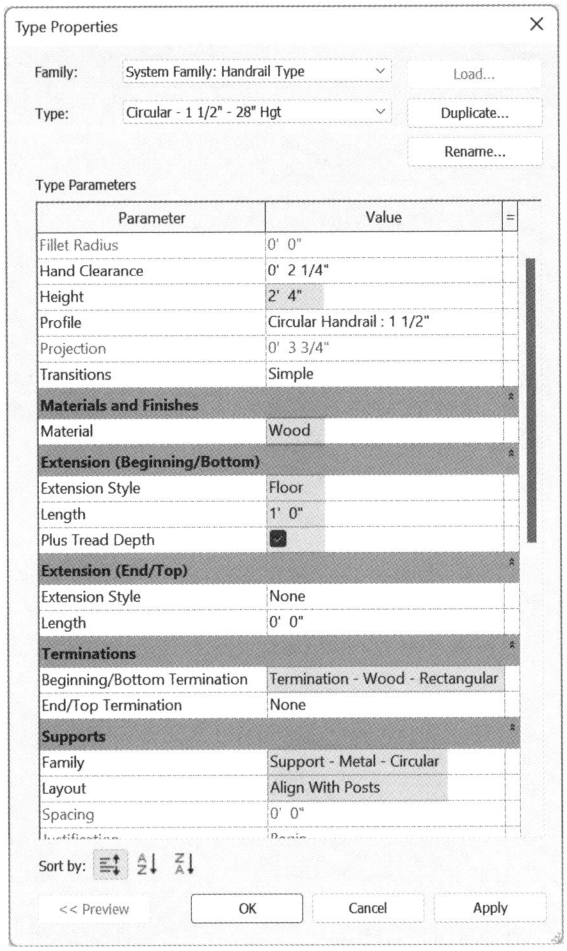

FIGURE 7-3.27 Lower handrail settings (i.e., Handrail 2)

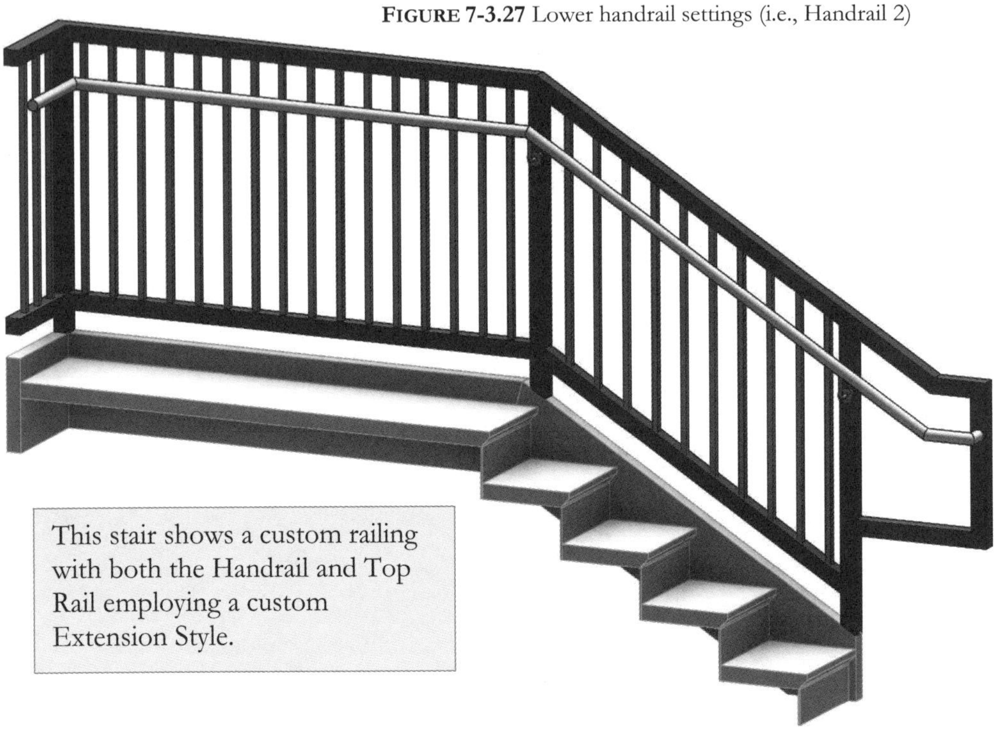

This stair shows a custom railing with both the Handrail and Top Rail employing a custom Extension Style.

Top Rail

The Top Rail is defined via a Railing's *Type Properties* as shown in Figure 7-3.28. Additional Top Rail types can be created by duplicating types listed in the *Project Browser*; **Families → Railings – Top Rail Type**. This is also where the height is defined.

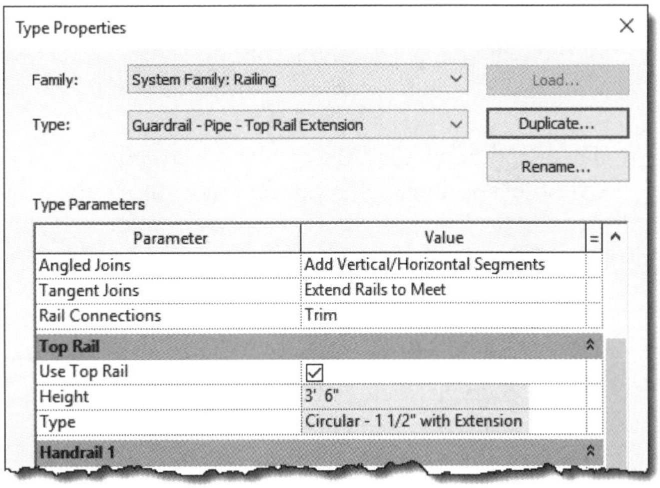

FIGURE 7-3.28 Top Rail defined in railing's type properties

The Top Rail has settings similar to the Handrail, but no supports, and can be adjusted separately from the Handrail. In the image below the Top Rail's **Extension Style** is set to **Post**. It can also be set to Wall, Floor or None just like the Handrail (Fig. 7-3.29).

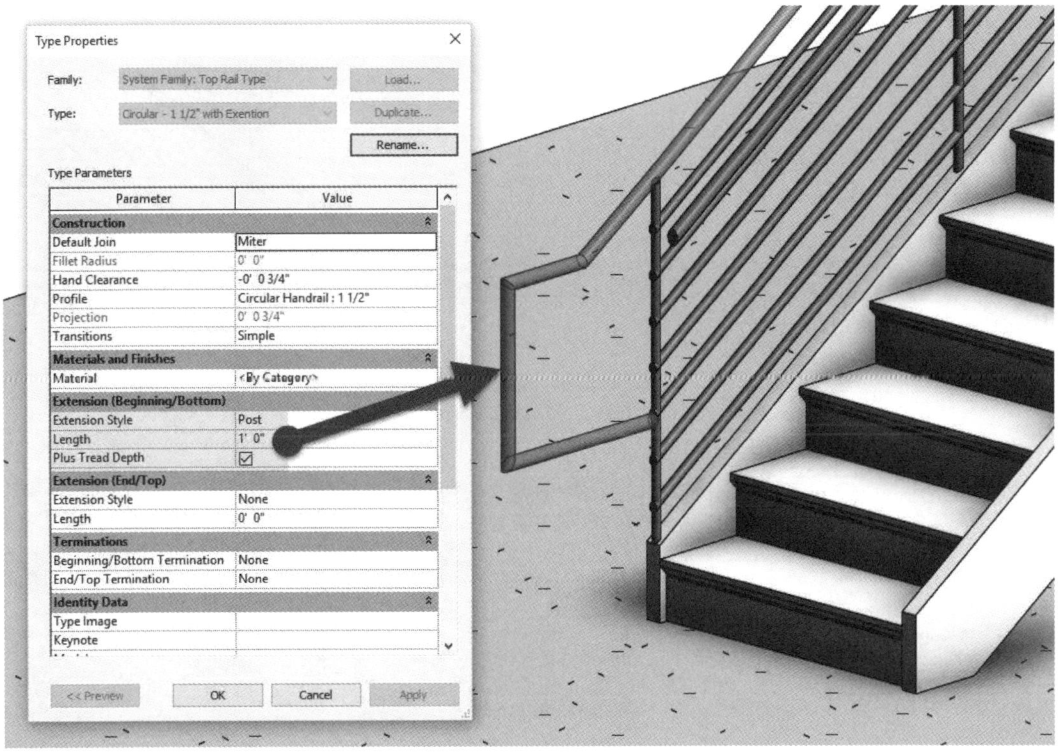

FIGURE 7-3.29 Top Rail extension style set to 'Post'

Remember that changes made to the Top Rail properties will affect all Railing types which use it. Notice the Top Rail type selected in Figure 7-3.28 is different than the Top Rail type specified in Figure 7-3.24 (also compare Top Rail pictures in the Handrail section).

Edit Rail (Top Rail or Handrail)

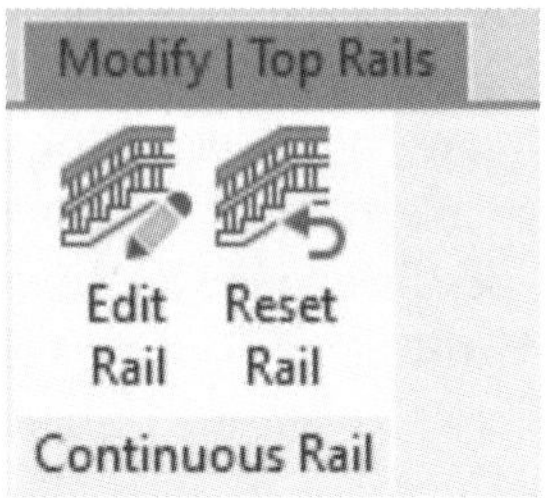

When a Handrail or Top Rail is selected, an option to edit the path of the railing appears on the Ribbon. This option only allows editing the path in a vertical plane aligned with the railing.

The Handrail or Top Rail can be selected by hovering the cursor over the Top Rail, being careful not to move the mouse, and then tapping the Tab key and clicking to select once highlighted. Once selected, the rail will be a transparent blue.

> **FYI:** Stairs upgraded from older Revit projects or template files (anything prior to Revit 2013) do not have the Top Rail and Handrail options. Those elements were defined in the Edit Rail structure dialog. Thus, they are not selectable elements within the railing. In this case, the railing would need to swap it out for a new supported type.

When the Extension Style options, Wall, Floor, Post and None, do not cover what you want, use the **Edit Rail** option. Clicking this from an elevation, section or 3D view allows a custom path to be defined.

The image to the right, Figure 7-3.30, shows the Top Rail path being modified. Notice the geometry appears as each line is sketched.

The custom result can be seen in Figure 7-3.31.

Unfortunately, at this time the railing cannot change planes/direction—to wrap around a column for example.

Selecting the Top Rail and clicking **Reset Rail** on the Ribbon will undo any changes.

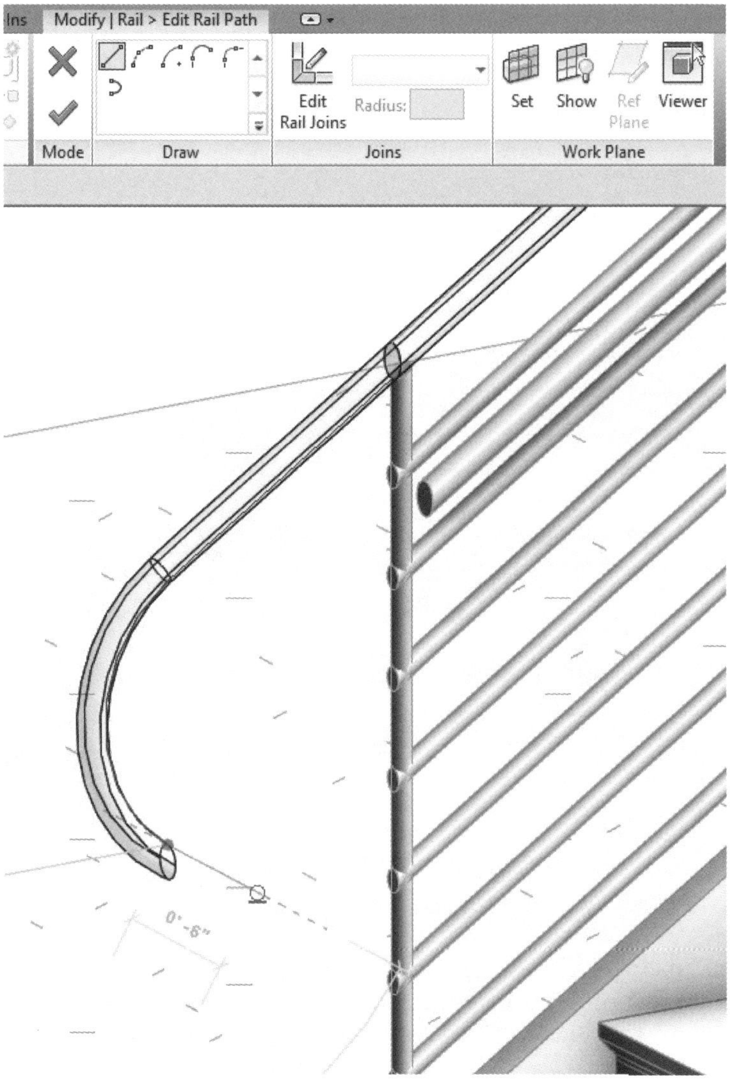

FIGURE 7-3.30 Editing the Top Rail path

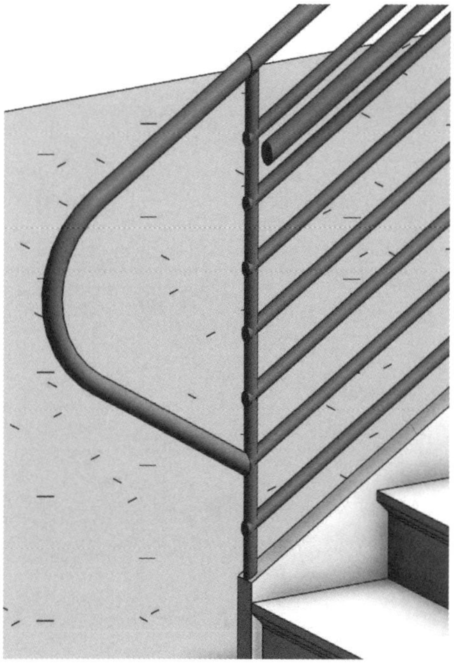

FIGURE 7-3.31 Custom Top Rail defined

FIGURE 7-3.32
Handrail only with supports at 6'-0" O.C. max.

Handrail Only

A railing or guardrail is not required when a stair, or ramp, is against a wall (Figure 7-3.32). In this case we just need a handrail without a railing. Unfortunately, this is not directly possible as there is no Handrail tool, just the Railing tool. Here is how this can be accomplished…

The first step is to **Duplicate** a railing—Guardrail – Rectangular is a good option as it requires fewer changes. In the new railing's Type Properties, set the **Top Rail** Use Top Rail to **unchecked** (Fig. 7-3.33). Next, click Edit for **Rail Structure** and Delete all rows. Finally, click Edit for **Baluster Placement** and set everything, Main pattern and posts, to **None** (Fig. 7-3.34).

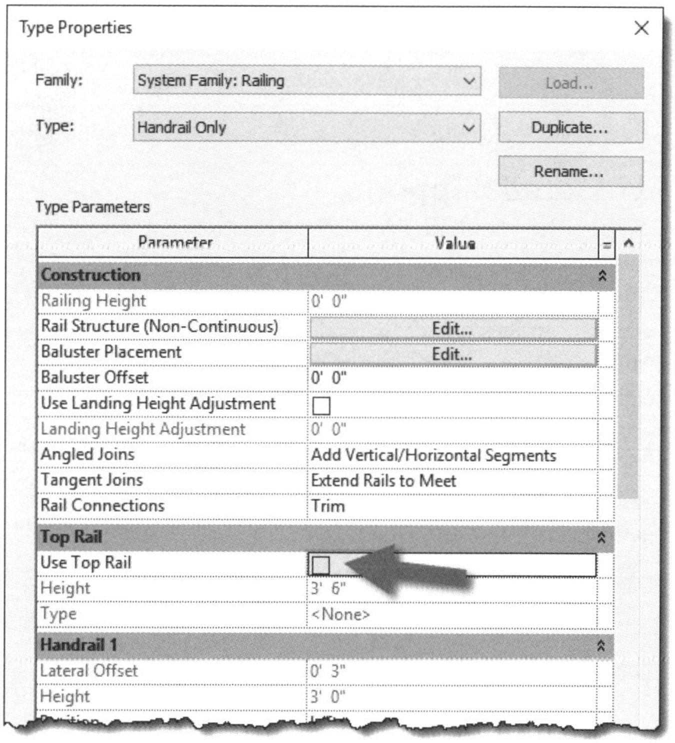

FIGURE 7-3.33 Omitting the Top Rail from a railing

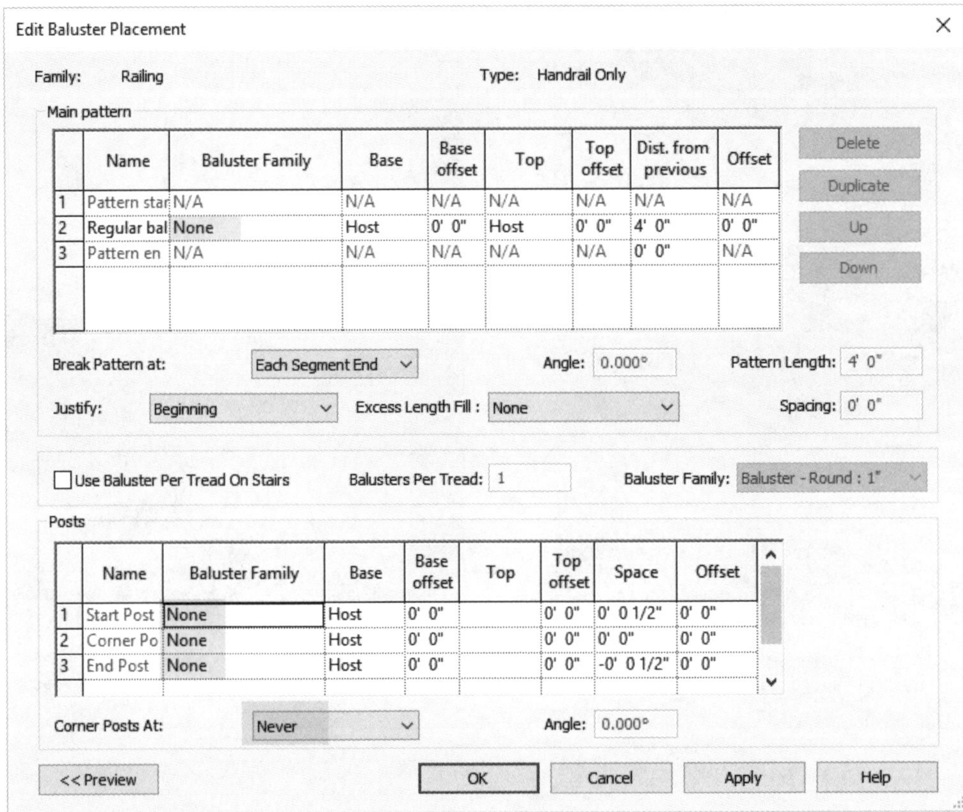

FIGURE 7-3.34 Omitting Balusters from a railing

Handrail Supports

Within the Handrail Type supports can be selected (Figure 7-3.35). The **Family** drop-down is based on special families currently loaded in the project file. The **Layout** option selected determines which of the remaining parameters are editable. In this example, Maximum Spacing causes the Spacing parameter to be active, but Justification and Number are inactive (i.e. greyed out).

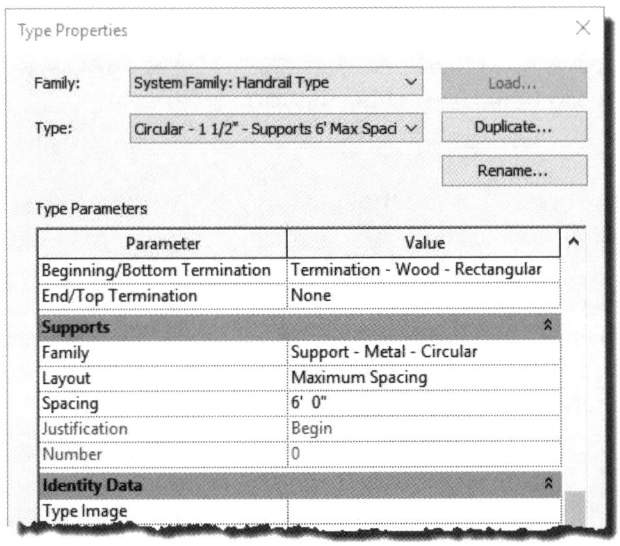

FIGURE 7-3.35 Handrail support settings

The automatically placed supports do not always land in the ideal position. Fortunately, they can be repositioned and even deleted individually. To modify a support it must be selected. To select a Support, hover the cursor over a support (don't move it) and then tap (not press) the Tab key until the Support highlights—and then click to select it. Select the pin icon to unpin that instance (Figure 7-3.36). It can now be moved or deleted as needed.

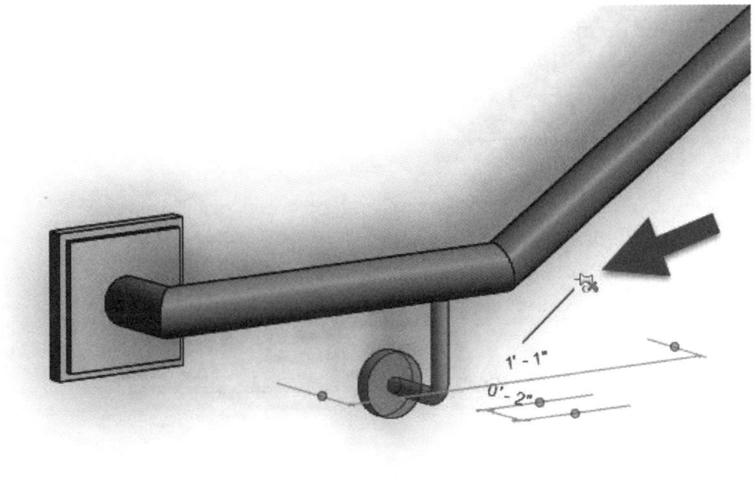

FIGURE 7-3.36 Support selected and un-pinned

Railing Hosting Opportunities

Revit has the ability to host railings to floors with modified points and, as shown below, the top of walls—even when they have been modified with Edit Profile. Railings can also be hosted by toposolids and roofs. Thus, a railing could be used to represent a fence on the site or lightning protection rods (using a highly customized railing type) on the roof.

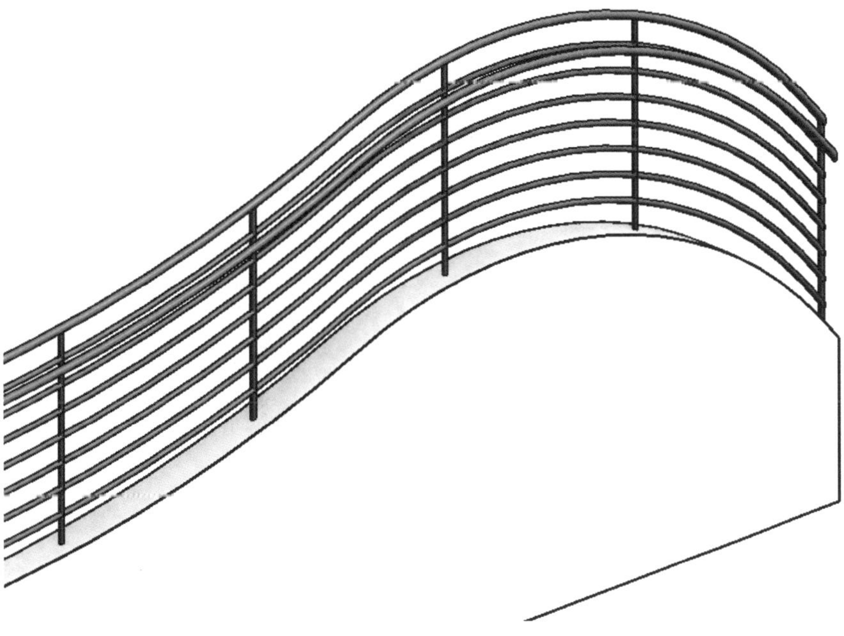

Sample Railing File

Make sure to examine the stair and railing sample file available with the provided Revit content; look in the **System Families** folder (click the *Imperial Library* shortcut on the left, in the Open dialog). While in this Revit project file, select a stair or railing and view its properties to see how it works. It is also possible to Copy/Paste selected examples into another open Revit project file. Download Autodesk content: https://autode.sk/30EJYkX

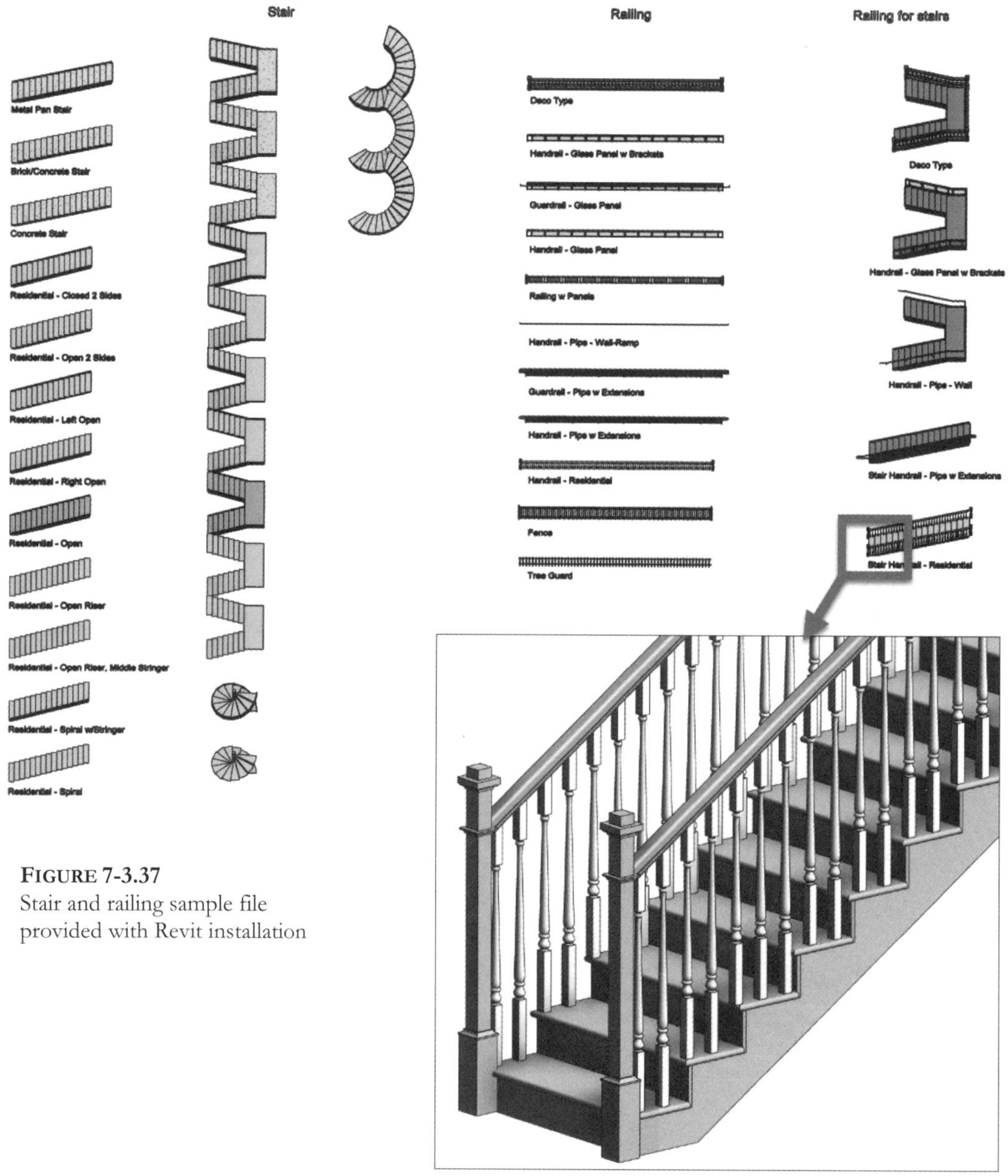

FIGURE 7-3.37
Stair and railing sample file provided with Revit installation

Exercise 7-4:
Ramps and Sloped Floors

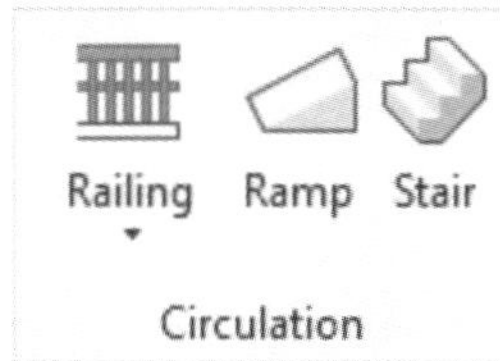

When two floors do not align vertically, or accessibility is required, a ramp must be provided. There are two main ways to model this in Revit. One is with the Ramp tool and the other is with the Floor tool. **For the most part the Ramp tool should never be used.** Rather, the Floor tool should be preferred as it generally works better as we shall see here.

The Ramp Tool:
First, we will review how the ramp tool works and then talk about its limitations.

The ramp tool is closely related to the original *Stair by Sketch* tool in how it works. Starting at the lower level in a plan-view, when the Ramp tool is started, Sketch mode is entered and the **Run** option is selected on the Ribbon. First, verify the **Base Level** and **Top Level** properties are set correctly—this determines the required horizontal distance. Picking points on the screen will define the center of the ramp (Figure 7-4.1). Based on the **Ramp Max Slope** setting (via Edit Type) the required length, in plan, is listed. **Landings** are automatically added between gaps as shown in the two images below (Figure 7-4.1 and 7-4.2). The sketch lines can be modified if needed. For example, maybe one side of the ramp runs along an angled or curved wall.

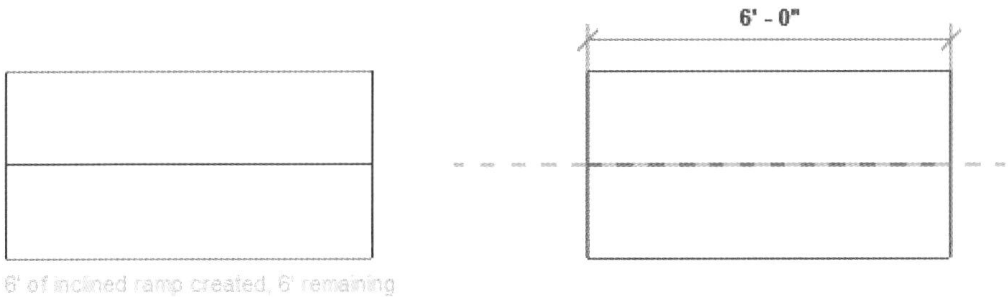

FIGURE 7-4.1 Ramp sketch mode; indicates length required based on vertical distance

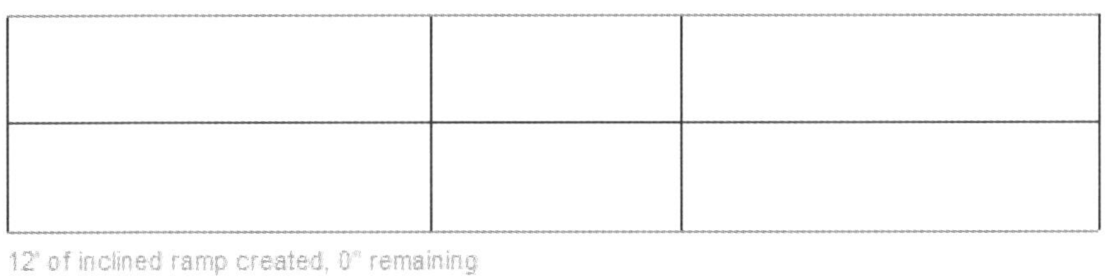

FIGURE 7-4.2 Ramp sketch mode; sketch complete with landing

Once the sketch is complete and the Finish (green check mark) is selected, the ramp is created as seen in Figure 7-4.3. By default this will include a railing on each side of the ramp.

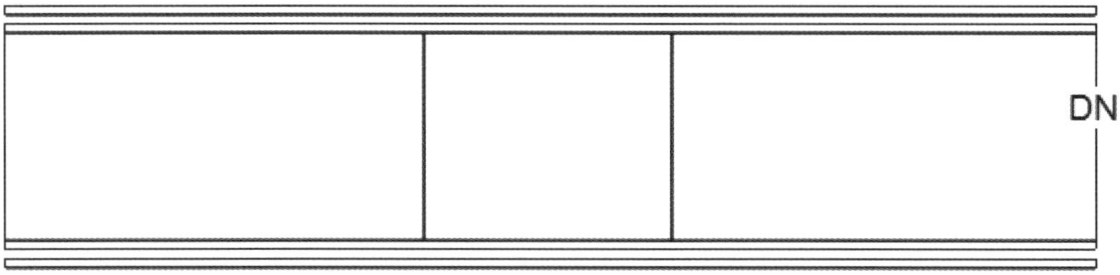

FIGURE 7-4.3 Ramp created including railings on each side

Looking at the ramp in 3D we notice the handrail is on the wrong side and the posts are half on, and half off, the ramp (Figure 7-4.4). Selecting the railings in plan (one at a time) and then clicking the **flip control-arrows** will move the handrail to the correct side. Also, with the railing selected, the **Tread/Stringer Offset** will reposition the railing.

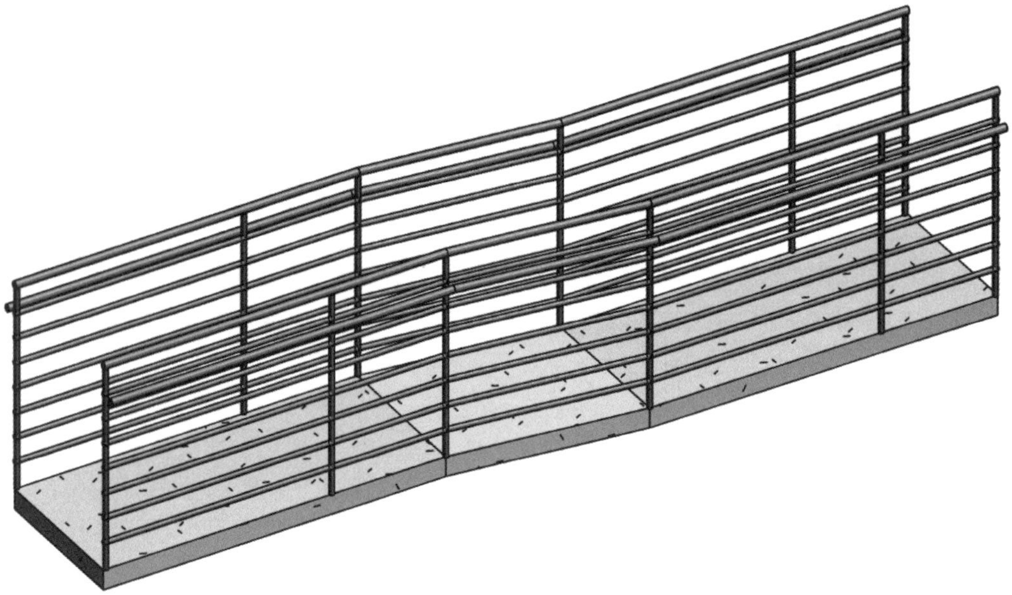

FIGURE 7-4.4 3D view of ramp

Most of the Instance (left) and Type (right) properties shown in Figure 7-4.5 are pretty straightforward. By default, Revit set the **Base Level** to match the level the current plan-view is based on and the **Top Level** to the next Level above. This usually works as a Level should generally be created for any surface you can walk on in a building. In this example, the Top Level was changed to match the Base Level and the Top Offset was modified to define the total vertical distance.

The Type property **Shape** determines the shape (or profile) of the ramp in section as seen in Figure 7-4.6, set to **Thick**, and Figure 7-4.7 set to **Solid**. Also notice the Ramp Max Slope (1/x) setting. This defines the horizontal distance required for every 1" of vertical rise. This is typically set based on building code and accessibility code requirements.

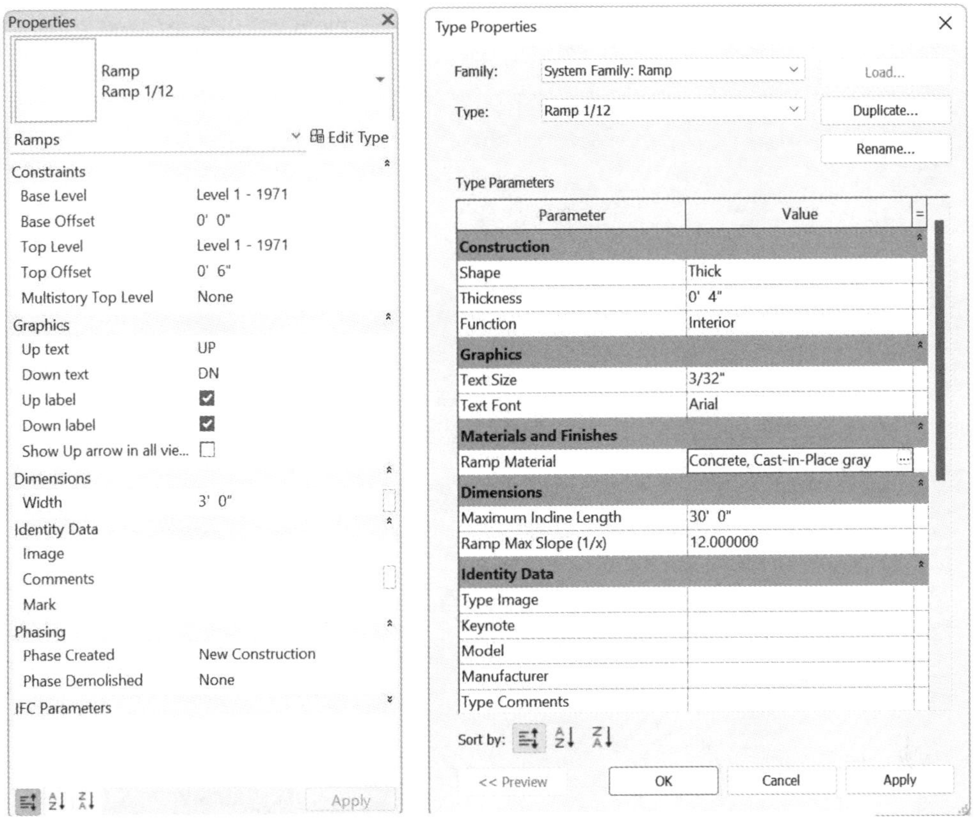

FIGURE 7-4.5 Ramp instance (left) and Type (right) properties

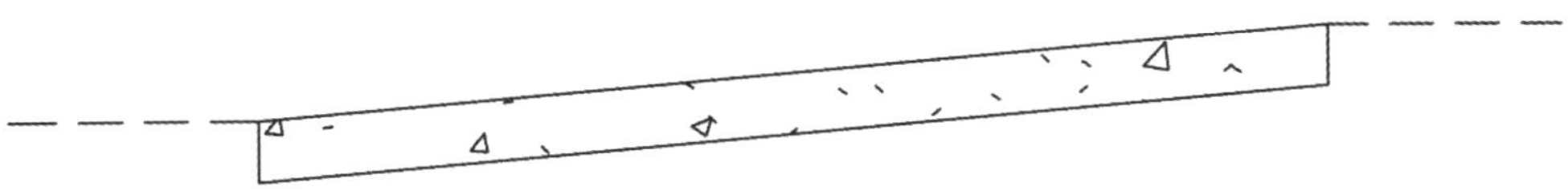

FIGURE 7-4.6 Ramp section with Shape properties set to Thick

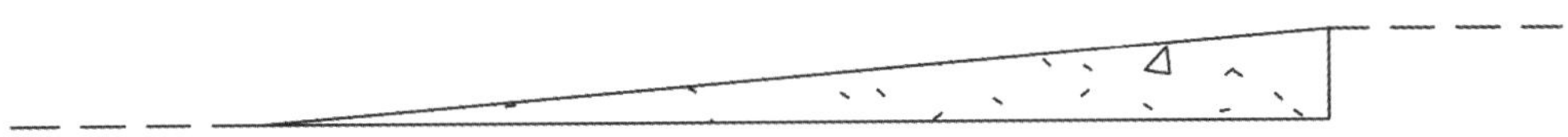

FIGURE 7-4.7 Ramp section with Shape properties set to Solid

Now that the basics of the Ramp tool have been covered, we will look at the limitations. The Ramp tool does not allow "Layers" of construction like the Floor tool does. Notice in Figure 7-4.5 that there is just one simple **Thick** property to define the thickness of the ramp. Thus, the ramp cannot look correct in both plan (Figure 7-4.8) and section (Figure 7-4.9), as there is only one material parameter for ramps. In previous versions of Revit, the **Spot Elevation** and **Spot Slope** annotation tools did not work on a Ramp element; they do now.

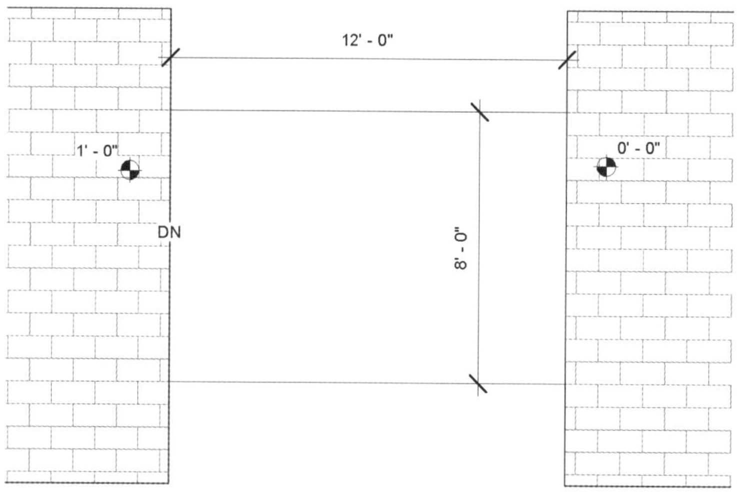

FIGURE 7-4.8 Ramp added between two floors – no floor finish or slope arrow

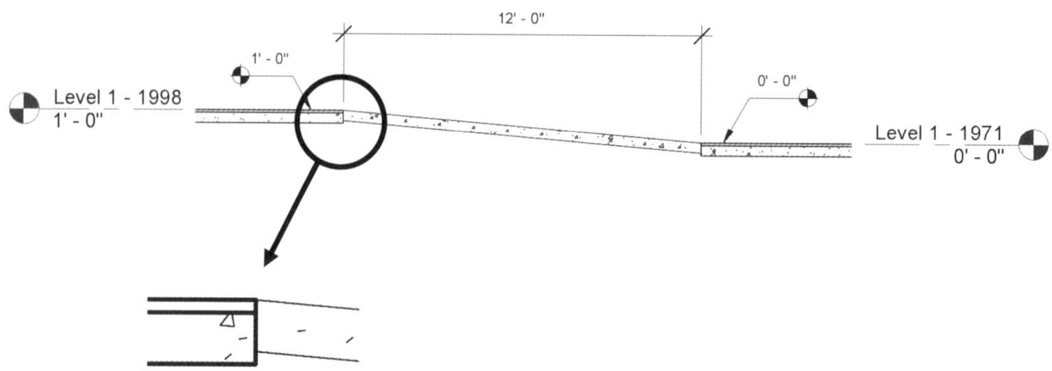

FIGURE 7-4.9 Ramp shown in section next to a concrete floor with a tile finish

The **Paint** tool can be used to apply a different material to the surface of the ramp, but the section and details still would not look correct. A Ramp cannot be joined to the adjacent floor construction as highlighted in the image above.

Sloped Floor:

An alternative to using the Ramp tool is to use the Floor tool and adjust it to slope.

First, we will look at the results of creating the same "ramp" as in the previous example. This Floor element can have multiple "Layers" of construction, including a separate surface finish. Additionally, we can apply a Spot Elevation and/or Spot Slope annotation as desired. The plan-view below has a Spot Slope element applied to indicate the slope and direction (Figure 7-4.10).

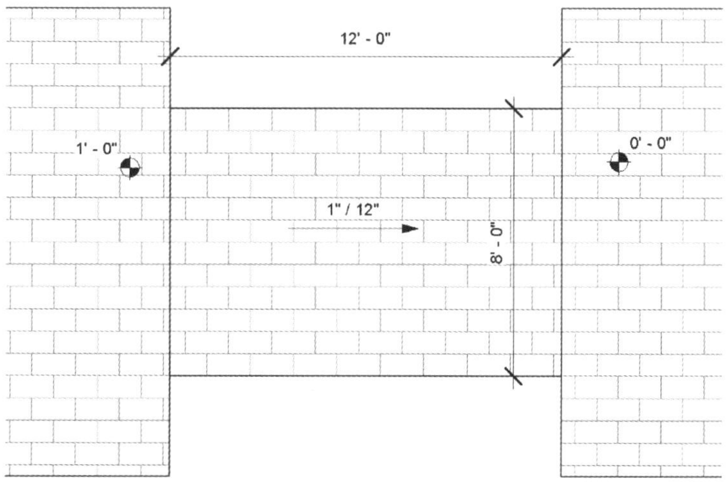

FIGURE 7-4.10 Sloped floor element added between two floors

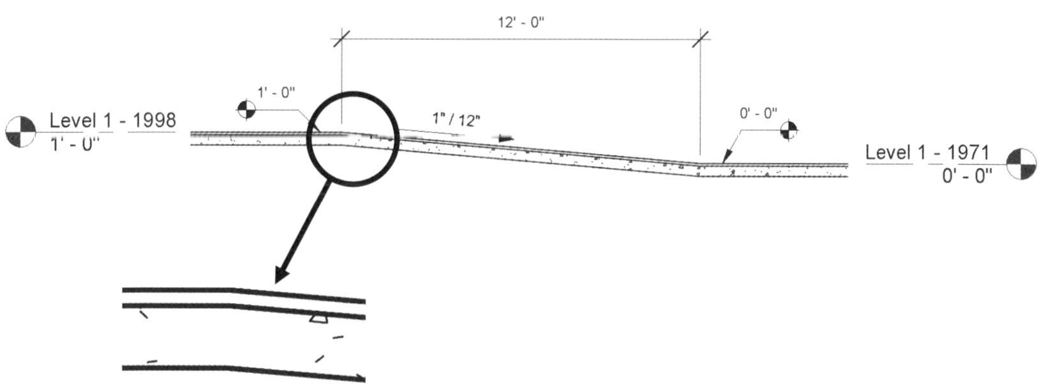

FIGURE 7-4.11 Sloped floor shown in section – joined to adjacent flat floor

As seen in the section above, the sloped floor joins nicely with the adjacent flat floor elements to create a continuous monolithic look that is common in this situation (Figure 7-4.11). Note that the Join command is used to achieve this look.

The only limitation to using a Floor rather than a Ramp element is a Railing cannot be added automatically. However, a Railing can be manually added and hosted to the floor.

Given the two examples, Ramp vs. Floor, it is generally preferred to use a Floor rather than a Ramp. Now we will look at how to create a sloped floor.

There are four ways to make a floor slope:

- Sketch line **defines slope**
- Sketch line **defines constant height** (preferred for existing conditions)
- **Slope Arrow** in sketch mode
- **Shape Editing** (generally avoid for simple ramps)

A sketch line, when selected, can be set to **Defines Slope** in the Properties Palette (Figure 7-4.12). For a ramp, only one edge needs to be set to Defines Slope. Once *Defines Slope* is selected, the Slope parameter may be modified; e.g., 1"/12".

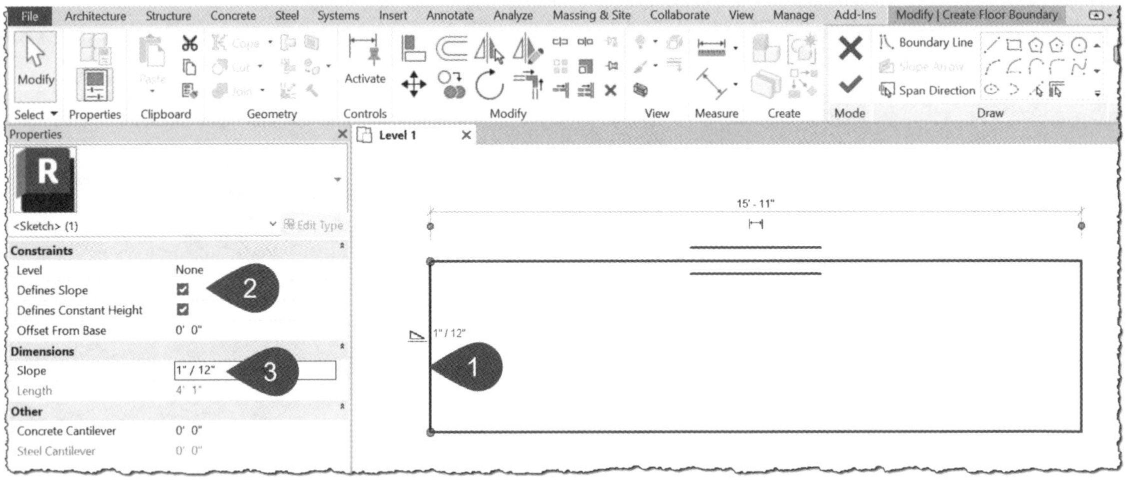

FIGURE 7-4.12 Using Defines Slope in floor sketch

When a sketch line is selected, while in sketch mode, there is a parameter called **Defines Constant Height** (Figure 7-4.13). Checking this box allows the **Offset From Base** to be modified. This value sets the specific height of that edit of the floor relative to the selected Level. This is helpful when documenting existing conditions and the slope is not known or not perfectly constructed per the original construction documents.

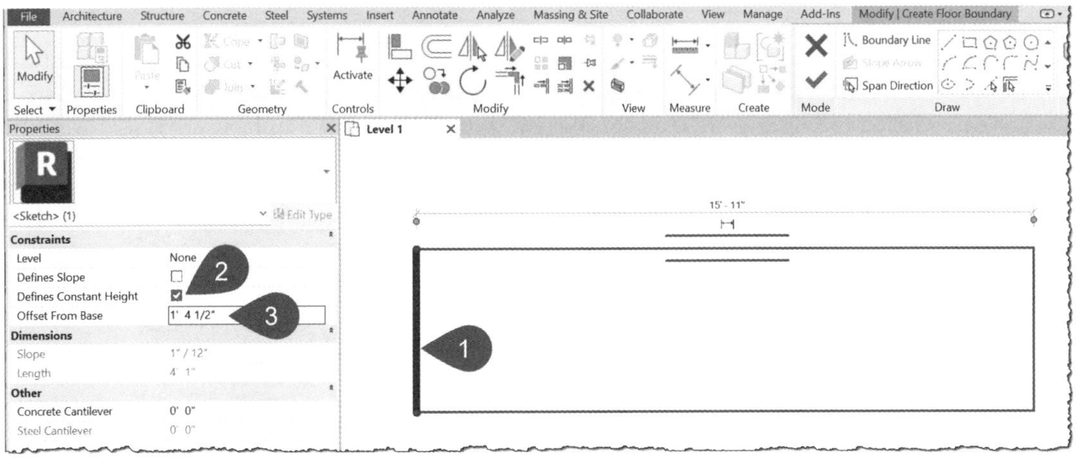

FIGURE 7-4.13 Using Defines Constant Height in floor sketch

The **Slope Arrow** option is easy to use while in sketch mode; simply select the Slope Arrow option on the Ribbon and point to point to define the direction the floor should slope (Figure 7-4.14). With the Slope Arrow selected, the Properties Palette lists the slope-related settings. Changing **Specify** to "Slope" allows the Slope parameter to be set; e.g., 1"/12".

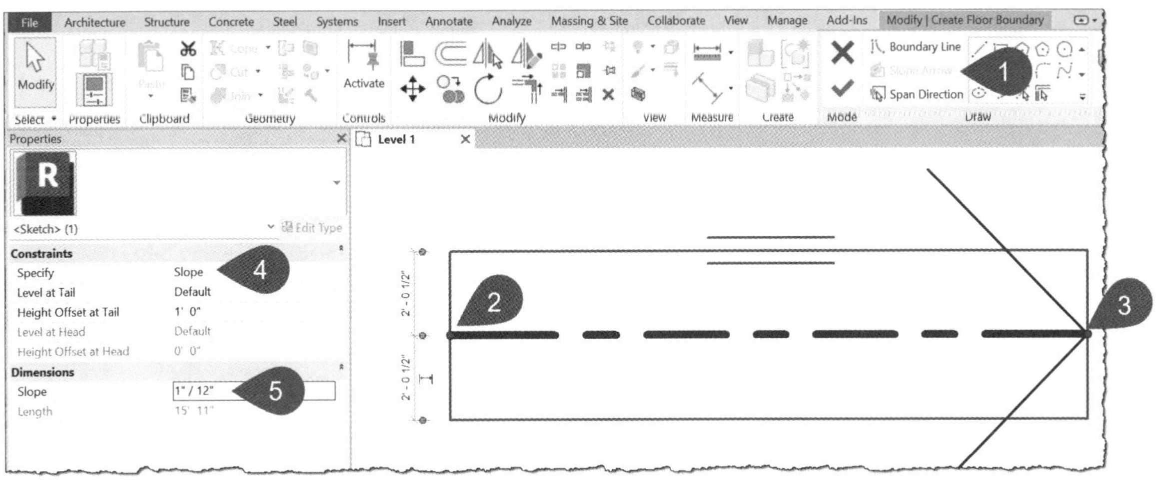

FIGURE 7-4.14 Using Slope Arrow in floor sketch

The **Shape Editing** feature is a little too complicated and should be avoided unless the surface warps or the bottom of the ramp needs to be flat. This feature is more for sloping a slab or roof around a floor/roof drain. To use this option, select the completed floor (not in sketch mode) and click the **Modify Sub Elements** tool on the Ribbon (Figure 7-4.15). Select one of the corner grips and then edit its offset value that appears next to the grip. Edit the grip for the other side of the ramp. Press Esc to finish the command.

If the bottom of the ramp needs to be flat, select the floor, go to Edit Type and then Edit Structure. Check the Varies option for each layer to have a flat bottom (Figure 7-4.15). The result can be seen in Figure 7-4.16. Note that the Varies setting will only affect floor instances that have their sub elements modified.

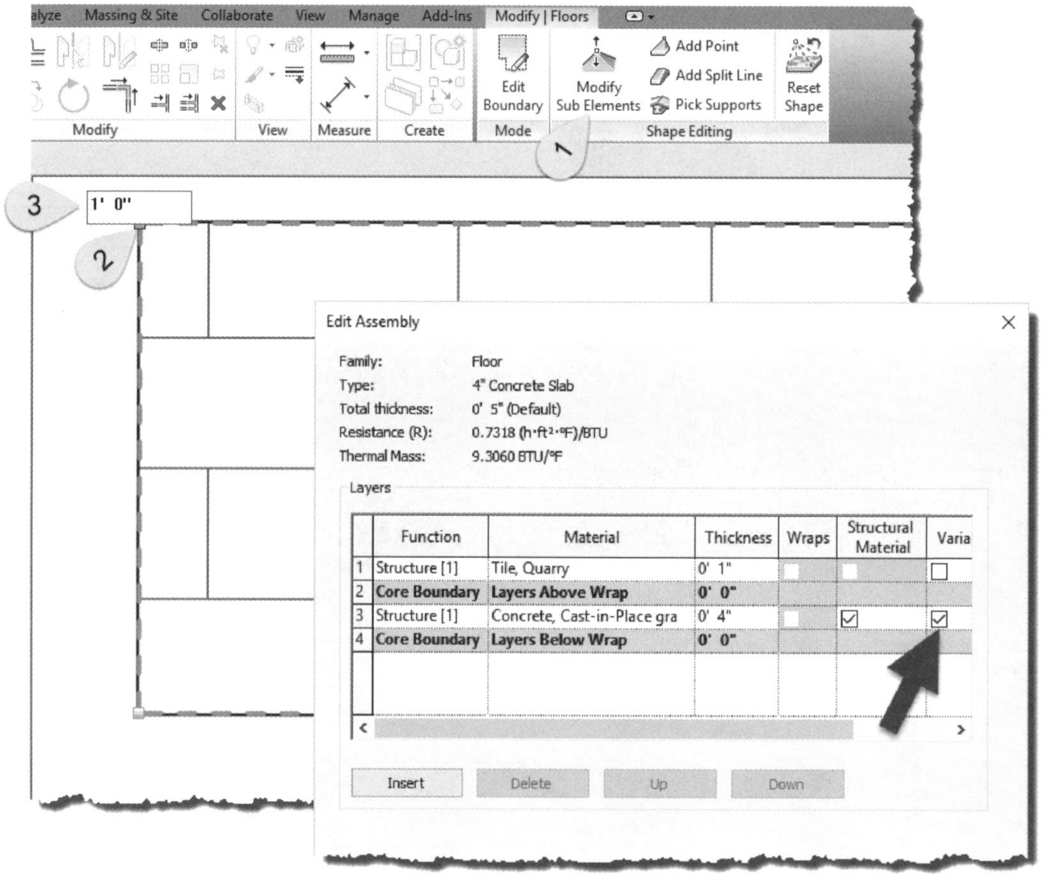

FIGURE 7-4.15 Modifying a floor's sub elements & floor structure dialog

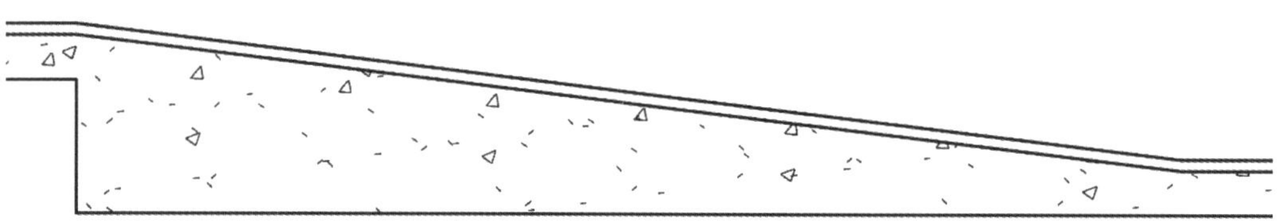

FIGURE 7-4.16 Floor with flat bottom

Exercise 7-5:
Elevators

Commercial buildings with more than one story often have an elevator for convenience and to comply with accessibility codes. This section will take a look at how they can be modeled within Revit.

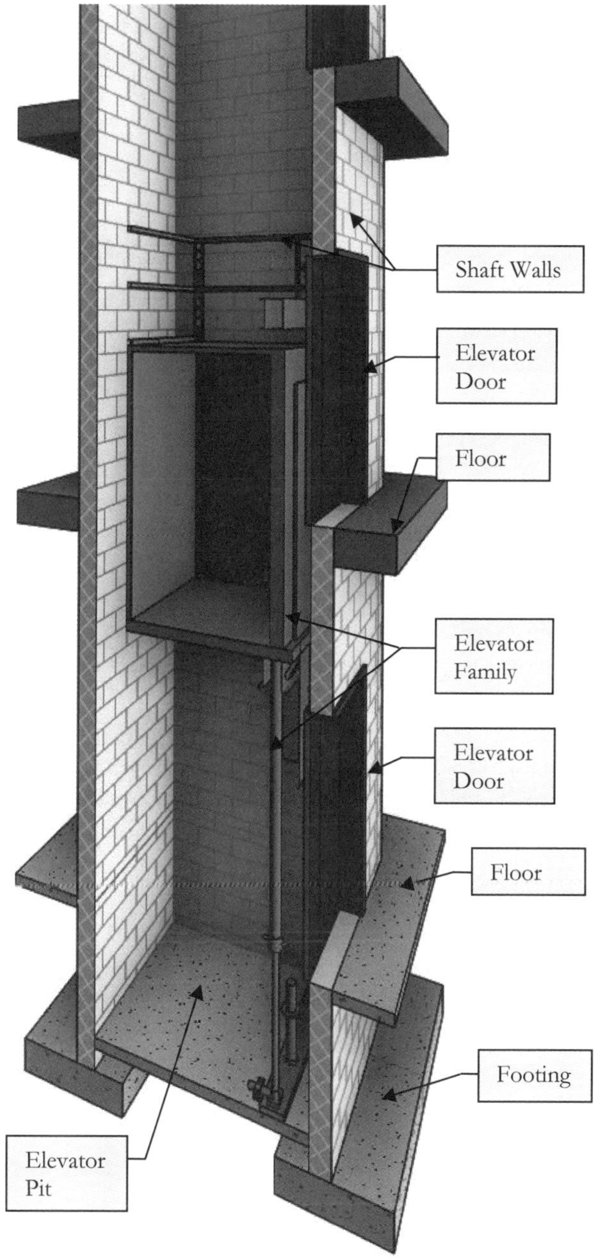

FIGURE 7-5.1 Elevator shaft cut away view

Shaft Walls:

First, an elevator is contained within a vertical shaft defined by four walls as seen in the image to the right (Figure 7-5.1). These walls are modeled using **Revit's wall tool**. These walls should be modeled as they will be built. In this example the masonry walls are bearing walls (i.e. they are structural and will support the floors and roof) so a single wall extends from the footing to the roof. If the walls are built on each floor, then separate walls should be created at each level. Also, if different finishes are required at each floor, then separate walls are added adjacent to the shaft walls.

The dimensions of the shaft are defined by the elevator manufacturer. The width and depth are derived from the "car" size and required tracks/rails. The height can vary depending on the type of elevator—this often includes a pit (an area below the lowest stop) and an overrun (space above the highest stop).

Shaft Openings:

It is important that the hole in the floor align vertically. The best way to ensure this is to use the **Shaft Opening tool**. This tool is a vertical extrusion which cuts each floor it comes in contact with. This is preferred over editing the sketch of each floor to define the opening—which would potentially be wrong at one or more floors. Depending on building construction, this shaft is either on the inside or the outside of the shaft walls. If inside, the floors will extend into the shaft walls.

Elevator Family:
The installed version of Revit does not come with any sample elevator content (except in the Metric Library folder).

The value in manufactured content is that it is the correct size and often has helpful features—for example, the family used on the previous page includes a box which defines the required shaft size, including pit depth and overrun. However, in the floor plan-views it does not follow the standard architectural graphics conventions for an elevator (whereas the generic one shown above does).

Another option is to create custom content. It is generic and parametric so it looks correct in plans and sections and is manually adjustable based on the elevator selected. There is a good example of a custom elevator family, including call buttons and indicator lights, in a thread at this location: http://www.revitforum.org/architecture-general-revit-questions/12417-elevators-what-do-you-do.html.

Yet another option is **DigiPara Elevatorarchitect**, which is a free Revit add-in. This tool includes several elevator manufacturers such as ThyssenKrupp, OTIS, KONE, Schindler and more. URL: http://www.digipara.com/.

Elevator Doors:
Elevators have several sets of doors. One set is associated with the elevator car while the rest are located on each floor the elevator stops at. The elevator cab door is represented in the elevator family. The doors at each floor are separate families individually placed at each floor.

Having separate elevator door families at each level will accommodate the various finishes at each level. **TIP:** when using multiple walls to represent the shaft wall and floor-specific finishes, use the join tool on those walls. This will cause the door family to cut through all walls.

Elevator Misc:
Elevators usually require an Elevator Equipment Room. This would be sized and positioned per the manufacturer's literature. If the elevator has a pit, it most likely requires a "pit ladder" for maintenance personnel to access the pit (this may have to be a custom family if one cannot be found).

Exercise 7-6:
Adding Utilitarian Stairs and Railings

In this exercise you will create a utilitarian stair in a stair shaft; this is a stair required for egress, with simple materials, and not intended to be primary circulation.

The Utilitarian Stair

The back stair is required for egress and is often referred to as a utilitarian stair due to the simple and durable finishes.

Utilitarian Stair Example
Durable, average cost stair with simple design

Utilitarian stairs are not readily visible and are primarily meant for emergency egress; their existence is primarily dictated by code. They certainly may be used as a means of vertical circulation within the building.

The finishes and light fixtures are simple, often painted CMU walls and surface mounted lights.

In stairs, building codes often require a gate at the ground level and at the upper level, if the stair continues to the roof. The reason for this is to help guide people in an emergency. Each floor in the utilitarian stair shaft looks the same, so it would be easy for a person, especially in a panicked state, to pass the ground level exit and continue down one or two more floors to the basement, extending their time in a dangerous situation. If the stair is used for normal, day-to-day, vertical circulation, some building officials will allow the gate to be placed on a magnetic hold-open which allows the gate to close in the event of a fire alarm system activation.

Most commercial codes also require that a sphere 4″ or larger not be able to pass through the guardrail. This has a large impact on design but creates a safe environment for the users; looking at the photo to the right, it is not difficult to see how older codes allowed for unsafe designs!

1. Make sure you are in the **Level 1** floor plan view.

2. **Zoom in** on the rear stair shaft (see image to right).

3. On the Architecture tab, select ***Stair → Stair***.

4. Ensure the *Type Selector* is set to ***Steel Pan Stair***.

5. On the *Ribbon*, set the *Location Line* to **Exterior Support: Right** and *Actual Run Width* to **3'-4"**, (Figure 7-6.2).

6. Position the cursor approximately as shown in **Figure 7-6.3**; you are selecting the start point for the first step. Make sure you are snapping to the wall with *Nearest*.

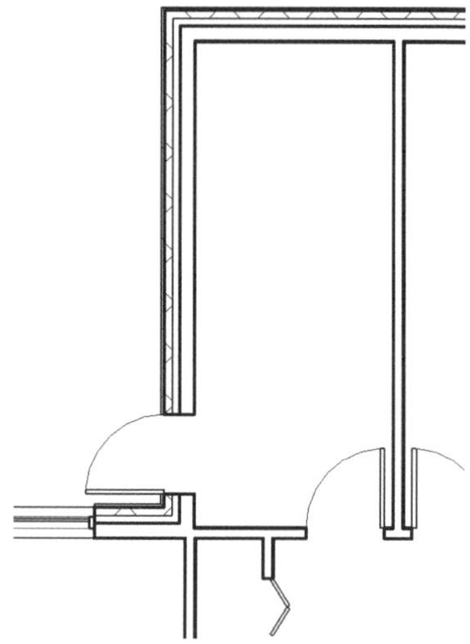

Rear stair shaft

7. Pick the second point as shown in Figure 7-6.4.

8. Pick the remaining points as shown in Figures 7-6.5 and 7-6.6.

9. Click **Finish Edit Mode**, i.e. the green check mark (Figure 7-6.2). Ignore any warnings about railings not being continuous at this point in the design.

Notice as you draw the stairs, Revit will display the number of risers drawn and the number of risers remaining to be drawn to reach the next level. If you click Finish Stairs, the green check mark, before drawing all the required risers, Revit will display an error message. You can leave the problem to be resolved later.

> **FYI:** *Revit has drawn the intermediate landings between levels. However, the landings at the main floor levels have not been created. Some projects extend the primary floor structure into the stair shaft to act as the landing for that level and also support the stair.*

The image to the right highlights the stair to be created in this section. Notice the handrail with wall brackets and that the guardrail extends along the edge of the level 2 floor.

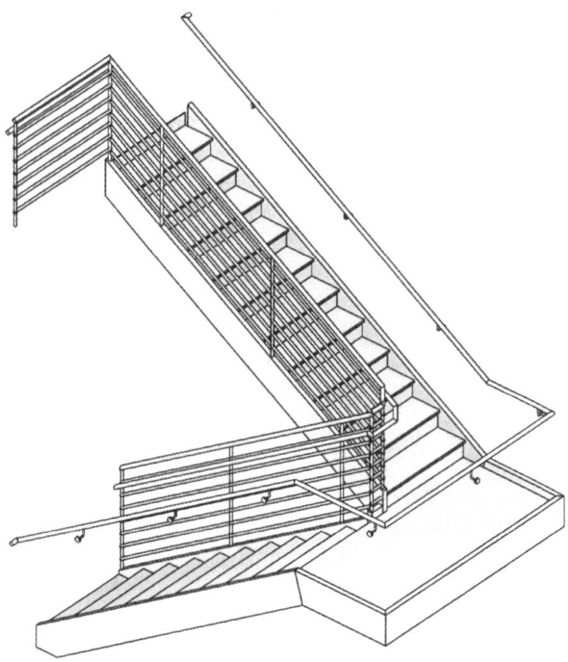

FIGURE 7-6.1 Stair and railings created in this section

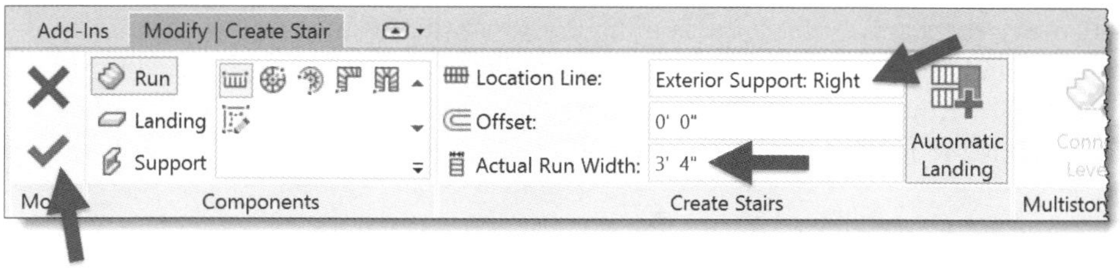

FIGURE 7-6.2 Finish Stair Sketch Button

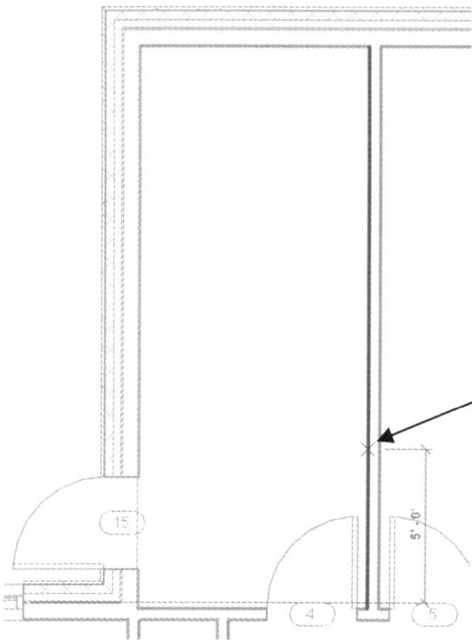

FIGURE 7-6.3 1st pick

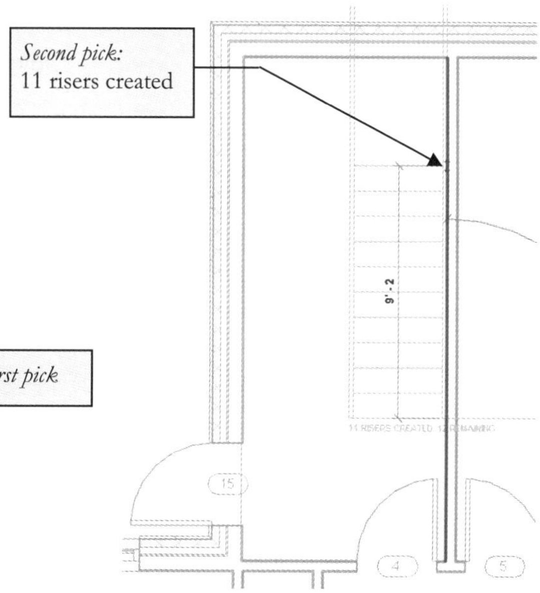

FIGURE 7-6.4 2nd pick

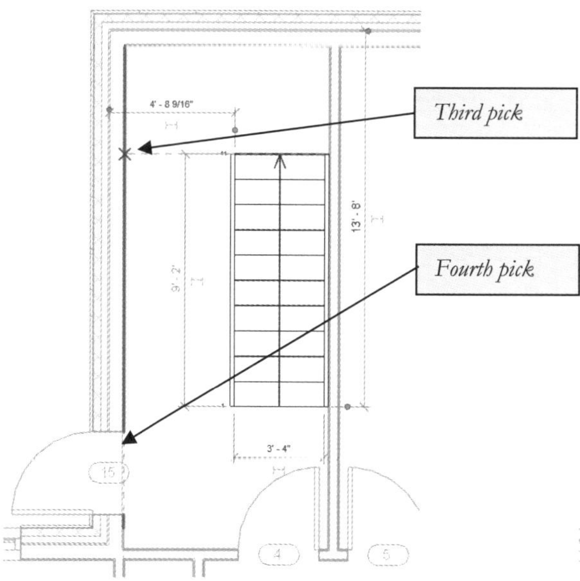

FIGURE 7-6.5 3rd and 4th picks

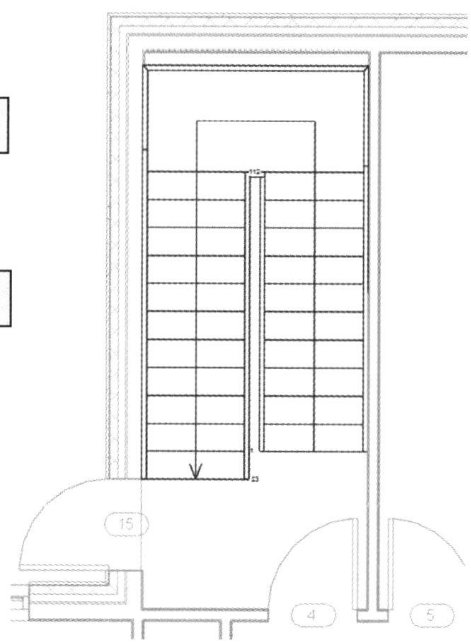

FIGURE 7-6.6 Finished (Level 1)

Next, you will move the stair north so the landing is against the exterior wall (with no gap). Another option would be to modify the landing, making it larger. In this case we will maintain what might be the code-minimum dimension (often the same dimension as the stair width – which is the Revit default).

10. Select the stair – a single click should select the entire stair and hosted railings.

11. Select the **Move** tool from the Modify tab.

12. Click to select on the northern-most dashed line, which represents the stringer/support, and then click perpendicular on the exterior wall – note the two arrows in Figure 7-6.7.

13. Figure 7-6.8 shows the stair in the correct position.

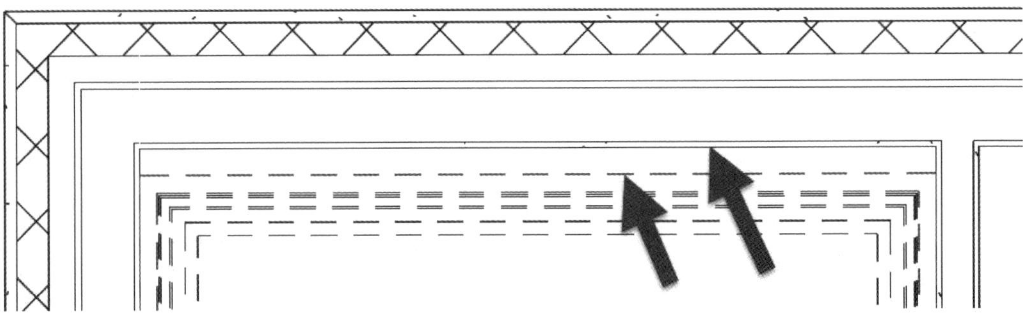

FIGURE 7-6.7 Moving stair north to align with exterior wall

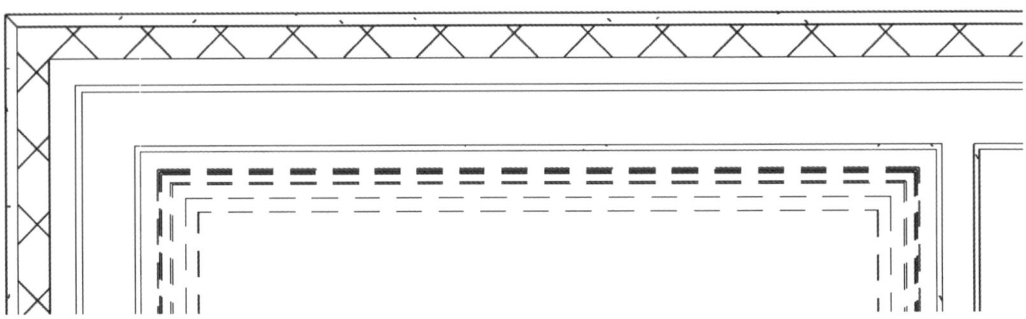

FIGURE 7-6.8 Stair moved north to align with exterior wall

Next you will make some adjustments to the railings and the level 2 floor.

14. Switch to the **Level 2 floor plan** view.

15. Adjust the **floor** so its edge aligns with the top of the stair (Figure 7-6.9); select the floor by its edge and click **Edit Boundary** on the Ribbon.

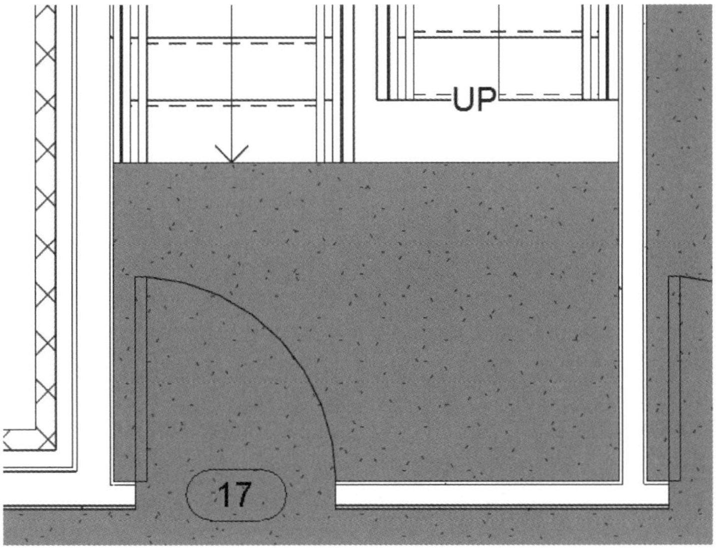

FIGURE 7-6.9 Adjust floor sketch to align with stair position

The outer railing is against a wall and therefore does not need to be a guardrail. Next, you will create a new railing type that consists of only a handrail and its supports.

16. Select the outer railing (adjacent to the walls) and change its *Type* to **Guardrail – Rectangular**. **FYI:** The "Guardrail – Pipe" option has several horizontal "rails" which would have to be deleted – so the "rectangular" option just saves a little editing time.

17. With the railing still selected, click **Edit Type**, select **Duplicate** and enter the new name: **Handrail Only** (Figure 7-6.10).

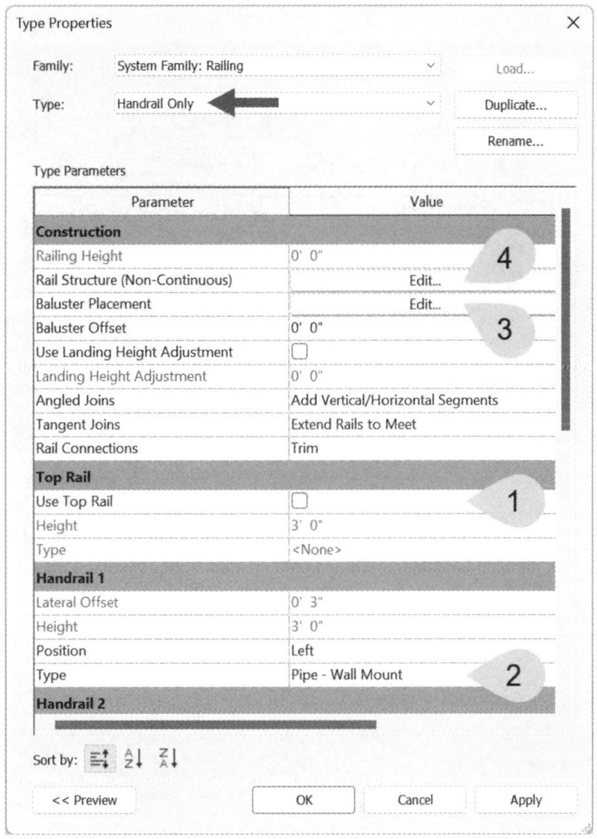

FIGURE 7-6.10 New handrail type; Handrail Only

18. Uncheck **Use Top Rail.**

19. Set **Handrail 1** Type to **Pipe – Wall Mount.**

20. Click the **Edit** button for **Baluster Placement** and set all "posts" to **None** (Figure 7-6.11). Click **OK** to close.

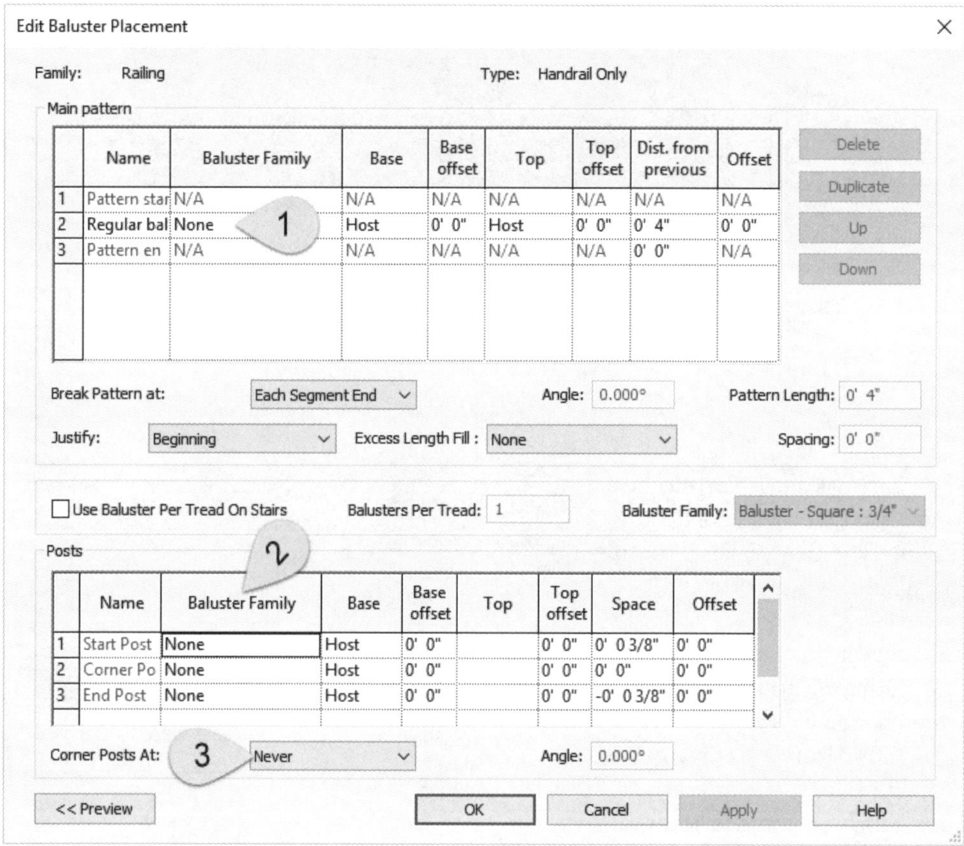

FIGURE 7-6.11 New handrail type; Handrail Only – modify Edit Baluster Placement dialog

21. Click the **Edit** button for **Rail Structure (Non-Continuous)** and make sure it contains no rails (i.e. the dialog is empty). Click **OK** to close.

22. Click **OK** to complete the modifications for the new Railing type.

Creating sections has not been covered yet, but if a section were cut through the stair we would see that both railings, *Guardrail - Rectangular* and *Handrail Only*, are not properly positioned (Figure 7-6.11). Each handrail has an Offset parameter (an instance parameter) which allows the entire railing to be repositioned as needed. The default offset value is 0'-1". A positive value moves the railing towards the center of the stair. The section indicates the railing needs to move in the opposite direction—thus a negative value is required. **FYI:** The values you are about to enter are the difference between the current value (0'-1") and the negative value the handrail/railing needs to move (i.e. -3"/-2" respectively).

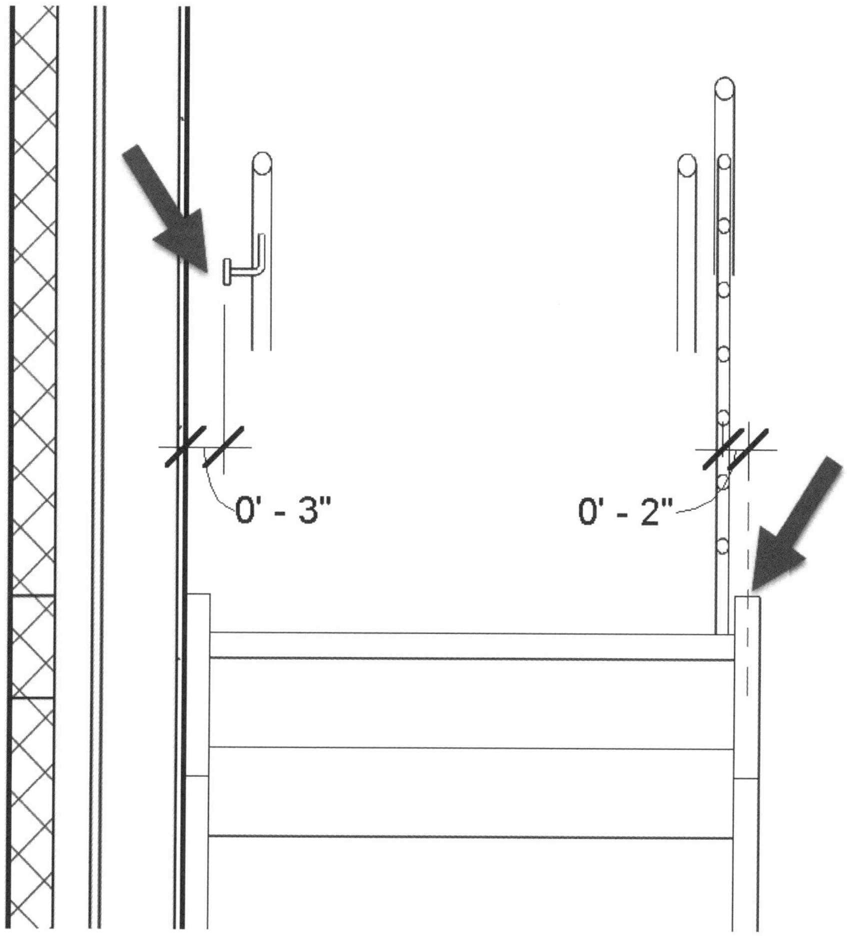

FIGURE 7-6.12 Default railing position needs to be adjusted

23. Select the inner railing, Guardrail – Pipe, and set the **Offset from Path** to **-0'-1"** in the Properties Palette. ***Tip:*** be sure to add the minus symbol.

24. Select the outer railing, Handrail Only, and set the **Offset from Path** to **-0'-2"** in the Properties Palette. ***Tip:*** be sure to add the minus symbol.

The railings are now positioned properly as shown in Figure 7-6.13. Notice the handrail wall brackets touch the wall (which they are attached to) and the posts of the guardrail are centered on the stringer (which they are welded to).

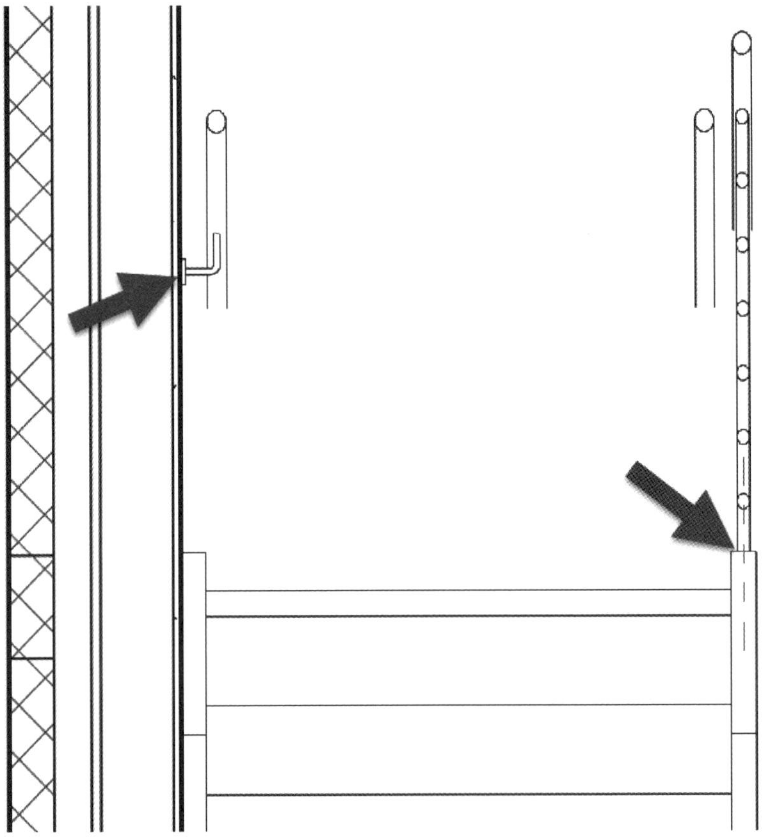

FIGURE 7-6.13 Railings repositioned relative to wall and stringer

Next we will adjust the handrail to return to the wall (this is required by building codes). Notice in Figure 7-6.14 that the handrail just stops at the edge of the first riser.

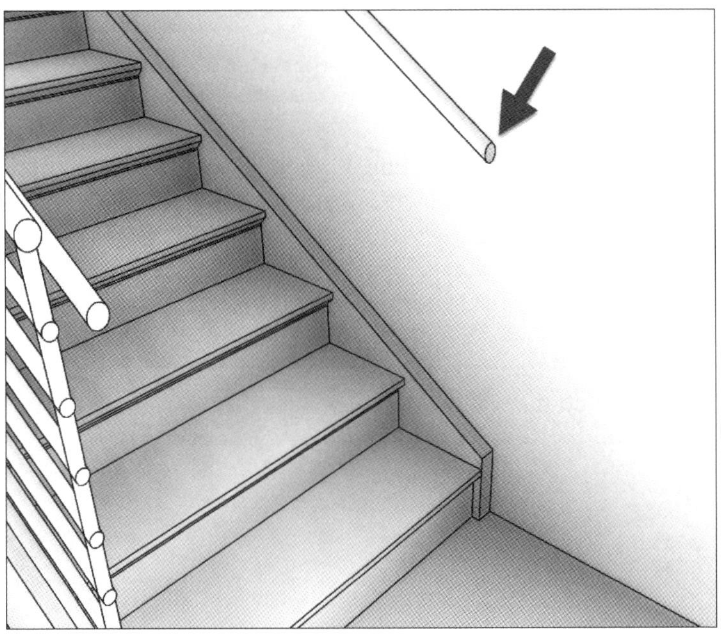

FIGURE 7-6.14 Railing needs to return to wall

25. In the *Project Browser*, expand **Families → Railings → Handrail Type**

26. Right-click on **Pipe – Wall Mount** and select **Type Properties** (Figure 7-6.15).

27. Set the **Extension Style**, for Extension (Beginning/Bottom), to **Wall** and check **Plus Tread Depth** (Figure 7-6.16).

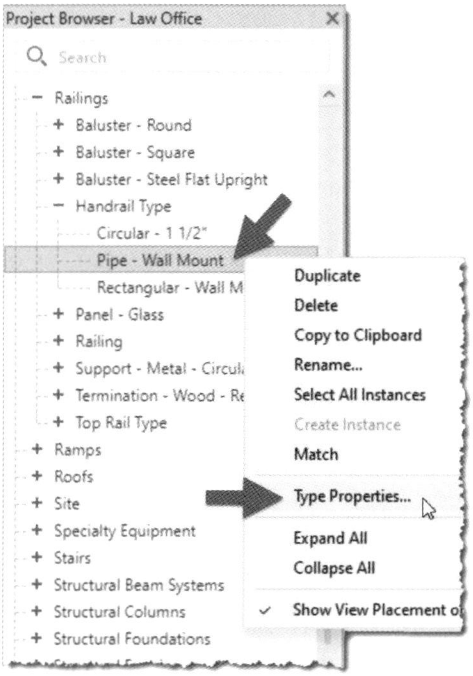

FIGURE 7-6.15 Modify handrail type

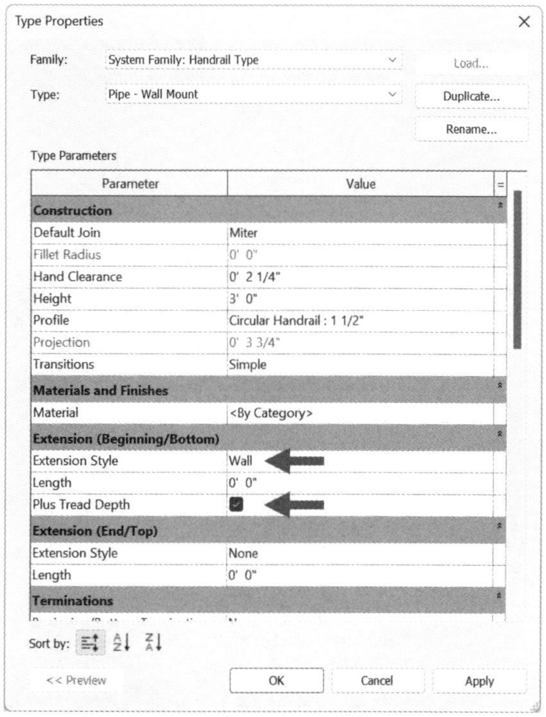

FIGURE 7-6.16 Handrail type properties

28. Click **OK** to complete the change.

The 3D camera view shown in Figure 7-6.17 shows the handrail returning to the wall. Also, Figure 7-6.18 shows the same thing in the Level 1 floor plan view. Notice the supports have been respaced. Note that supports can be selected, un-pinned, and then moved or deleted.

Similar adjustments can be made at the top of the stair and with the Top Rail.

FIGURE 7-6.17 Handrail now returns to wall

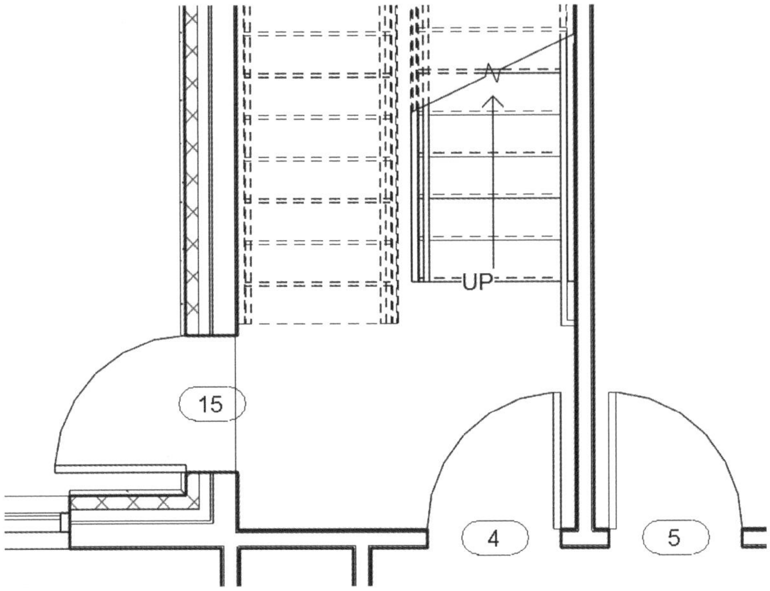

FIGURE 7-6.18 Plan view showing handrail now returns to wall

The last thing to do is extend the guardrail at the top of the stair at the open edge of the floor.

29. On the **Level 2** floor plan view, select the inner railing, Guardrail – Pipe, and click **Edit Path** on the *Ribbon.*

30. Sketch the additional line as shown in Figure 7-6.19.

31. Select the sketched line and set the *Slope* to **Flat** on the *Ribbon.*

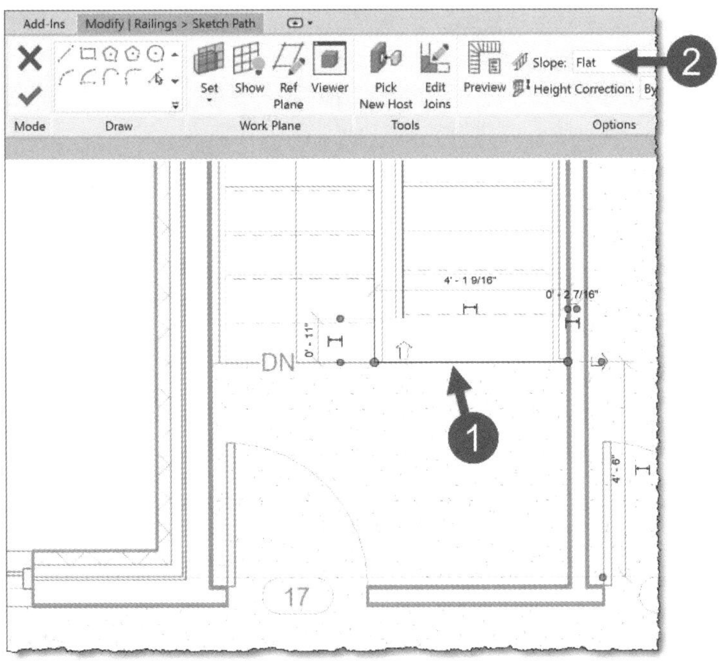

FIGURE 7-6.19 Modify railing sketch at Level 2

32. **Finish** the sketch by clicking the green check mark on the Ribbon.

33. **Save** your project file.

The image below shows the completed railing (Figure 7-6.20). The sketch line can be modified as needed to accommodate the intended attachment method—simply select the railing and click Edit Path to re-enter sketch mode and modify the path and position of the railing.

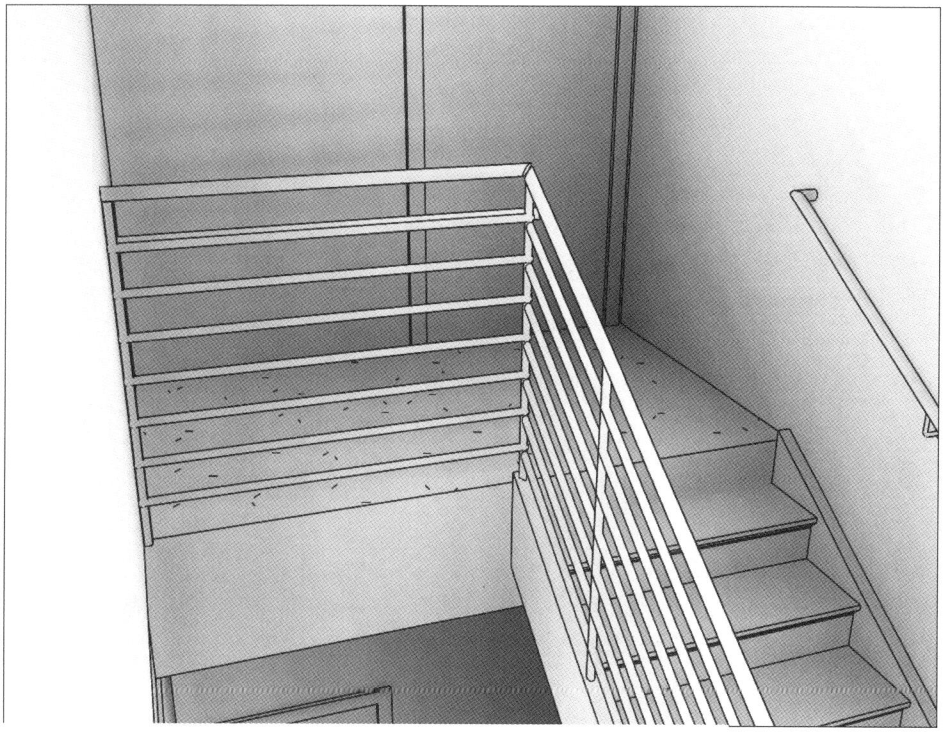

FIGURE 7-6.20 Stair railing extended along open floor edit in stair shaft

In the example above the stair railing was extended. This method allows the railing and handrail to return smoothly around the corner. However, sometimes the railing along the edge of the floor needs to be a separate Railing instance.

Exercise 7-7:
Open Stair and Railings

This exercise will cover the steps required to create a slightly more complicated stair and railing. This will be an open stair, i.e., not enclosed by walls, near the main entry.

Open Stair:

An open stair is often the primary stair used for vertical circulation in a building. This type of stair offers visual way-finding and can make an aesthetic statement for the building when well-located and designed. In our project, the open stair is located near the reception desk in the lobby so access to the upper level can be visually monitored.

Below is an example of a well-designed multi-story open stair. The railings are glass with a wood cap, the treads and risers are high quality terrazzo, and the walls are lined with wood panels. The stair is located next to windows which help the users know where they are in the building relative to the outside, helping with way-finding. The photo was taken through a large piece of glass that makes the stair visible at each floor within the building. In the event of a fire, the fire-shutters come down and close off this view!

OPEN STAIR EXAMPLE High quality stair with interesting design

The previous steps just walked you through the basics. This is all you would typically need to do early in a project. As the project is more refined and the walls stop moving, the stairs may be refined for stringer type and location, as well as landing size and shape.

1. In the Level 1 floor plan view, select the ***Stair*** tool.

2. Set the *Width* to **4′-0″** on the *Ribbon.*

Next, you will begin drawing a switchback stair similar to the one in the stair shaft. But, before you finish the stair sketch, you will modify the sketch lines at the landing. You will make it curved as in the image below (Figure 7-7.1).

The exact location of the stair is not important as the next chapter will have you reposition the stair once the floor is drawn.

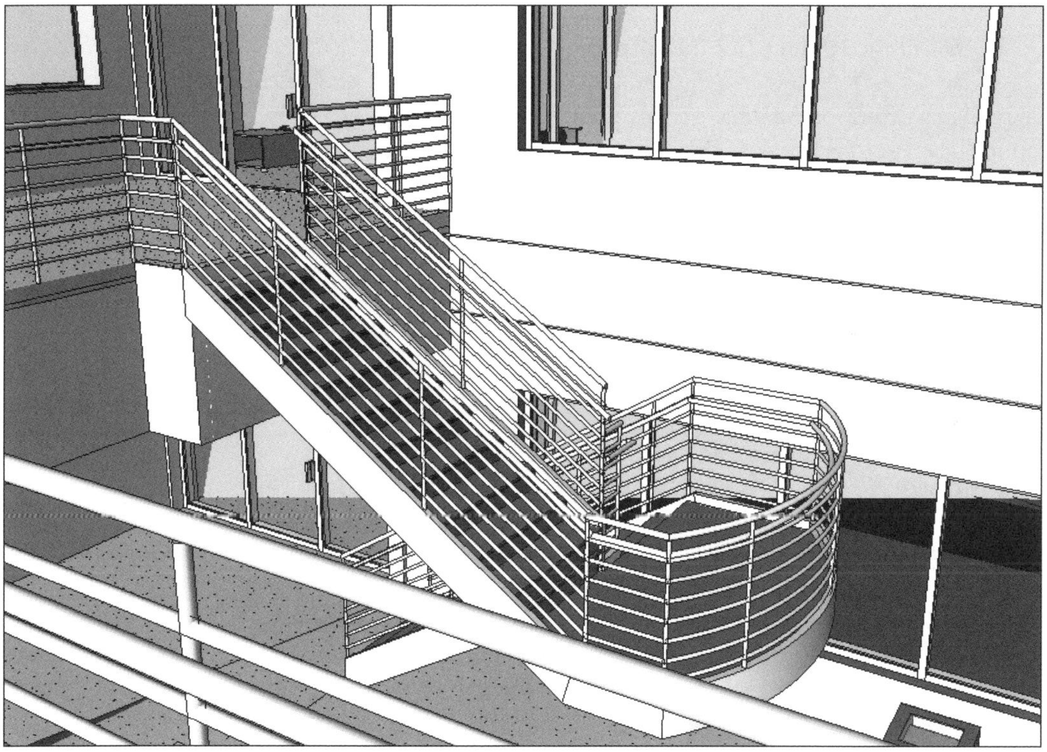

FIGURE 7-7.1 Landing modified to have curved edge and railing

3. Draw the **4′-0″** wide stair approximately as shown in Figure 7-7.2 (exact location not important at this point). Space between runs should be 1'-10".

The stair components shown in Figure 7-7.2 can be stretched, rotated and moved to adjust the footprint of the stair. This can be done until the stair sketch is finished. Once the stair is finished, you must select the stair and select *Edit Stairs* on the *Ribbon*; which places you back in *Sketch* mode and allows for additional edits.

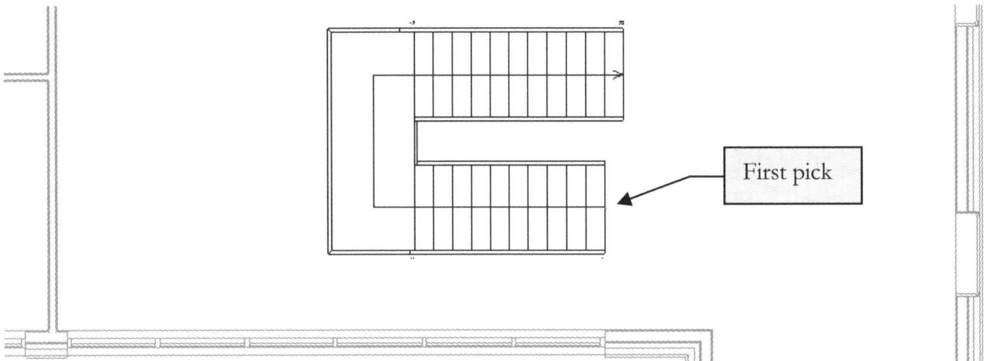

4. Select the landing, not the stringer (Figure 7-7.3).

The 3D stair components that are automatically created cannot be customized unless they are converted to a sketch-based object. The landing will be converted to a sketch-based element so the footprint can be modified.

5. Click **Convert** and then **Close** at the prompt.

6. With the landing still selected, click **Edit Sketch** from the *Ribbon*.

7. Select the vertical green sketch line on the left and delete it.

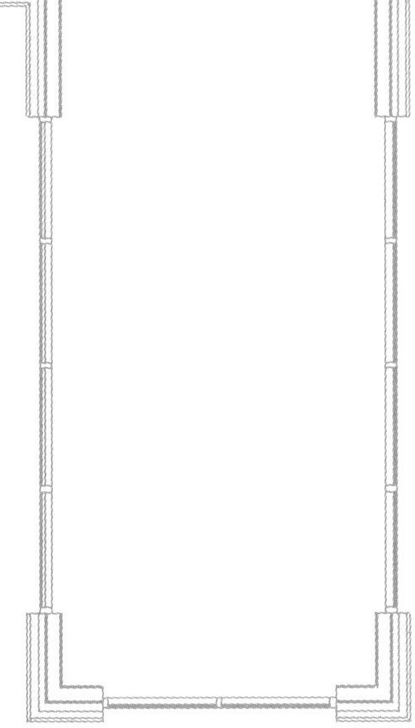

FIGURE 7-7.2
Stair layout in the lobby

8. In the *Draw* panel, on the *Ribbon*, select **Boundary** (Figure 7-7.4).

9. Select the *Start-End-Radius* ***Arc*** tool, also in the *Draw* panel.

10. Draw an arc similar to that shown in Figure 7-7.5. Exact dimensions are not important at this point.

11. Finish the stair sketch by clicking the **green checkmarks**.

12. Switch to the default **3D** view.

Notice the railing automatically followed the curved landing. In a later lesson you will add railings at the second level which ties into the stair railings.

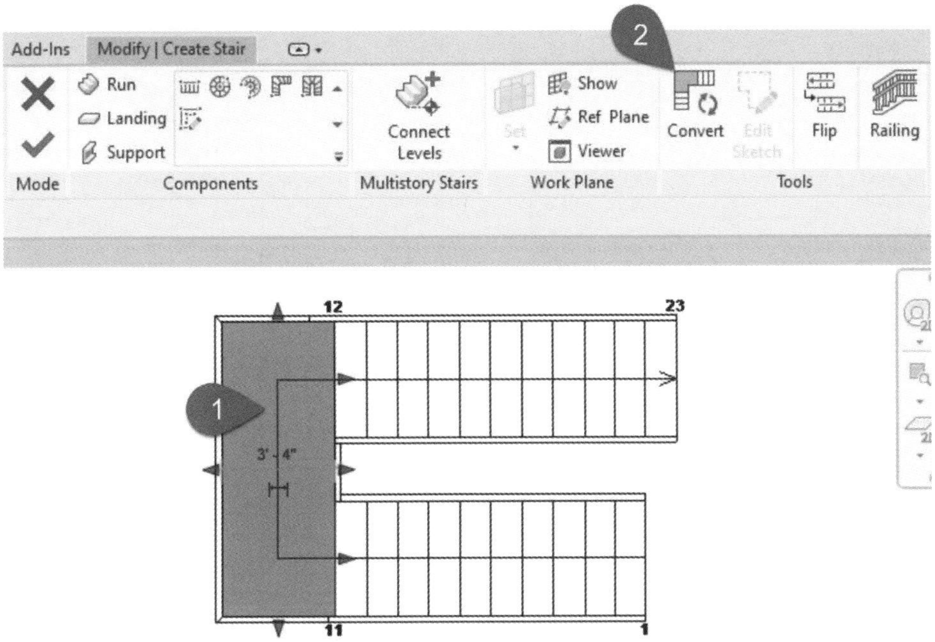

FIGURE 7-7.3 Select landing and convert to sketch to customize the footprint

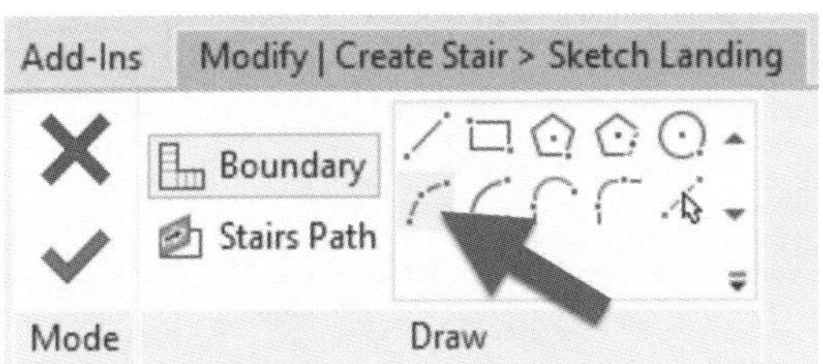

FIGURE 7-7.4 Edit landing boundary

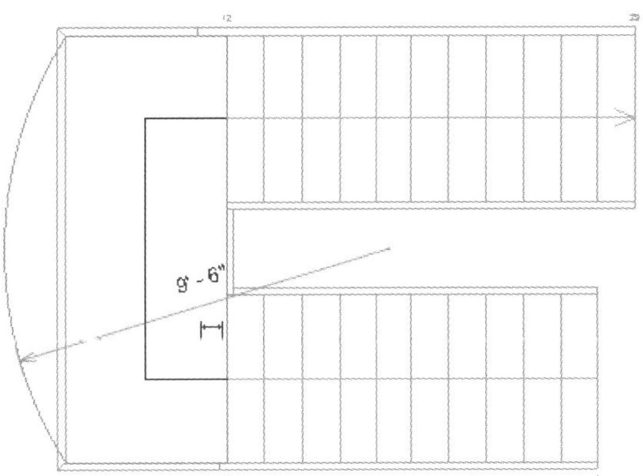

FIGURE 7-7.5 Curved line added at landing

Next, the stair will be moved into place to "connect" to the level 2 floor.

13. Switch to the **Level 2** floor plan view.

14. Select the stair (not railings) and, using **Move** and **Snaps**, position the stair as shown in Figure 7-7.6 relative to the level 2 floor element.

15. Select the inner railing, hosted on the stair, and edit its path as shown in Figure 7-7.7.
    a. Add two lines as pointed out
    b. Position the line **2"** in from the floor edge
    c. Set the *Slope* to **Flat** on the *Ribbon* for each line
    d. Click **Finish Edit Mode** (green checkmark) when done

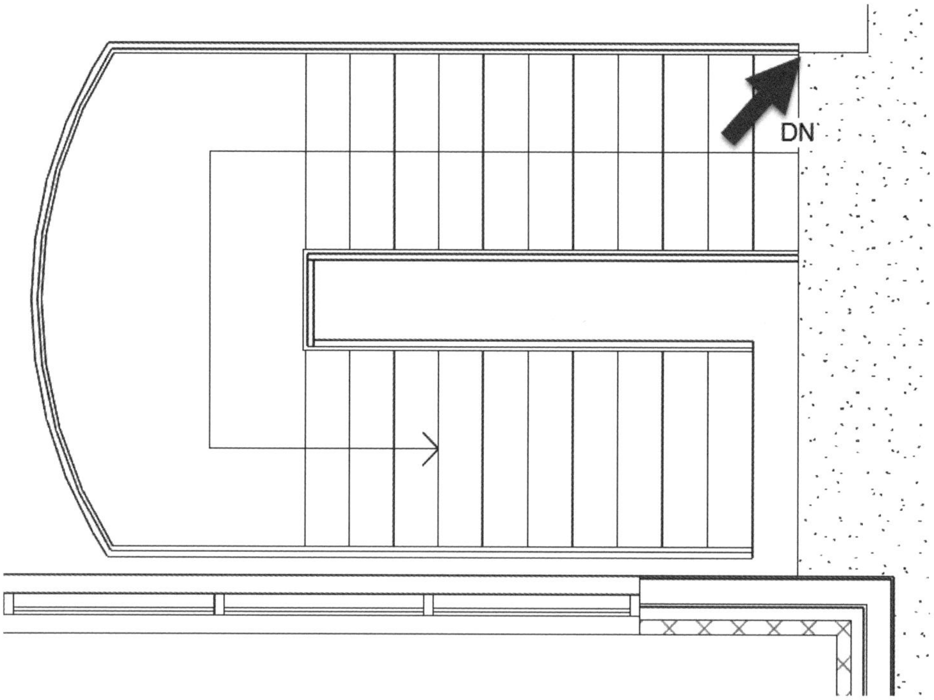

FIGURE 7-7.6 Open stair repositioned to align with Level 2 floor element

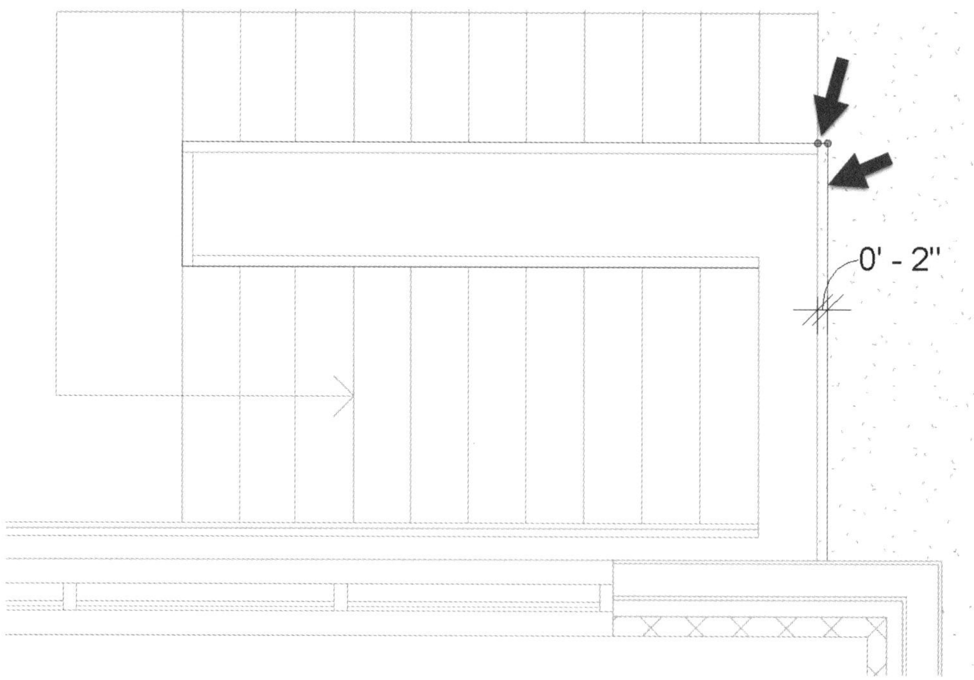

FIGURE 7-7.7 Editing the path of the inner railing

16. Edit the outer railing, hosted by the open stair, using similar steps to close off the level 2 floor edge as shown in Figure 7-7.9.

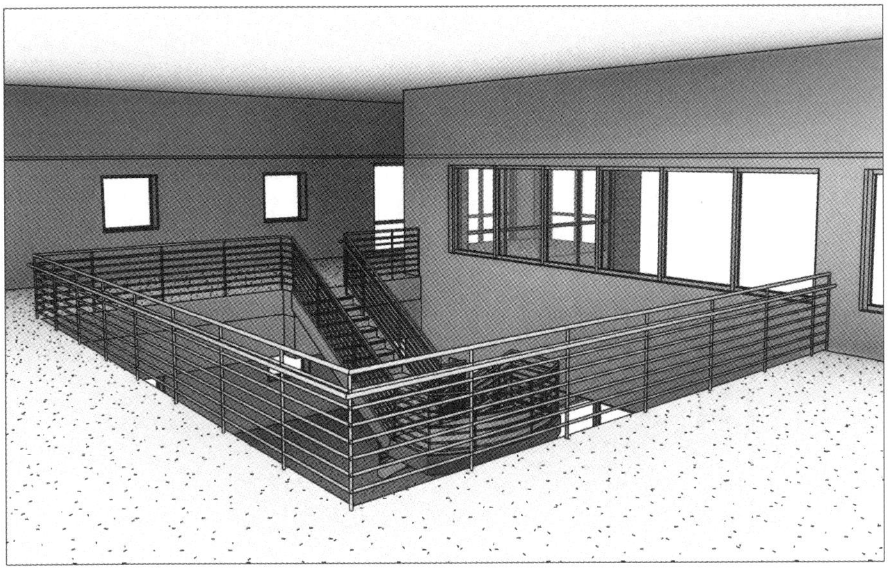

FIGURE 7-7.8 Stair railing extended along level 2 floor edge

The last task will be to modify the railing to achieve a different aesthetic look. To help visualize the changes, similar to the images on this page, add a camera view: **View→3D View→Camera**, and then pick two points in the Level 2 plan view. The first pick is where you are standing and the second is the direction you want to look. In the new camera view, turn off *Far Clip Active* in the Properties Palette. Project Browser lists the new view.

17. For the open stair, select the two railings and change the type to **Guardrail – Rectangular** via the *Type Selector.*

FIGURE 7-7.9 Stair railing type changed to Guardrail - Rectangular

As seen in the previous image, the new guardrail has a square top rail and smaller square balusters. This railing will be modified to have vertical supports which match the top rail dimensions. We will also add a horizontal element a few inches up from the floor as seen in the image below.

FIGURE 7-7.10 Railing style desired

The railing type "Guardrail – Rectangle" is not used anywhere else in the project so we can just modify it. If this type were used, we would want to duplicate the type before modifying it so as not to change a railing elsewhere in the same project. The utilitarian stair in the back will not be changed - it should still be set to "Guardrail – Pipe."

18. Select the two railings and set the instance parameter **Tread/Stringer Offset** to **-0'-1"** to center the railing on the stair stringer (Figure 7-7.11).

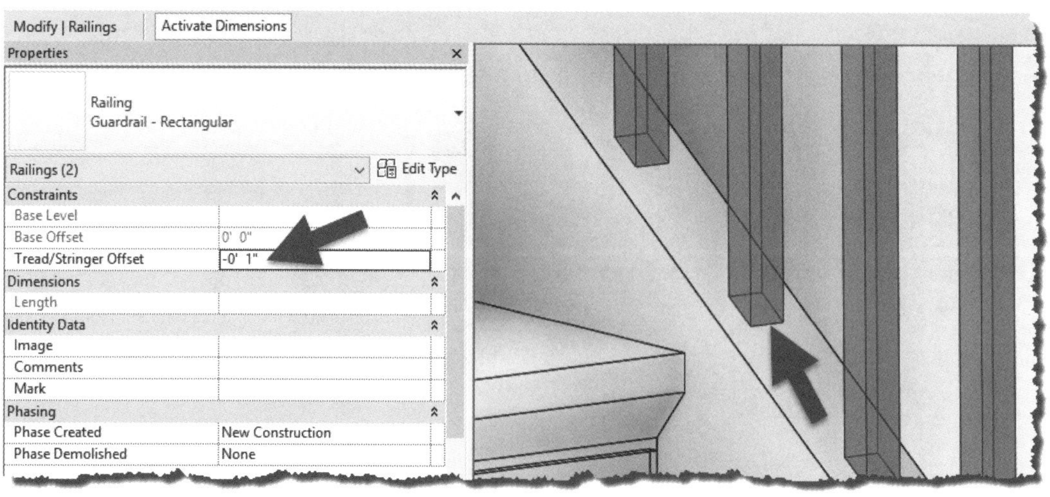

FIGURE 7-7.11 Centering railing on stair stringer

19. With one of the open stair railings selected, click **Edit Type** in the *Properties Palette.*

FIGURE 7-7.12
Bottom rail added

<u>**Horizontal Rail:**</u>

Next you will add a "horizontal" rail as seen in Figure 7-7.12. It is horizontal at floor/landing edges and sloped at stairs.

20. Click **Edit**, next to *Rail Structure.*
21. Click the **Insert** button (#1, Figure 7-7.13).
22. Make these changes (#2, Fig. 7-7.13):
    a. *Name:* **Bottom Rail**
    b. *Height:* **0'-7"**
    c. *Profile:* **Rect. Handrail: 2" x 2"**
23. Click **OK** once to close the *Edit Rails* dialog.

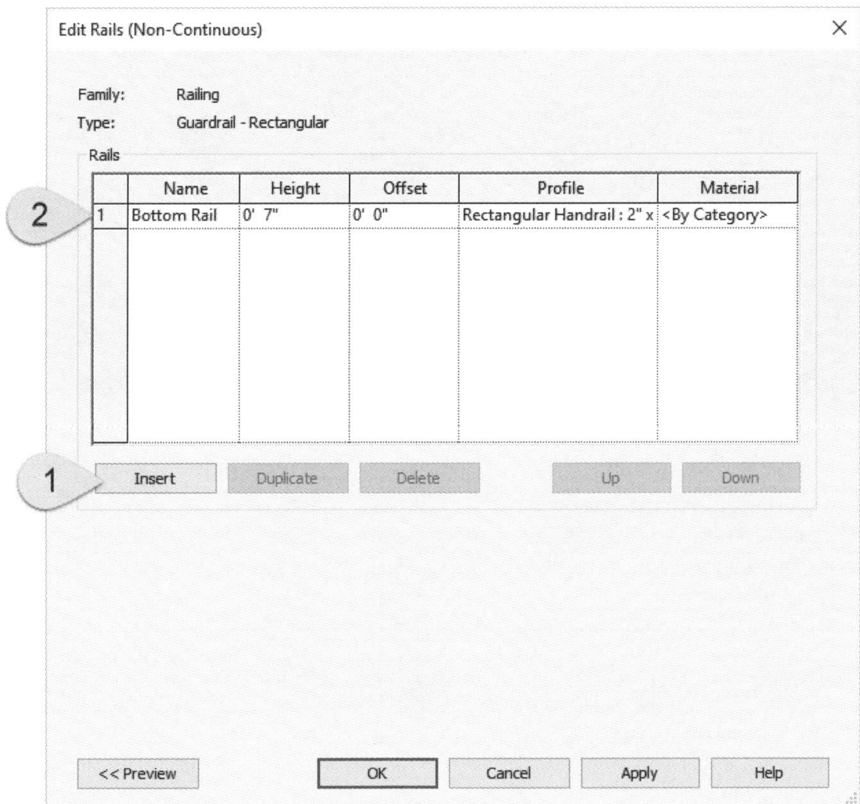

FIGURE 7-7.13 Adding "horizontal" rail to railing

Additional horizontal elements can be added following these same steps. Notice a *Material* can also be applied for each *Rail*, but if not specified here, the detail in **Manage→Object Styles** will be used. Notice in Figure 7-7.12 that the balusters extend through the new rail. You will correct that in a moment—the name we provided, <u>Bottom Rail</u>, will be used.

Start, End and Corner Posts:

The 3/4" balusters may not be strong enough to meet code requirements so we will add 2" square posts to the railing. First, we will add them at the ends (start and end) and corners; a corner is anywhere the railing changes direction—not just a 90 degree turn.

24. While still in the *Type Properties* dialog for Guardrail – Rectangular, click the **Edit** button for *Baluster Placement.*

25. Make the following edits (Figure 7-7.14):
    a. Edit the *Start, Corner and End Posts* to be **Baluster – Square: 2"**
    b. Edit the **Start Post** *Space*: **0'-1"**

26. Click **Apply**.

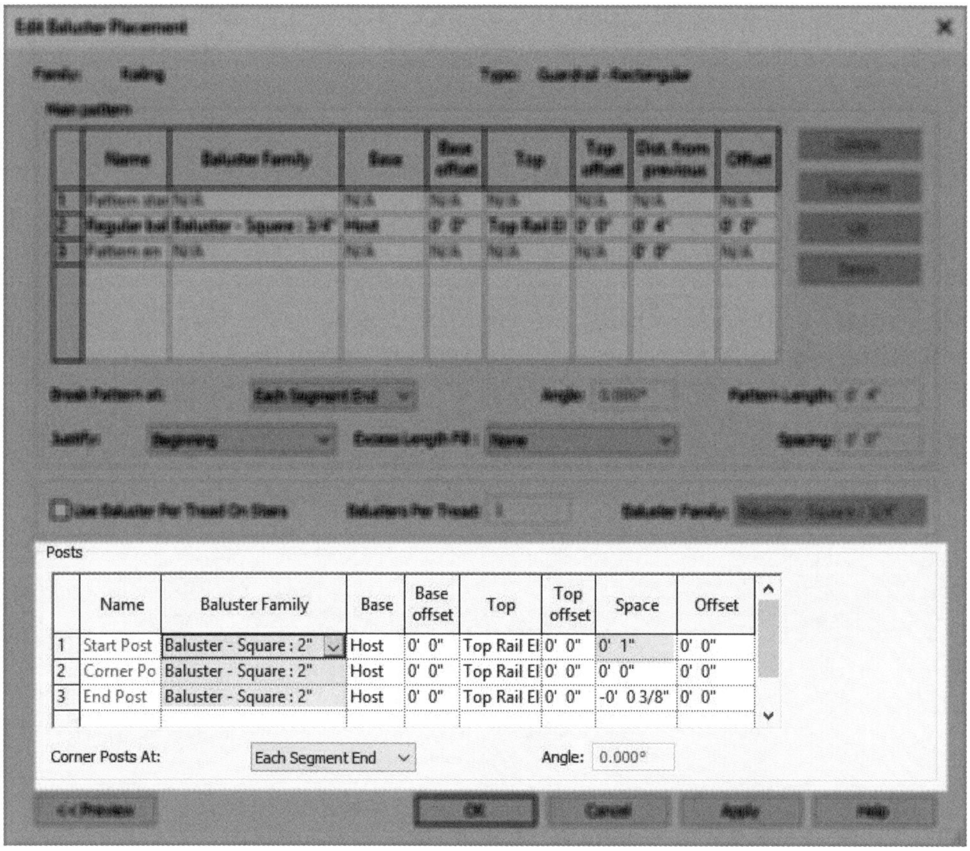

FIGURE 7-7.14 Edit Baluster Placement dialog; changing post family

Main Pattern:

The next step is to edit the "Main Pattern" area within the *Edit Baluster Placement* dialog. First, you will adjust the Balusters to start at the new Bottom Rail rather than the floor. Then several rows will be created to define a 4'-0" pattern which includes a 2" square post and several 3/4" square balusters.

27. While still in the *Edit Baluster Placement* dialog, in the *Main Pattern* section, change the **Base** option to **Bottom Rail** via the drop-down list (Figure 7-7.15).

    FYI: This option "Bottom Rail" comes from the name you provided in the *Rail Structure* dialog (Figure 7-7.13).

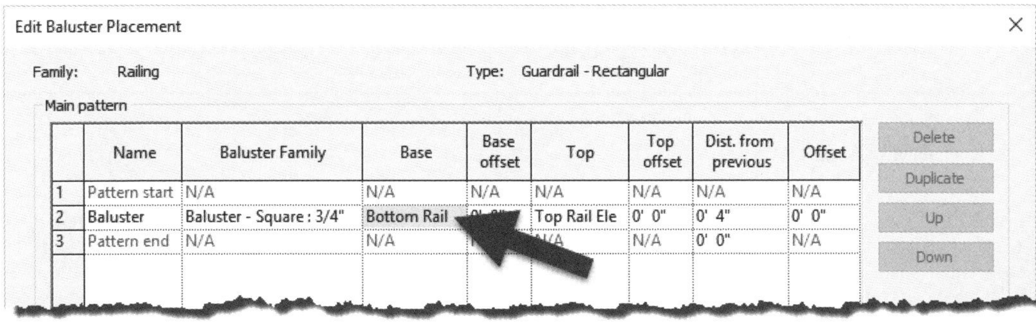

FIGURE 7-7.15 Edit Baluster Placement dialog; changing main pattern to start at new horizontal rail

28. Click **Apply**.

Notice the balusters now start at the new bottom rail rather than the floor (Figure 7-7.16). Now we want to add a 2" square post every 4'-0" along the railing. This requires we first add enough 3/4" balusters at the 4" spacing to equal 4'-0".

29. Duplicate the 3/4" baluster **10 times** as shown in Figure 7-7.17.

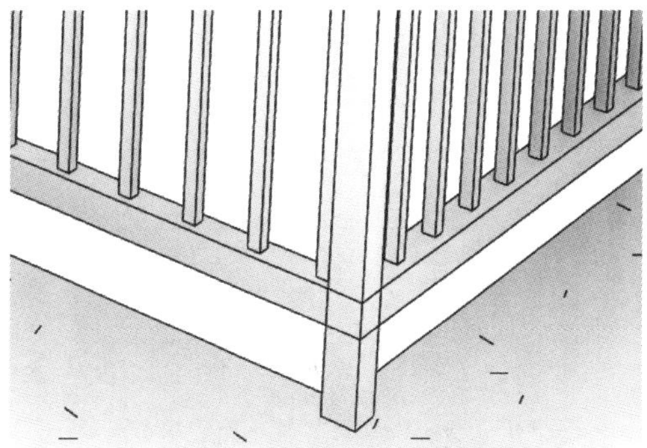

FIGURE 7-7.16 Result of current railing edits

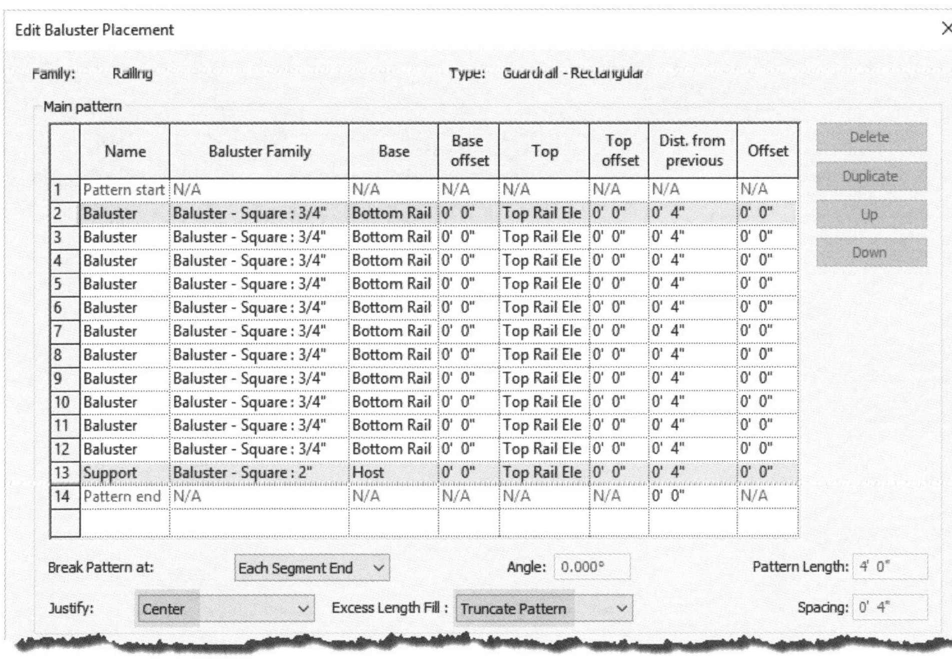

FIGURE 7-7.17 Edit Baluster Placement dialog; creating a 4'-0" pattern to include 2"

30. Duplicate the 3/4" baluster one more time and then change **Baluster Family** to **Baluster – Square: 2"** (Figure 7-7.17).

31. Change *Justify* to **Center**; this will center the pattern along each straight segment.

32. Set the *Excess Length Fill* to **Truncate Pattern** (Figure 7-7.17); this will repeat the pattern at the end when the total length is not perfectly divisible by 4'-0" (which will likely be most of the time).

33. Click **OK** to close all open dialog boxes.

The result should look similar to the next two images (Figure 7-7.18 & 19). The one problem with the bottom rail is that the spacing from the floor is too high for typical building codes in this example. The offset value we entered is both from the floor and the outside edge of the stair tread. If we lower the value the bottom rail is too close to the stair stringer. However, there is usually a steel plate of trim along the edge of the floor that would close this gap (that would be added as a separate element. The other option is to add the floor edge railing as a separate railing so the bottom rail could be adjusted via another railing type—but then the railing does not transition well between the stair and floor edge railing).

FIGURE 7-7.18 Modified railing result

FIGURE 7-7.19 Modified railing result

The final step is to modify the top rail and handrail extensions at the bottom of the stair. Remember to create new **camera views** as needed to see the changes you are making (per the steps outlined previously in this section).

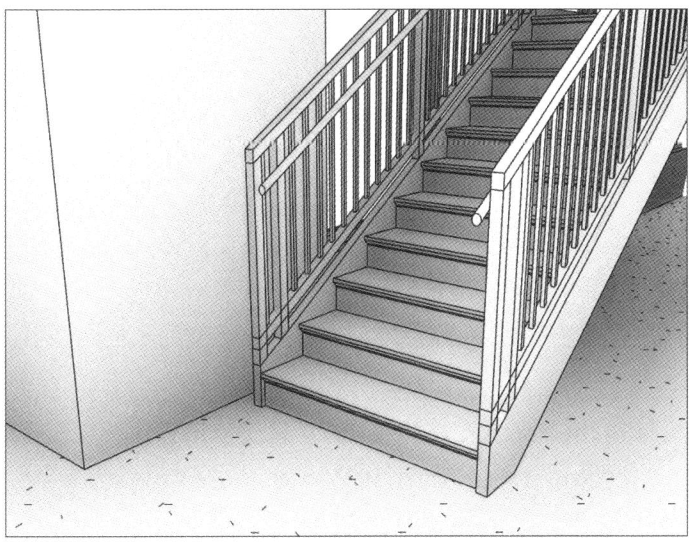

FIGURE 7-7.20 Default handrail condition at bottom of stairs

The default top rail and handrail start in alignment with the first tread (Figure 7-7.20). Most codes require the handrail to extend past the first step (sloped) a distance equal to one tread.

34. In a camera, 3d view, or section: select the **Top Rail**; hover the cursor over it and tap (not press) the **Tab** key until the Top Rail highlights and then click to select it.

35. Click **Edit Type** in the *Properties Palette.*

36. Make the following changes (Figure 7-7.21):
    a. Extension (Beginning/Bottom):
        i. Extension Style: **Post**
        ii. Length" **1'-0"**
        iii. Plus Tread Depth: **Checked**

37. Click **OK** to close the *Type Properties* dialog.

The Top Rail now extends one tread length at a slope, flattens out for 1'-0" and then returns to itself (i.e. the Post) as seen in Figure 7-7.22.

38. Select the **Handrail**; hover the cursor over it and tap (not press) the **Tab** key until the Handrail highlights and then click to select it.

39. Click **Edit Type** in the *Properties Palette.*

40. Make the following changes (Figure 7-7.23):
    a. Extension (Beginning/Bottom):
        i. Extension Style: **Wall**
        ii. Length" **0'-11"**
        iii. Plus Tread Depth: **Checked**
    b. Supports:
        i. Family: **Support – Metal – Circular**
        ii. Layout: **Align With Posts**

41. Click **OK** to close the *Type Properties* dialog. Click OK to any warnings.

The Handrail now extends one tread length at a slope, flattens out for 11 inches and then returns to the Top Rail (i.e. the Wall) as seen in Figure 7-7.24. The supports can be selected (via Tabbing) and moved/deleted when unpinned.

42. **Save** your Law Office project.

There are several limitations with stairs and railings, but understanding the ins and outs of what can be done allows the designer to get close and then let the details (i.e. 2D drafting views) cover the rest.

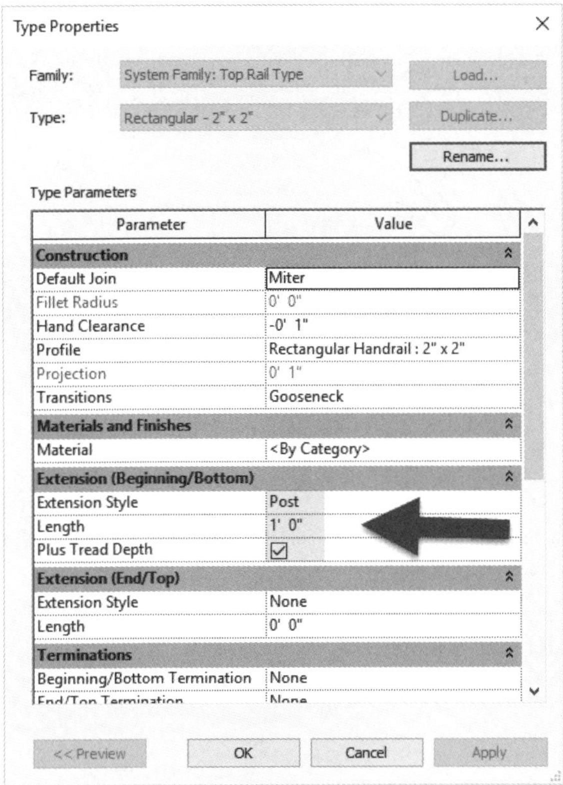

FIGURE 7-7.21 Editing Top Rail properties

FIGURE 7-7.22
Top Rail extension modified

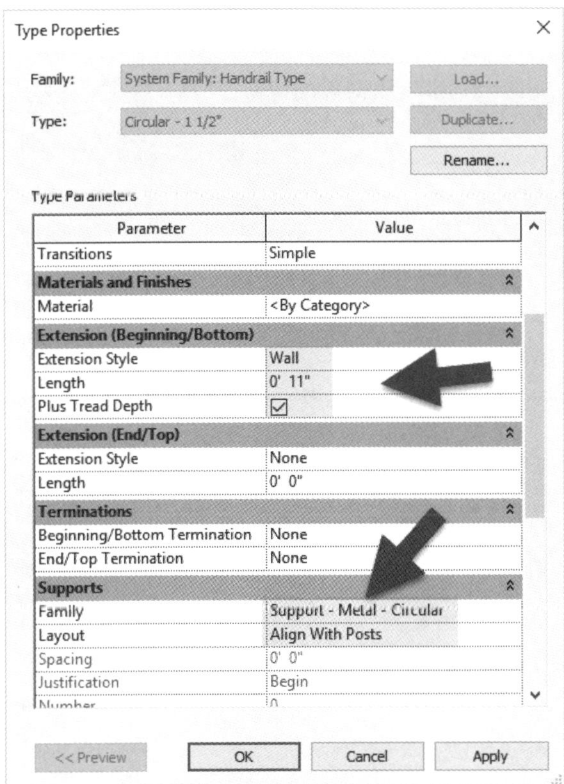

FIGURE 7-7.23 Editing Handrail properties

FIGURE 7-7.24
Handrail properties modified

Self-Exam:

The following questions can be used as a way to check your knowledge of this lesson. The answers can be found at the bottom of this page.

1. Stair landings are added automatically. (T/F)
2. A stair sample file can be downloaded from SDC Publications. (T/F)
3. Stairs and railings are shown as true 3D objects in plan views. (T/F)
4. A stair's railing cannot be deleted. (T/F)
5. Stair types are listed in the *Project Browser* under *Families.* (T/F)

Review Questions:

The following questions may be assigned by your instructor as a way to assess your knowledge of this section. Your instructor has the answers to the review questions.

1. Handrail supports can be moved or deleted. (T/F)
2. The riser is typically calculated to be as large as the building codes will allow. (T/F)
3. Stairs have multiple sub-categories which can be used to control stair visibility. (T/F)
4. To change a stair, select it and then click __________________ on the *Ribbon.*
5. A railing extending past the end of a stair run must always slope. (T/F)
6. To extend the stair's stringer you draw ___________________ lines.
7. Posts, within a railing instance, can be unpinned and repositioned. (T/F)
8. After starting the *Stair* tool, the first thing you need to do is set the _______ level and the ___________ level.
9. Railings can be modified to be shorter than the length of the stair. (T/F)
10. The riser height is based on the floor-to-floor height. (T/F)

SELF-EXAM ANSWERS:
1 – T, **2** – T, **3** – F, **4** – F, **5** – T

Lesson 8
Structural System

This chapter will introduce you to the structural features of Autodesk Revit. You will develop the structural model for the law office, placing grids, columns, beams, joists and footings. Finally, you will learn how to add annotations and tags that report the size of individual structural elements.

Exercise 8-1:
Introduction to Revit Structure

The image below shows the structural elements you will be adding in this chapter (except the roof structure). Keeping in line with the overall intent of this textbook, you will really just be skimming the surface of Revit's *Structural* features. For example, Revit can model concrete beams and columns, precast floors and roof planks, cross bracing, and rebar.

> *WARNING: This is strictly a fictitious project. Although some effort has been made to make the sizes of structural components realistic, this structure has not been designed by a structural engineer. There are many codes and design considerations that need to be made on a case-by-case basis.*

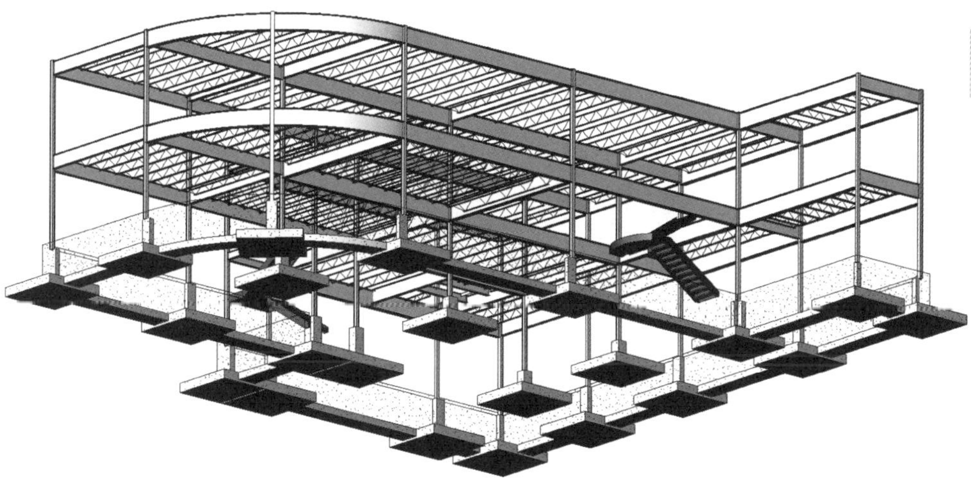

FIGURE 8-1.1 The completed structural model for the law office created in this chapter

In previous years Revit came in multiple versions: Revit Architecture, Revit Structure, Revit MEP, and an all-in-one version just called Revit. Now there is only one version that includes all features—it is just called Revit (or Autodesk Revit).

Listed below are a few of the highlights of Revit's structural features:

- 3D modeling of the entire structure
- Multi-user environment
    - Several people can be working on the same model when "worksharing" has been enabled (not covered in this book).
- Coordination with *Architecture* and *MEP*
    - Visually via 2D and 3D views
    - Using Interference Check feature
- 2D construction drawings generated in real-time from 3D model
    - Presentation drawings, including photo-realistic renderings
    - Construction Drawings (CD's phase)
        - Views can show true 3D geometry or single line
    - Construction Administration (CA phase)
        - Addendum
        - Architectural Supplemental Information (ASI)
        - Proposal Request (PR)
        - Change Order (CO)
- Schedules
    - Schedules are live lists of elements in the BIM.
- Design Options
    - Used to try different ideas for a structural design in the same area of a project (e.g., exposed cross-bracing vs. rigid structure)
    - Also used to manage bid alternates during CDs.
        - A bid alternate might be an extra 25′-0″ added to the wing of a building. The contractor provides a separate price for what it would cost to do that work.
- Phasing
    - Manage existing, new and future construction
- Several options to export to analysis programs
    - Export model to external program (e.g., Autodesk Robot Structural Analysis Professional, Autodesk A360 Structural Analysis, RISA, etc.)
- Export to industry standard shop drawing format (CIS/2)
    - Shop drawings are created and used by fabricators and contractors, once the design is done and the project has been bid.

Many of the highlights listed on the previous page are things that can benefit other disciplines. However, the list was generated with the structural engineer and technician in mind relative to the current software and processes used.

The Revit Platform

Whenever a project involves all three disciplines working in Revit, the same product version must be used. This is because Revit is not backwards compatible. It is not possible for the structural design team to use Revit *2025* while the architects and MEP engineers use Revit and Revit *2027*. The structural design team would have no way to link or view the architectural or MEP files; an older version of Revit has no way to read a newer file format.

Furthermore, it is not possible to *Save-As* to an older version of Revit, as can be done with other programs such as AutoCAD or Microsoft Word.

It is perfectly possible to have more than one version of Revit installed on your computer. You just need to make sure you are using the correct version for the project you are working on. If you accidentally open a project in the wrong version, you will get one of two clues:

- *Opening a 2025 file with Revit 2027:* You will see an upgrade message while the file is opened. It will also take longer to open due to the upgrade process. If you see this and did not intend to upgrade the file, simply close the file without saving. The upgraded file is only in your computer's RAM and is not committed to the hard drive until you Save.

- *Opening a 2027 file with Revit 2025:* This is an easy one as it is not possible. Revit will present you with a message indicating the file was created in a later version of Revit and cannot be opened.

Many firms will start new projects in the new version of Revit and finish any existing projects in the version it is currently in, which helps to avoid any potential upgrade issues. Sometimes, a project that is still in its early phases will be upgraded to a new version of Revit.

It should be pointed out that Autodesk releases periodic Revit updates. It is best if everyone on the design team is using the same build (i.e., 2027.0.1).

You will be looking at more specifics about the Revit *MEP* features in later chapters.

One Model or Linked Models

If the structural engineer is not in the same office, the linked scenario must be used as it is currently not practical to share models live over the internet (unless using Autodesk's BIM 360 cloud service). Linking does not work over the internet either (e.g. Google Drive, Dropbox, etc.); a copy of the model needs to be shared at regular intervals.

When all disciplines are in one office, on the same network, they could all work in the same Revit model, where each discipline uses Revit to manipulate the same Building Information Model (BIM). However, on large projects, the model is still typically split by discipline to improve performance due to software and hardware limitations. When a multi-discipline firm employs links, however, they are live and automatically updated when any one of the model files is opened.

In this book, you will employ the one-model approach. The process of linking and controlling the visibility of those links in the host file is beyond the scope of this text. Instead, you will focus your energy on the basic Revit tools for each discipline.

Ribbon – Structure tab:

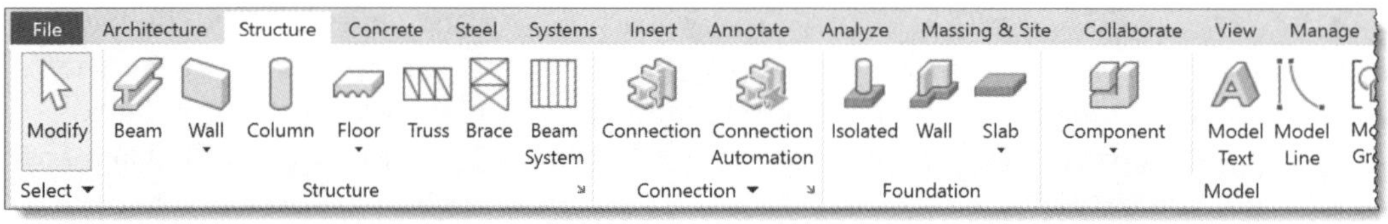

As can be seen from the image above, the *Structure* tab is laid out with the structural designer in mind. The very first tool is *Beam*, whereas *Wall* is the first tool on the *Architecture* tab. Also notice the panel names, *Structure*, *Foundation* and *Reinforcement*, are all discipline oriented.

Many tools are duplicates from those found on the *Architecture* tab; they even have the same icon. Duplicate tools, such as *Component, Openings, grids, etc.*, have the exact same programming code and create the same element which can then be edited by discipline using Revit.

Ribbon – Steel tab:

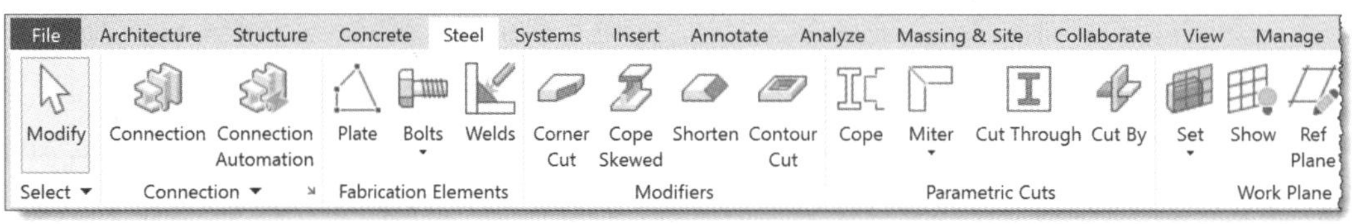

The Steel tab has more structural tools specific to structural steel design. These tools also work with **Autodesk Advance Steel**, an AutoCAD based application, used to create detailed fabrication/shop drawings and parts lists.

FYI: The Precast tab is not covered in this book and is typically not shown in screenshots.

Ribbon – Analyze tab:

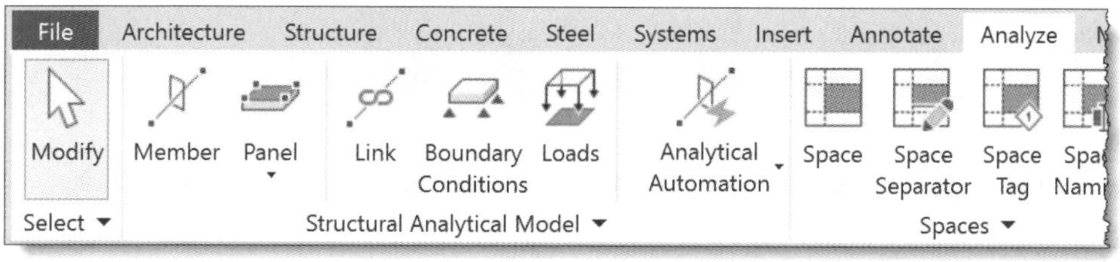

The *Analyze* tab reveals several tools which allow the structural engineer to specify various loads on the structure, once it has been modeled.

When structural elements are being drawn, Revit can optionally create the structural analytical model automatically. An example of this is shown to the right by single lines for each element that connects to each other, even though the 3D elements do not because a plate usually connects the beam to the column, so there is a gap in between.

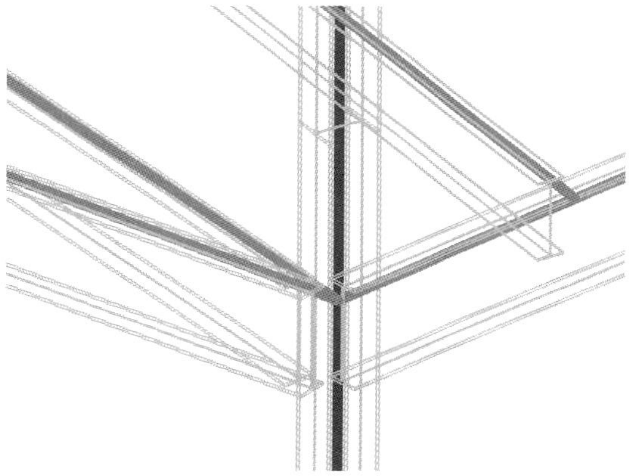

FIGURE 8-1.2 Analytical model lines

Revit provides tools to check the validity of the analytical model; e.g., *Check Supports* will notify you if a column does not have a footing under it!

The lines shown in Figure 8-1.2 can be hidden via the toggle on the *View Control Bar* (image to right) or by typing VV and clicking on the *Analytical Model Categories* tab (see image below).

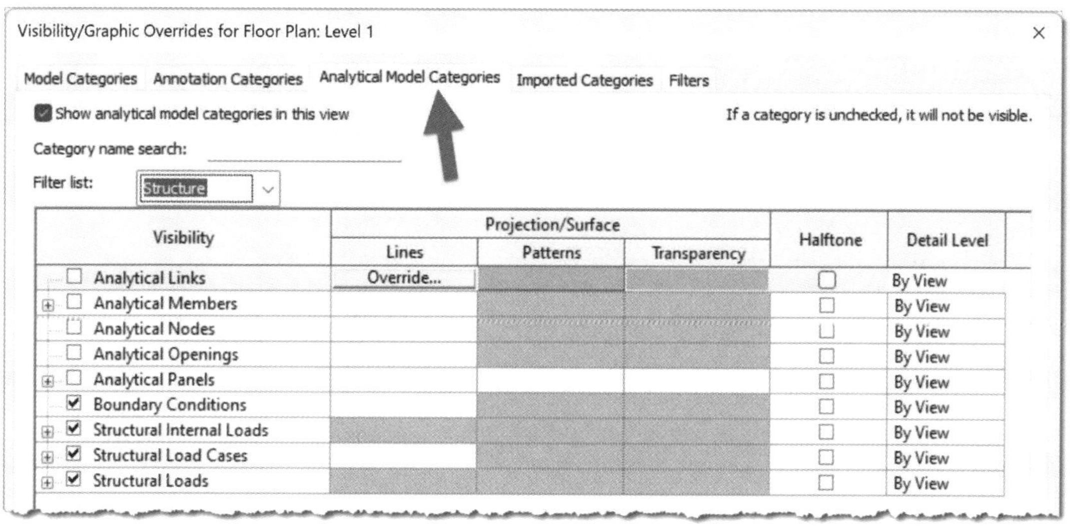

Structural Settings Dialog Box:

From the *Manage* tab, select *Structural Settings.*

Revit provides a *Structural Settings* dialog box that allows changes to be made in how the program works and displays structural elements. These settings only apply to the current project but apply to all views and schedules for that project.

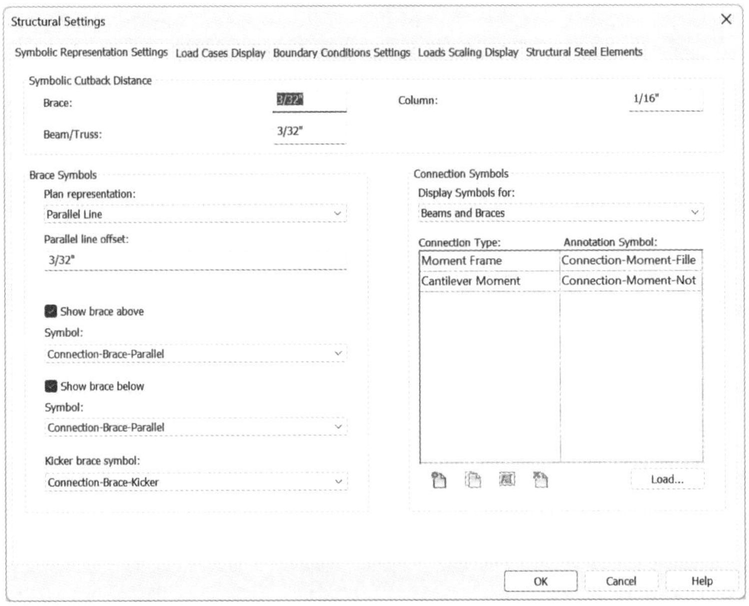

Do not make any changes in this dialog unless instructed to do so. This will help to ensure your drawings match those presented in the book.

Structural Content:

A vast array of industry standard beams, columns, joists, stiffeners and more are provided! Even some obsolete shapes are provided to aid in modeling existing structures. What is not provided can typically be modeled in Revit or the *Family Editor* as needed.

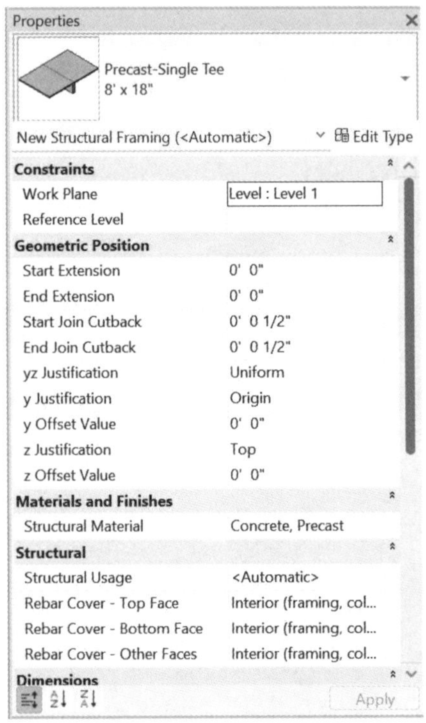

Structural Templates:

Revit provides only one template from which a new <u>structural</u> project can be started, compared to the four *Architecture* specific templates. This one template has all the basic views and components needed to start modeling a building's structure.

In an office environment, multiple templates may be needed if drastically different types of projects are worked on. For example, housing which is often wood framed and government which has specific annotation and dimensioning requirements.

Because you will be starting the structural model within the architectural model, you will not automatically have several important components ready to go. Not to worry, however, as the first thing you will do in the next exercise will be to import several elements from another project file, which will be based on the structural template.

Autodesk Revit Resources:

Autodesk's *Revit Help:*
http://help.autodesk.com/view/RVT/2027/ENU/

Autodesk's *Revit Structure Blog:*
https://revitstructureblog.wordpress.com/

Autodesk's *Revit Structure Discussion Group:*
https://forums.autodesk.com/t5/revit/ct-p/2003
(Click the link to Autodesk Revit *Structure.*)

Autodesk's *Subscription Website (for members only):*
accounts.autodesk.com

Exercise 8-2:
Creating Views and Loading Content

In this lesson, you will begin to prepare your BIM file for the structural modeling tasks. Although Revit provides a multi-discipline template, you will learn how to transfer settings between projects using the discipline-specific templates. To save time on future projects, the multi-discipline template is recommended.

The first steps in this lesson, therefore, will walk through the process of importing *Project Standards* from another file into your law office project. Once that has been done, you can then set up views in which to model and annotate the structural aspects of the building. These views will be similar to the floor plan views that currently exist for the architectural plans; they are defined by a horizontal slice or section through the building. The main difference is that various *Categories* will be turned off, such as casework, plumbing fixtures, etc., that are not directly relevant to the structure of the building.

Transfer Project Standards:

Revit provides a tool which allows various settings to be copied from one project to another; it is called *Transfer Project Standards*. In order to use this feature, two Revit project files need to be open. One is your law office project file and the other is a file that contains the settings you wish to import. You will start a new Revit structural project from a template file and use this file as the "standards" file; this file will not be used after this step is complete.

1. **Open** Revit.

2. Create a new file from the structural template; on the Home screen, select **New…** under the heading, Models, and then click the **Browse** button.

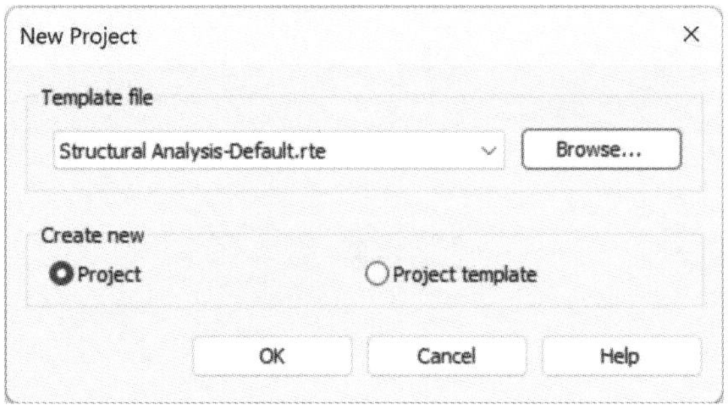

Revit only comes with one structural-specific template.

3. Select **Structural Analysis-Default** and then **Open** & **OK**.

   a. The file *should be* C:\ProgramData\Autodesk\RVT 2027\Templates\ US Imperial**Structural Analysis-Default.rte**.

You now have a new Revit project which is temporarily named Project 1.rvt. This will be the project from which you import various *Structural Settings* and *Families* into your law office project. Take a moment to notice the template is rather lean; it has no sheets and only a handful of views set up. A structural engineering department would take the time to set up an office standard template with sheets, families and views all ready to go for their most typical project to save time in the initial setup process.

4. **Open** your law office Revit project file and open the **Level 1 Floor Plan** view.
   You may wish to start this lesson from the data file provided online at SDCpublications.com. Make sure you select the file from the correct folder. See the inside front cover for more information.

Now that you have both files open, you will use the *Transfer Project Standards* tool to import several important things into the law office project file.

5. With the law office project file current (i.e., visible in the maximized drawing window), select **Manage → Settings → Transfer Project Standards**.

6. Make sure *Copy from* is set to **Project 1**, the file you just created. ***Tip:*** a Law Office model view needs to be current.

7. **<u>Important step</u>**: Click the **Check None** button to clear all the checked boxes.

8. After clicking *Check None* in the previous step, only check the boxes for the items listed below (Figure 8-2.1):

   TIP: If your list does not match the one below, you likely selected the wrong template file in step #3, above.

   a. Analytical Link Types
   b. Fabric *(select all three)*
   c. Foundation Slab Types
   d. Halftone and Underlay Settings
   e. Line Patterns
   f. Line Styles
   g. Load Types
   h. Materials
   i. Multi-Rebar Annotation Types
   j. Pad Types
   k. Rebar Cover Settings
   l. Rebar Types
   m. Reinforcement Settings
   n. Slab Edge Settings
   o. Structural Settings
   p. View Templates

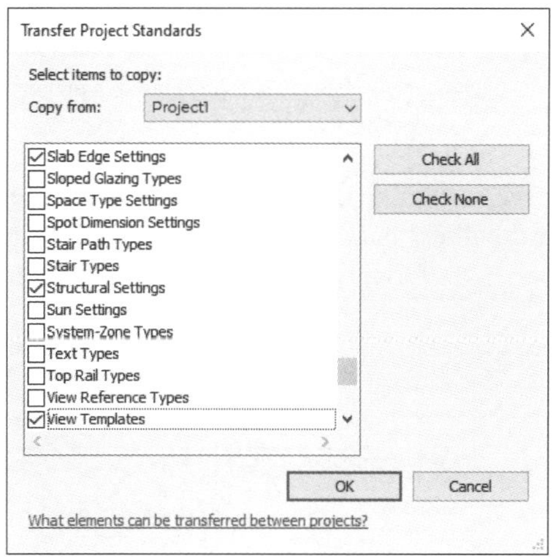

FIGURE 8-2.1 Transfer project settings

9. Click **OK** to import the selected items.

Because some items overlap, Revit prompts you about *Duplicated Types*; you can *Overwrite* or select *New Only*. Selecting "New Only" is safer if you are not sure what will be brought in by the template (or project file in this case). For the law office, you will use *Overwrite* to make sure you get all the structural settings and parameters needed.

10. Scroll down to see all the "duplicate types" so you have an idea what overlap there is; click **Overwrite** (see Figure 8-2.2).

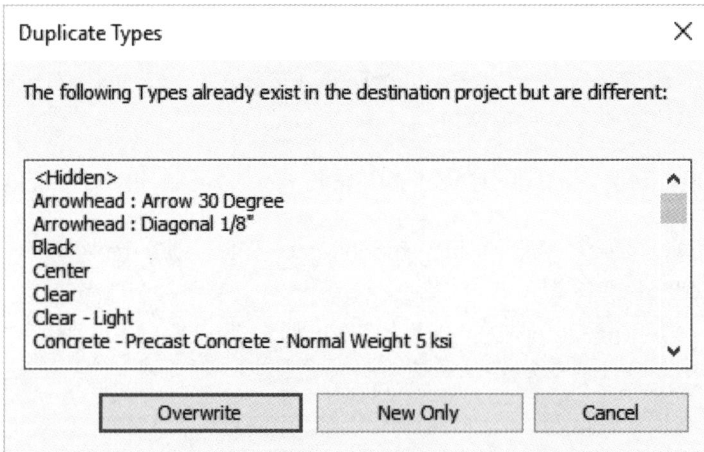

FIGURE 8-2.2 Transfer project settings; duplicate types warning

In the lower right corner of the screen, you may see a *Warning* prompt which can be ignored and will go away on its own. It is letting you know that some types have been renamed rather than overwritten to avoid conflicts (Figure 8-2.3).

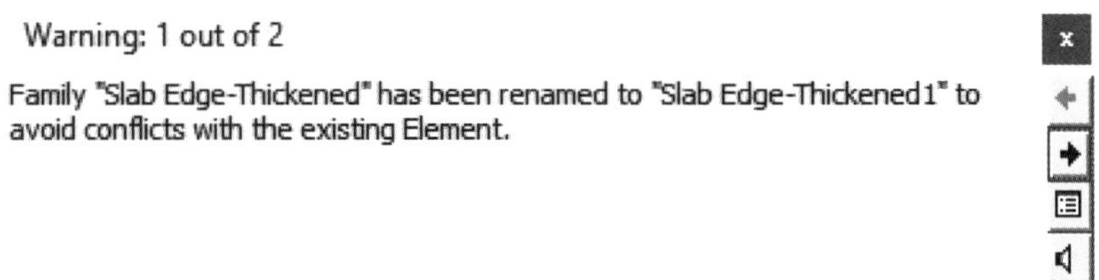

FIGURE 8-2.3 Warning message after transfer of standards

At this point you have many of the key settings loaded into your BIM file, such as *View Templates* and *Structural Settings*. A few items do not come across (e.g., boundary conditions and bracing symbols). However, that will not be a problem for this tutorial. **At this time you can close the temporary Project1 file without saving.**

Creating Structural Plan Views:

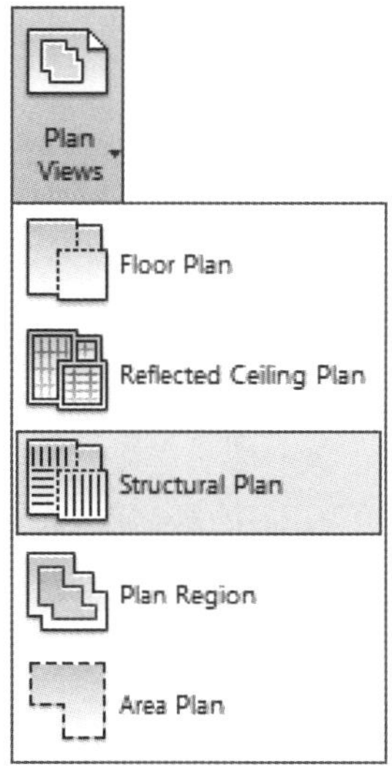

Next you will create three structural floor plan views:

- Level 1 – Structural Slab and Foundation Plan
- Level 2 – Structural Framing Plan
- Roof – Structural Framing Plan

After creating each of these views you will apply a **View Template**, which is a way to quickly adjust all the view-related parameters to a saved standard (i.e., a *View Template*).

11. While in the law office project, select **View → Create → Plan Views → Structural Plan**.

12. In the *New Plan* dialog box (Figure 8-2.4):

    a. Uncheck the *Do not duplicate existing views* option.

    b. *Select:* **Level 1**

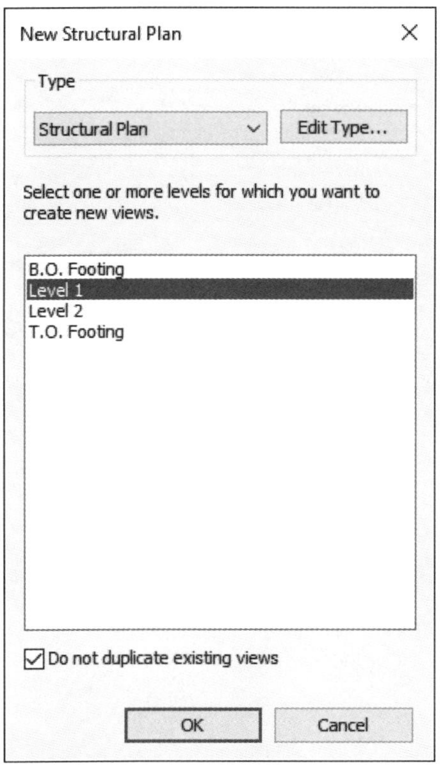

FIGURE 8-2.4 Creating a new plan view

13. Click **OK**.

At this point you have a new *View* created in the *Project Browser*. This view is in a new section, under *Views (all)*, called **Structural Plans** (Figure 8-2.5). Each view has separate notes and dimensions which is beneficial, because the structural drawings do not need to show a dimension from a wall to the edge of a countertop or sink.

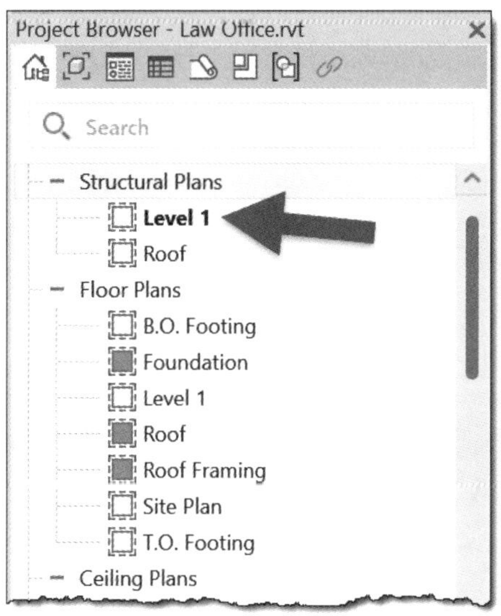

FIGURE 8-2.5 New structural plan created

Next, you will rename the *View* and apply a *View Template*.

14. In the *Project Browser*, right-click on **Level 1** *Structural Plans.*

15. Select **Rename** from the pop-up menu.

16. Enter: **Level 1 – Structural Slab and Foundation Plan.**

FYI: This is the name that will appear below the drawing when it is placed on a sheet.

17. Click **OK**.

18. Click **No** to the "Rename corresponding level and views" prompt.

It is best to rename views and levels manually; you do not typically want levels renamed to match the view name. All other disciplines see the same name; it should remain **Level 1**.

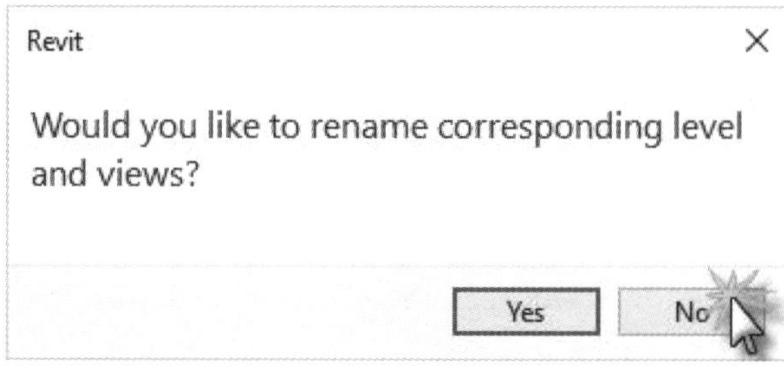

FIGURE 8-2.6 Rename level and views prompt; click No

View Templates:

Next, you will apply a *View Template* to your view so you know how to reset a view if it gets messed up at some point. You can also use this to update several views at once. First, you will change the current settings and then see how the view will be updated by applying a *View Template.*

19. Ensure nothing is selected and no commands are active so the *Properties Palette* is displaying the current view's properties.

    a. Set the **Discipline** to **Architectural** as shown in Figure 8-2.7.

    b. Set the *View Scale* to **1/4" = 1'-0"**

The *View Template* (you are about to apply to this view) will quickly correct the discipline setting.

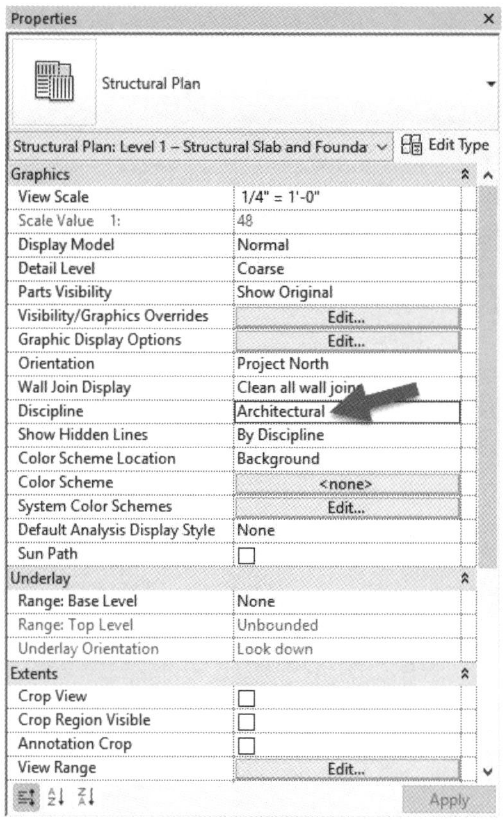

FIGURE 8-2.7 View properties – Structural Level 1

Next, you will look at the *View Range* settings. These control the location of the horizontal slice through the building.

20. With the ***Level 1 – Structural Slab and Foundation Plan*** view active, scroll down and click **Edit** next to *View Range* in the *Properties Palette.*

The ***View Range*** dialog has a significant role in what shows up in a plan view and what does not. In Revit *Structure*, things typically show up only when they fall at or below the *Cut plane*, and are above the *View Depth Level/Offset.* Search Revit's *Help System* for "view range" for a good description and graphics on these settings (Figure 8-2.8).

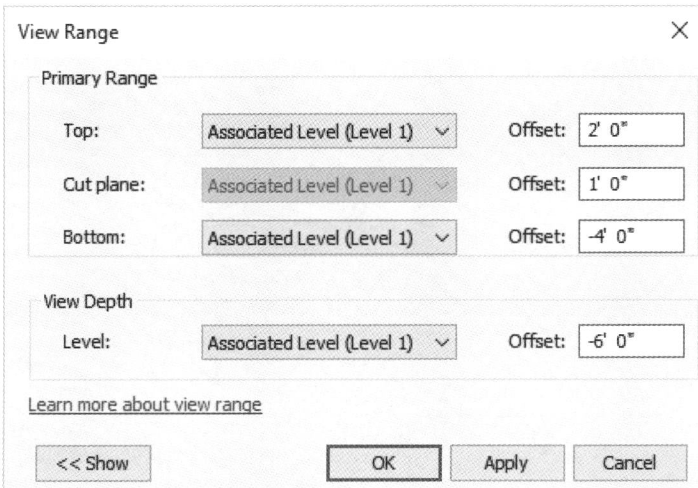

FIGURE 8-2.8 View Range – Structural Level 1

21. Click **Cancel** to close the *View Range* dialog without saving.

22. Type **VV** to open the *Visibility/Graphics Overrides* for the current view.

23. On the *Model Categories* tab, **check** all the disciplines in the *Filter list* drop-down (Figure 8-2.9).

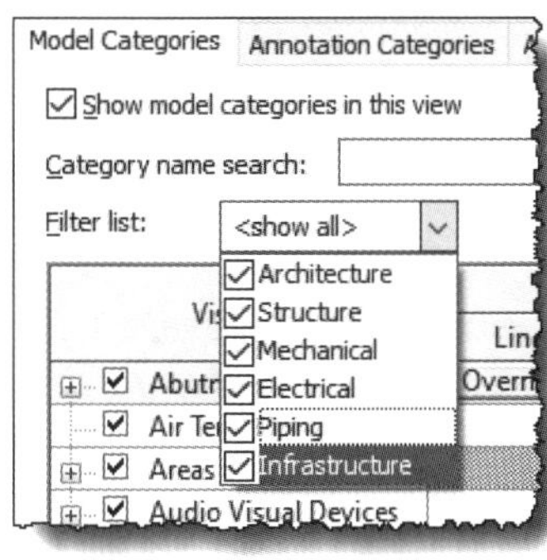

The ***Visibility/Graphics Overrides*** dialog (Figure 8-2.9) also has a significant role in what shows up and what does not in a view. The main thing to understand here is that the visibility of the items in these various categories can be controlled here for the current view, and only the current view. Unchecking *Casework* hides all the items that exist within that category, such as base and wall cabinets and custom casework such as reception desks, assuming they have been created with the correct *Category* setting. The *View Template* you are about to apply to this view will uncheck many of these *Categories.*

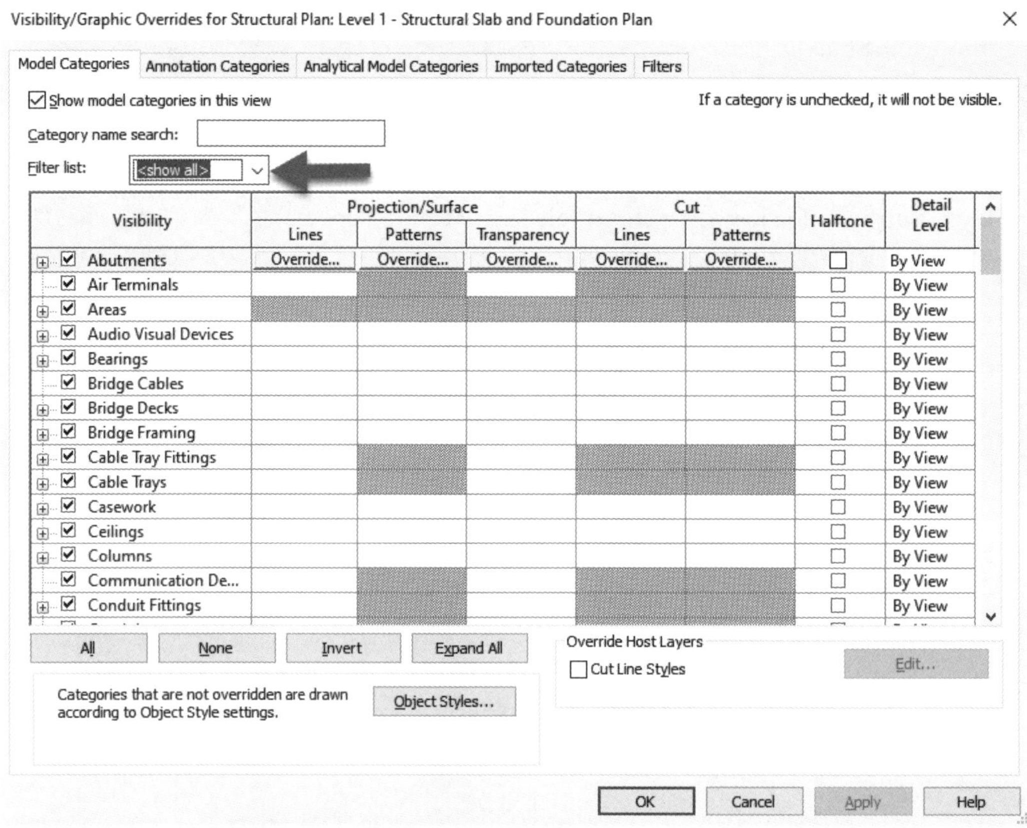

FIGURE 8-2.9 Visibility and Graphic Overrides – Structural Level 1

24. Click **Cancel** to close the *Visibility/ Graphic Overrides* dialog without saving.

Now you will apply the *View Template* and then review what it changes.

25. Right-click on ***Level 1 – Structural Slab and Foundation Plan*** in the *Project Browser* (see image to right).

26. Click **Apply Template Properties** from the pop-up menu.

27. On the left, select **Structural Foundation Plan**.

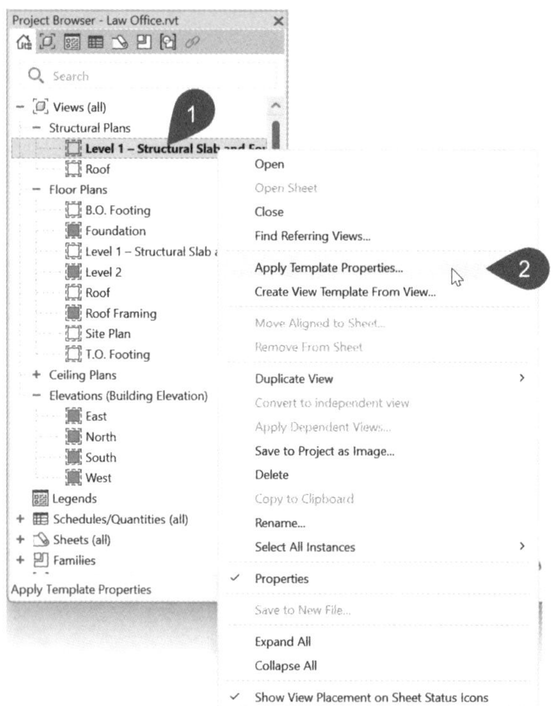

You are now in the *Apply View Template* dialog (Figure 8-2.10). Take a moment to observe all the settings it has stored and are about to be applied to the selected view, the one you right-clicked on.

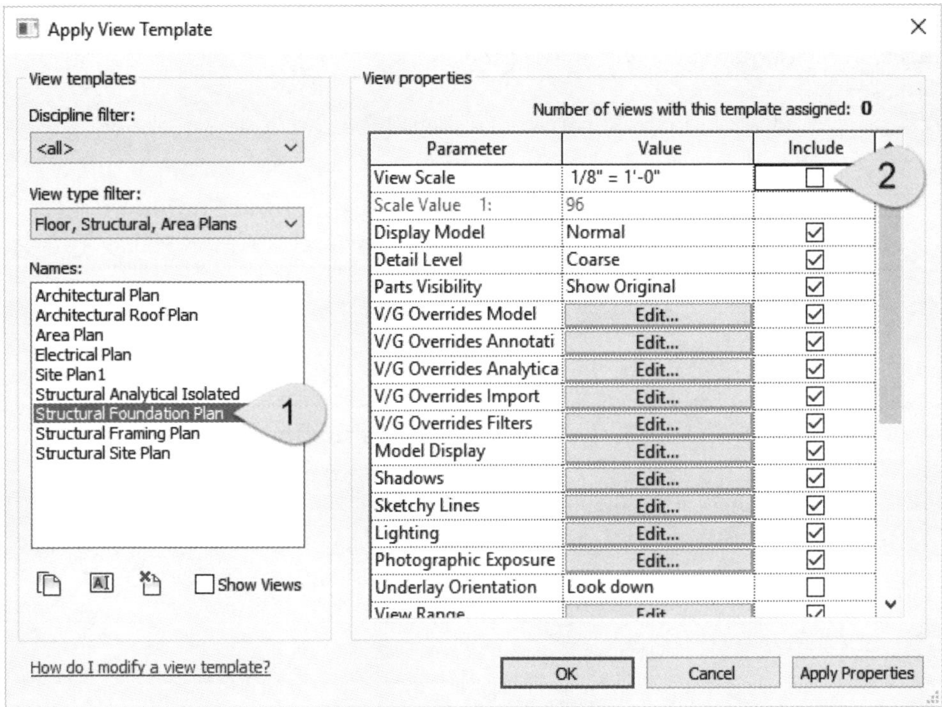

FIGURE 8-2.10 Apply View Template dialog – Structural Level 1

Notice the *View Scale* is set to ⅛"-1'-0." You know the scale needs to be ¼" = 1'-0" and you have already set that, so you will uncheck the *View Scale* so it is not included when the template is applied.

28. **Uncheck** *View Scale* (Figure 8-2.10) and then click **OK** to apply the *View Template*.

29. Type **VV** and turn off the *Doors* category.

The model visibility has now changed to mainly show the floor slab and stairs. All the walls, doors, etc., have been hidden in this view; they still exist, but are just not visible in this view.

Go back and review Steps 19-24 to compare the changes made to the *View Properties*, *View Range* and the *Visibility settings;* but don't change settings again.

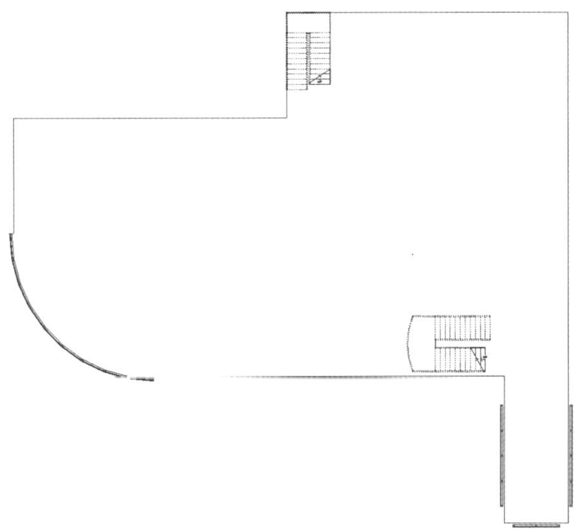

FIGURE 8-2.11 Result of applying view template

Next you will set up the two remaining views. It is expected that you will refer back to the previous steps if you need a review on the process.

30. Create/modify the following Structural Plans (*Tip:* Duplicate will not work):
    a. Create view: Level 2
        i. *Name:* **Level 2 – Structural Framing Plan**
        FYI: Do not rename levels
        ii. *Scale:* ¼″ = 1′-0″
        iii. *View Template to apply:* Structural Framing Plan (w/ scale unchecked)
        iv. *Visibility:* Hide Doors category
    b. Edit view: Roof
        i. *Name:* **Roof – Structural Framing Plan**
        FYI: Do not rename levels
        ii. *Scale:* ¼″ = 1′-0″
        iii. *View Template to apply:* Structural Framing Plan (w/ scale unchecked)

Loading Content:

Now that the structural views are set up and ready to go, you will look at how structural content is loaded into the project. The process is identical to how content is loaded using Revit's *Architectural* tools.

This section will just show you how to load a few elements. As you work through the rest of this chapter, you will have to load additional content; reference this information if needed.

31. Click **Insert → Load Autodesk Family** from the *Ribbon* (Figure 8-2.12).

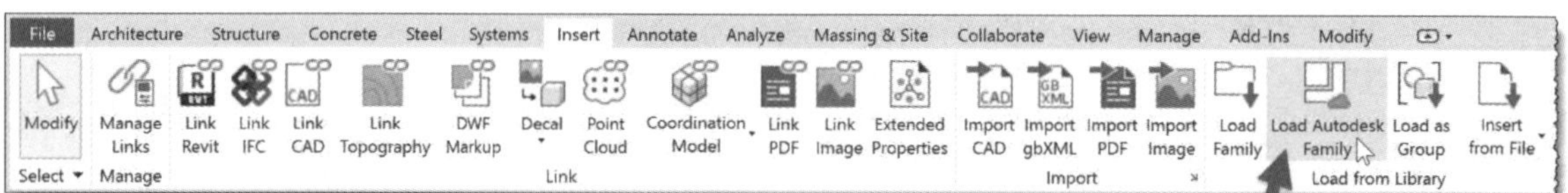

FIGURE 8-2.12 Loading content

Revit brings you to the online content library, thus **an internet connection is required** to load this content. Alternatively, the Autodesk content may be downloaded manually per the instructions in chapter 1.

> *FYI: Revit provides two major sets of content: Imperial (feet and inches) and Metric.*

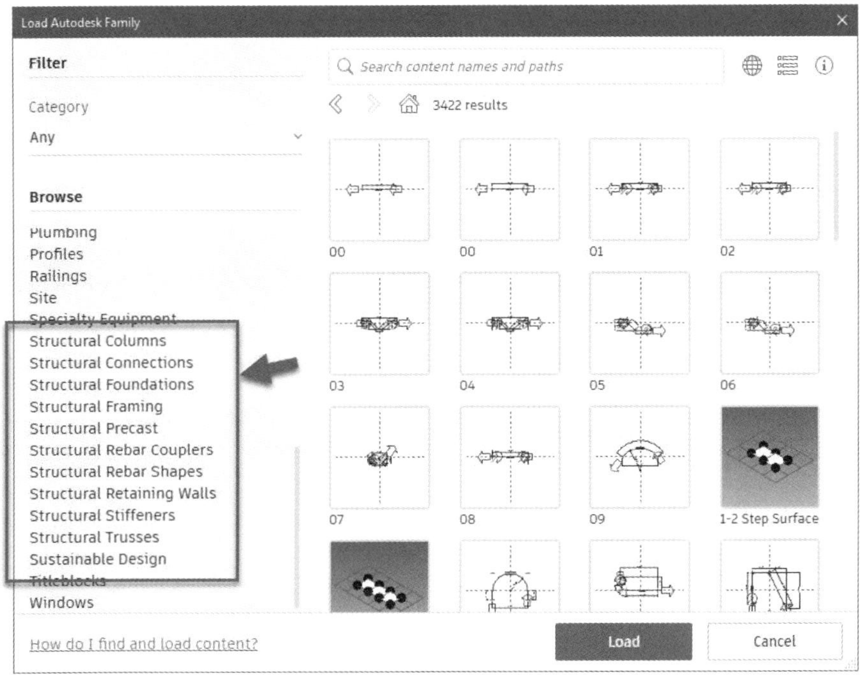

FIGURE 8-2.13 Loading content

Most everything needed by the structural engineer or technician is in the *Structural* folders.

32. Click on the **Structural** categories to explore them and then click All Results to back out of the current sub-category.

Notice the sub-categories listed in the *Structural* Columns category are named to describe each one's contents; see list to right.

First, you will load a steel column.

33. Click the **Structural Columns** sub-category to open it.

Notice the *Structural Columns* category is also broken down further into types of material; see list to right.

34. Click the **Steel** folder to open it.

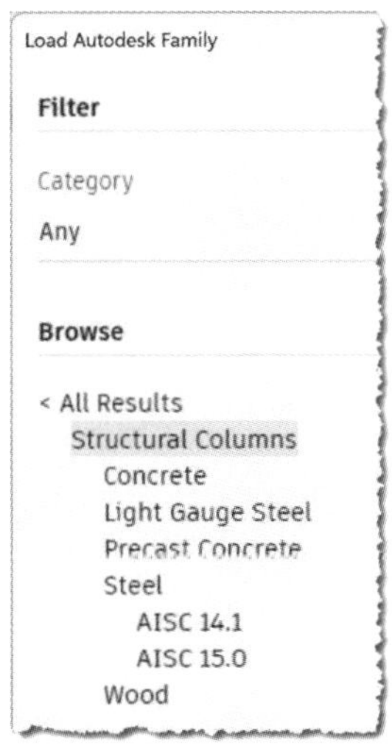

Structural Column sub-categories

You now have the choice of several types of steel column *Families* (Figure 8-2.14). Even though there are only a few *Families* listed here, they represent hundreds of column sizes. Each column has several *Types* defined for the various standard sizes available in the USA.

> ***FYI:** A* Type *is a group of parameters with specific values entered for a parametric family. See Chapter 18 for more on Families and Types.*

Most *Families* load all the *Types* associated with them. For example, a table might have three sizes, each defined as a type. When the table is loaded into a project, all three types are loaded and are available for use by the designer.

With steel shapes, however, there are way too many *Types* to have them all loaded into the project. If they were, the file would be bogged down with excess data, and it would make finding the sizes you need more difficult.

Revit uses **Type Catalogs** to deal with *Families* that have a large set of *Types*. A *Type Catalog* is simply a list that is provided just after loading the family, from which you can choose one or more *Types* to be loaded from the family. Additional *Types* can be added later.

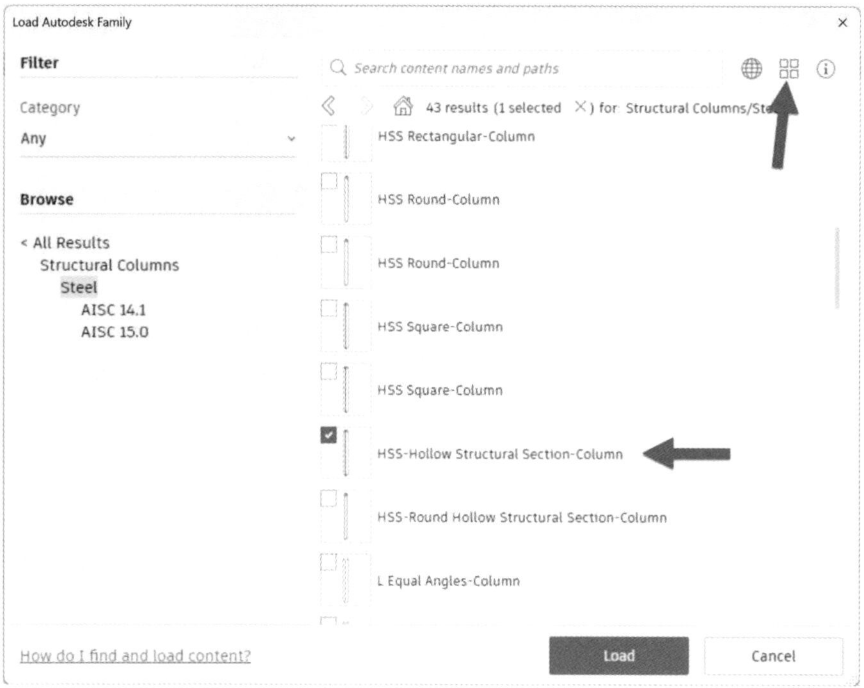

FIGURE 8-2.14 Loading content

35. Click the **HSS-Hollow Structural Section-Column.rfa** file and then click the **Load** button. Notice the listed content can be displayed in list format to make the file name easier to read.

You should now see the *Type Catalog*.

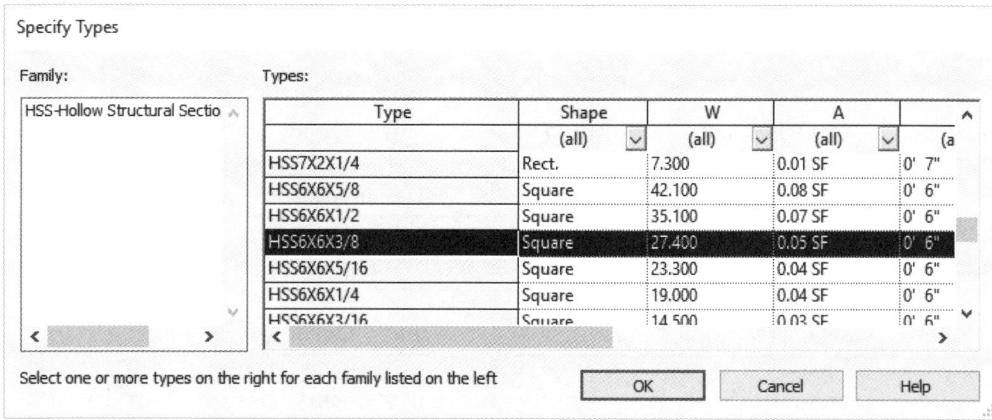

36. Scroll down and select the type name: **HSS6x6x3/8**.

37. Click **OK** to load it.

*TIP: Holding the **Ctrl** key allows you to select multiple Type names from the Type Catalog.*

You now have the **Hollow Structural Shape (HSS)** column loaded into your project and ready to be used as needed. You will use the same technique to load two beams and two bar joists.

38. Use the techniques just described to load the following content:
    a. Structural Framing → Steel → **K-Series Bar Joist-Rod Web.rfa**
        i. Types:
            - 16k5
            - 26k9
    b. Structural Framing → Steel → **W-Wide Flange.rfa**
        i. Types:
            - W24x55
            - W30x90

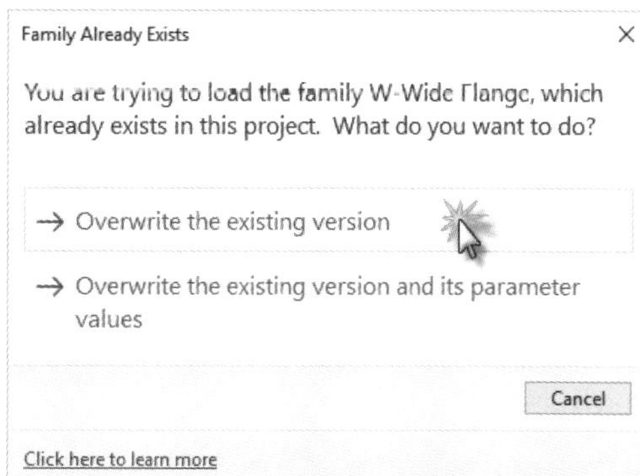

Any time a family already exists in a project, Revit gives you a prompt asking if you want to overwrite the version in the project, which may have been changed.

39. If prompted, click **Overwrite the existing version**.

40. **Save** your law office project.

Exercise 8-3:
Grids, Columns and Beams

In this exercise you will finally start placing some structural elements within the law office model. First, you will start with the grid layout; structural engineers do this with several rules-of-thumb in mind and experience. Once the grid is laid out with total spans and maximum depths of structural elements in mind, the columns can be placed. Finally, in this exercise, you will place the beams which span between the columns.

You will wrap this exercise up by creating a 3D view that only shows the building's structural elements. This is handy when the structural designer or technician wants to visualize and validate the structural model without the other building elements obscuring the view.

Location of Grids, Columns and Beams in Exterior Walls:

Placing a grid is simple and has been covered in one of the introductory chapters (see Exercise 2, Lesson 2-1). You will not align and lock these grids to the exterior wall as was done in that chapter because the grid line does not fall directly on any of the lines within the wall. The image below shows the typical location of the grid line relative to the exterior wall. *See the next page for a few comments regarding the image below.*

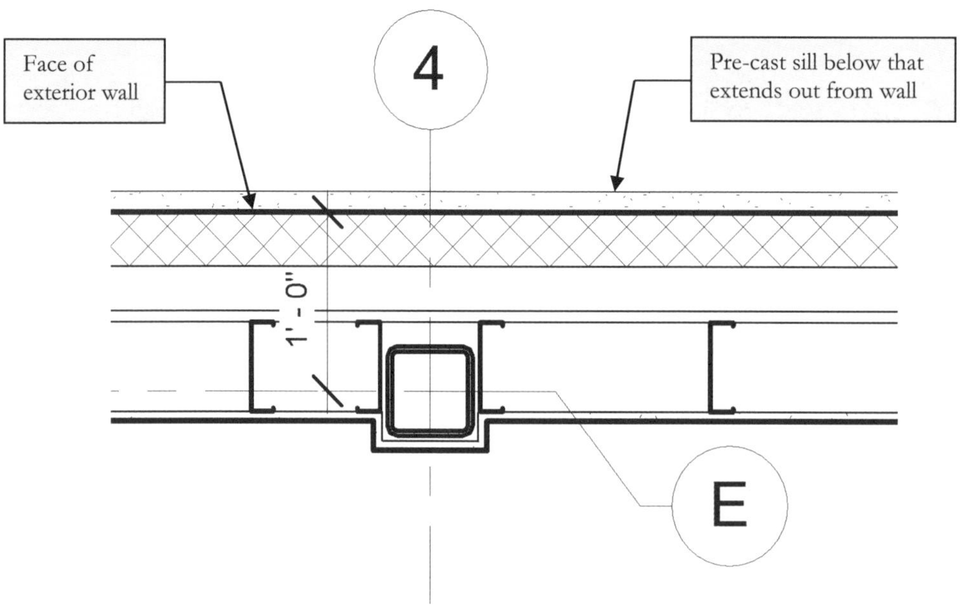

FIGURE 8-3.1 Typical location of column in exterior wall

DESIGN INTEGRATION TIP: Several things must be taken into consideration for the location of the columns in the exterior walls: ***1)*** *What is the column resting on? You have not drawn this yet; however, the column will be bearing on the foundation wall or a concrete pier, not the concrete slab on grade.* ***2)*** *Room for the insulation to pass by the column. This provides a thermal break which keeps the steel column from getting cold, or warm, depending on the climate, and causing condensation to occur.* ***3)*** *When the column pokes out into the room, as in our example, several things must be considered: 3**a)** Will this interrupt any heating system that may run along the base of the exterior wall? 3**b)** Will this interrupt any furniture system that needs to be placed up against these walls? 3**c)** Is this worth the extra labor involved? Adding gypsum board and metal furring costs more, as well as the floor and ceiling needing to be notched around these bumps in the walls.* ***4)*** *Does this design allow room for the electrical (power, data, or security) wires to pass by the column, say from one power outlet to the next?*

Notice in Figure 8-3.1 that the wall has an outermost line which represents a precast concrete sill; this can also be seen in Figure 8-3.2. Use caution when dimensioning to this wall, ensuring you do not pick this line rather than the main exterior face. This element within the wall is called a *Sweep*. Unfortunately, they cannot be hidden from the floor plan view, so you have to work around them.

Looking at Figure 8-3.2 one more time, notice the beams line up on the grids in addition to the columns. Therefore, the columns are also positioned to maintain the sheathing as it passes by the studs on the exterior side of the studs. As you can see, the beam just fits behind the sheathing. If the column were any closer to the exterior, the beams would poke out into the cold, or warm, air space.

FYI: In this tutorial you are using a prebuilt wall (i.e. a wall from the template) with several features in order to move things along and make for a nice-looking building. However, it would be a good idea to provide rigid insulation on the exterior side of the studs for a more uniform insulation barrier at the floor edges and structural locations.

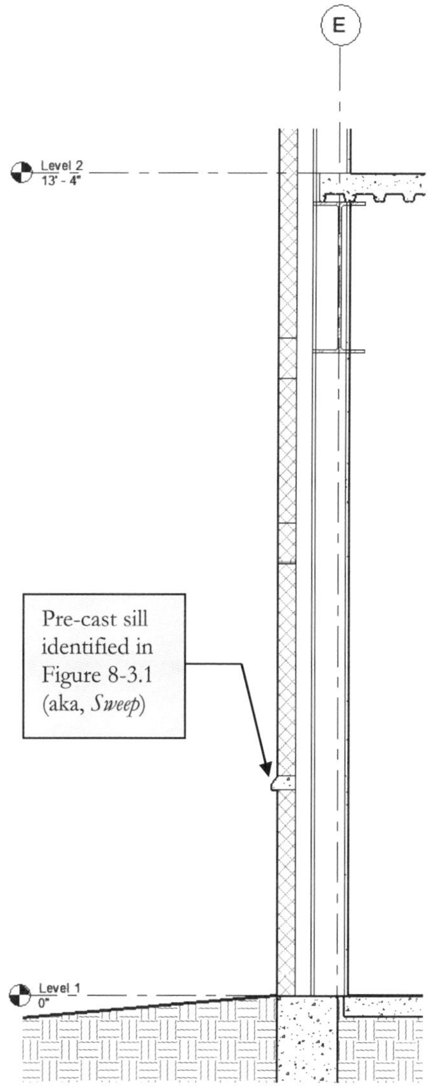

FIGURE 8-3.2
Typical exterior wall – notice profile

Laying Out the Grids:

You are now ready to start laying out the grids.

1. **Open** your law office model.

Next, you will temporarily switch to the architectural floor plan view so you can see the architect's exterior walls, which are needed in order to properly place the grids.

2. Switch to the **Architectural Level 1** floor plan view.

3. Use the ***Grid*** tool. See page 2-3, if needed, for more information.
    a. The *Grid* tool is identical in functionality across the Revit platform.

4. Layout the grid as shown in Figure 8-3.3.

    TIP: Draw a grid using the Align tool to position it along the exterior face of the exterior wall. Do not lock the alignment. Then Move the grid 1'-0" towards the interior to properly position the grid. Do not add the dimensions at this time.

    a. Make sure the grid's start and end points align as you sketch them so they lock. When locked, they will all move together when just one grid bubble or end point is moved.
    b. Use this as an opportunity to double-check the overall dimensions of your building. Many of the grids can be laid out based on the 1'-0" distance from the exterior face of the exterior wall rule we have established. Additionally, Figure 8-3.3 shows dimensions between each grid; this can be used to locate the remaining grids and verify dimensions.

Grids are usually laid out with numbers across the top and letters along one side. A few goals a structural engineer strives for are simplicity, repetition and consistency. If the spans are the same and the loads are the same, the structural members can usually be the same, thus making it more straightforward to design and build. However, these ideals are not always attainable for various reasons: code issues, dead load and live load variations and the architect's design.

In our project we have a design that does not afford a perfectly consistent and symmetrical grid layout due to the architect's design. This is not necessarily a bad thing, as steel can come in pretty much any length one needs. Also, on the second floor there is a law library which significantly increases the loads in that area, thus requiring deeper beams and joists.

Having various sizes on a project is still preferred over making everything the same, using more materials when not necessary and increasing the cost.

> ***FYI:*** *In the image below (Figure 8-3.3), you can see two dimensions with the word "**TYP.**" below them. First off, this is an abbreviation which should only be used if it has been defined in an abbreviation list somewhere in the set of documents. This abbreviation means "TYPICAL," and when used like this, lets the contractor know that any grid line near an exterior wall should be this same dimension (1'-0" in this case).*

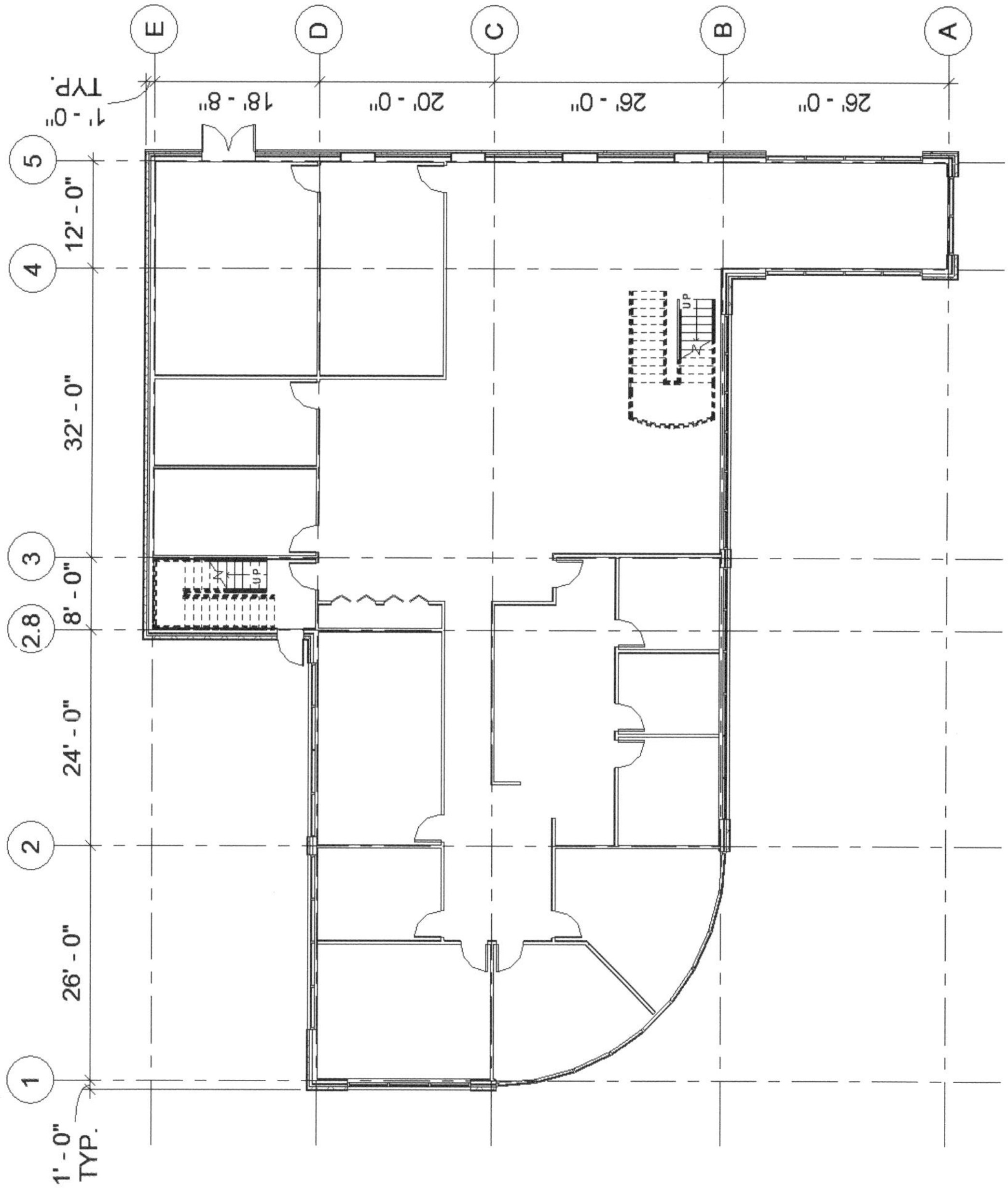

FIGURE 8-3.3
Grid numbers, letters and dimensions; image rotated on page to enlarge detail

The Various Options When a Grid is Selected:

When a grid is selected, a **small square box** shows up at each end (Figure 8-3.4). When the box is checked, a grid bubble shows up at that end. It is possible to have a grid bubble at both ends of the grid line; it is also possible to have the bubble turned off at each end.

The **padlock** shows that you properly aligned this end of the grid with the adjacent grids while sketching it, per the previous steps. Thus, when one grid end is repositioned, they will all move together. If one needed to move it apart from the others, you simply click on the *Padlock* to unlock it.

The **3D symbol** means, if you reposition the grid, the 3D plane this grid represents will move and possibly affect other views. If you click the 3D symbol, it becomes a 2D symbol and only the current view is adjusted. This only relates to changing the overall length of the grid in a view(s). If the grid is ever moved (in the other direction), the grid will always instantly update in all views; it is not possible for the same grid to be in two contradicting locations.

The small **circle grip** at the end of the grid line is what you click and drag on to reposition the end of the grid, the length. This can be hard to select if you are not zoomed in far enough.

Finally, the small "**break line**" symbol allows the grid head to be offset from the main grid line (see example in Figure 8-3.1). This is helpful when two grids are close to each other and would otherwise overlap. This option is often accidentally selected when trying to reposition the grid when zoomed out too far. If this happens, click *Undo*, zoom in and try again.

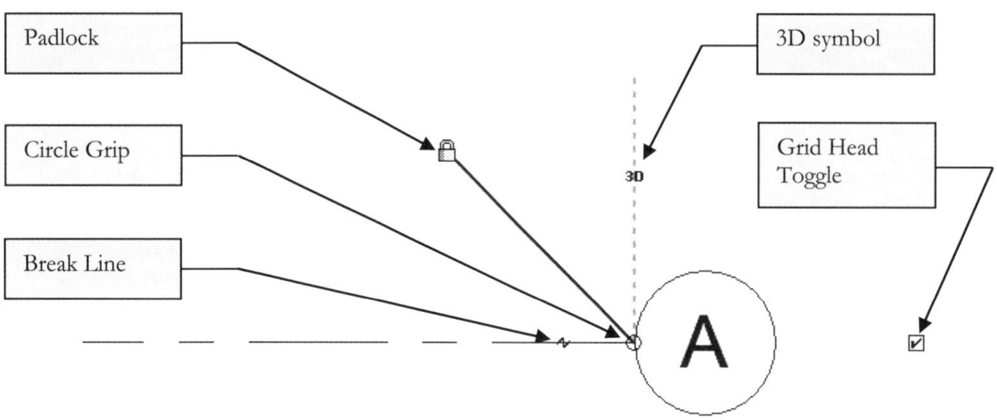

FIGURE 8-3.4 Various options when a grid line is selected

Grids are actually 3D planes that will show up in all views, plan, elevation and section, when a view's *Cut Plane* passes through a grid line plane. This will be covered more later, but for now you will simply explore the results.

5. Switch to the **Level 2 Architectural Floor Plan** view.

Notice the grids appear (Figure 8-3.5). Later, when you study elevations and sections, you will see grids automatically show up in those views as well.

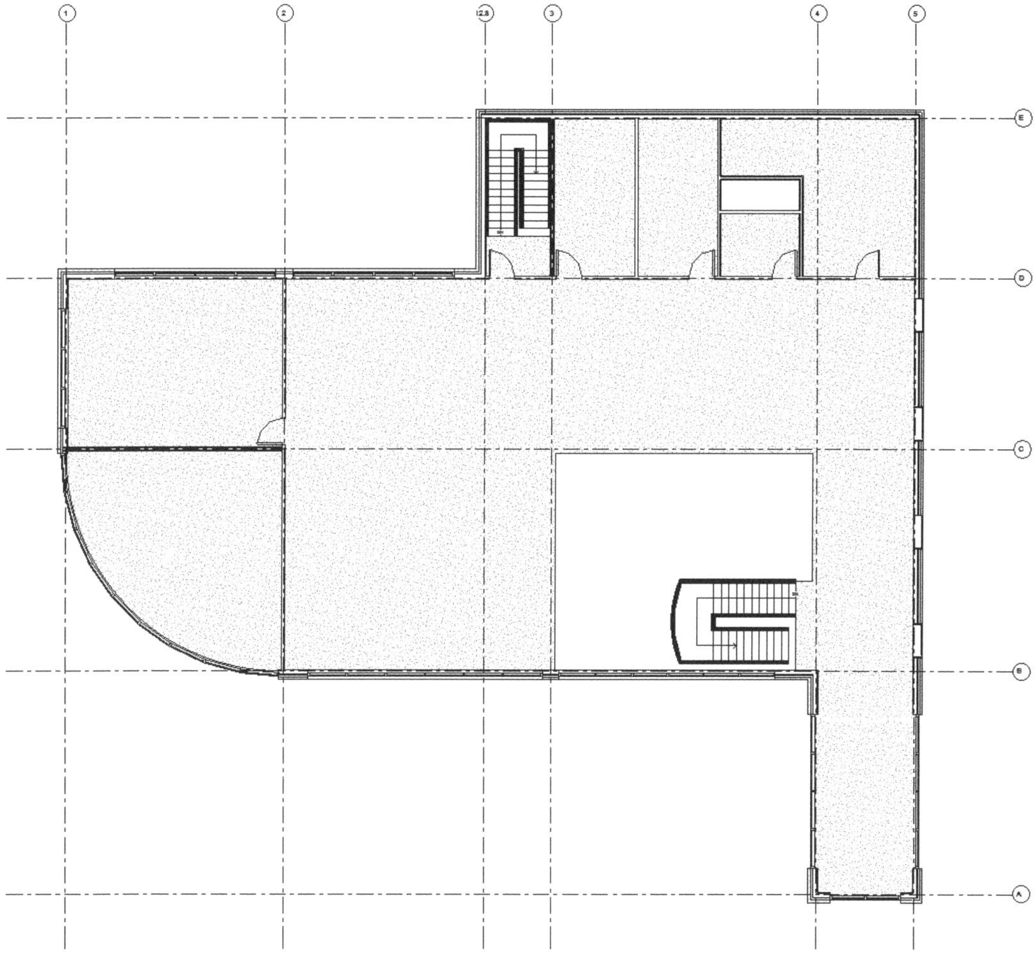

FIGURE 8-3.5
Level 2 Architectural Floor Plan view; grids automatically show up

Adding Columns:

Now that the grids have been placed you can begin to add structural columns; these columns will run from the Level 1 slab up to the roof. When modeling in Revit, you often need to model things the way they would be built. So, if the column size changed, you would need to stop and start a new column where the size change occurred. Say, for example, a tall building might have smaller and smaller columns the closer you get to the top because the load is getting lighter. Another consideration is column heights; they can only be so long before they do not fit on a truck; column splits are usually a few feet above the floor level.

6. Switch to the **Level 2 – Structural Framing Plan**.
7. Zoom in to the *intersection* of Grids **2** and **C**.
8. From the *Ribbon*, select **Structure → Structure → Column**.
    a. This is the *Structural Column* tool rather than *Architectural Column*.
9. Set the *Type Selector* to **HSS6x6x3/8** (Figure 8-3.6).
    a. *Family name:* HSS-Hollow Structural Section-Column
    b. Notice the “Depth” setting on the *Ribbon* (rather than “Height”)

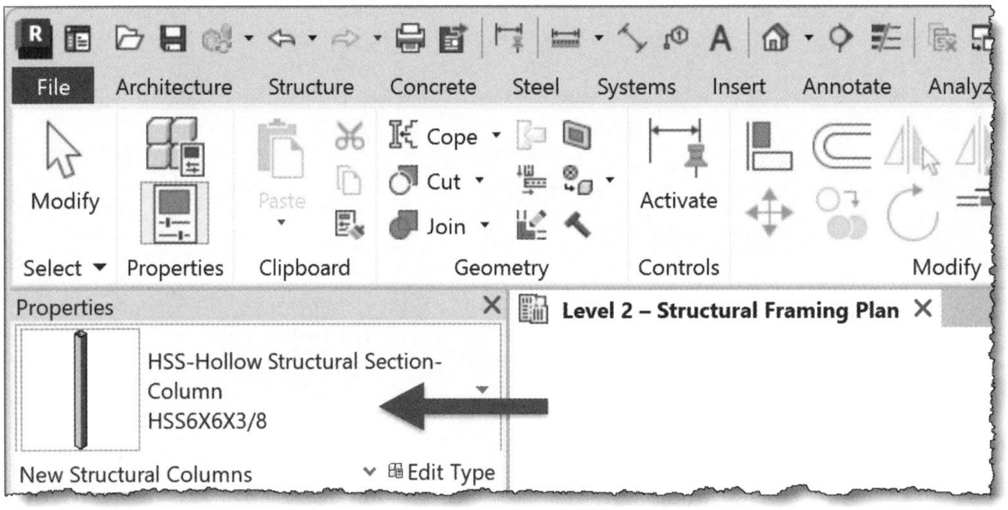

FIGURE 8-3.6 Options selected for placing first column

10. Click, using **Snaps**, at the intersection of Grids **2** and **C**.

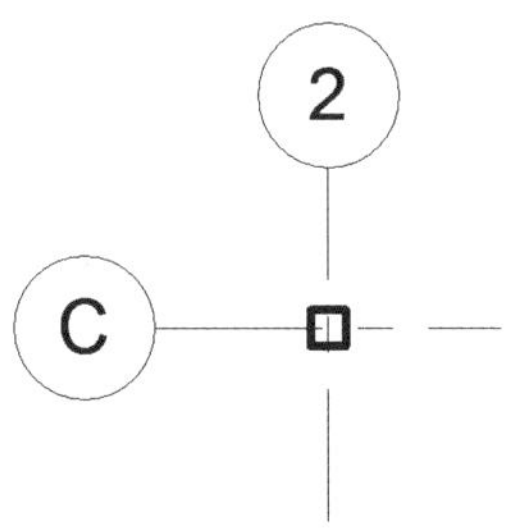

You have now added a structural column to the model! This column will show up in all views of the project. Next you will look at a few properties related to the column you just placed, before placing the remaining columns.

The first thing to note about columns is that they are placed from the top down, rather than the bottom up like walls. This is why you were instructed to switch to Level 2, rather than Level 1. Notice, back in Figure 8-3.6, that the depth of the column is listed on the *Options bar* rather than the height. Next, you will view the new column's properties to see this.

11. **Select** the new column in the **Level 2 Structural Plan** view.

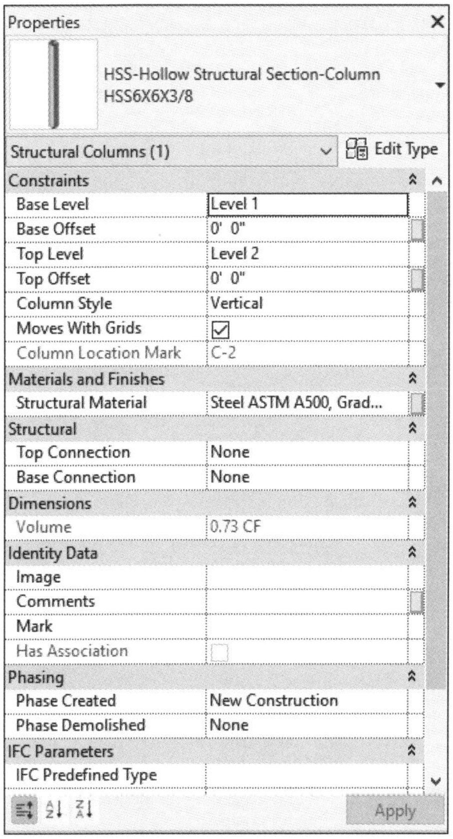

FIGURE 8-3.7 Instance properties for selected column

Note the information listed in the *Properties Palette.*

Notice, in Figure 8-3.7, that the *Base Level* is set to Level 1, per the *Options bar* when placed, and the *Top Level* is set to Level 2 per the current view.

Also, Revit is keeping track of the grid lines when the column falls directly on them. When "Moves With Grids" is checked, the columns will automatically follow a relocated grid.

Next you will change the *Top Level* to Roof, so the column fully extends from Level 1 up to the Roof level. You will also set the *Base Offset* to -8″ so the column starts below the slab-on-grade; this helps to hide the base plate.

12. Change the *Base Offset* to **-8″**. Be sure to add the minus sign.

13. Change the *Top Level* to **Roof**.

14. Click **Apply** or simply move your cursor back into the drawing window.

This new column will now show up on the **Level 2** architectural plan as well as the **Roof** structural plan. You will now add the remaining columns to the **Level 2 – Structural Framing Plan** view.

15. Place twenty additional columns.
    a. See Figure 8-3.8.
    b. A temporary circle has been added at each column location to help highlight them. Do not add this circle.
    c. Do not change the column height; this will be done later using the *Filter* tool.
    d. Notice not all grid intersections have a column.

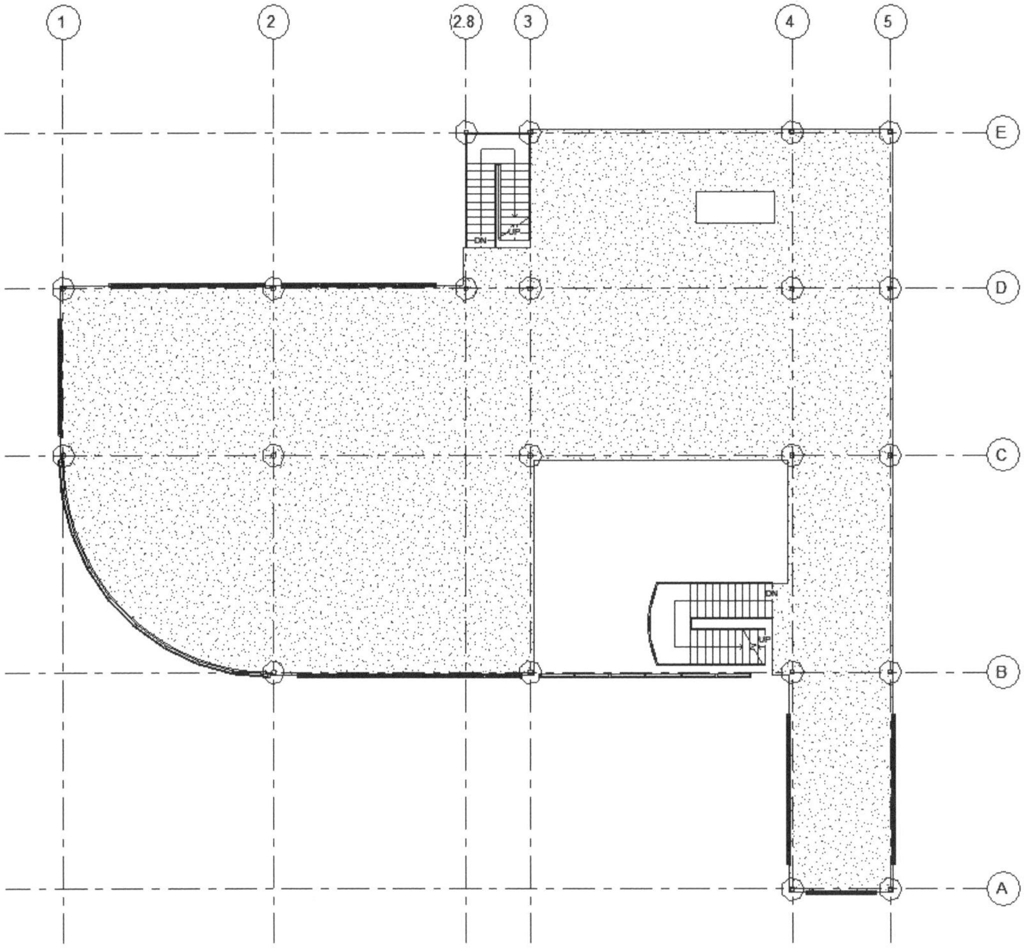

FIGURE 8-3.8 Level 2 – Structural Framing Plan; columns added

16. With all 21 columns placed, drag a selection window around the entire drawing which will select everything in the view.

Notice the total number of items that are currently selected is listed in the lower right. Immediately to the left of that is the *Filter* icon. The *Filter* tool allows you to narrow down your selection to a specific group of elements (i.e., doors, walls, columns, etc.). You will explore this next.

17. Click the ***Filter*** icon at the lower right corner of the window; see Figure 8-3.9.

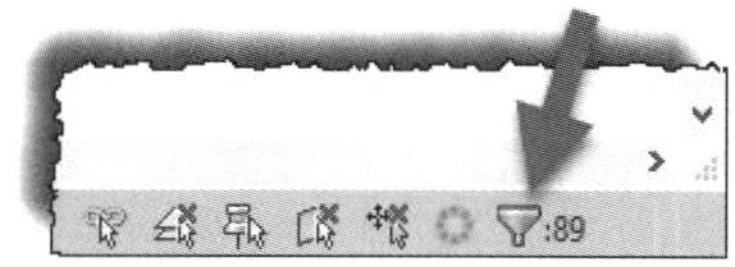

FIGURE 8-3.9
Filter icon and number of elements selected

18. Click the ***Check None*** button; see Figure 8-3.10.

19. Check the **Structural Columns** category; see Figure 8-3.10.

Clicking *Check None* and then selecting what you want is often faster than individually unchecking all the categories you do not want.

Notice a total count breakdown is listed to the right of each category. Only categories that have selected elements are listed; as you can see *Doors* is not listed but would be if any were selected.

20. Click **OK** to close the *Filter* dialog and change what is currently selected.

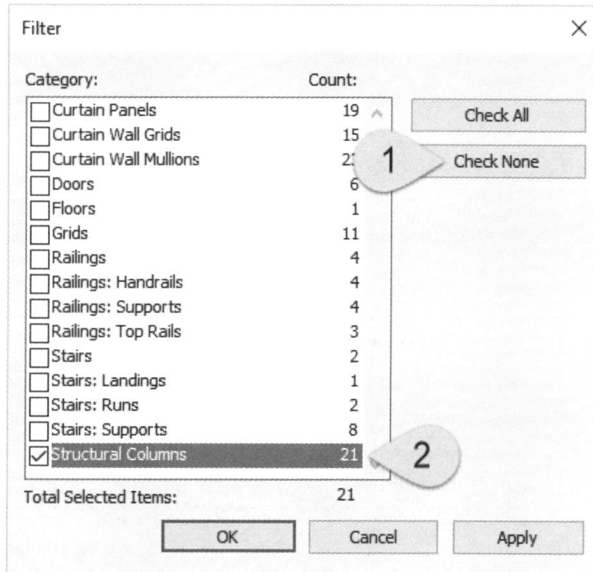

FIGURE 8-3.10
Filter dialog; various elements selected

Note that the lower right corner of the application window indicates that only 21 elements are now selected. Now that you have filtered elements down to just the *Structural Columns*, you can easily change the top and base settings.

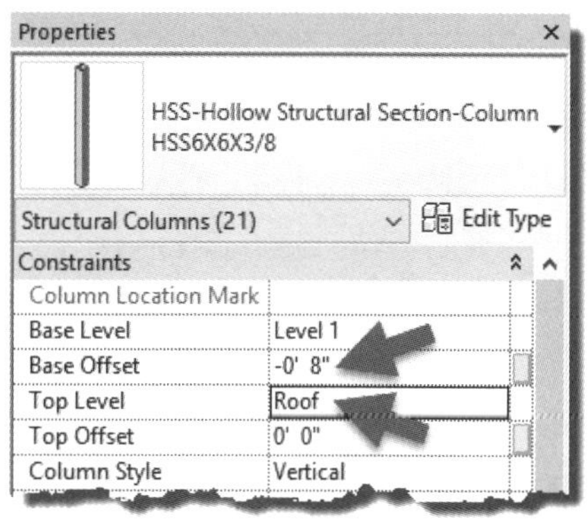

21. Per steps 12-14, do the following to the selected columns:

    a. Set the *Base offset* to **-8"** (be sure to add the minus sign).

    b. Set the *Top Level* to **Roof**.

The columns have been placed, as previously mentioned, based on maximum spans for the beams and joists and the architectural design. Often, the architects will agree to move their walls to accommodate a "cleaner" structural system layout; cleaner meaning whole foot dimensions without inches or fractions, standard bay sizes. A bay here is an area enclosed by four grids.

This tutorial started with the architectural walls on the correct location, so you will not have to move any walls to account for the newly added structural elements.

Controlling Visibility:

In this case, just before placing your first beam, you decide you want to turn off the curtain wall (i.e., glass openings) in the plan view to reduce confusion. These were not turned off by the *View Template* you had previously applied to this view.

22. In the **Level 2 – Structural Framing Plan**, type **VV**.

23. Set *Filter list* to **Show all**, if not already set. (See Figure 8-3.11.)

24. Uncheck the three "**Curtain**" categories, if not already turned off. (See Figure 8-3.11.)

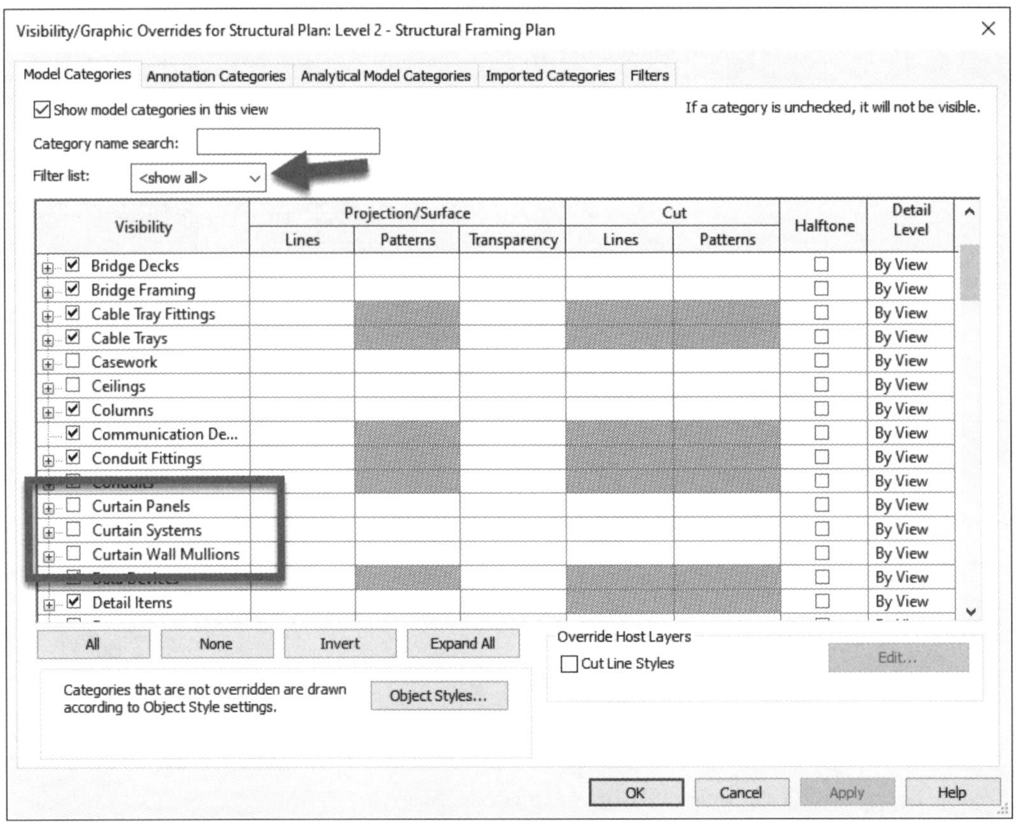

FIGURE 8-3.11 Visibility dialog; turning off the curtain walls

Placing Beams:

Now that the columns are placed, you can start adding beams between them. For now you will place them directly below the floor. However, later the vertical position of the beam will be adjusted downward when a bar joist is bearing on it (more on all this later). The first thing you will do is load a tag which will display the beam size for each member. The tag is added automatically as you model the structural framing members.

25. Per the steps outlined in the previous exercise, load the following family: Annotation\Structural\ **Structural Framing Tag.rfa**. (overwrite)

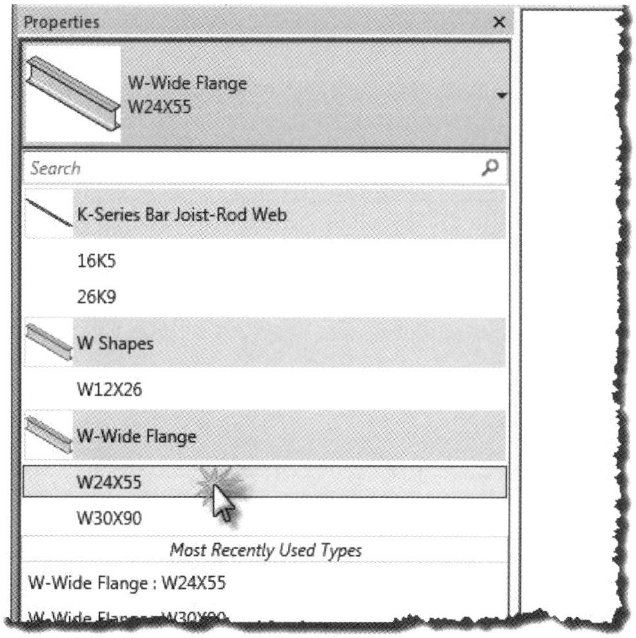

FIGURE 8-3.12 Beam tool active; picking a size via the type selector

26. Zoom in on Grid line **D**, between Grids **1** and **2**.
27. Select **Structure → Structure → Beam**.
28. Select **W24x55** from the *Type Selector*; see Figure 8-3.12.
    a. Make sure **Tag on Placement** is selected on the *Ribbon*.

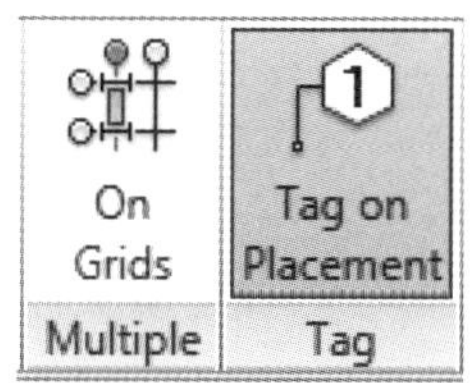

Any sizes needed, but not listed in the *Type Selector*, must be loaded per the instructions in the previous exercise. It is best to limit the number of steel shapes and sizes to those actually needed in the project. This should help reduce errors when selecting sizes and make finding what you want easier and faster.

By default, the top of the beam will align with the level associated with the placement view. The vertical position can be adjusted by adjusting the **z justification** and/or **z Offset Value** in properties.

Next, you will simply click at the midpoint of each column to place the beam. Because there is not an *Offset* option on the *Options bar*, you will adjust the vertical position of the beam after it is placed.

29. Click at the center of the columns at Grid intersections **D/1** and **D/2**.

The beam will be created and appear as shown below in Figure 8-3.13. Notice that a tag was placed above the beam, which indicates its size. This is because "Tag on Placement" was selected on the *Ribbon* when the beam was being placed into the model.

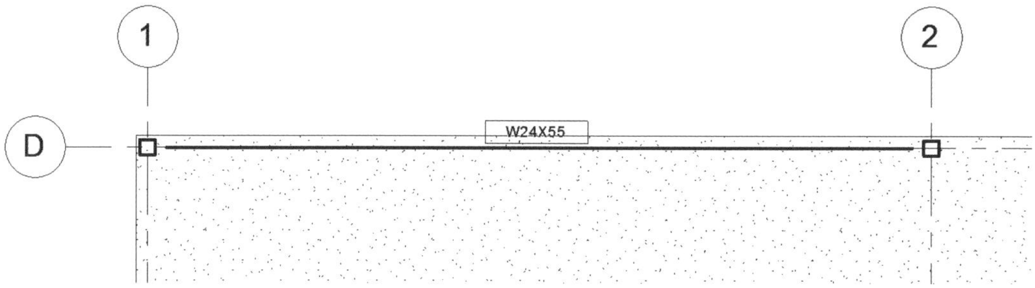

FIGURE 8-3.13 First beam placed

30. Press the **Esc** key twice or click **Modify** to deactivate the *Beam* tool.

It has been decided that the floor will be concrete over metal deck, at a total of 5½". The floors drawn by the architects, or you in Chapter 6, will be refined in the next chapter. This anticipated thickness will be used to reposition the beam vertically. Currently the top of the beam aligns with the top of the floor.

Additionally, some beams support bar joists, which in turn support the floor. The beams which support bar joists need to be lowered to accommodate the thickness of the bar joist at the bearing location. The beams which do not support bar joists, perhaps for frame rigidity, shear and edge of slab conditions, need to be directly below the slab.

The two typical beam conditions can be seen in the sections shown in Figures 8-3.14 and 8-3.15. Also, a snapshot of the completed structural framing plan shows the direction the joists are spanning (Figure 8-3.16).

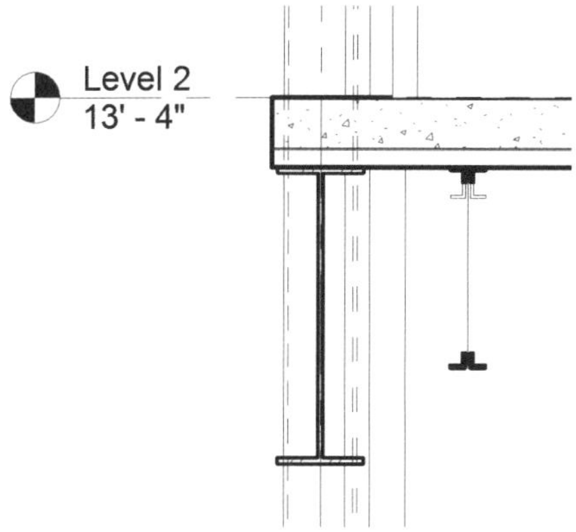

FIGURE 8-3.14 Beam parallel to bar joist

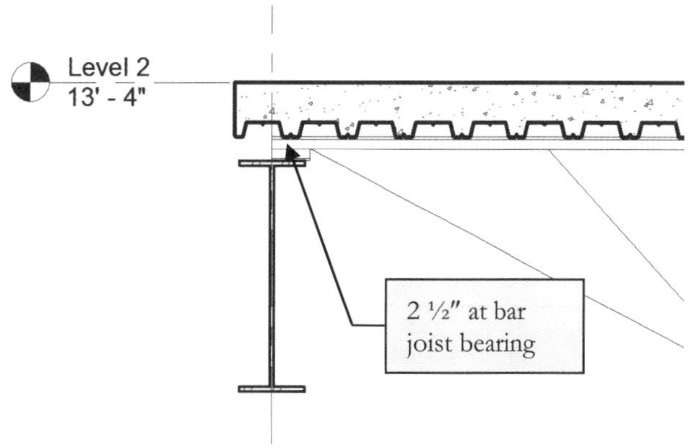

FIGURE 8-3.15 Beam supporting bar joist

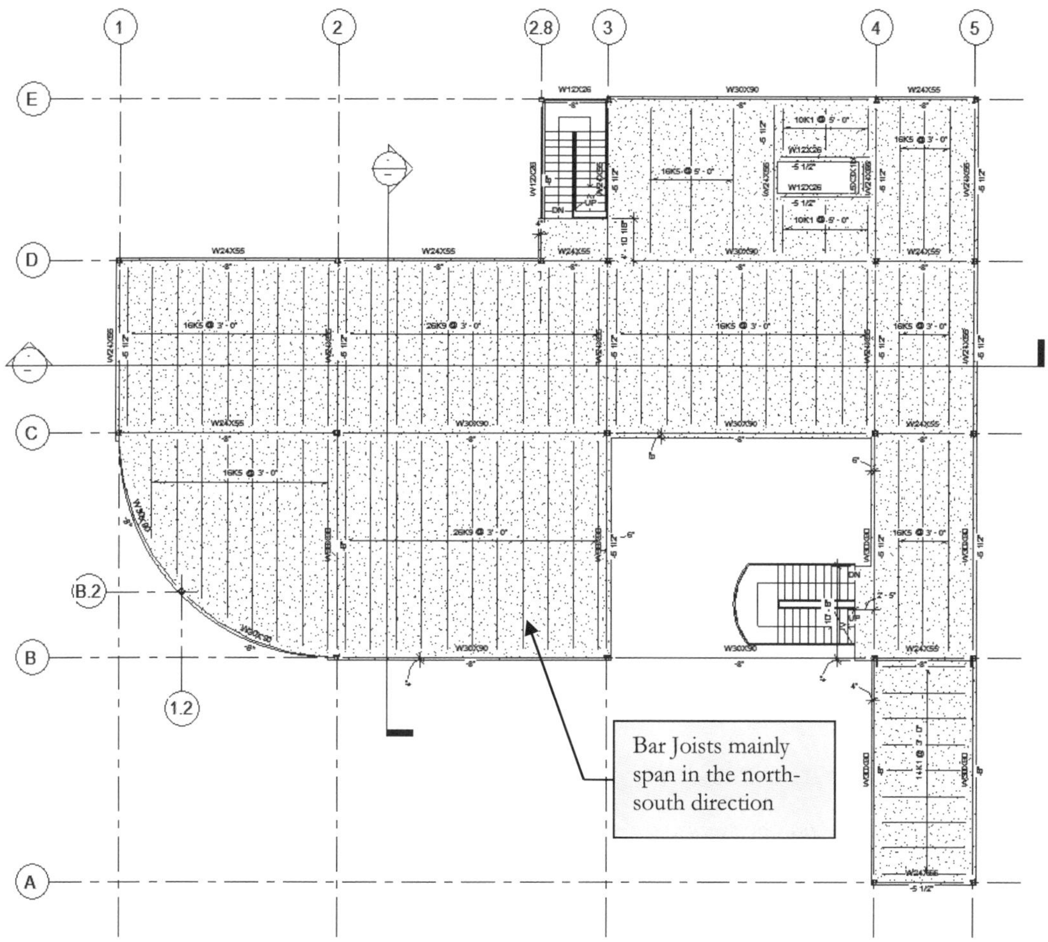

FIGURE 8-3.16 Snapshot of the completed Level 2 Structural Framing Plan, for reference only at this point. Note the direction of the bar joists which support the floor.

The image below shows the column at the intersection of Grid 1 and D; this is typically referred to as Grid 1/D.

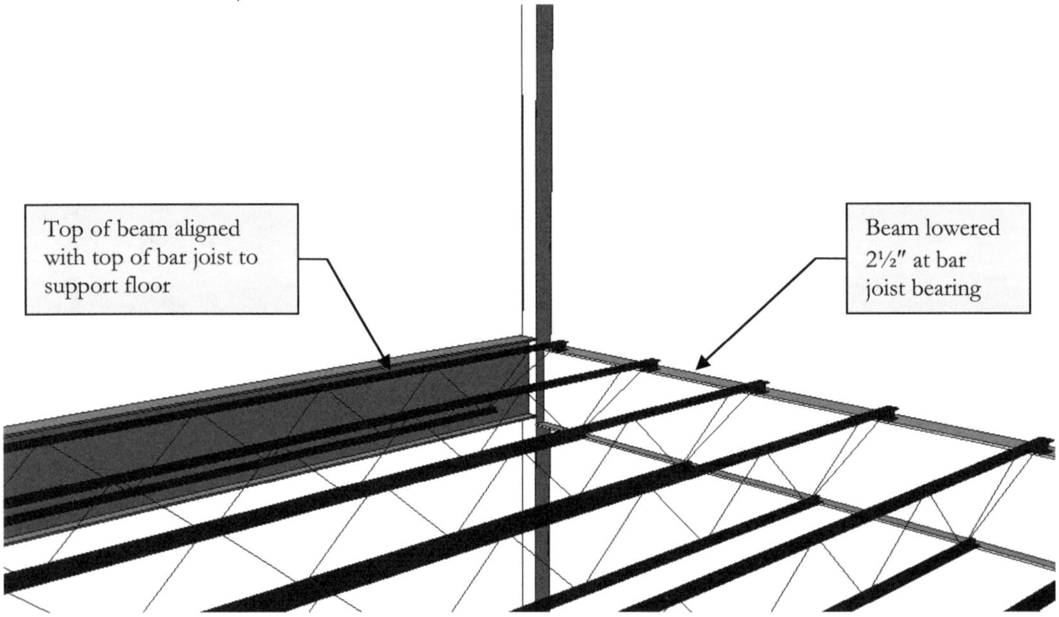

FIGURE 8-3.17 Perspective view of structural framing at Grid 1/D

Now that you know why the beam you just placed needs to be repositioned vertically, you will make that change.

31. Select the **Beam** and view its properties via the *Properties Palette* (Figure 8-3.18).

32. Change…
    a. *Start Level Offset* to **-0′ 8″**
    b. *End Level Offset* to **-0′ 8″**

33. Click **Apply** to commit the change.

34. With the beam still selected, see the image and comment on the next page.

Tip: if the beam does not slope, it is also possible to just edit the **z Offset Value**, rather than the two start/end offsets.

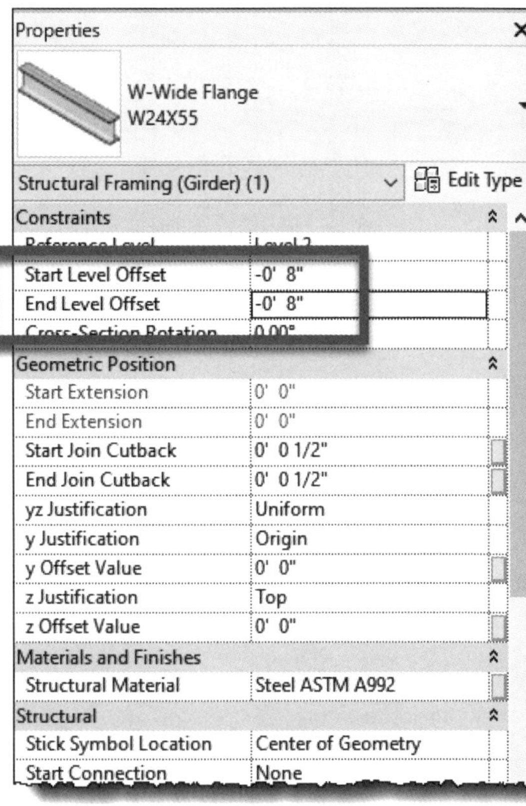

FIGURE 8-3.18 Beam properties

Note the following about the image below (Figure 8-3.19). When the beam is selected you see the elevation of the beam listed at each end. This text is blue, which means you can select it and edit it without needing to open the properties dialog. This is particularly handy for sloped beams.

However, the *Properties Palette* may be the better way to go once the bar joists have been placed. When changed via properties, Revit does not make any changes to the model until you click **Apply**. When you change the on-screen text at one end, it makes the change to that end immediately. Revit may pause as it calculates repositioning all the bar joists along a sloped beam. Then you wait again when the other end is modified. This is great when the beam does slope!

Finally, the triangular grips at each end allow you to manually adjust the one-line beam end location. When the view's *Detail Level* is set to *Coarse*, Revit will show a simplified version of the beam: a single line centered on the beam. At each end, the beam stops short of the column or wall to make the drawing more readable. This conforms to industry standard structural drafting techniques.

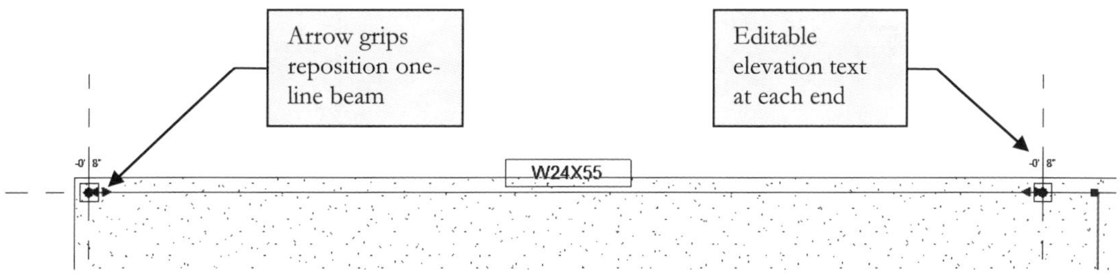

FIGURE 8-3.19 Beam selected in plan view, with "thin lines" toggled on via the *View* tab

The beam is now properly positioned to support the bar joists that will be added later.

Next you will place the remaining beams for this elevation on Level 2.

35. Place all the beams shown in Figure 8-3.20.
    a. All beams shown are at **-8."**
    b. Select the correct beam size via the *Type Selector.*
    c. Load additional beams sizes (e.g. W121x26 & W30x90) as needed per steps previously covered.

TIP: *Place all beams and then select them using the Filter tool and change the vertical positions all at once.*

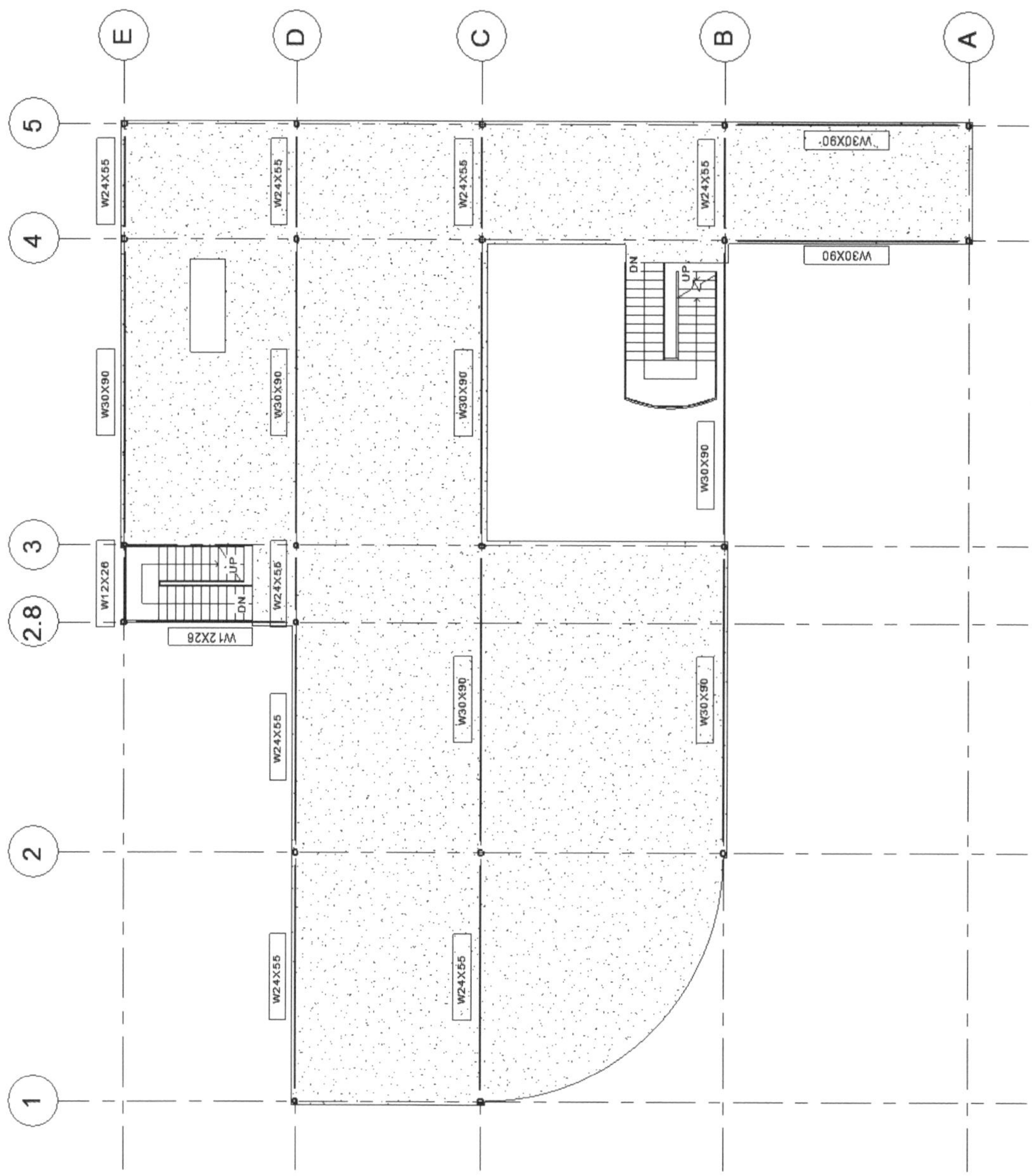

FIGURE 8-3.20 Level 2 beams with tops 8″ below the Level 2 plane; image rotated to increase size

Now that you have the beams that support bar joists placed, except at the curved wall, you will place the remaining beams which directly support the floor. Thus, the vertical offset will be 5½″, the thickness of the floor.

36. Place all the beams shown in Figure 8-3.21.

   a. All beams shown are at **-5½.″**

   b. All steps are similar to the previous step; however, *Filter* will not work because you do not want to change the -8″ beams.

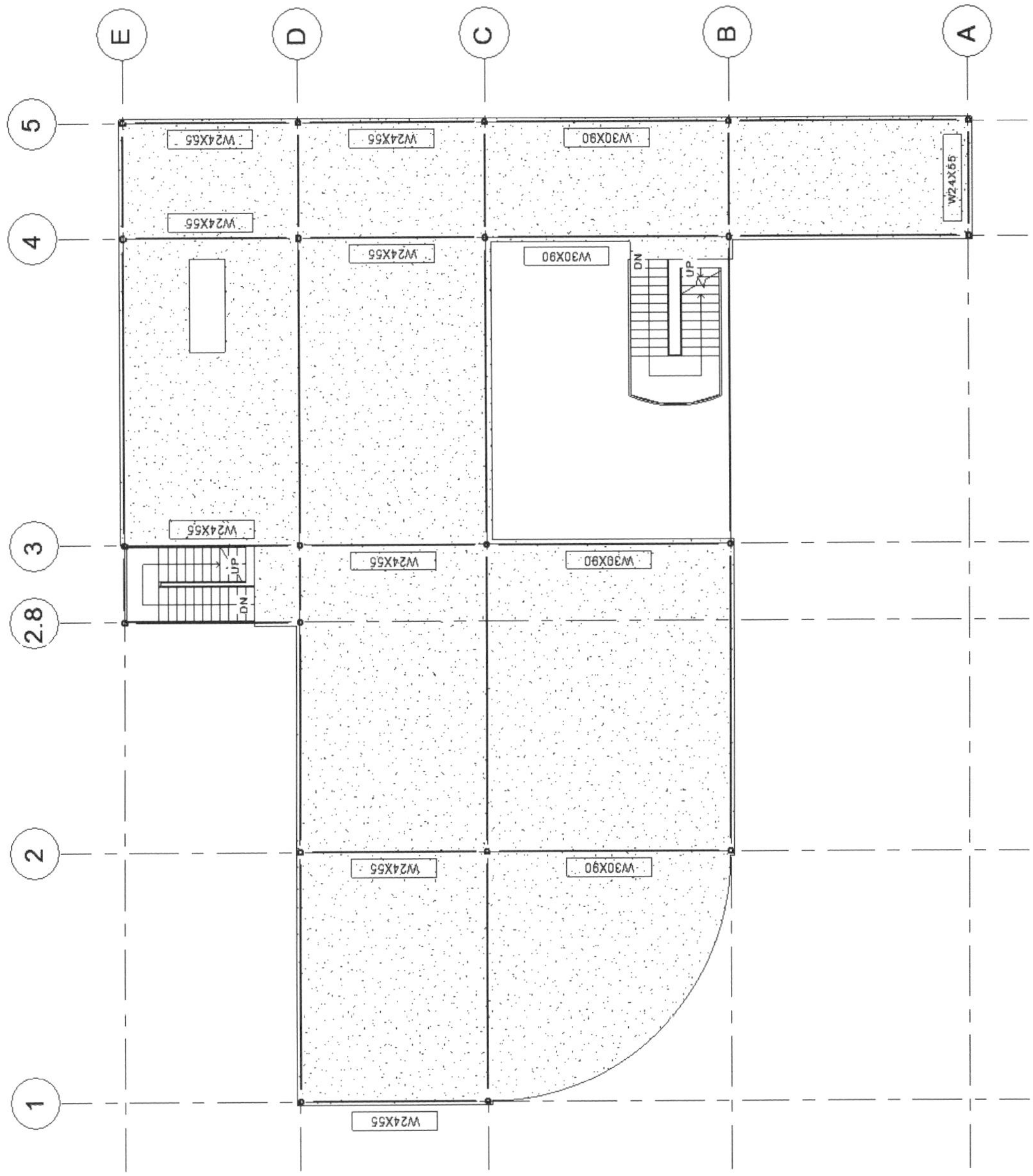

FIGURE 8-3.21 Level 2 beams with tops 5½″ below the Level 2 plane; image rotated to increase size, and the beam tags have been temporarily hidden for the beams placed in the previous step.

Beam tags are typically centered on the beam span in plan view and directly above it or to the left; this is Revit's default. Sometimes things such as notes or dimensions are in the way and the tag is not legible. It is possible to select the tag and move it (via the *Move* tool or by dragging it). The image above has a few such modifications: at both of the stairs and the floor opening in the Northeast corner of the building.

Next, you will add framing for the floor opening.

So far all your beams have been supported by columns. In the next steps you will place a few beams that are supported by other beams. Additionally, walls may support beams; the wall's parameter *Structural Usage* should be set to *Bearing* when supporting a beam; the default is non-bearing. Revit will automatically notify the user of this problem; see image to the right.

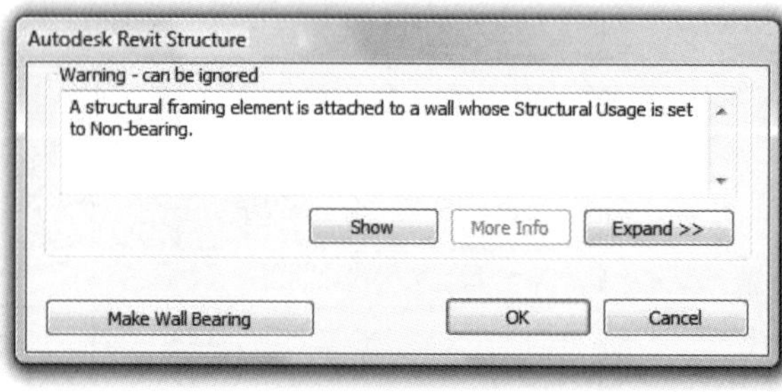

37. Place the W24x55 beam approximately as shown in Figure 8-3.22.
    a. Set the *Structural Usage* to **Girder** on the *Ribbon.*
    b. Snap to each of the previously placed beams.
    c. Revit may give you a prompt like the one shown above; simply click **OK** to ignore the warning.
    d. Move the beam down 5½″ via properties. Once lowered, drag the end grip back, and then drag it to the adjacent beam again. This will cause Revit to properly connect to the adjacent beam and clean up the connection graphically.

38. Select the beam and use the temporary dimensions to position it **12′-2″** from Grid 4. Remember, you can drag the grips to reposition the temporary dimensions so it goes from the beam to Grid 4.

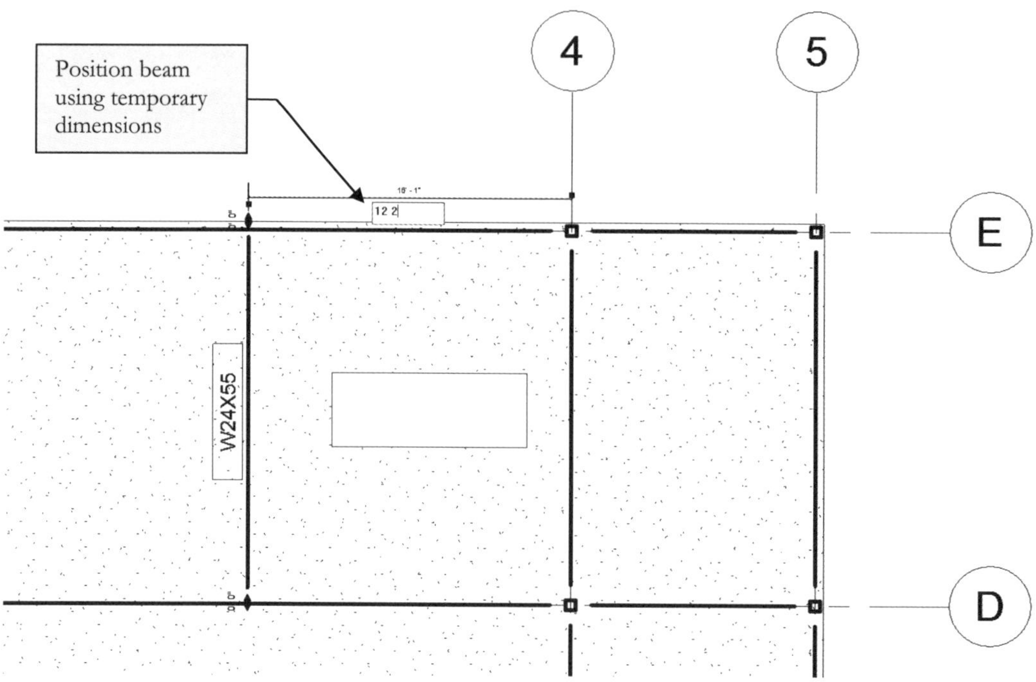

FIGURE 8-3.22 Beam is added near opening in floor and about to be repositioned via temporary dimensions

39. Draw the three remaining beams to support the floor opening:

    a. Position the center of the beam **5 13/16″** from the floor opening using the temporary dimensions.

    b. Set the elevation (i.e., offset) to **-8″** (beams) and **-5½″** (angle).

    c. Set the *Structural Usage* to **Girder**.

    d. You will need to load the angle **L5x3x1/4** before placing it: *Load Family* → Structural Framing\Steel\L-Angle.rfa

    e. Once the elevation is set properly, drag the beam endpoint to its support so it snaps to it.

    f. See Figure 8-3.23.

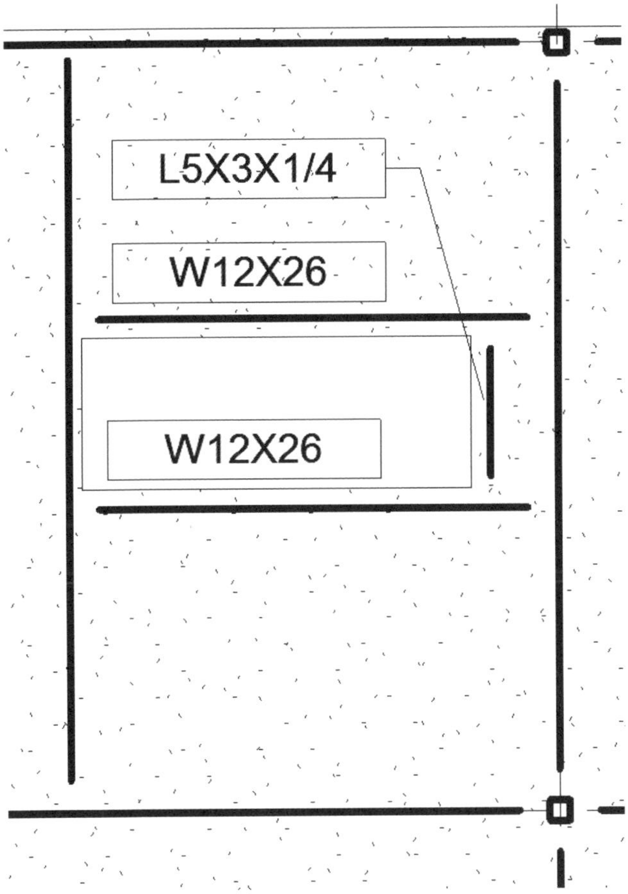

The *Structural Usage* determines the line weight of the line in *Coarse* mode. This setting also relates to structural analysis via the external programs that can import a Revit *Structure* model.

Notice, in this case, an angle is set to be a girder because it is holding up part of the floor, albeit a small portion with minimal load.

FYI: It is possible to add a permanent dimension from the floor opening to the beam and then load the dimension. This would cause the beam to automatically move with the floor opening.

FIGURE 8-3.23 Framing at floor opening

You will now add the curved beam, a column and two grids to finish off the Level 2 primary structure. The curved beam is too long, so a column is required at the midpoint. Rather than trying to locate the grids and column first, you will place the beam first. Then you can place the column centered on the beam, and place the grids based on the column location. Finally, you will split the beam at the new column location. This shows that things can typically be modeled in any order. There is not always one correct way to complete tasks.

40. Place the curved beam; see Figure 8-3.24.

    a. Select the ***Beam*** tool.

    b. On the *Ribbon*, select the ***Arc*** icon (Start-End-Radius).

    c. Set the size to **W30x90**.

    d. Pick the points in the order shown.

    e. Lower the beam to **-8.″**

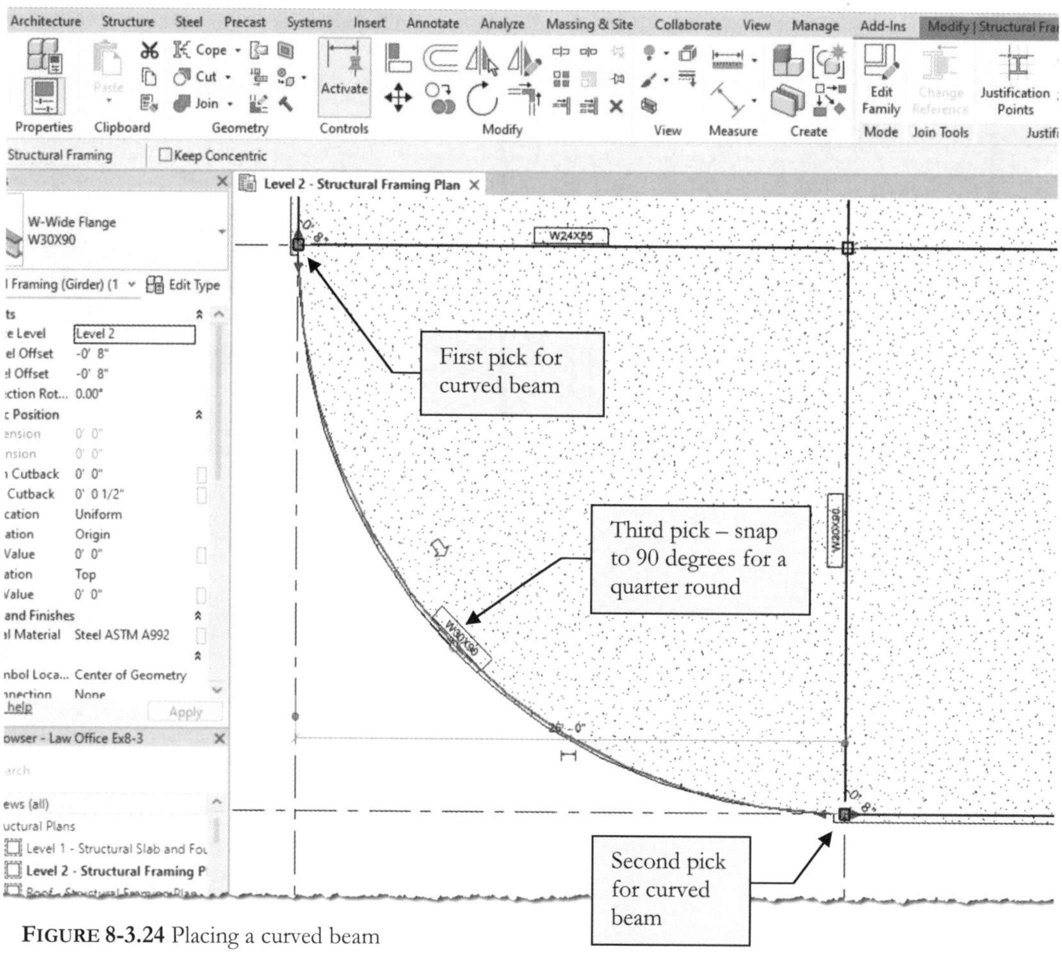

FIGURE 8-3.24 Placing a curved beam

For the next steps, see Figure 8-3.25.

41. Place a **column** at mid-span of the curved beam; use the midpoint snap.
    a. Use the same size HSS6x6x3/8 and top/bottom settings.
    b. *Bottom* at **-8"** and *Top* at **Roof**.

42. Select the column and then use the ***Rotate*** tool to rotate the column **45** degrees.

43. Add two **Grids**:
    a. Snap to the center of the column for the first point.
    b. Draw the grids as shown; adjust the endpoints.
    c. Change the grid number or letter as shown.

44. Split the **Beam**:
    a. Click **Modify → Edit → Split**.
    b. Click at the center of the column.

45. Delete the **beam tag** for the curved beam:
    a. Select it and press the Delete key.
    b. This tag will be added later.

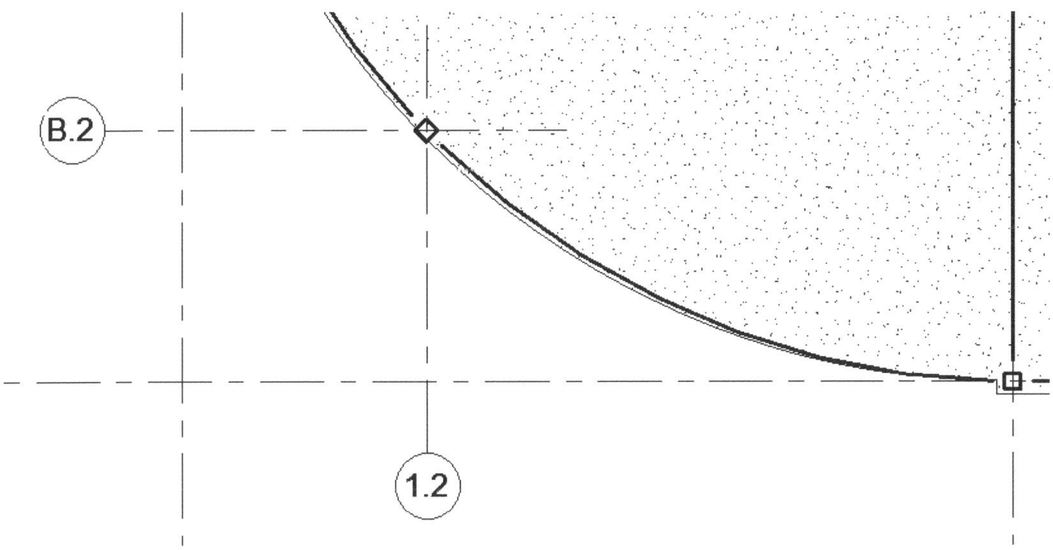

FIGURE 8-3.25 Adding a column and grids at mid-span of the curved beam

The roof is done in the same fashion as the *Level 2* floor framing. This information will be automatically added in a later chapter's file.

Exercise 8-4:
Floors and Bar Joist Layout

With the grids, columns and beams laid out, you can now focus on the floor and the structure that holds it up: the steel bar joists. The structural template has a few floor systems ready to go, and you already imported them into your project. In order for you to better understand how the floors work in Revit, you will modify the architectural floor previously created to have the proper structural representation. This process also illustrates that the architect's Revit geometry, from Schematic Design or Design Development phases, does not have to be discarded.

Level 2 Floor Construction:

Here you will modify the architect's Level 2 floor element to have the correct structural thickness and metal deck which spans the correct direction: perpendicular to the joists. If you recall, a temporary placeholder was added to the floor to represent the anticipated bar joist depth. This placeholder will be removed as the actual bar joists are about to be drawn.

1. **Open** the law office model, if not already open.
2. Load the following family: Profiles\Metal Deck**Form Deck_Composite.rfa**.
3. Switch to **Level 2 – Structural Framing Plan**, if needed.
4. Select the floor element; use the *Filter* tool if needed.
5. View the selected floor's type properties by clicking **Edit Type** from the *Properties Palette.*
6. Select **Edit**, next to the *Structure* parameter.
7. Make the following changes to the floor type's structure (Figure 8-4.1):
    a. Select Row 2 and change the thickness from 4″ to **5½.″**
    b. Select Row 5 and **Delete** the 1′-2″ thick finish layer.
    c. Change the *Function* of Row 3 to **Structural Deck [1]**.
    d. Once the previous step has been done, you now have access to the *Structural Deck Properties.* Do the following:
        i. *Deck Profile:* **Form Deck_Composite 1½″ x 6″**
        ii. *Deck Usage:* **Bound Layer Above**

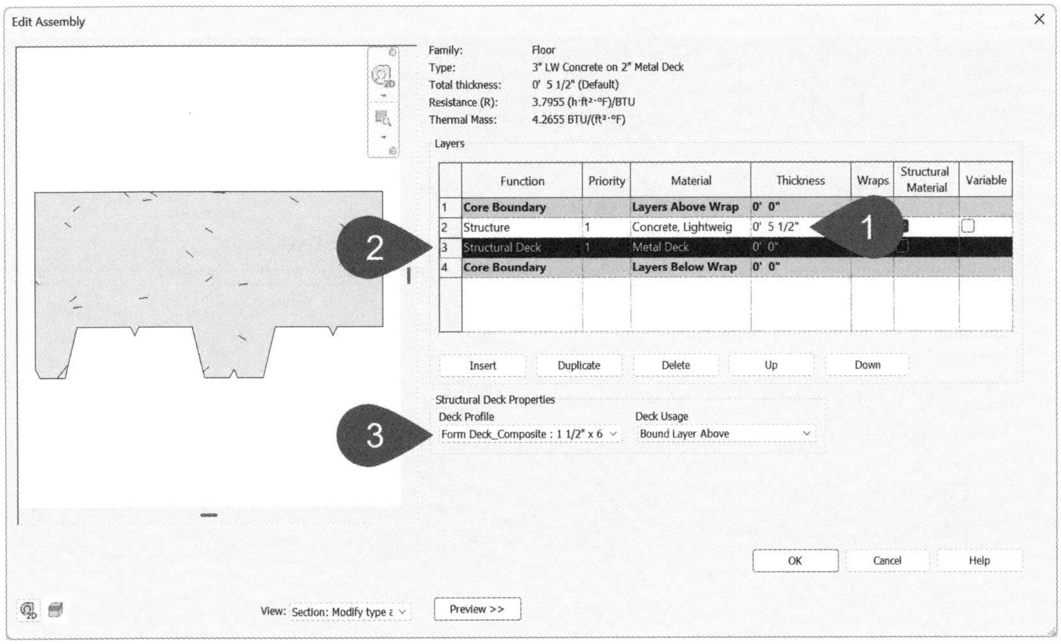

FIGURE 8-4.1 Editing the Level 2 floor construction

Notice in the preview above, the profile of the metal deck is visible in the preview window. It is important to show this profile in sections and details so the contractor knows which way the decking should be installed. The metal decking is only strong in one direction: that is the direction in which the flutes run. In the other direction the metal deck can actually bend to conform to a curved beam or roof. As you will see in a moment, Revit has a way in which you can specify the direction the decking runs.

In addition to selecting a deck profile, you also have a *Deck Usage* option in the lower right. The current setting is "bound layer above" which makes the metal deck exist within the overall thickness of the layer directly above it. (Only one exists in this example; it is concrete). The other option for *Deck Usage* is "standalone deck." This option makes the metal deck exist separately from the layer above; see the image to the right.

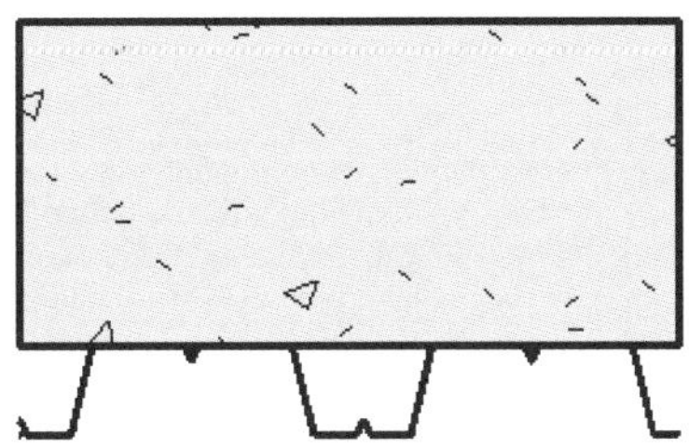

8. Select **OK** twice to close the open dialog boxes.

Next, you will add a *Span Direction* symbol which is used to indicate the direction the metal deck spans. The floor placed by the architects (in Revit *Architecture*) is an *Architectural Floor*. You will need to change it to a *Structural Floor* before it can be tagged. This is done by simply checking a box in the *Instance Properties* dialog box for the floor.

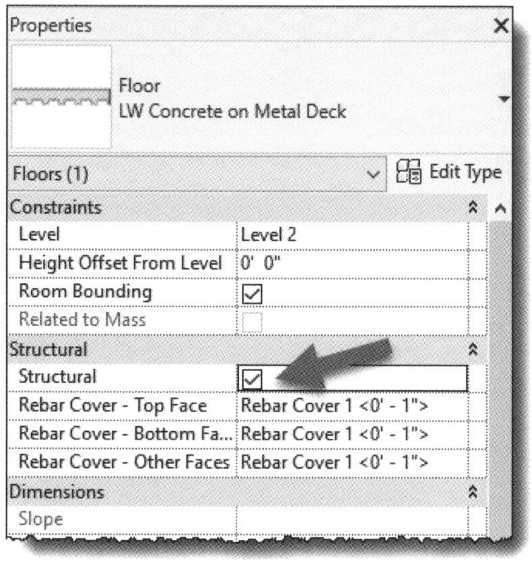

FIGURE 8-4.2 Level 2 floor's instance properties

9. **Select** the *Level 2* floor.

10. View its *Instance Properties* via the ***Properties Palette***.

11. **Check the box** next to the *Structural* parameter (Figure 8-4.2).

12. Click **Apply**.

13. Load the following family: Annotations\Structural**Span Direction.rfa**.

14. Select **Annotate → Symbol → Span Direction** from the *Ribbon*; see image to the right.

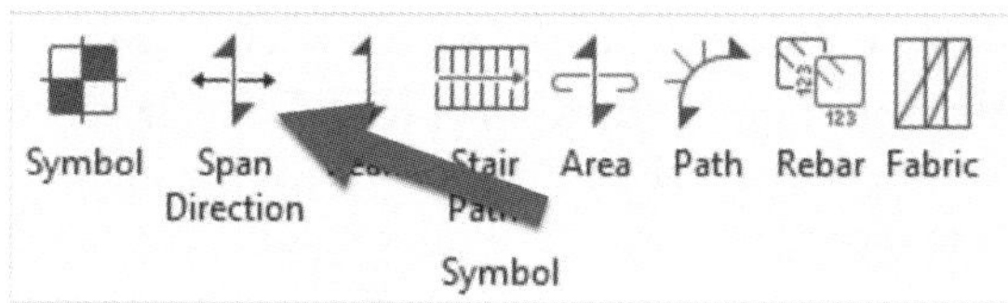

You have to select the edge of the structural floor before Revit can place the symbol.

15. **Click** the edge of the Level 2 floor.

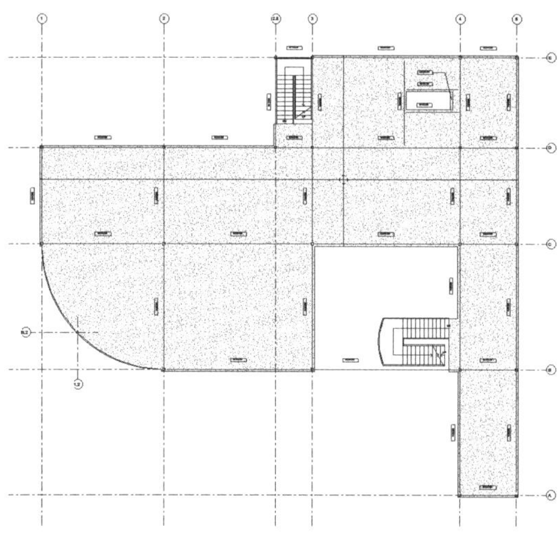

FIGURE 8-4.3 Level 2 span direction tag placed

16. **Click** anywhere within the middle of the floor (Figure 8-4.3).

17. Click **Modify** to finish the *Span Direction* tool.

The filled arrowheads indicate the direction the flutes run, and thus the span direction of the deck. In this example, the filled arrows should be on the left and the right. If not, you simply select the symbol and use the *Rotate* command. Also, when the symbol is selected, it can be moved so it does not obscure any text, tags or dimensions.

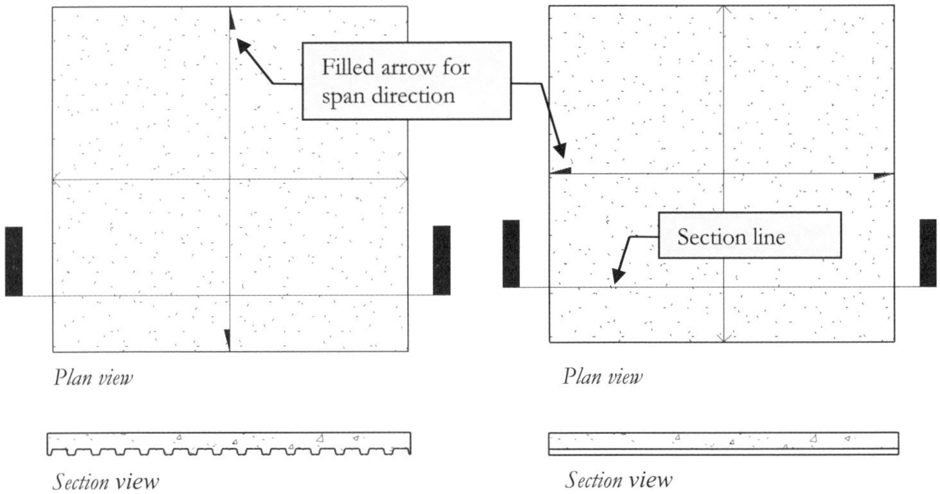

FIGURE 8-4.4 Span direction results

> ***FYI:*** *The* Span Direction *can also be adjusted while in* Sketch *mode for the floor. Click the* **Span Direction** *icon and then click a sketch line.*

The image above shows a clear example of the effect the *Span Direction* symbol has on the structural floor.

18. Ensure that the filled arrows are on the left and right, as in the example on the right in Figure 8-4.4. If not, select the symbol and use the *Rotate* tool to rotate it 90 degrees.

There is one more thing that has to be addressed before we can consider the Level 2 floor complete. Looking back at Figure 8-3.16, you can see the primary direction the bar joists span, which you will be drawing soon. This dictated the direction the metal deck should span, perpendicular to the joists. However, in the Southeastern corner of the building at the main entry, the joists turn 90 degrees to span the shorter direction and thus reduce the depth of the joist and amount of steel required. In this case, you need to break the floor element into two pieces so you can control the span direction independently for both areas.

19. Select the Level 2 floor element.
20. With the floor selected, click **Edit Boundary** on the *Ribbon.*
21. Modify the floor boundary so it stops at Grid **B**, as shown in Figure 8-4.5.
    a. Use *Trim* and *Delete* to edit the boundary.

> ***TIP:*** *Copy the linework for the portion of floor to be removed. This can then be pasted into the sketch of the new floor to be created in the next steps.*

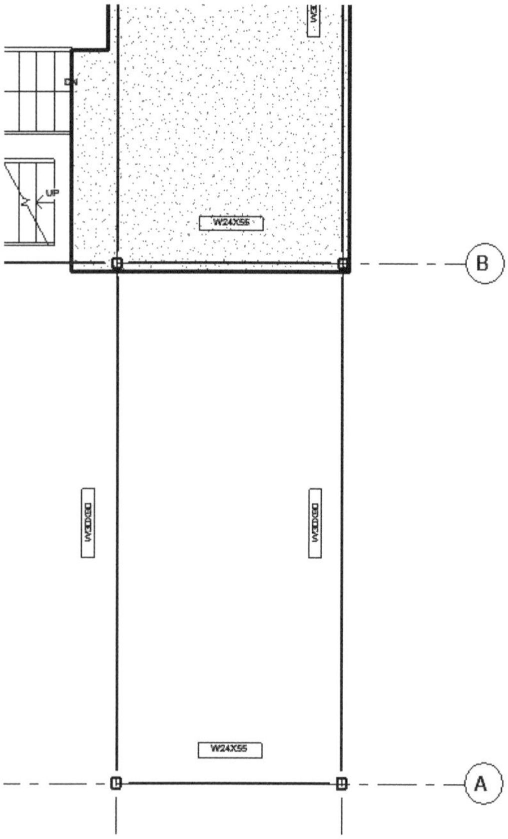

FIGURE 8-4.5 Revised floor boundary

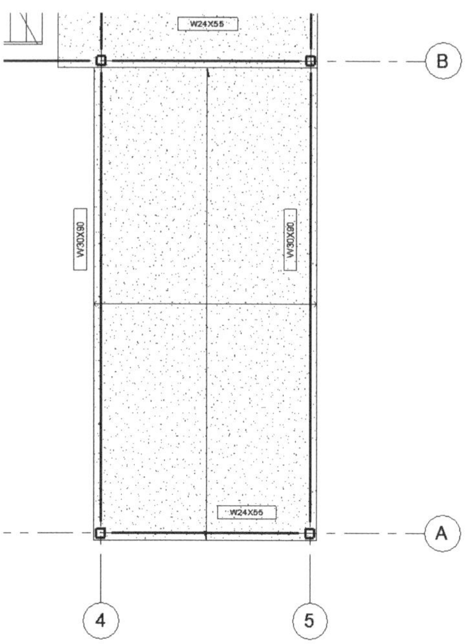

FIGURE 8-4.6 New floor added

22. Click green checkmark once the boundary has been updated; click **Don't attach** to both prompts.

The area between Grids A and B does not have a floor currently. You will create a new floor element for this area and adjust the Span Direction symbol appropriately.

23. Select Structure → Structure → Floor.

24. Sketch the boundary of the floor that was just deleted, making it the same 4⅝″ from the grid line to the edge of slab.

    a. If you copied the linework to the clipboard as suggested in Step 21, you can paste it by selecting *Paste → Aligned Current to View* from the *Ribbon.*

25. Once you have an enclosed boundary with no gaps or overlaps, click Finish Edit Mode (green checkmark) on the Ribbon.

26. Click **No** to any prompts.

Notice, when the structural floor is placed, a **Span Direction** symbol is automatically added (Figure 8-4.6).

27. If the filled arrows do not point North-South, opposite of the main floor, select it and Rotate it 90 degrees in either direction.

This wraps up the floor editing process. The roof is a similar process and the slab-on-grade, Level 1, is acceptable as-is.

Level 2 Floor Joists Using the Beam System Feature:

Now you will begin to place the bar joists. This is relatively easy as Revit provides a tool called *Beam Systems* that will fill an entire structural bay with bar joists, following predefined rules for spacing.

You will place bar joists in the Northwestern corner near Grids D/1. The joists will be spaced at 3′-0″ O.C. (on center) with any extra space being split at each end.

28. In the **Level 2 Structural Plan** view, **zoom in** to the Northwestern corner near Grids D/1.

29. Load the family: Annotation\Structural**Structural Beam System Tag.rfa**.

30. On the *Ribbon*, select **Structure → Structure → Beam System.**

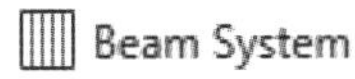

The *Ribbon* now displays the *Place Beam Structural System* contextual tab, and has several options to control what is modeled, joist size, and spacing. ***NOTE:*** *Revit thinks of any horizontal support member as a beam; its* Structural Usage *parameter defines how it is used, and* <u>Joist</u> *is one of those options.* You will be placing bar joists in the building to hold up the floor, but the *Beam System* tool will work equally well with I-joists, wide flange beams, dimensional lumber, or anything defined within the *Structural Framing* category.

31. Adjust the *Ribbon* and *Properties* to match Figure 8-4.7.
    a. *Tag on Placement:* **Selected**
    b. *Beam Type (drop-down):* **16k5**
    c. *Justification (drop-down):* **Center**
    d. *Layout Rule:* **Fixed Distance**
    e. *Fixed Spacing:* **3′-0″**
    f. *Tag style:* **System**

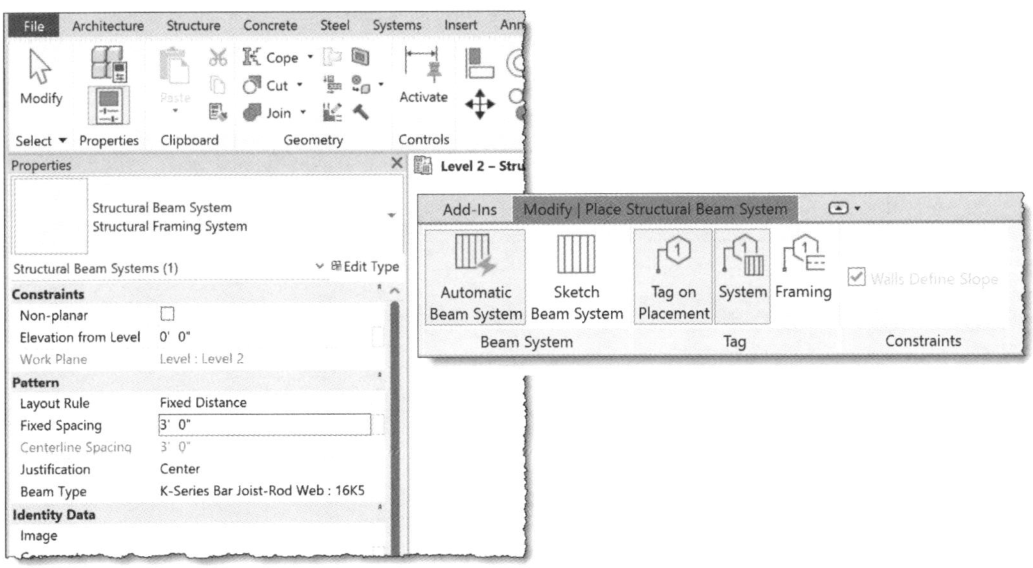

FIGURE 8-4.7 Beam system tool active; related settings

You loaded the 16k5 joist at the end of Exercise 8-2. Only families, specifically structural framing category families, loaded into the project will appear in the *Beam Type* list. If the structural member needed was not listed, you would have to click *Modify* to cancel the command and load the family.

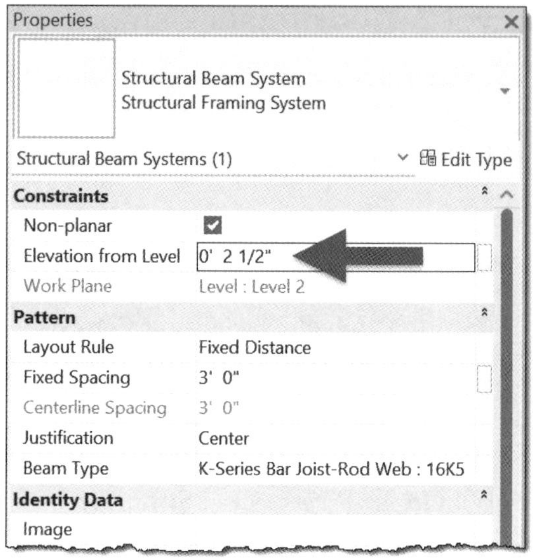

FIGURE 8-4.8 Instance properties for Beam System

Next you will adjust the elevation of the top of the joist; the reasoning for the number you enter will be provided momentarily.

32. View the ***Instance Properties*** of the *Beam System* you are about to place via the *Properties Palette.*

33. Check **Non-planar**, set the *Elevation from Level* to **2 ½"**, and click **Apply** (Figure 8-4.8).

Now for the easy part: you simply click one of the perimeter beams that defines a bay. The beam you select needs to be parallel to the span of the joists as you will learn in the next step.

34. DO NOT CLICK THE MOUSE BUTTON IN THIS STEP: **Hover** your cursor over the beam which runs along Grid 1 and notice the ghosted joist layout that appears; now **hover** your cursor over the Grid D beam to see the joist layout that would be created if you clicked on it.

35. **Click** the beam along Grid 1 as shown in Figure 8-4.9.

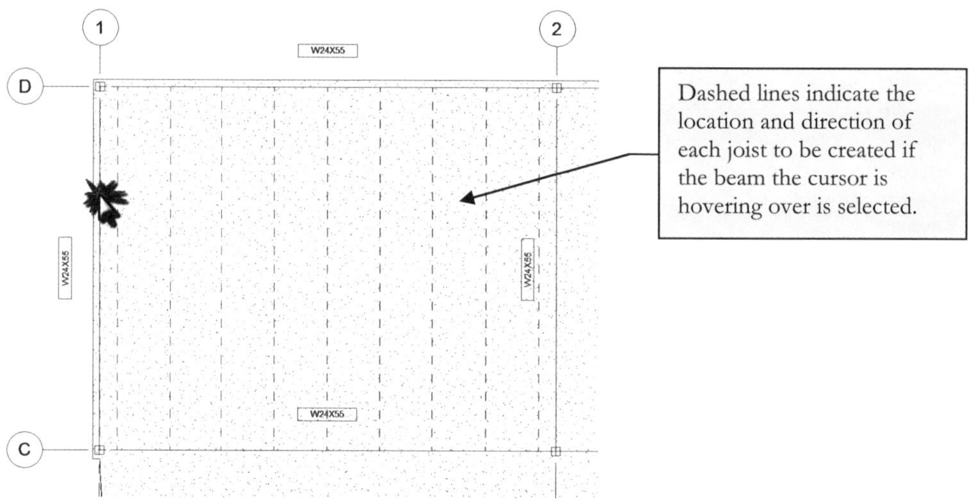

FIGURE 8-4.9 Creating a beam system for the bar joists

The *Beam System* is now created; see Figure 8-4.10. Notice the single-line representation provided for each joist with the ends stopping short of their supports to make things graphically clear; this is due to the *Detail Level* being set to *Coarse*. Also, a tag is provided indicating the joist size and spacing.

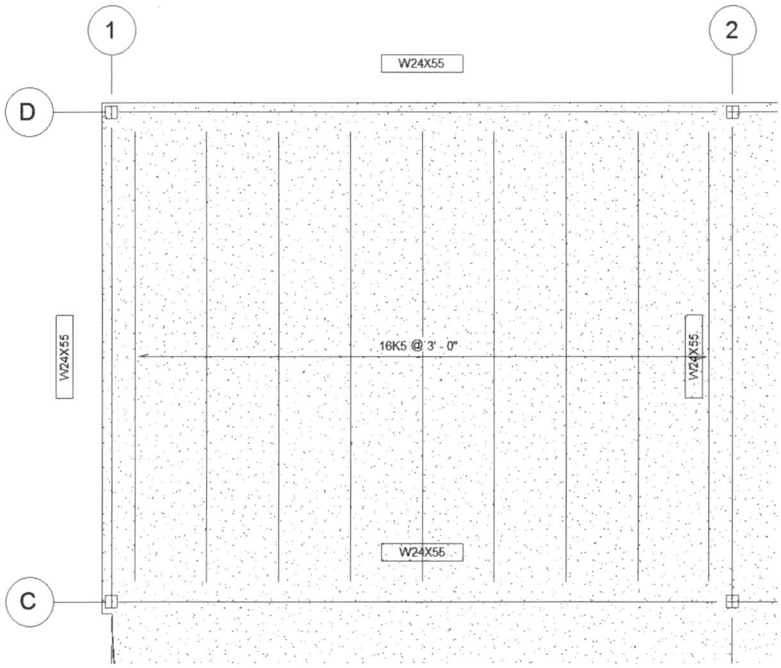

FIGURE 8-4.10 *Beam System* created

The figure below shows what things currently look like in section. You will learn how to create sections in a later chapter. Note: if Non-planar (aka 3D) was not checked, the bar joists would be 2.5" above the floor rather than above the beam (which is -8").

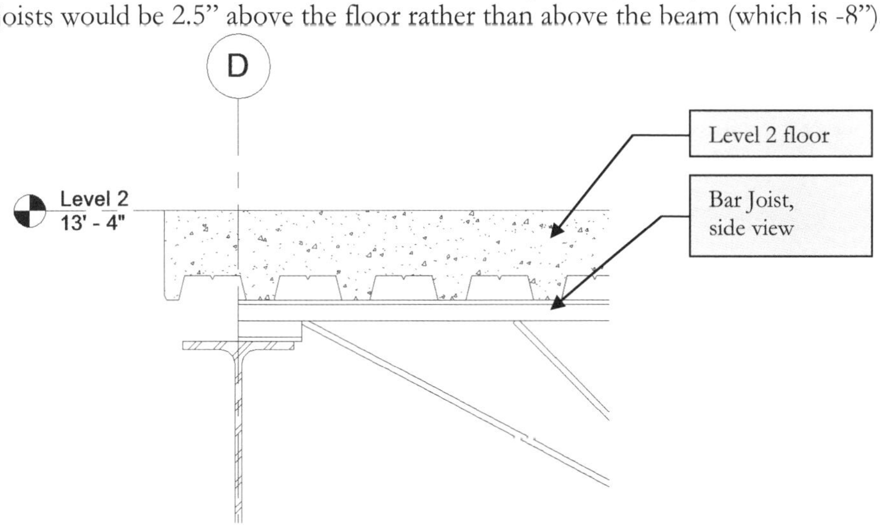

FIGURE 8-4.11 *Beam System* correctly positioned, section view

A bar joist typically only needs a minimal amount of bearing on a steel beam. However, sometimes the joist "seat," the bearing portion of the joist, needs to extend further to support the floor or another structural element. Although you will not do that in this tutorial, here is how it is done.

Each joist in the *Beam System* can be selected; it does not work if the entire *Beam System* itself is selected. Then you can view its *Instance Properties* (via the *Properties Palette*). There you may adjust the "start extension" and the "end extension." The image below has one extension set to 4″. You would have to select each joist to make this change. Having a start and end parameter allows you to individually control each end of the joist.

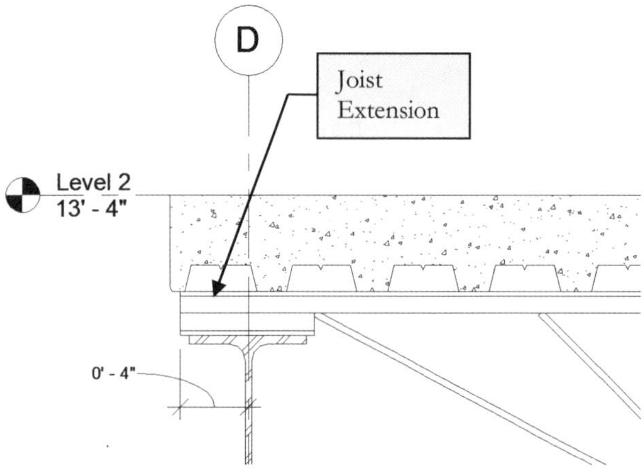

Construction	
Start Offset	0' 0"
Start Extension	0' 0"
End Offset	0' 0"
End Extension	0' 4"

FIGURE 8-4.12 Bar joist with joist extension

Now you will use the same technique to place the remaining *Beam Systems* throughout the second floor.

36. **Save** first, and then place the remaining *Beam Systems* for the information shown in Figure 8-4.13.
    a. The bay with the curved beam will take a few minutes for the *Beam System* to be created as each joist is a different size.
    b. Also, for the curved area, click *Delete Type* to continue when prompted (Figure 8-4.14).

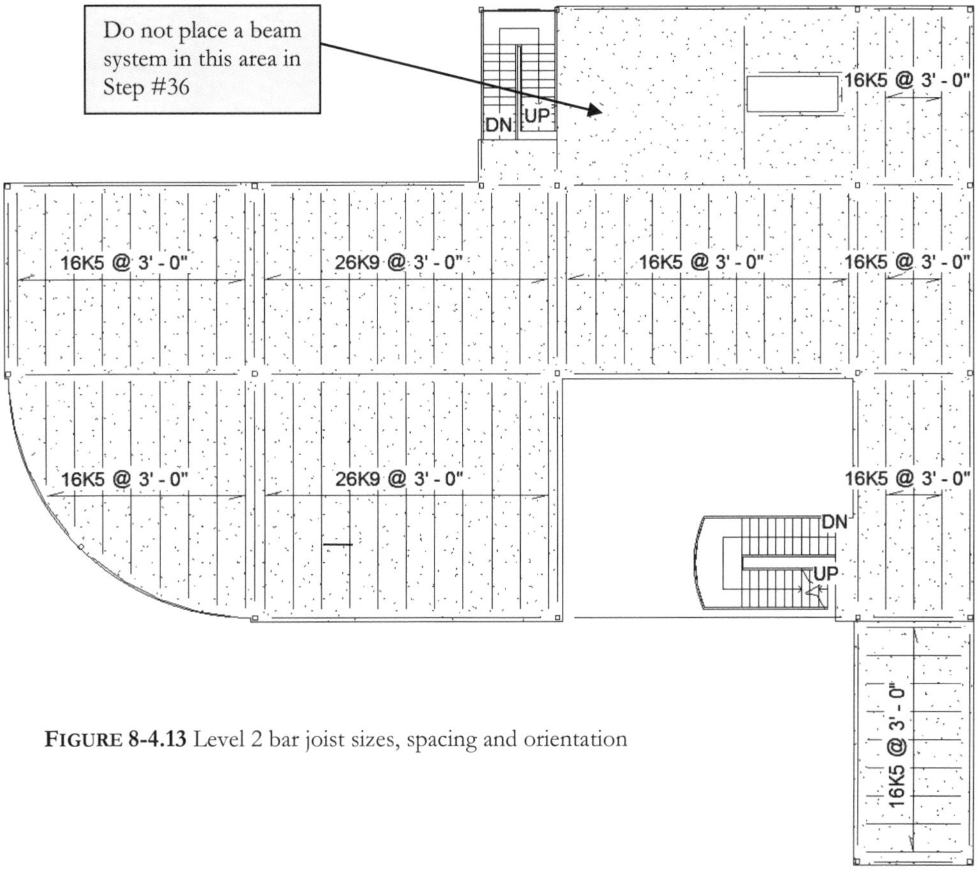

FIGURE 8-4.13 Level 2 bar joist sizes, spacing and orientation

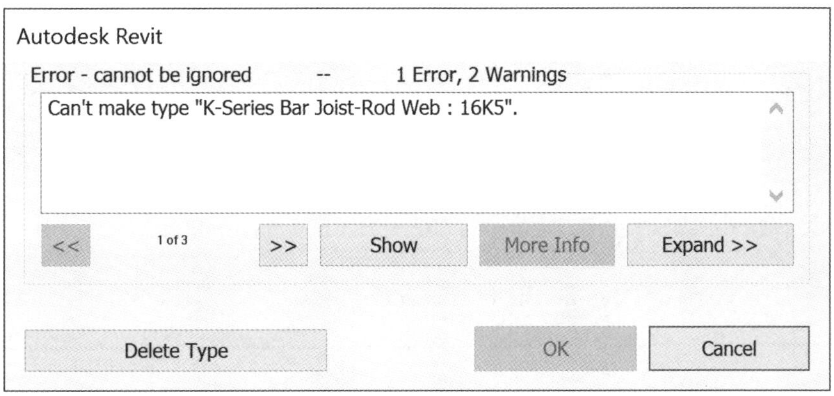

FIGURE 8-4.14 Warning message

Sketching the Perimeter of a Beam System:

The last area you will look at is near the Northeastern corner of the building, by the floor opening. You cannot use the one-click method here, as Revit will fill in the area from Grid 3 all the way past the floor opening to Grid 4. In this case, Revit provides a way in which you can sketch the perimeter of the *Beam System.*

37. Select the ***Beam System*** tool.

38. Click the ***Sketch Beam System*** button from the *Ribbon.*

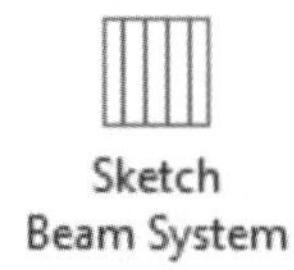

Rather than sketching new lines from scratch, you will use the *Pick Supports* options, which will force you to pick the beams that will define the perimeter of the *Beam System.*

39. Click the ***Pick Supports*** icon in the *Draw* panel of the *Ribbon* (Figure 8-4.15).

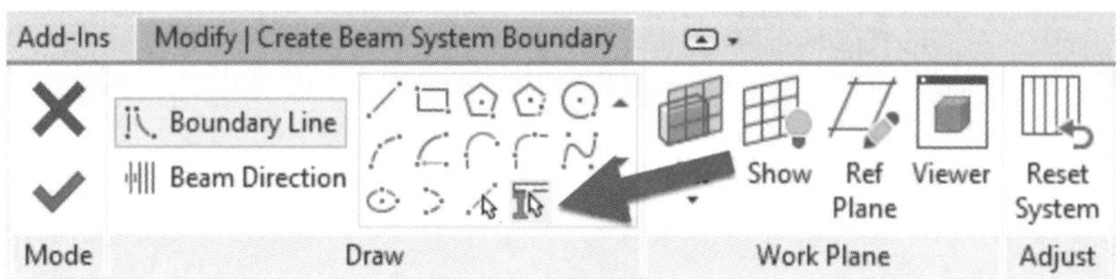

FIGURE 8-4.15 Ribbon: Beam system tool while in Sketch mode

Next, you will pick the four beams that define the perimeter of the area to receive joists.

40. Pick a vertical beam first (see highlighted beam in Figure 8-4.16); this defines the beam span. The beam span is defined by picking a beam parallel to the desired joist span.

41. Pick the other three beams to define the bay (Figure 8-4.17).

42. Use **Trim** to clean up the four corners.

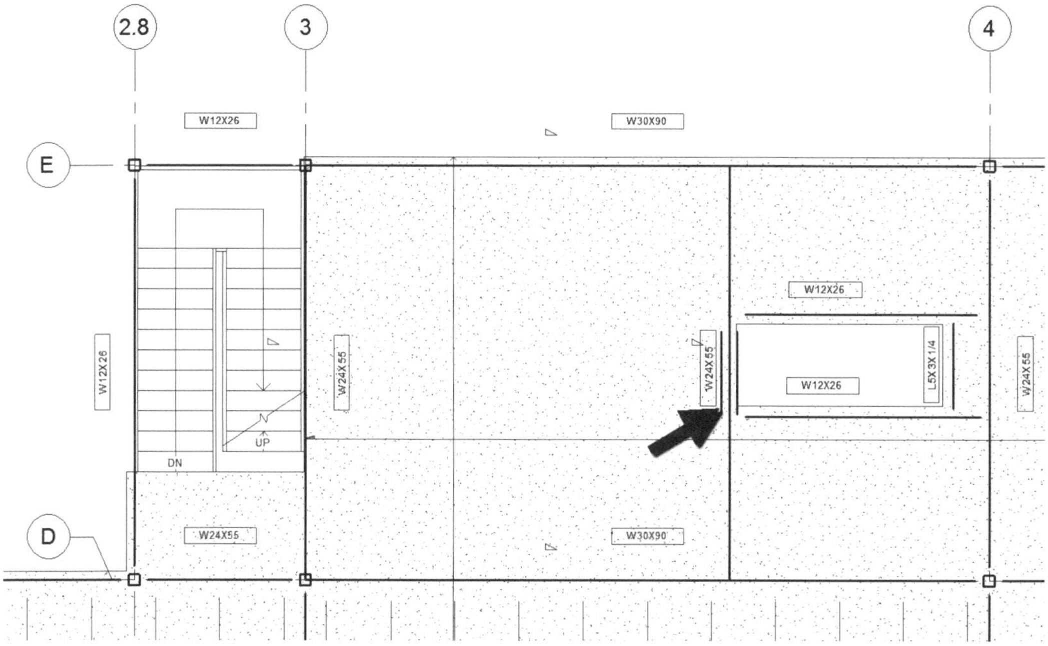

FIGURE 8-4.16 Beam System sketch mode; pick supports and trim used to define perimeter

43. Verify the following settings via the *Properties Palette*:

    a. *Elevation from Level =* **2 ½″**
    b. *Non-planar =* **checked**
    c. *Joist size =* **16k5**
    d. *Layout rule:* **Fixed Distance**
    e. *Fixed Spacing:* **3′-0″**
    f. See Figure 8-4.8.

    Tip: The beam system should have the same start and end offsets.

44. Click **Apply** if any changes have been made to the *Properties Palette.*

45. Click **Finish Edit Mode** (green check mark) to have Revit place the joists. 

The *Beam System* is now placed as desired in your Building Information Model (BIM), as you can see in Figure 8-4.17. You now only have two small areas to the East in which to place joists and Level 2 is then complete.

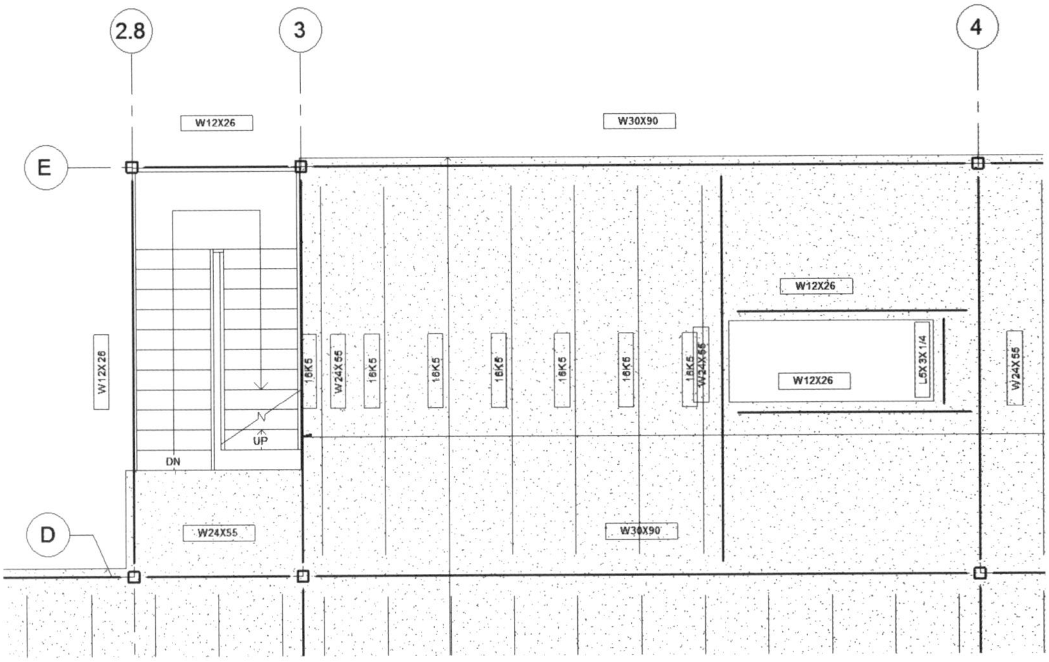

FIGURE 8-4.17 Beam System completed using the manual sketch technique

Revit does not give you the option to tag the *Beam System*. It only tags the individual beams, joists. This makes the plan cluttered, so we will delete them. In the next section, you will learn how to manually add beam and beam system tags when needed.

46. Select each joist tag and delete it by pressing the *Delete* key; do not delete the beam tags from the previous exercise.

    a. Select each tag one at a time and delete it, or select them all first, using the *Ctrl* key, and then delete them all at once.

A tag can be deleted at any time without worries. A tag only reports information contained within the element it is tagging; it contains no information itself. The point is, deleting a tag will not cause any information to be eradicated from the BIM. As you will see in the next exercise, tags can be added manually at any time.

Finally, you will place bar joists in the last two areas adjacent to the floor opening. You will need to load a new, smaller, bar joist size. If you tried to place one of the larger joists in this area you would get an error because the snap is too short and the joist too deep; Revit cannot build a valid joist given such conditions. Given the short span, the smaller joists are more appropriate.

47. Using techniques previously discussed, i.e., loading content and creating beam systems via sketching, place the remaining joists shown in Figure 8-4.18. Change the spacing to **3'-1"** to avoid joists being created right next to the adjacent beams.

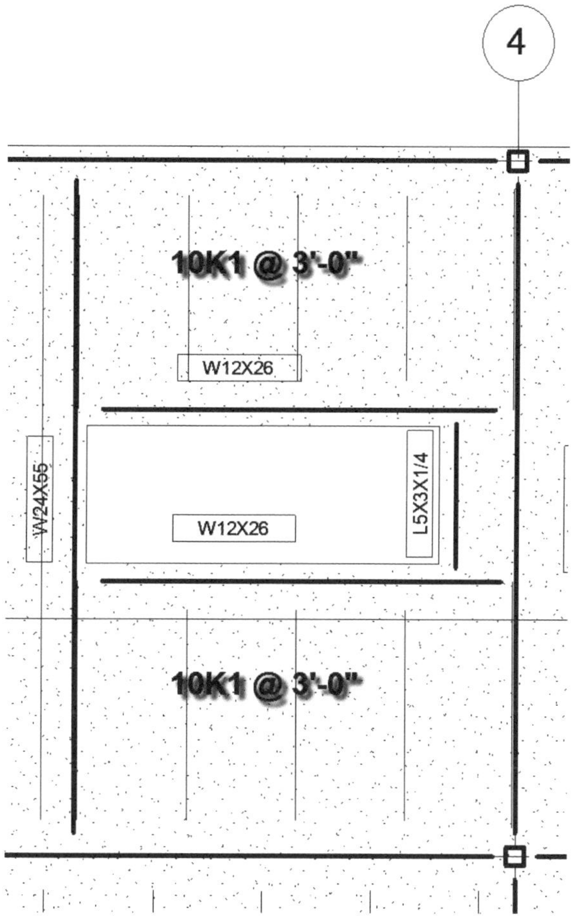

FIGURE 8-4.18 Beam Systems adjacent to the floor opening

The roof layout is pretty much the same process, with different joist sizes and spacing depending on the design requirements. The joists are often smaller and spaced further apart on the roof. This is because the roof can bounce more compared to a floor where people would feel uncomfortable and materials such as ceramic floor tile would crack. Sometimes snow loads, a dead load, would require similarly sized and spaced structural members.

> *NOTE: The remaining structure is provided in the chapter starter file for the next chapter. Be sure to start the next chapter with the provided chapter starter file.*

Exercise 8-5:
Foundations and Footings

This exercise will look at developing the building's below-grade structural elements, namely the foundations and footings. This information will be modeled and documented in the **Level 1 Structural Plan** view previously created.

1. **Start** Revit.

2. Switch to the **Level 1 – Structural Slab and Foundation** plan view.

Setting up the View:

The first thing you will do is set up the view; a few things need to be turned off. Plus, you will use a feature called "underlay" which lets you superimpose another plan over your current plan view. One trick here is that you can use the same level to see the architectural walls temporarily. You will use the exterior architectural walls to locate the foundation walls.

3. Type **VV** (do not press *Enter*) to access the *Visibility/Graphic Overrides* dialog for the current view.

4. Make the following changes to the *Model Categories* tab:
   a. **Check** *Show categories from all disciplines via the* Filter list if not already selected.
   b. **Uncheck** (i.e., turn off the visibility of):
      i. Curtain Panels
      ii. Curtain Systems
      iii. Curtain Wall Mullions
      iv. Floor
      v. Stairs

5. Click **OK**.

6. With nothing selected and no commands active, draw your attention to the *Properties Palette*, which is displaying the *View Properties* for the current view.
   a. Type **PP** to display the *Properties Palette* if it is not visible.

7. In the *Properties Palette*, in the *Underlay* section, set **Range: Base Level** to **Level 1**.

8. Make sure *Underlay Orientation* is set to **Look Down**.

9. Click **Apply** to apply the changes.

The plan should now look like Figure 8-5.1. Notice all the architectural walls for Level 1 are showing plus the Level 2 bar joists.

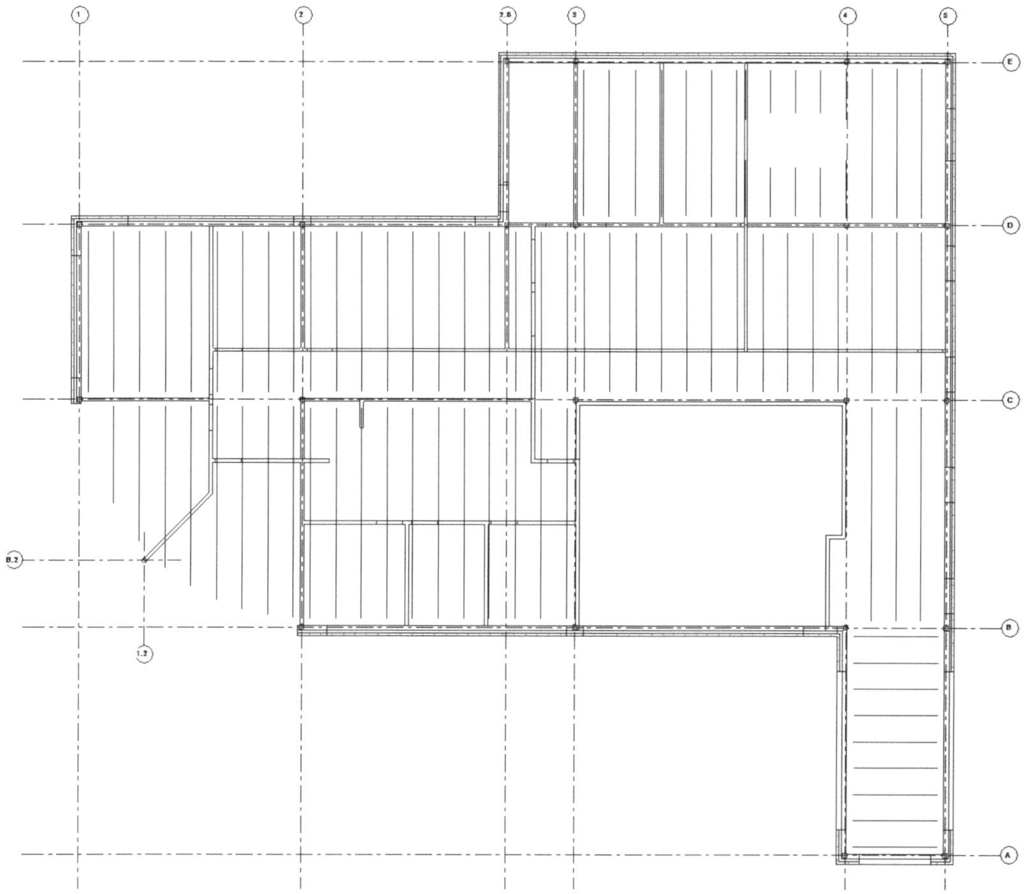

FIGURE 8-5.1 Level 1 structural plan with underlay setup

Foundation Walls:

Now you will draw the foundation walls around the perimeter of the building. Foundation walls are drawn using the *Wall* tool, and are drawn from the top down, like structural columns. The wall knows it is a foundation based on the *Type Parameter* Function, which is set to Foundation for the wall type you will be using.

10. Select **Structure → Structure → Wall** from the *Ribbon*.

11. Set the *Type Selector* to **Foundation – 12″ Concrete** (Figure 8-5.2).

12. Set the *Location Line* to **Finish Face: Exterior** on the *Properties Palette* (Figure 8-5.2).

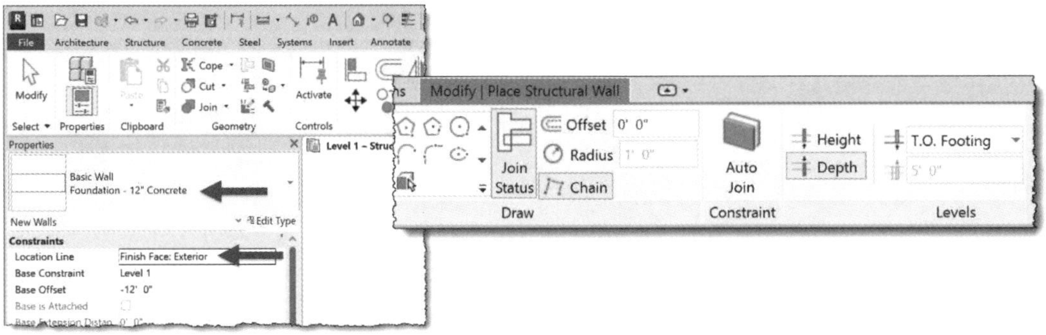

FIGURE 8-5.2 Wall tool – *Properties Palette* for foundation walls

Note in the image above, the wall *Depth* is being specified. In the next step you will ensure this is set to T.O. Footing (T.O. = top of). This will create a parametric relationship between the bottom of the foundation wall and the *Level Datum* named T.O. Footing. Thus, any change made to the T.O. Footing Level will automatically change the depth of all the foundation walls.

13. Make sure the *Depth* is set to **T.O. Footing** on the *Ribbon* (Figure 8-5.2).

14. Begin drawing the foundation wall around the perimeter of the building (Figure 8-5.3).
    a. Start at the point shown and work in a clockwise direction; if needed, press the spacebar to flip the wall to the correct side.
    b. Use *Snaps* and pick the inside and outside corners along the architectural exterior walls which are shown via the *Underlay.*
    c. When you reach the last straight wall segment, click the arc symbol in the *Draw* panel on the *Ribbon.*
    d. Draw the curved wall to close off the perimeter.

At this point you can turn off the *Underlay* as you only needed it to locate the foundation walls along the perimeter. The remaining foundations can be placed based on the steel column locations, which will remain visible in the view even after the *Underlay* is turned off.

15. Turn off the Level 1 *Underlay* by setting the option back to *None* in the view's *Properties.*

Your plan should now look like Figure 8-5.4, which shows the grids, columns and the newly added foundation walls.

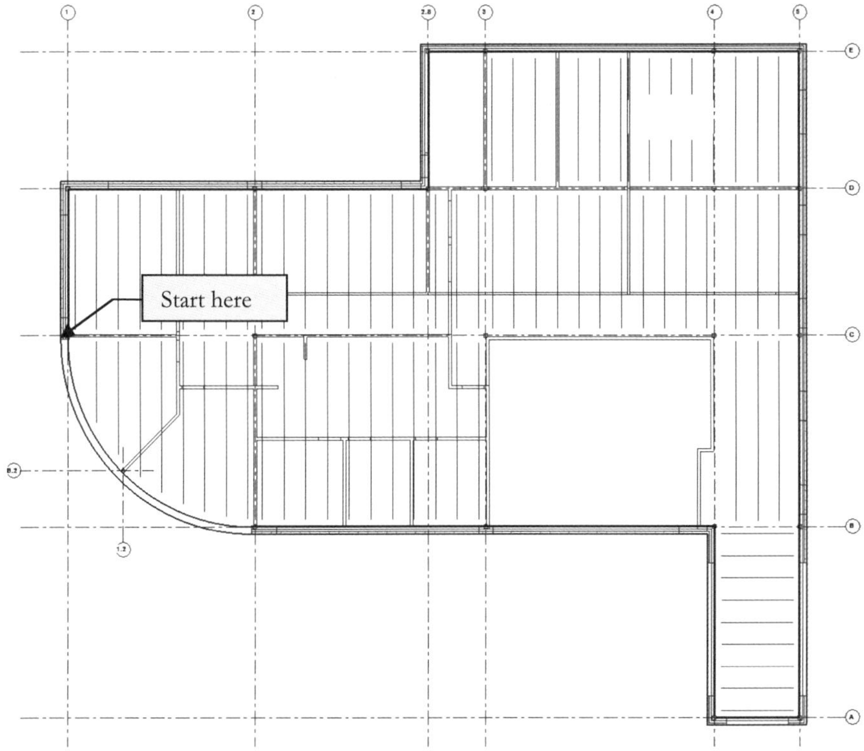

FIGURE 8-5.3 Level 1 slab and foundation plan; perimeter walls added

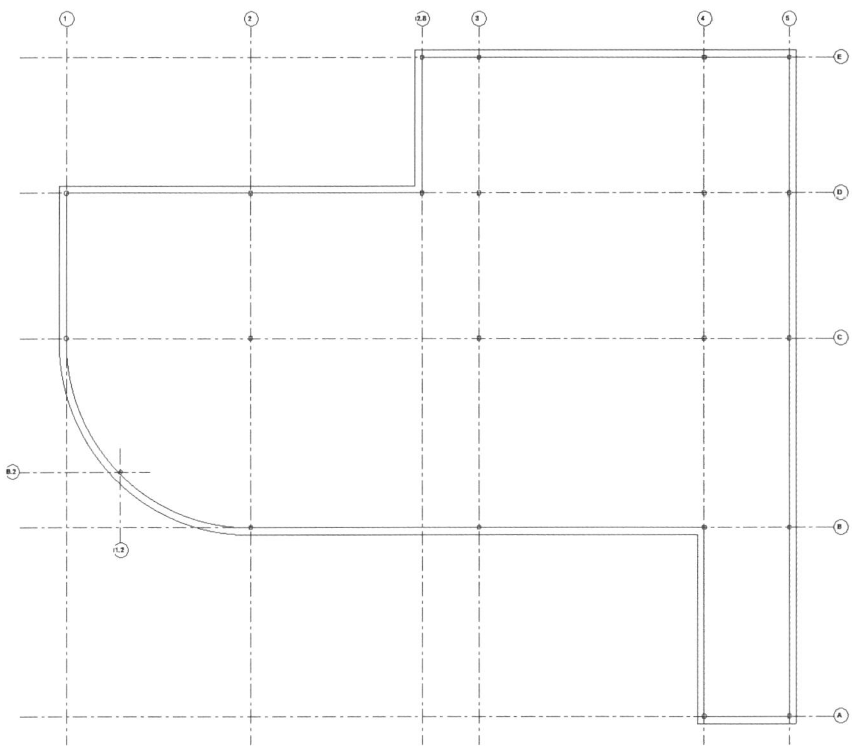

FIGURE 8-5.4 Level 1 slab and foundation plan; underlay turned off

Below Grade Concrete Columns (or Piers):

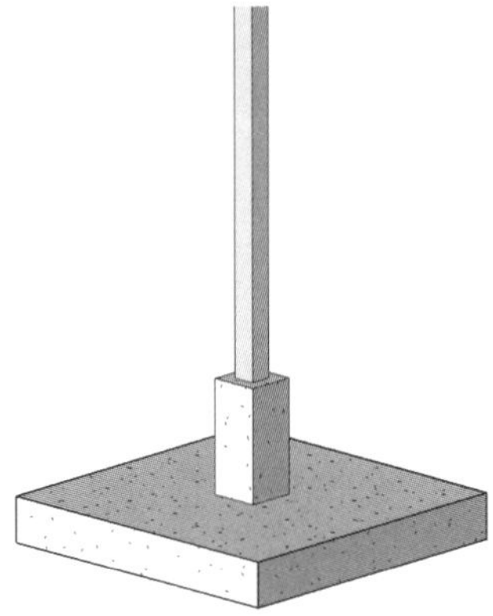

Next, you will add concrete footings below each steel column. This is done using the *Column* tool, the same one used to place the steel columns. But in this case, you will be placing concrete columns that extend below grade to footings.

Because the steel columns are not completely over the 12″ exterior foundation wall, you will have to add columns below them. These columns will be joined with the wall to properly represent the monolithic concrete pour. However, the column remains a separate element so it can be repositioned as needed.

You will also add isolated concrete columns at the interior locations. These would typically not be as deep as the exterior foundations because frost heave is not typically a concern. However, in this exercise you will place them at the same depth for simplicity.

All the concrete columns will be 18″x18″ and the top will be held 8″ below the Level 1 slab. The 8″ recess is to allow the Level 1 slab to wrap around the steel column and accommodate floor finishes.

16. Use **Load Autodesk Family** button on the *Ribbon.*

17. Browse to **Structural Columns\Concrete**.

18. Pick **Concrete-Square-Column** from the list, and select **Load**.

The family is now loaded with four *Types*: 12″x12″, 18″x18″, 24″x24″ and 30″x30″.

19. Select **Structure → Structural → Column** to activate the *Structural Column* tool.

20. Set the *Type Selector* to **18″x18″** <u>Concrete-Square-Column</u>.

21. Make sure the *Depth* setting on the *Ribbon* is set to **T.O. Footing**.

22. Snap to the center point of each steel column, to place a concrete column (Figure 8-5.5).

Your plan should now look like the image below (Figure 8-5.5). Notice how the column and the foundation wall automatically joined. When placing the columns, you did not have an option to lower the top of the column down 8″; you will do that next. This will create an unrealistic condition at the exterior walls that will not be addressed in this tutorial; typically, a notch or reveal would be added to make a consistent bearing area for the column and its bearing plate.

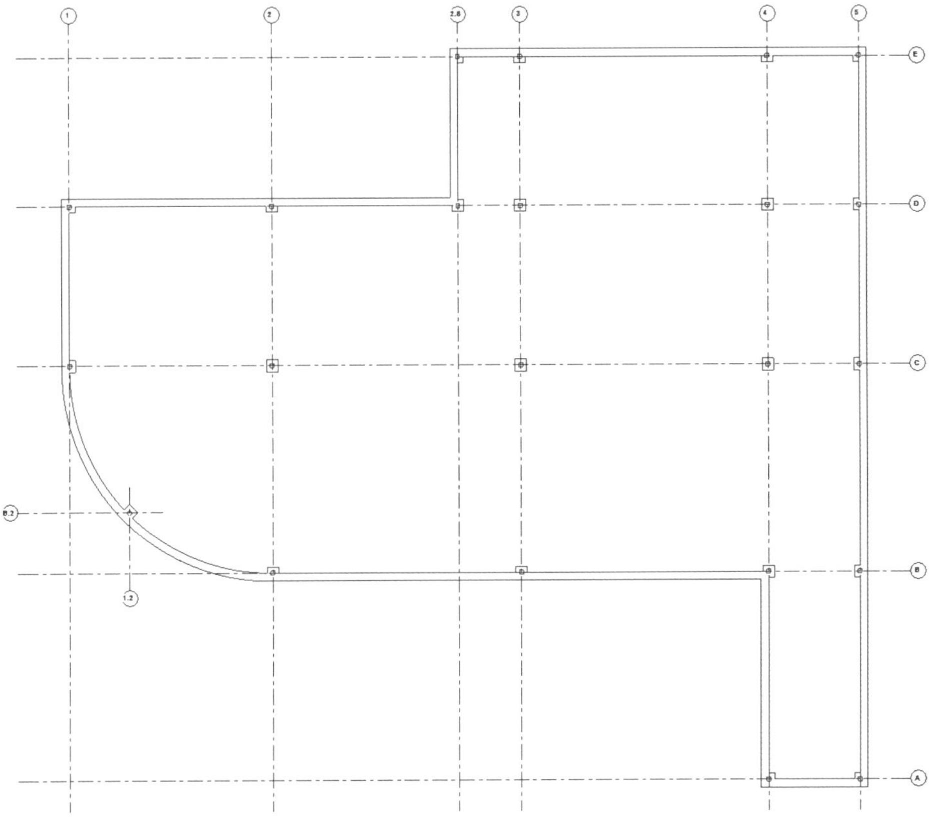

FIGURE 8-5.5 Level 1 slab and foundation plan; concrete columns added

23. Select and **Rotate** the concrete column (45 degrees) at the middle of the curved foundation wall (Figure 8-5.5).

24. Select one of the concrete columns.

25. Right-click and pick **Select all instances > In Entire Project** from the pop-up menu.

You now have all the concrete columns selected; notice the quantity of elements selected (22) is listed in the lower right.

> ***WARNING:*** *The "Select all instances > In Entire Project" command selected everything in the entire project, not just the current view! In this case, the current view contains all concrete columns in the project. So to be safe, you might have only selected the "Visible in View" option rather than "In Entire Project."*

26. With the concrete columns selected, note their *Instance Parameters* via the *Properties Palette.*

27. Set the *Top Offset* to **-8″**; be sure to add the minus symbol (see Figure 8-5.6).

FYI: When multiple elements are selected, you are changing them all at once here in the Instance Properties dialog.

28. Click **Apply** to commit the changes.

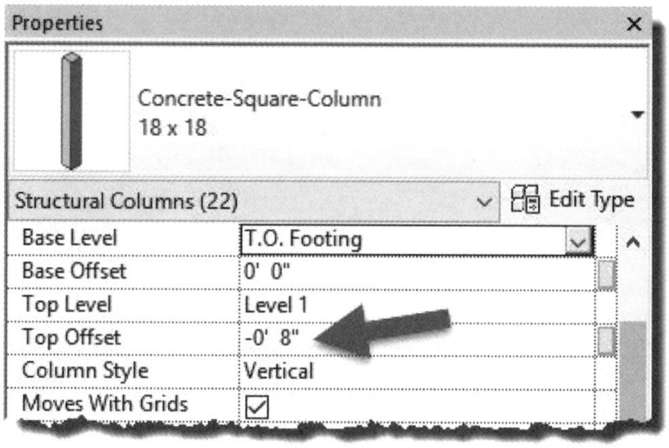

FIGURE 8-5.6
Changing top of concrete column elevation

Adding Footings (aka Foundations):

Now that you have all the below grade foundation walls and columns, you will add the footings, which spread out the load from the foundation walls on to the ground (aka, undisturbed or engineered soil). Revit provides a tool for this that nicely automates the process.

Wall Footings:

First you will add the continuous strip footing along the perimeter of the building, below the foundation wall. This footing will be 36″ wide and 12″ deep, centered on the 12″ foundation wall.

29. Switch to **B.O. Footing** plan view and select **Structure → Foundation → Wall** from the *Ribbon* (see the image to the right).

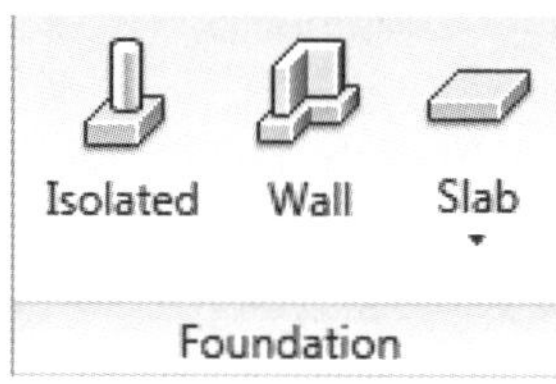

30. Make sure the *Type Selector* is set to **Bearing Footing – 36″ x 12″**.

31. Now simply click each foundation wall (Figure 8-5.7).

The footings have been added to the bottom of the foundation wall, at whatever depth it is, and centered on it. Later you will learn how to make the lines for the footings dashed.

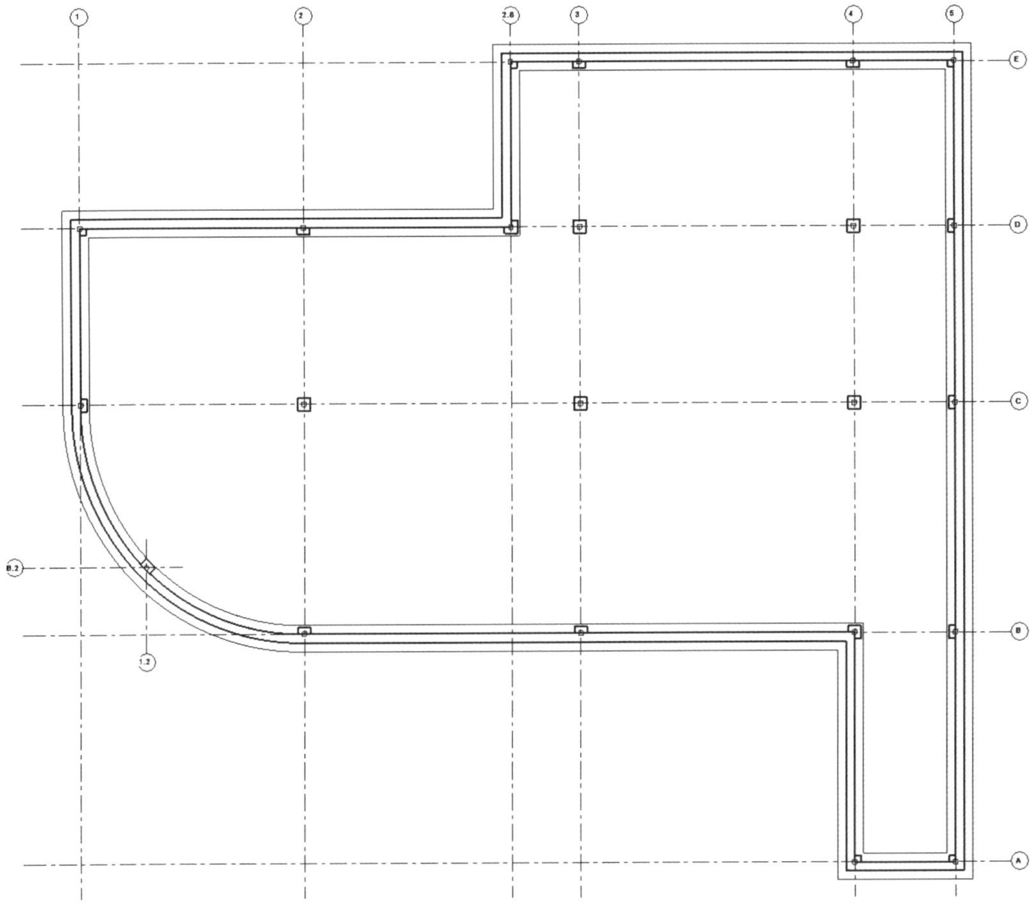

FIGURE 8-5.7 Level 1 slab and foundation plan; footings added

Isolated Footings:

Before placing the isolated footings you will switch to a different view. Revit will automatically look for a column at the point you pick and place the isolated foot at that column's bottom. However, in the **Level 1 Slab and Foundation Plan** view, it will only find the steel columns as they are the ones that pass through the Level 1 plane.

32. Switch to the **T.O. Footing** plan view.
    a. This is one of the architect's views (assuming you are the structural designer now); you can work in any view that is convenient and in your project.

Now you will add isolated footings below each column. These will be 9′-6″ x 9′-6″ x 1′-4″. Notice the thickness varies from the strip footing. When you place isolated footings below the perimeter columns, you will want the tops to align so the bearing plane is consistent.

33. Select **Structure → Foundation → Isolated** from the *Ribbon.*

Anytime the size or type you want is not listed, you need to duplicate an existing one and modify it to what you need. Next, you will make a new isolated footing type and adjust its size.

34. Click **Edit Type** via the *Properties Palette* to view the *Type Properties.*

35. Click **Duplicate**.

36. Type **9′-6″ x 9′-6″ x 1′-4″** and then click **OK**.

37. Adjust the *Width*, *Length*, and *Foundation Thickness* parameters accordingly; make them match the new type name you just created. See **Figure 8-5.8**.

38. Click **OK**.

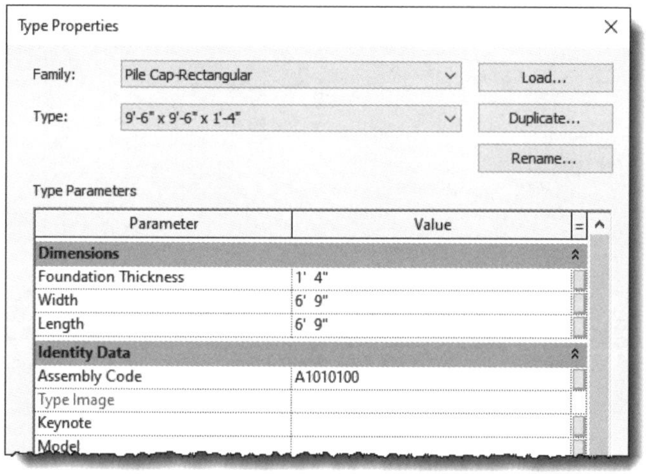

FIGURE 8-5.8 Isolated footing type properties

39. Click at the intersection of each grid line that has a concrete column.

TIP: Use the "At Column" option; remember to click Finish *when done.*

40. Switch back to the **Level 1 – Structural Slab and Foundation Plan** view.

41. Make sure the *Visual Style* is set to **Hidden Line**, via the *View Control Bar* or the *View Properties.*

The isolated footings are not shown yet, so the View Range will be adjusted in the followings steps to make the view look like Figure 8-5.9. Notice how the two footings, *isolated* and *wall*, clean up automatically. Because the depth varies, a dashed line is added between them. Also, *Isolated* footings that touch each other are joined to properly represent a monolithic pour.

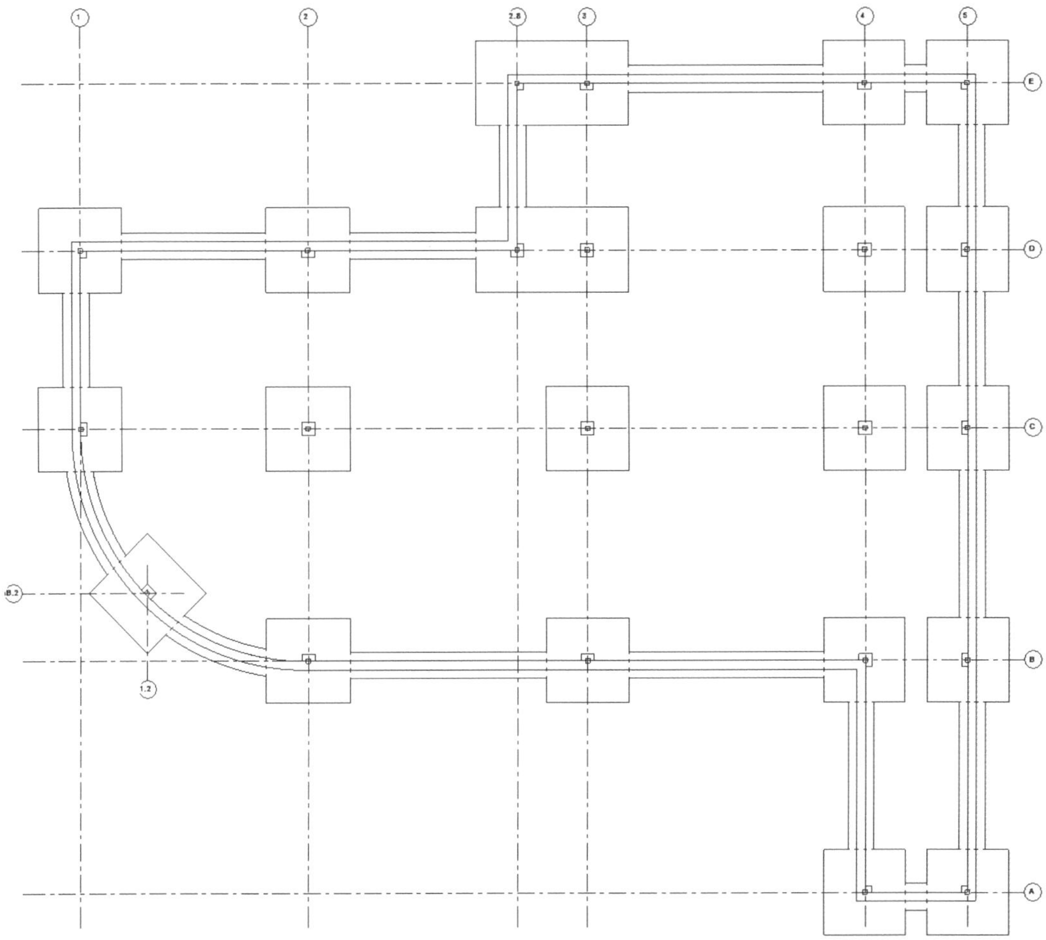

FIGURE 8-5.9 Isolated footings placed

View Range and View Depth Settings:

The final step in this exercise is to adjust the view so the footings are represented with dashed lines to distinguish them from the foundation walls. This is done with the *View Range* settings and the *Line Style* named <Beyond>.

First, you will be instructed to make the necessary changes and then an explanation will be given.

42. In the **Level 1 – Structural Slab and Foundation Plan** make sure nothing is selected and no commands are active.

43. Select **Edit** next to *View Range* in the *Properties Palette.*

44. Change the *Bottom* setting to **-1′-0″** and then change the *View Depth* to **-10'-0"** (see Figure 8-5.10).

FIGURE 8-5.10 View Range settings

45. Click **OK** to close the open dialog box.

You should not yet notice any change to your view.

46. On the *Ribbon*, click **Manage → Settings → Additional Settings → Lines Styles**.

47. Expand the *Lines* row if needed, by clicking the plus symbol to the left.

48. Change the *Line Pattern* for <Beyond> to **Hidden 1/8″** (Figure 8-5.11).

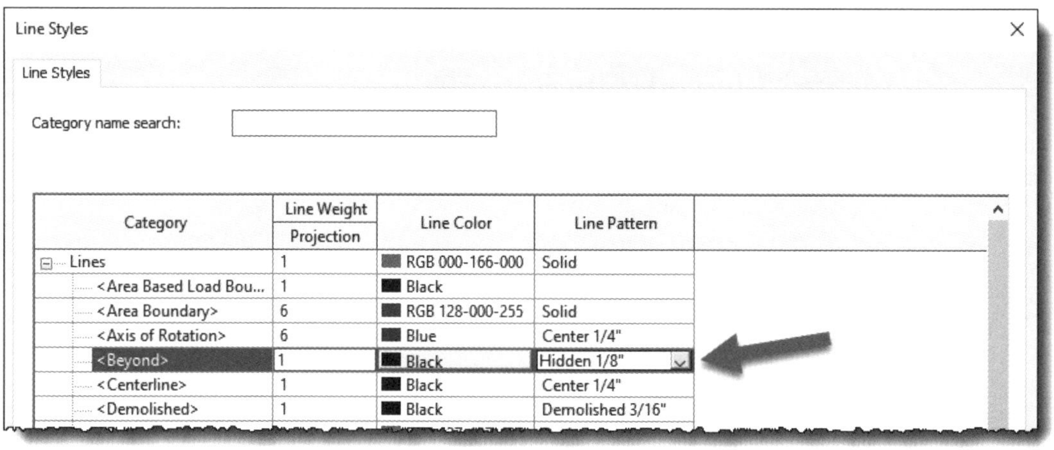

FIGURE 8-5.11 Line Style settings

49. Click **OK** to accept the changes.

Your plan should now look like Figure 8-5.12 below.

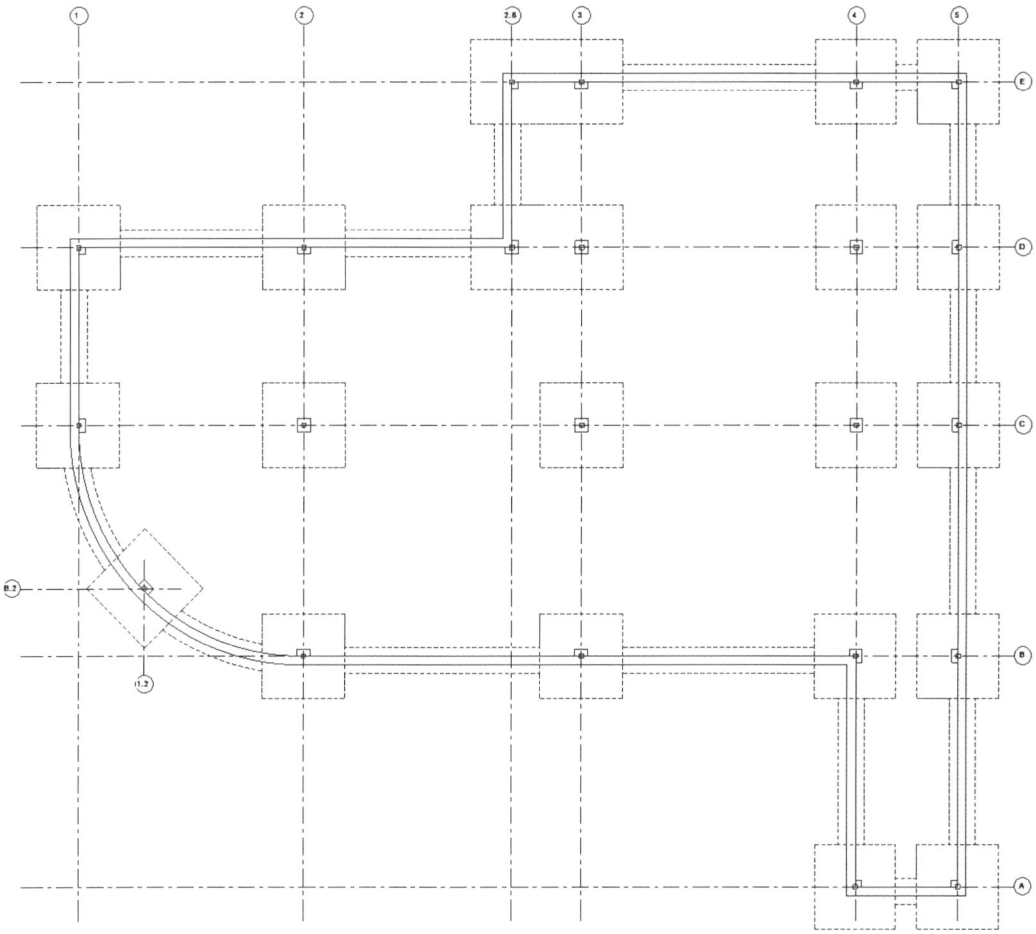

FIGURE 8-5.12 Level 1 – Structural Slab and Foundation Plan; footing now shown dashed

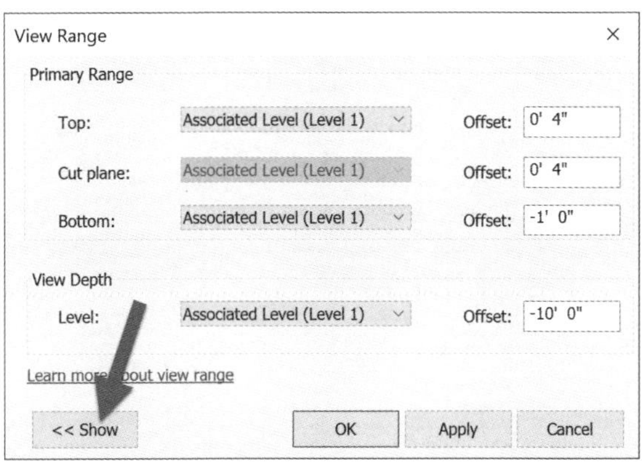

Now for the explanation on how this works. Every view has two settings, within the *View Range*, that deal with the bottom of the view: *Bottom* and *View Depth*. Often, they are both set to the same value, which is equal to the level. This is how Revit is able to show the 6th floor plan, for example, and not show everything else down to the basement, since it was told to stop looking at the level line.

Sometimes the Bottom setting is lowered to see beyond the level line in a plan view; for example, to show a recessed lobby or in the case of our example, to show the top of the concrete column.

Notice the image below which illustrates the two *View Range* items under consideration (Figure 8-5.13). The top of the concrete column is -8″ from Level 1 and the *Bottom* setting was set to -1′-0″. If the *Bottom* was set to 0′-0″ the concrete columns would not be visible in the plan view.

If the *View Depth* is set lower than the *Bottom*, in the *View Range*, the objects that occur between the bottom and the view depth, represented by the hatched area, have a special override applied to their linework. Revit has a special *Line Style* named "<beyond>" and its settings are applied to those lines.

The arrows in the image below point out the edges of elements, footings in this case, that will appear dashed due to them falling in the hatched area and the "<beyond>" line type being set to a dashed or hidden line pattern.

FYI: *The View Depth must be equal to or lower than the Bottom setting.*

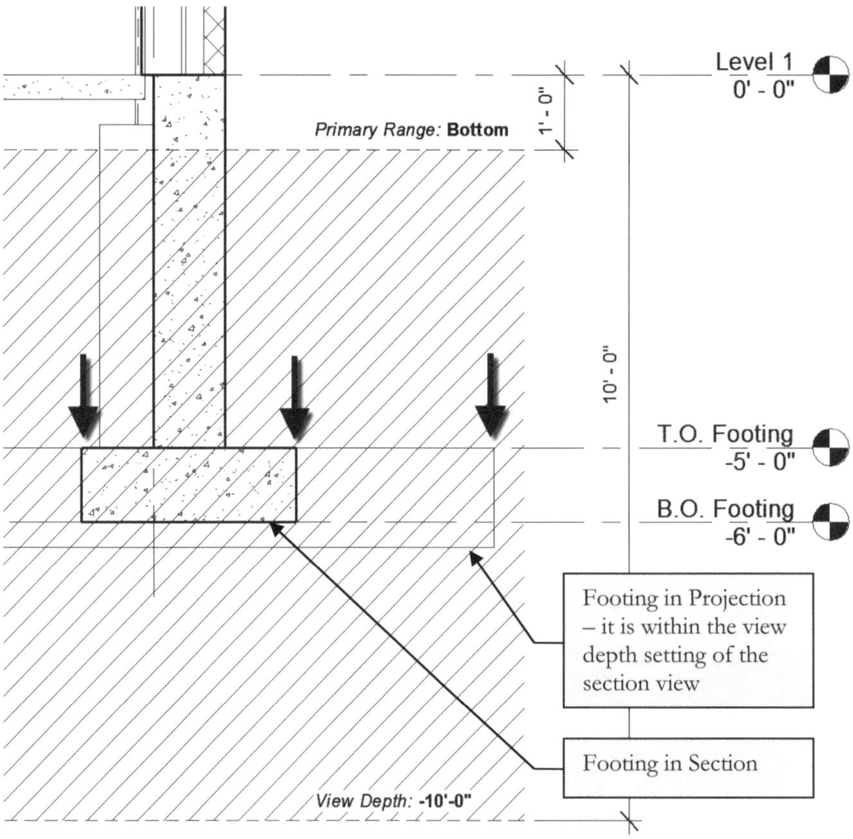

FIGURE 8-5.13 Section showing view range settings

Exercise 8-6:
Structural Annotation and Tags

In this last section specifically on Revit's *Structure* related workflows, you will look at a few of the tools used to annotate the structural plans. Addition of text, dimensions and tags is an important part of the design process. Revit makes these tasks simple and efficient. All of the dimensions and tags you will add automatically display the correct information because the data is coming directly from the Revit elements being referenced.

Even though this is the only chapter specifically devoted to Revit's *Structural* tools, it should be pointed out that many of the concepts covered in this book also apply to structural design and modeling. For example, creating sections and elevations works the same way in all disciplines working in Revit, as do the following:

- Elevations and Sections (Chapter 10)
- Placing stand-alone content (Chapter 11)
- Creating schedules (Chapter 12)
- Producing photo-realistic renderings (Chapter 15)
- Placing Views on Sheets (Chapter 16)
- Sheet index (Chapter 16)
- Phasing and Worksharing (Chapter 17)
- Creating custom Families (Chapter 18)

Dimensions:

Placing Dimensions is quick and simple in Revit; you select the *Aligned* dimension tool, select two elements you want to dimension between and click somewhere to position the dimension line and text. Anytime either of the elements move, Revit updates the dimension automatically. If either of the elements being dimensioned are deleted, the dimension is deleted. The dimension will be deleted even if the dimension is not visible in the current view. For example, if a grid is deleted in a section view, all of the dimensions to that grid will be deleted in the plan views.

Dimensions can be single or continuous; the image below shows one of each. The two 10′-0″ dimensions on the bottom are one element, not two; therefore, they move together and are quicker to place.

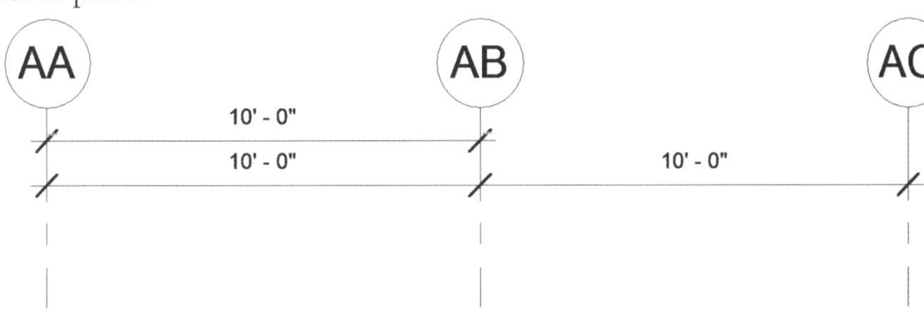

FIGURE 8-6.1 Dimensions; single or continuous

One more important thing to know about dimensions is that they are view specific; in fact, everything on the *Annotate* tab is view specific. This means the notes, dimensions and tags will only show up in the view they were created in, which makes sense; you do not want the structural beam tags showing up in the architect's floor plans or their door tags and notes about scribing a cabinet to a wall showing up in the structural plans. Only 3D elements show up in all views. Annotation is considered a 2D element.

Now you will dimension the grids in the **Level 2 – Structural Framing Plan** view.

1. **Open** your law office model.

2. Switch to the **Level 2 – Structural Framing Plan** view.

3. Select **Annotate → Dimension → Aligned** from the *Ribbon.*

4. Select Grid 1 and Grid 5 (first 2 of 3 picks required).

5. Select a spot just below the grid bubbles to locate the string of dimensions (pick 3 of 3). See Figure 8-6.2.

    a. The dimension should read **102′-0.″**

    ***FYI:** The last pick cannot be near something that is dimensional, as Revit will just place another witness line there rather than place the dimension. If you accidentally pick something, you pick it again to toggle that witness line off and then pick your final point away from it.*

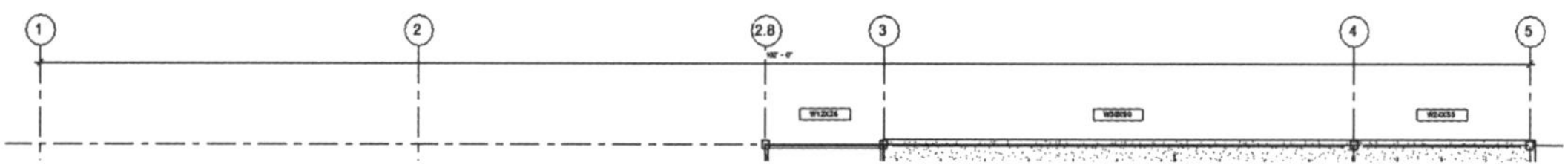

FIGURE 8-6.2 Overall dimension placed

Now you will add a second dimension line showing the major sections of the North side of the building.

6. Using the ***Aligned*** dimension tool again, pick Grid lines 1, 2.8 and 5 (first 3 of 4 picks). See Figure 8-6.3.

7. For your final pick, click near the previous dimension, but wait until you find the snap position where Revit indicates the standard distance between dimensions.

    a. The dimensions should read **50′-0″** and **52′-0″** respectively.

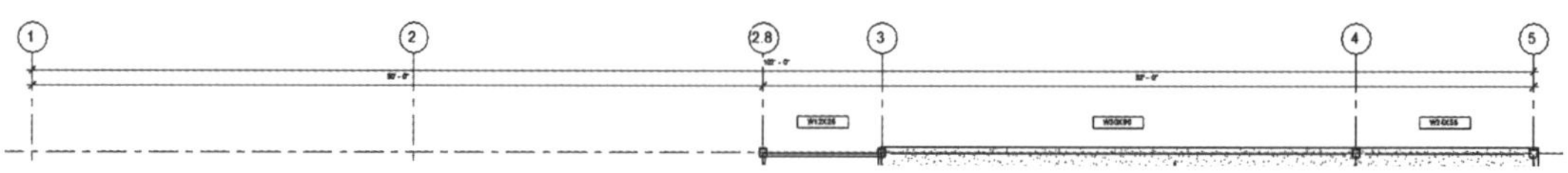

FIGURE 8-6.3 Second dimension placed

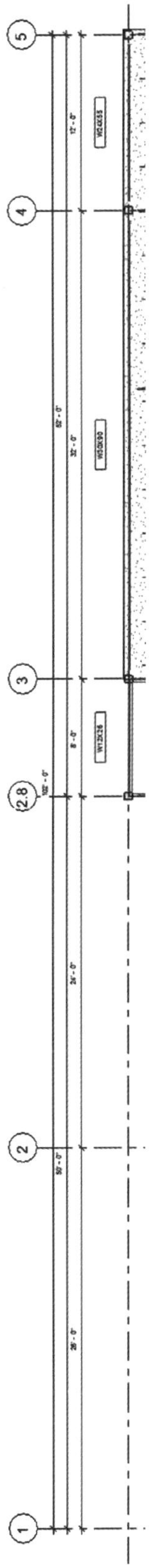

Next, you will create one more string of dimensions which locate each individual grid in the project.

8. Dimension each grid line as shown in Figure 8-6.4, placing the string at the standard spacing location.
    a. The dimensions should read, from left to right:
        i. 26′-0″
        ii. 24′-0″
        iii. 8′-0″
        iv. 32′-0″
        v. 12′-0″

If any of your dimensions do not work, you may go back and double check your previous work. However, if you are using the chapter starter files from the online files provided with this book, you should not have any problems.

Now you will place dimensions along the East side of the building.

9. Place the dimensions as shown in Figure 8-6.5.

Note how the dimensions automatically rotate to align with the elements being dimensioned, grids in this case. You would need to use the *Linear* dimension tool if you want to force the dimension to be vertical or horizontal for angled elements.

Dimensions can be selected and deleted at any time; this has no effect on the elements being dimensioned. Dimensions can also be hidden in any view via the "VV" shortcut.

FIGURE 8-6.4 Third dimension placed - image rotated to increase size

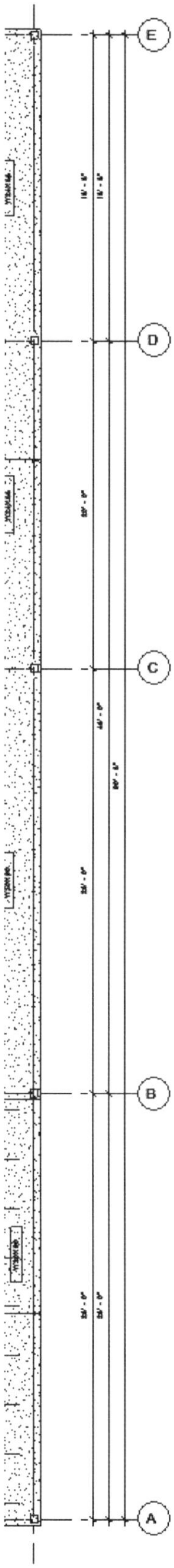

10. Add two dimensions to locate the grids near the curved beams as shown in Figure 8-6.6.

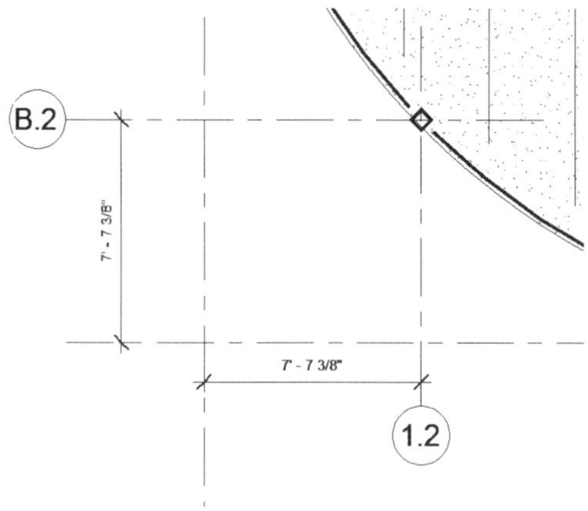

FIGURE 8-6.6 Dimension near curved beam

Even though the dimensions do not show up in the other plan views, you will want them in each of the structural plans. Next, you will learn how to quickly copy the dimensions from one view to another. This only works when there is something there for the Revit dimensions to latch onto. Your grids are, of course, consistent in each view so this method will work.

11. Select all the dimensions just placed in this exercise, by holding the Ctrl key and selecting them, or use the Filter feature.

12. Select **Copy** in the Clipboard panel of the Ribbon, not the Copy icon on the Modify panel.

13. Switch to the **Level 1 – Structural Slab and Foundation Plan** view.

14. Select **Modify → Clipboard → Paste → Aligned to Current View**.

The dimensions are now placed in the current view; you did not have to place them manually!

15. Adjust the grid bubble location so no dimensions are overlapping the large spread footings.

FIGURE 8-6.5 Additional dimension placed

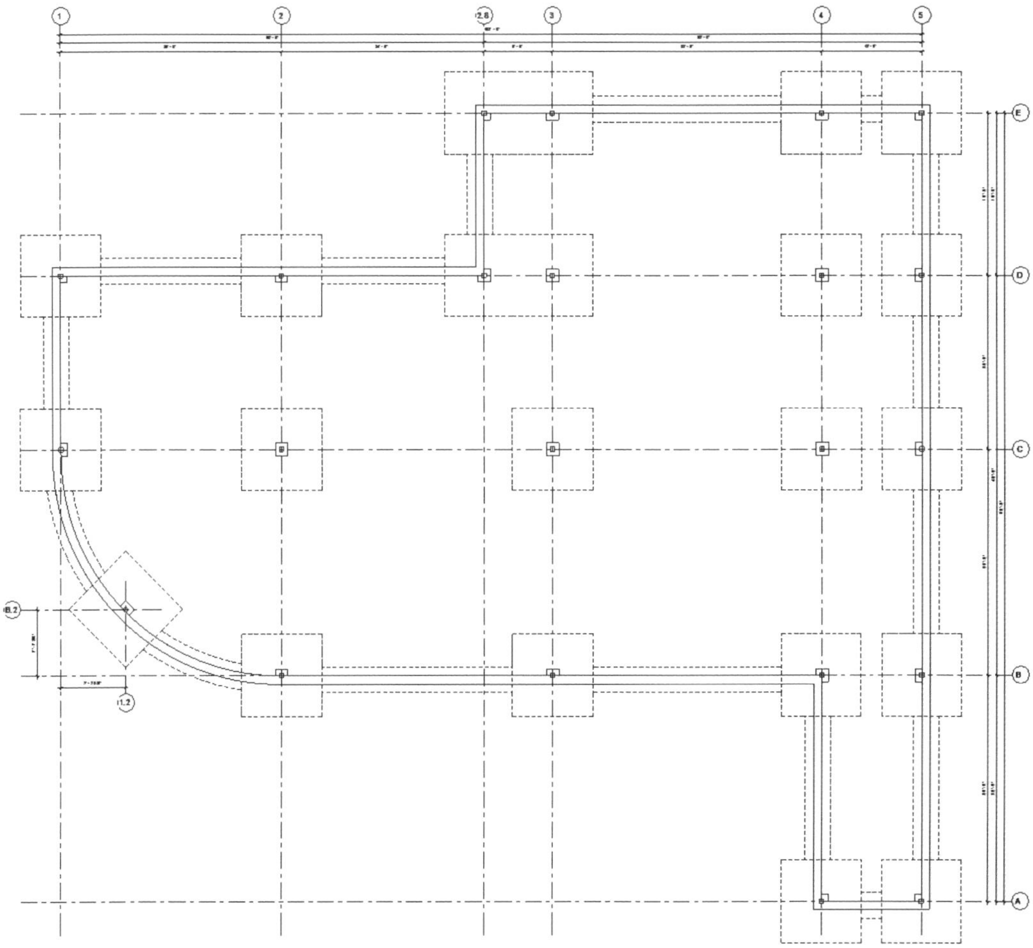

FIGURE 8-6.7 Dimension copied to another view

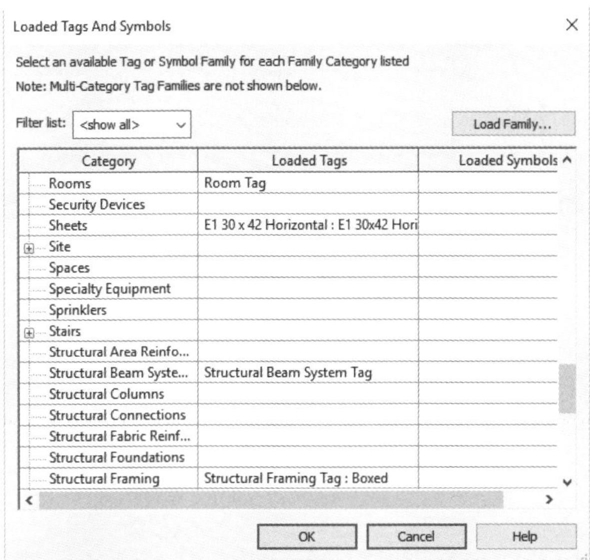

FIGURE 8-6.8 Loaded tags and symbols dialog

Placing Tags:

Most elements in Revit can be tagged. Each element category has its own tag family option, which means beams can have a different looking tag than footings; they can also display different information. Not all tags are loaded for every element. You may find that after trying to tag something, a tag for that type of element is not loaded and you have to use the *Load Family* tool to get one.

It is possible to have more than one tag for each element. You can use the *Loaded Tags And Symbols* tool, in the *Tag* panel fly out, to specify which tag is the default; see Figure 8-6.8. Whenever a tag is selected you can swap it with other loaded tags within the tagged elements category. As an example, you may want most beam tags to simply list the beam size. However, some may want to list camber, studs, etc. You may have several tags loaded which can report this information in the tag. One element can even have more than one tag.

Tags can be deleted at any time without losing information. All information displayed by a tag is coming from the element which it tags.

16. Switch to the **Level 2 – Structural Framing Plan** view.

17. Select **Annotate → Tag → Tag by Category** from the *Ribbon*.

18. **Uncheck Leader** on the *Ribbon*.

    a. We do not want a line with an arrow from the tag to the element.

19. Pick one of the curved beams in the Southwestern corner of the building; be careful not to select the floor as it can be tagged as well.

The tag is automatically placed at the midpoint of the curved beam, and rotated to align with the beam at that point. The tag can be selected and repositioned to avoid overlapping of text and geometry (Figure 8-6.9).

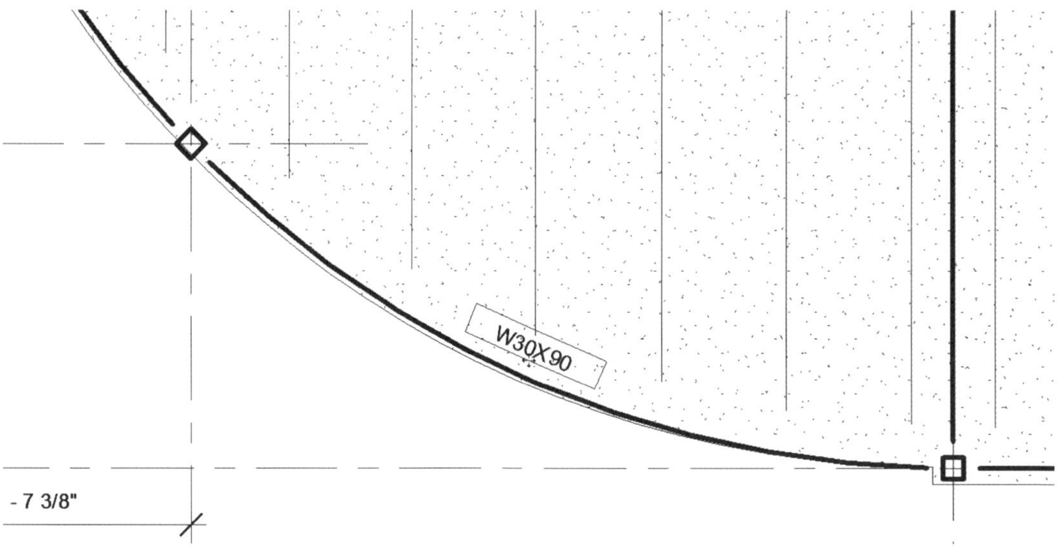

FIGURE 8-6.9 Beam tag placed; the tag is currently selected

20. Place a tag for the other curved beam.

Next you will place *Beam System* symbols. These will be added around the floor opening in the Northeastern corner of the plan.

21. Zoom into the area at Grids 3/4 and E/D.

22. Select **Annotate → Symbol → Beam** from the *Ribbon*.

23. Hover over the *Beam System* until it highlights with heavy dashed lines as in Figure 8-6.10, and then **click**.

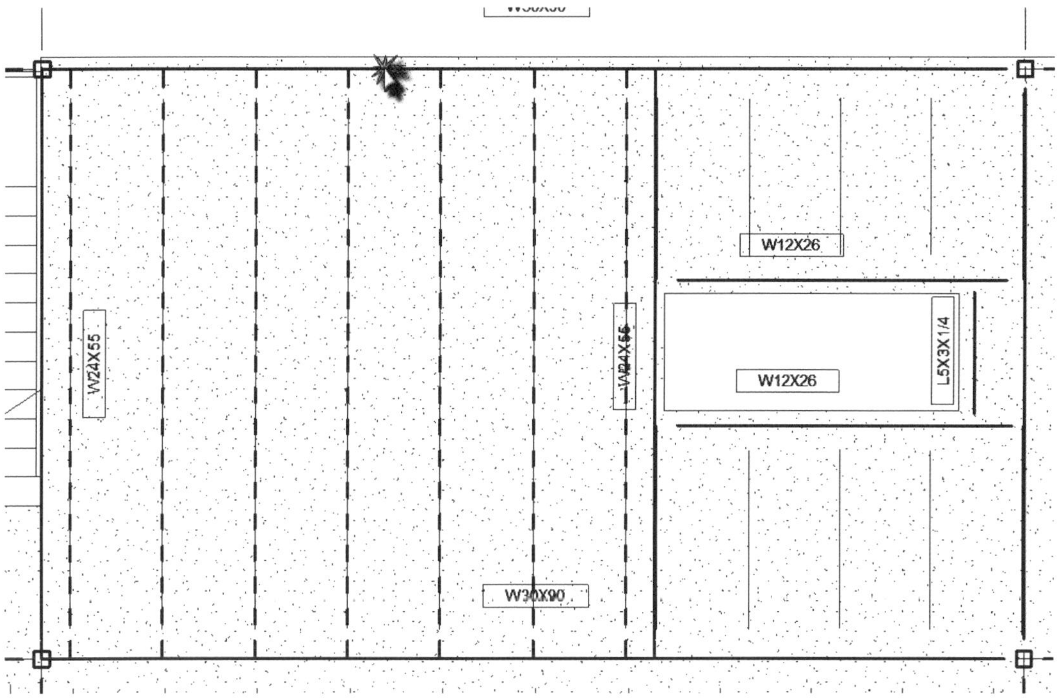

FIGURE 8-6.10 Placing a beam system symbol

24. Now click anywhere near the center of the *Beam System* to position the symbol; do not overlap the beam tags at the perimeter.

25. Repeat these steps for the two smaller beams to the right (if needed).

The Beam System symbol is now placed as shown in Figure 8-6.11.

Like tags, beam system symbols can also be selected and then moved or deleted. The size of the text and arrows for all tags, dimensions and symbols updates automatically whenever the view scale is changed.

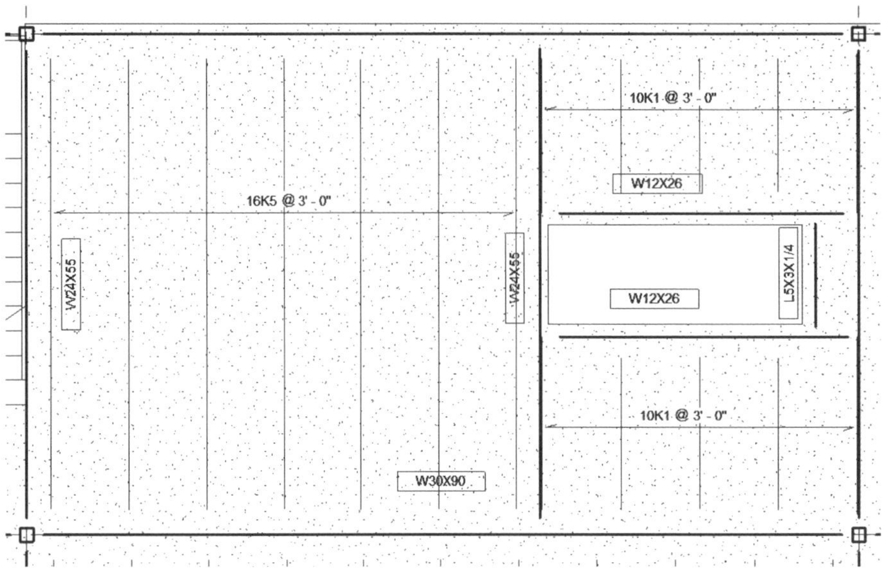

FIGURE 8-6.11 Beam system symbols placed

This is all the time that will be devoted to annotation specifically in Revit *Structure*. There are several other aspects that could be covered but fall outside of the scope of this textbook. For example, it is possible to set up a spot elevation that will report the elevation of the beam relative to the finished floor level. This information could be added directly to the beam tag.

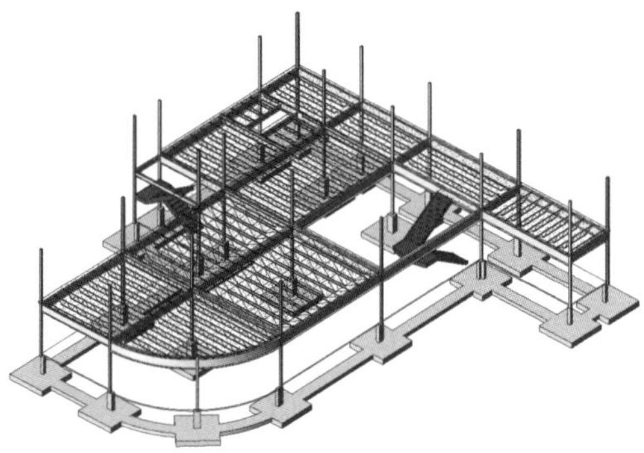

Setting Up a 3D Structural Model View:

It would be useful to set up a 3D view just for the structural portion of the model. Follow these steps if you would like to do so:

- Right-click and duplicate the ***Default 3D View***, named {3D}.
- Rename the view to **Structural 3D View**.
- Change the *Discipline* to **Structural** in the *Properties Palette.*
- Type **VV**.
- Turn off everything except the "structural" categories; make sure the "Show categories from all disciplines" option near the bottom is checked.
    - Leave floors and stairs on as well.
    - Set the *Transparent* option to 75 for the *Floors.*

That is it; you now have a permanent 3D view for the structural BIM.

26. **Save** and **back up** your work.

Self-Exam:

The following questions can be used as a way to check your knowledge of this lesson. The answers can be found at the bottom of this page.

1. *Revit 2025* cannot open *Revit 2027* projects. (T/F)
2. When you load a beam, every possible size is loaded. (T/F)
3. Tags can be automatically added when placing a beam. (T/F)
4. Use the ______________ tool to narrow down the current selection.
5. The _____________________ controls what part of the building a view is cutting through.

Review Questions:

The following questions may be assigned by your instructor as a way to assess your knowledge of this section. Your instructor has the answers to the review questions.

1. Revit *Structure* cannot create curved beams. (T/F)
2. Revit's structural tools are available to anyone with the Revit software. (T/F)
3. The *Transfer Project Standards* feature can be used to import several structural settings into a project. (T/F)
4. Structural floor elements can show the profile of metal deck in sections. (T/F)
5. A *Type Catalog* allows you to select and load only the types you want from a family which contains a large number of types. (T/F)
6. Revit columns can only extend from one floor to the next. (T/F)
7. When a grid is selected, if the icon near it says 2D, it will only move the grid bubble location in the current view. (T/F)
8. Use a _______________________ to quickly lay out the joists in a structural bay.
9. Beam elevations need to be changed to accommodate joist bearing conditions. (T/F)
10. It is not a good idea to delete tags as important information may be lost. (T/F)

SELF-EXAM ANSWERS:
1 - T, **2** – F, **3** - T, **4** - Filter, **5** – View Range

Notes:

Lesson 9
Annotation:

This chapter covers annotations in Revit: text, dimensions, tags, shared parameters, and keynotes. In print, the drawings are often insufficient to convey the design intent. These tools enable effective communication for those using the final printed drawings to both bid and build the building. Several of the chapters following this one will utilize many of these concepts.

All the tools covered in this chapter are found on the Annotate tab. Three of the tools on this tab are also on the Quick Access Toolbar because they are used often: **Dimension**, **Tag by Category**, and **Text**.

TIP: All the tools on the Annotate tab are 2D and view-specific.

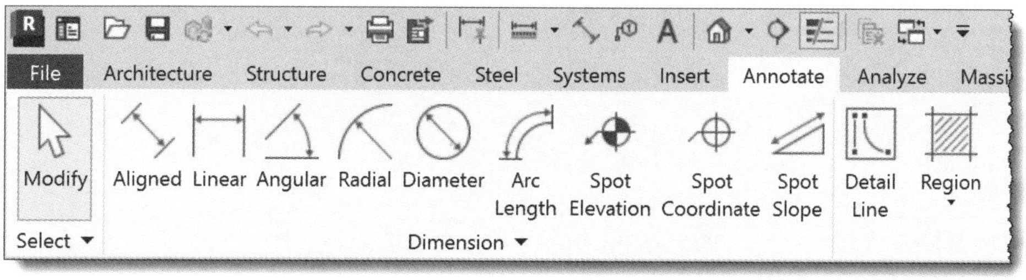

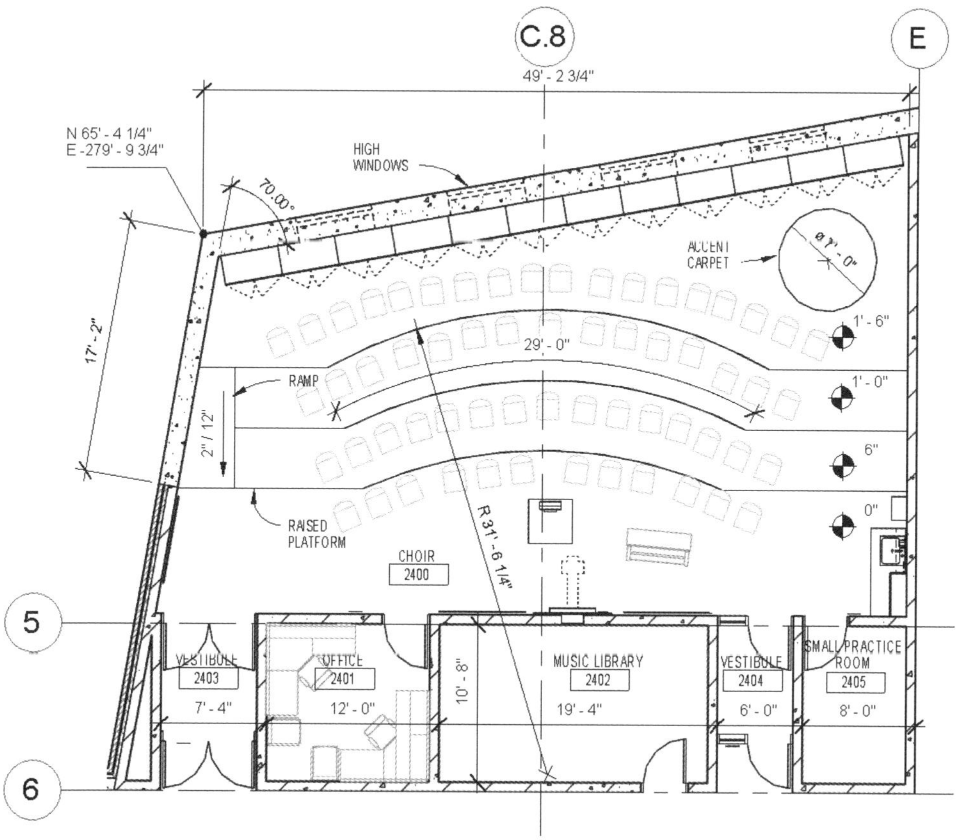

Exercise 9-1:
Text

This section covers placing notes using the **Text** command in Revit. We will also look at Revit's **Spell Check** and **Find/Replace** tools, including their limitations.

The first thing to know about the text tool is that it should be used as little as possible! Rather, dynamic tags, keynotes, and dimensions are preferred over static text to ensure the information is correct. Text will not update or move when something in the model changes—especially if the text is not visible or in the view where the model is being changed.

That said, the text command is still necessary and is often used in Revit.

Steps to add new Text to a view:

- Start the **Text** command
- Verify the **Text Style**
- Define the starting point; **click** *or* **click and drag**
- **Type** the desired text, typically without pressing *Enter*
- **Click away** from the text to finish the command

Steps to edit existing text:

- Select the text
- Click again to enter edit mode

Text

The Text tool can be started from the **Quick Access Toolbar**, the **Annotate** tab, or by typing **TX** on the keyboard.

The first step is to consider the current text type in the Type Selector (Figure 9-1.1). When creating new text types, the name of a text type should, at a minimum, contain the size and font name. The size is the **actual size on the printed page,** regardless of the drawing scale.

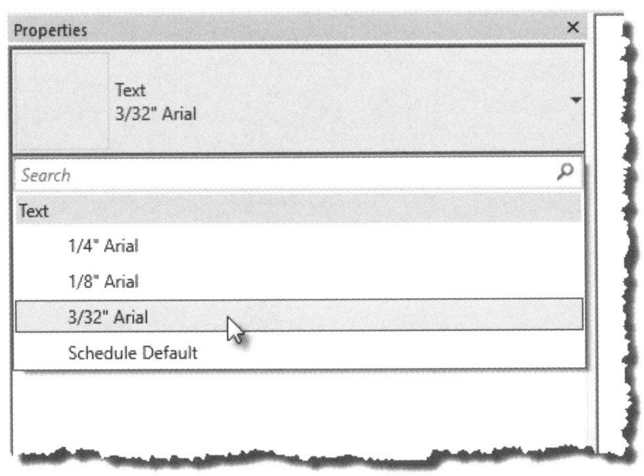

FIGURE 9-1.1 Type selector with text command active

There are additional steps that are optional, but at this point, you could click or click and drag within the drawing window and start typing your desired note.

Here is the difference between the **click** and **click and drag** options when starting text:

- **Click**: Defines the starting point for new text. No automatic return to next line while typing. An Enter must be pressed to start a new line; this is called a "hard return" in the word processing world.
- **Click and Drag**: This defines a windowed area where text will be entered. The height is not really important. The width determines when a line automatically returns to the next line while typing. Using this method allows paragraphs to be easily adjusted by dragging an edge of the selected textbox.

As long as "hard returns" are not used, the textbox width and number of rows adjust dynamically. To adjust the textbox, select the text, then use the round grip on the right (See Figure 9-1.2) to reposition it via click-and-drag with the left mouse button.

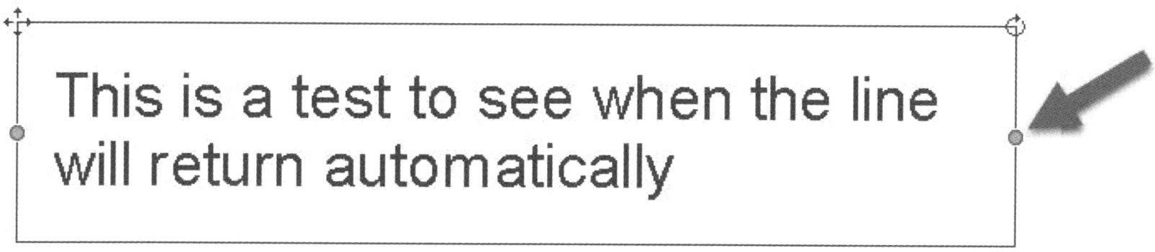

FIGURE 9-1.2 Selecting text and adjusting width of the textbox

The image to the right, Figure 9-1.3, shows the result of adjusting the width of the textbox—the text element went from two lines to four.

If an Enter is pressed at the end of each line of text when originally typed, the text will not automatically adjust as just described. An example of this can be seen in the following two images, Figure 9-1.4 & 5. Note that in some cases, this is desirable to ensure the text's formatting is not changed.

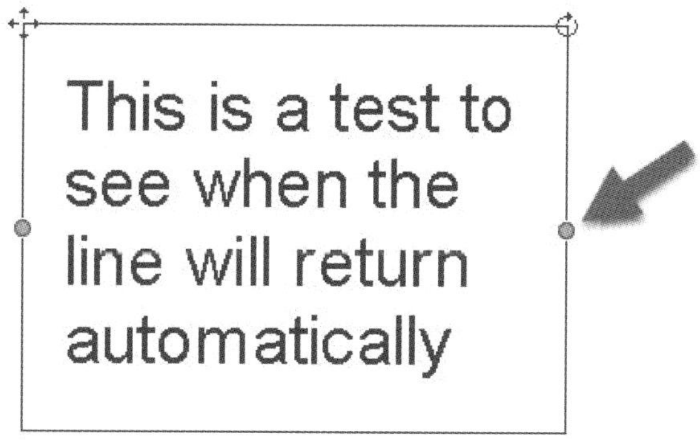

FIGURE 9-1.3 Text width adjusted

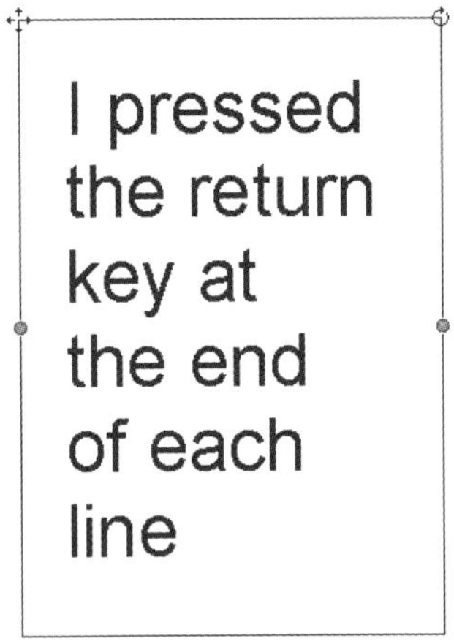

FIGURE 9-1.4
Text with hard returns

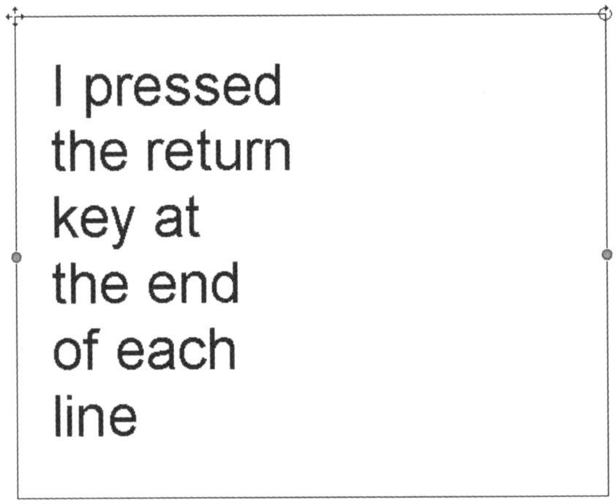

FIGURE 9-1.5
Text does not adjust when textbox width is modified

Keep in mind that this text tool is strictly 2D and view-specific. If the same text is required in multiple views, it either needs to be retyped or copied and pasted. However, for general notes that might appear on all floor plan sheets, a Legend View can be used.

Revit has a separate tool, on the Architecture tab, called **Model Text** for instances when 3D text is needed within the model. Model text is usually associated with something built by the contractor or manufacturer, such as a sign or the building's address.

Text Placement & Formatting Options

In addition to the basic topics covered, there are several options for text placement. These adjustments can be applied when creating the text initially or at any time later.

The formatting options are mainly found on the Ribbon immediately after activating the Text command.

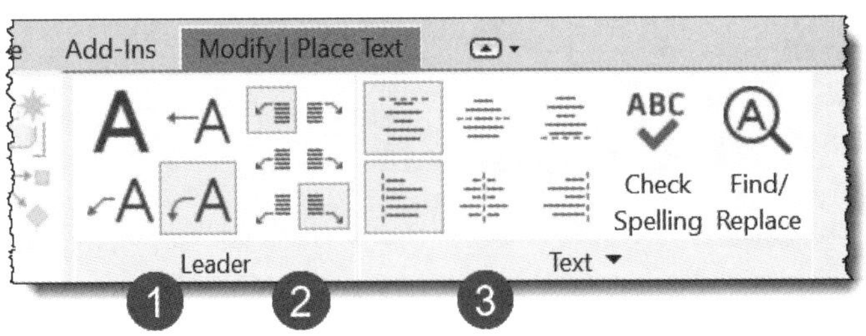

FIGURE 9-1.6 Formatting options on the Ribbon while creating text

The formatting options identified in the image are:

1. Leader options
2. Leader position options
3. Text Justification/Alignment

Leader Options

A leader is a line that extends from the text, with an arrow at its end, used to point to something in the drawing.

The default option, when using the text command, is no leader. This is the highlighted option in the upper left.

The remaining three options determine the graphical appearance of the leader: one segment, two segments, or curved, as seen in Figure 9-1.7. Often, a design firm will standardize on one of these three options for a consistent look.

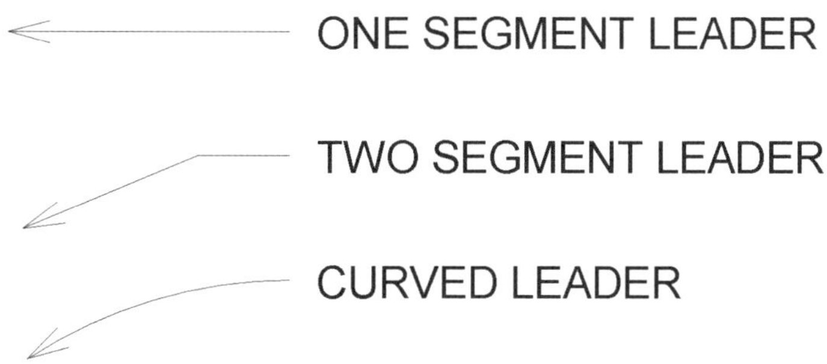

FIGURE 9-1.7 Leader formatting options

Here are the steps to include a leader with text:

- Start the **Text** command
- Select text type via **Type Selector**
- Select **Leader** option
- Specify **leader location** (2-3 picks)
- **Type** text
- Click **Close**, or click away from text, to finish

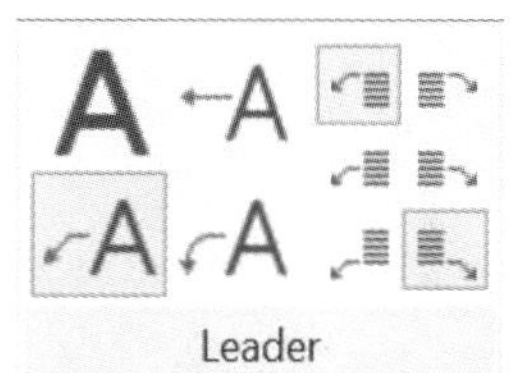

Leader Options

Once text with a leader is created, it can be selected and modified later if needed. In the next image, Figure 9-1.8, notice the two **circle grips** associated with the leader: at the arrow (magenta-colored grip) and the change in direction of the line (yellow-colored grip); the other two circle grips are for the textbox as previously described in this section. These two grips can be repositioned by clicking and dragging the left mouse button.

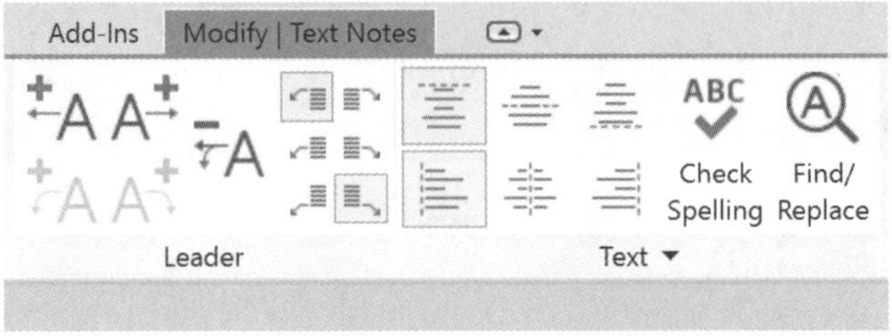

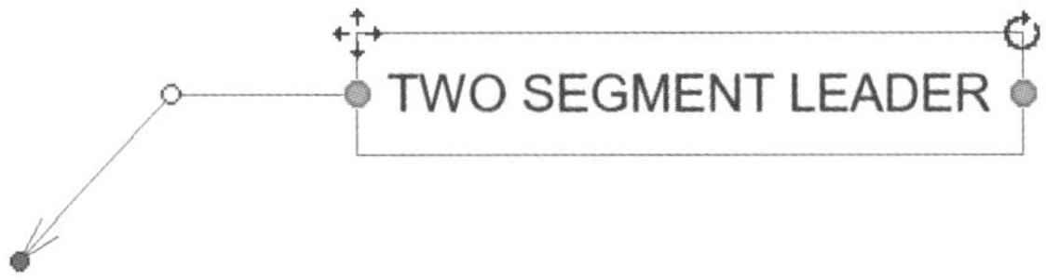

FIGURE 9-1.8 Text with leader selected; notice leader grips and Ribbon options

When text is selected, the Ribbon displays slightly different options for leaders as seen in the image above. It is possible to have multiple leaders (i.e., arrows) coming off the text—denoted by the green "plus" symbol. In the next image, Figure 9-1.9, a second leader was added on the left, and another on the right. It is not possible to have both curved and straight leader lines for the same text element. In this example, the curved leader options are grayed out as seen in Figure 9-1.8.

FIGURE 9-1.9 Multiple leaders added

Back in Figure 9-1.8, notice that leaders can be removed, even to the point where the text has no leaders. The one catch with the **remove leader** option is that they can only be removed in the reverse order in which they were added.

The **Leader Arrowhead** can be changed graphically (i.e., solid dot, loop leader, etc.). This will be covered in the section on Managing Text Types, as this setting is in the Type Properties for the text itself.

> ***Good to know…***
> Text can be placed in **any view** and on **sheets**. The only exception is that the Text command does not work in schedule views.
>
> Text can also be in a **Group**. When the group only has elements from the Annotate tab, it is a Detail Group. When the group also contains model elements, the text is in an Attached Detail Group. When a Model Group is placed, selecting it gives the option to add the Attached Detail Group.

Leader Position Options

These six toggles control the position of the leader relative to the text as seen in the two images below (Figures 9-1.10 and 11). These options also appear in the Properties Palette when text is selected, called **Left Attachment** and **Right Attachment**.

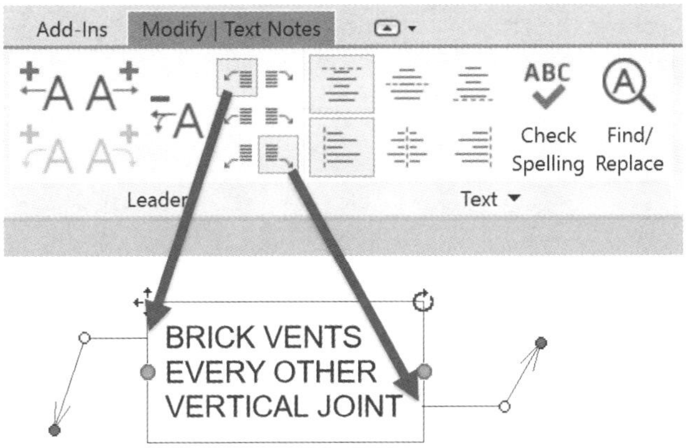

FIGURE 9-1.10 Leader position toggles – example A

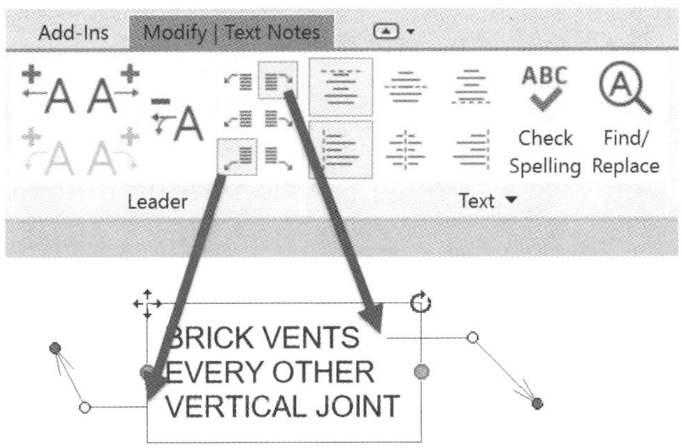

FIGURE 9-1.11 Leader position toggles – example B

Similar to a leader type, design firms will often select a standard that everyone is expected to follow so construction documents look consistent.

Text Justification
When text is selected, there are three options for horizontal justification on the Ribbon: Left, Center, and Right. The results are shown in the three images in Figure 9-1.12.

This option also appears in the Properties Palette when text is selected, called **Horizontal Align**. Keep in mind that all options in the Property Palette are instance parameters—meaning they only apply to the instance(s) selected. Thus, each text entity in Revit can have different settings.

Text Formatting
The next section to cover is the options to make text Bold, Italic, or Underlined.

These options do not appear in the Properties Palette because they can be applied to individual words (or even individual characters). In the example below, the word "Brick" is bold, "other" is italicized, and "vertical" is underlined.

If all the text is selected and set to one of these three options, any future edits will also retain these settings.

FYI: Notice the formatting options are different when editing the text, compared to when the text element is simply selected.

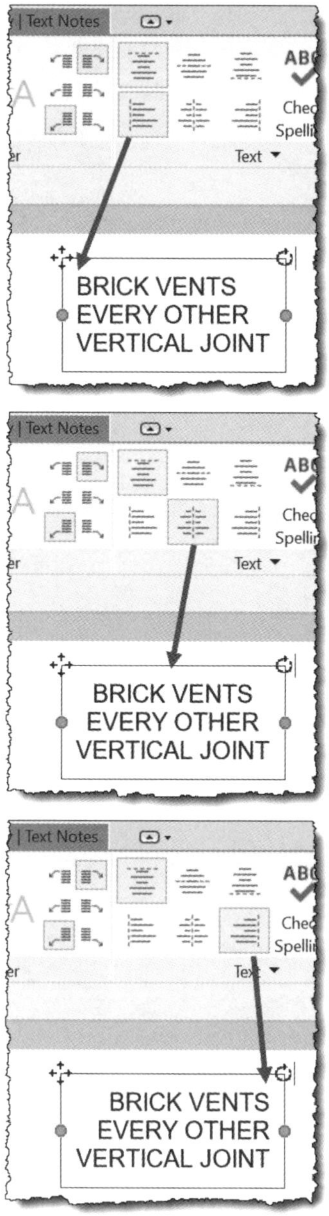

FIGURE 9-1.12 Text justification options

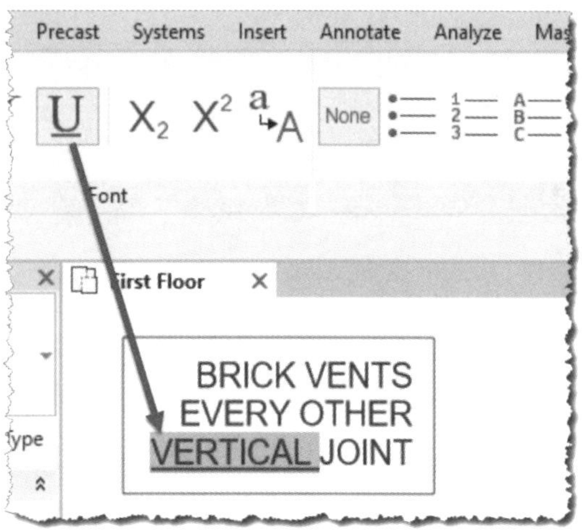

FIGURE 9-1.13 Text formatting

Text Formatting

The next section to cover is the **List** options on the Paragraph panel. This feature is only available while editing the textbox contents; to do so, select the text and click it to enter edit mode.

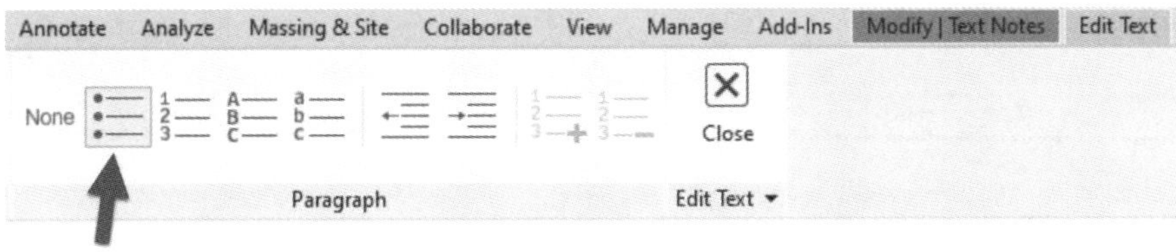

- 4" FACE BRICK
- 1" AIR SPACE
- 3" RIGID INSULATION
- 8" CONCRETE MASONRY UNIT (CMU)
- 3 5/8" MTL STUDS AT 16" O.C.
- 5/8" GYP BD

1. 4" FACE BRICK
2. 1" AIR SPACE
3. 3" RIGID INSULATION
4. 8" CONCRETE MASONRY UNIT (CMU)
5. 3 5/8" MTL STUDS AT 16" O.C.
6. 5/8" GYP BD

a. 4" FACE BRICK
b. 1" AIR SPACE
c. 3" RIGID INSULATION
d. 8" CONCRETE MASONRY UNIT (CMU)
e. 3 5/8" MTL STUDS AT 16" O.C.
f. 5/8" GYP BD

A. 4" FACE BRICK
B. 1" AIR SPACE
C. 3" RIGID INSULATION
D. 8" CONCRETE MASONRY UNIT (CMU)
E. 3 5/8" MTL STUDS AT 16" O.C.
F. 5/8" GYP BD

FIGURE 9-1.14 Four options to define a line within text

This is one case where you must press Enter to force the following text to a new line and automatically generate a list (i.e., bullet, letter, or number).

Clicking the **Increase Indent** tool will indent the list as shown below (Figure 9-1.15). To undo this later, click in that row and select **Decrease Indent**. There does not appear to be a way to change the indented list spacing. Using the backspace key, then indenting again, creates an indent without a number/letter.

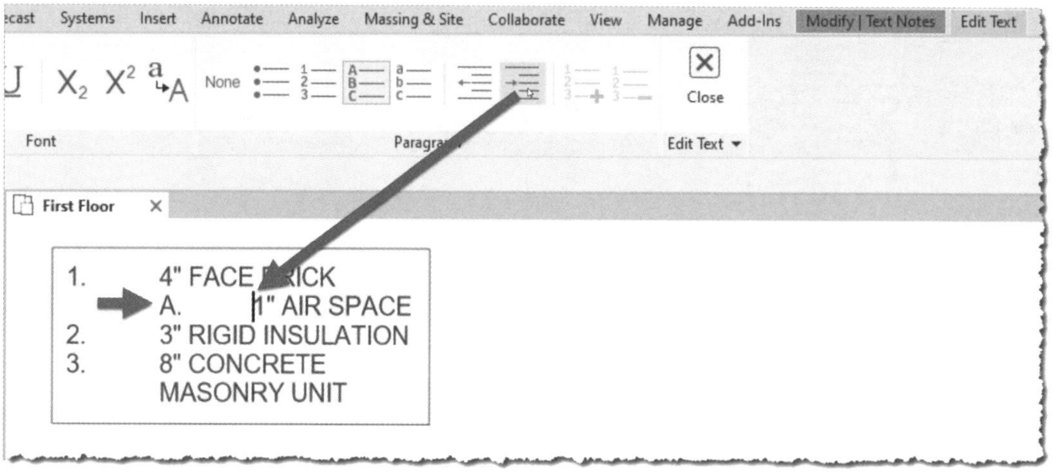

FIGURE 9-1.15 Indenting within a list

Clicking within the first row and selecting the plus or minus icons lets you change the starting number/letter of the list.

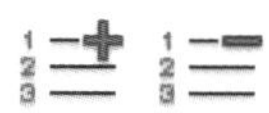

The text formatting options also allow for **subscript** and **superscript** as shown in the example below (Figure 9-1.16).

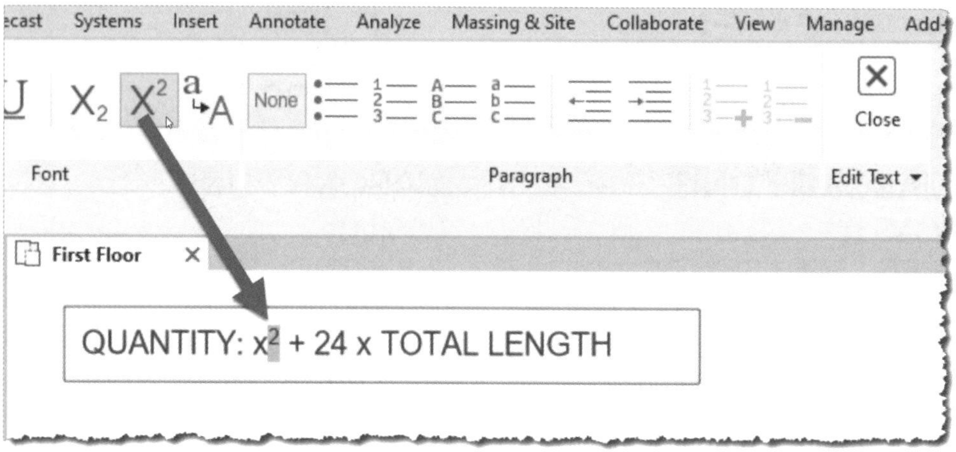

FIGURE 9-1.16 Superscript example

Also, notice the **All Caps** icon; clicking it will change the selected text to all uppercase. When this feature is used, Revit remembers the original formatting; toggling off the All Caps feature later restores the original formatting.

Managing Text Types

When using the text tool, the options in the Type Selector are determined by **Text Types** defined in the current project. Most design firms will have all the Text Types they need defined within their template.

There are two ways to access the text type properties. One is to start the Text command and then click **Edit Type** in the Properties Palette. The other is to click the arrow in the Text panel on the Annotate tab, as shown in the image below.

The **Type Properties**, as shown in the example to the right (Figure 9-1.17), are self-explanatory. Below is a brief description of each.

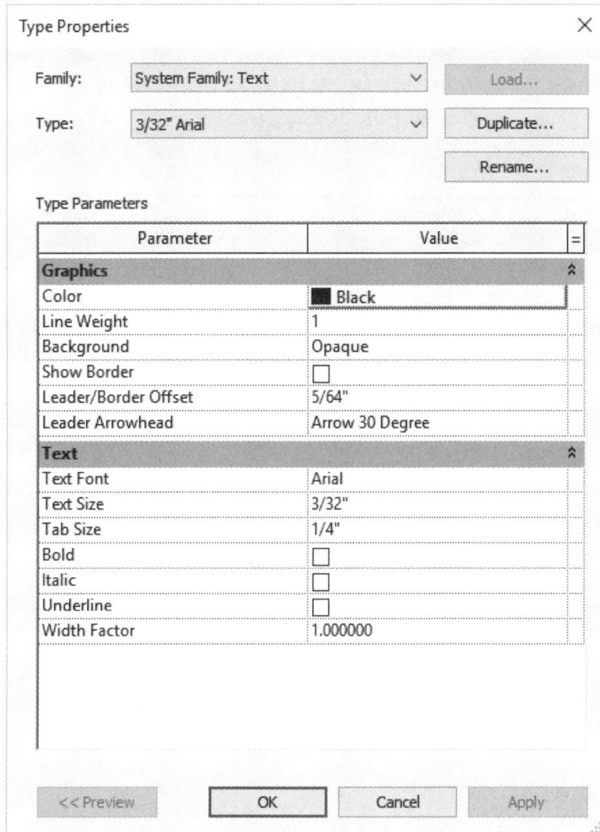

FIGURE 9-1.17 Text type properties

Command	*What it does…*
Color	This can affect printing, so it is often set to black.
Line Weight	This is only for the leader.
Background	*Toggle:* Opaque or Transparent
Show Border	*Check box:* Show or Hide
Leader/Border Offset	Space between text and border and leader – helpful when Background is set to Opaque.
Leader Arrowhead	Select from a list of predefined arrow types
Text Font	Select from a list of installed fonts on your computer
Text Size	Size of text on the printed page
Tab Size	Size of space when Tab is pressed (size on printed paper)
Bold	Default setting – can be changed while in edit mode
Italic	Default setting – can be changed while in edit mode
Underline	Default setting – can be changed while in edit mode
Width Factor	Adjusts the overall width of a line of text

Colors

The color applies to the text and the leader. The color is often set to black. If any other color is used, this can affect printing. For example, any color becomes a shade of gray when printed to a black-and-white printer—similar to printing a document from Microsoft Word, where green text is a darker shade of gray than yellow text. In the Print dialog, there is an option to print all colors as Black Lines, which can make colored text black. However, this also overrides gray lines and fill patterns.

Custom Fonts

Be careful using custom fonts installed on your computer, as others who do not have those fonts will likely not see the formatting the same as intended. Custom fonts can come from installing other software, such as Adobe InDesign. In fact, Autodesk also installs several custom fonts that are supposed to match some of the special SHX fonts that come with AutoCAD.

Custom Fonts

It is not possible to create custom arrowheads. However, the list of arrowheads is based on styles defined here: **Manage → Additional Settings → Arrowheads**. This provides many options for how these items look.

Width Factor

Some firms use a Width Factor like 0.75, 0.85, or similar to squish the text and fit more information on a sheet. Getting any narrower than this makes the text hard to read. This option actually changes the proportions of each letter, not just the space between them.

Misc.

Note that Text does not have a phase setting. Thus, the phase filters and overrides do not apply to text. It is sometimes desired to have text noting existing elements, such as ductwork, in a shade of gray rather than solid, and to reserve black for new elements.

Check Spelling

Revit has a tool that checks spelling. Keep in mind this only works on text created with the Text command and only for the current view. Revit cannot check the spelling of text in keynotes, tags, or families. Neither can it check the entire project.

The Spell Check tool can be found on the Annotate tab or on the Ribbon when text is selected. When Spell Check is selected, the dialog to the right appears if there are any misspellings found (Figure 9-1.18).

When Revit encounters a word not in the dictionary, it provides a list of possible correct words. Often, the first suggestion is the right one. If not, select from the list.

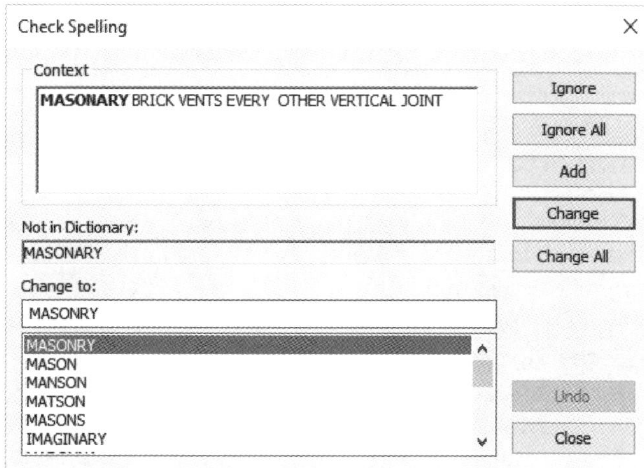

FIGURE 9-1.18 Check Spelling dialog

Clicking the **Change** button will correct the highlighted word. Clicking **Change All** will change all of the words with this same misspelling in the current view.

Sometimes Revit flags a word that isn't misspelled. This might be a company name, your name, a product name, or an industry abbreviation. In this case, one might select the **Add** option to add the word to the custom dictionary, so you don't have to deal with this every time you run spell check.

The image on the right shows the settings for the Spell Check engine. The options are self-explanatory. In an office, consider placing the custom dictionary on the server and pointing all users to it.

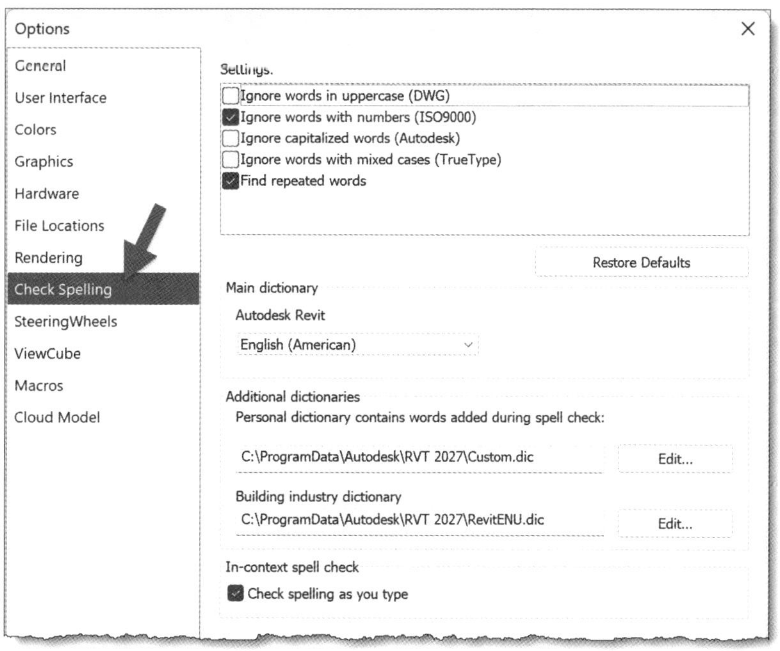

FIGURE 9-1.19 Check Spelling in Options dialog

Don't totally rely on Spell Check. A word may be spelled correctly but still be the wrong word. For example:

- Fill the **whole** with concrete and trowel level and smooth.
- Fill the **hole** with concrete and trowel level and smooth.

In this example, the word "whole" is wrong but spelled correctly. Also, keep in mind that Revit does not have a grammar-check system like popular word processing programs.

Find/Replace

Revit has a tool that lets you find or replace words within a view. Keep in mind, this only works on text created with the Text command. Revit cannot find or replace text in keynotes, tags, or families. Unlike the spelling tool, this tool can search the entire project.

When this tool is selected, the dialog to the right appears (Figure 9-1.20).

In this example, the current view is being searched for the brand name Sheetrock, so it can be replaced with the generic industry-standard term, **Gypsum Board**.

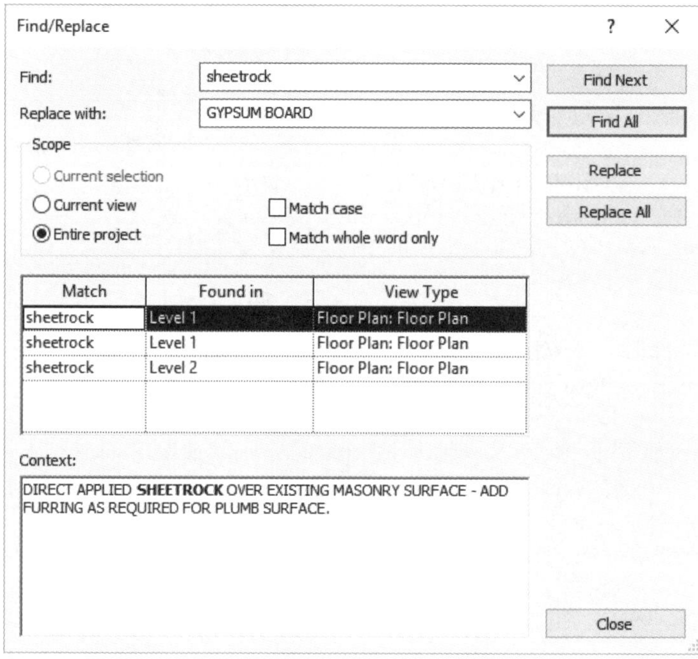

FIGURE 9-1.20 Find/Replace dialog

Selecting **Entire project** and then clicking **Find All** tells Revit to list all matches in the middle section of the dialog. For each row, you can click to select and see the context in which the found word(s) is used.

When items are found, the **Replace** or **Replace All** buttons can be used to swap out the text in one location or all. When clicking Replace, only the selected row is replaced.

This tool can be used to just find something and not replace it. For example, on a large project with hundreds of views in the Project Browser, using Find/Replace to search for details containing the word "roof drain" can significantly speed up locating the desired drawing.

Replacing a Text Type

In addition to replacing content within a text element, you can also replace the text type. For example, some imported details use a different font, and you want everything to match and be consistent. This is not really associated with the Find/Replace tool, but it is important to know how to accomplish this task.

> Replacing a Text Type within a view or project:
> - **Select** one text element within the project
> - **Right-click** (Fig. 9-1.21)
> - Pick **Select All Instances →**
>   - Visible in View
>   - In Entire Project
> - Select a different type from the **Type Selector**

This procedure will replace all the text in either the current view or the entire project. Even text that has been hidden with the "Hide in View" right-click option will be changed.

When a specific text type is selected, the selection count in the lower-right corner of the Revit window indicates the total number of elements selected (Figure 9-1.22). This can be used as a quick double check before replacing the text type. For example, if the intent was to replace only a few rogue text instances but the count was several hundred, this would be a clue that another view uses this text type and perhaps should not be changed, as it was created by someone else on the project. This can be especially true if multiple disciplines are working in the same project.

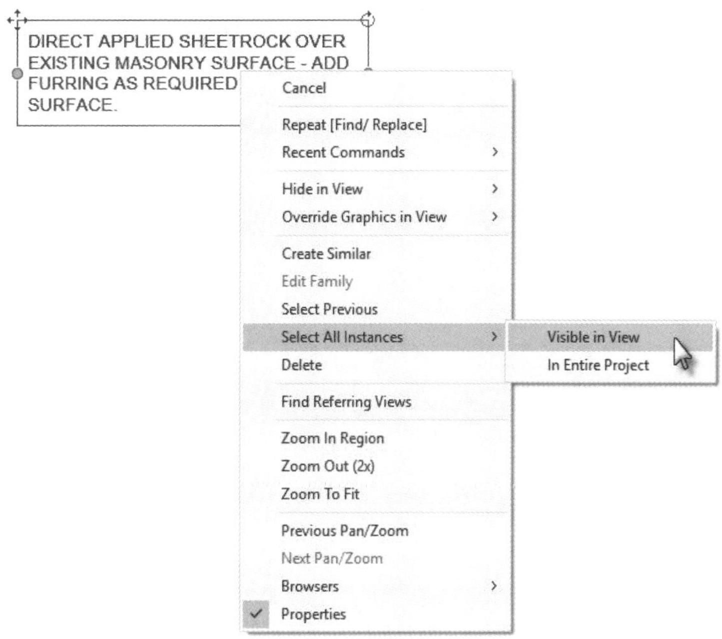

FIGURE 9-1.21 Select all instances via right-click

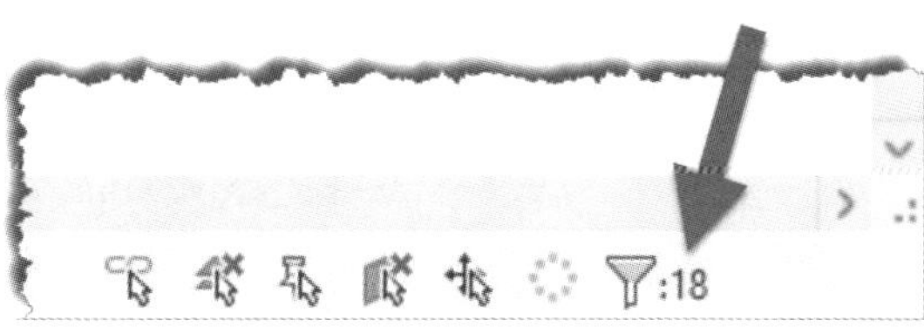

Exercise 9-2:
Dimensions

This exercise will cover the ins and outs of dimensioning in Revit.

The first thing to understand about dimensions is that they are 2D and view-specific—like all commands on the Annotate tab.

Dimension elements have an association with the thing(s) being dimensioned. If that thing(s) is deleted, the dimension will also be deleted, even if the dimension is not visible in the current view. For example, if a wall is deleted from a 3D view, then any dimensions associated with that wall, in a floor plan view, which may not even be open, will be deleted.

Because dimensions are associated with specific elements in the model, it is important to ensure the correct elements are selected when placing a dimension. In a floor plan, for example, the place to click to add a dimension may have several elements stacked on top of each other: grid line, wall edge, floor edge, window edge, and wall sweep. It may be necessary to tap the Tab key to cycle through the options and select the correct item (while tabbing, the highlighted element will appear in the status bar at the bottom of the screen).

Each dimension command will be covered in the order they appear on the Annotate tab, as seen in the image below.

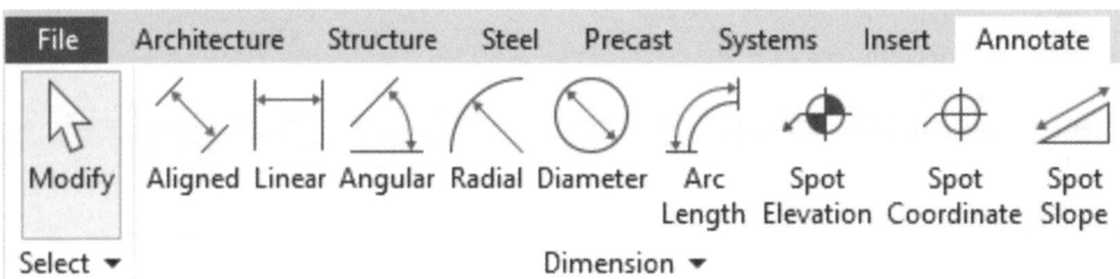

Command	*What it does (see image on next page)…*
1. *Aligned*	Most used dimension tool; dimension between parallel references (e.g., walls or ducts) or multiple points
2. *Linear*	Dimensions between points and always horizontal or vertical
3. *Angular*	Measures the angle between two references
4. *Radial*	Indicates the radius of a curved line or element
5. *Diameter*	Indicates the diameter of an arc or circle
6. *Arc Length*	Measures the length of a line/element along a curve
7. *Spot Elevation*	Lists the elevation at a selected point, on an element (e.g., floor, ceiling, toposolid)
8. *Spot Coordinate*	Indicates the N/S and E/W position of a selected point
9. *Spot Slope*	Used to indicate the slope of a ramp in plan or the pitch of a roof in elevation

The following floor plan example shows each dimension type used. This is a middle school choir room with various conditions in terms of dimensions, such as angled walls, curved lines, and multiple floor elevations.

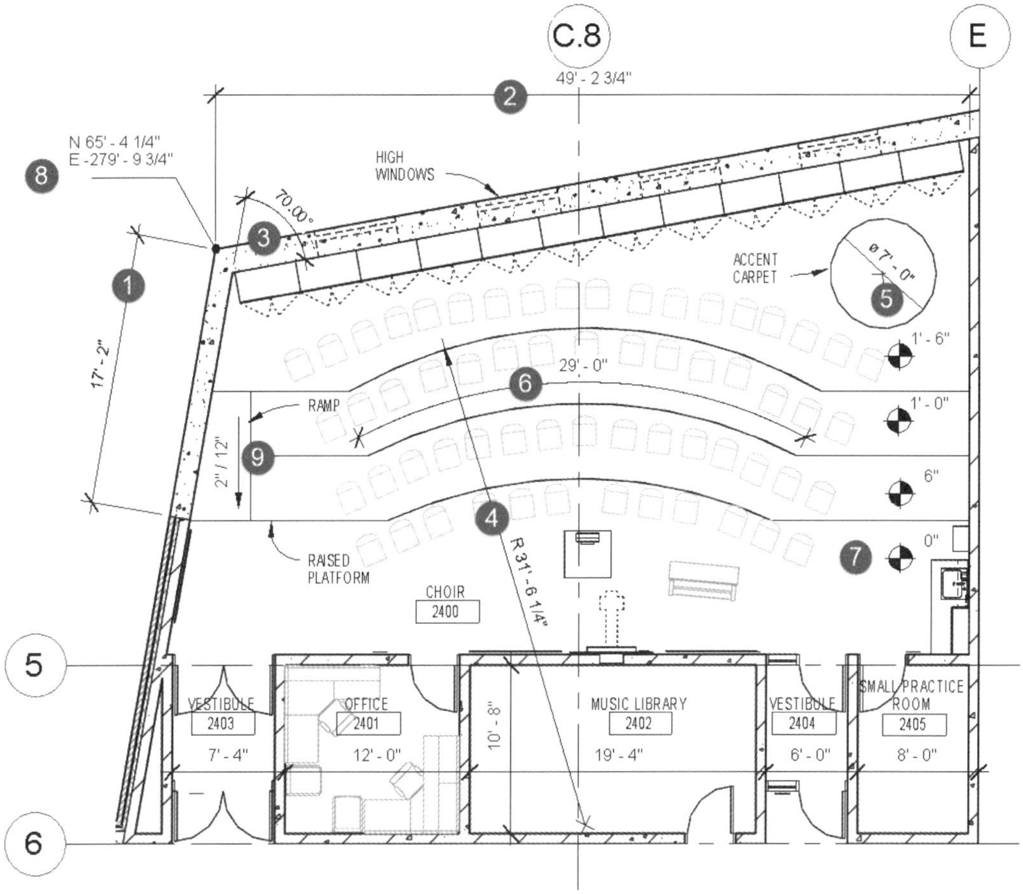

FIGURE 9-2.1 Example floor plan used for dimensioning study

Aligned - Dimension

This dimension tool is the most used of the dimension tools, and for this reason, it is also located on the Quick Access Toolbar (QAT).

Steps to add Aligned dimensions:

- Review **Type Selector** and **Ribbon** options
- **Select first reference**
    - o Click on the element ***or***
    - o Press tab to select a specific reference or intersection
- **Select second reference**
- Optional: Select additional references (creates a dimension string)
- **Click away** from anything dimensionable to finish the command

The **Align** dimension tool can create angled, horizontal, and vertical dimensions. When the tool is first started, the default "Prefer" option is to select **Wall Centerlines**, as indicated on the Ribbon. Clicking a wall starts a dimension line perpendicular to it. The second point could then be another wall at the same angle, or the endpoint or intersection of lines.

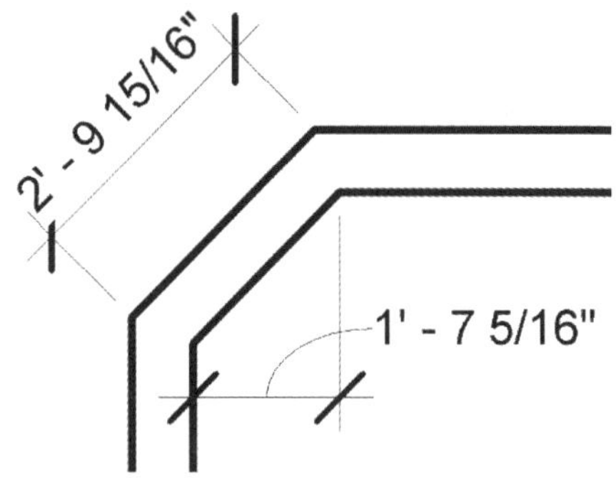

In the example to the right, if the vertical wall is rotated, the dimension will rotate with it. If the dimension must remain horizontal, use the Linear dimension option.

The image below shows the User Interface while the Aligned dimension tool is active.

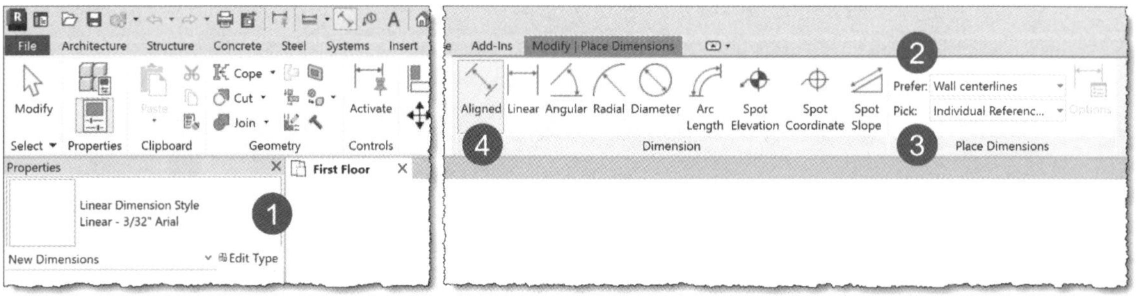

FIGURE 9-2.2 Using the Aligned dimension tool

Here is a description of the numbered items in the image above:

1. Type Selector
2. Selection Preference
3. Individual or Automatic Dimension
4. Switch to another dimension tool

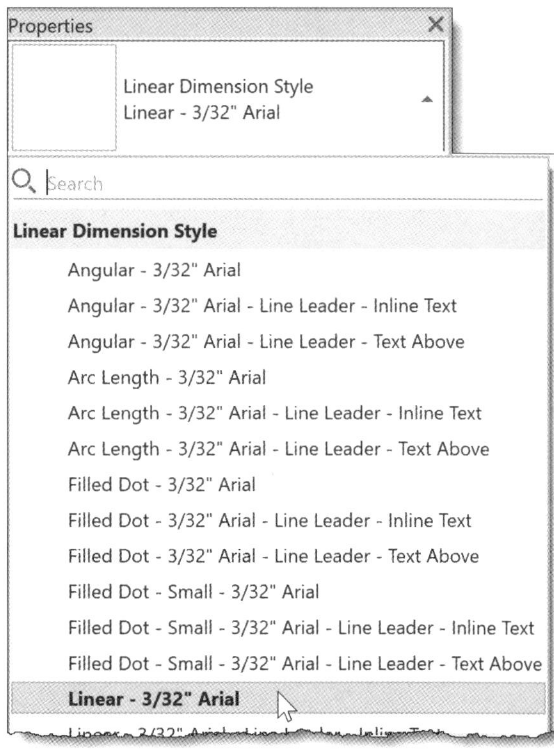

FIGURE 9-2.3 Selecting a dimension type

<u>Type Selector:</u>
Once the dimension tool is active, select the desired **Type** from the *Type Selector* (Figure 9-2.3). This list will vary depending on the template the project was started with and any modifications made.

Selection Preference:
The default is **Wall Centerlines**, which means that, even when zoomed way out, just clicking a wall will reference its centerline. The other options listed (Figure 9-2.4) are self-explanatory. Another option, rather than changing this drop-down list, is to hover the cursor over the desired face, e.g., **Wall faces**, and then tap the Tab key until that face is highlighted, and then click. This can save time by avoiding the need to keep moving the cursor all the way up to the Ribbon and changing the formal setting.

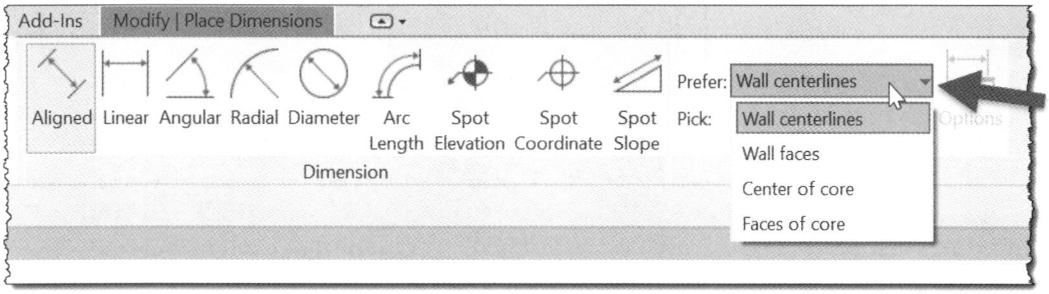

FIGURE 9-2.4 Specify the selection preference for dimensions

Individual versus Automatic Dimensions:
Revit defaults to the **Individual References** option so the designer can deliberately select each reference to dimension to (Figure 9-2.5).

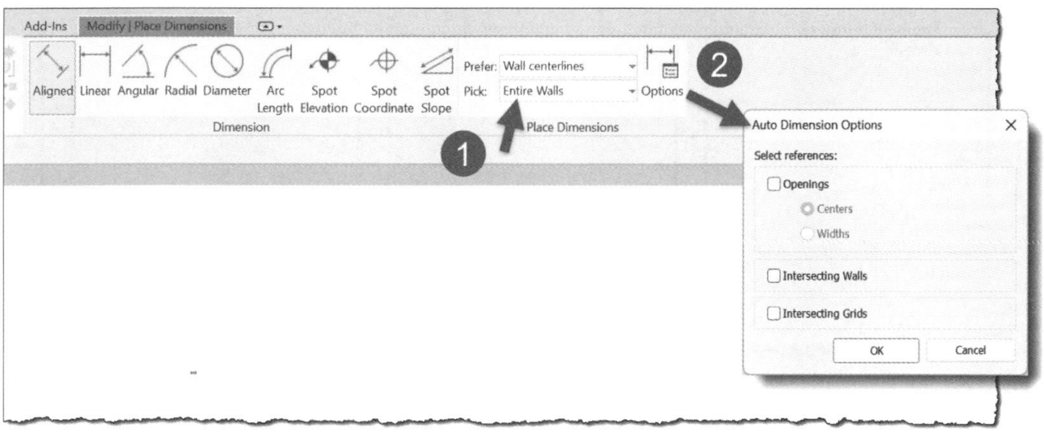

FIGURE 9-2.5 Specify individual or automatic dimensioning

Switching this option to **Entire Wall**, by default, will just add a dimension for the entire length of a selected wall. If **Wall Faces** is selected as well, the overall dimension is created as shown in the next image (Figure 9-2.6). Again, this dimension was created by simply clicking on the wall (with the door and windows); one click to specify the reference and another to position the line.

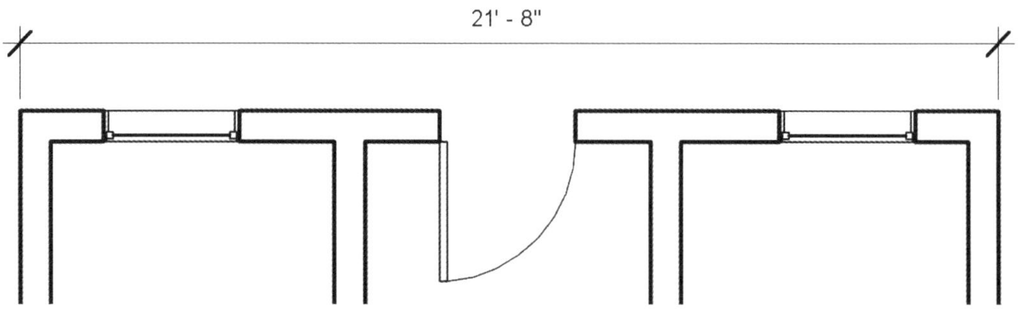

FIGURE 9-2.6 Automatic dimension created – example 1

When the **Entire Wall** option is selected, the **Options** button becomes active. Clicking this presents several options as shown in Figure 9-2.5. On the *Ribbon*, with *Pick* set to **Wall Centerlines** and the *Auto Dimension Options* dialog set to **Openings\Centerlines** and **Intersecting Walls**, the string of dimensions shown below is automatically created (Fig 9-2.7).

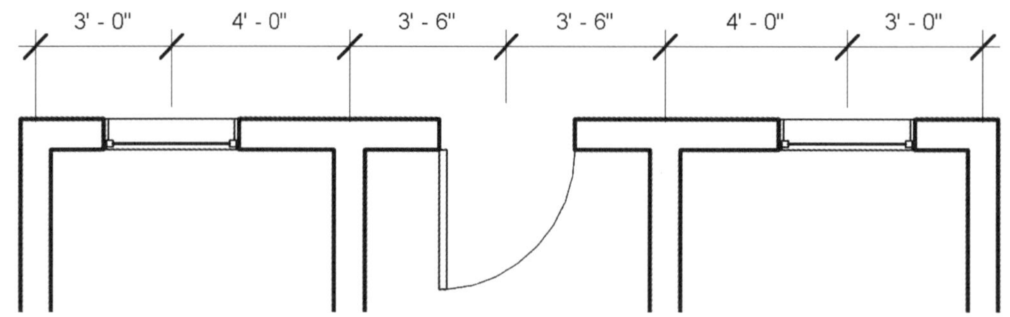

FIGURE 9-2.7 Automatic dimension created – example 2

In the next example (Figure 9-2.8), with the *Prefer* set to **Wall Faces** and the *Auto Dimension Options* dialog set to **Openings\Width** and **Intersecting Walls**, the string of dimensions shown below is automatically created.

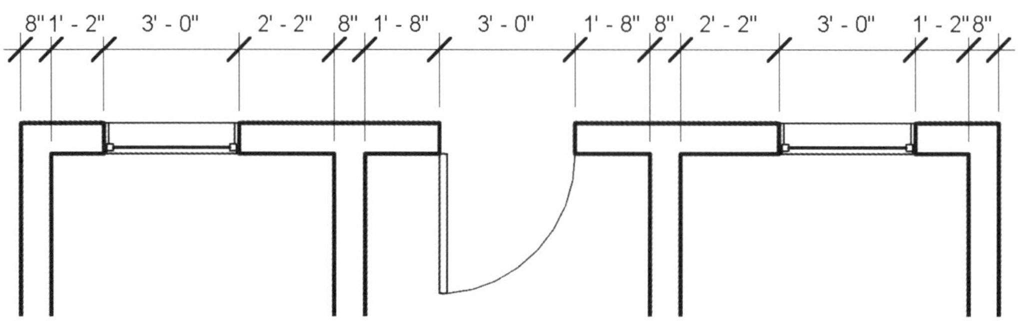

FIGURE 9-2.8 Automatic dimension created – example 3

Linear - Dimension
Use this tool to force Revit to maintain horizontal and vertical dimension segments or strings.

Steps to add Linear dimensions:

- Review **Type Selector** selection
- **Select first reference**
  - Intersection of walls and/or grids ***or***
  - Press tab to select a specific reference or intersection
- **Select second reference**
- Optional: Select additional reference
- **Click away** from anything dimensionable to finish command

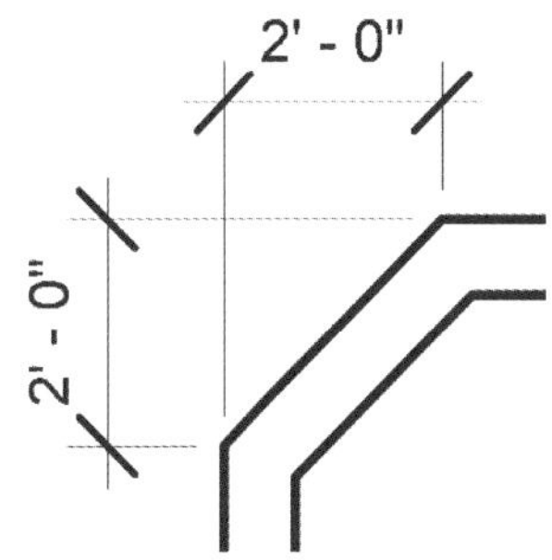

This tool will automatically pick points rather than the element's face. In the example shown to the right, after selecting the two points to be dimensioned, the direction the mouse is moved (up or left) determines whether the dimension is horizontal or vertical—pressing the Space Bar also toggles between the two orientations.

If the model is adjusted, these dimensions will automatically update regardless of which view they are in. Similarly, if one of these elements is deleted, these dimensions will also be deleted.

Angular - Dimension
Use this tool to indicate the angle between two references.

Steps to add Angular dimensions:

- Review **Type Selector** and **Ribbon** selections
- **Select first reference**
- **Select second reference**
- **Click** to place the location of the dimension line and text

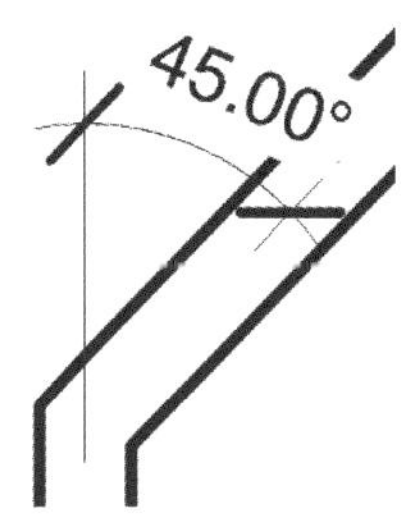

Using the angular tool provides a way to measure the angle between two elements. In the example to the right, the dimension could be in three different positions: one where it is, one in the lower right and the larger obtuse angle on the left.

If the two references are modified the angular dimension will update no matter which view it is in.

Radius - Dimension
Use this tool to indicate the radius of an arc or circular reference. This can be the edge of a floor, wall, duct, or detail lines.

Steps to add a Radius dimension:
- Review **Type Selector** and **Ribbon** selections
- **Select the reference**
- **Click** to place the location of the dimension line and text

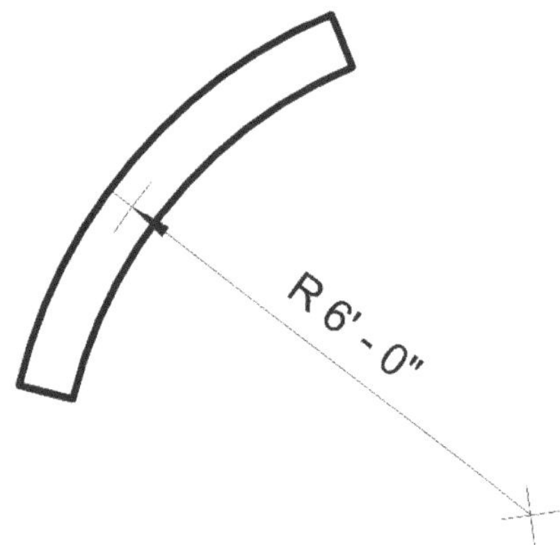

By default, the Radius dimension extends to the center point of the arc or circle. If a plan view is cropped, and Annotation Crop is active for the view, the center point must be visible within the cropped area.

Once the Radius is placed, the radius dimension can be selected, and the grip at the center point can be repositioned closer to the arc. Additionally, you can turn off the Center Mark symbol in the Type properties. However, in some cases, the center mark itself should be dimensioned so the contractor can accurately position the element within the building.

Diameter - Dimension
Use this tool to indicate the diameter of an arc or circular reference. This can be the edge of a floor, wall, duct, or detail lines.

Steps to add a Diameter dimension:
- Review **Type Selector** and **Ribbon** selections
- **Select the reference**
- **Click** to place the location of the dimension line and text

Arc Length - Dimension
Use this tool to measure the length of a line along a curved reference. This can be the edge of a floor, wall, duct, or detail lines.

Steps to add an Arc Length dimension:
- Review **Type Selector** and **Ribbon** selections
- **Select the reference**
- **Click** to place the location of the dimension line and text

Spot Elevation - Dimension

Use this tool to indicate the elevation of a surface.

> Steps to add a Spot Elevation dimension:
> - Review **Type Selector** and **Ribbon** selections
> - **Select the reference**
> - **Click** to place the location of the text and leader

The elevation listed is based on one of three options as listed below. This is a Type Property called Elevation Base. Thus, it is possible to use all three options, even right next to each other.

Elevation Base options for a Spot Elevation type:

- Project Base Point
- Survey Point
- Relative

Project Base Point:

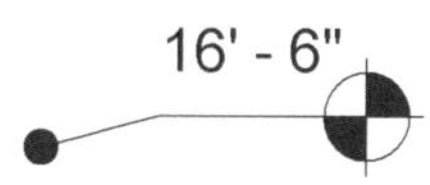

This option is related to the **level datum** numbers in the project. For example, the default templates that come with Revit set Level 1 to an elevation of 0'-0". In this example, all Spot Elevations set to Project Base Point will be relative to 0'-0" within a project.

Survey Point:

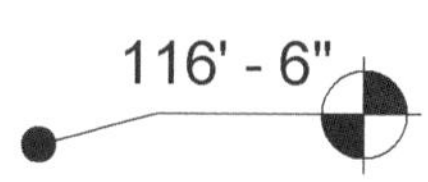

The Survey Base point is an **alternate coordinate system** used to align with the actual position on earth and elevation above sea level. Thus, any Spot Elevation set to Survey Point will display a value relative to the Survey Point settings. For example, where the Level 1 floor's Project Base Point is set to 0'-0" (or 100'-0"), the Survey value for Level 1 might be 650'-0" to match the elevation numbers shown for the contours on the Civil Engineer's grading plan. Revit can track both coordinate systems within the context of the Spot Elevation tool.

Relative:

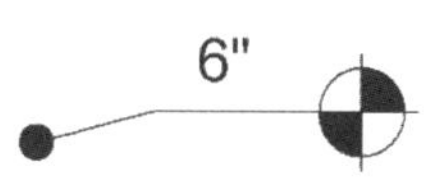

When a Spot Elevation has the Elevation Base set to Relative, the values listed are related to the plan view in which they are placed.

Spot Coordinate

Use this tool to indicate the North/South, East/West position of a point within the model.

Steps to add a Spot Coordinate dimension:

- Review **Type Selector** and **Ribbon** selections
- **Select the reference point**
- **Click** to place the location of the text and leader

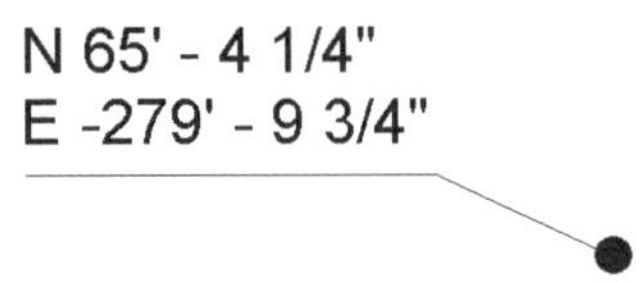

This feature can be used to indicate the positions of one or more building corners on the site. This is usually relative to a predefined Survey Point, which is relative to a benchmark or municipal coordinate system. On a typical commercial project, this information is provided only on the civil drawings and is therefore not required in the Revit model or documents.

Similar to the Spot Elevation tool, the Spot Coordinate can also be set to Relative or Project Base Point. This could be used to position items within the project, but it is not commonly used because the contractor or installer would need a direct line of sight between the two points.

Spot Slope
Use this tool to indicate the **Slope** in a floor plan view or the roof **Pitch** in an elevation view.

Steps to add a Spot Elevation dimension:
- Review **Type Selector** and **Ribbon** selections
- **Click** to both select a reference and place the location of the dimension element

Plan views:
In a plan view, the Spot Slope can indicate the slope of a sloped floor or a ramp.

Elevation View:
In an elevation view, the Spot Slope can be used to indicate the pitch of a roof, as shown in the example to the right.

TIP: When placing the Spot Elevation on a hip roof, in elevation, use the Tab key to select the correct surface. By default, the hip line is selected, which has a different slope from the roof face itself.

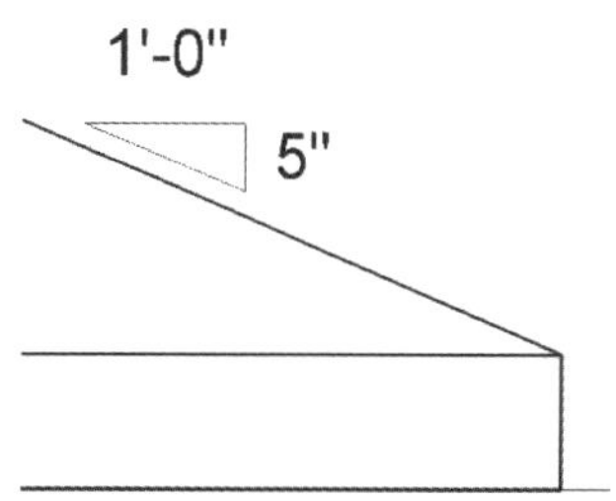

The Spot Slope element has an Instance Parameter in the Properties Palette that toggles between Arrow and Triangle, the two options shown above.

Modifying a Dimension

When dimensions need to be modified, there are a few things to keep in mind.

Ways to Modify a Dimension:
- Edit Witness Lines
- Modify text
- Reposition text
- Lock a Dimension
- Drive the location of geometry
- Change type

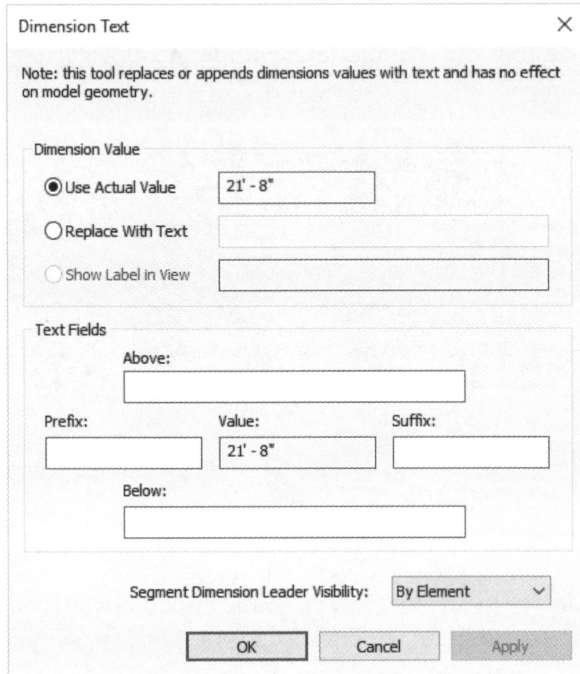

FIGURE 9-2.9 Dimension Text dialog

<u>Edit Witness Lines:</u>
After a dimension is placed, a wall or opening may be added, and rather than deleting a dimension string and adding a new one, Revit provides the **Edit Witness Lines** tool. Simply select a dimension and click the Edit Witness Line button from the Ribbon. Once active, click new references to **add witness lines** and click existing references to **remove witness lines**.

<u>Modify text:</u>
When a dimension is selected, clicking the dimension value opens the Dimension Text dialog (Figure 9-2.9).

Figure 9-2.10 shows the relative position of each of the "text fields."

When **Replace With Text** is selected, the dimension value can be replaced with text. For example, "PAINT WALL" or "EXISTING CORRIDOR WIDTH – VERIFY IN FIELD."

Revit will not allow a dimension value in the text replacement box. The main reason for this restriction is to prevent faking dimensions rather than adjusting the model.

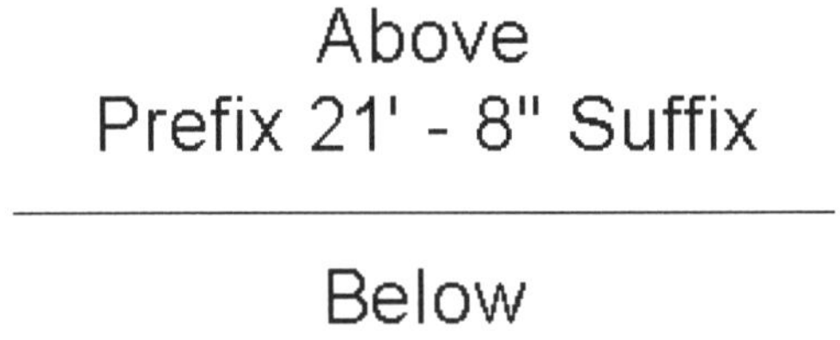

FIGURE 9-2.10 Dimension text field positions

Reposition text:
When a dimension is selected, clicking and dragging on the text grip allows the text to be repositioned.

When the text is moved past one of the witness lines, Revit will add a leader by default as shown to the right (Figure 9-2.11). Right-clicking on a dimension reveals related commands on the pop-up menu (Figure 9-2.12); selecting **Reset Dimension Text Position** will move the text back to the original location.

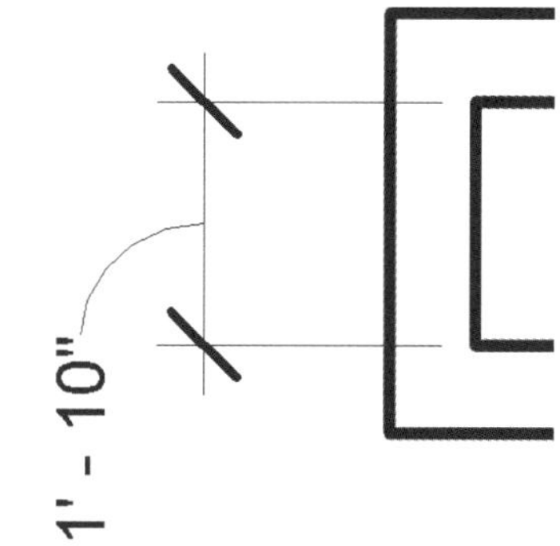

FIGURE 9-2.11 Dimension Text leader

Lock a Dimension:
When a dimension is selected, clicking the lock icon (Figure 9-2.13) will prevent that dimension value from changing. This will not prevent model elements from moving, but to maintain the dimension value, both reference elements will move. For example, if a dimension is locked between two walls which define a corridor, moving one wall will move the other wall to ensure the corridor width does not change.

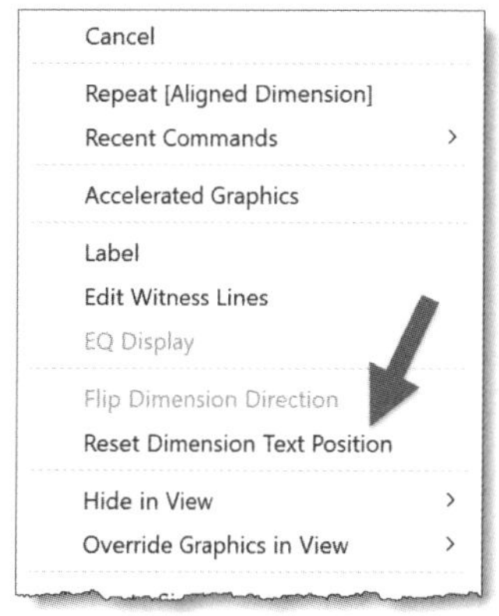

FIGURE 9-2.12 Right-click options

When elements are selected which are in some way constrained, Revit will show the lock symbol. This is true even if the locked dimension is not visible in the current view (Figure 9-2.14). Clicking this icon will unlock the constraint.

When a locked dimension is deleted, Revit asks if the constraint should also be removed. Thus, it is possible to delete the dimension but leave the constraint in place.

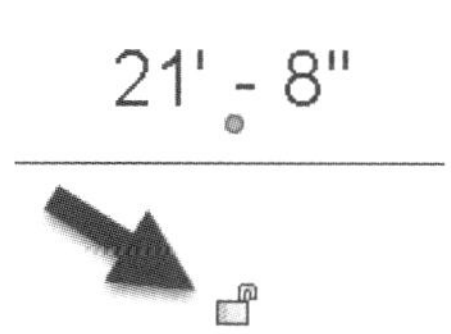

FIGURE 9-2.13 Dimension selected

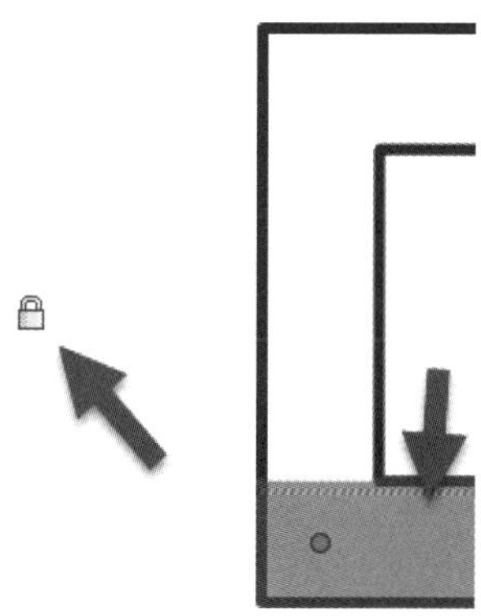

FIGURE 9-2.14 Locked element

Drive the location of geometry:
Like temporary dimensions, permanent dimensions can also be used to reposition geometry, such as walls, ducts, and more. The key is to select the element to be repositioned first, then click the dimension text. A common mistake is selecting the dimension directly and then clicking the text. This only opens the Dimension Text dialog. Also, consider that Revit would not know which referenced element to move if just selecting the dimension and not the element: move the left one, move the right element, or both equally?

TIP: A temporary dimension can be turned into a permanent dimension by clicking the "dimension icon" below the temporary dimension text, pointed out in Figure 9-2.15.

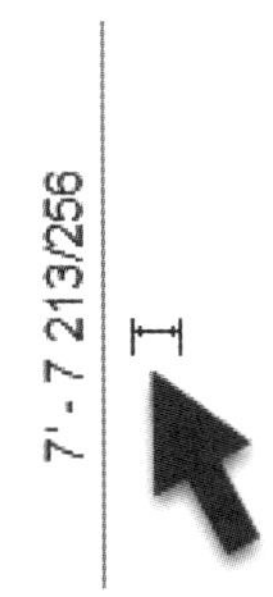

FIGURE 9-2.15 Temporary dimension selected

Change Dimension Type:
When a dimension is selected, click the Type Selector and select from the available options. Changing the type can affect the graphic appearance, the rounding, and when alternate units appear (e.g., metric).

Create and Modify Dimension Types

Sometimes it is necessary to modify a dimension type to match a design firm's graphical standard or a client requirement. Revit allows dimension types to be created and modified. Use caution when changing a dimension type, as all dimensions of that type will be updated in the current project. These changes will not affect any other projects or templates.

To modify existing types, either start the dimension command and click Edit Type or select one of the "Types" options in the extended panel area of the dimension panel on the Annotate tab (Figure 9-2.16).

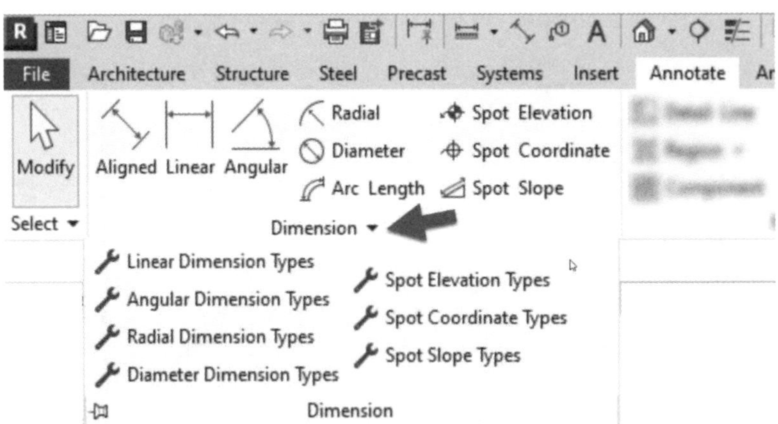

FIGURE 9-2.16 Editing Dimension types

To create a new Type, click the **Duplicate** option in the Type Properties dialog.

Figure 9-2.17 shows the various options that can be changed.

One option is **Units Format**. Selecting this option opens the Format dialog shown in Figure 9-2.18. Notice that a dimension style can be tied to the Project Units as set on the Manage tab. Un-checking this option allows this dimension style to round in a specific way and do a few other things, like "Suppress 0 feet:" and control the symbol (e.g., monetary symbol).

Setting up all the dimension styles typically needed in a template file will save a lot of time and help enforce a firm's standards.

TIP: To see how many instances use a specific dimension style in a project, select one and then right-click and pick Select All Instances → In Entire Project. The total number of selected items will be displayed in the lower-right corner of the screen, next to the filter icon on the status bar.

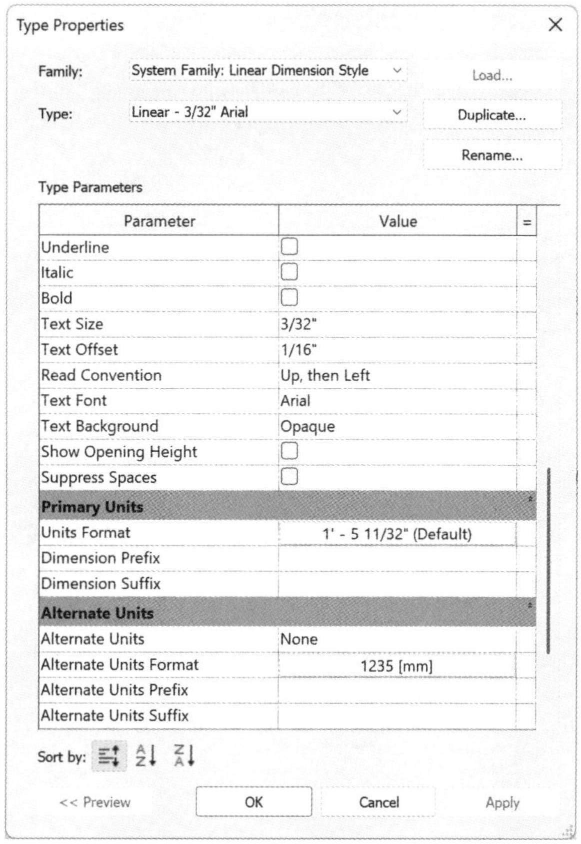

FIGURE 9-2.17 Dimension type properties

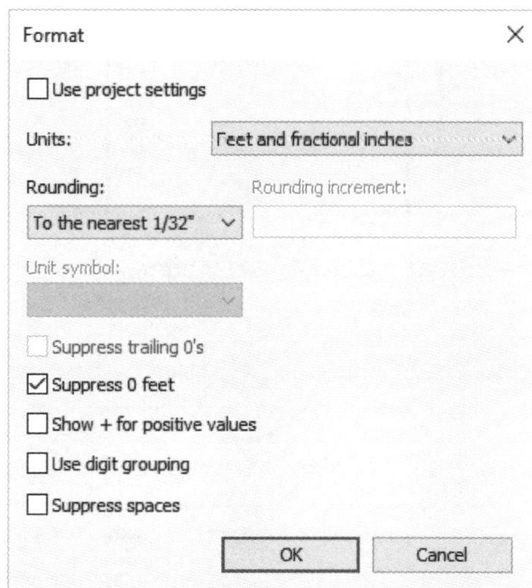

FIGURE 9-2.18 Dimension unit format

Dimension Equality

When a dimension string is selected, an **EQ** symbol appears with a red slash through it as seen in Figure 9-2.19. Clicking this toggle will make all dimension segments in that string equally spaced between the two ends.

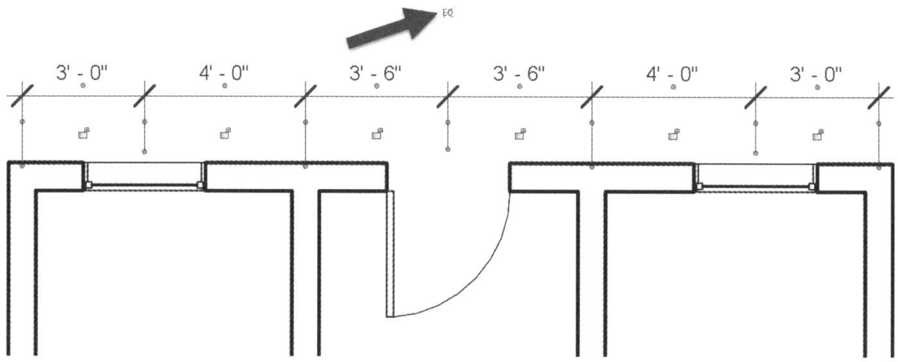

FIGURE 9-2.19 Dimension string selected and EQ symbol pointed

The image below (Figure 9-2.20) shows the result of clicking the EQ icon; the walls, windows, and door all moved with the now equally spaced witness lines. Notice the EQ icon no longer has a slash through it. If one of the end walls is moved, all elements are moved to maintain equal spacing. Setting the Dimension's **Equality Display** property to Value shows the dimension value rather than the "EQ" abbreviation.

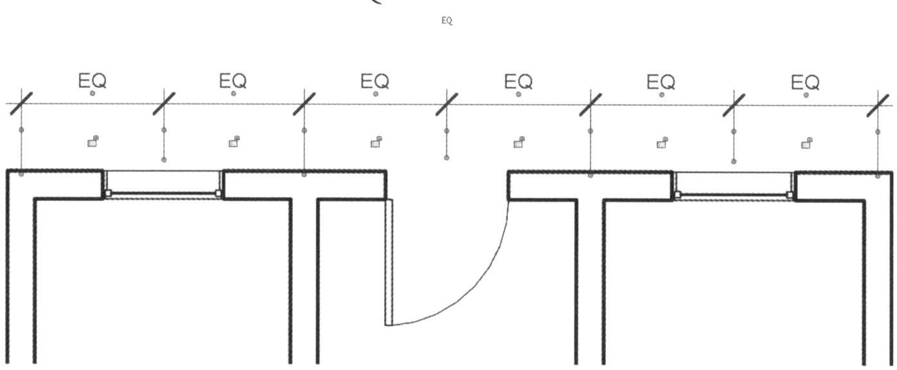

FIGURE 9-2.20 Dimension string with equality activated

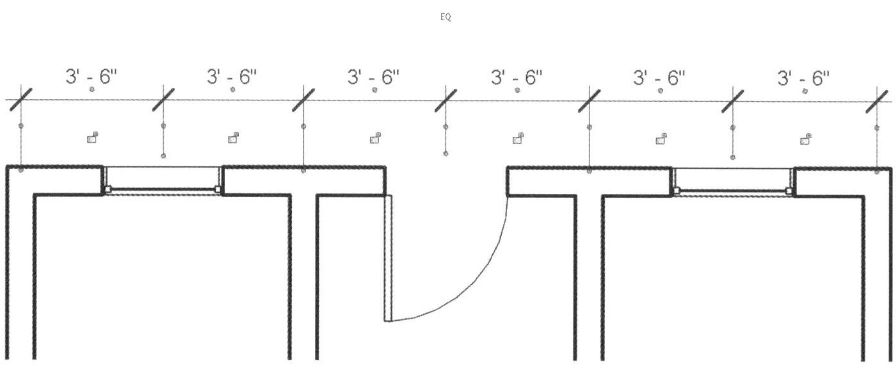

FIGURE 9-2.21 Dimension string with equality activated and dimension value shown

Exercise 9-3:
Tagging

This section will study how **tags** work in Revit. This is an important feature in Revit, one that designers use extensively. This feature is often used on furniture, doors, windows, casework, and ductwork, as well as many other elements within the Revit model.

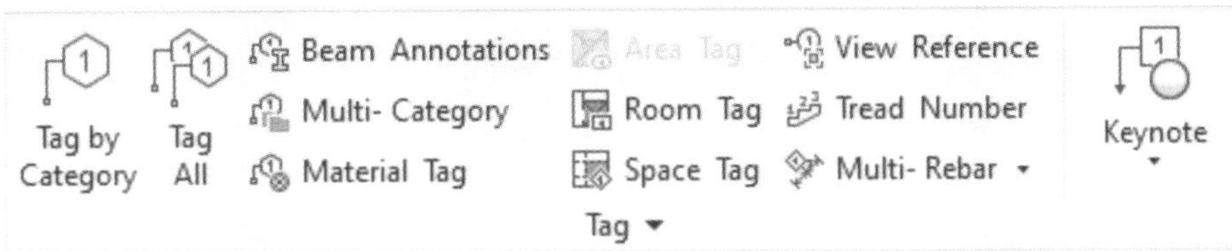

The basic premise of a *tag* is to be able to textually represent, in a drawing view, information found within an element, that is, an *Instance* or *Type Parameter*. One example found in nearly every set of construction documents is the door tag. This Revit tag has been set up to list the contents of a specific door's ***Mark*** parameter, which is an *Instance Parameter*.

The process to tag an element is simple:

- Select the ***Tag by Category*** tool from the *Quick Access Toolbar*.
- Adjust the settings on the *Ribbon* if needed.
- Click the element(s) to be tagged.

  FYI: Different tags are placed based on the category of the element selected.
- Click the *Modify* button or press the Esc key when done.

A *tag* is view-specific, meaning that if you add it to the Level 1 Finish Plan, it will not automatically appear in the **Level 1 Furniture Plan**. If you want the tag to appear in two Level 1 plan views, you need to add it twice. *(TIP: Use Copy/Paste.)* The advantage is that you can adjust the tag location independently in each view. One view may show furniture, and the other floor finishes. Each view might require the tag to be in a different location to keep it readable.

Tags are dependent on the element selected during placement. You cannot simply move a tag near another similar element and expect Revit to recognize this change. Similarly, if an element is deleted, the tag will also be removed from the model, even if the tag is in another view in the project.

The image below has several tags added to a floor plan view. All the listed information is coming from the properties of the elements that have been tagged. For example, the "M1" tag within the diamond shape is listing the wall type (i.e., *Type Mark*). Because the wall tag(s) is/are listing a *Type Parameter*, all wall instances of that type will report the same value, i.e., "M1." The door number "1" reports the element's Mark value, which is an *Instance Parameter*. Therefore, each door instance may have a different number. Notice some tags have the *Leader* option turned on. This is especially helpful if the tag is outside the room. Any 3D element visible in a view may be tagged, even the floor. In this case, the *Floor Tag* reports the *Type Name* listed in the *Type Selector*. The leader can be modified to have an arrow or a dot.

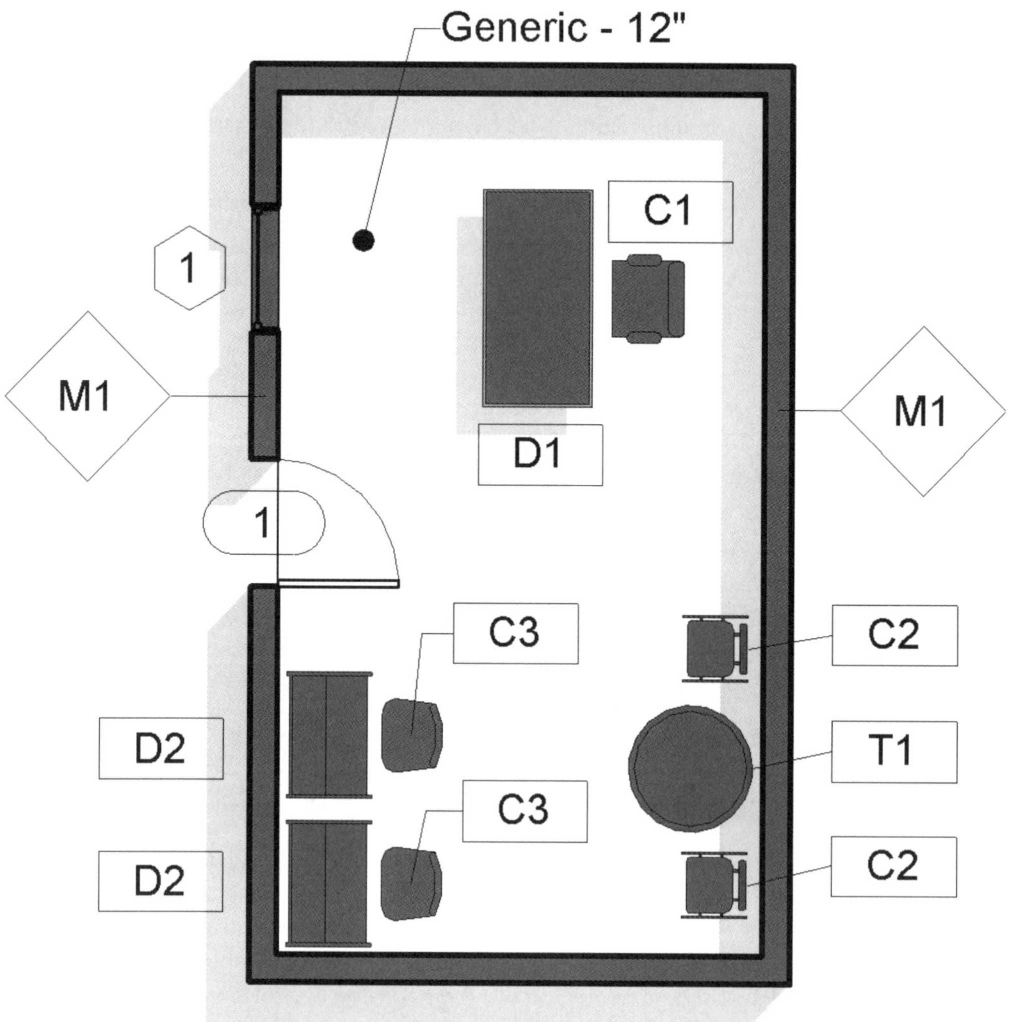

FIGURE 9-3.1 Floor plan with tags added

All of these tags were placed using the same tool: *Tag by Category*. Later, you will learn how to specify which tag gets used for each category (e.g., walls, furniture, floors, windows, etc.).

The section/interior elevation below (Figure 9-3.2) shows many of the same elements tagged as in the floor plan view above. If the wall's *Type Mark* is changed, the wall *Tag* will be instantly updated in all views: plans, elevations, sections, and schedules.

The tags had to be manually added to this view. They are not added here automatically just because you added one in the floor plan view, unlike when you add a section mark (where the section appears in other views automatically). If the view is deleted from the project, all these tags will automatically be deleted.

Some tags can actually report multiple parameter values found within an element. For example, the ***Ceiling Tag*** used in this example lists the *Type Name* and the ceiling height, and includes fixed text that reads "A.F.F.". Many tags can be selected and directly edited, which actually changes the values within the element. Changing the 8′-0″ ceiling height will change the ceiling position vertically.

It is possible to tag an element multiple times. You could add the same tag multiple times. In the example below, you could place a ***Wall Tag*** on each side of the door. You can also add different tags that report different information from the same element. The ***Wall Tag*** "M1" and the ***Material Tag*** "PT-1" are two separate tags that extract different information from the same wall.

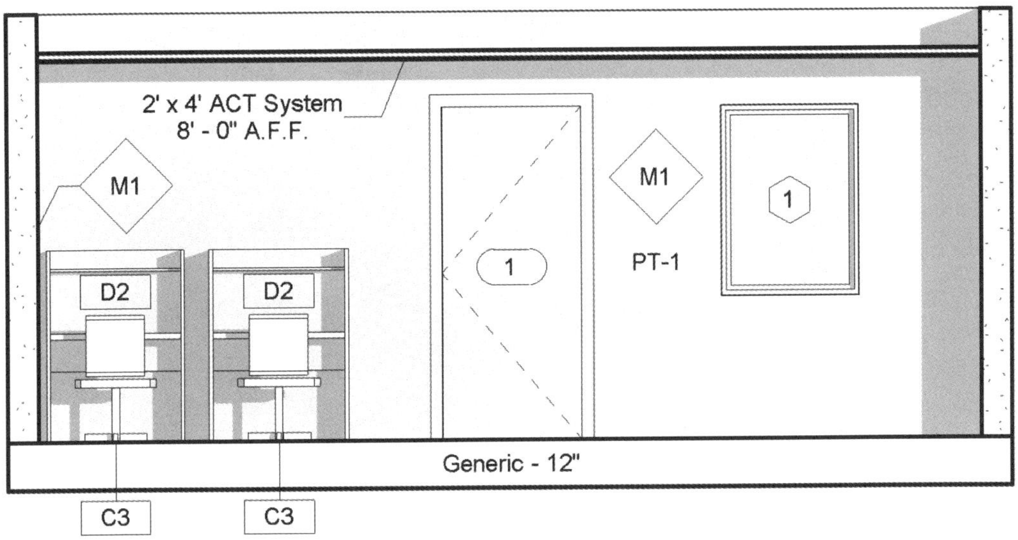

FIGURE 9-3.2 Section / interior elevation with tags added

Most design firms spend a little time adjusting the provided tags to make the text a little smaller and modify or delete the line work. This can easily be done by selecting a tag and then clicking ***Edit Family*** on the *Ribbon*. Revised tags can then be loaded back into the project and/or saved to a company template for future use.

It is also possible to add tags in 3D views (Figure 9-3.3b). Before tagging a 3D view, you must ***Lock*** it (Figure 9-3.3a) to prevent changing the view and interfering with the position of the tags relative to the elements being tagged.

FIGURE 9 3.3A Locking a 3D view

When the *Leader* option is off, the tag is placed at the center of the selected element. This initial position is not always desirable (e.g., note the D1 and C1 tags below), and you must move each tag so it is readable.

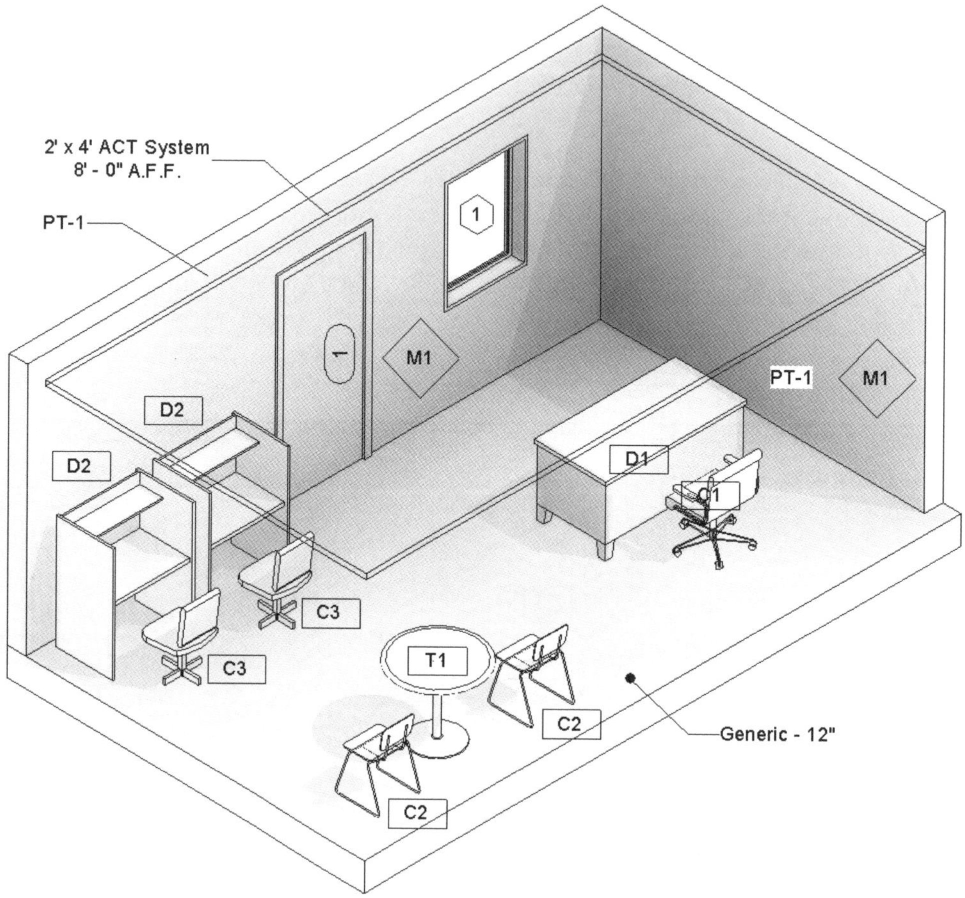

FIGURE 9-3.3B Locked 3D view with tags added

It is not possible to add *Room Tags* to 3D views.

It is helpful to understand where the information displayed in tags is stored. It is often necessary to change these values. In Figure 9-3.4, you can see that "PT-1" is the *Description* for the *Material* assigned to the wall type.

> ***TIP:*** *To find the* Material *assigned to a specific wall type: Select the wall → Edit Type → Edit Structure → observe the Material column.*

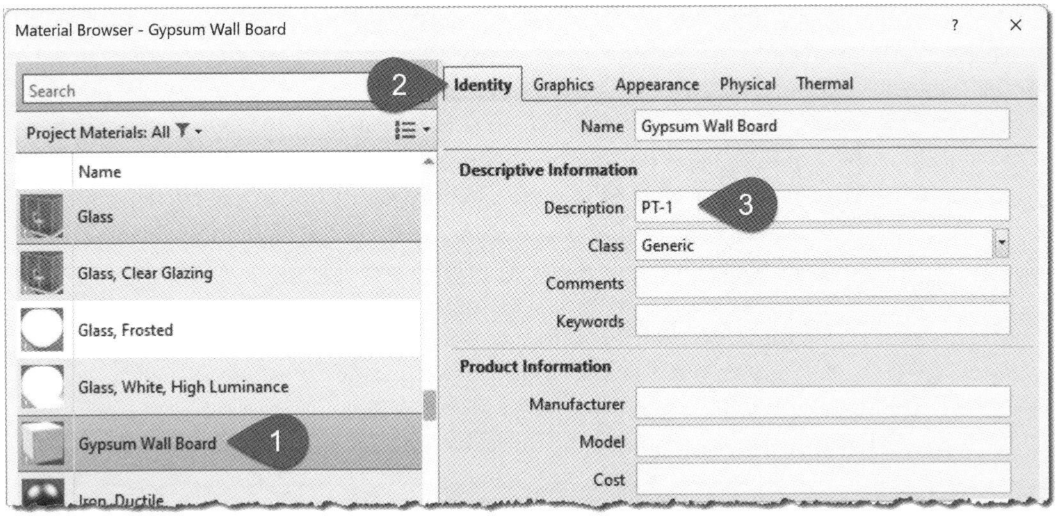

FIGURE 9-3.4 Material description value used in Material Tag

FYI: In the image above, the preview icons on the left with a gold triangle in the lower left corner are legacy materials, which are superseded by newer, physically accurate materials. However, many design firms still exclusively use the legacy materials.

A wall's *Type Mark* is found in the *Type Properties* dialog; select a wall → *Edit Type* from the *Properties Palette*. Notice in Figure 9-3.5 that the *Type Mark* is set to "M1." If you were to edit this value, all the tags for this wall will be updated instantly.

Seeing as all the information displayed in a tag is only stored in the element being tagged, you will never lose any information by deleting a tag.

> *FYI: A tag will move with the element even if the element is moved in another view where the tag is not visible.*

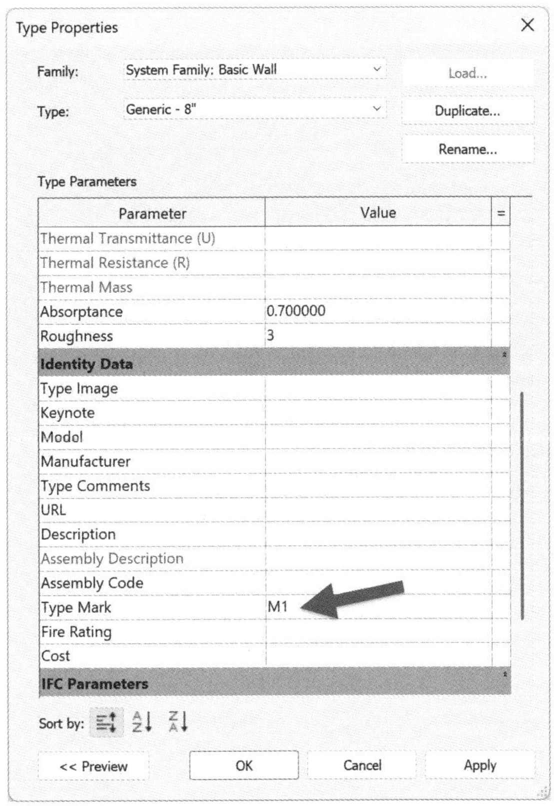

FIGURE 9-3.5 Selected wall's *Type Mark* value used in wall tag

The image below (Figure 9-3.6) shows the settings available on the *Ribbon* when the *Tag* tool is active.

- The tag orientation can be ***Horizontal, Vertical, or Model*** *(the latter may be rotated).*
- Clicking the **Loaded Tags and Symbols** button allows you to specify which tags are used when multiple tags for the same category are loaded in the current project.
- Selecting the ***Leader Line*** option draws a line between the tag and the element.
    - Leader End options:
        - *Attached End:* the leader always touches the tagged element.
        - *Free End:* allows you to move the end of the leader.
        - *Leader Start* is similar, but only adjustable after placement via the properties palette.
- **Leader Length**: This determines the initial length of the leader.

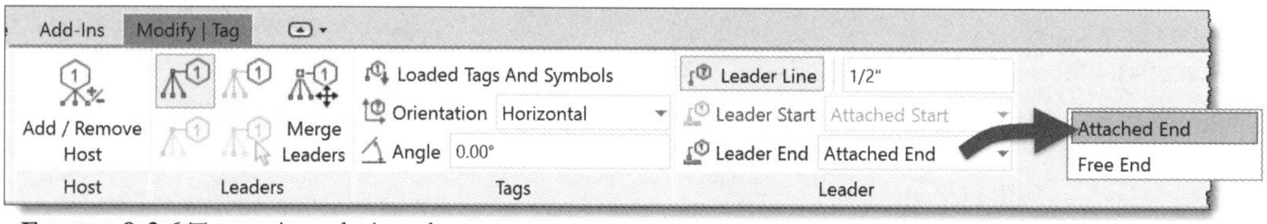

FIGURE 9-3.6 Tag options during placement

When clicking the *Loaded Tags and Symbols* button, you get the ***Loaded Tags and Symbols*** dialog as shown in Figure 9-3.7.

Notice that some categories do not have a tag family loaded. If you tried to tag a *Casework* element, Revit would prompt you to load a tag.

Clicking a tag name in the Loaded Tags column lets you select from multiple tag types/families loaded in the current project.

If you use one tag type in plan views and another in elevation views, you could open this dialog just before tagging in plan views, then adjust it again before tagging in elevation views.

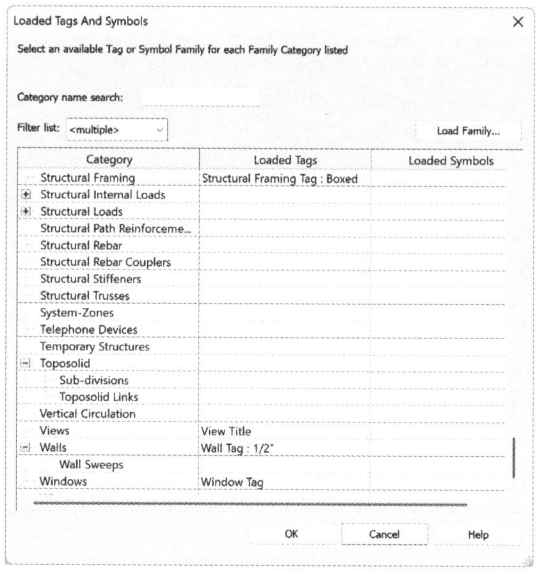

FIGURE 9-3.7 Loaded tags dialog

FYI: It is possible to let Revit place the default tag, then select the placed tag and swap it out via the Type Selector.

TIP: If you want to swap several tags with another type: Select one of the tags → right-click → **Select All Instances** *and then pick either* **Visible in View** *or* **In Entire Project**. *You now have all the tags selected and can pick something else via the* Type Selector.

The reader should be aware that some tags may be automatically added when content is added to the model. For example, when placing a window, the *Ribbon* has a toggle called ***Tag on Placement*** (Figure 9-3.8). When this option is selected (which it is NOT by default), a door tag is placed next to every door. Note that the tag is added only to the current view, which could be an elevation, a plan, etc.

You typically want this option off in the early design stages, since the tags will just get in the way as things move around. Also, existing elements are not usually tagged; thus, you would toggle this option off, so you do not have to come back and delete the tag later.

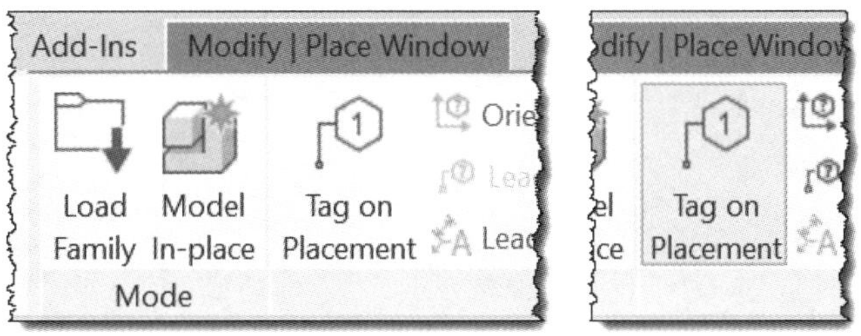

FIGURE 9-3.8 Tag on Placement option; **off** (shown on left) and **on** (on right)

If you did not add tags or some were deleted along the way, you will need to add them later. The easiest way to do this is to use the Tag All tool; it used to be called *Tag All Not Tagged*. When you use this tool, you can add a door tag to every door in the current view that does not already have a door tag. This is great for large projects with hundreds of doors, and you want to make sure you do not miss any. You may still have to go around and rotate and reposition a few tags, but overall, this is much faster!

Before concluding this introduction to tags, we will briefly look at how tags are created. If you select a tag and click Edit Family on the Ribbon, you will open the tag for editing in the *Family Editor*. Keep in mind that your project is still open in addition to the tag family.

If you select a furniture tag and edit it, you will see text (sample value shown) and four lines (Figure 9-3.9). Here, the lines can be selected and deleted if desired. Also, you can select the text, then click Edit Type to change its properties (e.g., height, font, width factor, etc.).

If you select the text and then click the ***Edit Label*** option on the *Ribbon*, you can change the parameter being reported, or report multiple parameters (Figure 9-3.9).

TIP: *Open a tag family, edit it, and then do a* Save-As *to make a new tag type.*

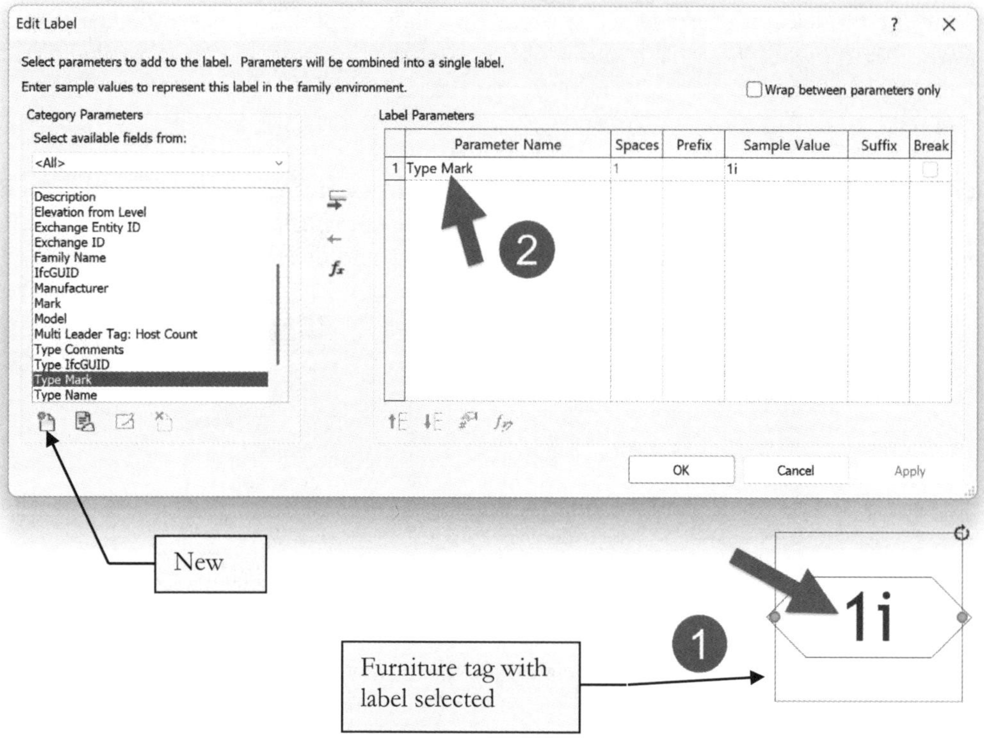

FIGURE 9-3.9 Editing a tag label in the family editor

In the *Edit Label* dialog above, you can click the **New** icon in the lower-left corner to load a Shared Parameter, which lets you create a tag that reports custom information. See the next section for more on this topic. Also, several icons to the right of the "New" icon is the *Edit Parameter's Units Format* tool that allows you to override the formatting for numeric parameters (Figure 9-3.10).

This concludes the introduction on using tags in Revit. The next section continues this discussion with a more advanced concept called *Shared Parameters*.

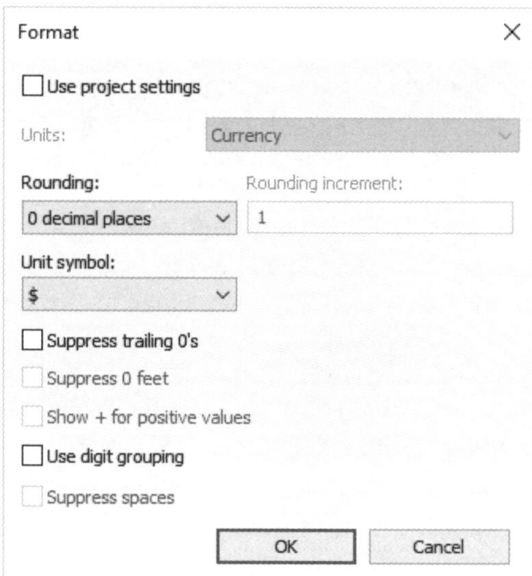

FIGURE 9-3.10 Editing a label's format

Exercise 9-4:
Shared Parameters

FYI: You will not be using Shared Parameters in the tutorial, but this information is essential for a designer to be proficient and properly leverage Revit's power.

Introduction

Revit has many features that are unique when compared to other building design programs; one of these is *Shared Parameters*. The main idea behind Shared Parameters is to manage parameters across multiple projects, schedules, families, and template files. This feature allows Revit to recognize that you are referring to the same piece of information across multiple unconnected files. Here, we will cover the basics of setting up Shared Parameters, common problems encountered, and a few related tips and tricks.

The main reason for using ***Shared Parameters*** is to display custom information in tags; however, there are a few other uses that will be mentioned later. In contrast, a ***Project Parameter*** is slightly easier to make in a project, but cannot appear in a tag; Revit has no way of knowing that the parameter created in the family, the info to be tagged, and the parameter created in the tag are the same bit of information. Both *Project* and *Shared Parameters* may appear in schedules.

The image below illustrates the concept of a common storage container (i.e., the Shared Parameter file) from which uniquely coded parameters can be loaded into content, annotations, and projects. This creates a connected common thread between several otherwise disconnected files.

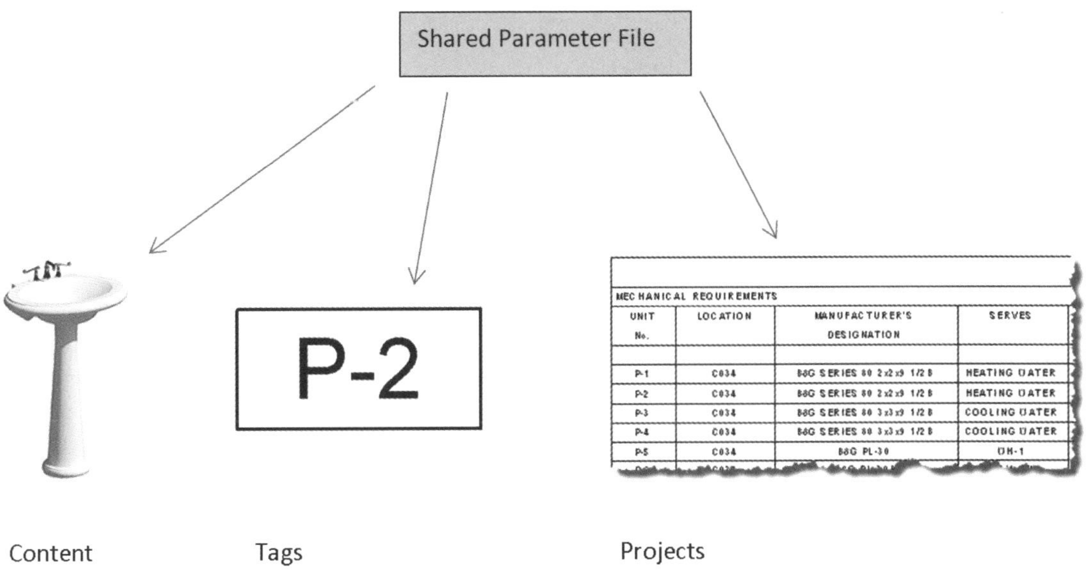

Shared Parameter File

Creating a *Shared Parameter* is fairly straightforward, but afterwards, managing them can be troublesome. Select **Manage → Shared Parameters** from the *Ribbon* to open the *Shared Parameters* dialog box (Figure 9-4.1). This dialog basically modifies a simple **text file**, which should not be edited manually. If a text file has not yet been created, you will need to select the ***Create*** button and provide a file name and location for your *Shared Parameter* file.

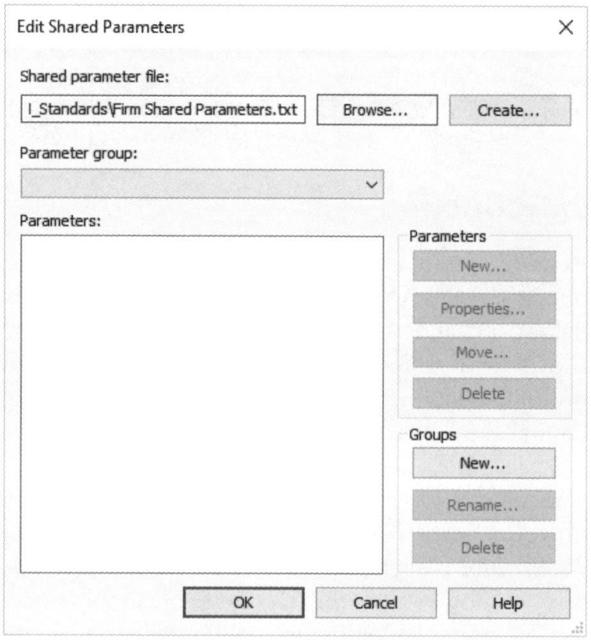

FIGURE 9-4.1 Edit Shared Parameters dialog

It is important to keep in mind that this file will be the main record of all your *Shared Parameters*. From this file, you create *Shared Parameters* within Projects, Templates, and Families. Therefore, it is ideal to only maintain one file for the entire firm, even if you have multiple locations. Of course, there is always an exception to the rule. This single file should be stored on the server, and the software deployment should be set up to automatically point user computers to the *Shared Parameters* file. This can also be done manually by clicking the *Browse* button in the *Shared Parameters* dialog.

Once a *Shared Parameter* is loaded into a project, template, or family, the text file is no longer referenced. So you technically do not need to send this file with your project file when transmitting to a consultant or contractor.

The file name should be simple and easy to find. Create a new text file for each version of Revit you are using; include the version number in the file name. Some newer parameter types will cause older versions of the software to reject the text file.

Creating a Shared Parameter

Open the *Shared Parameters* dialog box. Here you can easily create *Groups* and *Parameters*. *Groups* are simply containers, somewhat like folders, used to organize the multitude of parameters you will likely create over time. When starting from scratch, you must first create at least one *Group* before creating your first *Shared Parameter*.

To create a new *Group*, click the ***New*** button under the *Groups* heading. In a multi-disciplinary firm, you should have at least one group for each discipline. Parameters can be moved around later, so do not worry about that too much at first.

Click the ***New*** button under the *Parameters* heading to create a new parameter in the current *Group*. You only need to provide three pieces of information:

- Name
- Discipline
- Type of Parameter
- Tooltip (optional)

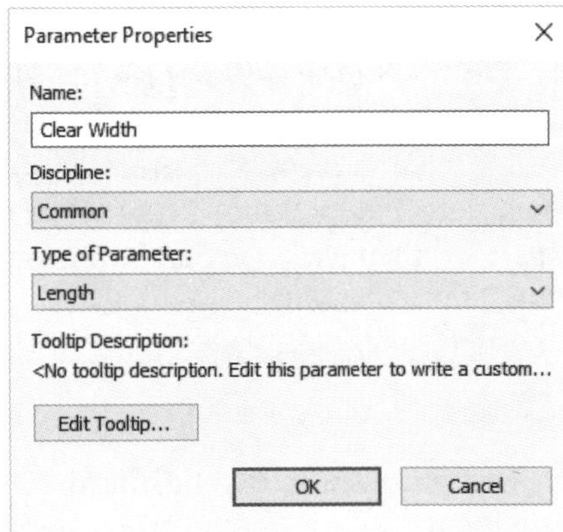

FIGURE 9-4.2 Setting Parameter Properties

In this example, see the image to the right (Figure 9-4.2). We will create a parameter called "Clear Width," which will be used in our door families (but can be used with other categories, as this is not specified at this level). The other standard options, such as *Instance* versus *Type*, are assigned when the parameter is set up in the project or family.

The **Discipline** option changes the options available in the *Type of Parameter* drop-down. The **Type of Parameter** drop-down lets Revit know what type of information will be stored in the parameter you are creating. Many programming languages require parameters to be declared before they are used and cannot be altered later. Revit is, in this sense, a graphical programming language.

The **Edit Tooltip** button allows an optional description of the parameter to be entered. Anyone working in the project will see the description when they hover their cursor over the parameter in the Properties Palette or Edit Type dialog.

When a new *Shared Parameter* is created, a unique code is assigned to it. The image below (Figure 9-4.3) shows the code created for the "Clear Width" parameter just created. For this reason, it is not possible to simply create another *Shared Parameters* file a few months from now and have it work the same.

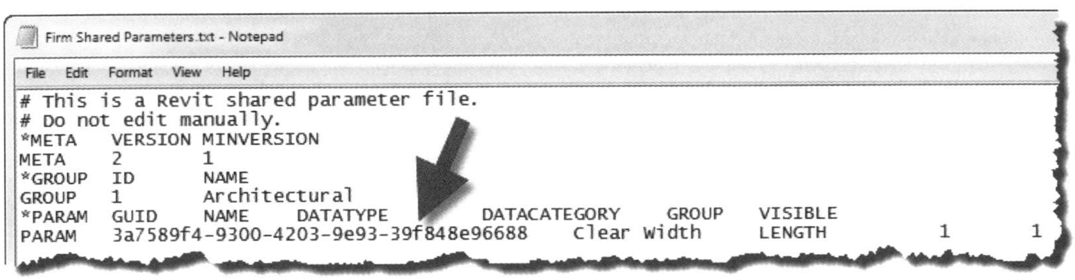

FIGURE 9-4.3 Shared Parameters text file

Creating a Shared Parameter in a Family

Now that you have created the framework for your *Shared Parameters*, i.e., the text file, you can begin to create parameters within content; the next section covers creating *Shared Parameters* in project files.

Open a family file – in this example, we will open the **Door - Single – Panel.rfa** file (download via Load Revit Family). Select the ***Family Types*** icon. Click the ***New Parameter*** icon on the lower-left (Figure 9-4.5). Now select the *Shared parameter*, then click the ***Select*** button (Figure 9-4.4). This will open the previously created shared parameter text file. Select "Clear Width" and then **OK**.

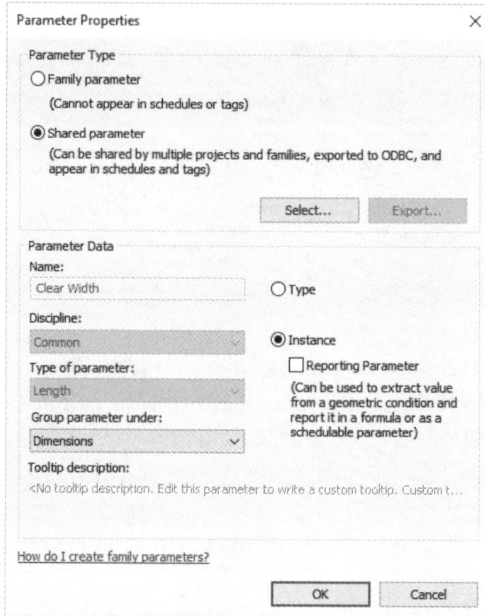

FIGURE 9-4.4 Parameter properties

Now you only have two bits of information left to provide. Is the parameter *Type* or *Instance*, and what is the "Group parameter under" option? This controls which section the parameter shows up under in the *Properties Palette.*

Notice how the bits of information specified in the *Shared Parameters* file are grayed out here. They cannot be changed, as doing so would create discrepancies between families and project files. Thus, this information is hard-wired.

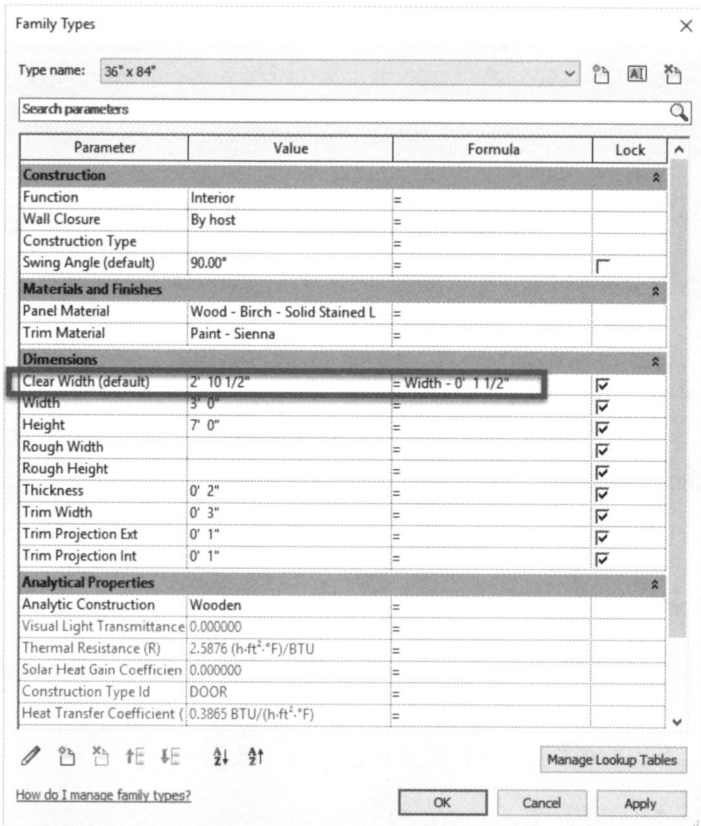

FIGURE 9-4.5 Family Types in family editor environment

Once the parameter has been created in the family, it can be used just like a *Family Parameter.* In this example, we created a formula to subtract the frame stops and the hinge/door imposition on the opening (Figure 9-4.5). Keep in mind that this value can now appear in a custom tag, if desired, listing the clear width for each door in a floor plan. Maybe the code official has required this. Using *Shared Parameters* is the only way to achieve this short of using "dumb text", that is, text manually typed which does not change automatically.

Next, we will look at creating a door tag that lists the clear width. This is similar to the steps just covered for the door family, since a tag is also a family. The only difference is that this parameter will be associated with a *Label.*

Note that the following steps are not required for the tutorial in this book: Open the default **Door Tag** family from within a Revit project (right-click it in the Project Browser and select Edit). Do a *Save As* and rename the file to **Door Tag – Clear Width.rfa**. Delete the linework, if desired. Select the text and click the *Edit Label* button on the *Ribbon.* In the *Edit Label* dialog, create a new parameter by clicking the icon in the lower-left corner; see the image below. Your only option here is to select a *Shared Parameter*; as previously mentioned, only *Shared Parameters* can be tagged. Once the new parameter is loaded, click to move it to the right side of the dialog, in the *Label Parameters* column. Next, select the original *Mark* parameter and remove it. Finally, edit the *Sample Value* to something like 2′-10″; this is what appears in the family to give you an idea of what the tag will look like in the project.

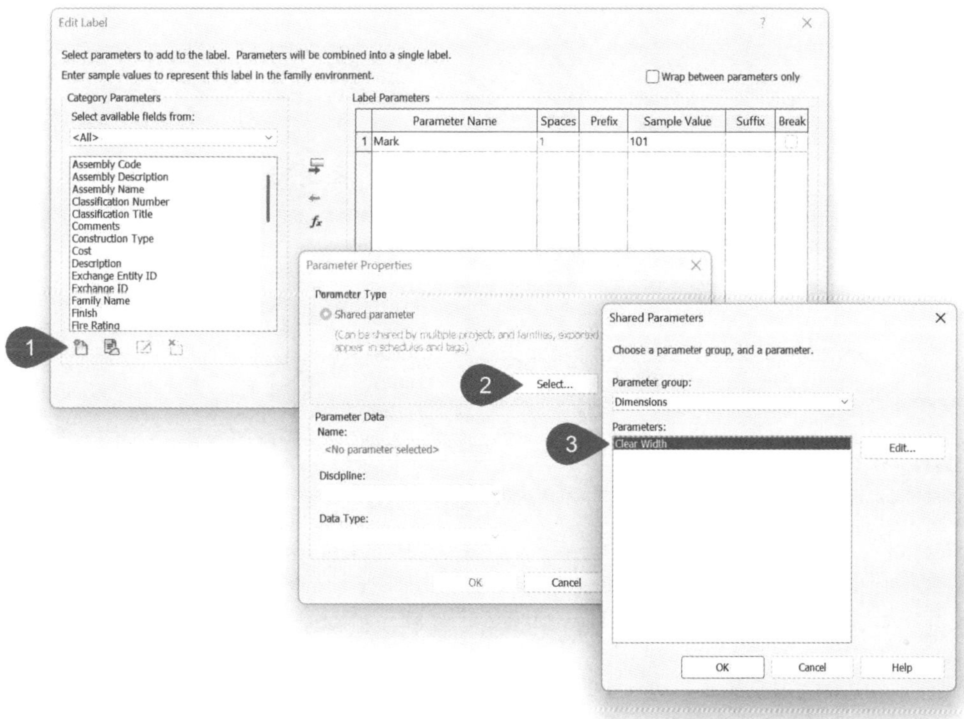

> *FYI: The* Mark *parameter could be left in the tag if you wanted both the* Mark *and* Clear Width *to appear together. The other option is to use two separate tags that can be moved independently. Keep in mind that it is possible to tag the same element multiple times. In this case, you would have two door tags on the same door, each tag being a different type.*

Load your new door and door tag families into a new project file. In the next section, you will see how these work in the project environment.

Using Shared Parameters in a Project

Now that you have your content and tags set up, you can use them in the project. First, draw a wall, then place an instance of the Single–Flush door (turn off *Tag on Placement*). Select the door and notice that the Clear Width parameter appears in the *Properties Palette*; it is an *Instance Parameter*. Add another door to the right of this one and change the width to 30″ via the *Type Selector*. Notice the *Clear Width* value has changed.

Next, you will tag the two doors. Select the ***Tag by Category*** icon from the *Quick Access Toolbar*. Uncheck the *Leader* option and select each door. Next, select each door tag, swap it with your new *Clear Width* option in the Type Selector, then set it to *Vertical* via the *Ribbon*.

> *TIP: If the text does not fit on one line, you have to go back into the family, increase the text box width, and reload the family into the project.*

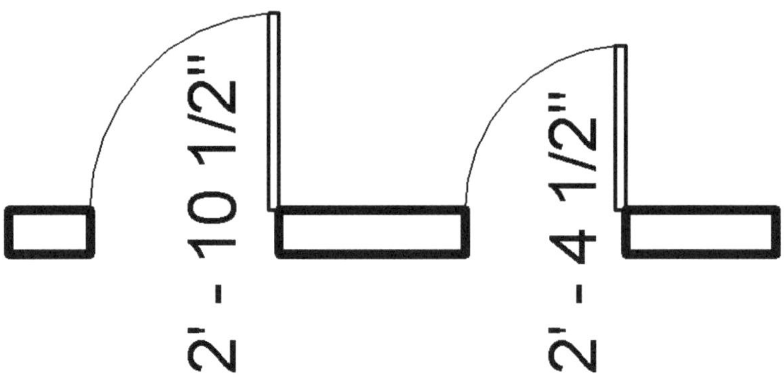

Things to Know

Only content that contains the *Shared Parameters* will display the parameter placeholder in a project. Try loading another door family (e.g., *Double–Flush*) into your test project without changing it in any way. Place an instance and then notice that the *Clear Width* option does not appear in the *Properties Palette*. This means that all content must have the Shared Parameter added in the family editor. It is possible to create a *Project Parameter* in the project/template file (that is based on a shared parameter) but you have to specify *Instance* or *Type*. If this varies, you cannot use a *Project Parameter*. The *Project Parameter* takes precedence and will change the loaded content.

Selectively associating parameters with content is a great trick when dealing with categories that have a variety of inputs, such as *Furniture* or *Mechanical Equipment*. Only loading *Shared*

Parameters into file cabinets or Air Handling Units (AHUs) will prevent those parameters from appearing in your lounge chairs or VAV boxes.

> ***FYI:*** *This also works with* Family Parameters, *but this information cannot be tagged or scheduled.*

Dealing with Problems

A number of problems can be created when *Shared Parameters* are not managed properly. The most common is when two separate *Shared Parameters* are created with the same name. This often happens when new users delete or otherwise lose a *Shared Parameter* file. They then try to recreate it manually, unaware that the previously mentioned unique code is different, and Revit will treat it as a different *Shared Parameter.* The first place this problem typically shows up is when a schedule in the project has blank spaces, even though the content (placed in the model) contains information. In this case, the schedule uses a specific version of the Shared Parameter, and only content that uses that same version appears in that schedule.

The fix for this problem is to open the bad content and re-associate the parameters with the correct *Shared Parameter.* It is not necessary to delete the bad parameter, which is good, as this could cause problems with existing formulas.

If you get content from another firm you are working with and they have used *Shared Parameters,* it is possible to export those parameters from the *Family Editor* into your *Shared Parameter* file. They will initially be located in the *Exported Parameters* group but can then be moved to a more appropriate location. This allows the unique code to be recreated in your project or content.

If you have a *Shared Parameter* with the same name as another firm's *Shared Parameter,* and you are working on the same model, that is a problem. You will have to decide whose version to use. There are third-party tools that can be used to add and modify Shared Parameters in batches of families.

Conclusion

Using *Shared Parameters* is essential to take full advantage of Revit's powerful features. Like any sophisticated tool, it takes a little effort to fully understand the feature and its nuances. Once you have harnessed the power of the feature and implemented it within your firm's content and templates, you can be much more productive and have less potential for errors and omissions on your projects.

Exercise 9-5:
Keynoting

This exercise will present an overview of the keynoting system in Revit. There are no steps to be applied to the project in this section.

Hybrid Method

A simple way to manage keyed notes is to use a custom Symbol family with a symbol and descriptive text, where the text visibility can be controlled per family instance. The keyed notes are placed in views with the text hidden, and the same keyed notes are also placed in a legend (or drafting view) with the text visible.

Notice in the plan view below that the keyed note is selected and that the custom instance parameter **Description Visible** is toggled off (Figure 9-5.1).

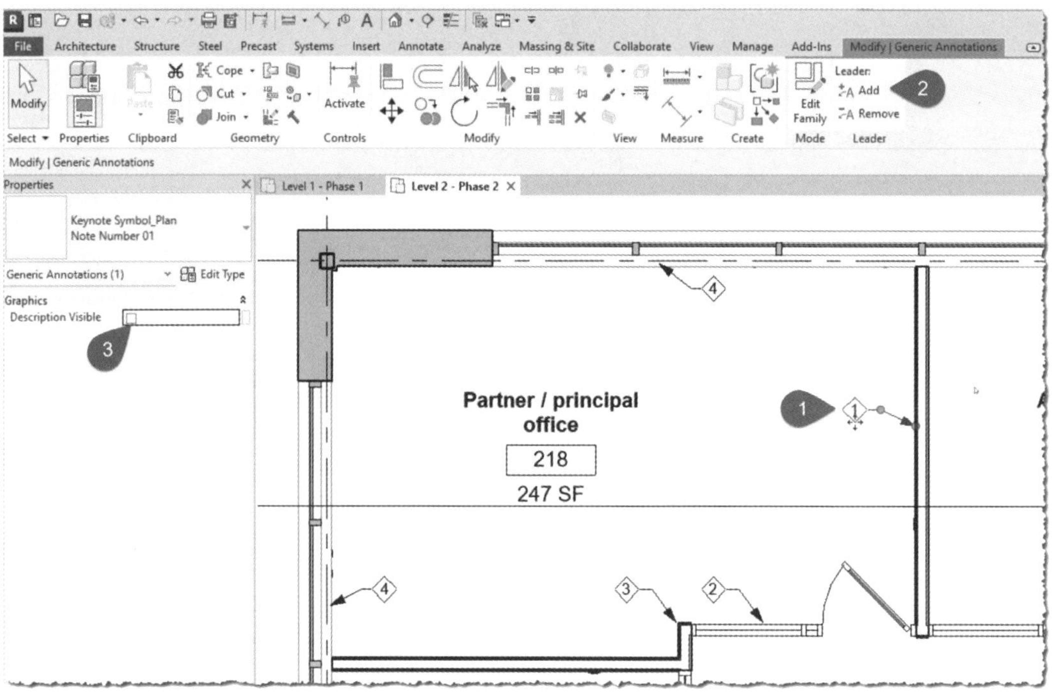

FIGURE 9-5.1 Keyed note in a floor plan view with 'Description Visible' toggled off

The next image shows the same family placed and then selected in a Legend view. In this view, the **Description Visible** is checked (Figure 9-5.2).

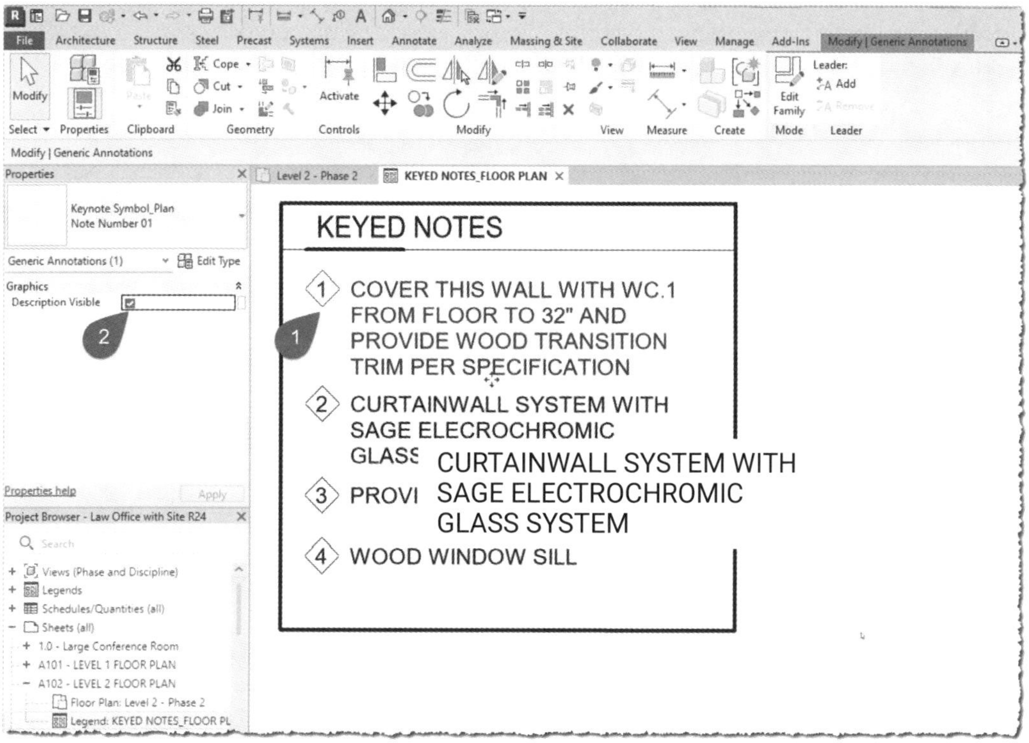

FIGURE 9-5.2 Keyed note in a legend view with 'Description Visible' toggled on

The image to the right shows the type properties for keyed note number 1. Notice the Keynote and Description are type parameters. This helps prevent someone from using the same number multiple times, each with a different description.

This method requires a different family for each plan type: e.g., Plan, Finish, Demo, Code, etc. Each family has one type for each note.

FYI: This example uses the **Multiline** parameter.

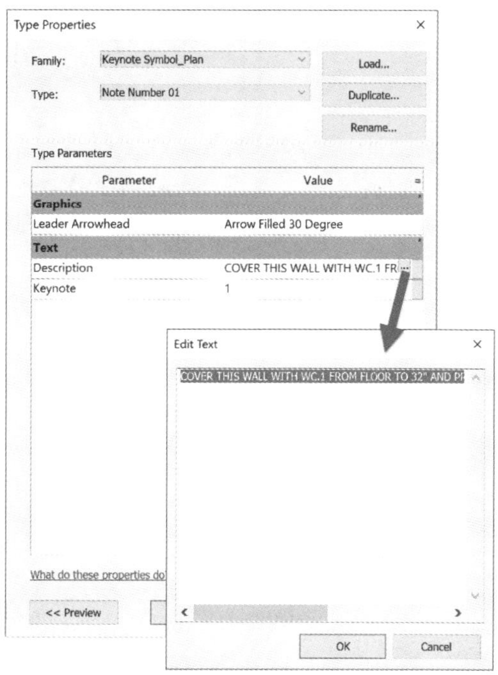

FIGURE 9-5.3 Type properties for selected keynote

Material Keynotes

We often want to identify a material in the model with "smart" text. In this case, we are talking about a Revit material defined within a **System Family** (e.g., Wall, Ceiling, Floor), a **Loadable Family** (e.g., Furniture, Casework, Doors, etc.), or **Painted** on a surface (which overrides the material defined in the Family).

There are two ways to identify materials within a Revit model (Figure 9-5.4):

- **Material Keynote**
- **Material Tag**

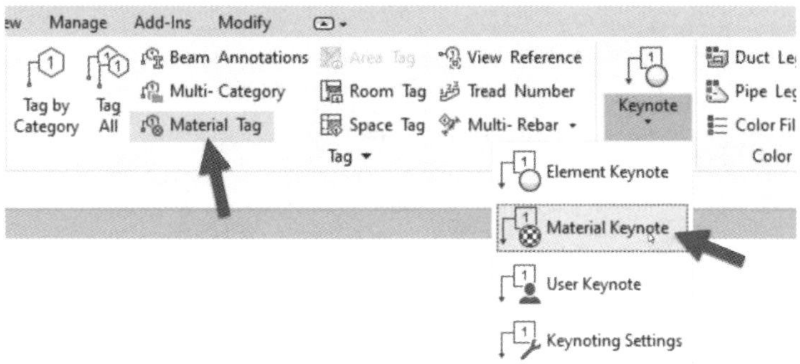

FIGURE 9-5.4 Material keynote and tag tools on the Annotate tab

FYI: It should be pointed out that even though we can define multiple materials for some elements, e.g., several layers within a wall (Brick, Insulation, Studs, Gypsum Board, etc.), we can only keynote/tag a material visible in a view—i.e., we can click on it. Materials hidden within a wall or equipment family cannot be tagged.

The two examples, Material Keynote and Material Tag, are shown in the image below—referencing the wall and the wall/base cabinets (Figure 9-5.5). The boxed text is a Keynote, and the adjacent text is a Material Tag.

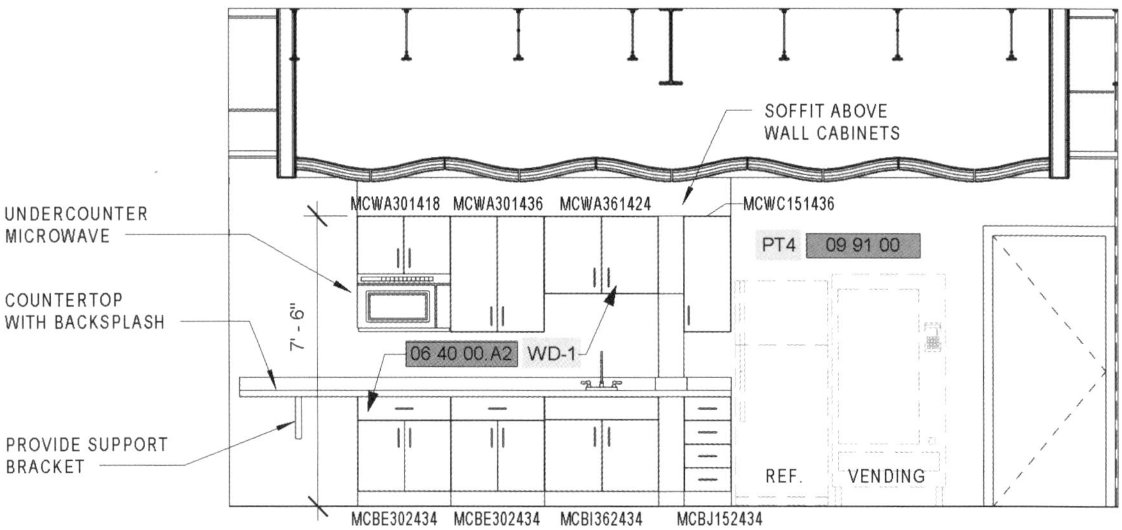

FIGURE 9-5.5 Material keynote applied to two elements (wall and cabinets)

Both values represented in the previous image are defined within the Material Browser as seen in the image below (Figure 9-5.6).

- Material Keynote → **Keynote**
    - o *The value must be selected from the Keynote file (more on this later)*
- Material Tag → **Mark**
    - o *The user can enter any value here*

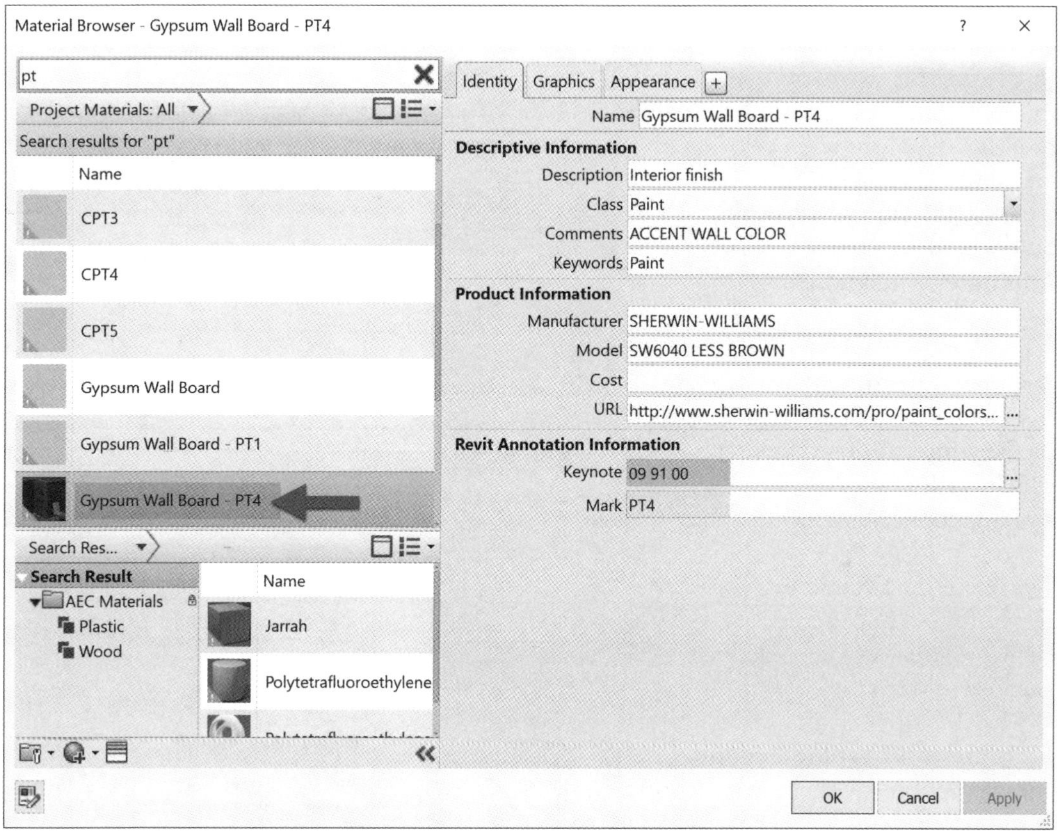

FIGURE 9-5.6 Annotation information within a Revit material

When either of these methods is used, the tags will update automatically if the family/type is changed (which also changes the material) or if a different material is painted on the elements being tagged.

When a Material is copied, the Keynote value is also copied (i.e. same keynote value is listed for the new material); however, the Mark value is not. The latter is preferred if you want to ensure the same value is not used for multiple materials.

Element Keynotes

Keynotes can be used to nearly eliminate "dumb" text in Revit. Here, we will quickly cover the basics of how keynotes work and then move on.

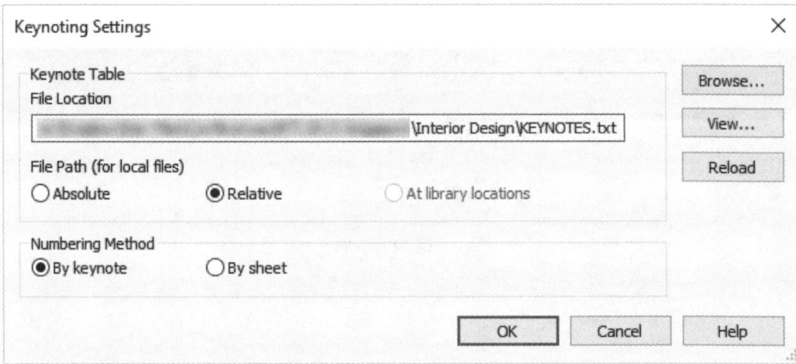

FIGURE 9-5.7 Keynoting settings dialog

First, the keynote information is stored in a simple text file (more on this in a minute). A Revit project can only reference one keynote file. The location of this file is defined in the **Keynoting Settings** file (Figure 9-5.7) via **Annotate → Keynotes**.

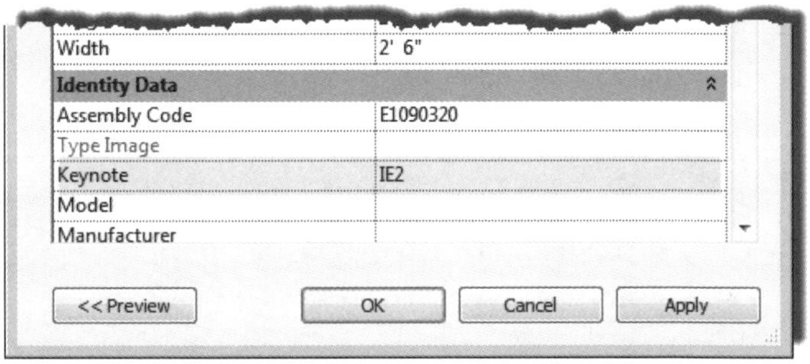

FIGURE 9-5.8 Keynote type parameter

Second, every model-based element in Revit has a **Keynote** type parameter (Figure 9-5.8). Editing this field opens the **Keynotes** dialog (Figure 9-5.9), which is a list based on the aforementioned external text file.

Third, use the **Element Keynote** tool to "tag" an element based on the predefined keynote value.

Fifth, create a **Keynote Legend** and place it on any sheets with keynoted views.

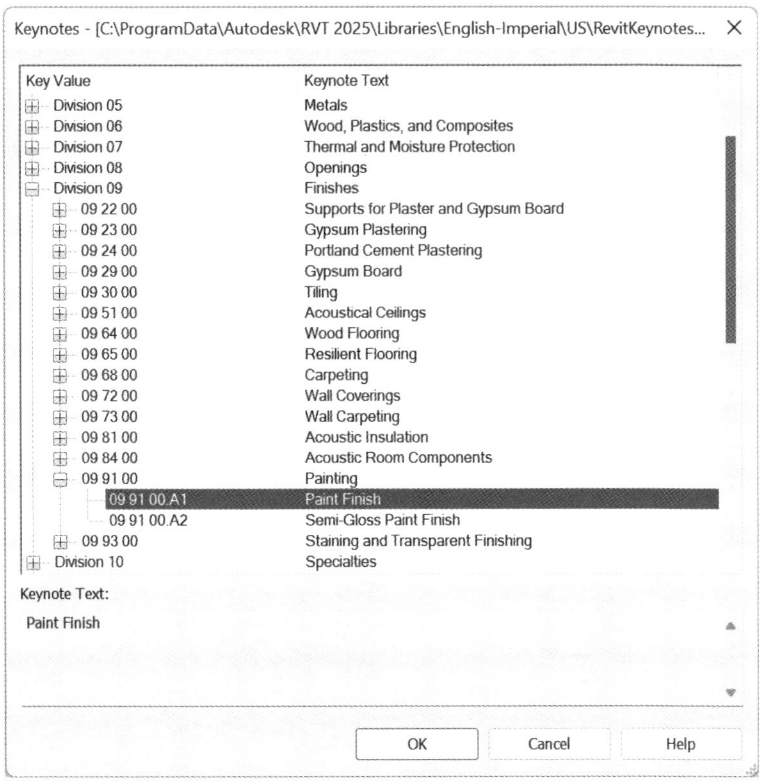

FIGURE 9-5.9 Keynotes dialog as viewed from within Revit

The result is shown in the sheet view below (Figure 9-5.10). The default keynote tag shows the keynote number, which corresponds to the same number and description in the legend. The result is "clean" looking drawings without excessive text.

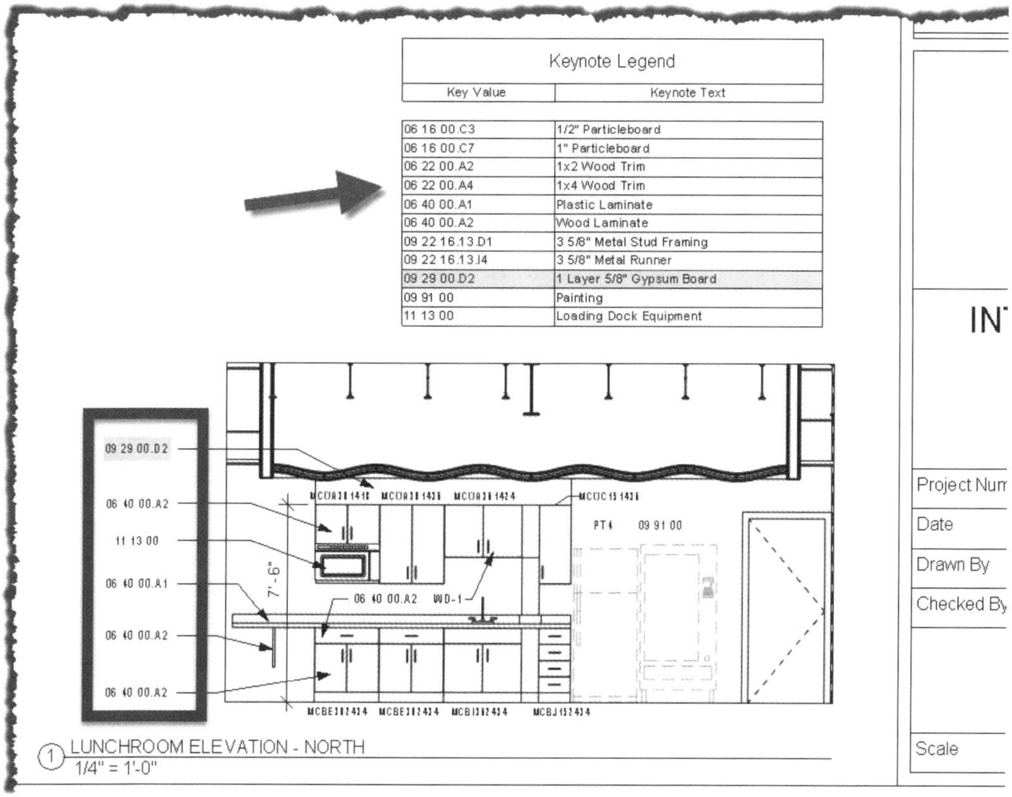

FIGURE 9-5.10 Example of a keynote legend and a view with keynotes

The keynote legend will only list keynotes that actually appear on a given sheet. Opening the keynote legend view directly will show all keynotes in the project. Keep in mind that the keynote legend lists only items that have been keynoted with the Keynote tool. It will not list a keynote just because an element's type property has a keynote value applied.

TIP: Use a Filter in Schedule Properties to limit the list if needed.

This concludes a basic overview of how keynotes work in Revit – with an emphasis on how they work out-of-the-box (OOTB). Next, we will look at a variation on this system that uses "normal" notes rather than product category numbers.

For this alternate method, we will start by creating a custom keynote file. Simply create an empty file using Microsoft Notepad and save it somewhere in your project folder (Figure 9-5.11).

To better understand the format of this file, note the following:

1. **Group definition**
    - unique number
    - descriptive text
2. **Keynote number**
3. **Keynote text**
4. **Group identifier**

The keynote text file must be stored on the server, accessible to all users (not necessarily with edit rights).

Results below explained on the next page…

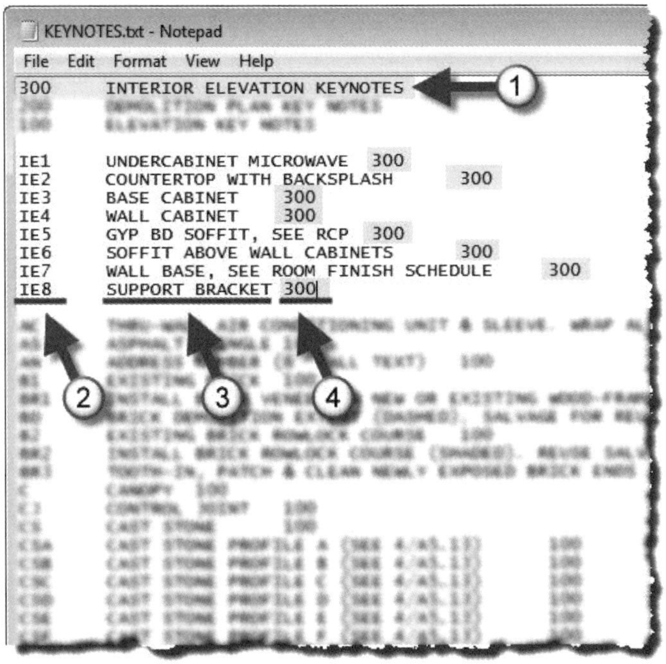

FIGURE 9-5.11 Anatomy of a keynote file

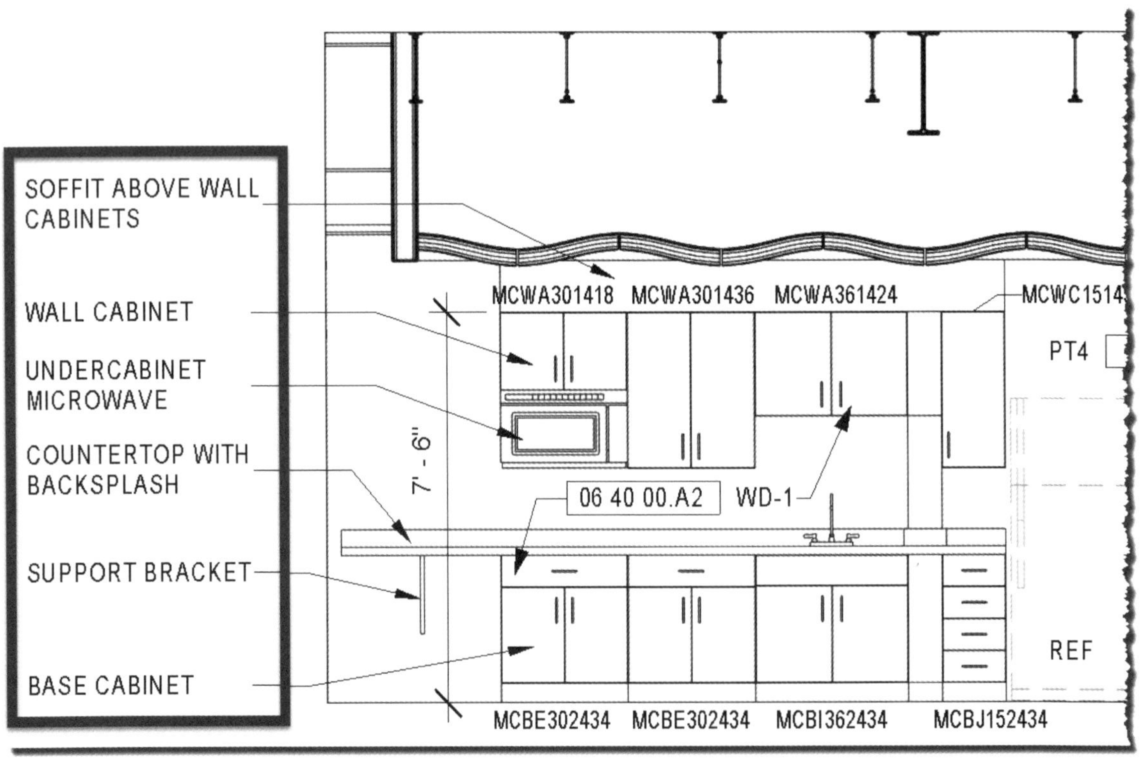

FIGURE 9-5.12 Keynotes added to elements in elevation - no "dumb" text

The elevation shown on the previous page includes Element Keynotes. The default Keynote tag has type properties to hide the keynote number & box and show the keynote number.

All the elements in the model have firm-approved standard notes applied to the Keynote type property. This information can be prepopulated in the content library (i.e., Revit families) to streamline production and ensure consistency across the firm.

Keynote Manager + Add-in for Revit

One challenge with maintaining the keynoting system in Revit is that the text file can only be edited by one person at a time. Also, after changes are made, they must be manually reloaded (note the Reload button in the Keynoting Settings dialog) to see them in the current Revit session (Figure 9-5.12).

Using **Keynote Manager +**, a third-party add-in for Revit, can help. This tool has the following features:

- Multiple users
- Auto reload
- Spellcheck
- Indicates keynotes used in the project (with house icon)
- Auto sequencing
- Add comments and URL links

FYI: To store the additional comments and external links, a same-named XML file is created right next to the keynote file.

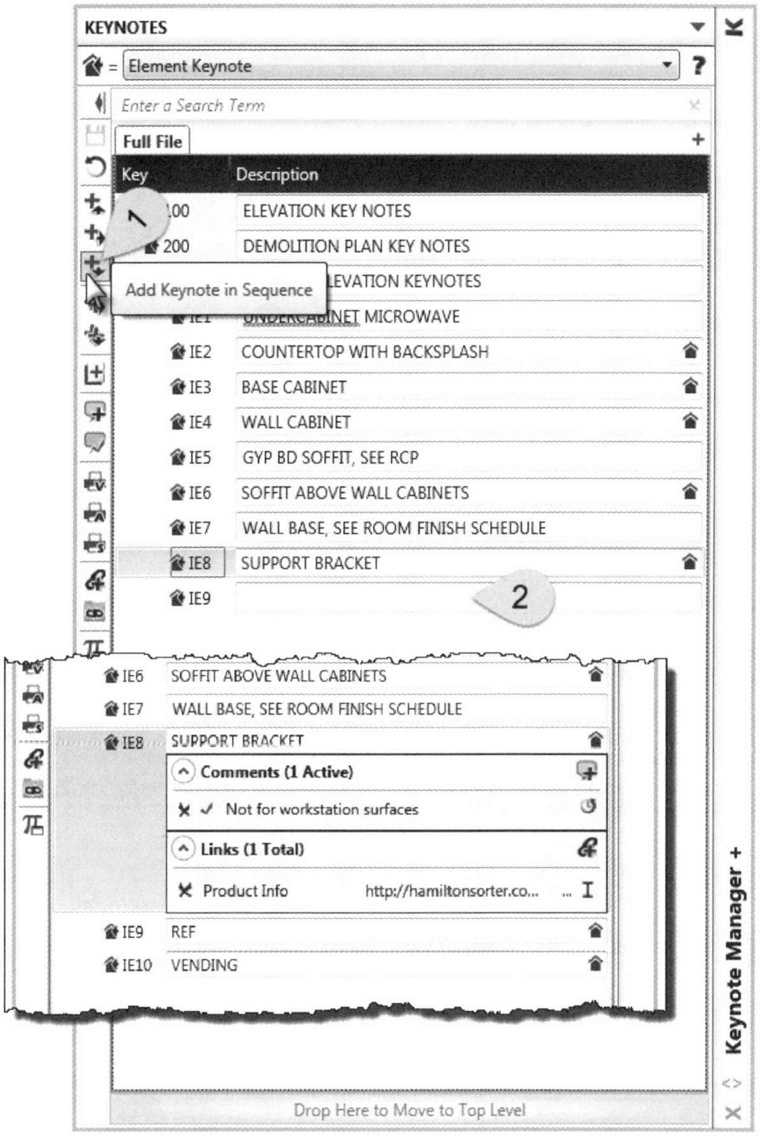

FIGURE 9-5.13 Keynote manager palette in Revit

Be sure to check out **Keynote Manager** by Revolution Design, Inc., for a powerful add-in that simplifies the use of Keynotes in Revit.
URL: http://revolutiondesign.biz/products/keynote-manager/features/

User Keynotes

User Keynotes work the same way as Element Keynotes, with one exception…

When the **User Keynote** tool is selected, the user is prompted to select an element to keynote. Next, a selection must be made from the keynote list (i.e., the text file).

Although this adds some flexibility to the process, it also provides an opportunity to select the wrong keynote. In the example below (Figure 9-5.14), the selected base cabinet is tagged with three keynotes (highlighted in yellow). One is an **Element Keynote**, and two are **User Keynotes**—both user keynotes indicate something completely different.

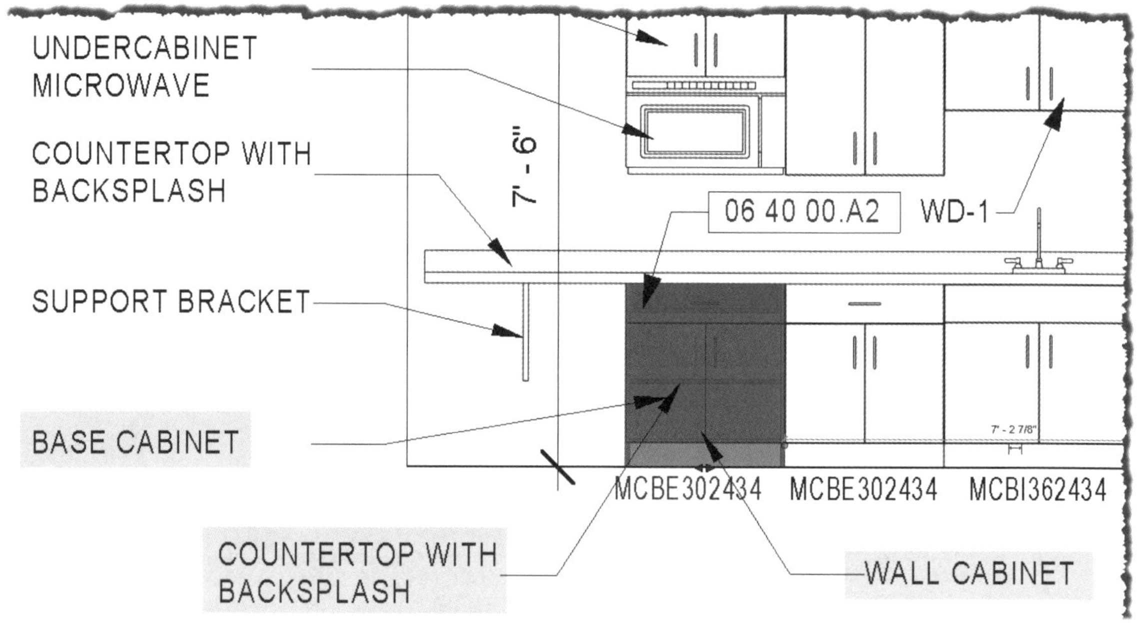

FIGURE 9-5.14 Multiple user keynotes applied to a single model element

Used correctly, the User Keynote tool can be helpful. However, those who use it must be trained and pick carefully each time they use it.

Self-Exam:

The following questions can be used as a way to check your knowledge of this lesson. The answers can be found at the bottom of this page.

1. Deleting a dimension with equality toggled on will always also delete the constraint in the model. (T/F)
2. To move an element, simply click on the dimension and edit the text. (T/F)
3. Material Keynote and Material Tag are the two ways to annotate a material. (T/F)
4. Pressing Enter in a text element limits the ability to modify using the text box grips and have the number of rows adjust. (T/F)
5. To measure the length along a curved line, use this dimension tool:

   ______________________________ .

Review Questions:

The following questions may be assigned by your instructor as a way to assess your knowledge of this section. Your instructor has the answers to the review questions.

1. A dimension string set to Equality can only display 'EQ' and not the actual dimension value. (T/F)
2. A single text element can have both curved and straight leaders. (T/F)
3. Spell check only works on text elements, not tags or keynotes. (T/F)
4. The use of basic text should be minimized. (T/F)
5. The same element can be tagged more than once, even in the same view. (T/F)
6. Use a Linear dimension to ensure a dimension remains horizontal. (T/F)
7. Revit's keynoting system requires an external text file. (T/F)
8. Text leaders can only be removed in the reverse order they were added. (T/F)
9. Revit can dimension all the openings in a wall at once. (T/F)
10. A 'user keynote' presents an opportunity for user error by selecting the wrong item from a list each time this tool is used. (T/F)

SELF-EXAM ANSWERS:
1 – F, **2** – F, **3** – T, **4** – T, **5** – Arc Length

Notes:

Lesson 10
Elevations, Sections, and Details

This lesson will cover interior and exterior elevations as well as sections. The default template you started with already has the four main exterior elevations set up for you. You will investigate how Revit generates elevations and the role the elevation tag plays in that process. Finally, you will learn how to link in AutoCAD drawings to reuse legacy details in Revit.

Exercise 10-1:
Exterior Elevations

Setting Up an Exterior Elevation:

Even though you already have the main exterior elevations established, you will go through the steps necessary to set one up. Many projects have more than four exterior elevations, so all exterior surfaces are elevated.

1. Open the **Chapter 10 starter file from the online files** to ensure you have the complete structural system in your project. ***WARNING:*** Your model will be incomplete if you do not start with the provided online file.

2. After opening the online file from SDCpublications.com, not your copy of the Law Office file, switch to your **Level 1** floor plan view, aka *Level 1*.

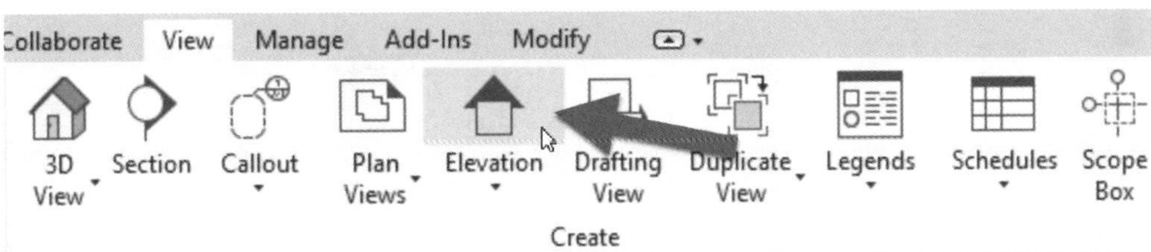

3. Select **View → Create → Elevation**.

4. Make sure the *Type Selector* is set to *Elevation:* **Building Elevation** and then place the elevation tag in plan view as shown in Figure 10-1.1.

   NOTE: As you move the cursor around the screen, the Elevation Tag automatically turns to point at the building.

You now have an elevation added to the *Project Browser* in the *Elevations* category. **The first thing you should do after placing an elevation is rename it**; the default name is not very descriptive. These generic names would get very confusing on larger projects with dozens of views.

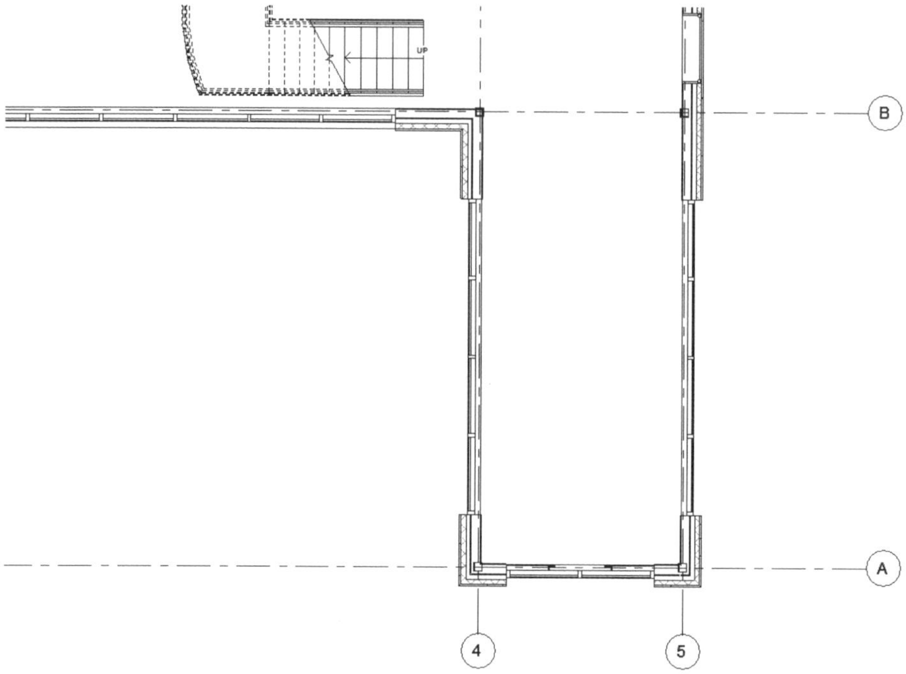

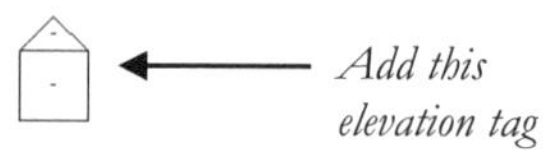

FIGURE 10-1.1 Added elevation tag

5. Right-click on the view name and select **Rename** (Figure 10-1.2).

6. Type: **South – Main Entry**.

The name should be fairly descriptive so you can tell where the elevation is just by the name in the *Project Browser*.

7. Double-click on **South – Main Entry** in the *Project Browser*.

The elevation may not look correct right away. You will adjust this in the next step. Notice, though, that an elevation was created simply by placing an *Elevation Tag* in plan view.

8. Switch back to the **Level 1** plan view.

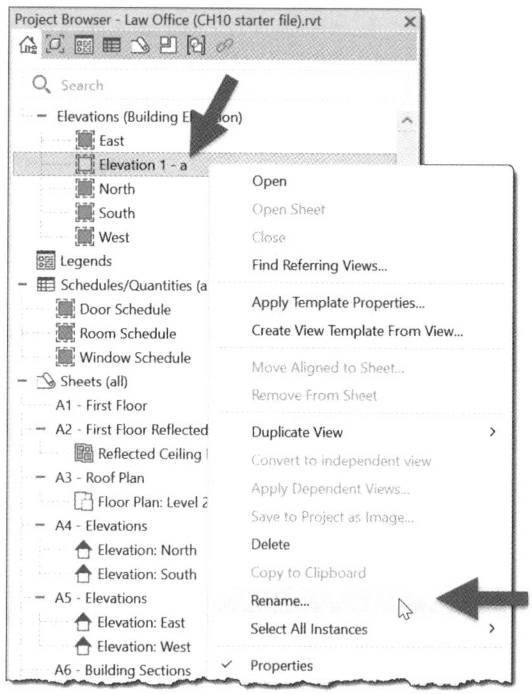

FIGURE 10-1.2 Renaming new view name

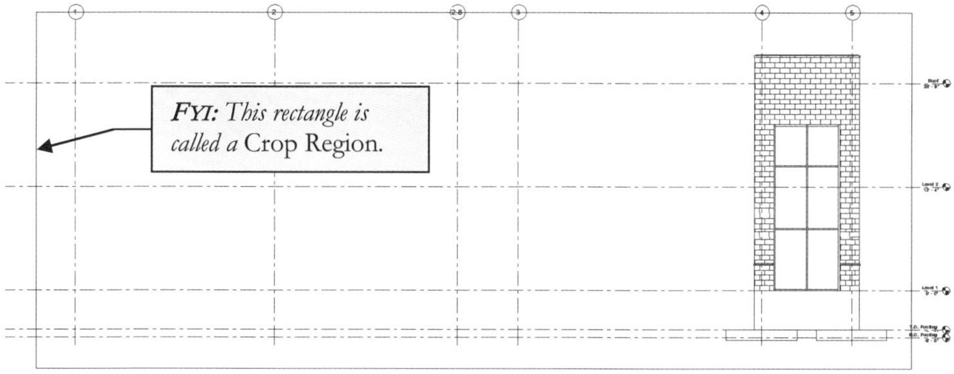

FIGURE 10-1.3 New exterior elevation view – initial state

Next you will study the options associated with the *Elevation Tag*. This, in part, controls what is seen in the elevation.

9. The *Elevation Tag* has two parts: the pointing triangle and the square center. Each part will highlight as you move the cursor over it. **Select the square center part**.

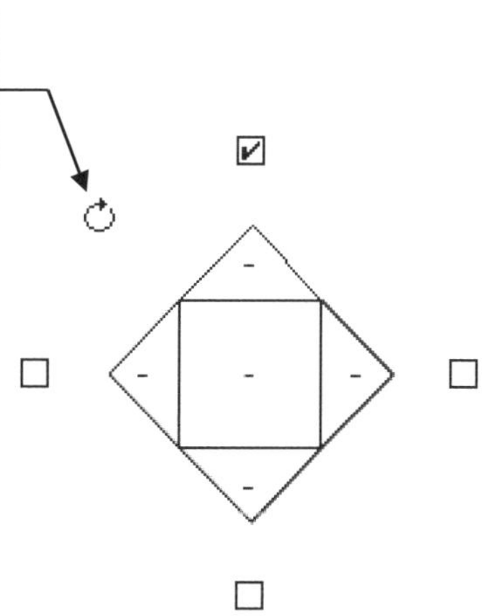

FIGURE 10-1.4 Selected elevation tag

You should now see the symbol shown on the right (Figure 10-1.4).

View direction boxes:
The checked box indicates which way the elevation tag is looking. You can check, or uncheck, the other boxes. Do NOT do that at this time. Each checked box adds another view name to the *Project Browser*.

Rotation control:
This control allows you to look perpendicular to an angled wall in plan, for example.

INTERIOR ELEVATIONS:

When adding the elevation tag to the floor plan you should select "Interior Elevation" from the *Type Selector*. This will use a different symbol to help distinguish the interior tags from the exterior tags in the plan views. Also, the interior and exterior views are separated in the *Project Browser*, making it easier to manage views as the project continues to develop. You will be looking at Interior Elevations in the next exercise.

10. Press the **ESC** key to unselect the elevation tag.

11. Select the pointed portion of the elevation tag.

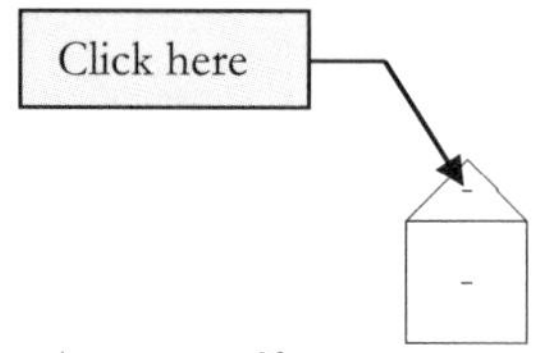

Your elevation tag should look similar to Figure 10-1.5.

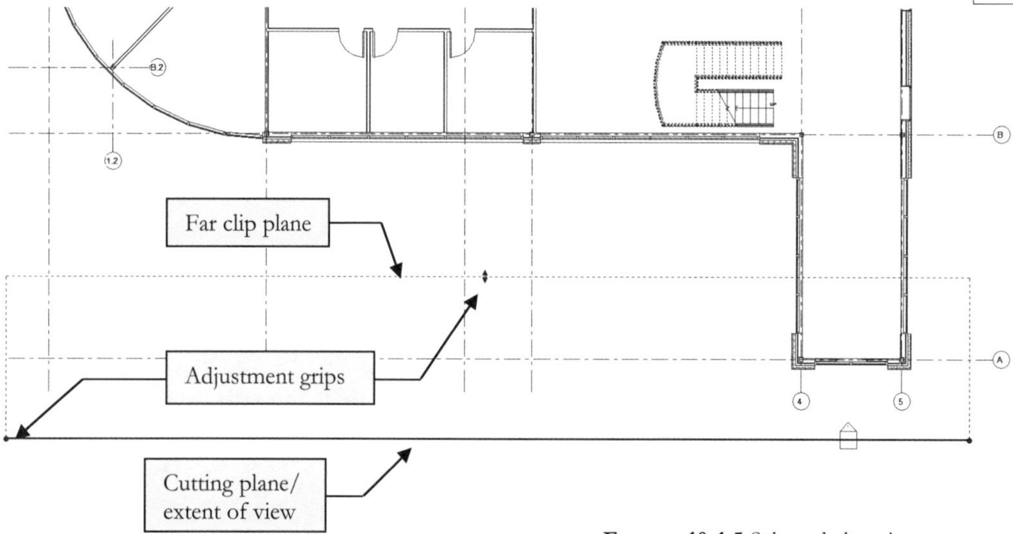

FIGURE 10-1.5 Selected elevation tag

The elevation tag, as selected in Figure 10-1.5, has several features for controlling how the elevation looks. Here is a quick explanation:

- **Cutting plane/extent of view line:** This controls how much of the 3D model is elevated from left to right (i.e., the width of the elevation). This list also acts like a section line in that nothing behind this line will show up.

- **Far clip plane:** This controls how far into the 3D model the elevation view can see. This can be turned off in the elevation's *View Properties*, not the plan's *View Properties*, making the view depth unlimited; the next page covers this more.

- **Adjustment grips:** You can drag these with the mouse to control the features mentioned above. These values can also be controlled in the elevation's *View Properties.*

Notice how the "extent of view" line was created to match the width of the building. You will be adjusting this later to only see the entry wall.

12. Select the view label **South – Main Entry** in the *Project Browser*; the *Properties Palette* now shows the selected view's *View Properties.*

You have several options in the *Properties* window (Figure 10-1.6). Under the heading *Extents,* notice the three Crop/Clipping options—these control the following:

- **Crop View**: This crops the width and height of the view in elevation. *Adjusting the width of the cropping window in elevation also adjusts the "extent of view" control in plan view.*

- **Crop Region Visible**: This displays a rectangle in the elevation view indicating the extent of the cropping window, described above. *When selected in elevation view, the rectangle can be adjusted with the adjustment grips.* See Figure 10-1.3.

- **Far Clipping**: If this is turned off, Revit will draw everything visible in the 3D model, within the extent of view.

You will manipulate some of these controls next.

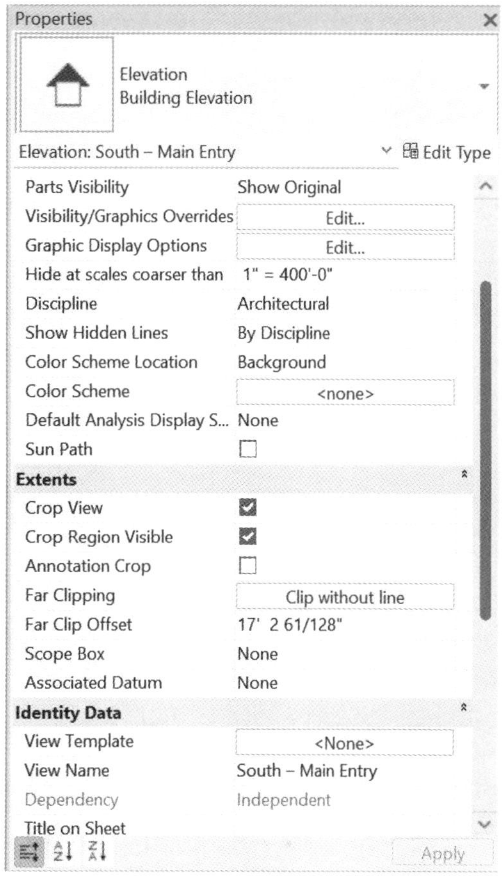

FIGURE 10-1.6 South – Main Entry view properties

13. With the elevation tag still selected, as in Figure 10-1.5, drag or move the "cutting plane/extent of view" line up **into** the main entry as shown in Figure 10-1.7. Do not move the tag itself.

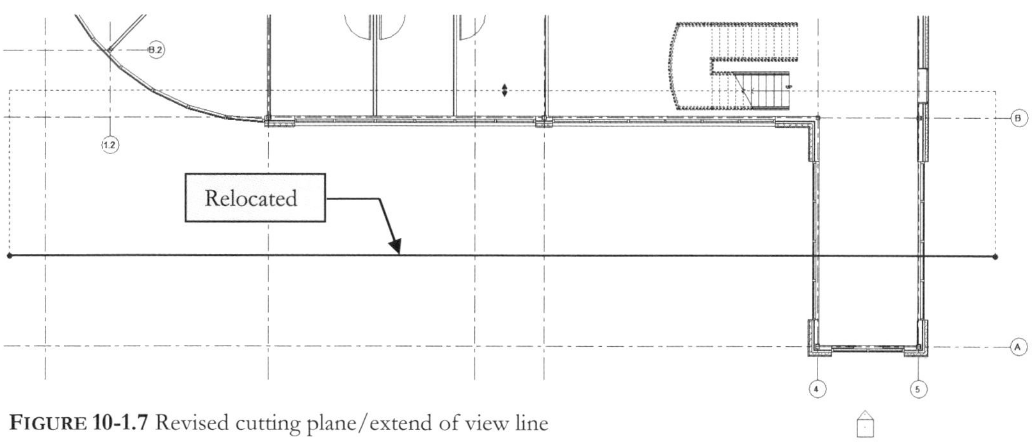

FIGURE 10-1.7 Revised cutting plane/extend of view line

14. Now switch to the *elevation view*: **South – Main Entry**.

Your elevation should look similar to Figure 10-1.8. If required, click on the cropping window and resize it to match this image.

The main entry wall and roof are now displayed in section because of the location of the "cutting plane" line in plan. Notice the steel beams and joists!

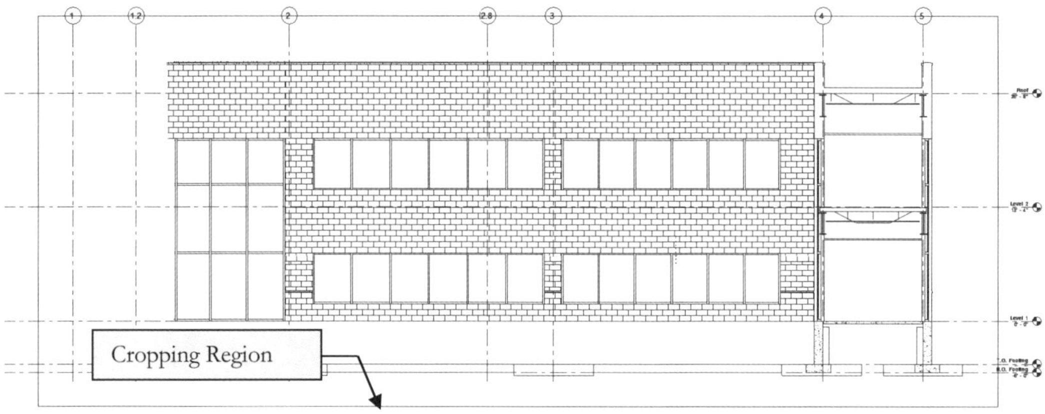

FIGURE 10-1.8 Elevation with cutting plane through main entry at Grids 4 and 5

As you can see, the grid lines appear automatically in the elevations, as do the level datums. Take a minute to observe how the far clip plane controls the visibility of Grid line **1.2** between Figures 10-1.3 and 10-1.8. It must be intersecting the grid lines in plan for it to show up in elevation; compare Figures 10-1.5 and 10-1.7. This is good as it just clutters the drawing to see grid lines that have nothing to do with this part of the drawing.

Notice that the curved wall near Grid **1** is not fully visible. This is not related to the cropping region shown in Figure 10-1.8. Rather, it is related to the "Far Clip Plane" set in the plan view, or in the view's properties.

15. Adjust the "Far Clip Plane" in the **Level 1 Architectural Plan** view so that the entire building shows in the **South – Main Entry** view.

    TIP: *Click on the grip and drag the "far clip plane" North until it is past the Grid line **C**, which is at the middle of the building.*

Now, when you switch back to the "South – Main Entry" elevation view, you should see the entire building.

> ***DESIGN INTEGRATION TIP:*** *When working on one model with multiple disciplines it is important to set the discipline parameters correctly in an elevation view's properties. This will prevent it from showing up in the structural floor plans, for example.*

Next, you will adjust the *Elevation Tag* to set up an enlarged elevation for the main entry area's South wall.

16. In the **Level 1 Architectural Plan** view, adjust the *Elevation Tag* to show only the main entry wall (Figure 10-1.9).
    - The *Cutting Plane/Extent of View* line is moved South so it is outside of the building footprint.
    - Use the left and right grips to shorten the same line.

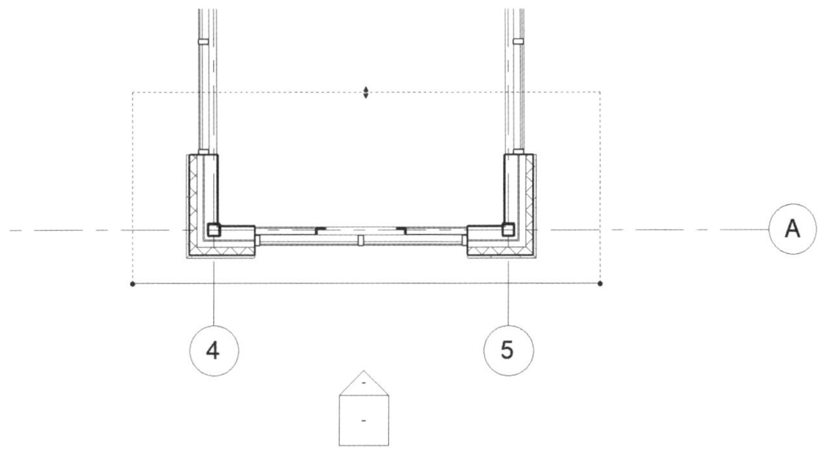

FIGURE 10-1.9 Main Entry wall enlarged elevation

17. Switch to **South – Main Entry** view to see the enlarged elevation you are setting up (Figure 10-1.10).

18. Make sure the **View Scale** is set to **½" = 1'-0"** on the *View Control Bar* at the bottom of the screen.

Notice how the level datum symbols are now smaller; *Undo* and try it again if you missed it.

19. Click the ***Hide Crop Region*** icon on the *View Control Bar* to make the *Crop Region* disappear.

Once you modify the view constraints in plan view (Figure 10-1.9) and you switch to the new elevation view, you can click on the *Crop Region* and use the grips to make the view wider.

When you drag the *Crop Region* to the right, the *Grids* and *Level Datum* move so they do not overlap the elevation. This is another example of Revit taking the busy work out of designing a building!

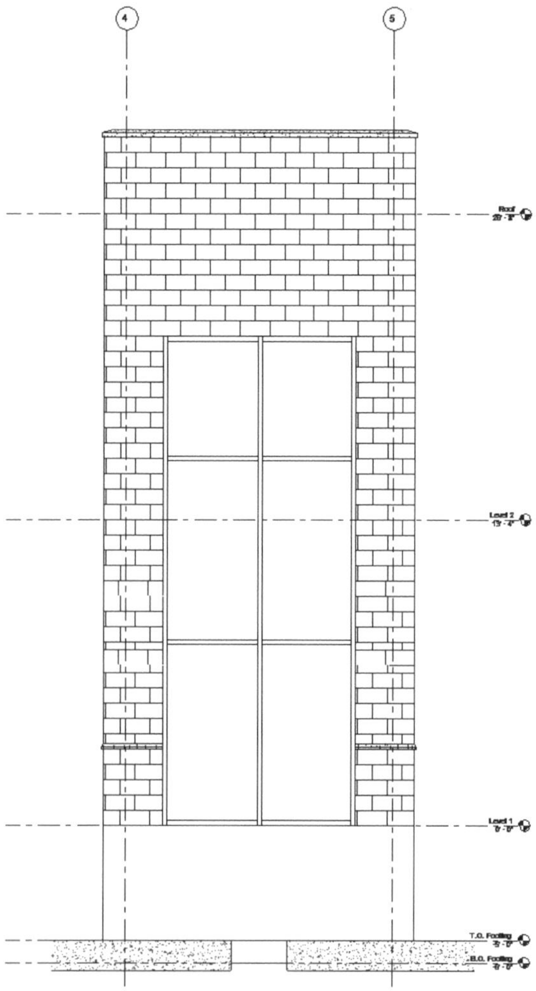

Crop Region, visibility should be turned off in Step #19.

ENLARGED ELEVATION:
An enlarged elevation like this might be used to dimension various items like the curtain wall, signage size and location, special accents, etc. The scale would typically be larger than the full South elevation so you can fit more notes and dimensions.

This view might be placed on a sheet with the other elevations or any sheet where you can find room.

FIGURE 10-1.10 Main Entry wall elevation

Modify an Exterior Elevation:

The purpose of the following steps is to demonstrate that changes can be made anywhere, and all other drawings are automatically updated.

20. Open the **East** exterior elevation view.

21. Select the fixed window in the upper right, near Grid **D**.

You will copy the window to the right so the *Level 2* storage room in the Northeastern corner of the building has some natural daylight.

22. **Copy** the selected window **12′-8″** to the North, i.e., to the right in this view (Figure 10-1.11).

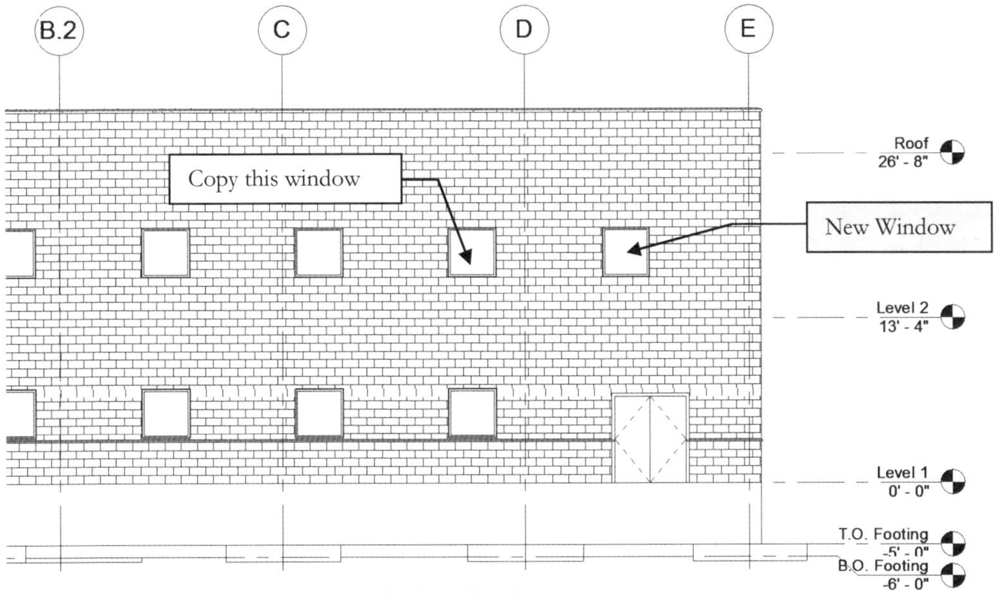

FIGURE 10-1.11 Modifying windows on the East elevation

Now you will switch to the **Level 2** plan view to see your changes.

23. Switch to the **Level 2 Architectural Plan** view and zoom in on the Northeastern area (Figure 10-1.12).

Notice how the windows in plan have changed to match the modifications you just made to the exterior elevations? This only makes sense, seeing as both the floor plan and the exterior elevation are projected 2D views of the same 3D model. Both views are directly manipulating the 3D model.

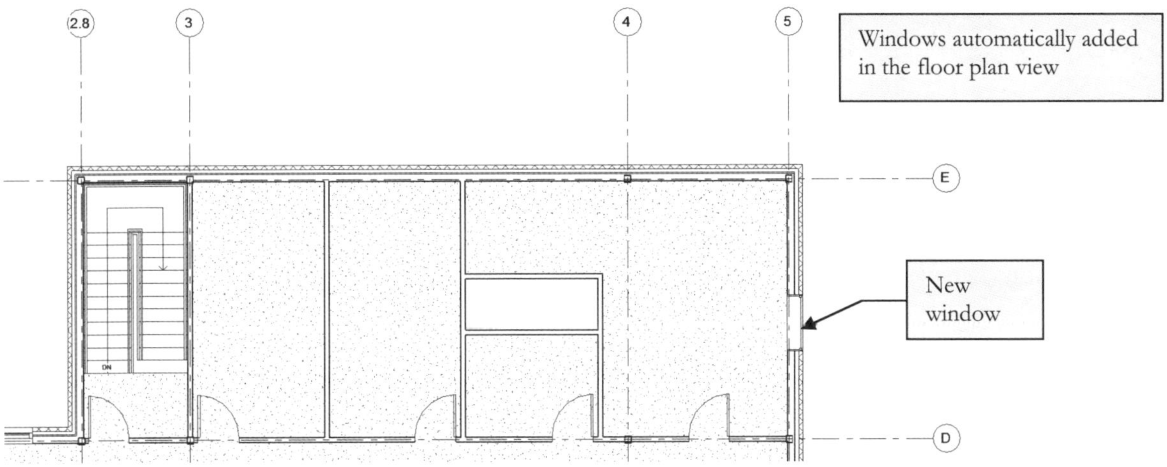

FIGURE 10-1.12 Window automatically added to the plan view

Next, you will insert a window in elevation using the *Window* command and look at a coordination issue with the structural design.

24. Switch to the **North** exterior elevation view.

25. Select the ***Window*** tool from the *Ribbon.*

Notice, with the window selected for placement, you have the usual listening dimensions helping you accurately place the window. As you move the window around, you should see a dashed horizontal green line indicating the default sill height, although you can deviate from this in elevation views.

26. From the *Type Selector* choose *Fixed:* **48"x48."**

27. Place a window as shown in **Figure 10-1.13**:

- Place the window at Level 2.
- Make sure the bottom of the window snaps to the dashed, cyan colored sill line.
- The window should be approximately centered on Grid 4.

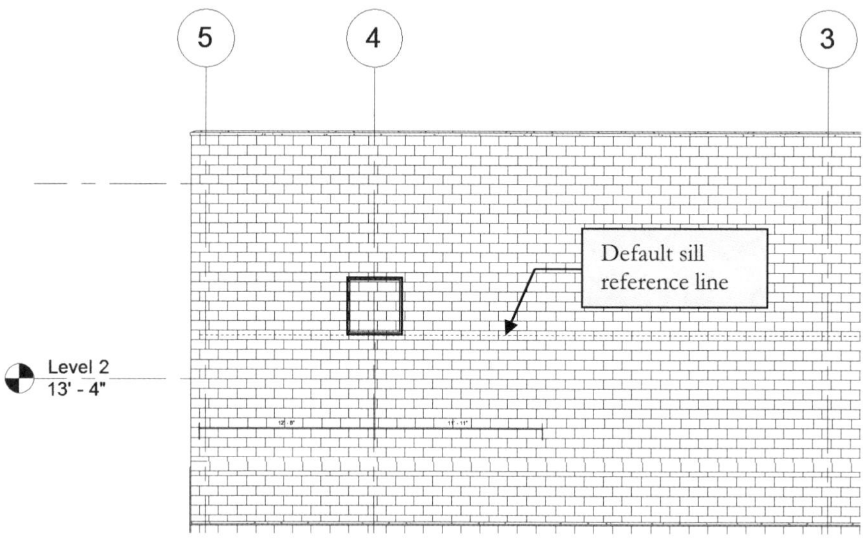

FIGURE 10-1.13 Placing a window on the North elevation

You now placed a window so that it conflicts with a column. Unfortunately, Revit does not tell you that the conflict exists; Revit will warn you if a newly placed window conflicts with a perpendicular interior wall. In this case you will visually be alerted to the conflict in both plan and elevation. Another way to discover this type of conflict is by running the **Interference Check** on the *Collaborate* tab, having Revit look for any windows which occupy the same space as any structural columns.

28. Zoom in on the new window and notice the structural column that is clearly visible (Figure 10-1.14).

29. Switch to the **Level 2 Architectural Plan** view to see the problem (Figure 10-1.15).

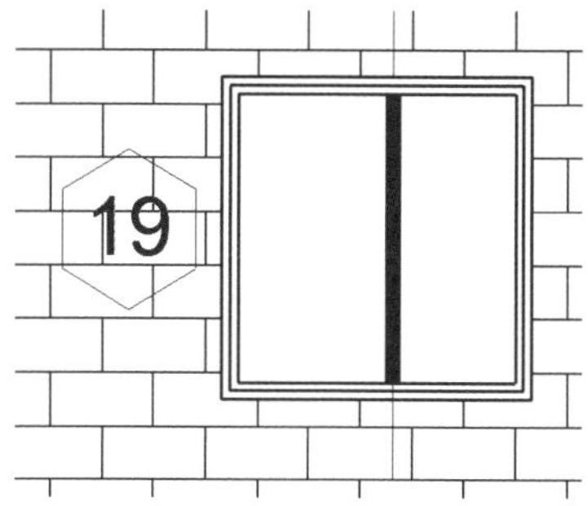

FIGURE 10-1.14
New window with column visible

Notice the column and window clearly conflict with each other. At this point you would need to move the window, delete the window or change the structural design, which is likely not practical for one window. In the next step you will delete the window from the floor plan view which, of course, will update the elevation.

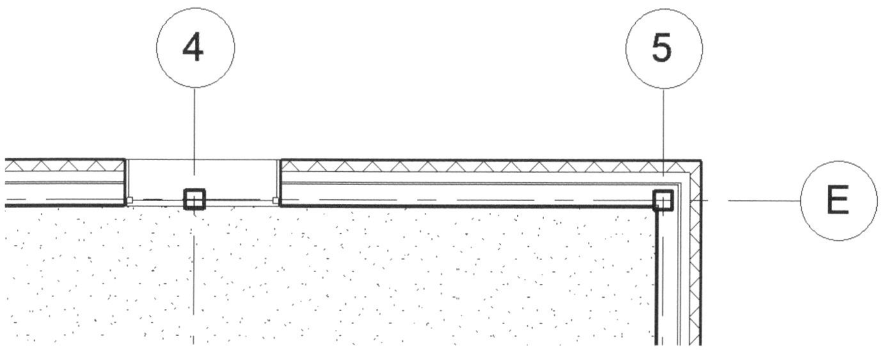

FIGURE 10-1.15 New window with column visible; plan view

30. While in plan view, select the new window and **Delete** it.

31. **Save** your BIM file.

TIP: Turning on shadows via the View Control Bar can make your 2D elevation view look more interesting; see image below. However, this makes working in the view very slow!

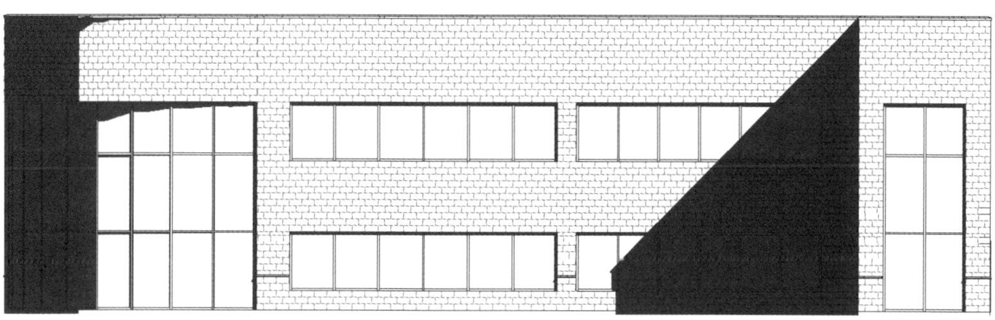

FIGURE 10-1.16 South elevation with shadows turned on

Exercise 10-2:
Interior Elevations

Creating interior elevations is very much like exterior elevations. In fact, you use the same tool. The main difference is that you are placing the elevation tag inside the building rather than on the exterior.

Adding an Interior Elevation Tag:

1. Open your law office project from the previous section.

2. Switch to the ***Level 1 Architectural Floor Plan*** view, if necessary.

3. Select the ***Elevation*** tool.

In the next step you will place an elevation tag. Before clicking to place the tag, try moving it around to see how Revit automatically turns the tag to point at the closest wall.

4. Select *Elevation:* **Interior Elevation** and then place an elevation tag looking East (i.e., to the right), as shown (Figure 10-2.1).

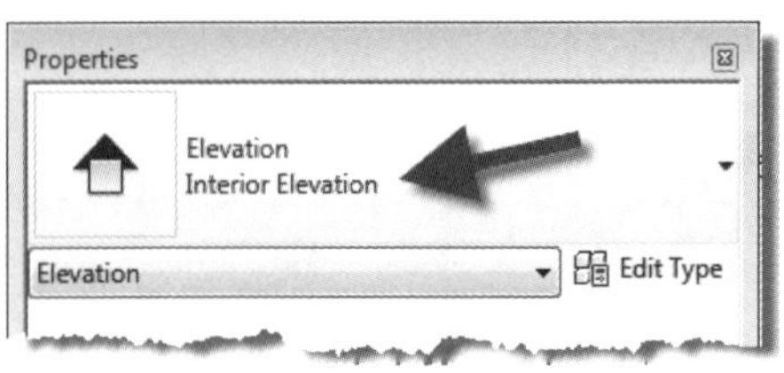

REMEMBER: *The first thing you should do after adding an Elevation Tag is to give it an appropriate name in the Project Browser list.*

5. Change the name of the elevation to **Lobby and Entry - East**.

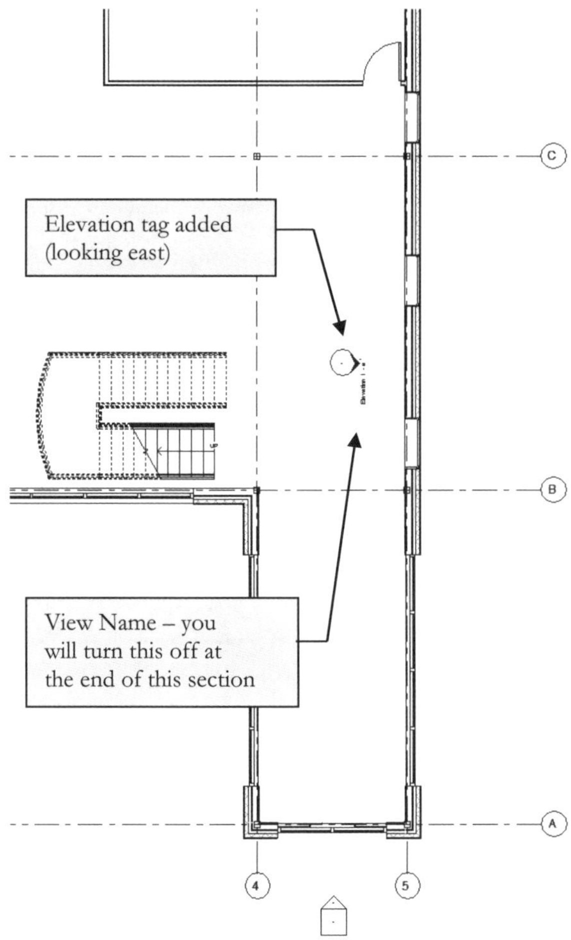

FIGURE 10-2.1 Level 1: Elevation tag added; Lobby / Entry

6. Switch to the **Lobby and Entry – East** view.

    TIP: *Try double-clicking on the elevation tag (the pointing portion).*

Initially, your elevation should look something like Figure 10-2.2; if not, you will be adjusting it momentarily so do not worry. Next you will adjust this view. Notice how Revit automatically controls the lineweights of elements in section versus elements in elevations.

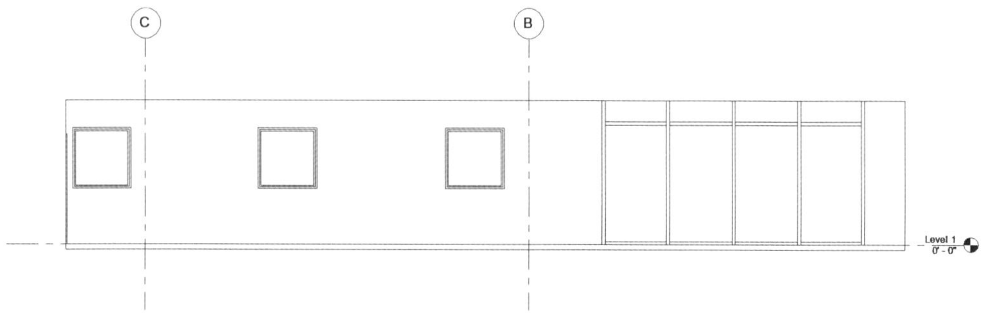

FIGURE 10-2.2 Lobby and Entry – East, initial view

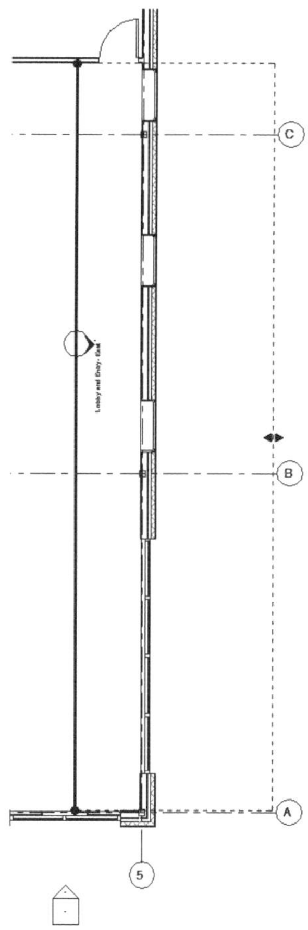

7. Switch back to the **Level 1** plan view.

8. Pick the pointed portion of the *Elevation Tag* so you see the view graphic control options (Figure 10-2.3).

You should compare the two drawings on this page, Figures 10-2.2 and 10-2.3, to see how the control lines in the plan view dictate what is generated or visible in the elevation view, for both width and depth.

Revit automatically found the left and right walls, the floor and ceiling in the elevation view.

Notice the *Far Clip Plane* is also accessible. If you cannot see the windows in the elevation view that means the *Far Clip Plane* needs to be moved farther to the right.

FIGURE 10-2.3 Elevation tag selected

FYI: The elevation tags are used to reference the sheet and drawing number so the client or contractor can find the desired elevation quickly while looking at the floor plans. It is interesting to know that Revit automatically fills in the elevation tag when the elevation is placed on a sheet and will update it if the elevation moves or sheet number changes.

9. Switch back to the **Lobby and Entry - East** view.

Just to try adjusting the *Crop Region* to see various results, you will extend the top upward to see the second floor.

10. Select the *Crop Region* and drag the upper middle grip upwards to increase the view size vertically (Figure 10-2.4).

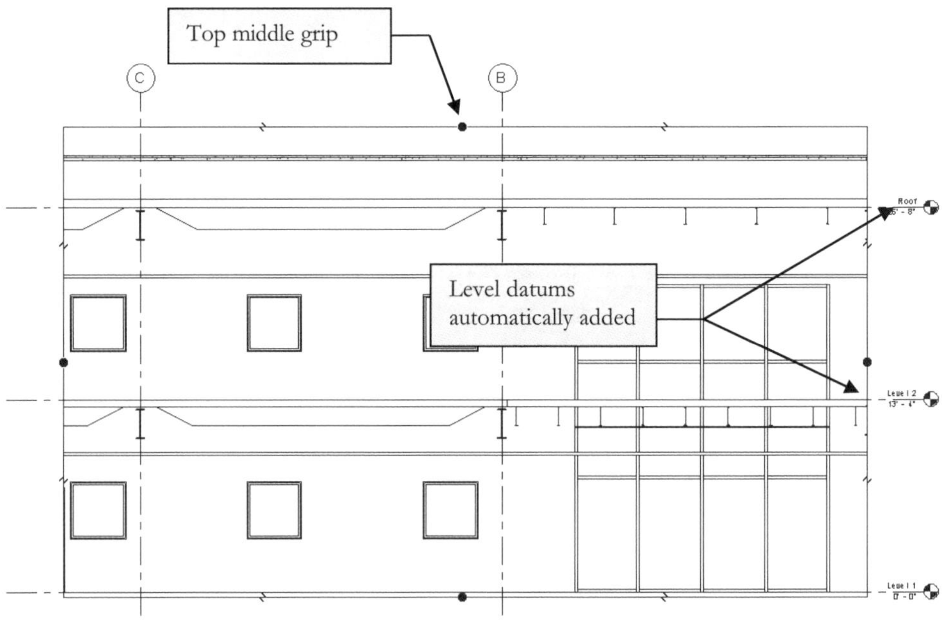

FIGURE 10-2.4 Lobby and Entry - East elevation; crop region selected and modified

Here you are getting a sneak peek ahead to the sections portion of this book. Notice the beams and joists. Notice that additional level datum lines were added automatically as the view grew to include more vertical information (i.e., Level 2, Roof). Notice the *Grids* automatically extended with the *Crop Region.* Also, the bar joists would have more detail if the *Detail Level* were set higher on the *View Control Bar.*

11. Now select **Undo** to return to the previous view (Figure 10-2.2).

The Level 1 level datum is not necessary in this view, so you will remove it from this view.

> ***IMPORTANT:*** *You cannot simply delete the Level datum because it will actually delete all associated views from the entire project (i.e., floor and ceiling plan views). This will delete any model elements that are hosted by that level and any tags, notes and dimensions in that view.*

To remove a level datum, you select it and tell Revit to hide it in the current view. You will do this next.

12. Click on the horizontal line portion of the **Level 1** level datum.

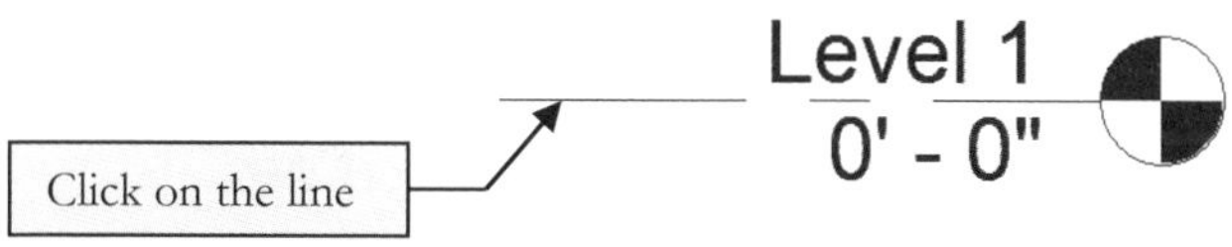

13. Right-click and select **Hide in View → Category** from the pop-up menu.

> ***TIP:*** *Selecting 'Element' would make only the selected level datum disappear from the current view.*

14. Adjust the bottom of the **Crop Region** to align with the Level 1 top-of-slab (horizontal line).

15. On the ***View Control Bar***, set:

    a. *View Scale* to: **¼"=1'-0"**, if needed.

    b. *Detail Level:* **Fine**

Your elevation should look like Figure 10-2.5.

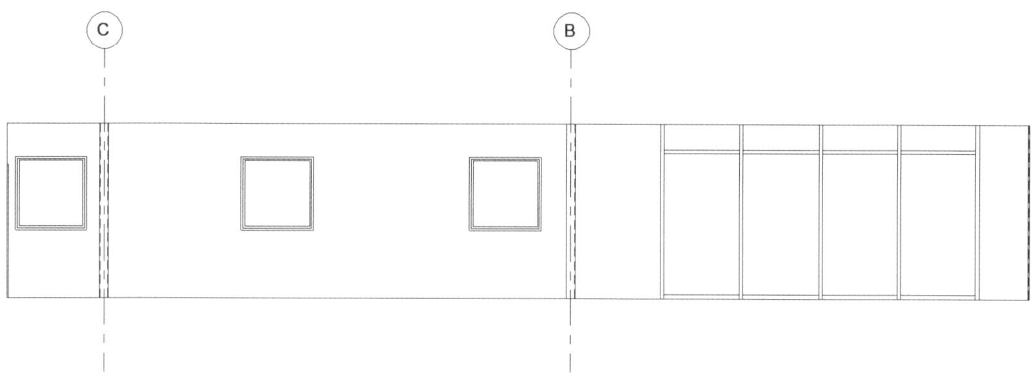

FIGURE 10-2.5 Lobby and Entry - East elevation

Notice in Figure 10-2.5 that the exterior columns are now showing. This has to do with changing the *Detail Level* from *Coarse* to *Fine.* In *Coarse* mode, Revit displays columns as stick figures and thus they were buried in the exterior wall. When the *Detail Level* was changed to *Fine* mode the actual 3D geometry of the selected steel shape is shown.

You can leave the crop window on to help define the perimeter of the elevation. You can also turn it off; however, some lines that are directly under the crop window might disappear.

> ***TIP:*** *If perimeter lines disappear when you print interior elevations, try unchecking "Hide Crop Regions" in the Print dialog and turn off the ones you do not want to see.*

Turning off the View Name on the Elevation Tag:

The interior elevation tag currently has the view name showing in plan view. You will turn this off as it is not required on the construction drawings.

16. Select **Manage → Settings → Additional Settings** (down-arrow)**→ Annotations → Elevation Tags**.

17. Set the *Type* to **½" Circle** (Figure 10-2.6).

18. Select **Elevation Mark Body_Circle: Filled Arrow** from the *Elevation Mark* drop-down list (Figure 10-2.6).

19. Click **OK** to close the dialog box.

The view name should now be gone from the *Elevation Tags* in the floor plan view.

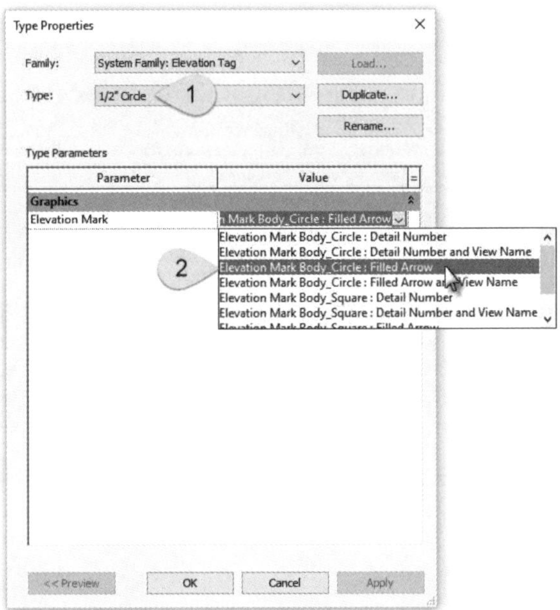

FIGURE 10-2.6 Adjusting the interior elevation tag

> ***FYI:*** *If you right-click on an elevation view name in the Project Browser, you will notice you can Duplicate the view (via Duplicate View → Duplicate). This is similar to how a floor plan is duplicated with one major variation: when an elevation view is duplicated, Revit actually just copies another elevation tag on top of the one being duplicated in the plan view. This is because each elevation view requires its own elevation tag. If two views could exist based on one elevation tag, then Revit would not know how to fill in the drawing number and sheet number if both views are placed on a sheet.*

Exercise 10-3:
Building Sections

Sections are one of the main communication tools in a set of architectural drawings. They help the builder understand vertical relationships. With traditional drafting techniques, architectural sections can occasionally contradict other drawings, such as mechanical or structural drawings. One example is a beam shown on the section is smaller than what the structural drawings call for; this creates a problem in the field when the duct does not fit in the ceiling space. The ceiling gets lowered and/or the duct gets smaller, ultimately compromising the design to a certain degree.

Revit takes great steps toward eliminating these types of conflicts. Sections, like plans and elevations, are generated from the 3D model. So it is virtually impossible to have a conflict between the various discipline's drawings. As many architects and structural, mechanical and electrical engineers are starting to share Revit models for even greater coordination, this is helping to eliminate conflicts and redundancy in drawing.

Similar to elevation tags, placing the section graphics in a plan view actually generates the section view. You will learn how to do this next.

Placing Section Marks:

1. Open your law office model.
2. Switch to **Level 1** plan view.

3. Select **View → Create → Section**.

   Tip: The Section tool can also be found on the quick access toolbar.

4. Draw a **Section** mark as shown in Figure 10-3.1. Start on the left side in this case. Use the *Move* tool if needed to accurately adjust the section after insertion.

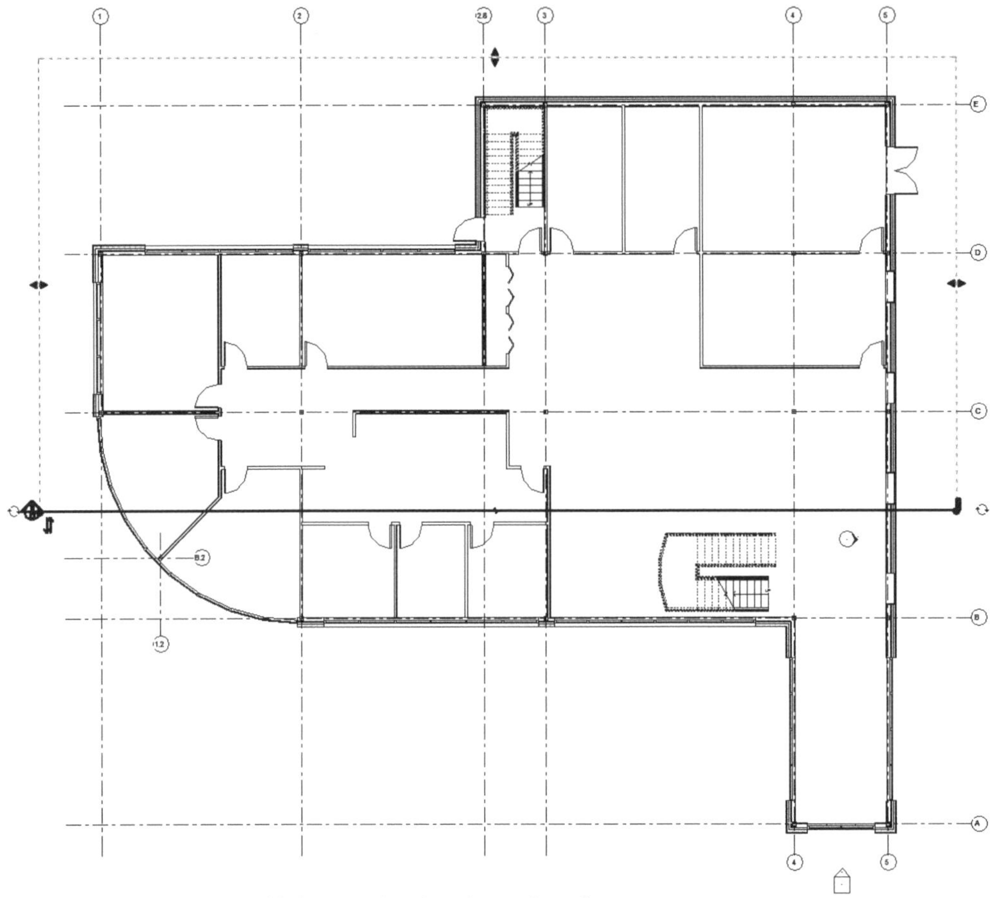

FIGURE 10-3.1 Section added to Level 1 plan view (selected)

You can see that the *Far Clip Plane* location in the plan view is out past the building perimeter; this means you will see everything (Figure 10-3.1). Anything passing through the section line is in section; everything else you see is in elevation. Revit calls it "projection." Everything behind the section is omitted from the view. Figure 10-3.2 also shows the *Crop Region.*

The image below lists the additional terms related to the *Section Mark* graphics in the plan view, as compared to *Elevation Tags.*

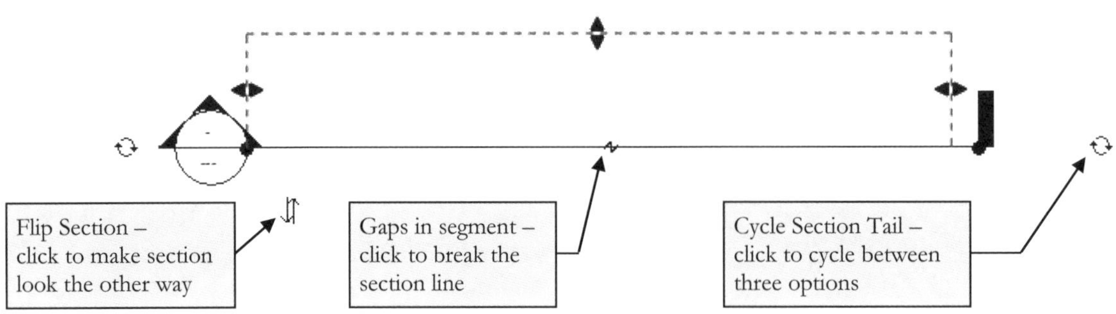

The *Section* tool is almost exactly like the *Elevation* tool. The only differences are the graphics in plan and the location in the *Project Browser*. Other than that they both function the same; they can show things in elevation or projection, and in section.

Notice, in the *Project Browser*, that a new category has been created: Sections (building Section). If you expand this category, you will see the new section view listed; it is called *Section 1*. You should always rename any new view right after creating it. This will help with navigation and when it comes time to place views on sheets for printing.

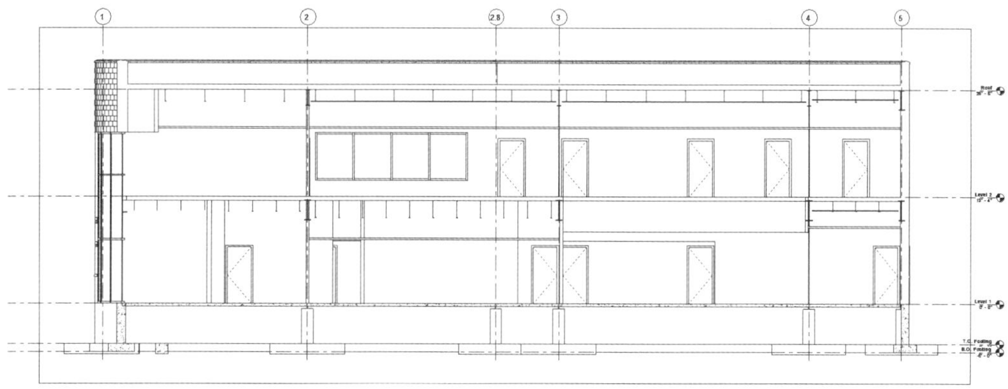

FIGURE 10-3.2 Initial Longitudinal section view

5. Rename section view *Section 1* to **Longitudinal Section**.

6. Switch to the new section view, **Longitudinal Section**.

   TIP: *Double-click on the section bubble head to open that view. The section needs to be unselected first; double-click on the blue part.*

7. On the *View Control Bar* change:

   a. *Detail Level* is set to **Medium**.

   b. **Hide Crop Region**.

8. Zoom in to the upper right corner to see the detail available in this section view, near the intersection of the Roof level datum and grid line 5. (See Figure 10-3.3.)

Notice the steel beams and bar joists in section. The metal roof decking extends into the wall but the layers above it do not; this is related to the roof's core material and the "extend to wall core" option you selected when creating the roof. You can also see the ceiling in the section; they are at the specified height and are the correct thickness. Finally, notice the elements in elevation (or projection): doors, beams and the parapet at the North exterior wall.

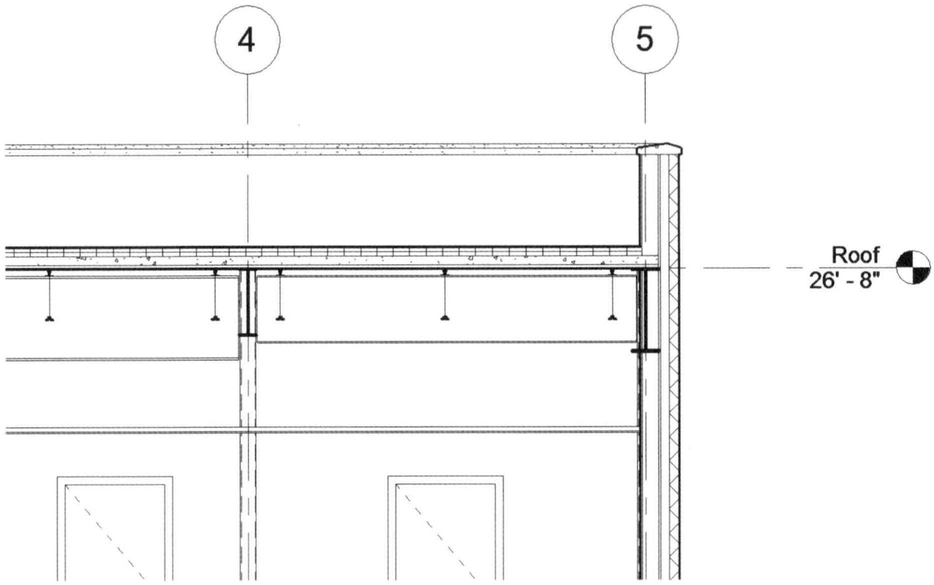

FIGURE 10-3.3 Longitudinal section view enlarged to show detail

9. Create another **Section** as shown in **Figure 10-3.4**.

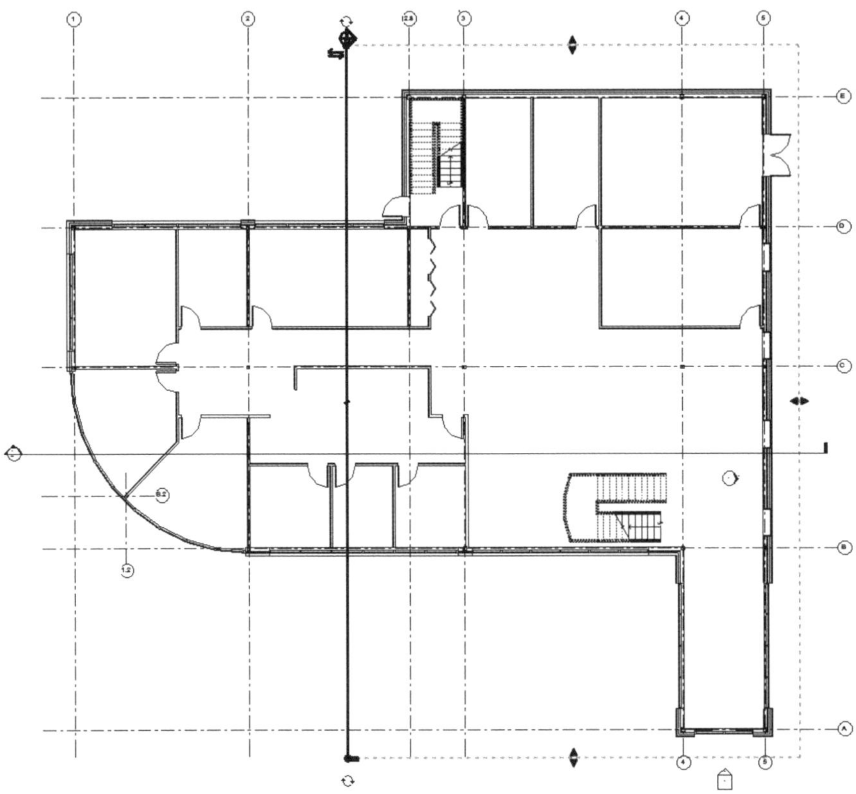

FIGURE 10-3.4 Cross section added looking East

10. Rename the new section view to **Cross Section 1** in the *Project Browser.*

11. Switch to the **Cross Section 1** view.

12. Set the *Detail Level* to **Medium** and turn off the **Crop Region** visibility via the *View Control Bar* (Figure 10-3.5).

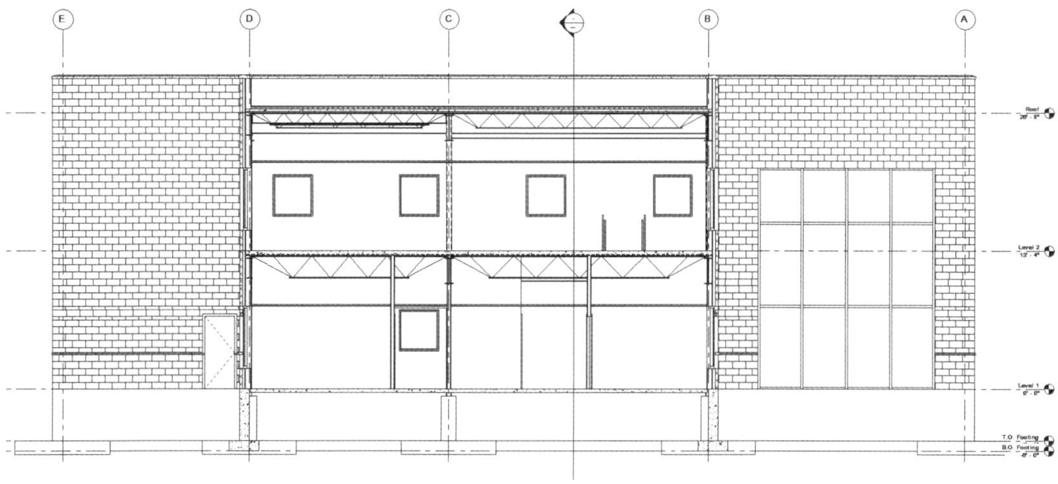

FIGURE 10-3.5 Cross Section 1

Revit automatically displays heavier lines for objects that are in section than for objects beyond the cutting plane and shown in elevation.

Also, with the *Detail Level* set to **Medium**, the walls and floors are hatched to represent the material in section.

Notice that the *Longitudinal Section* mark is automatically displayed in the *Cross Section 1* view. If you switch to the *Longitudinal Section* view you will see the *Cross Section 1* mark. Keeping with Revit's philosophy of change anything anywhere, you can select the section mark in the other section view and adjust its various properties, like the *Far Clip Plane.*

> ***FYI:*** *In any view that has a Section Mark in it, you can double-click on the round reference bubble to quickly switch to that section view. However, the section cannot be selected; the section head is dark blue when not selected.*

Making Modifications in the Model:

At this point you will take a look at making changes to the *Building Information Model* within your newly created *Cross Section* view. Currently, you will add the double doors to the main entry area, within the curtain wall.

13. Zoom into the curtain wall shown in elevation, between Grids A and B.

14. Select the vertical mullion shown in Figure 10-3.6.

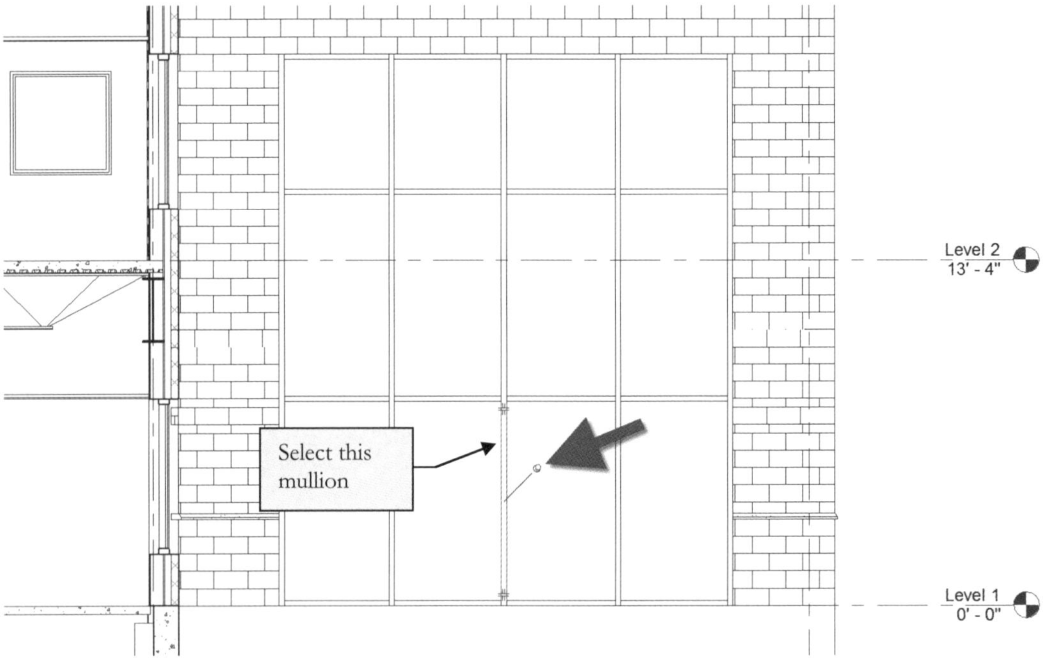

FIGURE 10-3.6 Cross Section 1 – main entry curtain wall area

This curtain wall was previously created using a wall type with rules that automatically added the vertical and horizontal mullions. If the width or height of the curtain wall were to be changed, the rules would automatically add or remove mullions and change their spacing. Because of this, all the mullions are pinned to prevent accidental changes.

In this case, we want to delete the vertical mullion and the two horizontal mullions below it on the ground. This is making room for the double doors about to be added.

> ***FYI:** Mullions start and stop automatically at each cell, or area of glass. That is why you are able to select just one as in the figure above.*

15. Click the **Pinned** symbol pointed out in Figure 10-3.6 to unpin the selected mullion.

16. Press the **Delete** key on the keyboard to delete the selected mullion.

17. **Delete** the two horizontal mullions, at the floor, as shown in Figure 10-3.7 below, per the previous steps.

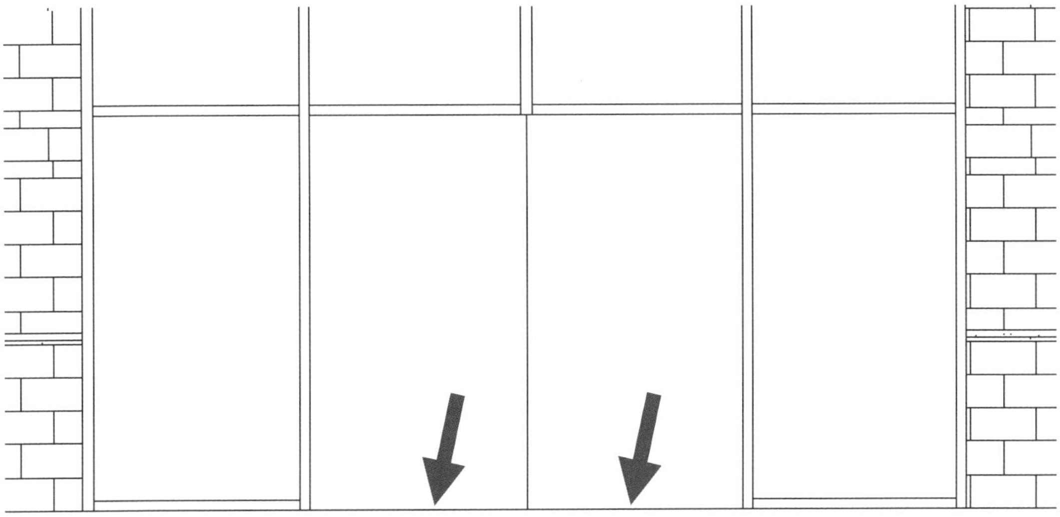

FIGURE 10-3.7 Cross Section 1 – main entry curtain wall area; three mullions deleted

Next you will need to remove a portion of the *Curtain Grid* to create one large *Curtain Panel* where the double door will go.

18. Select the vertical ***Curtain Grid***; hover your cursor until the heavy dashed line appears and then click on it. See Figure 10-3.8.

19. **Unpin** the *Curtain Grid* and then, with the *Curtain Grid* selected, click **Add/ Remove Segments** from the *Ribbon*.

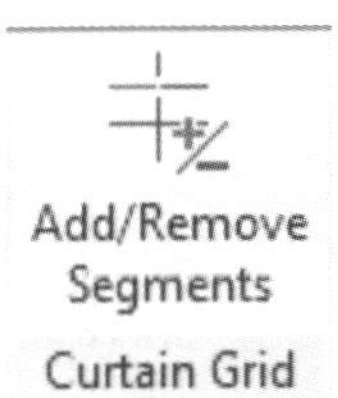

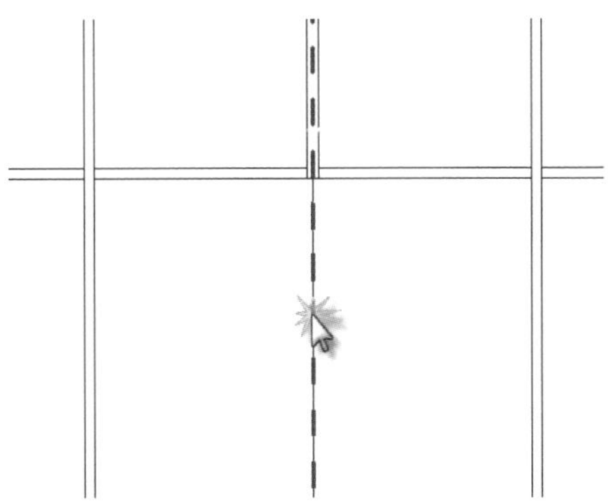

FIGURE 10-3.8 Selecting the curtain grid

You can now remove the selected portion of the *Curtain Grid.* When a portion of grid is removed, the *Curtain Panel* changes from two to one.

20. Click the same location again, shown in Figure 10-3.8.

21. Click **Modify** to finish the current operation.

Your double door opening should now look like Figure 10-3.9.

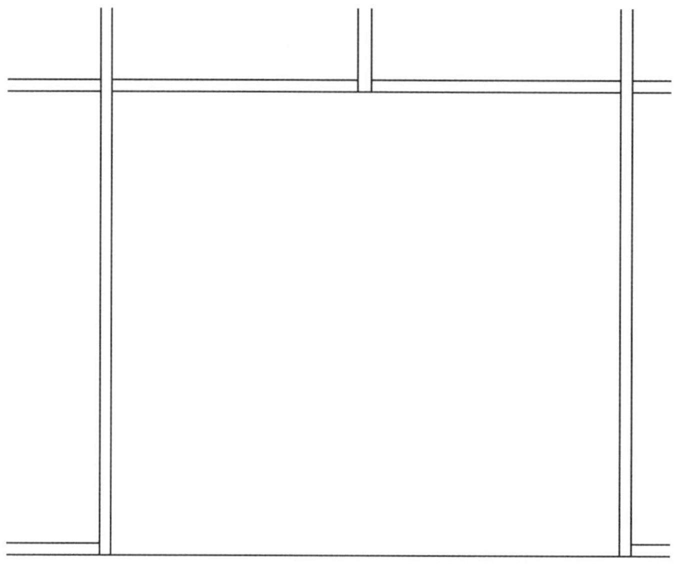

FIGURE 10-3.9 Mullions and curtain grid removed for double doors

Now you will add the double doors. To do this you select the *Curtain Panel.* This may require tapping the **Tab** button to cycle through the various elements below your cursor. Then select the double door family from the *Type Selector.*

22. Hover your cursor over the perimeter of the *Curtain Panel* and "tap" the **Tab** key, without moving the cursor, until the *Curtain Panel* highlights as in Figure 10-3.10.

23. Once the *Curtain Panel* is highlighted, click to select it.

24. Click the **pinned** symbol to **unpin** it.

You will now select the double door family you previously loaded from the *Element Type Selector.* Notice, you can also swap out the current panel for any of the standard Revit wall types as well.

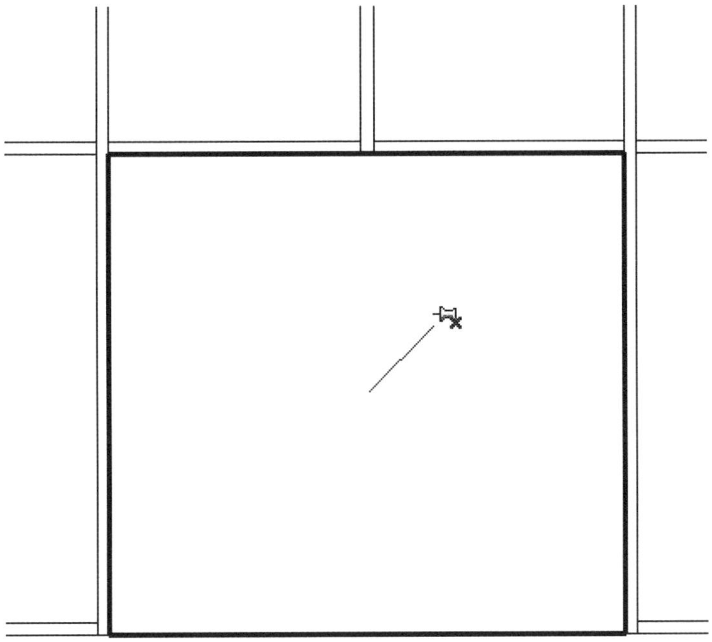

FIGURE 10-3.10 Curtain panel selected and un-pinned

25. With the *Curtain Panel* selected, pick **Store Front Double Door** from the *Type Selector.*

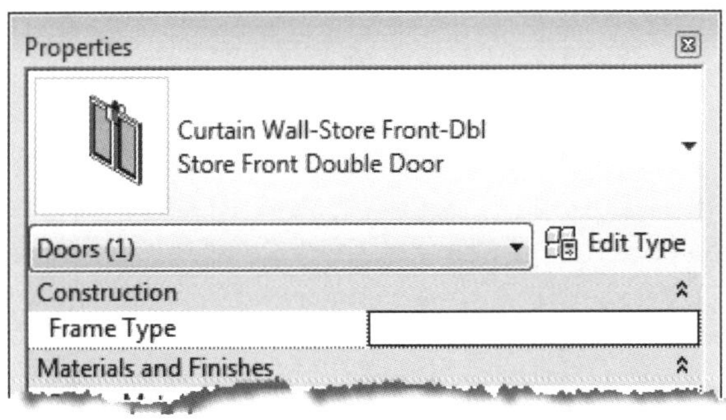

Your curtain wall should now look like the image below. The only thing you have to do now is verify the door swing in the plan view.

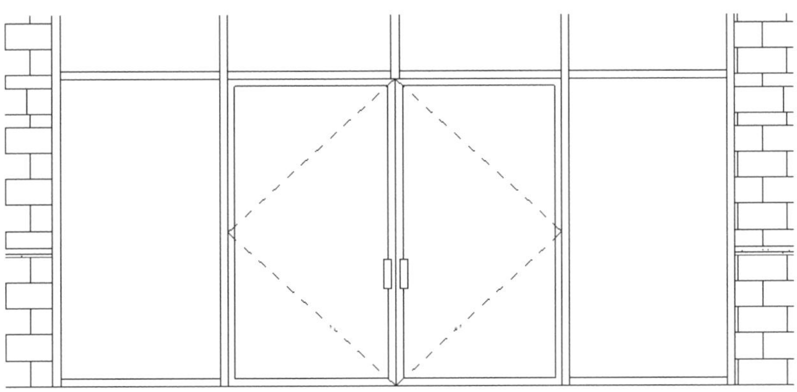

FIGURE 10-3.11 Double door added

The double door automatically stretches to fill the area contained by the *Curtain Panel.* This means the door may be too big or too small. Also, the double door is actually a special type of family for curtain walls, so it does not show up when using the *Door* tool. However, this door will show up in the *Door Schedule.*

26. Switch to the **Level 1 Architectural Floor Plan** view.

27. Zoom into the main entry area.

28. Verify the door swings in; if it does not:
    a. Select the door, using the **Tab** key if necessary.
    b. Click the *flip control* arrows to change the door swing.

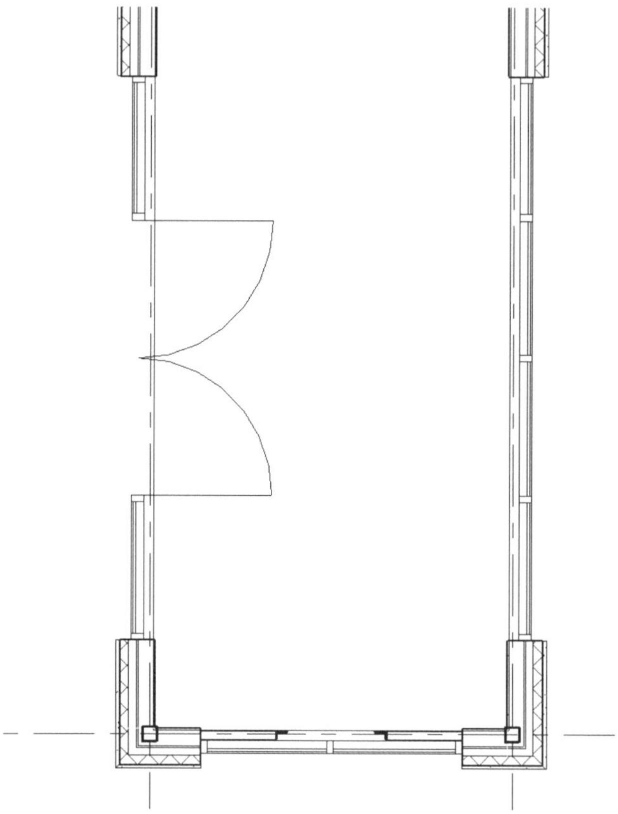

Obviously, codes vary on minimum door sizes and the direction in which the doors must swing in relation to building type and occupant load. We will leave things as they are for this tutorial.

If the door width needed to change, you would select the *Curtain Grid* on one side of the door and move it; this would automatically cause the mullions and panels to update, including the double door.

If the door swung out and the project was in a frost susceptible area, the structural engineers would need to add a concrete stoop.

FIGURE 10-3.12 Double door shown in plan

29. **Save** your project.

Exercise 10-4:
Wall Sections

So far, in the previous exercise, you have drawn building sections. Building sections are typically ⅛″ or ¼″ scale and light on detail and notes. Wall sections are drawn at a larger scale and have much more detail and annotations. You will look at setting up wall sections next.

Setting up the Wall Section View:

1. Open your law office file; do not forget to make backups.

2. Switch to the **Cross Section 1** view.

3. From the *View* tab on the *Ribbon*, click the ***Callout*** tool and then select *Section:* **Wall Section** from the *Type Selector.*

4. Place a **Callout** tag as shown in Figure 10-4.1.

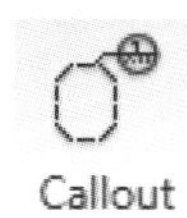

TIP: Pick in the upper left and then in the lower right (do not drag) to place the Callout tag.

TIP: You can use the control grips for the Callout tag to move the reference bubble, if desired, to move it away from notes/dimensions.

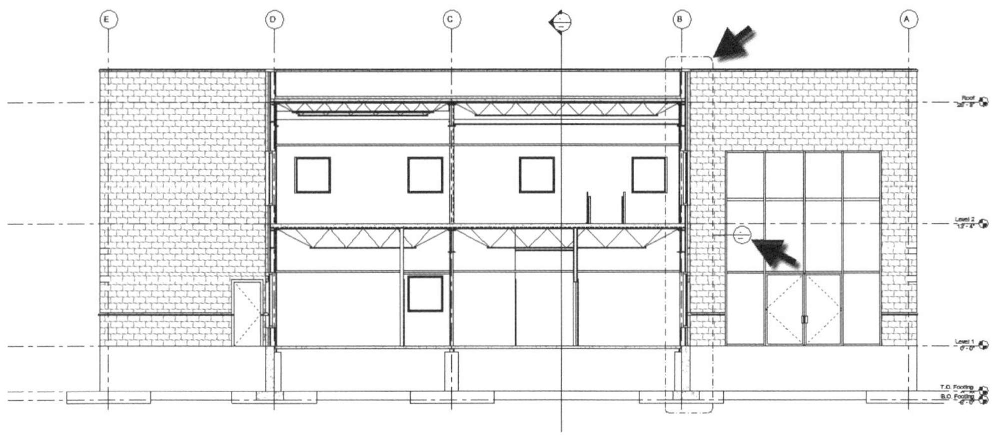

FIGURE 10-4.1 Cross Section 1 view with Callout added

5. Rename Cross Section 1 - Callout 1 to **Typical Wall Section**.

Notice that a view was added in the *Sections (Wall Section)* category of the *Project Browser.* Because *Callouts* are detail references of a section view, it is a good idea to keep the new callout view name similar to the name of the section.

It is possible to create a wall section using the same *Section* tool used in the previous exercise. However, *Callouts* differ from section views in that the callout is not referenced in every related view. This example is typical, in that the building sections are referenced from the plans and wall sections are referenced from the building sections. The floor plans can get pretty messy if you try to add too much information to them.

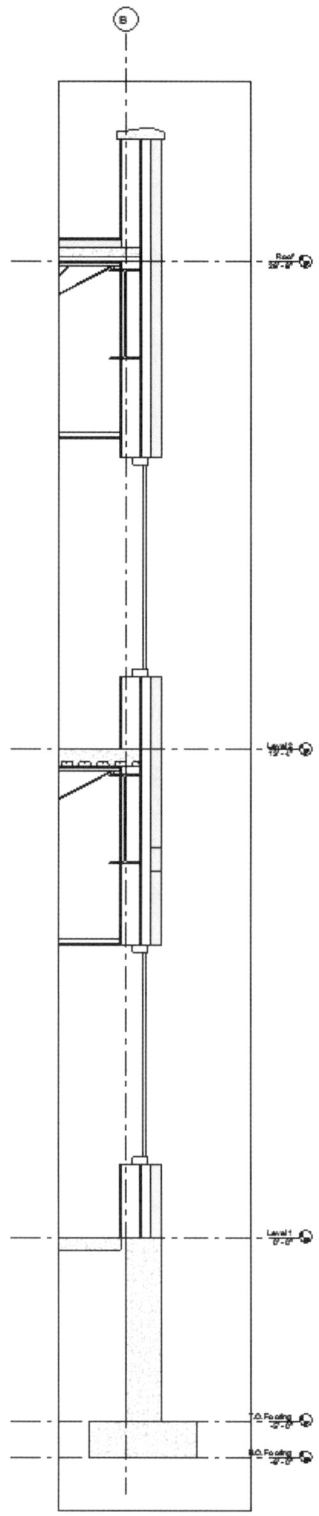

FIGURE 10-4.2 Typical Wall Section view

6. Double-click on the reference bubble portion of the *Callout* tag to open the **Typical Wall Section** view.

7. In the *Properties Palette* adjust the ***View Properties*** as follows:
    a. *Far clip settings:* **Independent**
    b. *Far clip offset:* **2′-0″**

Notice, down on the *View Control Bar*, that the scale is set to ½″ = 1′-0″. This affects the *Level* datum and any annotation you add.

8. On the *View Control Bar*, set the *View Scale* to **¾″ = 1′-0″** and the *Detail Level* to **Fine**.

Notice the level datum's size changed.

If you zoom in on a portion of the **Callout** view, you can see the detail added to the view. The wall's interior lines (i.e., veneer lines) are added and the materials in section are hatched. (See Figure 10-4.4; this is at the second floor line.)

As before, you can turn off and adjust the *Crop Region.*

9. On the *View Control Bar*, turn off the **Crop Region Visibility**; do not turn off cropping altogether. Also, set the *Detail Level* to **Fine**.

If you set the *Detail Level* to *Coarse*, you get just an outline of your structure. The *Coarse* setting is more appropriate for building sections than wall sections. Figure 10-4.3 is an example of the *Coarse* setting.

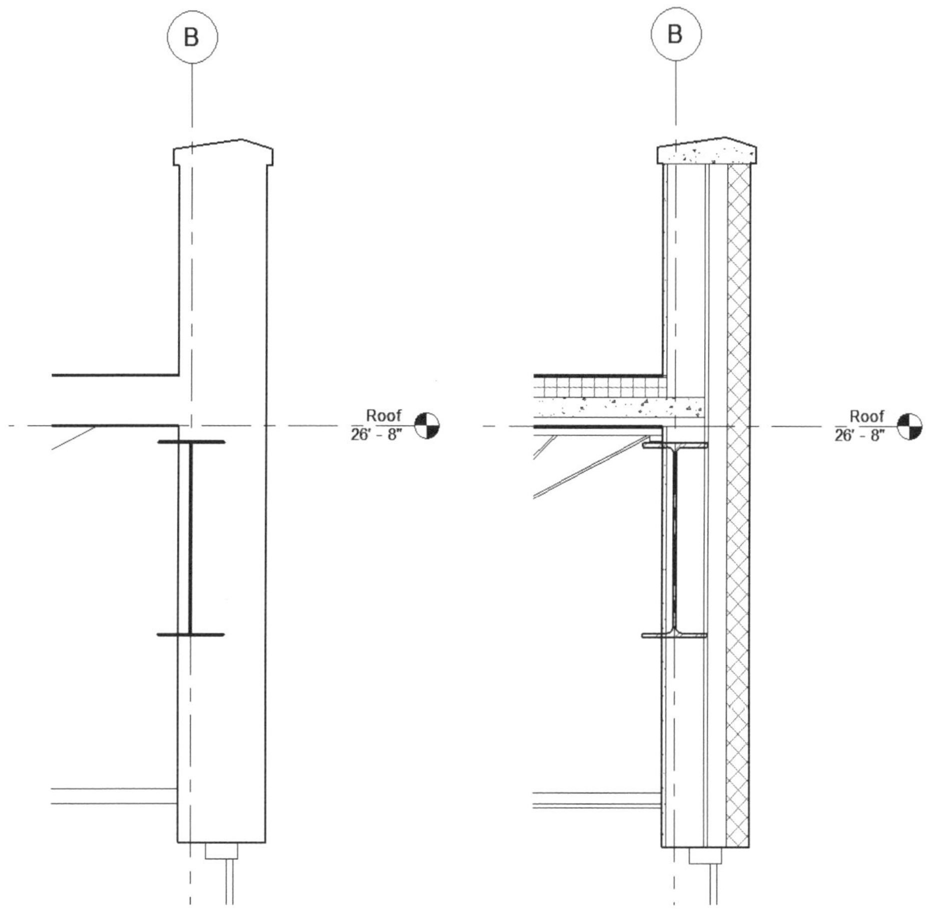

FIGURE 10-4.3 Detail level comparison – *Coarse* on left, *Fine* on right

Notice the steel beams and bar joists are shown as single-line representations in the *Coarse* detail level and the *Fine* view shows the true profile.

Add Notes and Dimensions:

Now you will add dimensions and text to the wall section. This process is the same for any view in Revit.

10. Add the dimension string as shown in **Figure 10-4.4**.

These dimensions are primarily for the masons laying up the CMU wall. Typically, when a window opening is dimensioned in a masonry wall, the dimension has the suffix M.O. This stands for Masonry Opening, clearly representing that the dimension identifies an opening in the wall. You will add the suffix next.

11. Select the dimension at the window opening.

12. Click directly on the blue dimension text (i.e., 6′-0″).

13. Type **M.O.** in the *Suffix* field and then click **OK** (Figure 10-4.5).

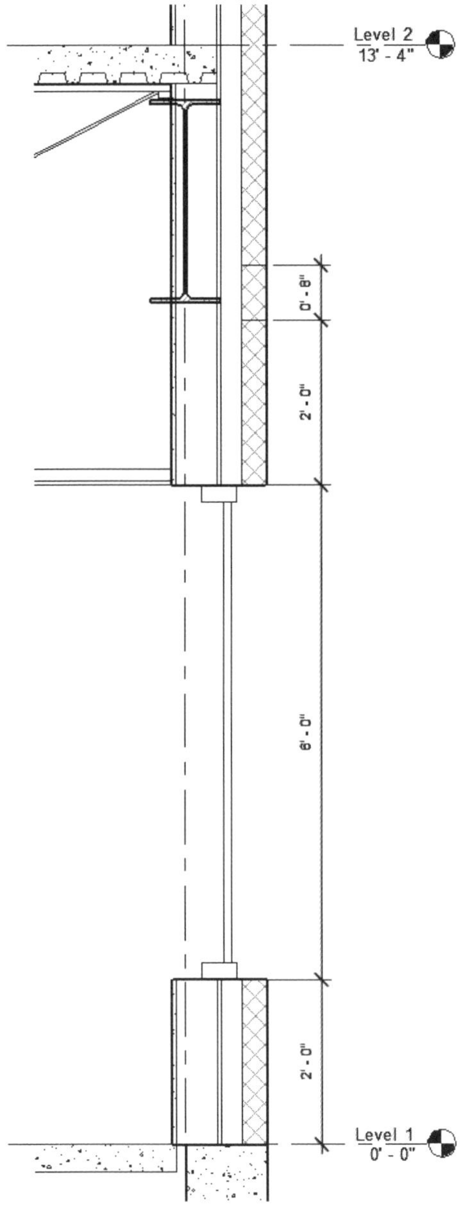

FIGURE 10-4.4 Added dimensions

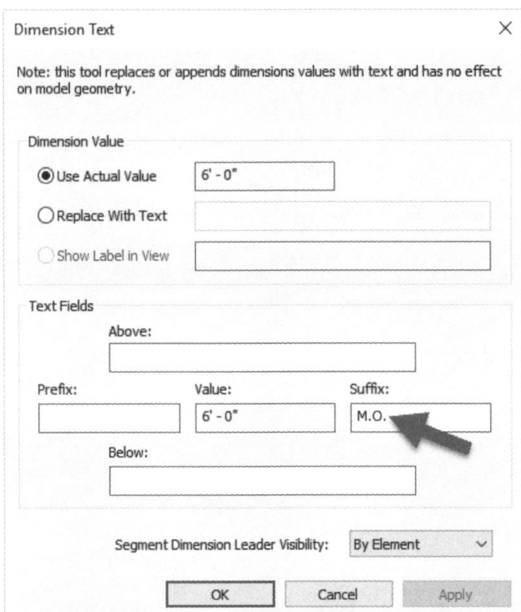

FIGURE 10-4.5 Selected dimension properties

Turn the *Crop Region* back on for a moment.

14. Turn on the **Crop Region** visibility, and then select it.

Notice the dashed line that shows around the *Crop Region*? It has its own set of positioning grips. This dashed lined area allows you to control the visibility of various elements in the current view, such as text. You will adjust the right-hand side so it will accommodate more text or notes. This can be toggled on or off in *View Properties* with the *Annotation Crop* option.

15. Drag the control grips for the vertical dashed line on the right as per **Figure 10-4.6**.

16. Turn the *Crop Region* off again.

17. Add the notes with leaders shown in Figure 10-4.7.
    a. The text style should be set to **3/32" Arial** via the *Type Selector* on the *Ribbon*, once in the *Text* command.

TIP: Select the Text tool and then one of the "Two Segments" Leader options on the Ribbon.

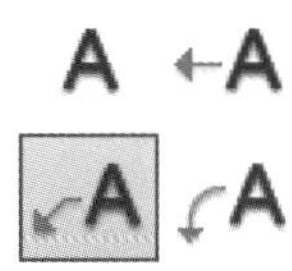

18. Select the text and use the grips and the justification buttons to make the text look like **Figure 10-4.7**.

Text will not automatically update like dimensions will. The leaders and arrows do not really know what they are pointing at. This needs to be manually adjusted if something moves.

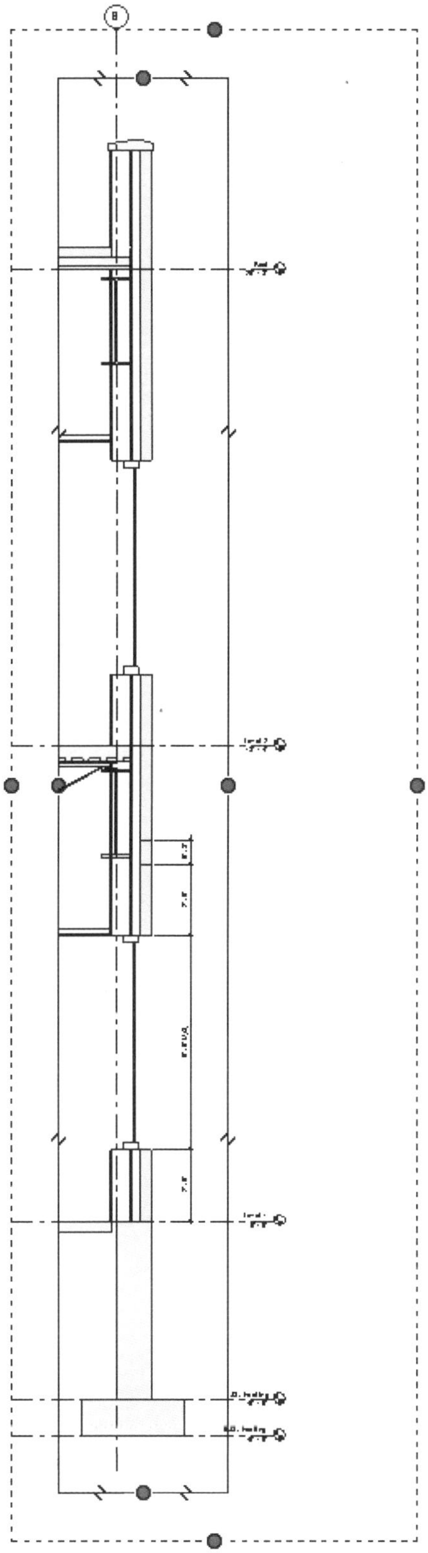

FIGURE 10-4.6 Crop Region edits

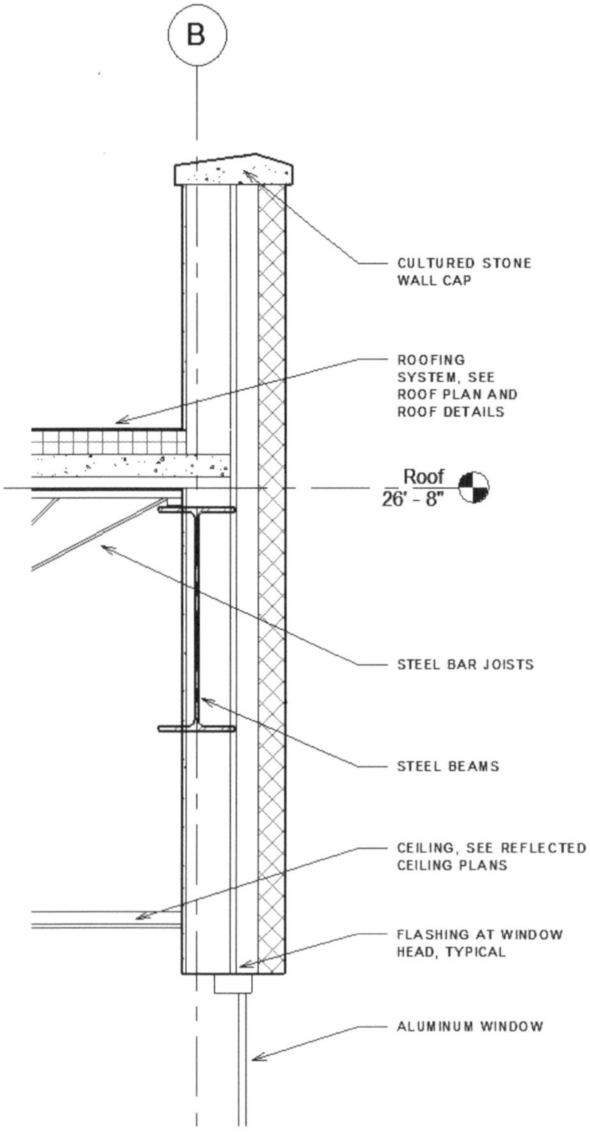

FIGURE 10-4.7 Notes added to wall section

Notes on **Notes**…

When placing the text with the *Two Segments* option, you should be able to snap to points on the screen that will make the notes align vertically within the drawing. The drawings look neater and more professional when the notes align.

It is not always possible, but when the arrow is generally perpendicular to the element it is pointing at, the drawing is easier to read.

All text in a set of construction documents (CDs) is typically uppercase. Some lowercase fonts can become hard to read, especially when the drawings are printed half-size, which is the preferred size for easy reference at one's desk.

Detail Lines are added to show things like the flashing above a window. Operating Revit would become too slow to use if every little thing was modeled.

TIP: *Adjust the Far Clip Plane if the bar joist is not visible – i.e., increase the value.*

Adding Detail Components:

Revit provides a way in which you can quickly add common 2D detail elements such as metal studs, dimensional lumber in section, anchor bolts, and wall base profiles to embellish your sections.

Next you will add just a few *Detail Components* so you have a basic understanding of how this feature is used.

You will add a metal stud runner track and batt insulation to the parapet wall.

19. Select **Annotate → Detail → Component → Detail Component**.

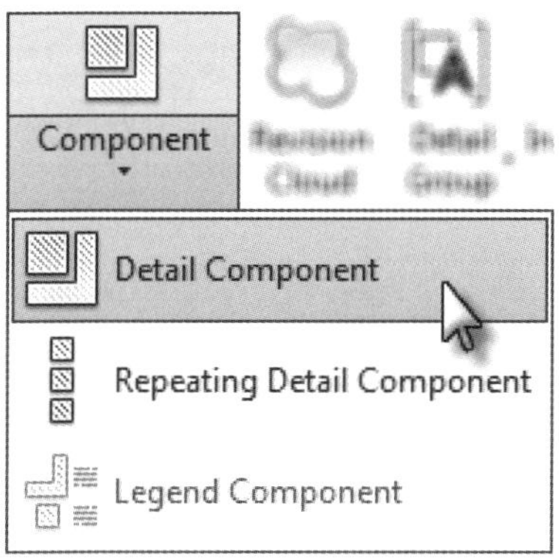

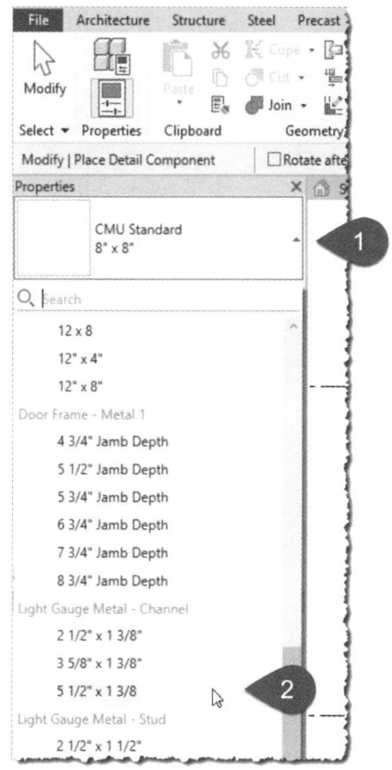

FIGURE 10-4.8
Detail Components

20. From the *Type Selector* pick *Light Gauge Metal - Channel:* **5 1/2" x 1 3/8** (Figure 10-4.8).

As you move the cursor around the screen, you will notice the *Detail Component* attached to your cursor will disappear whenever your cursor is outside of the *Crop Region.*

FYI: The light gauge channels are used in section, and the studs are used in plan views. The channels (aka, runner tracks) receive the studs at the top and bottom of the wall where they are screwed together.

21. Add the channels as shown in Figure 10-4.9.

TIP: When placing the metal stud or channel, you will need to press the spacebar to rotate and then move to properly position the element.

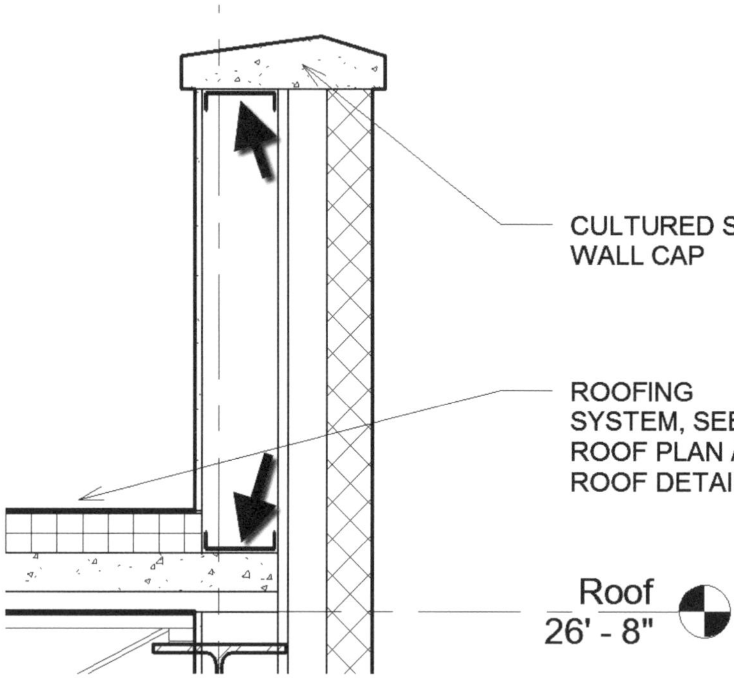

FIGURE 10-4.9 Typical Wall Section view; metal channels added

Detail Components can be copied once you have placed one in the view. Keep in mind that *Detail Components* are view specific and will not show up in any other view. You would have to repeat these steps in any other view in which they need to appear. Also, if the height of the parapet changes, the top channel you just placed will NOT automatically reposition itself unless you use the *Align* and *Lock* technique.

Next you will add the batt insulation (aka, fiberglass insulation), which occurs within the metal stud cavity.

22. Select **Annotation → Detail → Insulation.**

23. Enter **5 ½"** for the *Width* on the *Properties Palette.*

24. Pick the midpoint of the sill plate and the top plate to draw a line that represents the center of the insulation symbol; you can pick in either direction (Figure 10-4.10).

These techniques can be used to add batt insulation to the rest of the wall in this section, as well as runner tracks and window headers. A *Detail Component* would be used to represent rigid insulation if not already accounted for within the wall type.

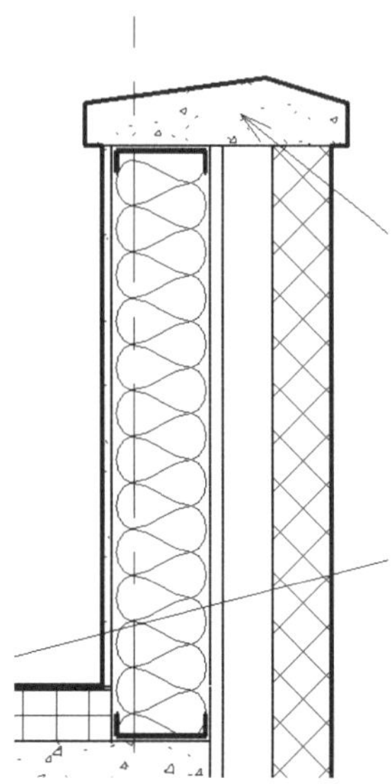

FIGURE 10-4.10
Insulation added

These tools just used are on the *Annotate* tab of the *Ribbon* because they are 2D graphics and only show up in the current view.

Drawing some elements like this, rather than modeling them three-dimensionally, can save time and system resources. A file could get very large if you tried to model everything. Of course, every time you skip drawing in 3D, you increase the chance of error. It takes a little experience to know when to model and when not to model.

Loading Additional Detail Components:

In addition to the *Detail Components* that are preloaded with the template file you started with, you can load more from the *Revit* content folder on your hard drive.

25. Select **Component → Detail Component** from the *Annotate* tab.

26. Click the **Load Autodesk Family** button from the *Ribbon.*

27. Click on the **Detail Items** category and then the following sub-categories: *Wood* and *Plastic\Architectural Woodwork\Wood Trim.*

28. Select the file named **Crown Molding-Section.rfa** and click **Load** (Figure 10-4.11).

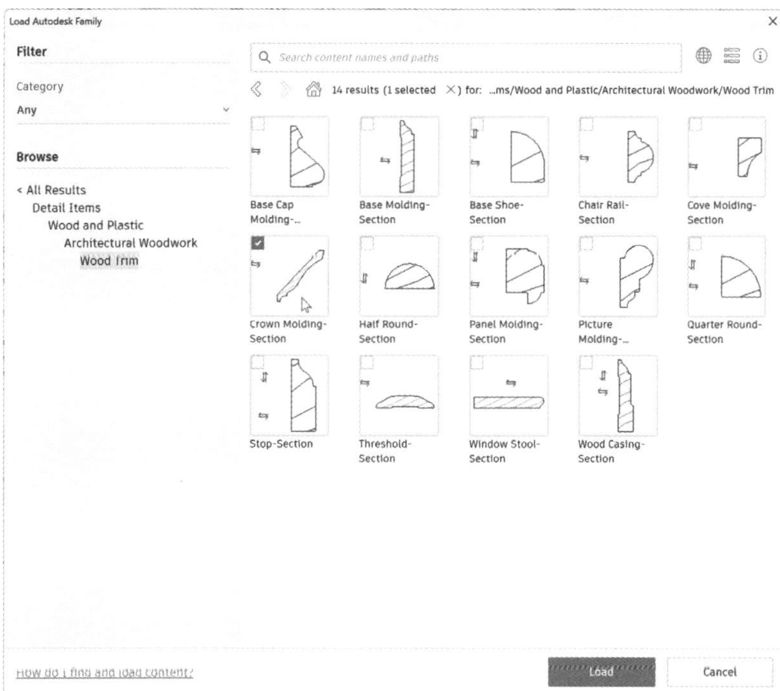

FIGURE 10-4.11 Load Detail Component dialog

You now have access to the newly imported crown molding. Take a minute to observe some of the other *Detail Components* that may be loaded into the project.

29. Place the **3/4" x 5 7/8"** crown molding at the Level 2 ceiling as shown in Figure 10-4.12. **Do not** press the *spacebar* to rotate before placing; you need to place it and then use the *Flip* icon when the element is selected.

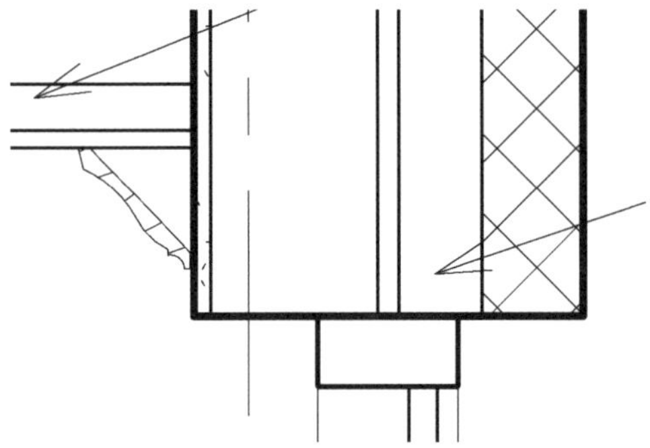

FIGURE 10-4.12 Crown molding placed at Level 2 ceiling

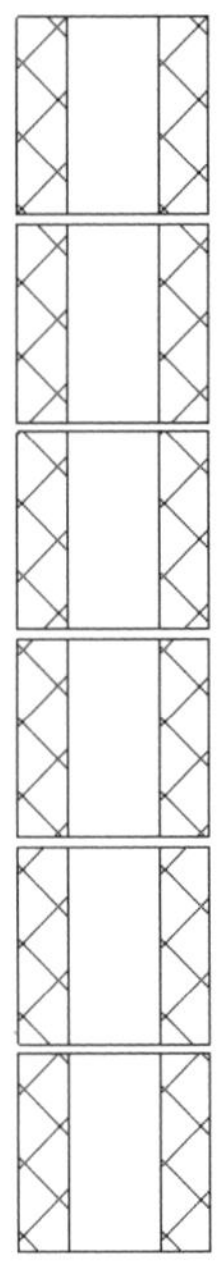

In addition to dimensions, text and detail components, you may also embellish your sections and elevations using *Detail Lines* and *Repeating Details*.

Detail Lines allow you to sketch anything you want. Sometimes you need to use the *Masking Region* to make portions of the model hidden.

A *Repeating Detail* allows you to pick two points on the screen and Revit will array a detail component between your two picks. For example, you can set up a Concrete Block (CMU) repeating detail and then pick the top and bottom of a section of wall to have CMU show up, as in the example image to the right. These have *Masking Regions* built into them so they hide the model linework below.

30. **Save** your project.

Exercise 10-5:
Details

This exercise shows you how to develop 2D details that are not tied to the 3D model in any way. Why would you want to do this, you might ask? Many design firms have developed detail libraries over the years for typical conditions. These details contain a significant amount of embodied knowledge of the firm as a whole. Many notes and dimensions have been added to address situations that have arisen and caused problems or cost the firm money. For example, a window head detail might show flashing that directs any moisture in the wall out – rather than into – the window or inside the building. Well, a note might have been added instructing the contractor to turn the flashing up at each side of the window to ensure moisture does not run off the end of the flashing and stay in the wall.

If every detail were a live cut through the model, the designer would have to spend the time adding all these notes and dimensions, and more importantly, try not to forget any, even if typing them from a printed reference page – similar to what you are doing with this book. (Have you missed anything yet, and had to go back and make a correction?) Furthermore, if a part of the model changes, the detail could be messed up. Or an item detailed from the live model might change and no longer be the typical condition.

As you can see, there are several reasons a design firm maintains and uses static 2D details.
NOTE: *Sometimes these details are used as starting points for similar details. This saves time, not having to start from scratch.*

It should also be pointed out that standard details should always be reviewed before "dumping" them into a project. If a note says, "Apply fireproofing to underside of metal roof deck," and your building has precast concrete plank, you need to change the note and the drawing. All other parts of the detail may perfectly match the project design you are working on.

Linking an AutoCAD Drawing

This first exercise will explore linking AutoCAD drawings into Revit when legacy details are required.

It is better to recreate these details in native Revit format rather than linking an AutoCAD drawing. Any external files linked to your BIM can slow it down and introduce corruption. This is especially true with site plans created in AutoCAD or AutoCAD Civil 3D. Site plans are often a great distance from the origin (i.e., 0,0,0 coordinate in an AutoCAD drawing) and this creates several issues.

In general, it is best to avoid AutoCAD DWG files within Revit. However, when required, they should always be Linked in, not *Imported*, and never *Exploded*. Importing DWG files makes them difficult to manage, and exploding them creates lots of extra text styles, fill patterns, and other items that clutter the BIM database.

1. Open ex10-4.rvt and **Save As ex10-5.rvt.**

AutoCAD DWG files can be linked directly into a plan view and used as underlays to sketch walls and place doors and windows when modeling an existing building in Revit that was drawn in a traditional CAD program.

In our example, we have a DWG file that contains a detail we want to reference and place on a sheet for our office building project. To do this, you create a *Drafting View* and link the CAD file into the drafting view. A *Drafting View* is a 2D drawing within the BIM project that has no direct relationship to the 3D model.

2. Click **View → Create → Drafting View** from the *Ribbon.*

Now you are prompted for a name and scale for the new drafting view; this can be changed later if needed.

3. Enter the following (Figure 10-5.1):

   a. *Name:* **Typical Roof Drain Detail**

   b. *Scale:* **1½″ = 1′-0″**

4. Click **OK** to create the new *Drafting View.*

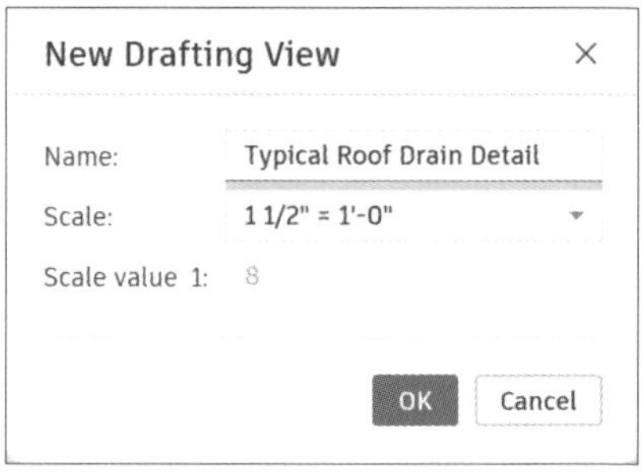

FIGURE 10-5.1 Creating a drafting view

You now have a new section, under *Views* in the *Project Browser*, called *Drafting Views* (Detail). Within this section is your new *Drafting View* – Typical Roof Drain Detail.

Within this new drafting view, you could begin sketching a detail from scratch using the various tools on the *Annotate* and *Modify* tabs. Or, in this example, you may link in a DWG file.

This roof drain detail is a good example of why 2D details are still useful in Revit, whether in DWG or native Revit format. As previously mentioned, many firms spend years developing standard details. These details include notes that have been added and edited as building materials change and problems arise. It would take a long time to cut a section of a 3D roof drain in the model and then add all the notes, if one can even remember what they are. Now, repeat this for 20 to 50 other items throughout the building project.

Next, you will link to the DWG file using the provided online file.

5. While in the newly created drafting view, select **Insert → Link → Link CAD** from the *Ribbon.*

6. Browse to the **DWG Files** folder within the files downloaded from the publisher's website.

7. Select the file **Typical Roof Drain Detail.DWG**.

8. Set the *Colors* options to **Black and White** (Figure 10-5.2).

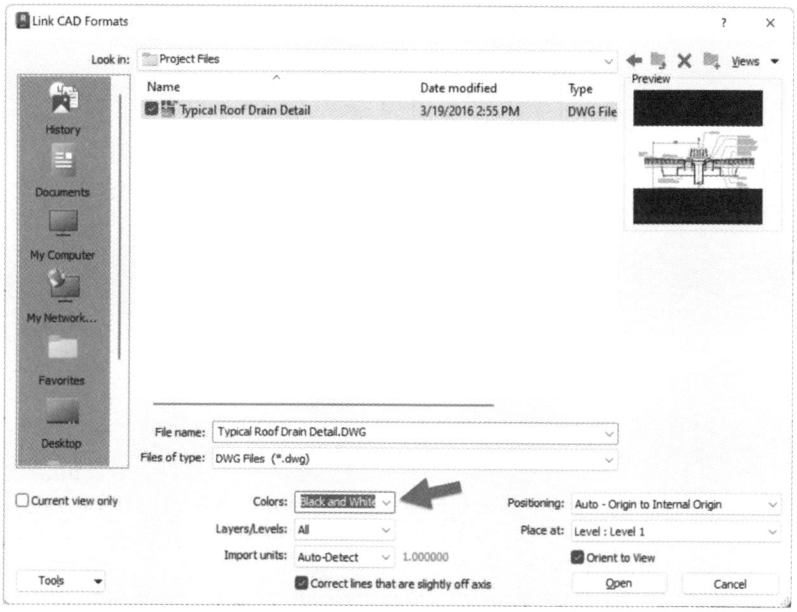

FIGURE 10-5.2 Linking an AutoCAD detail file

9. Click **Open** to place the linked AutoCAD DWG file.

10. Type **ZF** (for *Zoom Fit*) on the keyboard; do **not** press **Enter**.

You should now see the roof drain detail.

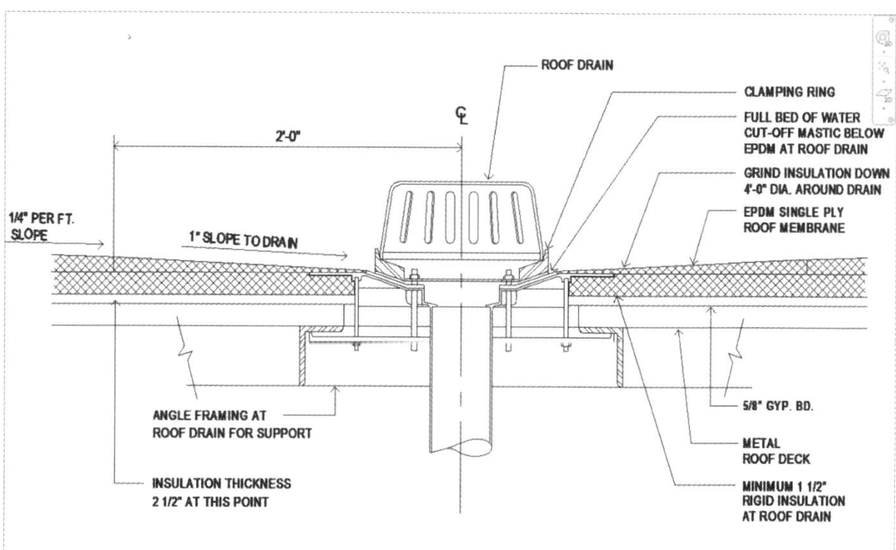

FIGURE 10-5.3 DWG file linked into drafting view

The drawing can be selected and moved around within the drafting view, but it cannot be edited. If you need to make changes to this drawing, you would have to do it in AutoCAD. Revit will automatically update any linked files when the project file is opened. It can also be done manually using the *Manage Links* tool.

When DWG files are linked into Revit, a specific set of line weights is used. These settings can be viewed by clicking the small arrow (i.e., the dialog launcher) in the lower-right corner of the *Import* panel on the *Insert* tab.

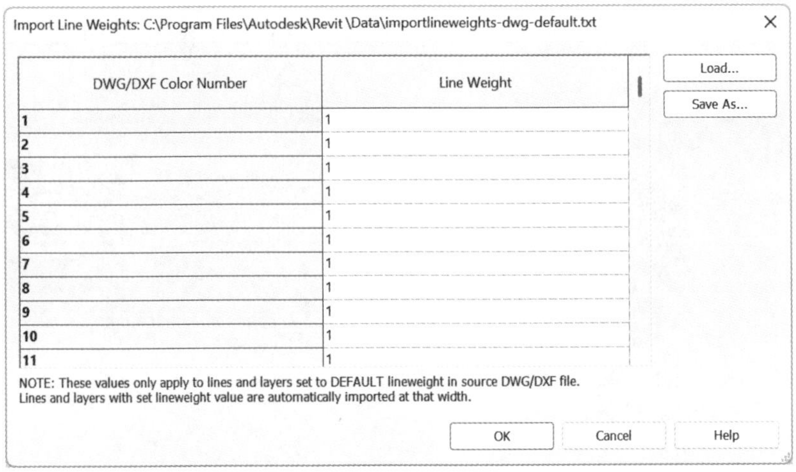

FIGURE 10-5.4 DWG color to Revit line weight conversion

Applying line weights is a one-time conversion process when the DWG file is linked in. Changing the line weight setting after a DWG has been linked in has no effect on it (only on new DWG files to be linked in).

> *TIP: Go to **Manage → Settings → Additional Settings → Line Weights** to see what each line weight number is equal to.*

If you type **VV** in the drafting view and then select the *Imported Categories* tab, you can see the AutoCAD *Layers* that exist in the imported DWG file (Figure 10-5.5). Unchecking a *Layer* will hide that information within the drafting view. You can also control the color and line weight of the lines on each *Layer*.

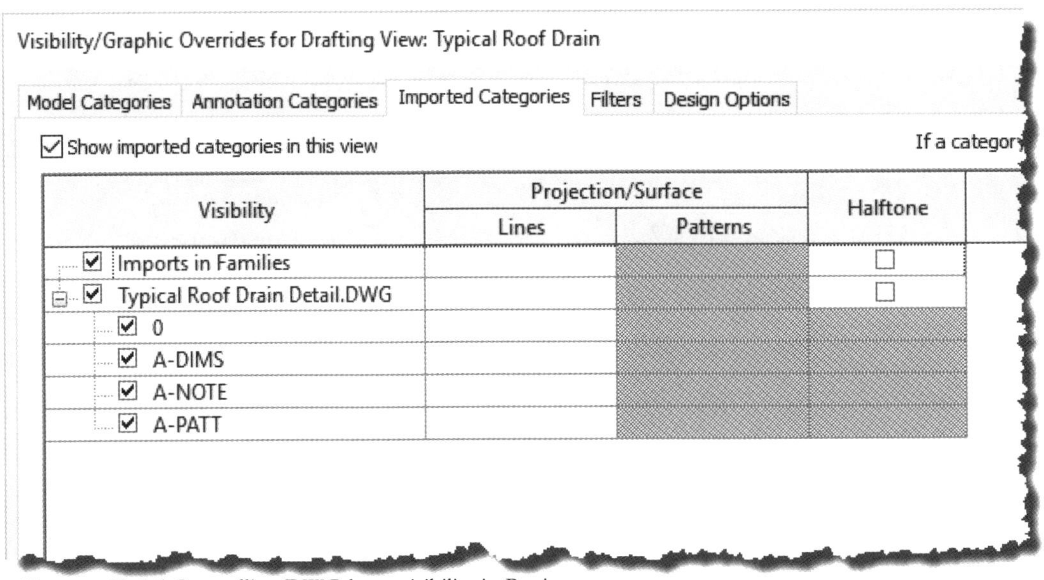

FIGURE 10-5.5 Controlling DWG layer visibility in Revit

Creating 2D Details

Autodesk Revit offers a wide range of 2D detail components for creating 2D details. These components allow for efficient detail drafting and design. Not every detail in Revit is generated from the 3D model; the amount of modeling required to achieve this is constrained by time, file size, and computing power. The following is an outline of the overall process; this will be followed by a few exercises for practice:

11. To create a 2D detail, one would create a **drafting view** via *View > Create > Drafting View*, providing a name and selecting a scale.
12. Once the *drafting view* has been created, **Detail Lines** and **Filled Regions** (via the *Annotate* tab) can be added.
13. In addition to *Detail Lines* and *Filled Regions*, one can insert pre-drawn items from the online Detail Library.
    a. Select **Load Autodesk Family** from the *Ribbon*. Or, use *Load Family* if content has been downloaded via https://autode.sk/30EJYkX.
    b. Select the **Detail Items folder** on the left.
    c. **Browse** to the desired folder; for example, *Metals→Steel Joists Framing → K-Series Bar Joist-Side.*
    d. Click **Load** to place the component.
    e. Select *Component > Detail Components* from the *Annotate* tab.
14. Add notes and dimensions to complete the 2D detail.

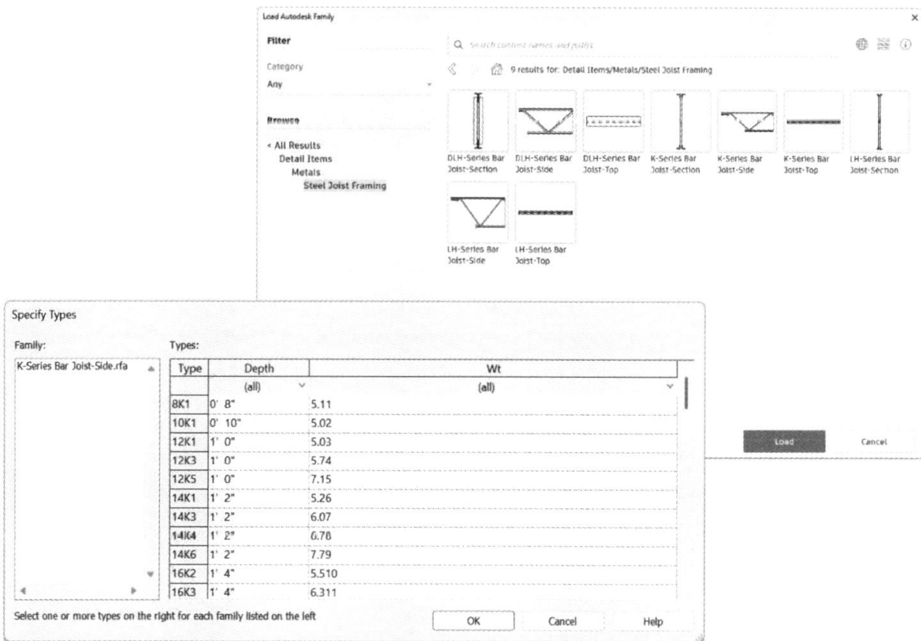

FIGURE 10-5.6
Loading detail components

Flooring Details

The first two details you will draw are simple details consisting of *Detail Lines*, *Filled Regions*, *Text,* and *Dimensions.*

You will draw a high-end terrazzo floor and wall base detail. This finish is poured in a liquid state, allowed to dry, and then polished to a smooth finish. The colors and aggregate options are virtually unlimited (for example, you could use a clear epoxy resin and place leaves within the flooring).

1. Per the steps previously covered in this section, create a new drafting view.
    a. *Name*: **Terrazzo Base Detail**
    b. *Scale*: **3″=1′-0″**

You will now draw the detail shown below. See the next page for specific steps.

Terrazzo floor example with brass inlay

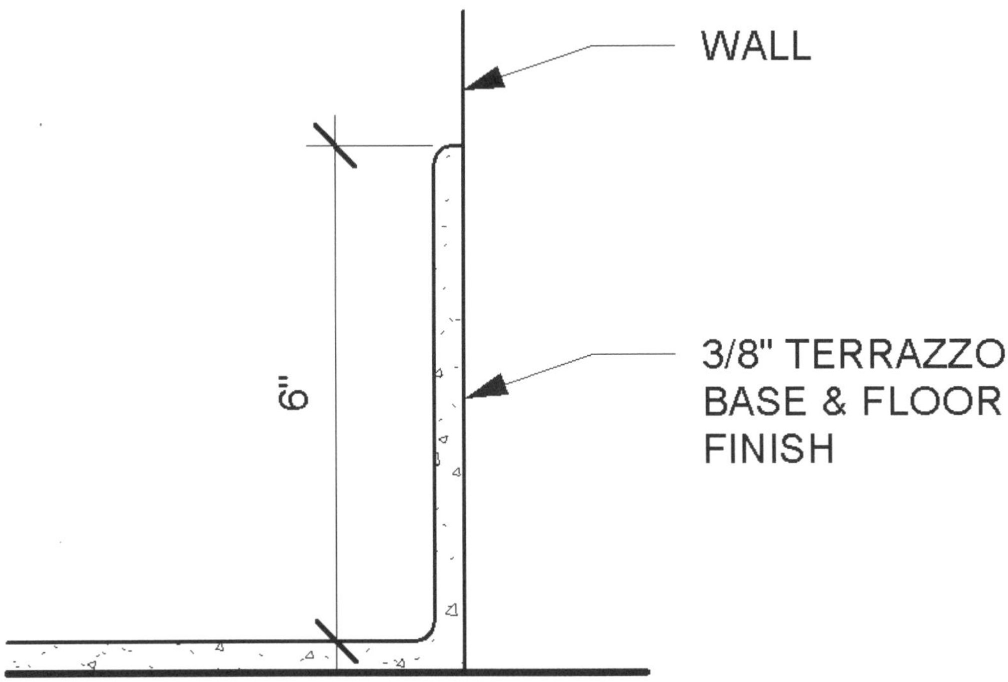

FIGURE 10-5.7 Terrazzo floor and wall base detail

2. Using the **Detail Lines** tool from the *Annotate* tab, draw the floor line **8″** long using **Wide Lines**.

FYI: The eight-inch dimension is random and does not represent anything other than a portion of the floor surface.

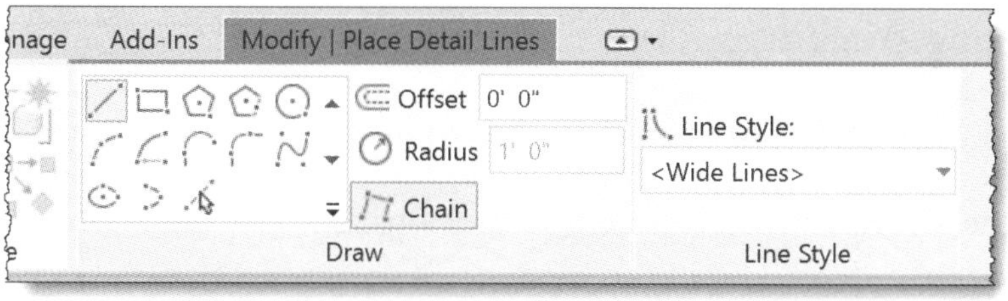

3. Draw a vertical line, also **8″** long, using the **Medium Lines** style. This line should be about 2″ from the right edge of the floor line (so your detail is generally proportional to the one in the book).

Next, you will offset the two lines just drawn to quickly create the terrazzo floor and base.

4. Select **Modify → Offset** on the *Ribbon.*

5. On the *Ribbon*, enter an offset value of **3/8″**.

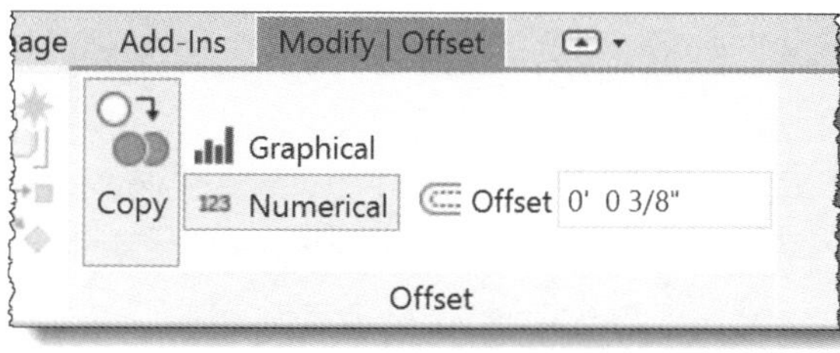

6. Pick the floor line when the preview line appears above the horizontal line.

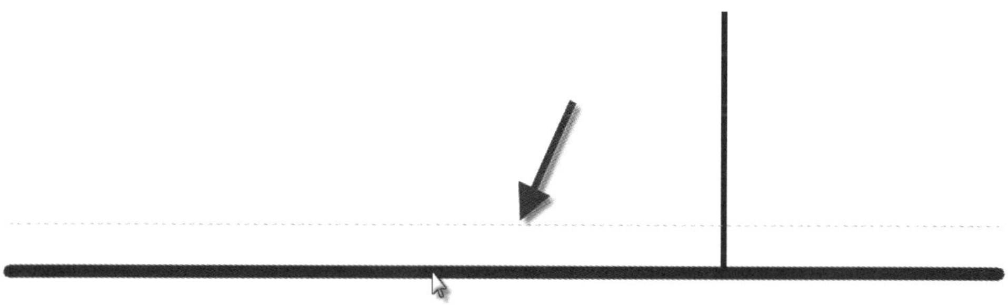

7. Now, **Offset** the vertical line **3/8″** to the left.

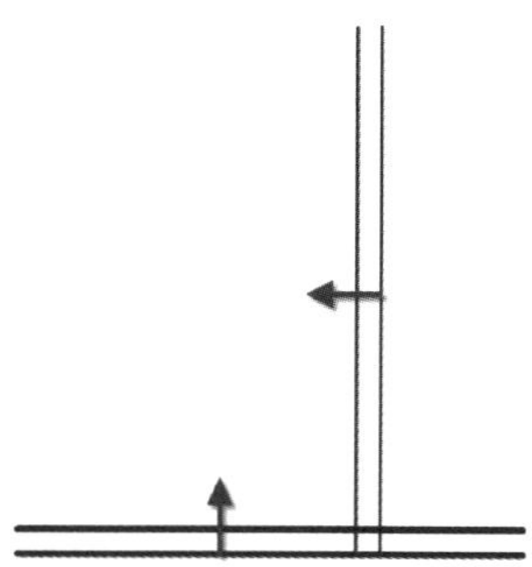

Your drawing should now look like the image to the right (less the arrows). Next, you will change the top horizontal line to a lighter line weight, offset it up 6″ to create the top of the wall base, and then use the *Fillet Arc* feature to round off the corners.

8. Select the top horizontal line and change the *Line Style* from *Wide Lines* to **Medium Lines** via the *Ribbon.*

9. **Offset** the top horizontal line upward **6"** inches.

10. Select the new horizontal line and then drag its right end grip over to the vertical line.

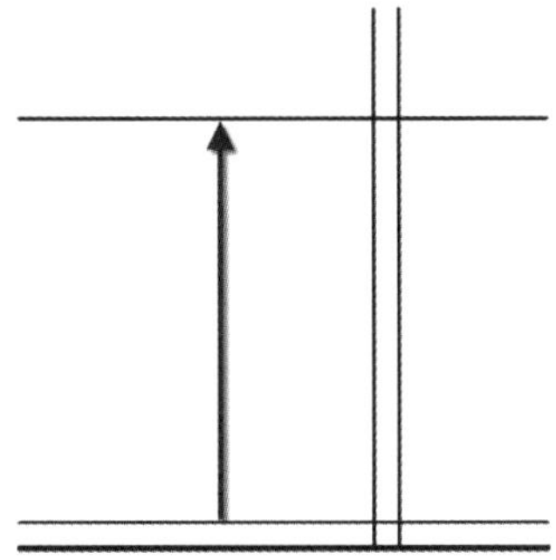

Next, you will trim and round the corners in one step.

11. Select the **Detail Line** tool from the *Annotate* tab.
    a. Select **Fillet Arc** from the *Draw* panel.
    b. Set the *Line Style* to **Medium Lines**.
    c. Check and set the *Radius* to **¼"**.

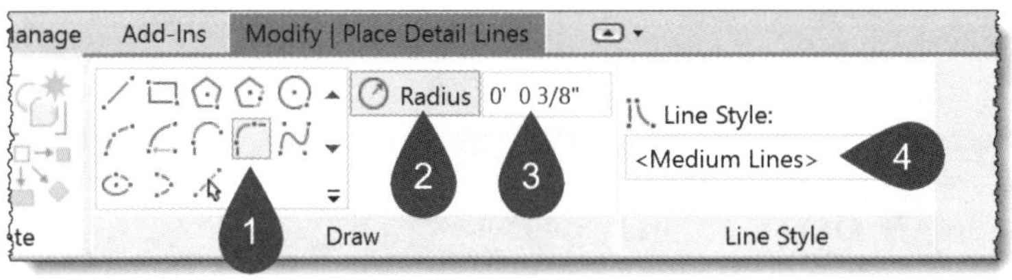

12. Click on the portion of the two lines you want to remain (see the two numbered clicks in the image to the right).

The line is now trimmed, and an arc has been added.

13. Repeat these steps to round off the top edge of the wall base.

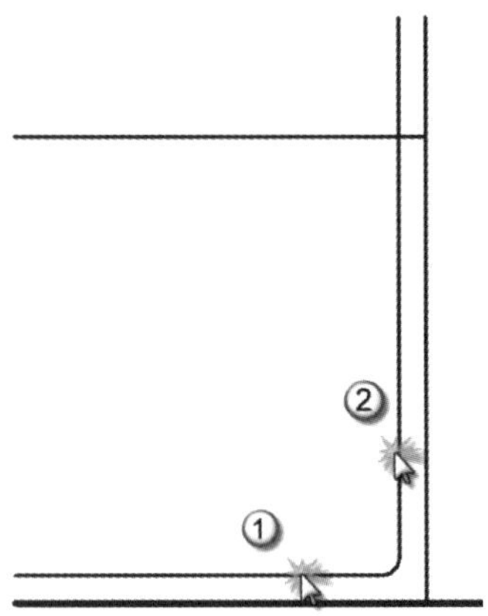

Next, you will add a *Filled Region* to represent the terrazzo material, with a pattern when viewed in a section. When creating the perimeter of a *Filled Region,* you also specify a *Line Style* (similar to the *Detail Line* tool). In this case, you will use *Thin Lines* for all but the left edge of the floor thickness. There, you will change the *Line Style* to an invisible line so as not to suggest a joint or the end of the flooring, but rather to indicate that the flooring material continues.

14. Select **Annotate → Detail → Region → Filled Region** from the *Ribbon.*
    a. Select the **Pick Lines** option from the *Draw* panel.
    b. Select **Thin Lines** from the *Lines Style* panel.

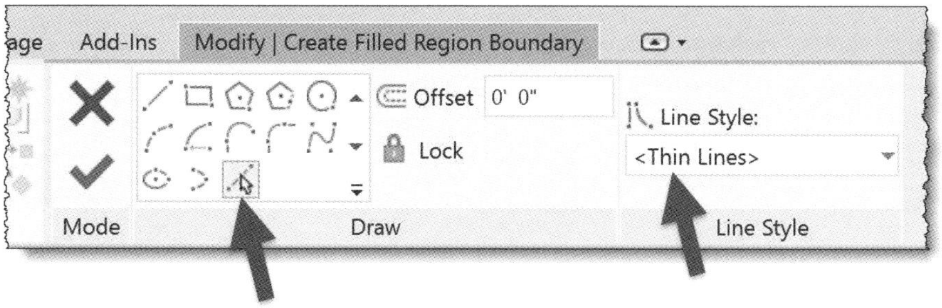

Selecting *Pick Lines* lets you quickly define the boundary of your Filled Region using lines already drawn. So, you simply click on a line rather than pick two points to define the start and endpoints of each edge. However, with the *Line* and *Arc* options, you could also snap to the endpoints of the previously drawn linework. The one drawback to using the *Pick Lines* option is that you will have to trim a few corners, since the Filled Region tool requires a clean perimeter (similar to the floor and roof tools).

15. Pick the five lines and two arcs that define the edges of the floor and wall base.

16. Switch to the **Line** option in the *Draw* panel and then set the *Line Style* to **<Invisible Lines>**.

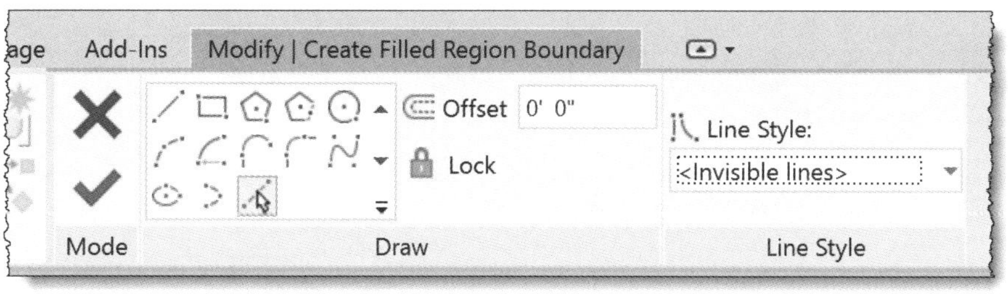

While in *Sketch Mode* (i.e., the green check mark and red X are visible) for the *Filled Region* tool, the invisible lines are not actually invisible. This allows you to select and modify them as needed.

17. Draw a line to close off the open edge of the flooring on the left-hand side.

18. Use the **Trim** tool to clean up the two corners where the lines run past.

19. Click the **green check mark** to finish the *Filled Region*.

Your drawing should look like the one shown to the right. The default pattern is a cross-hatch. You will change this next.

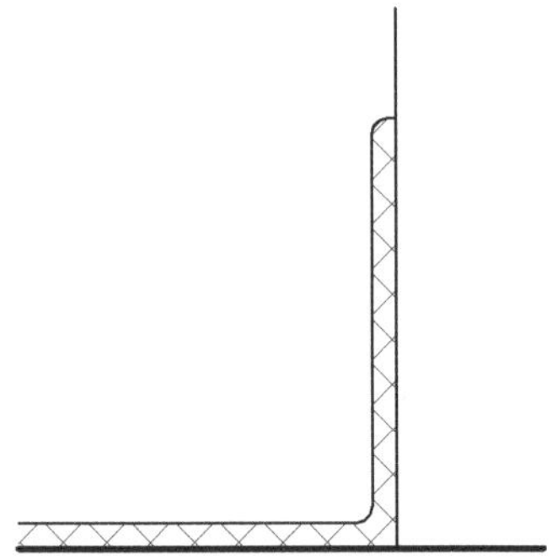

20. Select the *Filled Region*; you must click on one of the edges (and you may need to use *Tab*).

21. Expand the **Type Selector** to see the options currently available.

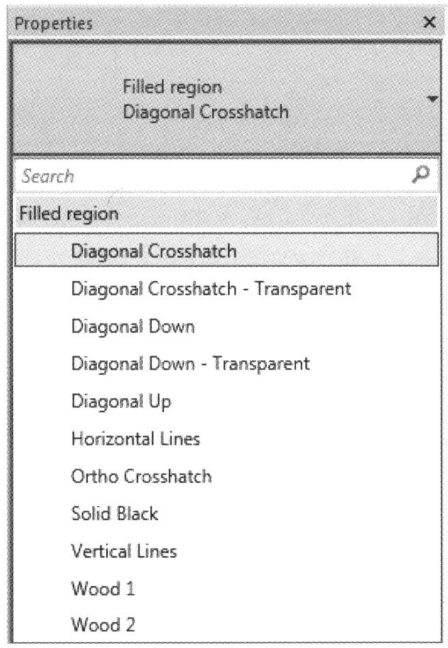

Looking at the list, we notice that concrete is not listed (which is what we decided we want). Next, you will learn how to add this.

22. Press **Esc** to close the *Type Selector*.

23. Click **Edit Type**.

24. Click **Duplicate**.

25. Enter **Concrete** for the name.

26. Click in the *Foreground Fill Pattern* field and then **click the icon** that appears to the right.

27. Select **Concrete** from the list and click **OK**.

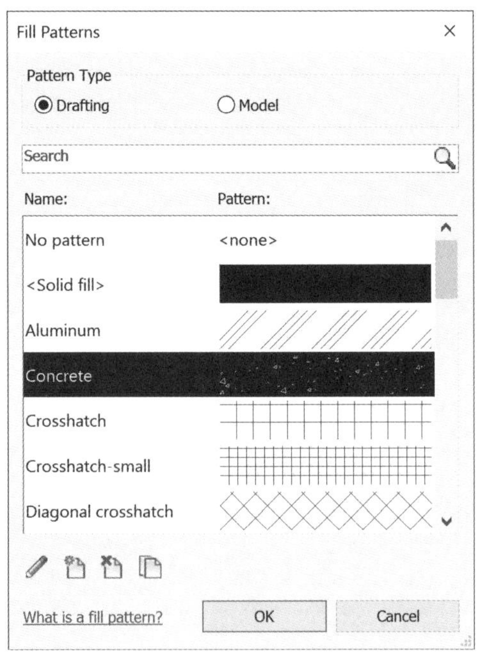

Notice the options to set the fill background to opaque or transparent, as well as the line weight setting.

28. Click **OK** to close the *Type Properties*.

Your terrazzo now has a concrete pattern. You can import additional fill patterns (using any AutoCAD hatch pattern file) or create custom ones with specific line spacing. This *Filled Region* tool can also be used in floor plans, for example, to highlight corridors or private office areas. When a *Filled Region* is selected, the area in square feet is displayed in the *Properties Palette*. Thus, you could quickly create a *Filled Region* to list the area, then delete it.

The last thing you will do is add the notes and dimensions. These will be the correct scale based on the *View Scale* setting (which should be 3″ = 1′-0″). Once you place the dimension, you will learn how to adjust the dimension style so the 0′ does not show up.

29. Add the dimension and two notes as shown.

30. Select the dimension.

31. Select **Edit Type**.

32. Click the button to the right of **Units Format**.

33. Uncheck **Use Project Settings**.

34. Check **Suppress 0 feet**.

35. Click **OK** twice to close both open dialog boxes.

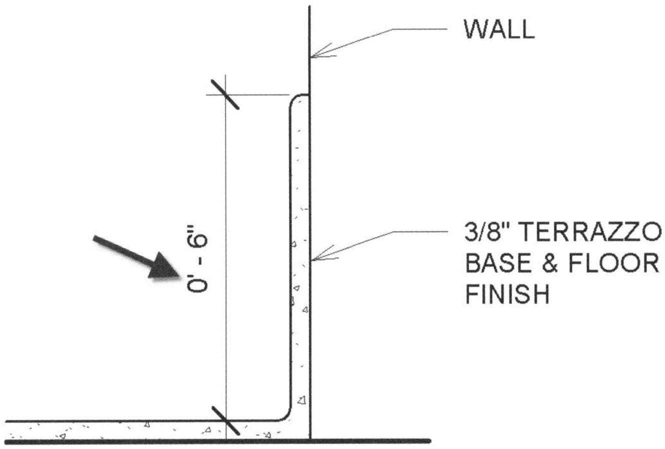

Your dimension should now only say 6″ rather than 0′-6″. Because you changed this in the *Type Properties*, the change will be applied to all dimensions (both previously saved and new). If you want to have both options, you would first need to *Duplicate* the dimension type, which is similar to creating new wall, door, and window types!

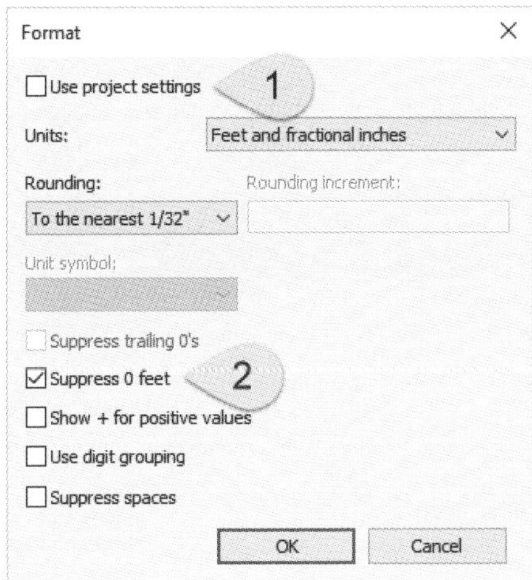

The last thing you will look at is adjusting the arrow style for the notes.

36. Select one of the notes.

37. Click **Edit Type**.

38. Change the *Leader Arrowhead* to **Arrow Filled 30 Degree**.

39. Click **OK**.

Your detail should now look similar to the one presented at the beginning of this exercise. This detail can now be placed on a sheet (covered in chapter 12). You can also export this detail and save it in a detail library that you and others in your firm can utilize. To export the detail, simply right-click on the view name in the *Project Browser* and select *Save to New File*. Place the file on a server so everyone can get at it. To load this file into another project select **Insert → Insert from File → Insert Views from File**.

Now you will draw another detail using the same tools and techniques. Keep in mind that every detail needs to go into its own *drafting view*. This is required for Revit to manage the reference bubbles on the sheets.

40. Create a new **drafting view**:
    a. *Name:* **Floor Transition Detail**
    b. *Scale:* **3″ = 1′-0″**

41. Draw the detail per the following guidelines:
    a. The detail will be plotted at 3″=1′-0″ (this determines the text and leader size).
    b. Tile pattern is **Diagonal Up–Small**; this requires a new *Fill Region* style (see the previous exercise for more information).
    c. The grout (i.e., area under tile) is to be hatched with **Sand – Dense**; this also requires a new *Fill Region* style.
    d. Draw the tile ¼″ thick and 4″ wide.
    e. The grout is ¼″ thick.
    f. The resilient flooring is shown ⅛″ thick.
    g. The solid surface (e.g., Corian) threshold is 1⅞″ wide; draw an arc between the two floor thicknesses.
    h. Hatch the threshold with the solid hatch:
        i. **Duplicate** the **Solid Black** *Filled Region* style.
        ii. Name the new style **Solid Gray**.
        iii. Set the **foreground pattern color** to a light gray (RGB color 192).
    i. The bottom concrete floor line is to be the heaviest line.

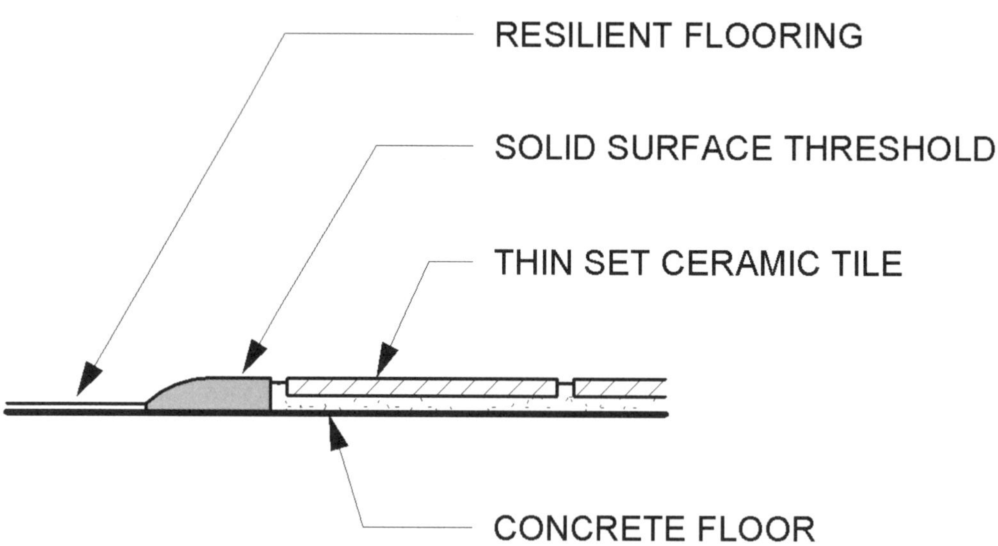

FIGURE 10-5.8 Floor transition detail: ceramic tile to resilient flooring

The previous drawing would typically occur in a door opening, and the location of the door would also be shown in the detail. This lets the contractor know that the threshold is to occur directly below the door slab.

Base Cabinet with Drawers

This section will dive right into drawing cabinet details. These are often based on industry standard dimensions, so many of the dimensions and material thicknesses can be omitted (assuming the project manual/specification covers this).

42. Create a **drafting view**:
    a. *Name:* **Base Cabinet Detail – Drawers**
    b. *Scale:* **1″ = 1′-0″**

Revit provides many *Detail Components* that aid in creating 2D details. Things such as side views of bar joists, section views of steel beams and angles, and more are available in the *Detail Component* library. The detail below takes advantage of three *Detail Components* which ship with Revit: particle board, lumber, and the countertop. The only things drawn with the *Detail Line* tool are the tops of the drawers, the drawer pulls (i.e., handles), and the heavy wall/floor lines.

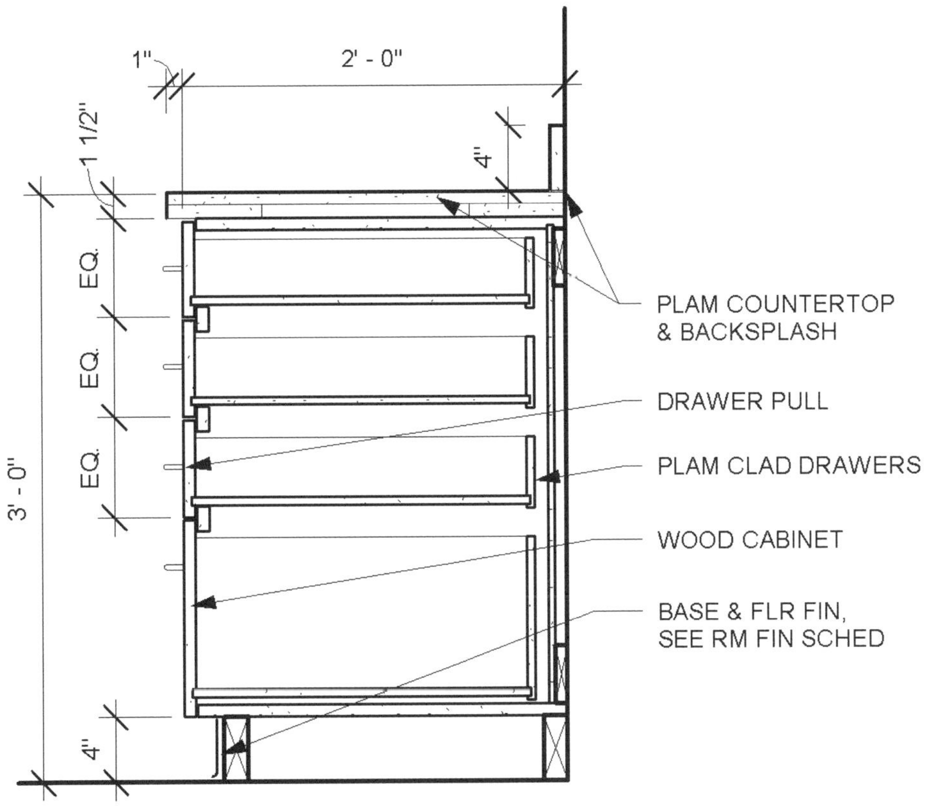

FIGURE 10-5.9 Cabinet section (with drawers)

43. Using the *Detail Line* tool, draw the floor and wall line, shown in the image to the right, using the **Wide Lines** style. (Do not add the dimensions.)

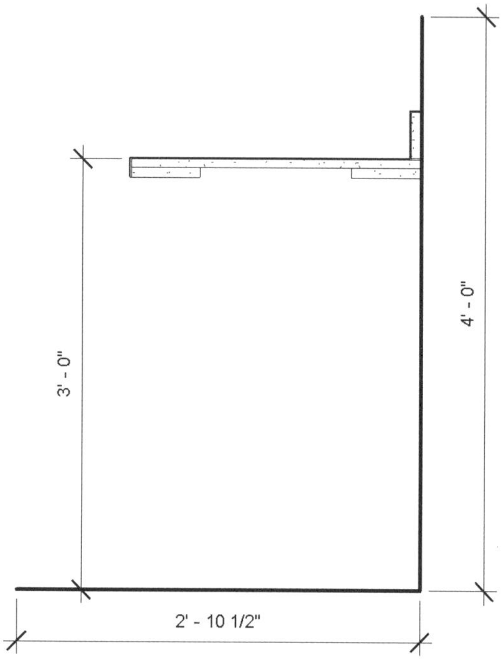

Next, you will load the countertop *Family* from the *Detail Component* library.

44. Select **Annotate → Detail → Component → Detail Component** from the *Ribbon.*

45. Click **Load Autodesk Family** from the *Insert* tab on the *Ribbon.*

46. Select the **Detail Items** section.

47. Now, browse to *Furnishings → Casework → Countertops.*

48. Select **Countertop-Section** and then click **Open.**

Countertop-Section with type *24″ Depth* is current, in the *Type Selector*, and ready to be placed.

49. Place the countertop as shown:
    a. Aligned with wall
    b. 3′-0″ above the floor (dimension to the line second from the top; the open heavy line is an exaggeration to highlight the added plastic laminate surface).
    c. With the countertop selected, adjust the values in the *Properties Palette*:
        i. *Backsplash Depth:* **0′ 1″**
        ii. *Counter Depth:* **2′-1″**
        iii. *Thickness:* **0′ 1⅝″**
    d. Do not add dimensions yet.

Be careful not to click on the grips when the countertop is selected, as this will adjust its dimensions; this is because the values are associated with an *instance parameter* rather than a *type parameter.*

Next, you will load and place the 2x lumber. The two on the floor are 4″ high, which are cut down from a 2x6. So you will load a 2x4 *Family* and then create a duplicate and adjust the height from 3½″ to 4″.

50. Per the step just covered, load **Nominal Cut Lumber-Section** from the following location: *Detail Item → Wood and Plastic → Wood Framing.*

To minimize the number of *Types* for the lumber *Family*, you are presented with the *Specify Types* dialog. This lets you pick just the sizes you want – more can be added later.

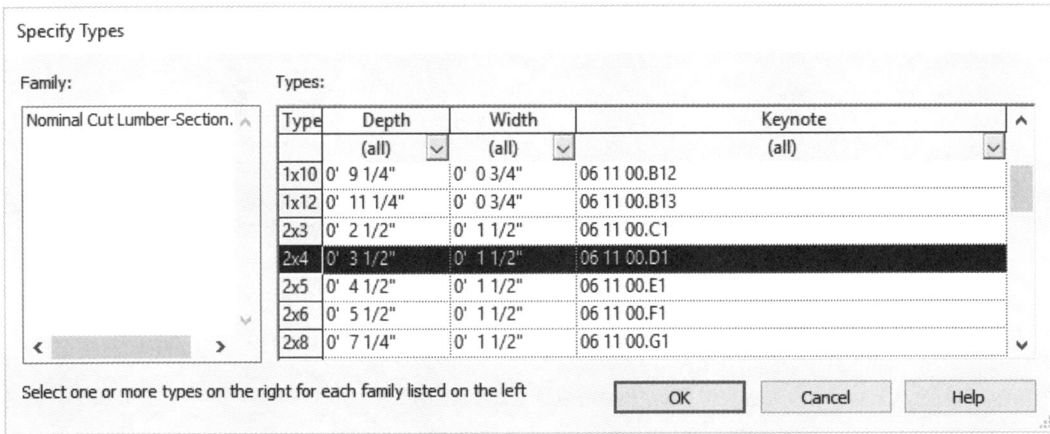

51. Hold the **Ctrl** key and select **1x4** and **2x4**, and then pick **OK**.

52. Select **2x4** in the *Type Selector*.

53. Click **Edit Type**.

54. Click **Duplicate**.

55. Enter **2x4 Base Cabinets** for the name.

56. Change the *Height* from 3½" to **4"**.

57. Click **OK** to close the *Type Properties*.

58. Place the two **2x4 Base Cabinet** detail components on the floor as shown in the image to the right. (Do not add the dimension.)

59. Place the two **1x4** components as shown.

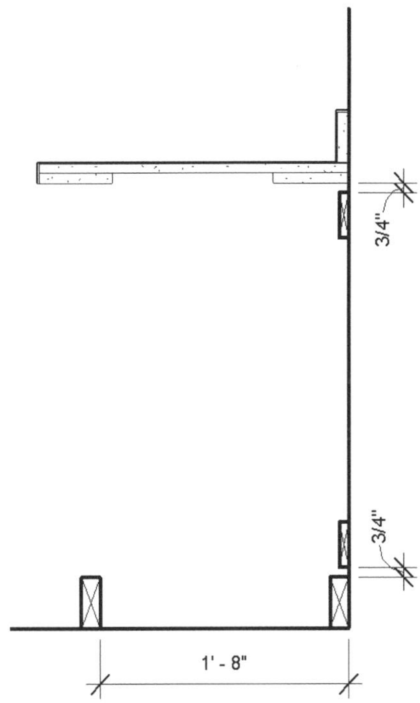

Next, you will load the detail component used to draw particle board. This *Family* is somewhat like the *Wall* tool. You pick two points and two lines, and a fill pattern is generated. The *Type Selector* also has a number of standard thicknesses ready to use.

60. Per the step just covered, load **Particle board-Section** from the following location: *Detail Items* → *Wood and Plastic* → *Sheathing*.

61. Select the **3/4″** type from the *Type Selector.*

62. Draw the two pieces of particle board shown in the image to the right; these are the top and bottom of the base cabinet. ***TIP:*** *Use the space bar to flip the thickness while drawing, if needed.*

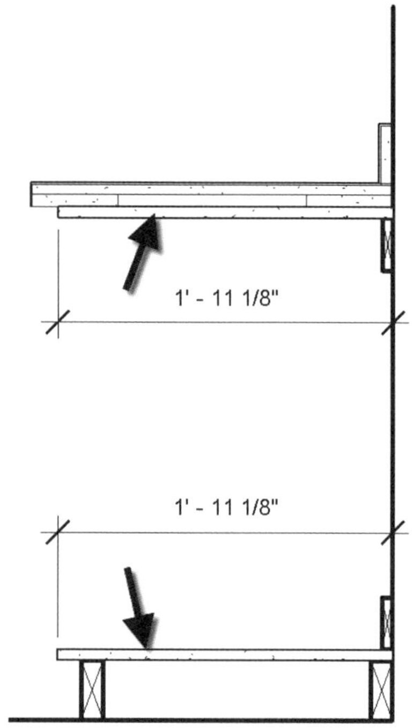

63. Draw the cabinet back; use the **3/8″** thickness option and extend it **1/4″** into the top and bottom boards. See image below. ***TIP:*** *Draw temporary detail lines, so you have a place to pick if needed. Delete them when done.*

The newest drawn particle board automatically shows up on top of any previously drawn particle board. This is how the notch is created. No trimming or erasing was required. If you need to change the overlap order, select the component and use the *Arrange* options on the *Ribbon*.

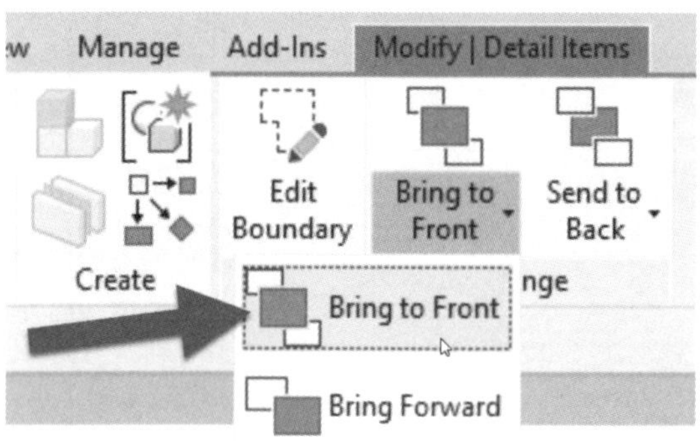

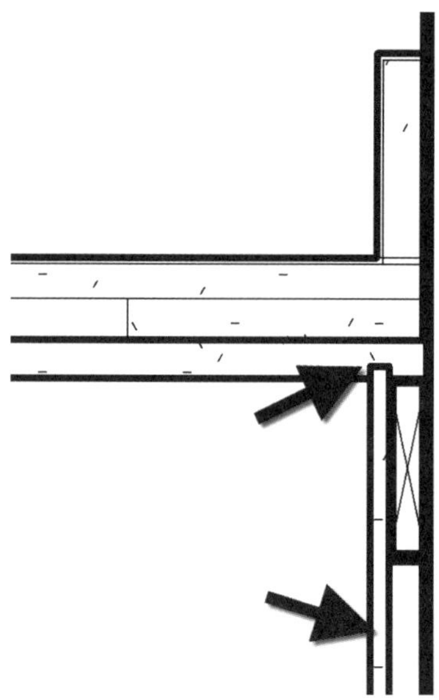

64. Draw the rest of the base cabinet using the techniques previously covered and the following information:

    a. The "EQ" dimensions are 6″.

    b. The drawer bottoms and backs are all ½″ particle board; everything else is ¾″.

    c. Use **Thin Lines** for the pulls and the top edge of the side drawer panel (seen in elevation in **Figure 10-5.9**). Use **Medium Lines** for the rubber base.

    d. Add dimensions not provided, which can be approximated; make it look like the image in the book as much as possible.

    e. Add all the notes and dimensions shown on the first image only.

Some things you should know about detailing

In the previous steps, you drew a typical detail showing a standard base cabinet with drawers. Interior designers occasionally draw these details, but more often, they simply review them for finishes.

The countertop material must match that specified in the **Project Manual** and intended for the project. For example, a PLAM (i.e., plastic laminate) countertop would not be appropriate for a laboratory where chemicals are used.

The base of the cabinet typically has the same wall base as the adjacent walls. For example, if the walls have a rubber base (also referred to as a resilient base), the toe-kick area of the base cabinet would also receive a rubber base; this is the type of base shown in the previous detail. If the project only had a ceramic tile wall base, you would show that.

The **notes for details** (or any drawing) should be simple, generic, and to the point. Notice in the previously drawn detail that the note for the base does not indicate whether the base is rubber, tile, or wood. This helps avoid contradictions with the room finish schedule. The note simply states that the cabinet and floor are to receive a finish and instructs the contractor to consult the Room Finish Schedule to determine the finish. This is particularly important in buildings with multiple variations in floor and base finishes.

Notes should not have any **proprietary or manufacturers' names** in them either. For example, you should not say "Sheetrock" in a note because this is the brand name; rather, you should use the generic term "gypsum board." Similarly, you would use the term "solid plastic" rather than "Corian" when referring to countertops or toilet partitions. In any event, whatever term you use on the drawings should be the same term used in the Project Manual!

One last comment: the *Construction Documents* set should never have **abbreviations** within the drawings that are not covered in the *Abbreviations* list, usually located on the title sheet. *Construction Documents* are legal, binding documents, which the contractor must follow to a "T." They should not have to guess as to what the designers meant in various notes all over the set of drawings. It is better to spell out every word, if possible, only abbreviating when space does not permit. You would not want a bunch of abbreviations in your bank loan or mortgage papers you were about to sign! Plus, undocumented abbreviations would probably not have much merit before a judge or arbitrator in a legal dispute!

65. Using the same steps just covered, draw the base cabinet shown below. Name the drafting view **Base Cabinet Detail**. The *Scale* is also **1″ = 1′-0″**.

    TIP: *Duplicate the Base Cabinet Detail – Drawer view and modify it to this detail; much of it is exactly the same.*

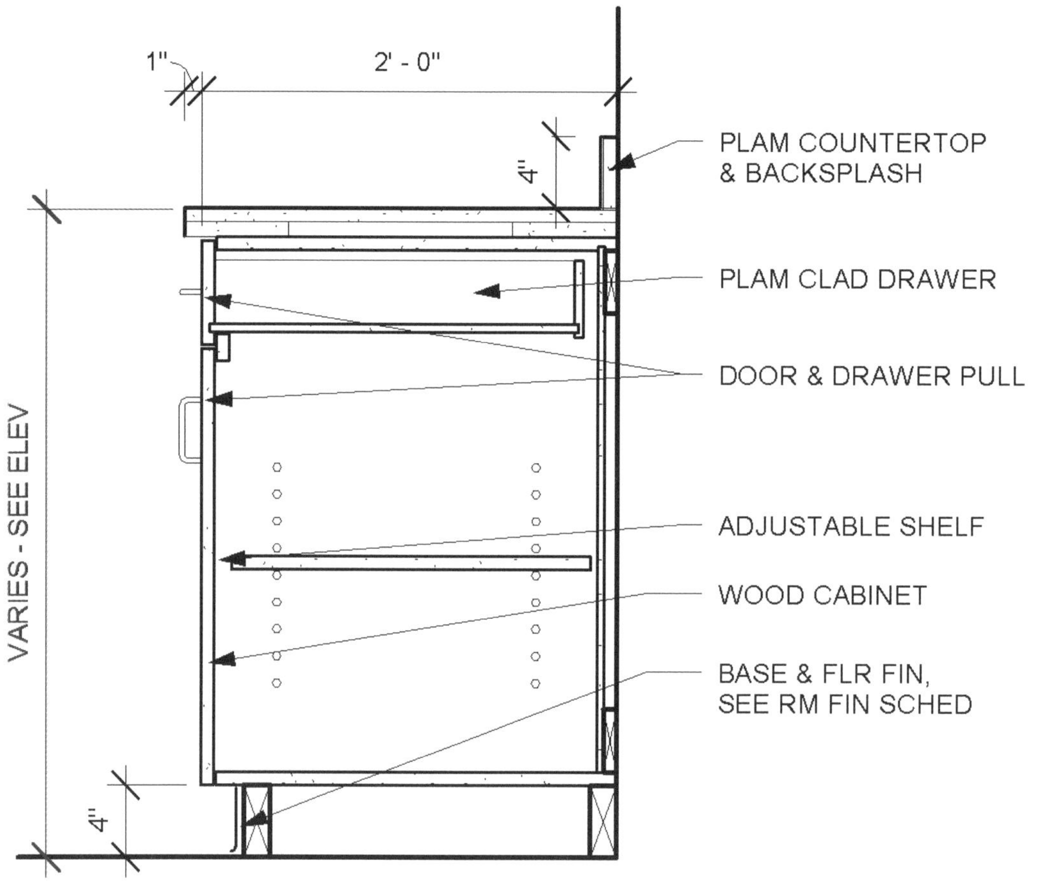

FIGURE 10-5.10 Cabinet section (door + drawer)

Cabinet details do not need to have every nook and cranny dimensioned, as they are standard items in the construction industry. Furthermore, the Project Manual usually references an industry standard that the contractor can use for typical dimensions, thicknesses, and wood grades.

The vertical dimension shown in the cabinet detail above says "VARIES - SEE ELEV." This notation, rather than an actual number, allows the detail to represent more than one condition. The interior elevations must have these dimensions, which may be the standard 36″ or the lower handicap-accessible height.

Ceiling Detail

Next, you will draw a typical recessed light trough detail at the ceiling. This is often used in commercial/public toilet rooms.

66. Create a new drafting view:
    a. *Name*: **Toilet Room Ceiling Detail**
    b. *Scale:* 1½″ = 1′-0″
    c. *See the next page for additional notes.*

67. Load the following *Detail Components* into your project:
    a. Finishes → Plaster and Gypsum Board → Supports → Non-Structural Metal Framing
        i. **Interior Metal Runner Channels-Section**
        ii. **Interior Metal Studs-Side**
    b. Finishes → Plaster and Gypsum Board → Gypsum Board → **Gypsum Wallboard-Section**
    c. Finishes → Ceilings → Acoustical Ceilings
        i. **Suspension Wall Angle-Section**
        ii. **Suspended Acoustic Ceiling-Square Edge-Section**

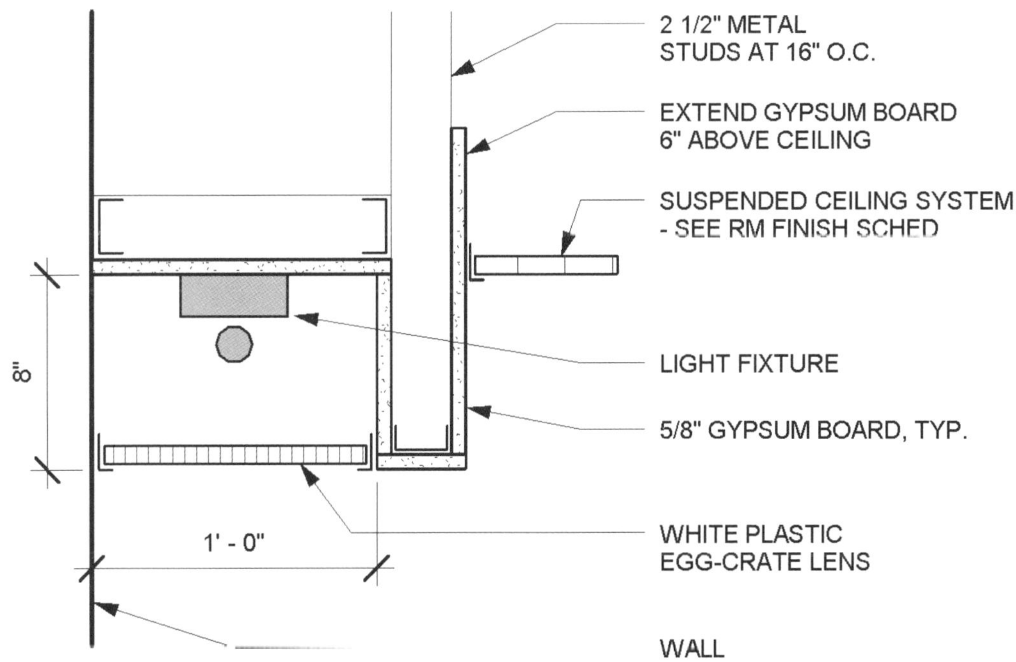

FIGURE 10-5.11 Ceiling detail

TIP: The notes in architectural details should align on one edge, as shown. Additionally, the leaders should not cross dimensions or other leaders unless it is totally unavoidable.

When using the *Detail Components,* you may occasionally run into challenges getting things to look exactly the way you want. For example, many firms have traditionally shown gypsum board as continuous, without indicating the joints. Most contractors understand this, and the designer usually does not want to imply the gypsum board is installed in a specific way or order. However, the *Detail Component* feature forces these edge lines to appear. Unfortunately, we **cannot** use the *Linework* tool to make some lines in a Detail Component invisible.

Another problem you will run into when using *Detail Components* is that everything is drawn to true scale. You may think, "Isn't that a good thing?" Usually it is, but some things need to be exaggerated to be legible on the printed page. Take the metal stud runner, for example; when placed next to the *Gypsum Board* detail component, it is totally hidden because the gypsum line weight is heavier than the runner stud. The best thing to do is edit the Family so the runner stud has a heavier line weight and its thickness is exaggerated inward (without changing the overall width). However, this type of change is outside the scope of this exercise, so you will do the following:

68. Erase the runner stud *Detail Components* and draw **Detail Lines** using **Medium Lines** – in bounds from the gypsum board.

69. Make the light fixture **4½″ x 1¾″** with a 1″ circle for the light. Use the previously created **Solid Gray Fill Region**.

70. Sketch the egg-crate lens using **Detail Lines**. Create a new *Fill Region* using the **Vertical-Small** fill pattern.

71. Add the notes and dimensions shown.

Fixed Student Desk at Raised Seating Classroom

This is a continuous student desk in a classroom setting.

72. Create a new Drafting View:
    a. *Name:* **Fixed Student Desk**
    b. *Scale:* **1½″ = 1′-0″**
    c. *See the next page for additional comments*

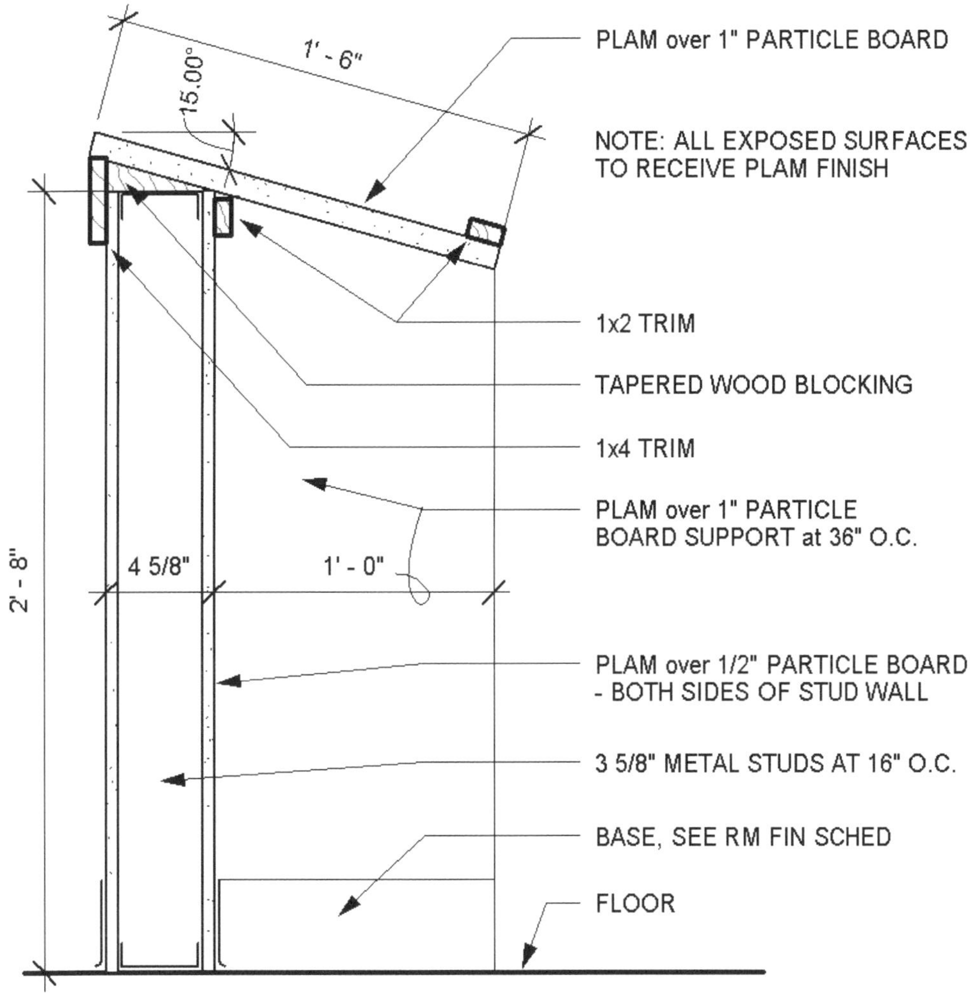

FIGURE 10-5.12 Fixed desk detail

73. Load the following **detail component**:
    a. Wood and Plastic\Millwork\Standard Millwork-Section
        i. Load the **1x2** and **1x4** sizes.

74. Develop the fixed student desk following these guidelines:
    a. All particle board and trim to be Detail Components.
    b. Tapered wood blocking to have **Wood 2** *Fill Pattern.*
    c. The curvy line pointing to the 1′-0″ dimension should be drawn like this:
        i. First, add the "PLAM" note using a regular leader;
        ii. Use the **Detail Line** tool;
        iii. Select the **Spline** *Draw* option;
        iv. Set the *Line Style* to **Thin**;
        v. Sketch the curvy line starting at the corner of the leader.
    d. Add a horizontal Detail Line at the top of the sloped work surface so you have something to pick when adding the angle dimension.

Some of the *Detail Components* have odd line weights when placed side-by-side. Both the wood trim and particle board are in section, so they should be the same line weight. You would have to edit the family to make this change, which will not be covered at this time.

Using the Keynotes Feature

The content that ships with Revit, both 2D and 3D, has a default keynote value assigned to it. Keynotes are used to save space and make details look neater; they are reference numbers rather than full notes, and an adjacent legend lists what each number means. This legend is for all the details on a sheet. You will learn how this works next. You will make a copy of the *Fixed Student Desk*, add keynotes, and then create a keynote legend.

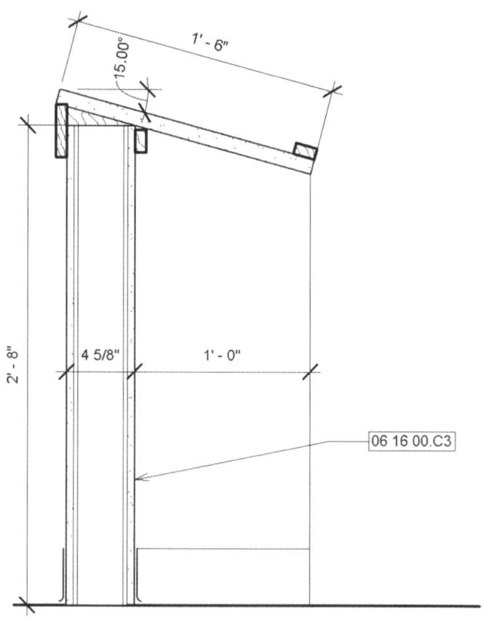

75. Right-click on the **Fixed Student Desk** item in the *Project Browser.*

76. Select **Duplicate → Duplicated with Detailing**.

77. Rename the new view **Fixed Student Desk – Keynotes**.

78. **Erase all the notes**, but leave the dimensions.

79. Select ANNOTATE → Keynote → Keynote Settings.

80. Browse to the provided text file: **RevitKeynotes_ Imperial_2004.txt** (see next image)

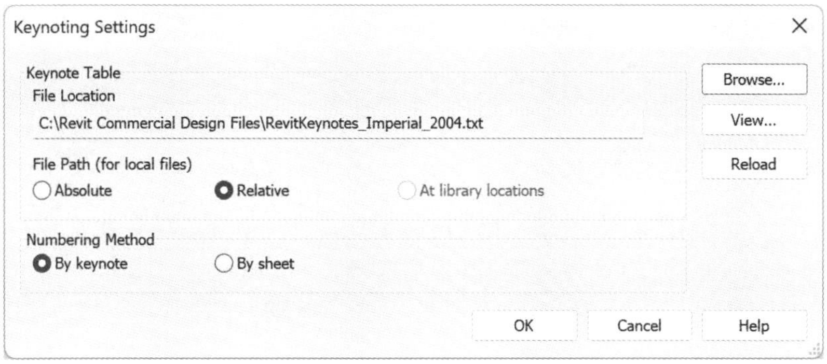

81. Select **Annotate → Tag → Keynote** from the *Ribbon*.

82. With the *Keynote* tool active, click the ½″ particle board shown in Figure 10-5.13; you will see it highlight just before selecting it.

83. Click two additional points to define a leader and text location, just like placing text with a leader.

You now have a keyed note placed in your drawing. This only works on *Detail Components* (in drafting views) and not *Detail Lines,* as they are too generic. Next, you will see where this keynote notation is coming from.

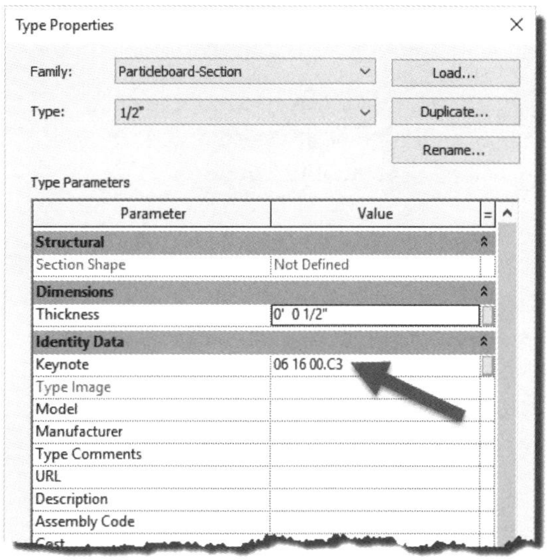

FIGURE 10-5.13 Keynote added

84. Select the ½″ particle board; go to its *Type Properties*.

Notice the *Keynote* value listed. This was defined in the *Family* you loaded. Next, you will view the *keynote text file* to see how a family could be changed to "mean" something else. You might change a family directly or create a duplicate *Type* first.

85. Click in the cell listing the *Keynote.*

86. Click the **small icon** that appears to the right (not in the "equals" column).

You now see a rather extensive listing of

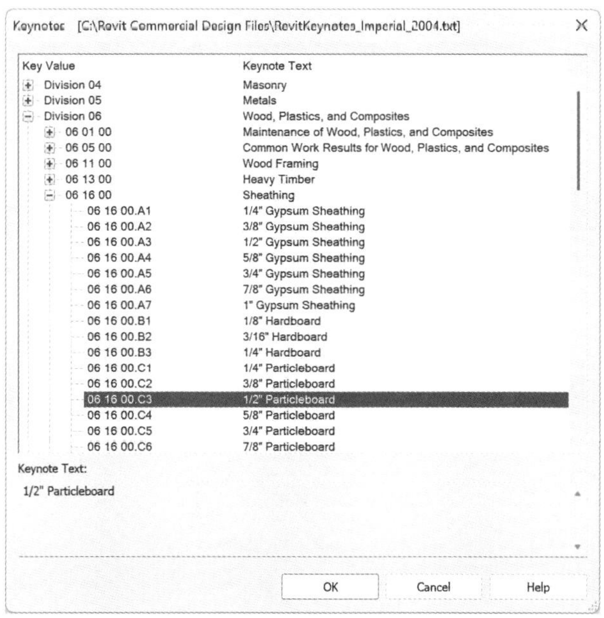

keyed notes (see the last image on the previous page). Take a minute to explore the various sections and descriptions for the keynote references.

87. After reviewing the keynote text file, click **Cancel**.

88. Click **OK** to close the *Type Properties* dialog.

The last thing to learn is how to create the **Keynote Legend**. This legend can be added to any sheet with keynotes. If the "By sheet" option is selected in the dialog box shown to the right, only keynotes actually found on that specific sheet will be listed.

89. From the *View* tab, select **Legend → Keynote Legend**.

90. Click **OK** to accept the name **Keynote Legend**.

91. Click **OK** to accept the default properties and to create the legend.

You should now see the *Keynote Legend* shown below.

***FYI:** Make sure the* numbering method *is still set to* By keynote *in order to see all the keynotes at this time.*

Later, in Chapter 12, you will learn how to place views on sheets.

Keynote Legend	
Key Value	Keynote Text
06 16 00.	1/2" Particleboard
06 16 00.	1" Particleboard
06 22 00.	1x2 Wood Trim
06 22 00.	1x4 Wood Trim
09 22 16.	3 5/8" Metal Stud Framing
09 22 16.	3 5/8" Metal Runner
09 29 00.	5/8" Gypsum Wallboard

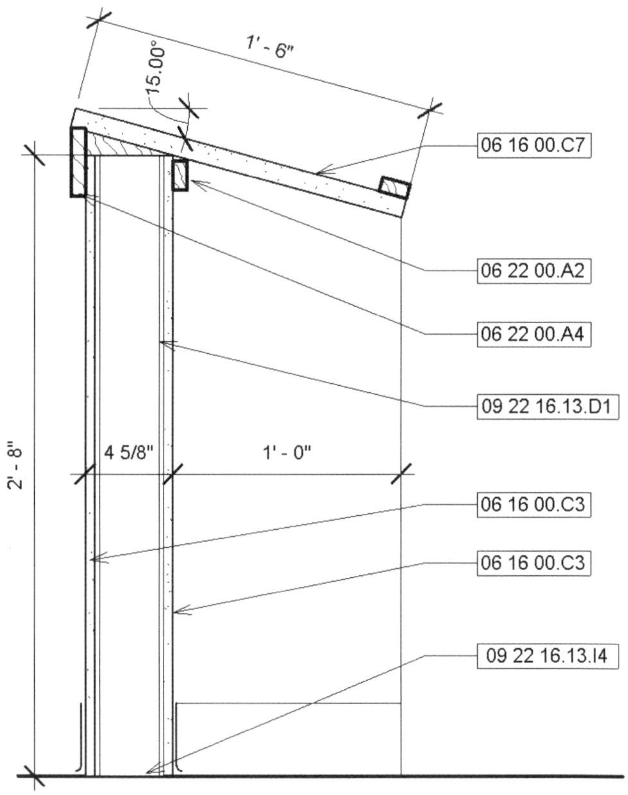

92. Add the remaining keynotes and then **Save**.

Finally, you can create elevations and sections that reference a drafting view rather than a true view of the model. This is another one of those places where you are breaking the intelligence of Revit's drawing sheet and number coordination.

To do this, you select the *Elevation* or *Section* tool, and rather than picking points in the drawing right away, you select a view that already exists in the project from the *Ribbon* options. Even though you have not placed any roof drains, you could switch to the **Roof** plan view and add a section mark that references the roof drain detail.

The following steps do not need to be performed at this time:

93. Switch to the **Roof** floor plan view.
94. Select the **Section** tool on the *View* tab.
95. On the *Ribbon,* adjust the following settings (Figure 10-5.14):
    a. *Type Selector:* **Detail View: Detail**
    b. *Reference other view:* **check**
    c. *Reference other view drop-down list:* **Typical Roof Drain Detail**

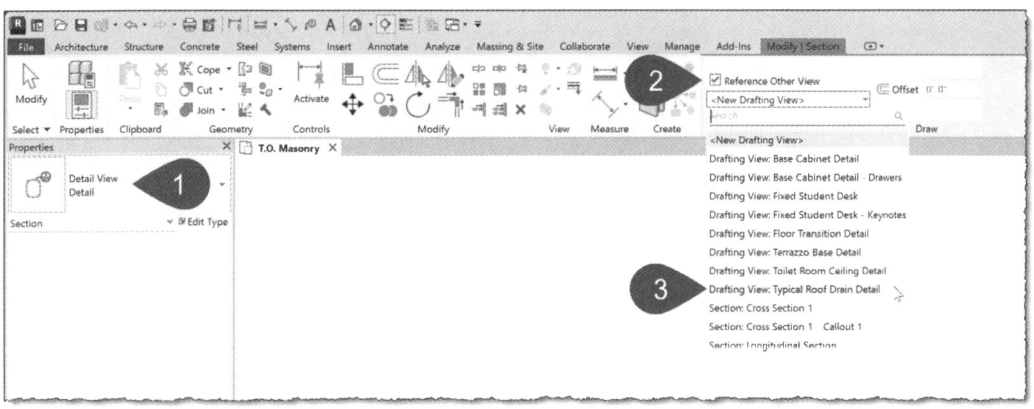

FIGURE 10-5.14 Placing a section that references the roof drain detail

96. Pick two points, roughly as shown in the image to the right.

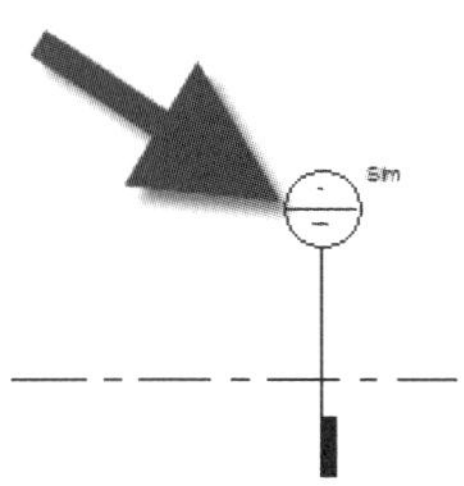

Try double-clicking on the blue bubble head; it should bring you to the roof drain detail. Once the detail is placed on a sheet, the bubble head will be automatically filled out!

97. Save as **10-5.rvt**.

Self-Exam:

The following questions can be used as a way to check your knowledge of this lesson. The answers can be found at the bottom of the page.

1. The plan is updated automatically when an elevation is modified, but not the other way around. (T/F)
2. You can use the *Elevation* tool to place both interior and exterior elevations. (T/F)
3. You can rename elevation views to better manage them. (T/F)
4. You have to resize the Level datum and annotations after changing a view's scale. (T/F)
5. The controls for the section mark (when selected) are similar to the controls for the elevation tag. (T/F)

Review Questions:

The following questions may be assigned by your instructor as a way to assess your knowledge of this section. Your instructor has the answers to the review questions.

1. The visibility of the crop window can be controlled. (T/F)
2. You have to manually adjust the lineweights in the elevations. (T/F)
3. As you move the cursor around the building, during placement, the elevation tag turns to point at the building. (T/F)
4. When a section mark is added to a view, all the other related views automatically get a section mark added to them. (T/F)
5. You cannot adjust the "extent of view" (width) using the crop window. (T/F)
6. What is the first thing you should do after placing an elevation tag?

   ____

7. Although they make the drawing look very interesting, using

   the ___________________ feature can cause Revit to run extremely slow.

8. It is possible to modify objects (like doors, windows and ceilings) in section views. (T/F)
9. You need to adjust the ______________________ to see objects, in elevation, that are a distance back from the main elevation.
10. AutoCAD DWG files should never be exploded. (T/F)

SELF-EXAM ANSWERS:
1 – F, **2** – T, **3** – T, **4** – F, **5** – T

Lesson 11
Interior Design

This lesson explores the various interior developments of a floor plan, such as toilet room layouts, cabinets, casework, and furniture design. Additionally, you will look at adding a guardrail and furring at the exposed structural steel columns. The rendered image below shows how Revit can be used to create an attractive, easy to understand presentation drawing of the building's interior design.

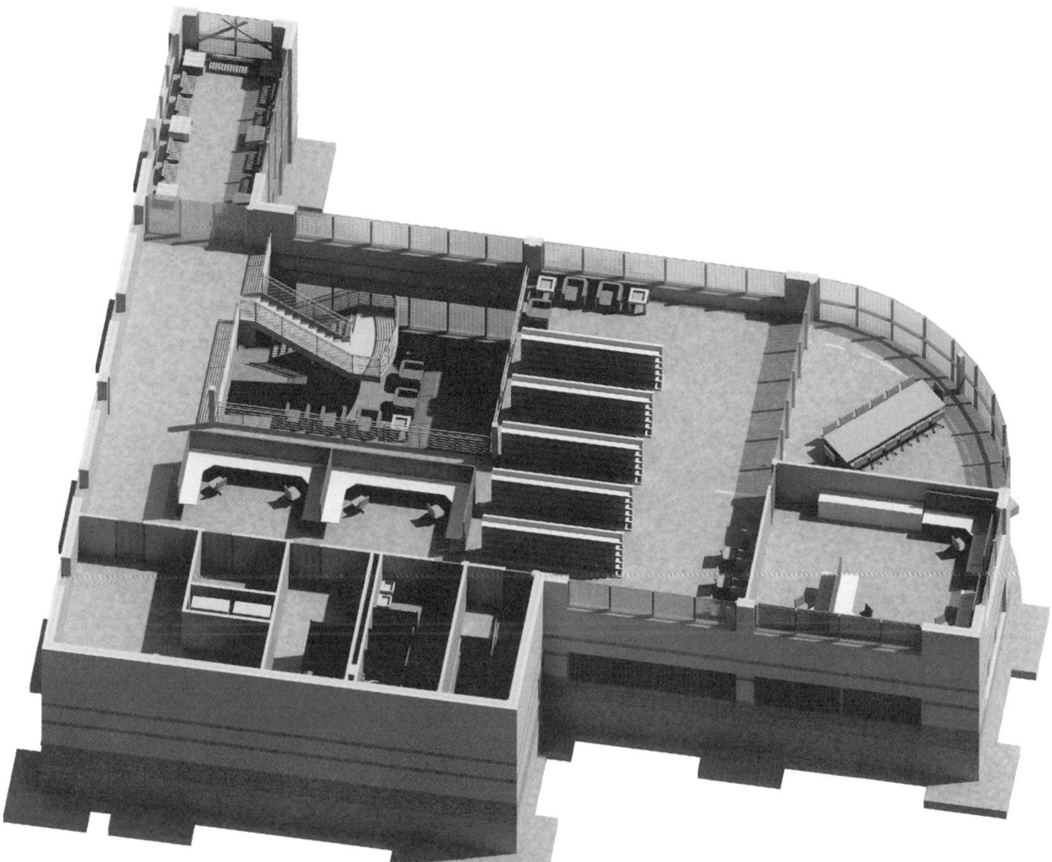

Exercise 11-1:
Toilet Room Layouts

There are several important factors in laying out a toilet room. The primary consideration typically is accessibility; that is, complying with local, state and federal accessibility codes so that people with various handicaps can easily access and use the toilet room facilities and the entire building in general.

Another consideration includes designed sight lines. It is undesirable for a person in the hallway to see any of the toilet fixtures when the door is being opened by someone entering that restroom space. It should be obvious that privacy, especially between males and females, should be expected in a toilet room design. Seeing the sinks or people washing their hands is not unacceptable but the designer needs to make sure the sight lines are not extended by the mirror above the sink. The design techniques employed to impede improper sight lines often take up a fair amount of floor space.

Another consideration has to do with the plumbing fixtures. It is important to have the correct type of fixture drawn and have it drawn at the correct size. Some of the code requirements are based on the clear space in front of the fixture; thus, the fixture needs to be the correct size in order to verify compliance. Also, whether the fixture is wall-hung or a floor mounted tank-type fixture is important; the mechanical engineer needs to know as they specify the fixture in the Project Manual. If the toilet is wall-hung, the wall needs to be thick enough to conceal the support bracket and the plumbing; the wall is even thicker when two toilets are back-to-back. From a designer standpoint, wall-hung toilets are often desirable in commercial buildings because they are easy to clean under and can be equipped with automatic flushing to help ensure a better experience for everyone!

Placing Plumbing Fixtures:

You will start this exercise by loading several components to be placed into your project. You can use either Revit *MEP* or Revit *Architecture* to place the plumbing fixtures. Often the architectural team places them as they are doing the initial toilet room design. However, the content between the *MEP* software and the architectural software is, unfortunately, not the same. The *MEP* content has special connectors on them that allow the *MEP* designers to connect water and sanitary piping to the element. Given this information, we will save a step and load our plumbing fixtures from the *MEP* content folders. You will do this using Revit *Architecture*, seeing as we have not covered Revit *MEP* yet.

Placing Plumbing fixtures

Image credit: Stabs, Wingate

1. Open Revit.

2. Open the **Law Office (CH11 starter file).rvt** file from the online files; save this file to your working folder.

3. Select **Insert → Load from Library → Load Autodesk Family**.

    a. Browse to the Plumbing\MEP category (Figure 11-1.1).

    b. If you are having trouble finding the *MEP* content, you can also browse to the following folder (if content has been manually downloaded):

    C:\ProgramData\Autodesk\RVT 2027\Libraries\English-Imperial

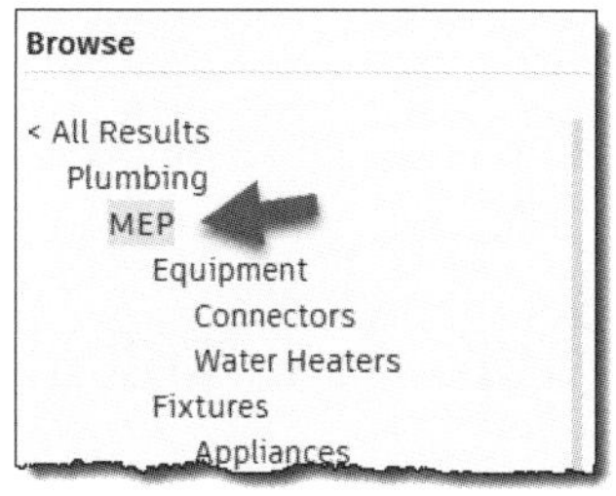

FIGURE 11-1.1 Plumbing\MEP

*FYI: The ProgramData folder is a **hidden** folder. In Windows Explorer: go to **Manage** (tab) **→ Options → Change Folder and Search Options**, and then on the **View** tab select "Show hidden files and folders and Drives."*

4. Load the following Revit *MEP Families* into your law office project:

    Plumbing\MEP\Fixtures folder…

    a. Water Closets**Water Closet - Flush Valve - Wall Mounted.rfa**

    b. Urinals**Urinal - Wall Hung.rfa**

    c. Lavatories**Lavatory – Wall Mounted.rfa**

5. Load the following *Families* into your law office project:

    Families\Interior Design folder from line files… (files provided with this book)

    a. **Grab Bar-3D.rfa**

    b. **Toilet Stall-Accessible-Front-Braced-3D.rfa**

    c. **Toilet Stall-Braced-3D.rfa**

    d. **Urinal Screen-3D.rfa**

TIP: All Families that are required for the law office project are located in the Families folder in the files downloaded from the publisher's website. This is helpful if the content was not installed with Revit.

The files you just loaded into your project represent various predefined *Families* that will be used to design the toilet room. It is also possible to create custom families for unusual conditions (see Chapter 18).

6. Switch to the **Level 1** architectural view.

Adding the Toilet Partitions

The toilet partitions offer privacy for toilets and urinals. They come in a few styles and materials. Styles range from floor-mounted to ceiling-hung; the latter offers better access to cleaning the floors, much like wall-hung toilets. Materials range from prefinished metal to solid phenolic core (i.e., plastic) to stainless steel.

The divider panels, pilasters and doors come in various thicknesses. However, each is typically drawn 1″ thick and is dimensioned to the center of the panel, so the thickness is not too important.

The example to the left shows a floor-mounted, overhead-braced toilet partition system.

Also, notice the urinal screen at the end of the countertop.

Floor drains are usually positioned beneath a toilet partition, so users do not have to walk over the slightly uneven surface.

Notice the accent floor tile that also takes into consideration the location of the toilet partitions.

Accessibility codes offer several layout options for toilet partitions. For example, if the door swings into the stall, more room is required in the stall to maintain the required clear floor space for the toilet fixture. Having a cheat sheet of several different layout options is a big help. Consult your local code for specifics.

The preceding image is very similar to the men's toilet room you are currently working on.

7. With the ***Component*** tool selected, pick **Toilet Stall-Accessible-Front-Braced-3D: 60" x 60" Clear** from the *Type Selector.*

8. Zoom in to the toilet room (east of the northern stair).

9. **Place** the toilet stall as shown and then move it into place using the ***Move*** (or *Align*) tool and your snaps (Figure 11-1.2).

    a. This is a *wall hosted* family, so it must be placed on a wall to exist in the project.

    b. Notice, when the toilet partition is selected, you have two flip controls which can be used to quickly change the orientation of the stall.

Once you move the toilet stall North, you will have your first stall in place.

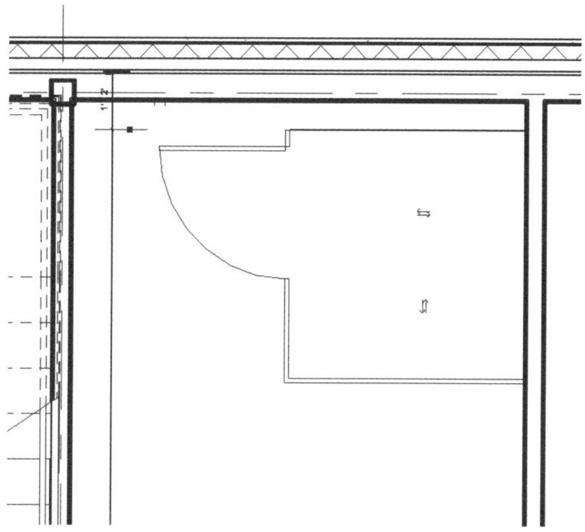

FIGURE 11-1.2 Accessible Toilet stall

Next, you will place two standard size toilet stalls.

10. Place two toilet stalls (**Toilet Stall-Braced-3D: 36" x 60" Clear**) as shown in Figure 11-1.3.

As with most projects, you will need to modify the model as you develop the design. In this case, we notice that toilets that are back-to-back and stacked on each floor will require a thicker wall to accommodate the fixture brackets as toilets are not supported by light gauge metal studs and larger piping. You will make this adjustment next.

For information on wall thicknesses behind double-hung toilets visit www.pdionline.org and review the publication *Minimum Space Requirements for Enclosed Plumbing Fixture Supports.*

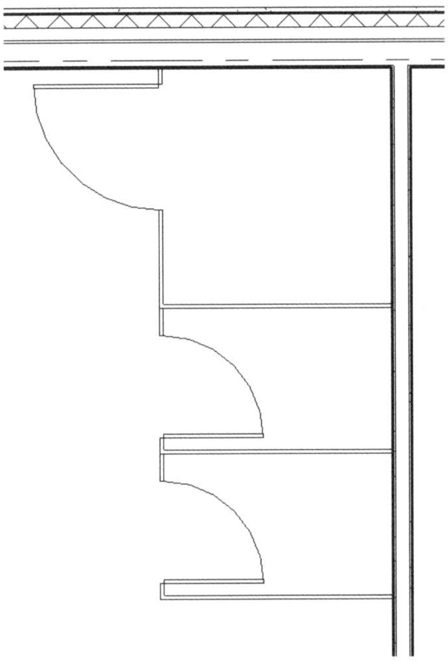

FIGURE 11-1.3 Std. Toilet stalls added

11. Select the middle wall and **Move** it **6″** to the West.

Notice how the toilet partitions moved with the wall because they are wall-hosted *Families*. The ceilings also adjusted.

12. Add an additional **4⅞″** gyp. bd. wall as shown in **Figure 11-1.4**.

In this case, you would not want to delete the original central wall and add two new walls. If you deleted the center wall, the wall-hosted content would also be deleted, and the ceilings would no longer update.

Next, you will adjust the *Location Line* of the two "wet walls" (i.e., walls that have plumbing behind them). This will help keep the finished face of the wall in the proper location when you adjust its thickness in the next few steps.

13. Select the two wet walls centered on the two toilet rooms and set the *Location Line* to **Finished Face: Exterior** via *Properties.*

14. Adjust the flip-control for each wall so they are positioned, in relation to the wall, as shown in Figure 11-1.4.

    FYI: You only see the flip-control when a single wall is selected.

15. Reposition the walls, if needed, so they match the dimensions shown in Figure 11-1.4; use the *Measure* and *Move* tools plus the temporary dimensions.

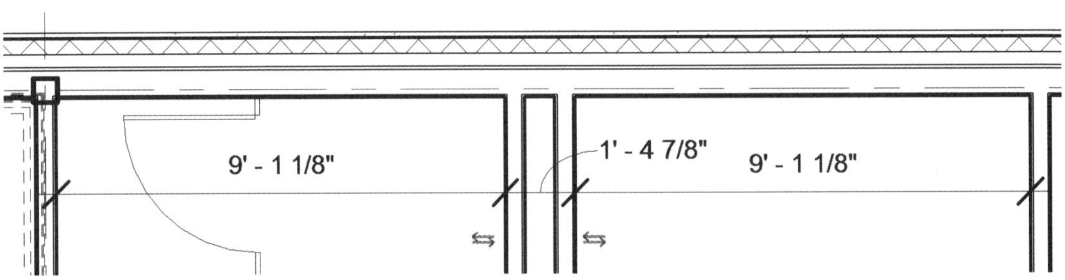

FIGURE 11-1.4 Toilet room wet-wall locations

Creating a Custom Wall Type

Now you will create a new wall type within your BIM project. The new wall type will be similar to the 4⅞″ stud wall, but it will only have gypsum board on one side of the wall.

Looking at Figure 11-1.5, you see the wall has gypsum board in the plumbing cavity, which is not appropriate. This would never be constructed this way, and if the BIM were used for quantity takeoff you would have too much gypsum board in the total.

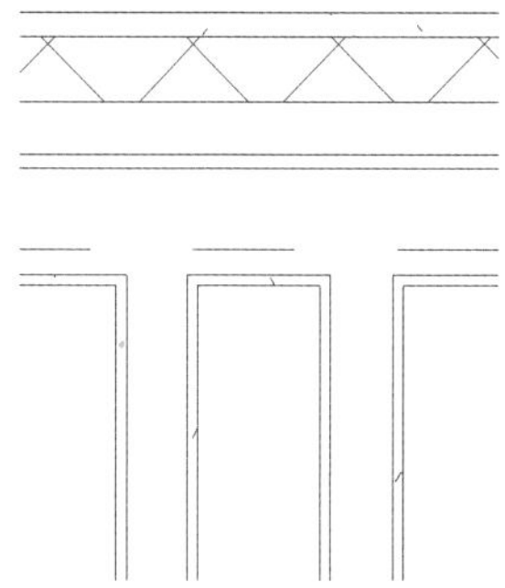

FIGURE 11-1.5
Toilet room wet wall

16. Select one of the two center toilet room wet walls.

17. Select **Edit Type** from the *Properties Palette.*

18. Click **Duplicate**.

19. Type: **Interior - 4 1/4″ Furring Partition**.

20. Click **OK**.

21. Click the **Edit** button next to the *Structure* parameter.

22. Click on **Row 5** to select it—the gypsum board *Layer* on the *Interior Side.*

23. Click the **Delete** button to remove the selected *Layer.*

Your *Edit Assembly* dialog should now look like Figure 11-1.6.

24. Click **OK** twice to close the open dialog boxes.

25. Select the other wet wall and change it to **Interior - 4 1/4″ Furring Partition** via the *Type Selector.*

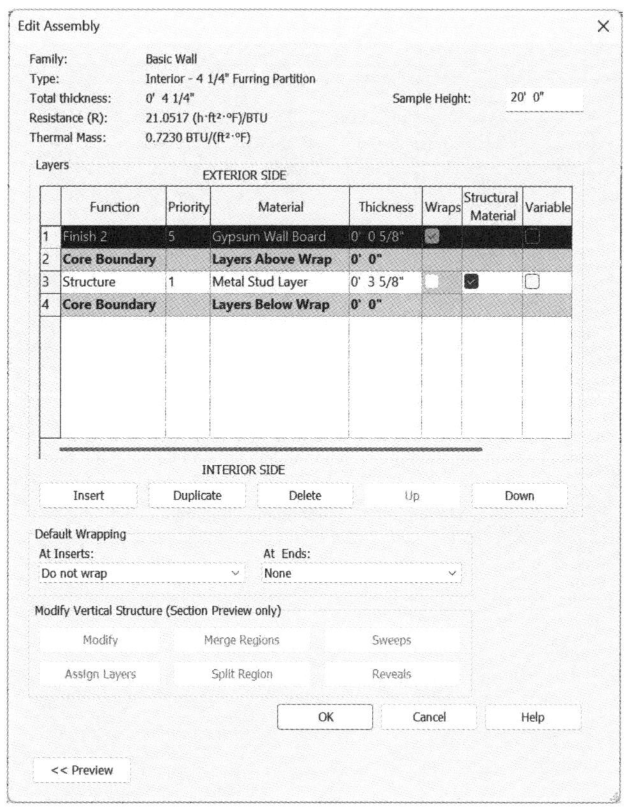

FIGURE 11-1.6 Edit wall configuration

Your two furring walls should now look like Figure 11-1.7. If the Location Line was not set properly, or the exterior side identified properly, the wall would have moved out of its proper position when you changed to a wall with a different thickness.

26. Use the *Measure* tool to ensure the walls are in the proper position; see Figure 11-1.4.

The exterior wall may have continuous gypsum board as shown. We will not modify that.

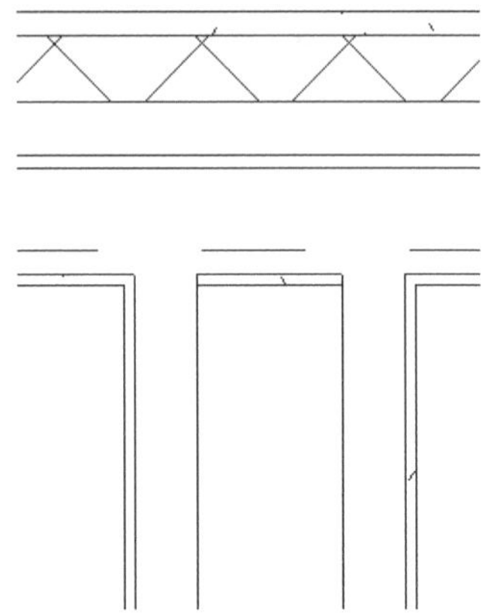

FIGURE 11-1.7
Toilet room wet wall revised

27. Add the additional components as shown in **Figure 11-1.8**.
    a. Note the family *name* is listed first and then the *Type*.
    b. The height (hgt) can be changed via the *Instance Properties*.

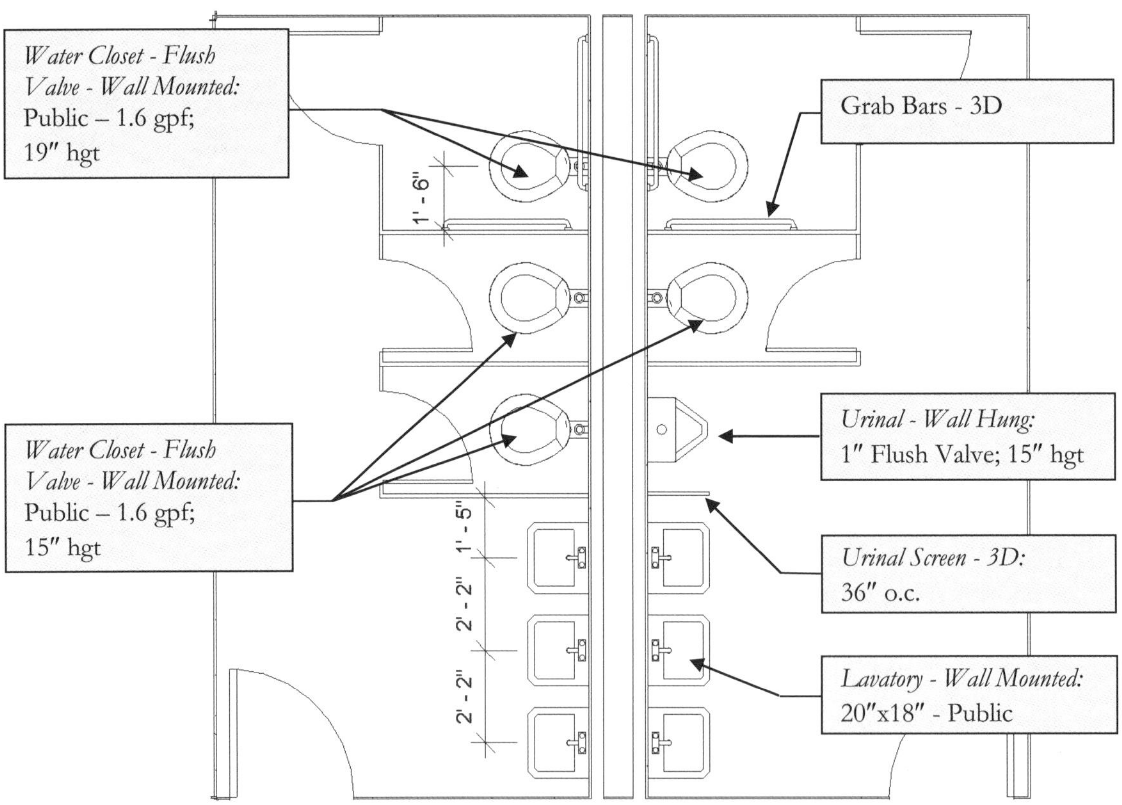

FIGURE 11-1.8 Toilet room layout

As mentioned previously, building codes vary by location. The toilets in the accessible stall area are usually mounted higher than the typical fixtures. When a room has more than one urinal, one is usually required to be mounted lower for accessibility and young children. Another example is that Minnesota requires a separate vertical grab bar above the horizontal grab bar on the wall next to the toilet; see Figure 11-1.9.

FIGURE 11-1.9 Grab bars

Creating a Group

Whenever you have a repeating arrangement of elements, you can create a **Group** and then copy the named *Group* around. When a change needs to be made to the *Group*, you change it in one place, and all the others automatically update.

You will select the entire toilet room layout and turn it into a *Group*. Then you will place a copy of that *Group* on Level 2.

28. Select the entire toilet room layout:
    a. 2 Wet walls
    b. 5 Toilets
    c. 5 Toilet partitions
    d. 6 Lavatories
    e. 1 Urinal
    f. 1 Urinal partition
    g. 2 Grab bars

29. With 22 elements selected, listed on the *Status Bar*, click the ***Create Group*** tool on the *Ribbon*.

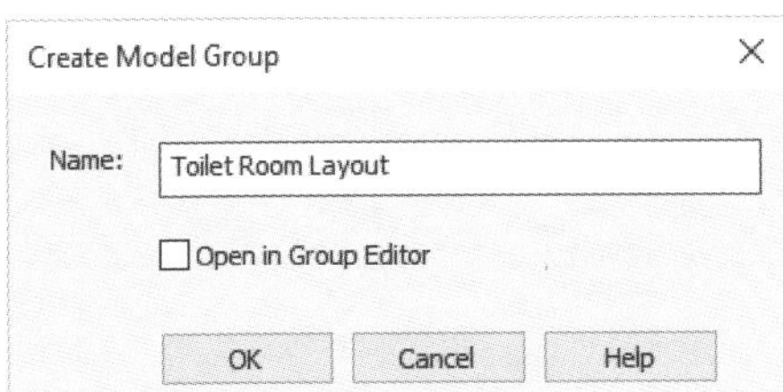

FIGURE 11-1.10 Naming a group

30. For the *Group Name* type: **Toilet Room Layout** (Figure 11-1.10).

31. Click **OK**.

You now have a *Group* which can be inserted on Level 2. However, you must do one more thing before doing that. You need to define the insertion point of the *Group*. By default, the insertion point for new groups is the center point of all the elements within the *Group*. This is fine for furniture groupings, but not for our toilet room layout where we do not want to have to move it around to find the correct location once placed.

32. Click to select the Toilet Room Layout group in the **Level 1 Architectural Floor Plan** view.

33. Click on the *Origin* icon and drag it to the upper-right corner of the men's toilet room as shown in Figure 11-1.11.

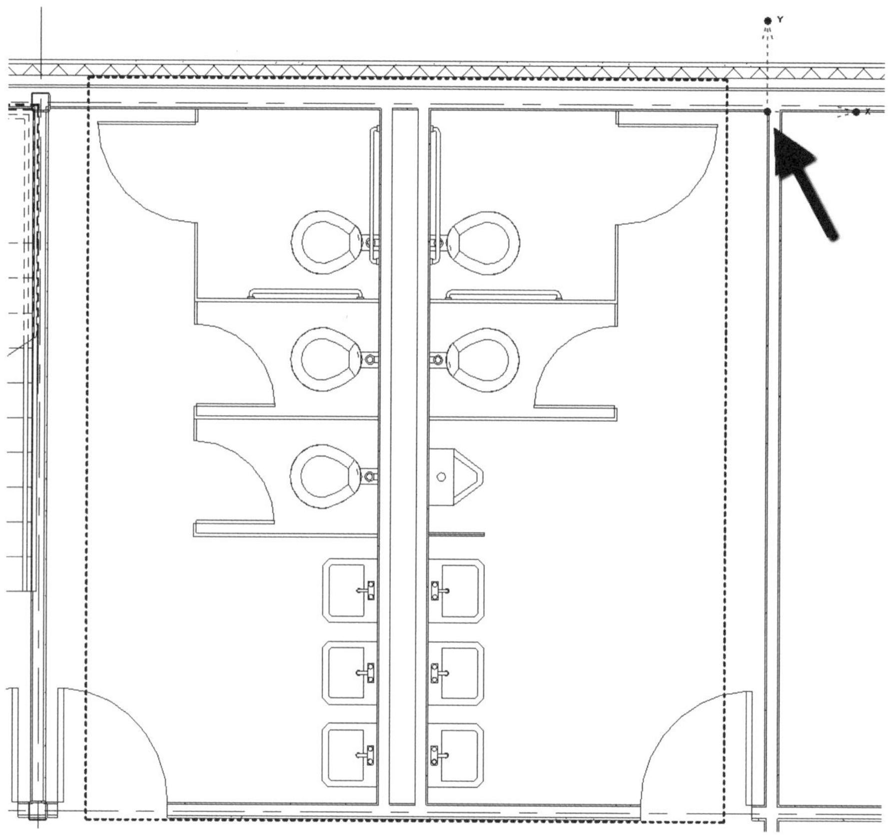

FIGURE 11-1.11 Repositioning the group's origin icon

Placing a Group

Now you will place a copy of your new Group on Level 2.

34. Switch to **Level 2** and zoom into the toilet room area.

35. Delete the original center wall between the two toilet rooms.

36. On the *Ribbon*, select **Architecture → Model → Model Group → Place Model Group** (Figure 11-1.12).

37. With your *Group* selected in the *Type Selector*, click the upper-right corner of the men's toilet room area to place the *Group*.

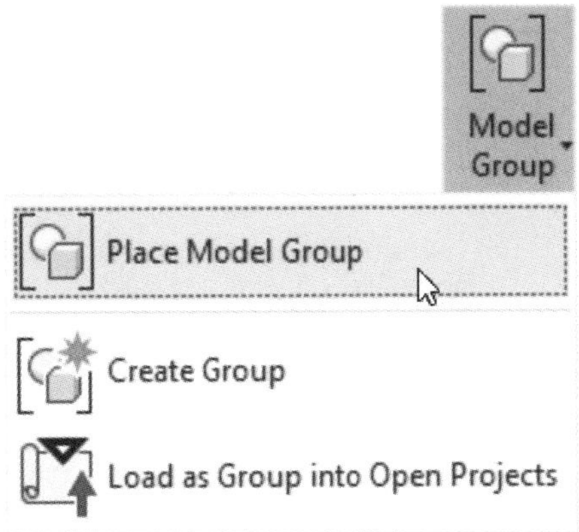

FIGURE 11-1.12 Place Model Group tool

You should now have a copy of your toilet room layout on Level 2! *Groups* can save a lot of time. See Figure 11-1.13.

To edit a *Group* you select it, and then click *Edit Group* on the *Ribbon*. When in *Edit Group* mode, the main model is grayed out so you can easily see what is in the *Group*. Once the changes are made, simply click *Finish Group* on the *Ribbon* and all instances of the *Group* are updated.

You will not make any changes to the *Group* at this time. If you decide to experiment, just *Undo* your changes before moving on.

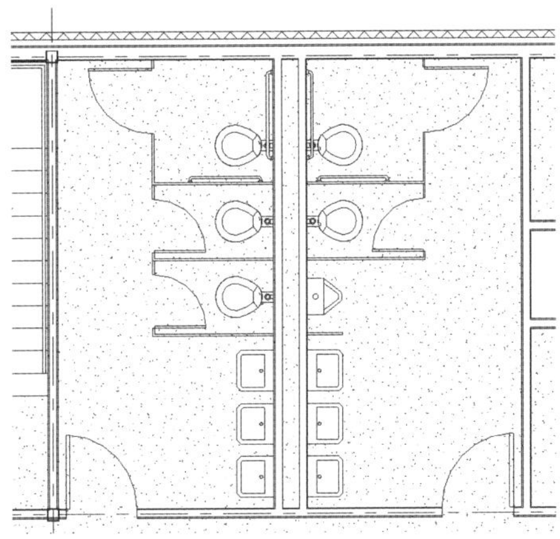

FIGURE 11-1.13 Group placed on Level 2

One challenge to using groups:

- The height of the walls cannot vary, so the floor-to-floor height must be the same if you have walls in the group.

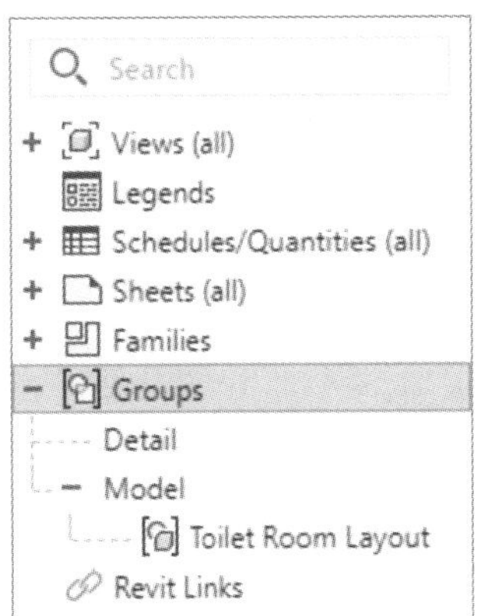

Near the bottom of the *Project Browser*, you will see a heading for *Groups*. You can find your *Group* listed there. If you right-click on the Group in the *Project Browser*, you can select *Save Group* to save a copy of the *Group* to its own file. This could be helpful if you needed to use this same layout in a multi-building project.

Interior Elevation View:

Next, you will set up an interior elevation view for the *Men's Toilet Room* using skills learned in previous chapters. You will also add a mirror above the sinks in elevation view.

38. Switch to **Level 1** and place an [interior] **Elevation** tag looking towards the wet wall, the wall with fixtures on it (Figure 11-1.14).

Notice again, how Revit automatically found the extents of the room when the elevation tag was placed in the plan view.

39. Rename the new view to **Men's Toilet – Typical** in the *Project Browser.*

40. Switch to the new view. Adjust the *Crop Region* so the concrete slab is not visible. Your view should look like Figure 11-1.15.

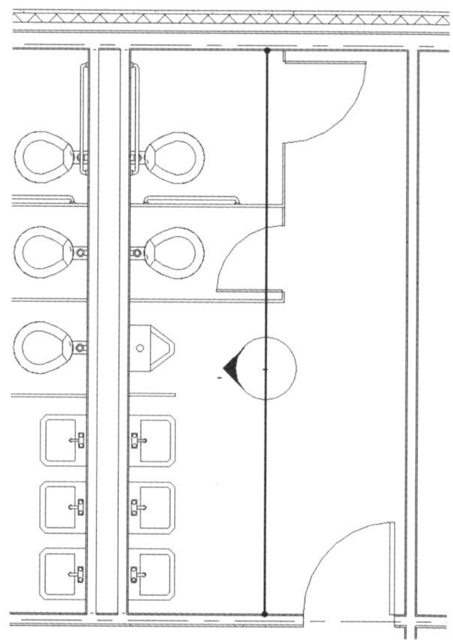

FIGURE 11-1.14 Elevation tag added

Your view should look like Figure 11-1.14. Notice how the lavatories (i.e., sinks) do not have faucets shown? This is because the *Detail Level* is not set to *Fine. Families* have the ability to be set up to show more or less detail as needed. The lower detail settings can make Revit run faster, but often the detail is needed to properly coordinate and annotate the drawings.

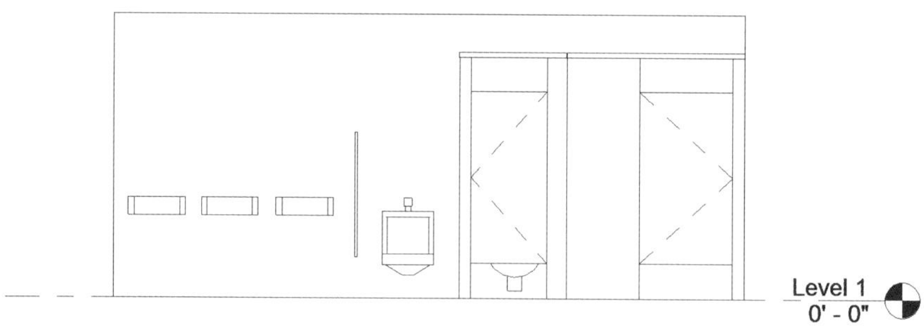

FIGURE 11-1.15 Men's Toilet – Typical initial view

41. Set the *Detail Level* to **Fine** and the *View Scale* to **½" = 1'-0"** on the *View Control Bar.*

You should now see the faucets. Next, you will edit the *Group* to add mirrors above the sinks. This will automatically update Level 2.

42. Load the component **Mirror.rfa** via Load Autodesk Family.

43. While in the interior elevation view, select any of the elements that are in the *Group*.

44. Select **Edit Group** from the *Ribbon*.

45. While still in the interior elevation view, place a **72″ x 48″ Mirror** on the wall above the sinks. Use the *Align* tool to align the mirror with the middle sink (Figure 11-1.16).

The mirror could only be added to the group because the wall it is to be placed on is in the same group.

46. Click **Finish** on the floating *Edit Group* panel (see image to right).

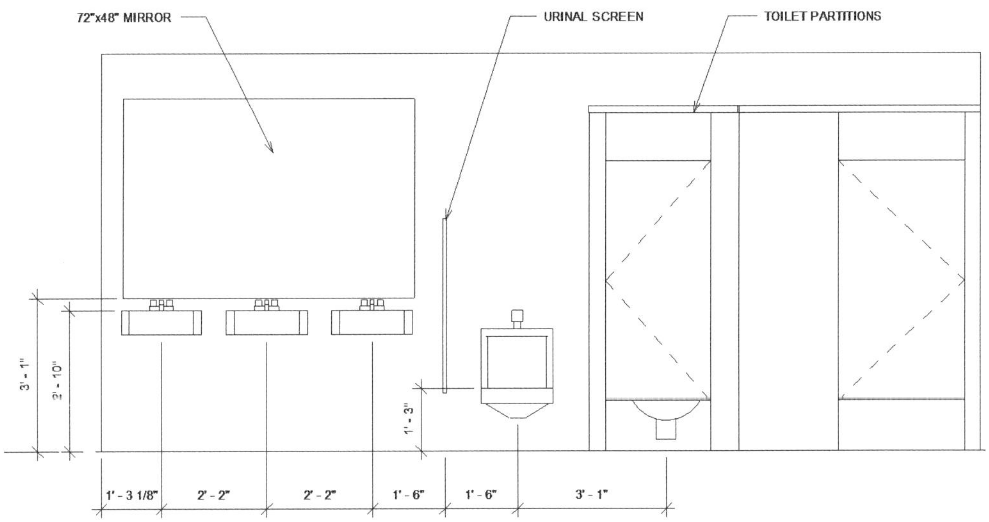

FIGURE 11-1.16 Updated interior elevation

47. Add the notes and dimensions per Figure 11-1.16. Adjust the heights and locations of the fixtures and components as required.

> ***FYI:*** *Keep in mind that many of the symbols that come with Revit, or any program for that matter, are not necessarily drawn or reviewed by an architect. The point is that the default values, such as mounting heights, may not meet ADA, national, state or local codes. Items like the mirror have a maximum height from the floor to the reflective surface that Revit's standard components may not comply with. However, as you apply local codes to these families, you can reuse them in the future.*

Adjusting the Reflected Ceiling Plan

Because you added a wall in the East toilet room, the definition of the room that the reflected ceiling plan uses is incorrect. You will adjust that next. You will have similar problems on Level 2 because you deleted a wall and then placed a *Group*.

48. Switch to the **Level 1** ceiling plan (Figure 11-1.17).

49. **Hide** the interior elevation tag from this view. Select its two components; right-click and select **Hide in View → Elements**.

50. Select the ceiling in the *Men's Toilet Room*, and then click **Edit Boundary** on the *Ribbon*.

    a. You may have to tap the **Tab** key to select the ceiling.

51. **Adjust** the left side of the ceiling to align with the new wall; when finished, click **Finish Ceiling** on the *Ribbon* (Figure 11-1.18).

Remember, deleting an element and then replacing it can cause problems!

52. Correct the ceilings on Level 2.

53. **Save** your project.

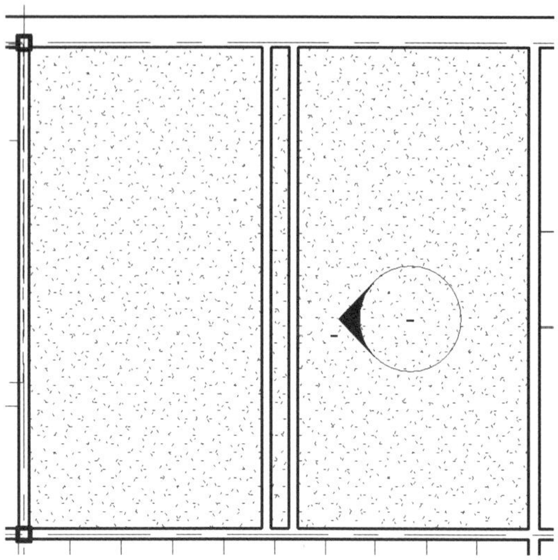

FIGURE 11-1.17 Level 1 RCP

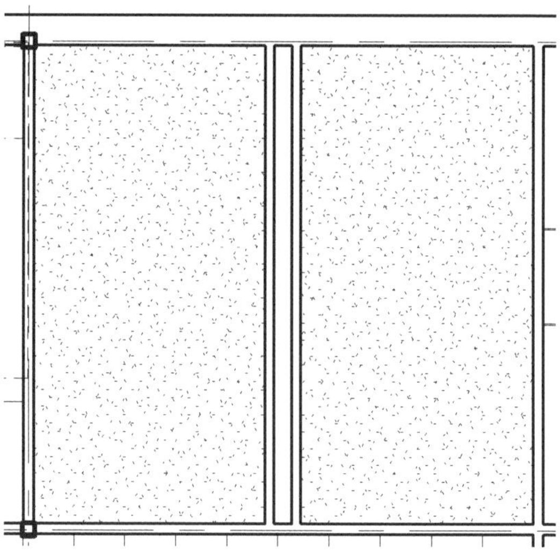

FIGURE 11-1.18 Revised Level 1 RCP

Exercise 11-2:
Cabinets

Introduction

This exercise covers the basic techniques used to add casework to your model. Casework is typically any built-in cabinets, countertops, desks, bars, etc., and is usually installed by a carpenter. This does not include systems furniture, or cubicles, which are sometimes attached to the wall.

Cabinets rendered in Revit

The architectural floor plans typically show the built-in items (i.e., casework) and the FFE Plan (furniture, fixtures and equipment) typically shows the moveable items. Furniture placement is covered in the next exercise.

The words "typical" and "usually" are used a lot because there is no exact science to how a set of drawings are put together. They can vary by country, state, city and even office.

Break Room Cabinets

Cabinets in a break room can vary quite a bit. The photo on the next page is similar to what you will be drawing next. The **base cabinets** are on the floor and are typically 24″ deep, but come in a variety of depths. The **wall cabinets** are attached to the wall and also come in various depths, 12″ and 14″ being the most common.

As you can see, the **electrical outlets** need to be coordinated with the electrical engineer; they need to be installed above the countertop and below the wall cabinets. When preparing the program, the designer should get a list of all the equipment required in each area. This will determine the number of outlets and locations. Often, items are overlooked or added later, creating an unsafe strain on the electrical system or requiring extension cords. For example, it is possible that the microwave shown in the photo was added by the users long after the design of the building; if the electrical system did not have enough capacity, it could make for an unsafe condition. If that were the case, a new outlet on another circuit would need to be added.

Notice two things about the wall cabinets: **1)** The cabinets have **under-counter lights** across the entire length. If this is desired by the client or designer, the electrical drawings need to be coordinated and the bottom of the cabinet recessed so the light fixture is not directly seen. **2)** The space between the top of the cabinet and the ceiling is filled in with studs and gypsum board for a clean, dust free finish, which is not always in the budget.

The cabinets in the break room often have plumbing to coordinate as well, for example, with a sink or dishwasher. When drawing plans, these items are roughly placed and then more refined later with interior elevations. With Revit both are automatically updated at the same time.

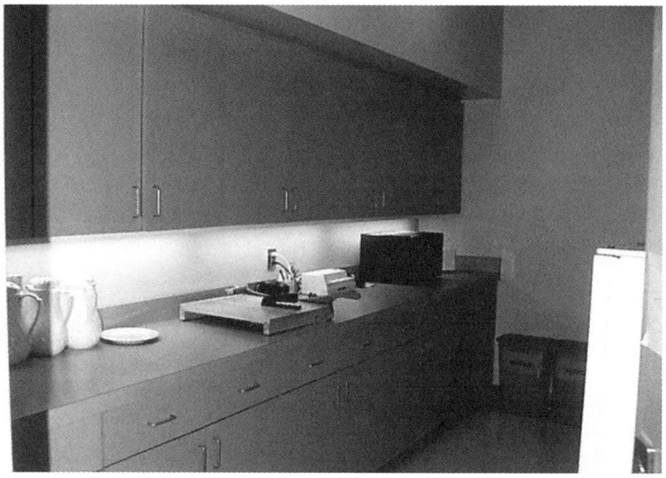

Example of typical work room cabinets; see comments on previous page

Placing Cabinets:

You will add base and wall cabinets in a break room on Level 1.

1. Open your law office BIM file.

2. Switch to **Level 1** view and zoom in to the area shown in Figure 11-2.1.

   TIP: Notice how the grids in the image below help locate what part of the plan is under consideration without the need to show the entire plan.

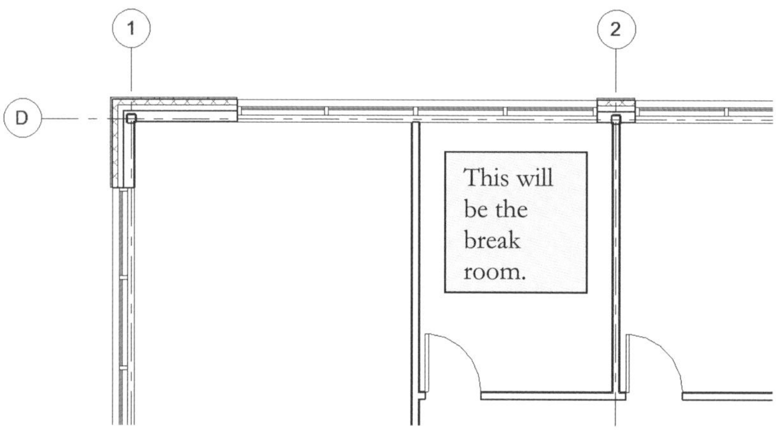

FIGURE 11-2.1 Level 1 – Northwestern corner

3. Load the following components into the project:

   (*sub-folder: Casework\Base Cabinets*):

   a. **Base Cabinet-4 Drawers**
   b. **Base Cabinet-Double Door Sink Unit**
   c. **Base Cabinet-Single Door**
   d. **Upper Cabinet-Double Door-Wall**

   TIP: You can load all four cabinets at once; just hold down the Ctrl key while you select them, and then click Open.

   (*load from provided SDC online Families folder*):

   e. **Refrigerator**
   f. **Law Office Counter Top w Sink Hole**

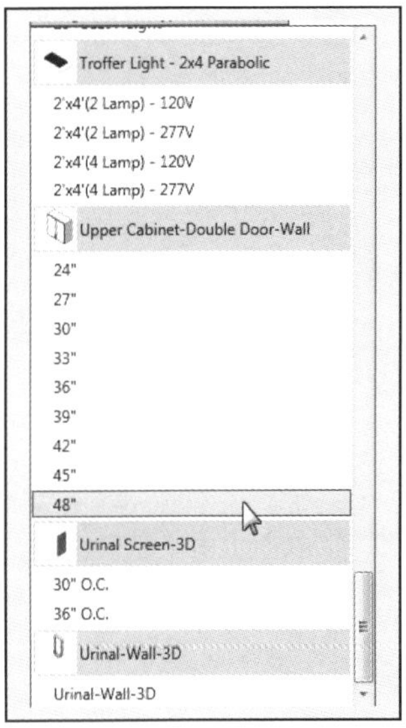

FYI: As with other components, such as doors and windows, Revit loads several types to represent the most valuable and useful sizes available.

Single and double door cabinets typically come in 3" increments, with different families having maximum and minimum sizes.

You are now ready to place the cabinets into your floor plan.

4. Select **Architecture → Component → Place a Component**, and then pick <u>*Base Cabinet-4 Drawers*</u>*:* **24"** from the *Type Selector.*

5. Place the cabinet as shown in **Figure 11-2.2**.

   TIP: The control arrows are on the front side of the cabinet; the cursor is on the back. Press the spacebar to rotate before clicking to place the element.

6. Place the other two base cabinets as shown in **Figure 11-2.3**, with a 24″ single door base cabinet in the middle and a 48″ sink base to the Northern end.

FIGURE 11-2.2 First base cabinet placed

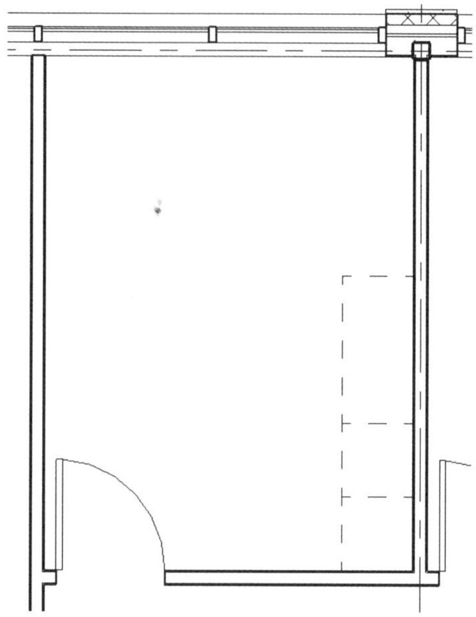

FIGURE 11-2.3 Three base cabinets placed

7. Add the four items as shown in Figure 11-2.4.

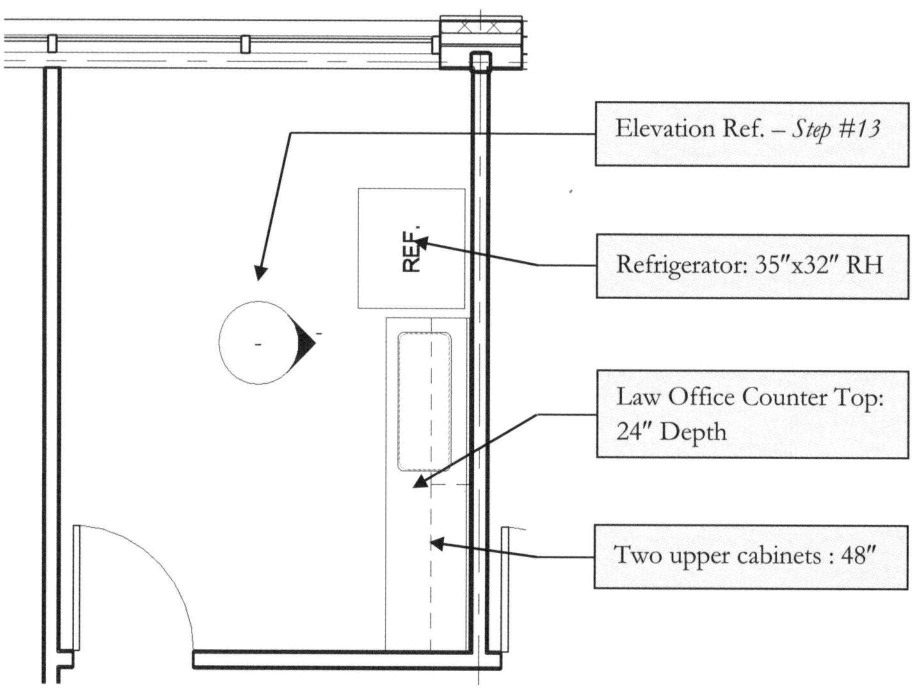

FIGURE 11-2.4 Break room plan view

> ***FYI:** The refrigerator has a hidden* Reference Line*, visible when the* Family *is selected, to help position the item the standard distance from the wall.*

Base cabinets are not hosted, which means they can be placed anywhere in the plan: against a wall or in the middle of a room as an island or peninsula. Uppers (wall) cabinets *are* wall hosted. Because wall cabinets are supported by walls, with rare exception, it makes sense that they be wall hosted similar to doors. When the wall moves, the upper cabinets will move with it; if the wall is deleted, the uppers will also be deleted. The base cabinets will not be moved if a wall is moved. This requires manual edits to the model. Both situations have pros and cons; for example, a group of wall cabinets cannot be easily moved to another wall, but a wall cabinet can be placed in an elevation view.

Placing the Sink:

Next you will be adding the sink. Similar to the previous exercise, you will be adding a sink from the Revit *MEP* content so it has the proper "connections" for the piping. None of the architectural content has these "connections" so we will not use them here.

The sink you are about to place is a **face** hosted component, which means it can be placed on any 3D face within the model. Much of the *MEP* content is *face* hosted because the other hosted types, e.g. walls, floor, and ceiling, do not work when linked models are used. Revit cannot find a wall through a link, but it can find a face.

The reason you loaded a custom countertop, and not one from the standard Revit library, is that it has been set up to properly work with *face based* families. The version that comes with Revit has the 3D geometry hidden in plan views, so a *face based* family cannot find a face.

When you placed the countertop and wall cabinets, they were located at a default height above the floor, which is set in the family. The nice thing about *face based* families is that they automatically stick to the face, no matter at what elevation it is. Therefore, you do not need to know the height of the countertop when placing the sink. And, of course, if the height of the countertop is adjusted later in the design, the sink will move with it.

8. Load the sink. See page 11-3 on loading *MEP* content.
    a. *MEP content folder:* **Plumbing Components\Fixtures\Sinks**
    b. *Family/File name:* **Sink - Kitchen - Double.rfa**

9. With the *Component* tool selected, pick:
    a. *Family:* **Sink – Kitchen – Double**
    b. *Type:* **42"x21" - Public**

10. On the *Ribbon*, select **Place on Face**; see image below.

FYI: The default option for face based family placement is "place on vertical face," which would be the side of the countertop.

11. Click anywhere on the countertop to place the sink.

12. Move the sink into position, centered on the hole in the countertop (Figure 11-2.5).

It is not really necessary to have a hole in the countertop at sink locations. This would only be required when cutting a section through it at the sink or when creating a rendering. Notice that the faucet is added separately, even though the *Family* has a hot and cold water connection built in.

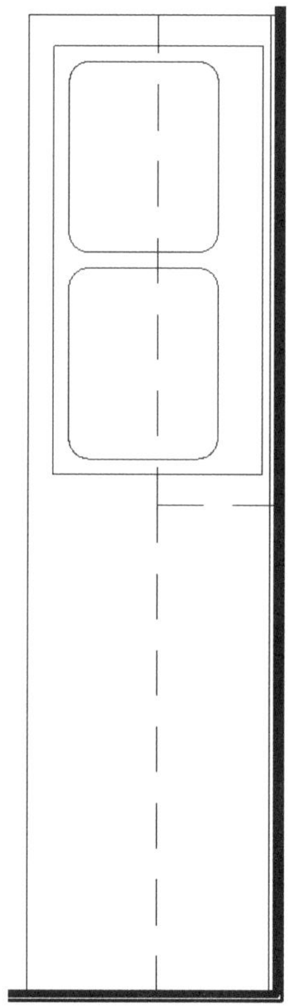

FIGURE 11-2.5 Sink added

Creating an Interior Elevation:

13. Add an interior elevation tag to set up the interior elevation view (Figure 11-2.4).

14. Rename the new elevation view to **Break Room (east)**.

15. Switch to the new view, **Break Room (east)**.

16. Adjust the **Crop Region** so the slab on grade is not visible.

17. Set the view scale to **½" = 1'-0."**

18. Set the *Detail Level* to **Fine** so the sink faucet is showing, via the *View Control Bar*.

Your drawing should look like **Figure 11-2.6**.

FYI: The wall cabinets are shown with dashed linework in plan because they occur above the floor plan cut plane. This helps to differentiate between wall and base cabinets.

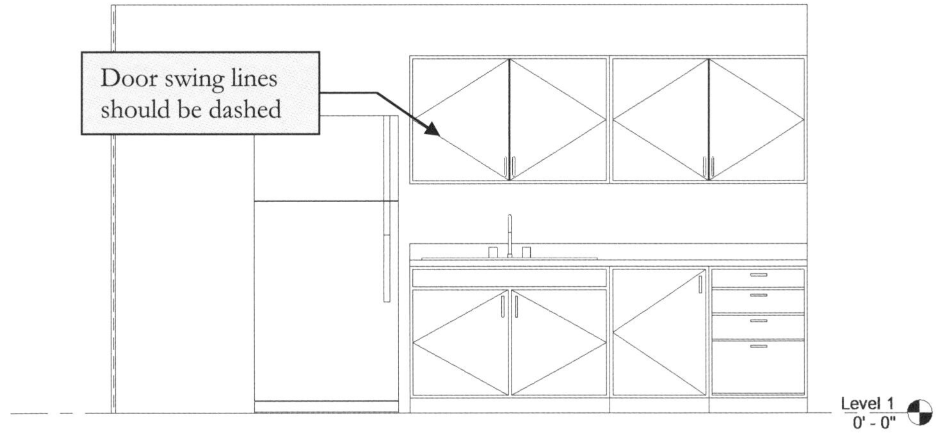

FIGURE 11-2.6 Interior elevation

Object Styles:

Next you will change the line type for the angled lines. These lines indicate the direction the cabinet doors open; they should be dashed. You could type "VV" and make the change for this view only. However, you will make the change from the *Manage* tab, on the *Ribbon*, and change this setting for every view!

19. Select **Manage → Settings → Object Styles** (Fig. 11-2.7).

Any changes made in the *Object Styles* dialog box automatically update all views in the project.

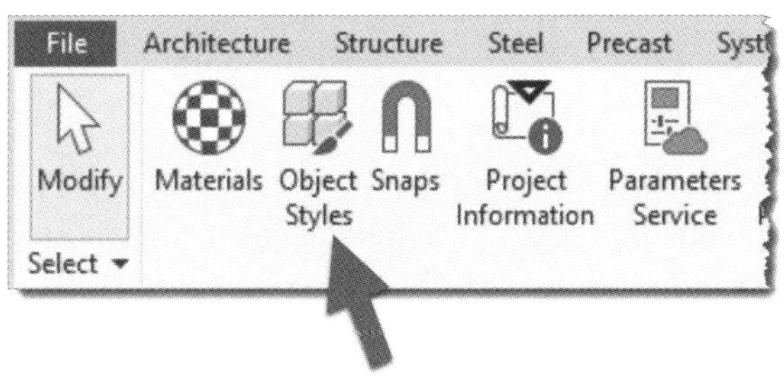

FIGURE 11-2.7 Object Styles tool

20. On the *Model* tab, expand the **Casework** section (Figure 11-2.8).

21. Change the *Line Pattern* for <u>Elevation Swing</u> (sub-category) to **Hidden 1/8"** (Figure 11-2.8).

22. Click **OK** to apply the changes.

Your angled lines should now be dashed (Figure 11-2.8). Setting up line weights and patterns in the *Object Styles* dialog is an important step in setting up an office template. Do not forget about the "Show categories from all disciplines" check box to see everything when needed.

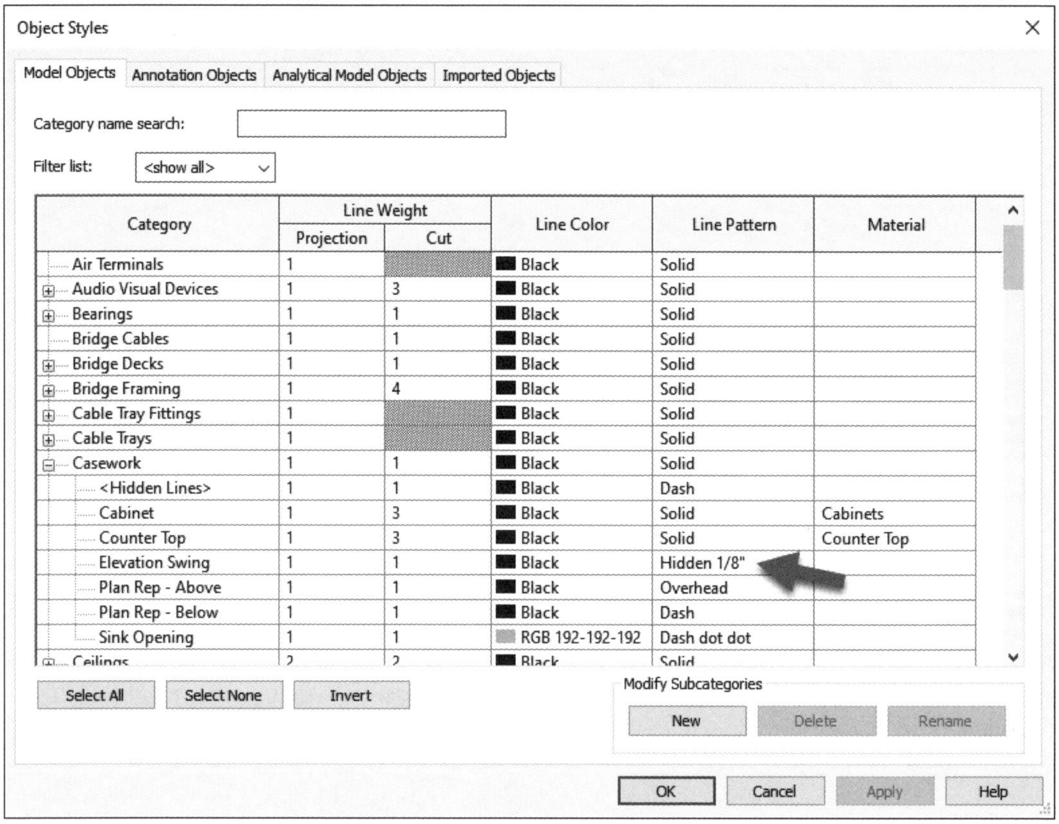

FIGURE 11-2.8 Object Styles dialog; Casework → Elevation Swing → Line Pattern changed

You will add notes and dimensions to the elevation. You can also add 2D linework to the elevation.

23. Add the notes and dimensions per Figure 11-2.9:

   a. All notes should be **3/32" Arial** text style.
      i. Use the proper justification and leader option to make the notes look like those shown.

   b. Dimensions should be **Linear - 3/32" Arial** and each string should be continuous, not individual dimensions.

   c. Use the ***Detail Line*** tool, on the *Annotate* tab, to draw the line on the wall behind the refrigerator indicating the vinyl base.

      i. Select the line and in the *Type Selector*, change the *Line Style* to **Thin Lines**.

      ii. Draw the line; snap to the endpoint of the base cabinet toe kick.

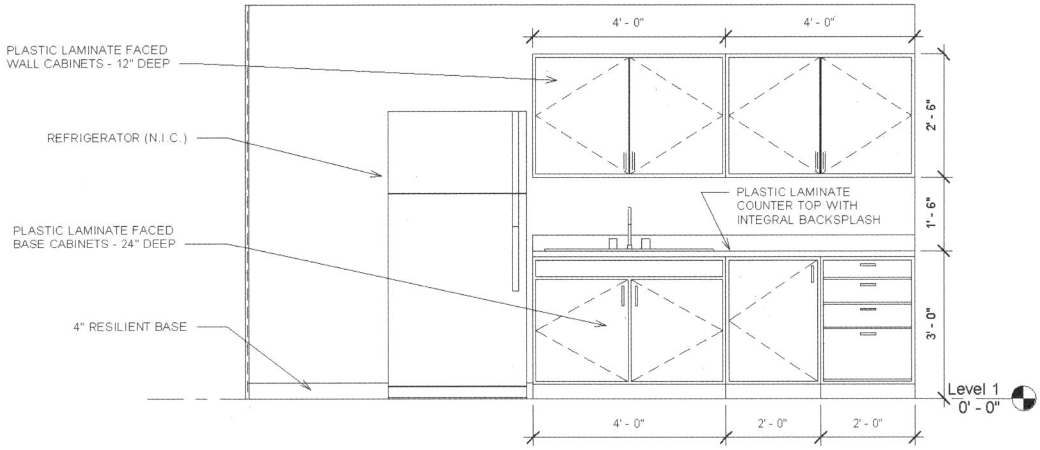

FIGURE 11-2.9 Interior elevation of Break Room with notes and dimensions added

> ***FYI:*** *The main difference between the* Model Line *tool on the Architecture tab and the* Detail Line *tool on the Annotate tab is this: Any linework drawn with the Model Line tool will show up on other views which see that surface. On the other hand, any linework drawn with the Detail Line tool will only show up in the view in which it was created.*
>
> *In other words, a Model Line is a 3D line and a Detail Line is a 2D line which is view specific. When drawing a Model Line you have to specify which plane you want to be sketching on, whereas the Detail Line does not care.*

It is possible to select a base or wall cabinet and swap it out with another cabinet via the *Type Selector*. When beginning to design a row of cabinets, it may be easier to place one base cabinet in plan and then switch to the elevation, copy the cabinet and swap it with the next cabinet needed, repeating these steps until done.

Notice how the countertop and wall cabinets were placed at the correct height. This was predefined in the family. If this same countertop was needed as a work surface at 30″, you could place it in plan and change the height via the element's *Instance Properties*, or simply move it in an elevation of section view.

Keep in mind these notes and dimensions may need to be manually adjusted if the cabinets are changed in another view, or this view.

Rather than dimensioning the width of the cabinets, it is also possible to tag them by category.

24. **Save** your project.

Exercise 11-3:
Furniture

This lesson will cover the steps required to lay out office furniture. The processes are identical to those previously covered for toilets and cabinets.

Loading the Necessary Families:

1. **Open** your law office project.

2. Select the *Component* tool and load the following items into the current project. ***TIP:*** *All content needed in this book is located on SDCpublications.com. You can speed up this step by loading everything from the online files as you can select multiple items at once when they are in the same folder.*

   Local Files *(i.e., Revit content on your hard drive, or using Load Autodesk Family)*

   a. Furniture System folder
      i. Work Station Cubicle
      ii. Storage Pedestal

   b. Furniture folders
      i. Cabinet-File 5 Drawer
      ii. Chair-Breuer
      iii. Chair-Desk
      iv. Chair-Executive
      v. Chair-Task Arms
      vi. Chair-Task
      vii. Credenza
      viii. Desk
      ix. Table-Coffee
      x. Table-Dining Round w Chairs

   c. Specialty Equipment\Classroom-Library folder
      i. Single Carrel
      ii. Stack Shelving

   Online Files *(see the inside front cover for more information)*

   a. FN - Admin Reception Desk (custom family)

   b. FN – Reception Desk (custom family)

   c. Table-Conference2 w Chairs

   Haworth Files *(from* www.Haworth.com *or the online files)*

   a. SLMS-FD01-8P (seating)

   b. SLMS-FD02-8P (seating)

   c. SLSE-SQ01-8P (lounge seating)

   d. SLSE-SQ02-8P (lounge seating)

   e. TOSE-SQW-BP (table)

These files represent various predefined families that will be used to design the offices.

TIP: You can set the View mode for the Open dialog box, which is displayed when you click Load Family. One option is Thumbnail mode; this displays a small thumbnail image for each file in the current folder. This makes it easier to see the many symbols and drawings that are available for insertion. Hold Ctrl *while spinning the mouse wheel to enlarge the previews; you might have to click within the preview pane first, to activate that area.*

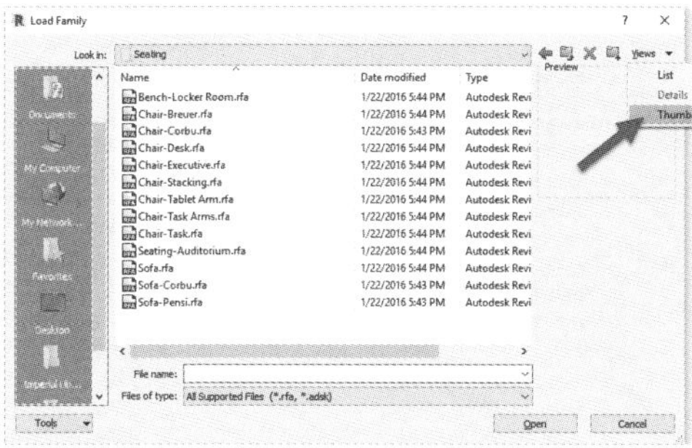

View set to Details mode

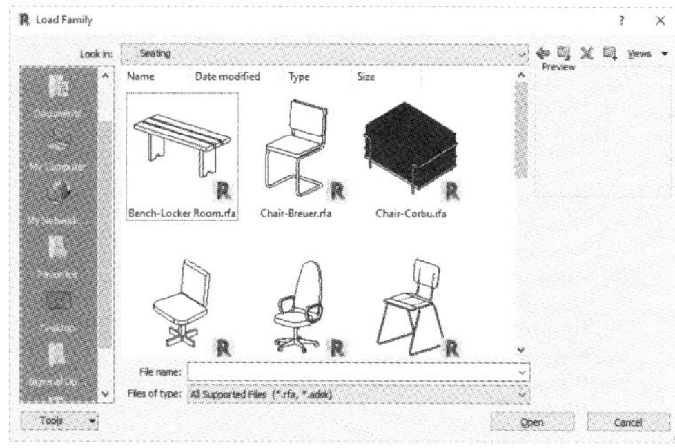

View set to Thumbnail mode

Designing the Office Furniture Layout:

3. The next two images of Level 1 and Level 2, Figures 11-3.1 and 11-3.2, show the furniture layout. Place the furniture as shown.

   TIP: Use snaps to assure accuracy; use Rotate and Mirror as required.

The two custom reception desks are examples of unique project related items that need to be created specifically for this project. You could not expect Autodesk to be able to create the infinite possibilities for you when it comes to content. Therefore, someone on the design team needs to be trained in creating content. In Chapter 18 of this book, an introduction to creating content is covered, but it just skims the surface. Chapter 5 covered a few basic concepts related to creating 2D families as well.

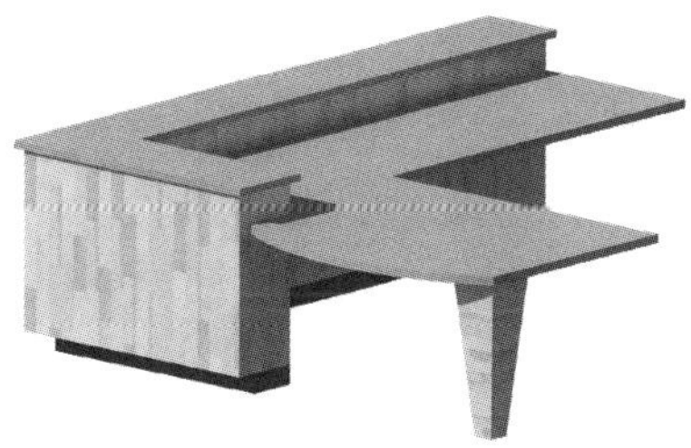

Custom Revit family

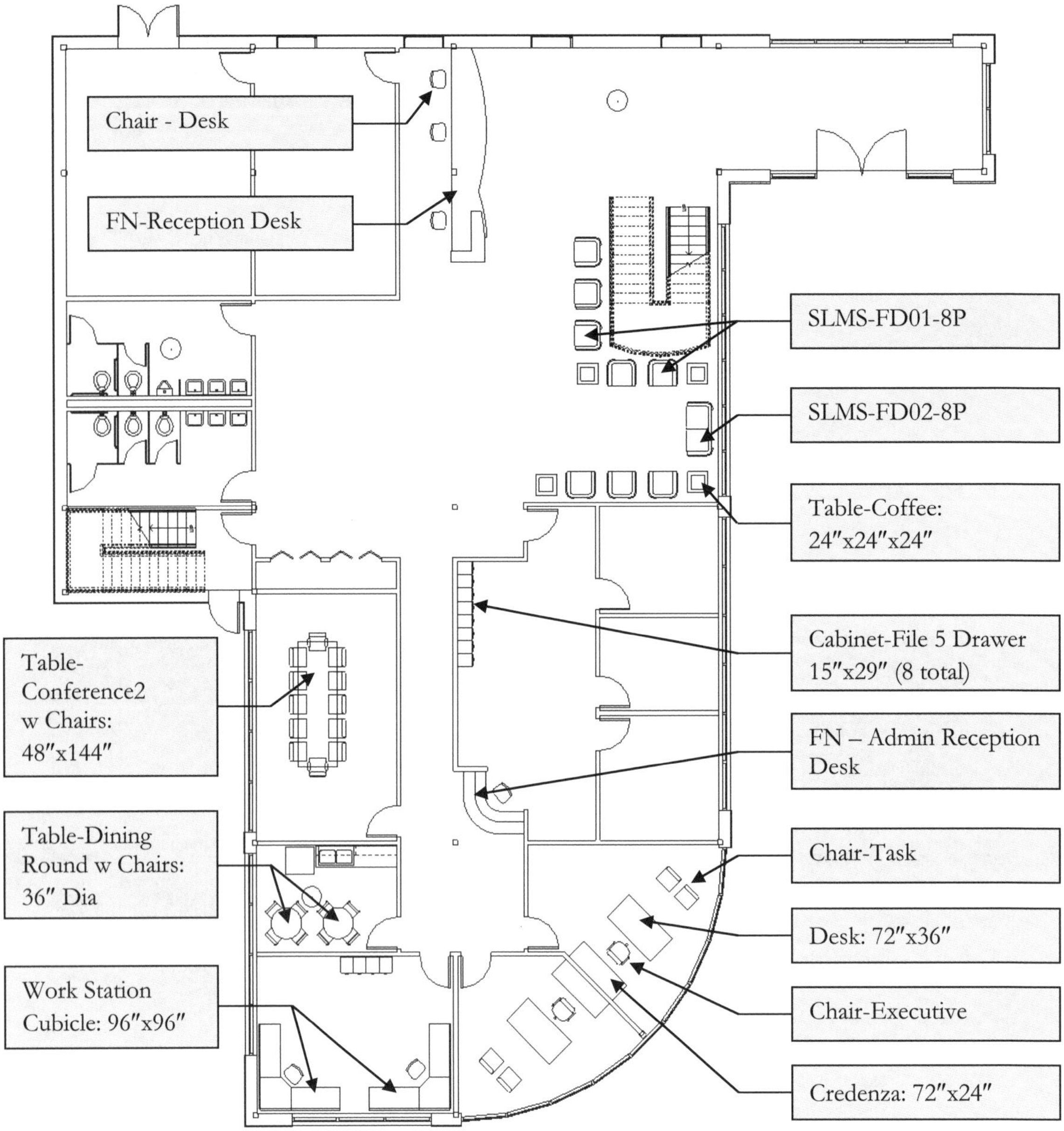

FIGURE 11-3.1 Level 1 furniture layout

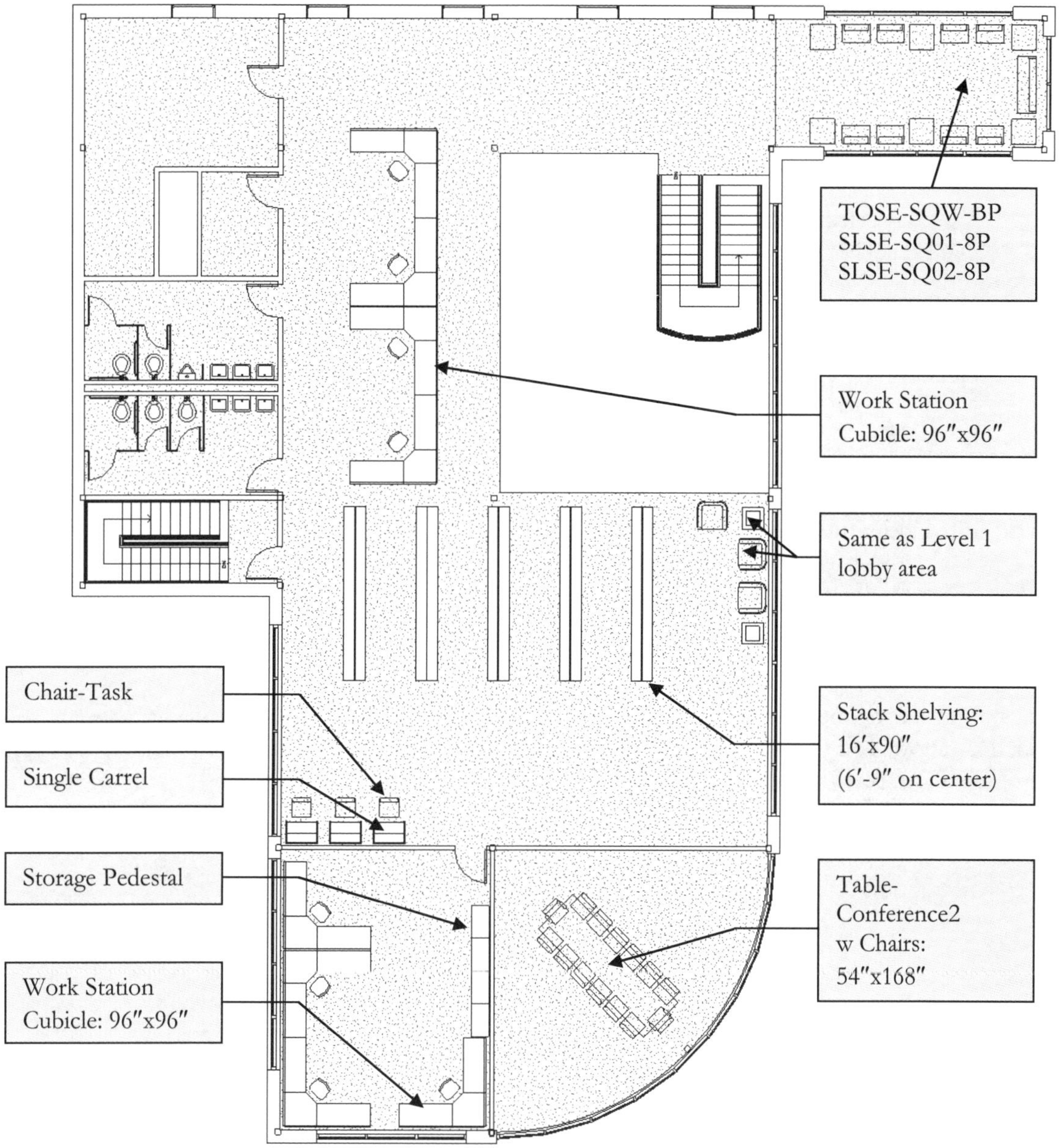

FIGURE 11-3.2 Level 2 furniture layout

3D view of Office Layout

Next you will look at a 3D view of your office area. This involves adjusting the visibility of the roof.

4. Switch to the **Default 3D** view.
    a. Try selecting the roof and notice it becomes transparent. This is a quick way to quickly verify something hidden behind another element.
5. Type **VV**.
6. Uncheck the *Ceiling*, *Roof* and *Structural Framing* categories.
7. Click **OK**.

Now the roof, ceilings and steel beams and joists should not be visible. You can also temporarily hide entire categories of individual elements in a view.

8. Select the East exterior wall. (Again, notice the selected item becomes transparent.)
9. Click the **Temporary Hide/Isolate** from the *View Control Bar*.

You should see the menu shown in Figure 11-3.3 show up next to the *Temporary Hide/Isolate* icon. This allows you to isolate an object so it is the only thing on the screen, or hide it so the object is temporarily invisible.

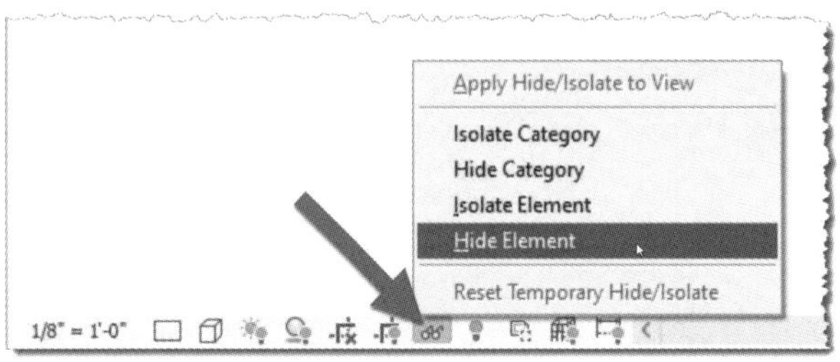

FIGURE 11-3.3 Hide/Isolate pop-up menu

10. Click **Hide Element** in the menu (Figure 11-3.3).

    FYI: This makes just the selected wall hidden; if you selected Hide Category, all the walls would be hidden.

Notice, while a *Temporary Hide/Isolate* is applied to a view, the perimeter of the view is highlighted with a heavy cyan line.

11. Adjust your **3D** view to look similar to **Figure 11-3.4** by clicking and dragging your mouse on the *ViewCube*.

You will now restore the original visibility settings for the **3D** view.

12. Click the *Hide/Isolate* icon and then select **Reset Temporary Hide/Isolate** from the pop-up up menu. (See Figure 11-3.3.)

    NOTE: *The* Temporary Hide/Isolate *feature is just meant to be a temporary control of element visibility while you are working on the model. If you want permanent results, you can click the "Apply Hide/Isolate to View" option. Also, to the right of the Hide/Isolate icon is the Reveal Hidden Elements icon, the light bulb icon, which will clearly show any elements that have been previously hidden.*

13. Reset the **3D** view's visibility settings so the roof, ceiling and structural framing are visible, via the *VV* shortcut.

14. **Save** your project.

    Notice the furniture and toilet rooms are represented in 3D.

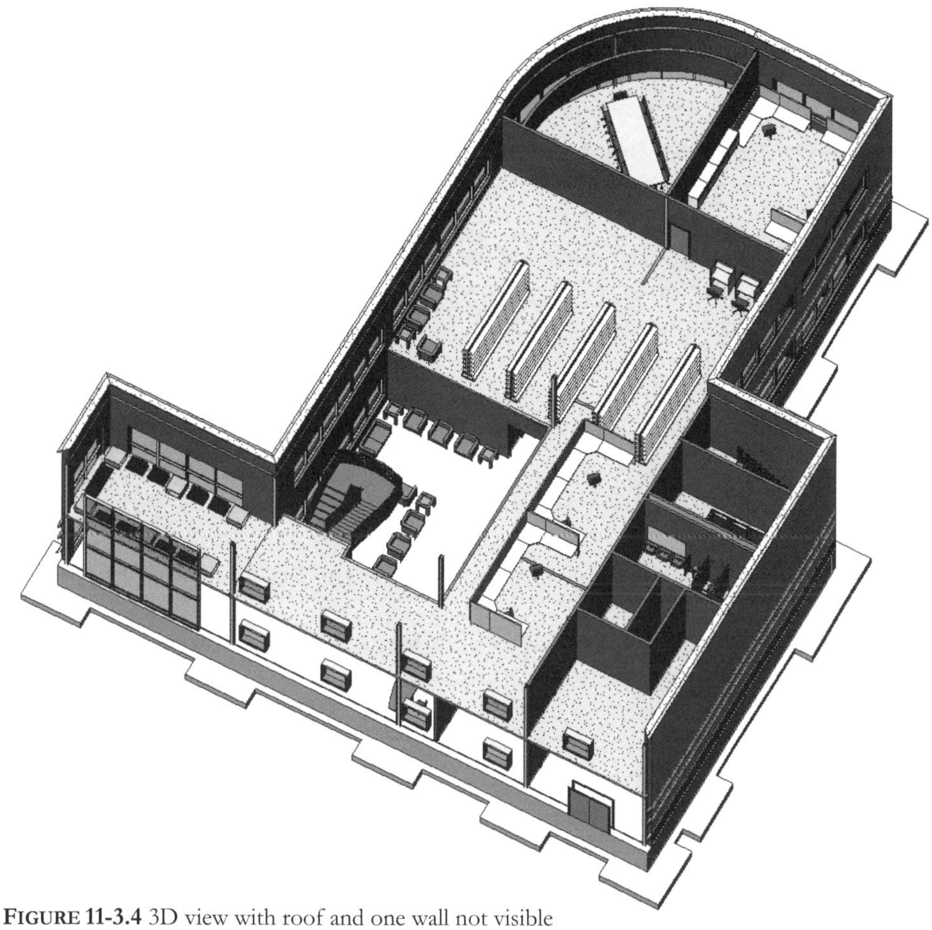

FIGURE 11-3.4 3D view with roof and one wall not visible

It is possible to save a copy of your **3D** view so you may leave it as shown in the image above. This would make it easy to refer back to this view. The view could also be placed on a sheet for presentation purposes.

Exercise 11-4:
Column Furring and Interior Curtain Wall

This lesson will cover the steps required to lay out guardrails at the second floor opening, add a finish at the columns and add three additional doors into the interior curtain wall.

Adding Column Furring:

First you will add *Architectural Columns* at each of the structural column locations. These columns will automatically take on the properties of the wall they are placed on; thus they will show the gypsum board wrapping around the column. Structural columns do not take on the properties of elements they are joined to like architectural columns.

1. Open your law office project file using Revit *Architecture*; remember to make backups!

2. Switch to the **Level 1 Architectural** view.

3. Select **Architecture → Build → Column → Column: Architectural** from the *Ribbon*.

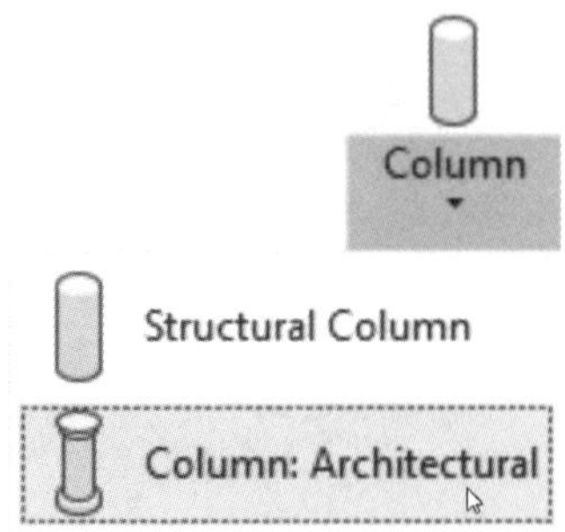

Looking at the *Type Selector*, you see there are three sizes available:

- 18″x18″
- 18″x24″
- 24″x24″

You will create a new type within the *Rectangular Column* family that is 8″x8″, which is the size we want to wrap around and conceal the columns.

4. While still in the *Architectural Column* tool, select **Edit Type** from the *Properties Palette.*

5. Click **Duplicate** in the upper right to create a new *Type.*

6. Enter **8″ x 8″** for the *Type* name (Figure 11-4.1).

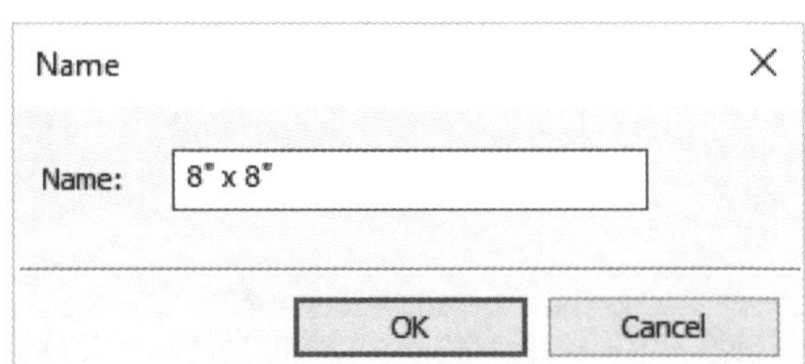

FIGURE 11-4.1 Enter type name

You now have a new *Type* within the *Rectangular Column* family, but you still need to adjust the new *Type's* parameters to be the correct size.

7. Change the *Width* and *Depth* parameters to **8″** (Figure 11-4.2).

8. Click **OK** to save the changes.

Now you are ready to place one of the columns.

9. **Zoom** in to the Northeastern corner of Level 1.

10. Click at the intersection of Grids 5 and E.

As you can see (Figure 11-4.3), the outline of the column is not really visible. It has blended in with the adjacent walls and now you have gypsum board that continues from the walls around the column.

In reality, this column may need to be a little larger to accommodate the metal furring which can range from ⅝″ channels to full 3⅝″, or larger, metal studs.

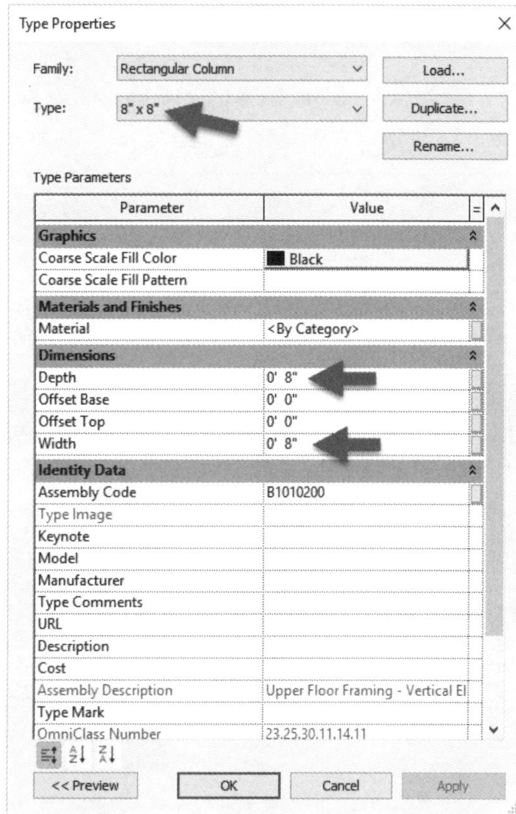

FIGURE 11-4.2 New type properties

Now you will repeat this process at every column location on each floor. You will not be given images to follow as the concept is straightforward.

11. Add the same *Architectural Column* at every column location on **both** levels.

Some of the architectural columns in the middle of the building, not near a wall, do not have gypsum board showing. You will use the *Join* tool to tell Revit that the column should take on the properties of the adjacent wall.

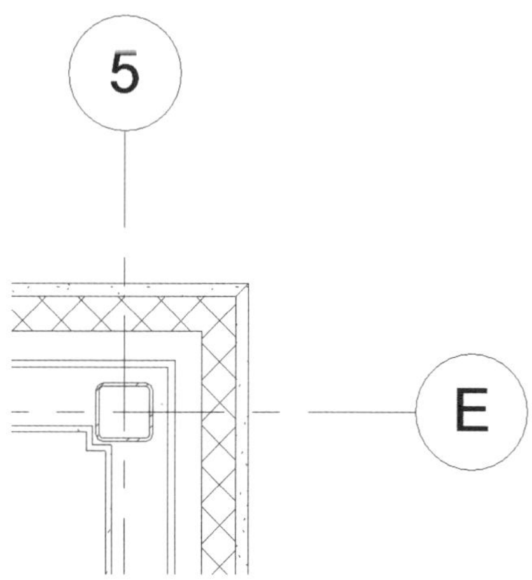

FIGURE 11-4.3 Architectural column added

12. On the *Ribbon*, select **Modify → Geometry → Join**.

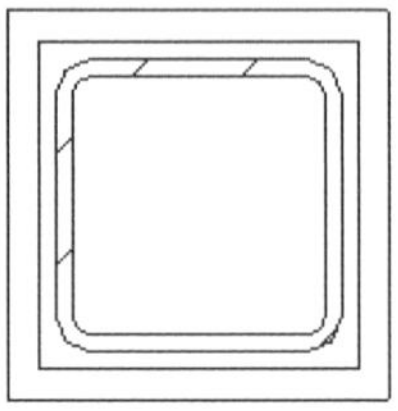

13. **Select** one of the architectural columns without gypsum board (e.g., Level 2 at Grids 4/C).

14. Now **select** any adjacent wall with gypsum board (to take on its properties).

15. Click **OK** to the warning about the joined elements not touching.

16. Repeat the previous steps as required so all the isolated columns have gypsum board as shown (walls that engage with a bulkhead above will not need this step).

All your steel columns are now hidden by a finish. The architectural columns go from the floor, of the view you placed them in, to the level above by default. Sometimes this furring stops just above the ceiling; in this case you adjust the height via the column's *Instance Properties*.

Interior Curtain Walls with Doors:

In this section you will add a curtain wall with a door at the main entry vestibule and directly above it, in what will be a meeting lounge. Finally, you will change an interior wall, in the Level 2 large conference room, from a stud wall to a curtain wall and add a door.

17. Zoom in to the Level 1 main entry area in the Southeastern corner of the building.

18. Select the ***Wall*** tool.

19. Set the *Type Selector* to *Curtain Wall:* **Storefront**.

20. With nothing selected, note the *Instance Properties* via the *Properties Palette.*

You will adjust the height of the curtain wall to stop at the ceiling.

21. Set the *Unconnected Height* to **9'-6."**

22. Click **Apply**.

23. Draw the curtain wall from right to left, directly on Grid line B, stopping short of the column furring on the west (see Figure 11-4.4).

The curtain wall wants to join to the exterior walls in a funny way at the corner condition on the West. Therefore, you will set the left side of the curtain wall so it does not join with other walls.

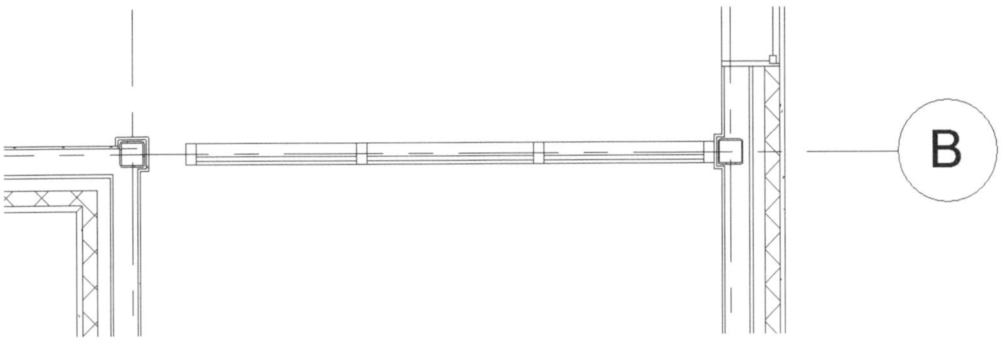

FIGURE 11-4.4 Interior curtain wall added; the West side is held back from the column furring

24. Click **Modify** or press **Esc** to end the *Wall* tool.
25. Select the interior curtain wall you just added; be sure to select the centerline which will appear when you cursor over it.
26. Right click on the blue dot on the West side of the wall.
27. Select **Disallow Join** from the pop-up menu (Figure 11-4.5).

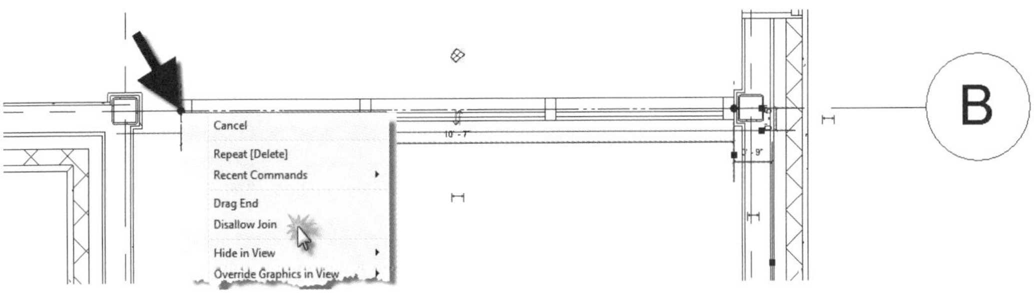

FIGURE 11-4.5 Wall selected; right-click on blue grip on the left to reveal menu

Now the wall will only go where you tell it. It will not try to join with the exterior wall and run past the column furring.

28. Drag the blue dot West to the column furring (Figure 11-4.6).

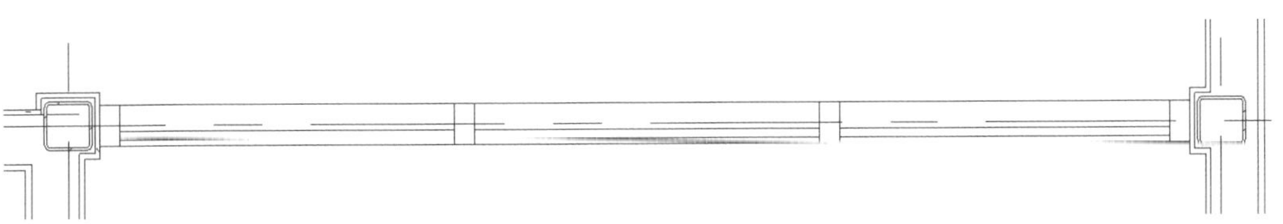

FIGURE 11-4.6 Interior curtain wall placed

Now you will place a door in the center position of the curtain wall. This can be done in plan or in elevation. You made edits in the building section view in a previous chapter; you will try it in the floor plan view this time.

First, you will delete the center mullion on the floor. You are only seeing the mullion on the floor because that is the only horizontal mullion below the cut plane of the current view.

29. Select the **center mullion** on the floor, and then click the ***pin*** icon to unpin it.

30. With the center mullion selected and unpinned, press the **Delete** key on the keyboard.

You are now ready to swap the glass panel out with a door.

31. Select the glass *Curtain Panel* (press **Tab** if required).

32. Click the ***pin*** icon to unpin it.

33. Select **Curtain Wall Sgl Glass** from the *Type Selector.*

34. With the door selected, again press **Tab** if required to select it, use the flip-controls to adjust the door's swing and hand as shown in Figure 11-4.7.

Now you will do the same thing in the same location on Level 2.

35. Following the steps just covered, place an 8′-6″ tall curtain wall along Grid B on Level 2 (Figure 11-4.8).

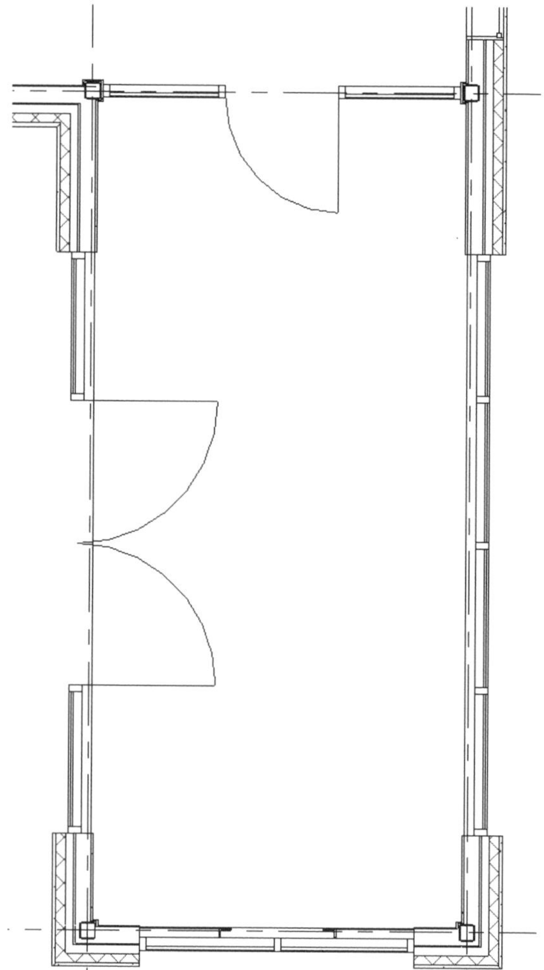

FIGURE 11-4.7 Interior door added

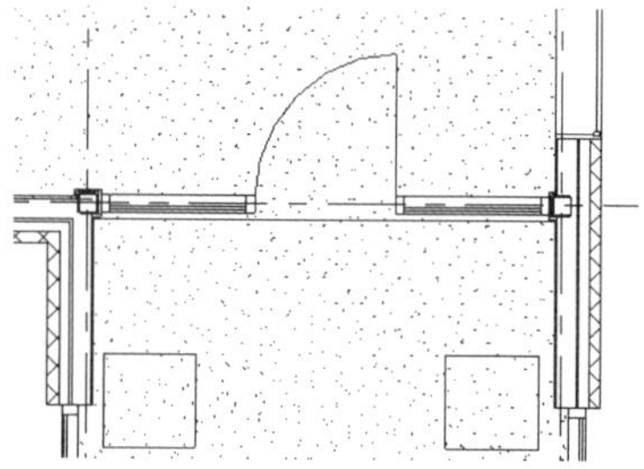

FIGURE 11-4.8 Level 2

Next, you will modify the East wall of the Level 2 *Conference Room* to be a curtain wall. This will let more light into the library area and make the space more dramatic.

The first thing you will need to do is split the wall so the East wall of the adjacent office space does not change from a stud wall. This process is typical anytime a change in wall construction occurs; you would not need to do this for a change in finish, such as paint or wall covering, unless you were tagging those materials directly off the wall. As you will see in the next chapter on schedules, you have to manually enter the finishes for each room. Unfortunately, they do not come from the wall types.

36. On Level 2, zoom in to the *Conference Room* with the curved wall.

37. Select **Modify → Edit → Split** from the *Ribbon.*

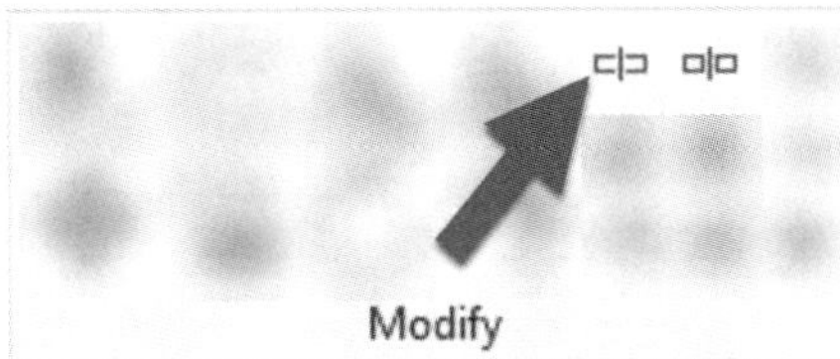

38. Click at the intersection of Grid 2/C with the wall highlighted, the wall that runs along Grid line 2, which is the one you will split.

You now have two walls where there was one. Next, you will select a wall of the *Conference Room* and swap it out with a curtain wall via the *Type Selector.*

39. Select the East wall of the Level 2 *Conference Room.*

40. Pick *Curtain Wall:* **Storefront** from the *Type Selector* (Figure 11-4.9).

Now you may get an error related to the end conditions, similar to the other two just placed.

41. Select **Delete Element(s)** if you get this warning.

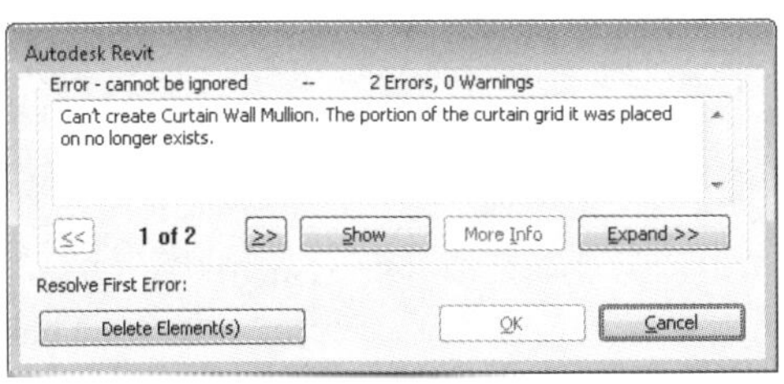

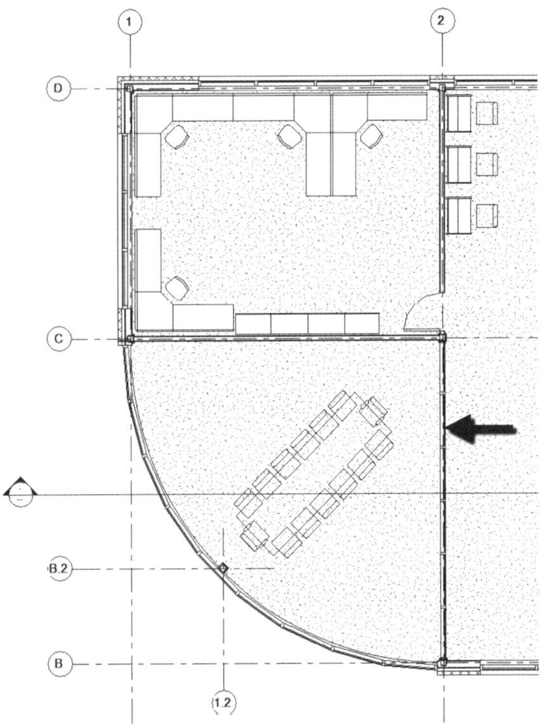

FIGURE 11-4.9 Wall changed to curtain wall

42. Select the curtain wall; right-click on each end grip and select **Disallow Join**.

43. **Drag** the end grips so they align with the column furring (Figure 11-4.10).

44. Add a door as shown in Figure 11-4.11 following techniques already covered.

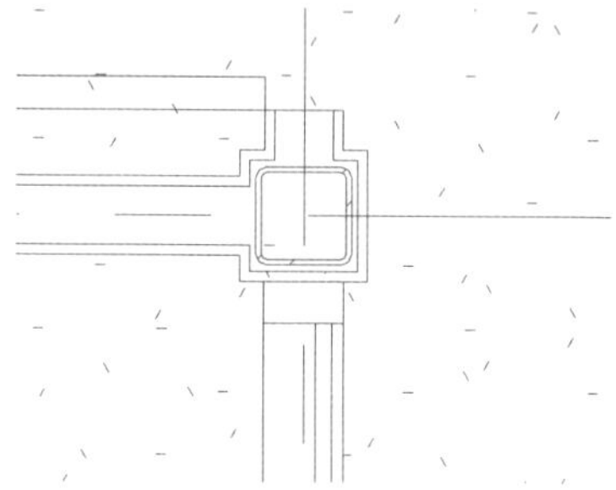

FIGURE 11-4.10
Curtain wall end condition

You now have a glass wall and a door into the Level 2 *Conference Room.*

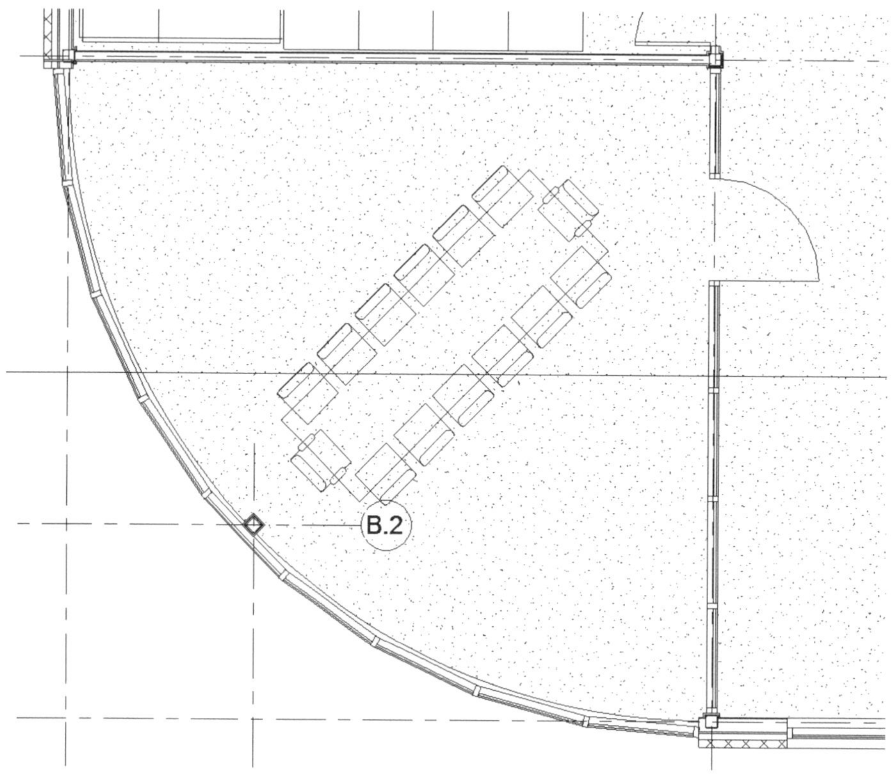

FIGURE 11-4.11 Door added to Curtain wall

The *Conference Room* wall would likely extend to the structure above to help control sound. Therefore, you would have to model a stud wall from the ceiling to the structure above. This can be drawn in the plan view if you know the dimensions above the floor, but you will not see it as it will be completely above the cut plane. You will not do this for our project, unless instructed to do so in a classroom setting.

Self-Exam:

The following questions can be used as a way to check your knowledge of this lesson. The answers can be found at the bottom of this page.

1. The toilet room fixtures are preloaded in the template file. (T/F)
2. Doors can be added to an interior curtain wall while in plan view. (T/F)
3. Revit content is not guaranteed to be in compliance with codes. (T/F)
4. You can draw 2D lines on the wall in an interior elevation view. (T/F)
5. Use the ____________ tool to copy the entire *Toilet Room* layout to another floor in the building; this will also allow for easy updates of all instances.

Review Questions:

The following questions may be assigned by your instructor as a way to assess your knowledge of this section. Your instructor has the answers to the review questions.

1. Revit *Architecture* content does not have the *MEP* "connections" for piping/ plumbing needed by the *MEP* "flavor" of Revit. (T/F)
2. Most of the time, Revit automatically updates the ceiling when walls are moved, but occasionally you have to manually make revisions. (T/F)
3. It is not possible to draw dimensions on an interior elevation view. (T/F)
4. Cabinets typically come in 4″ increments. (T/F)
5. Base cabinets automatically have a countertop on them. (T/F)
6. What can you adjust so the concrete slab does not show in elevation?

   ____

7. What type of component do you place around structural columns when you want the adjacent finish to wrap around it?

   ____

8. What is the current size of your Revit project?

   ____

9. What is the option you selected, when right-clicking on a selected wall's end-grip, so you could better control its endpoint location?

   ____

10. You use the ________ tool to make various components temporarily invisible.

SELF-EXAM ANSWERS:
1 – F, **2** – T, **3** – T, **4** – T, **5** – Group

Notes:

Lesson 12
Schedules

You will continue to learn the powerful features available in Revit. This includes the ability to create live schedules; you can delete a door number on a schedule and Revit will delete the corresponding door from the plan.

Exercise 12-1:
Rooms, Room Tags & Door Tags

This exercise will look at adding rooms, room tags and door tags to your plans. As you insert doors, Revit adds tags to them automatically. However, if you copy or mirror a door, you can lose the tag and have to add it manually.

Adding Rooms and Room Tags:

Revit has an element that can expand out in all directions and find the extents of a space: the floor, walls, ceiling, or roof. The element is called a **Room**. This element is used to hold information about each space within your building. For example, the *Room* element contains the square footage of a room as well as the column if "calculate volumes" is turned on.

The *Room* element also holds information like the room name and number, as well as finishes. Custom *Parameters* can be created, which would allow you to track virtually anything you want about each space.

Later in this chapter you will learn how to create a schedule listing the information contained in the *Room* object.

Rooms have to be manually added to each space. It is one of the few 3D elements you have to create in Revit that does not actually get built by the contractor. You only have to add a *Room* to a space once, and it does not matter which view you do it in; by default, the view you are in will also automatically get a *Room Tag*. Other views of that same space, like the electrical power plan, may need a *Room Tag* added, but not another *Room* element.

Be sure to read **Appendix D** on Revit's Rooms and Spaces.

You will be adding a *Room* and a *Room Tag* to each room on your Level 1 and Level 2 floor plans.

1. Open your law office file, or use the **Chapter 12** starter file from the online files.

The first thing you will do is make sure "Calculate Volumes" is turned on so the *Room* elements will extend up to the ceiling and not just use a default height.

2. Click the **Room & Area** panel fly-out on the *Architecture* tab of the *Ribbon* (Figure 12-1.1).

3. Select **Area and Volume Computations** as shown in Figure 12-1.2.

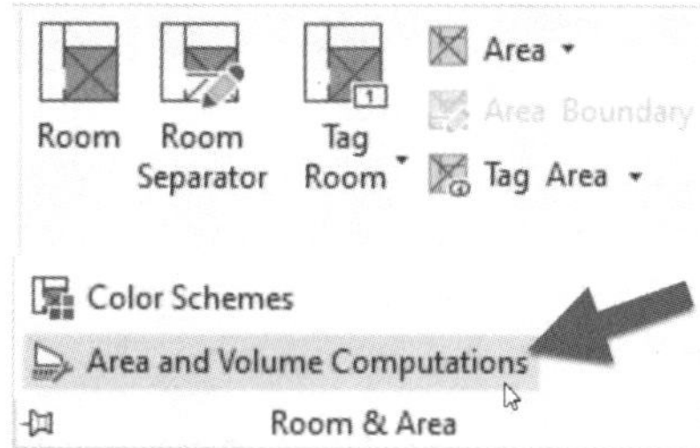

FIGURE 12-1.1 Panel fly-out

You are now ready to place your first *Room.*

4. Select **Architecture → Room & Area → Room**.

FIGURE 12-1.2 Setting Areas & volume

Placing a *Room* is similar to placing a *Ceiling* in the reflected ceiling plan; as you move your cursor over a room, the room perimeter highlights. When the room you want to place a *Room* element in is highlighted, you click to place it.

5. Click your cursor within the *Mechanical Room* (in the Northeastern corner) to place a ***Room***, which will also automatically place a *Room Tag* (Figure 12-1.3).

Notice, as you move your cursor around, an "X" appears within the space. This can help you determine if a space is properly enclosed by walls. Also, the intersection of the "X" is where *Room Tags* are initially located in other views.

While placing a *Room*, any spaces that already have *Rooms* will be indicated by the "X" and a light blue shade. This makes it easy to see which spaces still do not have *Rooms* placed in them.

Once the *Room* tool is ended, via **Modify** or **Esc**, the "X" and shade disappear.

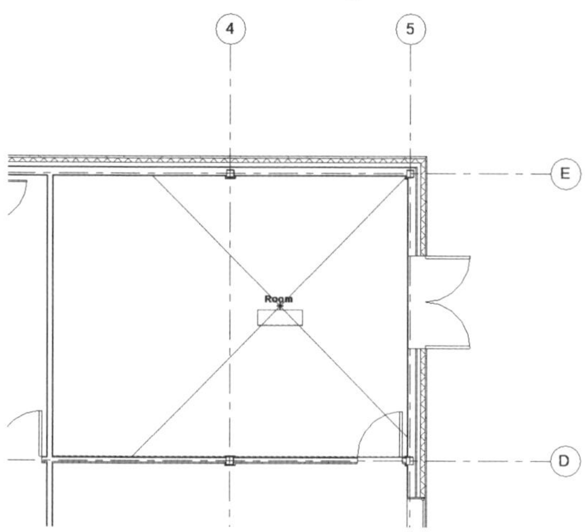

FIGURE 12-1.3 Room added to level 1 view

By default, Revit will simply label the space "Room" and number it "1"; you will change this to something different. Most commercial projects have a three-digit room number where the first digit equals the level; for example, the rooms on Level 1 will begin at number 100 and on Level 2 will begin at 200. Larger projects might have four-digit room numbers.

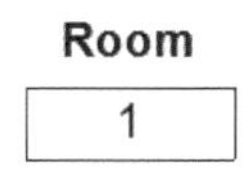

6. Press **Esc** or select **Modify** to cancel the *Room* command.

Next, you will change the room name and number. When you change the room number to 100, Revit will automatically make the next room placed "101." So, it is a good idea to place one room and then change the number so the remaining rooms do not need to be manually renumbered.

7. Click on the *Room Tag* you just placed to select it.

8. Now click on the room name label to change it; enter **MECH & ELEC ROOM**.
   TIP: Press Enter *or click away to finish typing.*

9. Now click on the room number to change it; enter **100**.

Adding Room Separation Lines:

Sometimes, you need to identify an area that is not totally enclosed by walls. For example, the Level 1 hallway would typically have its own room tag, separate from the main lobby area. However, if you place a *Room*, it would fill both spaces. Revit has a special line you can draw called a Room Separation Line, which will act like a wall, similar to a *Room Bounding* element.

10. **Zoom** in to the East end of the Level 1 hallway near Grids 3/C.

11. Select **Architecture → Room & Area → Room Separator**.

12. Draw a line as shown in Figure 12-1.5.

FIGURE 12-1.4
Room Separation Line

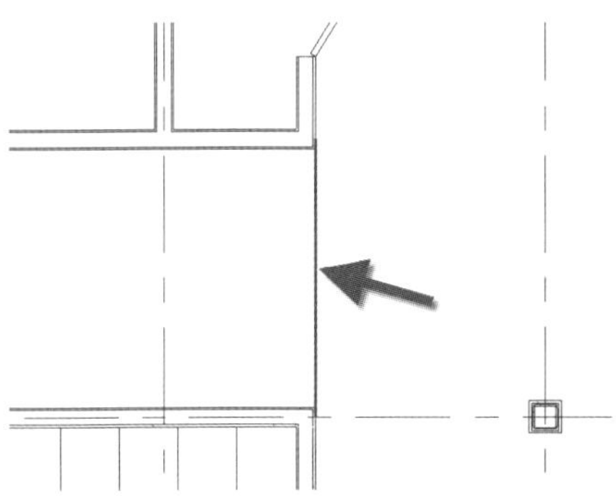

FIGURE 12-1.5 Room Separation Line added

A *Room Separation Line* acts like a wall when it comes to placing *Rooms*. This will not have any effect on ceilings.

These lines can be turned off via the "VV" shortcut: *Model Categories* tab → *Lines* → *<Room Separation>*.

Next, you will add *Room Separation Lines* at the reception desk and the two interior curtain walls along Grid B. The two curtain walls are a problem because we used the *Disallow Join* option to have better control over the curtain wall end conditions; this made a break in the *Room* boundary.

13. Add the ***Room Separation Lines*** shown in Figure 12-1.6.
    a. Do not add the dimension.
    b. Add the line just South of the interior curtain wall and the architectural columns to avoid any cleanup problems.

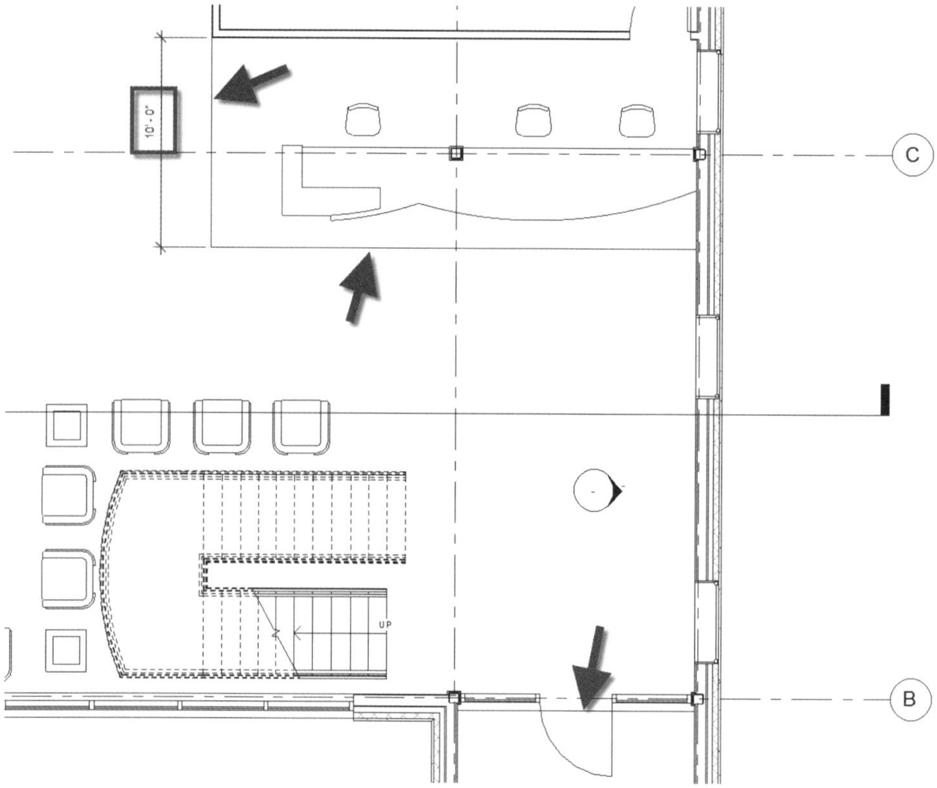

FIGURE 12-1.6 Additional Room Separation Lines added

14. Add two more ***Room Separation Lines***, on Level 1, at the <u>Admin Asst. Receptionist</u> area (Figure 12-1.7).
    a. Click from the face of the wall to the center of the structural column.

15. Switch to the **Level 2** Floor Plan (architectural) view.

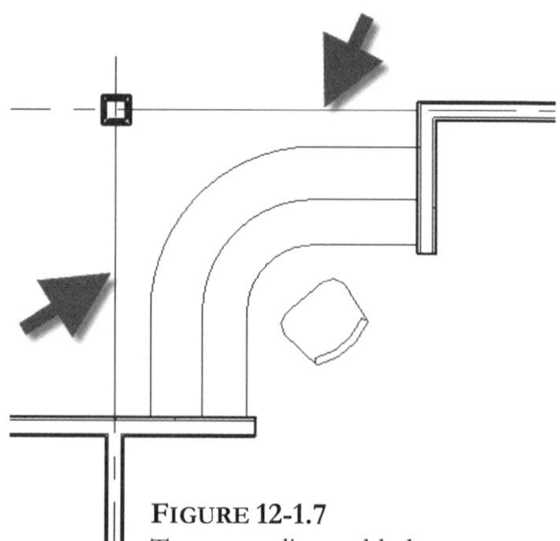

FIGURE 12-1.7
Two more lines added

16. Add the **four** *Room Separation Lines* shown in Figure 12-1.8.

   a. In this image, the lines are shown exaggerated because they overlap other linework.

   b. Pick at the center of the structural columns for the three lines around the opening in the floor.

   c. Draw the line just south of the interior curtain wall, just like on Level 1.

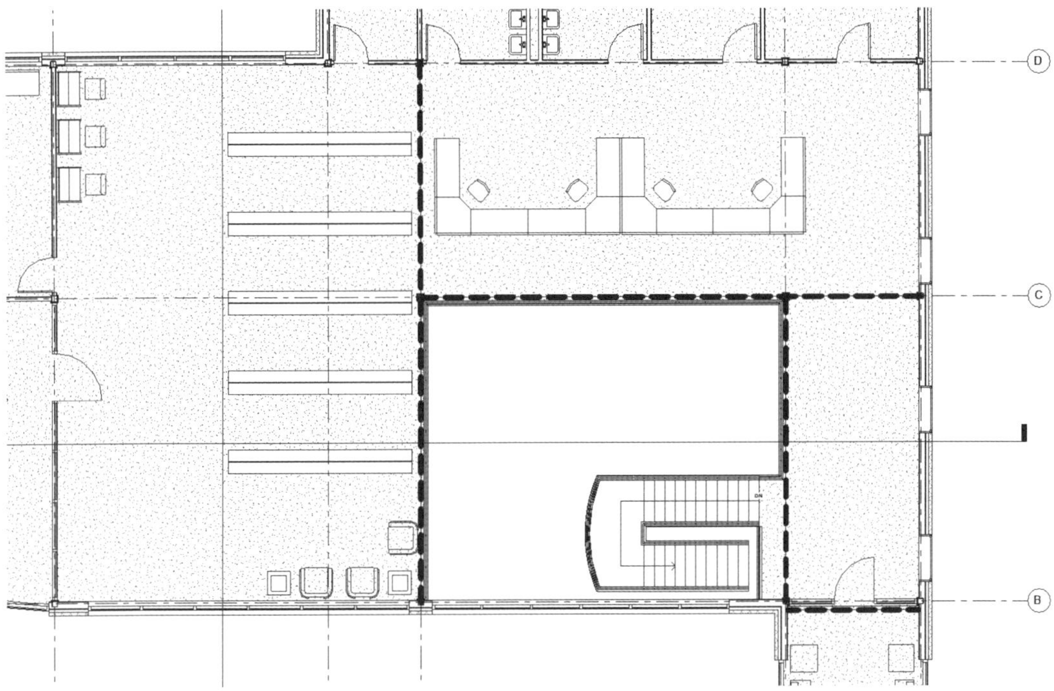

FIGURE 12-1.8 Level 2 Room Separation Lines added, shown as heavy dashed line

17. Using the ***Room*** tool, add *Rooms* for each space on Level 1 and Level 2; change the room name, and number if required, to match Figures 12-1.9 and 12-1.10.

   a. Where you click to place the *Room* is where the *Room Tag* is placed, so click where the *Room Tag* will not overlap other lines.

   b. North Stair: Place a *Room* on Level 1 and then skip Level 2 until Step #18.

   c. Coat Closet: Select the *Room Tag*, check "Leader Line" on the *Ribbon*, and then drag the *Room Tag* out of the room.

The view scale has been adjusted in the next two images to make it easier to read the room names and numbers. Also, several categories have been temporarily turned off for clarity. You should not do this because you need to make sure the room tags do not overlap anything.

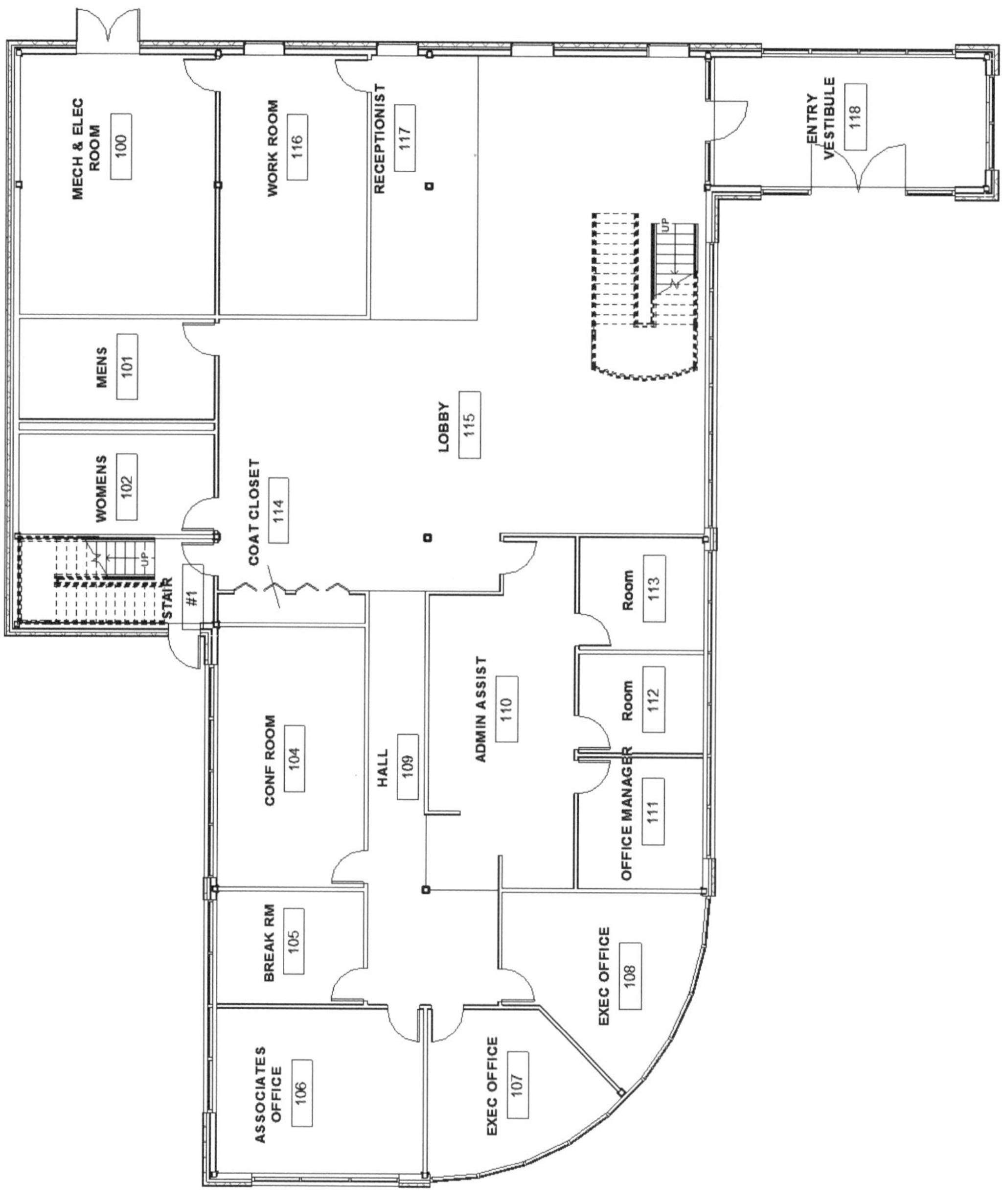

FIGURE 12-1.9 Level 1 room names and numbers; *image rotated on page to increase size*

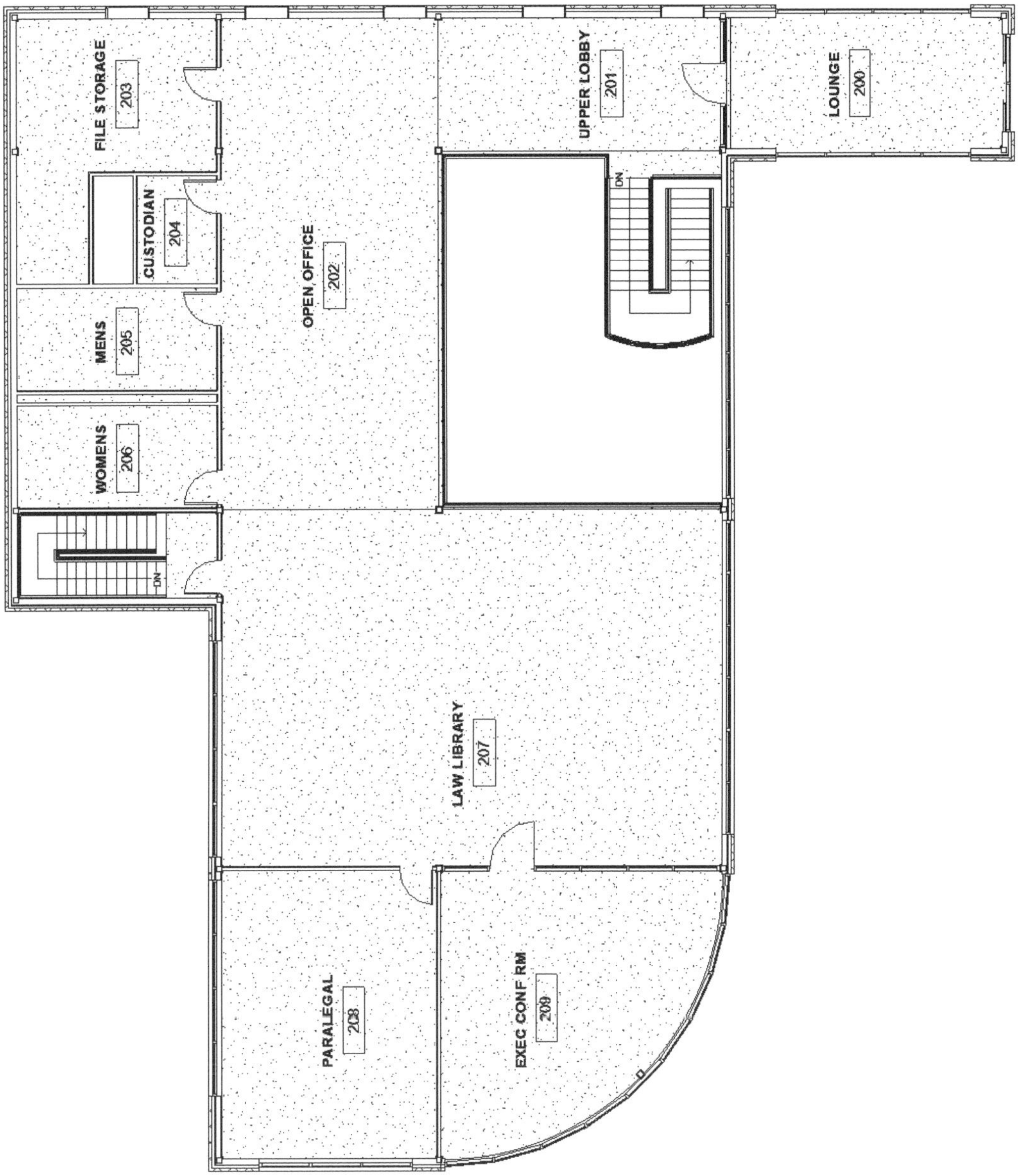

FIGURE 12-1.10 Level 2 room names and numbers; *image rotated on page to increase size*

Next, you will select the *Room* element on Level 1 and adjust its height. Then you can tag the same *Room* in the Level 2 view.

18. In the Level 1 view, select the *Room* element in *Stair #1*.

TIP: To select a Room, you need to move your cursor around the Room Tag until you see an "X" highlight, and then click to select it.

19. Change the room's *Limit Offset* to **26′-8″** in its *Instance Properties (Properties Palette).*

20. Click **Apply** to accept the change.

21. Switch to **Level 2** and zoom in to the North stair area.

22. Select **Architecture → Room & Area → Tag Room** from the *Ribbon.*

23. Click within the stair shaft; see Figure 12-1.11.

Notice how the room name and number fill out automatically. This is how you will add room tags in other plan views that do not already have them. As they are placed, they take on the properties of the previously placed rooms: room name and number in this case.

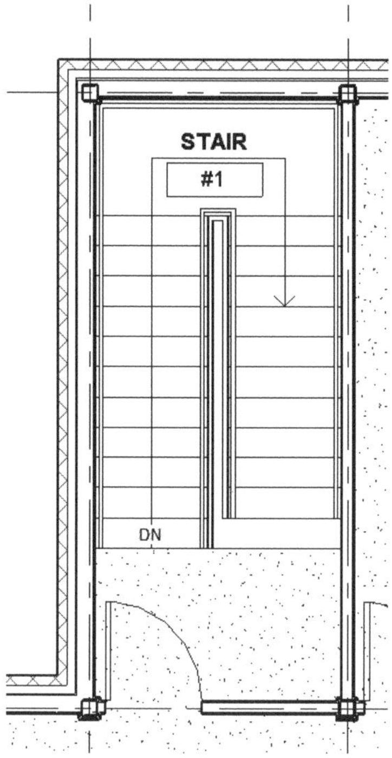

FIGURE 12-1.11
Level 2 with room tag added to stair

A *Room Tag* can display various information stored within the *Room* element. For example, if you select a *Room Tag*, not the *Room*, you can select a different tag *Type* from the *Type Selector.* The example below (Figure 12-1.12) shows a tag that reports the square footage of the space being tagged. Also, the tag *Type* can vary from view to view and even room to room. Try changing one and then change it back before continuing.

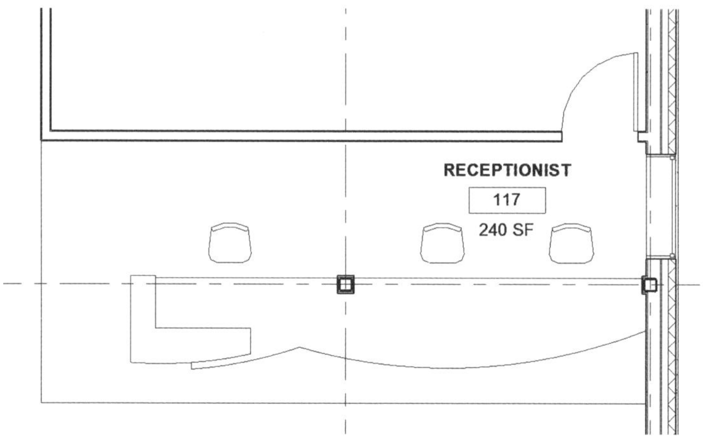

FIGURE 12-1.12 Room tag type that shows the area of a space

Adding Door Tags:

Next you will add *Door Tags* to any doors that are missing them. Additionally, you will adjust the door numbers to correspond to the room numbers.

Revit numbers the doors in the order they are placed into the drawing. This would make it difficult to locate a door by its door number if door number 1 was on Level 1 and door number 2 was on Level 3, etc.

Typically, a door number is the same as the room the door swings into. For example, if a door swung into an office numbered 304, the door number would also be 304. If the office has two doors into it, the doors would be numbered 304A and 304B.

24. Switch to **Level 1** view.

25. Select the **Annotate → Tag → Tag by Category** button on the *Ribbon* (Figure 12-1.13).

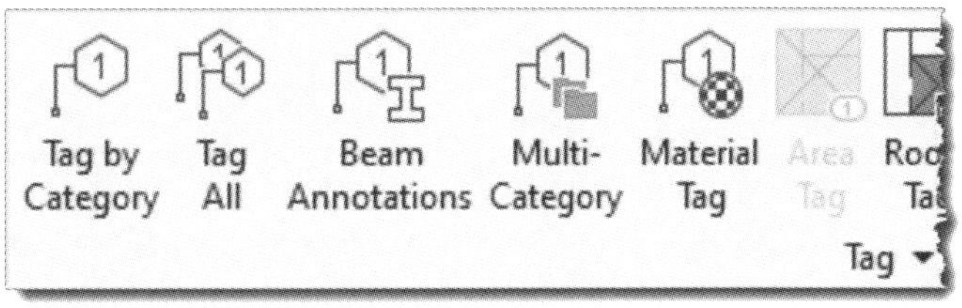

FIGURE 12-1.13 Annotate tab, Tag panel

Notice, as you move your cursor around the screen, Revit displays a tag, for items that can have tags, when the cursor is over it. When you click the mouse is when Revit actually places a tag.

26. **Unselect** the **Leader line** option on the *Ribbon.*

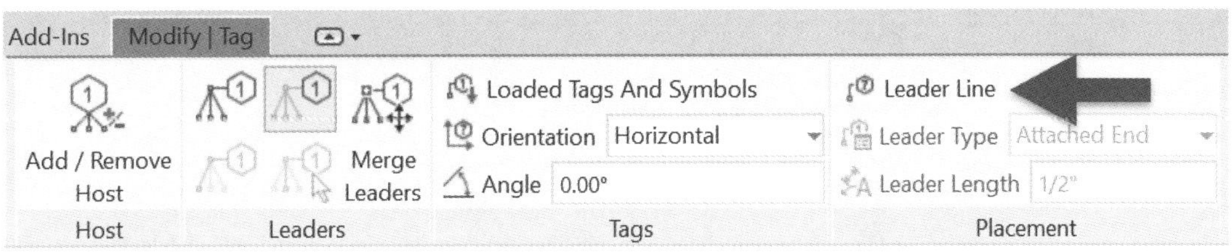

27. Place a *Door Tag* for each door that does not have a tag; do this for each level.

TIP: TAG ALL…

This tool allows you to quickly tag all the objects of a selected type (e.g., doors) at one time.

After selecting the tool, you select the type of object from a list and specify whether or not you want a leader. When you click OK, Revit tags all the untagged doors in that view.

28. Renumber all the *Door Tags* to correspond to the room they open into; do this for each level. See Figures 12-1.14 and 12-1.15.

REMEMBER: *Click Modify, select the Tag, and then click on the number to edit it.*

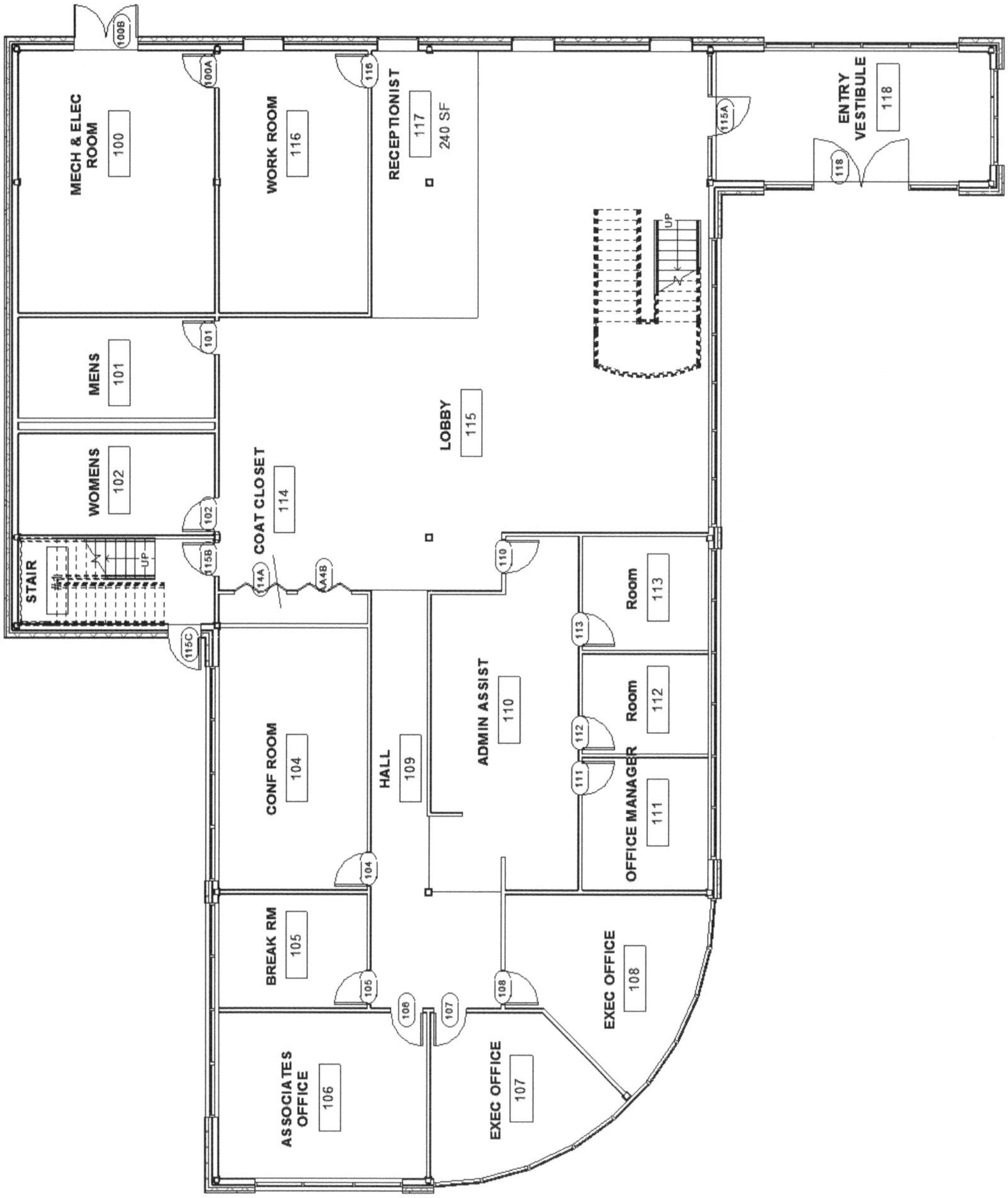

FIGURE 12-1.14 Level 1 *Door Tags* added and renumbered

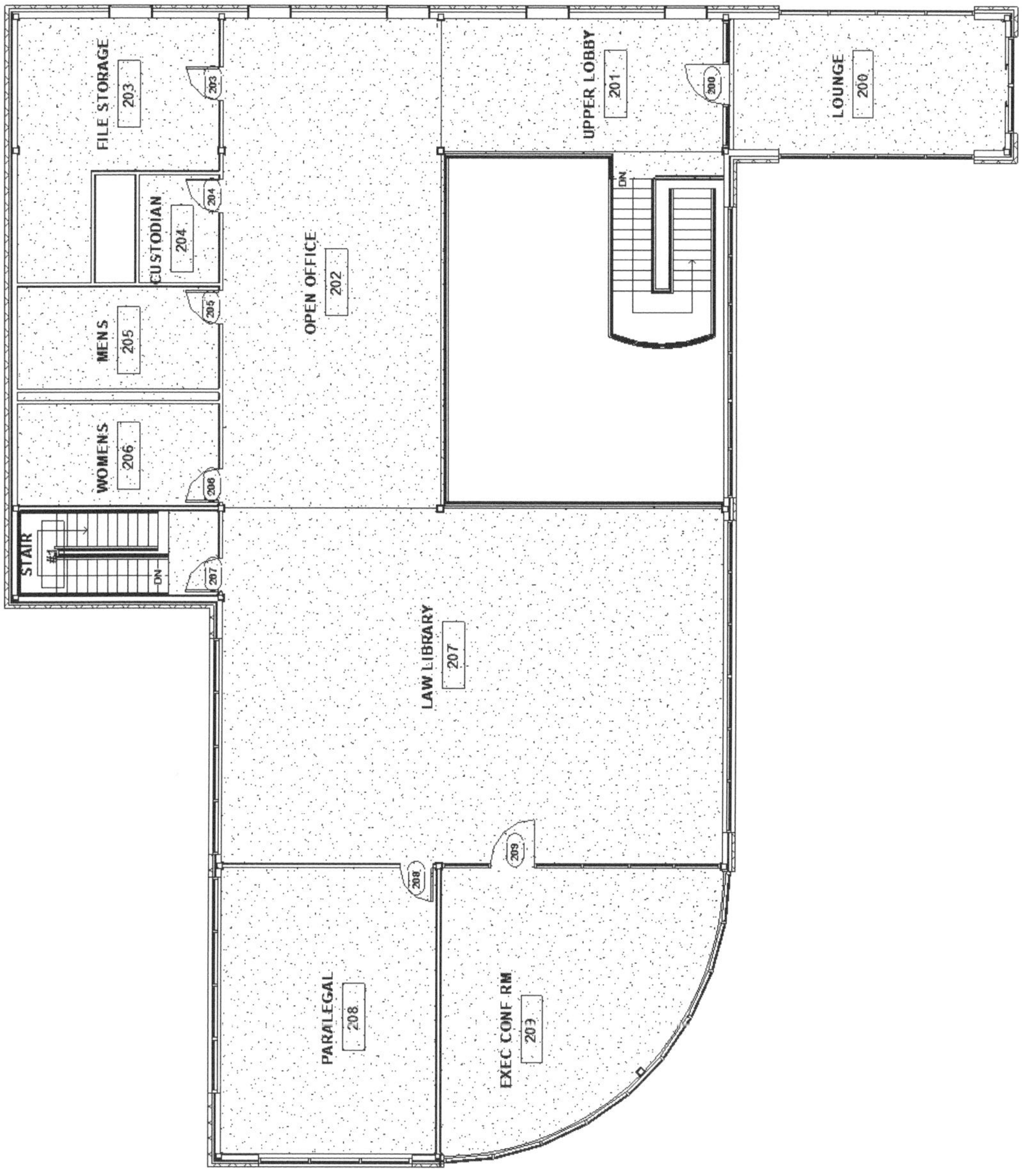

FIGURE 12-1.15 Level 2 *Door Tags* added and renumbered

29. **Save** your project.

Exercise 12-2:
Generate a Door Schedule

This exercise will look at creating a door schedule based on the information currently available in the building model.

Create a Door Schedule View:

A Door Schedule is simply another view of the building model. However, this view displays text/numerical data rather than graphical data. Just like a graphical view, if you change a Schedule view, it changes all the other related views. For example, if you delete a door number from the Schedule, the door is deleted from the plans and elevations.

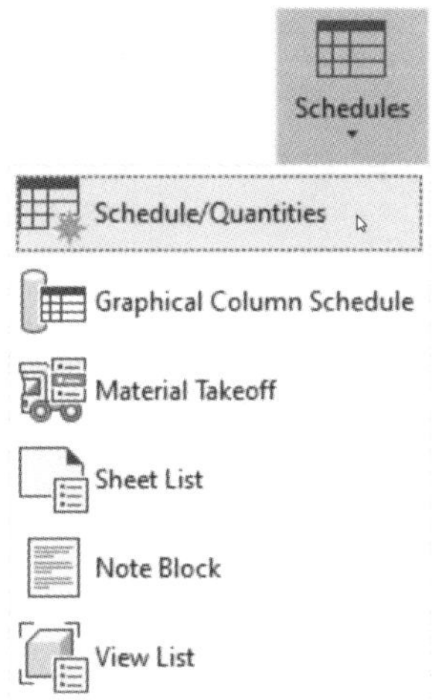

1. Open your law office *BIM* file.

2. Select **View → Create → Schedules →Schedule/ Quantities** button from the *Ribbon*.

3. Select **Doors** under *Category*.

4. Type **Law Office Door Schedule** for the *Name*.

5. Set the *Phase* to **New Construction**.

6. Click **OK** to create the schedule (Figure 12-2.1).

Your project already has a door schedule in it because it was pre-defined in the template. Thus, it would not really be necessary to create a door schedule. However, you need to understand how they are created to effectively modify and edit them.

You should now be in the *Schedule Properties* dialog where you specify what information is displayed in the schedule, how it is sorted and the text format.

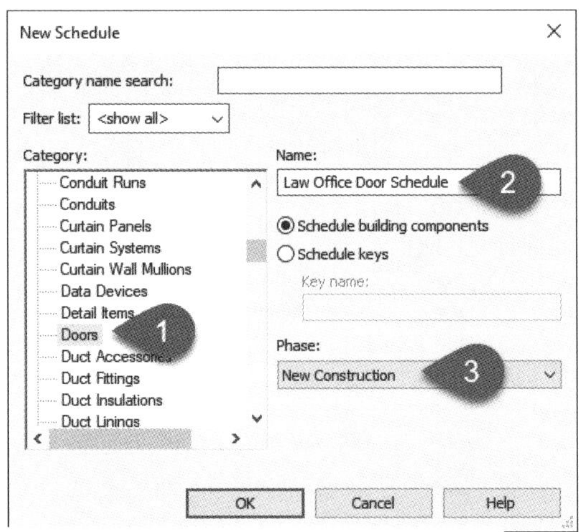

FIGURE 12-2.1 New Schedule dialog

7. On the ***Fields*** tab, add the information you want displayed in the schedule. Select the following (Figure 12-2.2):

   a. Mark *TIP: Click the Add → button each time.*

   b. Width

   c. Height

   d. Frame Material

   e. Frame Type

   f. Fire Rating

As noted in the dialog box, the fields added to the list on the right are in the order they will be in the **Schedule** view. Use the *Move Up* and *Move Down* buttons to adjust the order.

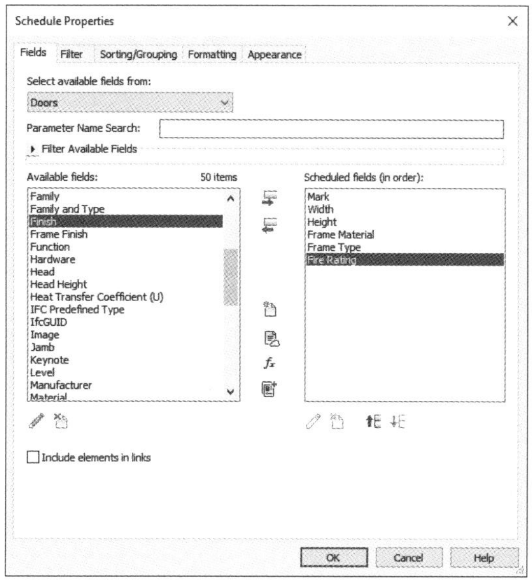

FIGURE 12-2.2 Schedule Properties – Fields

TIP: If you accidentally clicked OK *after the previous step, click one of the Edit buttons in the Properties Palette while the schedule view is active.*

8. On the ***Sorting/Grouping*** tab, set the schedule to be sorted by the **Mark** (i.e., door number) in ascending order (Figure 12-2.3).

*FYI: The **Formatting** and **Appearance tabs** allow you to adjust how the schedule looks. The formatting is not displayed until the schedule is placed on a plot sheet.*

Also, you cannot print a schedule unless it is on a sheet. Only views and sheets can be printed, not schedules or legends.

9. Click the **OK** button to generate the schedule view.

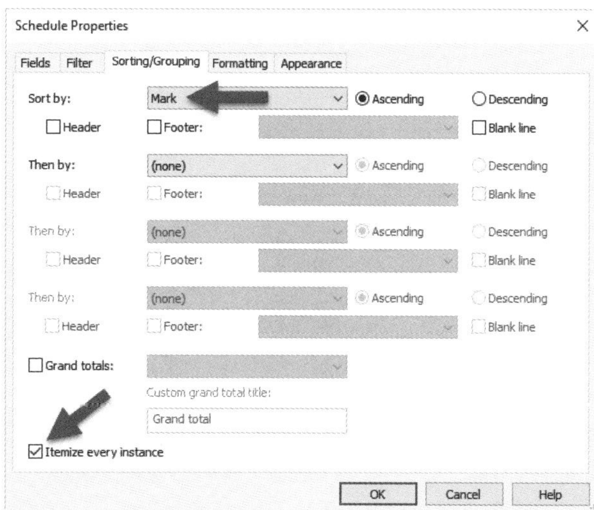

FIGURE 12-2.3 Schedule Properties – Sorting

You should now have a schedule similar to Figure 12-2.4.

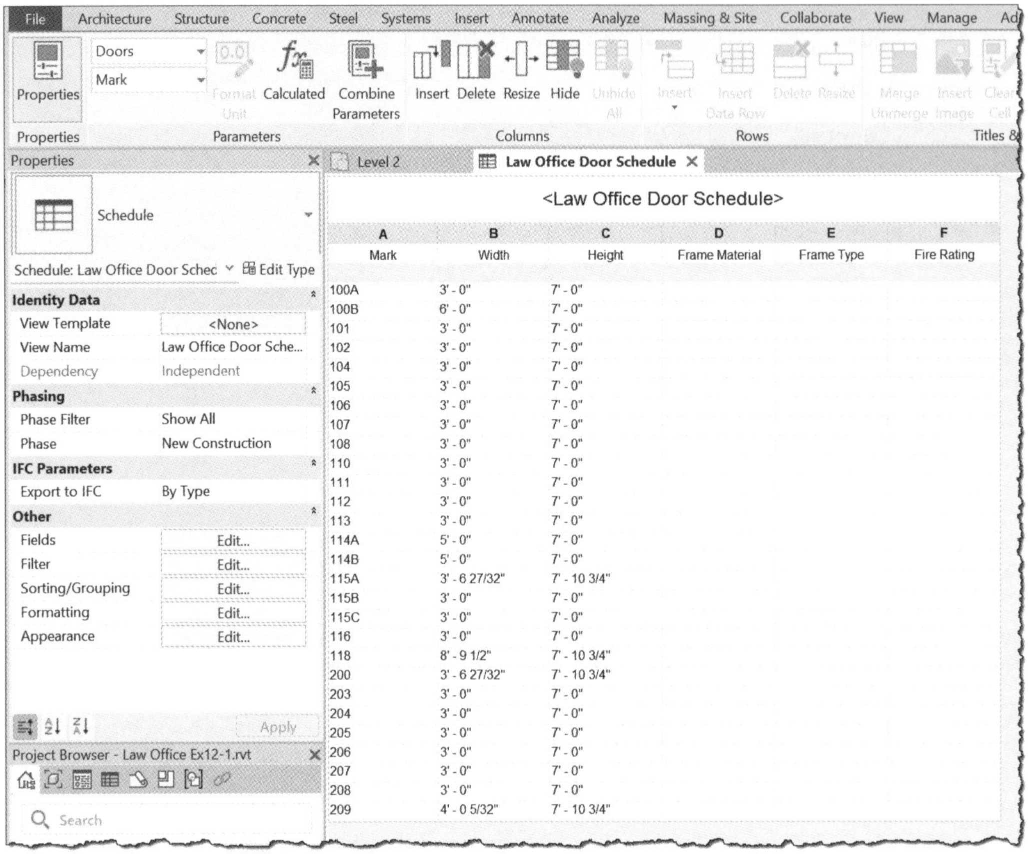

FIGURE 12-2.4 Door Schedule view

> *TIP: While in a schedule view, you can select **Application Menu → Export → Reports → Schedule** to create a text file (*.txt) that can be used in other programs like MS Excel.*

The example below is from a real Revit project; notice the detailed header information (i.e., grouped headers).

DOOR AND FRAME SCHEDULE													
DOOR NUMBER	DOOR				FRAME		DETAIL			GLAZING	FIRE RATING	HDWR GROUP	
	WIDTH	HEIGHT	MATL	TYPE	MATL	TYPE	HEAD	JAMB	SILL				
1000A	3' - 8"	7' - 2"	WD		HM		11/A8.01	11/A8.01					
1046	3' - 0"	7' - 2"	WD	D10	HM	F10	11/A8.01	11/A8.01 SIM				34	
1047A	6' - 0"	7' - 10"	ALUM	D15	ALUM	SF4	6/A8.01	6/A8.01	1/A8.01 SIM	1" INSUL		2	CARD READER N. LEAF
1047B	8' - 0"	7' - 2"	WD	D10	HM	F13	12/A8.01	11/A8.01 SIM			60 MIN	85	MAG HOLD OPENS
1050	3' - 0"	7' - 2"	WD	D10	HM	F21	8/A8.01	11/A8.01		1/4" TEMP		33	
1051	3' - 0"	7' - 2"	WD	D10	HM	F21	8/A8.01	11/A8.01		1/4" TEMP		33	
1052	3' - 0"	7' - 2"	WD	D10	HM	F21	8/A8.01	11/A8.01		1/4" TEMP		33	
1053	3' - 0"	7' - 2"	WD	D10	HM	F21	8/A8.01	11/A8.01		1/4" TEMP		33	
1054A	3' - 0"	7' - 2"	WD	D10	HM	F10	8/A8.01	11/A8.01		1/4" TEMP	-	34	
1054B	3' - 0"	7' - 2"	WD	D10	HM	F21	8/A8.01	11/A8.01		1/4" TEMP	-	33	
1055	3' - 0"	7' - 2"	WD	D10	HM	F21	8/A8.01	11/A8.01		1/4" TEMP	-	33	
1056A	3' - 0"	7' - 2"	WD	D10	HM	F10	9/A8.01	9/A8.01			20 MIN	33	
1056B	3' - 0"	7' - 2"	WD	D10	HM	F10	11/A8.01	11/A8.01			20 MIN	34	
1056C	3' - 0"	7' - 2"	WD	D10	HM	F10	20/A8.01	20/A8.01			20 MIN	33	
1057A	3' - 0"	7' - 2"	WD	D10	HM	F10	8/A8.01	11/A8.01			20 MIN	34	
1057B	3' - 0"	7' - 2"	WD	D10	HM	F30	9/A8.01	9/A8.01		1/4" TEMP	20 MIN	33	
1058A	3' - 0"	7' - 2"	WD	D10	HM	F10	9/A8.01	9/A8.01			-	33	

Image courtesy LHB

Next, you will see how adding a door to the plan automatically updates the door schedule. Likewise, deleting a door number from the schedule deletes the door from the plan.

10. Switch to the **Level 1** view.

11. Add a door as shown in **Figure 12-2.5**; number the door **104B**.

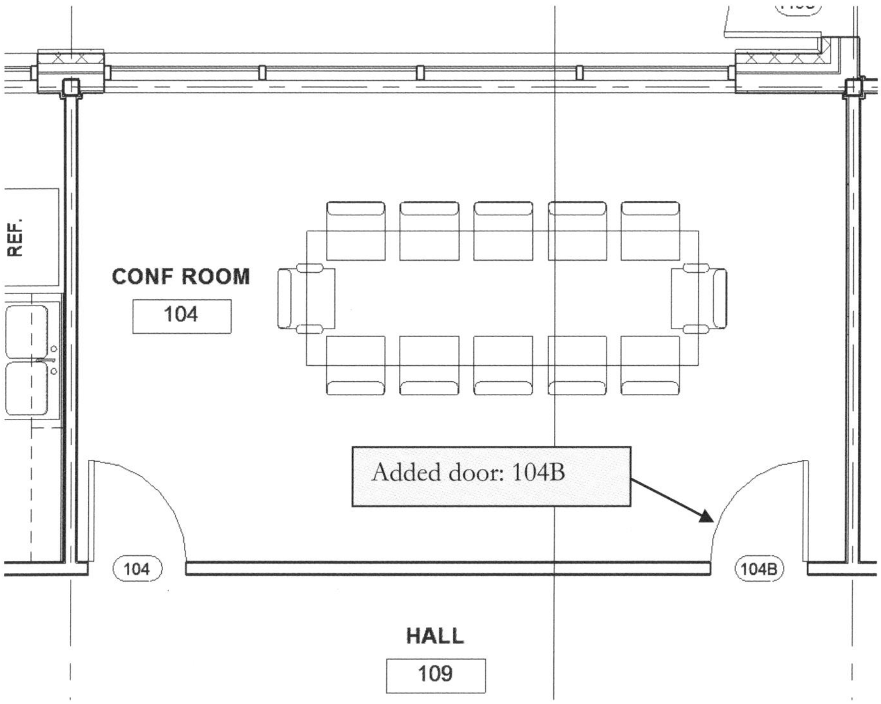

FIGURE 12-2.5 Level 1 – door added

12. Switch to the **Law Office Door Schedule** view, under *Schedules/ Quantities* in the *Project Browser*. Notice door *104B* was added (Figure 12-2.6).

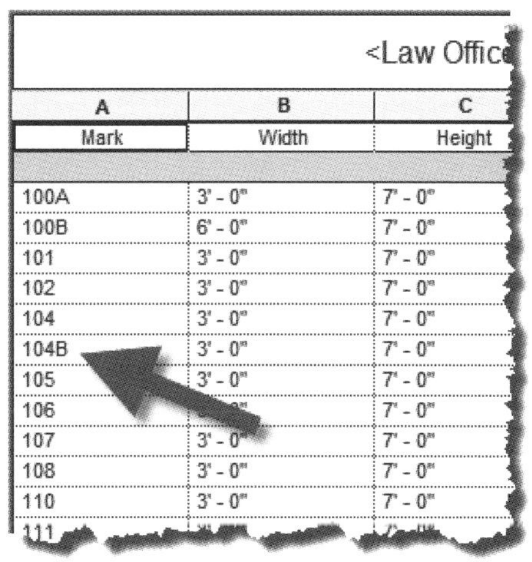

<Law Offic

A	B	C
Mark	Width	Height
100A	3' - 0"	7' - 0"
100B	6' - 0"	7' - 0"
101	3' - 0"	7' - 0"
102	3' - 0"	7' - 0"
104	3' - 0"	7' - 0"
104B	3' - 0"	7' - 0"
105	3' - 0"	7' - 0"
106	[illegible]	7' - 0"
107	3' - 0"	7' - 0"
108	3' - 0"	7' - 0"
110	3' - 0"	7' - 0"
111		

FIGURE 12-2.6 Updated door schedule

If you select the door (i.e., the row) in the schedule and then click *Highlight in model* on the *Ribbon* (Figure 12-2.7), Revit will switch to a plan view and zoom in on that door. This makes it easy to find a door that does not have a number or any door in an unknown location.

Next, you will delete door *104B* from the door schedule view.

13. Click in the cell with the number **104B**.

14. Now click the **Delete** (Row) button from the *Ribbon* (Figure 12-2.7).

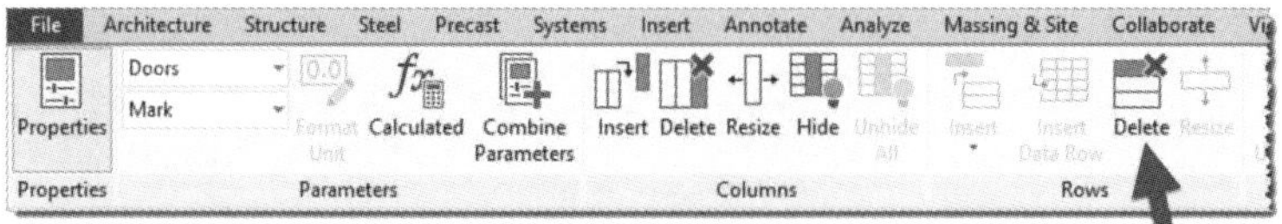

FIGURE 12-2.7 *Ribbon* for the door schedule view

You will get an alert. Revit is telling you that the actual door will be deleted from the project model (Figure 12-2.8).

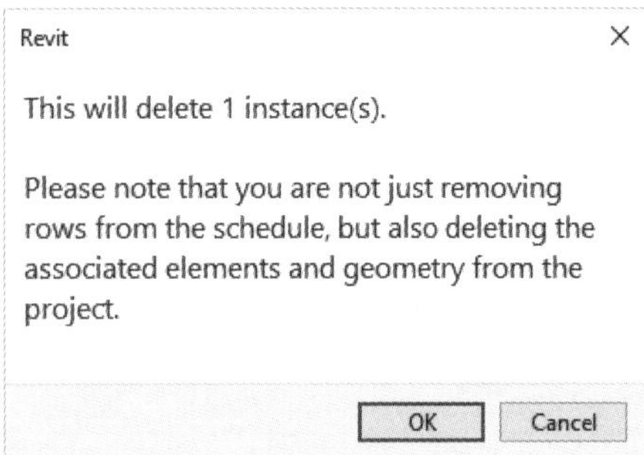

FIGURE 12-2.8 Revit alert message

15. Click **OK** to delete the door (Figure 12-2.8).

16. Switch back to the **Level 1** view and notice that door *104B* has been deleted from the project model.

17. **Save** your project.

> ***TIP:*** *The schedule view can be used to enter the information about each door. For example, you can enter the fire rating, the frame material, etc. This information is actually added to the Door object. If you switch to a plan view, select a door and view its properties; you will see all the information entered in the schedule for that door. You can also change the door number in the schedule.*

The image below shows a real Revit project with several doors; notice the door numbers match the room numbers. Also, the shaded walls are existing; Revit can manage phases very well.

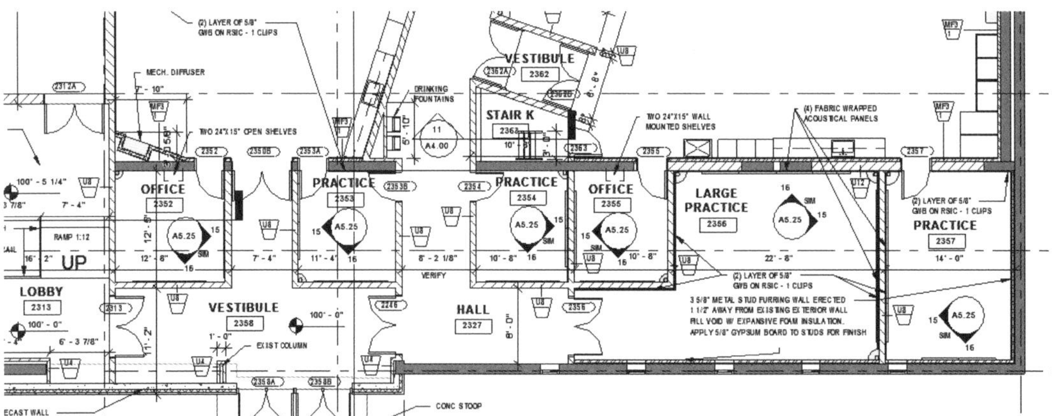

Image courtesy LHB (www.LHBcorp.com)

Exercise 12-3:
Generate a Room Finish Schedule

In this exercise you will create a room finish schedule. The process is similar to the previous exercise. You will also create a color-coded plan based on information associated with the *Room* element.

Create a Room Finish Schedule:

1. Open your Revit project.

2. Select **View → Create →** Schedule **→ Schedule/Quantities** button from the *Ribbon.*

3. Select **Rooms** under *Category.*

4. Type **Law Office Room Schedule** for the *Name.*

5. Set the *Phase* to **New Construction**.

6. Click **OK** to create the schedule (Figure 12-3.1).

7. In the ***Fields*** tab of the *Schedule Properties* dialog, add the following fields to be scheduled (Figure 12-3.2):
    a. Number
    b. Name
    c. Base Finish
    d. Floor Finish
    e. Wall Finish
    f. Ceiling Finish
    g. Area

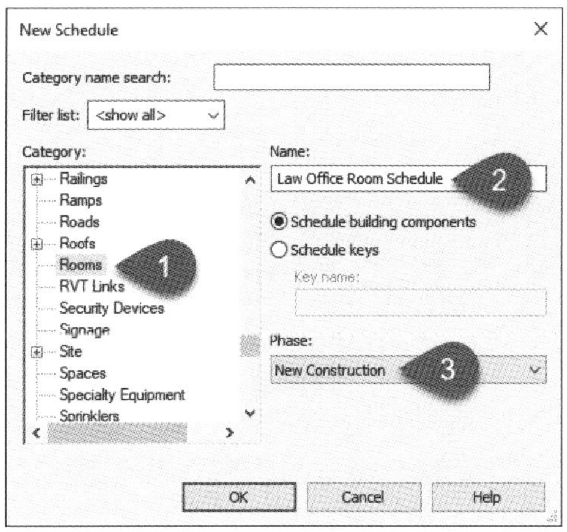

FIGURE 12-3.1 New Schedule dialog

Area is not typically listed on a Room Finish Schedule. However, you will add it to your schedule to see the various options Revit allows. It is possible to have multiple "room" schedules that list various things about the room.

8. On the ***Sorting/Grouping*** tab, set the schedule to be sorted by the ***Number*** field.

9. On the ***Appearance*** tab, set the *Title Text* to **1/8" Arial** (Figure 12-3.3).

10. Select **OK** to generate the Room Schedule.

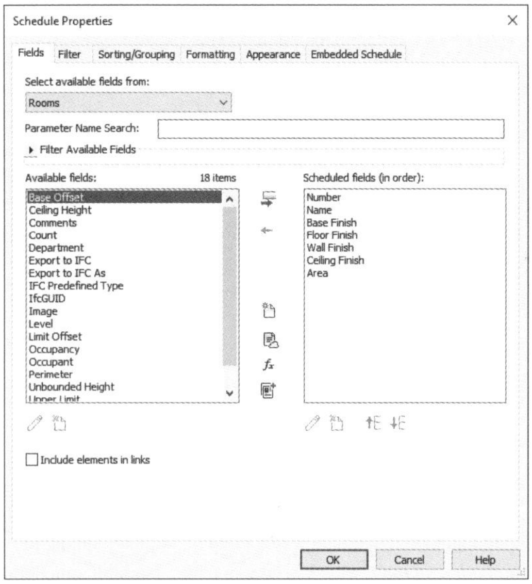

FIGURE 12-3.2
Schedule Properties - Fields

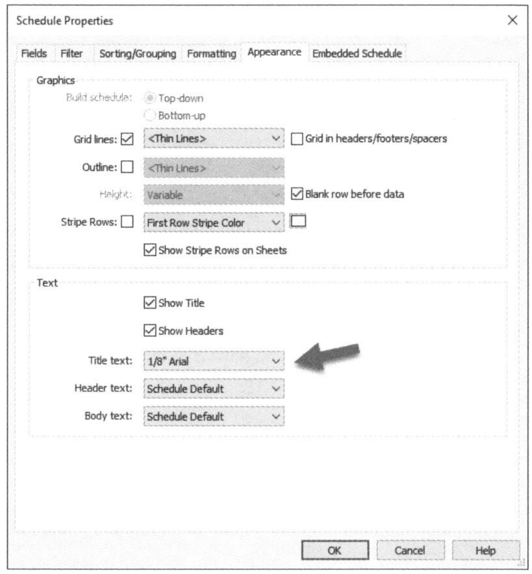

FIGURE 12-3.3
Schedule Properties - Appearance

Your schedule should look similar to the one to the right (Figure 12-3.4).

11. Resize the ***Name*** column so all the room names are visible. Place the cursor between *Name* and *Base Finish* and drag to the right until all the names are visible (Figure 12-3.4).

The formatting (i.e., *Bold* header text) will not show up until the schedule is placed on a plot sheet.

It is easy to add custom parameters that track something about the element being scheduled (rooms in this case). Simply click the Add Parameter button seen in Figure 12-3.2.

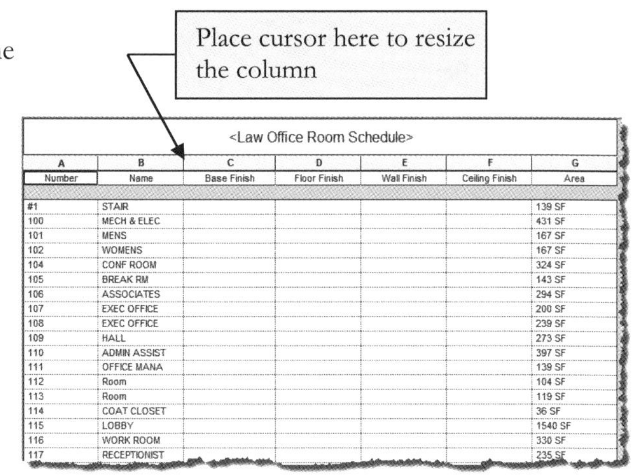

<Law Office Room Schedule>

A	B	C	D	E	F	G
Number	Name	Base Finish	Floor Finish	Wall Finish	Ceiling Finish	Area
#1	STAIR					139 SF
100	MECH & ELEC					431 SF
101	MENS					167 SF
102	WOMENS					167 SF
104	CONF ROOM					324 SF
105	BREAK RM					143 SF
106	ASSOCIATES					294 SF
107	EXEC OFFICE					200 SF
108	EXEC OFFICE					239 SF
109	HALL					273 SF
110	ADMIN ASSIST					397 SF
111	OFFICE MANA					139 SF
112	Room					104 SF
113	Room					119 SF
114	COAT CLOSET					36 SF
115	LOBBY					1540 SF
116	WORK ROOM					330 SF
117	RECEPTIONIST					235 SF

FIGURE 12-3.4 Room Schedule view

Modifying and Populating a Room Schedule:

Like the Door Schedule, the Room Schedule is a tabular view of the building model. So, you can change the room name or number on the schedule or in the plans.

12. In the **Law Office Room Schedule** view, change the name for room ***209*** (currently called *EXEC CONF RM*) to ***UPPER CONF ROOM***.

    TIP: *Click on the current room name and then click on the down-arrow that appears. This gives you a list of all the existing names in the current schedule; otherwise you can type a new name.*

13. Switch to the **Level 2** view to see the updated *Room Tag*.

You can quickly enter *Finish* information for several rooms at one time. You will do this next.

14. In the **Level 1** plan view, select the *Rooms* (not the *Room Tags*) for the offices shown – 4 total (Figure 12-3.5).

    REMEMBER: *Hold the Ctrl key down to select multiple objects.*

    TIP: *Move the cursor near the Room Tag but not over it to select the room; the large "X" will appear when the Room is selectable (see image below).*

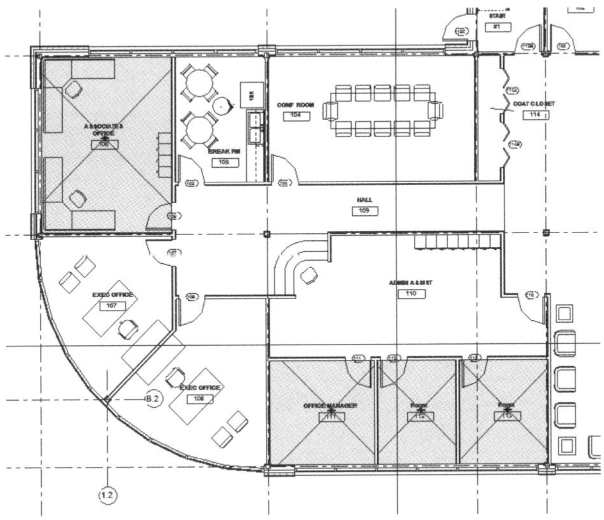

FIGURE 12-3.5 Level 1 rooms selected

15. Notice the parameters listed in the ***Properties Palette*** (aka, *Instance Properties*).

The *Parameters* listed here are the same as the *Fields* available for display in the Room Schedule. When more than one tag is displayed and a parameter is not the same, that value field is left blank. Otherwise, the values are displayed for the selected *Room*. Next you will enter values for the finishes.

16. Enter the following for the finishes (Figure 12-3.6):
    a. *Base Finish:* **WOOD**
    b. *Ceiling Finish:* **ACT-1** *(ACT = acoustic ceiling tile)*
    c. *Wall Finish:* **VWC-1***(VWC = vinyl wall covering)*
    d. *Floor Finish:* **CPT-1** *(CPT = carpet)*

17. Click **Apply**.

18. Switch back to the **Law Office Room Schedule** view to see the automatic updates (Figure 12-3.7).

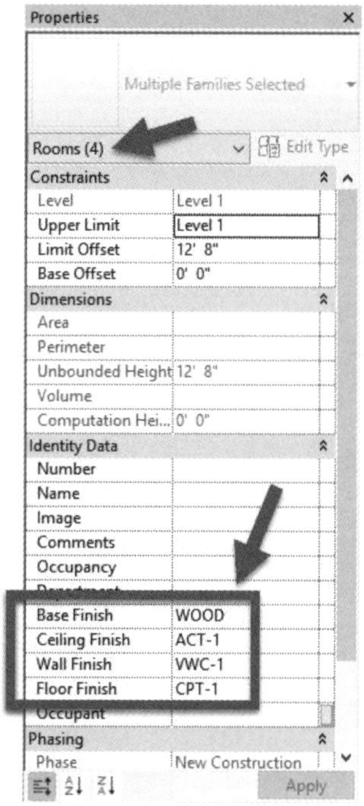

FIGURE 12-3.6
Element Properties – Room

You can also enter data directly into the **Room Schedule** view.

19. Enter the following data for the *Men's* and *Women's Toilet Rooms*:
    a. *Base:* **COVED CT**
    b. *Ceiling:* **GYP BD**
    c. *Wall:* **CT-2**
    d. *Floor:* **CT-1**

Hopefully, in the near future, Revit will be able to enter the finishes based on the wall, floor and ceiling types previously created!

> ***TIP:*** ***You can add fields and adjust formatting*** *anytime by right-clicking on the schedule view and selecting View Properties. This gives you the same options that were available when you created the schedule.*

<Law Office Room Schedule>

A	B	C	D	E	F	G
Number	Name	Base Finish	Floor Finish	Wall Finish	Ceiling Finish	Area
#1	STAIR					139 SF
100	MECH & ELEC ROOM					431 SF
101	MENS	COVED CT	CT-1	CT-2	GYP BD	166 SF
102	WOMENS	COVED CT	CT-1	CT-2	GYP BD	166 SF
104	CONF ROOM					329 SF
105	BREAK RM					143 SF
106	ASSOCIATES OFFICE	WOOD	CPT-1	VWC-1	ACT-1	294 SF
107	EXEC OFFICE					201 SF
108	EXEC OFFICE					238 SF
109	HALL					273 SF
110	ADMIN ASSIST					397 SF
111	OFFICE MANAGER	WOOD	CPT-1	VWC-1	ACT-1	139 SF
112	Room	WOOD	CPT-1	VWC-1	ACT-1	104 SF
113	Room	WOOD	CPT-1	VWC-1	ACT-1	119 SF
114	Room					36 SF

FIGURE 12-3.7 New data added to schedule

Setting Up a Color-Coded Floor Plan:

With the *Rooms* in place you can quickly set up color-coded floor plans. These are plans that indicate, with color, which rooms are *Offices*, *Circulation*, *Public*, etc., based on the room name in our example.

20. Right-click on the **Level 1** Floor Plans (architectural) view in the *Project Browser.*
21. Select **Duplicate View → Duplicate** (without detail) from the pop-up menu.
22. Rename the new view (*Copy of Level 1*) to **Level 1 – Color**.
23. Select **Annotate → Tag → Tag All**.
24. Select *Room Tags:* **Room Tag** from the list.

25. Click **OK**.

Now, all the rooms have a *Room Tag* in them!

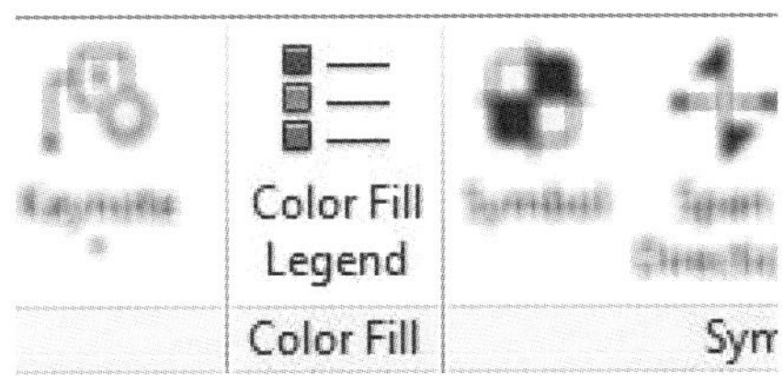

26. In the *New* view, select **Annotate → Color Fill Legend**.
27. Click just to the right side of the plan to place the *Legend Key*.
28. Select **Rooms** and **Name** and then **OK** to the following prompt (Figure 12-3.8).

You now have a color-coded plan where the colors are assigned by room *Name*; e.g., all the rooms named "*Office*" have the same color (Figure 12-3.9).

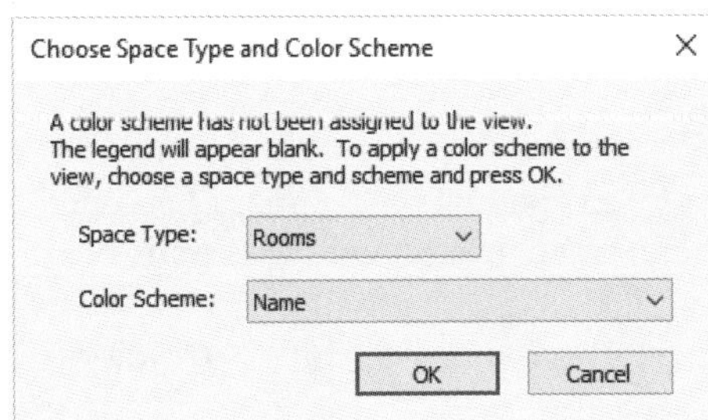

FIGURE 12-3.8 Color fill prompt

It is possible to sort by parameters other than *Name*. For example, you could sort by *Department*. However, you would need to enter department names first (e.g., *Partner*, *Associate*, *Staff*, *Public*, etc.).

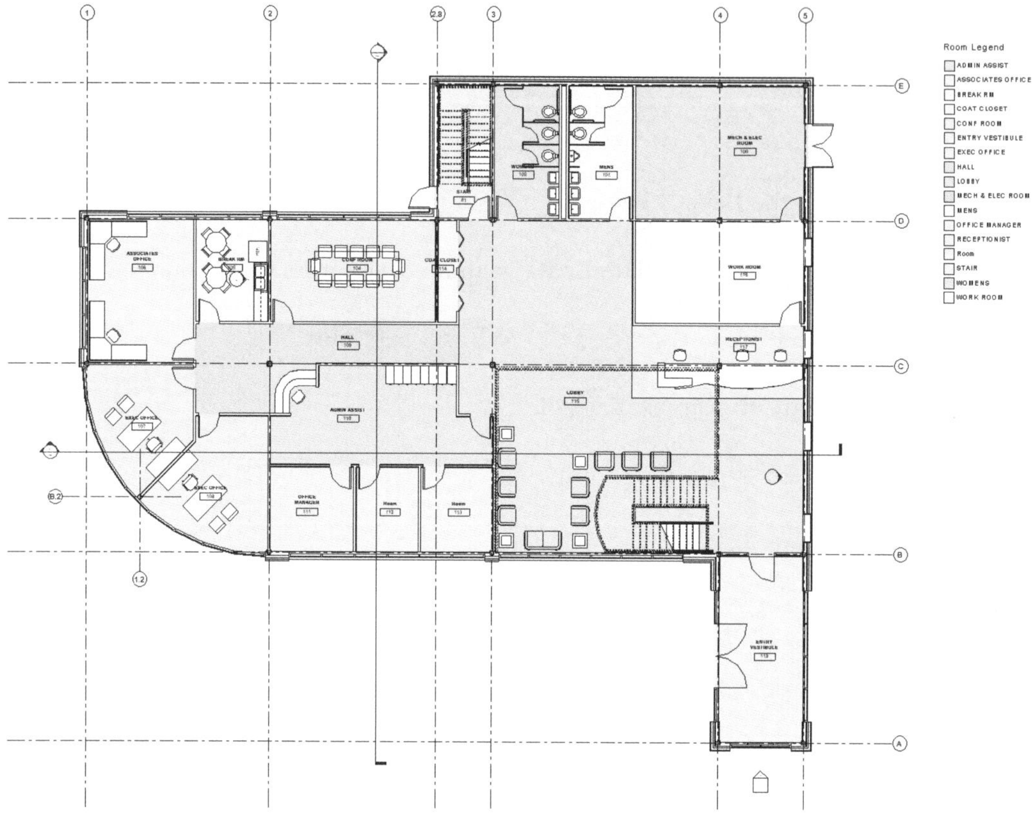

FIGURE 12-3.9 Color filled floor plan

> ***TIP:*** *Notice how the color coincides with the perimeter of the Room element previously placed. The room Separation Lines also control the room/color.*

Some furniture is white and other furniture is filled with the "fill" color of the room. The colored elements have the 3D geometry turned off in the plan view for increased performance. You will adjust this next.

29. Go to the **Level 1 – Color** view's *Properties* (*Properties Palette*).

30. Set the *Color Scheme Location* to **Foreground** and click **Apply**.

The colors are now consistent; the only drawback is the colors go to the center of the walls now.

31. Select the *Room Legend* shown in **Figure 12-3.9**.

32. Click **Edit Scheme** on the *Ribbon* (Figure 12-3.10).

FIGURE 12-3.10
Edit Scheme button

Each unique room name will get a different color. Before you finish, you will change one *Color* and one *Fill Pattern.*

33. Click on the *Color* for the **Lobby** (or the darkest color, which makes things within those rooms hard to see).

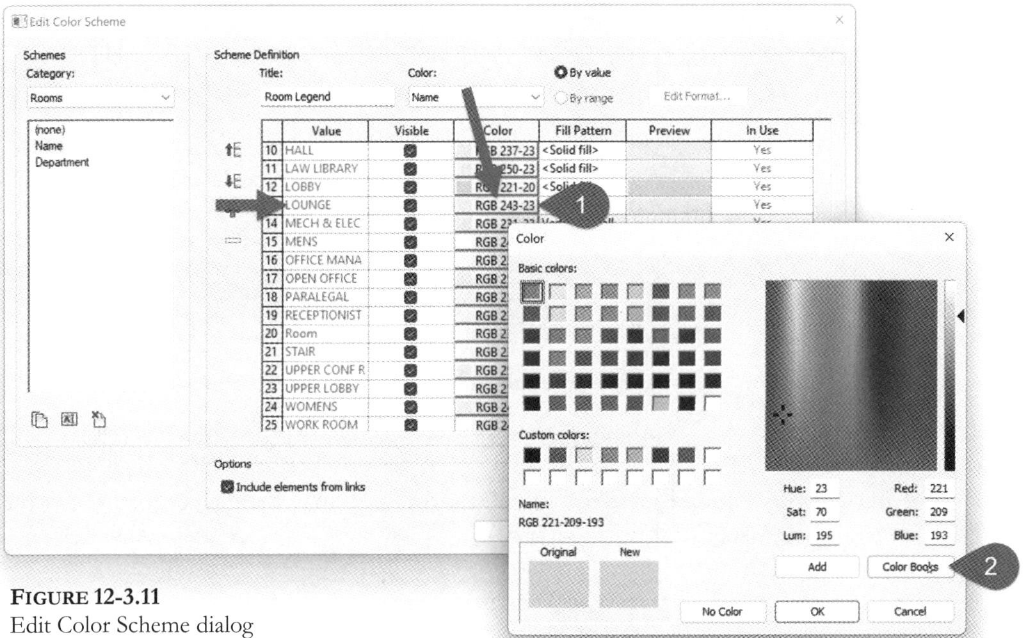

FIGURE 12-3.11
Edit Color Scheme dialog

FIGURE 12-3.12 Color selector

34. Click the **Color Books…** button to select a standard color (Figure 12-3.12).

35. Pick any color you like (Figure 12-3.13).

36. Click **OK** to accept.

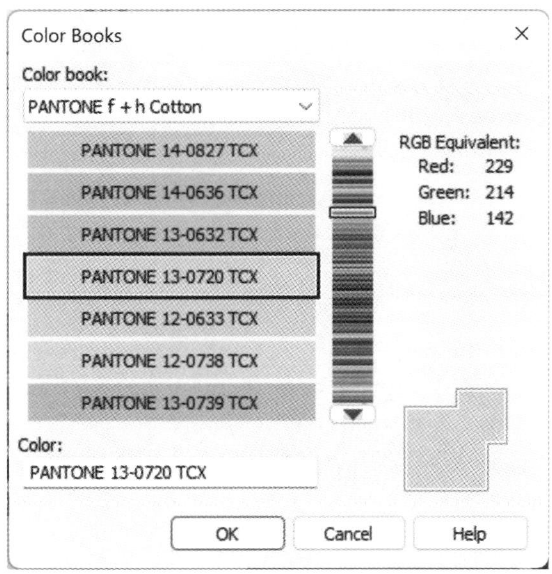

FIGURE 12-3.13 PANTONE Color selected

37. Now click on the *Fill Pattern* for the ***MECH & ELEC ROOM***.

38. Click the down-arrow and select **Vertical-small** from the list.

39. Click **OK**.

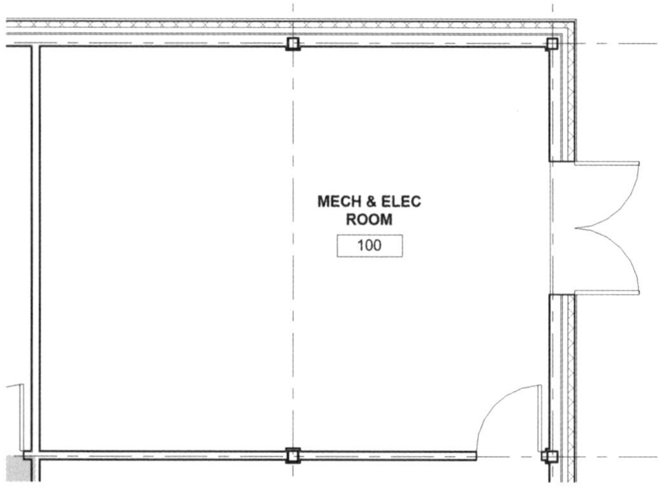

FIGURE 12-3.14 Fill pattern added to *MECH & ELEC ROOM*

Your mechanical room should look like Figure 12-3.14. You may need to darken the color if the lines are too hard to see (try printing it first).

40. Use the "VV" shortcut to turn off the *Sections* and *Elevations* in the **Level 1 – Color** view.

41. Follows the steps just covered to set up a **Level 2 – Color** view.

Your plan should now have the new color you selected for the *Lobby* and a hatch pattern in the *Mechanical Room*. Interior designers can create a color-filled plan based on the floor finishes. For example, all the rooms with *CPT-1* get one color and rooms with *CT-1* flooring get another color.

42. **Save** your project.

With the new "color" views set up, you can leave them in the project and refer back to them as needed. If you set up the colors in your main design views, you would likely need to remove the colors (*View Properties* → *Color Scheme* → *None*), making extra work when you needed the color view again.

Exercise 12-4:
Creating a Graphical Column Schedule

In this exercise you will create a column schedule. Revit can create a Column Schedule similar to the Door and Room Schedules just covered; most elements can be scheduled like this. Revit can create a graphical schedule of columns and their related grids. This type of schedule is typical industry practice for structural engineers on a set of Construction Documents (CDs).

Create a Column Schedule:

1. Open your Revit project

2. Select **View → Create → Schedules → Graphical Column Schedule** from the *Ribbon* (Figure 12-4.1).

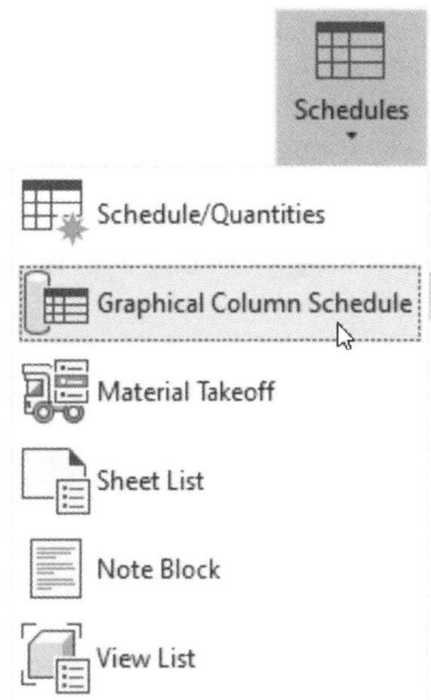

FIGURE 12-4.1
Create a graphical column schedule

You now have a Graphical Column Schedule (Figure 12-4.2) which can be placed on a sheet (to be covered in Chapter 16). Notice the grid intersections listed along the bottom. Also, each level is identified by horizontal lines within the schedules. The concrete foundation is shown, and then the steel. Some of the concrete columns look odd because they are missing the thickness for the foundation wall which passes by it. If you recall, you set the columns to start 8″ below the Level 1 floor slab; this can be seen and double-checked in this view.

The *Project Browser* now has a new category called *Graphical Column Schedules*. It is nice that the various categories only show up when something exists in that section; otherwise, the browser list would be unmanageable.

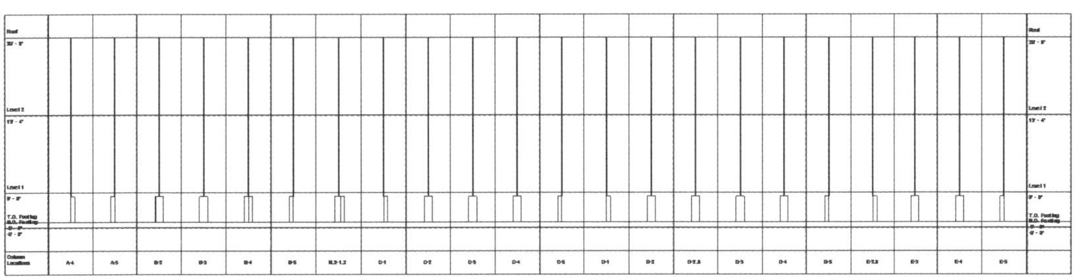

FIGURE 12-4.2 Graphical Column Schedule created

Next, you will look at a few ways in which you can control the graphics of the *Column Schedule.*

3. With the *Column Schedule* current, draw your attention to the *Properties Palette.*

4. Change both the *View Name* and the *Title* to **LAW OFFICE COLUMN SCHEDULE**.

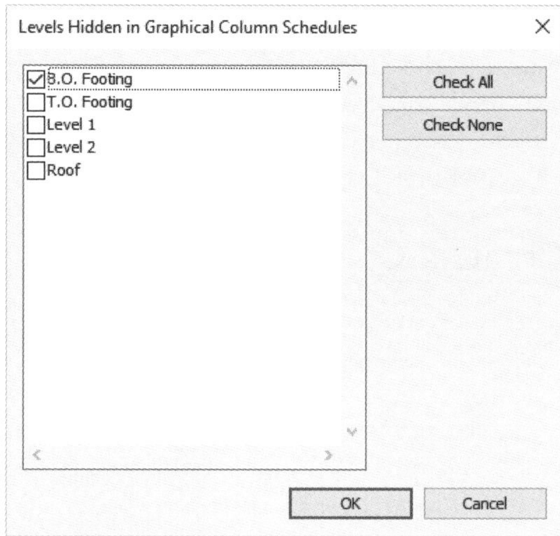

FIGURE 12-4.3 Hiding Levels

Revit allows you to hide levels that are not needed in the *Column Schedule*, for example, if someone on the design team added a level to manage the height of the top of masonry walls or window openings. It should be pointed out that *Level Datums* should only be used to define surfaces you walk on to avoid unintended issues. In this case, you will turn off the **B.O. Footing** level as it is not needed in this schedule.

5. Click **Edit** for *Hidden Levels.*

6. Check **B.O. Footing** and click **OK** (Figure 12-4.3).

7. Click **Edit** for *Material Types.*

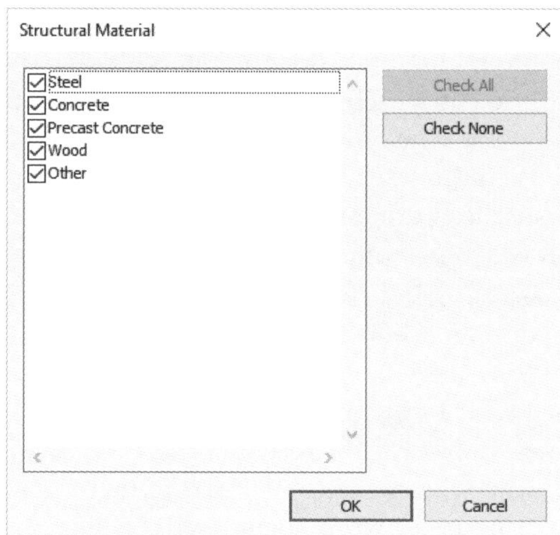

FIGURE 12-4.4 Structural materials

If you unchecked *Concrete* here, Revit would remove the concrete columns from the schedule (Figure 12-4.4). You will not make any changes at this time.

8. Click **OK** to close the *Structural Material* dialog without making any changes.

9. Click **Edit** for *Text Appearance.*

10. Set the *Title Text* to **Bold** (Figure 12-4.5).

11. Click **OK**.

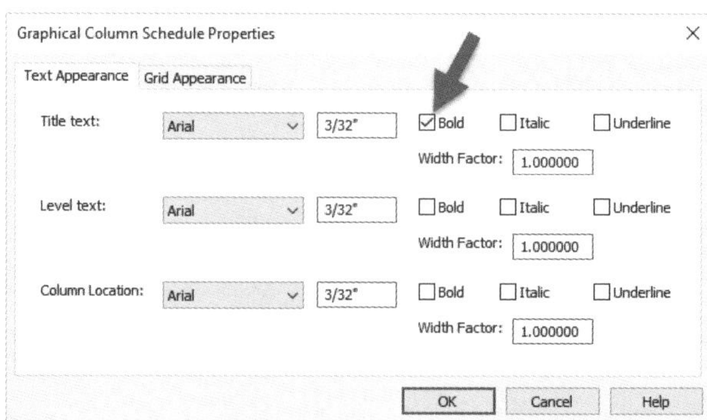

FIGURE 12-4.5 Text Appearance settings

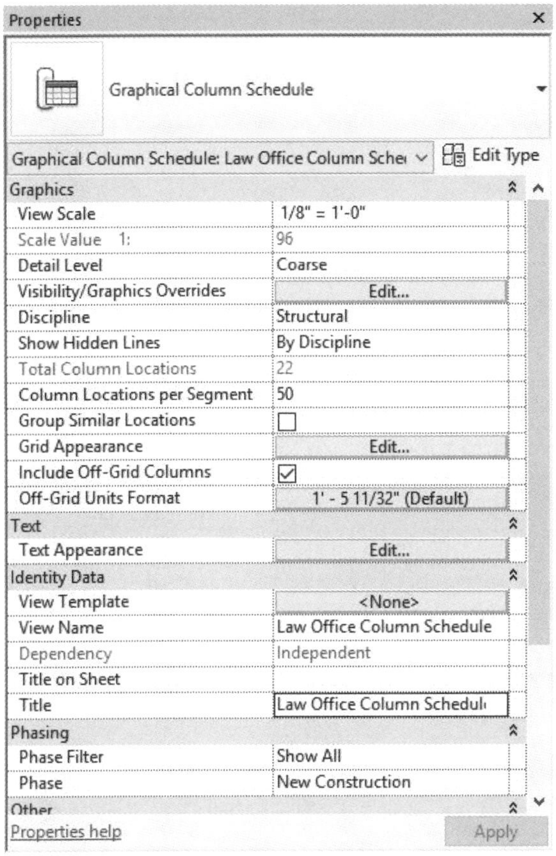

FIGURE 12-4.6 Graphical Column Schedule properties

Notice a few more things about the Column Schedule's *Properties* before closing it (Figure 12-4.6).

The total number of columns considered in the schedule is listed (22 in our example).

Also, *Include Off-Grid Columns* is checked. This will include columns that do not fall on any grid lines; most columns fall on grid lines as that is the main purpose of grid lines.

The *Group Similar Locations* option will show one graphical column for each column size and then list all the grid intersections below it. This makes the schedule smaller, but your project only has one column size so the schedule would actually be too small.

12. Click **Apply** to accept all the changes to the *Column Schedule.*

This completes the topic on *Graphical Column Schedules.*

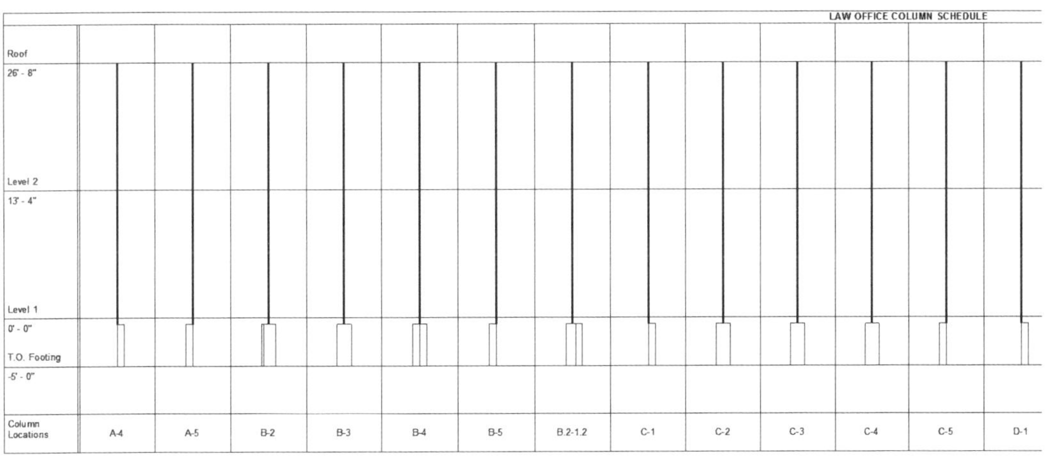

FIGURE 12-4.7 Graphical column schedule (partial view)

Self-Exam:

The following questions can be used as a way to check your knowledge of this lesson. The answers can be found at the bottom of this page.

1. Revit is referred to as a *Building Information Modeler (BIM)*. (T/F)
2. The area for a room is calculated when a *Room* element is placed. (T/F)
3. Revit can tag all the doors not currently tagged on a given level with the *Tag All* tool. (T/F)
4. You can add or remove various fields in a Door or Room Schedule. (T/F)
5. Use the ____________ tool to add color to the rooms in a plan view.

Review Questions:

The following questions may be assigned by your instructor as a way to assess your knowledge of this section. Your instructor has the answers to the review questions.

1. The schedule formatting only shows up when you place the schedule on a plot sheet. (T/F)
2. You can export your schedule to a file that can be used in MS Excel. (T/F)
3. A door can be deleted from the Door Schedule. (T/F)
4. A *Room Tag* can have a leader. (T/F)
5. It is not possible to add the finish information (i.e., base finish, wall finish) to multiple rooms at one time. (T/F)
6. When setting up a color scheme, you can adjust the color and the

   _________ pattern in the *Edit Scheme* dialog.
7. Use the ________________________ to adjust the various fields associated with each *Room* element in a plan view.
8. Most door schedules are sorted by the ___________ field.
9. What tool must you use to define a room boundary in an open area where the boundary you want is not completely defined by walls?

   ____
10. Revit automatically increments the room _________ as you place *Rooms*.

SELF-EXAM ANSWERS:
1 – T, **2** – T, **3** – T, **4** – T, **5** – Legend

Lesson 13
Mechanical System

This chapter will introduce you to the MEP features in Autodesk® Revit®. You will start the development of the ductwork and plumbing models for the law office, placing air terminals, ductwork, VAVs, water piping, waste piping, and more.

Exercise 13-1:
Introduction to Revit's Mechanical & Plumbing Tools

What is Revit MEP used for?

The image below shows the mechanical elements you will be adding in this chapter; you will actually just model a fraction of this. However, the next chapter's starter file will have all of this in it. Keeping in line with the overall intent of this textbook, you will really just be skimming the surface of what Revit's *MEP* tools can do. For example, Revit's *MEP* tools can size the ducts and do a total building heating and cooling loads calculation!

> *WARNING: This is strictly a fictitious project. Although some effort has been made to make the sizes of ducts and piping components realistic, this system has not been designed by a mechanical engineer. There are many codes and design considerations that need to be made on a case-by-case basis.*

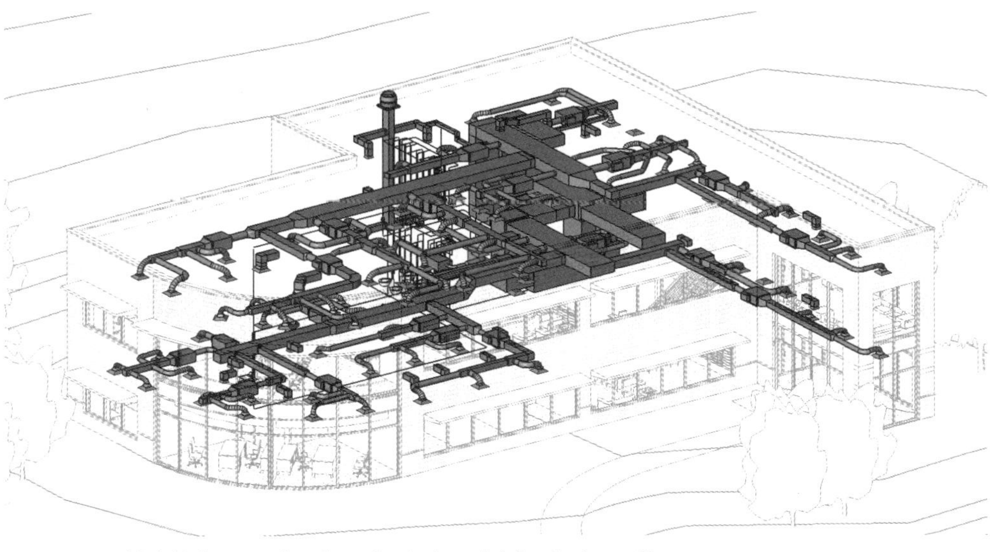

FIGURE 13-1.1 The completed mechanical model for the law office

Listed below are a few of the highlights of using Revit's MEP tools:

- 3D modeling of the entire mechanical system
- Multi-user environment
    - Several people can be working on the same model when "worksharing" has been enabled (though not covered in this book).
- Coordination with Architectural and Structural
    - Visually via 2D and 3D views
    - Interference Check feature
- 2D construction drawings generated in real-time from the 3D model
    - Construction Drawings (CDs phase)
        - Views can show true 3D geometry or single line representation.
            - Ducts are typically shown actual size.
            - Piping is often single line for clarity.
    - Construction Administration (CA phase)
        - Addendum
        - Architectural Supplemental Information (ASI)
        - Proposal Request (PR)
        - Change Order (CO)
- Schedules
    - Schedules are "live" lists of elements in the *BIM* file.
- Design Options
    - Used to try different ideas for a mechanical design in the same area of a project (e.g., exposed ductwork; round duct vs. rectangular duct)
    - Also used to manage bid alternates during CDs
        - A bid alternate might be an extra 25′-0″ added to the wing of a building. The contractor provides a separate price for what it would cost to do that work.
- Phasing
    - Manage existing, new and future construction
- Several options to export to analysis programs
    - Export model to external program (e.g., Autodesk Ecotect, IES Virtual Environment, etc.)

Many of the highlights listed above are things that can be utilized by all disciplines. However, the list was generated with the mechanical engineer and technician in mind relative to current processes used.

Ribbon – Systems Tab

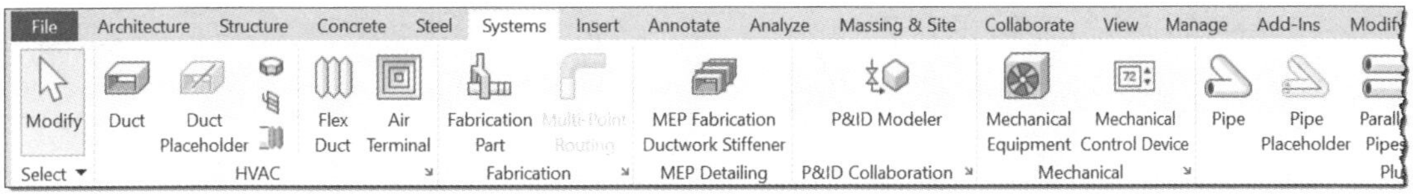

As can be seen from the image above, the *Systems* tab is laid out with the mechanical and electrical designer in mind. The very first tool is *Duct* (*Wall* is the first tool for Revit *Architecture*). Also notice the panel names: *HVAC*, *Mechanical* and *Electrical* are all MEP discipline oriented.

Many tools are duplicates from those found in Revit *Architecture*; they even have the same icon. Duplicate tools, such as *Stairs*, are the exact same programming code and create the same element, which would then be editable by any "flavor" of Revit.

The small down-arrow to the right of each panel title is what is called a ***dialog launcher***. On the *Systems* tab, they open either the *Electrical* or *Mechanical Settings* dialog.

Ribbon – Analyze Tab

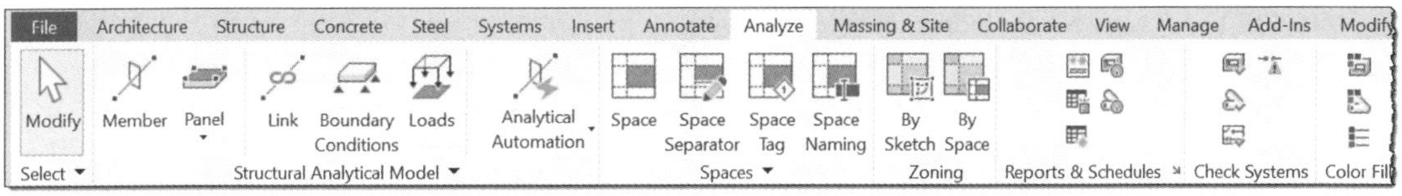

The *Analyze* tab reveals several tools which allow the mechanical and electrical designer to specify various loads on their designs once it has been modeled. The energy modeling tools can also be found on this tab.

Mechanical Settings Dialog Box

From the *Manage* tab, select *MEP Settings* → *Mechanical Settings* to reveal the *Mechanical Settings* dialog box; see Figure 13-1.2 below.

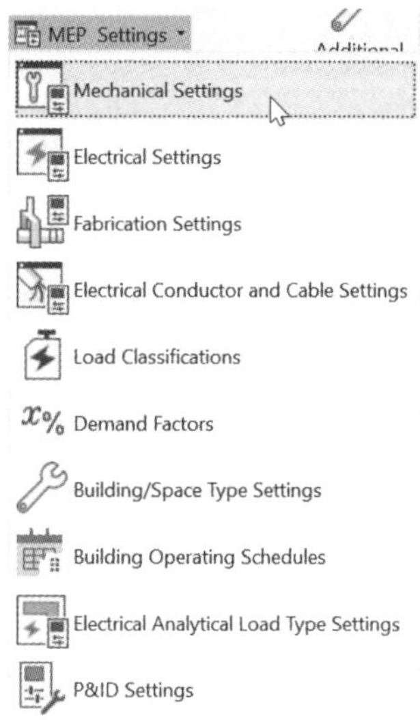

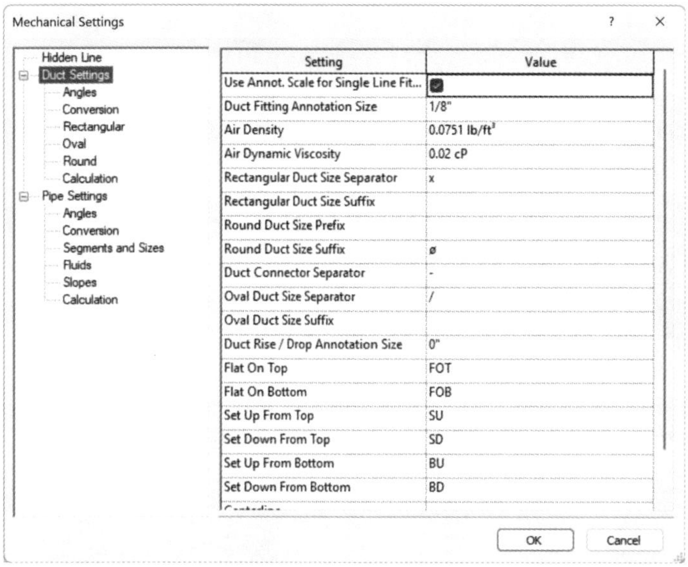

FIGURE 13-1.2 Revit MEP Mechanical Settings dialog

Revit provides a *Mechanical Settings* dialog box that allows changes to be made in how the program works and displays things; a related *Electrical Settings* dialog will be mentioned in the next chapter. These settings only apply to the current project but apply across the board to that project.

For this tutorial, do not make any changes in this dialog unless instructed to do so. This will help to ensure your drawings match those presented in the book.

MEP Content

A large array of industry-standard ducts, air terminals or diffusers, mechanical equipment, pipes, plumbing fixtures, and more are provided by Autodesk! New content is being added all the time by manufacturers via their websites. What is not provided can typically be modeled in Revit or the *Family Editor* as needed.

MEP Templates

Revit provides three templates from which a new MEP project can be started. One is specifically for mechanical (**Mechanical-Default.rte**), another is for electrical (**Electrical-default.rte**) and the third is for both in the same model (**Systems-Default.rte**). Yet another option is the Multi-Discipline template which can be used to host all disciplines, including architectural and structural (this is rarely used in practice).

The ideal setup is both mechanical and electrical in the same model. However, due to software and hardware limitations, in the realm of speed and performance, the two disciplines are sometimes split into separate models. Unfortunately, when the model is split, some functionality is lost as the electrical design team cannot connect to mechanical equipment, which requires electricity when it is in a linked file.

Because you will be starting the MEP model within the architectural model, you will not automatically have several important components ready to go. Not to worry, however, as the first thing you will do in the next exercise will be to import several settings from another project file, which will be based on the MEP mechanical template.

Autodesk Revit MEP Resources:

Autodesk's Revit Blog:
http://blogs.autodesk.com/revit/

Autodesk's Revit MEP Discussion Group:
forums.autodesk.com (also check out **Revitforum.org** and **AUGI.com**)
(and then click the links to *Autodesk Revit* → *Autodesk Revit MEP*)

Autodesk's Subscription Website:
manage.autodesk.com

The image below is a *Camera* view, at eye level, looking at the reception desk in the Level 1 *Lobby*. In 3D views, Revit *MEP* automatically makes the architectural and structural elements light gray and transparent so the MEP elements are highlighted. You will learn how to create *Camera* views in Chapter 15!

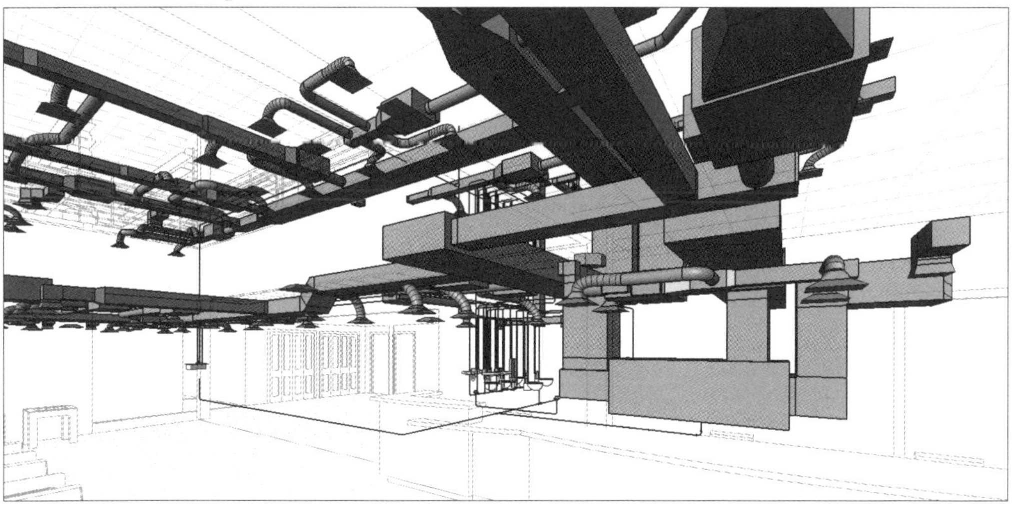

FIGURE 13-1.3 Camera view near the front reception desk

Exercise 13-2:
Creating Views and Loading Content

In this lesson you will begin to prepare your *BIM* file for the mechanical modeling tasks. One of the challenges with modeling everything in one model (versus separate models linked together) is that Autodesk does not provide a template specifically for this. A good starting template is provided for each discipline but not for a multi-discipline project.

The first steps in this lesson, therefore, will walk the reader through the process of importing *Project Standards* from another file into your law office project. Once that has been done, you can then set up views in which to model and annotate the mechanical aspects of the building. These views will be similar to the floor plan views that currently exist for the architectural and structural plans; they are defined by a horizontal slice through the building. The main difference is that various *Categories* will be turned off that are not directly relevant to the mechanical systems of the building.

Transfer Project Standards:

Revit provides a tool that allows various settings to be copied from one project to another; it is called *Transfer Project Standards*. This was first covered in Chapter 8. In order to use this feature, two Revit project files need to be opened. One is your law office project file, and the other is a file that contains the settings you wish to import. You will start a new Revit *MEP* project from a template file and use this file as the "standards" file; this file will not be used after this step is complete. The only reason this step is required is that the project was started from an architectural template, rather than one of the MEP templates.

1. **Open** Revit.
2. Create a new file from the **Systems-Default.rte** template. Select **Application menu → New → Project**; click **Browse**.
3. Click **OK** to create a new project.
   a. *The template file is located here*: C:\ProgramData\Autodesk\RVT 2027\Templates\English-Imperial**Systems-default.rte**

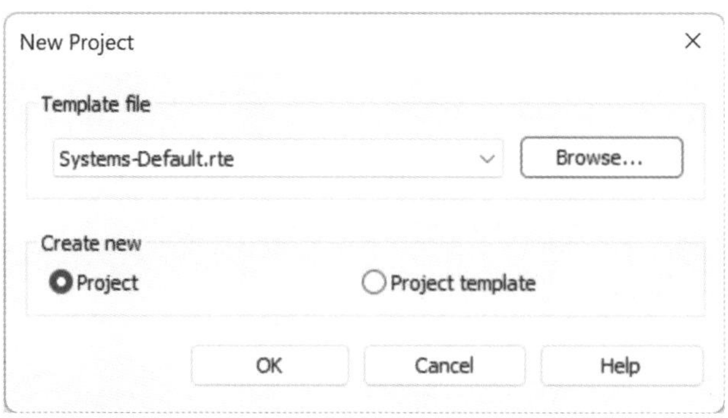

You now have a new Revit project which is temporarily named "Project1.rvt." This will be the project from which you import various MEP settings and families into your law office project. Take a moment to notice the template is rather lean; it has no sheets and several views set up. An MEP engineering department would take the time to set up an office standard template with sheets, families and views all ready to go for their most typical project to save time in the initial setup process.

4. **Open** your law office Revit project file using Revit *MEP*.
    a. Recommended: Start this lesson from the data file provided online—**Law Office (Chapter 13 starter file).rvt**

With both files open, you will use the *Transfer Project Standards* tool to import several important things into the law office project file.

5. With the law office project file current (i.e., visible in the maximized drawing window), select **Manage → Settings → Transfer Project Standards**.

6. Make sure *Copy from* is set to **Project1** (the file you just created).
7. Click the **Check None** button to clear all the checked boxes.
8. Check only the boxes for the items listed (Figure 13-2.1):
    a. Analytical Pipe Connection Types
    b. [3 items starting with] "**Cable Tray**"
    c. Circuit Naming Scheme
    d. [4 items starting with] "**Conduit**"
    e. Construction Types
    f. Distribution System
    g. [6 items starting with] "**Duct**"
    h. [3 items starting with] "**Electrical**"
    i. Filters
    j. [2 items starting with] "**Flex**"
    k. Fluid Types
    l. Halftone and underlay Settings
    m. Mechanical Equipment Sets
    n. MEP Hidden Line Settings
    o. [3 items starting with] "**Panel Schedule**"
    p. [*7 items that start with*] "**Pipe**" or "**Piping**"
    q. Space Type Settings
    r. System-Zone Types

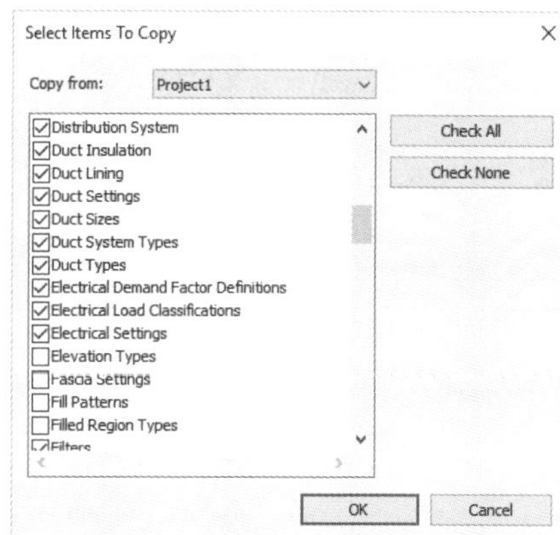

FIGURE 13-2.1 Transfer project settings

s. View Templates

t. Voltage Types

u. [6 items that start with] "**Wire**"

9. Click **OK** to import the selected items.

Because some items overlap, Revit prompts you about *Duplicate Types*; you can *Overwrite* or select *New Only*. Selecting *New Only* is safer if you are not sure what will be brought in by the template, or project file in this case. For the law office, you will use *Overwrite* to make sure you get all the MEP settings and parameters needed.

10. Scroll down to see all the "duplicate types" so you have an idea what overlap there is; click **OK/Overwrite** (see Figure 13-2.2).

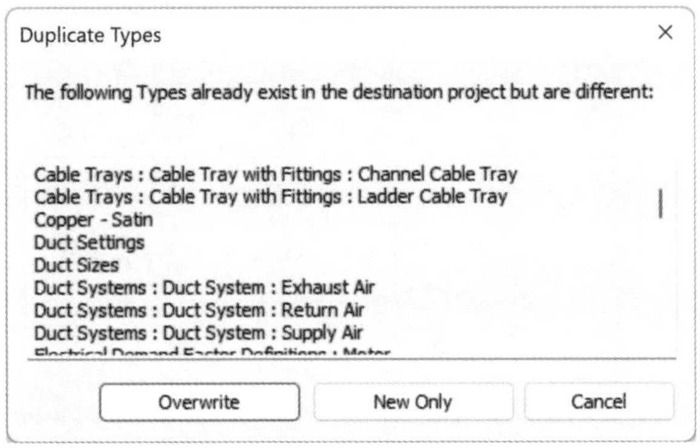

FIGURE 13-2.2
Transfer project settings; duplicate types warning

You now have many of the key settings loaded into your *BIM* file (e.g., *View Templates* and *Duct and Pipe Settings*). The settings you just brought into the model will accommodate both the mechanical chapter (this chapter) and the electrical chapter (the next chapter).

At this time you may close the temporary Project1 file without saving.

Creating Mechanical Plan Views

Next you will create the following floor plan views *(Level; View Template to use listed on right)*:

- Level 1 – HVAC Floor Plan *(Level 1; Mechanical Plan)*
- Level 2 – HVAC Floor Plan *(Level 2; Mechanical Plan)*
- Level 1 – Domestic Water Floor Plan *(Level 1; Plumbing Plan)*
- Level 2 – Domestic Water Floor Plan *(Level 2; Plumbing Plan)*
- Level 1 – Sanitary Floor Plan *(Level 1; Plumbing Plan)*
- Level 2 – Sanitary Floor Plan *(Level 2; Plumbing Plan)*
- Mechanical Roof Plan *(Roof; Mechanical Plan)*
- Under Slab Sanitary Plan *(Level 1; Plumbing Plan)*

FYI: Adjust the **View Range** *for the Under Slab Sanitary Plan view as follows:*
Bottom = *Level 1 @ 0'-0" and* View Depth = *Unlimited (rather than Level 1).*

Next you will create the following ceiling plan views *(use View Template listed)*:

- Level 1 – HVAC Ceiling Plan *(Level 1; Mechanical Ceiling)*
- Level 2 – HVAC Ceiling Plan *(Level 2; Mechanical Ceiling)*

After creating each of these views, you will apply a **View Template**, which is a way to quickly adjust all the view-related parameters to a saved standard (i.e., a *View Template*).

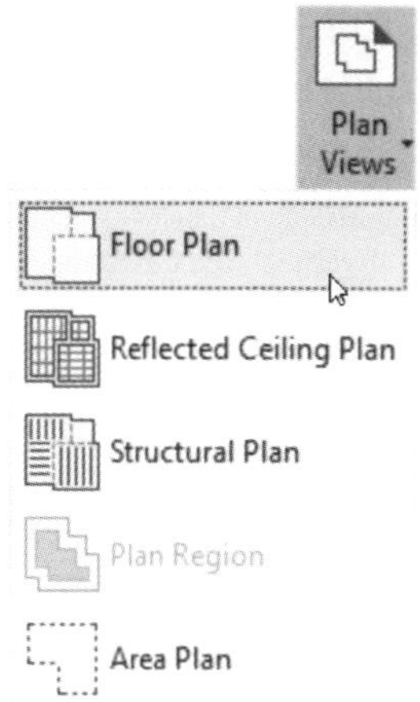

11. While in the law office project, select **View → Create → Plan Views → Floor Plan**.

12. **Uncheck** *Do not duplicate existing views.*

13. In the *New Floor Plan* dialog box, select:
    a. *Floor Plan Views:* **Level 1**
    b. *Click OK* (see Figure 13-2.3).

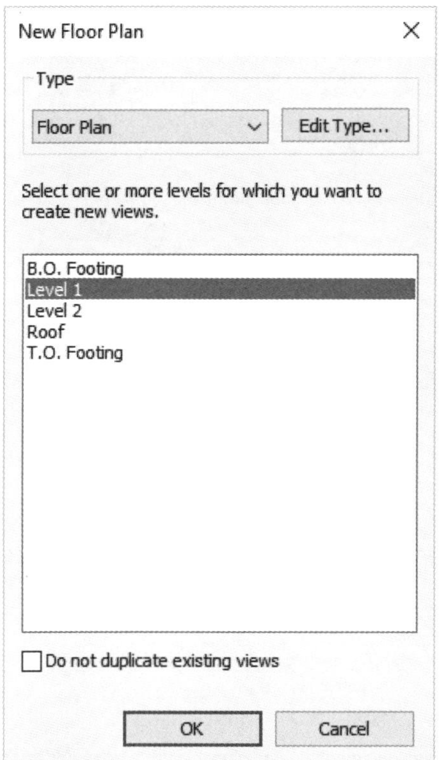

FIGURE 13-2.3 Creating new plan view

At this point, you have a new *View* created in the *Project Browser*. This view is in the *Floor Plans* section, under *Views (all)*; see Figure 13-2.4. When you change the *Discipline* and *Sub-Discipline*, and then adjust the *Project Browser* to sort by *Discipline*, the view will move to a new section in the *Project Browser*. This will make things more organized, especially when you have so many floor plan views.

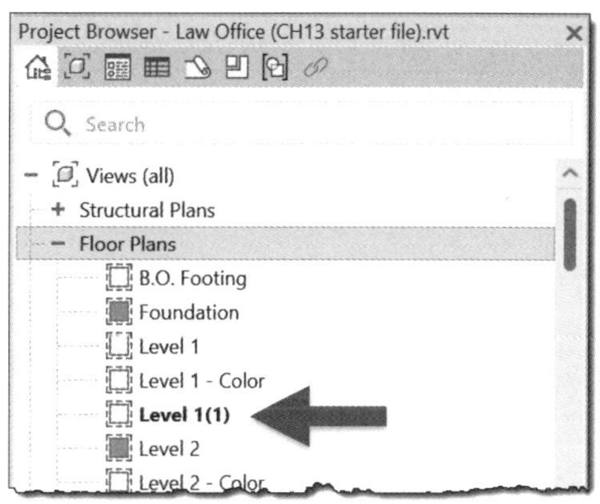

FIGURE 13-2.4 New plan view created

Next you will rename the *View* and apply a *View Template.*

14. In the *Project Browser*, right-click on **Floor Plans\Level 1(1)**.

15. Select **Rename** from the pop-up menu.

16. Type: **Level 1 – HVAC Floor Plan**.

    FYI: *This is the name that will appear below the drawing when it is placed on a sheet.*

17. Set the *View Scale* to **¼" = 1'-0"**

View Templates

Next, you will apply a *View Template* to your view so it is closer to what is needed for the design and documentation of an HVAC plan. First you will look at the current settings and how they will be changed by applying a *View Template.*

18. In the *Properties Palette*, adjust the *View Properties* so *Discipline* is set to **Architectural**, *Underlay* to **T.O. Footing** and clear the *Sub-Discipline.*

    FYI: *You are doing this so you can see that the* View Template *fixes these mistakes.*

Notice, in the *Properties Palette*, that *Discipline* is now set to *Architectural*, the *Sub-Discipline* is blank and an *Underlay* is active. The *View Template* will quickly correct these settings (Figure 13-2.5).

If you do not see the *Sub-Discipline* parameter, you need to revisit the steps on *Transfer Project Standards.*

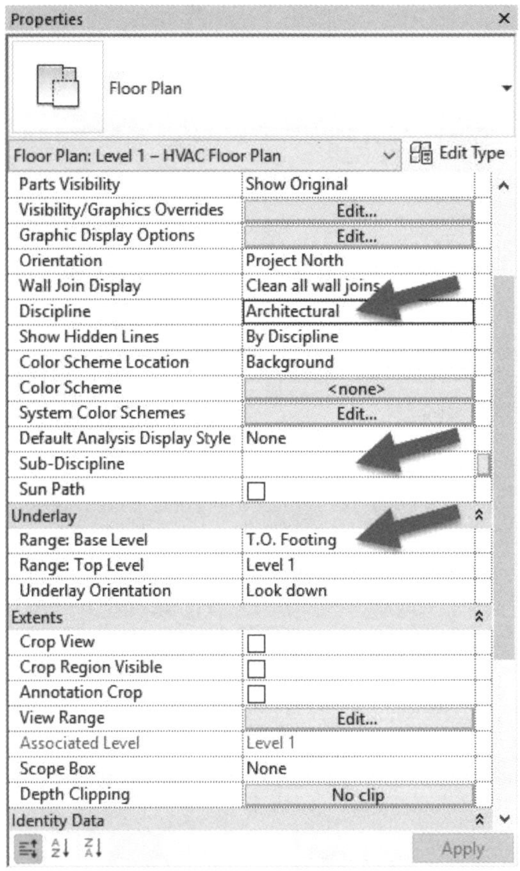

FIGURE 13-2.5 View Properties – HVAC Level 1

The ***View Range*** dialog has a significant role in what shows up in a plan view and what does not. In Revit *MEP*, things only show up in a view when they fall below the *Top View Range* and are above the *View Depth*. This is different from the architectural discipline setting where only things at or below the *Cut Plane* are shown. This is because most of the ductwork is above the ceiling, but the *Cut Plane* is similar to the architectural views so the doors and windows show up in the plan. The *Cut Plane* will have the same settings as the current architectural view you just copied; it is just the discipline setting that affects how the ductwork is shown.

The ***Visibility/Graphics Overrides*** dialog also has a significant role in what shows up and what does not in a view. The main thing to understand here is that the visibility of the items on these various categories can be controlled here for the current view, and only the current view. Unchecking *Casework* hides all the items that exist within that category, such as base and wall cabinets and custom casework such as reception desks (assuming they have been created with the correct *Category* setting). The *View Template* you are about to apply to this view will uncheck a few of these *Categories*. However, the HVAC plans need to see much of the architectural elements so they can design for them or around them, unlike the structural lesson in Chapter 8, where much of the architectural content was hidden because it does not typically have a direct effect on the structural design (e.g. casework, furniture, specialty equipment, etc.).

Now you will apply the *View Template* and then review what it changes.

19. Once again, right-click on **Level 1 – HVAC Floor Plan** in the *Project Browser.*

20. Click **Apply Template Properties** from the pop-up menu.

21. On the left, select **Mechanical Plan**.

You are now in the *Apply View Template* dialog (Figure 13-2.6). Take a moment to observe all the settings it has stored and which are about to be applied to the selected view (i.e., the one you right-clicked on).

Notice the *View Scale* is set to *⅛"-1'-0"*. You know the scale needs to be ¼" = 1'-0" and you have already set that. So you will uncheck the *View Scale* so it is not included when the template is applied.

22. **Uncheck** *View Scale* (Figure 13-2.6).

23. Click **OK** to apply the *View Template.*

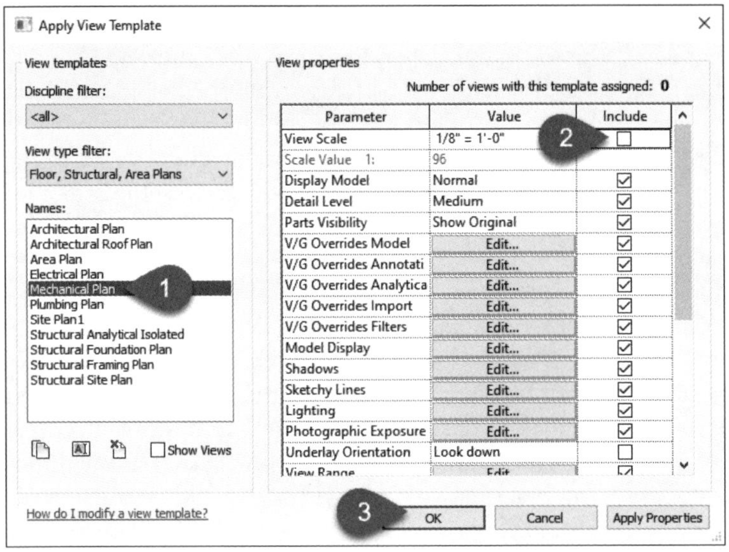

FIGURE 13-2.6 Apply View Template dialog – HVAC Level 1

The model visibility has now changed slightly (Figure 13-2.7). Notice how the architectural elements (i.e., walls, doors, furniture, etc.) are a light gray, and the plumbing fixtures are a medium black line so they stand out. Also, each discipline has its own set of section and elevation tags, so the architectural section marks and elevation tags have been hidden from this view.

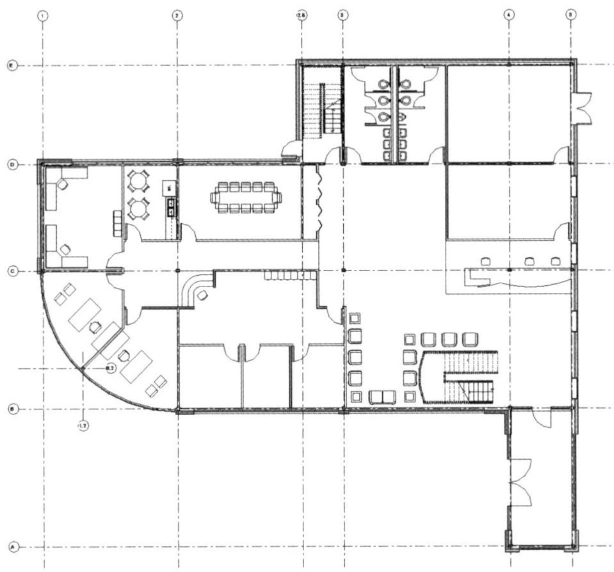

FIGURE 13-2.7 Result of applying view template

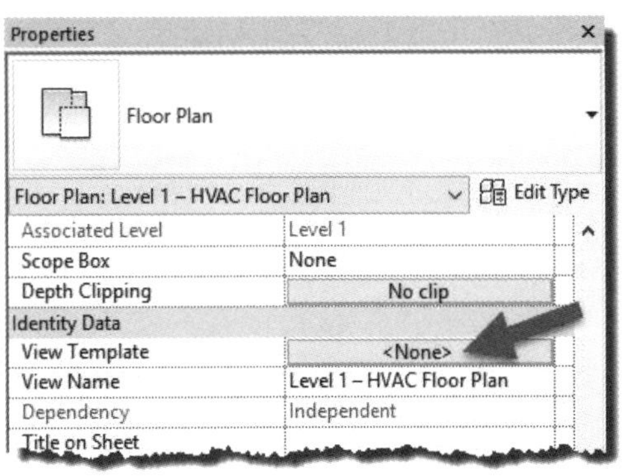

It is possible to assign a *View Template* to a view so it will automatically change if the *View Template* is adjusted later, per the button shown to the left. This is a good way to manage a large number of similar views, for example, a high rise with several similar floor plans. With a *View Template* assigned to each floor plan, making a change to the *View Template*, such as hiding the furniture, will update all views. Do not make any changes at this time.

Sort the Project Browser by Discipline:

The various views will be easier to manage if they are sorted by discipline and not just stored in the same section. You will change the *Project Browser* to accommodate this.

24. Click on the ***Views (all)*** heading at the top of the *Project Browser* to select it (Figure 13-2.8).

25. Now, in the Type Selector, pick ***Discipline*** from the drop-down list (Figure 13-2.8).

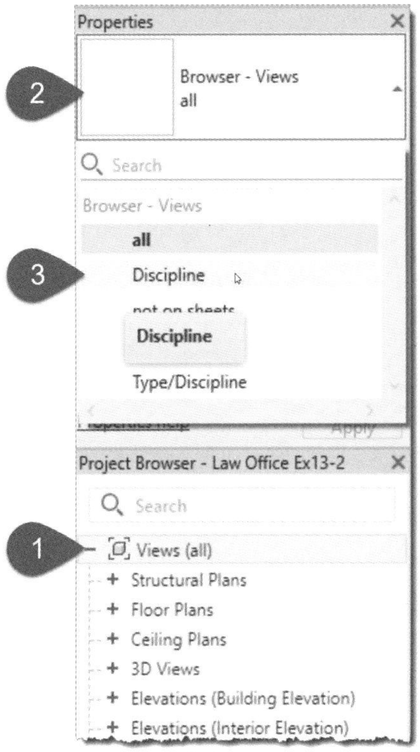

FIGURE 13-2.8
Project Browser properties

The *Project Browser* has now been changed to sort the views by its discipline setting (Figure 13-2.10). An MEP-only model would also sort by *Sub-Discipline* so the HVAC, Sanitary, etc., are in separate groups under the *Mechanical* heading.

In the following chapter, when you create the electrical views, a new *Electrical* heading will appear in the *Project Browser*.

Next, you will set up the remaining views. It is expected that you will refer back to the previous steps if you need a review of the process.

26. Create the remaining mechanical views, listed on page 13-10:
    a. Each to be **¼″ = 1′-0″**
    b. The *View Template* to be used is listed to the right, in parentheses, on page 13-10.
    c. Be sure to select *Reflected Ceiling Plan* when creating the ceiling plan views (compare to Step #11).

27. Verify the *View Properties* for each of the reflected ceiling plans has the *Underlay Orientation* set to **Look Up**.

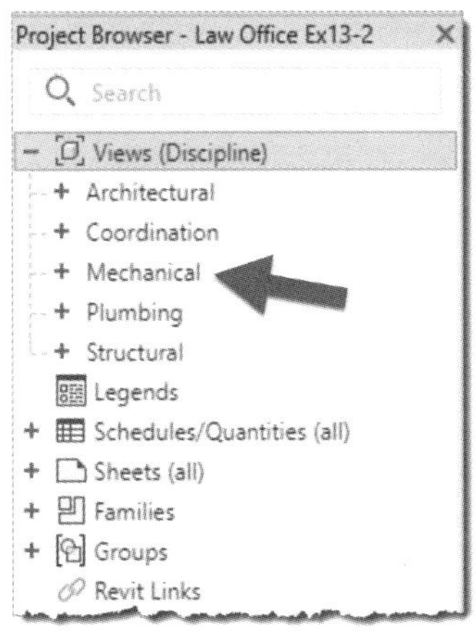

FIGURE 13-2.9
Project Browser by discipline

The previous step is important in making the view look correct. The ceilings will only show up if the *Underlay Orientation* is set correctly in a ceiling plan view.

Loading Content:

Now that the mechanical views are set up and ready to go, you will load some MEP content into the project. The process is identical to how content is loaded using Revit *Architecture* and *Revit Structure*.

This section will just show you how to load a few elements; as you work through the rest of this chapter you will have to load additional content, referencing this information if needed.

28. Use Load Autodesk Family to load the following MEP content:

    Mechanical\MEP\Air-Side Components\Air Terminals:
    - Exhaust Diffuser – Hosted
    - Louver – Extruded
    - Return Diffuser
    - Supply Diffuser

    Mechanical\MEP\Air-Side Components\Fans and Blowers:
    - Centrifugal Fan - Rooftop - Upblast

    Mechanical\MEP\Air-Side Components\Terminal Units:
    - VAV Unit - Fan Powered - Series Flow

    Plumbing\MEP\Fixtures\Drinking Fountains:
    - Drinking Fountain - Handicap

    Plumbing\MEP\Fixtures\Sinks:
    - Sink - Mop

    From online files at SDCpublications.com, provided with this book:
    - AHU-1 *(custom content)*
    - Water Heater *(standard Revit family; modified to be in correct category)*

You now have the content loaded that will be used to model the mechanical system, both ductwork and plumbing. You should only load content that you need, when you need it. Each family takes up space in the project, making the file on your hard drive larger. Additionally, once you start using those components in the project, the file gets larger. At this point in the book, your *BIM* file should be nearly 18MB.

29. **Save** your law office project.

Exercise 13-3:
Placing Air Terminals and the Air Handling Unit (AHU)

In this exercise you will start laying out ceiling **diffusers**, or air terminals. Just in case you are not sure what we are talking about, one is pointed out in the picture below (Figure 13-3.1). These can be either supply, return or exhaust diffusers. Some diffuser *Families* are hosted, meaning they attach to and move with the ceiling. Some diffusers are non-hosted and can be placed anywhere. Each has its pros and cons. A hosted diffuser will move with the ceiling, but this sudden relocation may wreak havoc on the ductwork layout. Also, the hosted diffusers cannot be placed until the ceilings have been placed. Non-hosted diffusers can be placed in rooms that are not intended to have a ceiling, and the solid ductwork is intended to support the diffuser. However, when placed in rooms with ceilings, you have to know the ceiling height. You will mainly be placing non-hosted diffusers (supply and return), but the exhaust air terminals will be hosted.

Finally, to close out this exercise, you will place a large piece of mechanical equipment called an **Air Handling Unit** (AHU). Sometimes these are placed on the roof, but you will be placing yours in the mechanical room on Level 1.

FIGURE 13-3.1 Diffuser (air terminal) example

Placing Non-Hosted Diffusers:

You will place supply diffusers in the *Associate's Office (106).*

1. **Open** your law office file using Revit *MEP.*

2. Switch to your **Level 1 – HVAC <u>Ceiling</u> Plan** view.

3. **Zoom** in to the *Associate's Office (# 106)* on Level 1, in the Northwestern corner.

To help the MEP designer from accidentally selecting architectural elements, Revit has a feature called Select Underlay Elements which is turned off by default. FYI: because the view has the discipline set to an MEP option (Mechanical in this case) the architectural elements are considered "underlay" elements, which is why they are grayed out as well.

4. Temporarily toggle on **Select underlay elements** (see image to right) and then click on the ceiling to select it.

5. Note the ceiling height is **8′-0″** as seen in the *Properties Palette.*

When working in the same model, it is possible to adjust the ceiling height by changing the ceiling height in the *Properties* dialog. But, if you are not involved in the architectural design, it is typically not acceptable for you, as a mechanical designer, to change the ceiling height. However, most mechanical designers work within the context of a linked architectural model, so it is not possible to change the ceiling height.

6. Select **Systems → HVAC → Air Terminal.**

7. Set the *Type Selector* to ***Supply Diffuser*** (family):
   24 x 24 Face 12 x 12 Connection (type name).

8. Set the *Elevation from Level* to **8′-0″** via the *Properties Palette.*

If you did not change the offset, Revit would give you a warning that the created element cannot be seen in the current view (Figure 13-3.2). This is because the diffuser was placed at the floor level (i.e., it is sitting on the floor) and therefore outside the *View Range.*

This warning can also occur if the category is turned off for the element you are placing in the current view. You can check this by typing *VV.*

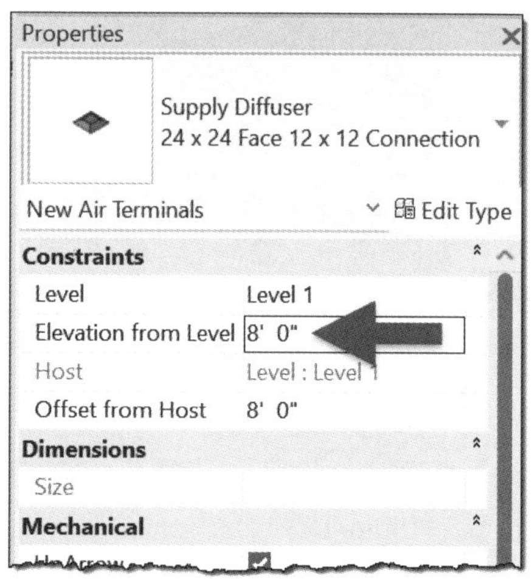

FIGURE 13-3.2
Diffuser offset from floor

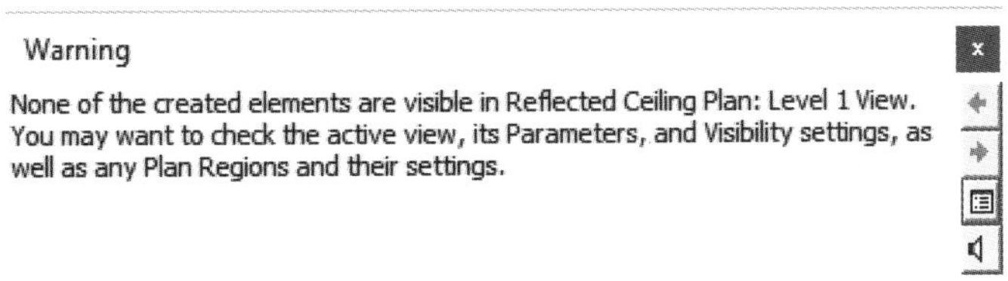

FIGURE 13-3.3 Not visible warning

You should now be able to see the diffuser in the Ceiling Plan view. Notice the arrows, which indicate that air is leaving the diffuser (supply) and not entering it (return). These arrows can be turned off one-by-one, so a corner condition could show air supply on only two sides.

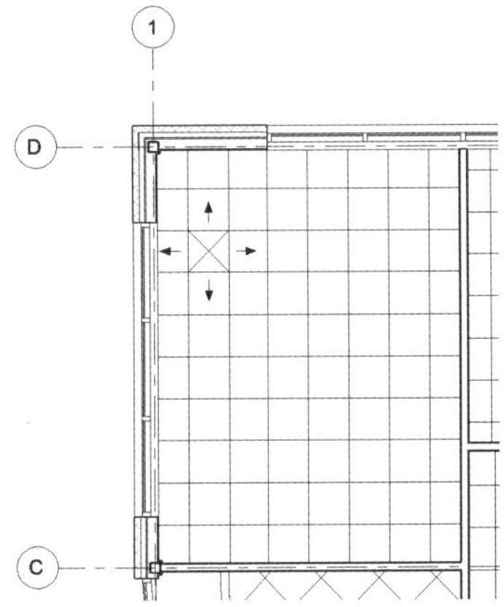

FIGURE 13-3.4 Diffuser placed

9. **Click** within the room to place the diffuser, and then use the ***Align*** command to reposition the diffuser as shown in Figure 13-3.4.
    a. Also reposition the ceiling grid if it does not match; simply select one of the ceiling grid lines and use the *Move* tool.

10. Now you can copy this diffuser to other three locations in the same room as shown in Figure 13-3.5.
    a. Select the diffuser, click *Copy* and then check *Multiple* on the *Ribbon*; click at the intersection of the ceiling grid lines.

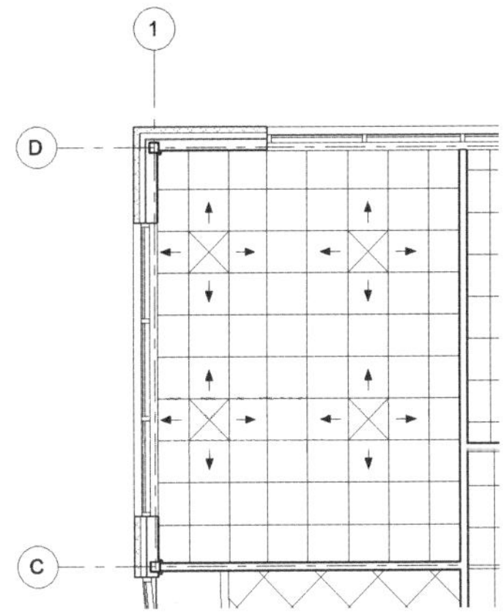

FIGURE 13-3.5 Diffuser copied

You can now use this technique to populate the entire **Level 1 Ceiling Plan** view.

11. Copy the diffuser to all other locations on Level 1 per Figure 13-3.6. Be sure to verify the ceiling height for each room and adjust the *Offset* parameter accordingly. ***FYI:*** the CFM value listed is adjusted in the next step.

The image to the right shows what the diffuser looks like when selected. Notice the small icon to the right indicates the selected item has a *Duct Connector*. Specifically, it lets the user know it's a supply connection which is 12″x12.″ A similar, but different, icon appears for return and exhaust diffusers.

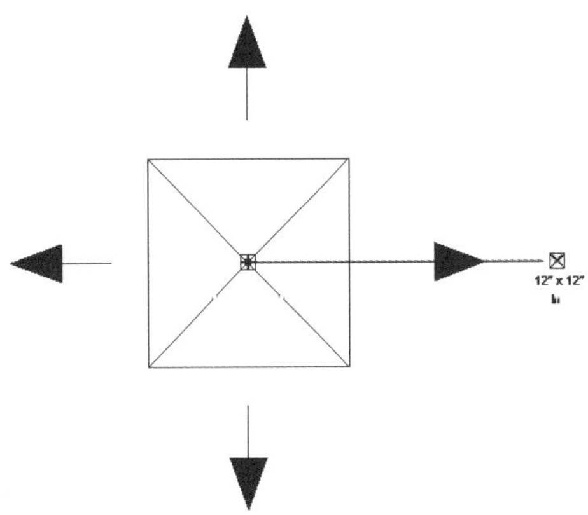

12. Select each diffuser and adjust the Flow (CFM) value in the *Properties Palette* to match that shown in Figure 13-3.6. The value shown is for each diffuser in the room.

    ***TIP:** Select all the diffusers in a room and then adjust the CFM.*

FIGURE 13-3.6 Level 1 supply diffuser layout and Flow inputs

You may refer back to Chapter 6 to verify the ceiling heights in addition to selecting them and viewing their properties. Another option is to add *Spot Elevations* (dimensions) to each ceiling in the **HVAC Ceiling Plan** view.

***TIP:** This will not work when the view is set to wireframe.*

13. Add the Level 2 diffusers and CFM as shown in Figure 13-3.7.

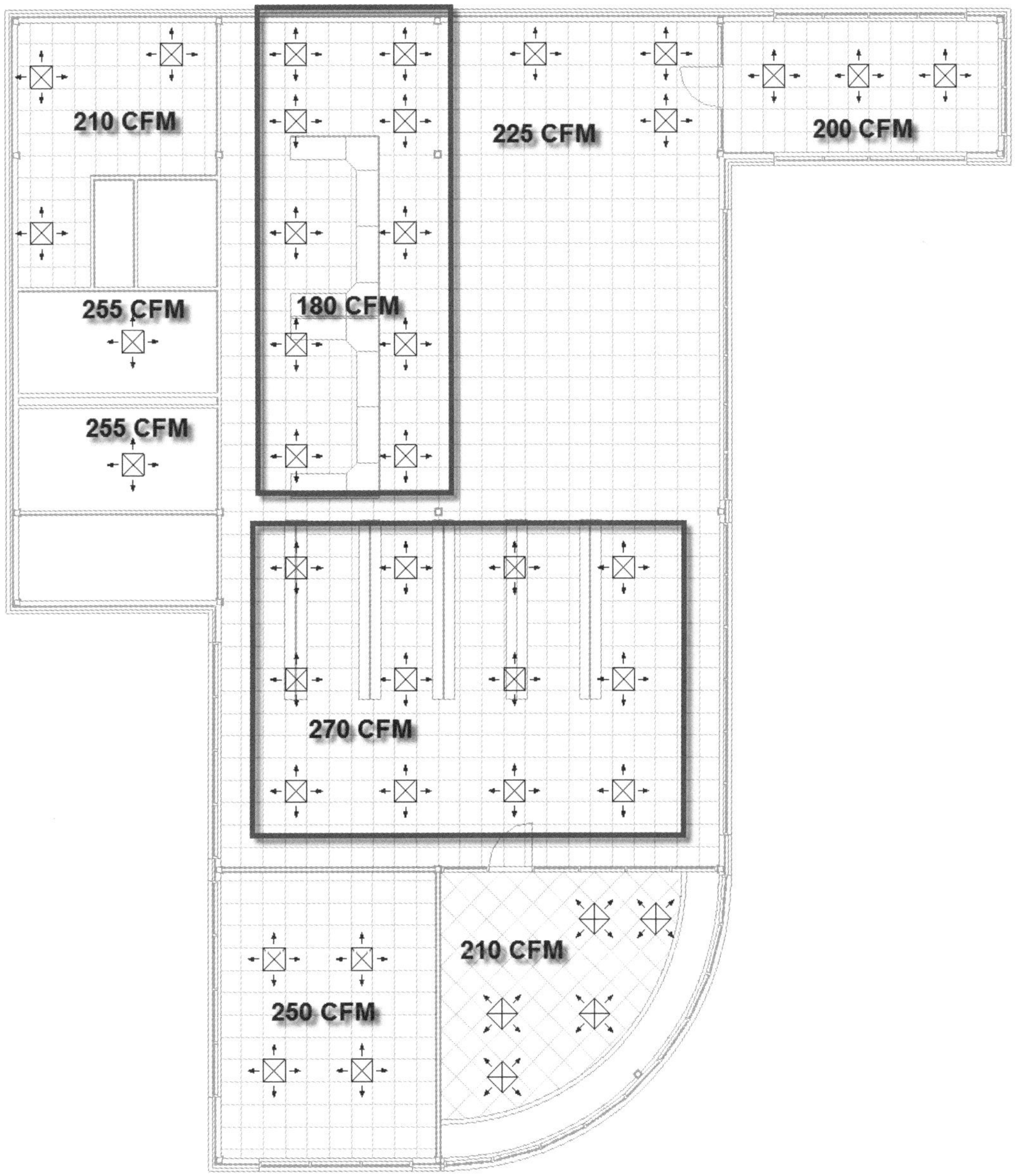

FIGURE 13-3.7 Level 2 supply diffuser layout

Diffusers are sized based on the number of them in a room and the size of the room. Having more at a lower CFM costs more due to the increased ductwork but is quieter due to the lower air pressure.

Return diffusers are placed the same way. Next you will place a *face* based exhaust diffuser in one of the toilet rooms. An exhaust system is different from a return air system in that the air is blown out of the building, whereas the return air is filtered and reused.

Placing Hosted Diffusers:

14. **Zoom** in to any one of the *Toilet Rooms* (in one of the **HVAC Ceiling Plans**).

15. Select the ***Air Terminal*** tool.

16. Select **Exhaust Diffuser - Hosted** from the *Type Selector.*

17. Set the **Placement** type to **Place on Face**; if not already selected. See image to the right.

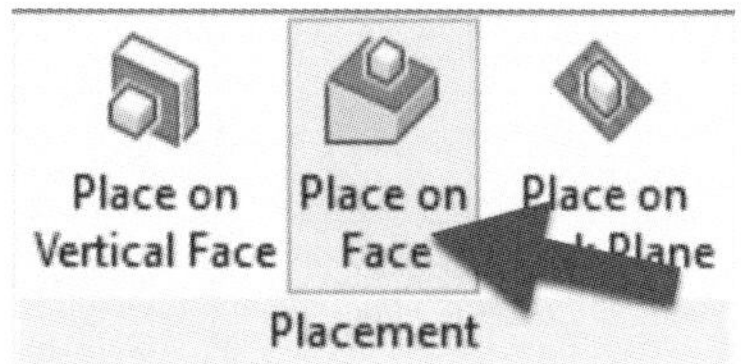

Next, you need to create a new *Type* for this family. It currently only has a 24″x24″ option; you need 12″x12″.

18. Click **Edit Type** from the *Properties Palette.*

19. Click **Duplicate**.

20. Type **12″ x 12″ Exhaust** and click **OK**.

21. Change the *Diffuser Width* to **1′-0.″**

22. Change the *Duct Width* to **10.″**

23. Click **OK** (Figure 13-3.8).

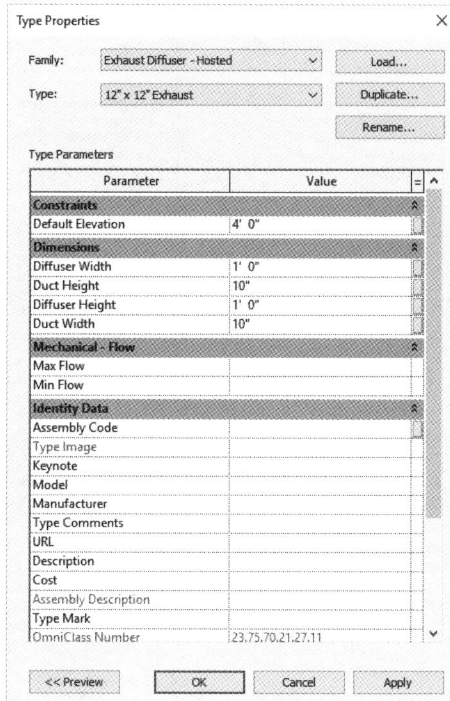

FIGURE 13-3.8 Exhaust diffuser properties

You now have a new exhaust diffuser size from which to choose. This was fast and easy due to the parametric nature of Revit's content.

24. Click within the Northern part of the *Toilet Room.*
    a. Notice the ceiling pre-highlights before you click to place the element.

25. Select the exhaust diffuser you just placed; view its *Instance Properties.*

26. **Uncheck** each of the four "arrow" options (Figure 13-3.9).

27. Set the exhaust *Flow (CFM)* to **225**.

Your exhaust diffuser should look like Figure 13-3.10.

28. Place a 12″x12″ exhaust diffuser in the other three *Toilet Rooms.*

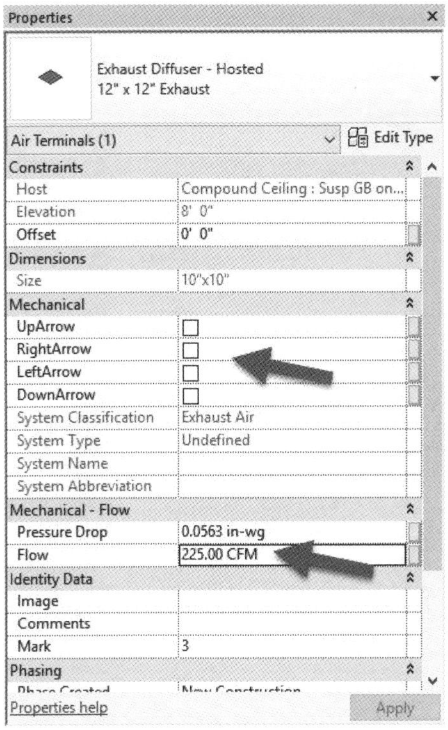

FIGURE 13-3.9 Exhaust diffuser properties

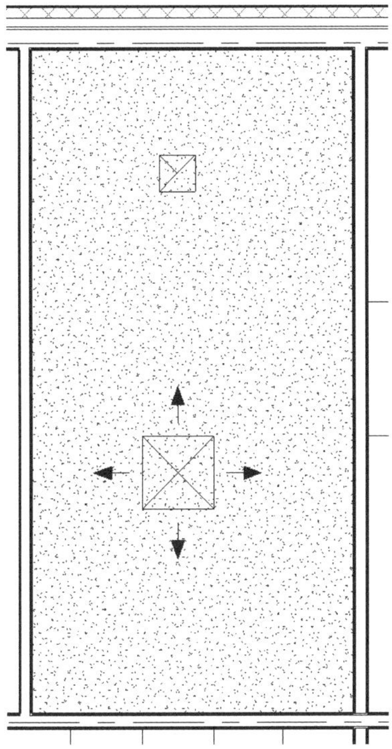

FIGURE 13-3.10 Exhaust diffuser placed

Placing the Air Handling Unit (AHU):

Now you will place the *AHU*, which is the same process for any *Mechanical Equipment* element (e.g., water heater, pump, etc.). The image on the following page (Figure 13-3.11) shows the item you will be placing. It is a simple 3D box which represents the size of the unit. It does not have to have all the minor bumps and recesses modeled, or the controls, as this will make the file size unnecessarily large. In the image, the *AHU* is selected. Whenever a family is selected that has MEP connectors, those connectors are made visible but only while the element is selected. Next to the connection icon is text that lists the duct/pipe size or voltage, depending on what type of connection it is: duct, plumbing or electrical. Right-clicking on one of these icons, and then selecting *Draw Duct (or Pipe/ Wire/Cable Tray/Conduit)* starts the proper tools (i.e., *Duct/Pipe/Wire/Cable Tray/ Conduit*) and sets it to the correct size to match the *Mechanical Equipment* to which you are connecting.

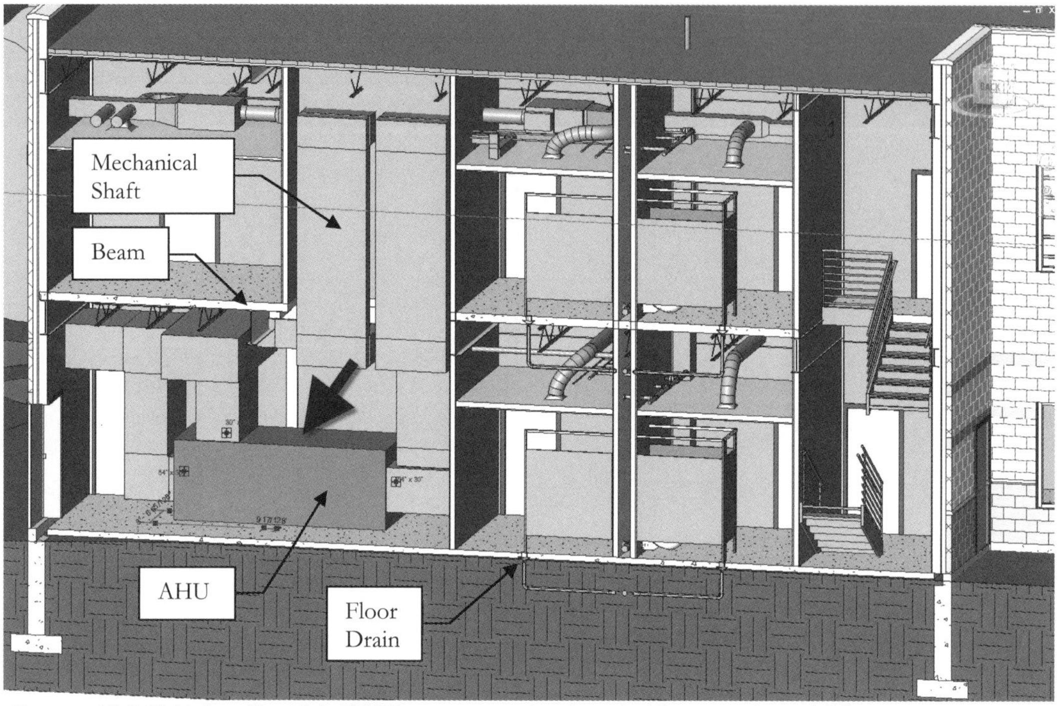

FIGURE 13-3.11 Air handling Unit (AHU); component is selected with connections visible

29. Zoom in to the *Mechanical Room* in the Northeastern corner of the **Level 1- HVAC Floor Plan**.

30. Select **Systems → Mechanical → Mechanical Equipment** tool on the *Ribbon*.
    a. Click **No** if prompted to load a tag.

31. Select **AHU-1** from the *Type Selector*. This was loaded from the provided online file in the previous exercise.

32. Click to place the AHU in the *Mechanical Room*; pick anywhere.

33. Adjust the location to match the dimensions shown in Figure 13-3.12. Do not add the dimensions (or, erase when done).

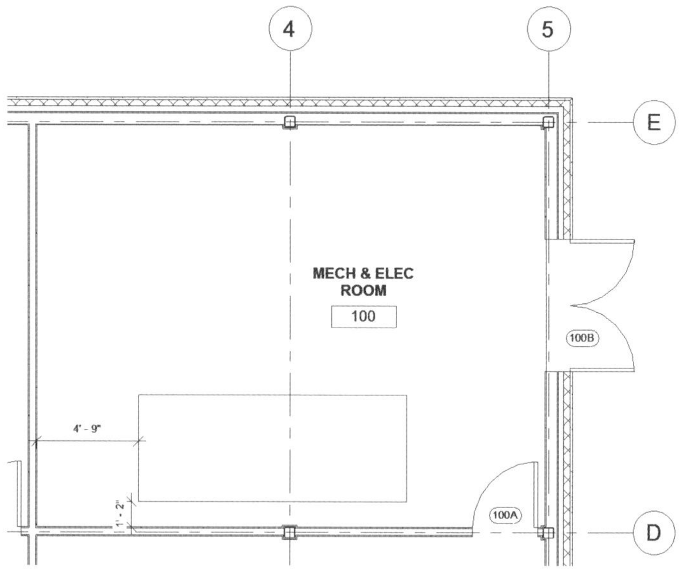

FIGURE 13-3.12 AHU placed. Do not add dimensions!

Finally, you will take a quick look at a few properties related to the AHU.

34. Click the AHU to select it in the **Level 1 – HVAC Floor Plan**.

As previously mentioned, when a family is selected that has MEP connections, they become visible. The square with the plus in it (⊞) represents a connection, and the text next to it indicates the size the ductwork needs to be when connecting to the equipment at that location.

The 30″x54″ connection is actually on the top of the AHU (Figure 13-3.13). A duct connects to the top at this location.

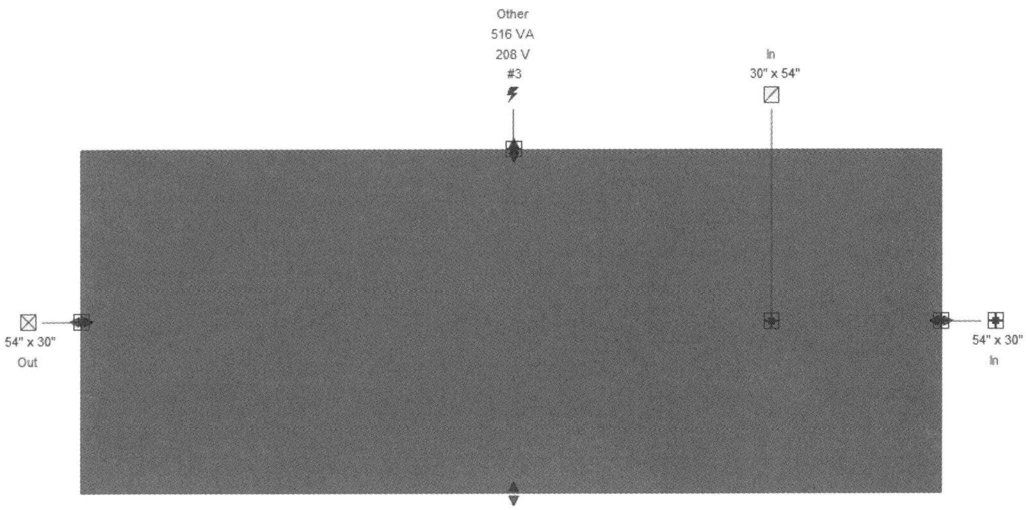

FIGURE 13-3.13 AHU selected in a plan view

35. View the AHU's ***Instance Properties***, via the *Properties Palette.*

Notice the AHU and connector dimensions are adjustable here. Also, notice the types of connections:

- SA = Supply Air
- RA = Return Air
- OA = Outside Air

36. **Save** your project.

FYI: It is possible to get more detailed families of mechanical equipment from some manufacturers. For an example, take a look at Daikin's website: *https://www.daikinapplied.com/resources/revit* .

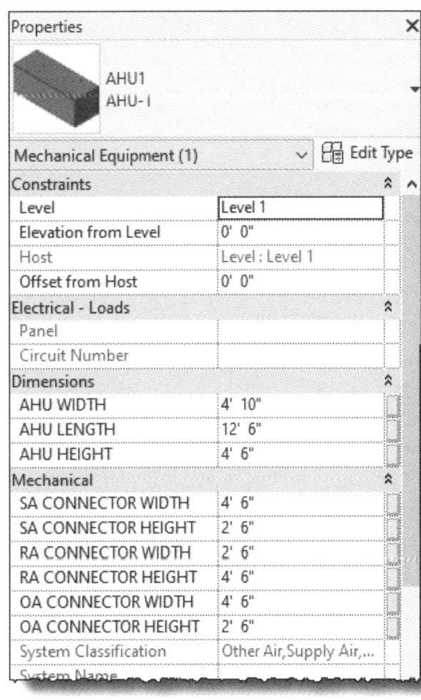

FIGURE 13-3.14 AHU instance properties

Exercise 13-4:
VAV Boxes, MEP Systems and Ductwork

With the diffusers in place, you will now look at placing *VAV* boxes and connect ductwork between the two. Due to the time involved in laying out the ductwork for the entire building, you will only do this to a few rooms so you understand how things work. The Chapter 14 starter file will have the ductwork for the entire building in it.

Placing a VAV Box:

A *Variable Air Volume* box (*VAV*) terminal unit allows the temperature to be efficiently controlled per room or per a group of rooms; each VAV box is connected to a thermostat, which lets it know what the heating/cooling need is. The AHU provides fresh air to the VAV boxes at a constant temperature, volume, humidity, etc. and the VAV box adjusts the air volume to meet the needs of the various spaces served. VAV boxes are typically hidden above the ceiling. You can do an internet search (type "VAV box") for more information on variable air volume terminal units.

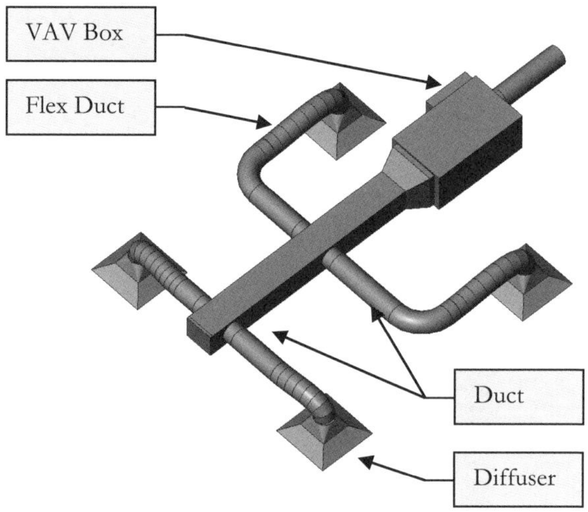

1. Switch to the **Level 1 – HVAC Floor Plan**.

Seeing as you know the VAV box will be placed on the floor and will not be visible in the Ceiling Plan view initially, you will work in the HVAC Floor Plan view. In fact, now that the diffusers are in the correct location relative to the ceiling grid, you can stay in the plan view to place mechanical equipment and draw ductwork.

2. **Zoom** in to the *Associate's Office*, Northwestern corner, again.

3. Select the ***Mechanical Equipment*** tool from the *Ribbon*.

    a. Click **No** if prompted to load a tag.

4. From the *Type Selector*, select *VAV Unit – Fan Powered – Series Flow:* **8."**

5. Set the *Offset* parameter to **8'-6"** in the *Properties Palette.*

6. Press the spacebar as needed to rotate the VAV box.

7. Click to place the element as shown in Figure 13-4.1.

Your model should look similar to Figure 13-4.1; the exact location of the VAV box is not important.

8. **Select** the VAV box.

9. Review its *Instance Properties.*

That is all there is to placing a VAV box. It will now show up in sections created by anyone on the design team. Next, you will place a few more units for more practice.

10. Use *Copy/Rotate* to place seven more VAV boxes as shown in Figure 13-4.2; move the two in the *Exec. Offices* up 1′-0″; you will have 8 total.

FYI: The view's Model Graphics Style has been set to Shading so the mechanical equipment is highlighted better.

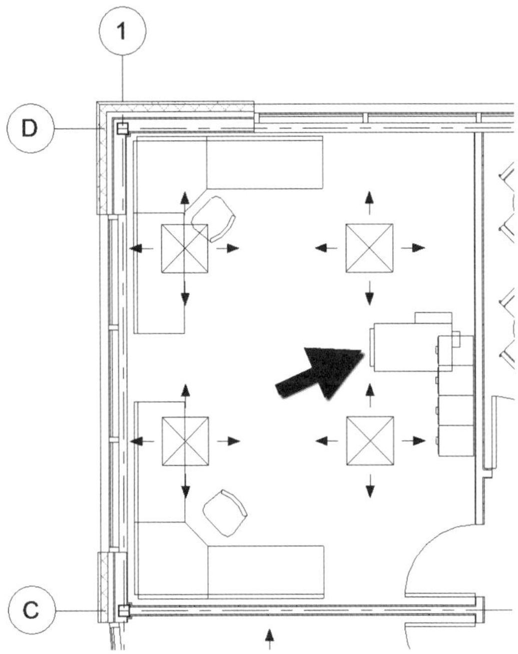

FIGURE 13-4.1 First VAV box placed

TIP: Clicking and dragging an element while holding the Ctrl key is a quick way to make a copy. Also, selecting an element and pressing the spacebar rotates it after it has been placed.

REMEMBER: You can use the arrow keys to nudge (i.e. move) selected elements.

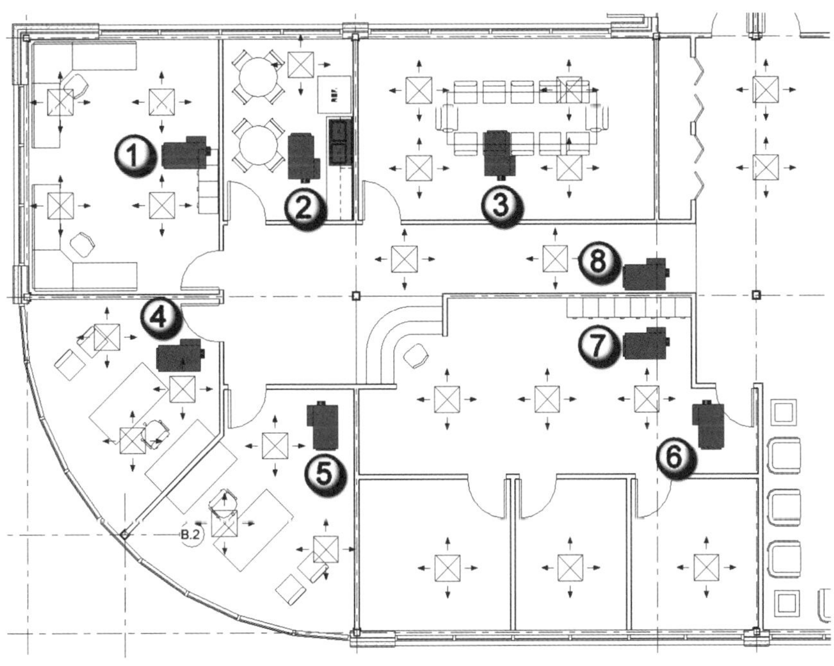

FIGURE 13-4.2
VAV box locations

Creating MEP Systems:

Now that you have the VAV boxes and diffusers placed, you can start to create *MEP Systems*. An *MEP System* is something Revit uses to understand the relationships between the various parts of an HVAC system. The term *MEP System* is specific to Revit and not used in the MEP construction industry.

Below are two examples of an *MEP System* and what they consist of:

- AHU-1 *(system name)*
  - AHU-1 *(Parent: Mechanical Equipment)*
  - One or more VAV boxes *(Child: elements served by parent)*

- VAV-1 *(system name)*
  - VAV-1 *(Parent: Mechanical Equipment)*
  - One or more Diffusers *(Child: elements served by parent)*

> ***FYI:*** *The terms "parent" and "child" are not Revit terms. They are just introduced here to better explain the concept.*

The process of creating a system is fairly simple. You select a "child" element in the project. From the *Ribbon*, you select the *Create Duct System* tool. Next, you give the *System* a name, and add additional child elements and pick the parent element. That is it.

11. Select one of the *diffusers* in the *Associate's Office*.

12. Select **Modify | Air Terminals → Create System → Duct** from the *Ribbon*.

13. Make the following modifications to the *Create Duct System* dialog, then click OK. (Figure 13-4.3).

    a. *System Type:* **Supply Air**
    b. *Name:* **VAV-1**
    c. *Open in System Editor:* **checked**

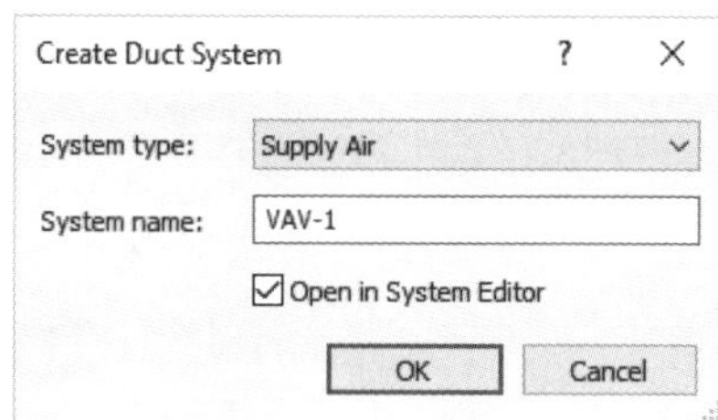

FIGURE 13-4.3 Create Duct System

Revit just created a system named VAV-1. The name is meant to match the name used to describe the "parent" element (the VAV box in this case) in the project. The system name should not be too generic, making it hard to find later once all the systems are created.

14. Notice the options on the *Ribbon* (see image below).

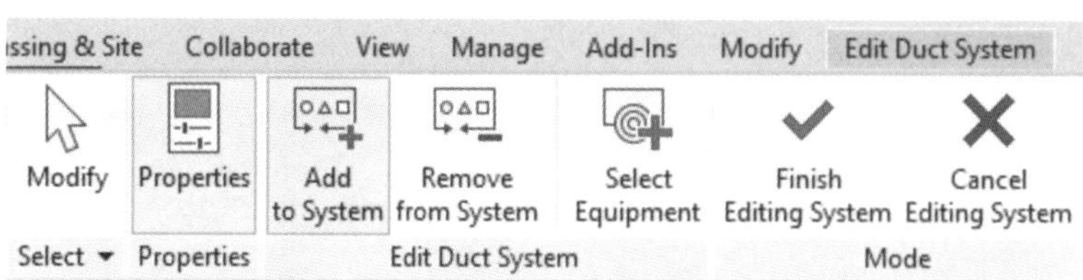

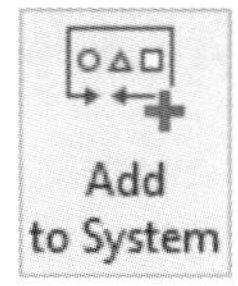

15. Click the ***Add to System*** button on the *Ribbon* (which should already be the default selection).

You are now in the *Add to System* mode. Thus, you can select the other diffusers in the room and add them to the *VAV-1* system.

16. Click to select the other three diffusers in the room to add them to the *System.*
    a. The diffusers will turn from gray lines to black lines when they are selected and considered part of the *System.*

17. Pick **Select Equipment** from the *Ribbon.*
18. Select the VAV box in the same room as the diffusers.

19. Click **Finish Editing System** on the *Ribbon.*

You have now created a *System*!

20. Create **seven** more *Systems* using the same naming convention and the numbers provided in Figure 13-4.2.
    a. *VAV-6* serves the three small offices to the South.
    b. *VAV-7* serves the diffusers in the same room as it.

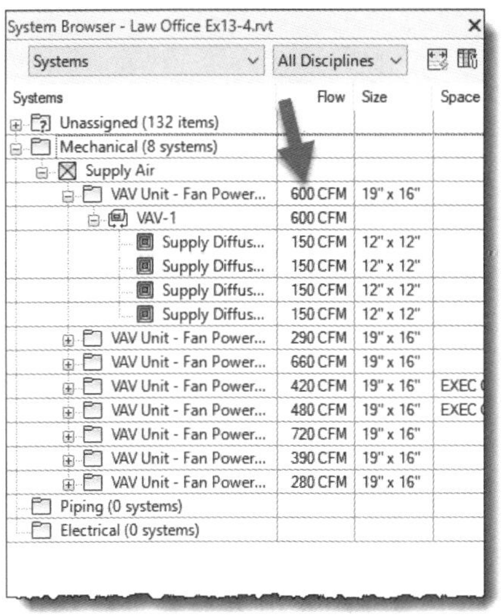

FIGURE 13-4.4 System Browser

Before moving on to the ductwork, you will look at a feature unique to Revit *MEP* that allows you to see the various systems in a list similar to the *Project Browser*; it is called the *System Browser.*

21. Select **View → User Interface → *System Browser.***

You should now see the *System Browser* on the right-hand side of the screen. If you expand the items as shown in the image to the left, you will see *VAV-1* and its total CFM, which is based on the values you entered into each diffuser (Figure 13-4.5).

Ultimately, you want the unassigned section to be empty so everything is on a *System.* If your numbers do not match the book, you should go back and double-check your CFM values.

FYI: The system totals shown above might not update until the project is closed and re-opened.

Adding Ductwork:

The following information will show how to draw the ductwork shown below. This will be an isolated example unrelated to the law office project.

- After selecting the *Duct* tool, you specify the duct *Width*, *Height*, and *Offset*, which is the distance off the floor to the center of the duct, on the *Properties Palette.*
- Next, you pick your **first** and **second** points in the model (Figure 13-4.5A).
- While still in the *Duct* tool, you change the *Properties Palette* settings.
- Now pick the **third** point (Figure 13-4.5A again). Notice the duct transition is automatically added.
- To make the duct go vertical, simply change the *Middle Elevation* (move the cursor back into the drawing window momentarily) and then click a fourth point. A duct will be drawn from the third point to the distance entered, above or below.

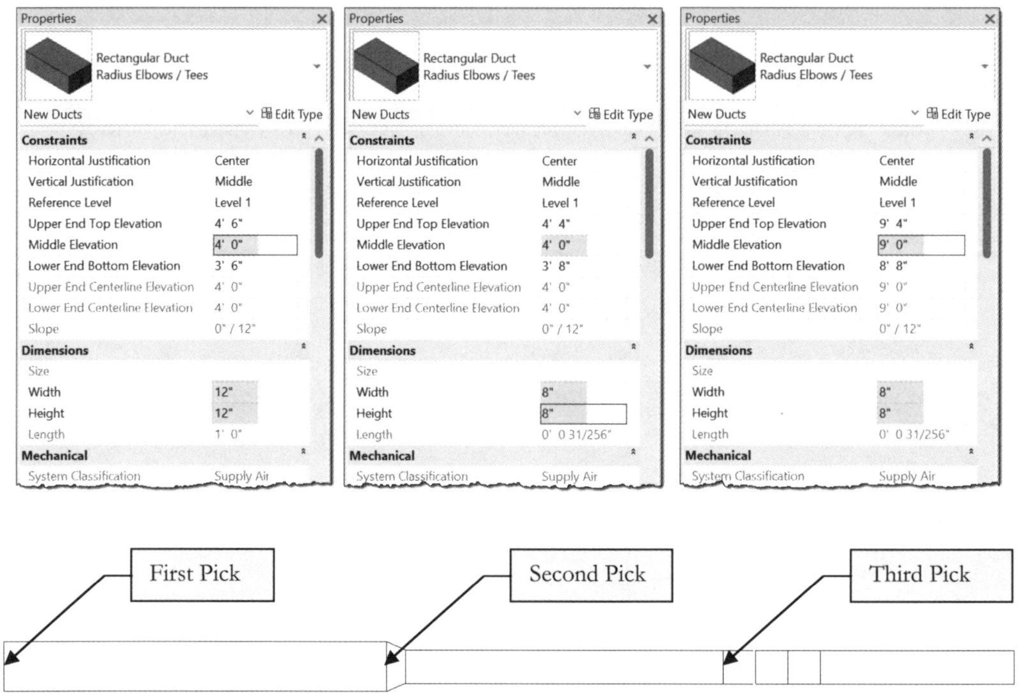

FIGURE 13-4.5A Modeling ductwork; plan view

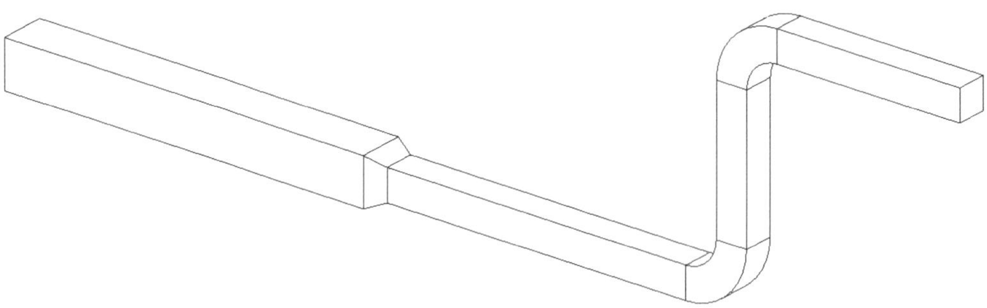

FIGURE 13-4.5B Modeling ductwork; 3D view

Now you will add some ductwork from the VAV box in the *Associate's Office* to the four diffusers.

22. In the **Level 1 – HVAC Floor Plan** view, zoom in to the *Associate's Office.*

23. Select the VAV box to reveal its connectors (Figure 13-4.6).

24. With the VAV selected, right-click on the 19″ x 16″ connector.

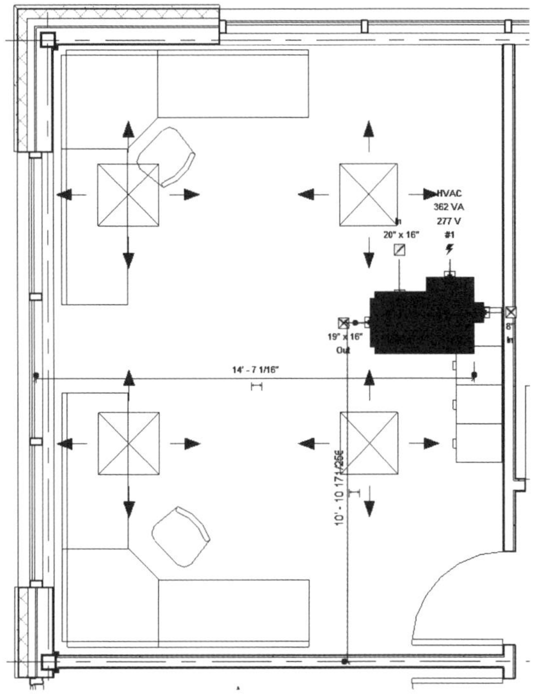

FIGURE 13-4.6 VAV box selected

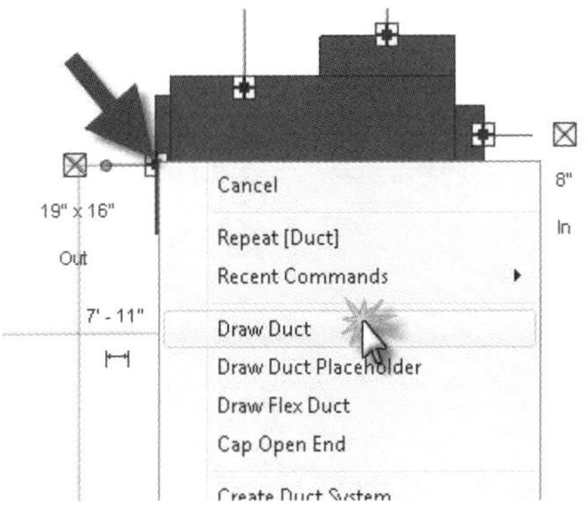

FIGURE 13-4.7 Right-click on connector

25. Select **Draw Duct** from the pop-up menu (Figure 13-4.7).

The *Duct* tool is automatically started, and the size and offset have been adjusted to match the connector size and elevation (see image to right).

26. Set the *Type Selector* to *Rectangular* **Duct: Mitered Elbows / Taps**.

27. Change the duct *Width* to **12″** and the *Height* to **10″** on the *Properties Palette* (changing the default setting shown to the right).

28. Click a point straight out from the connector, near the end of the diffuser (Figure 13-4.8).

29. Click **Modify** to finish the *Duct* tool.

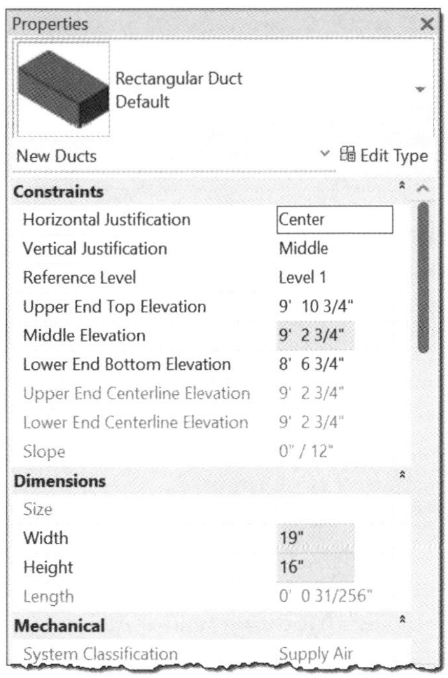

Initial duct settings

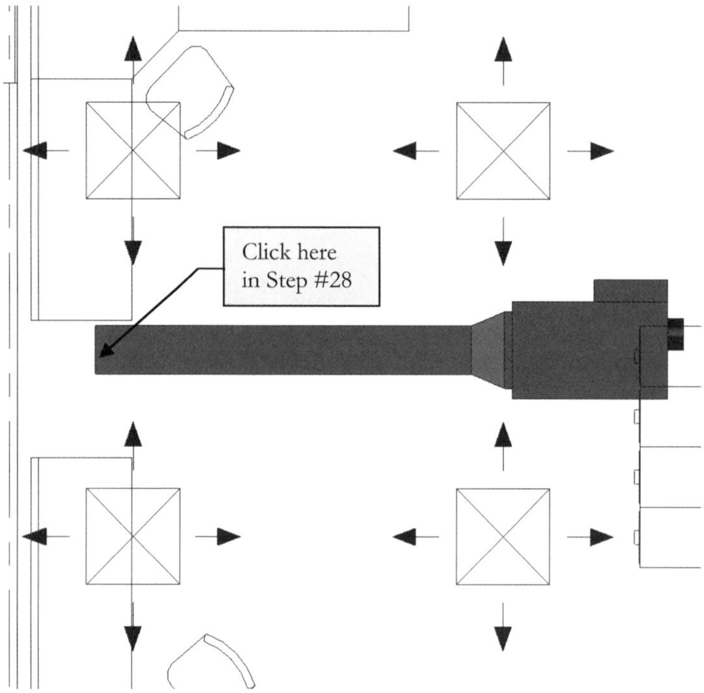

FIGURE 13-4.8 Drawing a duct off of the VAV

This is the main duct for this room/system. Next, you will draw branch ducts that come off of the "main" duct and head towards the *diffusers.*

30. Select the ***Duct*** tool from the *Systems* tab on the *Ribbon.*

31. Set the *Type Selector* to **Round Duct: Taps**.

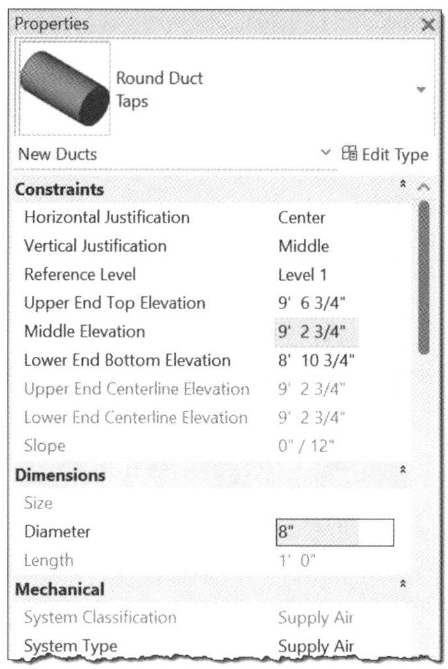

Notice that the Properties Palette changes to show a diameter instead of width and height.

32. Set the *Diameter* to **8″**; make sure the *Middle Elevation* is still **9′ 2 3/4″**.

33. Click the two points shown in Figure 13-4.9. ***TIP:*** Do not align the duct exactly with the air terminal, as this will generate a warning; offset it left or right slightly.

34. Click **Modify** to end the *Duct* tool.

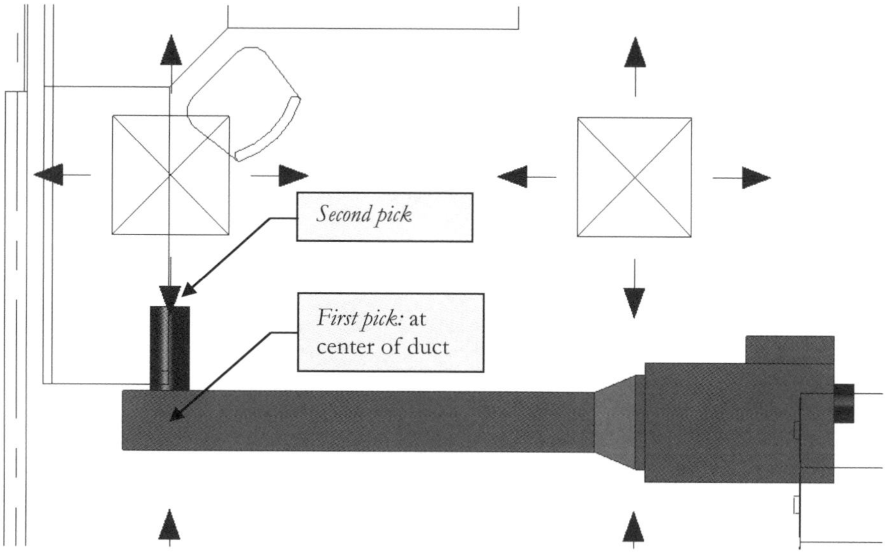

FIGURE 13-4.9 Drawing a branch duct

Next, you will draw another branch duct that turns the corner. Revit will automatically add an elbow at the corner, or duct fitting.

35. Similar to the previous steps, **Draw** an 8″ diameter branch duct by picking, approximately, the three points shown in Figure 13-4.10.

    TIP: *If you have trouble picking the third point, try clicking a little off center for the air terminal.*

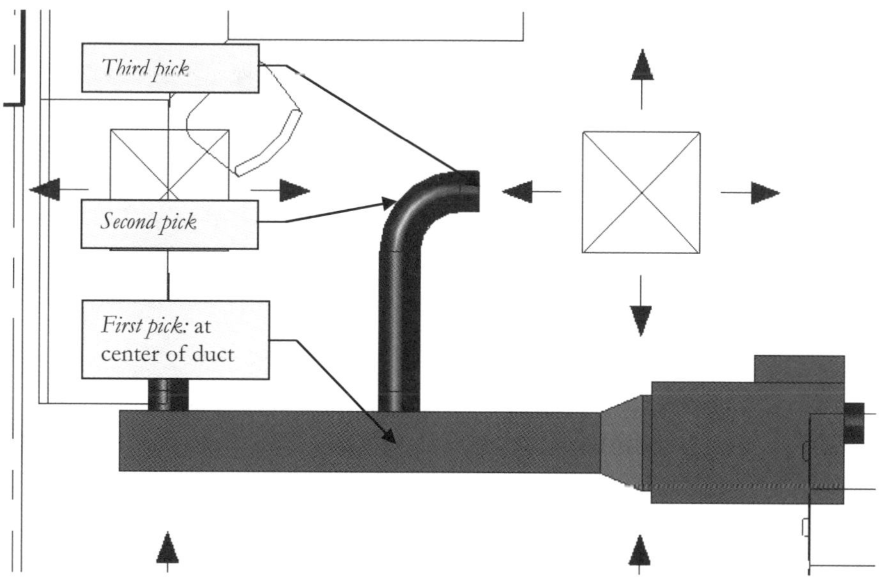

FIGURE 13-4.10 Drawing a branch duct with an elbow

Next, you will mirror the branch ductwork to the other side of the main duct.

36. **Select** the branch ductwork, including the round ducts, taps, and fittings (Figure 13-4.11).

37. Use the ***Mirror*** tool to mirror the selected elements about the center of the VAV box.

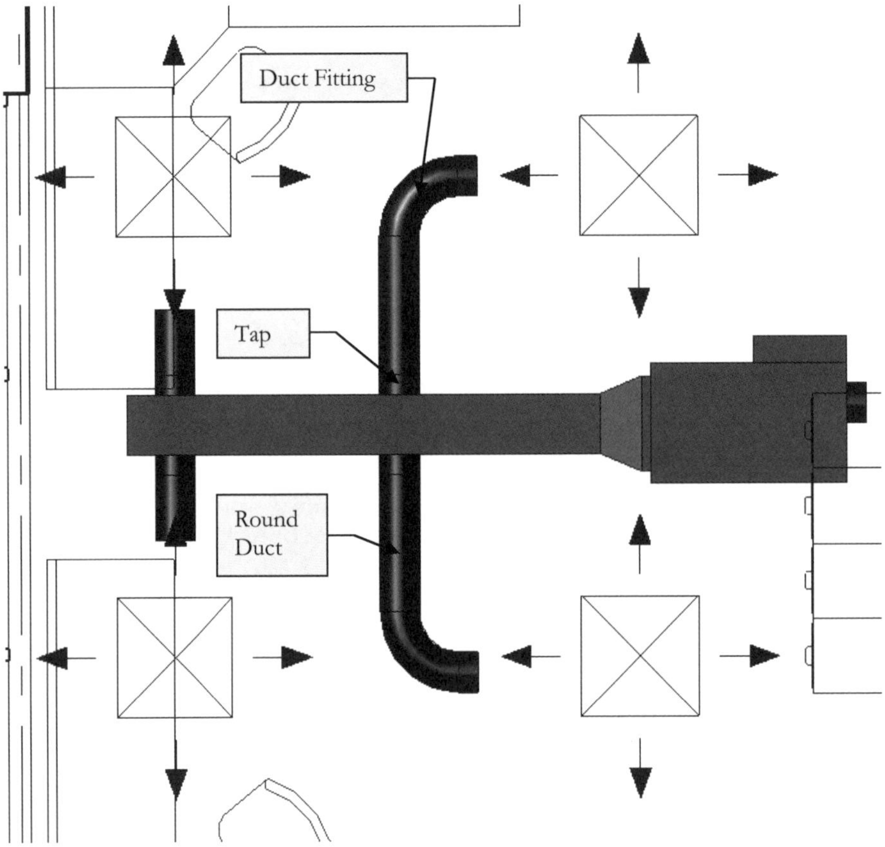

FIGURE 13-4.11 Mirrored "branch" ductwork about the VAV box

The next step will be to draw *Flex Duct* from the "solid" **duct** to the **diffuser**; things work best when drawn from in this order.

38. **Select** the "solid" round duct in the upper-left corner (Figure 13-4.12).

39. With the duct selected, **right-click** on the *connector* icon at the open end.

40. Pick **Draw Flex Duct** from the pop-up menu.

41. Notice the *Diameter* is automatically set to **8″** on the *Properties Palette.*

42. Pick at the <u>center</u> of the diffuser.

    a. Make sure you see the special "connector" snap before picking to ensure the flex duct gets connected to the duct "system" and is drawn at the right elevation.

FYI: *The connector on the diffuser is 12″x12″, so when you connect an 8″ diameter flex duct (as in this example), Revit automatically adds a transition fitting between the diffuser and the flex duct.*

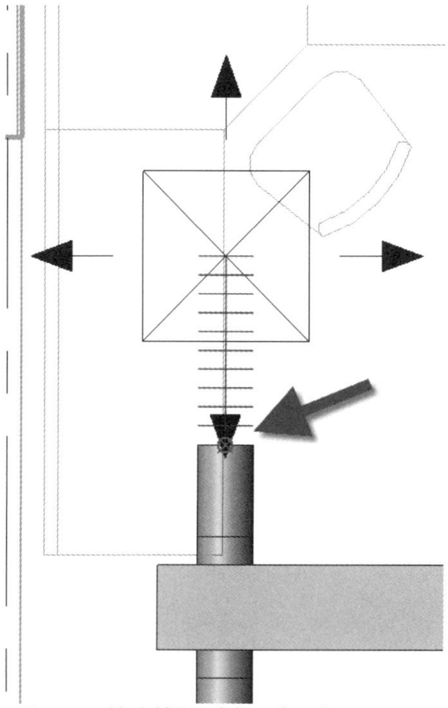

FIGURE 13-4.12 Modeling flex duct

43. Select **Modify**.

44. **Select** the flex duct.

45. View its *Instance Properties.*

46. Set the *Flex Pattern* to **Flex**.

47. **Repeat** the previous steps to add 8″ *Flex Duct* to the other three diffusers (Figure 13-4.13).

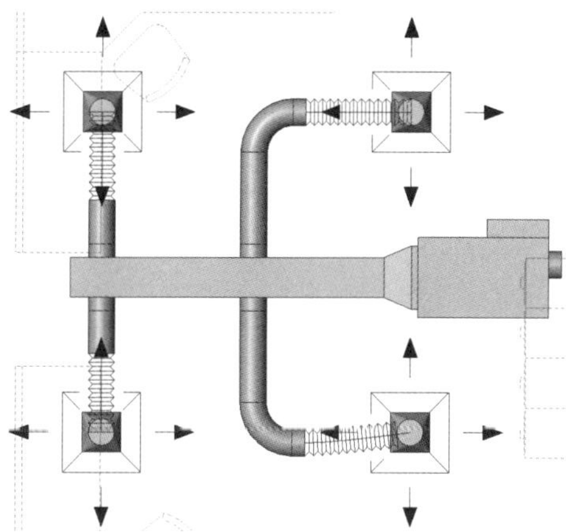

FIGURE 13-4.13 Modeling flex duct

The last thing you need to do to complete this system is to add an end cap to the open end of the main duct.

48. Load the following family:

    a. *Family name:* **Rectangular Endcap**

    b. *Folder:* Duct\Fittings\Rectangular\Caps

49. Select the main 12x10 duct.

50. Click the **Cap Open Ends** tool on the *Ribbon.*

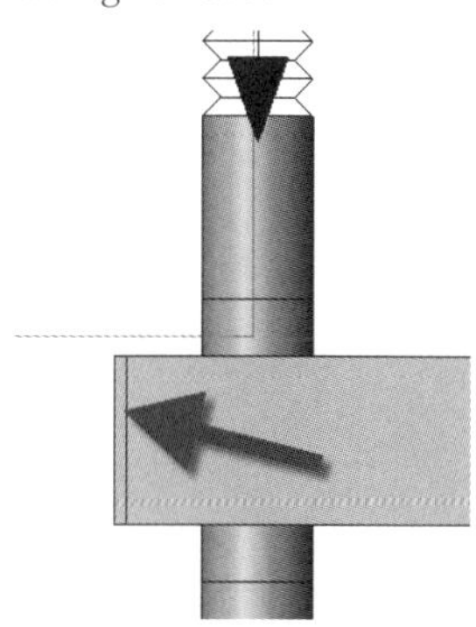

FIGURE 13-4.14 Endcap added

A cap is added to the open end of the duct (Figure 13-4.14).

Now with the system complete, you can select the VAV box and see the total CFM (outlet airflow parameter), 600CFM in this case, in the *Instance Properties*. This is a handy way to verify the system is complete. Another good test is to hover your cursor over any part of the system and press **Tab** until the entire system highlights; if you then click, it will select everything highlighted. When the entire system never highlights, then something is not properly connected. In this case you need to select one of the ducts near the problem area, pull its end back and then drag it back to the proper area, looking for the "connection" snap; you may even have to delete and redraw some elements. This can be tricky but gets easier with experience.

Now you will repeat the previous steps in order to complete the other ductwork systems.

51. Add the remaining ductwork at the other VAV box locations:
    a. Reference Figure 13-4.16.
    b. Make sure you use the duct with "taps" and not "tees."
    c. All "branch" ducts are 8″ diameter *Round Duct.*
        i. Exception: *Break Room* should be 10″ diameter.
    d. The "main" duct sizes vary; see image.

52. **Save** your project.

With the small amount of information covered in this chapter you can model the remaining portion of the building's HVAC system. However, due to space limitations in this book, you will not be expected to do so.

> ***DESIGN INTEGRATION:*** *If you switch to the cross section created earlier in the book, you will see the HVAC now added to the view (Figure 13-4.15). Here you can visually see there is enough space between the ceiling and the structure.*

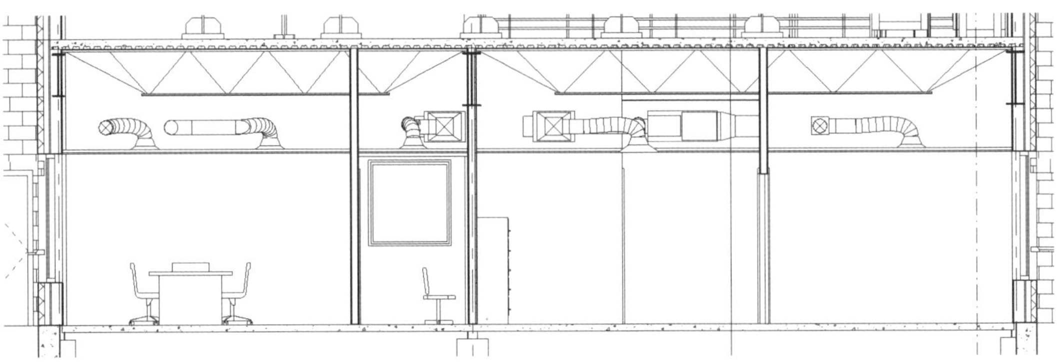

FIGURE 13-4.15 Ductwork now visible in the architectural cross section view

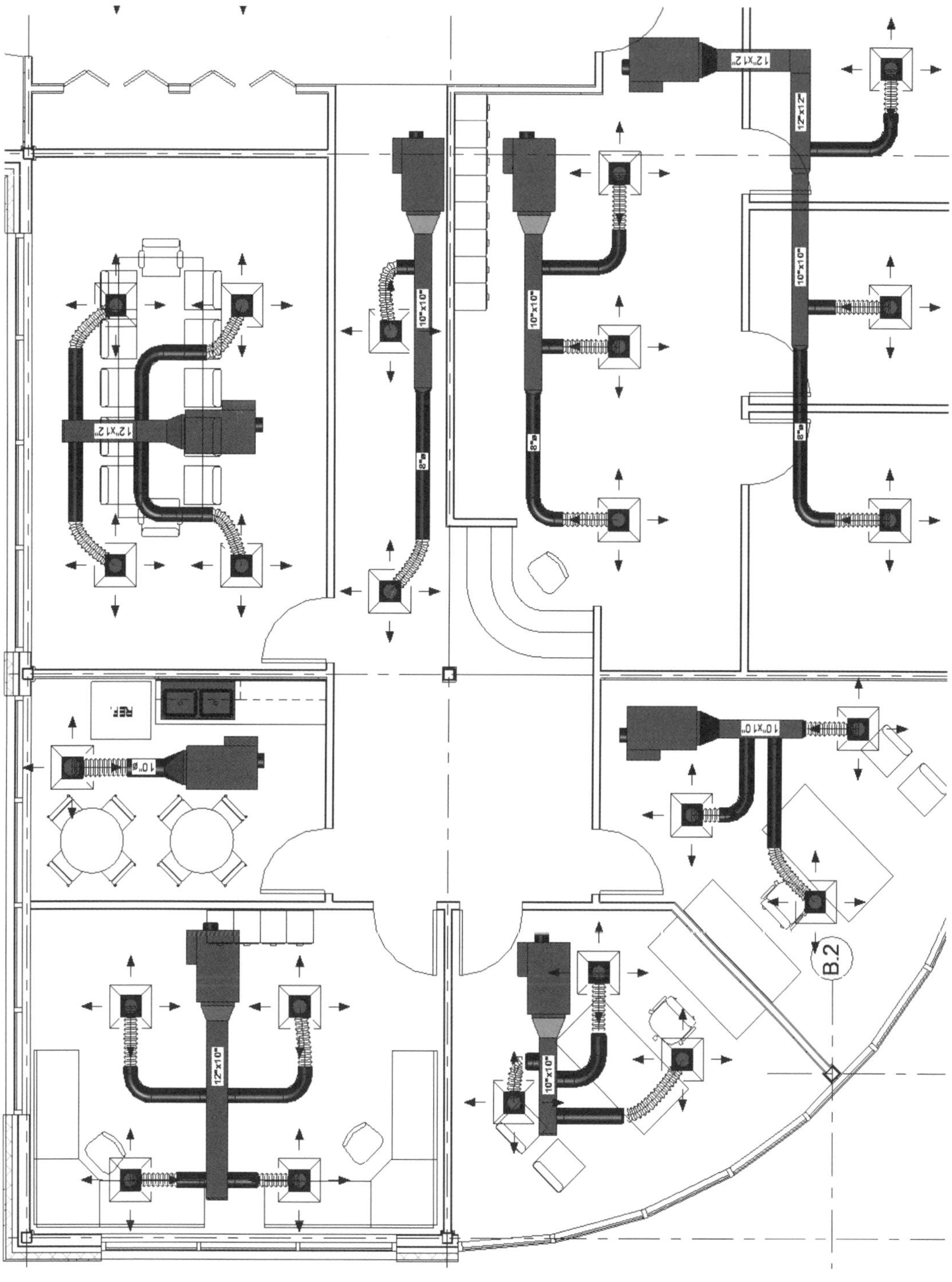

FIGURE 13-4.16 Ductwork added from each VAV box to the diffusers

Exercise 13-5:
Plumbing Layout

This short Exercise will review the *Plumbing* and *Piping* tools in Revit *MEP*. Autodesk has done a good job keeping steps similar between tasks. In fact, the steps to model piping are identical to laying out ductwork! Therefore, due to this fact and page limitations we will only place a water heater and connect piping to the sink in the *Break Room.*

The image below shows the entire piping and plumbing system for the law office. This data will be available in the Chapter 14 starter file (Figure 13-5.1).

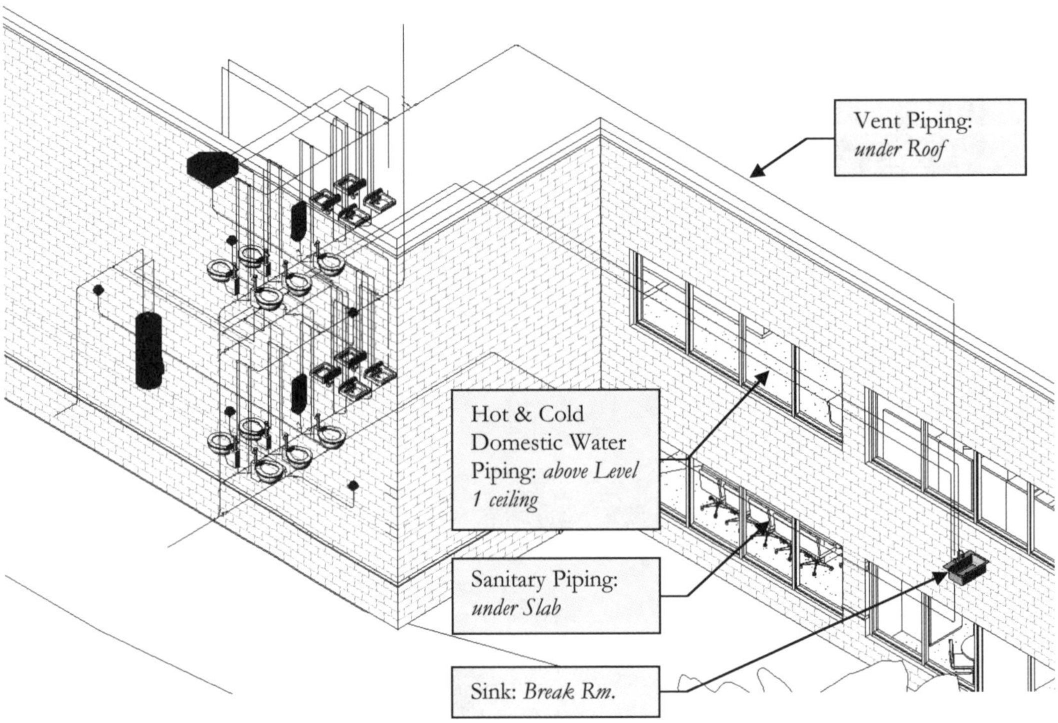

FIGURE 13-5.1 3D view of law office plumbing system

Placing the Water Heater:

1. **Start** Revit and open your Law Office project.

2. Switch to the **Level 1 – Domestic Water Floor Plan** view.

3. **Zoom** in to the *Mechanical and Electrical Room* in the Northeastern corner.

4. Select the ***Plumbing Equipment*** tool from the *Systems* tab on the *Ribbon*.

5. Select the **40 gallon** *Water Heater* from the *Type Selector*. If it is not listed, load it from the content provided with this book.

6. **Click** approximately as shown in Figure 13-5.2 to place the element.

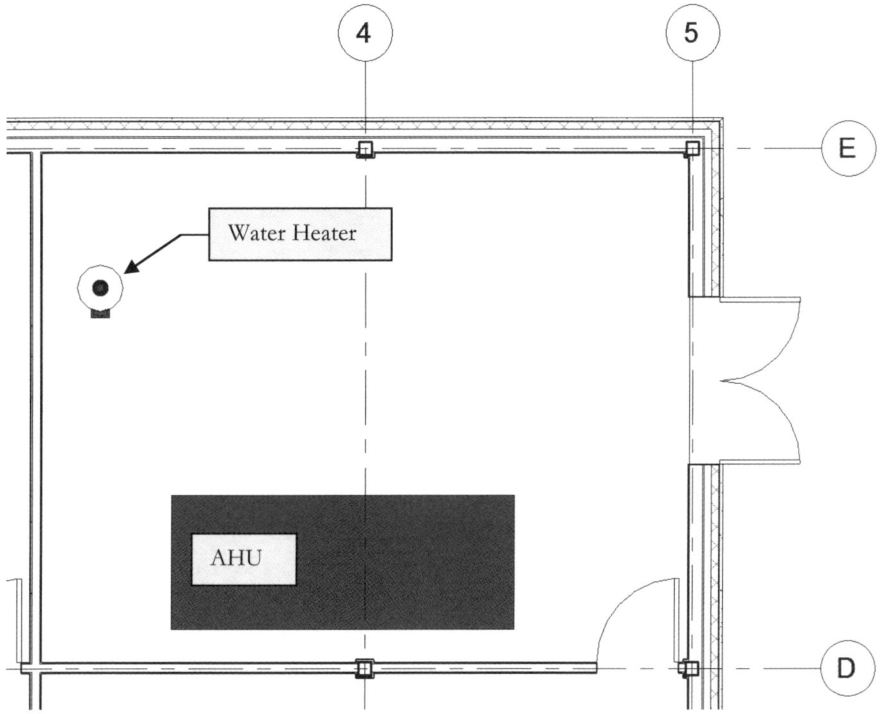

FIGURE 13-5.2 Level 1 – Domestic Water Floor Plan; water heater added

Immediately after the element is placed, it is selected. Notice all the connectors available (Figure 13-5.3). This one family has the three major types of connectors: duct, pipe, and power.

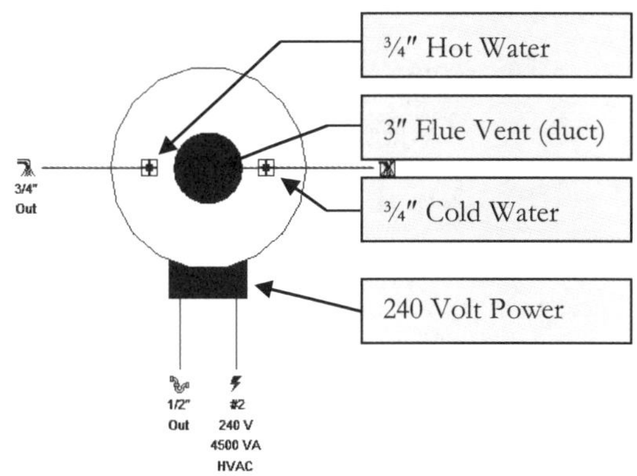

FIGURE 13-5.3 Water Heater connectors

7. Click **Modify** to finish the *Plumbing Equipment* tool.

The water heater that comes with Revit is set to be in the *Mechanical Equipment* category. The one you loaded from the online files has been changed to the *Plumbing Equipment* category so the water heater will show up if the *Mechanical Equipment* is hidden from the domestic water plan views; you would not typically want to see all the VAV boxes in this view. Turn the *Mechanical Equipment* category off if you want.

Piping Project Units:

Because you did not start from an MEP template, you need to change one setting so you are able to create pipes that are smaller than 1″ in diameter.

8. Select **Manage → Settings → Project Units** from the *Ribbon*.

9. Set the *Discipline* to **Piping** (Figure 13-5.4).

10. Click the button to the right of **Pipe Size**.

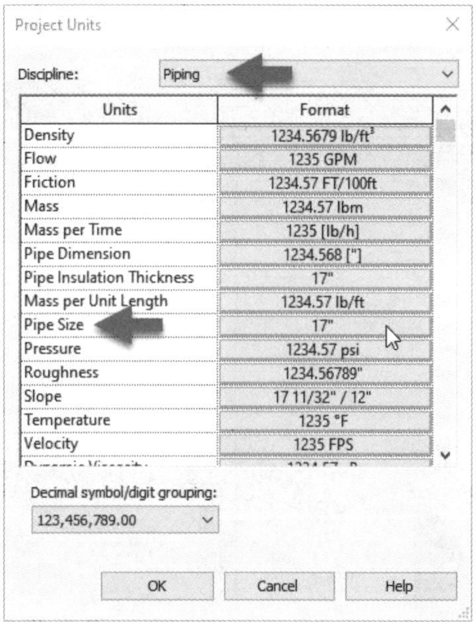

FIGURE 13-5.4 Project units; HVAC

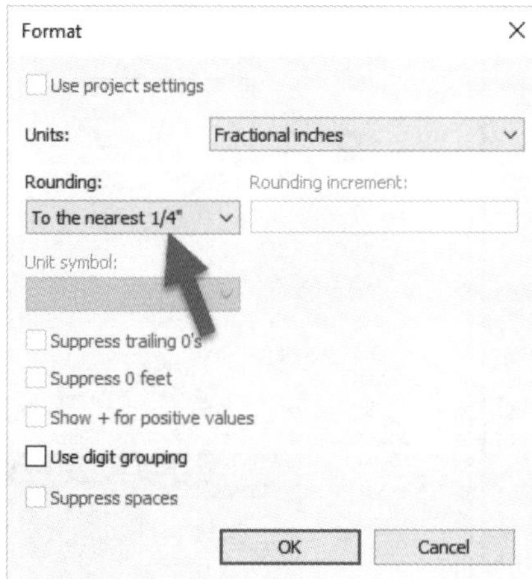

FIGURE 13-5.5 Project units: Format

11. Set the *Rounding* to **To the nearest 1/4″**.

12. Click **OK** twice to close the open dialog boxes.

Modeling Piping:

Now you will run hot and cold water piping from the *Mechanical Room* to the sink in the *Break Room*. Piping views usually have the *Detail Level* set to *Medium*, as this will make the pipe single line (the pipe's centerline) and the ducts are still two line (actual thickness). *Detail Level* of *Coarse* makes both ductwork and piping single line and *Fine* makes them both two line. Small pipe drawn with two lines bleeds together into one fat line and this also decreases model performance.

13. In the **Level 1 – Domestic Water Floor Plan** view, select the water heater.

14. **Right-click** on the hot water connector (see Figure 13-5.3).

15. Select **Draw Pipe** from the pop-up menu; set the *Type Selector* to **Standard**.

16. Set the *Middle Elevation* to **9′-8″** in *Properties*.

    a. Notice the pipe diameter is automatically set to ¾″ because you right clicked on the MEP connector on the water heater to start the command.

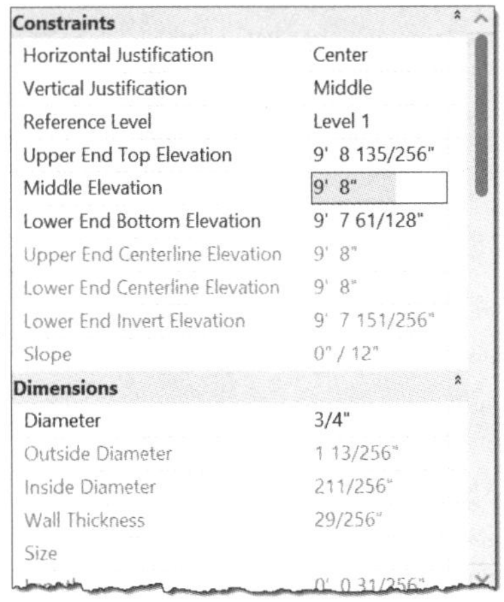

Notice, on the *Ribbon*, that you can specify a slope and Revit will automatically adjust the piping in the Z direction, that is, vertically, to maintain the required slope. This is used in sanitary and rain leader piping.

Now you need a vertical pipe up to 9′-8″, which is the height the hot water piping will run above the ceiling. Revit will automatically draw this vertical pipe for you when clicking away from the water heater (i.e., "second pick" in Figure 13-5.6).

17. Pick points 2 and 3 as shown in Figure 13-5.6; make sure the *Diameter* is **3/4″** and the *Middle Elevation* is still **9′-8″** on the *Properties Palette.*

You now have a vertical piece of pipe that goes from the water heater connector up to 9′-8″ above the floor.

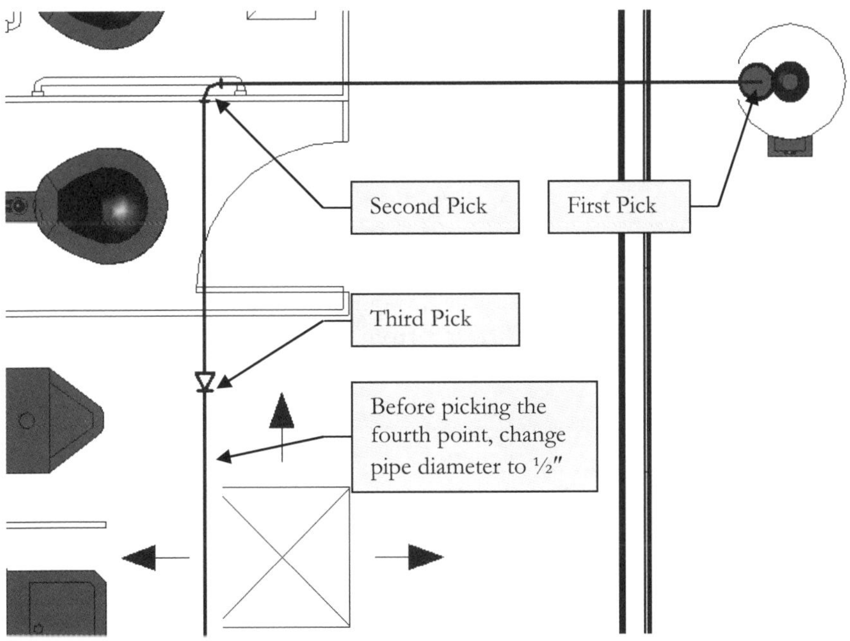

FIGURE 13-5.6 Hot water piping added

18. Set the *Diameter* to **½″** and leave the *Offset* at **9′-8.″**

19. Pick points 4 and 5 as shown in Figure 13-5.7.

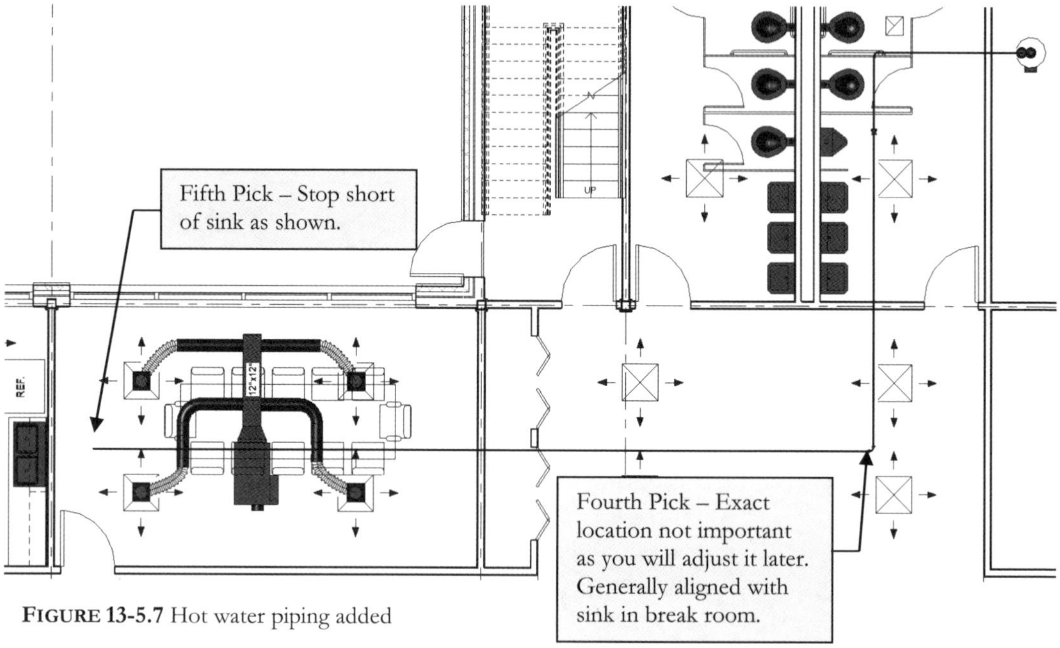

FIGURE 13-5.7 Hot water piping added

If you run the *Interference Check* from the *Collaborate* tab, you will see that the pipe conflicts with the VAV box in the *Conference Room* (comparing *Mechanical Equipment* to *Piping*)!

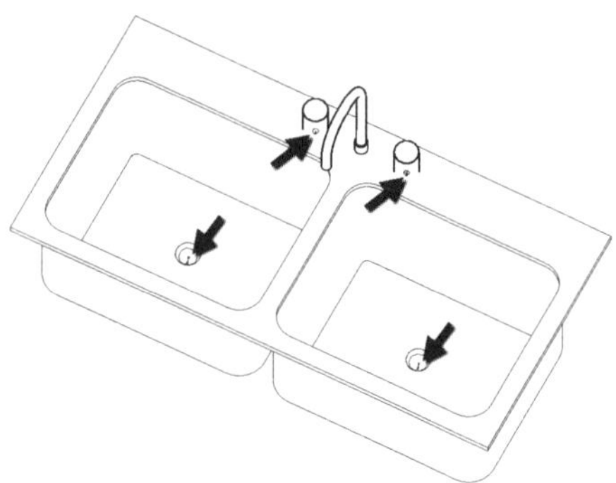

FIGURE 13-5.8 Sink family

Because you do not know the elevation of the hot water connector, it is easier to draw pipe from the sink to the pipe you just drew nearby. Another thing to note is that the connector is on a horizontal surface, so the pipe needs to drop down vertically and then over into the wall; see image to the left from the *Family Editor.* Finally, two connectors are provided for the sink drains.

20. Select the sink and then right-click on the hot water connector (Figure 13-5.9).

TIP: As you likely already know, the hot water is always on the left when you are facing the sink.

21. Click **Draw Pipe** from the menu.

22. Change the *Middle Elevation* to **2′-0″** on the *Properties Palette.*

23. *First Pick:* pick a point within the interior stud wall, directly to the east of the hot water connector. A vertical and horizontal pipe will be drawn.

24. Change the *Middle Elevation* to **9′-8″**. ***REMEMBER:*** *This is the same height as the pipe coming from the water heater.*

25. *Second Pick:* Click the endpoint of the pipe coming from the water heater. (If they do not align, follow the next step.)

26. If the pipe does not align with the pipe coming from the water heater (which it probably doesn't), your second pick should stop short of the previously drawn pipe so you can align it first. Use the ***Align*** tool to move the previously drawn pipe to align with the pipe coming from the sink. Finally, select one of the pipes and drag the endpoint over to the other (now aligned) pipe.

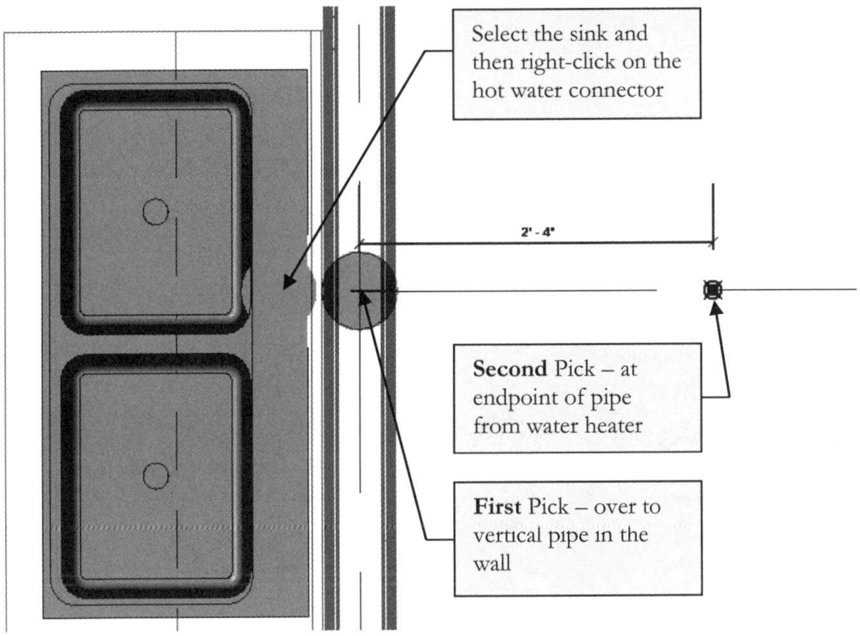

FIGURE 13-5.9 Sink piping

The two horizontal pipes at 9′-8″ will automatically clean up, so there will be no joint; when a union is needed, it needs to be manually added. Now you will add the cold water piping.

27. Use the same process to draw the cold water piping (Figure 13-5.10).
    a. Draw cold water from the water heater towards the North exterior wall. This will be the entry point for the building's water; middle elevation at **10′-0″**.
    b. Off of the water line just drawn, draw a ¾″ pipe as shown in Figure 13-5.10, heading towards the sink in the *Break Room.*
    c. Transition to a ½″ pipe next to the hot water transition.

The cold water is drawn 4″ above the hot water to avoid conflicts when they cross each other. Notice, when they do cross, the lower one is graphically interrupted (Figure 13-5.10). You may have to select the *Tee* and change it to a *Generic Tee* via the *Type Selector*.

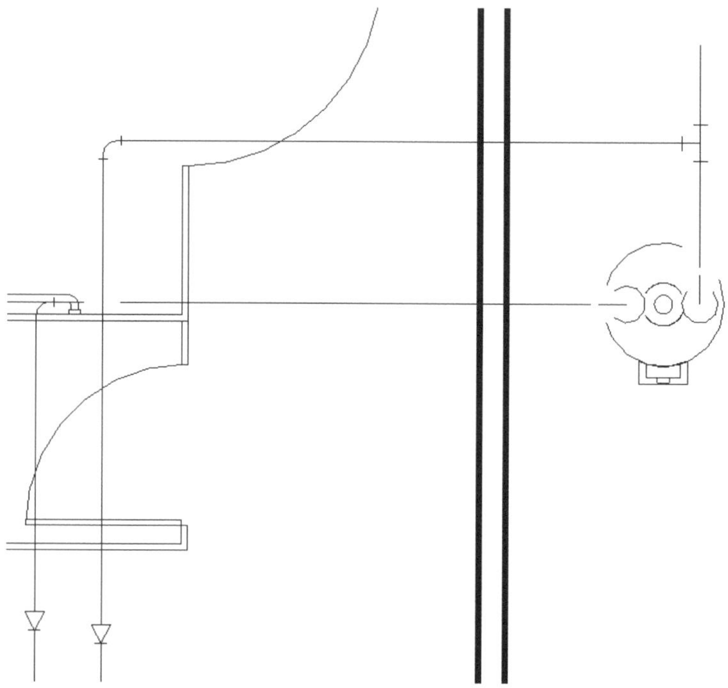

FIGURE 13-5.10 Cold water piping at 10′-0″

Below is a 3D view of the piping you have added to your law office project. You would continue this process to add drinking fountains, floor drains and the route piping to all connections. You should also create systems just like the examples in the HVAC exercise.

FIGURE 13-5.11 3D view of piping added to model

28. **Save** and **back up** your work to a flash drive or external hard drive.

Connect Into Feature

Revit MEP provides a tool to help simplify the process of connecting a family to a pipe or duct. If a family has a duct or pipe connector Revit will show the **Connect Into** tool on the *Ribbon* when that family ID is selected. If you select this tool, you can then select a nearby pipe or duct to connect to. What you select has to match the connector type; for example, if the family has a pipe connector you would select a nearby pipe. Revit will then automatically route pipe between the two. This may not always give the results desired and will not even work in some situations. But when it does work, it saves a lot of time.

When you select the **Connect Into** tool you will see the following prompt if the family has more than one connector in it (Figure 13-5.12). This lets Revit know which connector you wish to use within the family. Only connectors which do not already have anything connected to them will appear in this list.

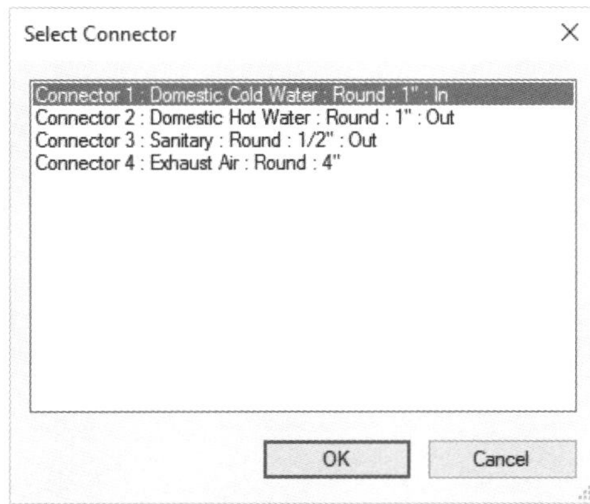

FIGURE 13-5.12 Prompt related to *Connect Into* tool

This tool is a little different than the **Generate Layout** tool which tries to do much more. The Generate Layout tool requires the elements be part of a *Duct* system, whereas the *Connect Into* tool does not. See Revit's help system for more on these tools.

System Browser

Be sure to take a look at the System Browser, **View → User Interface → System Browser**, again to see the Piping items listed there (Figure 13-5.13). Notice the three categories:

- Domestic Cold Water
- Domestic Hot Water
- Sanitary

This is a good way to track total flows and validate Revit's MEP connections. Anything listed under **Unassigned** is not properly connected.

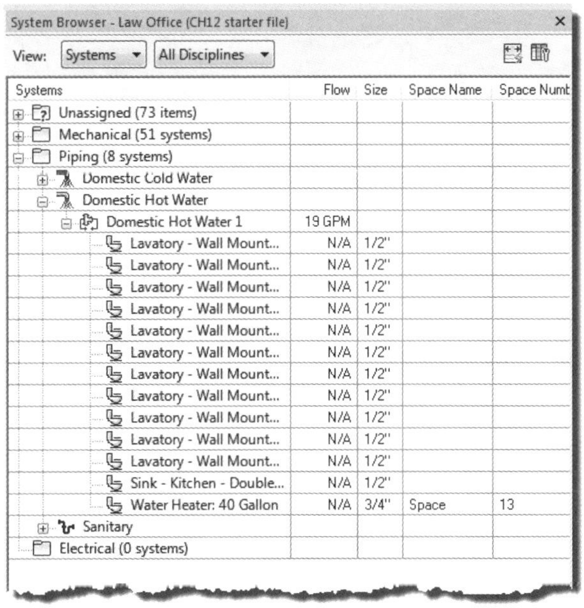

FIGURE 13-5.13 System Browser; showing piping

Self-Exam:

The following questions can be used as a way to check your knowledge of this lesson. The answers can be found at the bottom of this page.

1. Pressing the spacebar, while placing a component, rotates it. (T/F)
2. You can use *Transfer Project Settings* to import various settings from another project which is set up the right way. (T/F)
3. Modeling piping is very different from ductwork. (T/F)
4. In the ductwork view, set the ______________ to *Mechanical* so the architectural walls turn gray.
5. Ducts will show up as long as they are within the ____________________ .

Review Questions:

The following questions may be assigned by your instructor as a way to assess your knowledge of this section. Your instructor has the answers to the review questions.

1. Everyone on the design team must use the same release of Revit. (T/F)
2. You changed the *Project Browser* to sort by ________________.
3. Air terminals (i.e., diffusers) can be either hosted or non-hosted. (T/F)
4. Selecting several diffusers allows you to change the CFM at once. (T/F)
5. Which family did you place that has all three major types of connectors:

   (i.e., pipe, duct and power) ______________________ .
6. A *View Template* always changes the *View Scale*. (T/F)
7. Pressing the spacebar, while placing a component, mirrors it. (T/F)
8. A change in ______________________ was required in order to draw pipe smaller than 1" in diameter.
9. Duct and pipe elbows and transitions have to be added manually. (T/F)
10. Revit *MEP Systems* are used to understand the relationships between the various parts of an HVAC and plumbing system. (T/F)

SELF-EXAM ANSWERS:
1 - T, **2** - T, **3** - F, **4** - Discipline, **5** – View Range

Lesson 14
Electrical System

This chapter will introduce the electrical documentation capabilities of Autodesk Revit. You will develop the outlet and power panel layout as well as the lighting design.

Exercise 14-1:
Introduction to Revit MEP – Electrical

The previous chapter introduced the *User Interface* for Revit's *MEP* tools. If you have not reviewed that information, you may want to do so now.

Mechanical, HVAC, plumbing, and electrical engineers work closely together and are often in the same office.

In this chapter, you will add the views, content, and annotations required to document the electrical system. However, as in the previous chapters, you will not be covering any advanced concepts, such as wire sizing and load balancing at a power panel.

Starting with Revit MEP 2011, the software can create code-compliant panelboard schedules using the *Demand Factors* and *Load Classifications* functionality. Most electrical designs for buildings in the United States are based on the National Electrical Code (NEC). There are still things Revit cannot do, for example, arc-flash/short-circuit analysis and point-by-point lighting analysis. Other programs are still used for this, such as SKM Power Tools and ElumTools.

> *WARNING: This is strictly a fictitious project. Although some effort has been made to make the electrical design realistic, this system has not been designed by an electrical engineer. There are many codes and design considerations that need to be made on a case-by-case basis.*

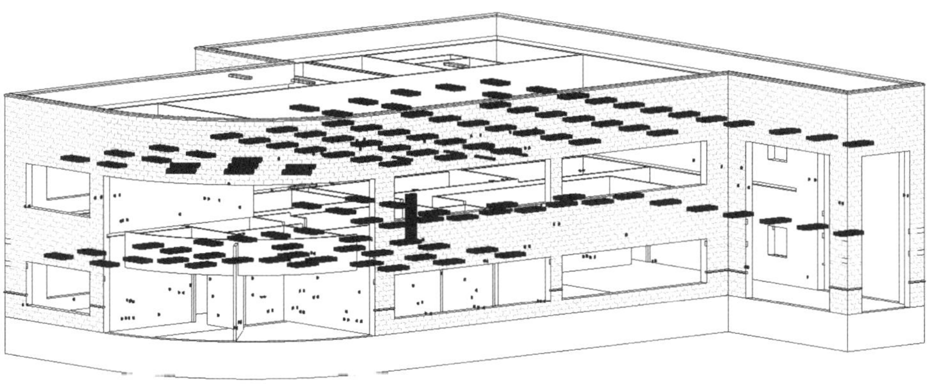

Exercise 14-2:
Creating Views and Loading Content

Most of the major MEP setup was done in the previous chapter with the ***Transfer Project Standards*** tool. If you have not done that yet, you should go to Chapter 13 and do so. You will set up views in which to model and annotate the electrical aspects of the building. These views will be similar to the floor plan views that currently exist for the architectural, mechanical, and structural plans.

1. **Open** the Chapter 14 starter file from the **online files** (see inside of front cover).
    a. The starter file has a more complete mechanical system compared to what was covered in the previous chapter.

Creating Mechanical Plan Views:

Next, you will create the following floor plan views *(using View Template listed to right)*:

- Level 1 – Power Floor Plan *(Electrical Plan)*
- Level 2 – Power Floor Plan *(Electrical Plan)*
- Level 1 – Systems Floor Plan *(Electrical Plan)*
- Level 2 – Systems Floor Plan *(Electrical Plan)*

Next, you will create the following ceiling plan views *(using View Template listed)*:

- Level 1 – Lighting Plan *(Electrical Ceiling)*
- Level 2 – Lighting Plan *(Electrical Ceiling)*

After creating each of these views, you will apply a **View Template**, which lets you quickly set all view-related parameters to a saved standard.

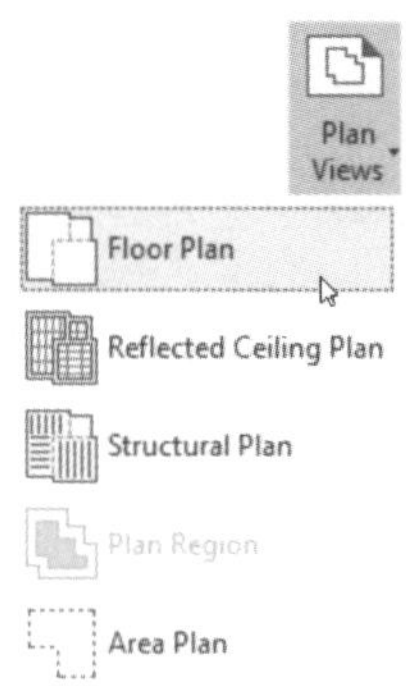

2. While in the law office project, select **View → Create → Plan Views → Floor Plan**.

3. **Uncheck** *Do not duplicate existing views.*

4. In the *New Plan* dialog box, select:
    a. *Floor Plan Views:* **Level 1**

5. Click **OK**.

Next you will rename the *View* and apply a *View Template.*

6. In the *Project Browser*, right-click on Coordination\Floor Plans**Level 1(1)**.
7. Select **Rename** from the pop-up menu.
8. Enter: **Level 1 – Power Floor Plan**.

   FYI: *This is the name that will appear below the drawing when it is placed on a sheet.*

9. Click **OK**.
10. Set the *View Scale* to **¼" = 1'-0"**.

View Templates:

Next, you will apply a *View Template* to your view so it is closer to what is needed for the design and documentation of an electrical power plan.

11. Once again, right-click on **Level 1 – Power Floor Plan** in the *Project Browser.*
12. Click **Apply Template Properties…** from the pop-up menu.
13. On the left, select **Electrical Plan**.

You are now in the *Apply View Template* dialog (compare to Figure 13-2.6). Take a moment to observe all the settings it has stored and are about to be applied to the selected view, the one you right-clicked on.

Notice the *View Scale* is set to ⅛"=1'-0". You know the scale needs to be ¼" = 1'-0" and you have already set that. You will uncheck the *View Scale* so it is not included when the template is applied.

14. **Uncheck** *View Scale.*
15. Click **OK** to apply the *View Template.*

Next, you will set up the remaining views. It is expected that you will refer back to the previous steps if you need a review of the process.

> ***POWER USER TIP:*** *A firm template file can have "placeholder" Revit Links loaded into it, one link for architectural and another for structural. This allows the View Templates to consider visibility settings for the linked files as well (e.g., hiding the architectural grid lines). When the actual architectural model is available, the placeholder link is swapped out using the* Manage Links *dialog and the* Reload From *tool therein.*

16. Create the remaining electrical views listed on page 14-2:

    a. Each should be **1/4" = 1'-0"**.

    b. The *View Template* to be used is listed to the right, in parentheses, on page 14-2.

    c. Be sure to select *Reflected Ceiling Plan* when creating the ceiling plan views; compare step 11.

17. Adjust the reflected ceiling plans as follows:

    a. Ensure *Underlay Orientation* is set to **Look Up** in the *View Properties.*

    b. Make sure the **Structural Framing** category is turned on (i.e., visible).

The previous step is important in making the view look correct. The ceilings will only show up if the *Underlay Orientation* is set correctly in a ceiling plan view.

Loading Content:

Now that the electrical views are set up and ready to go, you will load some MEP electrical content (i.e., *Families*) into the project. The process is identical to how content is loaded using Revit *Architecture* and Revit *Structure*. This section will just show you how to load a few elements. As you work through the rest of this chapter, you will have to load additional content, referencing this information if needed.

18. Load the following content via **Insert → Load Autodesk Family**:

    Annotation \Electrical
    - Electrical Device Circuit
    - Electrical Equipment Tag

    Electrical\MEP\Electrical Power\Distribution
    - Lighting and Appliance Panelboard - 208V MCB - Surface.
    - Combination Starter - Disconnect Switches

    Electrical\MEP\Electric Power\Terminals
    - Duplex Receptacle
    - Lighting Switches

You now have the content loaded that will be used to model the electrical system: power, systems and lighting. You should only load content that you need, when you need it. Again, each family takes up space in the project, making the file on your hard drive larger. Additionally, once you start using those components in the project, the file gets even larger.

At this point in the book, with all the mechanical modeled, your *BIM* file should be 28-32MB or more.

19. **Save** your law office project.

Spaces versus Rooms:

Revit's *MEP* tools are designed to use *Spaces* rather than *Rooms*. Both *Spaces* and *Rooms* work and behave exactly the same way in a project. The main reason to have two types of "room" elements has to do with the fact that most MEP models are in a separate file from the architectural model because of the size of the project and the engineers working in a different office and on a different server. Working over the internet is not an option with Revit.

In a Revit *MEP* model, the architectural model is linked in and the link's *Properties* are set to be "**room bounding**," which allows the *Spaces* to find the walls, floors and ceilings/roofs within the link. Then, when the *Space* has been placed in each room, the *Space* can automatically acquire several of the properties of the linked *Room*, such as room number, room name, area, and volume.

On the *Analyze* tab you will find the ***Space***, ***Space Separator*** and ***Space Tag*** tools. Revit has a nice feature: once in the *Space* tool, the *Ribbon* has a **Place Spaces Automatically** option. This will add a *Space* to every enclosed area, even chases, which is required for doing heating and cooling load calculations. Any *Space* not touching another *Space* is assumed to be an exterior wall.

Once Spaces are placed, you can use the ***Zone*** tool, on the *Analyze* tab, to group *Spaces* together into MEP *Zones*. This is the same idea as a building being divided into heating and cooling zones, by thermostat or furnace. It is then possible to add color to a plan view, highlighting each zone for a presentation drawing.

If the architects rename or renumber a *Room*, the MEP model will automatically be updated when the file is reopened. However, if the architects change layout of an area, you may have to add new *Spaces* or move them around. When a room size changes, the center of the "X" for the *Space* is what determines which room the *Space* is in. So, if two *Rooms* are adjusted in size, it could be that both *Spaces* end up in the same *Room*.

One of the main reasons for using *Spaces* in an MEP project is to be able to add *Room Tags* (i.e., *Space Tags*) which can be moved around so they do not overlap lights and ductwork. *Spaces* also hold engineering data such as total heating and cooling loads and lighting levels.

See ***Appendix D*** for more information on *Rooms* and *Spaces* in Revit.

Exercise 14-3:
Panelboard, Power Devices and MEP Systems

In this exercise, you will start laying out power devices (i.e., outlets) and panelboard (i.e., power panels with circuit breakers). The process is similar to the HVAC design; you place the components (e.g., outlets and light fixtures), create a system (i.e., a circuit), add components to the system, and select a panelboard for the circuit. Once finished, you can see the panel and its circuits nicely organized in the *System Browser*.

1. **Open** your law office project using Revit.

2. Switch to the **Level 1 – Power Floor Plan**.

Placing the Panelboard:

First you will place the *panelboard*, or *power panel*, in the *Mechanical and Electrical Room*. This is a *face based* family that you will place on the wall.

3. Select **Electrical Equipment** from the *Systems* tab (no tag required).

4. Select the *Lighting and Appliance Panelboard - 208V MCB - Surface* **- 400A** option from the *Type Selector*; make sure the placement option is **Place on Vertical Face**.

5. Place the panel as shown in Figure 14-3.1.

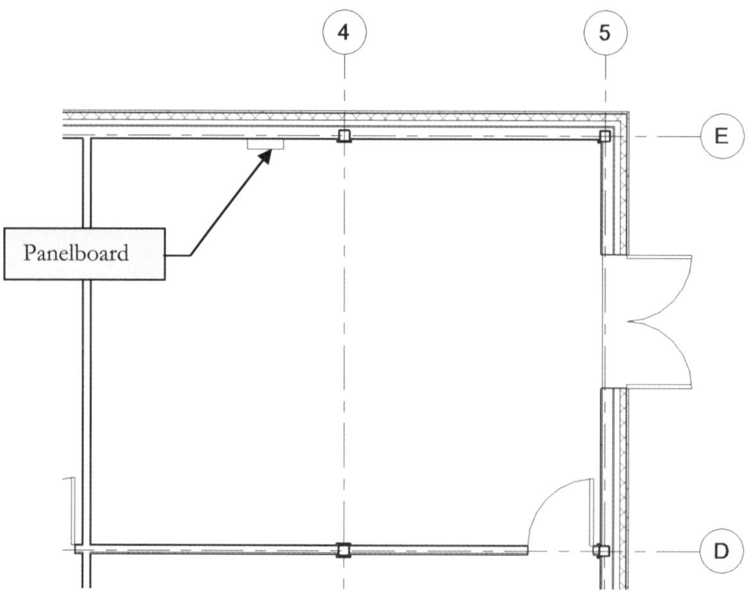

FIGURE 14-3.1 Panelboard placed in *Mechanical and Electrical Room*

Notice the *View Template* turned off all the ductwork and mechanical equipment to clean up the view so the electrical work is more easily read. However, this makes it hard to determine where the power panel should go. You cannot see the water heater, the AHU or the piping and ductwork. It might be better to leave that information on and make it all shaded gray like the architectural/structural. You can do this via the "VV" shortcut and check the halftone options to the right of any category. Do not do this now.

Distribution Systems:

The next thing you need to do is specify the power panel's *Distribution System*, which determines the types of things that can connect to this panel, such as outlets and lights versus high power industrial equipment.

In the *Electrical Settings* dialog you will see this is where the various *Distribution Systems* are defined (Figure 14-3.2). Notice the options: *Phase*, *Configuration*, number of *Wires* and *Voltage* information. The electrical settings also allow voltage definitions to be set up with max. and min. voltage. It is possible to *add* and *delete* systems as needed in this list, allowing a specialty firm to set things up correctly in their template for the kind of work they do.

The only thing you really need to know at this introductory level is that this feature does error checking by letting you know if you try to connect an electrical device to a circuit on a panel that is not compatible with it, meaning a sub-panel and transformer may be required which cost more time and money!

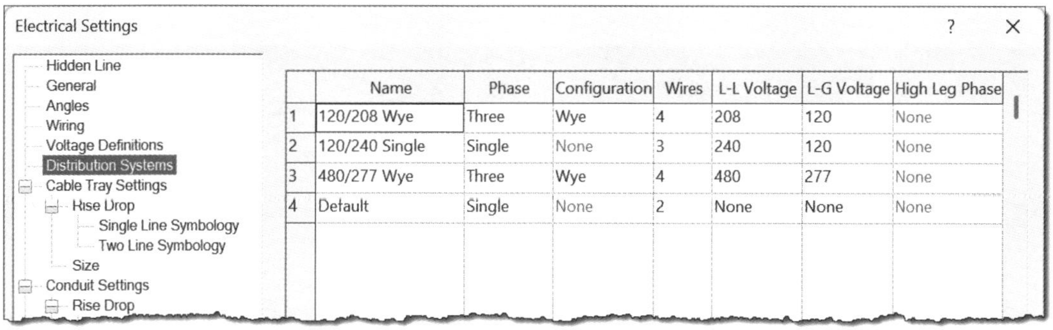

	Name	Phase	Configuration	Wires	L-L Voltage	L-G Voltage	High Leg Phase
1	120/208 Wye	Three	Wye	4	208	120	None
2	120/240 Single	Single	None	3	240	120	None
3	480/277 Wye	Three	Wye	4	480	277	None
4	Default	Single	None	2	None	None	None

FIGURE 14-3.2 Electrical settings: Distribution Systems

6. **Select** the panelboard you just placed.

7. Review its *Instance Properties* via the *Properties Palette.*

In the next step you will give the panelboard a name, specify a *Distribution System* and specify the number of circuits in the panel.

8. Set the following parameters:
    a. *Panel Name:* **Panel A**
    b. *Distribution System:* **120/208 Wye**
    c. *Max Single Pole Breakers:* **42**

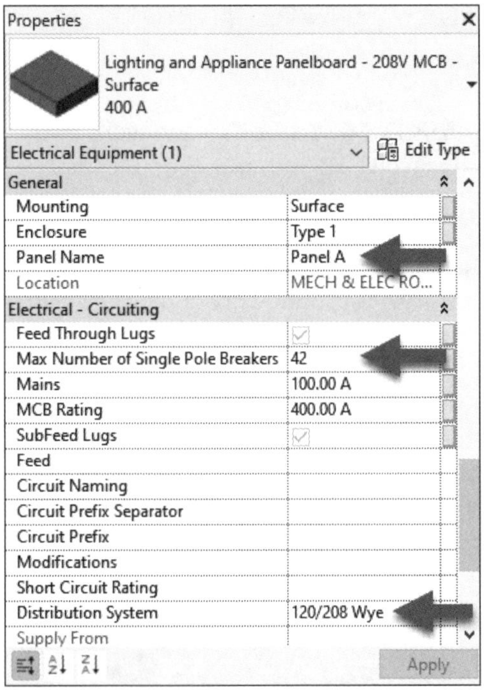

FIGURE 14-3.3 Panelboard properties

9. Click **Apply** to commit the changes to the panelboard.

Now that the panelboard is placed and set up properly, you can start placing outlets and light fixtures in the next *Exercise*. After the components are placed, you can then create the systems (i.e., circuits) and assign them to the panelboard.

It is generally possible to do the drafting part and not actually create the *MEP Systems* (i.e., circuits). However, this generates errors as the unassigned system has too many components on it. This warning is related to degraded model performance because Revit is constantly trying to cross-reference everything.

Placing Devices (i.e., Electrical Fixtures):

Now you will place several duplex outlets. The outlet families are *face based*, so they can go on any surface and then move with it. This will come in handy when you place the outlets on the *Reception Desk*, for example, as it is a custom family.

10. From the *Systems* tab, click the ***Device*** tool.
    a. Click the down arrow and select *Electrical Fixture.*
    b. Or, just click the upper part of the slip-button tool; notice the icon is the same.
    c. See the image to the right.
    d. Ensure **Tag on Placement** is unchecked (*Ribbon*).

11. Set the *Type Selector* to *Duplex Receptacle:* **Standard**.

12. Ensure **Place on Vertical Face** is selected.

13. Click to place an outlet on the East wall, as shown in Figure 14-3.4.

14. Click **Modify** to end the current command.

Face based families have the ability to show both 2D and 3D geometry; which one you see depends on which view you are in. The plan views show the 2D geometry that is the industry standard symbol for an electrical receptacle (i.e., outlet) in plan. This symbol is shown on the face of the wall, rather than in the wall where it would become obscured by the lines and hatching of the wall. Elevations and 3D views show the actual face plate, which helps to coordinate with other things like windows and cabinets.

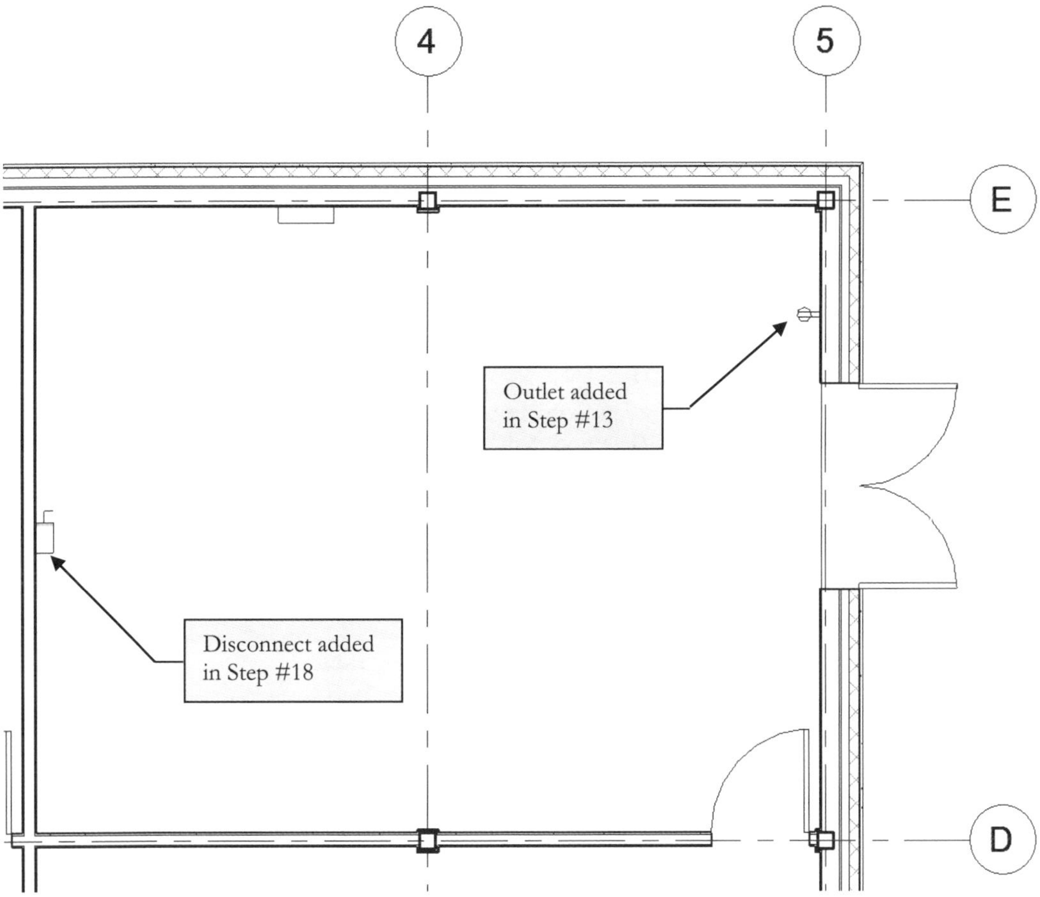

FIGURE 14-3.4 Placing an electrical fixture

Outlets are placed at a default height above the floor. The Revit-provided family has been set up to place the outlet at the standard 18″ above the floor (to the center of the face plate); this can be changed to comply with other codes and standards. In this case, we want 18″ and will manually change the few outlets that need to be at a different elevation.

The outlet you just placed needs to be 48″ *Above Finished Floor* (AFF) to comply with codes for outlets in mechanical and electrical rooms.

15. Select the outlet and **change** the *Elevation from Level* to **48″** in the *Properties Palette.* Be sure to add the inch symbol so it does not get moved to forty-eight feet above the floor!

Next you will place the remaining outlets for Level 1, except at the *Reception Desk.*

16. Place the outlets approximately as shown in Figure 14-3.5.
    a. All outlets are *Type* **Standard** except in the *Toilet Rooms* and above the counter in the *Break Room*, which are to be *Type* **GFCI**.
    b. All outlets are to be the standard 18″ AFF unless noted otherwise.
    c. If another face is getting in the way when placing an outlet (e.g., *Mirror*, *Admin Reception Desk*), place the outlet farther down the wall and then use the arrow keys to nudge it into place.
    d. The outlet in the center of the *Conference Room* is in the floor.
        i. Placement needs to be set to **Place on Face**.
        ii. Place the outlet away from the table and then move it to the center of the table; this will ensure you do not place the outlet on the face of the table rather than the floor.
        iii. In this case, both the face plate and 2D symbol appear.

Looking at the architect's interior elevation at the *Break Room*, image to the right, you can see the power receptacle is now showing. You may have to move a note out of the way for clarity. The outlet behind the refrigerator is not showing because the view *Discipline* is set to **Architectural** so the architectural elements are *not* transparent. Seeing the electrical fixtures in this architectural interior elevation is design integration in action!

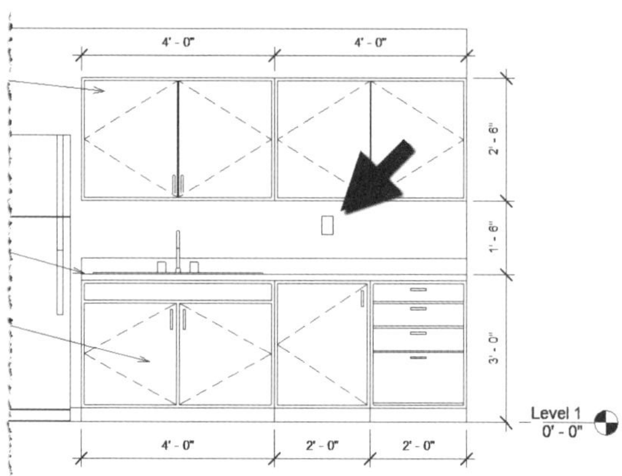

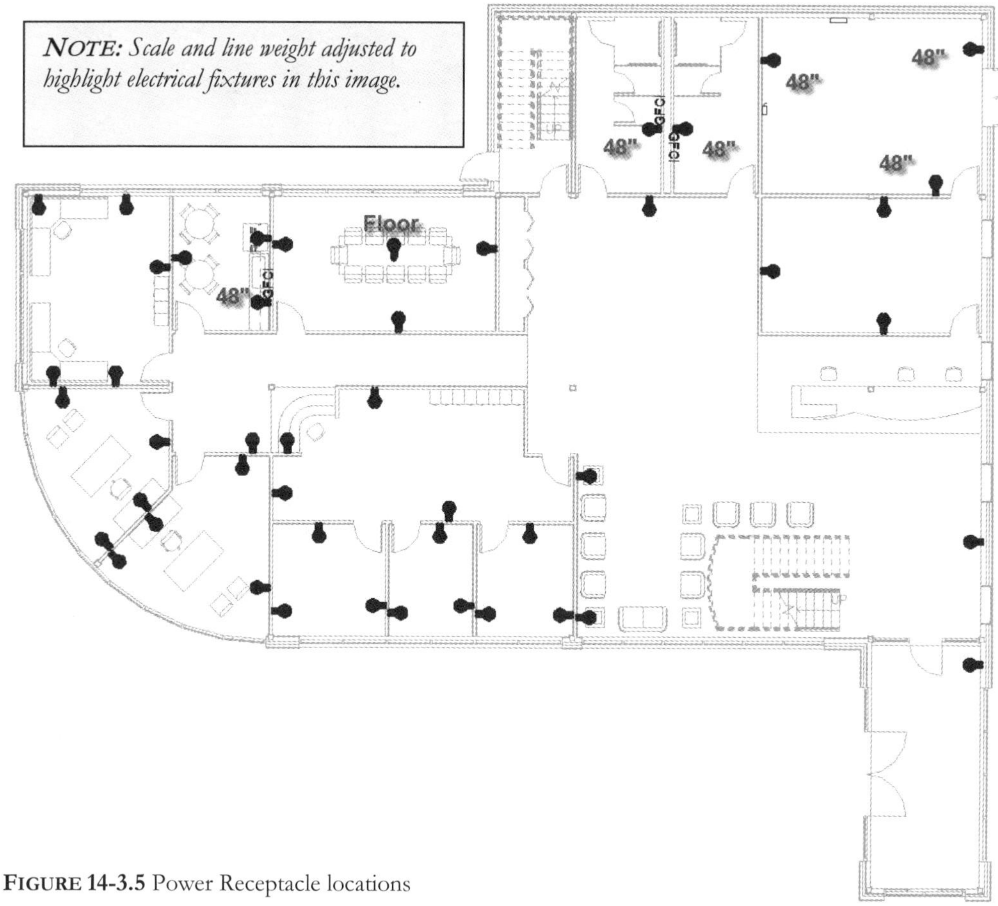

FIGURE 14-3.5 Power Receptacle locations

Placing the outlets at the *Reception Desk* is a little tricky because you cannot see the vertical surfaces that you will be placing them on; they are below the countertop. Therefore, you will create a temporary, or permanent if you wish, interior elevation looking at the back side of the *Reception Desk*. From here you can place the *face based* outlets easily, and then adjust the elevation via *Properties*.

17. Place the outlets at the *Reception Desk*. (See Figures 14-3.6 to 14-3.8.)
    a. Create an interior elevation. ***TIP:*** *Point at column when placing the elevation tag on plan.*
    b. Place outlets in new elevation view. If you have trouble, try placing them in a plan view with the *Visual Style* temporarily set to *Wireframe*.
    c. Adjust outlet elevation via *Properties Palette*.
    d. Delete the interior elevation tag, which will also delete the interior elevation view from the project. You can skip this step and leave the elevation tag in place if you wish.
    e. Make sure *Schedule Level* is set to **Level 1**.

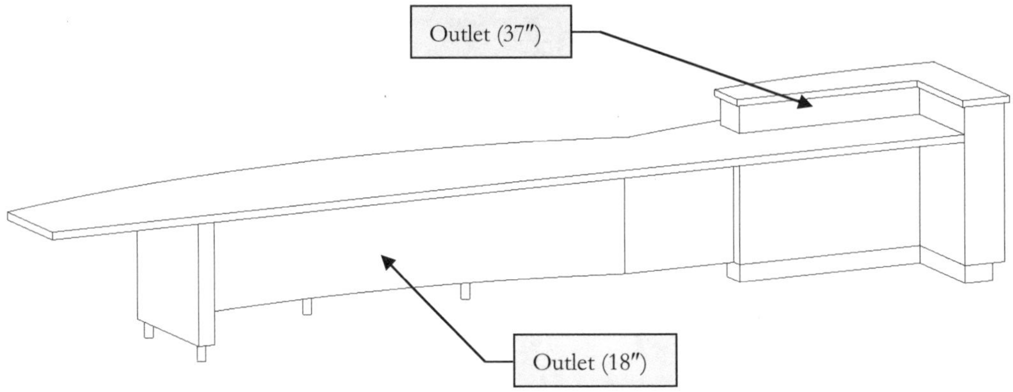

FIGURE 14-3.6 Outlets to be placed at reception desk

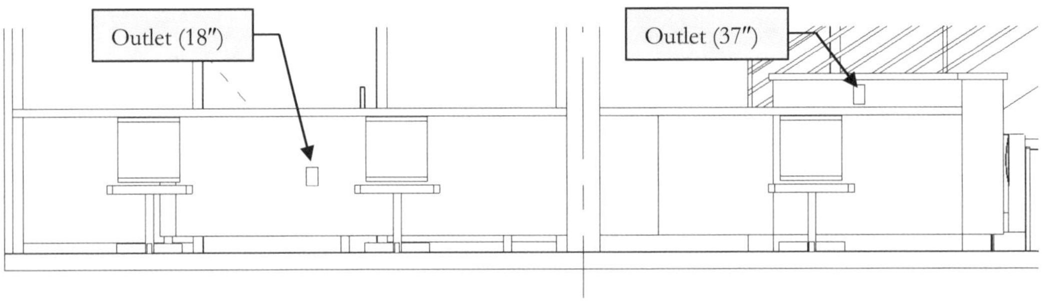

FIGURE 14-3.7 Outlets placed at *Reception Desk* (temporary interior elevation view created)

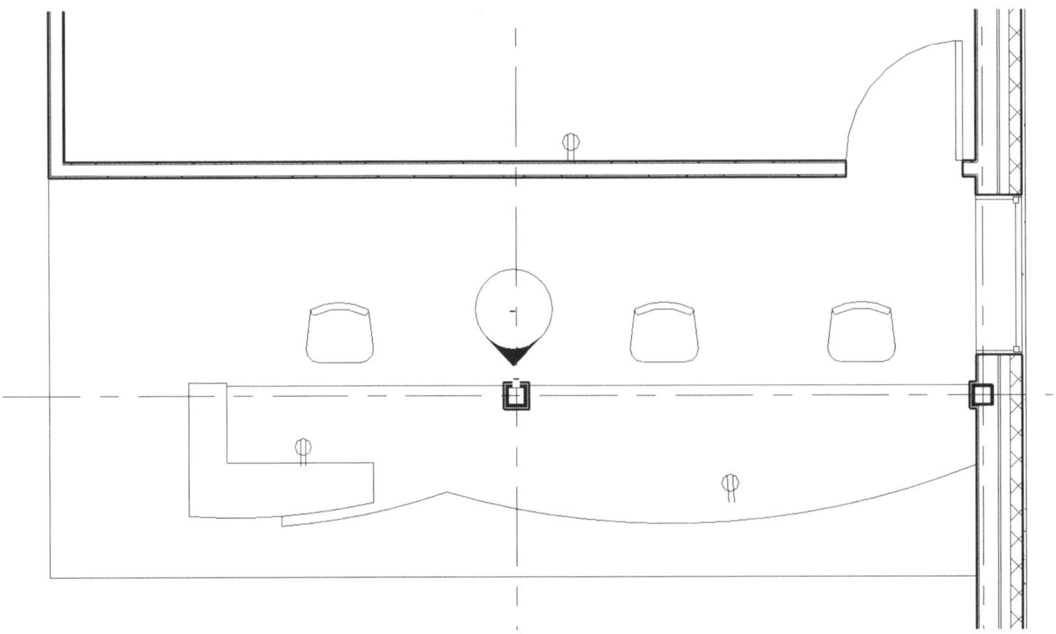

FIGURE 14-3.8 Level 1 Power Floor Plan view; outlets placed at *Reception Desk*

Notice how the outlets show up even though they are below the countertops (Figure 14-3.8). In the electrical and mechanical "disciplines," the architectural and structural elements are transparent.

Next, you will add a disconnect switch for the AHU. This allows the power to be shut off at the unit without the need to go to the panelboard.

18. Using the *Electrical Equipment* tool, place *Combination Starter - Disconnect Switches:* **208V – Size 1** family on the West wall of the Mechanical/Electrical Room (Figure 14-3.4).

    a. Select **Place on Vertical Face**. No tag is required.

You are now ready to place the Level 2 power devices.

19. Following the same instructions as Step 16, place the Level 2 outlets as shown in Figure 14-3.9.

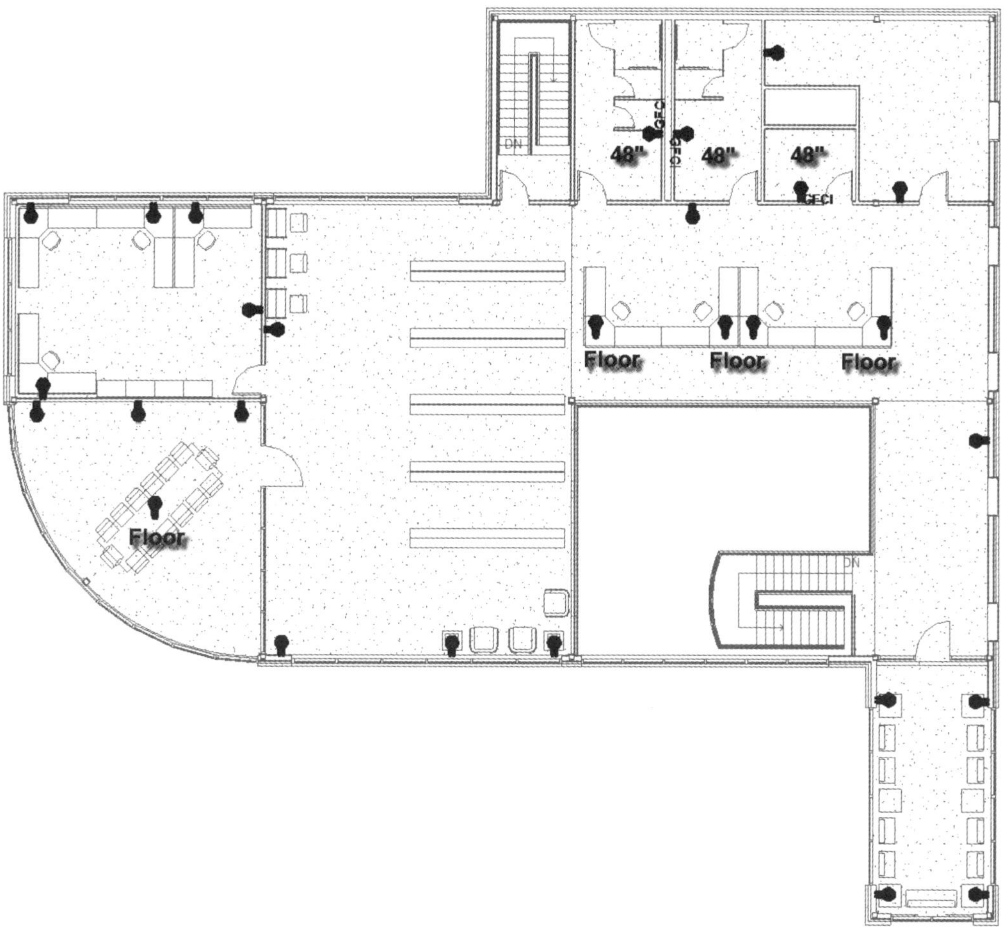

FIGURE 14-3.9 Level 2 power floor plan view; power receptacle locations

Next, you need to adjust the Level 1 Power Plan's *View Range* so the outlets in the floor above do not show up.

20. Switch to the **Level 1 Power Floor Plan** view.

21. With nothing selected and no commands active, note the ***View Properties*** via the *Properties Palette.*

22. **Edit** the *View Range.*

23. Change the *Top Offset* to **-1′-0″**; do not miss the minus symbol.

The floor outlets on Level 2 are now out of the Level 1 *View Range* and are therefore no longer visible.

Creating MEP Systems (i.e., Power Circuit):

In this section you will create an MEP *System* which is very similar to the process used with the HVAC design in the previous chapter.

24. **Zoom** in to the *Mechanical/Electrical Room* on Level 1.

25. Select one of the outlets (i.e., electrical fixture) in the *Mechanical/ Electrical Room.*

26. With the outlet selected, click the ***Power*** icon, within the *Create System* panel, on the *Ribbon.*

27. Click **Edit Circuit** on the *Ribbon.*

You are now in *Add to Circuit* mode.

28. Select the remaining four outlets shown in Figure 14-3.10.

29. Set the *Panel* drop-down on the *Ribbon* to **Panel A** (Figure 14-3.11).

30. Click **Finish Editing Circuit** on the *Ribbon* (i.e., green check mark).

You have just placed 5 outlets on the #1 circuit breaker in the power panel (Panel A).

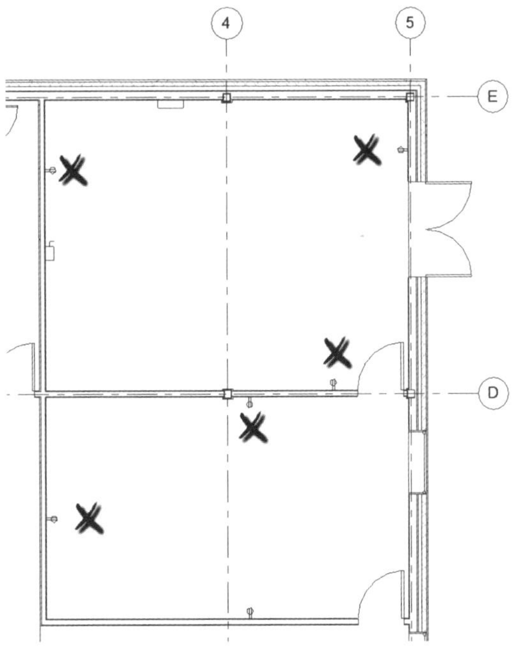

FIGURE 14-3.10 Outlets for circuit #1

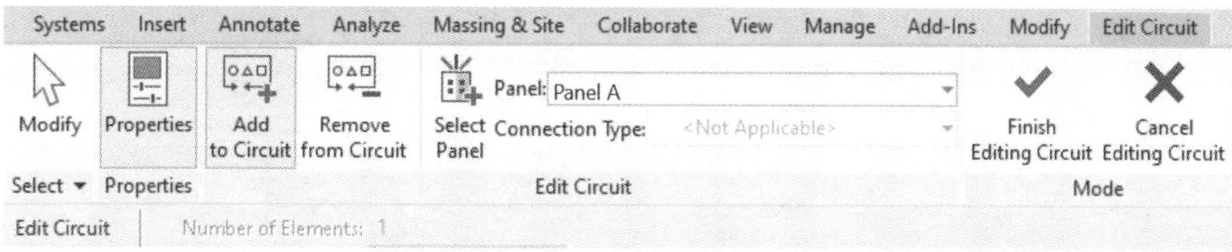

FIGURE 14-3.11 Power circuit; *Ribbon* settings

31. Select one of the outlets again and view its *Instance Properties (via the Properties Palette).*
    a. Notice the *Panel* and *Circuit* are now listed.

You will now add the remaining outlets to circuits. In the next exercise, you will also add the light fixtures to *power circuits* (i.e., MEP *Systems*) as well.

32. Following the previous step, create circuits in the order of the numbers shown; see Figures 14-3.12 and 14-3.13.
    a. See Step #34 after creating the second *Power System.*

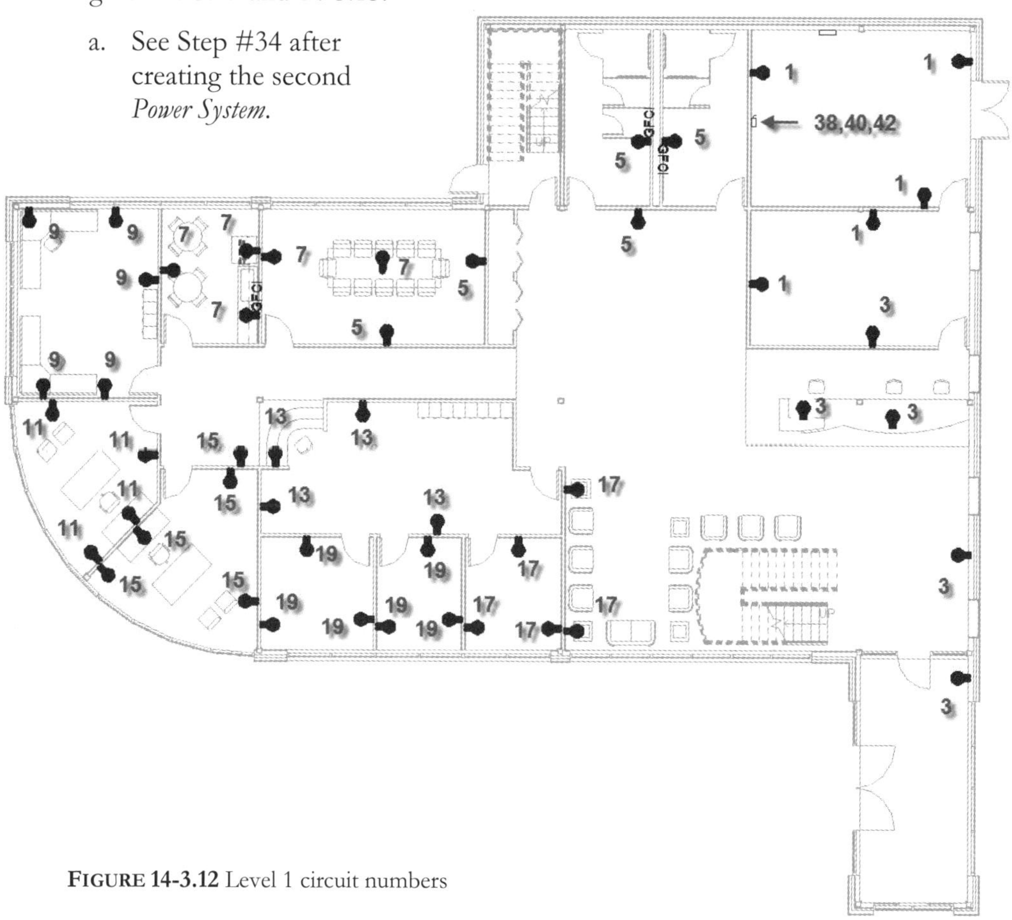

FIGURE 14-3.12 Level 1 circuit numbers

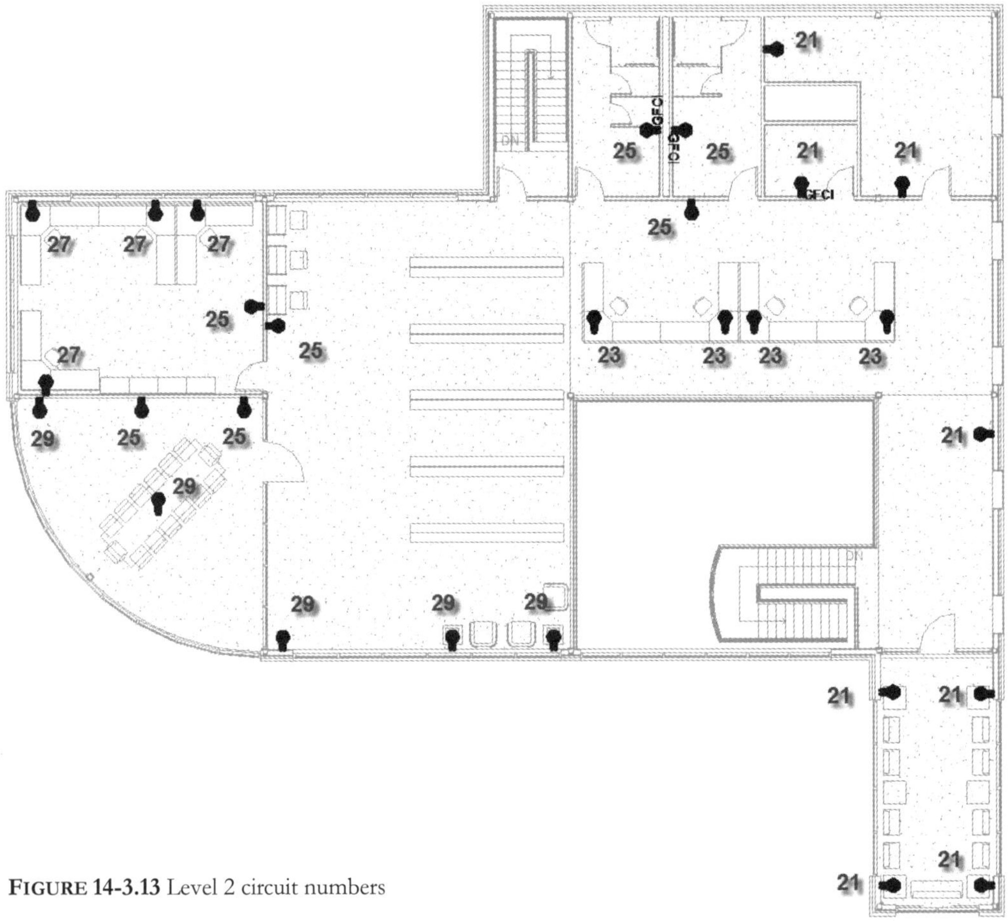

FIGURE 14-3.13 Level 2 circuit numbers

By default, Revit will select the next circuit available for you when creating a *Power System*. In our case we want to reserve all the even numbered circuits for the lighting system. So, when you create the second *Power System* and Revit places it on *Circuit number 2* in *Panel A*, you will need to manually move it to *Circuit 3*. The following steps show how to do this.

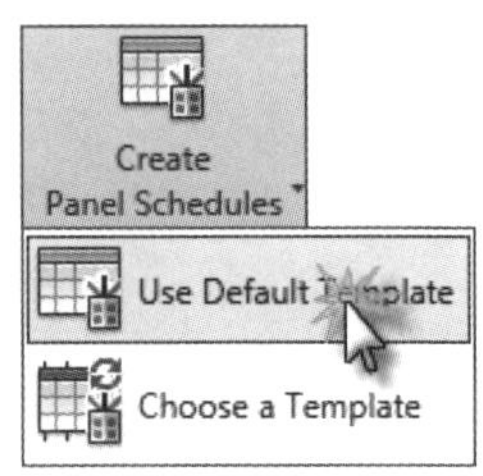

33. After creating the second *Power System*, select **Panel A** (family).

34. Click **Create Panel Schedules →Use Default Template** on the *Ribbon*.

35. Click in one of the "cells" for *Circuit 2*.

36. Click the ***Move Down*** button from the *Ribbon*.

37. Click the ***Move Across*** button. ***TIP:*** *Use* ***Move To*** *in place of Move Down/Across.*

38. Use these steps to properly position each circuit as they are created, then close the ***Panel Schedule*** view (Figure 14-3.15).

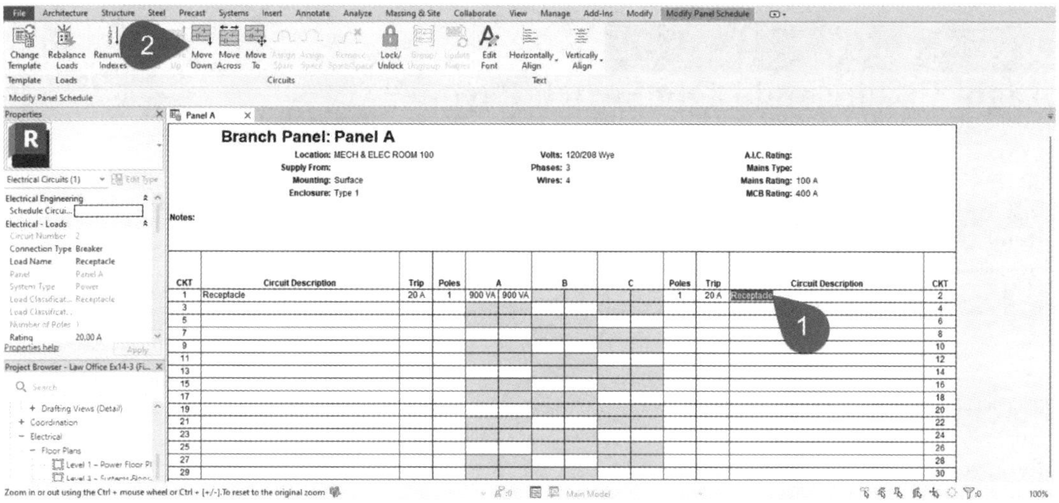

FIGURE 14-3.14 Editing circuit location for Panel A

The circuit is now moved from *2* to *3* (Figure 14-3.15). Notice the panel has 42 circuits, which you specified in the *Panel A Properties.*

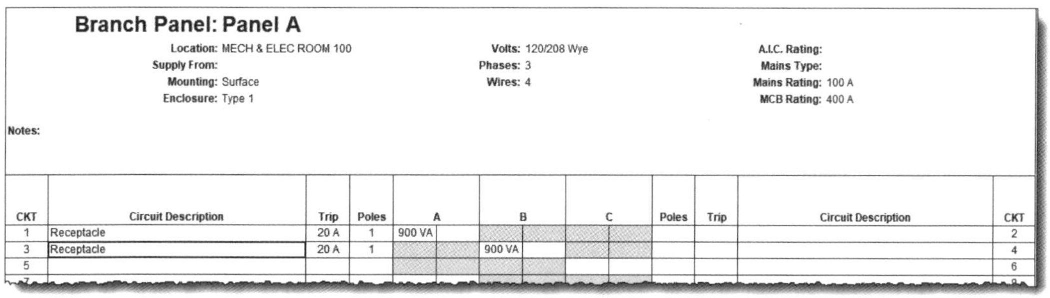

FIGURE 14-3.15 Circuit moved from slot 2 over to 3

The panel schedule can be accessed again via the *Project Browser*, under the *Panel Schedules* header, or by selecting the panel in the model and clicking the ***Edit Panel Schedule*** tool on the *Ribbon.*

This concludes the basic introduction to placing outlets, power panels and then creating circuits on the power panel for the outlets.

39. **Save** your project.

Exercise 14-4:
Light Fixture and Light Switch Layout

In this exercise you will place the light fixtures and create MEP *Systems* to specify which circuit specific lights are on.

1. Open your law office project using Revit *MEP*.

Placing Light Fixtures:

If you recall, you started your project from a Revit *Architecture* template. This template has 2x4 and a recessed can light fixture preloaded in it. Unfortunately, these families are not the same as the ones that come with Revit *MEP*; the parameters are slightly different. Also, the Revit *Architecture* families are *ceiling hosted*, whereas the Revit *MEP* light fixtures are *face based* families; Revit *MEP* content is standardized on *face based* content because it is the only type of "hosted" family that works when the architect's model is linked in, not in the same model as in our case.

First, you will delete *families* not needed from the project and then load the correct ones from the Revit *MEP* content library.

2. Expand the **Families** section in the *Project Browser*.

3. Expand the **Lighting Fixtures** section (Figure 14-4.1).

4. Right-click on the *Downlight* and *Troffer* families (separately) and select **Delete** to remove them from the law office project.

The two families and their *Types* are now removed from the project. You may do this with any family that is not required in your project. This can reduce the project file size and reduce errors. Do not delete any other families at this time.

5. Load the following families from the Revit *MEP* content library:
    a. Lighting\MEP\Internal:
        i. *Downlight – Recessed Can*
        ii. *Troffer Light – 2x4 Parabolic*

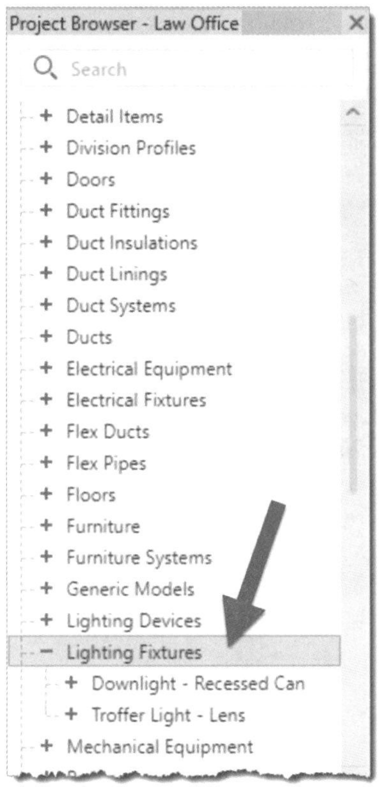

FIGURE 14-4.1
Project Browser;
Families\Lighting Fixture section

You are now ready to begin placing light fixtures. This will be done in the **Level 1 – Lighting Plans**. The 2x4 light fixture will actually snap to the ceiling grid, making it easier to place. The architectural light fixture does not snap to the ceiling grid.

6. **Open** the **Level 1 – Lighting Plan** view (which is a reflected ceiling plan view).

7. **Zoom** in to the *Associates Office* in the Northwestern corner.

8. In the view's *Properties*, double-check the following:
   a. *Visual Graphics Style:* Hidden Line (via *Graphic Display Options*)
   b. *Underlay Orientation:* Look Up
   c. *View Range:* Cut Plane = 7′-6″

9. Select the ***Lighting Fixture*** tool from the *Systems* tab on the *Ribbon*.

10. Select *Troffer Light – 2x4 Parabolic:* **2′x4′(2 Lamp) – 120V** from the *Type Selector*.

11. Click **Place on Face** from the *Placement* panel on the *Ribbon* (no tag required).

12. Move your cursor within the office, and then press the **spacebar** (on the keyboard) to rotate the fixture 90 degrees.

13. Place the fixture as shown in Figure 14-4.2.
    a. Make sure the fixture "snaps" to the grid before placing it; you may need to zoom in more.

14. Place the other three fixtures shown in Figure 14-4.2.

Next you will place the rest of the 2x4 fixtures on Level 1.

A nice thing about ***face based*** light fixtures, compared to *ceiling-hosted*, is that they can be placed on any face, not just a ceiling. In your back stair, you will be placing the fixture on the "face" of the underside of the floor above. Also, ceiling-hosted content does not work when the architectural model is linked in.

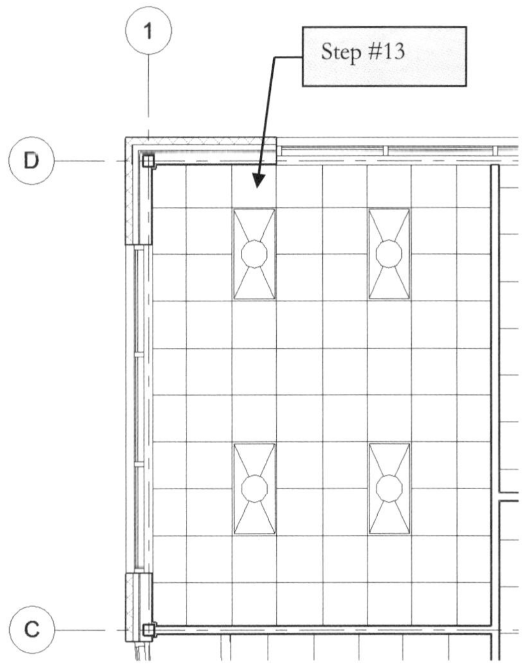

FIGURE 14-4.2 Light fixtures placed on Level 1

An important thing to know about ***faced based*** families is that you can **Copy** them from one room to another. If you do, the copied light fixture will become associated to the new ceiling if it is at the same height. If the light is copied to a location without a ceiling, or the ceiling is at a different height, it will become "not associated" meaning it has no Host. It is possible to select the light and use the *Pick New* tool and select a new host.

15. Place the remaining 2x4 light fixtures on Level 1 as shown in Figure 14-4.3.
    a. Load and use *Ceiling Light – Linear Box:* **1'x4'(1 Lamp) – 120V** in the North stairwell.
    b. Select each of the floor mounted outlets visible from Level 2 and then right-click and pick *Hide in View → Elements.*
    c. In the *Mechanical/Electrical Room*:
        i. Load and use the following family:
           Strip Lighting Fixtures: **4' 1 Lamp – 120**
        ii. Be sure to place the fixtures between the bar joists.

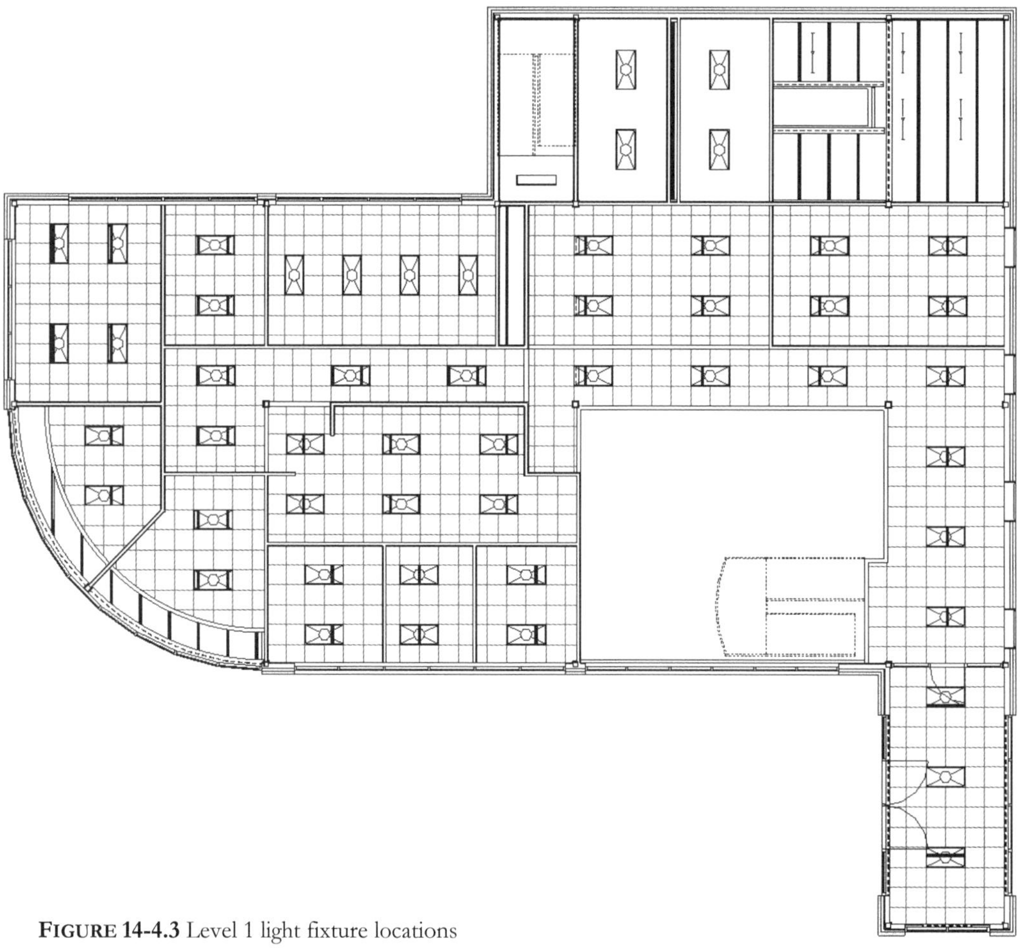

FIGURE 14-4.3 Level 1 light fixture locations

As you can see in the previous image, it is nice to have the bar joists visible when you can place the light fixtures so they will not conflict in rooms with no ceilings. It is rather odd that the bar joists are visible within the 2x4 light fixtures that are placed in ceilings (when a joist is directly above the fixture). This would be helpful if there was not enough space between the ceiling and the bar joist, but not in our case as we have plenty of room.

16. Place the Level 2 light fixtures as shown in Figure 14-4.4.
    a. Adjust the *Top Offset* and *View Depth* to **1′-0″** in the *View Range* to place the stairwell/custodian lights (on the underside of the roof face).
    b. Use *Ceiling Light – Linear Box:* **1′x4′(1 Lamp) – 120V** in the North stairwell and the *Custodian's Room.*
    c. Turn off the *Visibility* for the *Furniture Systems* and *Specialty_Equipment* categories. ***REMINDER:** Check "Architecture discipline."*

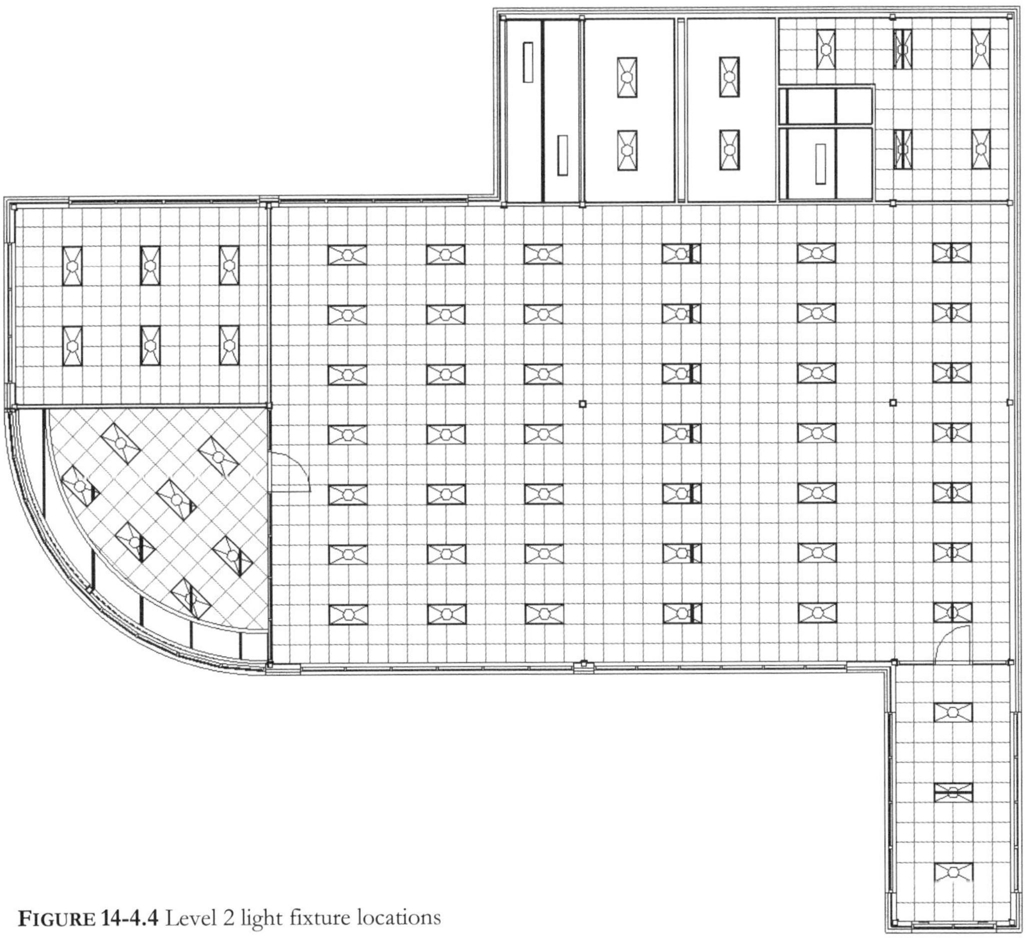

FIGURE 14-4.4 Level 2 light fixture locations

Now that you have all the light fixtures placed, you can connect them to circuits and light switches. First, you will place the light switches and then create the MEP *Systems.*

Placing Light Switches:

Now you will place the light switches. This is similar to placing the outlets. A rectangle will show up in the correct location in an elevation, but a symbol will show up in the plan view. If you recall, the *Cut Plane* for the ceiling plans is 7′-6″, which is above the 7′-0″ tall doors. Therefore, the doors do not appear in the Lighting Plan view. You will change this so the doors do show up as they are needed when placing light switches; they are typically on the latch side of the door. Additionally, if you want the light switches to show up in the Ceiling Plan view, the *Cut Plane* needs to be below the lowest light switch. The default light switch elevation is 4′-0″. Therefore, you will change the *Cut Plane* to 3′-6″.

17. Change the *Cut Plane* to **3′-6″** for both **Ceiling Lighting Plans**.

18. Turn off the *Casework*, *Furniture*, *Furniture Systems*, *Specialty Equipment* and *Structural Framing* categories to hide unnecessary information.

You should now be able to see the doors.

19. In the **Level 1 Lighting Plan** view, select **Systems → Electrical → Device (drop-down) → Lighting**

20. Set the *Type Selector* to *Lighting Switches:* **Single Pole** (load the family if needed).

21. Click on **Place on Vertical Face**, then click on the wall (in the *Associate's Office*) near the door to place the light switch as shown in Figure 14-4.5.

You now have a light switch at 4′-0″ above the floor. Now you will place the remaining light switches on Level 1.

22. Place the remaining light switches on Level 1 per Figure 14-4.6.
    a. All are to be **Single Pole** at the default **4′-0″** AFF. *Exception*: The switch near the main entry and the two near the North stair (the back door) are to be **Three Way** type switches.

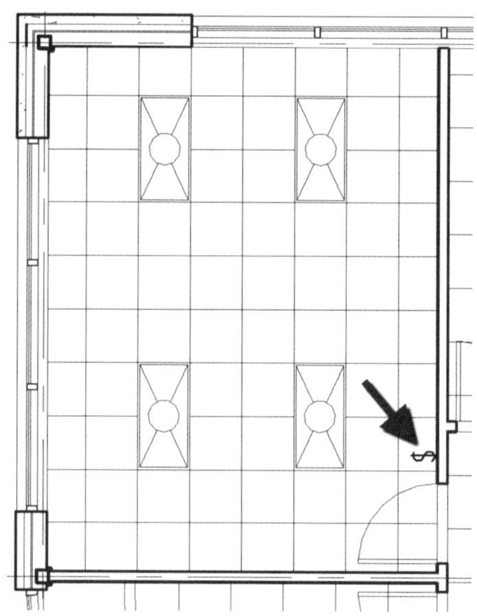

FIGURE 14-4.5 Level 1 light switch placed

23. Place the light switches on Level 2 per Figure 14-4.7.

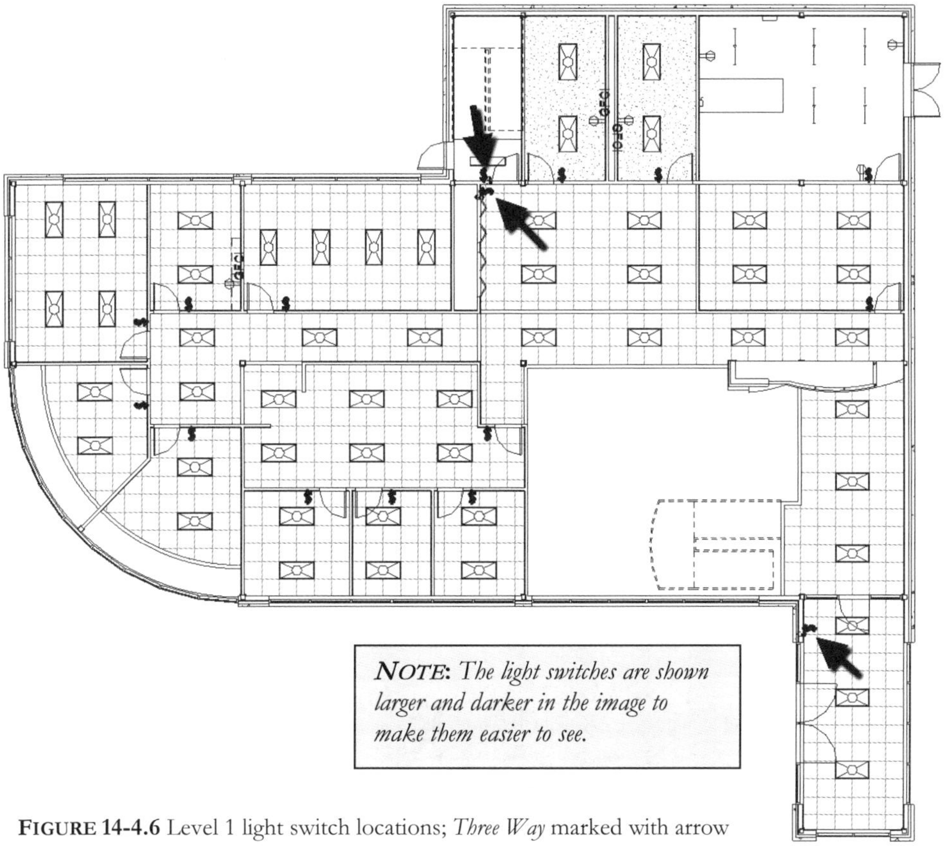

NOTE: *The light switches are shown larger and darker in the image to make them easier to see.*

FIGURE 14-4.6 Level 1 light switch locations; *Three Way* marked with arrow

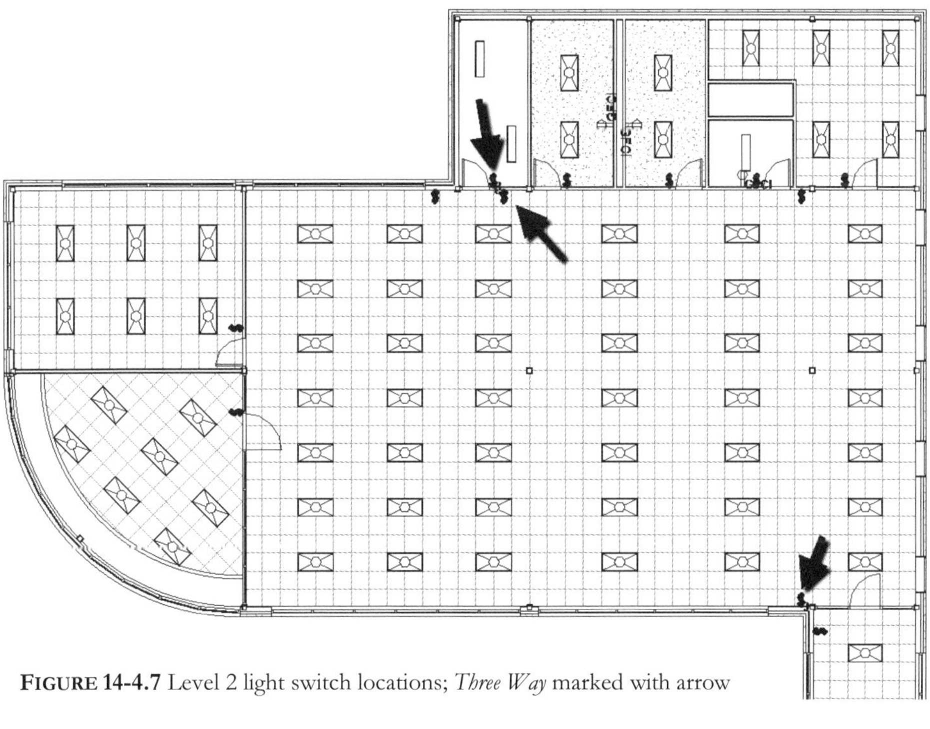

FIGURE 14-4.7 Level 2 light switch locations; *Three Way* marked with arrow

Creating MEP Systems (i.e., Power Circuit):

Now you will create the *power circuits* for the light fixtures.

24. Zoom in to the Level 1 *Associate's Office* (lighting plan).

25. Select one of the light fixtures and then click the ***Power*** tool on the *Ribbon.*

26. Select the ***Edit Circuit*** button.

27. Select **Panel A** from the *Panel* drop-down list on the *Ribbon.*

28. With the **Add to Circuit** option selected on the *Ribbon*, select the light fixtures shown in Figure 14-4.8 (bold looking with dashed line connecting them).

29. Click **Finish Editing Circuit** on the *Ribbon.*

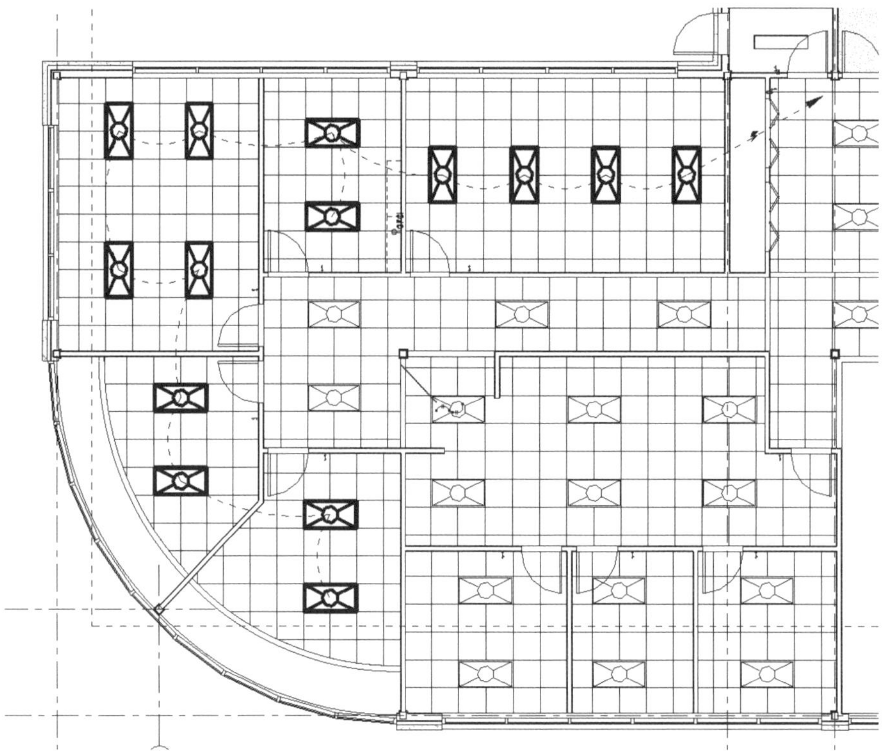

FIGURE 14-4.8 Level 1 light fixtures to go on circuit #6

If you hover over one of the light fixtures you just placed on a circuit and then press the **Tab** key on the keyboard, you will see several dashed arcs indicating which fixtures are on a circuit, as shown in Figure 14-4.8. If you then select the fixture, you can convert the temporary dashed arcs to *Wires*, which are lines that represent real wires the electrical contractor will install.

30. Per steps previously covered, move the new circuit to slot number *6* on *Panel A*.
TIP: Select the panel in plan and then click the Edit Panel Schedule *tool on the* Ribbon.

31. Create the remaining circuits for Levels 1 and 2 based on the circuit numbers shown in Figures 14-4.9 and 14-4.10.

    a. **Circuiting fixtures on different levels:** The lights in the *Level 2* stair shaft are on the same circuit as a few fixtures on *Level 1*. While in *Edit Circuit* mode on *Level 1*, simply switch to *Level 2*, click the ***Add to Circuit*** button on the *Ribbon* and select the desired lights on *Level 2*.

TIP: If you need to edit a circuit again after it has been created, select a light fixture already on the circuit and then, on the Electrical Circuits contextual tab on the Ribbon, select Edit Circuit.

FIGURE 14-4.9 Level 1 light fixture circuit numbers

As you can see, many more light fixtures can go on a circuit than can outlets. This is, of course, due to the electrical load placed on each, plus the fact that lights are a *fixed load* that can be accurately anticipated, whereas outlets can have many variations in load, like an electrical pencil sharpener versus an air conditioner. Revit will give a warning when the load on a circuit reaches capacity; try adding all the lights on Level 2 until you get the warning, and then *Undo*.

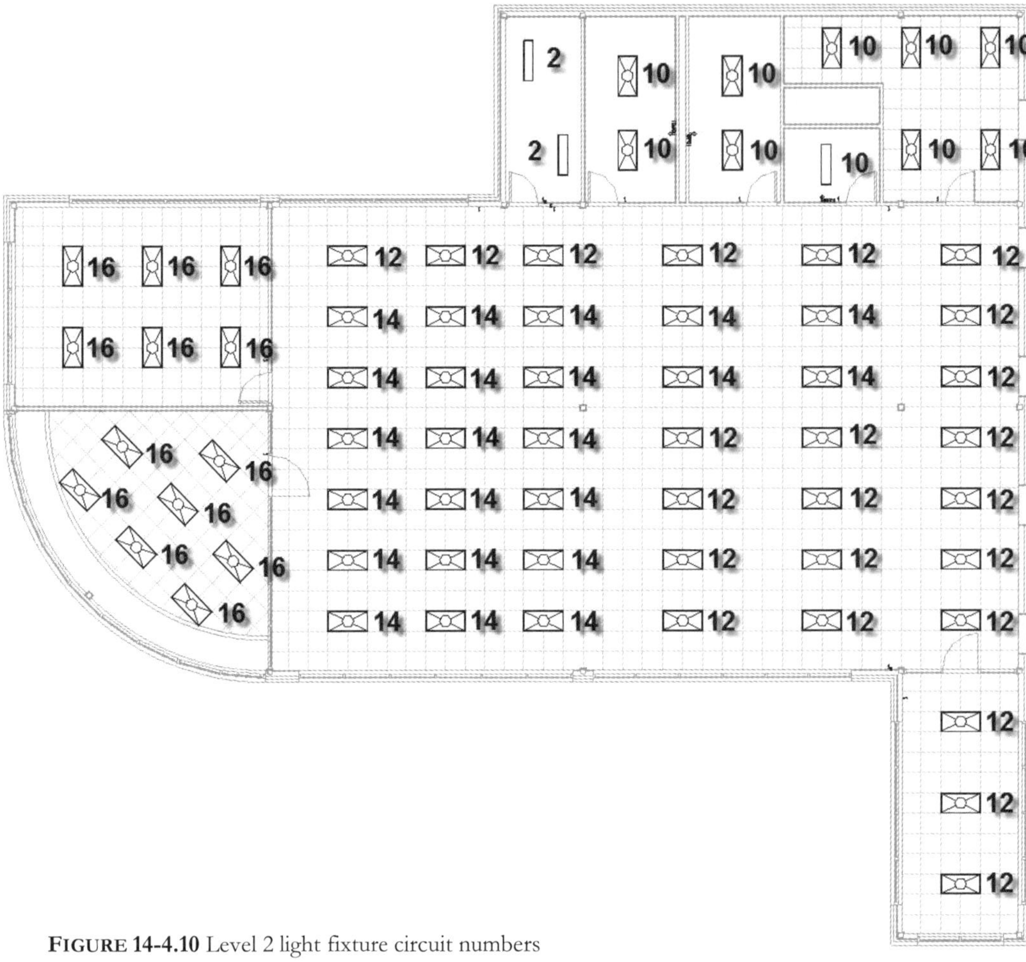

FIGURE 14-4.10 Level 2 light fixture circuit numbers

Creating MEP Systems (i.e., Switch System):

The final step in setting up the lighting system is to tell Revit which light fixtures are controlled by which light switches, or lighting device. The light fixtures on a circuit do not correlate to the lights controlled by a light switch. A circuit can support the operation of several rooms' worth of light fixtures, but each room typically has its own light switch.

32. On the **Level 1 Lighting Plan**, in the *Associate's Office* Northwestern corner, select one of the light fixtures.

33. Select the **Switch** button on the *Ribbon*.

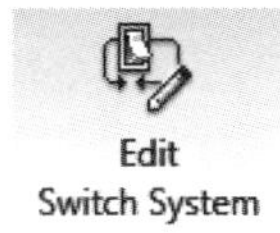

34. Select **Edit Switch System** from the *Ribbon.*

35. With **Add to System** highlighted on the *Ribbon*, pick the other three light fixtures in the room.

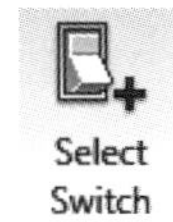

36. Click on the **Select Switch** button.

37. Select the light switch in the same room as the light fixtures.

38. Click **Finish Editing System**.

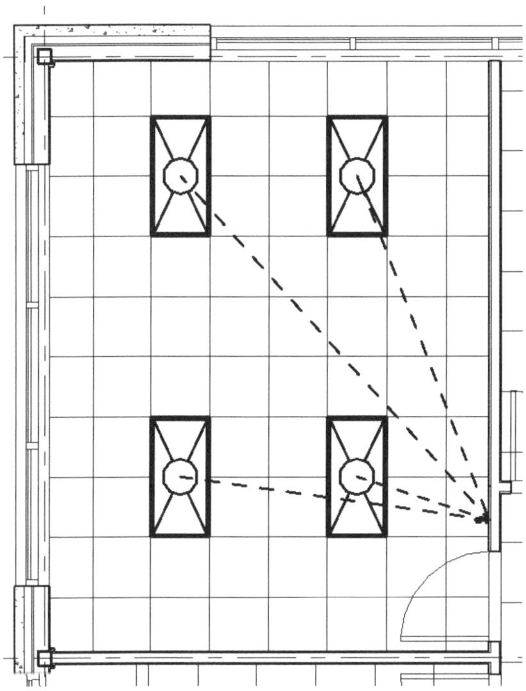

FIGURE 14-4.11 Light switch "connected" to lights

You have now told Revit which light switch controls the lights in the *Associate's Office.* If you hover over the light switch and then press the **Tab** key, you can see which lights are controlled by that switch (Figure 14-4.11).

Next, you will assign light switches to the remaining fixtures in the building.

FYI: Revit does not yet have the ability to manage multi switch systems such as three way or different bulbs within the same fixture. This must be managed manually with Shared Parameters (not covered in this text).

39. Create a *Switch System* for the remaining light fixtures in the building. Use your own judgment to decide which switches control which light fixtures.

Interference Check:

If you laid things out exactly as prescribed in the text, you will soon find there is a big problem. All the light fixtures were placed without coordinating the location of the HVAC diffusers. Many of the lights and diffusers overlap. It would have been best to have the diffuser *Visibility* turned on, but the *View Template* you used turns them off. You will use a Revit feature called *Interference Check* to reveal this hidden problem. This feature can be used to compare other categories as well, such as ducts and beams.

40. Select **Collaborate → Coordinate → Interference Check → Run Interference Check.**

41. Select **Lighting Fixtures** on the left and **Air Terminals** on the right (Figure 14-4.12).

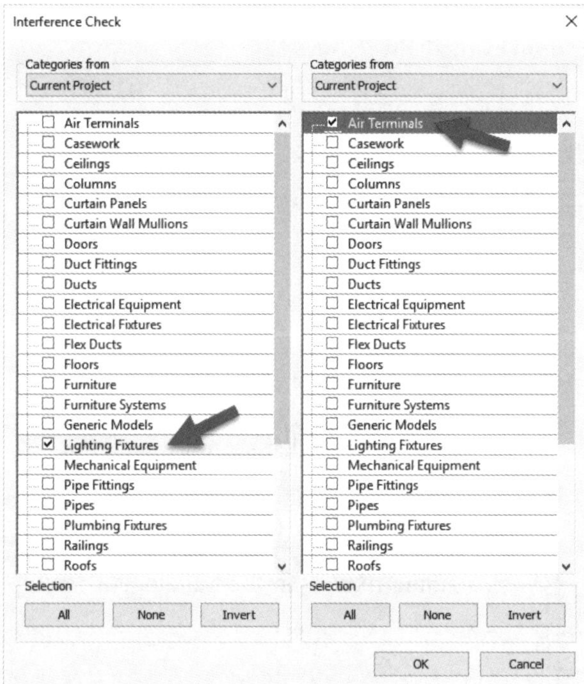

FIGURE 14-4.12 Interference Check dialog

42. Click **OK** to start the collision detection process.

Revit will show the results of the *Interference Check* (Figure 14-4.13). Each *air terminal* that conflicts with a *light fixture* is listed here. Expanding each will reveal the light fixture that is in conflict with it. With a listed light fixture or air terminal selected, you may click the **Show** button and Revit will switch to an appropriate view and zoom in on the element in question! When selected in the list, the element will highlight in the model, which is great if it is visible on the screen. Try it.

43. Click the **Close** button.

Next, you will turn on the *Air Terminal* category and set it to be a halftone so the *light fixtures* remain prominent in the **Lighting Plan** view.

44. Type **VV** in the **Level 1 Lighting Plan** view.

45. Check the **Air Terminal** *Category* to make it visible.

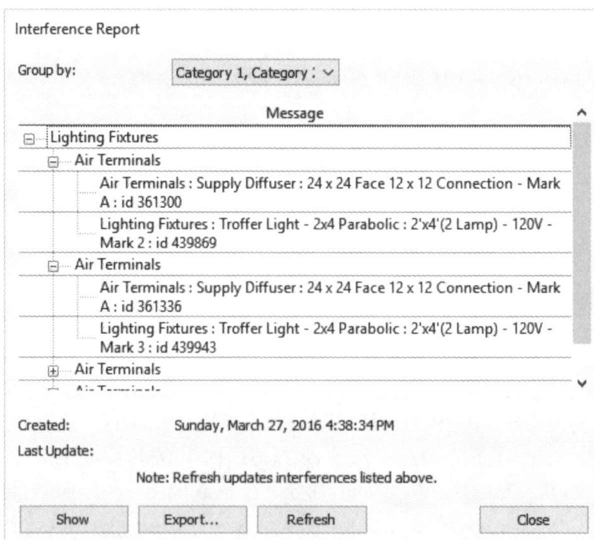

FIGURE 14-4.13 Interference Check results

46. Check the **Halftone** option to the right of the *Air Terminal* category.

47. Repeat these steps for the **Level 2 Lighting Plan** view.

48. Reposition any air terminals that are in conflict with the light fixtures.

The flex duct is forgiving when air terminals are repositioned. Setting the air terminals to be halftone allows the light fixtures to stand out in the lighting floor plan but maintain coordination. The image below shows the corrected lighting plan. The light fixtures have a custom tag which lists the fixture's circuit number and type.

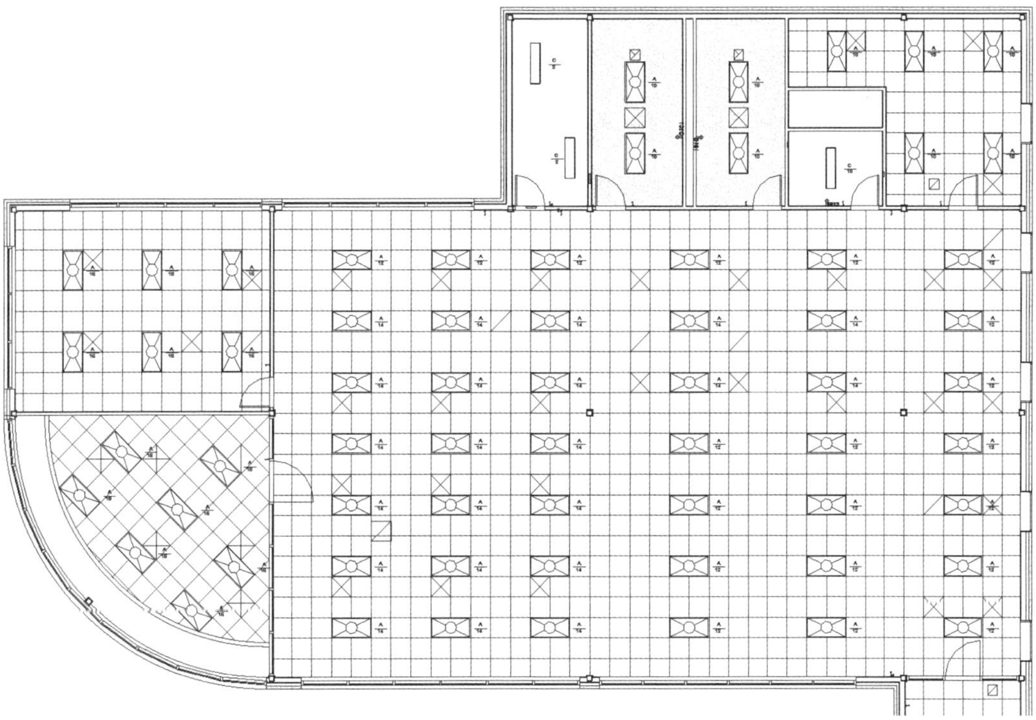

FIGURE 14-4.14 Corrected Level 2 lighting plan

That concludes the exercise on placing light fixtures, light switches and creating systems for them. The starter file for the next chapter will have tags added to each light fixture; it is a custom tag that lists the fixture *Type* and *Circuit* number.

49. **Save** your project!

Exercise 14-5:
Systems Layout

This short exercise will review the placement of system devices: data and phone in this case. Many phone systems are now VoIP (Voice over IP), which means they use the same connection as the computer network system. Therefore, in this case you will only place data devices. If you wanted to schedule the telephone system separately, you could load the telephone device families and place them and just consider the data type connections.

1. Open your law office project.

2. Switch to the **Level 1 – Systems Floor Plan** view.

3. Type "**VV**" and make the following changes:
   a. *Lighting Fixtures* category *Invisible*
   b. *Electrical Fixtures* set to *Halftone*
   c. *Lighting Devices* set to *Halftone*

The power devices, or outlets, are on the *Electrical Fixtures* category and the light switches are on the *Lighting Devices* category. Making these categories halftone allows them to be visible, and coordinated, but remain background information on the systems plans.

4. Repeat Step 3 for the **Level 2 Systems Floor Plan** view.

5. Zoom in to the *Associate's Office* in the **Level 1 – Systems Floor Plan** view.

Next, you will place a data device near each of the desks and on the East wall.

6. Select **Systems → Electrical → Device → Data.**

7. Click **No** and cancel the command (Figure 14-5.1).

8. Load Electrical\MEP\Information and Communication\Communication**Data Outlet.rfa**.
   a. Click **No** to load a tag, if prompted.

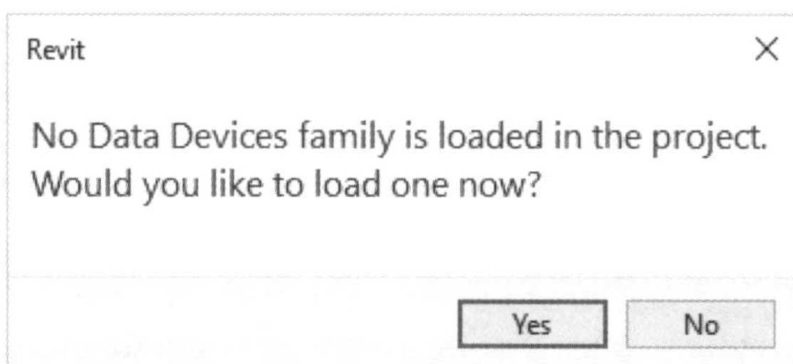

FIGURE 14-5.1 Prompt to load content

9. With **Place on Vertical Face** selected on the *Placement* panel, add the three *data outlets* as shown in Figure 14-5.2.

   TIP: *Be sure to zoom in and place the device on the wall and not on the face of the furniture.*

   a. Data devices are placed at a default 18″ above the floor like the power devices are; this can be changed via *Instance Properties.*

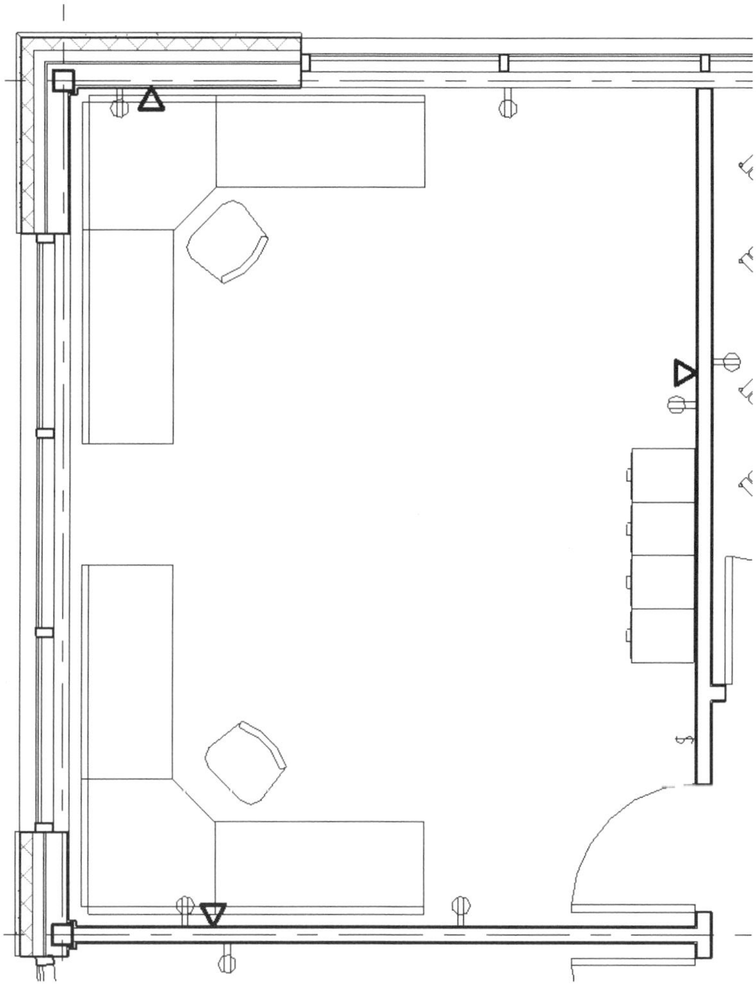

FIGURE 14-5.2 Three data outlets placed on walls

10. Using the process just covered, place outlets throughout the building in the **Systems Floor Plan** views.

11. You should open the **Power Floor Plan** views, make the *Data Devices* halftone and hide the light fixtures.

12. **Save** and **back up** your work.

Self-Exam:

The following questions can be used as a way to check your knowledge of this lesson. The answers can be found at the bottom of this page.

1. The electrical devices are *face based* in Revit *MEP*. (T/F)
2. Electrical devices placed in the electrical views will not automatically show up in the architect's views. (T/F)
3. Revit helps manage circuits in the power panels. (T/F)
4. The mechanical and electrical models have to be in separate files. (T/F)
5. What feature allows you to look for conflicts in your model:

   ______________________________.

Review Questions:

The following questions may be assigned by your instructor as a way to assess your knowledge of this section. Your instructor has the answers to the review questions.

1. The *Distribution System* is used to determine which elements can connect to which power panels. (T/F)
2. Mechanical and electrical engineers use the *MEP* "flavor" of Revit. (T/F)
3. *Face based* devices can only be placed on walls, not floors. (T/F)
4. Revit *Architecture* uses *Rooms* and Revit *MEP* uses *Spaces*. (T/F)
5. Deleting unneeded content from the project is recommended to keep file size down and reduce errors. (T/F)
6. The light fixtures you placed in this chapter will not move with the ceiling, similar to the air terminals. (T/F)
7. The electrical *View Templates* are perfect as is. (T/F)
8. A Panelboard has several limitations related to code compliance. (T/F)
9. Revit *MEP* automatically places an outlet on a circuit when it is placed. (T/F)
10. The various MEP devices have a default elevation they are placed at when in a plan view. (T/F)

SELF-EXAM ANSWERS:
1 – T, **2** – F, **3** – T, **4** – F, **5** – Interference Check

Lesson 15
Site and Renderings

In this chapter, you will take a look at Revit's photorealistic rendering abilities as well as the basic site development tools. Revit has a rendering technology called **Autodesk Raytracer**. Additionally, Autodesk offers several high-end rendering programs like *Autodesk 3DS Max* and *Autodesk Maya,* which work with Revit models in various ways, and the integration options improve with each new release.

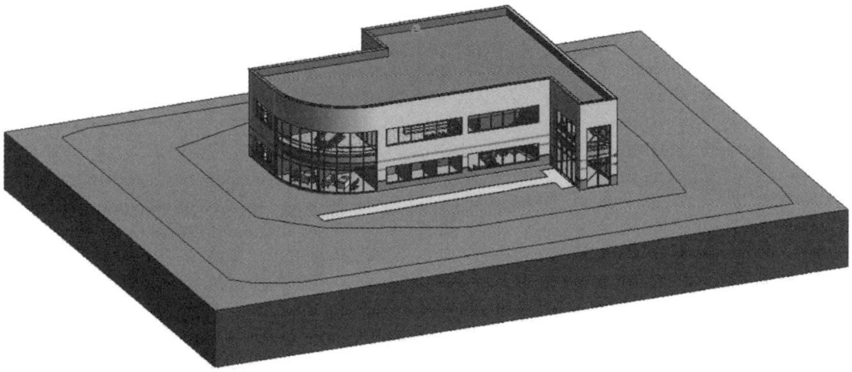

Exercise 15-1:
Site Tools

This lesson will give the reader a quick overview of the site tools available in Revit. The site tools are not intended to be an advanced site development package. Autodesk has other programs much more capable of developing complex sites such as AutoCAD Civil 3D 2027. These programs are used by professional Civil Engineers and Surveyors. The contours generated from these advanced civil CAD programs can be used to generate a topography object in Revit.

In this lesson you will create a topography object from scratch – you will also add a sidewalk.

Once the topography object (the topography object, or element, is a 3D mass that represents part *or* all of the site) is created the grade line will automatically show up in building and wall sections, exterior elevations and site plans. The sections even have the earth pattern filled in below the grade line.

As with other Revit elements you can select the object after it is created and set various properties for it, such as surface material, Phase, etc. One can also return to Sketch mode to refine or correct the surface – this is done in the same way most other Sketched objects are edited – by selecting the item and clicking *Edit* on the *Ribbon.*

Overview of Site Tools on the Ribbon:

Below is a brief description of what the site tools are used for. After this short review you will try a few of these tools on your residence project.

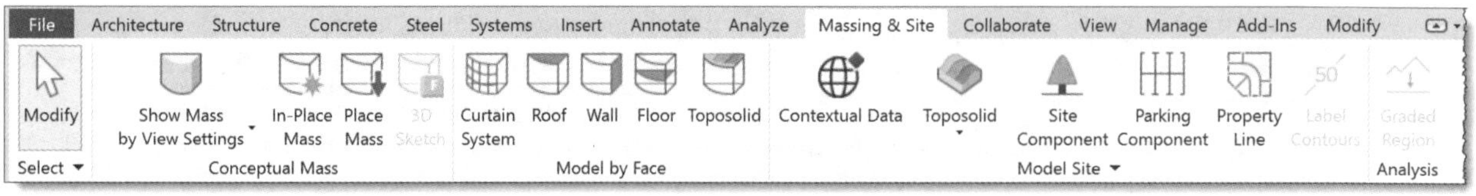

Toposolid: Creates a 3D surface by picking points, specifying the elevation of each point picked, or by using linework within a linked AutoCAD drawing that was created at the proper elevations.

These commands are only visible when a Toposolid is selected:

Sub-Divide: Allows an area to be defined within a previously drawn toposolid; the result is an area within the toposolid that can have a different material than the toposolid itself. The sub-division is still part of the toposolid and will move with it when relocated. If a subregion is selected and deleted, the original surface and properties for that area are revealed.

Simplify Toposolid: This command reduces the number of points used to define the surface. This can change the accuracy but may be required for complex surfaces.

Excavate: This command can be used to select floor or roof elements that will define an area to remove the toposolid (earth) above that area.

Site Component: Items like benches, dumpsters, etc., that are placed directly on the toposolid at the correct elevation at the point picked.

Parking Component: This is a parking stall layout that can be copied around to quickly lay out parking lots. Several types can be loaded which specify both size and angle.

Property Line: Creates property lines in plan views only.

Label Contours: Adds an elevation label to the selected contours.

FYI: Contours are automatically created based on the toposolid.

Graded Region: This tool is used to edit the grade of a toposolid that represents the existing site conditions and the designer wants to use Revit to design the new site conditions. This tool is generally only meant to be used once; when used it will copy the existing site conditions to a new phase and set the existing site to be demolished in the new construction phase. The newly copied site object can then be modified for the new site conditions.

Toposolid Smooth Shading: Found in the Model Site extended panel, it smooths the default faceted look of the surface but does not change the element.

The image below shows the additional Toposolid commands mentioned on the previous page (in the boxed area). These options are only visible on the Ribbon when a previously created Toposolid element is selected. Also, clicking on the **Shape Editing** panel title opens the expanded panel commands.

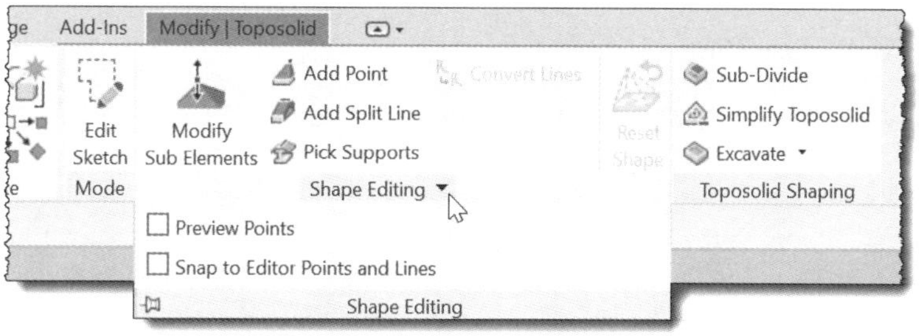

Site Settings:

Each Toposolid element created in a Revit model has its own *Contour Display* settings.

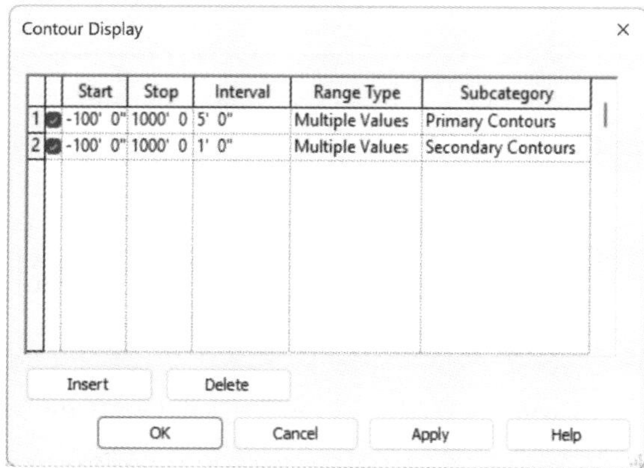

The ***Contour Display*** dialog is accessed via the Type Properties of a selected Toposolid element.

This dialog controls if the contours are displayed when the *toposolid* is visible, via the check box, and at what interval. If the *Interval* is set to 1′-0″ you will see contour lines that follow the ground's surface, and each line represents a vertical elevation change of 1′-0″ from the adjacent contour line. The contour lines alone do not tell you what direction the surface slopes in a plan view; this is why *Contour Labels* are important.

The default settings show primary and secondary contour lines. The **primary contour** lines occur every 5' vertically, in place of the **secondary contour** line in the same location. This is mainly a graphical setting that makes every fifth contour a thicker/darker line.

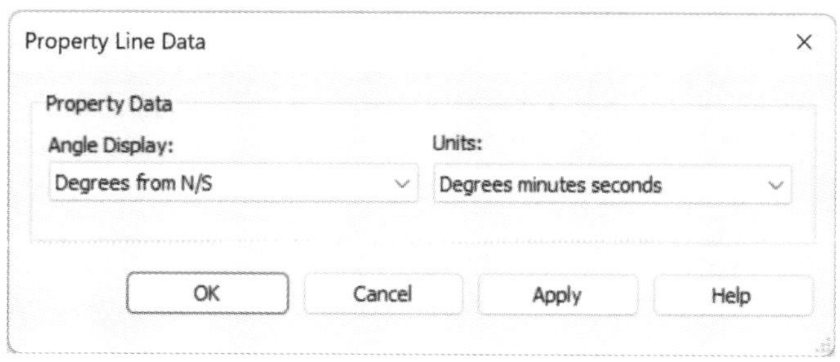

Property Line Data: This dialog controls how angles and lengths are displayed for information describing property lines.

The ***Property Line Data*** dialog is accessed from the down *arrow* next to the *Model Site* panel title.

Creating topography in Revit

1. Open your law office project.
   a. Or use the Chapter 15 starter file from the online files provided.

2. Switch to the **Site Plan** view.
   a. Adjust the category visibility so your view matches Figure 15-1.1. Also, set the *Detail Level* to *Fine*.

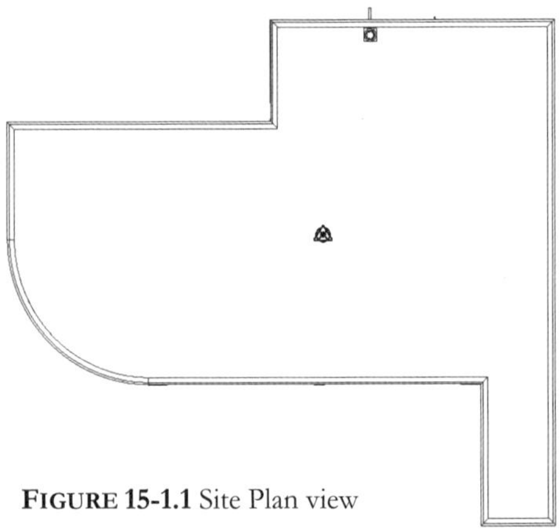

FIGURE 15-1.1 Site Plan view

Here you will basically see what appears to be a roof plan view of your project (Figure 15-1.1). This view has the visibility set such that you see the project from above, and the various "site" categories are turned on so they are automatically visible once they are created. Next, you will take a quick look at the *View Range* for this view so you understand how things are set up.

3. Type **VV**, and turn off **Communication Devices**, **Data Devices**, and **Grids** so they are not visible in the view.

4. In the *Properties Palette*, scroll down and select **Edit** next to *View Range*.

Here you can see the site is being viewed from 200′ above the first floor level, so your building/roof would have to be taller than that before it would be "cut" like a floor plan. The *View Depth* could be a problem here: on a steep site, the entire site will be seen if part of it passes through the specified *View Range*. However, items completely below the *View Range* will not be visible.

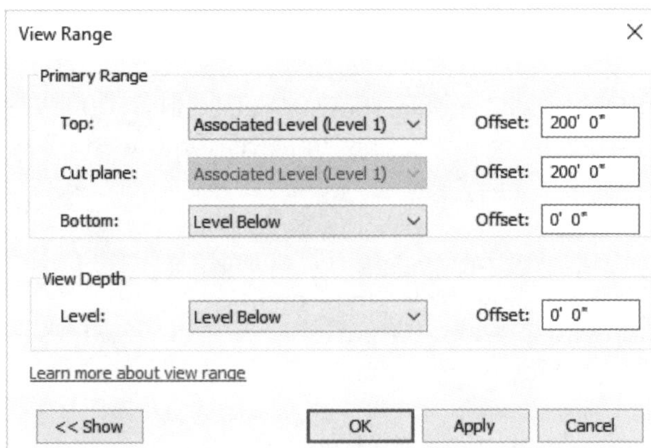

FIGURE 15-1.2 Site Plan view range settings

5. In the *View Depth* section, set the *Level* to **Unlimited**, and then click **OK**.

This change will ensure everything shows up on a steeper site.

You are now ready to create the site object. The element in Revit which represents the site is called *Toposolid.*

***TIP:** Structural engineers can use the toposolid tool to model ledge rock, which would aid in determining how deep foundations need to be.*

6. Select **Massing & Site → Model Site → Toposolid** from the *Ribbon.*

7. Using the Rectangle option on the Ribbon, sketch the boundary of the site as shown in Figure 15-1.3.

8. Click the **green checkmark** to finish the creation of the Toposolid. Click **Don't attach** when prompted.

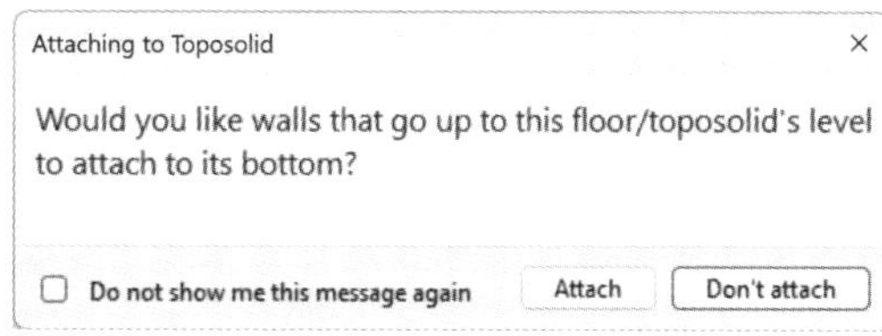

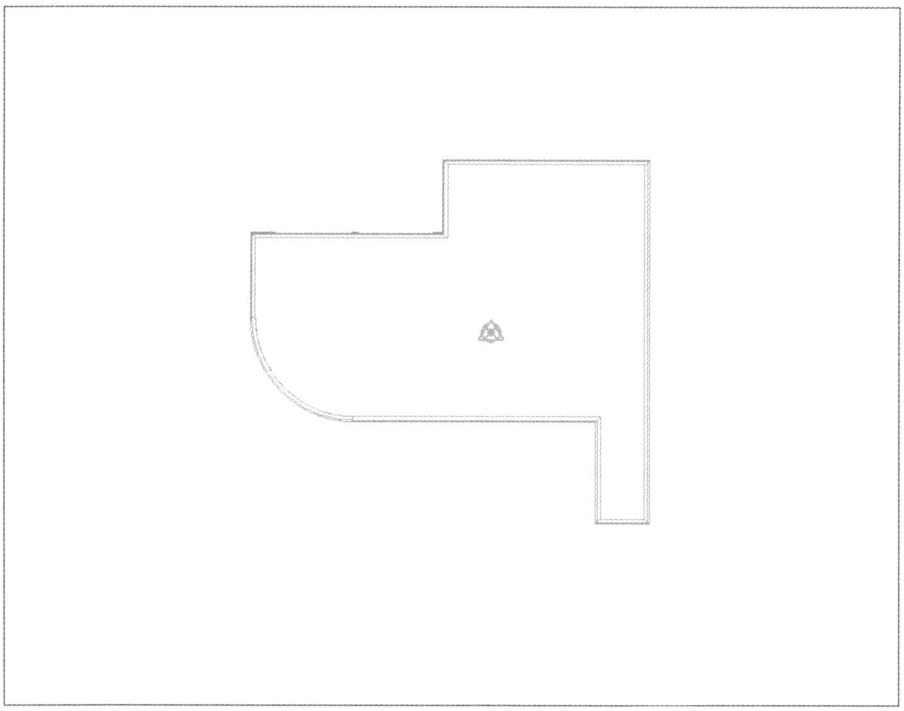

FIGURE 15-1.3 Boundary of site sketched using Toposolid tool

You now have a perfectly flat ground plane that is aligned with the level 1 floor. Next, you will increase the thickness of the Toposolid, move it down, and add points to warp/slope the surface so water drains away from the building.

Next, you will move the Toposolid down to the lowest anticipated level of the ground surface relative to the main level (Level 1) in the building. Then, points will be added within the boundary of the site, around the perimeter of the building, and the elevation of the point will be adjusted upward.

But, first, you will increase the thickness of the site object.

9. With the toposolid selected, click **Edit Type** in the properties palette.

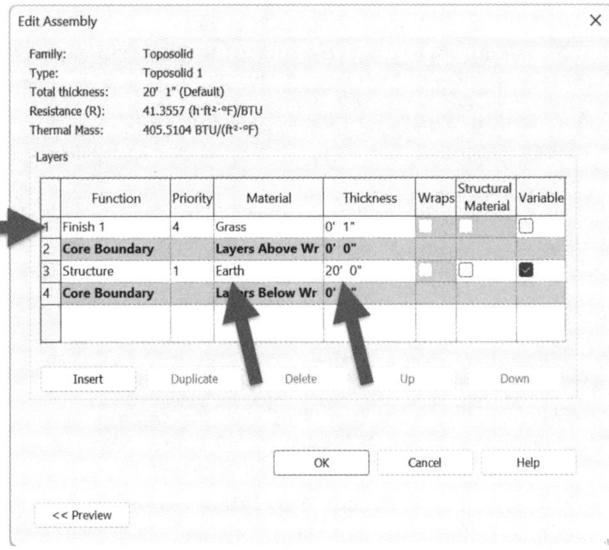

FIGURE 15-1.4 Toposolid type properties adjustment

10. Edit the Structure as follows (Figure 15-1.4):
    a. Material: **Earth**
    b. Thickness: **20'-0"**
    c. Insert Finish layer:
        i. Material: **Grass**
        ii. Thickness: **0'-1"**

11. With the Toposolid still selected, set the *Height Offset From Level* to **-2'-6"** (be sure to add the minus).

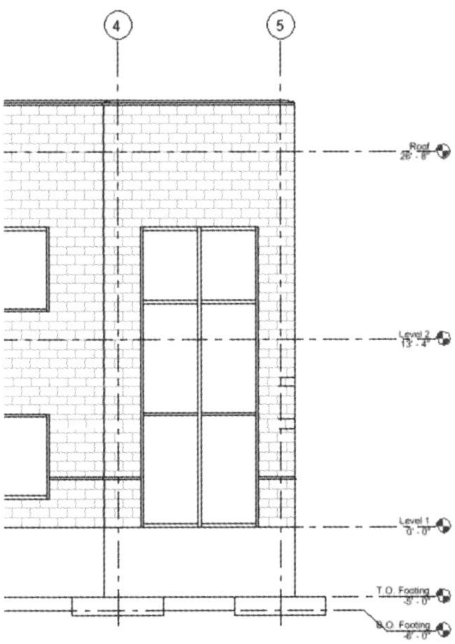

FIGURE 15-1.5 Partial South Elevation

Next, you will add points to adjust the surface.

The elevation you enter for each point should relate to the level datums set up in your project – for example, look at your South exterior elevation (Figure 15-1.5). Recall that the first floor is set to 0′-0″.

The only place you would want to add points at an elevation of -0′-1″ would be at the doors. Everywhere else should be at about -4″ so the grade does not rise higher than the top of the foundation wall and come into contact with the brick, and possibly block the weeps and brick vents.

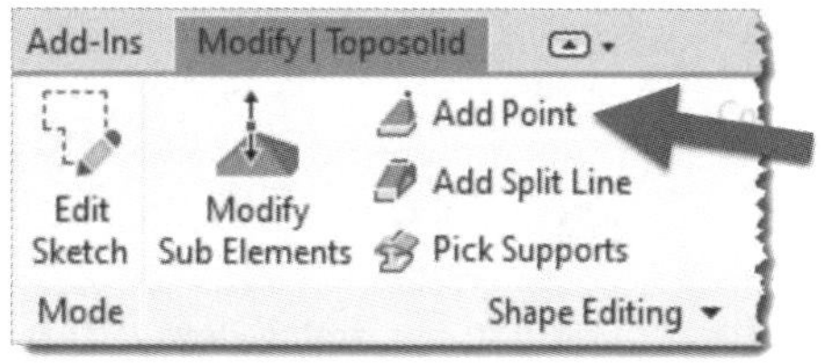

12. In the Site plan view, with the Toposolid selected, click the **Add Point** option on the Ribbon.

13. Pick the six points shown in Figure 15-1.6; these points are at the exterior door locations. Select each point and adjust the *Elevation* to **-0′-1″** (see image to right, remember to add the minus)

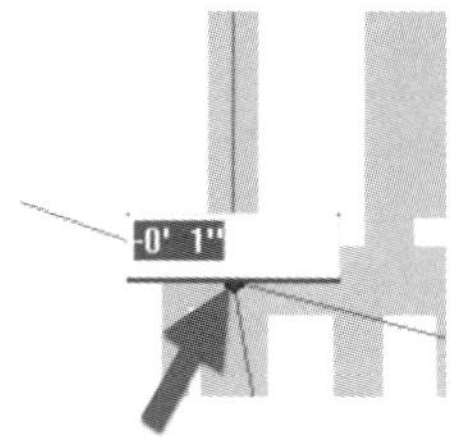

   a. If the points disappear, select the Toposolid and click **Modify Sub Elements** on the Ribbon to make them show up again.

14. Pick all the remaining inside and outside corners along the perimeter of the building which have not yet been selected. Change the *Elevation* to **-0′-4″** (don't forget the minus sign). ***Tip:*** Points can be copied.

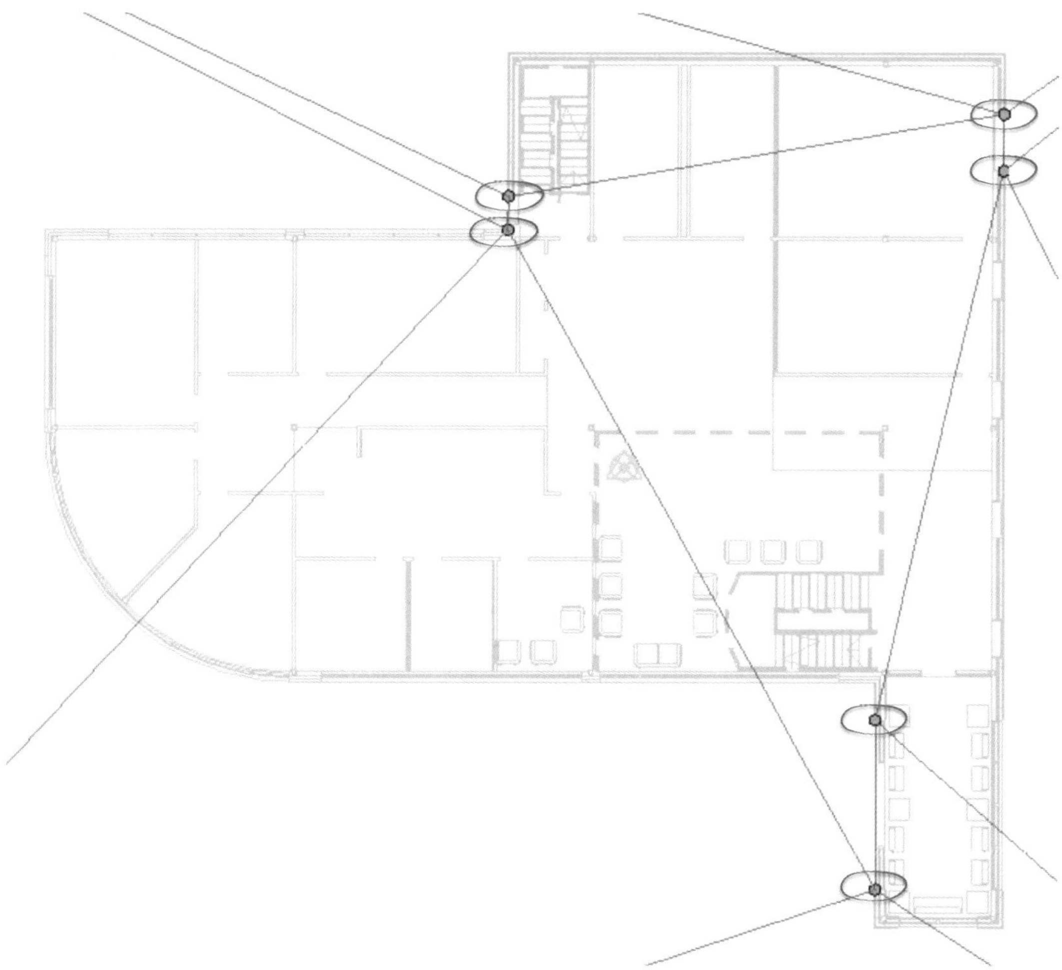

FIGURE 15-1.6 Site plan view – 6 points to be selected (elevation -0′-1″)

15. Click the **Modify** button to exit "edit mode" for the Toposolid element.

Revit has now modified the *Toposolid* based on the points you specified. The more points you add, the more refined and accurate the surface will be.

Ideally, you would use the *Toposolid* tool to create a surface from a surveyor's points file or contour lines drawn in an AutoCAD file – Revit can automatically generate surfaces from these sources, rather than you picking points. However, this process is beyond the scope of this tutorial.

16. Switch to the **3D view** to see your new ground surface (Figure 15-1.7).

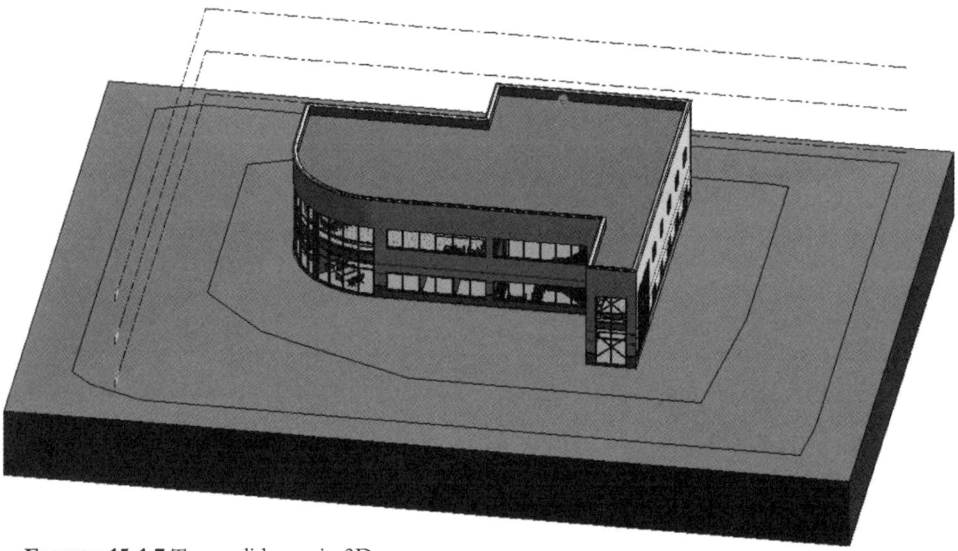

FIGURE 15-1.7 Toposolid seen in 3D

The toposolid is automatically added in sections and elevations (Figure 15-1.8). It may need to be turned off in other views.

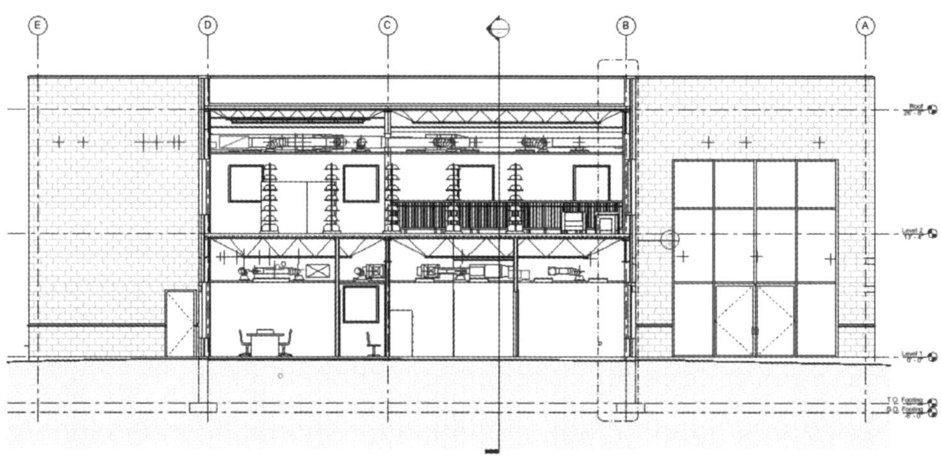

FIGURE 15-1.8 Section with ground pattern added

If your building has a basement or space partially below grade you will need to add an in-place Mass element to "stamp" out an area of the *Toposolid.* The Modify → Cut tool is used to remove the overlapping area between the Mass and the Toposolid. The Cut tool is also used when below-grade foundation walls and slabs overlap the Toposolid.
Next you will create a sidewalk to wrap up this lesson. You will use the *Sub-Divide* tool to create the sidewalk, which defines an area that is still part of the main site object.

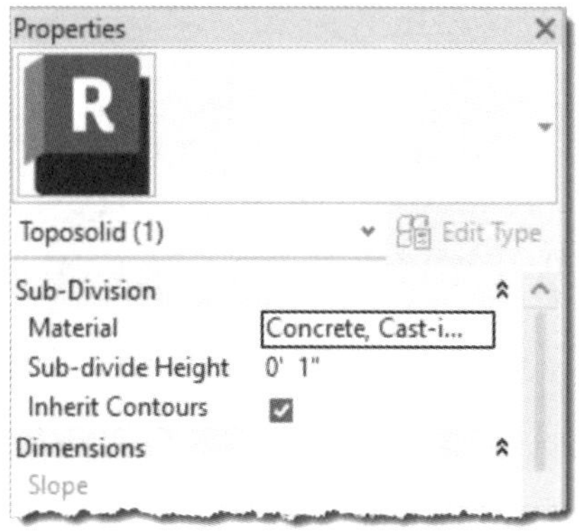

17. Switch back to the **Site** plan view.
18. Select the Toposolid, click the **Sub-Divide** tool (on the Ribbon), and then sketch the lines for the sidewalk (Figure 15-1.9).
19. Click the **green check mark** on the *Ribbon* to finish the *Subregion.*
20. Switch to the default **3D View** and select the new Sub-Division.
21. Adjust the *Sub-Divide Height* to **0'-1"** in Properties and pick a concrete material.

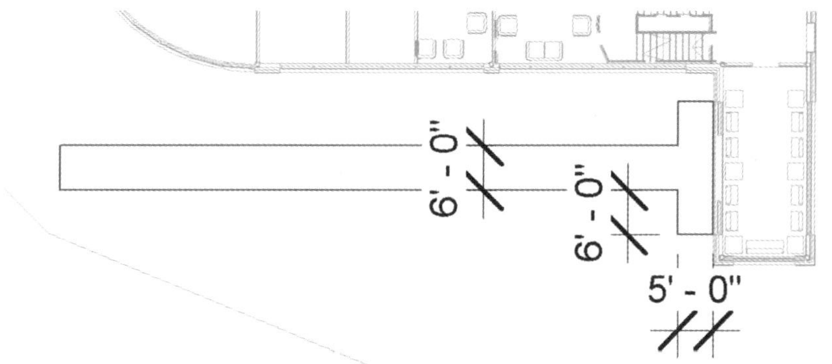

FIGURE 15-1.9 Partial site plan – closed sketch lines for sub-division

The sidewalk is now added to the Toposolid (Figure 15-1.10). If it is ever deleted, the toposolid will fill in the area as it was prior to adding the Sub-Division. Note that a Sub-Division can have a negative value, which results in a recessed area.

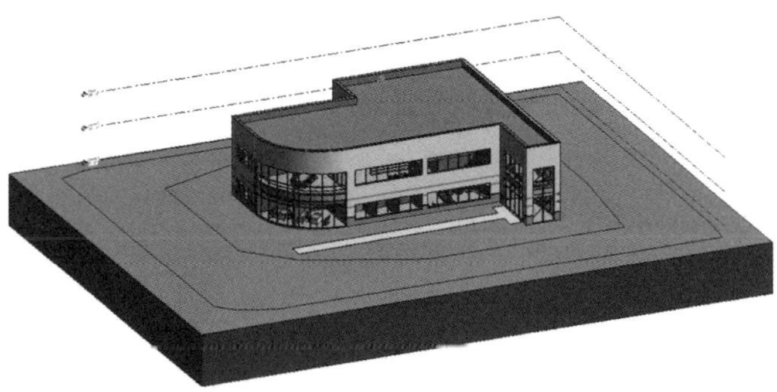

FIGURE 15-1.10 3D view with sidewalk added

That concludes this overview of the site tools provided within Revit. You now have everything modeled in your project so you can start to develop rendered images of your project for presentations.

Exercise 15-2:
Creating an Exterior Rendering

The first thing you will do in terms of rendering is set up a view. You will use the *Camera* tool to do this. This becomes a saved view that can be opened at any time from the *Project Browser.*

Creating a Camera View:

1. Open the **Level 1 Architectural** view, and then **Zoom to Fit** so you can see the entire plan (TIP: Type **ZF** on the keyboard).

2. Select **View → Create → 3D Views → Camera**.
   a. This tool is also available on the *Quick Access Toolbar.*

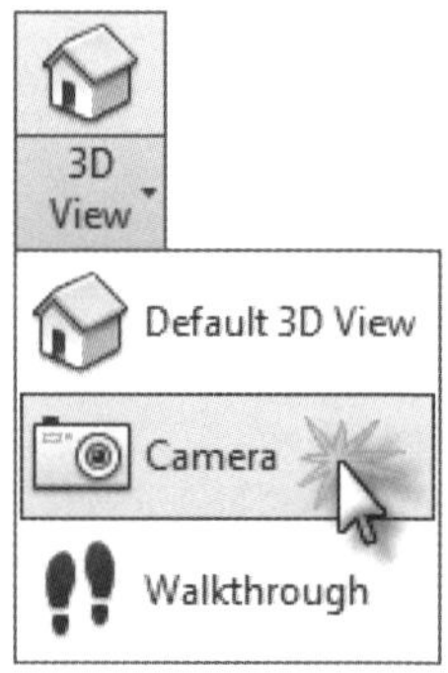

3. Click the mouse in the lower left corner of the screen to indicate the camera eye location (Figure 15-2.1).

   NOTE: Before you click, Revit *tells you it wants the eye location first on the* Status Bar.

4. Next, click near the Northeastern corner; see Figure 15-2.1 to specify the direction you wish to look.

Revit will automatically open a view window for the new camera. Take a minute to look at the view and make a mental note of what you see and don't see in the view (Figure 15-2.2).

On large projects (100MB or more in size) it can take several minutes for the camera view to open. The speed of your computer can dramatically improve performance. The CPU speed, the amount of RAM, and the quality of the graphics card are directly related to Revit's performance. Also, the graphics card's driver should be updated regularly to ensure optimal video performance. A new computer can come with a video driver that is one or two years old!

The image to the left shows the date of the video driver (i.e., Adapter) for a Windows 11-based computer. The driver is only a few months old, which is acceptable.

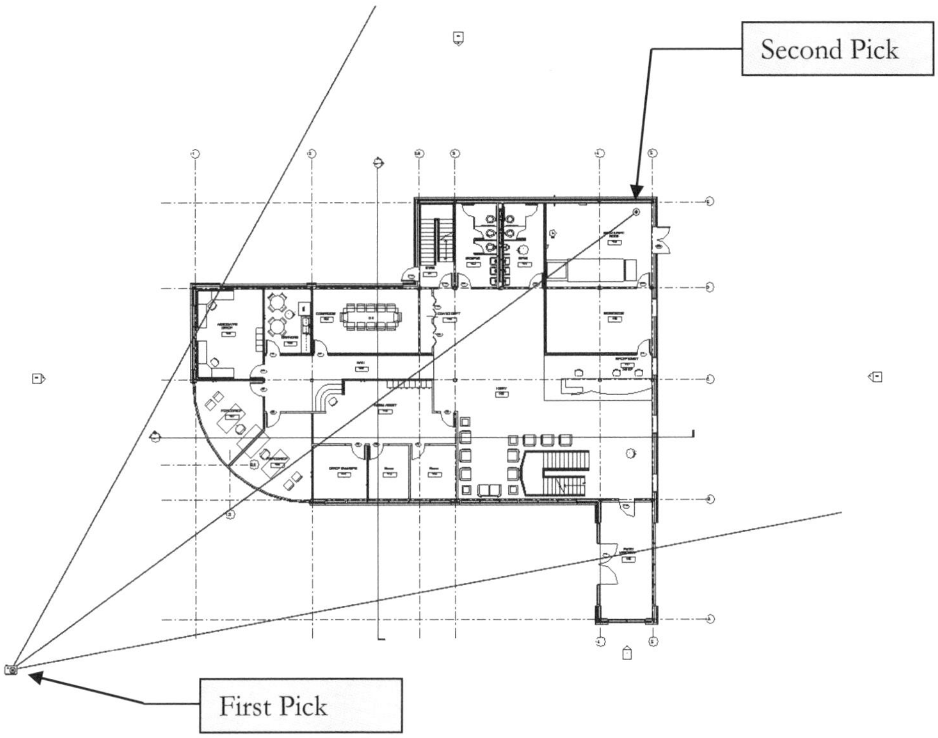

FIGURE 15-2.1 Placing a Camera in Level 1 plan view

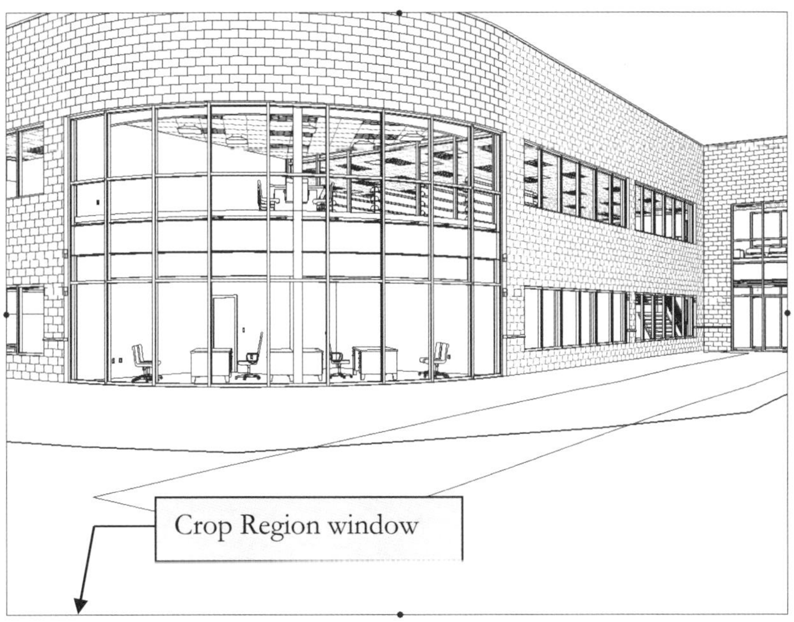

FIGURE 15-2.2 Initial Camera view

5. In **3D View 1** adjust the **Crop Region** to look similar to **Figure 15-2.3**.

This will be the view you render later in this exercise.

FIGURE 15-2.3 Revised camera – 3D View 1

Assigning Materials to Objects:

Materials are scanned images or computer-generated representations of the materials from which your building will be constructed.

Typically, materials are added while the project is being modeled. For example, when you create a material (using the *Materials* tool on the *Manage* tab), you can assign the material at that time. Of course, you can go back and add or change it later. Next, you will see the material assigned for the exterior masonry wall.

6. Switch to **Level 1 Plan** view.

7. Select an exterior wall somewhere in plan view.

8. In the *Properties Palette*, click **Edit Type…** and then click **Edit** *structure*.

9. Notice the material selected for the exterior finish is **Concrete Masonry Units**; click in that cell (Figure 15-2.4).

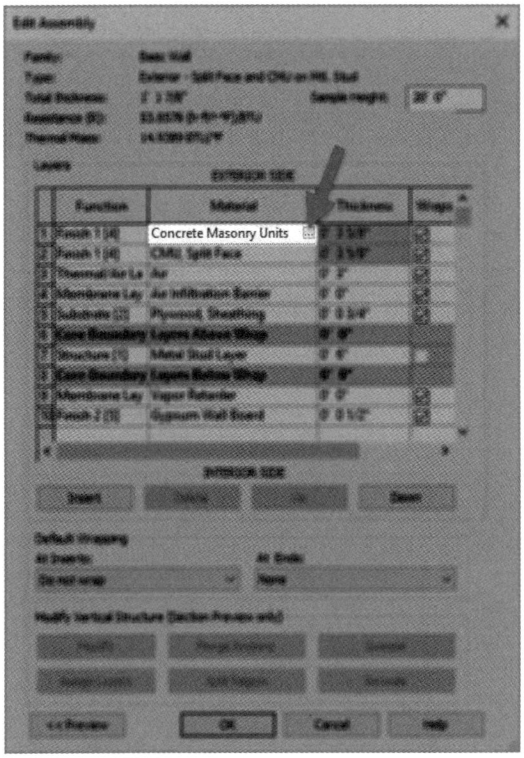

FIGURE 15-2.4 Exterior wall assembly

10. Click the "…" icon to the right of the label **Concrete Masonry Units**.

Now you will take a look at the definition of this material.

TIP: You can also get here via Manage (tab) → Materials *once you know which material is being used.*

You are now in the *Material Browser* dialog (Figure 15-2.5). You should notice that a *Texture* is already selected for the *Appearance* asset (Figure 15-2.6).

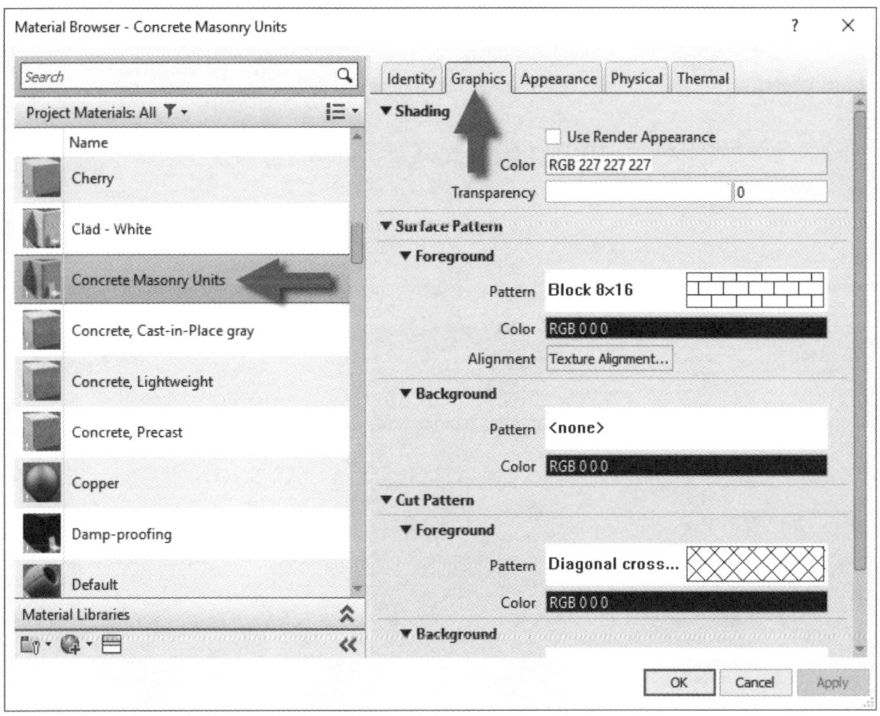

FIGURE 15-2.5 Materials dialog; initial view

11. Click the ***Appearance*** tab (Step 2 in Figure 15-2.6).

You will now see all the masonry graphics available in Revit's *Library* (Figure 15-2.6).

You can browse through the list and select any render graphics in the list to be assigned to the *Concrete Masonry Units* material in Revit. The graphic does not have to be CMU but would be confusing if something like brick were assigned to the *Concrete Masonry Units* material.

12. Click **Masonry** in the *Autodesk Library* section (Step #5, lower left of Figure 15-2.6). Take a few minutes to look at the various render graphics available; click on a few of the categories to narrow the options.

13. **Cancel** all open dialog boxes.

When you render any object (wall, ceiling, etc.) that has the material *Concrete Masonry Units* associated with it, it will have the light gray CMU image mapped on it.

If you need more than one CMU color, you duplicate the material listed in Figure 15-2.5 and assign another render appearance asset.

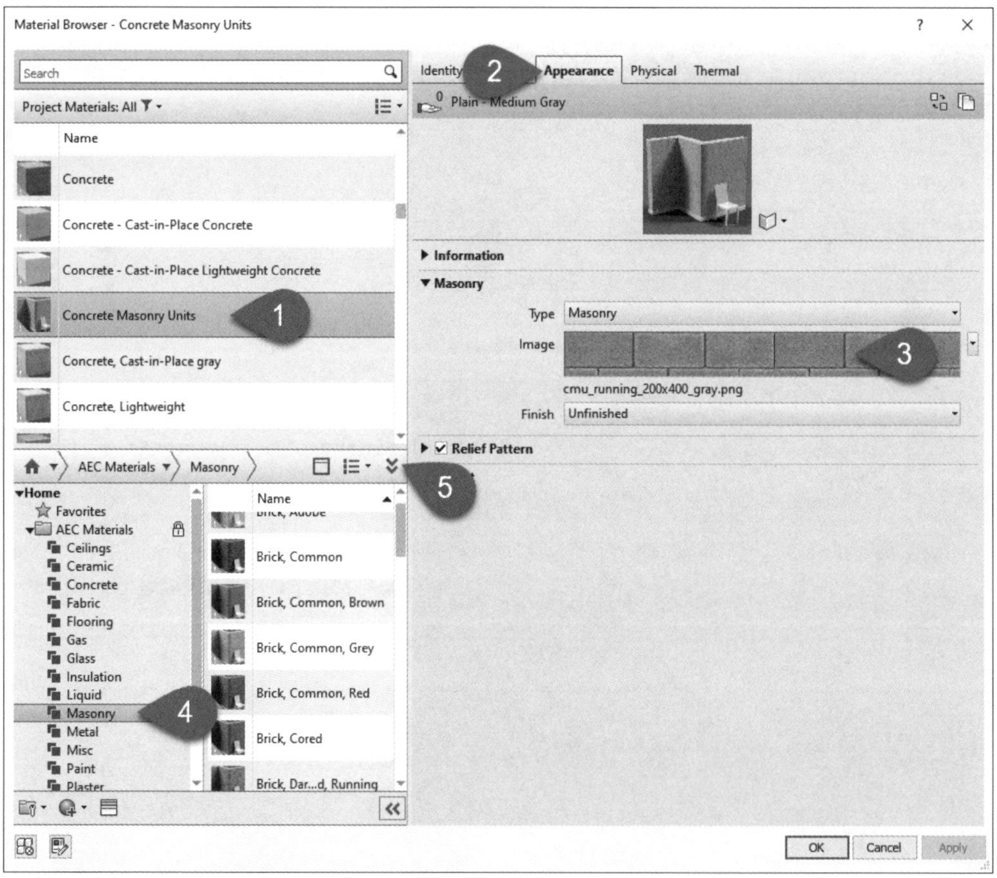

FIGURE 15-2.6 Revit's Render Appearance Library dialog – step #4

Next, you will look at the materials for the curtain wall. Both the mullions and the curtain panels, the glass in this case, have a material assigned to them.

14. Zoom in to one of the curtain wall elements.

15. Select one of the vertical mullions; hover and click only when the mullion highlights, tapping *Tab* if needed.

16. Open the **Type Properties** via the *Properties Palette.*

17. Notice the material for the mullion is set to **Aluminum** (Figure 15-2.7).

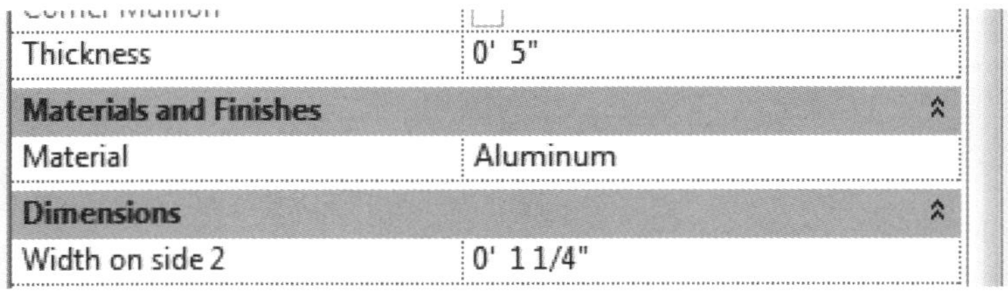

Thickness	0' 5"
Materials and Finishes	
Material	Aluminum
Dimensions	
Width on side 2	0' 1 1/4"

FIGURE 15-2.7 Mullion material

18. Click **OK** to close the open dialog.

Now you will look at the material for the *curtain panel.* To select the curtain panel, you will need to tap the *Tab* key in order to cycle through the options directly below the cursor.

19. Hover over the **curtain panel**, the glass, and tap the ***Tab*** key until it highlights; **click** to select it (Figure 15-2.8).

When the curtain panel is selected, you will see the lines change to the color blue and a push pin will appear indicating it is locked.

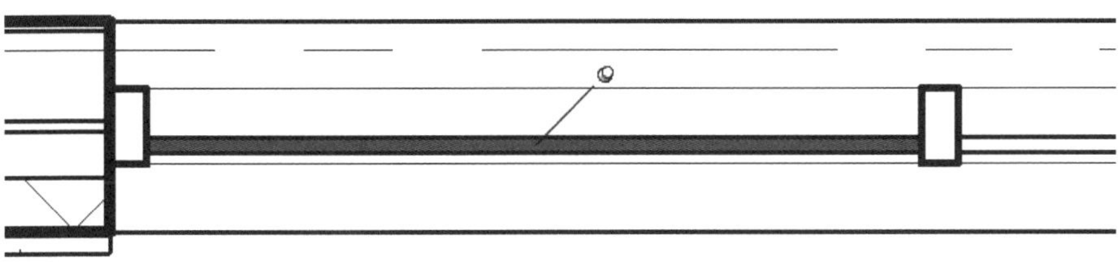

FIGURE 15-2.8 Select the Curtain Panel

20. View the curtain panel's **Type Properties**.

21. Notice the material is set to *Glass* (Figure 15-2.9).

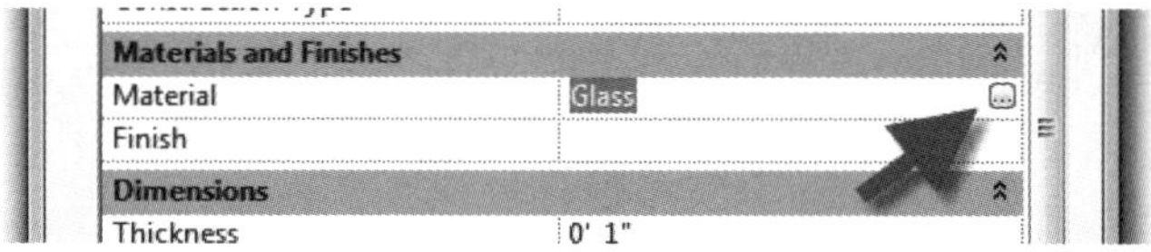

FIGURE 15-2.9 Curtain Panel material

22. Click on the material name **Glass** to select the cell.

23. Click the small button that appears to the right (Figure 15-2.9).

Notice for the *Graphics* asset (see Figure 15-2.10) the shading is set to a blue color with 75% transparency. This only relates to the shaded display styles and does not apply to rendered views. It is beneficial to check the *Use Render Appearance* option as the color in a shaded view will be automatically set to match the approximate color of the material that will be used for generating photorealistic renderings, i.e., the *Appearance* asset.

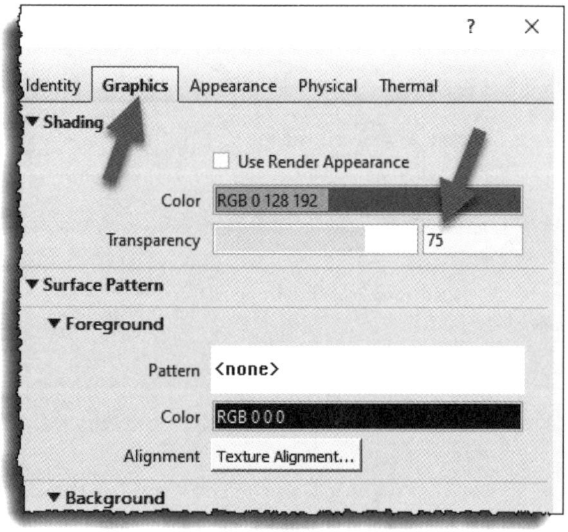

FIGURE 15-2.10 Editing material; Glass

24. Click *Use Render Appearance* option.

25. Switch to the ***Appearance*** tab.

We want to make sure that the render *Appearance* is not set to the generic, or just glass. You will select a reflective clear glazing next.

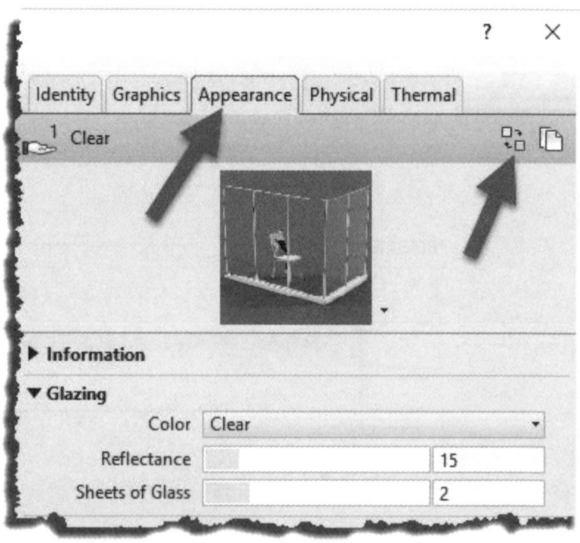

FIGURE 15-2.11A Replace this asset

26. Open the *Asset Browser* by clicking **Replace this asset** in the upper right (Fig. 15-2.11a).

27. Select the *Glazing* category (Figure 15-11A).

28. Select **Clear Reflective** from the options (Figure 15-4.11B).

It is best to select one of the "glazing" rendering *Appearances* for glass in windows and curtain walls. They are designed specifically for this situation and allow lighting calculations to work correctly if the model is exported to Autodesk *3DS Max Design.*

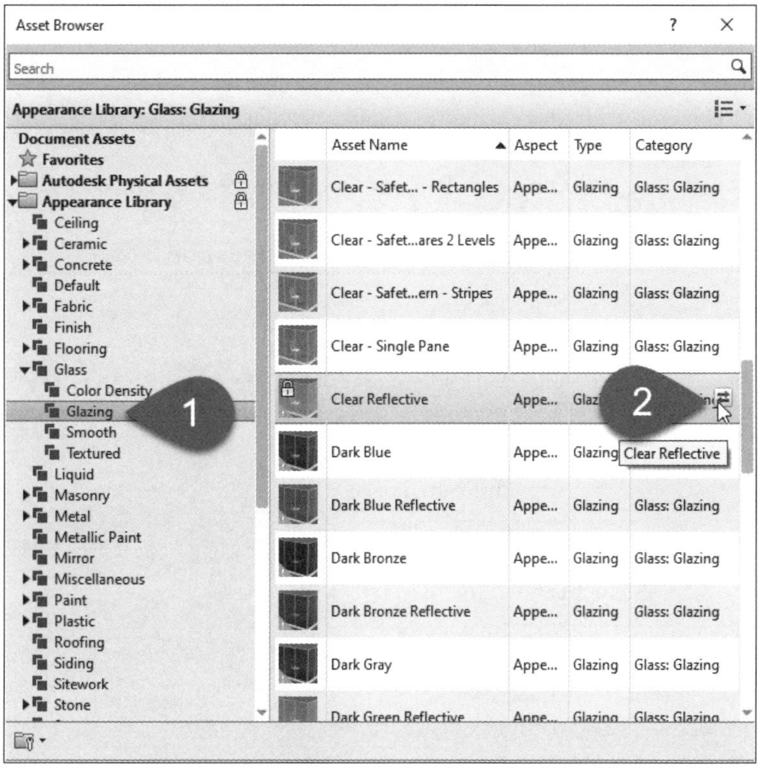

FIGURE 15-2.11B Asset browser

Notice, for the *Appearance* asset in the *Materials* dialog, that the number of sheets of glass is an option. Is your curtain wall double or triple glazed? Do not change this setting at this time. You should also notice the shading color changed on the *Graphics* tab to match the *Render Appearance* color.

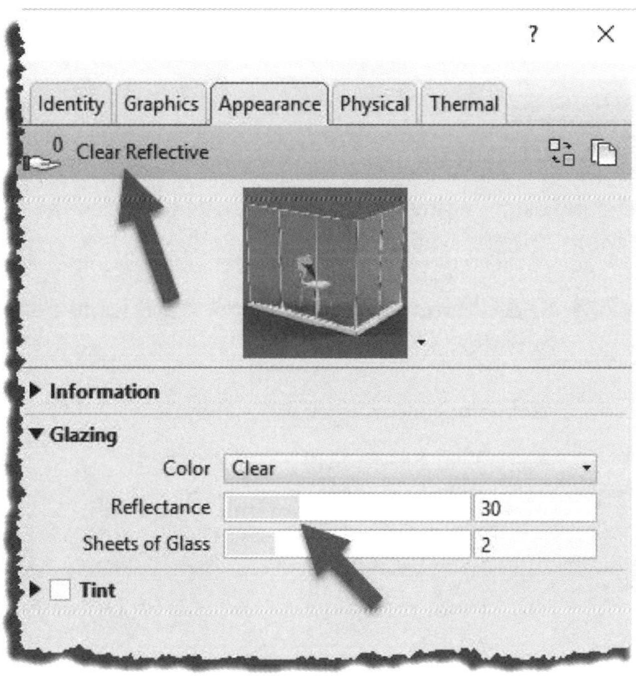

FIGURE 15-2.12 Asset properties

29. Click **OK** to close all open dialog boxes.

The way in which you just changed materials is the same for most elements.

Project Location:

A first step in setting up a rendering is to specify the location of the project on the Earth. This is important for accurate daylight studies.

30. Select **Manage → Project Location → Location**.

31. In the *Project Address* field, enter **Minneapolis, MN**.
    a. You may also enter your location if you wish.
    b. It is even possible to enter the actual street address.

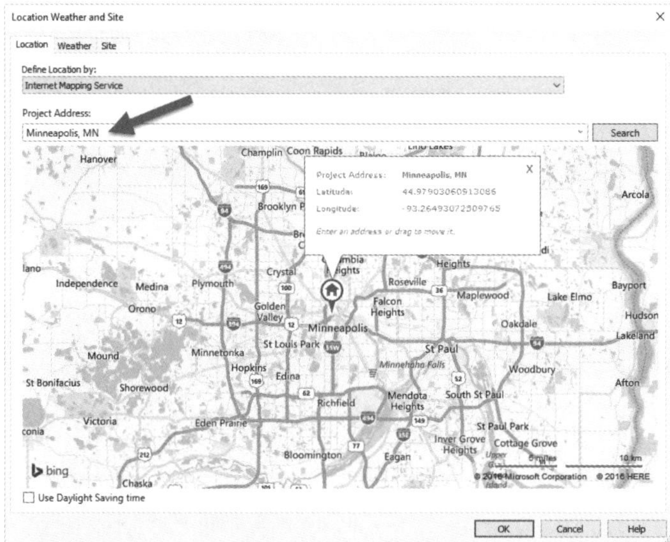

FIGURE 15-2.13 Location Weather and Site dialog

32. Press **Enter**.

You should now see an internet-based map of your project location, complete with longitude and latitude (Figure 15-2.13).

33. Click **OK**.

Sun Settings:

The next step in preparing a rendering is to define the sun settings. You will explore the various options available.

34. Select **Manage → Settings → Additional Settings** (*drop-down list icon*) **→ Sun Settings**.

35. Make the following changes (Figure 15-2.14)
    a. Solar Study: **Still**
    b. Select **Summer Solstice** on the left.
    c. Click the ***Duplicate*** icon in the lower left.
    d. Enter the following name: **Law Office 6-30 at 3pm**.
    e. **Uncheck** *Ground Plane at Level.*
    f. Adjust the Month, Day and Time to match the name just entered.
    g. Change the year to the current year.

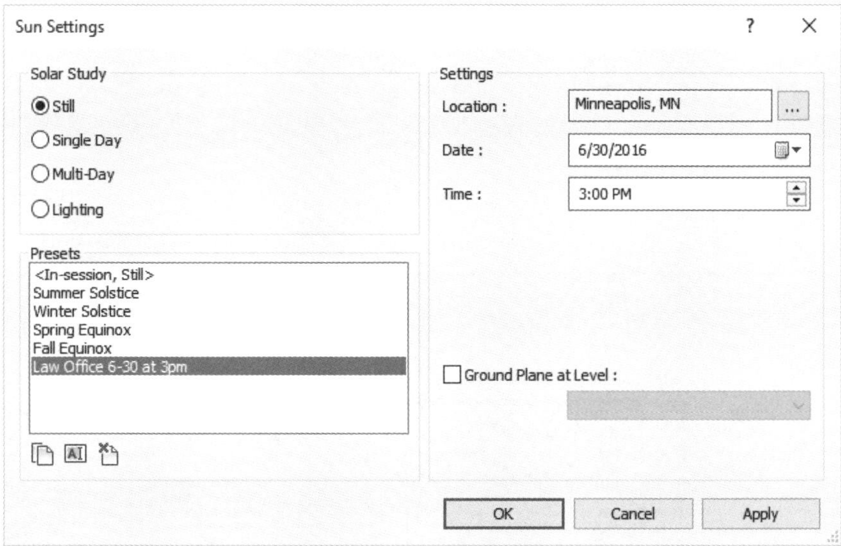

FIGURE 15-2.14 Sun Settings dialog

36. Click **OK** to close the dialog.

The previous sun settings apply to the entire project, not just the current view, which is the intent of the *Manage* tab. This means other views will have access to this new saved sun setting option. We turned off the *Ground Plane* because we have a toposurface for shadows to fall on… if we want ground shadows and don't have a ground surface, then that is when *Ground Plane* should be turned on.

Specifying True North:

Another important step in rendering sunlight is telling Revit what true north is. All architectural drawings assume a project north being straight up for convenience of design and drafting. To set True North, you do the following (but do not make any changes now):

- Switch to the **Site Plan** view.
- Set the *Orientation* to *True North* in the *View Properties.*
- Select **Position → Rotate True North** on the *Manage* tab.
- Rotate the model accordingly.

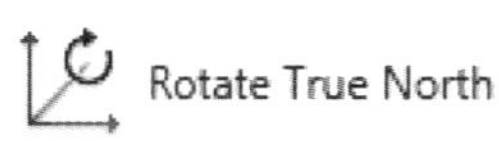

Properly setting True North will make the renderings more realistic and daylighting studies valid.

All views set to *Project North* will not be rotated. Do not modify *True North* at this time.

Placing Trees:

Next, you will place a few trees into your rendering. You will adjust their exact location so they are near the edge of the framed rendering so as not to cover too much of the building.

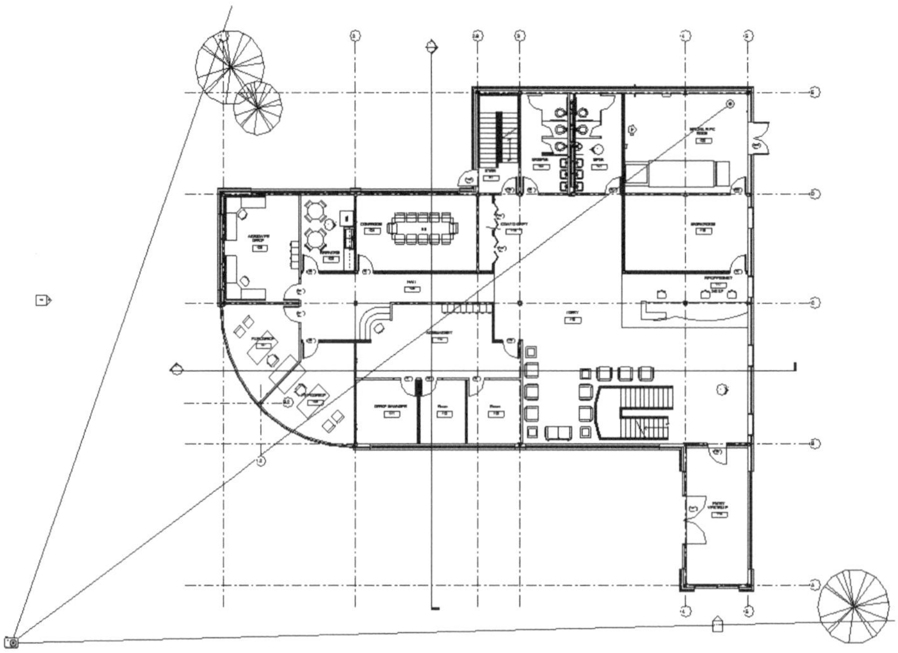

FIGURE 15-2.15 Level 1 with trees added

37. While still in the **Level 1 Plan** view, select **Architecture → Build → Component → Place a Component** from the *Ribbon. **FYI:** Click no for any tag prompt.*

38. Pick *RPC Tree – Deciduous:* **Largetooth Aspen 25′** from the *Type Selector* on the *Properties Palette.*

    ***FYI:** If the tree is not listed in the* Type Selector*, click Load Autodesk Family and load the Deciduous tree family from the Plantings folder.*

39. Place three trees as shown in **Figure 15-2.15**. One tree will be made smaller starting in Step #41.

    ***FYI:** While in the Level 1 Plan view, right-click on the 3D View 1 label in the Project Browser and select **Show Camera** to see the field of view.*

40. Adjust the trees in the plan view, reviewing the effects in the **3D View 1** view, so your 3D view is similar to Figure 15-2.16.

41. In the Level 1 Plan view, select the tree that is shown smaller in **Figure 15-2.15**.

42. Click **Edit Type** on the *Properties Palette,* and then click **Duplicate** and enter the name **Largetooth Aspen 18′**.

43. Change the *Plant Height* to **18′** (from 25′) and then click **OK** to close the open dialog boxes.

The previous three steps allow you to have a little more variety in the trees being placed. Otherwise, they would all be the same height, which is not very natural.

FIGURE 15-2.16 3D View 1 – with trees

Revit renderings can show a high level of detail if set up correctly. The images below show custom content created for use in projects. The content is accurate dimensionally and has materials assigned. The materials provided by Revit are high quality and help to create realistic renderings. Notice the transparent glass and reflections.

Images courtesy of LHB (www.LHBcorp.com)

Adding Exterior Sun Shades:

Controlling how the sunlight enters the building is an important part of an architectural design. In the next few steps you will add exterior sun shades to a few windows. This will block the hot sunlight during the summer months when it is high in the sky and allow it in during the winter months when the sun is low. This design technique can be validated in Revit by doing multiple renderings with various times and dates plugged in. Revit allows you to create animated sun studies as well!

44. Load the following two families from the files provided with this book:
    a. Renderings**Exterior Sun Shade**
    b. Renderings**Exterior Sun Shade – Curved Wall**

Exterior Sun Shade is a custom *face based* family. You will add it in an elevation view. The length can be adjusted via grips or element properties.

45. Switch to the West Elevation view.

46. Add the two sun shades to the curtain walls between Grids D and C via the ***Component*** tool (Figure 15-2.17).

47. Add five more sun shades, including one curved, at the windows shown in Figure 15-2.24. Adjust the length to match the window. Place the curved shade in plan view and then move it to the correct vertical position via an elevation view.

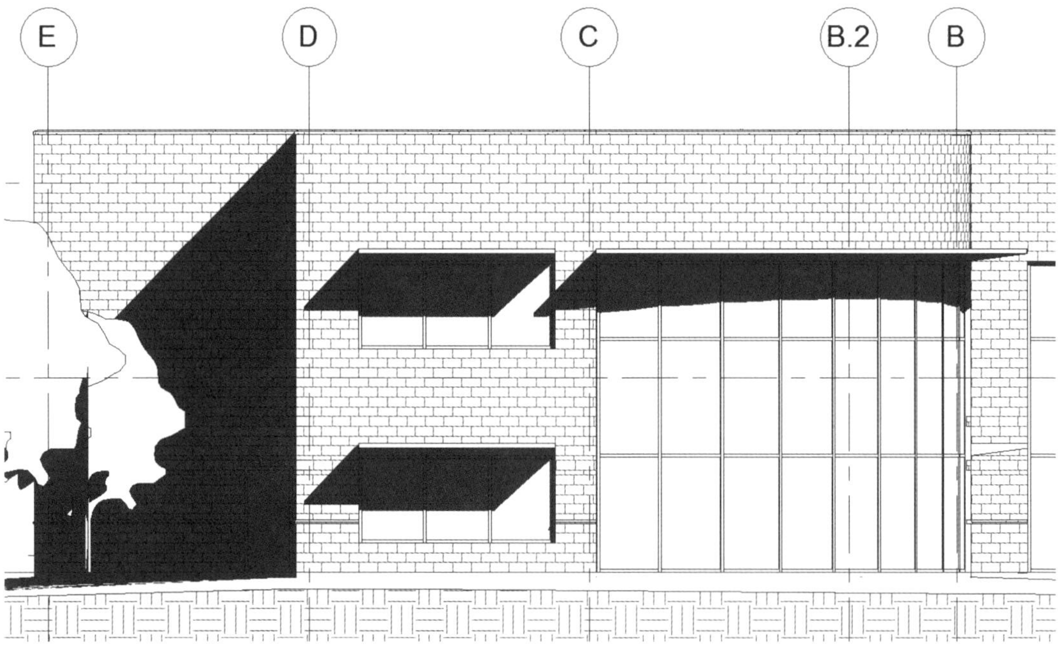

FIGURE 15-2.17 Sun shades added. Shadows turned on in 2D view

Setting up the Environment:

You have limited options for setting up the building's environment. If you need more control than what is provided directly in Revit, you will need to use another program such as Autodesk *3DS Max Design 2027* which is designed to work with Revit and can create extremely high-quality renderings and animations; it even has day lighting functionality that helps to validate LEED® (Leadership in Environmental and Energy Design) requirements.

48. Switch to your camera view: **3D View 1**

49. Select the ***Show Rendering Dialog*** icon on the *View Control Bar*; it looks like a teapot (Figure 15-2.18).

    FYI: *This icon is only visible when you are in a 3D view; the same is true for the Steering Wheel and View Cube.*

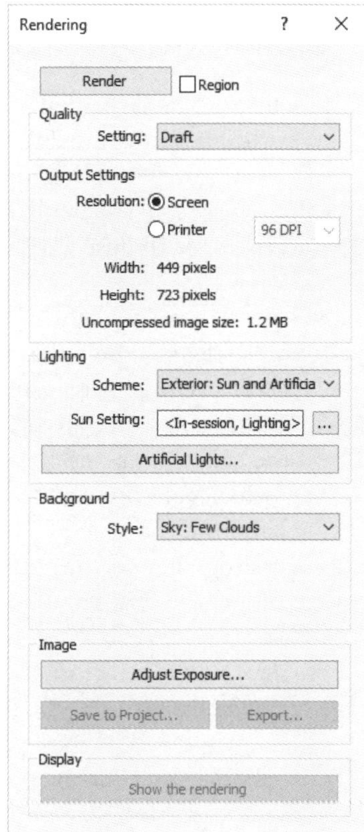

FIGURE 15-2.19 Rendering dialog

The *Rendering* dialog box is now open (Figure 15-2.19). This dialog box allows you to control the environmental settings you are about to explore and actually create the rendering.

FIGURE 15-2.18 Scene Selection dialog

50. In the *Lighting* section, click the down arrow next to *Scheme* to see the options. Select **Exterior: Sun and Artificial** when finished (Figure 15-2.20).

The lighting options are very simple choices: Is your rendering an interior or exterior rendering, and is the light source *Sun*, *Artificial* or both? You may have artificial lights, light fixtures like the ones you placed in the office, but still only desire a rendering solely based on the light provided by the sun. *Sun only* will be faster.

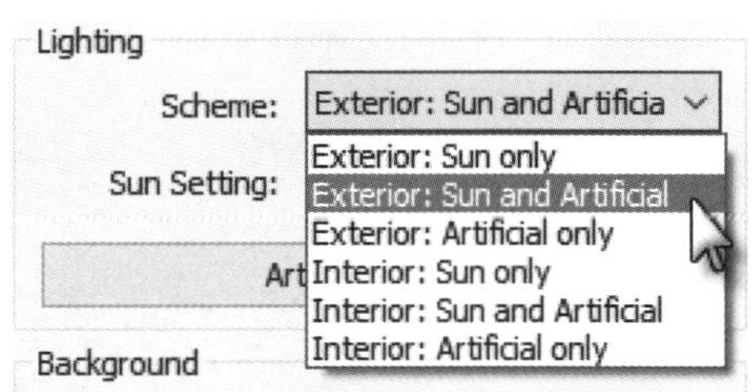

FIGURE 15-2.20 Lighting options

51. In the *Lighting* section, set the *Sun Setting* to <Still> **Law Office 6-30 at 3pm**. (This relates to the Figure 15-2.14 settings.)

    FYI: *In the Sun and Shadow Settings dialog box, Revit lets you set up various "scenes" which control time of day. Two examples would be:*
    - *Law Office Daytime, summer*
    - *Law Office Nighttime, window*

    Looking back at Figure 15-2.14, you would click Duplicate again and provide additional names. The names would then be available from the Sun drop-down list in the Render dialog box.

52. Click on the **Artificial Lighting** button (Figure 15-2.20).

You will now see a dialog similar to the one shown to the right (Figure 15-2.21).

You will see several 2x4 light fixtures. The light fixtures relate to the fixtures you inserted in the reflected ceiling plans using Revit's *MEP* tools. It is very convenient that you can place lights in the ceiling plan and have them ready to render whenever you need to (i.e., render and cast light into the scene!). Here you can group lights together so you can control which ones are on (e.g., exterior and interior lights).

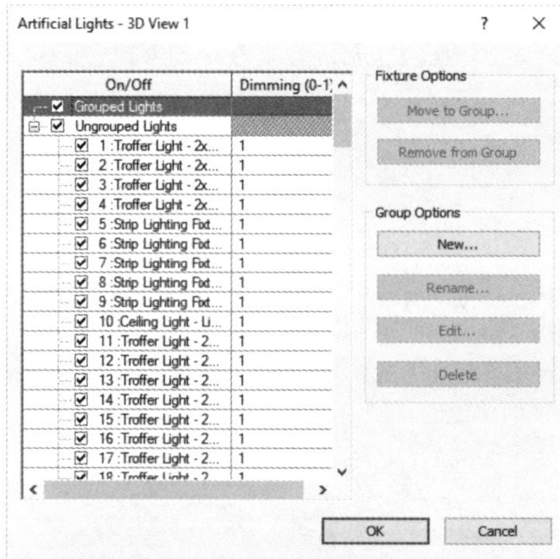

FIGURE 15-2.21 Scene Lighting dialog

53. Click **Cancel** to close the *Artificial Lighting* dialog.

54. Click the down-arrow next to *Style* in the *Background* area (Figure 15-2.22); if your options are different, verify the *Engine* setting above.

55. Select **Sky: Few Clouds**.

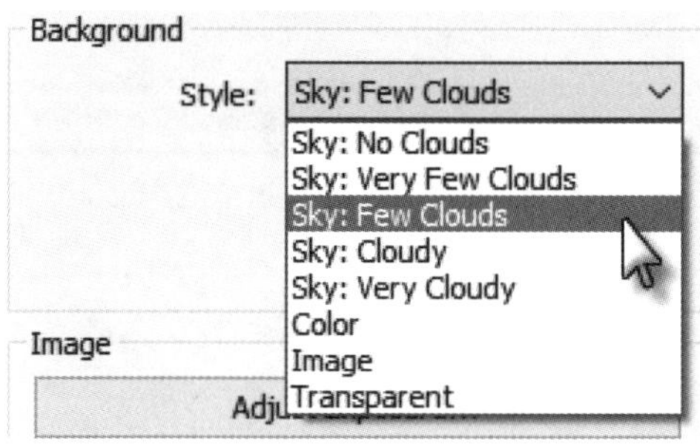

FIGURE 15-2.22 Background Style

Notice that for the background, one option is *Image*. This allows you to specify a photograph of the site, or one similar. It can prove difficult getting the perspective just right, but the end results can look as if you took a picture of the completed building.

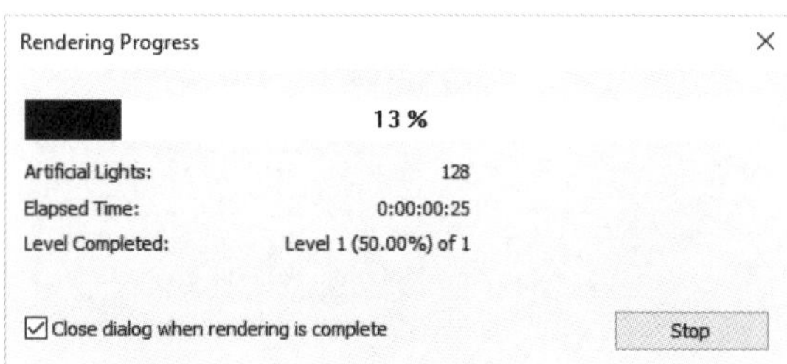

FIGURE 15-2.23 Rendering progress

56. Make sure the *Quality* is set to **Draft**.

FYI: *The time to process the rendering increases significantly as the quality level is raised.*

57. Click **Render** from the *Rendering* dialog box.

You will see a progress bar while the rendering is processing (Figure 15-2.23).

After a few minutes, depending on the speed of your computer, you should have a low quality rendered image similar to Figure 15-2.24 below. You can increase the quality of the image by adjusting the quality and resolution settings in the *Render* dialog. However, these higher settings require substantially more time to generate the rendering. The last step before saving the Revit project file is to save the rendered image to a file.

> ***FYI:*** *Each time you make changes to the model which would be visible from that view, you will have to re-render the view to get an updated image.*

Depending on exactly how your view was set up, you may be able to see light from one of the light figures. Also, notice the railing through the curtain wall; Revit has the glass in the windows set to be transparent!

FIGURE 15-2.24 Rendered view; low quality draft

58. From the *Rendering* dialog select **Export**.

> ***FYI:*** *The 'Save to Project' button saves the image within the Revit Project for placement on Sheets. This is convenient but does make the project size larger, so you should delete old ones from the Project Browser!*

59. Select a *location* and provide a *file name.*

60. Set the *Save As* type to **PNG**.

61. Click **Save**.

The image file you just saved can now be inserted into MS Word or Adobe Photoshop for editing.

The images below are examples of high-quality renderings that can be produced by Revit. These images were part of a design competition submittal which took First Place. The award was given by the Minnesota Chapter of the United States Green Building Council (USGBC). The design team included Wesley Stabs and Chris Wingate.

Realistic Display Setting:

In addition to *Shade* and *Hidden Line* display settings, you can also select ***Realistic***. This will show the render *Appearance* materials on your building without the need to do a full rendering. Although the shades and shadows are not nearly as realistic as a full rendering, turning on ***Ambient Shadows*** in the *Properties Palette > Graphic Display Options* comes pretty close. This is a great way to get an idea of how the materials look, but you will find it best to minimize the use of this setting as Revit will run much slower.

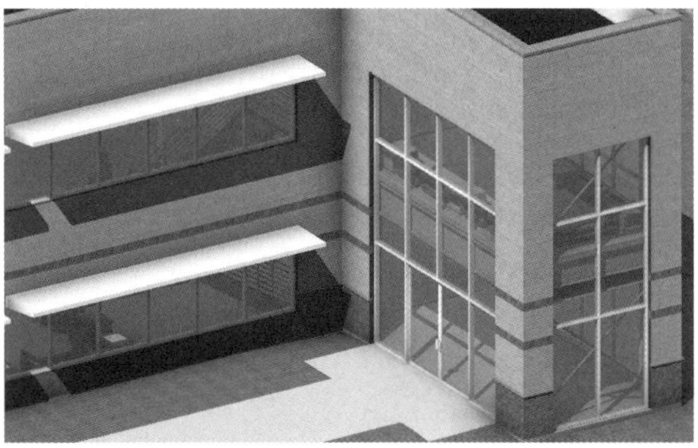

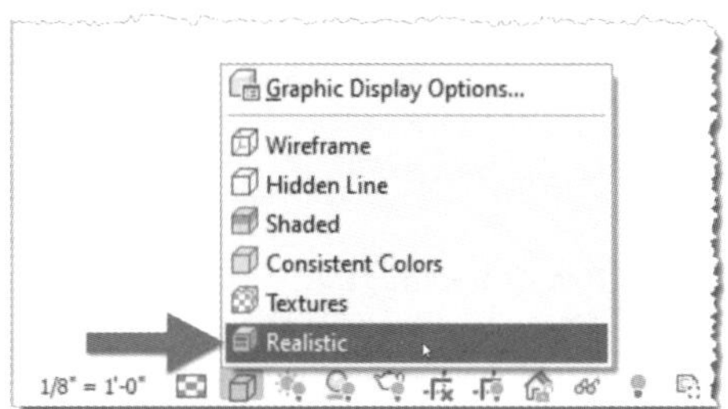

Duplicating a Material

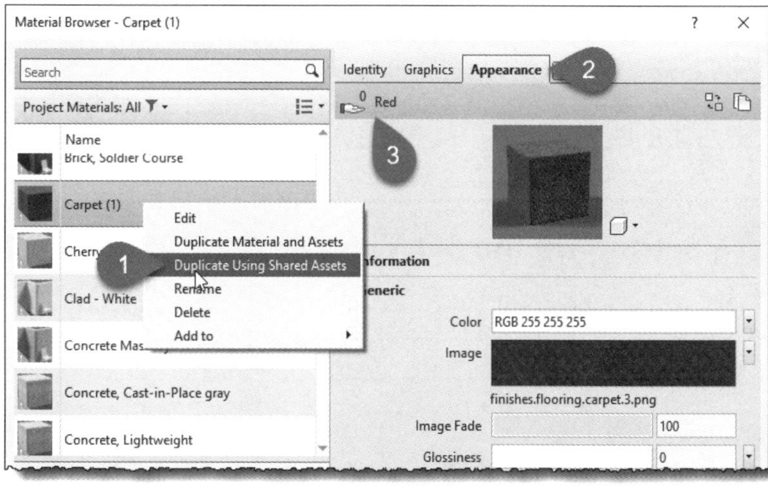

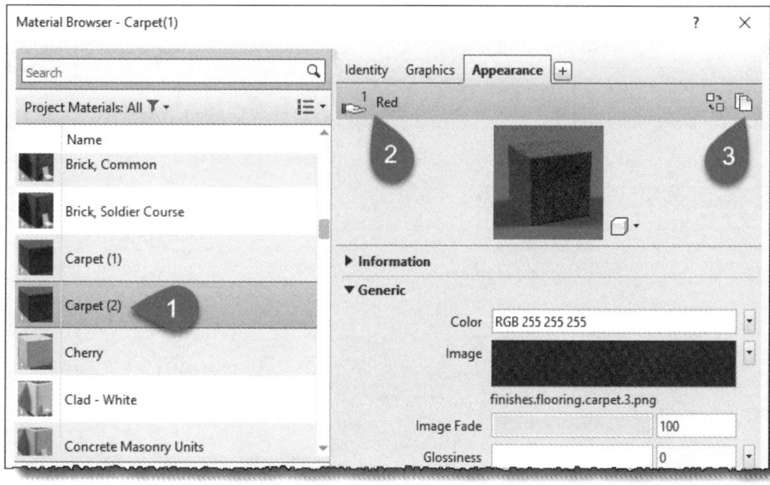

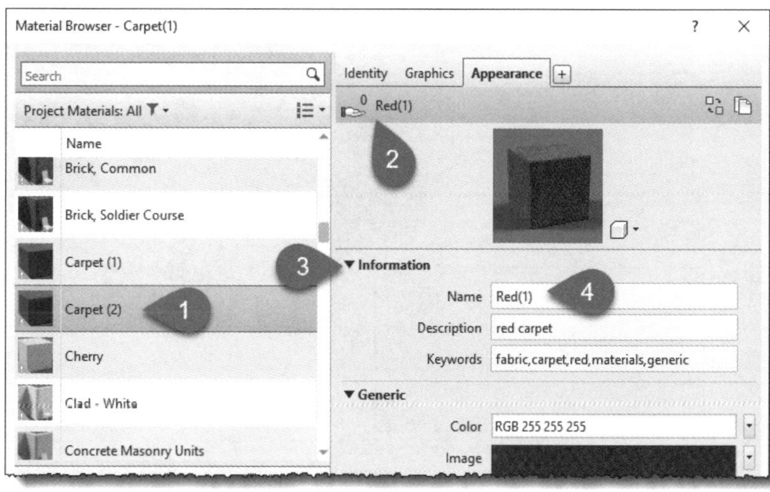

It is important to know how to properly duplicate a *Material* in your model so you do not unintentionally affect another *Material*. The information on this page is mainly for reference and does not need to be done in your model.

If you use **Duplicate Using Shared Assets** to duplicate a *Material* in your model, the **Appearance Asset** will be associated to the new *Material* AND the *Material* you copied it from! For example, in the image to the right, we will right-click on Carpet (1) and duplicate it. Before we duplicate it, notice the *Appearance Asset* named "RED" is not shared (#3 in the first image).

Once you have duplicated a *Material*, notice the two carpet materials, in this example, now indicate they both share the same *Appearance Asset*. Changing one will affect the other. Click the **Duplicate this asset** icon in the upper right (#3 in second image).

Once the *Appearance Asset* has been duplicated (third image), you can expand the information section and rename the asset. You can now make changes to this material without affecting other materials.

Tip: Use Duplicate Material and Assets to avoid these steps and the potential problem.

Exercise 15-3:
Rendering an Isometric in Section

This exercise will introduce you to a view tool called *Section Box*. This tool is not necessarily related to renderings, but the two features together can produce some interesting results.

Setting up the 3D View:

1. Open your law office file.

2. Switch to the ***Default 3D View*** via the ***3D*** icon on the *QAT (not to the* 3D View 1 *from Exercise 15-2).*

3. Make sure nothing is selected and note the ***View Properties*** in the *Properties Palette.*

4. Activate the **Section Box** parameter and then click **Apply**.

You should see a box appear around your building, similar to Figure 15-3.1. When selected, you can adjust the size of the box with its grips. Anything outside the box is not visible. This is a great way to study a particular area of your building while in an isometric view. You will experiment with this feature next.

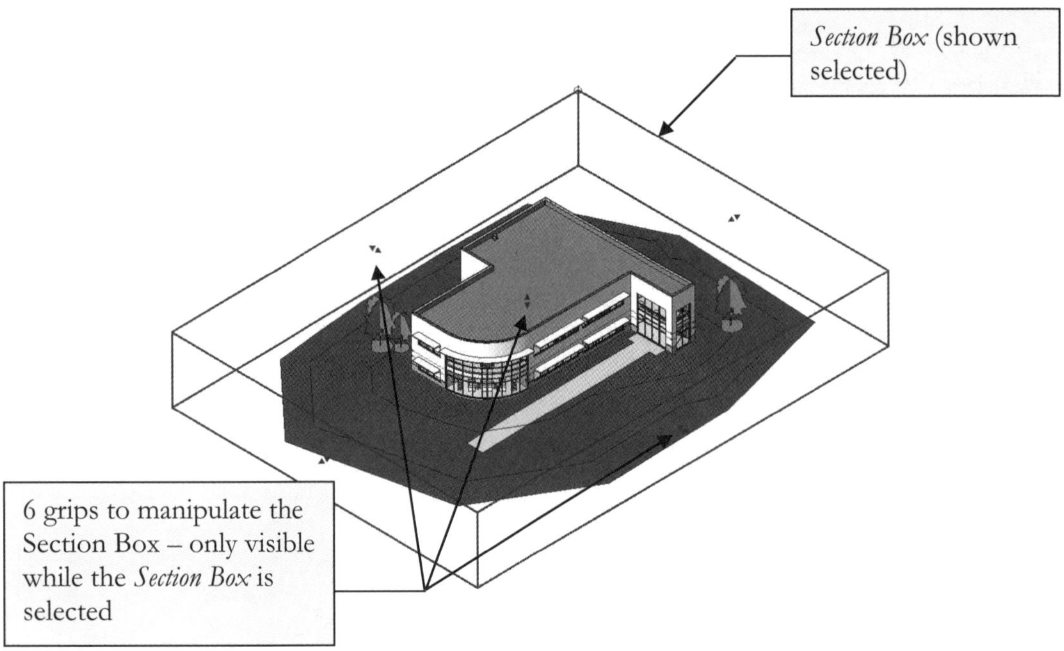

FIGURE 15-3.1 3D view with Section Box activated

5. To practice using the **Section Box**, drag the grips around until your view looks similar to **Figure 15-3.2**. *FYI: Grips only show when section box is selected.*

   TIP: This will require the ViewCube tool as well. Used to orbit the model.

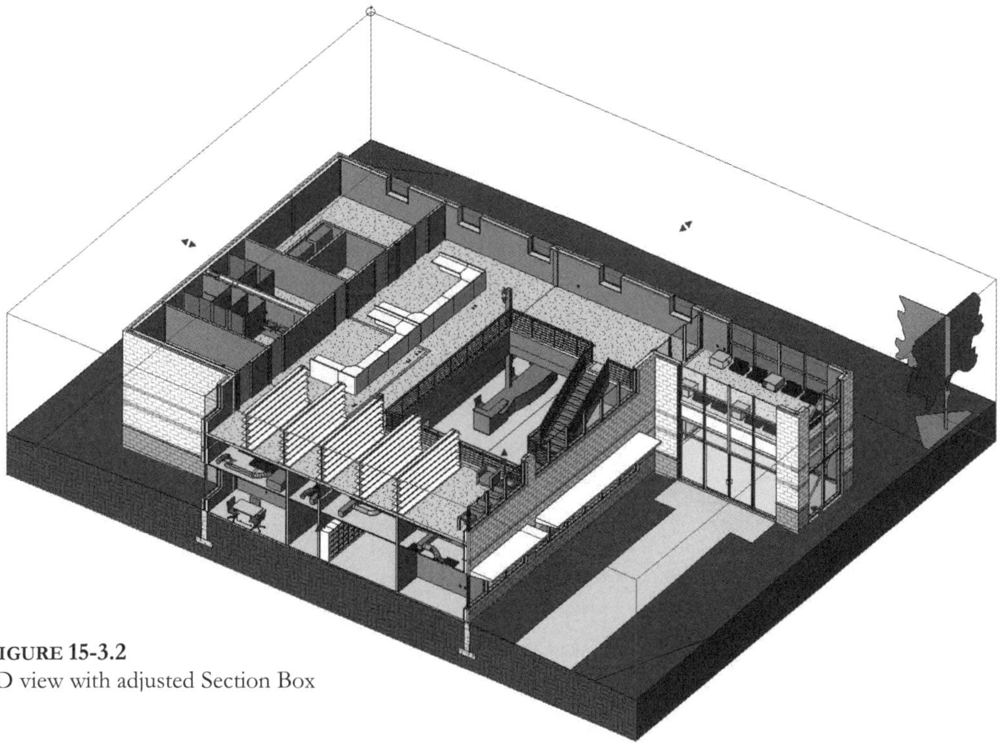

FIGURE 15-3.2
3D view with adjusted Section Box

This creates a very interesting view of the project. What client would have trouble understanding this drawing?

6. Select the ***Render*** icon.
   a. Select the *Scheme*: **Exterior: Sun only**.
   b. Set the *Sun Settings* to *Solar Type:* **Lighting** and *Presets:* **Sunlight from Top Left**.
   c. Background *Style* to **Color** (set the color to white).

7. Leave all other settings as they are and **Render** the view.

After a few minutes, the view is rendered and can be saved to the project so the image can be placed on a sheet, or exported and used in other applications such as PowerPoint.

Notice how the ground is rendered in section. Also, the ductwork is showing above the ceiling. Much of the model is gray because the various elements have the default material selected. If you take the time to specify a material for everything, you can generate another rendered image that is much better looking.

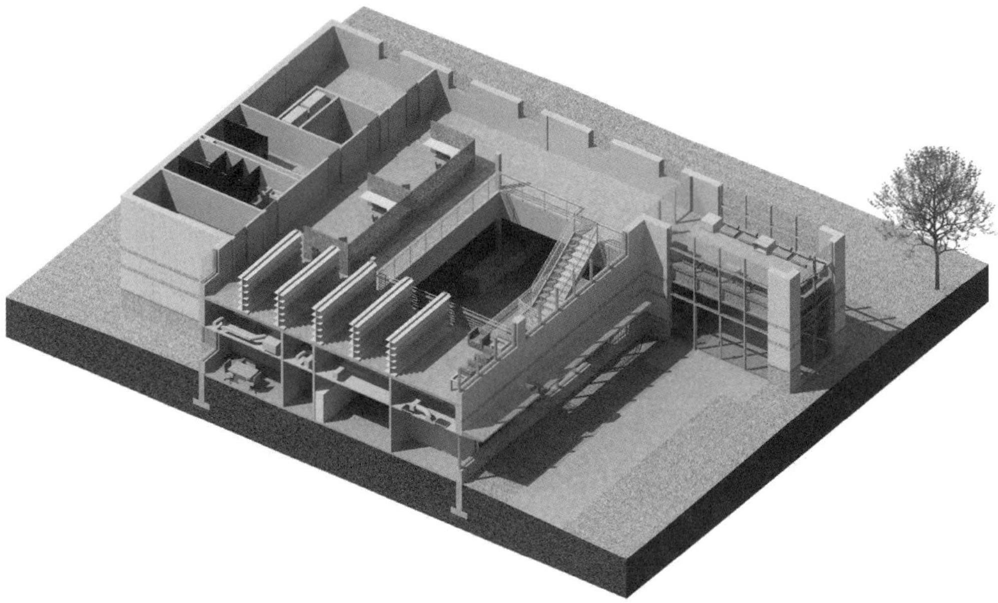

8. **Save** your project.

In the *Graphic Display Options* dialog for a given view you may turn on **Sketchy Lines** to make the view appear hand drawn. This technique is sometimes employed so the model does not look final. It suggests the design is preliminary and can still be changed. You do not need to make this change to your model at this time.

Exercise 15-4:
Creating an Interior Rendering

Creating an interior rendering is very similar to an exterior rendering. This exercise will walk you through the steps involved in creating a high-quality interior rendering.

Setting up the Camera View:

1. Open your law office project.

2. Open **Level 1** view.

3. From the *View* tab, select **3D View → Camera**.

4. Place the *Camera* as shown in **Figure 15-4.1**.

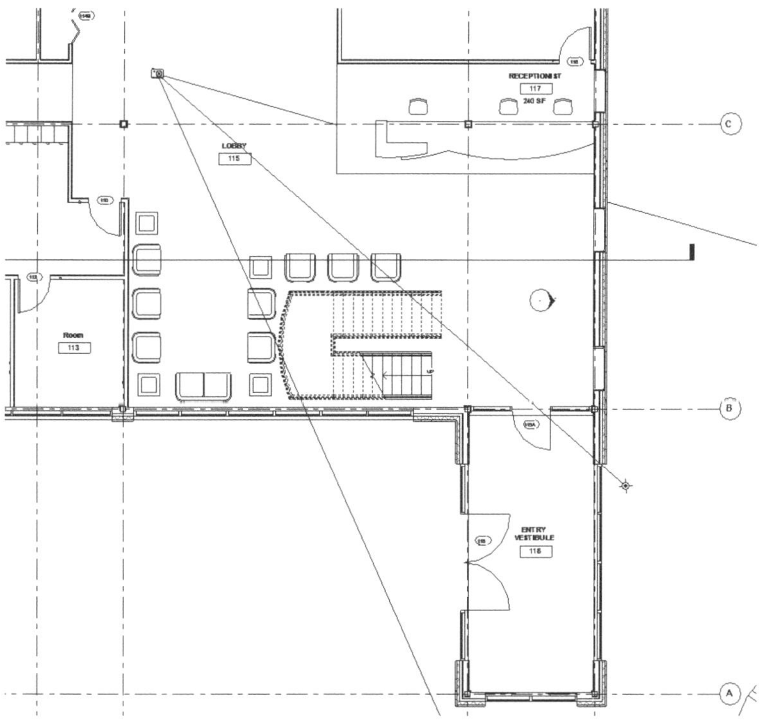

FIGURE 15-4.1 Camera placed – Level 1 view

Revit uses default heights for the camera and the target. These heights are based on the current level's floor elevation. These reference points can be edited via the camera properties.

Revit will automatically open the newly generated camera view. Your view should look similar to **Figure 15-4.2**.

FYI: Make sure you created the camera on Level 1 and picked the points in the correct order.

FIGURE 15-4.2 Initial interior camera view

5. Using the **Crop Region** rectangle, modify the view to look like **Figure 15-4.3**.

   TIP: You will have to switch to plan view to adjust the camera's depth of view to see the tree.

   REMINDER: If the camera does not show in plan view, right-click on the camera view label in the Project Browser and select Show Camera.

TIP: Turning on Consistent Colors *on the View Control Bar is a great way to visualize your design while trying to set up a view to be rendered. It does not have dark, hard-to-see surfaces as the Shaded option has. Turning on* Ambient Shadows *adds a nice sense of depth to the view as well.*

FIGURE 15-4.3 Modified interior camera; Hidden Line view with Ambient Shadows turned on

6. Switch back to **Level 1** to see the revised *camera* view settings.

Notice the field of view triangle is wider based on the changes to the *Crop Region* (Figure 15-4.4).

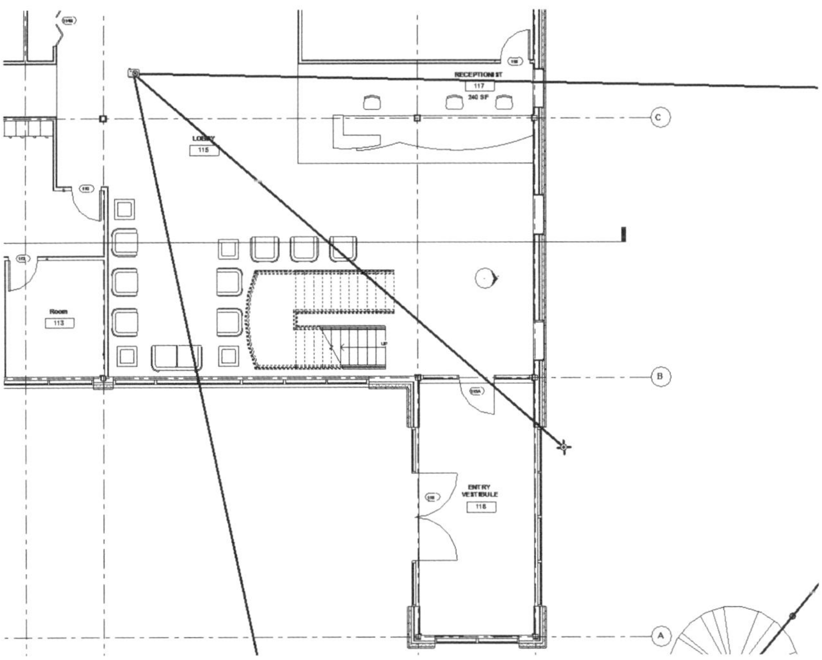

FIGURE 15-4.4 Modified camera – Level 1

Creating the Rendering:

Next you will render the view.

7. Switch back to your interior camera view, **3D View 2**.

8. Select **Show Render Dialog** from the *View Control Bar.*

9. Set the *Scheme* to **Interior: Sun and Artificial.**

   TIP: Be sure to select the "interior" option.

10. Set the *Sun* to **Law Office 6-30 at 3pm**.

11. Click **Render** to begin the rendering process.

This will take several minutes depending on the speed of your computer. When finished, the view should look similar to Figure 15-4.5.

12. Click **Export** from the *Rendering* dialog box to save the image to a file on your hard drive. Name the file **Lobby.png**.

You can now open the *Lobby.png* file in Adobe Photoshop or insert into a MS Word type program to manipulate or print.

To toggle back to the normal hidden view, click **Show the Model** from the *Rendering* dialog box.

There are many things you can do to make the rendering look even better. You can add interior props (e.g., pictures on the wall, and items on the countertop). You can adjust the *Sun* setting to nighttime and then render a night scene.

> *TIP: Setting the output to Printer rather than Screen allows you to generate a higher resolution image. Thus, between the Quality setting and the Output setting, you can create an extremely high-quality rendering, but it might take hours, if not days, to process!*

Revit also gives you the ability to set a material to be self-illuminating. This will allow you to make something look like it is lit up. You can also set a lamp shade to glow when a light source has been defined under it so it looks more realistic.

13. **Save** your project.

FIGURE 15-4.5 Rendered interior view

Be sure to check out **Appendix E**, from the online files, for an in-depth look at artificial and natural lighting design in Revit using **ElumTools** (Instructors can request free student access). ElumTools is a professional lighting design application.

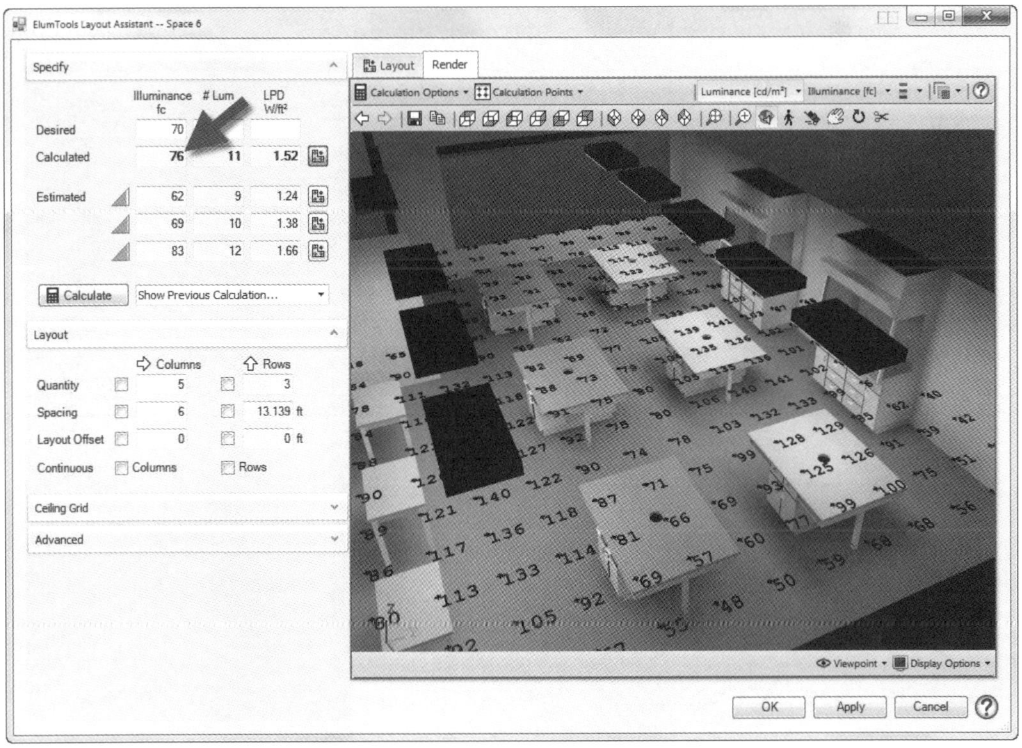

ElumTools lighting design add-in for Revit

Exercise 15-5:
Adding People to the Rendering

Revit provides a few RPC people to add to your renderings. These are files from a popular company that provides 3D photo content for use in renderings (http://www.archvision.com). You can buy this content in groupings, such as college students, or per item. In addition to people, they offer items like cars, plants, trees, office equipment, etc.

Loading Content into the Current Project:

1. Open your law office project.

2. Switch to **Level 1** view.

3. Click the **Load Autodesk Family** button on the *Ribbon.*

4. Browse to the **Entourage** folder and select both the **RPC Male** and **RPC Female** files and click **Load.**

5. Select **Component → Place a Component.**

6. Place two **Males** and one **Female** as shown in **Figure 15-5.1**.
   a. Change the Offset to 6′-4″ for the person on the stair landing.

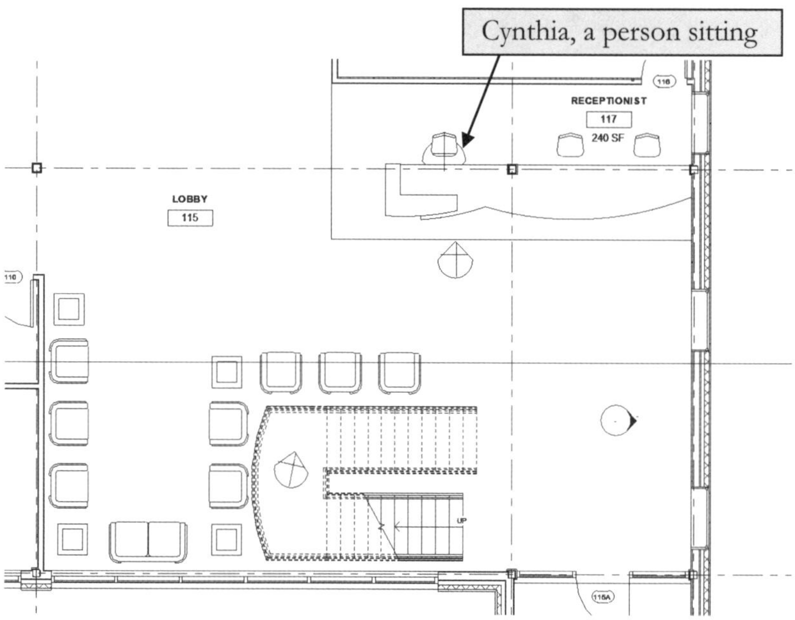

FIGURE 15-5.1 Level 1 – RPC people added

The line in the circle (Figure 15-5.1) represents the direction a person is looking. You simply rotate the object to make adjustments.

7. Select **Manage → Materials** from the *Ribbon.*

Next you will change the *Render Appearance* for the gypsum board so the walls are brighter. Any element in the building that uses the *Material* you are about to modify will be automatically updated.

8. Select **Gypsum Wall Board** from the *Materials* list.

9. Check the **Use Render Appearance** for shading option (*Graphics* tab).

10. Set the render *Appearance* to Wall Paint\ Matte\ **Flat -Antique White.** (replace asset)

11. **Close** the open dialog box.

12. Switch to your interior lobby camera view.

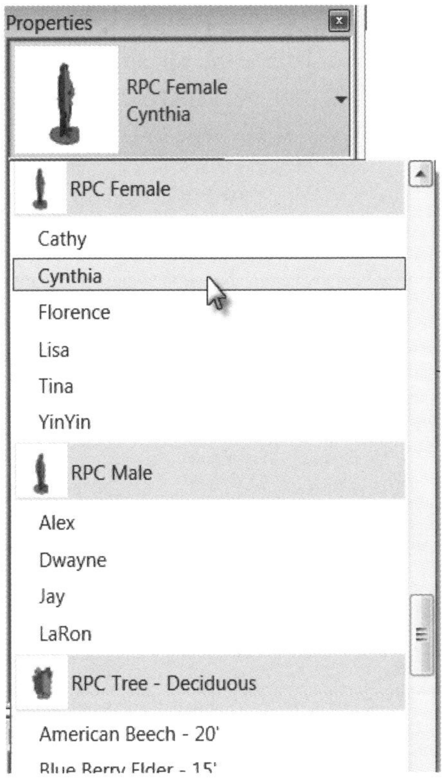

FIGURE 15-5.2 Type Selector

13. **Render** the lobby view with the settings previously used.

Your rendering should now have people in it and look similar to Figure 15-5.3.

FIGURE 15-5.3 Interior lobby view with people added rendered at High quality and 150dpi

Adding people and other "props" gives your model a sense of scale and makes it look a little more realistic. After all, architecture is for people. These objects can be viewed from any angle. Try a new camera view from a different angle to see how the people adjust to match the view and perspective, maybe from the second floor looking down to Level 1.

The RPC content looks generic in the model until it is rendered or the view is set to realistic.

14. **Save** your project.

FYI: As with other families and components, the more you add to your project, the bigger your project file becomes. It is a good idea to load only the items you need and delete the unused items via the Project Browser. Your project should be about 23MB at this point in the tutorial.

Sun Path

It is possible to turn on the feature called **Sun Path**. This shows the path of the sun over a day and a year. This is accessed from the *View Control Bar* while in a 3D view.

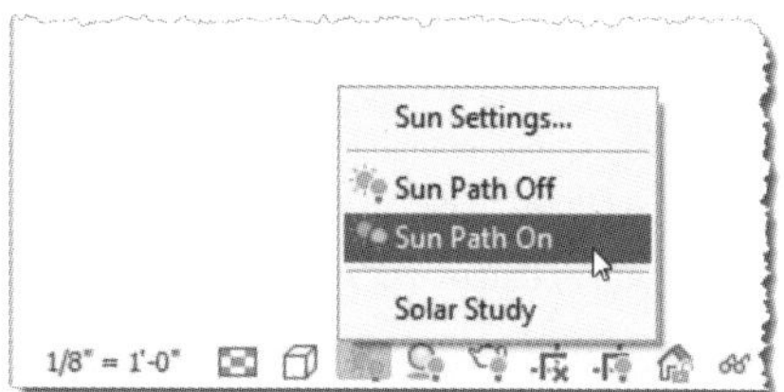

Once on, you can click and drag the sun along its daily or yearly path!

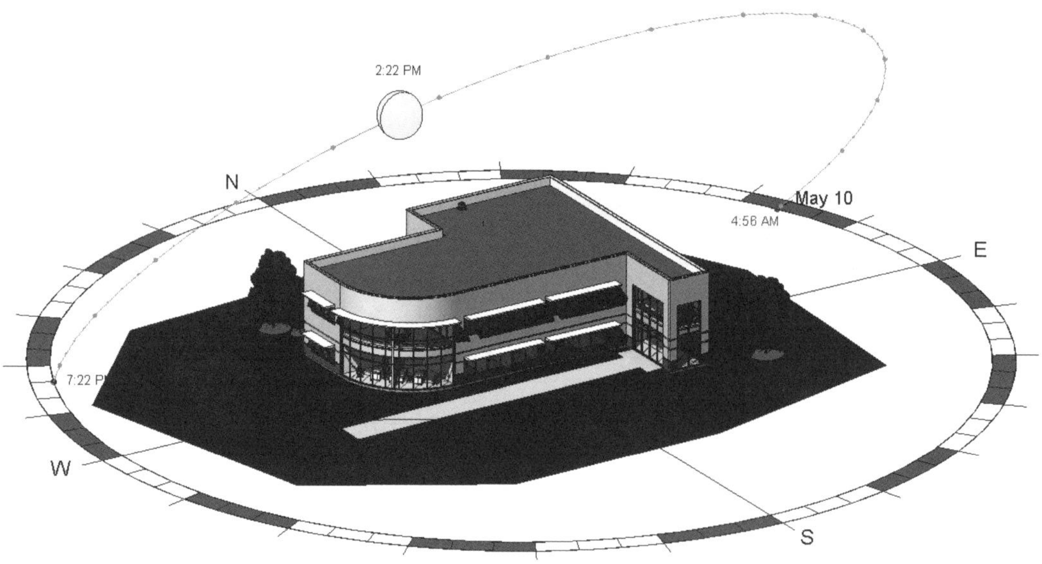

The first image below shows all the transportation content available through Archvision. When using their subscription option, you have access to all of their content (including people, trees and more). Using the Archvision Dashboard program (second image below), you simply drag and drop content into Revit. Students should contact Archvision about special student options. These elements work in Realistic views, renderings and A360 Cloud renderings.

Self-Exam:

The following questions can be used as a way to check your knowledge of this lesson. The answers can be found at the bottom of this page.

1. Creating a camera adds a view to the *Project Browser* list. (T/F)
2. Materials are defined in Revit's *Materials* dialog box. (T/F)
3. After inserting a light fixture, you need to adjust several settings before rendering and getting light from the fixture. (T/F)
4. The *Site* element shows up in section and elevation automatically. (T/F)
5. Use the ________________ tool to hide a large portion of the model.

Review Questions:

The following questions may be assigned by your instructor as a way to assess your knowledge of this section. Your instructor has the answers to the review questions.

1. You cannot "point" the people in a specific direction. (T/F)
2. You cannot get accurate lighting based on day/month/location. (T/F)
3. Adding components and families to your project does not make the project file bigger. (T/F)
4. Creating photo-realistic renderings can take a significant amount of time for your computer to process. (T/F)
5. The RPC people can only be viewed from one angle. (T/F)
6. Once a site element is created, it cannot be modified (T/F).
7. Adjust the _____________________ to make more of a camera view visible.
8. You use the _____________ tool to load and insert RPC people.
9. You can adjust the *Eye Elevation* of the camera via the camera's

   ______________________.
10. What is the file size of (completed) Exercise 15-5? _________________ MB

SELF-EXAM ANSWERS:
1 – T, **2** – T, **3** – F, **4** – T, **5** – Section Box

Lesson 16
Construction Documents Set

This lesson will look at bringing everything you have drawn thus far together onto sheets. The sheets, once set up, are ready for plotting. Basically, you place the various views you have created on sheets. The scale for each view is based on the scale you set when drawing that view, which is important to get right because it affects text and symbol sizes. When you finish setting up the sheets, you will have a set of drawings ready to print, either individually or all at once.

Exercise 16-1:
Setting Up a Sheet

Creating a Sheet View:

1. Open your law office project with Revit.

The template you started with already has several sheets set up and ready to use. A few of them even have views placed on them. You will learn how to create new sheets, place views on them, and modify the existing sheets to create a set of construction documents.

2. Select **View → Sheet Composition → Sheet**.

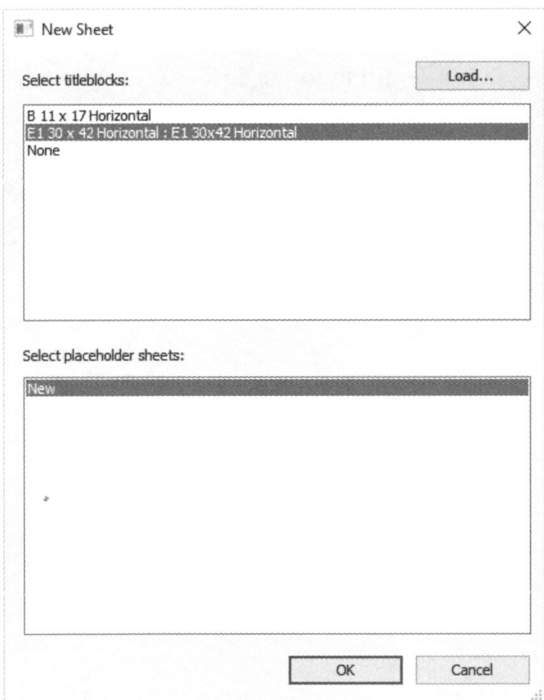

FIGURE 16-1.1 Select a Titleblock

Next, Revit will prompt you for a *Titleblock* to use. The template file you started with has two (Figure 16-1.1).

3. Select the **E1 30x42 Horizontal** titleblock and click **OK**.

That's it; you have created a new sheet that is ready to have views and/or schedules placed on it!

NOTE: *A new view shows up in the Project Browser under the heading Sheets. Once you get an entire CD set ready, this list can be very long.*

Revit also lets you create placeholder sheets which allow you to add sheets to the sheet index without the need to have a sheet show up in the *Project Browser*. This is helpful if a consultant, such as a food service designer, is not using Revit. This feature allows you to add those sheets to the sheet index. Placeholder sheets can also be added in the sheet list schedule by using the *New Row* tool on the *Ribbon*. Once a placeholder sheet exists, it can be turned into a real sheet by selecting from the lower list in the dialog (Figure 16-1.1).

FIGURE 16-1.2 Initial Titleblock view

4. **Zoom** in to the sheet number area (lower right corner).

5. Adjust the text to look similar to **Figure 16-1.3**.

TIP: *Select the Titleblock, hover the cursor over the text you wish to edit, and then click.*

> ***NOTE:*** *The time and date stamp helps to remember when a sheet was plotted, especially if you forget to update the date before printing.*

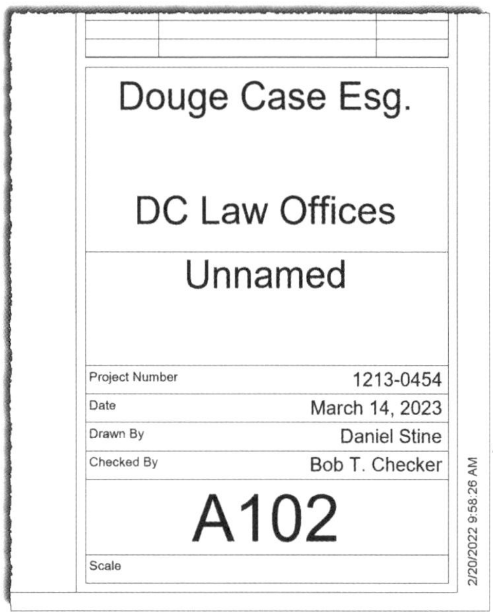

FIGURE 16-1.3 Revised Titleblock data

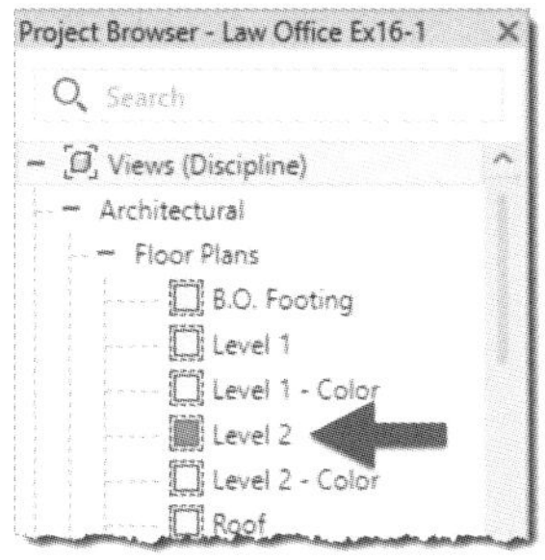

A filled box, in the *Project Browser*, indicates the view has been placed on a sheet (see image to the right). You cannot have the same view on two sheets. The Level 2 view is currently on the roof plan sheet (because Level 2 was renamed to Roof Plan previously). You will delete it so the Level 2 view can be placed on the proper sheet.

6. Switch to sheet **A3 – Roof Plan**, select the floor plan on the sheet and press the **Delete** key to remove it from the sheet. Notice the box is no longer filled in the *Project Browser*.

7. Switch back to sheet **A102** and **Zoom out** so you can see the entire sheet.

8. With the sheet fully visible, click and drag the architectural **Level 2** view (under floor plans) from the *Project Browser* onto the sheet view (Figure 16-1.4).

You will see a box that represents the extents of the view you are placing on the current sheet. Because the trees are visible and the elevation tags may be a distance away from your floor plan, the extents may be larger than the sheet. For now you will center the drawing on the sheet so the plan fits.

9. Move the cursor around until the box is somewhat centered on the sheet (this can be adjusted later at any time).

Your view should look similar to **Figure 16-1.4**.

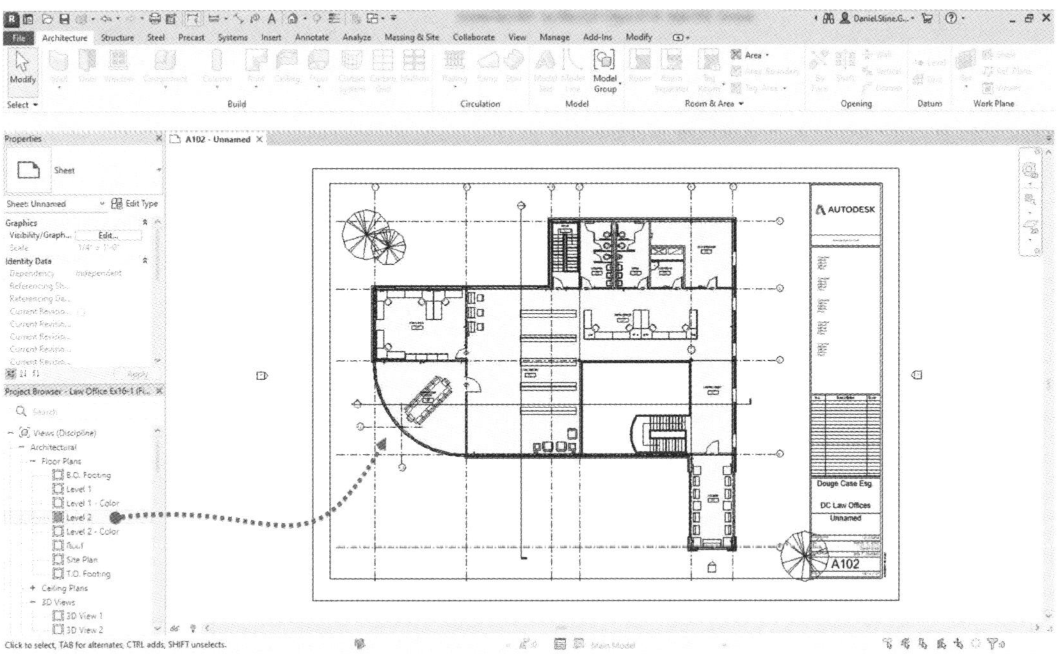

FIGURE 16-1.4 Sheet view with Level 2 added

10. Click the mouse in a "white" area (not on any lines) to deselect the Level 1 view. Notice the box goes away.

11. **Zoom In** on the lower left corner to view the drawing identification symbol that Revit automatically added (Figure 16-1.5).

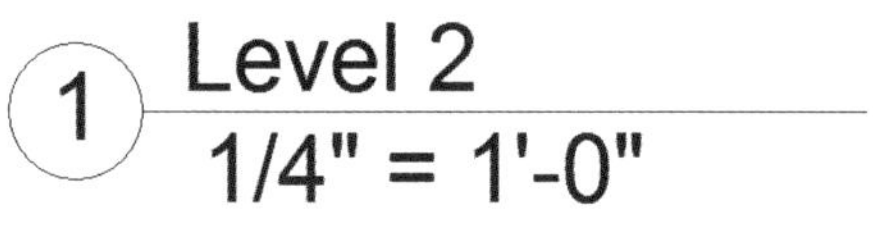

FIGURE 16-1.5 Drawing title

NOTE: The drawing number for this sheet is added. The next drawing you add to this sheet will be number 2.

The view name is listed. This is another reason to rename the views as you create them.

Also notice that the drawing scale is listed. Again, this comes from the scale setting for the Level 2 view.

12. **Zoom out** to see entire sheet again.

13. Move the drawing title below the floor plan. You need to click *Modify* first, so the floor plan is not selected.

    FYI: The title can only be moved when it is the only thing selected. The length of the title line can only be adjusted when the drawing is selected.

14. Switch back to the Level 2 view and turn off the *Planting* category via the **VV** shortcut.

    TIP: You can also right-click on the drawing in the sheet view and select Activate View to edit the view.

Setting Up the Exterior Elevations:

The project already has two sheets set up for the exterior elevations: sheets A4 and A5. These sheets already have the exterior elevations placed on them. This is done compliments of the template you started with. Looking at one of the sheets—you will notice two things (Figure 16-1.6). First, the drawings should be as large as possible to make them easier to read when printed. Ideally the plans and elevations would be the same scale. Secondly, the views will need to be cropped to the grade line so it does not extend off the page.

You will also notice in Figure 16-1.6 that the South elevation line cuts through the *Main Entry* area, creating a section view at that part of the building. If you did not want this, you would need to switch back to one of the plan views and select the point part of the South elevation tag and move it south so it does not cut through the building. In this case, you have a detailed elevation view of the portion missing, so you will not change it.

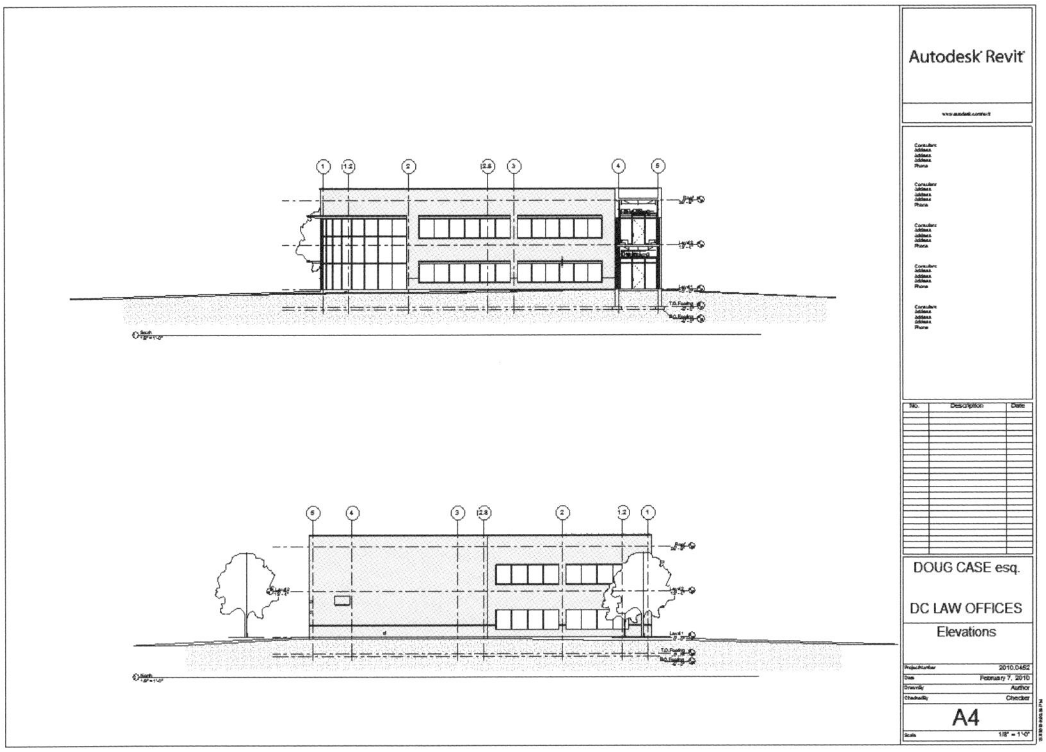

FIGURE 16-1.6 Initial layout of sheet A4 - Elevations

15. Switch to the **North elevation** view, not the sheet.

16. Change the scale to **1/4″ = 1′-0″**.

17. Hide the *Planting* category via "**VV**."

18. Toggle **on** *Crop Region* and *Crop Region Visibility* via the *View Control Bar.*

19. Adjust the *Crop Region* to be close to the building, as shown in Figure 16-1.7.

Notice how the levels for the footings are hidden when outside the *Crop Region.* Also, the levels and grids will move with the *Crop Region* when smaller than their extents. The *Crop Region* will print unless its visibility is turned off. You will do that next.

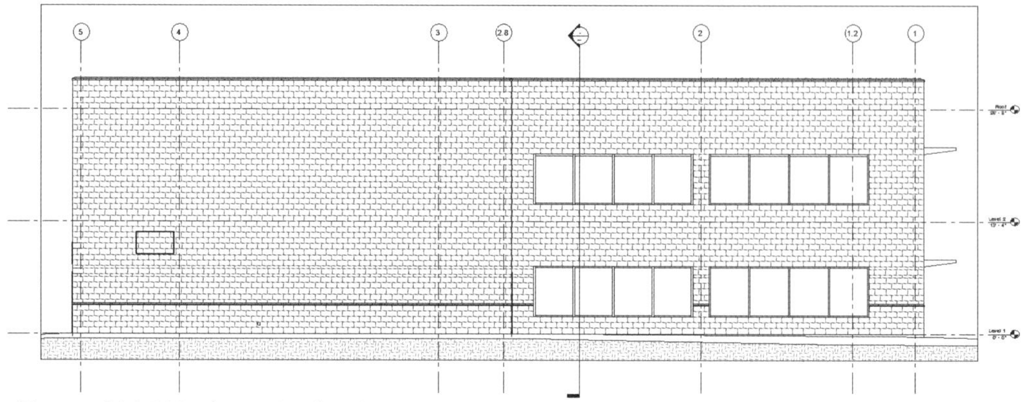

FIGURE 16-1.7 North exterior elevations

20. Click the *Crop Region Visibility* toggle, on the *View Control Bar*, to hide the *Crop Region.* But leave the view cropped.

21. Repeat these steps for the other three exterior elevation views.

22. Adjust the location of the elevations on sheets A4 and A5 as shown in Figure 16-1.8.

TIP: Sometimes it is easier to delete the view off the sheet and drag it back on from the Project Browser. This aligns the drawing title with the rescaled view. The entire view needs to be selected to adjust the length of the drawing title line. Select the drawing title to move it.

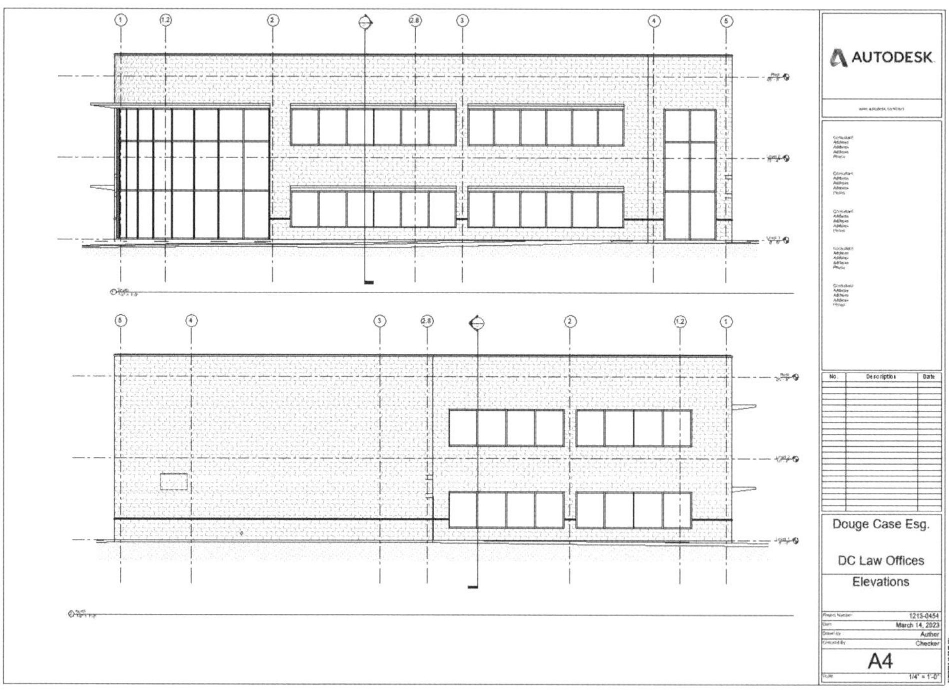

FIGURE 16-1.8 North exterior elevations

Now you will stop for a moment and notice that Revit is automatically referencing the drawings as you place them on sheets.

23. Switch to **Level 1** (see Figure 16-1.9).

Notice in Figure 16-1.9 that the number A5 represents the sheet number that the drawing can be found on. The number 1 (one) is the drawing number to look for on sheet A5.

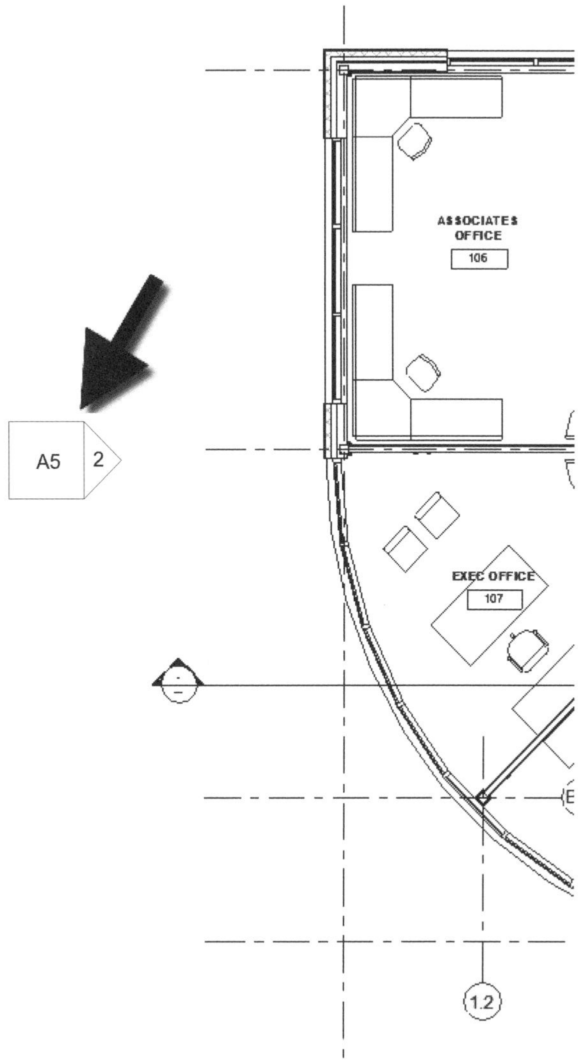

FIGURE 16-1.9
Level 1 – elevation Reference tag filled-in

Setting up Sections:

24. Switch to sheet **A9 - Building Sections**.

25. Add the two building sections as shown in **Figure 16-1.10**.

26. Switch to **Level 1 Plan** view and zoom in to the area shown in Figure 16-1.11.

Notice, again, that the reference bubbles are automatically filled in when the referenced view is placed on a sheet. If the drawing is moved to another sheet, the reference bubbles are automatically updated.

You can also see in Figure 16-1.9 that the reference bubbles on the building sections are filled in.

Because Revit keeps track of references automatically, a view in the *Project Browser* can only be placed on one sheet. The only exception is that *Legend* views can exist on multiple sheets. But they do not contain any elements from the 3D model and cannot be referenced. *Legend* views are for typical notes and 2D graphics that need to appear on multiple sheets.

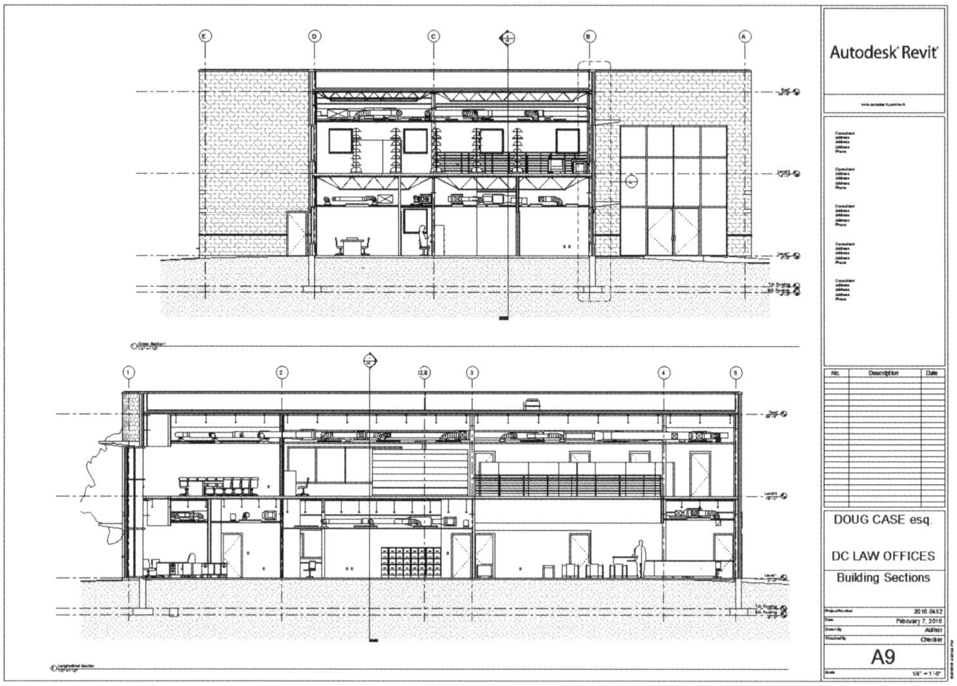

FIGURE 16-1.10 Sheet A9 - Building Sections

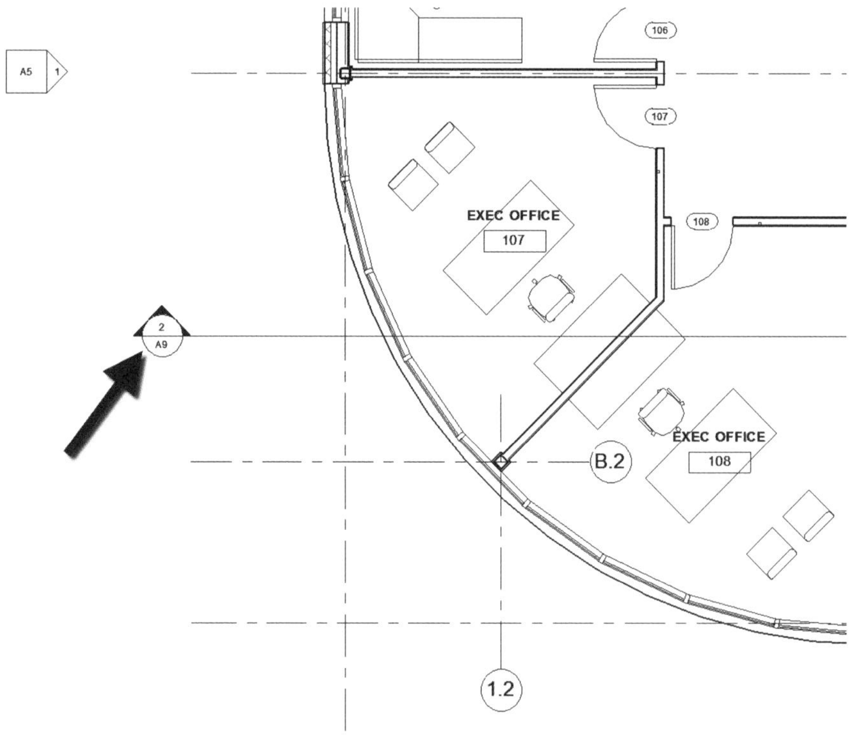

FIGURE 16-1.11 Section references automatically filled in

Set up the Remaining Sheets:

Next you set up sheets for the remaining views that have yet to be placed on a sheet. You will also renumber sheets as required.

27. Create the following sheets **and** place the appropriate views on them; the view name will generally match the sheet name:

    FYI: *Renumber any sheets as necessary; open the sheet and edit the sheet number, or edit via the sheet's properties. All plan views should be ¼" = 1'-0".*

    FYI: *Sheets marked with an asterisk will not have a view to place on it; they are mainly to fill out the sheet index in the next exercise.*

    Architectural Sheets
    - A101 Level 1 Floor Plan
    - A102 Level 2 Floor Plan
    - A103 Level 1 Reflected Ceiling Plan
    - A104 Level 2 Reflected Ceiling Plan
    - A105 Roof Plan
    - A200 Exterior Elevations
    - A201 Exterior Elevations
    - A300 Building Sections
    - A301 Building Sections*
    - A400 Wall Sections
    - A500 Interior Elevations
    - A600 Details
    - A800 Schedules

    Structural Sheets
    - S101 Level 1 Slab and Foundation Plan
    - S102 Level 2 Framing Plan
    - S103 Roof Framing Plan
    - S200 Structural Details*
    - S201 Structural Schedules

    Mechanical Sheets
    - M100 Under Slab Sanitary Plan
    - M101 Level 1 Sanitary Plan
    - M102 Level 2 Sanitary Plan
    - M201 Level 1 Domestic Water Plan
    - M202 Level 2 Domestic Water Plan
    - M301 Level 1 Ventilation Plan
    - M302 Level 2 Ventilation Plan

- M400 Mechanical Roof Plan*
- M500 Mechanical Schedules*
- M600 Domestic Water Riser Diagrams*
- M700 Sanitary Riser Diagrams*

Electrical Sheets

- E100 Electrical Site Plan*
- E101 Level 1 Lighting Plan
- E102 Level 2 Lighting Plan
- E201 Level 1 Power Plan
- E202 Level 2 Power Plan
- E301 Level 1 Systems Plan
- E302 Level 2 Systems Plan
- E400 Electrical Details*
- E500 Electrical Schedules
- E600 Single Line Diagrams*

> ***TIP:*** *Two sheets cannot have the same number.*
>
> *Sheets with views placed on them will have a plus sign next to the sheet name in the* Project Browser.

Question: On a large project with hundreds of views, how do I know for sure if I have placed every view on a sheet?

Answer: In addition to the filled squares in the Project Browser, Revit has a feature called *Browser Organization* that can hide all the views that have been placed on a sheet. You will try this next.

28. Take a general look at the *Project Browser* to see how many views are listed. (See Figure 16-1.13 on page 16-11.)

29. Select **Views (Discipline)** at the top of the *Project Browser* (Figure 16-1.12).

    TIP: *If you right-click here you have access to a search option where you can search the entire* Project Browser.

30. Select **Not on sheets** from the *Type Selector.*

31. Click **Apply**.

32. Notice the list in the *Project Browser* is now smaller. (See Figure 16-1.14 on page 16-11.)

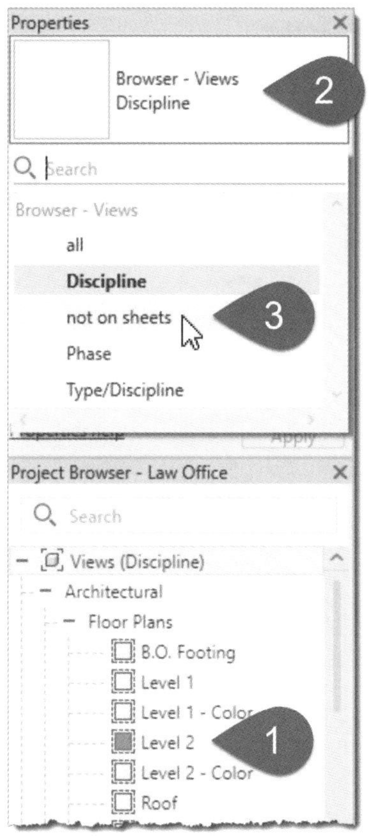

FIGURE 16-1.12 Project Browser and Properties Palette

The *Project Browser* now only shows drawing views that have not been placed onto a sheet. Of course, you could have a few views that do not need to be placed on a sheet, but this feature will help eliminate errors.

Next you will reset the *Project Browser.*

33. Switch the *Browser Organization* back to **Discipline** and click **Apply**.

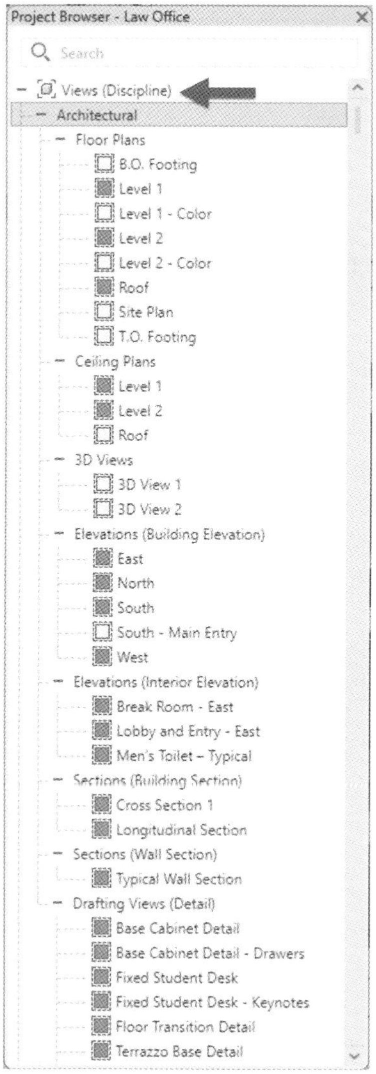

FIGURE 16-1.13
Project Browser; Views (Discipline)

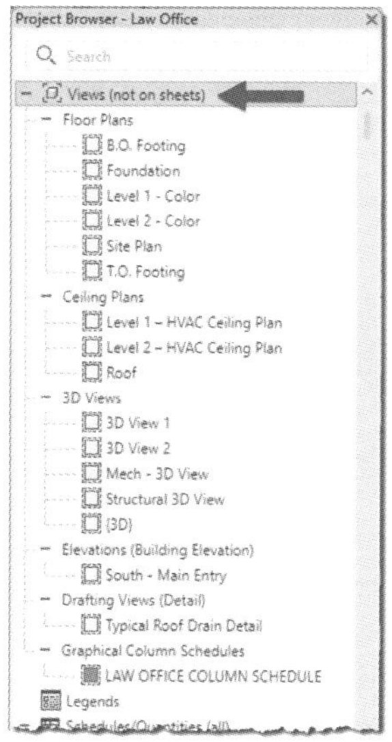

FIGURE 16-1.14
Project Browser; Views (not on sheets)

FIGURE 16-1.15
Project Browser; Sheets (All)

It is possible to customize the *Browser Organization* to sort views and sheets as needed.

34. **Save** your project.

Large Buildings – Matchlines and Dependent Views:

When the building floor plan is too large to fit on a single sheet you need to use the ***Matchline*** tool and the **Dependent Views** feature. Each can be used exclusive of the other, but they generally are used together. You will not do this for the book project, but the information is good to know.

The *Matchline* tool can be found on the *View* tab. It is similar to the *Grid* tool in that you add it in plan view, and it will show up in other plan views because it has a height. When the *Matchline* tool is selected, you enter *Sketch* mode. Here you can draw multiple lines which do not have to form a loop or even touch each other.

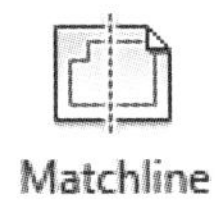

A *dependent view* is a view which is controlled by (i.e., dependent on) a main overall view but has its own *Crop Region*. A main view can have several *dependent views*. Any change made in *Visibility/Graphics Overrides* is made to the main view and each dependent view. The dependent view's *Crop Regions* generally coincide with the *Matchlines*. However, the *Crop Regions* can overlap.

Additionally, if *a dependent view's Crop Region* is rotated, the model actually rotates so the *Crop Window* stays square with the computer screen. However, the other dependent views and the main view are unaffected. This is great when a wing of the building is at an angle. Having that wing orthogonal with the computer screen makes it easier to work in that portion of the building and it fits better on the sheet in most cases.

To create a dependent view, you right-click on a floor plan view and select **Duplicate View > Duplicate as Dependent**. The image to the right shows the result in the ***Project Browser***, the **dependent views** are indented.

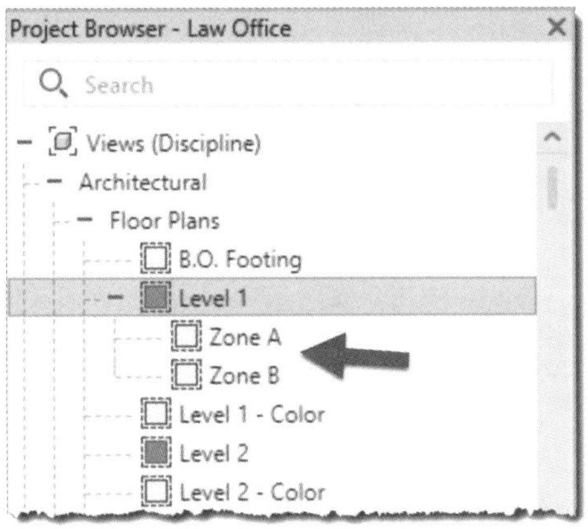

Once the *Matchline* is added and the dependent views are set up, you can add **View References** (from the *Annotate* tab) which indicate the sheet to flip to in order to see the drawing beyond the *Matchline.*

Finally, on large projects with multiple levels and floor plan views, you only have to set up the dependent views once (i.e., number and crop regions). With one plan set up, you right-click on the main view and select **Apply Dependent Views**. You will be prompted to select all the floor plan views for which you would like to have the dependent views created.

Exercise 16-2:
Sheet Index

Revit has the ability to create a sheet index automatically. You will study this now.

Creating a Drawing List Schedule:

1. Open your project.
2. Select **View → Create → Schedule → Sheet List**.

You are now in the *Sheet List* dialog box. This process is identical to creating schedules. Here you specify which fields you want in the sheet index and how to sort the list (Figure 16-2.1).

3. Add **Sheet Number** and **Sheet Name** to the right:
   a. Select the available field on the left.
   b. Click the **Add →** button in the center.
4. Click **OK**.

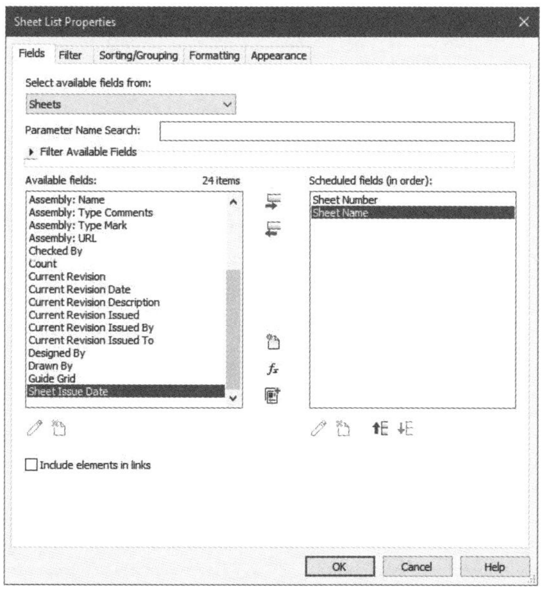

FIGURE 16-2.1
Drawing List Properties dialog; sheet number and name "added"

Now you should notice that the *Sheet Names* are cut off because the column is not wide enough. You will adjust this next.

5. Move your cursor over the right edge of the *Sheet List* schedule and click-and-drag to the right until you can see the entire name (Figure 16-2.2).

6. Edit **Sorting / Grouping** via the *Properties Palette* and sort the list by **Sheet Number**.

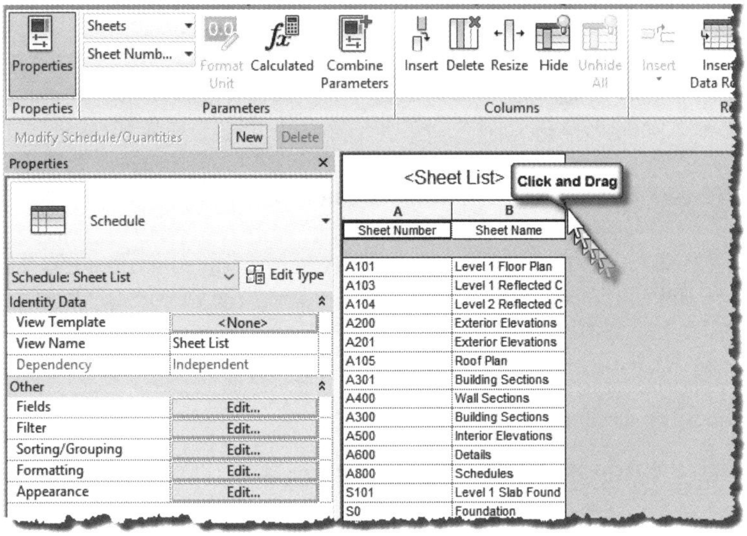

FIGURE 16-2.2
Sheet List view; notice sheet names are cut off in the right column

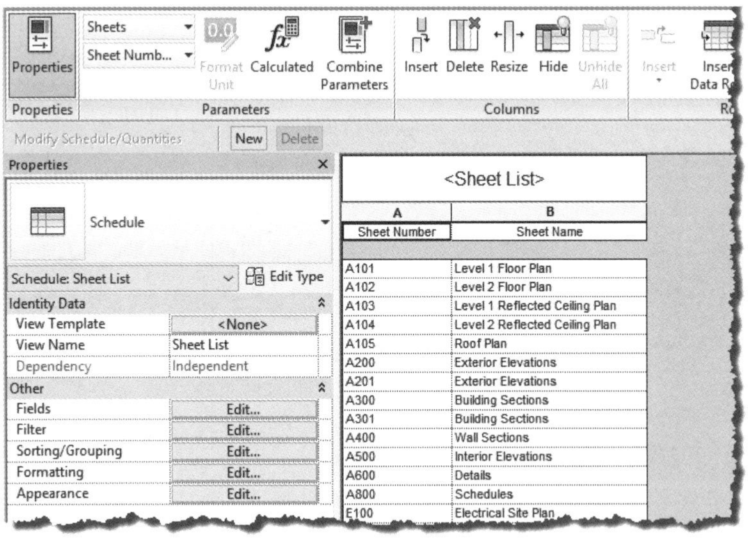

FIGURE 16-2.3
Sheet List view; sheet names are now visible and sorted by number

Setting Up a Title Sheet:

Now you will create a title sheet to place your sheet index on.

7. Create a new Sheet:
   a. Number: **T001**
   b. Name: **Title Sheet**

8. From the *Schedules/Quantities* category of the *Project Browser*, place the schedule named **Sheet List** on the *Title Sheet*. Once on the sheet, drag the "triangle" grip to adjust the column width.

Next you will place one of your rendered images that you saved to file (raster image). If you have not created a raster image, you should refer back to Lesson 15 and create one now (otherwise you can use any BMP or JPG file on your hard drive if necessary).

9. Select **Insert → Import → Import Image**.

10. Browse to your raster image file, select it and click **Open** to place the Image.

11. Click on your Title Sheet to locate the image.

Your sheet should look similar to Figure 16-2.4.

FYI: The text is added in the next step.

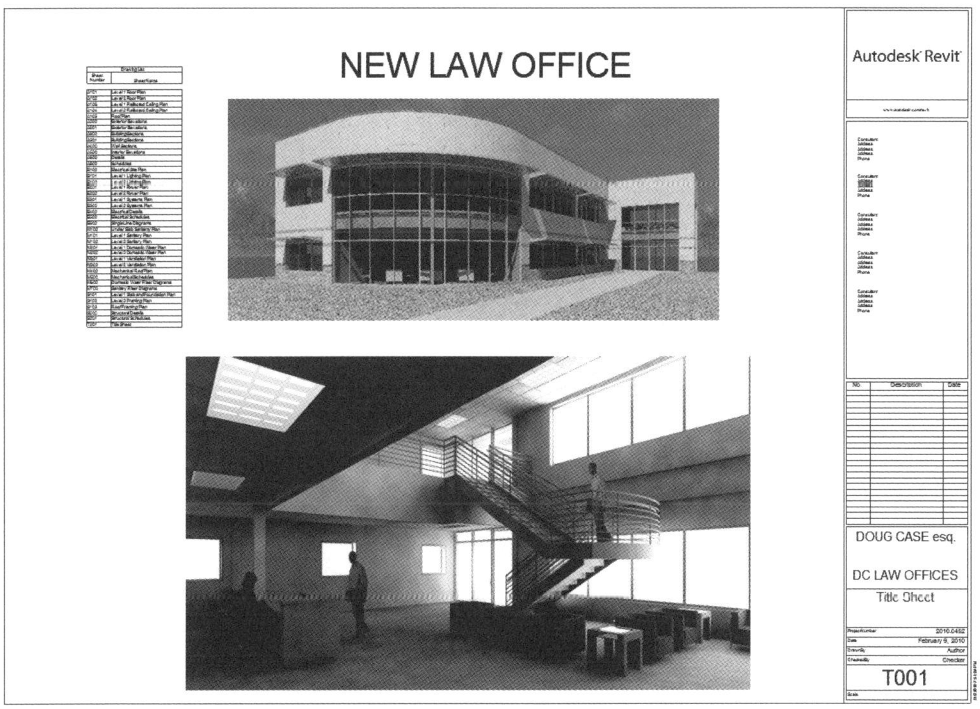

FIGURE 16-2.4 Sheet View: Title Sheet with sheet list, text and image added

12. Use the ***Text*** command to add the title shown in Figure 16-2.4.
    a. You will need to create a new text style and set the height to 1″.

When you have raster images in your project, you can manage them via the *Raster Images* dialog.

13. Select **Insert → Link → Manage Links.**

14. Click on one of the Images.

You are now in the *Manage Links* dialog which provides information about the image and allows you to delete it from the project (Figure 16-2.5).

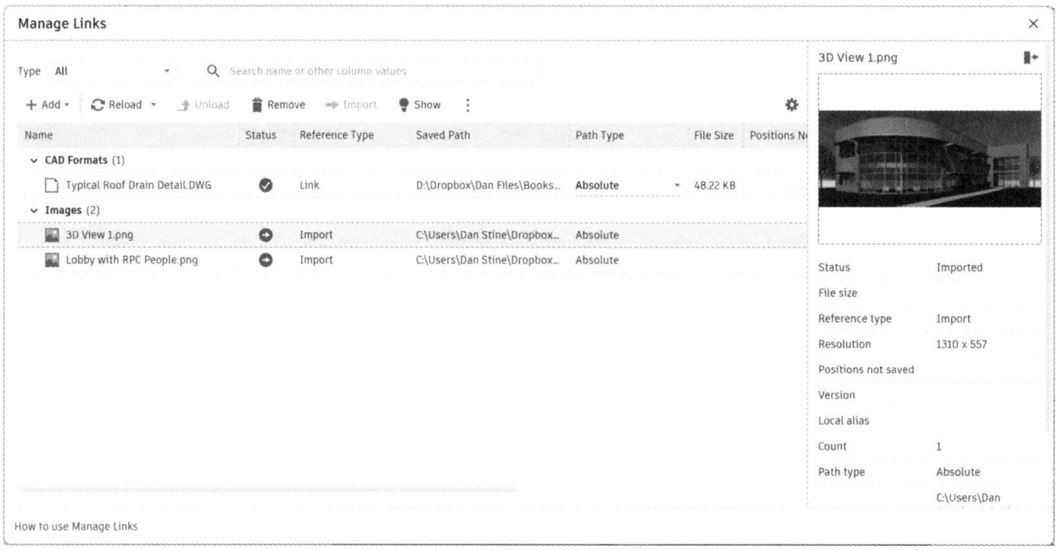

FIGURE 16-2.5 Raster Image dialog

TIP: You can create a custom parameter (via the Add Parameter button; see Figure 16-2.1) and then sort the sheet index schedule by that parameter. This allows you to force the "T" sheet to the top and the "E" sheets to the bottom.

15. Click **OK** to close the *Raster Images* dialog.

16. **Save** your project.

Exercise 16-3:
Printing a Set of Drawings

Revit has the ability to print an entire set of drawings, in addition to printing individual sheets. You will study this feature and a related process for creating redlines external to Revit and then referencing those markups back into Revit using a DWFx file.

Printing a Set of Drawings:

1. **Open** your project and then select **Application Menu → Print**.
2. Verify you have the correct printer selected (your options will vary).

   TIP: *If you have a PDF printer driver installed, select it to create PDF files.*

3. In the *Print Range* area, click the option **Selected views/sheets** (Figure 16-3.1).
4. Click the **Select…** button within the *Print Range* area.

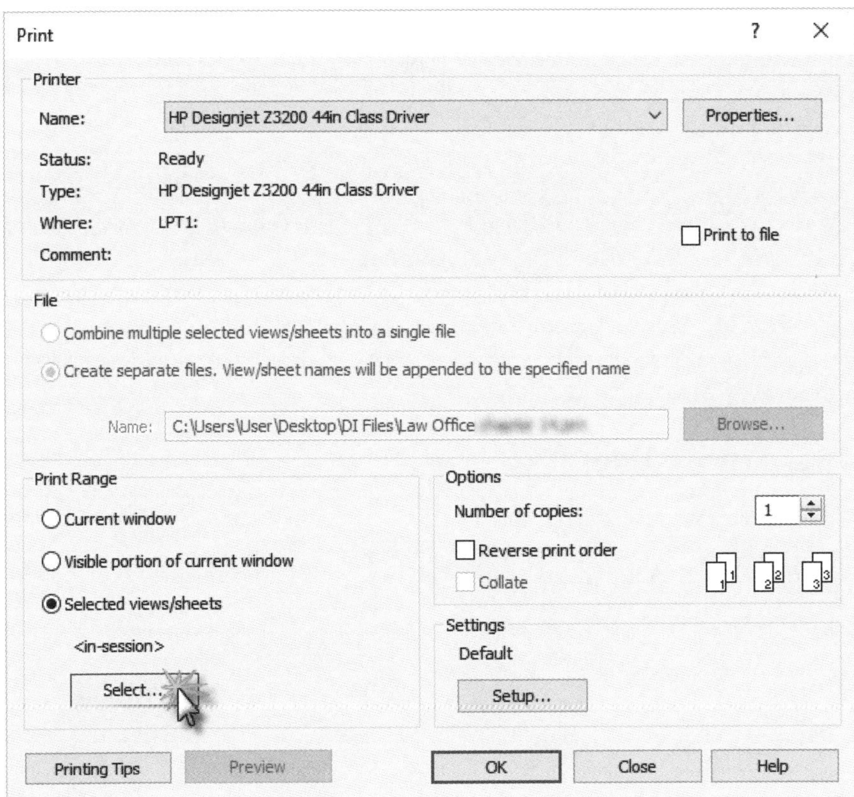

FIGURE 16-3.1 Print dialog box

You should now see a listing of all views and sheets (Figure 16-3.2).

Notice at the top you can *filter* for both **Sheets** and/or **Views**. Because you are printing a set of drawings, you will want to see only the sheets.

5. **Uncheck** the 2D/3D **Views** option.

The list is now limited to just sheets set up in your project.

6. Select all the *Sheets*.

7. Click **Select** to close the **View/Sheet Set** dialog.

   ***FYI:** Once you have selected the sheets to be plotted, you can save a Print Set. This will save the list of selected drawings to a name you choose. Then, the next time you need to print those sheets, you can select the name from the drop-down list at the top (Figure 16-3.2).*

   On very large projects (e.g., with 20 floor plan sheets), you could have a Plans *list saved, a* Laboratory Interior Elevations *list saved, etc.*

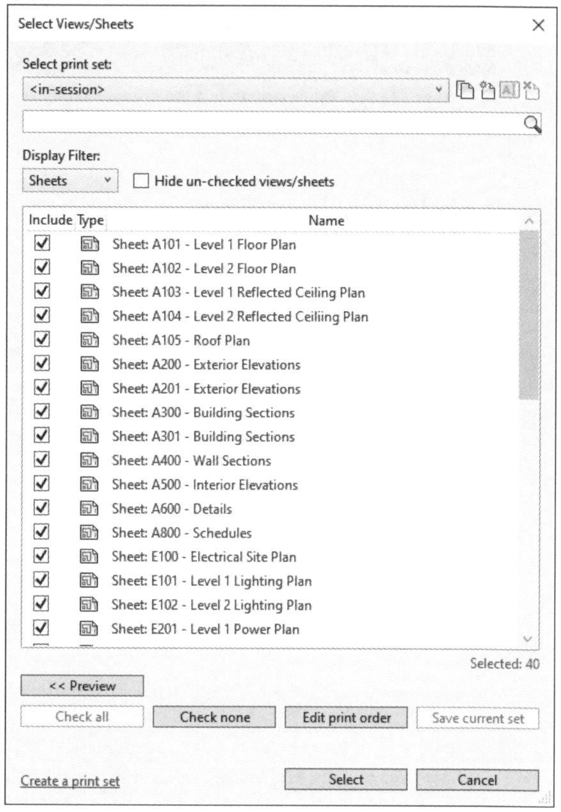

FIGURE 16-3.2 Selecting tool for printing

8. IF YOU ACTUALLY WANT TO PRINT A FULL SET OF DRAWINGS, you can do so now by clicking OK. Otherwise, click **Cancel**.

Autodesk can export to PDF. This tool can be found on the File tab, as shown in the image to the right. This is often the preferred format to send clients.

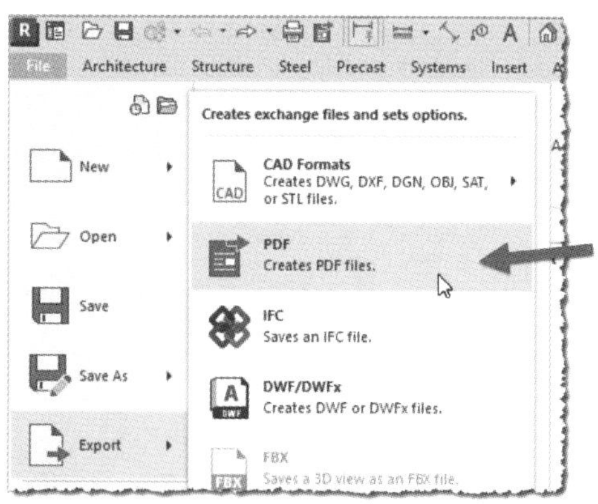

Exporting a 3D DWFx File:

The *3D DWFx* file is an easy way to share your project file with others without the need to give them your editable Revit file or the need for them to actually have Revit installed.

***NOTE:** You can download Revit from Autodesk's website, and run it in viewer mode (full Revit with no Save functionality) for free.* http://www.autodesk.com/products/design-review/overview.

The *3D DWFx* file is much smaller in file size than the original Revit file. Also, Autodesk Design Review is a *Viewer* that can be downloaded for free from www.autodesk.com/DWF.

9. Switch to your ***Default 3D*** view.
    a. You may need to go into *View Properties* and turn off the *Section Box* feature to see the entire model.

You must be in a 3D view for the *3D DWF* feature to work. If you are not in a 3D view, you will get *2D DWF* files:

10. Select **Application Menu → Export → DWF/DWFx.**

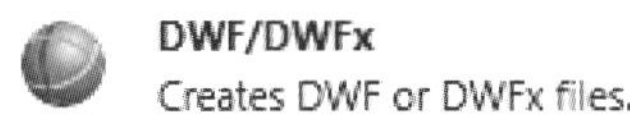

11. Click **Next…**: Specify a file name and location for the DWF file; click **OK**.

That's all you need to do to create the file. Now you can email it to the client or a product representative to get a more accurate cost estimate.

The *3D DWF* file is a meager 1MB, whereas the Revit *Project* file is 24MB. (Your file sizes will vary slightly based on factors like the number of families loaded, etc.) In most cases, an individual's networks and servers are set up so they cannot receive large files via email, so the 3D DWF is very useful.

You can access Design Review from *Start → All Programs → Autodesk → Autodesk Design Review 2017*. You can zoom, orbit and select objects. Notice the information displayed on the left when the front door is selected (see image below). Also notice, under the *Windows* heading, the sizes and quantities are listed.

> ***TIP:*** *Autodesk Design Review 2017 is a free download from Autodesk. This is their full-featured DWF viewer and markup utility!*

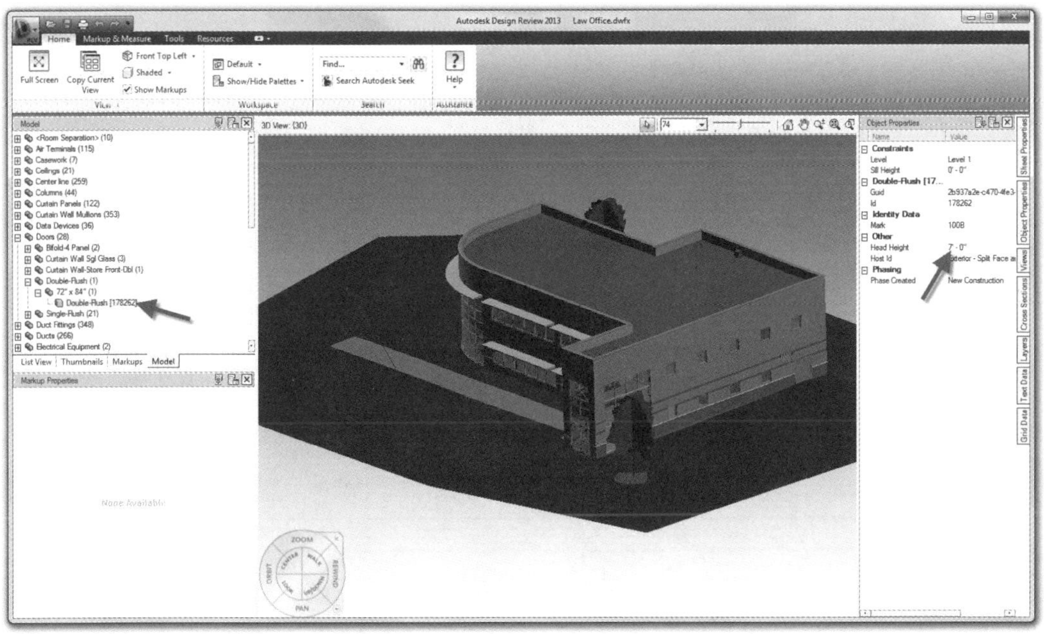

FIGURE 16-3.3 3D DWF in Autodesk Design Review

Exporting the sheets to a DWFx File:

It is also possible to create a DWFx file which represents some, or all, of the sheets in your project. This file is similar to a PDF file but is in Autodesk's proprietary format. However, as just mentioned, the view can be downloaded for free and includes markup tools which allow someone to add notes and revision clouds. The PDF format can have markups but requires Adobe Standard (or Professional), rather than just the viewer. The viewer is free, but Adobe Standard (or Professional) is not.

The following steps cover how to create a set of drawings in DWFx format.

12. Select **Application Menu → Export → DWF/DWFx**.

13. Do the following on the ***Views/Sheets*** tab (Figure 16-3.4):

    a. *Export:* **<In session view/sheet set>**

    b. *Show in list:* **Sheets in the model**

    c. Click the **Check All button**.

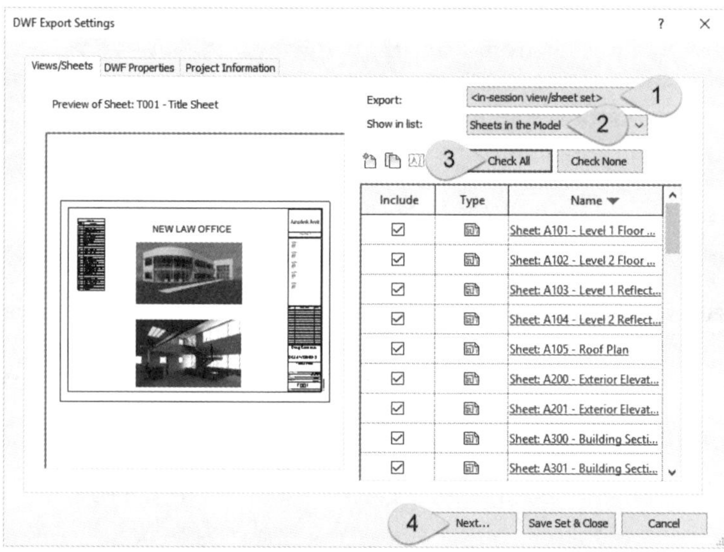

FIGURE 16-3.4 3D DWF export options

14. Review the options on the other two tabs (*DWF Properties* and *Project Information*), but do not make any additional changes at this time.

15. Click **Next**: Specify a file name and location for the DWFx file; click **OK**.

You now have a DWFx file with all the 2D sheets in it rather than a 3D model. This file can be used to print the project (either in an office/school or sent to a print shop). The file can also be an archive record of exactly what was sent out at each submittal point.

Next, you will take a quick look at the markup options in Autodesk *Design Review*.

16. Browse to the DWFx file just created and double click on it to open it.
    a. Or open *Design Review* and then use the ***Open*** command from the *Application* menu.

Notice, in Figure 16-3.5, the *Thumbnail* tab is selected on the left, which shows a small preview for each sheet in the file. Clicking on one of these previews opens that sheet in the larger viewing area.

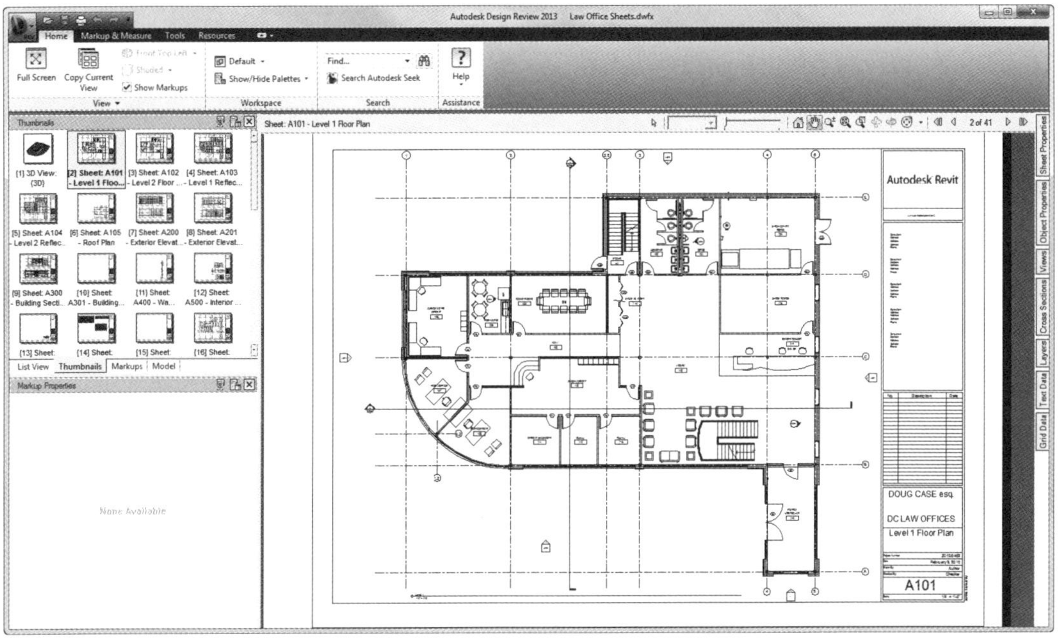

FIGURE 16-3.5 3D DWF sheets file

17. Make sure the *Level 1 Floor Plan*, **Sheet A101**, is selected.
18. Click the ***Markup and Measure*** tab on the *Ribbon*.
19. Use the ***Cloud***, ***Text*** and ***Line*** tools from the *Draw* panel to add the markups shown in Figure 16-3.6.
20. **Save** the DWFx file (via the *Quick Access Toolbar*).

One unique feature about doing markups in DWFx format, rather than PDF, is that the markups can be referenced back into Revit. This workflow is useful when a senior designer does not use Revit, or a client or contractor is providing feedback on the design and emailing the DWFx file back to you. You will see how this works next.

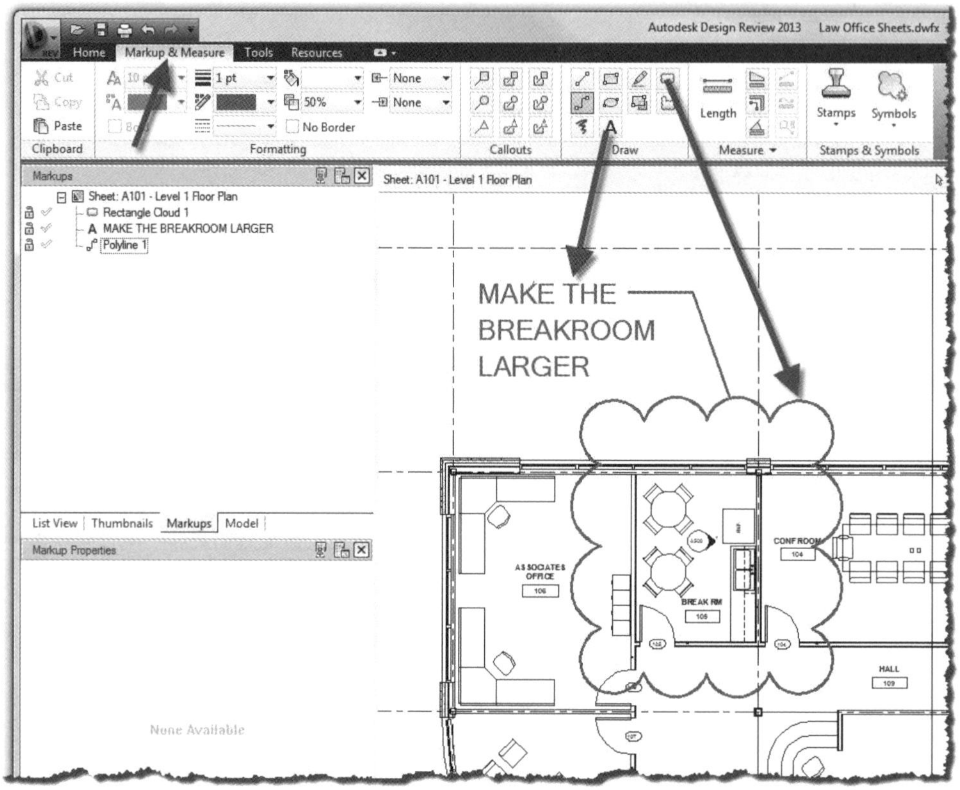

FIGURE 16-3.6 3D DWF sheets file with markups added

21. Open your Law Office file.

22. From the *Insert* tab, select **DWF Markup**.

23. Browse to your DWF sheet file with the markups.

24. Select the file and click **Open**.

25. Click **OK** (Figure 16-3.7).

26. Open **Sheet A101**.

Notice the markups added in *Design Review* are now in your Revit model (Figure 16-3.8).

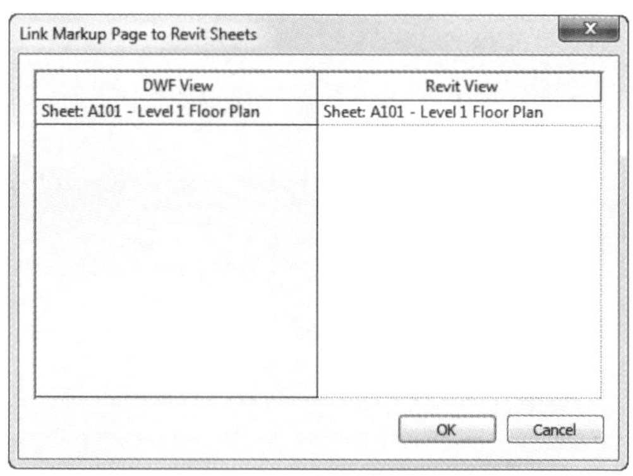

FIGURE 16-3.7 Import markup prompt

27. Select the *Revision* cloud in the sheet view (Figure 16-3.8).

Notice the *Properties Pallet* provides information about the origin of the markup and its current status (i.e., *None*, *Question*, *For Review* and *Done*).

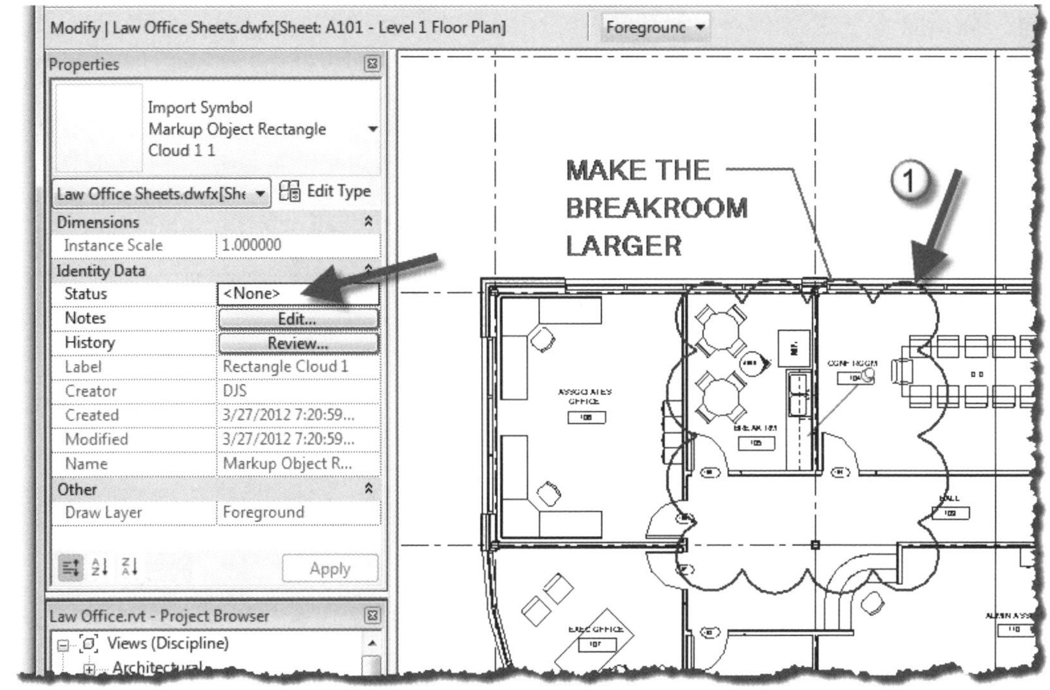

FIGURE 16-3.8 Markup overlay – revision cloud selected with properties shown

Follow these steps when you want to remove a *DWF Markup* link:

- **Manage → Manage Links**
- On the ***DWG Markup*** tab (Figure 16-3.9) select the markup and then click **Remove**.

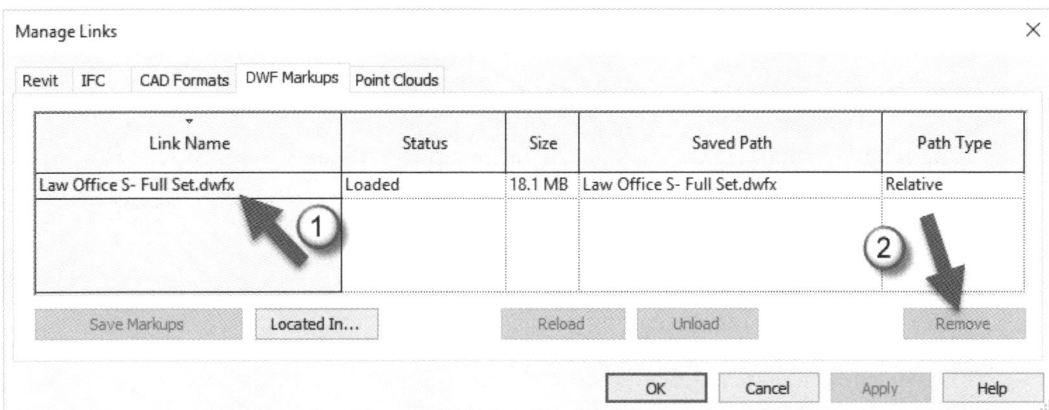

FIGURE 16-3.9 Markup overlay – revision cloud selected with properties shown

Autodesk User Certification Exam

Be sure to check out Appendix A for an overview of the official Autodesk User Certification Exam and the available study book and software, sold separately, from SDC Publications and this author.

Successfully passing this exam is a great addition to your resume and could help set you apart and help you land a great job. People who pass the official exam receive a certificate signed by the CEO of Autodesk, the makers of Revit.

Self-Exam:

The following questions can be used as a way to check your knowledge of this lesson. The answers can be found at the bottom of this page.

1. You have to manually fill in the reference bubbles after setting up the sheets. (T/F)
2. *DWF* files are much larger than the Revit file. (T/F)
3. It is possible to see a listing of only the views that have not been placed on a sheet via the *Project Browser*. (T/F)
4. You only have to enter your name on one titleblock, not all. (T/F)
5. Use the ____________ tool to create another drawing sheet.

Review Questions:

The following questions may be assigned by your instructor as a way to assess your knowledge of this section. Your instructor has the answers to the review questions.

1. You need to use a special command to edit text in the titleblock. (T/F)
2. The template you started with has only one Titleblock to choose from. (T/F)
3. You only have to enter the project name on one sheet, not all. (T/F)
4. The scale of a drawing placed on a sheet is determined by the scale set in that view's properties. (T/F)
5. You can save a list of drawing sheets to be plotted. (T/F)
6. You can be in any view when creating a *3D DWF* file. (T/F)
7. The reference bubbles will not automatically update if a drawing is moved to another sheet. (T/F)
8. On new sheets, the sheet number on the titleblock will increase by one from the previous sheet number. (T/F)
9. Image files cannot be placed on sheets. (T/F)
10. The *Sheet List* schedule never hides data. (T/F)

SELF-EXAM ANSWERS:
1 – F, **2** – F, **3** – T, **4** – F, **5** – Sheet

Index

Image below shows structural model created in Chapter 8.

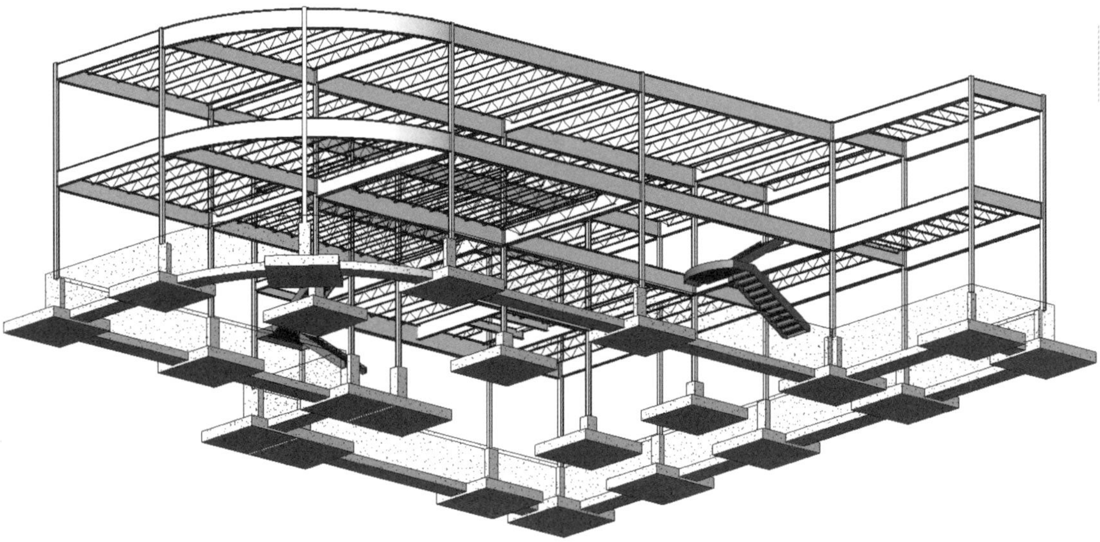

Autodesk User Certification Exam
Be sure to check out Appendix A for an overview of the official Autodesk User Certification Exam and the available study book and software, sold separately, from SDC Publications and this author.

Successfully passing this exam is a great addition to your resume and could help set you apart and help you land a great a job. People who pass the official exam receive a certificate signed by the CEO of Autodesk, the makers of Revit.